# A New Star-Rating System & Other Exciting News from Frommer's!

P9-DCZ-149

In our continuing effort to publish the savviest, most up-to-date, and most appealing travel guides available, we've added some great new features.

Frommer's guides now include a new **star-rating system.** Every hotel, restaurant, and attraction is rated from 0 to 3 stars to help you set priorities and organize your time.

We've also added **seven brand-new features** that point you to the great deals, in-the-know advice, and unique experiences that separate travelers from tourists. Throughout the guide, look for:

| | |
|---|---|
| ***Finds*** | Special finds—those places only insiders know about |
| ***Fun Fact*** | Fun facts—details that make travelers more informed and their trips more fun |
| ***Kids*** | Best bets for kids—advice for the whole family |
| ***Moments*** | Special moments—those experiences that memories are made of |
| ***Overrated*** | Places or experiences not worth your time or money |
| ***Tips*** | Insider tips—some great ways to save time and money |
| ***Value*** | Great values—where to get the best deals |

We've also added a **"What's New"** section in every guide—a timely crash course in what's hot and what's not in every destination we cover.

**Here's what the critics say about Frommer's:**

**"Amazingly easy to use. Very portable, very complete."**

*—Booklist*

**"Detailed, accurate, and easy-to-read information for all price ranges."**

*—Glamour Magazine*

**"Hotel information is close to encyclopedic."**

*—Des Moines Sunday Register*

**"Frommer's Guides have a way of giving you a real feel for a place."**

*—Knight Ridder Newspapers*

## Other Great Guides for Your Trip:

***Frommer's Munich & the Bavarian Alps***

***Frommer's Portable Berlin***

***Frommer's Portable Frankfurt***

***Frommer's Best-Loved Driving Tours of Germany***

***Frommer's Europe***

***Frommer's Europe from $70 a Day***

***Europe For Dummies***

Frommer's

POSTCARDS FROM

# Germany 2003

*Munich's Oktoberfest (which actually starts in late September) attracts millions of beer-lovers every year. See chapters 3 and 8.* © Barry Rowland/Tony Stone Images.

*The Brandenburg Gate, Berlin's most famous landmark, once marked the boundary between East and West Berlin. See chapter 4.* © *Tony Stone Images.*

*Sausages and beer: among the staples of the German diet.*
© *Dave Bartruff Photography.*

*Rothenburg is the most popular stop on the well-traveled Romantic Road. See chapter 7.*
*© Bob Krist Photography.*

*The Rhine is a popular and picturesque cruise-ship route. See chapter 14. © Hans Wolf/ The Image Bank.*

*The Karwendel Mountains, near Mittenwald, have some of Germany's best hiking trails. See chapter 9.* © *Werner H. Muller/Tony Stone Images.*

*Extravagantly painted facades, like this one in Mittenwald, are common sights in the towns of the Bavarian Alps. See chapter 9.* © *Kevin Galvin Photography.*

*Salt warehouses along the River Trave in Lübeck. See chapter 18.* © Dave G. Houser/Houserstock, Inc.

*A visit to "Mad" King Ludwig's Schloss Linderhof makes a good day trip from Munich or Oberammergau. See chapter 9.* © Greg Gawlowski/Photo 20-20.

*A colorful cafe in the spa town of Baden-Baden. See chapter 11.*
*© Bob Krist Photography.*

*The Black Forest has some of Germany's most scenic countryside. See chapter 11.*
*© Paul Trummer/The Image Bank.*

*Merchant homes along a canal in Hamburg. See chapter 17.* © *Lothar Reupert/The Image Bank.*

*Another side of Hamburg: the gaudy Reeperbahn, the city's red light district. See chapter 17.*
© *Romilly Lockyer/The Image Bank.*

*These half-timbered houses are in the Römerberg, the heart of old Frankfurt. See chapter 13.* © *Kevin Galvin Photography.*

*The best view of Heidelberg is from the Philosopher's Way, halfway up the hill on the north bank of the Neckar River. See chapter 12.* © *Bob Krist Photography.*

Frommer's®

# Germany

## 2003

by Darwin Porter & Danforth Prince

Wiley Publishing, Inc.

## About the Authors

Veteran travel writers **Darwin Porter** and **Danforth Prince** have written numerous best-selling Frommer's guides, notably to Germany, France, Italy, England, and Spain. Porter, who was bureau chief for the *Miami Herald* when he was 21, wrote the first Frommer's guide to Germany and has traveled extensively in the country. Prince, who began writing with Porter in 1982, worked for the Paris bureau of the *New York Times.*

Published by:

**Wiley Publishing, Inc.**
909 Third Ave.
New York, NY 10022

Copyright © 2003 Wiley Publishing, Inc., New York, New York. All rights reserved. No part of this publication may be reproduced, stored in a retrieval system or transmitted in any form or by any means, electronic, mechanical, photocopying, recording, scanning or otherwise, except as permitted under Sections 107 or 108 of the 1976 United States Copyright Act, without either the prior written permission of the Publisher, or authorization through payment of the appropriate per-copy fee to the Copyright Clearance Center, 222 Rosewood Drive, Danvers, MA 01923, (978) 750-8400, fax (978) 750-4744. Requests to the Publisher for permission should be addressed to the Legal Department, Wiley Publishing, Inc., 10475 Crosspoint Blvd., Indianapolis, IN 46256, (317) 572-3447, fax (317) 572-4447, E-Mail: permcoordinator@wiley.com.

Wiley and the Wiley Publishing logo are trademarks or registered trademarks of Wiley Publishing, Inc. in the United States and other countries and may not be used without written permission. Frommer's is a trademark or registered trademark of Arthur Frommer. Used under license. All other trademarks are the property of their respective owners. Wiley Publishing, Inc. is not associated with any product or vendor mentioned in this book.

ISBN 0-7645-6654-7
ISSN 1091-2827

Editor: Kendra L. Falkenstein
Production Editor: Ian Skinnari
Cartographer: Elizabeth Puhl
Photo Editor: Richard Fox
Production by Wiley Indianapolis Composition Services
Chapter 2 illustrations by Rashell Smith and Karl Brandt

Front cover photo: Neuschwanstein Castle.
Back cover photo: Looking out a window at Mittenwald's Fasching Carnival.

For information on our other products and services or to obtain technical support, please contact our Customer Care Department within the U.S. at 800-762-2974, outside the U.S. at 317-572-3993 or fax 317-572-4002.

Wiley also publishes its books in a variety of electronic formats. Some content that appears in print may not be available in electronic formats.

Manufactured in the United States of America

5 4 3 2

# Contents


**List of Maps** x

**What's New in Germany** 1

**1 The Best of Germany** 3

1 The Best Travel Experiences .....3
2 The Best Museums .....7
3 The Best Castles & Palaces .....8
4 The Best Cathedrals .....10
5 The Most Charming Small Villages .....10
6 The Best Driving Tours .....11
7 The Best Walks .....12
8 The Best Biking .....12
9 The Best Spas .....12
10 The Best Luxury Hotels .....13
11 The Best Small Inns & Hotels ...14
12 The Best Restaurants .....15
13 The Best Beer Halls & Taverns .....16
14 The Best Shopping .....16

**2 A Traveler's Guide to German Art & Architecture** 18

*by Reid Bramblett*

1 German Art 101 .....18
2 German Architecture 101 .....22

**3 Planning Your Trip to Germany** 30

1 The Regions in Brief .....30
2 Visitor Information .....34
*Destination: Germany—Red Alert Checklist* .....35
3 Entry Requirements & Customs . .35
4 Money .....36
*The U.S. Dollar, the British Pound & the Euro* .....36
5 When to Go .....37
*Germany Calendar of Events* ...38
6 Health & Insurance .....40
7 Tips for Travelers with Special Needs .....41
8 Getting There .....44
*What You Can Carry On—And What You Can't* .....45
9 Escorted Tours, Package Deals & Special Interest Vacations ....47
*Taking the Waters* .....50
*Germany for Jewish Visitors* ....52
10 Planning Your Trip Online .....53
11 Getting Around .....55
12 Tips on Accommodations .....58
13 Recommended Books .....59
*Fast Facts: Germany* .....60

**4 Berlin** 64

1 Orientation .....64
*Berlin Today & Tomorrow* .....66
*Neighborhoods in Brief* .....68
2 Getting Around .....72
*Fast Facts: Berlin* .....74
3 Where to Stay .....76
*Family-Friendly Hotels* .....80
4 Where to Dine .....90

*Family-Friendly Restaurants* ....91
5 Seeing the Sights .....103
*Sightseeing Suggestions for First-Time Visitors* .....103
*The Best Sightseeing Deal* ....103
*Frommer's Favorite Berlin Experiences* .....112
*A Death Camp: "A Guarantor of Memory"* .....121
6 Organized Tours .....124
7 Sports & Outdoor Pursuits ....126
8 Shopping .....127
*Treasures in the Barn District* .....130
9 Berlin After Dark .....134
*The Love Parade* .....135
*Life Is a Cabaret in Berlin* .....137
10 A Side Trip: Potsdam & Its Palaces .....145

## 5 Saxony & Thuringia 151

1 Weimar .....151
*Goethe Gets a Touch-Up* .....157
*The Thuringian Forest: Germany's Green Heart* .....161
2 Leipzig .....165
*Singing Through the Centuries: The St. Thomas Boys' Choir* ...169
3 Dresden .....177
4 Meissen .....193

## 6 Franconia & the German Danube 196

1 Bayreuth .....197
2 Bamberg .....202
3 Nürnberg (Nuremberg) .....207
*Albrecht Dürer & the German Renaissance* .....210
4 Regensburg .....217
5 Passau .....222
*Cruising the Danube* .....223
6 Ulm .....226

## 7 The Romantic Road 230

1 Würzburg .....230
2 Miltenberg .....238
3 Amorbach .....239
4 Bad Mergentheim .....240
5 Weikersheim .....242
6 Creglingen .....243
7 Rothenburg ob der Tauber ....244
8 Dinkelsbühl .....251
9 Nördlingen .....252
10 Donauwörth .....254
11 Augsburg .....255
12 Füssen .....260
13 Neuschwanstein & Hohenschwangau .....263
*The Fairy-Tale King* .....264

## 8 Munich 267

1 Orientation .....267
*Neighborhoods in Brief* .....270
2 Getting Around .....271
*Fast Facts: Munich* .....273
3 Where to Stay .....275
*Family-Friendly Hotels* .....278
4 Where to Dine .....283
*Family-Friendly Restaurants* ...287
*Beer Gardens* .....294
5 Seeing the Sights .....294

*Frommer's Favorite Munich Experiences* . . . . . .298
6 Organized Tours . . . . . .309
7 Sports & Outdoor Pursuits . . . .310
8 Shopping . . . . . .311
9 Munich After Dark . . . . . .315
*François Cuvilliés* . . . . . .317
10 Side Trips from Munich . . . . . .323

**9 The Bavarian Alps** 324

1 Berchtesgaden . . . . . .327
*Springtime for Hitler* . . . . . .332
2 Bad Reichenhall . . . . . .333
3 Chiemsee . . . . . .336
4 Bad Wiessee . . . . . .339
5 Mittenwald . . . . . .341
6 Garmisch-Partenkirchen . . . . . .343
*Hiking in the Bavarian Alps* . . .344
*A Dramatic Alpine Fantasy* . . . .346
7 Oberammergau . . . . . .350
*Shopping for Woodcarvings* . . .352

**10 Lake Constance (Bodensee)** 356

1 Lindau . . . . . .356
2 Friedrichshafen . . . . . .362
*Rebirth of the Zeppelin* . . . . . .363
3 Meersburg . . . . . .365
4 Konstanz (Constance) . . . . . .368
5 Reichenau . . . . . .372
6 Überlingen . . . . . .374
7 Ravensburg . . . . . .376

**11 The Black Forest (Schwarzwald)** 379

1 Freiburg im Breisgau . . . . . .379
*An Excursion to the Upper Black Forest* . . . . . .383
2 Badenweiler . . . . . .385
3 Titisee . . . . . .388
4 Triberg . . . . . .391
*Wunderhiking in the Black Forest* . . . . . .393
5 Freudenstadt . . . . . .393
6 Calw . . . . . .396
7 Pforzheim . . . . . .398
*Medieval Excursion from Pforzheim* . . . . . .399
8 Baden-Baden . . . . . .400
*The Town's Preoccupation: Ambling on the 'Ohs'* . . . . . .401

**12 Heidelberg, Stuttgart & the Neckar Valley** 408

1 Heidelberg . . . . . .408
2 Hirschhorn, Eberbach & Heilbrunn . . . . . .418
3 Stuttgart . . . . . .422
4 Tübingen . . . . . .430
5 Schwäbisch Hall . . . . . .432

**13 Frankfurt** 434

1 Orientation . . . . . .434
2 Getting Around . . . . . .438
*Fast Facts: Frankfurt* . . . . . .439
3 Where to Stay . . . . . .440
4 Where to Dine . . . . . .445
5 Seeing the Sights . . . . . .452

6 Sports & Outdoor Pursuits ....456
7 Shopping .....456
8 Frankfurt After Dark .....459
9 Side Trips from Frankfurt .....463
*Elvis in Bad Nauheim* .....473

## 14 The Rhineland 475

1 Speyer .....475
*Cruising the Rhine* .....478
2 Worms .....479
3 Mainz .....484
4 The Rheingau .....489
5 Koblenz .....492
6 Bonn .....495
7 Bad Godesberg .....502
8 Aachen (Aix-la-Chapelle) .....503
9 Cologne (Köln) .....507
*Beer Taverns* .....518
10 Düsseldorf .....521

## 15 The Mosel Valley 532

1 Cochem .....532
2 Beilstein .....535
3 Zell .....536
4 Traben-Trarbach .....537
5 Bernkastel-Kues .....538
6 Trier (Treves) .....540

## 16 Bremen, Lower Saxony & North Hesse 547

1 Bremen .....547
2 Lüneburg .....557
*The Lüneburg Heath* .....559
3 Celle .....560
4 Hannover .....562
5 Hameln .....568
6 Bad Pyrmont .....570
7 Goslar .....572
8 Göttingen .....575
9 Bad Wildungen .....579
10 The Fairy-Tale Road .....580

## 17 Hamburg 584

1 Orientation .....584
*Neighborhoods in Brief* .....586
*Fast Facts: Hamburg* .....587
2 Where to Stay .....588
3 Where to Dine .....596
4 Seeing the Sights .....600
5 Sports & Outdoor Pursuits ....604
6 Shopping .....604
7 Hamburg After Dark .....607
*Johnny & the Moondogs Invade Hamburg* .....609
*The Reeperbahn: A Walk on the Wild Side* .....610

## 18 Schleswig-Holstein 615

1 Lübeck .....615
2 Kiel .....622
3 Schleswig .....625
4 The Island of Sylt .....628
*A Disappearing Playground* ...629

**19 A Scenic Drive Along the Baltic** 633

1 Wismar .....633
2 Schwerin .....635
3 Rostock .....639
4 Stralsund .....642
5 Rügen .....644
*Storming the Gibraltar of the Baltic* .....646

**Appendix A: Germany in Depth** 647

1 History 101 .....647
*Dateline* .....647
2 In Pursuit of Musical Excellence .....653
3 A Taste of Germany .....655
*The Best of the Wurst* .....656
*O' Zapfstisl ("The Barrel Is Tapped")* .....658

**Appendix B: Useful Terms & Phrases** 661

1 Glossary .....661
2 Menu Terms .....662

**Index** 666

# List of Maps

Germany 4
Berlin Neighborhoods 70
Western Berlin Accommodations & Dining 78
Berlin-Mitte Accommodations & Dining 87
Attractions in Charlottenburg 105
Attractions in Berlin-Mitte 107
Attractions Around the Tiergarten 111
Potsdam 147
Saxony & Thuringia 153
Weimar 155
Leipzig 167
Dresden 179
The Zwinger 183
Franconia & the German Danube 199
Nürnberg 209
The Romantic Road 231
Würzburg 233
Rothenburg ob der Tauber 245
Augsburg 257
Munich Neighborhoods 268
Munich U-Bahn & S-Bahn 272
Central Munich Accommodations & Dining 276
Central Munich Attractions 296
Deutsches Museum 301
The Residenz 303
The Bavarian Alps 329
Lake Constance 357
The Black Forest 381
The Neckar Valley 409
Heidelberg 411
Stuttgart 423
Frankfurt 436
The Rhineland 477
Cologne (Köln) 509
Düsseldorf 523
The Mosel Valley 533
Lower Saxony & North Hesse 549
Bremen 551
Hamburg Accommodations & Dining 590
Attractions in Central Hamburg 601
Schleswig-Holstein 617
Driving Along the Baltic 635

## An Invitation to the Reader

In researching this book, we discovered many wonderful places—hotels, restaurants, shops, and more. We're sure you'll find others. Please tell us about them, so we can share the information with your fellow travelers in upcoming editions. If you were disappointed with a recommendation, we'd love to know that, too. Please write to:

*Frommer's Germany 2003*
Wiley Publishing, Inc. • 909 Third Ave. • New York, NY 10022

## An Additional Note

Please be advised that travel information is subject to change at any time—and this is especially true of prices. We therefore suggest that you write or call ahead for confirmation when making your travel plans. The authors, editors, and publisher cannot be held responsible for the experiences of readers while traveling. Your safety is important to us, however, so we encourage you to stay alert and be aware of your surroundings. Keep a close eye on cameras, purses, and wallets, all favorite targets of thieves and pickpockets.

### New! Frommer's Star Ratings & Icons

Every hotel, restaurant, and attraction listing in this guide has been ranked for quality, value, service, amenities, and special features using a star-rating scale. In country, state, and regional guides, we also rate towns and regions to help you narrow down your choices and budget your time accordingly. Hotels and restaurants in the Very Expensive and Expensive categories are rated on a scale of one (highly recommended) to three stars (exceptional). Those in the Moderate and Inexpensive categories rate from zero (recommended) to two stars (very highly recommended). Attractions, towns, and regions are rated according to the following scale: zero stars (recommended), one star (highly recommended), two stars (very highly recommended), and three stars (must-see).

In addition to the rating system, we also use seven icons to highlight insider information, useful tips, special bargains, hidden gems, memorable experiences, kid-friendly venues, places to avoid, and other useful information:

The following abbreviations are used for credit cards:

| | | | | | |
|---|---|---|---|---|---|
| AE | American Express | DISC | Discover | V | Visa |
| DC | Diners Club | MC | MasterCard | | |

## FROMMERS.COM

Now that you have the guidebook to a great trip, visit our website at **www.frommers.com** for travel information on nearly 2,500 destinations. With features updated regularly, we give you instant access to the most current trip-planning information available. At Frommers.com, you'll also find the best prices on airfares, accommodations, and car rentals—and you can even book travel online through our travel booking partners. At Frommers.com, you'll also find the following:

- Online updates to our most popular guidebooks
- Vacation sweepstakes and contest giveaways
- Newsletter highlighting the hottest travel trends
- Online travel message boards with featured travel discussions

# What's New in Germany

A unified, wealthy, industrial yet beautiful Germany awaits you, promising some of the most interesting travel experiences in Europe. Many of the country's historical and architectural treasures were lost during World War II, but much remains and much has been restored. In addition, German natural scenery, particularly in the Black Forest, the Mosel Valley, the Harz Mountains, and the Bavarian Alps, is a potent lure.

In the closing years of the 20th century, the country grew and changed at an astonishing pace, and the nation's capital was relocated from Bonn to Berlin. Berlin's refurbished Reichstag (which in the spring of 1999 became the seat of German Parliament) in many ways represents the changing mood of the nation, and its new glass dome glitters as a symbol of modernity. Berliners celebrated the Reichstag's rededication not with patriotic glory and pomp, but with an oompah band, meatballs, and beer. In the post-millennium, Germany abandoned its currency, the mark (for the euro), and unified itself with the countries of western Europe as never before.

For those who want to see history in the making, we recommend visiting Potsdam, Leipzig, Dresden, Meissen, and Weimar, all centers of East Germany before unification. Keep in mind, however, that although political developments have been fast-paced, the infrastructure of the eastern states has not fully risen to western German levels, and living standards here are still different from those in the former West Germany.

Other changes are also in the air. You'll find a preview of only a few of them below.

Finally, remember that though this guide is meant to help you decide where to go in Germany and how best to enjoy its charms, ultimately, the most gratifying rewards will be your own serendipitous discoveries—drinking beer in a yard shaded by chestnut trees, picnicking in a Bavarian meadow, or spending time chatting with a winemaker in the Mosel Valley. The German people are among the world's most sophisticated and interesting. You'll likely remember your experiences with them for years to come.

**BERLIN** For complete information on Berlin, see chapter 4, "Berlin."

**Accommodations** A new hotel just for women, **Hotel Intermezzo** (✆ **030/224890-96**), has opened only a 5-minute walk from the Brandenburg Gate and the Reichstag. The interior looks like a showroom for IKEA, and it's a most inviting haven. See p. 90 for more details.

**Restaurants** Some of the best cuisine in the capital is served at the new **Portalis** (✆ **030/20-45-54-96**), which is ultra-hip and avant-garde, offering the refined cuisine of France and the savory, sun-kissed food of the Mediterranean. Even jaded palates can be awakened here. See p. 98 for more details.

**DRESDEN** In this city of art and architecture on the Elbe, the **Rothenburger Hof** (✆ **0351/81260**) has been beautifully renovated and enjoys a regal position as a small luxury hotel. It first opened its doors in 1685. The latest incarnation is not a restored ancient monument, but a completely up-to-date 21st-century hotel with such facilities as a swimming pool and fitness center. See p. 186 for more details.

**MUNICH** For complete information on Munich, see chapter 8, "Munich."

**Accommodations** One of the Bavarian capital's most charming B&B-type hotels, **Hotel Biederstein** (✆ **089/3899970**), has opened near the English Garden. Newly renovated, it is decorated in a minimalist style and is charming with affordable prices. See p. 281 for more details.

**Restaurants** The place to be seen today is **Café Dukatz in the Literaturhaus** (✆ **089/291-9600**), which is the gathering place of the literati who come here to hang out, order coffee, or partake of an excellent international cuisine. See p. 289 for more details.

**OBERSALZBERG, THE BAVARIAN ALPS** In a controversial move, the site of Hitler's former alpine command center is being converted into a luxury hotel. Facing down protests that the resort might become a magnet for neo-Nazis, the Bavarian State Bank, the backers of the project, are moving ahead to give today's visitors the same mountain beauty and drama once enjoyed by the Nazi dictator and his mistress, Eva Braun. The Berghof where Hitler and Braun vacationed was destroyed by Allied air raids in 1945. See the "Springtime for Hitler" box on p. 332 for more details.

**BADEN-BADEN** In the Black Forest region of Germany, at the spa of Baden-Baden, a resort known for its cuisine, **Le Jardin de France** (✆ **07721/300-7860**) has opened and has become the finest dining room in the city. Adjacent to the landmark Baths of Caracalla, it accurately calls itself a "small corner of France set within Germany" and serves a finely honed conemporary French cuisine. See p. 406 for more details.

**COLOGNE** The stunningly upgraded **Museum Ludwig** (✆ **0221/2212-2382**) is today home to one of the world's largest collections of Picassos, thanks to a bequest of 774 works of this artist, including his famous 1923 *Harlequin* and his 1941 *Woman with Artichoke.* See p. 511 for more details.

**BERNKASTEL-KUES** Deep in the Mosel Valley outside this wine town, a restaurant has risen to become one of the most acclaimed in Germany. **Waldhotel Sonnora** (✆ **06578/98220**) serves a spectacular continental cuisine that attracts serious foodies from all over the country. See p. 539 for more details.

**BREMEN** The art gallery **Kunsthalle** (✆ **049/421-329080**) received worldwide headlines in the summer of 2001 when a treasure trove of art, including drawings by Rembrandt and Dürer, were returned to the museum after more than 50 years away. The missing art was looted in 1945 by Soviet troops and later stolen. Police finally recovered the art in a Brooklyn, New York apartment house. This museum has also long been known for its 19th- and 20th-century French art, including a lot of old masters. See p. 550 for more details.

**HAMBURG** A real discovery is the opening of the **Hotel Garni Mittelweg** (✆ **040/414-1010**) in the upscale residential neighborhood of Poseldorf, within a short stroll of the Aussenalster. In a converted 19-century home of a former rich merchant, the building was tastefully and comfortably converted into a family hotel, which charges affordable prices. See p. 595 for more details.

# 1

# The Best of Germany

Below you'll find our carefully compiled lists of the best that Germany has to offer, from castles and cathedrals to spas, restaurants, and sightseeing—and nearly everything else you'll want to see and do.

## 1 The Best Travel Experiences

- **Exploring the New Berlin:** Anyone who lived through the neuroses of the Cold War can't help but shudder at the memory of the Berlin Wall. Since reunification, civic planners, with almost manic enthusiasm, have demolished large sections of what once stood as a scar across the face of a defeated nation. The architectural changes and urban developments that are constantly updating the cityscape around Berlin's Friedrichstrasse and Potsdamer Platz can be confusing. But regardless of which renewal program is churning up rubble at the time of your visit, a pilgrimage through what used to be the most bitterly contested urban turf in Europe can't help but provoke powerful emotions. See chapter 4.
- **Spending a Midsummer's Night in a Biergarten:** When the temperature rises, head immediately for the unpretentious cheer of the nearest biergarten (everybody in Germany seems to have his or her favorite, so we're not even going to try to name the "best"). These watering holes, which often feature trellises, climbing vines, Chinese lanterns, and arbors, offer low-cost fun on soft summer nights. You can order platters of hearty food with your beer or bring your own picnic.
- **Cruising the Elbe, the Danube, and the Rhine:** This trio of rivers, along with their tributaries, dominated German commerce for hundreds of years. Today, an armada of tugboats, barges, and cruise ships still ply the muddy waters beside riverbanks lined with the historic majesty (and sometimes the industrial might) of Central Europe. Cruises begin and end at large cities of historic interest and last anywhere from 6 hours to 7 days. See **Sächsischer Dampfschiffahrt** in chapter 5, **Donau-Schiffahrt** in chapter 6, and **KD River Cruises** in chapter 14.
- **Boating on the Königssee:** A romantic poet would praise this lake, near Berchtesgaden in Bavaria, for the forest-covered mountains that surround its cold, deep, dark waters. The baroque chapels and fairy-tale hamlets on its shores supplement its natural grandeur. The boat you ride will be powered by very quiet electric motors, so that you can hear the extraordinary echoes that bounce off the rock faces. See p. 330.
- **Hiking in the Bavarian Alps:** In summer, alpine hiking is a major attraction in Germany. Hikers are able to observe firsthand a variety of wildlife, often including endangered species. Two of the best

# Germany

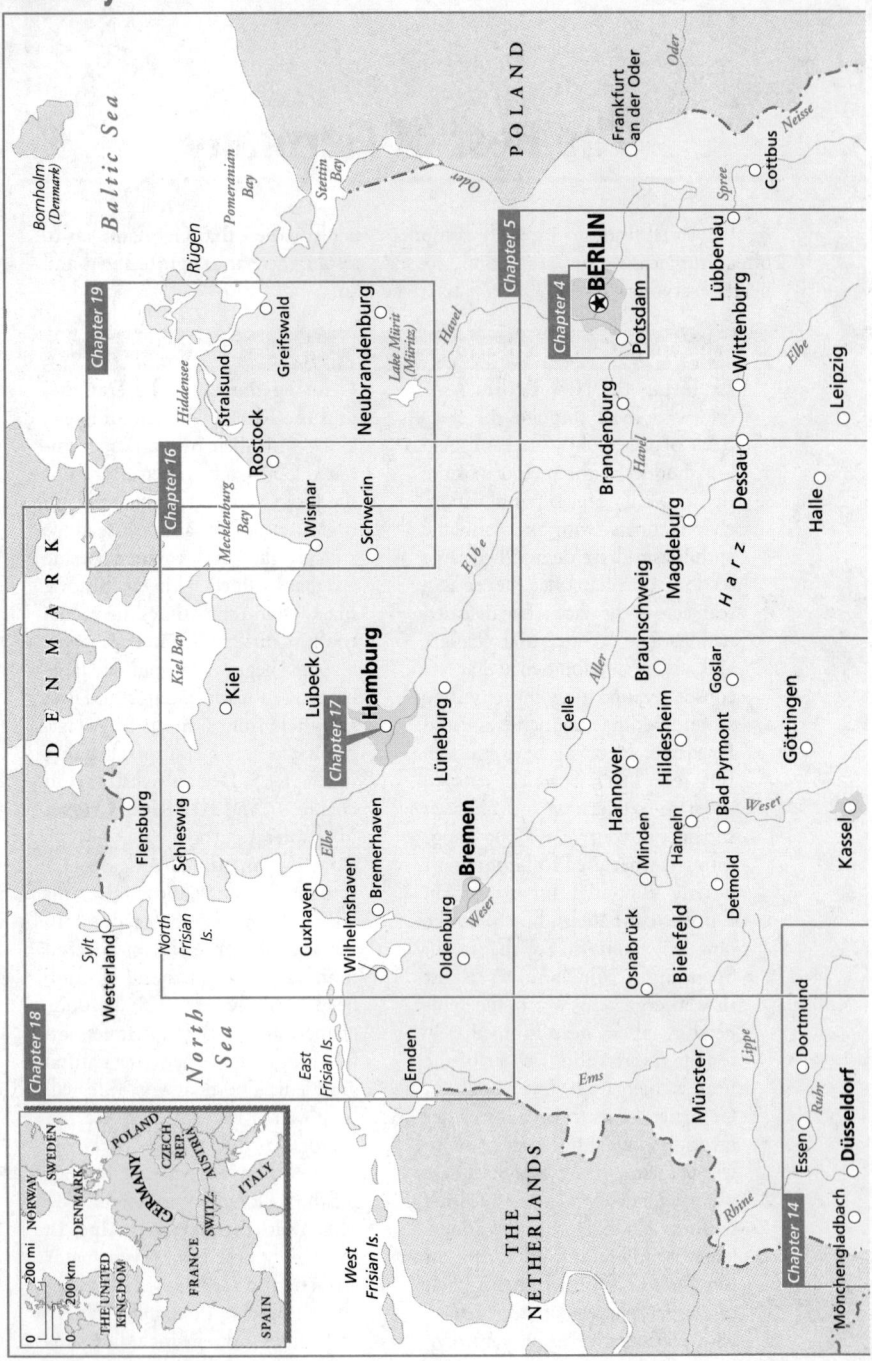
0 200 mi
0 200 km
NORWAY
SWEDEN
DENMARK
THE UNITED KINGDOM
POLAND
GERMANY
CZECH REP.
AUSTRIA
SWITZ.
FRANCE
ITALY
SPAIN
Chapter 18
Chapter 19
Chapter 16
Chapter 17
Chapter 5
Chapter 4
Chapter 14
Bornholm (Denmark)
Baltic Sea
Rügen
Pomeranian Bay
Stettin Bay
Oder
POLAND
Frankfurt an der Oder
Oder
Cottbus
Neisse
Spree
Lübbenau
Wittenburg
Elbe
Leipzig
Hiddensee
Stralsund
Greifswald
Rostock
Wismar
Schwerin
Neubrandenburg
Lake Müritz (Müritz)
Mecklenburg Bay
Havel
Brandenburg
Potsdam
BERLIN
Havel
Magdeburg
Dessau
Halle
Harz
Braunschweig
Goslar
Göttingen
Kassel
Hildesheim
Hameln
Bad Pyrmont
Detmold
Weser
Hannover
Minden
Celle
Aller
Osnabrück
Bielefeld
Münster
Lippe
Ems
Rhine
Ruhr
Essen
Dortmund
Düsseldorf
Mönchengladbach
THE NETHERLANDS
West Frisian Is.
Emden
East Frisian Is.
North Sea
Oldenburg
Bremen
Weser
Elbe
Lüneburg
Bremerhaven
Wilhelmshaven
Cuxhaven
Hamburg
Lübeck
Kiel
Kiel Bay
Schleswig
Flensburg
North Frisian Is.
Westerland
Sylt
DENMARK

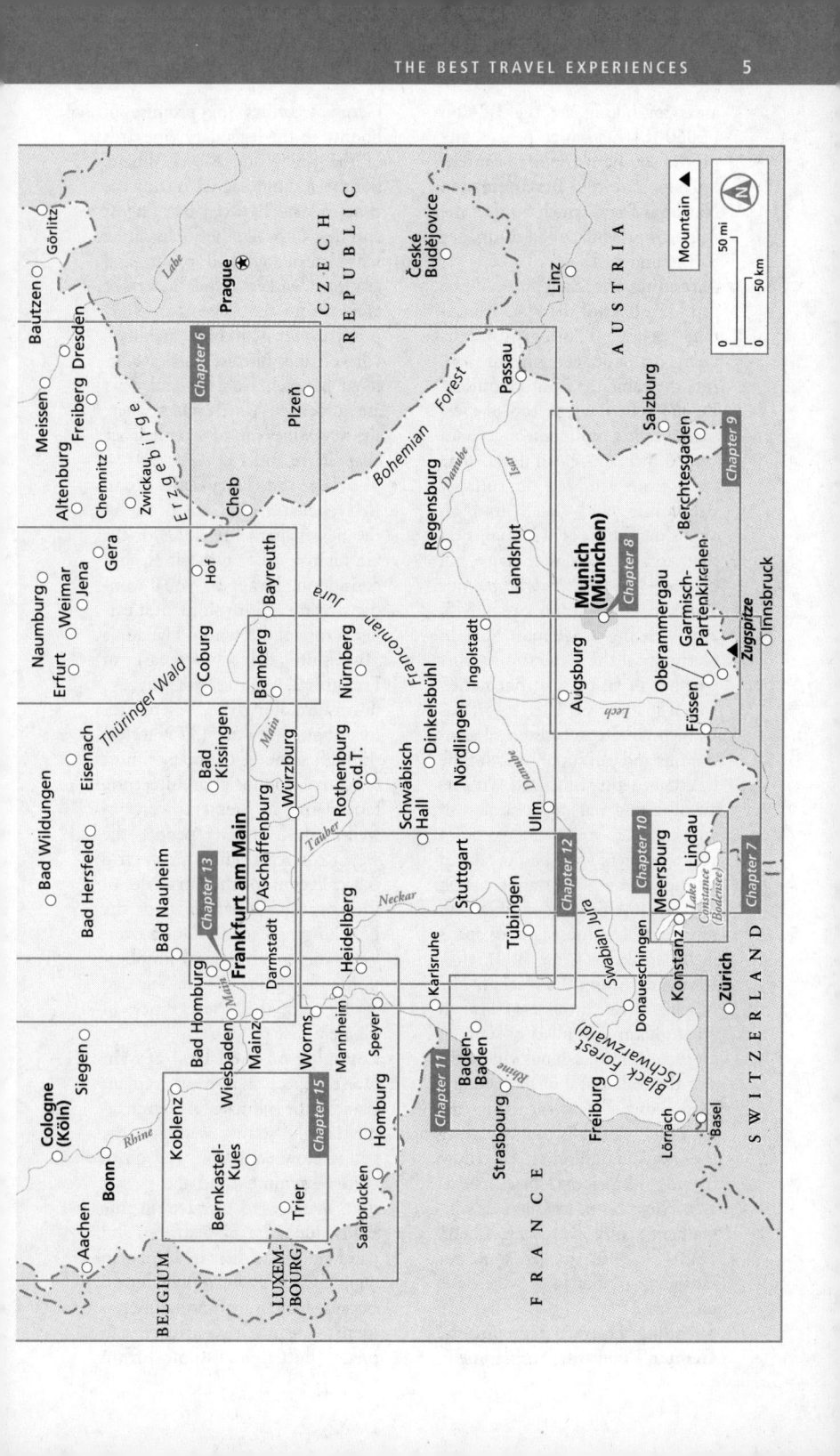
Görlitz
Bautzen
Meissen
Freiberg
Dresden
Altenburg
Chemnitz
Zwickau
Erzgebirge
Elbe
Prague
CZECH REPUBLIC
České Budějovice
Linz
AUSTRIA
Mountain
0 50 mi
0 50 km
N
Chapter 6
Cheb
Plzeň
Bohemian Forest
Passau
Salzburg
Naumburg
Erfurt
Weimar
Jena
Gera
Hof
Bayreuth
Coburg
Thüringer Wald
Jura
Franconian
Regensburg
Danube
Isar
Landshut
Munich (München)
Chapter 8
Berchtesgaden
Chapter 9
Garmisch-Partenkirchen
Oberammergau
Zugspitze
Innsbruck
Augsburg
Lech
Füssen
Bamberg
Nürnberg
Ingolstadt
Bad Kissingen
Main
Würzburg
Bad Wildungen
Eisenach
Bad Hersfeld
Bad Nauheim
Chapter 13
Frankfurt am Main
Aschaffenburg
Rothenburg o.d.T.
Tauber
Schwäbisch Hall
Dinkelsbühl
Nördlingen
Ulm
Stuttgart
Neckar
Chapter 12
Tübingen
Chapter 10
Meersburg
Lindau
Lake Constance (Bodensee)
Chapter 7
Konstanz
Zürich
Swabian Jura
Donaueschingen
Black Forest (Schwarzwald)
Freiburg
Lörrach
Basel
SWITZERLAND
Bad Homburg
Wiesbaden
Mainz
Darmstadt
Heidelberg
Worms
Mannheim
Speyer
Karlsruhe
Baden-Baden
Rhine
Strasbourg
Homburg
Saarbrücken
Chapter 11
FRANCE
Cologne (Köln)
Siegen
Bonn
Koblenz
Bernkastel-Kues
Trier
Chapter 15
Aachen
BELGIUM
LUXEMBOURG

areas for hiking are the 1,240m (4,060-ft.) **Eckbauer** peak, lying on the southern fringe of Partenkirchen and the **Berchtesgaden National Park,** which borders the Austrian province of Salzburg. See p. 324 and 344.

- **Ascending the Zugspitze:** If the gentle inclines of the Harz Mountains or the Thuringian forests aren't dramatic enough for you, ride the cable car from Garmisch-Partenkirchen to the top of Germany's tallest mountain at 2,963m (9,720 ft.) above sea level. The view from the top is suitably panoramic, and you'll find an appealing aura of German-ness that comes from the many hill climbers and trekkers who fan out across the hiking trails. See p. 345.
- **Experiencing a German Spa:** In Germany, the question isn't whether to visit a spa, but rather, which spa to visit? Each resort has its own virtues and historical associations and can supply a list of the health benefits associated with its awful-tasting waters. Regardless of your choice, you'll emerge from your treatment with a more relaxed attitude and a greater appreciation of German efficiency and German sensuality. The most famous spa is in Baden-Baden (see p. 400).
- **Motoring Along the Neckar:** The Neckar River meanders through about 80km (50 miles) of some of Germany's most famous vineyards. But the real appeal of the winding road along the water is in the medieval castles scattered along the way. Highlights en route include Heidelberg, Neckarsteinach, Hirschhorn, Eberbach, Zwingenberg, and Burg Hornberg. Don't forget to stop en route for samplings of the local wines. See chapter 12.
- **Spending Harvest Time in the German Vineyards:** Springtime in Germany brings the promise of bounty to the legendary vineyards of the Rhine and Mosel Valleys, but the autumn harvest is truly the time to visit. Between late August and mid-October, the banks of the rivers turn gold and russet, and armies of workers gather buckets of grapes from the rows of carefully pruned vines. Most of the medieval villages and historic castles scattered between Koblenz and Trier are associated with estates where the new wines can be sampled. See chapters 14 and 15.
- **Touring the Fairy-Tale Road (Märchenstrasse):** This is one of the newer marketing ideas of the German tourist authorities, but considering its appeal, you'll wonder why they didn't think of it earlier. From the town of Hanau (a 30-minute drive northeast of Frankfurt), the route zigzags northward along the Weser River for about 600km (375 miles) through some of Germany's most evocative folkloric architecture, terminating in Bremen. Scores of well-marked detours pepper the way. Required reading for the trip is a collection of the fairy tales of the Brothers Grimm and the Nibelungen legends. Don't overlook the psychological implications of Goldilocks, the Big Bad Wolf, and the Pied Piper of Hameln. See p. 580.
- **Lounging on the Island of Sylt:** Don't expect a lush or verdant island—the climate is temperamental, the setting is savage, the winds blow cold from the north even in summer, and the grasses that manage to survive in the sandy dunes are as weathered and sturdy as the soldiers in a Prussian regiment. Why is it wonderful? Because here, the no-nonsense residents of north Germany can preen, flutter, and show off to

each other, far from the strictures of their workplaces and the hardworking grind of their everyday lives. See p. 628.

## 2 The Best Museums

Financial prosperity, artistic flair, and academic curiosity have helped the Germans develop some of the finest museums anywhere.

- **Gemäldegalerie,** Berlin: This is one of Europe's leading art museums, with a celebrated collection of works from the 13th to the 18th centuries. The cavalcade of major European masters ranges from Botticelli and Breughel to Vermeer and Velásquez. Divided during the Cold War, since mid-1998 the collection has been reunited in one home. These days, the lighting and the displays are better than ever. See p. 110.
- **Pergamon Museum,** Berlin: Built in 1930 on an island in the Spree, this museum contains entirely reconstructed temples from ancient Assyria, Greece, Rome, and Sumer. And don't miss the sprawling exhibitions devoted to the ancient art of the Islamic world and the Far East either. See p. 109.
- **Zwinger,** Dresden: A vast rectangular esplanade flanked with pavilions, heroic statues, formal gardens, and galleries, this museum was designed for Augustus the Strong (Elector of Saxony and King of Poland) by his favorite architect, Pöppelmann (1662–1736). The destruction of the Zwinger (in the final days of World War II), one of Dresden's most beautiful buildings, was a great loss, though its postwar reconstruction was a triumph for the East German government. Among the treasures amassed inside are paintings, 18th-century Dresden porcelain, and an ornamental collection of antique weapons. See p. 182.
- **Deutsches Museum,** Munich: Since 1925, this museum has been one of the most important showcases of science and technology in the world. Occupying an island in the Isar River, it features many hands-on as well as historical exhibits. See p. 299.
- **Alte Pinakothek,** Munich: This massive and symmetrical building is one of the most visible in Munich, with a wraparound garden where urbanites like to walk during lunch hour. Inside is a staggering assortment of important paintings from every era, scattered over two sprawling floors of dignified splendor. See p. 298.
- **Dachau Concentration Camp Memorial Site,** Dachau, near Munich: Heinrich Himmler first organized Dachau as a concentration camp for enemies of the Reich in 1933. An escaped inmate, Joseph Rovan, described it as "implacable, perverted, an organization that was totally murderous, a marvelous machine for the debasement and dehumanizing of man." Today, it's one of the most poignant museums in the world. See p. 323.
- **Stadtische Galerie im Lenbachhaus,** Munich: Housed in the former villa of portrait painter Franz von Lenbach, this museum has a stunning and internationally renowned collection of modern art, including the Blaue Reiter ("Blue Rider") period, best represented by Kandinsky. It also has a rich collection of Gothic art works as well. See p. 305.
- **Gutenberg Museum,** Mainz: This museum is one of the most comprehensive tributes to printing and

publishing anywhere in the world. The bulky presses on which Johannes Gutenberg used movable type (42 lines per page) and two of the earliest Bibles ever printed are the primary displays here. There's also a historical rundown on the science and technologies that have dominated the printing industry ever since. See p. 485.

- **Museum Ludwig,** Cologne: This is the new home of one of the world's largest collections of the works of Pablo Picasso, equaled only by the Picasso museums of Barcelona and Paris. The museum's collection was beefed up when Irene Ludwig, widow of the late German art patron, Peter Ludwig, donated 774 works of Picasso's to the museum. See p. 511 for more details.
- **Wallraf-Richartz Museum/ Foundation Corboud,** Cologne: The oldest museum in Cologne presents one of Germany's grandest collections of art, from the 14th to the 19th centuries. The collection of gothic works alone is one of the finest in Europe, and the galleries are a virtual encyclopedia of art, from Flemish old masters to the French impressionists. See p. 512 for details.
- **Kunsthalle,** Hamburg: The leading art museum in Northern Germany, the Kunsthalle is one of the most important in Europe, with some 3,000 paintings in its treasure trove of art, along with some 400 sculptures. Some of its rare treasures date from the 14th century, including works by Bertram, the leading German master of the time. One section of the gallery also displays modern works, including art by such artists as Andy Warhol, Joseph Beuys, and Picasso. See p. 601.

## 3 The Best Castles & Palaces

During the Middle Ages, Germany was divided into many intensely competitive feudal states and principalities. This unstable atmosphere encouraged the construction of fortified castles. As hostilities died down, architects began to design for comfort, style, and prestige, adding large windows, gilded stucco and plaster, frescoes, and formal gardens. As a result, Germany is full of all kinds and styles of castles (*burg*) and palaces (*schloss*).

- **Sans Souci Palace,** Potsdam: Frederick the Great's retreat, where he came to read, listen to music, and generally renew his allegiance to the principles of the Enlightenment, is Germany's most successful blend of landscape and architecture. The more than 120ha (300 acres) of intricately landscaped gardens have enough pavilions, fountains, orangeries, and heroic statues to keep a visitor intrigued for days. The palace itself is an architectural highlight, approached by a terraced staircase of sublime beauty. See p. 147.
- **Schloss Wartburg,** Eisenach: Built between 1067 and the 16th century, this was the headquarters of the Landgraves of Thuringia, a center of patronage for the troubadours (*Minnesinger*) of Germany, and a place of refuge for Martin Luther, who completed his translation of the Bible within its massive walls. Wagner used it as inspiration for the setting of *Tannhäuser,* and Johann Sebastian Bach and Goethe both visited. Today, from its position on a rocky hilltop, it's a regional museum. See p. 164.
- **Residenz,** Würzburg: Built between 1720 and 1744 as the official residence of the powerful bishops of Würzburg, this is one of the most massive baroque

palaces in Germany. It combines a chapel (*Hofkirche*) with gardens, a gallery of paintings, frescoes by Tiepolo, and enough decoration to satisfy the most demanding taste for ornamentation. Also within its showrooms are a worthy collection of ancient Greek and Roman artifacts and valuable paintings from the 14th to the 19th century. See p. 234.

- **Neuschwanstein,** near Füssen: When the creators of California's Disneyland needed an inspiration for their fairy-tale castle, this is the model they picked. Neuschwanstein is the most lavishly romantic (and impractical) castle in the German-speaking world. A 19th-century theatrical set designer drew it up in a neofeudal style. The man who ordered its construction was (who else?) "Mad" King Ludwig II of Bavaria. See p. 265.
- **Hohenschwangau Castle,** near Füssen: It was completed in 1836 and built on the ruins of a 12th-century fortress. Its patron was the youthful prince regent, Maximilian II of Bavaria, who used it to indulge his taste for "troubadour romanticism" and the life of the English country manor. See p. 263.
- **Schloss Nymphenburg,** Munich: It was originally conceived and constructed between 1664 and 1674 as an Italian-inspired summer home for the Bavarian monarchs. Subsequent Bavarian kings added on to its structure until around 1780, by which time the building and its lavish park bore a close resemblance to the French palace at Versailles. A highlight of the interior is the green, gold, and white banqueting hall, whose frescoes and ornate stucco are among the most memorable in Bavaria. See p. 302.
- **Schloss Linderhof,** near Oberammergau: This palace was built in the 1870s as a teenage indulgence by Ludwig II. Its architects created a whimsically eclectic fantasy, inspired by Italian baroque architecture. In the surrounding park, Moorish pavilions and Mediterranean cascades appear against alpine vistas in combinations that are as startling as they are charming. See p. 354.
- **Altes Schloss,** Meersburg: Legend has it that this castle's cornerstone was laid by Dagobert, king of the Franks, in 628. The castle remained a Catholic stronghold even during the Protestant Reformation, housing bishops who appreciated its 3m- (10-ft.-) thick walls as a bulwark against the rising tempest around them. In the early 1800s, its owners threatened to tear the castle down, until a German Romantic, Baron Joseph von Lassberg, bought it and transformed it into a refuge for writers, poets, and painters. Although still mostly a private residence, many parts can be visited. See p. 366.
- **Heidelberg Castle,** Heidelberg: This castle originated as a Gothic-Renaissance masterpiece in the 1500s and was massively expanded as rival rulers competed for control of the Rhineland. After the French sacked and burned the town and the castle in 1689, it never regained its original glory. Today, the ruins brood in dignified severity from a position on a rocky hilltop high above the student revelry and taverns of the folkloric city below. See p. 410.
- **Burg Eltz,** Moselkern, near Cochem: Its multiple turrets and towers, which rise amid a thick forest near the Mosel River, evoke the chivalry and poetry of the Middle Ages. This is one of the best-preserved medieval castles in Germany. See p. 535.

## 4 The Best Cathedrals

- **Ulm Münster,** Ulm: The 161m (536-ft.) spire of this cathedral is the tallest in the world. Although its foundations were laid in 1377, this skyscraper wasn't completed vertically until 1890. See p. 227.
- **Kaiserdom (Imperial Cathedral),** Speyer: Partly because of their age, Romanesque churches are the most impressive symbols of early medieval Germany. This massive church, dating from 1030, has four bell towers, a cornerstone laid by one of Germany's earliest kings, Konrad II, and an undeniable sense of the (anonymous) architect's aesthetic links with the traditions of ancient Rome. See p. 204.
- **Dom St. Peter,** Worms: This church is a grand example of High Romanesque style; its oldest section dating from 1132. The Diet of Worms, held here in 1521, condemned the beliefs of the young Martin Luther and banished him to the far boundaries of the Holy Roman Empire. See p. 480.
- **Cologne Cathedral,** Cologne: Based on French Gothic models in Paris and Amiens, this cathedral was envisioned as one of the largest religious buildings in Christendom. It required 600 years to finish—work stopped for approximately 300 years (1560–1842), until the neo-Gothic fervor of the romantic age drove it to completion. In 1880, it was inaugurated with appropriate pomp and circumstance in the presence of the German kaiser. Today, its vast russet-colored bulk towers above the city, instantly recognizable from miles away. See p. 510.
- **Cathedral (Dom),** Aachen: Its size and the stonework dating from 1414 are deeply impressive, but even more so is the cathedral's association with the earliest of the German emperors, Charlemagne. He was crowned in an older building on this site in A.D. 800. The cathedral's treasury contains gem-encrusted Christian artifacts from the 10th century whose heft and barbaric glitter evoke pre-Christian Germania. See p. 504.

## 5 The Most Charming Small Villages

- **Quedlinburg:** Spared in part from the ravages of World War II, this Harz town still evokes the Middle Ages with its 1,600 half-timbered buildings, more than any other town in the country. Named a UNESCO World Heritage Site, Quedlinburg is a gem of yesterday and was an imperial residence for 2 centuries. Wander the cobblestone streets of the Altstadt (old town) for a journey back in time. See p. 175.
- **Meissen:** Some 26km (16 miles) north of Dresden, this is a romantic little town built along the banks of the River Elbe. It's celebrated for its porcelain, which carries a trademark of two crossed blue swords and is valued by collectors the world over. Even without its porcelain factory, the town merits a visit for its quiet charm, its old buildings, and its 15th-century castle. See p. 193.
- **Rothenburg**: If you have time for only one stop along the Romantic Road, make it Rothenburg ob der Tauber, which may be your only chance in life to see a still intact medieval walled city, on the Tauber River. Rothenburg exists

in a time capsule, even though in World War II, 40% of the town was destroyed. Luckily for you, locals quickly rebuilt their Altstadt in its former style to reclaim their glorious architectural past. If you have time for a second stop along the Romantic Road, try **Dinkelsbühl,** which is not as grand as the more celebrated Rothenburg, but because of this, it has far fewer tourists and therefore it manages to retain more old-time charm. See p. 244 and 251.

- **Mittenwald:** This town has long been celebrated as the most beautiful in the Bavarian Alps. Its magnificently decorated houses have painted facades and ornately carved gables. In the mid-17th century, it was known as "The Village of a Thousand Violins" because of the stringed instruments made here. See p. 341.
- **Lindau:** Dating from the 19th century, this former free imperial town of the Holy Roman Empire is like a fantasy of what a charming Bavarian lakeside village should look like, even if only in the movies. But this garden "city," under landmark protection, is for real. Lindau is enveloped by aquamarine waters, and one part of it is known as the "Gartenstadt," because of its luxuriant flowers and shrubs. See p. 356.
- **Rüdesheim:** The Rhine Valley's most popular wine town is set along the edge of the mighty river. Rüdesheim is known for its half-timbered buildings and its Drosselgasse, or "Thrush Lane," a narrow cobblestone lane stretching for 182m (200 yds.) and lined with wine taverns and cozy restaurants. See p. 489.
- **Cochem:** If you're seeking an idyllic medieval riverside town during your "grape tour" of the Mosel River valley, make it Cochem, famous for its towering castle, dating from 1027. On the left bank of the Mosel, Cochem lies in a picture-postcard setting of vineyards. Little inns serving a regional cuisine along with plenty of Mosel wine make Cochem highly desireable as an overnight stopover, and an alternative choice to the more commercial centers found along the nearby Rhine. See p. 532.

## 6 The Best Driving Tours

The appeal of the open road is a prominent part of German culture. Some of the best drives include:

- **The Romantic Road:** This well-traveled route, which stretches between the Main River and the beginning of the Bavarian Alps, is dotted with lovely medieval towns. See chapter 7.
- **Alpine Road (Deutsche Alpenstrasse):** Follow this road for more than 480km (300 miles) through the foothills of the Bavarian Alps. Scenic majesty and architectural charm combine for an unforgettable experience. See p. 326.
- **Upper Black Forest:** Fairy tales always seem to be more believable when you're in the Black Forest, and the twisting secondary roads that connect Freiburg with Lake Titisee pass through lots of charming scenery and architecture. See p. 383.
- **Mosel Valley:** The road along this Rhine tributary passes by some of the country's most famous vineyards. And, at least a half dozen of the cities en route are worth visiting. See chapter 15.

## 7 The Best Walks

- **The Royal Castle Walk:** For one of the grandest panoramas in all of the Alps (in any country), hike up to the Marienbrücke, the bridge that spans the Pöllat Gorge behind Neuschwanstein Castle. From there, if you're up to it, you can continue uphill for about an hour for an amazing view of "Mad" King Ludwig's fantasy castle. See p. 263.
- **Partnachklamm:** One of the most dramatic walks in all of the Bavarian Alps starts from the great winter sports resort of Garmisch-Partenkirchen. A signposted trail leads to the dramatic Partnachklamm Gorge. Carved from solid rock, the route passes two panoramic bottlenecks amid the thunder of falling water and clouds of spray. See p. 346.
- **Mainau Island:** A walk across the footbridge to Mainau, in Lake Constance, is like a visit to a tropical country. Mainau is filled with exotic plants collected by the Baden princes and members of the Royal House of Sweden. Tropical brushwood and other botanical wonders still thrive in this mild climate. You'll hardly believe you're in Germany. See p. 369.
- **Cochem:** The Reichsburg Castle, which towers over the little town of Cochem, can be reached on foot in about 15 minutes from the town's Markplatz, or market square. Although hardly an alpine climb, this walk is one of the most rewarding you'll find in Germany, with panoramas in all directions. See p. 532.

## 8 The Best Biking

- **Munich by Bike:** So many locals can be spotted riding bikes that Munich at first appears to be the biking capital of Germany. If you'd like to join in the fun, pick up a copy of the pamphlet *Rad-Touren für unsere Gäste* (available at the tourist office), which outlines itineraries for touring Munich by bike. See chapter 8.
- **Lake Constance:** Rent a bike at the train station in the former imperial town of Lindau and set out in any direction to enjoy the views of this beautiful lake. The Lindau tourist office will provide you with a map and suggestions for the best routes to follow. See chapter 10.
- **The Neckar Valley Cycle Path:** This signposted path allows you to follow the source of the Neckar, beginning in Villingen-Schwenningen and going all the way to the confluence of the Rhine at Mannheim. Instead of going the whole way, many visitors prefer to pick up a bicycle in Heidelberg and cycle along the riverbanks until they find a good spot for a picnic. See p. 410.
- **Lüneburg Heath:** This wild heath in northern Germany is one of the country's major natural attractions. (Some of Germany's greatest poets have waxed rhapsodic about this shrub-covered land.) Rent a bike and pick up a map at the Lüneburg tourist office and set out on your adventure. See p. 559.

## 9 The Best Spas

- **Bad Reichenhall:** Many spa lovers head for this remote corner of Bavaria to "take the waters." Europe's largest saline source was first tapped here in pre-Christian times. There's a definite 19th-century aura to the place. And though some of the hotels in the town are better than others, all have equal access to the spa and lie about a 5-minute walk from it. See chapter 9.

- **Baden-Baden:** There's no better spa in all of Germany, and certainly none more fashionable or famous. Baden-Baden is also the site of the country's most celebrated casino. The spa's been going strong ever since the leisure class of the 19th century discovered its healing waters, although the Roman legions of the emperor Caracalla had discovered the springs here long before that. As at Bad Reichenhall, all hotels, no matter what their price range, have equal access to the spa. See chapter 11.
- **Wiesbaden:** One of Germany's oldest cities, Wiesbaden attracted Roman legions to its hot springs and continues to lure today's fashionable traveler as well. It's not as chic as Baden-Baden, but Wiesbaden still has one of Germany's most elegant casinos and concert halls, along with two gourmet restaurants. In summer the beer garden at the Kurhaus is one of the most animated along the Rhine. See chapter 13.
- **Bad Homburg:** Bad Homburg lies at the foot of the Taunus Hills in a setting of medieval castles and luxuriant forests. There are more than 31 fountains in the town's Kurpark. The Bad Homburg Palace was once the summer residence of Prussian kings. See chapter 13.
- **Bad Nauheim:** What do Elvis Presley and William Randolph Hearst have in common? Both stayed at Bad Neuheim—the newspaper czar by choice, and Elvis by orders of the U.S. Army. The warm carbonic-acid springs are used in the treatment of heart and circulatory ailments and rheumatic diseases. See chapter 13.

## 10 The Best Luxury Hotels

German efficiency and cleanliness are legendary around the world, so it's not surprising that you can choose from a staggering number of well-managed hotels.

- **Grand Hotel Esplanade,** Berlin (✆ **030/25-47-80**): This strikingly contemporary hotel near several foreign embassies is one of the most prestigious and best in the German capital. With its collection of modern art, its spacious, cheerfully decorated rooms, and its first-class service, it is a prime address for the luxury-minded. See p. 77.
- **Four Seasons,** Berlin (✆ **800/332-3442** in the U.S., or 030/2-03-38): One of Germany's great luxury hotels, the Four Seasons is all about opulence, superb service, and comfort. It's discreet, tasteful, reliable, and a brilliant addition to the roster of luxury leaders in Germany's capital. See p. 86.
- **Hotel Elephant, Weimar** (✆ **03643/80-20**): This is one of Germany's most interesting hotels because of its age (over 300 years), its name, its 50-year survival in Germany's eastern zone, and its associations with such luminaries as Schiller, Liszt, and Goethe. Today, it's a cost-conscious treasure chest of German history. See p. 159.
- **Eisenhut,** Rothenburg ob der Tauber (✆ **09861/70-50**): This hotel's 16th-century walls and valuable collection of antiques enhance the appeal of the most authentic Renaissance town in Germany. See p. 248.
- **Kempinski Hotel Vier Jahreszeiten München,** Munich (✆**800/ 426-3135** in the U.S., or

089/2-12-50): Munich's most prestigious choice offers elegance and luxury. The wealthy and titled have checked in here for more than a century, enjoying the ambience, the antiques, the style, and the grace. See p. 278.

- **Bayerischer Hof & Palais Montgelas,** Munich (✆ **800/223-6800** in the U.S., or 089/2-12-00): This deluxe hotel and a 17th-century Bavarian palace are molded together to form Munich's version of the Waldorf-Astoria in New York. This is the only hotel in Munich to provide serious competition for the front-ranking Kempinski Hotel. See p. 275.
- **Der Kleine Prinz,** Baden-Baden (✆ **07221/34-66-00**): This hotel's director once helped manage the New York Hilton and the Waldorf-Astoria. Today, he and his wife run a century-old pair of neobaroque houses in the heart of Germany's most elegant resort, Baden-Baden. Der Kleine Prinz is among the most romantic of Germany's many Romantik Hotels. See p. 403.
- **Krone Assmannshausen,** Rüdesheim-Assmannshausen (✆ **06722/40-30**): Sprawling along the banks of the Rhine in an oversize, grange-like, gingerbread-laden fantasy, this hotel has witnessed the arrival of many important Germans (including Goethe) in its 400-year history. It also contains one of the best traditional restaurants in town. See p. 491.
- **Park Hotel Bremen,** Bremen (✆ **0421/3-40-80**): Designed like an aristocratic manor house, this hotel lies within a 200ha (500-acre) city park. With infusions of grand bourgeois grace and impeccable service, it embodies the carefully maintained elegance of this North German trading port. See p. 553.
- **Fürstenhof Celle,** Celle (✆ **05141/20-10**): This 17th-century manor, enlarged with half-timbered wings, stands out even in a town legendary for its medieval and Renaissance buildings. There's a cozy bar in the medieval cellar and one of the best dining rooms in Lower Saxony. See p. 561.
- **Vier Jahreszeiten,** Hamburg (✆ **800/223-6800** in the U.S. and Canada, or 040/3-49-40): Its dignified interior is as opulent as its 19th-century facade. This hotel's appeal is correctly aristocratic, but it still has a touch of the saltwater zestiness that has made Hamburg a great city. See p. 592.

## 11 The Best Small Inns & Hotels

- **Sorat Art'otel,** Berlin (✆ **030/88-44-70**): This hotel in the heart of Berlin is chic, discreet, and unique. The swirling action of the Ku'damm lies right outside the door, but inside, the decor is soothing and serene, the work of some of the continent's top designers. See p. 84.
- **Altstadt-Hotel Laubenwirt,** Passau (✆ **0851/33-70**): This inexpensive hotel stands at the convergence of three rivers—the Danube, the Ilz, and the Inn. But the hotel offers more than river views—it's comfortably and traditionally furnished, and its regional cuisine and convivial pub attract the locals. See p. 225.
- **Parkhotel Atlantic,** Heidelberg (✆ **06221/60-42-0**): This 24-room inn is on the wooded outskirts of Heidelberg, near the famous castle. Comfort and convenience are found in every room, and in the afternoon you can go

for long walks along the woodland trails surrounding the property. See p. 415.

- **Admiral Hotel,** Wiesbaden (✆ **0611/5-86-60**): A hotel of considerable charm (rooms are appealingly old-fashioned), the Admiral offers the best value in this trendy spa resort outside Frankfurt. See p. 467.
- **Gästehaus Englischer Garten,** Munich (✆ **089/383-94-10**): This is an oasis of charm and tranquility, close to the English Garden where buffed Munich lies out nude in the sun. The furnishings are in an old-fashioned Bavarian style, but the comfort is first-rate. See p. 282.
- **Antik-Hotel Bristol,** Cologne (✆ **0221/12-01-95**): In the heart of this cathedral city along the Rhine, this hotel is unique as it's filled with antiques, both country-rustic and town-house elegant, making the atmosphere both authentic and inviting. See p. 515.
- **Hanseatic Hotel,** Hamburg (✆ **040/48-57-72**): This little hotel evokes a prim and proper English gentleman's club. Rooms are one of a kind, often containing antiques. In summer, the owner can be spotted out front tending his flower garden, getting ready to welcome you. See p. 595.

## 12 The Best Restaurants

- **Rockendorf's Gourmet Restaurant,** Berlin (✆ **030/21-99-21-70**): During the latter days of the Cold War, this restaurant was often photographed as a symbol of the "good life" available within West Berlin. Since reunification, it has moved, but it is still elegant and refined, offering creative cuisine to a clientele that includes the most important movers and shakers in Germany. See p. 92.
- **Essigbrätlein,** Nürnberg (✆ **0911/22-51-31**): Food critics single this out as the best dining spot in Nürnberg, and we concur heartily. Its upscale Franconian and Continental cuisine is reason enough to go to the city in the first place. See p. 215.
- **Weinhaus Zum Stachel,** Würzburg (✆ **0931/5-27-70**): This is the oldest (ca. 1413) wine house in a town loaded with them. Food is good, portions are copious, the wine flows, and everyone has a wonderful time. This is old-time Deutschland at its most appealing. See p. 237
- **Tantris,** Munich (✆ **089/36-19-59-0**): Savvy German food critics have honored Tantris's Hans Haas as the country's top chef. He definitely serves some of the finest and most innovative food in Bavaria. See p. 292.
- **Seehotel Siber,** Constance (✆ **07531/6-30-44**): Bertold Siber remains one of the leading chefs of Germany, certainly without peer along the northern tier of Lake Constance. Both the service and the cuisine here exhibit amazing attention to detail. See p. 371.
- **Hanse Stube,** Cologne (✆ **0221/27-01**): Located in a landmark hotel, this restaurant lies on the same square as the fabled Rhineland cathedral. French cuisine in Cologne doesn't get any better in the city than it does here—the chefs reflect a prodigious talent in preparing a cuisine based only on the finest and freshest ingredients. See p. 516.
- **Victorian Restaurant,** Düsseldorf (✆ **0211/8-65-50-22**): Regulars know what a treasure they have in

this restaurant: Market-fresh ingredients and a steady hand in the kitchen produce award-winning traditional and modern food. See p. 528.

- **Waldhotel Sonnora**, outside Bernkastel-Kues (✆ **06578/9-82-20**): In the Mosel Valley, the Waldhotel Sonnora is one of the most justifiably acclaimed restaurants in the country. Be sure to make a reservation as far in advance as possible, and prepare yourself for a gastronomic adventure in continental cuisine. Herr Thieltges, the chef, told us, "We don't just serve dishes—rather, culinary masterpieces." And we agree. See p. 539.
- **Fischereihafen Restaurant,** Altona, near Hamburg (✆ **040/38-18-16**): Patrons from Tina Turner to Helmut Kohl have pronounced the food here delightful. From a window seat, you can overlook the boats that might have hauled in your sole, eel, turbot, herring, or flounder from the seas that very day. See p. 597.

## 13 The Best Beer Halls & Taverns

- **Auerbachs Keller,** Leipzig (✆ **0341/21-61-00**): The most famous tavern in eastern Germany, this is where Goethe staged the debate between Faust and Mephistopheles. The tavern dates from 1530 and has a series of murals evoking the Faust legend. See p. 172.
- **Hofbräuhaus am Platzl,** Munich (✆ **089/22-16-76**): The Hofbräuhaus is the world's most famous beer hall and can accommodate some 4,500 beer drinkers on any given night. Music from live bands and huge mugs of beer served at wooden tables combine to produce the best of Bavarian nighttime fun. See p. 318.
- **Zum Roten Ochsen,** Heidelberg (✆ **06221/2-09-77**): Over the years, "The Red Ox" has drawn beer drinkers from Mark Twain to Bismarck. Students have been getting plastered here since 1703, and the tradition continues just as strong as ever. See p. 517.
- **Ratskeller,** Göttingen (✆ **0551/5-64-33**): The beer in the town of Göttingen flows freely in many taverns, but this place is the most reliable (and it has good food, too). This 600-year-old spot lies in the cellar of the historic town hall and has served customers such as Otto von Bismarck and the Brothers Grimm. See p. 577.
- **Bayrisch Zell,** Hamburg (✆ **040/31-42-81**): It doesn't quite have the charm of the fabled Hofbräuhaus in Munich, but after all, this is northern Germany. The bustling place seats 1,200, and on many nights there seems to be a lot more people here. It's one of the safe places in the notorious St. Pauli district. See p. 613.

## 14 The Best Shopping

The best way to approach shopping here is to make it a part of your overall experience and not an end unto itself. Though Berlin and Munich are the major shopping centers in Germany, the rest of the country is OK—neither a shopper's mecca nor the bargain basement of Europe. Still, you can find some good buys here, such as:

- **Porcelain:** For centuries, Germany has been known for the quality of its porcelain. Names such as KPM, Rosenthal, and Meissen are household words.

KPM, for example, has been a Berlin tradition for more than 2 centuries. See shopping sections of various chapters.

- **Toys:** Nürnberg, the country's toy center, produces some of the most imaginative playthings in the world. See section 3, "Nürnberg," of chapter 6.
- **Handcrafts:** In the Bavarian Alps, woodcarvers still carry on their time-honored tradition. The best place to purchase woodcarvings is in the alpine village of Oberammergau. See p. 352.
- **Timepieces:** Corny though they may be, carved Black Forest cuckoo clocks remain an enduring favorite. See chapter 11.
- **Cutlery:** WMF (Württembergische-Metalwaren-Fabrik) and J. A. Henckels are two of the country's premier producers of fine cutlery. Their knives are expensive, but longtime users say they last forever. Both WMF and Henckels stores are found all over Germany.
- **Optical Products:** German precision is best exemplified in its microscopes, binoculars, and other such precisely calibrated products, and the world marketplace has spoken with its purchasing power, seeking out optical products from Germany. Many consumers consider German eyecare equipment and lenses the best in the world, and German supremacy is often recognized at world trade fairs. Never resting on its laurels, German optical companies continue into the 21st century, with breakthroughs in design and equipment ranging from colored contact lenses to the most sophisticated ophthalmic laser equipment.

# 2

# A Traveler's Guide to German Art & Architecture

*By Reid Bramblett*

Germany's art ranges from medieval, carved wood statues to Dürer prints to expressionist paintings; its architecture from Gothic cathedrals and riotous baroque chapels to neoclassical temples and Bauhaus buildings. This overview should help you make sense of it all.

## 1 German Art 101

### ROMANESQUE (11TH–12TH CENTURIES)

Artistic expression in early medieval Germany was largely church-related. Because Mass was said in Latin, the illiterate masses had to learn Bible lessons via ***bas reliefs*** (sculpture that projects slightly from a flat surface) and **wall paintings,** which told key tales to inspire faith in God and fear of sin.

The best examples of this period include:

- **Sculpture.** Scraps of surviving Romanesque sculpture are the superb 11th-century, carved wood doors on **Cologne's St. Maria im Kapitol** (p. 512), **Augsburg's Dom St. Maria** (p. 256), and the intricate *The Shrine of the Magi* reliquary (1182–1220) in **Cologne Cathedral** (p. 510).
- **Wall paintings.** Rare examples survive in **Trier's Rheinisches Landesmuseum** (p. 543) and **Cologne's St. Maria Lyskirchen** (p. 512).

### GOTHIC (13TH–15TH CENTURIES)

Late medieval German art continued to be largely ecclesiastical, including **stained glass, church facades,** and massive **wooden altarpieces** festooned with **statues** and **carvings.** In Gothic **painting** and **sculpture,** figures tended to be more natural looking than in the Romanesque, but remained highly stylized, with features and rhythmic gestures exaggerated for symbolic or emotional emphasis.

The best examples and artists include:

- **Stained glass.** This art was refined in **Cologne's St. Gereon's Sacristy, Ulm Müster,** and **Rothenburg's St. Jakobskirche** (p. 512, 227, and 246 respectively).
- **Stephan Lochner** (active 1400–51). High Gothic painter of gold backgrounds and dainty figures, Lochner was the premier artist of the School of Cologne, where he painted the **Cologne Cathedral's** *Altar of the City Patrons* (ca. 1440) and the **Wallraf-Richartz Museum's** *Madonna in the Rose Garden* (1450). See p. 510 and 512 respectively.
- **Bamberger Reiter.** This anonymous equestrian statue in **Bamberg's Kaiserdom** is a masterpiece of 13th-century sculpture (p. 204).
- **Tilman Riemenschneider** (1460–1531). Germany's genius Gothic woodcarver of languid figures draped in flowing, folded robes, he was the first to

refrain from painting his sculptures. Some of his best works remain in **Würzburg,** including statues in the **Mainfränkisches Fortress** (p. 233) and three sandstone tombs in the **Dom St. Kilian** (p. 233). His masterpieces are the *Tomb of Henry II* (1499–1513) in **Bamberg's Kaiserdom** (p. 204) and the massive altarpiece in **Creglingen's Herrgottskirche** (p. 244).

## RENAISSANCE (LATE 15TH–16TH CENTURIES)

Renaissance means "rebirth," in this case of classical ideals. During this time, humanist thinkers rediscovered the wisdom of ancient Greece and Rome, while artists strove for greater naturalism, using newly developed techniques (such as linear perspective) to achieve new heights of realism.

Though Germany enjoyed a few towering Renaissance masters such as Dürer, most Protestant Reformation movements played down the role of art in worship—some of the stricter sects outright condemned it as idolatry. This left private patronage as the main revenue stream for artists, which resulted in lots of portraits, and some landscapes from those working in Vienna in the early 1500s, but precious little else.

The German Renaissance masters include:

- **Albrecht Dürer** (1471–1528). Genius painter, superb illustrator, and one of the greatest draughtsman ever, Dürer was the most important Renaissance artist outside Italy. While he was influenced by Giovanni Bellini and admired Leonardo da Vinci, his art remained distinct, matching the scientific and geometric precepts of the Florentine Renaissance with a command of color learned in Venice, a Flemish eye for meticulous detail, and the emotional sensibility of the German Gothic. He was the first to paint standalone self-portraits (including one in **Munich's Alte Pinakothek;** p. 298) as well as watercolors and gouaches for their own sake rather than merely as sketches. More paintings grace **Berlin's Gemäldegalerie** (p. 110) and the **Germanisches Nationalmuseum** (p. 211) in his native **Nürnberg.** Also see the box on p. 210.
- **Matthis Grünewald** (1470–1528). Grünewald was a retro foil to Dürer, adopting and adapting Renaissance techniques and compositions to pump up the emotional intensity of his paintings, but stamping the look firmly Gothic. You can see his paintings in **Munich's Alte Pinakothek** (p. 298) and **Stuppach's Church** (p. 242).
- **Lucas Cranach the Elder** (1472–1553). Cranach melded Renaissance sensibilities with a still somewhat primitive, medieval look, but was always on the forefront of artistic movements. As a young artist in Vienna, he helped popularize landscape painting as a member of the Danube School (*Rest on the Flight into Egypt* [1504] in **Berlin's Gemäldegalerie;** p. 110), and invented the full-length portrait (*Duke of Saxony* [1514] and *The Duchess* [1514] in **Dresden's Gemäldegalerie Alte Meister,** in the Zwinger complex; p. 182). A personal friend of Martin Luther's (*Portrait of Martin Luther* in **Nürnberg's Germanisches Nationalmuseum;** p. 211), Cranach also did the woodcuts for the first German translation of the New Testament.
- **Hans Holbein the Younger** (1497–1543). Second only to Dürer in the German Renaissance, and one of the greatest portraitists ever, Holbein actually spent most of his career in Basel and later as a court painter in London. Germany preserves precious little of his work, but you can see the *Portrait of Georg Gisze* (1532) in **Berlin's Gemäldegalerie** (p. 110) and a Nativity in the **Freiburg Cathedral** (p. 380).

## BAROQUE & ROCOCO (16TH–18TH CENTURIES)

The **baroque** is more theatrical and decorative than the Renaissance, mixing a kind of super-realism based on the use of peasant models and the exaggerated *chiaroscuro* ("light and dark") of Italy's Caravaggio with compositional complexity and explosions of dynamic fury, movement, color, and figures. **Rococo** is this later baroque art gone awry, frothy and chaotic. Most baroque and rococo art in Germany consists of stuccoes and frescoes decorating the fabulous churches and don't really stand alone as works of art in their own right.

Artists from this period include:

- **Andreas Schlüter** (1660–1714). He came back from Italy crazy about baroque and proceeded to make sculptures in the style, which can now be found at Berlin's **Schloss Charlottenburg** (p. 104).
- **Balthazar Permoser** (1651–1732). He studied in Salzburg and Florence before bringing the baroque style of Italy's Bernini back with him to **Dresden,** where as court sculptor he created the stone pulpit in the **Katholische Hofkirche** (p. 181) and sculptures adorning the **Zwinger** (p. 182).

## ROMANTIC (19TH CENTURY)

The Romantics felt that the classically minded Renaissance had gotten it wrong and the overly exuberant German baroque was way over the top. The Gothic Middle Ages became their inspiration, and with a surge of Teutonic nationalist pride, the Brothers Grimm collected folk tales, builders created fantasy castles, and artists set up easels in the forests and on mountaintops. The Romantics had a suspicion of progress and a deep respect for nature, human rights, and the nobility of peasantry. Their paintings tended to be heroic, historic, dramatic, and beautiful.

The best examples from this period include:

- **Adam Elsheimer** (1578–1610). Elsheimer created tiny paintings that bridged the gap from late Renaissance *Mannerism* (a style characterized by twisting figures in exaggerated positions), through baroque, to proto-Romantic. His friend Rubens admired him for knitting figurative painting and landscape together so convincingly. His *Flight into Egypt* (1609) resides in **Munich's Alte Pinakothek** (p. 298).
- **Caspar David Friedrich** (1774–1840). Greatest of the German Romantics, Friedrich specialized in majestic landscapes of closely examined detail but dramatically exaggerated proportions, often with pro-Protestant/anti-Catholic overtones. **Dresden's Gemäldegalerie Alte Meister** in the Zwinger complex (p. 182) houses his famous *Cross in the Mountains* (1808), though he also has works in **Hamburg's Kunsthalle** (p. 601), **Berlin's Schloss Charlottenburg** (p. 104), and **Munich's Neue Pinakothek** (p. 305).

## EARLY 20TH CENTURY

Until Hitler, Germany was one of Europe's hotbeds of artistic activity, a crucible of the modern that gave rise to several important movements whose influences echoed throughout international 20th-century art. But the Nazis outlawed and confiscated what they called "degenerate" modern art (partly because many of the artists, including the expressionists, were pointedly anti-Aryan).

Almost all the artists listed below are represented at **Cologne's Museum Ludwig** (p. 511), save Höch and Grosz, who you can find at **Berlin's Neue Nationalgalerie** (p. 110) alongside Schmidt-Rottluff, Nolde, Dix, and Beckmann. At least one artist from every movement is at **Stuttgart's Staatsgalerie**

(p. 425), and there are also good modern collections at **Düsseldorf's Kunstsammlung Nordrhein-Westfalen** (p. 525) and **Dresden's Albertinum** (p. 181). **Pinakothek der Moderne** is strong on expressionist artists.

The major artists and movements of the early 20th century include:

- **Expressionism.** Very broadly, expressionism describes art in Germany up through World War I (and beyond) that abandoned realism and embraced, to varying degrees, exaggeration, visible artistry (thick paint, obvious brushstrokes, and strong colors), and most importantly abstraction—all to try to "express" the emotions or philosophy of the artist himself. Pure expressionism fell into two main groups:
  - **Die Brücke,** founded in 1905 Dresden, turned its back on the modernizing 20th century and contemporary cubist and futurist movements and sought inspiration instead in folk art, medieval examples, and "unspoiled" landscapes. Its greatest members were **Ernst Kirchner** (1880–1938) and **Karl Schmidt-Rottluff** (1884–1976), though impressionist **Emil Nolde** (1867–1956) also later joined for a while. They have their own **Brücke Museum,** Bussardsteig 9 (✆ **030/831-2029;** www.bruecke-museum.de), in Berlin. (Due to construction, the Brücke Museum is temporarily closed. Call or check their website to see if they've reopened when you want to go.)
  - **Der Blaue Reiter group** was set up in Munich in 1911 by Russian-born **Wassily Kandinsky** (1866–1944), **Franz Marc** (1880–1916), and **August Macke** (1887–1914) to oppose the cultural insularity and antimodern stance of Die Brücke. These "Blue Riders" embraced international elements, modern abstraction techniques, spontaneity (a lot of their stuff looks almost child-like—an assessment they would love to hear), and bright, vibrant color schemes to seek an emotional, visceral intensity in their work.
- **Dadaism.** Dada is a nonsense word adopted by a bunch of disillusioned artists in Zürich in 1916, but the movement quickly spread to Germany. Dadaists were by turns abstract, nihilistic (inviting gallery visitors to help destroy the art), and just generally anti-art (many made random collages of found materials).

  Its proponents included **Hannah Höch** (1889–1978), who collaged photographs and magazine cut-outs to make social statements; **George Grosz** (1893–1959), who was more strictly a painter, and later moved on to the Neue Sachlichkeit movement (below); and **Kurt Schwitters** (1887–1948), who later started his own splinter group called "Merz" which experimented with abstract and Russian constructivist elements.

  Both **Max Ernst** (1891–1976) and Alsatian **Jean "Hans" Arp** (1887–1966) started as Blaue Reiter expressionists and, after their dada collage period, ended up in Paris as surrealists (Ernst as a painter, Arp as a sculptor and painter of amorphous shapes).
- **Neue Sachlichkeit (New Objectivity).** This 1920s Berlin movement opposed the elitism and abstraction of the expressionists with caricature-filled depictions of harsh colors and harsher subjects (sex, violence, and the plight of the urban worker). Proponents included **Otto Dix** (1891–1969), who started as an expressionist but quickly became one of the most scathing and disturbing New Objectivity painters; **George Grosz** (see "Dadaism" above); and **Max Beckmann** (1884–1950) who also was originally an expressionist.

## POST–WORLD WAR II ART

Germany hasn't had any one style or school to define its art since World War II, though terms such as *neo-expressionism* (an anti-abstract, antiminimalist, anti-conceptual trend that grounds itself more in tradition and figurative art) are often bandied about. There have been, however, several important artists. All three listed below are represented in **Stuttgart's Statsgallerie** (p. 425) and **Bonn's Kunstmuseum** (p. 497). In addition, **Munich's Pinakothek der Moderne** has a Kiefer, and **Cologne's Museum Ludwig** (p. 511) has Beuys (as does **Düsseldorf's Kunstsammlung Nordrhein-Westfalen;** p. 525) and Baselitz.

Notable Post–World War II artists include:

- **Josef Beuys** (1921–86). An iconoclast and nonconformist who made constructivist sculpture from trash, he helped form the fluxus group (which rejected the growing commercial gallery scene), and participated in "happenings" of performance art (once, memorably, strutting around the stage lecturing on art to a dead rabbit in his hand).
- **Anselm Kiefer** (born 1945). Ignoring the 20th-century tendency for abstraction and minimalism, Kiefer made a return to huge, mixed-media figurative art often with a strong historical bent—the bleak landscape (and bleak national feelings) of post–World War II Germany.
- **Georg Baselitz** (born 1938). Baselitz is a figurative painter—and a sculptor, since the 1980s—and important neo-expressionist with a penchant for portraying people upside down.

## 2 German Architecture 101

When considering a building's design, particularly for structures built before the 20th century, keep in mind that very few buildings were actually built in one style. A large, expensive structure—such as a church, usually the most significant building in any town—often took centuries to complete, during which time tastes would change and plans would be altered. While each architectural era has its own distinctive features, some elements, general floor plans, and terms are common to many, or may appear near the end of one era and continue through several later ones.

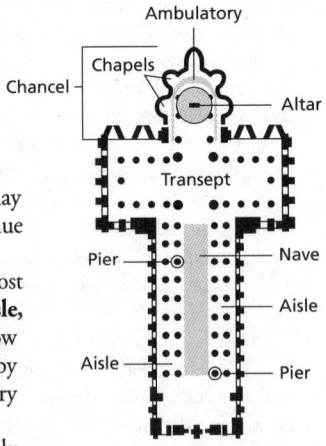

*Church Floor Plan*

From the Romanesque period on, most **churches** consist either of a single wide **aisle,** or a wide central **nave** flanked by two narrow aisles. The aisles are separated from the nave by a row of **columns,** or square stacks of masonry called **piers,** usually connected by **arches.**

This main nave/aisle assemblage is usually crossed by a perpendicular corridor called a **transept** near the far, east end of the church so that the floor plan looks like a **Latin cross** (shaped like a crucifix). The shorter, east arm of the nave is the holiest area, called the **chancel;** it often houses the stalls of the **choir** and the **altar.** If the far end of the chancel is rounded off, we call it an **apse.** An **ambulatory** is a curving corridor outside the altar and choir area, separating it from the ring of smaller chapels radiating off the chancel.

Some churches, especially after the Renaissance when mathematical proportion became important, were built on a **Greek cross** plan, each axis the same length like a giant +. By the baroque, funky shapes became popular, with churches built in the round or as ellipses, for example.

Very few buildings (especially churches) were built in only one particular style. Massive, expensive structures often took centuries to complete, during which time tastes would change and plans would be altered.

## ROMANESQUE (10TH–12TH CENTURIES)

Romanesque architects concentrated on building large churches with wide aisles to accommodate the masses. The Romanesque took its inspiration from ancient Rome (hence the name) where early Christians had adapted the *basilica* (ancient Roman law court buildings) to become churches.

### IDENTIFIABLE FEATURES

- **Rounded arches.** These load-bearing architectural devices allowed architects to open up wide naves and spaces, channeling all the weight of the stone walls and ceiling across the curve of the arch and down into the ground via the columns or *pilasters* (a shallow pier or rectangular column projecting only slightly from a wall).
- **Thick walls, infrequent and small windows, and huge piers.** These were necessary to support the weight of all that masonry, giving Romanesque churches a dark, somber, mysterious, and often oppressive feeling.
- **Tall towers on the facades.** Many Romanesque churches look a bit like fortresses with their squat, solid facade towers.
- **Dual chancels.** Several Romanesque churches have chancels at both the west and the east ends. The one on the west end is usually more ornate, having been built for the emperor and his court (a holdover from pre-Romanesque churches which often had a *Westwerk,* a tower on the west end where the imperial retinue could attend Mass without mixing with the masses).
- **Blind arcades.** A range of decorative arches carried on piers or columns and attached to a wall.
- **Dwarf gallery.** On the exterior (curving around the apse, decorating the facade, or running all along the walls—always up high), this is a line of small, open arches, like a tiny *loggia* (a room open on one or more sides).

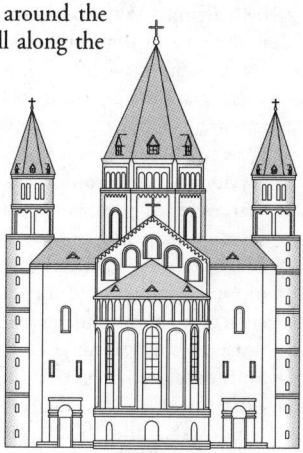

*Dom, Mainz*

### BEST EXAMPLES

- **Mainz's Dom.** Looking more like a castle fortress than a church, with two massive towers and four smaller ones, it sports chancels at both ends (p. 485).
- **Worms's Dom St. Peter.** Another fortress of God with a dual-chancel arrangement, it has two imposing facades sprouting rounded towers and dwarf galleries. Though the entrance is Gothic, the St. Anna chapel has Romanesque statues (p. 480).
- **Speyer's Kaiserdom.** The largest cathedral in Germany, this four-towered Romanesque basilica houses the largest and best Romanesque crypt in

Germany. Dwarf galleries and blind arcades ring the entire exterior. The nave's vaulting, however, was a first step toward the Gothic (p. 476).

## GOTHIC (13TH–16TH CENTURIES)

By the 12th century, engineering developments freed architects from constructing the heavy, thick walls of Romanesque structures. As a result, ceilings began to soar, walls to thin, and windows to proliferate.

Instead of dark, somber, relatively unadorned Romanesque interiors that forced the eyes of the faithful toward the altar, where the priest stood droning on in unintelligible Latin, the Gothic interior enticed the churchgoers' gaze upward to high ceilings filled with light. The priests still conducted Mass in Latin, but now peasants could "read" the Gothic comic books of stained-glass windows.

From the exterior, the squat and brooding Romanesque fortresses of God were replaced by graceful buttresses and soaring spires, which rose from town centers like beacons of religion.

German **Hallenkirche,** or "Hall Churches," spread from Westphalia throughout southern Germany. Their aisles and transept are about the same height as the nave, the whole ensemble almost as wide as it is tall, giving Hallenkirche an airy, boxy look.

### IDENTIFIABLE FEATURES

- **Pointed arches.** The most significant development of the Gothic era was the discovery that pointed arches could carry far more weight than rounded ones.
- **Cross vaults.** Instead of being flat, the square patch of ceiling between four columns arches up to a point in the center, creating four sail shapes, sort of like the underside of a pyramid. The X separating these four sails is often reinforced with ridges called **ribbing.** As the Gothic progressed, four-sided cross vaults became six-, eight-, or multisided as architects played with the angles.
- **Facade flanked by two towers.**
- **Flying buttresses.** These freestanding exterior pillars connected by graceful, thin arms of stone help channel the weight of the building and its roof out and down into the ground. To help counter the cross-forces involved in this engineering sleight of hand, the piers of buttresses are often topped by heavy pinnacles or statues.
- **Spires.** These pinnacles of masonry seem to defy gravity and reach toward heaven itself.
- **Gargoyles.** These wide-mouthed creatures are actually drain spouts.
- **Tracery.** These delicate, lacy spider webs of carved stone curlycues grace the pointy ends of windows and acute lower intersections of cross vaulting.
- **Stained glass.** Because pointy arches can carry more weight than rounded ones, windows could be larger and more numerous. They are often filled with Bible stories and symbolism writ in the colorful patterns of stained glass. Large, circular ones on facades and transepts ends are called **rose windows.**

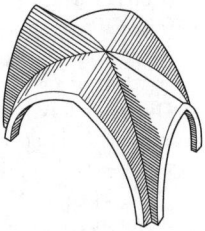

*Cross Vault*

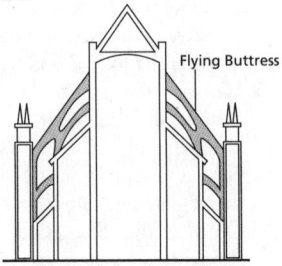


*Cross Section of a Gothic Church*

- **Choir screen.** Serving as the inner wall of the ambulatory and outer wall of the choir section, the choir screen is often decorated with carvings or tombs.
- **Half-timbered houses.** The Gothic era saw the rebuilding of German towns with houses made of exposed cross timbers with the triangular sections between them filled in with plaster, often painted.

### BEST EXAMPLES

- **Cologne Cathedral.** This is a hulk of a Gothic cathedral, and Germany's finest, at once massive and graceful. The facade is Germany's keynote example of flamboyant Gothic, the interior a soaring void of arches and light, impossibly huge. It also contains some fantastic Gothic stained glass, paintings, and carved choirs stalls (p. 510).
- **Freiburg Cathedral.** Built almost entirely during the Middle Ages, this cathedral is a remarkable Gothic construct, centered on an enormous single tower that comprises the facade (with its great gargoyles), and an extended chancel surrounded by a late Gothic ambulatory and radiating chapels (p. 380).

*Cologne Cathedral*

- **Ulm Münster.** Second in size only to Cologne's cathedral, Ulm's Münster sports the world's tallest spire—though it did take 500 years to complete, so the 1890 finishing is neo-Gothic. Inside, rather than a nave, there are five airy aisles with no transept (p. 227).
- **Hallenkirche.** The best of Germany's tall, airy Hall Churches are **Nördlingen's St. Georgskirche, Munich's Frauenkirche, Dinkelsbühl's Georgenkirche,** and **Nürnberg's St.-Lorenz-Kirche** (p. 253, 306, 251, and 212 respectively).
- **Backsteingotik (Northern Brick Gothic).** East of the Elbe and along the Baltic, the prevailing use of brick forced Gothic architecture to be simple and monumental. **Lübeck's** soaring **Marienkirche** and towering ***Rathaus*** (town hall) both served as models for other brick churches and secular architecture (p. 617), including **Schwerin Dom** (p. 637), and **Stralsund's St. Nikolaikirche** and **Rathaus** (p. 642 for both).
- **Gothic towns.** The best-preserved town centers with Gothic-style houses and buildings include **Rothenburg ob der Tauber, Goslar, Regensburg,** and **Tübingen** (p. 244, 572, 217, and 430 respectively).

## RENAISSANCE (LATE 15TH–MID-17TH CENTURIES)

Germany was so busy with the Reformation that the country had little time for the Renaissance, which really only had an effect in southern Germany (transalpine influences from Italy) and a few isolated examples in the far north (seepage from Flemish and Dutch neighbors).

### IDENTIFIABLE FEATURES

- **Italianate Renaissance.** Other than a close eye to the Renaissance ideals of proportion, symmetry, and the *Classical orders* (distinguished by the use of three column capitals: Corinthian, Ionic, and Doric), little specifically identifies Italianate Renaissance buildings.

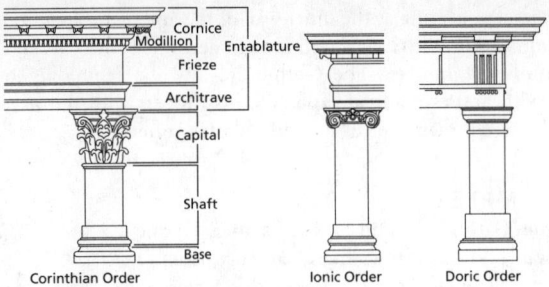


*Classical Orders*

- **Weser Renaissance.** This late–16th and early–17th century style was prevalent in Lower Saxony, distinguishable on houses by pinnacled *gables* (the triangular upper portion of a wall at the end of a pitched roof), heavy scrollwork, elaborate *dormers* (an upright window projecting from a sloping roof), rounded *pediments* (a low-pitched feature above a window, door, or pavilion), and decorative stone bands.

### BEST EXAMPLES

- **Michaelskirche, Munich.** The only solidly Renaissance church in Germany, built (1583–97) by the Jesuits to resemble their church in Rome, Michaelskirche has a harmonious statue-studded facade and a huge, cradle-vaulted single nave (p. 306).
- **Hameln.** The Pied Piper town has several fine Weser Renaissance houses, including the **Rattenfängerhaus, Hochzeitshaus,** and **Dempterscheshaus.**
- **Celle.** The preserved town center is Weser Renaissance, entirely built between the 16th and 18th centuries, including the moated **Herzogschloss Castle** (p. 560).

## BAROQUE & ROCOCO (17TH–18TH CENTURIES)

More than any other movement, the **baroque** aimed toward a seamless meshing of architecture and art. The stuccoes, sculptures, and paintings of this time were all carefully designed to complement each other—and the space itself—to create a unified whole. This effect was both aesthetic and narrative, the various art forms all working together to tell a single Biblical story (or, often, to subtly relate the deeds of the commissioning patron to great historic or Biblical events).

The German baroque only truly flourished in the south and in lower Saxony—especially in Catholic, Counter-Reformation areas—but these regions excelled at it, managing to make Germany's brand of over-the-top, baroque chaos work better perhaps than in any other country. Whereas **rococo** is usually used as a derogatory term for the baroque gone awry into the grotesque, in Germany the rococo actually succeeds (sometimes).

### IDENTIFIABLE FEATURES

- **Classical architecture rewritten with curves.** Baroque lines follow a complex geometry and interplay of concave and convex surfaces. The overall effect is to lighten the appearance of structures and add movement of line and vibrancy to the static look of the Renaissance.
- **Complex decoration.** Unlike the sometimes severe and austere designs of the Renaissance, the baroque was playful. Architects festooned structures and encrusted interiors with an excess of decorations—lots of ornate stuccowork,

pouty cherubs, airy frescoes, heavy gilding, twisting columns, multicolored marbles, and general frippery—all intended to liven things up.

- **Multiplying forms.** The baroque loved to pile up its forms and elements to create a rich, busy effect, breaking a pediment curve into segments so each would protrude further out than the last, or building up an architectural feature by stacking short sections of concave walls, each one curving to a different arc.

## BEST EXAMPLES

- **The Residenz, Würzburg** (1720–44). Balthasar Neumann (1687–1753) designed this sumptuous baroque palace, including the monumental staircase under the world's largest ceiling fresco by Italian master Tieoplo. The palace's chapel is textbook rococo. See p. 234.
- **Wieskirche, near Füssen** (1746–54). Dominikus Zimmermann (1685–1766) crafted this oval-planned rococo beauty in the middle of a cow pasture; he had it frescoed by his brother Johann Baptist. See p. 261.
- **Sans Souci Palace, Potsdam** (1744–1860). Frederick the Great's palace is one of Europe's best examples of rococo set amid one of the most intricately landscaped gardens in Prussia. See p. 147.
- **Cuvillié's Munich buildings.** Jean François de Cuvillié (1698–1767), a French dwarf, was originally the Elector of Bavaria's court jester until his talent for architecture was recognized. After schooling in France, he returned to **Munich** to craft its greatest rococo monuments, including the jewel box of the **Residenz's Alte Residenztheater** (p. 302), which now bears his name, and the facade of the baroque **Theatinerkirche.** His masterpiece is **Schloss Nymphenburg's Amalienburg** hunting lodge (p. 304), which became a model for palaces across Europe.

*Amalienburg, Schloss Nymphenburg*

## NEOCLASSICISM & ROMANTIC (MID-18TH–19TH CENTURIES)

As a backlash against the excesses of the baroque and rococo, by the middle of the 18th century, architects began turning to the austere simplicity and grandeur of the Classical Age and inaugurated the **neoclassical** style. Their work was inspired by the rediscovery of Pompeii and other ancient sites. However, many of their interiors continued to be rococo, though more muted than before.

The sterility of German **neoclassicism** didn't last long, however, and the 19th century left the increasing nationalist German society looking into its own past for inspiration, kicking off the neo-Gothic **romantic** movement.

### IDENTIFIABLE FEATURES

- **Neoclassical.** The classical ideals of mathematical proportion and symmetry, first rediscovered during the Renaissance, are neoclassical hallmarks. Of the classical orders, German neoclassicists preferred the austere, monumental Doric style for their temple-like buildings and massive colonnaded porticos.

- **Romantic.** Gothic fantasy is the only way to describe this style, which cranked up the defining aspects of the Gothic (spires, tracery, buttresses, and gargoyles) to higher and more dramatic levels than the Middle Ages ever imagined.

### BEST EXAMPLES

- **In Berlin.** The Prussians remade Berlin in a neoclassical image, starting with the **Brandenburger Tor** (p. 118) and moving on to the buildings of Karl Friedrich Schinkel (1781–1841), among which **Altes Museum, Schloss Charlottenhof,** and **Nikolaikirche** are his best (p. 108, 149, and 642 respectively). There's a museum devoted to him called the **Friedrichswerdersche Kirche-Schinkelmuseum** (p. 113).
- **In Munich.** Ludwig I had Leo von Kelnze lay out neoclassical structures across his "new Athens," including those surrounding **Königsplatz** (p. 298) and the nearby **Alte and Neue Pinakotheks** (p. 298 and 305).
- **Ludwig II's Bavarian fantasies.** Caught up in Wagner's dramatic operas set in the heroic Middle Ages, "Mad King" Ludwig II was the ultimate romantic, building for himself a series of faux medieval fairy-tale castles, including **Herrenchiemsee's Neues Schloss** (p. 337) and the incomparable fantasy of **Neuschwanstein Castle** (p. 265), a festival of banner-fluttering towers and battlements right out of a Brothers Grimm folk tale, its entire setting chosen solely for its picture postcard perfection.

*Neuschwanstein*

## 20TH-CENTURY GERMAN ARCHITECTURE

Germany's take on the early 20th-century Art Nouveau movement was called **Jugendstil.**

The **Bauhaus** was a 1920s avant-garde school of architecture led by **Walter Gropius** (1883–1969) that combined industrial age architecture with art and craft to create functional buildings and furnishings. Among its chief designers and institute teachers were Marcel Breuer, Wassily Kandinsky, Oskar Schlemmer, and Paul Klee. The Nazis closed the school down in 1933, though it was reborn in Chicago.

### IDENTIFIABLE FEATURES

- **Jugendstil.** This style reacted against the burgeoning culture of mass production by stressing the uniqueness of craft. Practitioners created asymmetrical, curvaceous designs based on organic inspiration (plants and flowers) and used such materials as wrought iron, stained glass, tile, and hand-painted wallpaper.
- **Bauhaus.** A use of right angles, concrete, and glass, and an absence of ornamentation characterize many Bauhaus structures, which otherwise share only a devotion to functionality. In design, the movement is famous for its early plastic and metal tube chairs.

### BEST EXAMPLES

- **Jugendstil.** Jugendstil houses and hotels exist across Germany, but the movement took its name from *Jugend* magazine published in the

**Schwabing district of Munich** (p. 271), where many buildings in the style survive. Munich is also home to the **Jugendstil Museum** in the Stuck-Villa, Prinzregentenstrasse 60 (✆ **089/45-55-51-25**), a hybrid neoclassical/Jugendstil (art nouveau) structure.

- **Bauhaus.** Bauhaus structures, too, pepper Germany in unobtrusive ways, often in city outskirts. One fine example includes Berlin's Die **Siemensstadt,** the first modern housing complex, built with long "slab" blocks, by Walter Gropius (the founder of the Bauhaus movement). Berlin also has the **Bauhaus-Archiv Museum für Gestaltung** (p. 110) devoted to Bauhaus drawings, photographs, and some design examples.

*Siemensstadt*

# 3

# Planning Your Trip to Germany

This chapter covers everything you need to know to make trip-planning a snap, from when to go to how to shop for the best airfare. Browse through it to get started and make sure you've touched all the bases.

## 1 The Regions in Brief

Germany lies in the heart of Europe, bordered by Switzerland and Austria to the south; France, Luxembourg, Belgium, and the Netherlands to the west; Denmark to the north; and Poland and the Czech Republic to the east. The country encompasses 356,216 square km (137,535 sq. miles) and has a population of about 80 million.

### BERLIN & POTSDAM

Berlin has once more taken its place as Germany's capital and cultural center. It beckons visitors with glorious museums, wonderful cultural offerings, and cutting-edge nightlife. Southwest of Berlin is Potsdam, with its famous palace and elegant gardens and parks, set in an idyllic landscape along the Havel River. See chapter 4.

### THURINGIA

Long a tourist mecca for workers from the Eastern Bloc countries, Thuringia, with its untouched villages, churches, and medieval fortress ruins is now being discovered by Westerners. If your idea of East Germany was nothing but grim industrial cities and cheap housing projects, be prepared for a surprise. Here you can still see the small towns once known to Luther, Bach, and Wagner. The region's densely forested mountains are prime hiking country. The cultural center, with many attractions, is the city of Weimar, once the bastion of such greats as Walter Gropius, Miës van der Rohe, Liszt, Goethe, and Schiller. See chapter 5.

### SAXONY: LEIPZIG & DRESDEN

Known for its annual trade fair that draws participants from around the world, Leipzig is the most important industrial center in the east after Berlin. But this city, once the home of Bach, is also a cultural treasure, with museums, old churches, and Thomanerchor (the famous boys' choir). For those who find Berlin too overwhelming, Leipzig offers an excellent alternative. See chapter 5.

But if it's a choice between Leipzig and Dresden, make it Dresden, still one of the most beautiful cities in Germany, though 80% of its center was destroyed in an infamous 1945 Allied air raid. Today, Dresden is bouncing back—and fast. See chapter 5.

### FRANCONIA & THE GERMAN DANUBE

Some of Germany's greatest medieval and Renaissance treasures came from this region, which gave the world such artists as Albrecht Dürer and Lucas Cranach The Elder. Come here to visit some of the most beautiful and historical towns in Germany, notably Regensburg, Bamberg, Nürnberg, and Bayreuth, where Wagner built his theater and created his Festspiel, the famous opera festival. But if you can only visit one town, head for Würzburg, Germany's baroque city. Located on the banks of the Main River, this glorious old city is overlooked by a fortified castle. Regensburg, 100km (62 miles) southeast of Nürnberg, is also worth a visit, though tourists often pass it by. It suffered no major bombings in World War II, and so remains one of the best-preserved cities in Germany. Nürnberg, although it holds much of interest today with its many preserved art treasures, was heavily bombed and had to be virtually rebuilt. The Danube, which flows through this region, isn't blue and doesn't have the allure, dramatic scenery, or castles of the Rhine, but it's worth exploring for its own quiet charm. See chapter 6.

## THE ROMANTIC ROAD

One of the most scenically beautiful but also one of the most overrun attractions in Germany, the Romantic Road (Romantische Strasse) winds its way south from Würzburg to the little town of Füssen at the foot of the Bavarian Alps. Along the way, Rothenburg ob der Tauber is one of the most splendidly preserved medieval towns in Europe, and as if that weren't enough, the road comes to an end at "Mad" King Ludwig's most fantastic creation: Neuschwanstein Castle. The idea of the "Romantic Road," originally a bit of PR hype to promote the area, was launched in 1950. It was such a success that the road is now clogged with traffic in summer, so the trip is best made in spring or autumn, before the tour buses arrive. (If you want an admittedly less scenic, but still charming, "romantic road," try the "Fairy-Tale Road" in Lower Saxony and North Hesse.) The region of the Romantic Road is known for its folk traditions, old-world charm, and unspoiled medieval towns still surrounded by their original walls. Despite its drawbacks, the road remains one of the most beautiful and interesting trails in all of Europe. See chapter 7.

## MUNICH & THE BAVARIAN ALPS

Rebuilt from the rubble of World War II, Munich is one of the most visited cities of Europe and probably the best place in Germany for old-fashioned fun. It should be included even on the briefest of itineraries. As chic and cosmopolitan as Frankfurt or Berlin, Munich is also kitschy in the best sense of Bavarian tradition. A night at the Hofbräuhaus, Germany's most fabled beer hall, with its liter mugs and oom-pah bands, will get you into the spirit of Munich life. After strolling through the Englischer Garten and having a glass of Bavarian wine in Schwabing (the legendary artists' district), you can tackle Munich's vast array of museums and palaces. Save time for the Deutsches Museum, the largest technological museum in the world. Munich also lies at the gateway to the Bavarian Alps. Shimmering alpine lakes, half-timbered houses frescoed with paintings, picture-postcard towns like Mittenwald and Oberammergau are all here, plus hiking, nature, wildlife, and alpine-ski trails in winter. See chapters 8 and 9.

## LAKE CONSTANCE (BODENSEE)

The 260km (162-mile) coastline of the Bodensee is shared with Austria and Switzerland, but Germany got the best part, the lake's beautiful northern rim. A boat trip on the Bodensee, although not comparable to a Rhine cruise, is a major attraction. The tour takes in castles as well as towns built on islands near the shoreline. The best center is Lindau at the southeastern part, near the Austrian border. Reached by a causeway, this island town has the most luxuriant growth of flowers and shrubs of any resort along the lake. But Konstanz, the largest city on the lake, also merits a visit, because it's one of the best-preserved major medieval cities in Germany. See chapter 10.

## THE BLACK FOREST (SCHWARZWALD)

This dense fir forest, filled with beauty, charm, and myth, actually receives more sunshine than most other forests in Germany. The major center of the region is Freiburg, but the most visited city is the elegant Baden-Baden resort. Black Forest cake and smoked ham might be reason enough to visit the area, but there are many other allures as well, including casino gambling, great spas, and plenty of hiking, bicycling, and cross-country skiing. Freiburg im Breisgau remains one of the most beautiful and historic towns in Germany and makes the best center for exploring the region. If you want a Black Forest cuckoo clock—just as good as the ones touted in Switzerland—head for Triberg. See chapter 11.

## HEIDELBERG & THE NECKAR VALLEY

Except for the Bavarian Alps, there is no more tranquil and scenic part of Germany than the Neckar Valley. The area's Burgenstrasse (Castle Road) has more castles than any comparable stretch along the mighty Rhine, and the Neckar River Valley is just as romantically charming as the more overrun Romantic Road. Allow time to take detours into hidden side valleys to see sleepy little towns, most often with a protective castle hovering over them. Heidelberg, the apotheosis of romantic Germany, needs no selling. This famous medieval university town with its historic castle perfectly captures the spirit of south Germany and has attracted poets and composers over the decades. Goethe and hard-to-impress Mark Twain both fell in love here—Goethe with a woman of striking beauty and the more cynical Twain with Heidelberg itself. Unfortunately, Heidelberg suffers from overcrowding, especially in July and August, when tourists descend by the busload. See chapter 12.

## STUTTGART & TUBINGEN

The capital of the state of Baden-Württemberg, Stuttgart is an industrial giant, headquarters of both Mercedes and Porsche. It's also a city of world-class museums and home to the acclaimed Stuttgart Ballet and Stuttgart State Opera. Its setting, surrounded by green hills with vineyards and orchards, is attractive, but the town isn't a serious contender for visitors when compared to Berlin or Munich. If you can give Stuttgart a day, fine. If not, head at once to nearby Tübingen, the ancient university city on the upper Neckar that has been compared favorably to Heidelberg. It doesn't have Heidelberg's grandeur (or its hordes of visitors), but we prefer its youthful air, its tranquility, and the quiet beauty of its half-timbered houses and alleyways. Don't worry about rushing around to see a lot of attractions—just soak up the old-time atmosphere. See chapter 12.

## FRANKFURT

Called "the Manhattan of Germany" because of its location on the Main River, Frankfurt is vibrant, dynamic, and flashy. This has earned it the dubious distinction of being the most Americanized city in Germany, maybe in Europe. You come here for the glitz and excitement of a major world player on the financial scene, the thriving, modern, and international metropolis, not for "Romantic Road" architecture. Our recommendation is that you treat it as a center worthy of at least two days of your time (it has any number of attractions), rather than just as a transit hub. For many visitors, Frankfurt is their introduction to Germany, in the way that New York is the entry to America for thousands. Like New York, Frankfurt is hardly typical of the country in which it sits, but that doesn't mean you can't have a good time here. It's very civilized and filled with artistic treasures—in fact, the metropolis spends more per year on the arts than any other city in Europe. When not attending the ballet, a Frankfurter might be found slugging down a few jugs of apple wine in the open-air taverns of Sachsenhausen on the city's Left Bank. See chapter 13.

## THE RHINELAND

After the Rhine's beginnings in the mountains of Switzerland as a narrow stream, this mighty river of legend flows for some 1,370km (850 miles) through one of the most picturesque and most industrialized regions of Europe. For 2,000 years it has been a major trade route. Bonn, Cologne, Düsseldorf, and Koblenz all lie on its banks. For most visitors, the number-one attraction is a romantic cruise down the Rhine, through gorges and past ancient castles, vineyards, and the fabled Lorelei. The most panoramic stretch is between Rüdesheim and Koblenz. Start your Rhine cruise at Rüdesheim, Germany's favorite wine village, about 72km (45 miles) west of Frankfurt. If you have time for only one Rhineland city, make it Cologne rather than the more commercialized Düsseldorf. Cologne is dominated by its famous cathedral, the largest in Germany, but this ancient city is also filled with dozens of other attractions, including restored Romanesque churches, striking Roman ruins, and the best modern-art galleries in the country. See chapter 14.

## THE MOSEL VALLEY

Known as La Moselle in nearby France, the Mosel River weaves a snake-like path through the mountains west of the Rhineland. It doesn't have the Rhine's dramatic scenery, but we somehow prefer it, with its vineyards, castles, and fortresses that attract far fewer visitors. The swift-moving Rhine is filled with commercial traffic, but the Mosel is slow-moving, tranquil, and inviting, dotted with sleepy wine towns where you can sample some of the world's greatest vintages. Trains rumble all night along the Rhine, but not on the Mosel. (The inevitable tour buses do get through, however.) The best time to visit is during the annual fall grape harvest, centering in Cochem or Bernkastel-Kues. We've saved the best of this area for last: Near the Luxembourg border lies Trier, one of Europe's most fascinating antiques and the oldest city in Germany; it existed 1,300 years before Rome. Trier is a virtual theme park of Roman culture and architecture. See chapter 15.

## LOWER SAXONY & NORTH HESSE: THE FAIRY-TALE ROAD

Hansel and Gretel, Rumpelstiltskin, the Pied Piper, and even Cinderella list their addresses as "The Fairy-Tale Road." Frankly, the Fairy-Tale Road isn't as architecturally splendid as the Romantic Road, but it's also not as crowded, and it does have a wealth of treasures for visitors interested in German lore and legend or lovers of the tales of the Brothers Grimm, who lived and worked here. The road begins at Hanau, just east of Frankfurt, and stretches for 595km (370 miles) north, coming to an end in Bremen. The trail passes through colorful towns with half-timbered buildings and past plenty of castles. Naturally, it's haunted by witches, goblins, and memories of the Pied Piper of Hameln. See chapter 16.

## HAMBURG

The port city of Hamburg is exhilarating. The Germans often say they go to Frankfurt "for the banking" but to Hamburg "to have a good time." This Hanseatic City along the Elbe River has been beautifully rebuilt after the devastation caused by bombers in World War II, especially the night of July 28, 1943. A city of lakes, parks, and tree-lined canals, it is more famous for the tall tales of its red-light district. But these steamy after-dark diversions are only a small part of what Hamburg is. Restored architectural masterpieces and historic churches give this industrial city of 2 million prestige and allure. The world press might still call Hamburg Germany's "capital of lust" because of all its sex clubs, but the city is also concerned with protecting its environment, with historical preservation, and being a city of art and intellectual pursuits. If you can, spend at least two days here. See chapter 17.

### SCHLESWIG-HOLSTEIN

This northwestern corridor of Germany, sandwiched between the North Sea and the Baltic, evokes bucolic Denmark to which it was linked before Bismarck's defeat of that Scandinavian country in 1867.

Germany's northernmost province is one of our favorites because of its offshore vacation islands and the chance it offers to escape from the industrialization of Northern Germany into acres upon acres of rolling green fields used for agriculture. Large areas are still forested, and there is enough moorland to delight a native of Yorkshire, England. The chief historical interest centers around the ancient merchant city of Lübeck, the former capital of the Hanseatic League and the hometown of Thomas Mann, the great German writer. Although heavily restored after World War II, Lübeck is loaded with attractions, and its Aldstadt (old town) has been designated a UNESCO World Heritage Site. The province is also home to Germany's most sophisticated seaside resort and its northernmost point, the island of Sylt, famed for its cosmopolitan atmosphere, its celebrities, and its climate of iodine-rich air and lots of rain. The port city of Kiel is short on charm because it was severely bombed in World War II, but the ancient stronghold of Schleswig invites wandering, exploring, and dreaming of the golden age of the Vikings. See chapter 18.

### THE BALTIC COAST

With the salt air and wind in your hair, you can head east from Schleswig-Holstein and travel all the way along the Baltic coast to the Polish border. During the Cold War, traveling this strip of coastal towns was made difficult by the East German authorities. But today, these beach towns eagerly welcome visitors from the West, finding them better tippers than they did the former hordes who used to descent on the Baltic from the Eastern Bloc Communist countries. A lighter, more fun-loving spirit has come to these towns that once were dull Communist watering holes for the masses. The region hasn't entirely thrown off its dark past, but restoration continues to turn this coastline into a vacation spot to compete with others in the country. There is hopeful talk of turning the district once again into the playground that it once was for the glitterati of the early 20th century. Wismar, Schwerin, Rostock, Stralsund, and Rügen make the best and most colorful centers. See chapter 19.

## 2 Visitor Information

Nearly all larger towns and all cities in Germany have tourist offices. The **German National Tourist Board** headquarters is at Beethovenstrasse 69, 60325 Frankfurt am Main (✆ **069/21-23-8800;** www.visits-to-Germany.com or www.germany-tourism.de).

**IN THE U.S.** 122 E. 42nd St., 52nd Floor, New York, NY 10168-0072 (✆ **800/637-1171;** 212/661-7200; fax 212/661-7174).

**IN CANADA** 2 Bloor St. E., Suite 3330, Toronto, ON M4W 3R8 (✆ **416/967-3381;** fax 416/967-4101).

### Destination: Germany—Red Alert Checklist

- Citizens of EU countries can cross into Germany for as long as they wish with a picture ID. Citizens of other countries must have a passport.
- Did you pack your camera and an extra set of camera batteries and purchase enough film? If you packed film in your checked baggage, did you invest in protective pouches to shield film from airport x-rays?
- Do you have a safe, accessible place to store money?
- Did you bring your ID cards that could entitle you to discounts such as AAA and AARP cards, student IDs, and so on?
- Did you bring emergency drug prescriptions and extra glasses and/or contact lenses?
- Do you have your credit-card pin numbers?
- Did you leave a copy of your itinerary with someone at home?

**IN THE U.K.** P.O. Box 2695, London W1A 3TN (✆ **020/7317-0908** or 020/7495-6129).

**IN AUSTRALIA** P.O. Box A980, Sydney, NSW 1235 (✆ **02/9267-8148;** fax 02/9267-9035).

## 3 Entry Requirements & Customs

### ENTRY REQUIREMENTS

Every U.S., Canadian, British, and Australian traveler entering Germany must hold a valid passport. You won't need a visa unless you're staying longer than 3 months. Safeguard your passport in an inconspicuous, inaccessible place like a money belt. If you lose your passport, visit the nearest consulate of your native country as soon as possible for a replacement. It is always a good idea to have a photocopy of your passport (stored separately from it) to expedite replacement.

### CUSTOMS

**WHAT YOU CAN BRING INTO GERMANY** In general, items required for personal and professional use or consumption may be brought in to Germany duty-free and without hassle. No duty is levied for a private car, provided that it is reported. You can also bring in gifts duty-free up to a total value of 180€ ($160.75).

The following items are permitted into Germany duty-free from non-EU (European Union) countries: 200 cigarettes; 1 liter of liquor above 44 proof, or 2 liters of liquor less than 44 proof, or 2 liters of wine; 50 grams of perfume and 0.25 liters of eau de cologne; 500 grams of coffee; and 100 grams of tea. From EU countries the duty-free limits are higher: 300 cigarettes; 1.5 liters of liquor above 44 proof, or 3 liters of liquor less than 44 proof, or 4 liters of wine; 75 grams of perfume and 0.375 liters of eau de cologne; 750 grams of coffee; and 150 grams of tea. Duty-free allowances are authorized only when the items are carried in the traveler's personal baggage.

**WHAT YOU CAN TAKE HOME** For information, **U.S. citizens** should contact the **U.S. Customs Service,** 1300 Pennsylvania Ave. NW, Washington, DC 20229 (✆ **877/287-8867**) and request the free pamphlet *Know Before You Go.* It's also available on the Web at www.customs.gov. (Click on "Traveler Information," then "Know Before You Go.")

For a clear summary of **Canadian** rules, write for the booklet *I Declare,* issued by the **Canada Customs and Review Agency** (✆ **800/461-9999** in Canada, or 204/983-3500; www.ccra-adrc.gc.ca).

**Citizens of the U.K.** should contact HM Customs & Excise at ✆ **0845/010-9000** (from outside the U.K., 020/8929-0152), or consult their website at www.hmce.gov.uk for information.

A helpful brochure for **Australian citizens,** available from Australian consulates or Customs offices, is *Know Before You Go.* For more information, call the **Australian Customs Service** at ✆ **1300/363-263,** or log on to www.customs.gov.au.

Citizens of **New Zealand** can have most of their questions answered in a free pamphlet available at New Zealand consulates and Customs offices: *New Zealand Customs Guide for Travellers, Notice no. 4.* For more information, contact **New Zealand Customs,** The Customhouse, 17–21 Whitmore St., Box 2218, Wellington (✆ **04/473-6099** or 0800/428-786; www.customs.govt.nz).

## 4 Money

The major cities of Germany are some of the world's most expensive. So if you want to see the country without breaking the bank, you may want to cut short your time in Frankfurt, Munich, or Berlin and concentrate on interesting regional capitals such as Freiburg in the Black Forest, where you can cut your travel cost by anywhere from 20% to 40%. You might also want to consider a rail pass.

Although prices in Germany are high, you generally get good value for your money. The inflation rate has remained low. Hotels are usually clean and comfortable, and restaurants generally offer good cuisine and ample portions made with quality ingredients. Trains are fast and on time, and most service personnel treat you with respect.

Many people come to Germany just for winter sports. The most expensive resorts are places like Garmisch-Partenkirchen. However, if you avoid the chic places, you can enjoy winter fun at a moderate cost. Some of the winter spots in the Bavarian Alps that haven't been overrun by the beautiful people give you great

### The U.S. Dollar, the British Pound & the Euro

In January of 2002, the largest money-changing operation in history led to the deliberate obsolescence of many of Europe's individual national currencies, including the German mark. In its place was substituted the euro, a currency based on the fiscal participation of a dozen nations of Europe.

**For American Readers:** At this writing, 1 euro equals approximately 89 US cents, and 1 US dollar equals approximately 1.12€. This was the rate of exchange used to calculate the dollar values, each of which was rounded to the nearest nickel, throughout this book.

**For British Readers:** At this writing, Great Britain still uses the pound sterling, with 1 euro equaling approximately 70 pence, and £1 equaling approximately 1.43€.

***Note:*** The relative value of the euro fluctuates against the US dollar, the pound sterling, and most of the world's other currencies, and its value might not be the same by the time you actually travel to Germany.

value for your money. And prices in a village next to a resort are often 30% lower than at the resort itself.

In Germany, many prices for children (generally defined as ages 6–17) are considerably lower than for adults. And fees for children under 6 are often waived entirely.

### THE EURO

The **euro,** the new single European currency, became the official currency of Germany and 11 other participating countries on **January 1, 1999.** The euro went into general circulation on **January 1, 2002.** Over a 2-month transition period, German mark banknotes and coins were withdrawn from circulation. The symbol of the euro is a stylized E: €. Its official abbreviation is "EUR."

It's a good idea to exchange at least some money—just enough to cover airport incidentals and transportation to your hotel—before you leave home, so you can avoid the less-favorable rates you'll get at airport currency exchange desks. Check with you local American Express or Thomas Cook office or your bank to see if you can exchange your home currency for euros there. American Express cardholders can order foreign currency over the phone at ✆ **800/807-6233.**

It's best to exchange currency or traveler's checks at a bank, not a currency exchange, hotel, or shop. Note the rates and ask about commission fees; it can sometimes pay to shop around and ask the right questions.

### ATMS

ATMs worldwide are linked to a network that most likely includes your bank at home. **Cirrus** (✆ **800/424-7787;** www.mastercard.com) and **PLUS** (✆ **800/843-7587;** www.visa.com) are the two most popular networks; call or check online for ATM locations at your destination. Be sure to check the daily withdrawal limit before you depart and ask whether you need a new PIN for use in Germany. Keep in mind that many European ATMs won't allow you to withdraw money from savings accounts, so be sure to transfer any funds you'll need to your checking account before leaving home.

### CREDIT CARDS

Credit cards are invaluable when traveling. They are a safe way to carry money and provide a convenient record of all your expenses. Keep in mind that though credit cards are widely accepted throughout Germany, they're still not accepted quite as commonly as in the U.S., especially in smaller towns.

You can also withdraw cash advances from your credit cards. At many banks, you don't even need to go to a teller; you can get a cash advance at the ATM if you know your PIN.

Almost every credit-card company has an emergency 800-number that you can call if your wallet or purse is stolen. The company may be able to wire you a cash advance off your credit card immediately, and in many places, can deliver an emergency credit card in a day or two. **Citicorp Visa's** U.S. emergency number is ✆ **800/645-6556;** 813/623-1709 in Canada. **American Express** cardholders and traveler's check holders should call ✆ **800/233-5439** for all money emergencies. **MasterCard** holders should call ✆ **800/307-7309.**

## 5 When to Go

The most popular tourist months are May to October, although winter travel to Germany is becoming increasingly popular, especially to the ski areas in the Bavarian Alps. Germany's climate varies widely. In the north, winters tend to be cold and rainy; summers are most agreeable. In the south and in the Alps, it can be very cold in the winter, especially in January, and very warm in

**Berlin's Average Daytime Temperature & Rainfall (inches)**

| | Jan | Feb | Mar | Apr | May | June | July | Aug | Sept | Oct | Nov | Dec |
|---|---|---|---|---|---|---|---|---|---|---|---|---|
| °F | 30 | 32 | 40 | 48 | 53 | 60 | 64 | 62 | 56 | 49 | 40 | 34 |
| °C | -1 | 0 | 4 | 9 | 12 | 16 | 18 | 17 | 13 | 9 | 4 | 1 |
| Rainfall | 2.2 | 1.6 | 1.2 | 1.6 | 2.3 | 2.9 | 3.2 | 2.7 | 2.2 | 1.6 | 2.4 | 1.9 |

**Frankfurt's Average Daytime Temperature & Rainfall (inches)**

| | Jan | Feb | Mar | Apr | May | June | July | Aug | Sept | Oct | Nov | Dec |
|---|---|---|---|---|---|---|---|---|---|---|---|---|
| °F | 34 | 36 | 42 | 49 | 57 | 63 | 66 | 66 | 58 | 50 | 41 | 35 |
| °C | 1 | 2 | 6 | 9 | 14 | 17 | 19 | 19 | 14 | 10 | 5 | 2 |
| Rainfall | 6.5 | 5.1 | 5.6 | 5.7 | 5.9 | 5.5 | 5 | 5.1 | 4.2 | 4.8 | 6.5 | 6 |

summer, but with cool, rainy days even in July and August. Spring and fall are often stretched out—in fact, we've enjoyed many a Bavarian-style "Indian summer" until late in October.

## HOLIDAYS

Public holidays are January 1 (New Year's Day), Easter (Good Friday and Easter Monday), May 1 (Labor Day), Ascension Day (10 days before Pentecost/Whitsunday, the 7th Sun after Easter), Whitmonday (day after PentecostWhitsunday), October 3 (Day of German Unity), November 17 (Day of Prayer and Repentance), and December 25 to 26 (Christmas). In addition, the following holidays are observed in some German states: January 6 (Epiphany), Corpus Christi (10 days after Pentecost), August 15 (Assumption), and November 1 (All Saints' Day).

## GERMANY CALENDAR OF EVENTS

Dates listed below are for 2003. All dates and events are subject to change. Contact the German National Tourist Board (see "Visitor Information," above) for more information. The Board publishes a free calendar of forthcoming events three times a year, in April, October, and January; the first two are half-yearly calendars and the last is a yearly preview. They give the dates of trade fairs and exhibitions, theatrical and musical performances, local folk festivals, sporting events, conferences, and congresses throughout Germany.

### January

**New Year's Day International Ski Jumping,** Garmisch-Partenkirchen. One of Europe's major winter sporting events. For more information, contact the tourist bureau on Dr.-Richard-Strauss-Platz (✆ **08821/18-0700**). January 1.

### February

**International Film Festival,** Berlin (at various theaters; announced in local newspapers). Stars, would-be stars, directors, and almost anyone with a film to peddle show up at this well-attended festival. It lasts for 1 week and is a showcase for the work of international film directors as well as the latest German films. Tickets can be purchased at any box office. Contact the **Full House Service** (✆ **030/25489-100**) or www.berlinale.de for more information. February 5 to 16.

**Ambiente.** This is one of the principal consumer-goods trade fairs of Europe. Its origins go back centuries. For information, contact the **Messe Frankfurt Gubh** (✆ **069/7-57-50;** fax 069/75-75-64-33; 770/984-8016 in the U.S.). February 27 to March 2.

**Fasching.** Carnival festivals take place throughout Germany, reaching their peak on the Tuesday (Mardi Gras) before Ash Wednesday (Feb 12). Particularly famous

Carnivals take place in Bonn, Cologne, Düsseldorf, and especially Munich.

### March

**Spring Fairs.** Highlights throughout Germany, especially in Augsburg, Münster, Nürnberg, Hamburg, and Stuttgart. Dates vary from year to year.

### April

**Walpurgis Festivals.** Celebrated in the Harz Mountains. Festivities occur on the night of April 30.

### May

**Hamburg Summer.** A whole series of cultural events, including concerts, plays, festivals, and special exhibitions throughout May, June, and July. For information, contact the **Hamburg Tourist Bureau,** im Hauptbahnhof (✆ **040/30-05-13-00**).

**International May Festival,** Wiesbaden. This city near Frankfurt hosts a premier cultural event—a series of artistic celebrations lasting 1 month. For information, contact the **Wiesbaden Tourist Office,** Rheinstrasse 15 (✆ **0611/1-72-97-98**).

**Red Wine Festival,** Rüdesheim/Assmannshausen. This is held in Assmannshausen, the Rhine village most famous for red wines. For information, contact the **Rüdesheim Tourist Bureau,** Rheinstrasse 16 (✆ **06722/29-62**). May 23 to 26.

### June

**Floodlighting of the Castle,** Heidelberg. Fireworks enliven the display in this storied university city. For more information, contact the **Heidelberg Tourist Bureau,** Pavillon am Hauptbahnhof (✆ **06221/1-42-20**). June 4, July 9, and September 3.

**Mozart Festival,** Würzburg. Aficionados of the composer flock to this major cultural event in the baroque city of Würzburg. For more information, contact **Tourismus Zentrale** im Würzburg-Palais, am Congress-Centrum (✆ **0931/37-33-35**). May 31 to July 5.

### July

**Freiburg Wine Tasting.** Local residents and visitors enjoy the first vintages from grapes grown in the Black Forest district. For more information, contact the **Freiburg Tourist Bureau,** Rotteckring 14 (✆ **0761/388-18-80**). Early July.

See **Floodlighting of the Castle,** Heidelberg, under June, above.

**Richard Wagner Festival.** Bayreuth Festspielhaus. One of Europe's two or three major opera events, this festival takes place in the composer's Festspielhaus in Bayreuth, the capital of upper Franconia. Note that opera tickets often must be booked years in advance. For information, contact Festival Administration, **Bayreuther Festspiele,** Am Festspiele, 95445 Bayreuth (✆ **0921/7-87-80;** www.festspiele.de). Late July to late August.

### September

See **Floodlighting of the Castle,** Heidelberg, under June, above.

**Oktoberfest,** Munich. Germany's most famous festival happens mainly in September, not October. Millions show up, and hotels are packed. Most activities are at Theresienwiese, where local breweries sponsor gigantic tents that can hold up to 6,000 beer drinkers. Contact the **Munich Tourist Bureau** (✆ **089/2-33-03-00**) or www.muenchen-tourist.de for particulars, or just show up. Always reserve hotel rooms well in advance. Mid-September to the first Sunday in October.

**Berliner Festwochen.** One of the high points on the cultural calendar of Germany, the Berlin Festival brings an international array of performing artists to Berlin. It features opera and symphony performances as well as major theatrical presentations. Contact the **Berlin Tourist Information Office** (✆ **030/25-00-25**). Early September to mid-October.

### October

**Frankfurt Book Fair.** A major international event for publishers, book dealers, agents, and authors. Contact the **Frankfurt Tourist Office** (✆ **069/21-23-87-08**) or www.frankfurt-bookfair.com. October 8 to 13.

### November

**Jazz-Fest Berlin.** This annual festival, staged at the Philharmonie, attracts some of the world's finest jazz artists, ranging from traditional to experimental. Contact the **Berlin Tourist Information Office** (✆ **030/25-00-25**) for more information. Early November.

**Winter Dom,** Hamburg. An annual amusement fair (sometimes called Hamburg Dom) at the Heiligengeistfeld. For more information, contact the **Hamburg Tourist Bureau,** im Hauptbahnhof (✆ **040/30-05-13-00**). November 8 to December 6.

### December

**Christmas Fair,** Mainz. Mainz stages its Christmas fair on the Rhine for the 4 weeks preceding Christmas. For more information, contact the **Mainz Tourist Bureau,** Vruckenturm am Rathaus (✆ **06131/28-62-10**). Other German towns hold Christmas fairs in November.

## 6 Health & Insurance

### TRAVEL INSURANCE AT A GLANCE

Since Germany for most of us is far from home, and a number of things could go wrong—lost luggage, trip cancellation, a medical emergency—consider the following types of insurance.

Check your existing insurance policies before you buy travel insurance to cover trip cancellation, lost luggage, medical expenses, or car-rental insurance. You're likely to have partial or complete coverage. But if you need some, ask your travel agent about a comprehensive package. The cost of travel insurance varies widely, depending on the cost and length of your trip, your age and overall health, and the type of trip you're taking. Insurance for extreme sports or adventure travel, for example, will cost more than coverage for a European cruise. Some insurers provide packages for specialty vacations, such as skiing or backpacking. More dangerous activities may be excluded from basic policies.

For information, contact one of the following popular insurers:

- **Access America** (✆ 800/284-8300; www.accessamerica.com)
- **Travel Guard International** (✆ 800/826-1300; www.travelguard.com)
- **Travel Insured International** (✆ 800/243-3174; www.travelinsured.com)
- **Travelex Insurance Services** (✆ 800/228-9792; www.travelex-insurance.com)

### MEDICAL INSURANCE

Most health-insurance policies cover you if you get sick away from home—but check, particularly if you're insured by an HMO. With the exception of certain HMOs and Medicare/Medicaid, your medical insurance should cover medical treatment—even hospital care—overseas. However, most out-of-country hospitals make you pay your bills up front, and send you a refund after you've returned home and filed the necessary paperwork.

Members of **Blue Cross/Blue Shield** can now use their cards at select hospitals in most major cities worldwide (✆ **800/810-BLUE** or www.bluecares.com for a list of hospitals).

If you require additional insurance, try one of the following companies:

- **MEDEX International,** 9515 Deereco Rd., Timonium, MD 21093-5375 (✆ **888/MEDEX-00** or 410/453-6300; fax 410/453-6301; www.medexassist.com).
- **Travel Assistance International** (✆ **800/821-2828;** www.travelassistance.com), 9200 Keystone Crossing, Suite 300, Indianapolis, IN 46240 (for general information on services, call the company's Worldwide Assistance Services, Inc., at ✆ **800/777-8710**).

The cost of travel medical insurance varies widely. Check your existing policies before you buy additional coverage. Also, check to see if your medical insurance covers you for emergency medical evacuation. If you have to buy a one-way same-day ticket home and forfeit your nonrefundable round-trip ticket, you may be out big money.

### CAR-RENTAL INSURANCE (LOSS/DAMAGE WAIVER OR COLLISION DAMAGE WAIVER)

Before leaving home, check if your personal auto-insurance policy covers you while in Germany. If not, check the rental-company policy as well as your credit-card coverage. Is your destination covered? Are other drivers covered? How much liability is covered if a passenger is injured? (If you rely on your credit card for coverage, you may want to bring a second credit card with you, as damages may be charged to your card and you may find yourself stranded with no money.) Car-rental insurance costs about $20 a day.

### THE HEALTHY TRAVELER

German medical facilities are among the best in the world. If a medical emergency arises, your hotel staff can usually put you in touch with a reliable doctor. If not, contact your embassy or consulate; each one maintains a list of English-speaking doctors. Medical and hospital services aren't free, so be sure that you have appropriate insurance coverage before you travel. The water is safe to drink throughout Germany; however, do not drink the water in mountain streams, regardless of how clear and pure it looks.

### WHAT TO DO IF YOU GET SICK AWAY FROM HOME

If you worry about getting sick away from home, consider purchasing **medical travel insurance** and carry your ID card in your purse or wallet. In most cases, your existing health plan will provide the coverage you need. See the section on insurance earlier in this chapter for more information.

Pack prescription medications in your carry-on luggage. Carry written prescriptions in generic, not brand-name form, and dispense all prescription medications from their original vials. Also bring along copies of your prescriptions in case you lose your pills or run out.

## 7 Tips for Travelers with Special Needs

### TIPS FOR TRAVELERS WITH DISABILITIES

Germany is one of the better countries for travelers with disabilities. In all the large cities, there are excellent facilities. The local tourist offices can issue permits for drivers to allow them access to disabled parking areas. Older, smaller towns may pose more of a problem, however, especially where the streets are cobblestone.

In any case, a disability shouldn't stop anyone from traveling. There are more resources out there than ever before.

### AGENCIES/OPERATORS

- **Flying Wheels Travel (✆ 800/535-6790;** www.flyingwheelstravel.com) offers escorted tours and cruises that emphasize sports and private tours in minivans with lifts.
- **Access Adventures (✆ 716/889-9096**), a Rochester, New York–based agency, offers customized itineraries for a variety of travelers with disabilities.
- **Accessible Journeys (✆ 800/TINGLES** or 610/521-0339; www.disabilitytravel.com) caters specifically to slow walkers and wheelchair travelers and their families and friends.

### ORGANIZATIONS

- **The Moss Rehab Hospital (✆ 215/456-9603;** www.mossresourcenet.org) provides friendly, helpful phone assistance through its **Travel Information Service.**
- **The Society for Accessible Travel and Hospitality (✆ 212/447-7284;** fax 212-725-8253; www.sath.org) offers a wealth of travel resources for all types of disabilities and informed recommendations on destinations, access guides, travel agents, tour operators, vehicle rentals, and companion services. Annual membership costs $45 for adults; $30 for seniors and students.

### PUBLICATIONS

- **Mobility International USA (✆ 541/343-1284;** www.miusa.org) publishes *A World of Options,* a 658-page book of resources, covering everything from biking trips to scuba outfitters, and a biannual newsletter, *Over the Rainbow.* Annual membership is $35.
- **Twin Peaks Press (✆ 360/694-2462**) publishes travel-related books for travelers with special needs.

## GAY & LESBIAN TRAVELERS

Although Germany is one of the "gayest" countries of Europe, there is also prejudice and hostility here. Violence against gays and foreigners (especially nonwhite) is not unknown. On the other hand, homosexuality is widely accepted by a vast number of the country's millions, especially young people. All major cities have a wide and varied gay and lesbian nightlife. Keep in mind western Germany is far more gay-friendly than the more isolated outposts of the former East Germany. The legal minimum age for consensual homosexual sex is 18.

Before you go, consider picking up a copy of ***Frommer's Gay & Lesbian Europe,*** which contains a chapter on Berlin.

**The International Gay & Lesbian Travel Association (IGLTA) (✆ 800/448-8550** or 954/776-2626; fax 954/776-3303; www.iglta.org), with around 1,200 members, links travelers with appropriate gay-friendly service organizations or tour specialists. It offers quarterly newsletters, marketing mailings, and a membership directory. Most members are gay or lesbian businesses, but individuals can join for $200 yearly, plus a $100 administration fee for new members. Members are kept informed of gay and gay-friendly hoteliers, tour operators, and airline and cruise-line representatives. Contact the IGLTA for a list of its member agencies, who will be tied into IGLTA's information resources.

### AGENCIES/OPERATORS

- **Above and Beyond Tours (✆ 800/397-2681;** www.aboveandbeyondtours.com) offers gay and lesbian tours worldwide and is the exclusive gay and lesbian tour operator for United Airlines.
- **Now, Voyager (✆ 800/255-6951;** www.nowvoyager.com) is a San Francisco–based gay-owned and operated travel service.

### PUBLICATIONS

- ***Out and About*** (✆ **800/929-2268** or 415-644-8044; www.outandabout.com) offers guidebooks and a newsletter 10 times a year packed with solid information on the global gay and lesbian scene.
- ***Spartacus International Gay Guide*** and ***Odysseus*** are good, annual English-language guidebooks focused on gay men, with some information for lesbians. You can get them from most gay and lesbian bookstores, or order them from **Giovanni's Room** bookstore, 1145 Pine St., Philadelphia, PA 19107 (✆ **215/923-2960;** www.giovannisroom.com).
- ***Gay Travel A to Z: The World of Gay & Lesbian Travel Options at Your Fingertips,*** by Marianne Ferrari (Ferrari Publications; Box 35575, Phoenix, AZ 85069), is a very good gay and lesbian guidebook series.

## SENIOR TRAVELERS

Mention the fact that you're a senior citizen when you first make your travel reservations. Most airlines and many hotels offer discounts for seniors. In most cities, people over the age of 60 qualify for reduced admission to theaters, museums, and other attractions, as well as discounted fares on public transportation.

Members of **AARP** (formerly known as the American Association of Retired Persons), 601 E St. NW, Washington, DC 20049 (✆ **800/424-3410** or 202/434-2277; www.aarp.org), get discounts on hotels, airfares, and car rentals. AARP offers members a wide range of benefits, including *Modern Maturity* magazine and a monthly newsletter. Anyone over 50 can join.

### AGENCIES/OPERATORS

- **Grand Circle Travel** (✆ **800/221-2610** or 617/350-7500; www.gct.com), offers package deals for the 50-plus market, mostly of the tour-bus variety, with free trips thrown in for those who organize groups of 10 or more.
- **Elderhostel** (✆ **877/426-8056;** www.elderhostel.org), arranges study programs for those aged 55 and over (and a spouse or companion of any age) in the U.S. and in more than 80 countries around the world. Most courses last 5 to 7 days in the U.S. (2–4 weeks abroad), and many include airfare, accommodations in university dormitories or modest inns, meals, and tuition.
- **Interhostel** (✆ **800/733-9753;** www.learn.unh.edu/interhostel), organized by the University of New Hampshire, also offers educational travel for seniors. On these escorted tours, the days are packed with seminars, lectures, and field trips, with sightseeing led by academic experts. **Interhostel** takes travelers 50 and over (with companions over 40), and offers 1- and 2-week trips, mostly international.
- **Elder Travelers,** 1615 Smelter Ave., Black Eagle, MT 59414; (www.eldertravelers.com), aids those who are more than 50 years old, like to travel and to meet people. Their stated purpose is to provide members with "zero cost lodging" anywhere in the world, including Germany, as senior citizens are hooked up with their counterpart hosts in the lands in which they travel. For $40 annually, subscriptions are given to their informative newsletter, which provides links to the best travel data sites worldwide. For more information on this unique group, seek them out at www.eldertravelers.com.
- **Vantage Deluxe World Travel,** 90 Canal St., Boston, MA 02114

(✆ **800/322-6677,** or 617/878-6000), for some 2 decades has taken thousands of mature travelers on out-of-the-extraordinary travel experiences in various European countries, including Germany. Travel is on luxurious river cruises and fully escorted land tours. Groups are deliberately kept small. For more details, contact www.vantagetravel.com/trips/landTours.asp.

### PUBLICATIONS

- ***101 Tips for the Mature Traveler*** is available from Grand Circle Travel (✆ **800/221-2610** or 617/350-7500; fax 617/346-6700).
- ***The 50+ Traveler's Guidebook*** (St. Martin's Press).
- ***Unbelievably Good Deals and Great Adventures That You Absolutely Can't Get Unless You're Over 50*** (Contemporary Publishing Co.).

## 8 Getting There

### BY PLANE

**Lufthansa** (✆ **800/645-3880;** 01/803-803-803; www.lufthansa.com) operates the most frequent service and flies to the greatest number of Germany's airports. From North America, Lufthansa serves 16 gateway cities. In any season, there are more than 100 weekly flights from these cities to Germany. The largest of the gateways is the New York City area, where flights depart from both JFK and Newark airports. Lufthansa has an alliance with **United Airlines** and **Air Canada** to provide seamless air service to Germany and other parts of the globe from North America. Dubbed "Star Alliance," the union allows cross-airline benefits, including travel on one or all of these airlines on one ticket and frequent-flier credit to the participating airline of your choice.

**American Airlines** (✆ **800/443-7300;** www.aa.com) flies nonstop to Frankfurt daily and American's flights connect easily with ongoing flights to many other German cities on Lufthansa or British Airways. **Continental Airlines** (✆ **800/231-0856;** www.continental.com) offers daily nonstop service to Frankfurt and Düsseldorf. From the Delta Flight Center at JFK airport in New York, **Delta Airlines** (✆ **800/241-4141;** www.delta.com) offers daily service to both Frankfurt and (via Brussels) Hamburg. Delta is especially strong in service to Germany from its home base in Atlanta. **United Airlines** (✆ **800/241-6522;** www.val.com) offers daily nonstops to Frankfurt, and because of the Star Alliance, discussed above, all German flights by Lufthansa or Air Canada will also be honored as a part of a United ticket. **US Airways** ✆ **800/428-4322**) also flies to Frankfurt daily (from North Carolina).

From London, **British Airways** (✆ **0845/773-3377** U.K.; www.british-airways.com) and **Lufthansa** (✆ **0845/773-7747** in the U.K.) are the most convenient carriers to the major German cities, including Düsseldorf, Cologne, Frankfurt, Munich, and Berlin. It also services Bremen, Hannover, and Stuttgart. **British Midland** (✆ **0870/607-0555** in London, or 0345/554-554 in the U.K.) has two daily flights to Cologne, four daily to Frankfurt, and one daily to Dresden.

### NEW AIR TRAVEL SECURITY MEASURES

In the wake of the terrorist attacks of September 11, 2001, the airline industry began implementing sweeping security measures in airports. Expect a lengthy check-in process and extensive delays. Although regulations vary from airline to airline, you can expedite the process by taking the following steps:

- **Arrive early.** Arrive at the airport at least 2 hours before your scheduled flight.
- **Don't count on curbside check-in.** Some airlines and airports have stopped curbside check-in altogether, whereas others offer it on a limited basis. For up-to-date information on specific regulations and implementations, check with the individual airline.
- **Be sure to carry plenty of documentation.** A government-issued photo ID (federal, state, or local) is now required. You may need to show this at various checkpoints. With an E-ticket, you may be required to have with you printed confirmation of purchase, and perhaps even the credit card with which you bought your ticket. This varies from airline to airline, so call ahead to make sure you have the proper documentation. And be sure that your ID is **up-to-date;** an expired driver's license, for example, may keep you from boarding the plane altogether.
- **Know what you can carry on—and what you can't.** Travelers in the United States are now limited to one carry-on bag, plus one personal bag (such as a purse or a briefcase). The Transportation Security Administration (TSA) has also issued a list of newly restricted carry-on items; see the box "What You Can Carry On—and What You Can't."
- **Prepare to be searched.** Expect spot-checks. Electronic items, such as a laptop or cellphone, should be readied for additional screening. Limit the metal items you wear on your person.
- **No ticket, no gate access.** Only ticketed passengers will be allowed beyond the screener checkpoints, except for those people with specific medical or parental needs.

## FLYING FOR LESS: TIPS FOR GETTING THE BEST AIRFARE

Passengers within the same airplane cabin are rarely paying the same fare. Passengers who can book their ticket

### Tips What You Can Carry On—And What You Can't

The Transportation Security Administration (TSA), the government agency that now handles all aspects of airport security, has devised new restrictions for carry-on baggage, not only to expedite the screening process but to prevent potential weapons from passing through airport security. Passengers are now limited to bringing just one carry-on bag and one personal item onto the aircraft (previous regulations allowed two carry-on bags and one personal item, like a briefcase or a purse). For more information, go to the TSA's website, www.tsa.gov. The agency has released an updated list of items passengers are not allowed to carry onto an aircraft:

**Not permitted:** knives and box cutters, corkscrews, straight razors, metal scissors, golf clubs, baseball bats, pool cues, hockey sticks, ski poles, and ice picks.

**Permitted:** nail clippers, nail files, tweezers, eyelash curlers, safety razors (including disposable razors), syringes (with documented proof of medical need), walking canes, and umbrellas (must be inspected first).

long in advance, who can stay over Saturday night, or who are willing to travel on a Tuesday, Wednesday, or Thursday after 7pm, will pay a fraction of the full fare. Here are a few other easy ways to save.

- **Consolidators,** also known as bucket shops, are a good place to find low fares. Consolidators buy seats in bulk from the airlines and then sell them back to the public at prices usually below even the airlines' discounted rates. Their small ads usually run in Sunday newspaper travel sections. And before you pay, request a confirmation number from the consolidator and then call the airline to confirm your seat. Be aware that bucket shop tickets are usually nonrefundable or rigged with stiff cancellation penalties, often as high as 50% to 75% of the ticket price. Protect yourself by paying with a credit card rather than cash. Keep in mind that if there's an airline sale going on, or if it's high season, you can often get the same or better rates by contacting the airlines directly, so do some comparison shopping before you buy. Also check out the name of the airline; you may not want to fly on some obscure Third World airline, even if you're saving $10. And check whether you're flying on a charter or a scheduled airline; the latter is more expensive but more reliable.
- **Council Travel** (✆ **800/226-8624;** www.counciltravel.com) and **STA Travel** (✆ **800/781-4040;** www.sta.travel.com) cater especially to young travelers, but their bargain-basement prices are available to people of all ages. **The TravelHub** (✆ **888/AIR-FARE;** www.travelhub.com) represents nearly 1,000 travel agencies, many of whom offer consolidator and discount fares. Other reliable consolidators include **1-800-FLY-CHEAP** (www.1800flycheap.com); **TFI Tours International** (✆ **800-745-8000** or 212/736-1140; www.lowestprice.com), which serves as a clearinghouse for unused seats; or "rebators" such as **Travel Avenue** (✆ **800/333-3335;** www.travelavenue.com) and the **Smart Traveller** (✆ **800/448-3338** in the U.S. or 305/448-3338), which rebate part of their commissions to you.
- Search **the Internet** for cheap fares. Great last-minute deals are available through free weekly e-mail services provided directly by the airlines.
- Join a travel club such as **Moment's Notice** (✆ **718/234-6295;** www.moments-notice.com) or **Sears Discount Travel Club** (✆ **800/433-9383,** or 800/255-1487 to join; www.travelersadvantage.com), which supply unsold tickets at discounted prices. You pay an annual membership fee to get the club's hot-line number. Of course, you're limited to what's available, so you have to be flexible.
- Join **frequent-flier clubs.** It's best to accrue miles on one program, so you can rack up free flights and achieve elite status faster. But it makes sense to open as many accounts as possible, no matter how seldom you fly a particular airline. It's free, and you'll get the best choice of seats, faster response to phone inquiries, and prompter service if your luggage is stolen, your flight is canceled or delayed, or if you want to change your seat.

## GETTING THERE BY TRAIN

Many passengers, especially holders of the **Eurailpass,** travel to Germany by train from other European cities. (See "Getting Around," later in this chapter, for information on purchasing the Eurailpass and other rail passes.)

**British Rail** runs four trains a day to Germany from Victoria Station in **London,** going by way of the Ramsgate–Ostend ferry or jetfoil. Two trains depart from London's Liverpool Street Station, via Harwich–Hook of Holland. Most trains change at Cologne for destinations elsewhere in Germany. Tickets can be purchased through British Rail travel centers in London (✆ **877/677-1066** in the U.K., or 0845/748-4950). See "By the Chunnel," below, for information about the Eurostar service running between London and Brussels via the Channel Tunnel.

Train journeys can be lengthy. If you go by jetfoil, Cologne is 9½ hours away from London; by Dover–Ostend ferry, it's 12½ hours; and via the Ramsgate–Ostend ferry, it's 13 hours. Berlin can be reached in about 20 hours. Travel from London to Munich, depending on the connection, can take from 18 to 22 hours; it's often cheaper to fly than to take the train.

### BY CAR & FERRY

If you want to bring your car over from England, you face a choice of ports from which you'll continue on driving to Germany. **P & O Stenna Lines** (✆ **0870/600-0611** in the U.K.; www.posl.com), has 30 to 35 ferryboat crossings a day, depending on the season, between Dover and Calais. The crossing can take as little as 1 hour and 15 minutes. Once in Calais, the drive to Cologne takes about 3 hours. Other options involve passage from Harwich to the Hook of Holland, a sea crossing of about 8 hours. You can also take your car via the Chunnel (see below).

### BY THE CHUNNEL

The $15-billion **Channel Tunnel** (or "Chunnel"), one of the great engineering feats of all time, is the first link between Britain and the Continent since the Ice Age. The tunnel was built beneath the seabed through a layer of impermeable chalk marl and sealed with a reinforced concrete lining. The 50km (31-mile) journey between Britain and France takes 35 minutes, although actual time in the Chunnel is only 19 minutes. Once on the Continent, you can connect to Germany fairly easily.

**Rail Europe** sells tickets on the **Eurostar** direct train service between London and Paris or Brussels (✆ **877-257-2887;** www.eurostar.com). In the U.K., make reservations for **Eurostar** at ✆ **0870/530-0003;** in Paris at ✆ **08-36-35-35-39;** and in the U.S. at ✆ **800/848-7245.** The train operates 24 hours a day, 365 days a year, running every 15 minutes during peak travel times and at least once an hour at night.

The tunnel also accommodates passenger cars, charter buses, taxis, and motorcycles from Folkestone to Calais. Tickets may be purchased at the tollbooth. Contact **Eurotunnel** (✆ **800/4-EURAIL** in the U.S. and Canada; 08705/35-35-35 in the U.K.).

## 9 Escorted Tours, Package Deals & Special Interest Vacations

Before you start your search for the lowest airfare, you may want to consider booking your flight as part of a travel package such as an escorted tour or a package tour. What you lose in adventure, you'll gain in time and money saved when you book accommodations, and maybe even food and entertainment, along with your flight.

### PACKAGE TOURS FOR INDEPENDENT TRAVELERS

Package tours are not the same thing as escorted tours. With a package tour, you travel independently but pay a group rate. Packages usually include airfare, a choice of hotels, and car rentals, and packagers often offer several options at different prices. In many cases, a package that includes airfare, hotel, and transportation to and from the airport will cost you less than just the hotel alone would have, had you booked it yourself. That's because packages are sold in bulk to tour operators—who resell them to the public at a cost that drastically undercuts standard rates.

## ESCORTED TOURS (TRIPS WITH GUIDES)

Escorted Tours are structured group tours, with a group leader. The price usually includes everything from airfare to hotels, meals, tours, admission costs, and local transportation.

## RECOMMENDED ESCORTED TOUR OPERTORS

**American Express Travel** (✆ **800/941-2639** in the U.S. and Canada) is one of the biggest tour operators in the world. Its offerings are comprehensive, and unescorted customized package tours are available, too.

**Brendan Tours** (✆ **800/421-8446**) has a selection of 9- to 15-day tours. **Caravan Tours** (✆ **800/227-2826;** www.caravantours.com) offers tours of southern Germany and Austria, many of which begin and end in Berlin. Accommodations are at the better hotels, and rates include everything except airfare. **Collette Vacations** ✆ **800/832-4656;** www.collettevacations.com) has an Apline Countries tour that covers southern Germany, Austria, and Switzerland. **Globus & Cosmos Tours** (✆ **800/338-7092;** www.globusandcosmos.com) offers 16-day tours of various parts of Germany. It also has a budget branch that offers tours at lower rates; all are escorted. **Maupintour** (✆ **800/255-4266;** www.maupintour.com) has a selection of upscale tours, such as a Rhine River tour of Berlin, Dresden, Meissen, Nurnberg, and Heidelberg, or an 18-day tour that goes from Vienna to Amsterdam. **Tauck World Discovery** (✆ **800/468-2825;** www.tauck.com) has a wide selection of escorted tours, such as the 14-day Romantic Germany tour from Frankfurt to Berlin, with stops in Dresden, Heidelberg, and Oberammergau. Most meals are included in the rates, but airfare is extra.

Two companies offer super-deluxe tours (with prices to match). **Abercrombie & Kent** (✆ **800/323-7308** or 630/954-2944; www.abercrombiekent.com) provides group tours to various areas of Germany and will customize them to suit your needs. **Travcoa** (✆ **800/992-2003;** www.travcoa.com) offers top-of-the-line coach tours, such as a 16-day tour of Ludwig's castles and the Romantic Road, which begins in Munich and ends in Strasbourg, France.

## BY CRUISE

Germany's premier cruise carrier is **KD River Cruises of Europe.** For information, contact them at 323 Geary St., Suite 603, San Francisco, CA 94102 (✆ **800/858-8587** or 415/392-8817), or 2500 Westchester Ave., Suite 113, Purchase, NY 10577 (✆ **800/346-6525**).

Luxury 8- to 10-day cruises on the Rhine, Main, and Danube rivers are also available through **Euro Cruises,** 33 Little W. 12th St., New York, NY 10014 (✆ **800/688-3876;** www.eurocruises.com). These cruises feature optional shore excursions. All cabins have twin beds and windows. **Jody Lexow Yacht Charters** rents hotel barges (including crew, food, and beverages) and smaller self-drive craft for touring the canals and rivers of Germany. For additional information, contact 26 Coddington Wharf, Newport, RI 02840 (✆ **800/662-2628;** www.judylexowyachtcharters.com). **Etoile de Champagne,** 88 Broad St., Boston, MA 02110 (✆ **800/280-1492;** www.etoilechampagne.com), can arrange a 6-night luxury barge cruise that runs from Trier to Koblenz, with daily excursion stops along the way.

Groups of 12 to 16 people can arrange 7- to 14-day tours of European breweries, both well-known and off the beaten track, through **MIR Corporation** (✆ **800/424-7289;** www.mircorp.com). The tours begin in many European cities.

## SPECIAL INTEREST VACATIONS

**Himalayan Travel,** 8 Berkshire Place, Danbury, CT 06810 (✆ **800/225-2380;** 800/743-2349; www.himalayantravelinc.com) has a variety of German adventure trips, including hiking, walking, trekking, and cycling tours of such areas as the Black Forest, Bavaria, and King Ludwig's Trail. The tours are self-guided, and luggage is transported by van from one hotel to the next. Rates include accommodations in two- and three-star hotels and some meals, but not airfare.

**Europe Express,** 1940 116th Ave. NE, Bellevue, WA 98004 (✆ **800/426-3615;** www.europeexpress.com), offers a variety of self-guided walking and biking tours as well as cross-country skiing trips throughout Germany. It covers such areas as the Black Forest and King Ludwig's Trail, and will customize your trip if you wish.

## BIKING

Pedaling through the Bavarian countryside is the way to go for many visitors. You can bike through green valleys and past rivers, such as the Danube, while enjoying rural landscapes and life in German villages. **Allgemeiner Deutscher Fahrrad-Club,** P.O. Box 107747; Hellerallee 23, 28077, Bremen (✆ **0421/34-62-90**), offers complete information on biking in Germany. For more information on touring Germany by bike, see "Getting Around," later in this chapter.

For the past 2 decades, **Class. Adventures,** P.O. Box 143, Hamlin, NY 14464 (✆ **800/777-8090** or 585-964-8488); fax 585/964-7297 has offered bike tours of such areas as the Romantic Road. **Euro-Bike and Walking Tours,** P.O. Box 990, DeKalb, IL 60115 (✆ **800/321-6060,** or 815/758-8851; fax 815/758-8822; www.eurobike.com), has a full range of bicycling and walking tours of Bavaria, as well as a 9-day biking tour of Germany, Switzerland, and France. The upscale outfitter **Butterfield & Robinson,** 70 Bond St., Suite 300 Toronto, ON, Canada M5B 1X3 (✆ **800/678-1147,** or 416/864-1354; fax 416/864-0541; www.butterfield.com), offers a new biking trip along the Romantic Road and along the banks of the Main, Tauber, and Neckar rivers.

Dozens of companies in Britain offer guided cycling tours. One of the best is the **Cyclists Touring Club,** 69 Meadrow, Godalming, Surrey GU7 3HS (✆ **01483/417-217;** www.ctc.org.uk). It charges £27 ($40.50) a year for membership.

## GOLF

Most German golf courses welcome visiting players who are members of courses at home. Weekday greens fees are usually around 38€ ($33.95), rising to as much as 52€ ($46.45) on Saturday and Sunday. For information about the various golf courses in Germany, write to the **Deutscher Golf/Verband,** Victoriastrasse 16, 65185 Wiesbaden (✆ **0611/99-02-00**).

Here are a few of the country's best places to golf. The Swabian region of Allgäu has several good courses. The **Golf Club Oberstaufen und Steibis** (✆ **08386/85-29**), at Oberstaufen, is an 18-hole golf course close to a forest and nature park. Oftrerschwang, a small, charmingly peaceful resort on

## king the Waters

any other country in Europe, Germany has developed the spa process to a high art. The heyday of German spa construction coincided with the rise of the bourgeoisie in the 19th century, when a lavish series of resorts was built around the dozens of mineral springs bubbling from the soil. Many of these springs had been known since the Middle Ages, or even Roman times, and to each was attributed specific cures for arthritis, gout, infertility, hypertension, and gynecological problems. (The German word *Ku—Kurort* means "spa"—is derived from the Latin *cura,* meaning "care.") Going to a spa became an intensely ritualized social experience.

There are basically four types of spas.

1. **Mineral & Thermal Spas/Springs.** Springs with at least 1 gram of dissolved mineral substances per liter of natural water are designated "mineral springs." If the water emerges from the ground at a temperature of 20°C (68°F) or more, it's called a "thermal spring." The treatment provided in mineral and thermal springs is as varied as the composition of the waters. Some of these waters are suitable for bathing.
2. **Climatic Health Resorts.** These health resorts lie in densely wooded areas permeated with fresh air. Climatic therapy consists of open-air kinesitherapy and constitutional walks along paths.
3. **Seaside Spas & Health Resorts.** Seawater and mud from coastal shallows are much used in therapeutic treatments, often for treating circulatory disorders and cardiac defects, for rehabilitation after operations, and for skin diseases and other treatments.
4. **Kneipp (Hydropathic) Spas & Health Resorts.** This treatment was first developed by Sebastian Kneipp in 1849. It's based on a strengthening of the body's intrinsic immune system and on developing a proper macrobiotic rhythm. Warm water relaxes, cold water stimulates, and a natural way of life brings harmony—this is the basic Kneipp formula. Treatments consist of the following: (1) hydrotherapy for exercising the vascular and circulatory systems and for strengthening the immune system; (2) consumption of natural basic whole foods to ensure regular metabolism; (3) use of medicinal herbs to activate self-health powers; (4) physical training and kinesitherapy to improve cardiac activity and blood circulation; and

the scenically beautiful Tiefenberger Moor, has **Golf Club Sonnenalp** (✆ **08321/27-20**). A good 18-hole course is found at **Golf Bodensee** (✆ **08389/89190**) on Lake Constance in southern Germany. Farther north, the city of Augsburg has an 18-hole course at **Golf Augsburg** (✆ **08234/56-21**).

## HIKING & MOUNTAIN CLIMBING

These sports are popular in the German uplands. It's estimated that there are more than 80,000 marked hiking and mountain-walking tracks in the country. The **Verband Deutscher Gebirgs- und Wandervereine,** Wilhelmshöher Alle 157–159, 34121

(5) adjustment therapy to ensure a balanced way of life and a harmony of mind and body.

Don't expect frenzied nightlife or nonstop activities at a spa. Spas try to pad the emotional edges of life for their clientele and provide a soothing and unruffled environment that almost anyone can appreciate. Enjoy a leisurely meal in one of the resort's airy and elegantly formal restaurants, preferably one that overlooks a sprawling flower garden. Sit in a cafe, perhaps with a glass of wine, and watch the rituals of the prosperous bourgeoisie. And, if you choose, elect a spa treatment.

There are more than 300 health resorts in Germany today. The word *Bad* before the name in any town (for example, Bad Godesberg or Bad Orb) is a sure sign that the town has some sort of ritualized process for taking the waters. Most spa directors insist on a brief medical checkup—performed on-site by resident doctors—before any treatment can begin.

In our view, no spa in Germany tops **Baden-Baden** in the Black Forest. Baden-Baden has everything—not only the waters at its opulent Kurhaus, but also Germany's best casino. There are more sightseeing attractions than at any other spa in Germany, more deluxe hotels (plenty of stars and political figures come here), and better food.

Another fabled spa, though somewhat less grand than Baden-Baden, is **Wiesbaden,** which is located outside Frankfurt, in the shelter of the Rhine and the Taunus Mountains. It has one of the finest open-air thermal pools in the country, and its thermal baths include both indoor and outdoor pools, along with endless massage rooms and solariums.

After Wiesbaden and Baden-Baden, the other leading spas fall off a bit, attracting mostly those interested in specific cures. For example, **Bad Reichenhall** in the Bavarian Alps is known for its saline waters, and has a good reputation for the treatment of respiratory problems, skin ailments, and rheumatism. **Bad Kissingen** is known for mud baths, seawater Jacuzzis, and saunas—but it's a bit dull when stacked up against its more glamorous siblings. **Bad Homburg,** in the foothills of the Taunus Mountains, is long past its 19th-century heyday, but it still enjoys a reputation for the treatment of heart and circulatory diseases.

Regardless of the various medical claims made at the spas of Germany, the real reason to go to any spa, in our view, is to momentarily escape the stress of everyday life.

Kassel (✆ **0561/938-730**), services the trails and offers details not only about trails but also about shelters, huts, and addresses of hiking associations in the various regions. The **Deutsche Alpenverein,** Von-Kahr-Strasse 2–4, 80997 Munich (✆ **089/14-00-30**), owns and operates 50 huts in and around the Alps that are open to all mountaineers. This association also maintains a 15,000km (9,500-mile) network of alpine trails.

The best **alpine hiking** is in the Bavarian Alps, especially the 1,235m (4,060-ft.) Eckbauer, on the southern fringe of Partenkirchen. The tourist office will supply hiking maps and details (see chapter 9). Another great

## Germany for Jewish Visitors

In the last few years, Jews in Eastern Europe have decreased in population because of immigration; the Jewish populations in some Western countries have also decreased because of intermarriage. Germany's Jewish population, on the other hand, is slowly increasing, mostly through immigration. It's estimated that there are between 40,000 and 80,000 Jews now living in the country, a figure that's nowhere near the prewar high of 500,000, but that still represents significant growth. The most prominent of the new arrivals are from the ex-Soviet Union. Some 70% of Jews in such cities as Bremen and Hamburg are native Russian speakers.

Berlin's Jewish community is the largest. Its 10,000 to 20,000 members are well-served by several kosher restaurants, a Jewish high school, the new Mendelssohn Center at nearby Potsdam University, and both a weekly and monthly paper. Other important Jewish communities are located in Frankfurt (7,000), Munich (3,000), Düsseldorf (2,000), Stuttgart (1,600), Cologne (1,500), and Hamburg (1,500). Another 75 smaller communities are scattered throughout the country.

While anti-Semitism has not disappeared completely, in general, postwar Germany has worked hard to confront its past—far more so than Austria, for example. Some 30 museums today deal with Jewish issues, and former concentration camp sites display their grisly reminders to visitors. German high schools include Holocaust studies in their curriculum. In politics, there are about 80 extreme-right groups, 20 or so classified as neo-Nazi, with maybe 65,000 members, but this is in a country of more than 80 million people.

Berlin has the country's highest concentration of places of interest to Jewish visitors. The Jüdischer Friedhof at Weisensee, a suburb of Berlin, was Europe's largest Jewish cemetery, and today contains around 110,000 graves and a memorial to Jews murdered in the Nazi era. A darker sight is the chillingly elegant Wannsee Villa, overlooking the Wannsee (lake), where the "Final Solution" was formally proposed in January 1942. The most hopeful landmark is the newly renovated Oranienburger Strasse Synagogue. Unlike the other five Berlin synagogues, this glorious and immense Moorish-style structure operates only as a memorial and museum. Berlin also has two museums dedicated to the city's Jews and many monuments, such as the Wives of Jewish Husbands Memorial, dedicated to the hundreds of non-Jewish women who demonstrated outside Gestapo headquarters in February 1943 after their husbands had been arrested.

place for hiking is **Berchtesgaden National Park,** Kurgarten, Maximilianstrasse 1, Berchtesgaden (✆ **08652/22-07**), bordering the Austrian province of Salzburg (see chapter 9). This park also offers the best-organized hikes and will hook you up with various groups offering hikes.

## WINTER SPORTS

More than 300 winter-sports resorts operate in the German Alps and wooded hill country such as the Harz

Mountains and the Black Forest. In addition to outstanding ski slopes, trails, lifts, jumps, toboggan slides, and skating rinks, many larger resorts also offer ice hockey, ice boating, and bobsledding. Curling is very popular as well, especially in upper Bavaria. The Olympic sports facilities at Garmisch-Partenkirchen enjoy international renown, as do the ski jumps of Oberstdorf and the artificial-ice speed-skating rink at Inzell. More than 250 ski lifts are found in the German Alps, the Black Forest, and the Harz Mountains. Information on winter-sports facilities is available from local tourist bureaus and the offices of the German National Tourist Board (see "Visitor Information," earlier in this chapter).

**Garmisch-Partenkirchen** (see chapter 9), is Germany's most famous winter sports center. Set in beautiful alpine scenery, this picturesque resort is close to Zugspitze, Germany's highest mountain. A mountain railway and a cable car can take you to the peak. In the town itself is the Olympic Ice Stadium, built in 1936, and the Ski Stadium, which has two jumps and a slalom course. Skiers of every level will be satisfied with the slopes on the mountain above the town. For information, contact the **Verkehrsamt** on Richard-Strauss-Platz (✆ **08821/18-0700**).

## 10 Planning Your Trip Online

Researching and booking your trip online can save time and money. Then again, it may not. It is simply not true that you always get the best deal online. Most booking engines do not include schedules and prices for budget airlines, and from time to time you'll get a better last-minute price by calling the airline directly, so it's best to call the airline to see if you can do better before booking online.

On the plus side, Internet users today can tap into the same travel-planning databases that were once accessible only to travel agents—and do it at the same speed. Sites such as **Frommers.com, Travelocity.com, Expedia.com,** and **Orbitz.com** allow consumers to comparison shop for airfares, access special bargains, book flights, and reserve hotel rooms and rental cars.

But don't fire your travel agent just yet. Although online booking sites offer tips and hard data to help you bargain shop, they cannot endow you with the hard-earned experience that makes a seasoned, reliable travel agent an invaluable resource, even in the Internet age. And for consumers with a complex itinerary, a trusty travel agent is still the best way to arrange the most direct flights to and from the best airports.

Still, there's no denying the Internet's emergence as a powerful tool in researching and plotting travel time. The benefits of researching your trip online can be well worth the effort.

**Last-minute specials,** such as weekend deals or Internet-only fares, are offered by airlines to fill empty seats. Most of these are announced on Tuesday or Wednesday and must be purchased online. They are only valid for travel that weekend, but some can be booked weeks or months in advance. Sign up for weekly e-mail alerts at airline websites or check megasites that compile comprehensive lists of last-minute specials, such as **Smarter Living** (smarterliving.com) or **WebFlyer** (www.webflyer.com).

Some sites, such as Expedia.com, will send you **e-mail notification** when a cheap fare becomes available to your favorite destination. Some will also tell you when fares to a particular destination are lowest.

### TRAVEL-PLANNING & BOOKING SITES

Keep in mind that because several airlines are no longer willing to pay commissions on tickets sold by online travel agencies, these agencies may either add a $10 surcharge to your bill if you book on that carrier—or neglect to offer those carriers' schedules.

The list of sites below is selective, not comprehensive. Some sites will have evolved or disappeared by the time you read this.

- **Frommer's** (www.frommers.com) is an excellent travel-planning resource. We're a little biased, of course, but we think you'll find the travel tips, reviews, monthly vacation giveaways, and online-booking capabilities thoroughly indispensable. Among the special features are our popular **Message Boards,** where Frommer's readers post queries and share advice (sometimes even our authors show up to answer questions); **Frommers.com Newsletter,** for the latest travel bargains and inside travel secrets; and Frommer's **Destinations Section,** where you'll get expert travel tips, hotel and dining recommendations, and advice on the sights to see for more than 2,500 destinations around the globe.
- **Travelocity** (www.travelocity.com or www.frommers.travelocity.com) and **Expedia** (www.expedia.com) are among the most popular sites, each offering an excellent range of options. Travelers search by destination, dates, and cost.
- **Orbitz** (www.orbitz.com) is a popular site launched by United, Delta, Northwest, American, and Continental Airlines. With this site, you're granted access to the largest data bank of low rates, airline tickets, rental cars, hotels, vacation packages, and other travel products. You get, among other offerings, available fares from more than 450 airlines.
- **Qixo** (www.qixo.com) is another powerful search engine that allows you to search for flights and accommodations from some 20 airline and travel-planning sites (such as Travelocity) at once. Qixo sorts results by price.
- **Priceline** (www.priceline.com) lets you "name your price" for airline tickets, hotel rooms, and rental cars. For airline tickets, you can't say what time you want to fly—you have to accept any flight between 6am and 10pm on the dates you've selected, and you may have to make one or more stopovers. Tickets are nonrefundable, and no frequent-flier miles are awarded.

## OUR FAVORITE GERMAN WEBSITES

If you open a site that's in German and it's all Greek to you, don't panic. Many of them provide English translations. Look for the little British or American flag, or for the word *English.*

- The **German National Tourist Board** site (www.germany-tourism.de) gives you an online tour of several quaint, window box filled cities and highlights attractions for educational excursions, romantic vacations, or youth trips. You can also access facts on weather, transportation, events, and so forth. A new, related site (www.visits-to-germany.com) designed especially for United States travelers lets you design and price specific itineraries and vacation packages to Germany.
- The **Hotelguide Germany IHA Hotel Association** (www.hotels-germany.com) lets you book a room at any of more than 750 German hotels through this site. Conduct a search according to location and amenity preferences, or check out the page of special offers for accommodations conducive to family travel, cultural activities, sports, biking, special events, or last-minute travel.

- Get started on the appealing, if daunting, task of eating in Germany with the help of the **Gastroscout.com** site (www.eat-germany.net). Search for a schnitzel-filled *Gasthaus* or other eatery by city, price, ethnicity, child-friendliness, wheelchair accessibility, or any of a slew of other criteria. If you're not sure what it is you're searching for, recommendations are listed.
- The **Berlin.de** site (www.berlin.de) offers an online hotel reservation service, a virtual ticket counter for all kinds of shows and cultural events, and a large photo gallery for virtual sightseeing. The site also offers special packages and lots of information for travelers with special needs (such as families and travelers with disabilities).
- The **Munich Tourist Office** site (www.munich-tourist.de) offers information about the city's history, economy, places of interest (museums, parks, churches, and so on), and accommodations. There's also an entire section devoted to Oktoberfest.

## 11 Getting Around

### BY PLANE

From Frankfurt, most **Lufthansa** (✆ **800/645-3880**) destinations in Germany can be reached in an average of 50 minutes, with at least four flights daily.

All German cities with commercial airports have an airport shuttle service, offering reduced fares and fast connections between the city center and the airport. Departure points are usually the airlines' town offices and the city's main rail terminal. Luggage can be checked at the DB (Deutsche Bahn/GermanRail) baggage counter at the airport for delivery to the railroad station at your ultimate destination.

### BY TRAIN

Whether you travel first or second class, you'll find that the trains of **GermanRail (DB Rail)** deserve their good reputation for comfort, cleanliness, and punctuality. All are modern and fast. Both first- and second-class trains carry smoker and nonsmoker compartments. A snack bar or a dining car, serving German and international cuisine as well as good wine and beer, can usually be found on all trains except locals.

For city sightseeing, you can leave your baggage in a locker or check it at the station's baggage counter. In many cities, GermanRail provides door-to-door baggage service, allowing passengers to have luggage picked up at or delivered to their hotels. Accompanying baggage can be checked for a nominal fee. Suitcases, baby carriages, skis, bicycles, and steamer trunks are permitted as baggage. Insurance policies of various kinds, including a travel medical plan, are also available.

About 20,000 **InterCity (IC)** passenger trains offer express service every hour between most large and medium-size German cities. IC trains have adjustable cushioned seats and individual reading lights, and often offer telephone and secretarial services. Bars, lounges, and dining rooms are available, too. A network of **EuroCity (EC)** trains connecting Germany with 13 other countries offers the same high standards of service as those of IC.

Germany's high-speed rail network, known as **InterCity Express (ICE)** trains, is among the fastest in Europe, reaching speeds of 265 kmph (165mph). One of these trains runs from Hamburg via Würzburg and Nürnberg to Munich; another from Frankfurt via Stuttgart to Munich; and yet another from Berlin via Frankfurt to Munich. Each train makes stops along the way. ICE significantly reduces travel time, making transits north to south across the country easily possible in the course of a single day. Some 200 east-west connections have been added to the GermanRail timetable to link the Deutsche Bundesbahn (west) and the Deutsche Reichsbahn (east). Additional connections make Leipzig and Dresden more accessible.

**InterCity Night (ICN)**—one of the most comfortable night trains in Europe—operates between Berlin and Bonn and Berlin and Munich. Even though the train doesn't depart until 10 or 11pm, you may board as early as 8 or 8:30pm. Arrival the next morning is between 6:55 and 7:55am, and you have the option of remaining aboard until 9 or 9:30am.

The ICN offers first and tourist class. Sleeping accommodations in first class include single or double compartments with shower and toilet, and they are equipped with key cards, phones for wake-up service, luggage storage, and other amenities. Tourist class offers open seating with sleeperettes (reclining seats). The ICN is equipped with a restaurant and bistro car, and breakfast buffet is included in the first-class fare. For an extra cost, a limited menu for dinner is offered. Advance reservations are mandatory for all sleeping accommodations.

DER Rail issues tickets for the ICN and also makes reservations. Eurail and GermanRail pass holders are accepted on this train but have to pay for the seat or sleeper reservation and also for meals. Youth-pass holders are only accepted in tourist class. Children under the age of 4 travel free, provided they do not require a separate seat; those between 4 and 12 are charged half fare.

Before leaving for Germany, you can get complete details about the **German Federal Railroad** and the many plans it offers, as well as information about Eurailpasses, at Raileurope (✆ **800/848-7245;** www.raileurope.com).

**GERMANRAIL TOURIST PASSES**

You can buy a **GermanRail Pass** from a travel agent before you leave home. The pass allows 4 days of travel in 1 month and costs $260 first class or $180 second class. Additional days cost $32 first class and $22 second class.

A youth version of the same pass, valid only for persons under 26 years of age and available only in second class, costs $142 for 4 days in 1 month, $156 for 5 days in 1 month, $166 for 6 days in 1 month, $180 for 7 days in 1 month, $192 for 8 days in 1 month, $204 for 9 days in 1 month, and $216 for 10 days in 1 month. Another bargain is a **Twinpass,** for two adults traveling together. This pass costs $390 for 4 days in 1 month for first class or $270 for second class.

The passes also entitle the bearer to additional benefits, such as free or discounted travel on selected bus routes operated by Deutsche Touring/Europabus, including destinations not serviced by trains, or excursions along particularly scenic highways such as the Romantic Road and the Castle Road. The pass also includes free travel on **KD German Line steamers** (day trips only) along the Rhine, Main, and Mosel rivers.

These passes are most conveniently available from **Rail Europe** (✆ **800/4-EURAIL** in the U.S., or 800/361-RAIL in Canada). Rail Europe can also arrange cost-effective "Rail and Drive" packages that combine a certain number of days on the train with a certain number of days in a rental car. Here's an example of how it might work: Ride the train from Frankfurt to Munich, spend 3 days exploring the city, then rent a car for a 2-day excursion to Berchtesgaden and the Bavarian Alps. The GermanRail Flexipass is also sold by **DER Travel** (✆ **800/782-2424;** www.der.com in the U.S. and Canada) and by **CIT Tours**

(✆ **800/248-7245;** www.cittours.com.au in the U.S. and Canada, or 847/318-7101 in Chicago).

**WHERE TO BUY RAIL PASSES** Travel agents in all towns and railway agents in major North American cities sell all these tickets, but the biggest supplier is **Rail Europe** (✆ **800/848-7245;** www.raileurope.com), which can also give you informational brochures.

Many different rail passes are available in the U.K. for travel in Britain and continental Europe. Stop in at the **International Rail Centre,** Victoria Station, London SWIV 1JY (✆ **0870/5848-840** in the U.K.). Some of the most popular passes, including Inter-Rail and Euro Youth, are offered only to travelers under 26 years of age; these allow unlimited second-class travel through most European countries.

## BY CAR

British travelers who want to bring their own cars over should see "Getting There," earlier in this chapter.

Competition in the European car-rental industry is fierce, so make sure you comparison shop. You can make reservations by calling these toll-free numbers: **Avis** (✆ **800/331-1212**), **Budget** (✆ **800/527-0700**), **Hertz** (✆ **800/654-3001**), **Kemwel Holiday Autos** (✆ **800/678-0678**), and **Auto Europe** (✆ **800/223-5555**). Cars can often be rented at one German city and returned at another for no additional charge.

There are some advantages to **prepaying rentals** in dollars before leaving the United States. You get an easy-to-understand net price (which you have to prepay at least 14 days before departure by credit card), the rental process is more streamlined, and you can avoid unpleasant surprises caused by sudden unfavorable changes in currency exchange rates. Remember, however, that if you opt to prepay and your plans change, you'll have to go through some rather complicated paperwork (and, in some cases, have to pay a penalty of around $25) for changing or canceling a prepaid contract.

**GASOLINE** Gasoline is readily available throughout Germany, and service stations appear frequently along the Autobahns. The cheapest gasoline is at stations marked SB-TANKEN (self-service), but remember that gas will always be much more expensive than in the U.S. A liter (about a fourth of a gallon) costs .75€ to 2€ (65¢–$1.80). Gasoline pumps labeled BLEIFREI offer unleaded gas.

**DRIVING RULES** In Germany, you drive on the right side of the road. Both front-seat and back-seat passengers are required to wear safety belts. Children cannot ride in the front seat.

Easy-to-understand international road signs are posted, but U.S. travelers should remember that road signs are in kilometers, not miles. In congested areas, the speed limit is about 50 kmph (around 30 mph). On all other roads except the Autobahns, the speed limit is 100 kmph (about 60 mph).

In theory, there is no speed limit on the Autobahns (in the left, fast lane), but many drivers going too fast report that they have been stopped by the police and fined on the spot. So reasonable caution is recommended here, for safety if not other reasons. A German driver on the Autobahn can be a ferocious creature, and you may prefer the slow lane. The government recommends an Autobahn speed limit of 130 kmph (80 mph).

*Note:* Drinking while driving is a very serious offense in Germany. Be sure to keep any alcoholic beverages in the trunk or some other storage area.

**BREAKDOWNS/ASSISTANCE** The major automobile club in Germany is **Automobilclub von Deutschland (AvD),** Lyoner Strasse 16, 60329 Frankfurt (✆ **069/6-60-60**). If you have a breakdown on the Autobahn, you can call from an emergency phone, each of which is spaced about a mile apart. On secondary roads, go to the nearest phone. If you don't belong to an auto club, call ✆ **01802/222-222.** In English, ask for "road service assistance." Emergency assistance is free, but you pay for parts or materials.

**MAPS** The best maps, available at all major bookstores throughout Germany, are published by **Michelin,** which offers various regional maps. **Hallweg** also offers good maps.

**DRIVER'S LICENSES** American drivers, and those from EU countries, need only a domestic license to drive. However, both in Germany and throughout the rest of Europe, you must also have an international insurance certificate, known as a green card (*carte verte*). Any car-rental agency will automatically provide one of these as a standard part of the rental contract, but it's a good idea to double-check all documents at the time of rental, just to be sure that you can identify the card if asked by border patrol or the police.

### BY BUS

An excellent, efficient bus network services Germany. Many buses are operated by **Bahnbus,** which is owned by the railway. These are integrated to complement the rail service. Bus service in Germany is particularly convenient during slow periods of rail service, normally around midday and on Saturday and Sunday. German post offices often operate local bus services (contact local post offices for schedules and prices).

The most popular bus ride is along the Romantic Road (see chapter 7), where special green-and-white buses carry tourists regularly from town to town. For more information, ask a travel agent or call **Deutsche Touring GmbH,** Amrömerhof 17, Frankfurt (✆ **069/79030**).

### BY BOAT

Perhaps Germany's most beautiful features are its lakes and rivers. The mighty Rhine is the country's most traveled waterway. German cruise ships also run on the Main River between Mainz and Frankfurt; on the Danube from Nürnberg to Linz (Austria), going on to Vienna and Budapest; and on the Mosel between Cochem and Trier.

**KD River Cruises of Europe,** 323 Geary St., Suite 603, San Francisco, CA 94102 (✆ **800/858-8587** or 415/392-8817), or 2500 Westchester Ave., Suite 113, Purchase, NY 10577 (✆ **800/346-6525**), operates the most services. Eurailpasses are valid for most KD excursions. The company also offers luxury cruises, the most popular being a 5-day cruise along the Rhine from Amsterdam to Basel or vice versa.

## 12 Tips on Accommodations

In general, Germany has one of the highest standards of innkeeping in the world. However, many of the hotels in the eastern section of Germany—once geared to tourism from the old Eastern Bloc countries—are not of the same standard as those in the west.

Hotels range from palaces of luxury and comfort to plain country inns and simple guesthouses (*Gasthäuser*), with a huge variation in rates. The cheapest accommodation is in pensions (*Fremdenheime*) or rooms in private homes (look for a sign saying ZIMMER FREI, meaning there's a room for rent). Hotels listed as *garni* provide no meals other than breakfast.

When you don't have time to make reservations on your own, you can call **Travel Interlink** at ✆ **800/888-5898;** www.travelinterlink.com. Also, tourist offices will often book you into a room for a small charge.

## 13 Recommended Books

### BIOGRAPHY

Riefenstahl, Leni. *Leni Riefenstahl: A Memoir.* St. Martin's Press, 1993. This autobiography by the aging photographer and former film director has been both praised and condemned by critics. Known as the "Führer's moviemaker" because of her 1934 Nazi propaganda film, *The Triumph of the Will,* Riefenstahl has been the subject of lurid speculation concerning her personal and professional life. She answers her critics in this account of her life.

Taylor, A.J.P. *Bismarck: The Man and the Statesman.* Random House, 1967. This is the story of the "Iron Chancellor," who was instrumental in unifying the German states into the German Empire.

Trevor-Roper, Hugh. *The Last Days of Hitler.* Macmillan, 1986. This is an insightful reconstruction of the twilight of the Third Reich.

### FICTION

Goethe, Johann Wolfgang von. *The Sorrows of Young Werther.* Random House, 1990. This is required reading for every German schoolchild. Goethe explored the theme of suicide in this early epistolary novella.

Grass, Günter. *Dog Years* (Harcourt Brace Jovanovich, 1989), *The Tin Drum* (Random House, 1990), and *The Flounder* (Harcourt Brace Jovanovich, 1989). Grass's works deal with the German psyche coming to terms with the dreadful legacy of Nazism and World War II. His latest book, *The Call of the Toad* (Harcourt Brace Jovanovich, 1993), is a good read—part love story and part political lampoon.

Hesse, Hermann. *Narcissus and Goldmund.* Batman, 1981. This book tells the story of two monks in Germany in the Middle Ages.

Isherwood, Christopher. *The Berlin Stories.* New Directions, 1954. Isherwood lived in Berlin from 1929 to 1933. His most famous story was "Good-Bye to Berlin," which became the source of the stage and film versions of *Cabaret.*

Mann, Thomas. *The Magic Mountain.* Random House, 1969. This is Mann's most celebrated masterpiece.

Nebenzal, Harold. *Café Berlin.* Avon, 1994. Nebenzal has attracted a lot of world attention with this kaleidoscopic work, his first novel. Its intrigue unfolds against the backdrop of the 1930s nightlife of Berlin.

Remarque, Erich Maria. *All Quiet on the Western Front.* Fawcett, 1987. This is a classic novel of World War I.

### FOLKLORE & LEGENDS

Grimm, Jacob, and Wilhelm Grimm. *Complete Grimm Tales.* Pantheon, 1974. This is the world's most famous collection of folktales, with a cast of characters that includes everybody from Little Red Riding Hood to Tom Thumb.

*The Nibelungenlied.* Penguin, 1965. Every school kid in Germany reads this great epic poem which details the exploits of Siegfried and Kriemhild and the fall of the Burgundians. The Nibelungenlied is characterized by the violence of its emotions and its uncompromising emphasis on vengeance. The mystery is, who wrote it? It is believed that some unknown Danubian poet penned the work at the dawn of the 13th century. Too bad his name isn't known; otherwise, he'd be celebrated as one of Europe's great epic writers. Richard Wagner drew upon this prose epic for his Ring Cycle, although he used other Norse legends as well.

### HISTORY

Ash, Timothy Garton, *In Europe's Name: Germany and the Divided Continent.* Random House, 1993. This book tells a tale filled with paradoxes and ironies of how a divided Germany achieved unification. Ash, a British journalist and scholar, drew part of his information from declassified files of East Germany's secret police.

Darnton, Robert. *Berlin Journal 1989–90.* W. W. Norton, 1991. This American scholar writes of the near-bloodless revolution that led to the unification of Germany.

Large, David Clay, *Berlin.* Basic Books, 2000. In this controversial and caustic survey of Berlin since 1871, the author claims that, "no other place has so dramatically encapsulated the highs and lows of our modern human experience" as Berlin. From the days of Bismarck to its position as "capital of the Cold War," Berlin the city is painted in vivid strokes in this absorbing tale of triumph and defeat.

Schneider, Peter. *The German Comedy: Scenes of Life After the Wall,* translated by Leigh Hafrey and Philip Boehm. Farrar, Straus & Giroux, 1992. Comic absurdities surrounding the collapse of the Wall fill this book, but Schneider (author of *The Wall Jumper*) also explores resurgent anti-Semitism and how Germans are coping with the flood of refugees from the east.

Shirer, William L. *The Rise and Fall of the Third Reich: A History of Nazi Germany.* Simon & Schuster, 1959–60. This story has never been told better—the complete saga of Hitler's empire from beginning to end.

West, Rebecca. *A Train of Powder.* Viking, 1955. This English novelist and historian covered the Nürnberg Trials for the *Daily Telegraph.* She provides a keen insight into the moral and legal judgments rendered there.

## TRAVEL

Twain, Mark. *A Triumph Abroad.* Hippocrene Books, 1989. The American humorist's travels through Germany are comically detailed here. Read also his comments on "The Awful German Language."

### *FAST FACTS:* Germany

*Business Hours* Most **banks** are open Monday to Friday 8:30am to 1pm and 2:30 to 4pm (Thurs to 5:30pm). Money exchanges at airports and border-crossing points are generally open daily from 6am to 10pm. Exchanges at border railroad stations are kept open for arrivals of all international trains. Most **businesses** are open Monday to Friday from 9am to 5pm and on Saturday from 9am to 1pm. Store hours can vary from town to town, but **shops** are generally open Monday to Friday 9 or 10am to 6 or 6:30pm (to 8:30pm on Thurs). Saturday hours are generally from 9am to 1 or 2pm, except on the first Saturday of the month, when stores may remain open until 4pm.

*Drug Laws* Penalties for illegal drug possession in Germany are severe. You could go to jail or be deported immediately.

*Drugstores* Pharmaceuticals are sold at an *Apotheke.* For cosmetics, go to a *Drogerie.* German pharmacies take turns staying open nights, on Sundays, and on holidays, and each *Apotheke* posts a list of those that are open off-hours.

*Electricity* In most places the electricity is 220 volts AC (50 cycles). A transformer and a plug that fits the German socket will be needed for your U.S. appliances. Many leading hotels will supply these.

*Embassies & Consulates* The following embassies and consulates are all located in Berlin. The embassy of the **United States** is in Dahlem at Clayallee 170 (✆ **030/832-92-33;** U-Bahn: Dahlem-Dorf), open Monday to Friday 8:30am to 3pm. The **U.K. Embassy** is at Under den Linden 32–34 (✆ **030/20-18-40;** U-Bahn: Under den Linden), open Monday to Friday 9am to 4pm. The **Australian Embassy** is at Friedrichstrasse 200 (✆ **030/880-08-80;** U-Bahn: Uhlandstrasse), open Monday to Friday 9am to noon. The **Canadian Embassy** is at Friedrichstrasse 95 (✆ **030/20-31-20;** U-Bahn: Friedrichstrasse), open Monday to Friday 9am to noon. The **Irish Embassy** is at Friedrichstrasse 200 (✆ **030/22-07-20;** U-Bahn: Uhlandstrasse), open Monday to Friday 9:30am to noon and 2:30 to 3:45pm. The **New Zealand Embassy** is at Friedrichstrasse 60 (✆ **030/206-210;** U-Bahn: Friedrichstrasse), open Monday to Friday at 9am to 1pm and 2 to 5:30pm. The **South African Embassy** is at Friedrichstrasse 60 (✆ **030/22-07-30;** U-Bahn: Friedrichstrasse), open Monday to Friday 9am noon.

*Emergencies* Throughout Germany the emergency number for **police** is ✆ **110;** for fire or to call an ambulance, dial ✆ **112.**

*Liquor Laws* As in many European countries, drinking laws are flexible, enforced only if a problem develops. Officially, you must be 18 to consume any kind of alcoholic beverage. Bars and cafes rarely request proof of age. Drinking while driving, however, is treated as a very serious offense.

*Mail* General delivery—mark it POSTE RESTANTE—can be used in any major town or city in Germany. You can pick up your mail upon presentation of a valid identity card or passport. Street mailboxes are painted yellow. It costs 1.50€ ($1.35) for the first 5 grams (about ⅕ oz.) to send an airmail letter to the United States or Canada, and 1€ (90¢) for postcards. To mail a package, go to one of the larger post offices, preferably the main branch in the area. All letters to the U.K. cost .55€ (50¢)

*Police* Throughout the country, dial ✆ **110** for emergencies.

*Restrooms* Use the word *Toilette* (pronounced twah-*leh*-teh). Women's toilets are usually marked with an "F" for *Frauen,* and men's toilets with an "H" for *Herren.* Germany, frankly, doesn't have enough public toilets, except in transportation centers. The locals have to rely on bars, cafes, or restaurants—and using them isn't always appreciated if you're not a paying customer. Toilets often have attendants who expect a small tip; if you need soap and a towel, give something extra.

*Safety* Germany is a reasonably safe country in which to travel, although neo-Nazi skinheads, especially in the eastern part of the country, have sometimes attacked black or Asian travelers. One of the most dangerous places, especially at night, is around the large railway stations in such cities as Frankfurt, Munich, Berlin, and Hamburg. Some beer halls get especially rowdy late at night.

*Taxes* As a member of the European Union, Germany imposes a tax on most goods and services known as a **value-added tax (VAT),** or in German, *Mehrwertsteuer.* Nearly everything is taxed at 15%, including vital necessities such as gas and luxury items such as jewelry. VAT is included in the prices of restaurants and hotels. Note that goods for sale, such as cameras, also have the 15% tax already factored into the price; but the listed prices of services, such as getting a mechanic to fix your car, don't include VAT, so an extra 15% will be tacked on to the bill. Stores that display a "Tax Free" sticker will issue you a Tax-Free Shopping Check at the time of purchase. When leaving the country, have your check stamped by the German Customs Service as your proof of legal export. You can then get a cash refund at one of the Tax-Free Shopping Service offices in the major airports and many train stations, even at some of the bigger ferry terminals. Otherwise, you must send the checks to Tax-Free Shopping Service, Mengstrasse 19, 23552 Lübeck, Germany. If you want the payment to be credited to your bankcard or your bank account, mention this. There is no airport departure tax in Germany.

*Telephone* The country code for Germany is 49. To call Germany from the United States, dial the international access code 011, then 49, then the city code, then the regular phone number. ***The phone numbers listed in this book are to be used within Germany; when calling from abroad, omit the initial 0 in the city code.***

Local and long-distance calls may be placed from all post offices and coin-operated public telephone booths. The unit charge is 15€ (15¢). More than half the phones in Germany require an advance-payment telephone card from **Telekom,** the German telephone company. Phone cards are sold at post offices and newsstands; they cost 6€ to 25€ ($5.35–$22.35). Rates are measured in units rather than minutes. The farther the distance, the more units are consumed. For example, a 3-minute call to the United States costs 41 units. Telephone calls made through hotel switchboards can double, triple, or even quadruple the regular charge. Therefore, try to make your calls outside your hotel at a pay phone or post office. Post offices can also send faxes for you.

German phone numbers are not standard and come in various formats. In some places, numbers have as few as three digits. In cities, one building's number may have 5 digits whereas the phone next door might have 9 digits. Germans also often hyphenate their numbers differently. But since all the area codes are the same, these various configurations should have little affect on your phone usage once you get used to the fact that numbers are inconsistent and vary from place to place.

To call the U.S. or Canada from Germany, dial 01, followed by the country code (1), then the area code, and then the number. Alternatively, you can dial the various telecommunication companies in the States for cheaper rates. From Germany, the access for **AT&T** is ✆ **0800-888-00-10;** for **MCI** ✆ **0800-888-8000;** and for **Sprint** ✆ **0800-888-0013. USA Direct** can be used with all telephone cards and for collect calls. The number from Germany is ✆ **01-30-00-10. Canada Direct** can be used with Bell Telephone Cards and for collect calls. This number from Germany is ✆ **01-30-00-14.**

If you're calling from a public pay phone in Germany, you must deposit the basic local rate.

*Time* Germany operates on Central European time (CET), which means that the country is 6 hours ahead of eastern standard time (EST) in the United States and 1 hour ahead of Greenwich mean time (GMT). Summer daylight saving time begins in Germany in April and ends in September—there's a slight difference in the dates from year to year—so there may be a period in early spring and in the fall when there's a 7-hour difference between EST and CET. Always check if you're traveling during these periods—especially if you need to catch a plane.

*Tipping* If a restaurant bill says *Bedienung,* that means a service charge has already been added, so just round up to the nearest Euro.

If not, add 10% to 15%. Round up to the nearest mark for taxis. Bellhops get 1€ (90¢) per bag, as does the doorperson at your hotel, restaurant, or nightclub. Room-cleaning staffs get small tips in Germany, as do concierges who perform some special favors such as obtaining hard-to-get theater or opera tickets. Tip hairdressers or barbers 5% to 10%.

# 4

# Berlin

Berlin's history is dark, not only as Hitler's nerve center of Nazi horror, but also as the battleground of the Cold War. But with its field of new skyscrapers and hip clubs and fashion boutiques, post-millennium Berlin is recasting itself as the continent's new capital of cool.

However, make no mistake, Berlin is not exactly escaping the past, as the opening of the new Jewish Museum (Jüdisches Museum Berlin), a paean to German Jewry, testifies. Instead, Berlin is reconciling itself to its notorious history and moving with confidence into its future. As one hip young Berliner, Joachim Stressmann, told us: "We don't know where we're going, but we know where we've been, and no one wants to go back there."

The reunited city of Berlin is once again the capital of Germany. Berlin was almost bombed out of existence during World War II; its streets reduced to piles of rubble, its parks to muddy swampland. But the optimistic spirit and strength of will of the remarkable Berliners enabled them to survive not only the wartime destruction of their city, but also its postwar division, symbolized by the Berlin Wall.

Today, structures of steel and glass tower over streets where before only piles of rubble lay, and parks and gardens are again lush. Nonetheless, even in the daily whirl of working, shopping, and dining along the Ku'damm, Berliners encounter reminders of less happy days. At the end of the street stands the Kaiser Wilhelm Memorial Church, with only the shell of the old neo-Romanesque bell tower remaining. In striking contrast is the new church, constructed west of the old tower in 1961, and nicknamed "lipstick and powderbox" by Berliners because of its futuristic design.

Before the war, the section of the city that became East Berlin was the cultural and political heart of Germany, where the best museums, the finest churches, and the most important boulevards lay. The walled-in East Berliners turned to restoring their important museums, theaters, and landmarks (especially in the Berlin-Mitte section), while the West Berliners built entirely new museums and cultural centers. This contrast between the two parts of city is still evident today, though east and west are coming together more and more within the immense, fascinating whole that is Berlin.

## 1 Orientation

### ARRIVING

**BY PLANE** **Tegel** is the city's busiest airport, serving most flights from the west. Historic **Tempelhof** (made famous as the city's lifeline during the Berlin Airlift) has declined in importance, although it's still used for flights from Basel, Brussels, Copenhagen, Prague, and many cities within Germany. **Schönefeld,** the airport in the eastern sector, is used primarily by Russian and eastern European airlines. Private bus shuttles among the three airports operate constantly, so you can make connecting flights at a different airport. For information on any of the three airports call ✆ **0180/500-01-86** or visit www.berlin-airport.de/PubEnglish.

**Lufthansa** (✆ **800/645-3880;** www.Lufthansa-usa.com) offers direct flights from Washington, D.C. to Berlin. Otherwise transatlantic passengers from other cities are routed to its hubs at Frankfurt and Munich.

**Delta** (✆ **800/241-4141;** www.delta.com) has flights to Berlin-Tegel in the evening from New York's JFK airport and from Atlanta. However, daily flights, depending on the season or on business, are not always a sure thing, so you'll need to check with a travel agent or the airline itself.

The best and most convenient service into Berlin is available aboard **British Airways (BA)** (✆ **800/247-9297;** www.britishairways.com), which efficiently funnels dozens of daily flights from North America to Germany, including five a day into Berlin-Tegel, through its vast terminals at London-Heathrow. Connections to Berlin are excellent from at least 40 gateways in the U.S. and Canada, more than that offered by any other airline. Frequent transatlantic price wars keep fares to Berlin aboard BA lower than you might have thought, especially in off-season. Stopovers in London can be arranged at minimal cost, and deeply discounted hotel packages are available in either Berlin or London, at rates that are significantly less than what you'd have paid if you'd arranged them yourself. And if you opt for passage in Business Class (BA calls it Club Class), you'll ride on the most comfortable, and one of the largest, airline seats in the industry, in a configuration that can be transformed into something approaching a bed.

**Berlin-Tegel Airport** (✆ **01805/000186;** www.berlin-airport.de/PubEnglish) is 8km (5 miles) northwest of the city center. Public transportation by bus, taxi, or U-Bahn is convenient to all points in the city. BVG buses X9 and 109 run every 10 to 15 minutes from the airport to Bahnhof Zoo in Berlin's center, departing from outside the arrival hall; a one-way fare is 2.40€ ($2.15). A taxi to the city center costs 20€ to 22€ ($17.85–$19.65) and takes 20 minutes. No porters are available for luggage handling, but pushcarts are free.

The main terminal has a **visitor information counter** where you can get a free map of the city. The counter is open daily 5am to 10pm. Facilities at the terminal include money-exchange centers, luggage-storage facilities (and locker rentals), a police station, auto-rental kiosks, dining facilities, and a first-aid center. Shops sell gifts, film, and travel paraphernalia.

**Berlin-Schönefeld Airport** (✆ **01805/000186;** www.berlin-airport.de/PubEnglish), once the main airport for East Berlin, now receives many flights from Asia, as well as Russia and other European countries. It lies in Brandenburg, 19km (12 miles) southeast of the city center. The city center is a 55-minute ride on the S-Bahn. You can also take bus 171 from the airport to Rudow, where you transfer to the U-Bahn. Either means of transport costs 3€ ($2.70).

**Berlin-Tempelhof Airport** (✆ **01805/000186;** www.berlin-airport.de/PubEnglish) is the city's oldest airport, 6km (4 miles) southeast of the city center. Tempelhof now receives several flights a day from German and European cities. Take the U-Bahn or bus 119. All bus trips from Tempelhof into the center cost 2.80€ ($2.50).

**BY TRAIN** As Berlin strengthens its role as capital, increasing numbers of trains are speeding their way into town. All points of the country, especially Frankfurt, Munich, and Bonn, maintain excellent rail connections, with high-tech, high-speed improvements being made to the country's railway system

## Berlin Today & Tomorrow

Berlin is living up to its reputation as a dynamic, exciting hub of activity as never before. The city's nightlife is among Europe's best and wildest. And now that the German government has been transferred here from Bonn, Berlin is bidding to become the reborn capital not only of Germany, but of all Europe.

As befits a new capital, the city is undergoing a major face-lift. More than $120 billion has been invested in new streets, buildings, and railways. The former East Berlin is rapidly being restored and gentrified, particularly in the **Mitte** (central) district. Here, new luxury hotels and shopping arcades compete with the litter of the Kurfürstendamm (street). The opening of the Hotel Adlon (p. 88), overlooking the Brandenburg Gate, is particularly notable, because it evokes the restoration of Unter den Linden and the return to some of its pre-war glory, since Adlon, at one time, was the most important hotel in Berlin, perhaps in all of Germany. **Prenzlauer Berg,** a blue-collar eastern neighborhood that escaped the worst of the wartime bombing, is becoming a chic district of cafes and boutiques. The downside of all this for Berliners has been the sharp increase in real-estate prices, as well as the inconvenience of living in the world's largest construction site.

Many of Berlin's famous buildings have also been restored. The rebuilt **Reichstag** (p. 119) has a glittering glass dome; upon the building stands not the old glowering imperial hunter, but the national symbol, the eagle (locals refer affectionately to the statue as "the fat hen"). The Oranienburger Strasse **synagogue** (also known as **Neue Synagoge Berlin-Centrum Judaicum/The New Synagogue**), wrecked on Kristallnacht and finished off by Allied bombers, has been rebuilt in all its splendor. Likewise, **Berliner Dom (Berlin Cathedral)** and the five state museums on **Museum Island** (Museumsinsel; p. 68) have been returned to their original glory.

Visitors, unfortunately, often overlook Berlin's **natural attractions.** Few metropolitan areas are blessed with as many gardens, lakes, woodlands, and parks—these cover an amazing one-third of the city. First-time visitors are often surprised to learn that small farms with fields and meadows still exist within the city limits.

virtually all the time. One recent major improvement is that Berlin and the great port of Hamburg are now 15 minutes closer thanks to high-speed (250kmph/155 mph) InterCity Express service (the trip is now 2 hours and 8 minutes). Since reunification, Berlin has improved the facilities of railway stations in both the western zone (Bahnhof Zoologischer Garten) and eastern zone (Berlin Ostbahnhof), installing improved S-Bahn links to interconnect them. The station you'll use depends on the destination or origin of your train, or the location of your hotel within the city. Some, but not all, trains make arrivals and departures from both stations. A third station, Berlin Lichtenberg, within the city's eastern half, is used for trains pulling in from small towns. For information about any railway station, call ✆ **01805/996633.**

**BY BUS (COACH)** Regularly scheduled buses operate from 250 German and continental cities, including Frankfurt, Hamburg, and Munich. Long-distance bus companies servicing Berlin include **Autokraft GmbH, Haru-Reisen,** and **Bayern Express & P. Köhn** (✆ **030/8-60-96-0** or 030/8-60-21-1).

Arrivals and departures are at the **ZOB Omnibusbahnhof am Funkturm,** Masurenalle, Charlottenburg. Taxis and bus connections are available at the station, U-Bahn at the nearby Kaiserdamm station.

**BY CAR** From Frankfurt, take the E451 north until it connects with the E40 going northeast. Follow this Autobahn past Jena and then head north on the E51 into Berlin. From Nürnberg, also take the E51 into Berlin. From Dresden, take the E55 north to Berlin. Expect heavy traffic on the Autobahns on weekends and sunny days when everybody is out touring.

## VISITOR INFORMATION

For visitor information and hotel bookings, head for the **Berlin Tourist Information Center,** Europa Center (near Memorial Church); the entrance is on the Budapesterstrasse side. It's open Monday to Saturday 8:30am to 8:30pm and Sunday 10am to 6:30pm. There's also a branch at the south wing of the Brandenburg Gate, open daily 9:30am to 6pm. Neither branch accepts telephone calls from the general public. Instead, dial ✆ **030/25-00-25** for hotel reservations within Germany. If you're calling from outside of Germany, you'll have to access a different number: ✆ **01805/75-40-40.** The cheapest and most up-to-date way to access tourist information about Berlin is on the Internet at www.berlin-tourism.de.

## CITY LAYOUT

Berlin is one of the largest and most complex cities in Europe. Because it's so spread out, you'll need to depend on public transportation. No visitor should try to explore more than two neighborhoods a day, even superficially.

The center of activity in the western part of Berlin is the 4km (2½-mile) long **Kurfürstendamm,** called the Ku'damm by Berliners, who seem to have a habit of irreverently renaming every street and building in the city. Along this wide boulevard you'll find the best hotels, restaurants, theaters, cafes, nightclubs, shops, and department stores. It's the most elegant and fashionable spot in Berlin, but, like much of the city, it combines chic with sleaze in places. Walkers can stop off at one of the popular cafes lining the boulevard.

### *Tips* Finding an Address

As for the numbering of streets in Berlin, keep in mind that the city sometimes assists you by posting the range of numbers that appears within any particular block, at least within major arteries such as the Kurfürstendamm. These numbers appear on the street signs themselves, which is a great help in finding a particular number on long boulevards. You won't find these numbers on street signs of smaller streets, however. Although some streets are numbered with the odds on one side and the evens on the other, many (including the Ku'damm) are numbered consecutively up one side of the street and back down the other. ***Warning:*** The names of some eastern Berlin streets and squares with links to the old East German regime have been changed.

From the Ku'damm you can take Hardenbergstrasse, which crosses Bismarckstrasse and becomes Otto-Suhr-Allee, which will lead to the **Schloss Charlottenburg** area and its museums, a major sightseeing area. The **Dahlem Museums** are in the southwest of the city, often reached by going along Hohenzollerndamm.

The huge **Tiergarten** is the city's largest park. Running through it is **Strasse des 17 Juni,** which leads to the famed **Brandenburg Gate** (just south of the Reichstag). On the southwestern fringe of the Tiergarten is the **Berlin Zoo.**

The Brandenburg Gate is the start of eastern Berlin's most celebrated street, **Unter den Linden,** the cultural heart of Berlin before World War II. It runs from west to east, leading to **Museumsinsel (Museum Island),** where the most outstanding museums of eastern Berlin, including the Pergamon Museum, are situated.

Unter den Linden crosses another major artery, **Friedrichstrasse.** If you continue south along Friedrichstrasse, you'll reach the former location of **Checkpoint Charlie,** a famous border site of the Cold War days. No longer a checkpoint, it now has a little museum devoted to memories of the Berlin Wall.

Unter den Linden continues east until it reaches **Alexanderplatz,** the center of eastern Berlin, with its towering television tower (Fernsehturm). A short walk away is the newly restored **Nikolaiviertel (Nikolai Quarter),** a neighborhood of bars, restaurants, and shops that evoke life in the prewar days.

**MAPS** Good maps of Berlin can be purchased at bookstores or news kiosks, such as the Europa Press Center (a magazine and newspaper store in the Europa Center). One of the best maps is the **Falk** map, which offers full-color detail and comprehensive indexes (consequently, it's sometimes awkward to unfold and refold). Be sure to obtain an up-to-date map showing the most recent changes.

## NEIGHBORHOODS IN BRIEF

Visitors who knew Berlin during the Cold War are amazed at the way traffic now zips between sectors that once were rigidly segregated by border guards. Today, your taxi will blithely drive beneath the Brandenburg Gate or along the Friedrichstrasse, without regard to barriers that once used to be virtually impenetrable. Names you're likely to hear as you navigate your way through the reunited city include the following:

### In the Western Zone

**Charlottenburg** Despite being renamed by Berlin wits as Klamottenburg (Ragsville) after the bombings of World War II, this is still the wealthiest and most densely commercialized district of western Berlin. Its centerpiece is Charlottenburg Palace. One of the most interesting subdivisions of Charlottenburg is the neighborhood around **Savignyplatz,** a tree-lined square a short walk north of the western zone's most visible boulevard, Kurfürstendamm. Lining its edges and the streets nearby are a profusion of bars, shops, and restaurants, an engaging aura of permissiveness, and an awareness that this is the bastion of the city's prosperous bourgeoisie.

**Dahlem** Now the university district, Dahlem was originally established as an independent village to the southwest of Berlin's center.

**Ku'damm** In the 1950s and '60s, during the early stages of the Cold War, the Ku'damm emerged as a rough-and-tumble boomtown, bristling with boxy-looking new constructions, and permeated with a maverick sense of parvenu novelty. Since reunification, when vast neighborhoods within Mitte opened for real-estate speculation and instant gentrification, the Ku'damm has reinvented itself as a bastion of capitalistic and corporate conservatism, with a distinct sense of old and established money that's waiting for public perceptions to grow bored with the novelties that have been associated with the opening of the former East Berlin. The poignancies of the Weimar Republic and the Cold War are not lost, however, even upon the corporate sponsors of the big-money real-estate ventures that line the Ku'damm. If you look at the Hochhaus entrance of the Europa Center, on the Tauentzienstrasse side, whose glossy chrome-trimmed interior decor might remind you of an airport waiting lounge, you'll find a plaque honoring the long-ago site of the private home of Weimar statesman Gustav Stresemann, which used to stand at 12A Tauentzienstrasse. Immediately adjacent to that plaque is an artfully graffitized chunk of the former Berlin Wall, encased in Plexiglas like an irreplaceable work of ancient archaeology. It is dedicated to the people who lost their lives trying to escape over the Wall during the peak of the Cold War.

**Grunewald** Many newcomers are surprised by the sheer sprawl of Grunewald's 49 sq. km (19 sq. miles) of verdant forest. The area serves as a green lung for the urbanites of Berlin. It lies southwest of the city center.

**Hansaviertel** This neighborhood, northwest of Tiergarten park, contains a series of residential buildings designed by different architects (including Le Corbusier, Walter Gropius, and Alvar Aalto).

**Kreuzberg** Originally built during the 19th century to house the workers of a rapidly industrializing Prussia, this has traditionally been the poorest and most overcrowded of Berlin's districts. Today, at least 35% of its population is composed of guest workers from Turkey, the former Yugoslavia, and Greece. Prior to the city's reunification, the district evolved into the headquarters for the city's artistic counterculture. Since reunification, however, the fast-changing neighborhoods within Mitte, especially Hackescher Höfe (see below) have offered stiff competition.

**Schöneberg** Like Kreuzberg, it was originally an independent suburb of workers' housing, but after the war it was rebuilt as a solidly middle-class neighborhood that also happens to include the densest concentration of gay bars and clubs (between Nollendorfplatz and Victoria-Luise-Platz).

**Spandau** Set near the junction of the Spree and Havel rivers, about 10km (6 miles) northwest of the city center, Spandau boasts a history of medieval grandeur. Though it merged with Berlin in 1920, its Altstadt (old city) is still intact. The legendary Spandau prison was demolished in the early 1990s.

**Tiergarten** The name Tiergarten (which means "Animal Garden") refers both to a massive urban park and, to the park's north, a residential district of the same name. The park was originally intended as a backdrop to the grand avenues laid out by the German kaisers. The neighborhood contains the Brandenburg Gate, the German Reichstag (Parliament), the Berlin Zoo, and some of the city's grandest museums.

### In The Eastern Zone

**Mitte (Center)** Closed to capitalist investment for nearly 50 years, this monumental district in the heart of Berlin is the one that's on every speculator's mind these days. It was originally conceived as the

# Berlin Neighborhoods

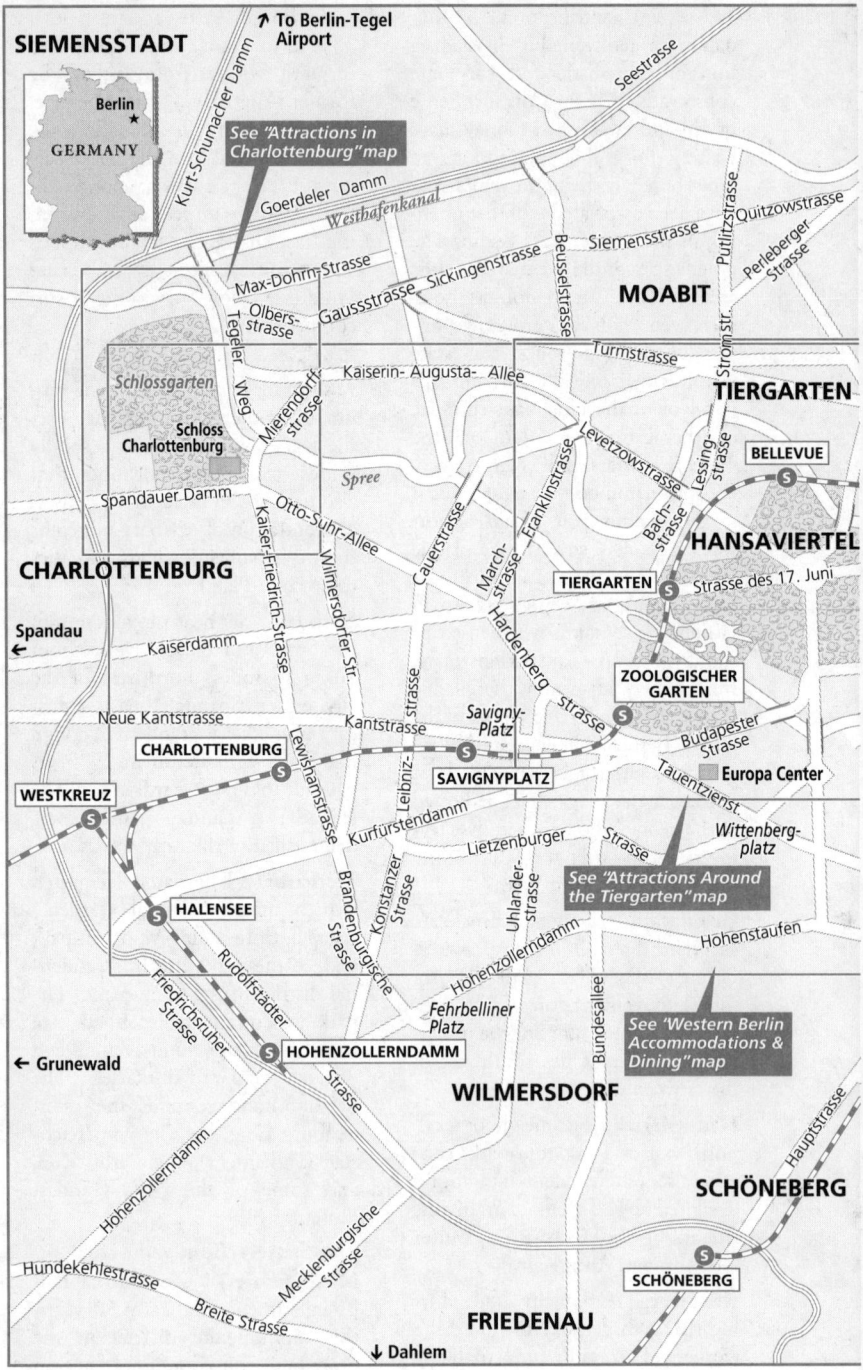

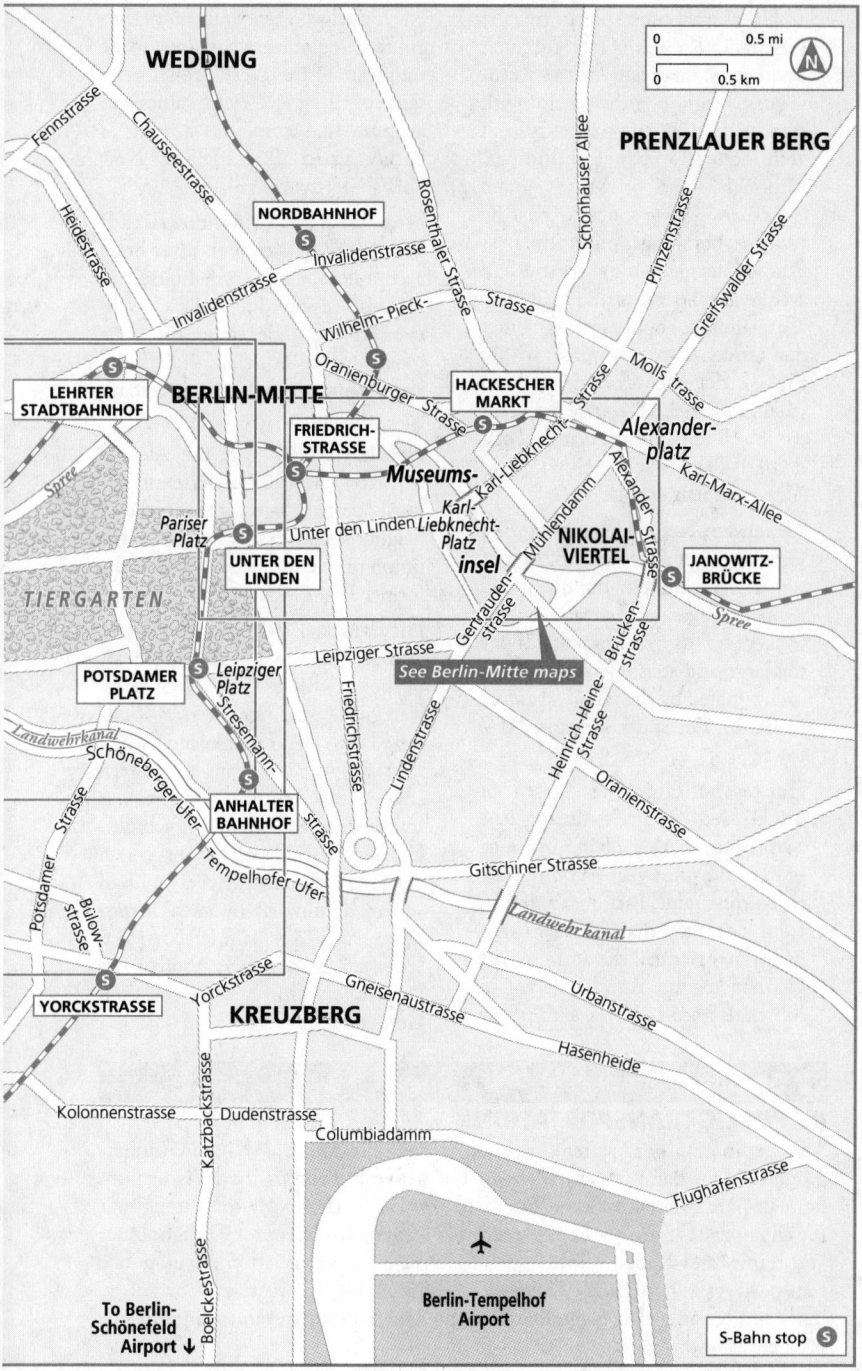
0 0.5 mi
0 0.5 km
N
WEDDING
PRENZLAUER BERG
Fennstrasse
Chausseestrasse
Heidestrasse
NORDBAHNHOF
Invalidenstrasse
Invalidenstrasse
Rosenthaler Strasse
Schönhauser Allee
Prinzenstrasse
Greifswalder Strasse
Wilhelm-Pieck-Strasse
Oranienburger Strasse
Mollstrasse
LEHRTER STADTBAHNHOF
BERLIN-MITTE
HACKESCHER MARKT
FRIEDRICH-STRASSE
Alexander-platz
Karl-Liebknecht-Strasse
Museums-insel
Karl-Liebknecht-Platz
Karl-Marx-Allee
Spree
Pariser Platz
Unter den Linden
Mühlendamm
NIKOLAI-VIERTEL
Alexander Strasse
JANOWITZ-BRÜCKE
UNTER DEN LINDEN
TIERGARTEN
Gertrauden-strasse
Brücken-strasse
Spree
Leipziger Strasse
See Berlin-Mitte maps
POTSDAMER PLATZ
Leipziger Platz
Stresemann-strasse
Friedrichstrasse
Lindenstrasse
Heinrich-Heine-Strasse
Landwehrkanal
Schöneberger Ufer
ANHALTER BAHNHOF
Oranienstrasse
Potsdamer Strasse
Tempelhofer Ufer
Gitschiner Strasse
Bülow-strasse
Landwehrkanal
Yorckstrasse
YORCKSTRASSE
KREUZBERG
Gneisenaustrasse
Urbanstrasse
Hasenheide
Katzbackstrasse
Kolonnenstrasse
Dudenstrasse
Columbiadamm
Flughafenstrasse
Boeckestrasse
Berlin-Tempelhof Airport
To Berlin-Schönefeld Airport ↓
S-Bahn stop S

architectural centerpiece by the Prussian Kaisers. Its fortunes declined dramatically as the Communist regime infused it with starkly angular monuments and architecturally banal buildings. Although some of Mitte's grand structures were destroyed by wartime bombings, unification has exposed its remaining artistic and architectural treasures. The district's most famous boulevard is Unter den Linden. Famous squares within the district include Pariser Platz (the monumental square adjacent to the Brandenburg Gate), Potsdamer Platz (see below), and Alexanderplatz (see below).

**Alexanderplatz** The former East German regime threw up lots of rather ugly modern buildings and defined Alexanderplatz as the centerpiece of its government. Today the large and sterile-looking square is dominated by the tallest structure in Berlin, the Sputnik-inspired TV tower.

**Hackesche Höfe** A warren of brick-sided factories during the 19th century, it's evolving into one of the city's most visible counterculture strongholds. Part of this derives from the fact that it wasn't too badly mangled by the former East German regime. Another factor in its renaissance involves a thirst by cutting-edge, often youthful Berliners to re-colonize what used to be the heart of the DDR. You'll get a sense of rising real-estate values and an aura that combines aspects of Paris's Latin Quarter and New York's Greenwich Village.

**Museumsinsel (Museum Island)** This island in the Spree River hosts a complex of museums housed in neoclassical buildings that always seem to be under renovation. Its most famous museum, the Pergamon, contains magnificent reconstructions of ancient temples.

**Nikolaiviertel** Near the Alexanderplatz, the Nikolaiviertel is the most perfectly restored medieval neighborhood in Berlin, and a triumph of the restoration skills of the former East German regime.

**Potsdamer Platz** Before World War II, this was the thriving heart of Berlin. Blasted into rubble by wartime bombings, it was bulldozed into a "no man's land" when the Wall went up on its western edge. After reunification, it was transformed into the biggest building site in Europe, out of which emerged a glittering, hyper-modern square dominated by such corporate giants as Daimler-Chrysler. It's often cited as a symbol of the corporate culture of a reunited Germany.

## 2 Getting Around

### BY PUBLIC TRANSPORTATION

The Berlin transport system consists of buses, trams, and U-Bahn (underground) and S-Bahn (elevated) trains. The network is run by the **BVG** or Public Transport Company Berlin-Brandenburg. Public transportation throughout the city operates from about 4:30am to 12:30am daily (except for 62 night buses and trams, and U-Bahn lines U-9 and U-12). For information about public transport, call ✆ **030/29-71-9843** or 030/19-449 or visit www.bvg.de/e_index.html. For a plan of Berlin's **U-Bahn and S-Bahn system,** see the inside back cover of this guide.

The **BVG standard ticket** (*Einzelfahrschein*) costs 2.10€ ($1.90) and is valid for 2 hours of transportation in all directions, transfers included. A 24-hour ticket for the whole city costs from 6.10€ ($5.45). Only standard tickets are sold on buses. Tram tickets must be purchased in advance. All tickets should be kept until the end of the journey; otherwise you'll be liable for a fine of 40€ ($35.70). Unless you buy a day pass, don't forget to time-punch your ticket into one of the small red boxes prominently posted at the entrance to city buses and underground stations.

If you're going to be in Berlin for 3 days, you can purchase for 18€ ($16.05) a **Berlin-Potsdam WelcomeCard,** which entitles holders to 72 free hours on public transportation in Berlin and Brandenburg. You'll also get free admission or a price reduction of up to 50% on sightseeing tours, museums, and other attractions, and a 25% reduction at 10 theaters as well. The card is sold at many hotels, visitor information centers, and public-transportation sales points. It's valid for one adult and three children under the age of 14.

Two **excursion bus lines** make some beautiful scenic spots accessible. Bus 218 operates from the Theodor-Heuss-Platz U-Bahn station (near the radio tower) via Schildhorn, Grunewald Tower, and Wannsee Beach to the Wannsee S-Bahn station, and bus 216 runs from the Wannsee S-Bahn station to Pfaueninsel via Moorlake.

## BY TAXI

Taxis cruise restlessly along the major boulevards, indicating their availability by an illuminated roof light. The meter begins ticking at 2.50€ ($2.25). A 1€ (90¢) supplement is added if you call a cab to a specific address by phone. Within the city center, each kilometer costs around 1.53€ ($1.35), depending on the time of day. Prolonged taxi rides that you arrange to distant suburbs are factored at a per-kilometer rate of 1.02€ (90¢). Staff members at hotels and restaurants can easily summon a cab for you, in some cases simply by throwing a switch on their phone. Otherwise, dial toll-free, within Berlin, ✆ **0800/217-6544.** If that doesn't work, try 030/21-02-02, 030/41-01-31-87, or 030/69-022.

## BY CAR

U.S. rental companies have outlets in Berlin. If possible, you should make reservations in advance. You'll find **Hertz** at Berlin-Tegel Airport (✆ **030/41-70-46-74**) and at Budapesterstrasse 39 (✆ **030/2-61-10-53**). **Avis** is also at Berlin-Tegel (✆ **030/4-10-13-148**) and at Budapesterstrasse 41 (✆ **030/23-09-370**).

But in general, touring Berlin by car is not recommended. Traffic is heavy, and parking is very difficult to come by. Use the excellent public transportation network instead.

**PARKING** If you're driving into Berlin, chances are that you'll want to safely store your car once you arrive. Many hotels offer parking facilities; otherwise, you'll find parking garages that remain open throughout the day and night. Those located near the Ku'damm and the Europa Center include the **Parkhaus Metropol,** Joachimstaler Strasse 14–19; **Parkhaus Los-Angeles-Platz,** Augsburger Strasse 30; **Parkhaus Europa Center,** Nürnberger Strasse 5–7; and the **Parkhaus am Zoo,** Budapesterstrasse 38. Charges start at 2€ ($1.80) per hour.

**CITY DRIVING** One problem that often infuriates drivers in Berlin is that it's almost impossible to turn left on major avenues (except at major intersections in the east), because of the positioning of metal barriers and tram lines. Oversize signs tell you to drive straight on. Drivers have to make a right-hand turn, swing around the block, and then proceed straight across the tram lines wherever a traffic light will allow.

## BY BICYCLE

Bicycling in Berlin's crushing traffic is not a very appealing prospect, but you might want to rent a bike to explore the city's outlying parks and forests. Both the U-Bahn and S-Bahn provide specific compartments for bicycles for an extra 2.55€ ($2.30). Transport of bicycles, however, is not permitted during rush hour: Monday to Friday before 9am and again in the afternoon between 2 and 5:30pm. In the city and suburbs, try to confine your bicycling to cycle zones, delineated with solid red lines running between the pedestrian sidewalks and the traffic lanes.

A good place for bike rentals is **Fahrradstation,** Readrathstrasse 40–41 (✆ **030/28-38-4848;** S-Bahn: Hackescher Markt), open Monday to Friday 8am to 8pm, Saturday and Sunday 10am to 4pm. A 24-hour rental costs from 11€ to 16€ ($9.80–$14.30) on up.

## *FAST FACTS:* Berlin

*American Express* Amex offices include locations at Bayreutherstrasse 37–38 (✆ **030/2149830;** U-Bahn: Wittenbergplatz), open Monday to Friday 9am to 7pm and Saturday 10am to 1pm; Alte Potsdamer Strasse 7 (✆ **030/25297474;** U-Bahn: Hüttenweg), open Monday to Friday 9:30am to 8pm and Saturday 9:30am to 4pm; Am Borsigturm 2 (✆ **030/43402060;** U-Bahn: Borischverger), open Monday to Friday 9:30am to 8pm and Saturday 9:30am to 4pm; and Friedrichstrasse 172 (✆ **030/2017400;** U-bahn: Friedrichstrasse), open Monday to Friday 9am to 7pm and Saturday 10am to 2pm.

*Business Hours* Most **banks** are open Monday to Friday 9am to either 1 or 3pm. Most other **businesses** and **stores** are open Monday to Friday 9 or 10am to either 6 or 6:30pm and Saturday 9am to 2pm. On *langer Samstag,* the first Saturday of the month, shops stay open until 4 or 6pm. Some stores close late on Thursday (usually 8:30pm).

*Currency Exchange* You can exchange money at all airports, at major department stores, at any bank, and at American Express offices (see above) and other currency exchange outlets. There is also a currency exchange office at the Bahnhof Zoo; it's open Monday to Saturday from 8am to 9pm and on Sunday from 10am to 6pm. ATM machines proliferate in Berlin at virtually every branch of the Dresdner or Deutsche Bank, post offices, and railway stations. Two particularly convenient branches with 24-hour ATM service are **Deutsche Bank** at Wittenbergplatz (U-Bahn: Wittenbergplatz) and **Dresdner Bank** at Kurfürstendamm 237 (U-Bahn: Kurfürstendamm).

*Dentists/Doctors* The Berlin tourist office in the Europa Center (✆ **030/264-7480;** U-Bahn: Kurfürstendamm) keeps a list of English-speaking dentists and doctors in Berlin. For an emergency doctor, call ✆ **030/31-00-31;** for an emergency dentist, call ✆ **030/890-04-333.**

*Drugstores* If you need a pharmacy (*Apotheke*) at night, go to one on any corner and look for a sign in the window giving the address of the nearest pharmacy with nighttime hours (such postings are required by law). For a centrally located pharmacy, go to **Europa–Apotheke,** Tauentzienstrasse

9–12 (✆ **030/2-61-41-42;** U-Bahn: Kurfürstendamm), located near the Europa Center; it's open Monday to Friday 9am to 8pm and Saturday 9am to 4pm. In Mitte, a few steps from Unter den Linden, and maintaining the same hours, is the **Dorotheenstadtische Apotheke,** Friedrichstrasse 151 (✆ **030/204-4817;** U-Bahn: Friedrichstrasse).

*Embassies & Consulates* See "Fast Facts: Germany," in chapter 3.

*Emergencies* To call the police, dial ✆ **110.** To report a fire or to summon an ambulance, dial ✆ **112.**

*Hospitals* Hotel employees are usually familiar with the locations of the nearest hospital emergency room. In an emergency, call ✆ **112** for an ambulance.

*Hot Lines* If you're the victim of rape or sexual assault, call **LARA,** Tempelhoferufer 14 (✆ **030/216-88-88**). For problems relating to drug use or drug addiction, call the drug help line at ✆ **030/1-92-37.** Gays seeking legal or health-related advice should call **Schwüles Uberfall** (✆ **030/216-33-36**). Gays can also call the **Café Positif** (✆ **030/216-8654**) for advice about AIDS and its treatment and prevention; and **Man-o-Meter** (✆ **030/216-8008**) for information about anything to do with gay life or gay events in Berlin or the rest of Germany. All of the above are staffed with some English speakers.

*Internet Access* You can get internet access all over town—ask at your hotel for the one closest to you. For a good place in the center of town, visit **Karstadt Sports,** Joachimstaler 5–6 (✆ **030/8802-41-89;** U-Bahn: Bahnhof Zoologisher Garten). Open Monday to Saturday 10am to 8pm.

*Laundry/Dry Cleaning* Deluxe and first-class hotels offer laundry service, but prices tend to be high. You'll find laundromats (*Wascherei*) and dry-cleaning outlets (*Reiningung*) all over town. One that's relatively convenient is **Wascherei Lindenberg,** Curtius Strasse 13–14 (✆ **030/833-1056;** S-Bahn Lichterfelder West). Otherwise, ask at your hotel for additional options.

*Lost Property* For items lost on the bus or U-Bahn, go to **BVG Fündbüro,** Frauenhoferstrasse 33–36 (✆ **030/25-62-30-40;** U-Bahn: Ernst-Reuter-Platz); open Monday to Thursday 9am to 6pm and Friday 9am to 2pm. For items lost on the S-Bahn, go to **Deutsches Bahn AG/8-Bahn Berlin GmbH,** Mittelstrasse 20 (✆ **030/2-97-296-12;** U-Bahn: Friedrichstrasse), Monday, Wednesday, or Thursday 10am to 4pm, Tuesday 10am to 6pm, or Friday 8am to noon. The general lost-property office, **Zentrales Fündbüro,** is at Platz der Luftbrücke 6 (✆ **030/69-95;** U-Bahn: Platz der Luftbrücke). Hours are Monday and Tuesday 7:30am to 2pm, Wednesday noon to 6:30pm, and Friday 7:30am to noon.

*Post Office* The post office at Budapester Strasse 42 (U-Bahn/S-Bahn: Zoologischer Garten) is open Monday to Saturday 8am to midnight, Sunday and holidays 10am to midnight. If you have mail sent there, have it marked *Hauptpostlagernd,* Postamt 120, Bahnhof Zoo, 10612 Berlin. An equivalently large post office in the city's eastern side is at Friedrichshain, Strasse der Pariser Commune 8–10 (U-Bahn: Oranienberger Strasse). It's open Monday to Friday 7am to 9pm and Saturday 8am to 8pm. For information about postal services, call ✆ **0180/55-555.**

*Radio* Radio programs in English can be heard on 87.9 FM (or 94 on cable) and 1197 AM for the American Forces Network, and on 30 FM (87.6 on cable) for the BBC.

*Restrooms* A restroom is called a *Toilette* and is often labeled WC, with either F (for *Frauen,* "women") or H (for *Herren,* "men"). Public facilities are found throughout Berlin and at all terminals, including the Europa Center on Tauentzienstrasse. It's customary to tip attendants at least .25€ (20¢).

*Safety* One unfortunate side effect of reunification has been an increase in muggings, bank robberies, hate crimes, and car break-ins. Residents of Berlin sometimes feel unsafe at night, especially in the dimly lit streets of Kreuzberg. Nonetheless, Berlin is still much safer than most large American cities. In case of a robbery or an attack, report the problem immediately to the police. You'll need a police report for any insurance claims.

*Taxis* See "Getting Around," earlier in this chapter.

*Telegrams/Fax* These can be sent from the post office (see "Post Office," above).

*Water* The tap water in Berlin, as in all German cities, is safe to drink. However, most Berliners prefer to ask for bottled water, either carbonated or noncarbonated.

*Weather* For a report on Berlin weather, call ✆ **0190/270-641.** The cost is .75€ (65¢) per minute.

## 3 Where to Stay

Berlin is the scene of frequent international trade fairs, conferences, and festivals, and during these times, vacancies in the city will be hard to find. The greatest concentration of hotels, from the cheapest digs to the most expensive, lies in the center near the **Kurfürstendamm** (Ku'damm), the main boulevard of western Berlin. Most good-value pensions and small hotels are in the western part of the city; note that many such accommodations are in older buildings where plumbing is rarely state-of-the-art.

The business convention crowd still anchors primarily in the west, as do the hordes of summer visitors on whirlwind tours of Europe. **Eastern Berlin** often attracts Germans from other parts of the country who want a glimpse of the Berlin that was shut away behind the Wall for so long. The eastern sector still doesn't have the visitor structure and facilities of the west, although several first-class and deluxe hotels have opened there, notably the Grand, Adlon, and Hilton.

Travelers can also head for hotels in **Grunewald,** close to nature in the Grunewald Forest, or **Charlottenburg,** near Olympic Park. If you like biking, jogging, and breathing fresh air and don't mind the commute into central Berlin for shopping and attractions, you'll enjoy both these areas.

Tegel Airport is only 20 minutes from Berlin by taxi, but if you have a very early departure or late arrival, and want the added security of an airport hotel, you can check into **Novotel Berlin Airport,** Kurt-Schumacher-Damm 202, 13405 Orsteil-Reinickendorf (✆ **030/41060;** fax 030/4106700). Doubles are medium-size and furnished in standard motel-chain format. The rate for a double is 130€ ($116.10), dropping to 78€ ($69.65) on Friday and Saturday. There's also a restaurant on-site, plus a free shuttle service that runs back and forth between the hotel and airport. American Express, Diners Club, MasterCard, and Visa are accepted.

## ON OR NEAR THE KURFÜRSTENDAMM

### VERY EXPENSIVE

**Grand Hotel Esplanade** ★★★ Strikingly contemporary, this *luxe* hotel lies in a quiet and verdant neighborhood near several foreign embassies, some concert halls, and the massively expanding Potsdamer Platz. Thanks to river views and a swath of park, you might get the feeling that you're far from the city. It competes effectively with other Berlin hotels in its class, with a well-conceived collection of modern art. It is, in fact, the hyper-contemporary alternative to the more traditional Kempinski (see below). The starkly contemporary, bright, sun-flooded, and cheerful rooms pay strict attention to sound insulation. Bathrooms are generously sized with shower-tub combinations. Corner rooms are among the most spacious and have some of the best views of the surrounding area.

Lützowufer 15, 10785 Berlin. ✆ **030/25-47-80.** Fax 030/2-54-78-82-22. www.esplanade.de. 386 units. 250€–306€ ($223.25–$273.25) double; from 422€ ($376.85) suite. AE, DC, MC, V. Parking 16€ ($14.30). U-Bahn: Kurfürstenstrasse, Nollendorfplatz, or Wittenbergplatz. **Amenities:** 3 restaurants; 2 bars; pool; fitness center; 3 saunas; solarium; salon; room service; massage; babysitting; laundry/dry cleaning. *In room*: A/C, TV, minibar, hair dryer, safe.

**Kempinski Hotel Bristol Berlin** ★★★ This hotel reigns as one of Berlin's most prestigious and visible hotels, enjoying a reputation equivalent to some of the best hotels in the world. But the emergence of such luxe Berlin Mitte properties as Adlon and Four Seasons (see later in this chapter) has shaken the Kempinski crown. It occupies a bulky, boxy-looking building that was originally erected during the peak of the Cold War, but whose interior has benefited from ongoing improvements and renovations. The staff is superbly trained and the shamelessly rich-looking decor is more opulent and better designed than that of many comparably priced competitors. Rooms contain high-quality reproductions of English and continental antiques, enough insulation to retain an almost reverential hush, and spacious bathrooms with shower-tub combinations. Overall, this is the most opulent hotel in what used to be defined as Berlin's Western Zone.

Kurfürstendamm 2, 10719 Berlin. ✆ **800/426-3135** in the U.S., or 030/88-43-40. Fax 030/883-6075. www.kempinskiberlin.de/english/. 301 units. 242.75€–275.95€ ($216.80–$246.40) double; 367.90€ ($328.55) suite. AE, DISC, MC, V. Parking 17.90€ ($16). U-Bahn: Kurfürstendamm. **Amenities:** 3 restaurants; bar; lounge; pool; fitness center; sauna; room service; babysitting; laundry/dry cleaning. *In room*: A/C, TV, minibar, hair dryer.

**Steigenberger Berlin** ★★ One of Berlin's most visible luxury hotels lies on a formal, gracefully proportioned plaza a few steps from the Kaiser Wilhelm Memorial Church. Originally built behind a nondescript facade in 1981, it caters to a demanding clientele of relatively conservative clients. This place represents western Berlin's sense of the status quo more visibly than virtually any other hotel in town. Public areas are large, well-designed, open spaces with high ceilings. Overall, expect a sense of bustling conservatism, plush and contemporary

---

*Tips* **Dialing Germany**

Remember that the phone numbers in this book contain an initial 0 in the German city code. That 0 is only used within Germany. Omit it when calling from abroad.

---

# Western Berlin Accommodations & Dining

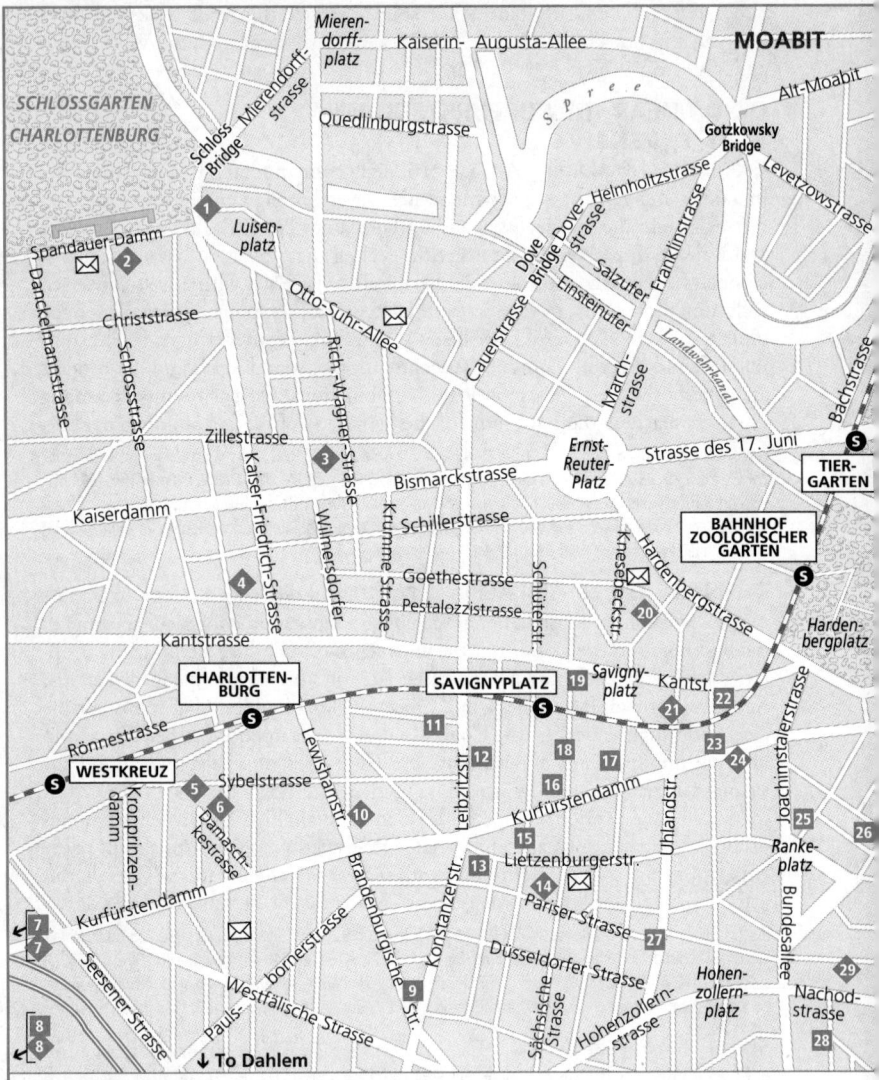


**ACCOMMODATIONS ■**

Ambassador Berlin **39**
Arco Hotel **30**
Art Nouveau **12**
Artemesia **9**
Bleibtreu Hotel **18**
Bogota **15**
Brandenburger Hof/Relais & Châteaux **26**
City Pension Alexandra **16**
Grand Hotel Esplanade **37**
Grand Hyatt Berlin **36**
Hecker's Hotel **17**
Hotel Crystal **19**
Hotel Domus **27**
Hotel Palace Berlin **33**
Hotel-Pension Bregenz **13**
Hotel Sylter Hof Berlin **38**
Kempenski Hotel Bristol Berlin **23**
Kronprinz Berlin **7**
Pension München **28**
Pension Niebuhr **11**
Pension Nürnberger Eck **30**
Regent Schlosshotel Berlin **8**
Savoy **22**
Sorat Art'otel **25**
Steigenberger Berlin **31**

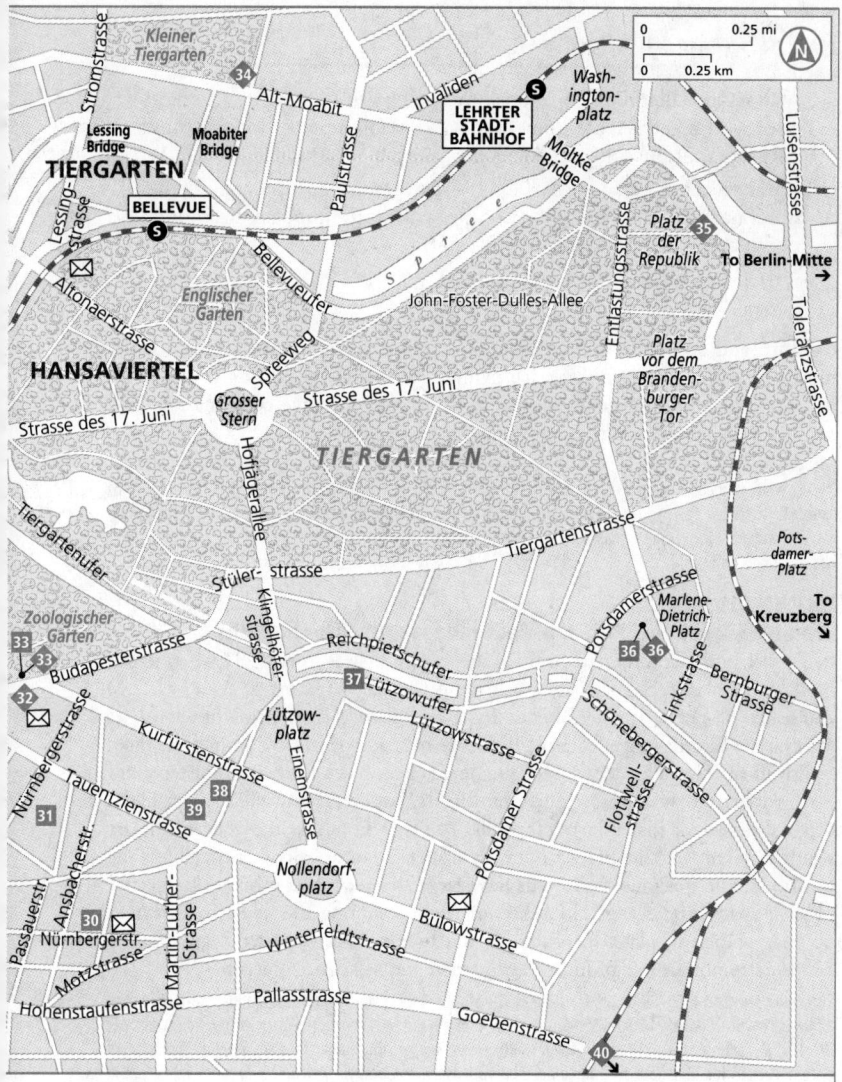


**DINING**

Alt-Luxemburg **4**
Ana e Bruno **2**
Bamberger Reiter **29**
Bierhaus Luisen-Bräu **1**
Daitokai **32**
Ernst-August **6**
First Floor **33**
Funkturm Restaurant **8**
Hard Rock Café **24**
Harlekin **36**
Kaefer's Restaurant Dachgarten **35**
Lubitsch **14**
Marjellchen **10**
Paris Bar **21**
Paris-Moskau **34**
Ponte Vecchio **3**
Restaurant Mario **20**
Rockendorf's Gourmet Restaurant **40**
Seidler Restaurant **5**
Vivaldi **7**
Vox **36**

Post Office
S-Bahn stop

### Kids Family-Friendly Hotels

**Ambassador Berlin** (p. 84) Kids love the eighth-floor heated tropical pool with a retractable dome and a waterfall. Rooms, for the most part, are spacious and exceedingly comfortable for families.

**Hotel Palace Berlin** (p. 83) For the family traveling upmarket, this hotel near the zoo is a good choice, with both indoor and outdoor pools, and a helpful family-friendly staff.

comfort, and corporate Europe at its most deeply entrenched. Rooms, for the most part, are medium in size, each maintained in good condition with a tasteful modern decor and generous-size beds. Bathrooms have combination tubs and showers, makeup mirrors, and robes.

Los-Angeles-Platz 1, 10789 Berlin. ✆ **800/223-5652** in the U.S. and Canada, or 030/21-27-0. Fax 030/2-12-71-17. www.steigenberger.de. 397 units. 220€–330€ ($196.45–$294.70) double; from 435€ ($388.45) suite. AE, DC, MC, V. Parking 16€ ($14.30). U-Bahn: Kurfürstendamm. **Amenities:** 2 restaurants; 2 bars; pool; sauna; solarium; room service; massage; babysitting; laundry/dry cleaning. *In room*: A/C, TV, dataport, minibar, hair dryer, safe.

## EXPENSIVE

**Brandenburger Hof/Relais & Châteaux** ★★★ This hotel lies on a dignified street in the commercial heart of the city and dates from 1991 when it was built in the classic Bauhaus style beloved by so many Germans. As a Relais & Châteaux property, it offers better food and service than most hotels of its pricerange. Rooms range from medium-size to spacious and are among the most stylish in the city. The decor, with torchère lamps, black leather upholstery, and platform beds, may appear a touch minimalist, but everybody will appreciate the original artworks that adorn the walls. Another bonus is the state-of-the-art security system and the French doors that open up onto balconies on all but the top floor. The spacious bathrooms have large shower/tub combinations, plenty of shelf space, and scales. Housekeeping here is among the finest in Berlin. A popular gathering place for guests is the hotel's "Wintergarten," an unusual combination of an Italian monastery garden and a Japanese garden.

Eislebener Strasse 14, 10789 Berlin. ✆ **030/21-40-50.** Fax 030/21-40-51-00. www.brandenburger-hof.com. 82 units. 240€–280€ ($214.30–$250.05) double; from 450€ ($401.85) suite. Rates include breakfast. AE, DC, MC, V. Parking 16€ ($14.30). U-Bahn: Kurfürstendamm or Augsburger Strasse; S-Bahn: Zoologischer Garten. **Amenities:** 2 restaurants; piano bar; spa; room service, laundry/dry cleaning. *In room*: TV, dataport, minibar, hair dryer, safe.

**Savoy** ★ If you don't demand grand, full-service facilities, this might be the hotel for you. Built in 1929, the quiet, unassuming Savoy is a reliable and durable favorite. It's better than many in its category, and although it has lost some of its old-Berlin flavor, it remains the choice for the die-hard traditionalist. Its beautifully furnished rooms and luxurious suites come complete with generous desk space, upholstered armchairs, cocktail tables, and spotlessly kept bathrooms with shower-tub combinations.

Fasanenstrasse 9–10, 10623 Berlin. ✆ **800/223-5652** in the U.S. and Canada, or 030/31-10-30. Fax 030/31-10-33-33. www.hotel-savoy.com. 125 units. 156.35€–241.20€ ($139.60–$215.40) double; from 265.70€ ($237.25) suite. Children under 13 stay free in parents' room. Rates include breakfast. AE, DC, MC, V. U-Bahn: Kurfürstendamm. **Amenities:** Restaurant; bar; fitness center; sauna; room service; babysitting; laundry. *In room*: TV, minibar, hair dryer, safe.

## MODERATE

**Art Nouveau** On the fourth floor of an Art Nouveau apartment house, this little known hotel is an atmospheric choice. Even the elevator is a historic gem of the upmarket and desirable neighborhood. Established in the late 1970s, Art Nouveau was fully renovated in 1998. The well-furnished and comfortable rooms are pleasantly decorated and high ceilinged and are filled with excellent beds and well-kept bathrooms equipped with shower-tub combinations. Rooms in the rear are more tranquil except when the schoolyard is full of children at play. There's an honor bar in the lobby where guests keep track of their own drinks. A generous breakfast is the only meal served.

Leibnizstrasse 59, D-10629 Berlin. ✆ **030/327-74-40.** Fax 030/327-74-40. www.hotelartnouveau.de. 15 units. 107.30€ ($95.80) double; 173.75€ ($155.15) suite. Rates include breakfast. AE, MC, V. U-Bahn: Adenauerplatz. *In room:* TV, dataport, hair dryer.

**Artemisia** *Finds* This hotel *for women only* occupies the fourth and fifth floors of a residential building with an elevator. In cold weather, there's often a cozy fire in one of the sitting rooms. Women's conferences and consciousness-raising sessions sometimes take place here. Rooms are medium in size and meticulously maintained, each with a good-size shower or bath. Children, including boys up to age 14, can stay here with their mothers.

Brandenburgischestrasse 18 (near the Ku'damm), 10707 Berlin. ✆ **030/8-73-89-05.** Fax 030/8-61-86-53. www.frauenhotel-berlin.de. 12 units, 10 with shower or bath. 89€ ($79.50) double without shower or bath; 104€ ($92.85) double with shower or bath. Children under 8 stay free in mother's room. Rates include continental breakfast. AE, DC, MC, V. Free parking. U-Bahn: Konstanzerstrasse. **Amenities:** Breakfast room; bar; lounge. *In room:* TV, hair dryer.

**Bleibtreu Hotel** ★ The facade of this trend-conscious hotel isn't easily recognizable from the street, as the tiny lobby is accessible via an alleyway that leads past an avant-garde garden and a big-windowed set of dining and drinking facilities. The setting is the labyrinthine premises of what was built long ago as a Jugendstil-era apartment house. Rooms are small, minimalist, and furnished in carefully chosen natural materials. Extras include dataports and cordless phones. Bathrooms are cramped but well designed, and equipped with showers. Tables spill from the cafe into the tiny garden, where shrubs and flowers are surrounded with smooth-polished pieces of colored glass—a definite conversation piece.

Bleibtreustrasse 31 (1 block south of the Kurfürstendamm). ✆ **030/88474-0** or 800/223-5652 for reservations in the U.S. and Canada. Fax 030/88474-444. www.bleibtreu.com. 60 units. 78.85€–218.70€ ($70.40–$195.30) double. Rates include breakfast. AE, MC, V. S-Bahn: Savignyplatz. **Amenities:** Restaurant; bar; cafe; lounge; room service; laundry. *In room:* TV, dataport, minibar, hair dryer, safe.

**Hotel Domus** *Value* Clean, streamlined, and unpretentious, this government-rated three-star hotel dates from 1975. It was created from an older core whose elaborate detailing couldn't be salvaged. The result is an enduringly stylish, uncluttered piece of architecture that rises from a prestigious neighborhood a few blocks from the Ku'damm. It's a favorite of business travelers, who appreciate its good value and respectability. As such, it has a high proportion of single rooms, which cost 79€ to 89€ ($70.55–$79.50). Rooms are well designed, well scrubbed, and although not particularly large, very comfortable, each with a neat, shower-only bathroom. There are virtually no extras on-site, and other than breakfast and a drink that the receptionist might sell you within the lobby, no meals are served. But overall, it's a worthy, albeit simple choice, with good value and a helpful staff.

Uhlandstrasse 49, D-10719 Berlin. ✆ **030/880-3440.** Fax 030/880344-44. www.hotel-domus-berlin.de. 71 units. 115€–130€ ($102.70–$116.10) double; 140.50€ ($125.45) suite. Discounts sometimes available

Fri–Sun, depending on bookings. AE, DC, MC, V. Parking 5.10€ ($4.55). U-Bahn: Hohenzollernplatz or Spichernstrasse. **Amenities:** Breakfast room; lounge. *In room:* TV, hair dryer.

**Kronprinz Berlin** This hotel is located away from Berlin's center at the far western edge of the Ku'damm. In spite of its many discreet charms and features, it remains relatively little known or publicized. All rooms have balconies and fine appointments (often tasteful reproductions of antiques). If you want a little extra comfort, ask for one of the Bel-Etage rooms. All units are equipped with compact bathrooms, many with tub-and-shower combination. Many guests congregate in the garden under the chestnut trees in summer.

Kronprinzendamm 1, 10711 Berlin. ✆ **030/89-60-30.** Fax 030/8-93-12-15. www.kronprinz-hotel.de. 80 units. 140€ ($125) double; 215€ ($192) suite. Children 12 and under stay free in parents' room. Rates include buffet breakfast. AE, DC, MC, V. Free parking. U-Bahn: Adenauerplatz. Bus: 104, 110, 119, 129, or 219. **Amenities:** Breakfast room; bar; babysitting; laundry/dry cleaning. *In room:* TV, dataport, minibar, hair dryer, safe.

## INEXPENSIVE

**Bogota** Since 1964, this hotel has been a local favorite for the frugal traveler when a quartet of four separate hotels on four floors were combined into a cohesive whole. Typical for older Berlin apartment houses, bedrooms come in various shapes and sizes, but all of them have been recently restored.

The building more or less withstood WWII bombardments. Constructed in 1911, it had been a famous address known for its frequent parties, at which a young Benny Goodman appeared on occasion. The famous entrepreneur, Oskar Skaller, lived here and was known for his collection of Impressionists, including paintings by van Gogh.

What is now the lounge and TV room was once the office of the infamous director, Hans Hinkel, of the Reich Chamber of Culture. Charlie Chaplin named the title character in his film, *The Great Dictator,* after Hinkel. Bedrooms are well cared for and comfortable, the best opening onto an inner courtyard. Bathrooms with shower units are small but efficiently organized.

Schlüstrasse 45, 10707 Berlin. ✆ **030/8-81-50-01.** Fax 030/8-83-58-87. www.hotelbogota.de. 125 units, 60 with bathroom (12 with shower but no toilet). 69€ ($61.60) double without bath; 77€ ($68.75) double with shower but no toilet; 94€–98€ ($83.95–$87.50) double with bath. Rates include continental breakfast. AE, DC, MC, V. Parking 10€ ($8.95). U-Bahn: Adenauerplatz or Uhlandstr. S-Bahn: Savignyplatz. **Amenities:** Breakfast room; lounge. *In room:* TV, hair dryer.

**City Pension Alexandra** This three-floor hotel is comfortable, centrally located, and quiet. The building dates from 1900 and was converted into a hotel in the 1920s. Certain rooms are lined with photographs of old Berlin—perfect for acquainting yourself with what to look for as you tour the streets of the city. Most rooms have modern furniture and well-kept baths with shower units; some are more classic.

Wielandstrasse 32, 10629 Berlin. ✆ **030/8-81-21-07.** Fax 030/88-57-78-18. www.alexandra-berlin.de. 9 units, 4 with shower only. 69€ ($61.60) double with shower only; 99€ ($88.40) double with bath. Rates include buffet breakfast. AE, MC, V. S-Bahn: Savignyplatz. **Amenities:** Breakfast room; lounge; babysitting; laundry. *In room:* TV, hair dryer.

**Hotel Crystal** In a 19th-century building, the hotel rises six floors with an elevator. It's owned and operated by American John Schwarzrock and his German wife, Dorothée, who are always glad to welcome American visitors. The very basic rooms are comfortable and extremely clean, with eclectic furniture that you might think was gathered piecemeal.

Kantstrasse 144, 10623 Berlin. ✆ **030/312-90-47.** Fax 030/3-12-64-65. 33 units, 21 with bathroom (5 with shower only). 47€ ($41.95) double without bath; 62€ ($55.35) double with shower only; 66.50€ ($59.40) double with bath. Rates include breakfast. AE, MC, V. Parking free. S-Bahn: Savignyplatz. **Amenities:** Breakfast room; bar. *In room:* Hair dryer.

**Hotel-Pension Bregenz** This dignified pension occupies the fourth and sunniest floor of a four-story, century-old apartment building, accessible by elevator. The owner, Mr. Zimmermann, works hard to maintain the cleanliness and charm of his comfortably furnished, relatively large rooms. Double doors help to minimize noise from the public corridors. The staff gladly assists guests in reserving tickets for shows and tours.

Bregenzer Strasse 5, 10707 Berlin. ✆ **030/8-81-43-07.** Fax 030/8-82-40-09. 14 units, 10 with bath. 58.75€ ($52.45) double without bath, 86.85€ ($77.55) double with bath. Rates include breakfast. AE, MC, V. Parking 2.55€ ($2.30). U-Bahn: Adenauerplatz. S-Bahn: Savignyplatz. **Amenities:** Breakfast room; lounge. *In room:* TV, minibar, hair dryer, safe.

**Pension München** This pension occupies only part of the third floor of a massive four-story elevator building erected as an apartment house in 1908. It offers a simple but tasteful decor of modern furnishings accented with fresh flowers. Rooms are clean, with contemporary furniture and prints and engravings by local artists. Each comes with a compact, shower-only bathroom. Look for sculptures by the owner in some of the public areas. ***Note:*** If there are no rooms available, you're likely to be recommended to a similar pension, **Pension Güntzel** (✆ **030/8-57-90-20**), on the building's street level and cellar.

Guntzelstrasse 62 (close to Bayerischer Platz), 10717 Berlin. ✆ **030/8-57-91-20.** Fax 030/85-79-12-22. www.hotel-pension-muenchen-in-berlin.de. 8 units. 75€ ($67) double with bath. AE, DC, MC, V. On-street parking available. U-Bahn: Guntzelstrasse. *In room:* TV.

**Pension Niebuhr** Clean, safe, and sophisticated, this gay-friendly hotel occupies one and a half floors of a century-old apartment building. Willi Heidasch is your amiable host, maintaining simple but clean rooms, seven with phone and TV. Beds are a bit worn but still have comfort in them, and shower bathrooms are small. Paintings by aspiring Berlin artists (many for sale) decorate the public areas. About half the clientele is gay, a percentage that's growing, according to the owner.

Niebuhrstrasse 74, 10629 Berlin. ✆ **030/3-24-95-95.** Fax 030/3-24-80-21. www.pension-niebuhr.de. 12 units, 7 with bathroom. 63€ ($56.25) double without bath; 89€ ($79.50) double with bath. Rates include breakfast. AE, MC, V. Parking 3€ ($2.70). S-Bahn: Savignyplatz. **Amenities:** Breakfast room; lounge; room service. *In room:* TV.

**Pension Nürnberger Eck** This reliable pension is refreshingly old-fashioned. It occupies the second floor of a four-story building on a relatively quiet side street. Rooms are large, with high ceilings, massive doors, and in many cases, reproductions of Biedermeier-style furniture, including comfortable beds with soft mattresses, plus small shower bathrooms. This is the kind of place where Sally Bowles from *Cabaret* might have stayed.

Nürnberger Strasse 24a (near the Europa Center), 10789 Berlin. ✆ **030/2-35-17-80.** Fax 030/235-178-99. 8 units, 5 with bathroom. 70€ ($62.50) double without bath; 92€ ($82.15) double with bath. MC, V. Rates include breakfast. Parking 6.15€ ($5.50). U-Bahn: Augsburgerstrasse. **Amenities:** Breakfast room; lounge. *In room:* TV.

## NEAR THE MEMORIAL CHURCH & ZOO

### VERY EXPENSIVE

**Hotel Palace Berlin** ★★ *Kids* Although it isn't at the level of the Kempinski or the Grand Hotel Esplanade, this well-managed hotel outranks such landmarks as the Berlin Hilton and the Steigenberger Berlin. Don't be surprised by its boxy exterior (ca. 1968) that rises immediately adjacent to the equally boxy-looking Europa Center. Inside, thanks to dozens of improvements made throughout the 1990s, the setting is very comfortable, and at times even opulent. Rooms range in size from medium to spacious. All have fine beds, superb lighting, quality carpeting, and conservatively traditional styling. The best of the lot are those that benefited from a radical upgrade in the late 1990s. Known as "new deluxe rooms," they're for the most part on the third, fourth, and fifth floors. About 90 of the rooms, usually on the seventh and part of the sixth floor, are set aside for nonsmokers. Most bathrooms feature tub-shower combinations. The glamorous in-house restaurant, First Floor, is the only gourmet deluxe restaurant in Berlin that's open every day for lunch and dinner. Families will appreciate this hotel's proximity to the zoo as well as the fact that many of the rooms are spacious enough to accommodate extra beds and because children under 12, who share a room with their parents, can stay at no extra charge.

Budapesterstrasse 45, 10787 Berlin. ✆ **800/457-4000** in the U.S. and Canada, or 030/2-50-20. Fax 030/2-502-1161. www.palace.de. 282 units. 249.90€–291.25€ ($223.15–$260.10) double; from 325€ ($290.25) suite. AE, DC, MC, V. Parking 15.35€ ($13.70). U-Bahn: Zoologischer Garten. **Amenities:** 3 restaurants; 2 bars; room service; massage; babysitting; laundry/dry cleaning. Immediately adjacent to the hotel, in the separately managed Thermen and Europa Center, hotel guests enjoy free use of 2 swimming pools, exercise equipment, saunas, and steam baths. *In room:* A/C, TV, minibar, hair dryer, safe.

## EXPENSIVE

**Ambassador Berlin** ★ *Kids* This hotel is an attractive choice if you'd like to lodge near the Ku'damm. The heated tropical pool on the eighth floor, with its retractable dome and a waterfall, is an unusual feature, attracting the family trade. Rooms are, for the most part, spacious and exceedingly comfortable and include traditional furnishings. Bathrooms are rather small, and only a fifth have showers; the rest have tubs. Soundproof windows are always a relief in noisy central Berlin, and nonsmokers get a floor to themselves. The hotel is sometimes overrun with large groups.

Bayreutherstrasse 42–43, 10787 Berlin. ✆ **030/21-90-20.** Fax 030/21-90-23-80. www.sorat.de. 199 units. 105€–174€ ($93.75–$155.40) double; 195€ ($174.15) suite. Rates include buffet breakfast. AE, DC, MC, V. Parking 13€ ($11.60). U-Bahn: Wittenbergplatz. **Amenities:** Restaurant; 2 bars; pool; sauna; solarium; massage; babysitting; laundry. *In room:* A/C, TV, minibar, hair dryer.

**Hecker's Hotel** For years this establishment enjoyed a reputation as a small, private hotel, but now it's expanded. Although not in the same league as the Sorat (see below), this is still a winning choice. It's conveniently located near the Ku'damm and the many bars, cafes, and restaurants around Savignyplatz. The original 42 rooms are smaller than the newer units, which are medium-size. The rather severe and somewhat somber modern style may not suit everyone—certainly not those seeking romantic ambience. Each unit comes with a compact, shower-only bathroom. There is a sterility here but also up-to-date comfort and top-notch maintenance.

Grolmanstrasse 35 (near the Ku'damm), 10623 Berlin. ✆ **030/8-89-00.** Fax 030/8-89-02-60. www.heckers-hotel.com. 69 units. 143.10€–194.20€ ($127.80–$173.40) double; 229.95€–347.50€ ($205.35–$310.30) suite. Rates include breakfast. AE, DC, MC, V. Parking 10.20€ ($9.10). U-Bahn: Uhlandstrasse. Bus: 109 from Berlin-Tegel Airport to Uhlandstrasse. **Amenities:** Restaurant; bar; car rental; room service. *In room:* TV, minibar, hair dryer, safe.

**Sorat Art'otel** ★ Chic, discreet, and avant-garde, the Sorat is unlike any other Berlin hotel. The location is ideal, in the heart of cosmopolitan Berlin, with the Ku'damm action virtually outside the front door. The decor, strictly minimalist, includes touches from top designers. You'll find Philippe Starck bar stools, Arne Jacobsen chairs, and artwork by Berliner Wolf Vostell. Modernists will be at home here, amid chrome-legged furnishings and pedestal tables that look like cable spools. Traditionalists might not be so pleased. Rooms are all comfortable, with soundproofing, large beds, and tasteful lighting. Bathrooms are generous in size with shower-tub combinations. The service here is among Berlin's finest.

Joachimstalerstrasse 28–29 (near the Ku'damm), 10719 Berlin. ✆ **030/88-44-70.** Fax 030/88-44-77-00. www.sorat-hotels.com. 133 units. 217.20€–232.50€ ($193.95–$207.60) double. Rates include buffet breakfast. AE, DC, MC, V. U-Bahn: Kurfürstendamm. **Amenities:** Restaurant; lounge; room service; laundry. *In room*: AC, TV, minibar, hair dryer.

### MODERATE

**Hotel Sylter Hof Berlin** This hotel, built in 1966, offers rich trappings at good prices. The main lounges are warmly decorated in Louis XV style, with chandeliers, provincial chairs, and antiques. Well-maintained rooms—mostly singles—may be too small for most tastes but are good for business travelers. All the compact, tiled bathrooms are equipped with shower-tub combinations. The staff pays special attention to your comfort.

Kurfürstenstrasse 114–116, 10787 Berlin. ✆ **030/2-12-00.** Fax 030/2-14-28-26. www.wylterhof-berlin.de. 161 units. 137.95€ ($123.20) double; from 171.70€ ($153.35) suite. Rates include buffet breakfast. AE, DC, MC, V. Parking 10.20€ ($9.10). U-Bahn: Wittenbergplatz. Bus: 100 or X9. **Amenities:** Breakfast room; bar; lounge; nightclub; room service. *In room*: TV, minibar, hair dryer.

### INEXPENSIVE

**Arco Hotel** Although some of its competitors are more visible and more heavily promoted, this is one of the most consistently reliable and fairly priced gay hotels in Berlin. It occupies part of a former old-Berlin apartment building that was completely renovated in 1999. Rooms are mostly white, well scrubbed, and well organized, with tasteful albeit simple artwork and furnishings. Each comes with a small, shower bathroom. There's a garden in back, site of breakfasts during clement weather. A polite and hardworking staff is alert to the location of emerging neighborhood bars and restaurants, many of whose owners recommend this place. Much of its business derives from repeat guests from as far away as Los Angeles.

Geisbergstrasse 30, D-10777 Berlin. ✆ **030/23-51-480.** Fax 030/21-47-51-78. www.arco-hotel.de. 22 units. 82€–92€ ($73.25–$82.15) double. Rates include breakfast. AE, DC, MC, V. U-Bahn: Viktoria-Luise-Platz or Nollendorferplatz. **Amenities:** Breakfast room; lounge. *In room*: TV, hair dryer, safe.

## IN GRUNEWALD

### VERY EXPENSIVE

**Regent Schlosshotel Berlin** ★★★ With only 54 gem-like rooms, this is one of the most historic and plushest hotels in Berlin. It was built in the 19th century by a friend and advisor of Kaiser Wilhelm II, who entertained him from time to time on the premises. For anyone who can afford it and prefers a stay in the city's verdant suburbs, the experience can be elegant, historic, and charming. Service is superb and invariably cheerful. Although changes have been made to the decor, its original inspiration was by German-born fashion superstar Karl Lagerfeld. The structure's monumental staircase, minstrel's gallery, and other Belle Epoque trappings remain, but Mr. Lagerfeld's contributions have added an undeniable gloss to the hotel's interior. Beds are sumptuous, with great pillows, fine linen, and elegant fabrics. Bathrooms have shower-and-tub combos, plush towels, radiantly heated floors, slippers, scales, and robes.

Brahmsstrasse 10, 14193 Berlin-Grunewald. ✆ **800/545-4000** in U.S. and Canada, or 030/895-840. Fax 030/895-84800. www.regenthotels.com. 54 units. 335€–395€ ($299.15–$352.75) double; from 500€, ($446.50) suite. AE, DC, MC, V. S-Bahn: Grunewald. **Amenities:** 2 restaurants; bar; health club; spa; sauna; salon; room service; massage; babysitting; laundry/dry cleaning. *In room:* A/C, TV/VCR, dataport, stereo and CD player, minibar, hair dryer, safe.

## IN BERLIN-MITTE

### VERY EXPENSIVE

**Berlin Hilton** ★ The Four Seasons and Westin Grand are finer hotels, attracting some of the Hilton's former clients, but this durable landmark is still going strong. Set within one of the city's most expensive and desirable neighborhoods (Gendarmenmarkt), this deluxe hotel was the first to open in what was East Berlin following the collapse of the Berlin Wall. Today, it's the third largest hotel in the city and one of the most popular. The seven-floor hotel contains enough accessories and facilities to keep you jumping for a week. Thanks to all the visual distraction in the lobby, there's even a vague sense that you might be in a resort hotel that's eager to cater to the needs of both large groups and business travelers alike. Rooms are conservatively modern and very comfortable, with double-glazed windows, comfortable beds, bedside controls, and well-equipped bathrooms with tub-shower combos. At least half overlook the twin churches of the dramatic Gendarmenmarkt.

Mohrenstrasse 30, 10117 Berlin. ✆ **800/445-8667** in the U.S. and Canada, or 030/2-02-30. Fax 030/20-23-42-69. www.hilton.com. 598 units. 210€–400€ ($187.55–$357.20) double; 270€–920€ ($241.10–$821.55) suite. Special weekend packages available. AE, MC, V. Parking 13€ ($11.60). U-Bahn: Stadtmitte. **Amenities:** 4 restaurants; 3 bars; nightclub; pool; health spa; Jacuzzi; sauna; bowling alley; room service; babysitting; laundry. *In room:* A/C, TV, minibar, hair dryer, safe.

**Four Seasons** ★★★ This hotel lacks the historical pedigree of its major competitor, the newly rebuilt Adlon, but the Four Seasons is Berlin's most sumptuous address. One of Berlin's most opulent hotels, it was built in 1996 on the site of a bombed-out parking lot about a block from the Gendarmenmarkt. From the look of things, you'd never realize the venue is new, as everything about it evokes Versailles and an undeniable sense of well-established and very plush prosperity. Decor, illuminated with light from two separate courtyards, includes Viennese crystal chandeliers and antiques from throughout Europe, giving you the sense that you've entered a private and very upscale home. Rooms are furnished with timeless taste and elegance, with very large bathrooms, each with walk-in showers, deep tubs, and a relentlessly upscale selection of toiletries.

Charlottenstrasse 49, 10117 Berlin. ✆ **800/332-3442** in the U.S., or 030/2-03-38. Fax 030/203-36-009. www.fourseasons.com. 204 units. 224.85€–342.90€ ($200.80–$306.20) double; from 379.65€ ($339.05) suite. AE, DC, MC, V. Parking 22€ ($19.65). U-Bahn: Französische Strasse. **Amenities:** Restaurant; bar; health club; room service; massage; babysitting; laundry/dry cleaning. *In room:* A/C, TV, minibar, hair dryer, safe.

**Grand Hyatt Berlin** ★★★ This is the most exciting, best-designed, and most iconoclastic hotel in Berlin, a government-rated five-star mecca. Don't expect rococo frills: Interior designer Hannes Wettstein permeated this hotel with a minimalist simplicity that might remind you of a Zen temple. Ceilings soar toward surreal-looking inverted pyramids, upstairs hallways run off into futuristic-looking infinities, and light derives from rambling expanses of glass or translucent slabs of alabaster. The large and sunflooded rooms are among the hotel's best features. Suites are often commandeered by fashion photographers as backgrounds for cutting-edge fashion layouts. *Hint:* For a surcharge of 51.10€ ($45.65), you can upgrade your accommodation to the Regency Club. There, the value of free

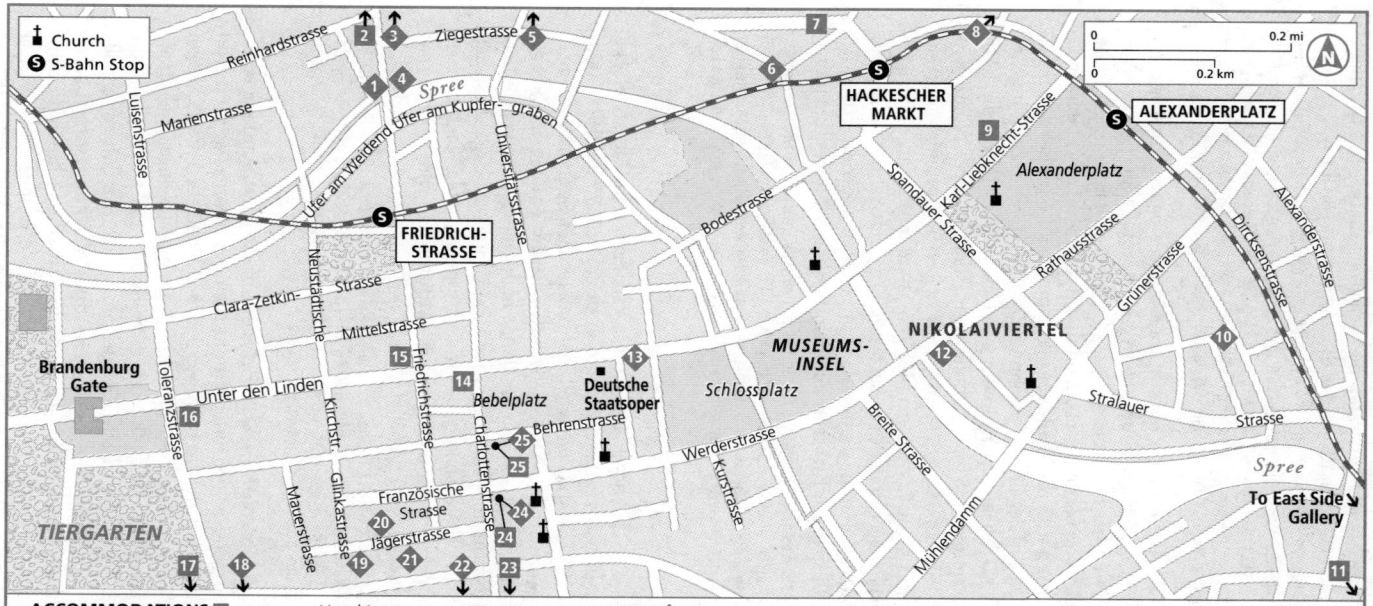


**ACCOMMODATIONS ■**
Alexander Plaza **9**
Berlin Hilton **23**
Dorint am Gendarmarkt **24**
Four Seasons **25**
Hotel Adlon **16**
Hotel Hackescher Markt **7**
Hotel Intermezzo **17**
Hotel Luisenhof **11**
Hotel Unter Linden **15**
Maritim Pro Arte **2**
Westin Grand Hotel **14**

**DINING ◆**
Aigner **24**
Alexanderkeller **12**
Die Weltbühne **8**
Dressler **13**
Französischer Hof **19**
Ganymed **1**
Guy **20**
Keller Restaurant im Brecht-Haus-Berlin **3**
La Gaiola **6**
Langhans **22**
Mutter Hoppe **12**
Oren **5**
Portalis **18**
Restaurant Vau **21**
Schwarzengraben **8**
The Seasons Restaurant **25**
StäV **4**
Zur Letzten Instanz **10**

breakfasts, afternoon tea, evening cocktail hour, daytime snacks, and enhanced services will more than compensate you for the supplement you'll pay.

Marlene-Dietrich-Platz 2, D-10785 Berlin. ✆ **030/25-53-12-34.** Fax 030/25-53-12-35. www.hyatt.com. 340 units. 210€–285€ ($187.55–$254.50) double; 51.10€ ($45.65) supplement, per room, for upgrade to Regency Club; from 325€, ($290.25) suite. AE, DC, MC, V. Parking 6€ ($5.35). U-Bahn: Potsdamer Platz. **Amenities:** 2 restaurants; bar; cafe; pool; tennis court; health club; sauna; room service; laundry/dry cleaning; computer rental. *In room:* A/C, TV, dataport, Sony Playstation, minibar, hair dryer, safe.

**Hotel Adlon** ★★★ Berlin's most historic hotel is now a phoenix freshly risen from the ashes of 1945. Only the Four Seasons (see above) is a more sumptuous address in Berlin. No other hotel sits as close to the Brandenburg Gate, at the top of an avenue that's reasserting its claim on the city's sense of chic. Grand and historic, and permeated with the legends of the glamour and tragedies that befell it during various eras of its life, it was originally built by legendary hotelier Lorenz Adlon in 1907, then reopened with a well-publicized flourish in 1997 after a massive expenditure of funds. Public areas, some of them illuminated with lavishly detailed stained-glass domes, contain coffered ceilings, mosaics, inlaid paneling, and lots of Carrara marble. Rooms are mostly large and have lots of state-of-the-art electronic extras, such as CD players. Those on the top floor offer the best views but are a bit more cramped and lack some extras. All come equipped with spacious bathrooms containing shower-tub combinations.

Unter den Linden 77, 10117 Berlin. ✆ **800/426-3135** in the U.S., or 030/22-61-0. Fax 030/22-61-1116. www.hotel-adlon.de. 337 units. 275.95€–357.70€ ($246.40–$319.45) double; from 459.90€ ($410.70) suite. AE, DC, MC, V. Parking 23€ ($20.55) per day. S-Bahn: Unter den Linden. **Amenities:** 3 restaurants; bar; pool; health club; spa services; room service; babysitting; laundry/dry cleaning. *In room:* A/C, TV, minibar, hair dryer, safe.

## EXPENSIVE

**Alexander Plaza** ★ This hotel is set a short walk from both Alexanderplatz and the historic district of Hackescher Höfe. It originated around 1900 as an office building. In 1997, it was converted into one of the neighborhood's most charming and best-managed hotels. A labyrinth of hallways open into rooms with unique floor plans. Each has parquet floors, high ceilings, and neo-Biedermeier blond-wood furniture. The "executive rooms" are very large. Low-end rooms are smaller and less dramatic, but still very comfortable. Each midsize unit comes with a private bathroom equipped with tub and shower. The staff here is among the most attentive in Berlin.

Rosenstrasse 1, D-10178 Berlin. ✆ **800/223-5652** for reservations in North America, or 030/240-010. Fax 030/240-01-777. www.alexander-plaza.com. 92 units. 150€–180€ ($133.95–$160.75) double; 195€–235€ ($174.15–$209.85) suite. S-Bahn: Hackescher Markt. **Amenities:** Restaurant; bar; health club; sauna; solarium; steamroom; room service. *In room:* A/C, TV, minibar, hair dryer.

**Dorint am Gendarmenmarkt** ★★ This is one of the latest boutique hotels to open, and it's so good it lures visitors from such old favorites as the Berlin Hilton. The shell that contains this hotel was designed by the then–East German government in 1981 as a youth hostel, and set behind a faux-Jugendstil facade that has since then been declared a historic monument. After reunification, the Dorint chain carefully converted the structure into an upscale hotel of artfully simple, Zen-like minimalism. The result is a soothing blend of high-tech accessories and a restful kind of neutrality, all of it adminstered in a hip and upbeat way that usually appeals to anyone working in the field of media, the arts, or high-tech science. Small and choice, and presenting an ultra-hip version of "new Berlin" to the antique setting of the Gendarmenmarkt, it's one of the genuinely unusual upscale hotels in Berlin. Every room is different, but the best overlook the Gendarmenmarkt from behind tiny balconies. Most units have a shower unit.

Charlottenstrasse 50–52, D-10117 Berlin. ✆ **030/20375-0.** Fax 030/20375-100. www.dorint.com. 92 units. 174€–304€ ($155.40–$271.45) double; 235€–600€ ($209.85–$535.80) suite. AE, DC, MC, V. U-Bahn: Stadtmitte. **Amenities:** Restaurant; cafe; health club; sauna; steamroom; meditation room; room service; laundry. *In room*: A/C, TV, dataport, minibar, hair dryer, safe.

**Maritim Pro Arte** ★ This is a more *luxe* version of Sorat Art'otel (p. 84). Set about a block from Unter den Linden, this hotel was built as an avant-garde architectural showcase in the mid-1970s by the then East German government. Today, despite frequent renovations, it still evokes a jazzy, "moderno," and vaguely dated kind of architecture that features lots of chrome and stainless steel. There's a bustle here, however, thanks in part to a hardworking and polite staff, and a regular clientele of business clients and conventioneers. Avant-garde artwork is exhibited throughout, and Phillipe Starck created some of the furniture. Rooms are individually designed, soothing, uncluttered, and comfortable. Most provide a fax outlet and all have reclining chairs. Each unit comes with a good-size private bathroom with tub and shower.

Friedrichstrasse 151–153 (across from Friedrichstrasse station), 10117 Berlin. ✆ **030/2-03-35.** Fax 030/20-33-42-09. www.maritim.de. 403 units. 168€–238€ ($150–$212.55) double; from 300€ ($267.90) suite. AE, DC, MC, V. Parking 15€ ($13.40). S-Bahn: Friedrichstrasse. **Amenities:** 3 restaurants; bar; pool; fitness studio; sauna; solarium; room service; babysitting; laundry. *In room*: A/C, TV, minibar, hair dryer, safe.

**Westin Grand Hotel** ★★★ This is a monument to "capitalistic decadence," as they used to say during the Cold War era, but amazingly, it was first constructed on socialist soil by the then-communist East German government. Now under management by the Westin group, and devoid of its original sense of stiffness, it's one of Berlin's finest hotels, though it pales in comparison to its major rival, the Four Seasons. Belle Epoque features blend with contemporary styling. Rooms, radically renovated and upgraded in 1998, come in a wide range of styles, from beautifully appointed standard doubles all the way up to the lush-looking Schinkel Suite. Beds contain wonderfully soft linens, down pillows, and comforters. Other features include terry-cloth robes, combination tub and shower, and fresh flowers.

Friedrichstrasse 158–164, 10117 Berlin. ✆ **800/843-3311** in the U.S., or 030/2-02-70. Fax 030/20-27-33-62. www.westin-grand.com. 364 units. 286.15€–301.50€ ($255.55–$269.25) double; 454.80€ ($406.15) suite. AE, DC, MC, V. Parking 13€ ($11.60). U-Bahn: Französische Strasse. S-Bahn: Friedrichstrasse. **Amenities:** Restaurant; bar; lounge; pool; fitness club; sauna; solarium; salon; room service; massage; babysitting; laundry/dry cleaning. *In room*: A/C, TV, minibar, hair dryer, safe.

## MODERATE

**Hotel Hackescher Markt** ★ You'd never know this nugget of charm was newly built in 1998, as everything about it evokes a late–19th century landmark. Inside, there's a quiet, flagstone-and-ivy covered courtyard that clients use for reading, and a polite and helpful staff that knows virtually everything about what's happening in the hotel's cutting-edge neighborhood. There's a bar on street level where hipsters might feel supremely comfortable, and where live music is often presented in the evenings. Rooms are soothing, partially oak-paneled, and outfitted with comfortable and practical furniture. Standard singles tend to be just a bit small—a better bet might be one of the more upscale doubles. Bathrooms have heated floors, and combination tub and shower. Some guests appreciate the romantic overtones of rooms on the uppermost floor, whose walls are angled thanks to the building's mansard roof.

Grosse Präsidentenstrasse 8, D-10178 Berlin. ✆ **030/28-00-30.** Fax 030/28-00-31-11. www.hackescher-markt.com. 31 units. 132.85€–168.65€ ($118.65–$150.60) double; 173.75€–199.30€ ($155.15–$177.95) suite. AE, MC, V. U-Bahn: Hackescher Markt. **Amenities:** Restaurant; bar; room service; laundry. *In room:* TV, minibar, hair dryer, safe.

**Hotel Intermezzo** *Finds* In the center of a quiet street, this hotel *for women only* lies only a 5-minute walk from the Brandenburg Gate, the Reichstag, and Unter den Linden. The back of the hotel looks onto the landmark Potsdamer Platz and the new Sony Centre. In other words, you couldn't be more central in Berlin. The interior design looks like a showroom at IKEA. Bedrooms are attractively and comfortably furnished, each with a tidy shower. Female guests meet like-minded souls in the breakfast room, which looks like it was transplanted from a Swedish B&B to Berlin. A freshly made and excellent buffet is prepared every morning. The hotel is a clean, well maintained, and inviting haven for women, especially those traveling alone. Most guests are solo travelers.

An der Kolonnade 14, 10117 Berlin. ✆ **030/224-890.** Fax 030/224-890-97. www.hotelintermezzo.de. 16 units. 40€ ($35.70) single; 67€ ($59.85) double; 85€ ($75.90) triple; 114€ ($101.80) quad. Children up to 12 23€ ($20.55). Boys allowed up to 12. AE, MC, V. S-Bahn: Potsdamer Platz. **Amnenities:** Breakfast room. *In room:* TV, hair dryer.

**Hotel Luisenhof** ★ This is one of the most desirable small hotels in eastern Berlin. It lies within a severely dignified house, built in 1822. Its five floors of high-ceilinged rooms have been outfitted in a conservative and traditional style, a welcome escape from modern Berlin. The upgraded units range in size from small to spacious, but all are equipped with fine beds and individual fax machines. Bathrooms, though small, are beautifully appointed, most with a tub and shower. The neighborhood around this hotel, like many other parts of the once-dour eastern zone, is undergoing a rapid renovation.

Köpenicker Strasse 92, 10179 Berlin. ✆ **030/2-41-59-06.** Fax 030/2-79-29-83. www.luisenhof.de. 27 units. 135.40€–180€ ($120.90–$160.75) double; 190€–250€ ($169.65–$223.25) suite. Rates include breakfast. AE, DC, MC, V. Parking 8€ ($7.15). U-Bahn: Märkisches Museum. **Amenities:** Restaurant; room service; laundry/dry cleaning. *In room:* TV, minibar, hair dryer.

**Hotel Unter den Linden** An architectural fright erected by Cold War commies, this hotel is softening under capitalist control. The location, at the corner of Unter den Linden and Friedrichstrasse, is almost unbeatable for Berlin Mitte convenience. You can walk out the door and stroll over to the Reichstag or the Brandenburger Tor. It's banal but affordable. Its guestrooms are comfortable and a bit small, each with newly installed plumbing including shower-only bathrooms.

Unter den Linden 14, 10117 Berlin. ✆ **030/238-110.** Fax 030/238-11-100. 331 units. 118€–163€ ($105.35–$145.55) double. Rates include breakfast. AE, DC, MC, V. U-Bahn: Friedrichstrasse. **Amenities:** Breakfast salon; bistro bar with summer terrace; room service; laundry. *In room:* TV.

## 4 Where to Dine

If it's true that optimism and appetite go hand in hand, Berliners must be among the most optimistic people in Europe. But just because Berliners like to eat, doesn't mean that they like to spend a lot on food. Locals know that you can often have a memorable dinner here in an unheralded wine restaurant or sidewalk cafe. Rising food costs in the east, however, mean that in the new Berlin, the eastern section can no longer be viewed as a bargain basement in the food department.

### Kids Family-Friendly Restaurants

**Funkturm Restaurant** (p. 96) Kids delight in ascending this radio tower on Messedam, open daily 10:30am to 11:30pm. The food at the restaurant is good, and later you can go to the observation platform for a truly grand view. The elevator costs 3.05€ ($2.70) for adults, 1.55€ ($1.40) for children.

**Hard Rock Cafe** (p. 94) After enough sauerkraut and wurst, kids may want a familiar American hamburger, and this place dispenses them by the truckload.

If a restaurant bill says *Bedienung,* that means a service charge has already been added, so just round up to the nearest euro.

Examples of typical dishes are the Berliner *Schlachteplatte* (cold plate); pigs' trotters cooked with sauerkraut and pea purée; and *Eisbein* (pickled knuckle of pork with sauerkraut). Venison, wildfowl, and wild boar also appear frequently, as do carp and trout, along with an infinite variety of sausages.

But Berlin does not limit itself to traditional cuisine. A new wave of restaurants has swept across the city, from east to west. More and more are going ethnic, serving everything from Indonesian or French to Thai or Japanese. Eastern European wines are now almost as popular as those from Germany itself.

See the maps "Western Berlin Accommodations & Dining" (p. 78) and "Berlin-Mitte Accommodations & Dining" (p. 87) for restaurant locations.

## ON OR NEAR THE KURFÜRSTENDAMM

### VERY EXPENSIVE

**Bamberger Reiter** ★★★ CONTINENTAL Bamberger Reiter, serving French, German, and Austrian dishes in the style of *neue Deutsche Küche,* is still the choice of savvy local foodies. Don't judge it by its location in an undistinguished 19th-century apartment house. The decor evokes old Germany, with lots of mirrors and fresh flowers. The quality is beyond question here—only Rockendorf's or Alt-Luxemburg can even pretend to have better food. The menu changes daily according to the availability of fresh ingredients and the inspiration of the chef, but might include a roulade of quail, bass with Riesling sauce, lamb with beans and potato croutons, and date strudel with almond ice cream. German seafood aficionados go here for the fresh fish, which is caught with hook and line—not netted, which is believed to encourage a fresher catch. The wine list is enormous, with a dozen varieties of champagne alone.

Regensburgerstrasse 7. ✆ **030/2-18-42-82.** Reservations required. Main courses 17.90€–30.65€ ($16–$27.35); 4- or 5-course fixed-price menu 44.95€–49.05€ ($40.15–$43.80). AE, DC, MC, V. Tues–Sat 5:30pm–1am (last order 10:30pm). U-Bahn: Spichernstrasse.

**Harlekin** ★★ FRENCH/INTERNATIONAL This is among the top three restaurants of Berlin, ranking up there with First Floor (see below) and Bamberger Reiter (see above). This restaurant's rise to prominence chagrined jealous chefs at old favorites like the Kempinski. The menu is perfectly balanced between tradition and innovation. For example, appetizers are likely to include such dishes as calves' consommé with crayfish or osso buco consommé with lobster Spätzle. For your main course, you might be won over by the saddle of lamb baked in a spring roll or turbot roasted with mixed root vegetables. All dishes are made with fresh local produce and are perfectly prepared. Set menus are always delightful and often pleasantly surprising.

In the Grand Hotel Esplanade, Lützowufer. ✆ **030/25-47-88-58.** Reservations recommended. Main courses 23€–30.65€ ($20.55–$27.35); 4–-6-course menu 66.45€–84.30€ ($59.35–$75.30). AE, DC, MC, V. Tues–Sat 6:30–11pm. Closed July. U-Bahn: Nollendorfplatz or Wittenbergplatz.

**Rockendorf's Gourmet Restaurant** ★★★ CONTINENTAL After 25 years in a villa in north Berlin, Rockendorf's, one of the best known of all the city's restaurants, delights gourmets in its new quarters behind the landmark KaDeWe department store, near the Europa Center. This new 35- to 40-seat Art Deco restaurant mounts a serious challenge to frontrunners Bamberger Reiter and Alt-Luxemburg. Chef Siegfried Rockendorf achieves a happy wedding between nouvelle cuisine and classic specialties. Perhaps you'll try his memorable fresh jellied aspic with cucumber sauce. Sometimes the combinations appear startling but are delightful—take the very creamy and very light turnip soup with lobster. Other choice plates include a filet of turbot in Ricard sauce, and goose-meat paté in Sauterne with cranberries. The service is exquisitely refined—attentive without being cloying. Everything is served on fine porcelain. Some of Germany's most visible names in show biz, journalism, and politics come here.

> *Tips* **A Map Note**
>
> For restaurants located in western Berlin, see the "Western Berlin Accommodations & Dining" map on p. 78–79.

The complex also contains a 30-seat cocktail/aperitif bar; a folkloric *gutbürgerlich* (suggests old-fashioned, cozy, and homestyle—the German equivalent of soul food) restaurant, Restaurant Berliner Original, wherein main courses cost from 14€ to 22.45€ ($12.50–$20.05); and a Bistro & Café that's also a pastry emporium for very elaborate baked goods, where pastries, snacks, and small platters cost from 7.15€ to 16.35€ ($6.40–$14.60). Berliner Original is decorated in a country alpine style, and the cafe in ersatz Jugendstil. The Berliner Original is open daily 11:30am to 2pm and 7 to 10pm, and the bistro/cafe is open daily 10am to 10pm.

Passauerstrasse 5–7. ✆ **030/21-99-21-70.** Reservations required. Main courses 22.55€–40.90€ ($20.15–$36.50). AE, DC, MC, V. Mon–Sat noon–2pm and 7–10pm. Closed last 2 weeks in July. U-Bahn: Wittenbergplatz.

### EXPENSIVE

**Paris Bar** ★ FRENCH This French bistro has been a local favorite since it cheered up the postwar years in dismal bombed-out Berlin. It's crowded with elbow-to-elbow tables like a Montmartre tourist trap but is a genuinely pleasing little place on the see-and-be-seen circuit, close to the Theater des Westens. The food is invariably fresh and well prepared, but not particularly innovative.

Kantstrasse 152 (between Savignyplatz and Fasenenstrasse). ✆ **030/3-13-80-52.** Reservations recommended. Main courses 12.80€–24.55€ ($11.45–$21.90). AE. Daily noon–1am. U-Bahn: Uhlandstrasse.

### MODERATE

**Kaefer's Restaurant Dachgarten** CONTINENTAL When a team of cutting-edge architects redesigned the most famous building in Berlin, the Reichstag (Parliament House), they added a restaurant on the uppermost floor, just behind the soaring metallic dome that has inspired so many photographs. The setting is metallic-looking and edgy. Lines to get in here can be overwhelming, mingling sightseers and diners in the same queues, so here's our advice on how to short-circuit the potential wait: Phone in advance for a dining reservation, and note the reservation number an attendant will give you. Head for the Reichstag's handicapped entrance on the building's west side, facing the Platz der Republik, give the attendant your number, then ride an elevator directly to the restaurant, avoiding the lines of sightseers coming just to admire the building's dome.

Included in the price of your meal will be a close-up view of the dome and the rest of the building's interior. Frankly, a visit here might best be configured at breakfast, when there's a business-like aura that's consistent with this building's august role as a Teutonic icon. Views sweep from the dining room out over what used to be known as East Berlin. The lunch menu is more "Berliner" than the Continental/Asian evening menu. Lunchtime menus include house-style meatballs with cole slaw and potato salad; grilled steaks and wursts. Dinners are a bit more exotic, focusing on dishes like fried filet of duck with Austrian-style scalloped potatoes and Asian asparagus and water chestnuts, and filet of turbot with a purée of truffles and herb-flavored risotto.

In the Reichstag, Platz der Republik. ✆ **030/2262-9933.** Reservations necessary. Breakfast 10€–14€ ($8.95–$12.50) per person. Lunch main courses 12€–17€ ($10.70–$15.20); dinner main courses 13€–23€ ($11.60–$20.55). Fixed-price lunch 27€ ($24.10); fixed-price dinner 39€–62€ ($34.85–$55.35). AE, DC, MC, V. Daily 9–11am; 11:30am–2:30pm and 6:30–9:30pm (last food order). S-Bahn: Unter den Linden.

**Marjellchen** ★ EAST PRUSSIAN This is the only restaurant in Berlin specializing in the cuisine of Germany's long-lost province of East Prussia, along with the cuisines of Pomerania and Silesia. Ramona Azzaro, whose East Prussian mother taught her many of the region's famous recipes, is the creative force here. Amid a Bismarckian ambience of vested waiters and oil lamps, you can enjoy a savory version of red-beet soup with strips of beef, East Prussian potato soup with shrimp and bacon, *Falscher Gänsebraten* (pork spare ribs stuffed with prunes and bread crumbs "as if the cook had prepared a goose"), marinated elk, and *Mecklenburger Kümmelfleisch* (lamb with chives and onions). This is the type of food Goethe or Schiller liked; perhaps you'll be a convert, too. Of course, Marjellchen isn't the place to go if you want to keep tabs on the cholesterol intake.

Mommsenstrasse 9. ✆ **030/8-83-26-76.** Reservations required. Main courses 10.20€–20.45€ ($9.10–$18.25). AE, DC, MC, V. Mon–Sat 5pm–midnight. Closed Dec 23–24, and 31. U-Bahn: Adenauerplatz or Uhlandstrasse.

**Restaurant Mario** NORTHERN ITALIAN Here you'll find Berlin's most imaginative northern Italian food. The innovative chefs shop for the best and most market-fresh ingredients. Begin with a platter of the most delectable antipasti in town. At least two different kinds of pastas are offered nightly, including a favorite made with a green-pepper pesto. Also on hand are more traditional dishes such as chicken breast stuffed with mozzarella and herbs, tantalizing herb-seasoned lamb cutlets, and fresh fish simply grilled and perfectly seasoned.

Carmerstrasse 2. ✆ **030/3-12-31-15.** Reservations recommended. Main courses 10.20€–17.90€ ($9.10–$16); fixed-price menus 12.80€–33.20€ ($11.45–$29.65). AE, MC, V. Mon–Fri noon–midnight; Sat 4pm–1am. S-Bahn: Savignyplatz.

**Seidler Restaurant** GERMAN This restaurant enjoys a reputation as a select dining spot and social center. Your host, Mr. Seidler, has a devoted local following among theater and media personalities. The chef believes in strong flavors and good hearty cookery. Savor the *Kohlroulade,* a stuffed cabbage roll—few chefs would want to compete with it. The *Tafelspitz,* boiled beef with vegetables, would have pleased Emperor Josef of Austria (it was his favorite dish). Another highlight is the rack of lamb with honey onions and rosemary potatoes. Look also for market-fresh daily specials. The ambience is that of a Berlin bistro, charmingly cluttered with kitsch from all over the world.

Damaschkestrasse 26. ✆ **030/3-23-14-04.** Reservations required. Main courses 7€–19€ ($6.25–$16.95). MC. Mon–Sat 5pm–midnight. U-Bahn: Adenauerplatz.

### INEXPENSIVE

**Hard Rock Cafe** *Kids* AMERICAN This is the local branch of the familiar worldwide chain that mingles rock-'n'-roll nostalgia with American food. Menu choices range from a veggie burger to a "pig" sandwich (hickory smoked pork barbecue) that you might find in rural Georgia. The food is unexceptional, but service is friendly, and most kids will be happy to eat here.

Meinekestrasse 21. ✆ **030/88-46-20.** Reservations accepted for groups of 10 or more. Main courses 8.20€–18.90€ ($7.30–$16.90). AE, MC, V. Sun–Thurs noon–midnight; Fri–Sat noon–1am. U-Bahn: Kurfürstendamm.

**Lubitsch** CONTINENTAL Lubitsch is deeply entrenched in the consciousness of many local residents, and it's considered in some quarters to have a degree of conservative chic. That reputation was enhanced in 1999 when Chancellor Schröder dropped in for lunch and a photo-op, causing ripples of energy to reverberate through the neighborhood. Menu items include lots of cafe drinks, with glasses of wine priced at 4.50€ to 7€ ($4–$6.25), and steaming pots of afternoon tea, but if you drop in for a meal, expect platters of chicken curry salad with roasted potatoes; Berlin-style potato soup; braised chicken with salad and fresh vegetables; a roulade of suckling pig; and Nürnberger-style *wursts.* Count on a not so friendly staff, a black-and-white decor with Thonet-style chairs, and a somewhat arrogant environment that despite its drawbacks, is very, very *Berliner.*

Bleibtreustrasse 47. ✆ **030/882-37-56.** Reservations not necessary. Main courses 5.10€–17.90€ ($4.55–$16). AE, DC, MC, V. Mon–Sat 9:30am–midnight; Sun 4pm–midnight. U-Bahn: Kurfürstendamm.

## NEAR THE MEMORIAL CHURCH & ZOO

### VERY EXPENSIVE

**First Floor** ★★★ REGIONAL GERMAN/FRENCH This is the showcase restaurant of the Palace Berlin Hotel. Located near the Tiergarten and set one floor above street level, it features a perfectly orchestrated service and setting that revolves around the cuisine of a master chef. Winning our praise are such dishes as a terrine of veal with arugala-flavored butter; sophisticated variations of Bresse chicken; guinea fowl stuffed with foie gras and served with a truffled vinaigrette sauce; a cassolette of lobster and broad beans in a style vaguely influenced by the culinary precepts of southwestern France; filet of sole with champagne sauce; and a mascarpone mousse with lavender-scented honey.

In the Palace Berlin Hotel, Budapesterstrasse 45. ✆ **030/25-02-10-20.** Reservations recommended. Main courses 25.55€–38.35€ ($22.80–$34.25). Fixed-price menus 40.90€ ($36.50) lunch only; 66.45€–102.20€ ($59.35–$91.25) lunch and dinner. AE, DC, MC, V. Daily noon–2pm and 8–11pm. U-Bahn: Zoologischer Garten.

### EXPENSIVE

**Daitokai** ★ JAPANESE Think of this restaurant as a less-institutionalized Benihana's where vermilion carp lanterns illuminate the labyrinth of reflecting pools. Chefs prepare the meals before your eyes at several long tables. This teppanyaki restaurant offers some of the city's finest grilled steak—tender, juicy, and never overcooked. The seafood and vegetables are served with an artistic flair, and the fish is always fresh and beautifully presented: They never skimp on quality here. The flawless service features kindly, almost overly polite waitresses in kimonos. To dine here inexpensively and still eat well, take advantage of the set luncheons.

Europa Center. ✆ **030/2-61-80-99.** Reservations recommended. Main courses 19.50€–28.50€ ($17.40–$25.45); fixed-price meals 55.27€–80.80€ ($49.35–$72.15). AE, DC, MC, V. Tues–Sun noon–2:30pm and 6–10:30pm. U-Bahn: Kurfürstendamm.

## NEAR THE TIERGARTEN

### VERY EXPENSIVE

**Paris-Moskau** ★ INTERNATIONAL The grand days of the 19th century are alive and well at this restaurant in the beautiful Tiergarten area, where good dining spots are scarce. The menu features both classic and more cutting-edge dishes. The fresh tomato soup is excellent. Some of the dishes are mundane—the grilled filet of beef in mushroom sauce comes to mind—but other lighter dishes with delicate seasonings are delightful. We recommend the grilled North Sea salmon with herbs accompanied by basil-flavored noodles. The chef should market his recipe for saffron sauce, which accompanies several dishes. You'll receive attentive service from the formally dressed staff.

Alt-Moabit 141. ✆ **030/3-94-20-81.** Reservations recommended. Main courses 18.90€–24.55€ ($16.90–$21.90); fixed-price menus 53.65€–79.20€ ($47.90–$70.75). No credit cards. Daily 6–11:30pm. S-Bahn: Bellevue.

## IN GREATER CHARLOTTENBURG

### VERY EXPENSIVE

**Alt-Luxemburg** ★★★ CONTINENTAL Bamberger Reiter is still the leader among Berlin restaurants, but Alt-Luxemburg is nipping at its heels. Karl Wannemacher is one of the outstanding chefs of Germany. Try the honey-glazed duck breast or the saddle of venison with juniper sauce. His Bavarian cream of eel and sturgeon terrine is also excellent. For dessert, don't miss the memorable semolina dumplings with orange ragout or the orange sorbet. The service is both unpretentious and gracious. The dark paneling, evenly spaced mirrors, antique chandeliers, and old-fashioned ambience create a Belle Epoque aura.

Windscheidstrasse 31. ✆ **030/3-23-87-30.** Reservations required. Fixed-price 4-course menu 66.45€ ($59.35); 5-course menu 74.10€ ($66.15). AE, DC, MC, V. Mon–Sat 5–11pm. U-Bahn: Sophie-Charlotte-Platz.

### EXPENSIVE

**Ana e Bruno** ★ ITALIAN This is one of Berlin's most charming Italian restaurants. Ana and Bruno turn out a delectable cuisine that takes full advantage of the freshest ingredients and produce in any season. *Nuova cucina* is emphasized here more strongly than traditional Italian classics, and the chefs like to experiment. The combinations of food offer delicious flavors and the creations a harmonious medley. Expect dishes such as a radicchio-studded pasta with perfectly cooked shrimp or an Italian filet of veal with a tuna sauce. Regular customers and gourmets keen on experimenting always seem satisfied with the results. A large wine selection, mostly reasonable in price, complements the menu.

Sophie-Charlotten-Strasse 101. ✆ **030/325-71-10.** Reservations recommended. Main courses 32€–34€ ($28.60–$30.35); fixed-price menus 67€–99€ ($59.85–$88.40). AE, V. Tues–Fri 6:30–10:30pm. U-Bahn: Bismarckstrasse.

### MODERATE

**Bierhaus Luisen-Bräu** GERMAN One of the city's largest breweries, Luisen-Bräu dates from 1987. The decor includes enormous stainless-steel vats of the fermenting brew, from which the waiters refill your mug. There is no subtlety of cuisine here; it's robust and hearty fare. You serve yourself from a long buffet table. The seating is indoor or outdoor, depending on the season, at long picnic tables that encourage a sense of beer-hall *Bruderschaft* (camaraderie).

Luisenplatz 1, Charlottenburg (close to Charlottenburg Palace). ✆ **030/3-41-93-88.** Reservations recommended on weekends. Salads, snacks, and platters 5.10€–12.80€ ($4.55–$11.45). MC, V. Sun–Thurs 9am–1am; Fri–Sat 9am–2am. U-Bahn: Richard-Wagner-Platz.

**Ernst-August** FRENCH/INTERNATIONAL Although outclassed by dozens of grander establishments, this restaurant still maintains a special niche. It's the type of place a local might take a friend from out of town. The setting is quiet and unobtrusive. Antique bric-a-brac adorn the walls. The chef might prepare one of two variations of hare, a longtime German favorite in which he takes a special pride. Even a simple rump steak gets care and attention here.

Sybelstrasse 16. ✆ **030/3-24-55-76.** Reservations required. Main courses 12.80€–19.40€ ($11.45–$17.30). No credit cards. Wed–Sun 6:30pm–1am (kitchen stops serving hot food at midnight). Closed July 15–Aug 15. U-Bahn: Adenauerplatz.

**Funkturm Restaurant** *Kids* INTERNATIONAL This restaurant at the radio tower's 65m (213-ft.) midway point provides both good food and sweeping, high-altitude views. You'll first have to pay 1.50€ ($1.35) for the elevator ride up. Inside the restaurant's metallic, glossy interior, every table sits near a window, which is entertaining for kids. Menu items include saddle of lamb with vegetables, pepper steak, and seafood. If you just want to enjoy the view without the food, consider paying 3€ ($2.70) for a ride up to the observation platform near the top of the 136m- (446-ft.-) high tower. The higher platform is open daily 10am to 11:30pm. For information about the tower and its upper-tier observation platform, call ✆ **030/30-38-0996.**

Messedamm 22. ✆ **030/303-829-96.** Reservations not necessary. Fixed-price lunch 19€ ($16.95); fixed-price dinner 29€ ($25.90). Main course 9€–18€ ($8.05–$16.05). AE, DC, MC, V. Tues–Sun 11:30am–11pm. U-Bahn: Kaiserdamm.

**Ponte Vecchio** ★ TUSCAN We've dined here many times before and were moderately pleased, but the kitchen is so improved that we now view it as the finest Italian restaurant in Berlin. Market-fresh ingredients produce a winning cuisine with a Tuscan focus. If you don't opt for the excellent fresh fish of the day, you'll find any number of other tempting dishes, such as several variations of veal. Shellfish is deftly handled according to Tuscan style, with fresh basil and olive oil. For pasta that's succulent, savory, and spicy, we'd recommend the *penne all'arrabiata,* that old Roman favorite.

Spielhagenstrasse 3. ✆ **030/3-42-19-99.** Reservations required. Main courses 18€–35€ ($16.05–$31.25). DC. Wed–Mon 6:30–11pm. Closed 4 weeks in summer. U-Bahn: Bismarckstrasse.

## IN GRUNEWALD

### VERY EXPENSIVE

**Vivaldi** ★ INTERNATIONAL This restaurant is the culinary showcase of one of the most unusual small hotels in Berlin, a neo-Renaissance palace built in 1912 by an advisor to Kaiser Wilhelm II. Vivaldi serves, with panache, some of the most elegant hotel food in Berlin, within a paneled and antique-strewn setting that's as grand as anything you're likely to find in Europe. Most diners opt for one of two fixed-price menus, although there's also a limited a la carte list. A clear soup of lentils with smoked duck breast might be followed by gratinated oysters and scallops resting on a bed of spinach salad. Turbot that's braised with green asparagus, U.S. filet of beef in red wine sauce and venison with black Perigord truffles are triumphs of subtle flavors. Service is impeccable. For dessert, consider a honey and clementine parfait.

In the Regent Schlosshotel Berlin, Brahmsstrasse 10. ✆ **030/89-58-40.** Reservations recommended. Main courses 24€–33.20€ ($21.45–$29.65). Fixed-price 4-course dinner 80€ ($71.45); fixed-price 7-course dinner 101€ ($90.20). AE, DC, MC, V. Tues–Fri 6–10:30pm. S-Bahn: Grunewald.

## IN BERLIN-MITTE

### EXPENSIVE

**Guy** ★ INTERNATIONAL This is gastronomy as theater. You'll understand this as you proceed to any of three separate balconies, each supporting at least one row of artfully decorated tables. The overall effect can be compared to the balconies of an old-fashioned opera house, where sight lines tend to focus on whatever's happening on the stage, or on the occupants of other balconies. Don't expect beer and schnitzels, as the cuisine is very *haute,* even to the point of seeming experimental. The menu changes frequently but might include a medley of marinated quail and goose liver; mussels served on a purée of arugula; lobster and sweetbreads cooked in puff pastry with tarragon-flavored cream sauce; and braised breast of goose with a roulade of potatoes and herbs. If you're in the mood for strong doses of *Gemütlichkeit* (comfort), ask for one of the limited number of tables within its cozy wine cellar. During clement weather, there's additional seating on the terrace in front.

Jägerstrasse 59–60. ✆ **030/20-94-26-00.** Reservations recommended. Main courses 24.55€–28.60€ ($21.90–$25.55). Fixed-price lunch 14.80€–19.95€ ($13.20–$17.80); fixed-price dinner 50.60€–73.05€ ($45.20–$65.25). AE, DC, MC, V. Mon–Fri noon–3pm and 6pm–1am; Sat 6pm–1am. U-Bahn: Stadtmitte or Französischer Strasse.

**Langhans** ★★ MODERN INTERNATIONAL Few other restaurants combine the culinary traditions of Italy and Japan with such skill and style. Named after the 18th-century designer of the Brandenburg Gate and created by Detlef Bernhardt, a German-born longtime resident of Japan, it occupies two floors of a grandly proportioned building that flanks the Gendarmenmarkt. Downstairs is a convival and hip bar loaded with well-dressed patrons, some of whom munch on Spanish-inspired tapas. The most visible culinary zest, however, is upstairs, within a long, minimalist dining room whose views sweep simultaneously out over the twin domes of the square's two churches and a panorama of the brightly lit kitchen. Here, an international team produces dishes whose flavors are as intriguing as they are delicious. The frequently changing menu may include lemongrass-and-coconut soup with shrimp; carpaccio of veal with sesame and arugula; spaghettini with salmon caviar, Japanese wakame, and lemongrass; braised dorado with green curry and mango; and a superb version of free-range hen with ginger-flavored risotto and sukiyaki sauce. Desserts, as well as virtually everything else on the menu, change frequently, but if it's available you'd probably be richly satisfied with a pear charlotte with tonkabean ice cream.

Charlottenstrasse 59. ✆ **030/20-94-50-70.** Reservations recommended. Main courses 19.95€–24.55€ ($17.80–$21.90); fixed-price menu 40.90€–46€ ($36.50–$41.10). AE, MC, V. Mon–Sat 10am–2am. U-Bahn: Stadtmitte.

**Portalis** ★★ *Finds* FRENCH/MEDITERRANEAN This is one of the best examples in Berlin of the avant-garde, worldly, sophisticated, and hip restaurants that have imported ideas from sunnier, usually Mediterranean, climes. Don't be fooled by its resemblance to a bistro: the cuisine is far more ambitious than that. The color scheme meshes earth tones with dark grays, cherrywood floors, black leather, stainless steel, and uplighting, all of which combine into an artful showcase for the avant-garde cuisine. Textures here are light, without extravagant use of cream or butter, well suited to palates and waitlines that might have been jaded with too frequent an exposure to a constant diet of *mitteleuropaïsche* (food of Central Europe) cuisine. Examples of the food produced by high-energy chef Volker Drkosch change with the seasons, but might include scallops with fresh peas and kohlrabi; a perfectly braised filet of sole with spinach, polenta-stuffed ravioli, and morels; sorbets might be flavored with the juice of prickly pear or obscure French cheeses; and tempuras might include lobster flavored with lemongrass. Freshwater crayfish, when available, might be simply but flavorfully seared and seasoned only with salt, pepper, and butter. Expect a scattering of well-heeled *Berliner* insiders here, including politicians and personalities from the stage and screen.

Kronenstrasse 55–58. ✆ **030/20-45-54-96.** Reservations recommended. Main courses 24€–28€ ($21.45–$25); fixed-price lunch menu 27€ ($24.10); fixed-price dinner menu 61€–76€ ($54.45–$67.85). AE, DC, MC, V. Tues–Fri noon–2pm and 6:30–11pm. U-Bahn: Stadtmitte.

**Restaurant Vau** ★★ INTERNATIONAL This restaurant is the culinary showcase of chef Kolja Kleeburg. You can select from a menu based on fresh and seasonal ingredients. Choices include terrine of salmon and morels with rocket salad; smoked sturgeon with white beans and caviar; aspic of suckling pig with sauerkraut; salad with marinated red mullet, mint, and almonds; crisp-fried duck with marjoram; ribs of suckling lamb with thyme-flavored polenta; and desserts such as Woodruff soup with champagne-flavored ice cream. The wine list is international and well chosen.

Jägerstrasse 54. ✆ **030/202-9730.** Reservations recommended. Lunch main courses 10.20€ ($9.10) each; dinner main courses 24.55€–34.75€ ($21.90–$31.05). Fixed-price 4-course dinner 69€–117€ ($61.60–$104.50). AE, DC, MC, V. Mon–Sat noon–2:30pm and 7–10:30pm. U-Bahn: Hausvoigteiplatz.

**Schwarzengraben** ★ CONTINENTAL This is the watering hole of the Berlin *Schickeria* or chic crowd. One Berlin paper defined these trendies as "media honchos and their overblond dates." The see-and-be-seen scene might be more important than the cuisine, but two Italian brothers, Ivo and Rudolf Girolo, succeed admirably with super-fresh ingredients that are well prepared. Sea bass is baked between slices of eggplant, and it's a most credible dish, as is the Italian gnocchi with sausage and green olives. "Black Crows" (its English name) evokes a SoHo-style restaurant in New York. Remarkably, the kitchen is prepared to make on short notice a total of 300 pasta dishes. There are also 150 fish recipes the chefs know by heart. There are even 20 different types of salami that can rest on your plate. Our dining companion for the evening hailed the gnocchi with rabbit ragout and truffles as "orgasmic." We're fond of the duck and rabbit pastele. The main dining is upstairs; downstairs for whisky and cigars.

Neue Schonhauswer Schonhauser Strasse 13. ✆ **030/2839-1698.** Reservations recommended. Main courses 10€–23€ ($8.95–$20.55). AE, MC, V. Daily 10am–3:30pm and 6–11:30pm. U-Bahn: Weinmeister.

**Vox** ★ INTERNATIONAL/SUSHI This is one of the most exciting and creative restaurants in Berlin, far outshining any competition within the vast architectural complex at Potsdamer Platz. One of Switzerland's best design teams created the minimalist decor, with lots of visual emphasis on a mostly stainless steel, open-to-view kitchen. Here, a team of uniformed chefs concoct artfully presented platters of braised goose liver with apple-flavored vinaigrette; filet of lamb cooked in a wood-burning oven with goat cheese, pepper oil, and Mediterranean vegetables; rotisserie-cooked breast of Barbary duck with mango chutney; and roasted sturgeon on a frothy sauce of white rosemary. The culinary philosophy here combines Mediterranean with Asian cuisines in ways you might not expect. One corner of the restaurant features the best sushi bar in Berlin. The venue is enhanced by an attentive and very hip staff, some of whom shuttle between the restaurant and a stylish cocktail lounge that features jazz and blues every night beginning at 10pm. During clement weather, tables spill out onto the terrace, beneath verdant rows of linden trees.

> **Tips A Map Note**
>
> For restaurants located in Berlin-Mitte, see the "Berlin-Mitte Accommodations & Dining" map on p. 87.

In the Grand Hyatt Berlin, Marlene-Dietrich-Platz 2. ✆ **030/25-53-12-34.** Reservations recommended. Lunch main courses 12.80€–18.40€ ($11.45–$16.45); dinner main courses 26€–31€ ($23.20–$27.70); platters of sushi 11€–20€ ($9.80–$17.85). AE, DC, MC, V. Daily noon–2pm and 6:30pm–midnight. U-Bahn: Potsdamer Platz.

## MODERATE

**Aigner** CONTINENTAL Habsburg Austria lives on here. In the late 1990s, the Dorint chain bought the furnishings from one of Vienna's oldest cafes, the Aigner, and moved them into the ground floor of one of Berlin's newest hotels. The result is a black-and-white Jugendstil setting replete with Thonet chairs. There's a lot of ambience here, thanks partly to a location that overlooks the Gendarmenmarkt, and a staff that provides old-fashioned service with a modern flair. The restaurant's signature dish is *Tafelspitz,* the boiled-beef-with-horseradish dish. Here, it's served in a big brass kettle with both haunch and shoulder of beef, with lots of soup, vegetables, savoy cabbage, crème fraîche, and apple-flavored horseradish. Other choices include baked and crusty pike-perch; carpaccio of octopus; Wiener schnitzel; and filet of codfish with white beans and chorizo.

In the Das Hotel am Gendarmenmarkt, Charlottenstrasse 50–52. D-10117 Berlin. ✆ **030/20375-0.** Reservations recommended. Main courses 16.50€–23€ ($14.75–$20.55). AE, DC, MC, V. Daily noon–11:30pm. U-Bahn: Stadtmitte.

**Die Weltbühne** INTERNATIONAL/MEDITERRANEAN This emerging restaurant maintains a bar—one of the longest in Berlin—where you're likely to get so distracted with visual input that you might find it hard to eventually move into dinner. You'll be glad you did, however, when you taste the well-flavored and sophisticated food that's churned out by chef Jens Heier. The dining room is divided into semiprivate banquette areas outlined in hardwood paneling, forest green upholstery, elaborate Murano-glass chandeliers, and vague references to Bauhaus. Cuisine is superb, based on a changing set of visions influenced by the season and the inspiration of the chef. Examples include a galette of rabbit with arugula salad; carpaccio of duck breast with Parmesan and vinegar; a salad of green asparagus with paprika mousse; mussels with baby onion risotto; and filet of turbot with ratatouille, potato-filled ravioli, and champagne sauce. A particularly appealing dessert is a kirsch-flavored praline with Campari-grapefruit sorbet.

Gormannstrasse 14. ✆ **030/280-094-40.** Reservations recommended. Main courses 14.50€–22€ ($12.95–$19.65). AE, MC, V. Daily 6pm–12:30am. U-Bahn: Rosenthalerplatz.

**Französischer Hof** *Value* GERMAN If you want a reasonable meal in a relaxed atmosphere, this is the place. Französischer Hof fills two floors connected by a Belle Epoque staircase, evoking a century-old Parisian bistro. The kitchen may not be the finest, but ingredients are fresh and deftly handled. One recent memorable dinner included roast duck breast with calvados along with zucchini and potato pancakes. You can begin with the delectable selection of fish canapés. Saddle of lamb is always admirably done, although you may prefer the rather theatrical flambéed filet Stroganoff with almond-studded dumplings.

Jagerstrasse 56. ✆ **030/2-04-35-70.** Reservations recommended. Main courses 10€–18€ ($8.95–$16.05). AE, DC, MC, V. Daily noon–midnight. Closed Dec 24. U-Bahn: Hausvogteiplatz.

**Ganymed** GERMAN/INTERNATIONAL There's nothing trendy or immediately fashionable about this restaurant, which occupied these premises beginning in 1929, and which stalwartly continued doing business within East Berlin throughout the Cold War. The setting includes two formal dining rooms, one with an ornate plaster ceiling of great beauty; the other a more modern, big-windowed affair that overlooks the Spree. Food arrives in worthy portions, with plenty of flavor, albeit without too much concern for modern culinary fancies or trends. Examples include the house assortment of appetizers (*Vorspeisen*), laden high with smoked fish, smoked ham, stuffed dumplings, and fish mousse; goose liver terrine; Eisbein—the pork shank specialty of 19th-century Berlin; schnitzels made from organically raised veal; mussels in choron sauce; and breast of pheasant wrapped in Black Forest cured ham.

Schiffbauerdamm 5. ✆ **030/28-59-90-46.** Reservations recommended. Main courses 10€–17€ ($8.95–$15.20). Fixed-price menus 25€–48€ ($22.35–$42.85). AE, MC. Mon–Sat 5pm–1am; Sun noon–1am. U-Bahn: Friedrichstrasse.

**The Seasons Restaurant** INTERNATIONAL One of the most appealing hotel dining rooms in Berlin exudes a sense of prosperity, thanks to a decor that might have been inspired by Versailles, a sheathing of carefully oiled and partially gilded oak, an open fireplace, and a color scheme of champagne and brown. Despite the upscale decor, the restaurant maintains a deliberately reasonable price-to-value ratio. An impeccably trained staff offers elaborate versions of tuna carpaccio with sesame; smoked breast of pheasant with wild mushrooms, black nuts, and farmer's salad; filet and liver of veal with truffled mashed potatoes and glazed apples; and quail stuffed with goose liver baked in a clay pot. Consider prefacing a meal here with a drink in the hotel's supremely elegant bar.

In the Four Seasons Hotel, Charlottenstrasse 49. ✆ **030/2-03-38.** Reservations recommended. Lunch main courses 17€–24€ ($15.20–$21.45); dinner main courses 26€–32€ ($23.20–$28.60); fixed-price menu 55€–62€ ($49.10–$55.35). AE, MC, V. Daily noon–2:30pm and 6:30–10:30pm. U-Bahn: Französische Strasse.

**Zur Letzten Instanz** GERMAN Reputedly, this is Berlin's oldest restaurant, dating from 1525. Zur Letzten Instanz has supposedly been frequented by everybody from Napoléon to Beethoven. Prisoners used to stop off here for one last beer before going to jail. The place is located on two floors of a baroque building just outside the crumbling brick wall that once ringed medieval Berlin. Double doors open on a series of small woodsy rooms, one with a bar and ceramic *Kachelofen* (stove). At the back, a circular staircase leads to another series of rooms, where every evening at 6pm, food and wine (no beer) are served. The menu is old-fashioned, mainly limited to good, hearty fare in the best of the Grandmother Berlin tradition of staples.

Waisenstrasse 14–16 (near the Alexanderplatz). ✆ **030/2-42-55-28.** Soup 5€–7€ ($4.45–$6.25); main courses 11€–16€ ($9.80–$14.30); fixed-price dinner from 19€–27€ ($16.95–$24.10). AE, DC, MC, V. Mon–Sat noon–1am; Sun noon–11pm. U-Bahn: Klosterstrasse.

## INEXPENSIVE

**Alexanderkeller** GERMAN This reasonably priced, unpretentious restaurant is a lunchtime favorite of neighborhood residents and office workers. The generous meals might include filet of roast beef served with potatoes and artichoke hearts; filet of zander with parsley and new potatoes; or roast pork with red-wine sauce. Food is rich and the meat dishes heavy, but the people in this area love this type of food.

In the cellar of the Hotel Luisenhof, Köpenicker Strasse 92. ✆ **030/2-75-01-42.** Main courses 11€–25€ ($9.80–$22.35). MC, V. Daily 10am–midnight. U-Bahn: Märkisches Museum.

**Dressler** CONTINENTAL No other bistro along Unter den Linden recreates as successfully Berlin's prewar decor and style. Designed to resemble an arts-conscious bistro of the sort that might have amused and entertained tuxedo-clad clients in the 1920s, it's set behind a wine-colored facade, and outfitted with leather banquettes, black-and-white tile floors, mirrors, and film memorabilia from the great days of early German cinema. Waiters scurry around with vests and aprons, carrying trays of everything from caviar to strudel, as well as three kinds of oysters and hefty portions of lobster salad. You can always drop in to ogle the racks of elegant pastries, consuming them with steaming pots of tea or coffee. Otherwise, more substantial menu items include turbot with champagne vinaigrette; pheasant breast with Riesling sauce; local salmon trout with white wine sauce and braised endive; stuffed breast of veal; and calf's liver with apples.

Unter den Linden 39. ✆ **030/204-44-22.** Reservations recommended. Main courses 13.80€–23€ ($12.30–$20.55). AE, DC, MC, V. Daily 8am–midnight. S-Bahn: Unter den Linden.

**Keller-Restaurant im Brecht-Haus-Berlin** SOUTH GERMAN/-AUSTRIAN This is a dining oddity, since this is the only restaurant in Germany in the house of a world-famous German writer. From 1953 until his death in 1956, Bertolt Brecht lived here with his wife, Helene Weigel. Today the building houses the Brecht-Weigel-Museum (see "Exploring Berlin-Mitte," later in this chapter). The restaurant downstairs, with white plaster and exposed stone, is decorated with photographs of the playwright's family, friends, and theatrical productions. No one will mind if you just stop in for a glass or two of wine—the place specializes in eastern German wines, as well as French and New World wines. Traditional south German and Austrian food is also served, such as an Austrian recipe for *Fleisch Laberln,* meatballs made from minced pork, beef, green beans, and bacon and served with dumplings. In good weather, the seating area includes an enclosed courtyard upstairs.

Chausseestrasse 125. ✆ **030/2-82-38-43.** Reservations recommended. Main courses 8€–15€ ($7.15–$13.40). AE, DC, MC, V. Daily 6pm–midnight, and from May–Oct 11am–3pm and 6pm–midnight. U-Bahn: Zinnowitzer Strasse.

**La Gaiola** ITALIAN The owner of this restaurant, an Italian immigrant, wanted to bring the rich flavor of his country's cuisine to Berlin and has done so admirably. Food is served in generous portions. We're especially fond of the fresh seafood or the pasta with sautéed calamari. Two of our favorite dishes include the halibut sautéed or grilled and the lobster ravioli, which is only featured on weekends.

Monbijouplatz 11–12. ✆ **030/28-53-98-90.** Reservations recommended. Main courses 11€–15€ ($9.80–$13.40). AE, MC, V. Daily 6pm–1am. U-Bahn: Hackescher Markt.

**Mutter Hoppe** *Value* GERMAN This cozy, wood-paneled restaurant still serves the solid Teutonic cuisine favored by a quasi-legendary matriarch (Mother Hoppe) who used to churn out vast amounts of food to members of her extended family and entourage. Within a quartet of old-fashioned dining rooms, you'll enjoy heaping portions of such rib-sticking fare as sauerbraten with roasted potatoes; creamy goulash with wild mushrooms; filet of zander with dill-flavored cream sauce; and braised filet of pork in mushroom-flavored cream sauce. Wine is available, but most guests opt for a foaming mug of beer.

Rathausstrasse 21, Nikolaiviertel. ✆ **030/241-56-25.** Reservations recommended. Main courses 8.20€–17.90€ ($7.30–$16). MC, V. Daily 11:30am–midnight. U-Bahn/S-Bahn: Alexanderplatz.

**Oren** ISRAELI/ARABIC You'll notice a similarity in architecture between this restaurant and the massive reconstruction of the Oranienburger synagogue, next door. The cream-colored, high-ceilinged premises are owned by, and rented from, Berlin's Jewish community. The savory aromas of old-fashioned Jewish cooking permeate the restaurant. As such, the site tends to exert a powerful and immediate emotional appeal on customers, 90% of whom are visitors making a pilgrimage to the nearby synagogue. Prices are reasonable, and the vegetarian and fish platters are both wholesome and plentiful. The menu includes cream of garlic soup; vegetarian platters with hollandaise or choron sauce; filet of zander with fresh cucumber salad; falafel with hummus, tahini, olives, and pita; cold gefilte fish with red-beet salad; smoked trout; and a ragout of zucchini and mushroom with herbed rice. Red or white meat almost never appears on the menu.

Oranienburger Strasse 28. ✆ **030/282-8228.** Reservations recommended. Main courses 9€–25€ ($8.05–$22.35). AE, MC, V. Mon–Thurs noon–1am; Fri–Sat 10am–2am; Sun 10am–1am. S-Bahn: Oranienburger Tor or Hackescher Markt.

**StäV** ★ *Finds* RHENISH For years, this upscale tavern entertained the politicians and journalists whose business involved the day-to-day running of the German government from Germany's former capital of Bonn. Although at first its owners opposesd the re-inauguration of Berlin as the German capital, when the switch was made, they valiantly pulled out of the Rhineland and followed their clientele to new digs within a 5-minute walk of the Brandenburg Gate, near the Friedrichstrasse Bahnhof. Don't come here imagining that all you'll get is a taste of noodles, Sauerbraten, and Rhinelander kitsch. Dining next to you, you'll find some of the most politically savvy and astute elected officials, journalists, and bureaucrats in Berlin. They line the walls of this high-energy place, creating—in the words of the owners—a minimuseum of German politics during the government's "exile" in the Rhineland. The only beer served is Kölsch, a brew more closely associated with the Rhineland than any other beer. Rhenish food items include a mass of apples, onions, and blood sausage known as *Himmel and Ärd* (heaven and hell), braised beef with pumpernickel and raisin sauce; and Rhenish sauerbraten with noodles. Other items, many influenced by the cullinary traditions of Berlin, include braised liver with bacon and onions, a crisp version of Alsatian pizza known as *Flammenküche*, and potato cakes topped with apples and shredded beets or with smoked salmon and sour cream.

8 Schiffbauerdamm. ✆ **030/282-3965.** Reservations recommended. Main courses 8.20€–12.50€ ($7.30–$11.15); fixed-price menu 15€–18€ ($13.40–$16.05). AE, DC, MC, V. Daily 11am–1am. U-Bahn: Friedrichstrasse.

## 5 Seeing the Sights

### SIGHTSEEING SUGGESTIONS FOR FIRST-TIME VISITORS

**If You Have 1 Day** Get up early and visit the **Brandenburg Gate,** symbol of Berlin, then walk down **Unter den Linden** and have coffee and pastry at one of the cafes along the edges off this boulevard. Visit the **Gemäldegalerie** to see some of the world's greatest masterpieces. Afterward, go to **Charlottenburg Palace** and its museums to view the celebrated bust of Queen Nefertiti in the **Ägyptisches Museum.** In the evening, walk along the Kurfürstendamm, visit the **Kaiser Wilhelm Memorial Church,** and dine in a local restaurant.

**If You Have 2 Days** On Day 2, visit the **Pergamon Museum** on Museum Island; be sure to see the Pergamon Altar. Explore the **National Gallery** and the **Jewish Museum,** then head for Alexanderplatz. Take the elevator up for a view from its TV tower, before exploring the **Nikolai Quarter** on foot.

**If You Have 3 Days** On Day 3, go to **Potsdam** (see "A Side Trip: Potsdam & Its Palaces" later in this chapter).

**If You Have 4 or 5 Days** On Day 4, take a walk through the restored Nikolai Quarter. In the afternoon return to Charlottenburg Palace and explore the **Historical Apartments,** and in the evening visit the **Europa Center** for drinks and dinner. On Day 5, see some of the sights you might have missed. Take some walks through Berlin and stop at the Cold War's **Checkpoint Charlie,** with its museum. If time remains, visit the **Berlin Zoo,** stroll through the **Tiergarten,** and attend a cabaret in the evening.

#### The Best Sightseeing Deal

At all state-owned museums you can purchase a *Tageskarte* for 4.10€ ($3.65), allowing you entry to all of the state-owned museums on the same day. A 3-day card for 8.20€ ($7.30) allows entry to all state-owned museums for 3 consecutive days. Admission will be higher for special exhibitions. The card can be purchased at any state-owned museum.

Take advantage of free admission to all the state museums on the first Sunday of every month, including the Pergamon, Alte Nationalgalerie, Altes Museum, Ägyptisches Museum, Gemäldegalerie, Neue Nationalgalerie, Sammlung Berggruen, and the Museum for Gegenwart at Hamburger Bahnhof. Just remember, you won't be the only one doing so.

## THE TOP MUSEUMS

The great art collections of old Berlin suffered during and after World War II. Although many paintings were saved by being stored in salt mines, many larger works were destroyed by fire. Part of the surviving art stayed in the east, including a wealth of ancient treasures that remind us of the leading role played by German archaeologists during the 19th and early 20th centuries. The paintings that turned up in the west and were passed from nation to nation in the late 1940s have nearly all been returned to Berlin.

### CHARLOTTENBURG PALACE & MUSEUMS

Charlottenburg lies just west of the Tiergarten. Plan on spending the day here, because the area contains several museums as well as the royal apartments. After seeing the main attractions, you can enjoy a ramble through **Schlossgarten Charlottenburg.** These formal gardens look much as they did in the 18th century. A grove of cypresses leads to a lake with swans and other waterfowl.

North of the palace stands the **Mausoleum,** which holds the tombs of King Friedrich Wilhelm II and Queen Luise, sculptured by Rauch, as well as several other interesting funerary monuments of the Prussian royal family.

**Ägyptisches Museum** ★ The western Berlin branch of the Egyptian Museum is housed in the palace's east guardhouse. It's worth the trip just to see the famous colored bust of Queen Nefertiti, which dates from about 1360 B.C. and was discovered in 1912. The bust, stunning in every way, is all by itself in a dark first-floor room, illuminated by a spotlight. It's believed that the bust never left the studio in which it was created but served always as a model for other portraits of the queen. In addition, look for the head of Queen Tiy, the world-famous head of a priest in green stone, and the monumental Kalabasha Gateway, built by Emperor Augustus around 30 B.C. Other displays feature jewelry, papyrus, tools, and weapons, as well as objects relating to the Egyptian belief in the afterlife.

Schloss-strasse 70. ✆ **030/343-5730.** Admission 4.10€ ($3.65) adults, 2.05€ ($1.85) children; free admission 1st Sun of each month. Tues–Fri 10am–6pm; Sat–Sun 11am–6pm. U-Bahn: Sophie-Charlotte-Platz or Richard-Wagner-Platz.

**Bröhan Museum** Berlin's finest collection of Jugendstil (German Art Nouveau) is found here. When Professor Bröhan started the collection, Jugendstil was viewed as having little merit. It's a different story today. The objects include glass, furnishings, silver and gold, paintings, and vases. The outstanding porcelain collection ranges from Gallé to Sèvres and Meissen to Royal Copenhagen.

Schloss-strasse 1A. ✆ **030/32-69-06-00.** Admission 5.10€ ($4.55); 2.55€ ($2.30) students and children. Tues–Sun 10am–6pm (until 8pm on Wed). U-Bahn: Sophie-Charlotte-Platz or Richard-Wagner-Platz.

**Schloss Charlottenburg** ★★ Schloss Charlottenburg, one of the finest examples of baroque architecture in Germany, was built by Sophie Charlotte. This beautiful and intelligent woman, a patron of philosophy and the arts, was the wife of Friedrich I, crowned as the first king in Prussia (as opposed to "of") in 1701. He nearly bankrupted the state with his extravagant ways.

The residence was begun as a summer palace but got out of hand, eventually growing into the massive structure you see today. When you pass through the heavy iron gates and enter the courtyard, you'll immediately encounter a baroque equestrian statue of Friedrich I himself, by Andreas Schlüter. The main entrance to the palace is directly behind, marked by the 48m- (157-ft.-) high cupola capped by a gilded statue of Fortune. Inside, you'll find a columned

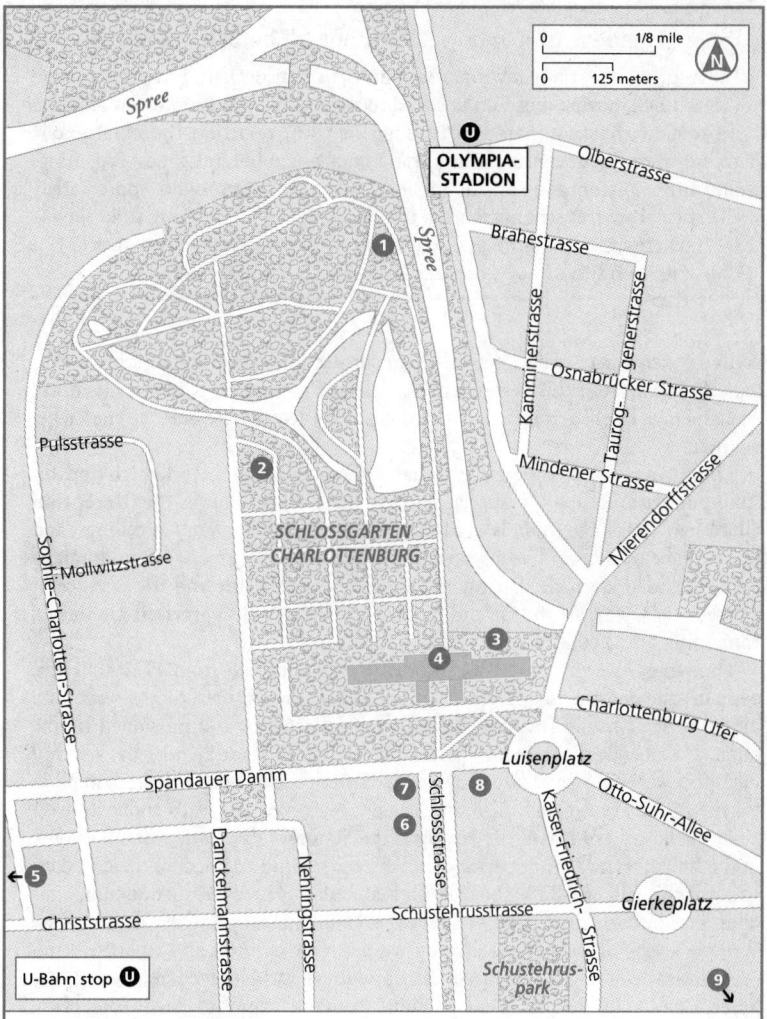

Ägyptisches Museum **8**
Belvedere **1**
Bröhan Museum **6**
Dahlemer Museen **9**
Die Sammlung Berggruen: Picasso und Seine Zeit **7**
Mausoleum **2**
Olympia Stadion **5**
Schinkel Pavilion **3**
Schloss Charlottenburg **4**

### Tips Preview of Coming Attractions: The Brücke Museum

Some of our all-time favorite German artists, especially Ernst Kirchner (1880-1938), have a museum devoted to their work. ***Die Brücke*** was an art movement that originated in Dresden in 1905, rejecting the emerging trends of the 20th century and turning once again to landscapes, folk art, and other retrograde sources for inspiration. For those who appreciate the special art this school created, the opening of this museum, sometime in 2003 (there may be delays), could prove to be a hot museum ticket. Check its web site at www.bruecke-museum.de for more details.

rotunda with stucco reliefs depicting the virtues of Prussian princes in mythological terms. From this vestibule, you can take guided tours of the Historical Apartments. English translations of the guide's lecture are sold at the ticket counter.

The main wing of the palace contains the apartments of Friedrich and his "philosopher queen." Of special interest in this section is the **Reception Chamber.** This large room is decorated with frieze panels, vaulted ceilings, and mirror-paneled niches. The tapestries on the walls (1730) are based on Plutarch's *Lives;* included are such classical scenes as Pericles in battle and the sacrifice of Theseus on Delos. At the far end of the west wing is the **Porcelain Chamber,** containing a fine collection of Chinese porcelain.

The **wing,** known as the Knobelsdorff-Flügel and built from 1740 to 1746, contains the apartments of Friedrich the Great. Today these rooms serve as a museum of paintings, many of which were collected or commissioned by the king. The King's finest paintings are on the upper floor. Works by Watteau include *The Trade Sign of the Art Dealer Gersaint,* purchased by Friedrich in 1745 for the palace's music hall. Also note the decoration on the walls and ceilings.

At the far eastern end of the Schloss is the **Schinkel Pavillon,** a summerhouse in the Italian style. Karl Friedrich Schinkel, the leading architect of the day, constructed this villa in 1825. Today it holds a small but noteworthy museum, containing paintings, drawings, and sketches from the early 1800s. Some of the sketches are by Schinkel himself, who was both an architect and an artist.

At the far end of Schlossgarten Charlottenburg is the **Belvedere,** close to the Spree River. This former royal teahouse contains exquisite Berlin porcelain, much of it from the 1700s.

Luisenplatz. ✆ **030/32-09-1275.** Combination ticket for all buildings and historical rooms 7.65€ ($6.85) adults, 5.10€ ($4.55) children under 14. English translation of guide's lecture on sale at the ticket counter. Palace Tues–Fri 9am–5pm; Sat–Sun 10am–5pm; Museum Tues–Fri 10am–6pm; Sat–Sun 11am–6pm. U-Bahn: Sophie-Charlotte-Platz or Richard-Wagner-Platz.

## MUSEUMINSEL MUSEUMS

**Alte Nationalgalerie** ★ This museum is known for its collection of 19th-century German as well as French Impressionists art. The museum also has the world's largest collection of the works of one of the best known of all Berlin artists, Adolph von Menzel (1815–1905). We especially like his *Das Balkonzimmer.* Other paintings include a galaxy of art representing the romantic and classical movements as well as the Biedermeier era, the latter especially well represented by Caspar David Friedrich and Schinkel. Allow at least an hour and a half to take in canvasses by everybody from Pissarro to Cézanne, from Delacroix to Degas, and from van Gogh to Monet. We are especially fond

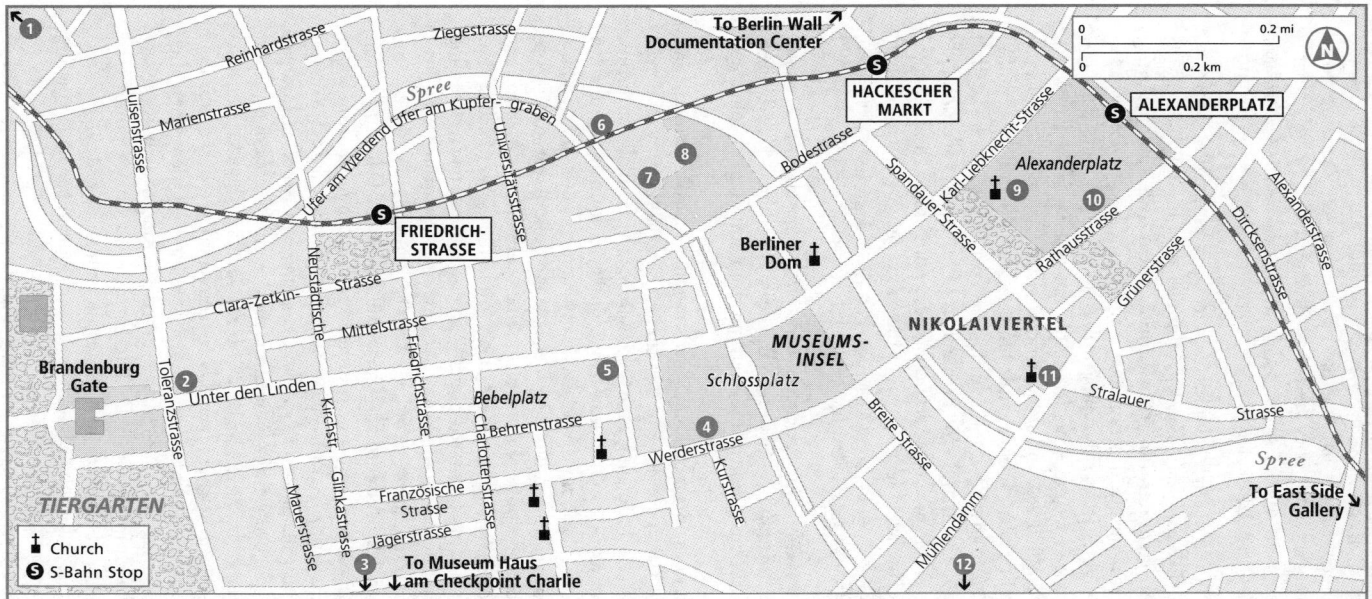


Alte Nationalgalerie **8**
Altes Museum **6**
Brecht-Weigel-Museum **1**
Deutsches Historisches Museum **2**
Deutsche Staatsoper **5**
Fernsehturm (TV Tower) **10**
Friedrichwerdersche Kirche-Schinkelmuseum **4**
Jüdisches Museum **12**
Marienkirche **9**
Museum Haus am Checkpoint Charlie **3**
Nikolaikirche **11**
Pergamon Museum **7**

of the works of Max Liebermann and Max Beckmann. The collection would have been far greater than it is had not the Nazis either sold or destroyed so many early–20th century works they viewed as "degenerate."

Museumsinsel. ✆ **030/20905555.** Admission 6€ ($5.35) adults, 3€ ($2.70) children. Tues–Sun 10am–6pm. S-Bahn: Hackescher Markt. Tram: 1, 2, 3, 4, 5, 6, or 53.

**Altes Museum** Karl Friedrich Schinkel, the city's greatest architect, designed this structure, which resembles a Greek Corinthian temple, in 1822. On its main floor is the **Antikensammlung (Museum of [Greek and Roman] Antiquities),** a collection of antique decorative art. Some of the finest Greek vases of the black-and-red-figures style, from the 6th to the 4th century B.C., are here. The best-known vase is a large Athenian amphora (wine jar) found in Vulci, Etruria. It dates from 490 B.C. and shows a satyr with a lyre and the god Hermes. One of several excellent bronze statuettes, the Zeus of Dodone (470 B.C.) shows the god about to cast a bolt of lightning. You can also see a rare portrait of Cleopatra (from Alexandria). In the Brandenburg-Prussian art collection is an exceptional bronze statue of the goddess Luna descending through an "arch of the sky." The Prussians called it "the pearl of the collection."

Bodestrasse 1–3, Museumsinsel. ✆ **030/20-90-50.** Admission 6€ ($5.35) adults, 3€ ($2.70) children. Tues–Sun 10am–6pm. U-Bahn/S-Bahn: Friedrichstrasse. Bus: 100 to Lustgarten.

**Dahlemer Museen** ★★ After extensive reorganizing, this complex of museums, occupying one mammoth structure in the heart of Dahlem's Freie Universität, contains institutions devoted to everything from ethnological collections to Far Eastern Art.

Occupying most of the main building is the **Ethnologisches Museum** ★★★, which is the one to visit if you have to skip the rest. This is the greatest ethnological collection on earth, totaling some 500,000 artifacts from all continents, even prehistoric America. Art and artifacts are displayed from Africa, the Far East, the South Seas, and South America. Many of the figures are ritualistic masks and are grotesquely beautiful. The Incan, Mayan, and Aztec stone sculpture alone equal the collections of some of the finest museums of Mexico. The best part is the collection of authentic boats from the South Pacific. The museum displays an intriguing assemblage of pre-Columbian relics, including gold objects and antiquities from Peru. The museum's Department of Music allows visitors to hear folk music recordings from around the globe.

In the same complex, **Museum für Ostasiatische Kunst** (Museum of Far Eastern Art) ★★ is a gem of a museum devoted primarily to Japan, Korea, and China, with artifacts dating back to as far as 3000 B.C. Launched in 1906 as the first Far Eastern museum of art in Germany, this museum is one of Europe's finest in presenting an overview of some of the most exquisite ecclesiastical and decorative art to come out of the Far East. It is the equal of or better than similar collections in Paris. In essence, the museum represents the loot acquired during a massive "shopping expedition" the Germans took to the Orient where they even managed to garner the 17th-century imperial throne of China, all lacquered and inlaid with mother-of-pearl. The Japanese woodblock prints, each seemingly more exquisite than the next, are reason enough to visit.

Germany's greatest collection of Indian art is on exhibit in the same building at the **Museum für Indische Kunst,** covering a span of 40 centuries. It's an international parade of some of the finest art and artifacts from the world of Buddhism, representing collections from such lands as Burma, Thailand, Indonesia, Nepal, and Tibet.

### *Moments* A New Wall

Berliners aren't likely to forget the **Berlin Wall** any time soon, but just in case, their government has reconstructed a partial stretch of the wall at Bernauer Strasse and Ackerstrasse (U-Bahn: Bernauer Strasse), at a cost of 1.43 million € ($1.3 million). The 70m- (230-ft.-) long memorial consists of two walls that include some of the fragments of the original wall (those fragments not bulldozed away or carried off by souvenir hunters). The memorial is mostly made of mirror-like stainless steel. Slits allow visitors to peer through. A steel plaque reads "In memory of the division of the city from 13 August 1961 to 9 November 1989." Critics have called the construction "a sanitized memorial," claiming it does little to depict the 255 people shot trying to escape its predecessor.

Outside the Dahlem museum complex, but only a 5-minute walk away, **Museum Europäischer Kulturen** (✆ **030/83901-279**) is devoted to the German people themselves—not the aristocrats but the middle class and the peasant stock who built the country. It is a true "museum of the people." The exhibits go back 4 centuries, tracing how artisans and homemakers lived and worked. Household items are displayed along with primitive industrial equipment such as a utensil for turning flax into linen. Furnishings, clothing, pottery, and even items used in religious observances are shown, along with some fun and whimsical exhibits, including depictions of pop culture from the 1950s through the '80s.

Lansstrasse 8. ✆ **030/83011.** Admission 2€ ($1.80) adults, 1€ (90¢) students and children. Tues–Fri 9am–6pm, Sat–Sun 11am–6pm. U-Bahn to Dahlem-Dorf.

**Pergamon Museum** ★★★ Pergamon Museum houses several departments, but if you have time for only one exhibit, go to the **Department of Greek and Roman Antiquities,** housed in the north and east wings of the museum, and enter the central hall to see the **Pergamon Altar** ★★★ (180–160 B.C.), which is so large that it has a huge room all to itself. Some 27 steps lead from the museum floor up to the colonnade. Most fascinating is the frieze around the base. It shows the struggle of the Olympian gods against the Titans and is strikingly alive, with figures that project as much as a foot from the background. If you explore further, you'll find a Roman market gate discovered in Miletus as well as sculptures from many Greek and Roman cities, including a statue of a goddess holding a pomegranate (575 B.C.), found in southern Attica, where it had been buried for 2,000 years. It was so well preserved that flecks of the original paint are still visible on her garments.

The **Near East Museum** ★, in the south wing, contains one of the largest collections anywhere of antiquities from ancient Babylonia, Persia, and Assyria. Among the exhibits is the Processional Way of Babylon with the Ishtar Gate, dating from 580 B.C., and the throne room of Nebuchadnezzar. Cuneiform clay tablets document a civilization that created ceramics, glass, and metal objects while Europe was still overrun with primitive tribes. The museum's upper level is devoted to the **Museum of Islamic Art.** Of special interest are the miniatures, carpets, and woodcarvings.

Kupfergraben, Museumsinsel. ✆ **030/20-90-50.** Admission 4.10€ ($3.65) adults, 2.05€ ($1.85) children; free admission 1st Sun of each month. Tues–Fri 10am–6pm; Sat–Sun 11am–6pm. U-Bahn/S-Bahn: Friedrichstrasse. Tram: 1, 2, 3, 4, 5, 13, 15, or 53.

## TIERGARTEN MUSEUMS

**Bauhaus-Archiv Museum für Gestaltung (Bauhaus Design Museum)** The Bauhaus Museum houses a permanent exhibition of photos and architectural designs relating to the Bauhaus school. Even if you're not a student of architecture, this museum is fascinating; it will bring you closer to the ideas and concepts that inspired modern design.

Klingelhoferstrasse 14. ✆ **030/2-54-00-20.** Admission 4€ ($3.55) adults, 2€ ($1.80) children under 12. Wed–Mon 10am–5pm. U-Bahn: Nollendorfplatz.

**Gemäldegalerie (Picture Gallery)** ★★★ This is one of Germany's greatest art museums. Several rooms are devoted to early German masters, with panels from altarpieces dating from the 13th to 15th centuries. Note the panel, *The Virgin Enthroned with Child* (1350), surrounded by angels that resemble the demons in the works of Hieronymus Bosch. Eight paintings make up the Dürer collection, including several portraits.

Most of the great European masters are represented. The Italian collection contains five Raphael Madonnas, along with works by Titian (*The Girl with a Bowl of Fruit*), Fra Filippo Lippi, Botticelli, and Correggio (*Leda with the Swan*). There are early Netherlandish paintings from the 15th and 16th centuries (van Eyck, van der Weyden, Bosch, and Brueghel) as well. Several galleries are devoted to 17th-century Flemish and Dutch masters, with no fewer than 15 works by Rembrandt, such as his famous *Head of Christ. The Man with the Golden Helmet,* long famous as a priceless Rembrandt, was proven in 1986 to be by another hand. This remarkable painting is now accepted as a fine independent original.

Mattäiskirchplatz 4. ✆ **030/20-90-55-55.** Admission 6€ ($5.35) adults, 3€ ($2.70) children. Tues–Fri 10am–6pm; Sat–Sun 11am–6pm. U-Bahn: Kurfürstenstrasse, then bus 148. Bus: 129 from Ku'damm (plus a 4-min. walk).

**Kunstgewerbemuseum (Museum of Decorative Arts)** This museum displays applied arts and crafts from the Middle Ages through the 20th century. Its outstanding exhibition is the Guelph Treasure, a collection of medieval church articles in gold and silver. The basement rooms show contemporary design from the Bauhaus school to Charles Eames and Memphis. Venetian glass, Italian majolica, German Renaissance goldsmiths' work, and 18th-century porcelain figurines are also displayed. Notable are such Art Nouveau works as a translucent opal-and-enamel box by Eugène Feuillâtre. There's a cafeteria inside, open from 10am to 4:30pm.

Matthäikirchplatz (opposite the Philharmonie), Tiergartenstrasse 6. ✆ **030/2-66-29-02.** Admission 3€ ($2.70) adults, 1.50€ ($1.35) children. Tues–Fri 10am–6pm; Sat–Sun 11am–6pm. U-Bahn: Kurfürstenstrasse. S-Bahn: Potsdamer Platz.

**Neue Nationalgalerie (Staatliche Museum zu Berlin)** ★ In its modern glass-and-steel home designed by Ludwig Mies van der Rohe (1886–1969), the Neue Nationalgalerie is a sequel of sorts to the art at Dahlem. It contains a continually growing collection of modern European and American art. Here you'll find works of 19th-century artists, with a concentration on French impressionists. German art starts with Adolph von Menzel's paintings from about 1850. The 20th-century collection includes works by Max Beckmann and Edvard Munch and E. L. Kirchner's *Brandenburger Tor* (1929), as well as paintings by Bacon, Picasso, Ernst, Klee, and American artists such as Barnett Newman. There's food service in the cafe on the ground floor, open 10:30am to 5:45pm.

# Attractions Around the Tiergarten

Aquarium **13**
Bauhaus-Archiv Museum für Gestaltung **12**
Brandenburger Tor **5**
Deutsche Guggenheim Berlin **4**
Erotik-Museum **16**
Europa Center **17**
Filmmuseum Berlin **11**
Gemäldegalerie **9**
Kaiser-Wilhelm Gedächtniskirche **15**
Käthe Kollwitz Museum **16**
Kongresshalle **2**
Kunstgewerbemuseum **8**
Märkisches Museum **16**
Martin-Gropius-Bau **6**
Museum für Gegenwart **1**
Neue Nationalgalerie **10**
Philharmonie **7**
Reichstag **3**
Schöneberg Rathaus **16**
The Story of Berlin **16**
Zoologischer Garten Berlin **14**

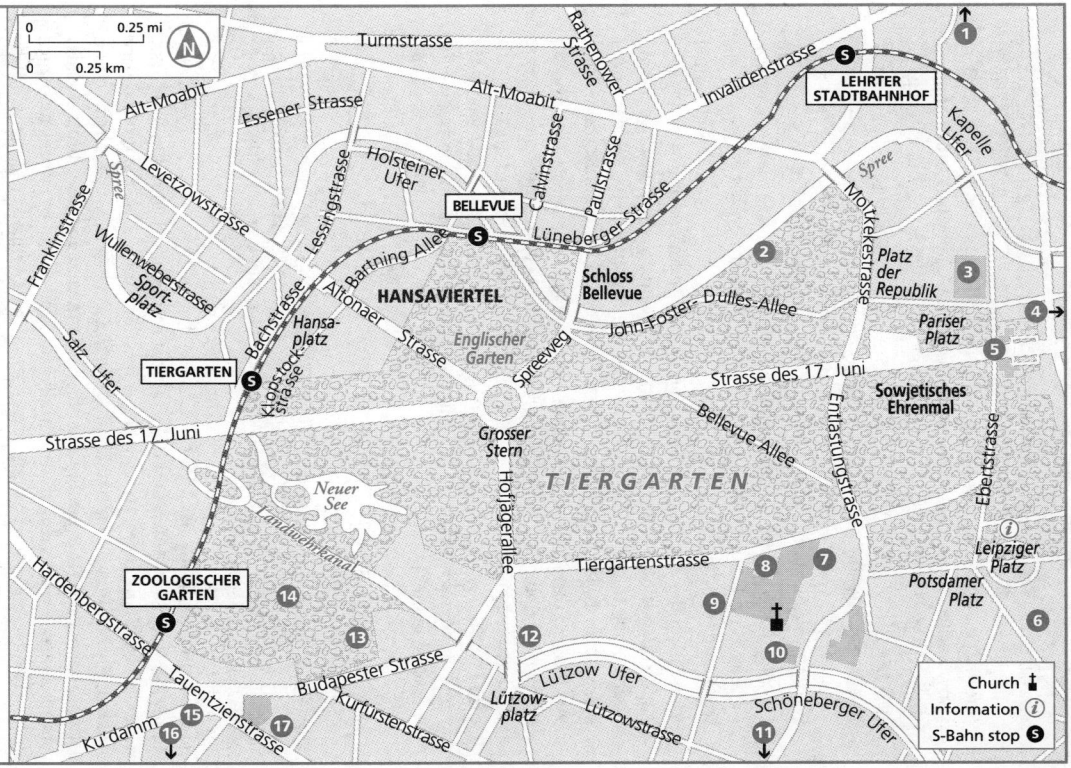

### *Moments* Frommer's Favorite Berlin Experiences

**Strolling along Unter den Linden and the Kurfürstendamm.** You can't know Berlin until you've strolled the Ku'damm, that glossy, store-lined showcase of Western capitalism or Unter den Linden, the Prussian centerpiece of the Berlin-Mitte district.

**Kneipen Crawling.** This is the Berlin version of "pub crawling." Whether you want breakfast or a beer at 4am, there's always a Kneipe waiting to claim you, no matter what neighborhood you're in.

**Looking for a Touch of Culture.** The baton of the late Herbert von Karajan is no longer raised, but the Berlin Philharmonic is still one of the world's leading orchestras.

**Wandering the Nikolai Quarter.** A symbol of Berlin's desire to bounce back after war damage, this charming 16th-century neighborhood has been completely rebuilt. Period taverns and churches make it ideal for a leisurely stroll down narrow streets illuminated by gas lanterns.

**Picnicking in the Tiergarten.** What better place for a picnic than the former hunting grounds of the Prussian electors? Wander through this 167 hectare (412-acre) park until you find the ideal spot, but first stop off at Kaufhaus des Westens (KaDeWe; p. 131) sixth-floor food emporium at Wittgenbergplatz, 20 minutes away, for the makings of a memorable meal.

Potsdamerstrasse 50 (just south of the Tiergarten). ✆ **030/2-66-26-62.** Permanent collection 4.10€ ($3.65) adults, 2.05€ ($1.85) children and students; temporary exhibitions 3.60€ ($3.20). Tues–Fri 10am–6pm; Sat–Sun 11am–8pm. Closed Jan 1, Dec 24–25 and 31, and the Tues after Easter and Whitsunday. U-Bahn: Kurfürstenstrasse. S-Bahn: Potsdamer Platz.

## OTHER MUSEUMS & SIGHTS

**Deutsche Guggenheim Berlin** ★ This state-of-the-art museum is devoted to modern and contemporary art. The exhibition space is on the ground floor of the newly restored Berlin branch of Deutsche Bank. The Guggenheim Foundation presents several exhibitions at this site annually and also displays newly commissioned works created specifically for this space by world-renowned artists. The bank supports young artists from the German-speaking world by purchasing their work and displaying them throughout the company's offices and public spaces. Exhibitions have ranged from the most avant-garde of modern artists to Picasso, Cézanne, and Andy Warhol.

Unter den Linden 13–15 (at the intersection with Charlottenstrasse). ✆ **030/20-20-93-0.** www.deutsche-guggenheim-berlin.de. Admission 3€ ($2.70) adults, 2€ ($1.80) children. Daily 11am–8pm; Thurs till 10pm. S-Bahn: Unter den Linden.

**Die Sammlung Berggruen: Picasso und Seine Zeit (The Berggruen Collection: Picasso and His Era)** ★ This unusual private museum displays the awesome collection of respected art and antiques dealer Heinz Berggruen. A native of Berlin who fled the Nazis in 1936, Berggruen later established a mini-empire of antique dealerships in Paris and California before returning, with his collection, to his native home in 1996. Sometime during your visit, there's a good chance that 80-year-old Mr. Berggruen, who has an apartment nearby, will be conducting a lecture on his favorite painter or spontaneously strolling among his paintings. The setting is a renovated army barracks designed by noted architect August Stütler in 1859. Although most of the collection is devoted to Picasso, there are also works by Cézanne, Braque, Klee, and van Gogh. The Picasso collection alone, which covers all his major periods, is worth the trip.

Schlosstrasse 1 (entrance across from the Egyptian Museum, in Charlottenburg). ✆ **030/830-1466.** Admission 6.15€ ($5.50) adults, 2.05€ ($1.85) students and children. Tues–Fri 10am–6pm; Sat–Sun 11am–6pm. Closed Mon. U-Bahn: Richard-Wagner Platz, followed by a 10-min. walk.

**Erotik-Museum** This "museum" lies on the corner of the seediest looking block in Berlin. You start out on the third floor and work your way down. Believe it or not, this is now Berlin's fifth most visited museum. The museum shelters some 5,000 sexual artifacts from around the world, including many Indian and Asian miniatures of erotic positions, even large carved phalli from Bali, along with such relics as African fertility masks. Life-size dioramas explore such topics as S&M and festishism. There are some Chinese wedding tiles from the 18th and 19th centuries that were supposed to provide sexual education to a newly married couple. The museum in its exhibits also honors the "queen of the Rubber Willy" herself, Beate Uhse, a household name in Germany. Her life is documented from her Luftwaffe days to pictures of her at the helm of a large speedboat. This septuagenarian opened the world's first shop devoted to "marital hygiene," ultimately championing the right to sell contraceptives. Today she still heads the world's largest sex-related merchandising business. Downstairs are video cabins filled with middle-aged men in raincoats and a "sex superstore."

Joachimstaler Strasse 4. ✆ **030/886-06-66.** Admission 5€ ($4.45), 4€ ($3.55) students and seniors. Daily 9am–midnight. U-Bahn/S-Bahn: Zoologischer Garten.

**Filmmuseum Berlin** ★ A thematic and chronological tour through the saga of the much-troubled German cinema is on show here. The link between Berlin and Hollywood is one of the main focuses of the collection, which is supplemented with special exhibitions. Currently the museum also owns some 9,000 German and foreign films, both silents and talkies. The collection here owns a million stills of scenes, portraits, and productions along with 30,000 screenplays, 20,000 posters, and 60,000 film programs. Germany's only world-class star, Marlene Dietrich, comes alive again in one wing. Berlin acquired part of her extensive estate of memorabilia in 1993. On display are such costumes as her famous "naked" pearl dress that gave the illusion of transparency and the swan's down coat designed by Jean Louis. Photos, costumes, props, letters, and documents recall the remarkable life of this diva who startled the world with her performance in Josef von Sternberg's *Der Blaue Engel* in 1930. Highlights of other films include props from *The Cabinet of Dr. Caligari*, the most famous German film of the Weimar Republic. One room is devoted to the controversial Leni Riefenstahl, the star director of the fascist era whose key films *Triumph des Willens* and *Olympia* established her as one of the world's major filmmakers and the leading exponent of Nazi propaganda.

Postdamer Strasse 2. ✆ **030/300-903-0.** www.filmmuseum-berlin.de. Admission 6.15€ ($5.50) adults, 4.10€ ($3.65) students, children, and senior citizens. Tues–Wed, Fri–Sun 10am–6pm; Thurs 10am–8pm. U-Bahn/S-Bahn: Potsdamer Platz.

**Friedrichswerdersche Kirche–Schinkelmuseum** This annex of the Nationalgalerie is located in the deconsecrated Friedrichswerdersche Kirche, which was designed in 1828 by Karl Friedrich Schinkel (1781–1841). It lies close to Unter den Linden, not far from the State Opera House. The twin

Gothic portals of the old church shelter a bronze of St. Michael slaying a dragon. Inside, the museum is devoted to the memory of Schinkel, who designed many of Berlin's great palaces, churches, and monuments. Memorabilia and documents record his great accomplishments. There are also exhibitions of neoclassical sculptures, portraits, and tombs by Johann Gottfried Schadow, Christian Daniel Rauch, Friedrich Tieck, and Berthel Thorvaldsen, the Danish sculptor.

Werderstrasse (at the corner of Niederlagstrasse). ✆ **030/2-08-13-23.** Admission 2.10€ ($1.90) adults, 1€ (90¢) children. Tues–Sun 10am–6pm. U-Bahn: Hausvogteiplatz.

**Jüdisches Museum Berlin (Jewish Musum Berlin)** ★★ The most talked about museum in Berlin, the Jewish Museum is housed in a building that is one of the most spectacular in the entire city. Called "the silver lightning bolt," it was designed by architect Daniel Libeskiind. To some viewers, the building suggests a shattered Star of David by its building plan and the scarring in the zinc-plated facade. Odd-shaped windows are haphazardly embedded in the building's exterior.

Inside, the spaces are designed to make the visitor uneasy and disoriented, simulating the feeling of those who were exiled. A vast hollow cuts through the museum to mark what is gone. When the exhibits reach the rise of the Third Reich, the hall's walls, ceiling, and floor close in as the visitor proceeds. A chillingly hollow Holocaust Void, a dark, windowless chamber, evokes much that was lost.

The exhibits concentrate on three themes: Judaism and Jewish life, the devastating effects of the Holocaust, and the post–World War II rebuilding of Jewish life in Germany.

Europe's largest Jewish Museum presents the panorama of German-Jewish history, its cultural achievements and its horror. The history of German Jewry is portrayed through objects, works of art, and documentation.

The roots of this museum were in an older museum opened in 1933 shortly before Hitler's rise to power. That collection of art and Judaica was shut down by the Gestapo in 1938, and all of its holdings were confiscated.

The on-site Liebermanns Restaurant features a world cuisine, with an emphasis on Jewish recipes—all strictly kosher.

Lindenstrasse 9–14. ✆ **030/25-99-33.** www.jmberlin.de. Admission 5€ ($4.55); students and seniors 2.50€ ($2.25); kids 5 and under free. Family ticket 10€ ($9.10) for 2 adults and up to 4 children. Mon 10am–10pm, must arrive by 9pm; Tues–Sun 10am–8pm, must arrive by 7pm. Closed on December 24, Rosh Hashana, and Yom Kippur. U-Bahn: Hallesches Tor or Kochstrasse.

**Kaiser-Wilhelm Gedächtniskirche (Kaiser Wilhelm Memorial Church)** There is no more evocative site in the western sector of Berlin to remind us of the horrors of war. The massive red sandstone church that originally stood here was dedicated in 1895 as a memorial to Kaiser Wilhelm II. In 1945, during the closing months of World War II, a bomb dropped by an Allied plane blasted it to pieces, leaving only a few gutted walls and the shell of the neo-Romanesque bell tower. After the war, West Berliners decided to leave the artfully evocative ruins as a reminder of the era's suffering and devastation. In 1961, directly at the base of the ruined building, they erected a small-scale modern church designed by Egon Eierman. Always irreverent, Berliners, noting the avant-garde architecture and geometric design of the new church, nicknamed it "the lipstick and powder box." Its octagonal hall is lit solely by thousands of colored glass windows set into a honeycomb framework. On its premises, you can visit a small museum with exhibitions and photographs documenting the history of the original church and the destructive ravages of war. The new church can hold up to 1,200 worshippers, and 10-minute religious services—conceived for office workers heading home—are held there every day at 5:30 and at 6pm. Between June and August, English-language services are conducted daily at 9am, and free organ concerts are presented here every Saturday, year-round, at 6pm.

Breit-Scheidplatz. ✆ **030/218-50-23.** Free admission. Ruined church Mon–Sat 10am–4pm; new church daily 9am–7pm. U-bahn: Zoologischer Garten or Kurfürstendamm.

**Käthe-Kollwitz-Museum** ★ This museum has been called a personalized revolt against the agonies of war. Many works express the sorrow of wartime separation of mother and child, inspired in part by the artist's loss of a son in World War I and a grandson during World War II. Berlin-born Käthe Kollwitz (1867–1945) was an ardent pacifist and socialist whose works were banned by the Nazis. The first woman ever elected to the Prussian Academy of the Arts, she resigned her position in 1933 to protest Hitler's rise to power. Her husband, Karl Kollwitz, was a physician who chose to practice among the poor on a working-class street (now called Kollwitzstrasse). In 1943, Allied bombing drove Käthe to the countryside near Dresden, where she died in 1945, a guest of the former royal family of Saxony in their castle at Moritzburg.

The lower floors of the museum are devoted to woodcuts and lithographs, the upper floors to particularly poignant sculptures. ***Note:*** The collection is closed twice a year for special exhibits.

Fasanenstrasse 24. ✆ **030/8-82-52-10.** Admission 5€ ($4.45) adults, 2.30€ ($2.05) children and students. Wed–Mon 11am–6pm. U-Bahn: Kurfürstendamm or Uhlandstrasse.

**Märkisches Museum** The full cultural history of Berlin is displayed in one of the most prominent buildings on the banks of the Spree; 42 rooms contain collections of artifacts from excavations, plus such art treasures as Slav silver and Bronze Age finds. You can learn about Berlin's theaters and literature, the arts in Berlin and Brandenburg, and the life and work of Berlin artisans. Most visitors like the array of mechanical musical instruments that can be played Wednesday 3 to 4pm and Sunday 11am to noon, for an extra 1€ (90¢).

Am Källnischen Park 5. ✆ **030/30-86-60.** Admission 4.10€ ($3.65) adults, 2.05€ ($1.85) children. Tues–Sun 10am–6pm. U-Bahn: Märkisches Museum. Bus: 147, 240, or 265.

**Martin-Gropius-Bau** When this gallery opened in 1981, the *New York Times* called it one of the "most dramatic museums in the world." It contains the **Museum Berlinische Galerie,** with works of art, architecture, and photography from the 19th and 20th centuries; the **Jewish Museum;** and the **Werkbund Archiv.** On the ground floor are changing exhibitions. The building lies near the site of the former Berlin Wall, and its eastern section opens onto the leveled former Gestapo headquarters. It's fascinating to look at the adjoining building with its unrestored exterior terra-cotta friezes—some damaged, some destroyed, and some left intact. The building itself is interesting architecturally, as it was one of the first big commissions that the Bauhaus guru, Walter Gropius, ever designed. Because the possibilities are always changing, you'll never be sure what you're going to see here; the center has been acclaimed for staging some of Berlin's major art and history exhibitions, so, chances are, you won't be disappointed.

Stresemannstrasse 110. ✆ **030/25-48-60.** Admission 6€ ($5.35) adults, 3€ ($2.70) children. Tues–Sun 10am–8pm. U-Bahn: Potsdamer Platz. S-Bahn: Anhalter Bahnhof.

**Museum für Gegenwart** This Museum of Contemporary Art opened in 1996 north of the Spree River in the old Hamburger Bahnhof, the oldest train station in Berlin. The structure was the terminus of the 290km (180-mile) train run from Hamburg. Today, the 19th-century station no longer receives trains but is a premier storehouse of postwar art, a sort of Musée d'Orsay of Berlin. Traces of its former function are still evident, including the high roof designed for steam engines. The modern art on display is some of the finest in Germany; the nucleus of the collection was donated by the Berlin collector Erich Marx (no relation to Karl Marx). You can view everything from Andy Warhol's now legendary Mao to an audiovisual Joseph Beuys archive. The museum houses one of the best collections of the work of Cy Twombly in the world because the curator, Heiner Bastian, was once his assistant. Other works are by Rauschenberg, Lichtenstein, and the recently deceased Dan Flavin. Beuys is also represented by 450 drawings.

Invalidenstrasse 50–51. ✆ **030/20-90-55-55.** www.smpk.de/hbf/e/s.html. Admission 4.10€ ($3.65) adults, 2.05€ ($1.85) children. Tues–Wed, Fri 10am–6pm; Thurs 10am–10pm; Sat–Sun 11am–6pm. U-Bahn: Zinnowitzer Strasse. Bus: 157, 245, 248, or 340.

**Museum Haus am Checkpoint Charlie** Exhibits in this small building evoke the tragic events connected with the former Berlin Wall. You can see some of the instruments of escape used by East Germans, including chairlifts, false passports, hot-air balloons, and even a minisub. Photos document the construction of the wall, the establishment of escape tunnels, and the postwar history of both parts of Berlin from 1945 until today, including the airlift of 1948 to 1949. One of the most moving exhibits is the display on the staircase of drawings by school children, who, in 1961 to 1962, were asked to depict both halves of Germany in one picture.

Friedrichstrasse 44. ✆ **030/253-7250.** Admission 5.10€ ($4.55) adults, 2.55€ ($2.30) children and students. Daily 9am–10pm. U-Bahn: Kochstrasse. Bus: 129.

**Olympia-Stadion** Built in 1936 by Werner March for the XI Summer Olympic Games, the Olympia-Stadion, which seats 100,000 people, was the first in Europe to supply all the facilities necessary for modern sports. Hitler expected to see his "master race" run off with all the medals in the 1936 Olympics, but his hopes were dashed when an African-American, Jesse Owens, took four golds for the U.S. team.

The stadium area covers a total of 136ha (330 acres), but the main attraction is the arena. The playing field in its center lies 14m (47 ft.) below ground level. For a panoramic view of Berlin, take the elevator to the top of the 80m (260-ft.) platform, where the Olympic bell hangs. Sporting or cultural events are still presented here about once a week during spring, summer, and autumn. For ticket sales and information for sporting events within the stadium, call **Herta-BSC (Herta-Berlin Soccer Club)** at ✆ **030/3-00-92-80.** For information about the occasional live concerts, call **Conzert Concept** at ✆ **030/81-07-50.**

Olympischer Platz 3. ✆ **030/30-06-33.** Admission 1€ (90¢). June–Sept daily 9am–5pm; off-season daily 9am–4pm. U-Bahn: Olympia-Stadion.

**Schöneberg Rathaus** This former political and administrative center of West Berlin is of special interest to Americans. It was the scene of John F. Kennedy's memorable (if grammatically shaky) "Ich bin ein Berliner" speech on June 26, 1963. Berliners have renamed the square around the building the John-F.-Kennedy-Platz. From the 72m- (237-ft.-) high tower, a Liberty Bell replica is rung every day at noon. This Freedom Bell, a gift from the American people in 1950, symbolized U.S. support for the West Berliners during the Cold War. The document chamber contains a testimonial bearing the signatures of 17 million Americans who gave their moral support to the struggle.

America Online Keyword: Travel

**Booked seat 6A, open return.**

**Rented red 4-wheel drive.**

**Reserved cabin, no running water.**

**Discovered space.**

With over 700 airlines, 50,000 hotels, 50 rental car companies and 5,000 cruise and vacation packages, you can create the perfect getaway for you. Choose the car, the room, even the ground you walk on.

**Travelocity.com**
A Sabre Company
**Go Virtually Anywhere.**

Travelocity,® Travelocity.com® and the Travelocity skyline logo are trademarks and/or servicemarks of Travelocity.com L.P., and Sabre® is a trademark of an affiliate of Sabre Inc. © 2002 Travelocity.com L.P. All rights reserved.

© 2002 Yahoo! Inc.

**Book your air, hotel, and transportation all in one place.**

Hotel or hostel? Cruise or canoe? Car? Plane? Camel? Wherever you're going, visit Yahoo! Travel and get total control over your arrangements. Even choose your seat assignment. So. One hump or two? travel.yahoo.com

powered by COMPAQ

YAHOO!
Travel

Do You YAHOO!?

John-F.-Kennedy-Platz. ✆ **030/75-600.** Free admission. Daily 9am–6pm. Tower closed Nov–Mar. U-Bahn: Rathaus Schöneberg.

**The Story of Berlin** This multimedia extravaganza portrays 8 centuries of the city's history through photos, films, sounds, and colorful displays. Beginning with the founding of Berlin in 1237, it chronicles the plague, the Thirty Years' War, Frederick the Great's reign, military life, the Industrial Revolution and the working poor, the Golden 1920s, World War II, divided Berlin during the Cold War, and the fall of the Wall. Lights flash in a media blitz as you enter the display on the fall of the Wall, making you feel like one of the first East Berliners to wonderingly cross to the West. Conclude your tour on the 14th floor with a panoramic view over today's Berlin. Allow at least 2 hours to see the museum. Though the displays are a bit jarring and the historical information is too jumbled to be truly educational, the museum does leave a lasting impression.

Ku'damm-Karree, Kurfürstendamm 207–208 (at the corner of Uhlandstrasse). ✆ **01805/99-20-10.** Admission 9.30€ ($8.30) adults, 7.50€ ($6.70) students/children, 21€ ($18.75) families. Daily 10am–8pm (you must enter by 6pm). S-Bahn: Ulandstrasse.

## EXPLORING BERLIN-MITTE

The best street for strolling in eastern Berlin is the famous **Unter den Linden,** beginning at Brandenburg Gate.

**Alexanderplatz,** named for Russian Czar Alexander I, was the center of activity in the old East Berlin. This square has brightened considerably since reunification, though aesthetically speaking it's got a long way to go. Neon lights and bright murals now coexist alongside the dull and fading GDR-era structures, and street musicians and small markets give the area new life.

The massive 335m (1,100-ft.) **Fernsehturm (TV tower)** on Alexanderplatz is the second-highest structure in Europe. It's worthwhile to take the 60-second elevator ride to the observation platform, 186m (610 ft.) above the city. From this isolated vantage you can clearly distinguish most landmarks, and on the floor above, you can enjoy cake and coffee in the revolving Tele-Café. The elevator to the top costs 4.50€ ($4) for adults and 2€ ($1.80) for children. The tower is open daily March to October 9am to 1am, and November to February daily 10am to midnight.

At the foot of the Fernsehturm stands Berlin's second-oldest church, the brick Gothic **Marienkirche (St. Mary's Church),** Karl-Liebknecht-Strasse 8 (✆ **030/2-42-44-67**), dating from the 15th century. Inside you can see the painting *Der Totentanz* (*The Dance of Death*), painted in 1475 then discovered in 1860 beneath a layer of whitewash in the church's entrance hall. Also worth seeing is

### *Moments* Night of Shame

Best visited at night, as it is more evocative then, **Bebelplatz** is a square along Unter den Linden, in Belin-Mitte, approached just before you reach Staatsoper. Here is an eloquent memorial to the notorious Nazi book burning that took place here on the night of May 10, 1933. Through a window set in the pavement, you can look below to a small library lined with empty bookshelves. Some 25,000 books were burned, all by authors considered enemies of the Third Reich. Nearby is a plaque with the prophetic words of the poet, Heinrich Heine. In 1820 he wrote, "Where books are burned, in the end people will burn."

the marble baroque pulpit carved by Andreas Schlüter (1703). The cross on the top of the church annoyed the Communist rulers of the former East Germany—its golden form was always reflected in the windows of the Fernsehturm. The church is open Monday to Thursday 10am to noon and 1 to 4pm, Friday to Sunday noon to 4pm. Free tours are offered Monday to Thursday at 1pm and Sunday at 11:45am.

**Brandenburger Tor (Brandenburg Gate)** ★★ This triumphal arch—now restored—stands in the very heart of Berlin, and once was the symbol of the divided city. In the heyday of East Germany, the structure was integrated into the Berlin Wall, which followed a north-south axis as it made its wicked way to the Potsdamer Platz. Six Doric columns hold up an entablature that was inspired by the Propylaea of the Parthenon at Athens. Surrounded by the famous and much photographed Quadriga of Gottfried Schadow from 1793, the gate was designed by Carl Gotthard Langhans in 1789. Napoléon liked the original Quadriga so much he ordered them taken down and shipped to Paris, but they were returned to Berlin in 1814. In Berlin's heyday before World War II, the gate marked the grand western extremity of the "main street," Unter den Linden. In the Room of Silence, built into one of the guardhouses, visitors still gather to meditate and reflect on Germany's past.

Unter den Linden. Free admission. Room of Silence daily 11am–6pm. S-Bahn: Unter den Linden. Bus: 100.

**Brecht-Weigel-Museum** This building was occupied by poet and playwright Bertolt Brecht (1898–1956) and his wife, noted actress Helene Weigel (1900–72), from 1953 until their deaths. Brecht, who lived in the United States during World War II, returned to East Berlin after the war. Here he created his own "epic theater" company, the acclaimed Berliner Ensemble. The museum is in an old apartment house. It displays the artists' living and working rooms and the Brecht and Weigel archives, containing 350,000 manuscripts, typescripts, and collections of his printed works, press cuttings, and playbills. An attendant guides all visitors around the museum. There's a restaurant downstairs (see "Where to Dine," earlier in this chapter).

Chausseestrasse 125. ✆ **030/282-99-16.** Admission 4.50€ ($4) adults, 2.25€ ($2) children and students. Tues–Wed and Fri 10–11:30am; Thurs 10am–noon and 5–6:30pm; Sat 9:30am–1:30pm; Sun 11am–6pm. Visits by guided tour only. U-Bahn: Zinnowitzer Strasse.

**Deutsches Historisches Museum** The big museum news coming out of Berlin will be the reopening of this museum some time in 2003 (no firm date is set). From the Neanderthals to the Nazis, the whole saga of German history is presented. The collection includes extensive posters and documents of the history of the workers' movement as well as a few remains from the former

---

***Moments*** **In Memory of . . .**

At the corner of Lewetzov and Jagow streets is a **Jewish War Memorial** to the many Berliners who were deported—mostly to their deaths—from 1941 until the end of the war in 1945. The memorial is a life-size sculpture of a freight car with victims being dragged into it. Behind it is a 15m (50-ft.) structure listing the dates of the various death trains and the number of prisoners shipped out. The memorial stands on the site of a former synagogue destroyed by the Nazis.

---

### The Heartbeat of Berlin

The Potsdamer Platz Arcades contain 140 specialty shops, restaurants, and cafes, inviting you to shop and relax in a civilized urban atmosphere. One of the most visited attractions at the center includes the **Sony Center am Potsdamer Platz** (✆ **030/20-94-54-00**), with two cinemas—the CineStar Multiplex and the Cinestar IMAX 3D. The 10-story office building offers a panoramic view that embraces the Philharmonie, the Kulturforum, and the Tiergarten. Around Marlene-Deitrich-Platz, prominent companies offer a whole range of leisure and entertainment facilities. They include the Berlin IMAX-Theater, the Stella Musical-Theater, the Grand Hyatt Hotel, the Madison City Suites, the Berlin Casino, and the Cine-Max cinema center.

Zeughaus (arsenal) collection, which before World War II had been the largest collection of militaria from the history of Brandenburg and Prussia. The museum also owns tons of the old GDR communist art (naturally all the workers are depicted with smiling faces). There will be a permanent exhibition on German history in the main building, with temporary exhibitions in an annex.

Under den Linden 2. ✆ **030/20-30-40.** Call to confirm its opening, times of visit, and admission. U-Bahn: Friedrichstrasse.

**Reichstag (Parliament)** ★ The night of February 17, 1933, was a date that lives in infamy in Germany history. On that night, a fire broke out in the seat of the German house of parliament, the Reichstag. It was obviously set by the Nazis on orders of Hitler, but the German Communist Party was blamed. That was all the excuse Hitler's troops needed to begin mass arrests of "dissidents and enemies of the lawful government." Because of this mysterious fire, democracy came to an end in Germany. The Reichstag was in for even greater punishment as it faced massive allied bombardment in World War II.

Today it's come back and is once again the home of the country's parliament in the wake of the collapse of the Berlin Wall and subsequent reunification in 1990. The building still evokes the neo-Renaissance style it had when it opened in 1894. Today, it's crowned by a new glass dome designed by Sir Norman Foster, the famous English architect. You can go through the west gate for an elevator ride up to the dome, where a sweeping vista of Berlin opens before you. There's both an observation platform and a rooftop restaurant (but the view is better than the food).

Platz der Republik 1. ✆ **030/2273-2152.** Free admission. Daily 8am–midnight (last entrance at 10pm). S-Bahn: Unter den Linden. Bus: 100.

## THE HISTORIC NIKOLAI QUARTER

The historic **Nikolaiviertel** (U-Bahn: Klosterstrasse) was restored in time for the city's 750th anniversary in 1987. Here, on the banks of the Spree River, is where Berlin was born. Many of the medieval and baroque buildings in the neighborhood were completely and authentically reconstructed after World War II. Subsequently, some of the city's old flavor has been recaptured here.

The area is named for the **Nikolaikirche (Church of St. Nicholas),** Nikolaikirchplatz, off Spandauerstrasse (✆ **030/24-00-20**). The church, the oldest in Berlin, was originally constructed in the 14th century on the remains of a 13th-century Romanesque church. The restored building now displays the finds of postwar archaeological digs; during the reconstruction, 800-year-old skeletons were found. It's open Sunday 2 to 4pm and Saturday noon to 3pm; a visit can be arranged on weekdays if you call in advance. Admission to the church is free, but admission to the tower is 1€ (90¢).

## OTHER ARCHITECTURAL SIGHTS

Just north of the Tiergarten is the **Hansaviertel,** or Hansa Quarter (U-Bahn: Hansaplatz). The architecture of this area (no specific address) was an outgrowth of the great INTERBAU 1957 (International Builder's Exhibition), when architects from 22 nations designed buildings for the totally destroyed quarter. The diversity here is exciting: 50 architects took part, including Gropius, Niemeyer, and Duttman.

Le Corbusier also submitted a design for an apartment house for INTERBAU 1957, but the structure was so gigantic that it had to be built near the **Olympic Stadium** (U-Bahn: Olympia-Stadion). The **Corbusier House,** called *Strahlende Stadt* (radiant city), is one of Europe's largest housing complexes—its 530 apartments can house up to 1,400 people. Typical of the architect's style, this tremendous building rests on stilts.

The architects of rebuilt Berlin were also encouraged to design centers for the performing arts. One of the most controversial projects was the **Kongresshalle (Congress Hall),** on John-Foster-Dulles-Allee, in the Tiergarten, just west of Brandenburg Gate (S-Bahn: Unter den Linden). This building was conceived as the American contribution to INTERBAU 1957. The reinforced concrete structure has an 18m- (60-ft.-) high vaulted ceiling that reminds some viewers of an oversize flying saucer. Berliners immediately christened it "The Pregnant Oyster." The building today is used mainly for conventions. More successful was the **Philharmonie,** new home of the Berlin Philharmonic, at Matthäikirchstrasse, and its adjacent chamber-music hall, next to the Tiergarten. The tent-like roof arches up in a bold curve, and the gold-colored facade glitters.

Berlin's tallest building sits in the midst of the city's busiest area. The 22-story **Europa Center,** just across the plaza from the Kaiser Wilhelm Memorial Church at Breitscheidplatz (U-Bahn: Kurfürstendamm), is the largest self-contained shopping center and entertainment complex in Europe. This town-within-a-town opened in 1965 on the site of the legendary Romanisches Café, once a gathering place for actors, writers, and artists in the flamboyant 1920s. Berliners dubbed it "Pepper's Manhattan," after its owner, K. H. Pepper. In addition to three levels of shops, restaurants, nightclubs, bars, and cinemas, it contains dozens of offices, a parking garage, and an observation roof. At the Tauentzienstrasse entrance, you can find two pieces of the former Berlin Wall. The building is open daily 9am to midnight (to 10pm in winter). Admission to the observation roof is 2€ ($1.80).

## SIGHTS IN THE ENVIRONS

**Berliner Dom** The cathedral of Berlin took some devastating hits in the British serial bombardments of Berlin in 1940, but it was restored to some of its former glory in the post-war decades, reopening in 1993. Unlike many European capitals where the cathedral is among the top two or three attractions, you can safely miss Berlin's Dom without feeling cultural deprivation. That said, the best way for an overview of this 19th-century cathedral is from the Dome Gallery ★, reached after climbing 270 steps. From here, you get a good glimpse of the Dom's ceiling and the rest of its much-restored interior. The reconstruction of this cathedral into its classic form was completed in 1822. Its most

## A Death Camp: "A Guarantor of Memory"

A grim sight, and a place of misery and death, the notorious **Sachsenhausen Concentration Camp,** built in the summer of 1936, is open to the public north of Berlin. More than 200,000 prisoners—Jews, gypsies, homosexuals, communists, and intellectuals—were imprisoned here until 1945.

The SS, under Heinrich Himmler, practiced methods of mass killing here later used in other Nazi death camps. Torture and medical experiments (on both live and dead bodies) were the norm here as prisoners were methodically exterminated, including Stalin's oldest son. The Soviets imprisoned everyone from former Nazi functionaries to its own Russian soldiers who had contacted sexually transmitted diseases in Germany.

The foundations of "Station Z" (where exterminations occurred) remain, along with "Jewish only" barracks which were torched by rightists in 1992 and reconstructed. Types of brutal punishment are depicted in a jail block, along with many evocative reminders such as hair shorn from prisoners and an open can of Zyklon B inside a glass case. There's even a display of counterfeit British and American money made by the Nazis. You're greeted by a monument with red triangles worn by political prisoners.

The legacy of horror didn't end with the so-called "liberation" of 1945. The Soviet Secret Police then turned the camp into a prison, and some 12,000 inmates died here from 1945 until 1950 when the camp shut down. Mass graves from the Soviet era were discovered here in 1990. A museum has opened to document the double atrocities of two totalitarian regimes.

Sachsenhausen Concentration Camp (Strasse der Nationen 22, Oranienburg; ✆ **03301/803715**) is open April through September Tuesday to Sunday 8:30am to 6pm, October through March Tuesday to Sunday 8:30am to 4:30pm. Admission is free. Take Oranienburg S-Bahn to the end (trip time: 40 min.), then a 20-minute walk.

notable features include a gilded wall altar with the 12 apostles by Karl Friedrich Schinkel, and the magnificent Sauer organ containing 7,000 pipes.

The stained-glass windows are especially stunning, depicting such scenes as the Resurrection, as symbolized by an Angel holding a palm branch. The tombstones of Prussian royals are displayed in the crypt; the most impressive tombs being those of Frederick I and his queen, Sophie Charlotte. ***Tip:*** The best time to visit is for one of the organ concerts, conducted year-round, usually on Saturday at 6pm. An announcement is printed within the church listing hours of all ecclesiastical and musical events.

In the Lustgarten, Museum Island. ✆ **030/202-69-136.** Admission 4.10€ ($3.65) adults, 2.05€ ($1.85) students/seniors. Free for ages 13 and under. Mon–Sat 9am–7pm, Sun noon–7pm (until 6pm in winter). S-Ban: Alexanderplatz or Hackescher Markt.

**Haus der Wannsee-Konferenz** This was the site of one of the most notorious conferences in history: a meeting of Nazi bureaucrats and SS officials to plan the annihilation of European Jewry. The minutes of the conference were kept by Adolf Eichmann, the sallow-faced SS functionary who later mapped out transport logistics for sending millions of Jews to their deaths.

The villa is now a memorial to the Holocaust. It includes a selection of photographs of men, women, and children who were sent to concentration camps. This exhibit is not for the squeamish. Nearly all the pictures on display are official Nazi photographs, including some of Nazi medical experiments. As noted at the trials at Nürnberg, "No government in history ever did a better job of photographing and documenting its crimes against humanity."

Am Grossen Wannsee 56. ✆ **030/80-50-01-0.** www.ghwk.de/engl/kopfengl.htm. Free admission. Daily 10am–6pm. S-Bahn: Wannsee, then bus 114.

**Jüdischer Friedhof (Jewish Cemetery)** This famous Jewish cemetery was opened in 1880. It contains 110,000 graves of Jewish residents of Berlin. Many distinguished artists, musicians, and scientists, as well as religious leaders, are buried here. Some tombs are of Jewish soldiers who fought for Germany in World War I. A memorial honors Jewish victims murdered during the Nazi era. You may have a hard time finding the cemetery on your own, so we recommend a taxi.

Herbert-Baumstrasse, Weissensee (a suburb east of Berlin). ✆ **030/9-25-33-30.** Mar–Nov daily 8am–5pm; Dec–Feb Mon–Thurs 8am–4pm, Fri 8am–3pm. Tram: 23 or 24, or taxi.

**Neue Synagoge Berlin-Centrum Judaicum (The New Synagogue)** Originally consecrated on Rosh Hashanah in 1866 and capped with what's remembered as one of the most spectacular domes in Berlin, this synagogue was vandalized in 1938 during Kristallnacht, torched by Berliners in 1944, blasted by Allied bombs in 1945, and finally, after about a decade of further deterioration, demolished by the Communist East Germans in the 1950s. During its heyday, with 3,200 seats and a design inspired by the Moorish architecture of the Alhambra in Granada, Spain, it was the largest synagogue in Germany. In recent times, it was partially rebuilt, and capped with a gilded dome that's visible for many surrounding blocks. Inside, there's a replica, using some of the original carvings, of some of the original synagogue's entrance vestibules and anterooms, within which are exhibitions detailing the events that transpired in this building since its original construction. The bulk of the synagogue was never rebuilt. In its place is a gravel-covered plot of land where markers indicate the original layout of the building. If you visit you'll gain a disturbing and unnerving insight into the destruction of a way of life that used to be, and a sense of the passion with which Berlin's Jewish and German communities commemorate the memory of their murdered kinfolk.

Oranienburgerstrasse 31. ✆ **030/880-28-316.** www.cjudaicum.de/. Admission 2.55€ ($2.30) adults, 1.55€ ($1.40) for children under 14. Sun–Thurs 10am–6pm; Fri 10am–2pm. Last entrance 30 min. before closing. S-Bahn: Oranienburger Tor or Hackescher Markt.

**Spandauer Zitadelle (Spandau Citadel)** This citadel stands at the confluence of the Spree and Havel rivers in northwestern Berlin. The Hohenzollern electors of Brandenburg used it as a summer residence, and in time it became the chief military center of Prussia. The citadel has been besieged by everybody from the French to the Prussians. The Juliusturm (Julius Tower) and the Palas, constructed in the 13th to 15th centuries, are the oldest buildings in Berlin still standing. The main building, accessible by footbridge, houses a local-history museum.

Am Juliusturm. ✆ **030/354-944-200.** Admission 2.50€ ($2.25) adults, 1.50€ ($1.35) students. Tues–Fri 9am–5pm; Sat–Sun 10am–5pm. U-Bahn: Zitadelle.

## BERLIN'S PARKS & ZOO

The huge **Botanischer Garten (Botanical Garden),** Königin-Luise-Strasse 6–8 (✆ **030/83-85-01-11;** www.bgbm.org/BGBM/; S-Bahn: Botanischer Garten or Rathaus Steglitz), near the Dahlem Museums, contains vast collections of European and exotic plants. The big palm house is one of the largest in the world. There's a large arboretum here as well as several special collections, such as a garden for blind visitors and another with water plants. Admission is 4€ ($3.55) for adults, 2€ ($1.80) for children, and free for children under 6. The gardens are open daily 9am to 8pm April and August; 9am to 9pm May, June, and July; 9am to 7pm September; 9am to 6pm March and October; 9am to 5pm February; and 9am to 4pm November, December, and January; the museum is open daily, year-round from 10am to 6pm.

The **Tiergarten** ★ is the largest green space in central Berlin, covering 2.5 sq. km. (just under 1 sq. mile), with more than 23km (14 miles) of meandering walkways. It was originally laid out as a private park for the electors of Prussia by a leading landscape architect of the day, Peter Josef Lenné. The park was devastated during World War II, then the trees that remained were chopped down for fuel as Berliners shivered through the winter of 1945–46. Beginning in 1955, trees were replanted, and walkways, canals, ponds, and flowerbeds were restored to their original patterns. The park is popular with joggers and (sometimes nude) sunbathers. Inside the park is the Berlin Zoo (see below).

Among the park's monuments is the **Siegessäule (Victory Column),** a golden goddess of victory perched atop a soaring red-granite pedestal. The monument stands in the center of the wide boulevard (Strasse des 17 Juni) that neatly bisects the park. A 48m- (157-ft.-) high observation platform can be reached by a climb up a 290-step spiral staircase. It's open on Monday 3 to 6pm and Tuesday to Sunday 9:30am to 6:30pm. Admission is 1€ (90¢) for adults and .50€ (45¢) for children. For information, call ✆ **030/391-29-61.**

**Zoologischer Garten Berlin (Berlin Zoo-Aquarium)** ★, Hardenbergplatz 8 (✆ **030/25-40-10;** U-Bahn/S-Bahn: Zoologischer Garten), founded in 1844, is Germany's oldest zoo. It occupies almost the entire southwest corner of the Tiergarten. Until World War II, the zoo boasted thousands of animals—many were familiar to Berliners by nickname. By the end of 1945, however,

### *Kids* Fun for Kids

Children love the **Berlin Zoo-Aquarium** (see above). Its most famous residents, the giant pandas, are perennial favorites. The zoo also has playgrounds and a children's section, where the animals welcome a cuddle. Another place to take the kids is **Grips-Theater,** Altonaerstrasse 22 (✆ **030/39-74-74-77;** U-Bahn: Hansaplatz), known for its bright, breezy productions. Children are sure to enjoy the music and dancing (if not the simple German-language dialogue). Tickets cost 8.50€ ($7.60) for students and persons under 16, and 15€ ($13.40) for adults. Call to ask about current productions. Most performances begin at 7:30pm, although there are some matinees as well, depending on the production. The theater is closed from late June to mid-August.

only 91 had survived. Today, more than 13,000 animals live here, many of them in large, open natural habitats. The most valuable residents are the giant pandas. The zoo also has Europe's most modern birdhouse, with more than 550 species.

The **aquarium** is as impressive as the adjacent zoo, with more than 9,000 fish, reptiles, amphibians, insects, and other creatures. Crocodiles, Komodo dragons, and tuataras inhabit the terrarium within. You can walk on a bridge over the reptile pit. There's also a large collection of snakes, lizards, and turtles. The "hippoquarium" is a new attraction.

Admission to the zoo is 7.65€ ($6.85) for adults and 3.85€ ($3.45) for children; to the aquarium, 7.15€ ($6.40) for adults and 3.85€ ($3.45) for children. A combined ticket costs 12.25€ ($10.95) for adults and 6.15€ ($5.50) for children. The zoo is open April to October daily 9am to 6:30pm; November to March daily 9am to 5pm. The aquarium is open year-round daily 9am to 6pm.

## 6 Organized Tours

### WALKING TOURS

For an excellent introduction to Berlin and its history, try one of the walking tours offered by **Berlin Walks** (✆ **030/301-9194** or e-mail: BerlinWalks@compuserve.com for information). "Discover Berlin" is a 3-hour introductory tour that takes you past the New Synagogue, the Reichstag, and the Brandenburg Gate, among other major sites. This walk starts daily at 10am and 2:30pm (in winter at 10am only). "Infamous Third Reich Sites" focuses on the sites of major Nazi buildings in central Berlin, such as Goebbels' Propaganda Ministry and Hitler's New Reichschancellery; it starts at 10am on Saturdays, Sundays, Tuesdays, and Thursdays in summer, less frequently in the off-season. "Jewish Life in Berlin" takes you through the pre-war Jewish community; sights include the Old Cemetery and the former Boys' School. The tour starts at 10am Monday and Thursday, April to mid-October. For all tours, reservations are unnecessary—simply meet the guide, who will be wearing a Berlin Walks badge, outside the main entrance to Bahnhof Zoologischer Garten (Zoo Station), at the top of the taxi stand. Tours last from 2½ to 3 hours and cost 8.20€ ($7.30) for those under 26 and 10.20€ ($9.10) for everyone else. This summer, Berlin Walks will be inaugurating a new 5-hour tour to Potsdam, starting every Wednesday and Saturday at 9am; meet at the same place.

### BUS TOURS

Berlin is a far-flung metropolis whose interesting neighborhoods are often separated by extended areas of parks, monumental boulevards, and Cold War wastelands. Because of these factors, organized bus tours can be the best way to navigate the city.

Some of the best are operated by **Severin+Kühn,** Kurfürstendamm 216 (✆ **030/88-04-190;** U-Bahn: Kurfürstendamm), located on the second floor of a building across from the Kempinski Hotel. This agency offers a half-dozen tours of Berlin and its environs. Their 2-hour "12-Stops-City Tour" departs daily every half hour April to October 10am to 4pm and November to March 10am to 3pm. Tickets cost 17.90€ ($16) per person. The tour passes 12 important stops in Berlin, including the Europa Center, the Brandenburg Gate, and Potsdammer Platz, provides taped audio commentary in eight languages, and offers the option of getting on and off the bus at any point during the hour. Retain your ticket stub to reboard the bus.

**Severin+Kühn** also offers the 3-hour "Big Berlin Tour," which departs at 10am and 2pm daily and costs 20€ ($17.85) per person. This tour incorporates more sites than the 12-Stops-City Tour. All tours include a live guide who delivers commentaries in both German and English.

One of the most interesting tours visits Potsdam, site of the famed World War II conference and of Sans Souci Palace, former residence of Frederick the Great. The price is 33.50€ ($29.90) per person. Departures are Tuesday to Sunday at 10am, May to September; and Saturday and Sunday at 2:15pm, April to October.

## BOAT TOURS

It may not be the obvious choice for transportation in Berlin, but a boat ride can offer visitors a good change of pace. The networks of canals that bisect the plains of what used to be known as Prussia were an engineering marvel when they were completed in the 19th century. Today, transport through the lakes, locks, and canals around Berlin retains its nostalgic allure, and affords unusual vistas that aren't available from the windows of more conventional modes of transport. Berliners boast that their city has more bridges than Venice. Local waterways include the Spree and Havel rivers—ranging in size from narrow channels to large lakes—as well as many canals. You can take short tours that offer close-up views of the city or daylong adventures along the Spree and Havel; the latter often turn into beer-drinking fests.

> **IMPRESSIONS**
>
> *"Eight times the size of Paris, Berlin is a work-in-progress, poised to challenge bourgeois Paris as a younger, more dynamic fulcrum for Europe's creative community."*
>
> —James Sherwood

The city's best-known boat operator is **Stern- und Kreisschiffahrt,** Pushkinallee 60–70 (✆ **030/5-36-36-00**). Since Germany's reunification, the company has absorbed the piers and ferryboats of its former East German counterparts. "Historische Stadtfahrt" is a ride along the banks of the Spree, the river that helped build Berlin. Two-, 3-, and 4-hour tours (in German only) depart at 10am and 2pm from a quay near Berlin's cathedral, Am Palast Ufer. These trips offer good views of the Reichstag, the Pergamon Museum, the Königliche Bibliothek (Royal Library), and the monumental heart of the former East Berlin. The tours lasting 1 hour cost 8€ ($7.15) per person; tours lasting 2 hours cost 10€ ($8.95); tours lasting 4 hours are 15€ ($13.40).

Stern- und Kreisschiffahrt also has a cruising yacht, *Moby Dick,* a whale-shaped boat that usually sails along the waters of the Eglersee and looks like something that might have been developed by the staff at Disneyland. It departs from a point near the Alt-Tegel U-Bahn station, on the city's northwestern edge. Walk for about 10 minutes through the suburb of Tegel to the Greenwich Promenade, and then to the Stern- und Kreisschiffahrt pier. Boats head southward from Tegel, passing along the Havel River and many of its lakes. Reservations are usually necessary for all boat rides described here. Rides operate only April to either late October or early December, depending on the tour. Prices and actual itineraries change seasonally; call for more details.

## 7 Sports & Outdoor Pursuits

### BIKING

The best place to rent bikes in Berlin is at **Fahradstation,** GmbH, an outfit that maintains hundreds of bicycles and at least two locations within central Berlin. Two of their most central locations include Rosenthalerstrasse 40–41 (✆ **030/28-38-48-48;** S-Bahn: Hackescher Markt), in Hackescher Höfe, and Bergmannstrasse 9 (✆ **030/215-1566;** U-Bahn: Platz de Luftbrüke), in Kreuzberg. Rentals cost 15€ ($13.40) per day or 35€ ($31.25) per week, plus a one-time insurance fee of 3€ ($2.70). The city maintains a labyrinth of bike paths, marked by red bricks on the walkways, through the central core of Berlin and in its parks, especially the Tiergarten. The best places for biking are the Tiergarten in central Berlin, and farther afield in the Grunewald Forest (S-Bahn: Grunewald).

### JOGGING

Head for the vast and verdant leafiness of the **Grunewald,** on the city's western edge, which is crisscrossed with pedestrian and bike paths. This area is appropriate for very long endurance tests. Closer to the center is the **Tiergarten,** which allows you to soak up a little history on your morning jog thanks to its many monuments and memorials. The grounds of **Schloss Charlottenburg** are also good for jogging.

### SPECTATOR SPORTS

Among Berliners, **füssball (soccer)** is the most popular sport. For information about which teams are playing, ask your hotel receptionist, or refer to a daily newspaper or the weekly magazine *Berlin Programm.*

### SWIMMING & SAUNAS

Berlin has dozens of pools. One of the best equipped is the **S.E.Z. Landsberger,** Landsberger Allee 77 (✆ **030/421-820;** U-Bahn: Alexanderplatz). Here you'll find a swimming pool, a diving pool, a wave pool, an assortment of waterfalls, a jet pool, sauna and solarium facilities, a weight room, about half a dozen restaurants and snack bars, and a bowling alley. The cost is 5.50€ ($4.90) for adults and 2.50€ ($2.25) for children for 2 hours of swimming.

A worthy competitor (just east of Tempelhof Airport) is the **Club Paradise,** Buschkrugallee 64 (✆ **030/6-06-60-60;** U-Bahn: Grenzallee), which has indoor and outdoor pools, saunas, a steam room, solariums, and a 120m (393½-ft.) water slide. Its latest attraction, called "Crazy River," sends you down a river in water tubes. A 4-hour pass costs 10.75€ ($9.60) for adults and 8.20€ ($7.30) for children ages 2 to 12. It's open daily 10am to 11pm.

Perched on the top floor of the Europa Center's parking garage (*Parkhaus Europa Center*), you'll find a health and exercise club called **Thermen,** Nürnberger Strasse 9 (✆ **030/2-61-60-32;** U-Bahn: Wittenbergplatz), offering an array of heated pools, saunas, massage facilities, and solariums. A full-day pass costs 18€ ($16.05), but if you want to limit your exposure to just 3 hours, you'll pay 7€ ($6.25) for arrivals between 10am and 9pm, and 16€ ($14.30) if you arrive between 9pm and closing. Both men and women share the same saunas. If you just want to use the pool, and bypass the saunas and exercise facilities, you'll pay 8€ ($7.15) for a 2-hour immersion, regardless of the time of day. Massages cost 22€ ($19.65) for 30 minutes. Hours are Monday to Saturday 10am to midnight and Sunday 10am to 9pm.

For outdoor swimming during the hot months, head to one of Europe's largest lake beaches at **Wannsee.** Take the S-Bahn to Nikolaisee and follow the hordes of bathers heading toward the water's edge.

### TENNIS & SQUASH

At **Sports Treffe,** Buschkrugallee 84 (✆ **030/6-06-60-11;** U-Bahn: Grenzall), indoor courts rent for 27€ ($24.10) for a 1-hour session, depending on when you play. There are also five squash courts that each rent for around 18€ ($16.05) for a 1-hour session. Somewhat closer to Berlin's center is the **Squash & Tennis Center,** Treuenbrietzenerstrasse 36 (✆ **030/4-15-30-11;** U-Bahn: Wittenau, then bus 124 or X-21), which has similar rates. There are also courts in the **Preussen Park,** Kamenzerstrasse 34, Lankwitz (✆ **030/7-75-10-51;** U-Bahn: Mariendorfer), open 24 hours a day year-round with rates beginning at 18€ ($16.05) per hour.

## 8 Shopping

The **Ku'damm** (or Kurfürstendamm) is the Fifth Avenue of Berlin. It's filled with quality stores but also has outlets hustling cheap souvenirs and T-shirts. Although Berliners themselves shop on the Ku'damm, many prefer the specialty stores on the side streets, especially between **Breitscheidplatz** and **Olivaer Platz.** You might also want to check out **Am Zoo** and **Kantstrasse.**

Another major shopping street is the **Tauentzienstrasse** and the streets that intersect it: **Marburger, Ranke,** and **Nürnberger.** This area offers a wide array of stores, many specializing in German fashions for women. Stores here are often cheaper than on the Ku'damm. Also on Tauentzienstrasse (near the Ku'damm) is Berlin's major indoor shopping center, the **Europa Center** (✆ **030/3-48-00-88**), with around 75 shops, as well as restaurants and cafes. At the end of this street lies the **KaDeWe,** the classiest department store in Berlin and the biggest in continental Europe.

A new, upmarket version of the Europa Center is the **Uhland-Passage,** at Uhlandstrasse 170, which has some of the best boutiques and big-name stores in Berlin. Shoppers interested in quality at any price should head to **Kempinski Plaza,** Uhlandstrasse 181–183, a pocket of posh with some of the most exclusive boutiques in the city. Haute-couture women's clothing is a special feature here. More trendy and avant-garde boutiques are found along **Bleibtreustrasse.**

If it's serious bargains you're looking for, head to **Wilmersdorferstrasse.** Here you'll find a vast number of discount stores, although some of the merchandise is second-rate. Try to avoid Saturday morning, when it's often impossibly overcrowded.

In eastern Berlin, not that long ago, you couldn't find much to buy except a few souvenirs. All that is changed now. The main street, **Friedrichstrasse,** offers some of Berlin's most elegant shopping. Upmarket boutiques—selling everything from quality women's fashions to Meissen porcelain—are found along **Unter den Linden.** The cheaper stores in eastern Berlin are around the rather bleak-looking **Alexanderplatz.** Many specialty and clothing shops are found in the **Nikolai Quarter.** The largest shopping mall in eastern Berlin, with outlets offering a little bit of everything, is at the **Berliner Markthalle,** at the corner of Rosa-Luxemburg-Strasse and Karl-Liebknecht-Strasse.

Most stores in Berlin are open Monday to Friday 9 or 10am to 6 or 6:30pm. Many stay open late on Thursday evenings, often to 8:30pm. Saturday hours are usually 9 or 10am to 2pm.

## ANTIQUES

**Astoria** Astoria, whose buyers frequently scour the antique markets of France, England, and Germany, pays homage to the decorative objects of the 1920s and 1930s. You'll find antique mirrors, lamps, tables, and jewelry here, as well as a handful of reproductions. Bleibtreustrasse 42. ✆ **030/8-83-81-81.** S-Bahn: Savignyplatz.

**Harmel's** Most of Harmel's inventory was gathered in England and France, a commentary on the relative scarcity of genuine German antiques because of wartime bombing. The carefully chosen collection stresses furniture, jewelry, and accessories from the Victorian and Edwardian eras. Damaschkestrasse 24. ✆ **030/3-24-22-92.** U-Bahn: Adenauerplatz.

**Kunstsalon** Don't expect everything in this shop to be tasteful. Instead, you'll find the kind of rococo art objects that Liberace might have used in a stage set, or that a hip Berliner nightclub or brothel might buy as a means of creating instant kitsch. Everything is a cast-off from previous productions of the Komische Oper (Comic Opera), including both the stage props and the costumes. Come here for the wigs, gowns, and waistcoats that clothed the partyers during *The Merry Widow,* the candelabra that lit up Violetta when she died in *Traviata,* and the associated trash and treasures that evoke smiles from virtually anyone who understands their origin. The store also sells CDs, posters, and reproductions of rare portraits of Garbo, Dietrich, and Charlie Chaplin with Pola Negri during a holiday they enjoyed at the nearby Adlon Hotel in 1929. Unter den Linden 41. ✆ **030/20-45-02-03.** S-Bahn: Under den Linden.

**L. & M. Lee** This is one of several sophisticated antiques stores on the Kurfürstendamm's eastern end. The inventory includes mostly German-made porcelain, silver, and glass from the early 20th century, and an assortment of 19th-century pieces from other European countries. Kurfürstendamm 32. ✆ **030/8-81-73-33.** U-Bahn: Kurfürstendamm.

**Stilbruch Antiquitäten & Schmuck** It's far from being the largest antique store in Berlin, but something about its dense inventories of Biedermeier-era furniture, tableware, and jewelry might appeal to your sense of schmaltz and nostalgia. Owner Margareta Wojcieszak makes sure that objects are beeswaxed or polished to a high sheen. Everything seems to evoke a story about other places, other priorities, and other eras. Bleibtreustrasse 49. ✆ **030/312-83-04.** S-Bahn: Savignyplatz.

## ART GALLERIES

**Galerie Brusberg** One of Germany's most visible and influential art galleries, Galerie Brusberg was established in 1958 by Dieter Brusberg. The gallery has handled the work of Max Ernst, Salvador Dalí, Paul Delvaux, Henri Laurens, Pablo Picasso, and René Magritte, plus German artists Altenbourg, Antes, and Klapheck. Long before unification, it promoted painters of the old Eastern bloc, notably Bernhard Heisig, Harald Metzkes, and Werner Töbke. No one will mind if you drop in just for a look. Kurfürstendamm 213. ✆ **030/8-82-76-82.** U-Bahn: Uhlandstrasse.

**Galerie Pels-Leusden and Villa Grisebach Auktionen** This building, constructed in the 1880s by architect Hans Grisebach as his private home, is a historic monument in its own right. Two floors are devoted to 19th- and 20th-century art, mainly German. Prices begin at around 100€ ($89.30) for the least expensive lithograph, and go much higher. The building also functions as headquarters and display area for an auction house. Sales are held every spring and fall. Fasanenstrasse 25. ✆ **030/8-85-91-50.** U-Bahn: Uhlandstrasse.

**Prüss & Ochs Gallery** This gallery's setting resembles a fortress from the Industrial Revolution. It's built of red brick that's accessible via a labyrinth of alleyways that lead in from one of the oldest and most historic streets in the neighborhood. Art exhibitions change regularly, but regardless of what the temporary venue is, it's likely to be as offbeat and iconoclastic as the arts scene in Berlin itself. The company's main branch is in arts-conscious Cologne; this one gives the sense of exploring the artistic frontiers of Berlin, with special emphasis on counterculture art that's being produced in Asia and the Balkans. Sophienstrasse 18. ✆ **030/28391-387.** U-Bahn: Weinmeisterstrasse.

## BOOKSHOPS

This literate and culture-conscious city boasts lots of bookshops catering to a multilingual clientele. For English and American literature and recent periodicals, go to the **British Bookshop,** Mauerstrasse 83–84 (✆ **030/2-38-46-80;** U-Bahn: Stadtmitte). An outfit richly stocked with works from German publishing houses is **Literaturhaus Berlin,** Fasanenstrasse 23 (✆ **030/8-87-28-60;** U-Bahn: Uhlandstrasse). The leading gay bookstore of Berlin, containing both erotica and upscale literature in several different languages, is **Prince Eisenherz,** Bleibtreustrasse 52 (✆ **030/3-13-99-36;** S-Bahn: Savignyplatz).

## CHINA & PORCELAIN

**KPM** This prestigious emporium was founded in 1763, when Frederick the Great invested his personal funds in a lackluster porcelain factory, elevated it to royal status, and gave it a new name: **Königliche Porzellan-Manufaktur (Royal Porcelain Factory).** It was Prussia's answer to Meissen in Saxony. Since then, the factory has become world-famous for its artistry and delicacy. Each exquisite, hand-painted, hand-decorated item is carefully packed for shipment to virtually anywhere in the world. Patterns are based for the most part on traditional 18th- and 19th-century designs. All objects carry a distinctive official signature, an imperial orb, and the letters KPM. There's also an array of high-quality trinkets for visitors.

You can also visit the **factory** itself at Wegelystrasse 1 (✆ **030/39-00-90;** U-Bahn: Tiergarten). Guided tours let you look at the craftsmanship of the employees, and you can also buy pieces here. Tours are provided once a day from Monday to Thursday at 10am. The charge is 2.55€ ($2.30), which is applied to any purchase. Children under 16 are prohibited, as are video cameras and photography. Kurfürstendamm 27 in the Kempinski Hotel Bristol. ✆ **030/88-67-21-10.** U-Bahn: Kurfürstendamm.

**Meissener Porzellan** This is one of the most famous porcelain outlets in Europe. It offers the finest array of exquisite Meissen dinner plates in Berlin, and also displays and sells sculptures and chandeliers. For information on a Meissen factory tour, see chapter 5. Kurfürstendamm 26A. ✆ **030/88-68-35-30.** U-Bahn: Kurfürstendamm.

**Rosenthal** Head here for contemporary Rosenthal designs from Bavaria. In addition to Rosenthal porcelain, you'll find Boda glassware and elegantly modern tableware. Kurfürstendamm 226. ✆ **030/8-85-63-40.** U-Bahn: Kurfürstendamm.

## *Finds* Treasures in the Barn District

At the very heart and soul of Berlin's fashion and art revival is the Scheulenviertel, or "barn district" (S-Bahn: Hackescher Markt). The name comes from a period in the 17th century when hay barns were built far from the city center for fear of fires. In time the city's growth overtook the area, and it became Berlin's Jewish quarter. For some reason, many of its oldest buildings survived World War II bombing assaults.

The remains of a grand 1909 shopping arcade—which occupies most of the block formed by Oranienburger, Rosenthaler, Grosse Hamburger Strasse, and Sophienstrasse—have been turned into a series of galleries, studios, and theaters. Worth a visit is **Tacheles,** Oranienburger Strasse 53–56 (✆ **030/282-61-85;** S-Bahn: Hackescher Markt), or "talking turkey" in Yiddish. It's an alternative arts center. One of the several cutting-edge shops in the immediate Hackesche Hofe neighborhood includes **Lisa D.,** Hackescher Hofe–Hof 4, Rosenthalerstrasse 40–41 (✆ **030/282-9061;** S-Bahn: Hackescher Markt), a sought-after designer whose women's clothing has been favored in Berlin and New York for a long time. Clothing includes a sophisticated multicolored mixture of sportswear, office wear, and evening wear, with an of-the-minute emphasis on stripes.

The more prestigious galleries are found along Auguststrasse. **Galerie Wohnmaschine,** Tucholskystrasse 34–36 (✆ **030/3087-20-15),** became the area's first gallery when it opened in 1988. Some of the best artists in the city are on exhibit here, most of them of a conceptual or minimalist bent. One of the most prestigious and respected of these galleries is viewed today as a pioneer that made its way eastward within a few weeks of reunification: **Eigen & Art Gerd Harry Lybke,** Auguststrasse 26 (✆ **030/28-31-002;** U-Bahn: Rosenthaler Platz; S-Bahn: Oranienburger Strasse). They represent a roster of artists that include, among others, Leo Rauch and Carsten Nicolai.

Other shopping highlights include **Tools & Gallery,** Rosenthaler Strasse 44–45 (✆ **030/2859-9343;** U-Bahn: Weinmeisterstrasse), which sells both formal and elegantly casual clothing for both sexes, including exclusive labels such as Givenchy, Balenciaga, and Kenzo. **Johanna Petzoldt,** Sophienstrasse 9 (✆ **030/282-6754;** U-Bahn: Weinmeisterstrasse), sells handcrafts from the old Erzebirg region, including wooden toys and assorted curiosities, such as scenes fitted into a matchbox.

## DEPARTMENT STORES

**Galeries Lafayette** Paris in Berlin is found at this modern department store, right off Friedrichstrasse, designed by Jean Nouvel with a spectacular interior. The opening of this store has made Friedrichstrasse, the "street of spies" in the Cold War era, one of the most fashionable shopping areas in Eastern Europe. Its French food department evokes what is meant by dying and going to heaven. Franzoesische Strasse 23. ✆ **030/2094-8000.** U-Bahn: Franzoesische Strasse.

**Kaufhaus des Westens (KaDeWe)** This huge luxury department store, known popularly as KaDeWe (pronounced kah-day-vay), was established some 90 years ago. It's best known for its sixth-floor food department, where more than 1,000 varieties of German sausages are displayed along with delicacies from all over the world. Sit-down counters are available. After fortifying yourself here, you can explore the six floors of merchandise. KaDeWe is more than a department store—one shopper called it a "collection of first-class specialty shops." Tauentzienstrasse 21. ✆ **030/2-12-10.** U-Bahn: Kurfürstendamm or Wittenbergplatz.

**Wertheim** This centrally located store is good for travel aids and general basics. It sells perfumes, clothing for the entire family, jewelry, electrical devices, household goods, photography supplies, and souvenirs. It also has a shoe-repair section. Shoppers can fuel up at a large restaurant with a grand view over half the city. Kurfürstendamm 231. ✆ **030/88-00-30.** U-Bahn: Kurfürstendamm.

## FASHION

**Anette Peterman** This shop is noteworthy because of its limited number of carefully chosen dresses, each of which is displayed, and priced, like an art object in its own right. Sheer, shimmering, and undeniably sexy, they're the kind of design that might be worn to dinner at a posh Schlosshotel in the country. Bleibtreustrasse 49. ✆ **030/323-2556.** S-Bahn: Savignyplatz.

**Bleibgrün** It's small, its fashionable, and it's sought after by well-dressed and well-heeled women from Berlin and its suburbs. And best of all, the staff is charming and helpful. Come here for access to things that are terribly chic and contemporary, including dresses by Jean-Paul Gaultier, Paul Smith, Marithé François Girbaud, and a handful of other currently fashionable trend-setters. Bleibtreustrasse 30. ✆ **030/885-0080.** S-Bahn: Savignyplatz.

**Bogner Zenker-Berlin** This three-story shop has sold garments to three generations of clients. Its selection of women's clothing includes everything from formal evening gowns to sportswear. Many of the items are made in Germany, Austria, or Italy. Kurfürstendamm 45. ✆ **030/8-81-10-00.** S-Bahn: Savignyplatz.

**Chaapeaux Hutmode Berlin** There are only about 10 hatmakers left in Berlin today, and of those 10, only two or three have earned the respect and patronage of the city's couture crowd. This is the most appealing of the lot and also the most whimsical. Andrea Curti, owner and designer, draws her inspirations from vintage fashion magazines, old movies, and anything that looked good on Greta Garbo. The result is an artfully arranged inventory of veiled, feathered, or minimalist hats. Come here with a sense of glamour, a sense of humor, a sense of theatricality, and some open-ended ideas about what makes you look good. Bleibtreustrasse 51. ✆ **030/312-09-13.** S-Bahn: Savignyplatz.

**Modenhaus Horn** Berlin is one of the world's most fashion-conscious cities, and here you'll see examples of what's *au courant* for chic women. Kurfürstendamm 213. ✆ **030/8-81-40-55.** U-Bahn: Kurfürstendamm.

**Sonia Rykiel** This stylish showcase is the only shop in Germany devoted exclusively to Ms. Rykiel, the successful French fashion mogul. She designed the store's interior herself. ***Beware:*** Even a Sonia Rykiel T-shirt is expensive. There's both a children's shop and a women's shop. Kurfürstendamm 186. ✆ **030/8-82-17-74** for women, or 030/882-28-85 for children. U-Bahn: Adenauerplatz.

**To Die For** Clothing here follows trends so obsessively that you're likely to find inventories configured exclusively in tones of gray, black, and apple green.

These examples are guaranteed to change before your visit, but unless you're relatively fit and in good shape, don't expect to find anything suitable. For any man or woman who's relatively thin, you might find whatever you need to assimilate yourself into many of Mitte's emerging bars and clubs. Neue Schönhauser Strasse 10. ✆ **030/28-38-68-34.** S-Bahn: Hackescher Platz.

**Triebel** This elegant store offers everything you might need for a weekend retreat at a private hunting lodge, such as clothing, shoes, boots, or sporting equipment. If you dream of looking like the lord of a Bavarian manor in a loden coat and feather-trimmed hat, or if you've been invited on a spontaneous fox-hunt, come here first. The inventory includes a selection of hunting rifles and shooting equipment. Schönwalder Strasse 12, Spandau. ✆ **030/3-35-50-01.** U-Bahn: Rathaus Spandau. S-Bahn: Spandau.

**Werner Scherer** The arrival of this upscale menswear emporium symbolized to some extent the rebirth of the Unter den Linden as a glamorous shopping destination. Set on the street level of the Adlon Hotel, it's the showplace of Munich-based designer Werner Scherer, who makes the kind of clothes that millionaires love to buy. Expect access to the best-made shirts we've ever seen, silk neckties, and curiosities that include bomber jackets crafted from a mixture of silk and linen, and buttery soft black leather coats. Despite its high prices, the shop does a roaring business with the glam crowd, many of whom wouldn't consider buying their shirts anywhere else. Unter den Linden 77. ✆ **030/22-67-98-93.** S-Bahn: Unter den Linden.

## JEWELRY

**Galerie Lalique** One of the more unusual jewelry stores in Berlin, this emporium stocks the original designs of about 50 German-based designers. Most pieces are modern interpretations, using diamonds and other precious stones. Even though the store's name is similar to that of the French glass designer, no crystal or glassware is sold here. Bleibtreustrasse 47. ✆ **030/8-81-97-62.** S-Bahn: Savignyplatz.

**Treykorn** This outlet displays the most avant-garde jewelry in Berlin. Owners Andreas and Sabine Treykorn provide a showcase for more than three dozen of the boldest and often most controversial jewelry artisans in the city. Although some pieces sell in the thousands, there are many more reasonable selections as well. Savignyplatz 13-Passage. ✆ **030/312-4275.** S-Bahn: Savignyplatz.

**Wurzbacher** Everything this small store sells is crafted on-site from either gold or platinum, often with accents of precious or semiprecious stones. Most designs are modern and streamlined. Some pieces are noteworthy for their heft. Most of the jewelry here is for women, although a scattering of rings, tie clips, and cuff links are for men. Kurfürstendamm 36. ✆ **030/8-83-38-92.** U-Bahn: Uhlandstrasse. S-Bahn: Savignyplatz.

## KITCHENWARE

**VMF** Its inventory is a restaurant owner's fantasy, with appealing kitchen gadgets that cooks will love. Be warned that most appliances here are incompatible with North American electric current. But if you're interested in glassware (from Nachtmann and Eich), stoneware, kitchen cutlery, or Hummel and Goebel porcelain figurines, you'll find this place fascinating. Kurfürstendamm 229. ✆ **030/8-82-39-41.** U-Bahn: Kurfürstendamm.

## MARKETS

**Antik & Flohmarkt** You might want to check out the finds at this flea market in the S-Bahn station. Some 60 vendors try to tempt buyers with assorted bric-a-brac, including brassware and World War II mementos. Friedrichstrasse S-Bahn station, Berlin-Mitte. ✆ **030/2-08-26-45.** U-Bahn/S-Bahn: Friedrichstrasse.

**Berliner Trödelmarkt** This flea market lies near the corner of the Bachstrasse and the Strasse des 17 Juni, at the western edge of the Tiergarten, adjacent to the Tiergarten S-Bahn station. It's the favorite weekend shopping spot of countless Berliners, who come here to find an appropriate piece of nostalgia, a battered semi-antique, or used clothing. The market is held every Saturday and Sunday 10am to 5pm. Strasse des 17 Juni. ✆ **030/26-55-00-96.** S-Bahn: Tiergarten.

## MILITARY FIGURES

**Berliner Zinnfiguren** A mecca for collectors since 1934, this shop carries an impressive inventory of German-language books on military history and more than 10,000 different pewter figurines of soldiers from many different imperial armies, up to the Franco-Prussian War of 1870. Also included are hand-painted models of Roman and ancient Greek foot soldiers. Flat, hand-painted pewter figures are sold only in sets of 12 or more and cost from 80€ to 150€ ($71.45–$133.95); fully detailed depictions of Prussian soldiers from the 1870s can range as high as 130€ to 160€ ($116.10–$142.90) each, or even 1,000€ ($893) for special pieces. Knesebeckstrasse 88. ✆ **030/315-700-0.** S-Bahn: Savignyplatz.

## MUSIC

**Musik Riedel** Most of the professional musicians of Berlin have a working familiarity with the layout of this well-established store, as it's been selling musical instruments and sheet music since 1910. Regardless of how esoteric, you're likely to find the score to whatever it is that interests you—sometimes in used folios that have some historic interest in their own right. They also have a good selection of CDs. Uhlandstrasse 38. ✆ **030/882-7395.** U-Bahn: Uhlandstrasse.

## PERFUME

**Harry Lehmann** This is the kind of shop where German mothers and grandmothers might have bought their perfume between the two world wars. Don't expect a standardized list of the big names you'd find at a duty-free airport shop. Most scents here are family recipes, distilled from flowers, grasses, and leaves. The reasonable prices might surprise you—10g (.35 oz.) for as little as 3€ ($2.70). Coming here is a cheap and amusing way to experience the scents of a Prussian spring. Kantstrasse 106. ✆ **030/3-24-35-82.** U-Bahn: Wildersdorferstrasse.

## PUNK MEMORABILIA

**Kaufhaus Schrill** Few other stores mingle a sense of junkiness and kitsch with such artful abandon. Its stocks would gladden any punk-rocker's heart, especially if he or she were on the lookout for Elvis-era memorabilia, hair barrettes that glow in the dark, and jewelry that might appeal to Courtney Love for her date with a group of bikers. Don't come here expecting anything tasteful—that isn't its style. Partly because of that, and partly because the place evokes a vivid sense of the long-ago rebelliousness of the '60s, the place is something of an icon for disaffected, or counterculture, youth. Bleibtreustrasse 46. ✆ **030/882-40-48.** S-Bahn: Savignyplatz.

## SCULPTURE

**Gipsformerei der Staatlichen Museen Preussischer Kulturbesitz (Plaster Works of the State Museums of Prussia)** This company has duplicated the world's great sculptures as plaster casts since 1819. Today, there's an inventory of more than 6,500 of them, everything from busts of Queen Nefertiti to a faithful reproduction of the Farnese Bull. Prices begin at 12.80€ ($11.45). Objects can be crated and shipped around the world. Sophie-Charlotte-Strasse 17. ✆ **030/3267690.** S-Bahn: Westend.

## SHOPPING ARCADES

One of the many surprising aspects of the rebuilt and redesigned Postsdamer Platz is the **Potsdamer Platz Arkaden** (U-Bahn/S-Bahn: Potsdamer Platz), one of the most comprehensive shopping malls in Berlin. In a deliberate rejoinder to more outdated Ku'damm malls, such as the Europa Center, it contains at least 100 shops, with more being added all the time, scattered over three levels. Lots of the stores offer cost-cutting clothing and housewares, but two whose inventories are attractive to foreign short-term visitors include **The Museum Company** (✆ **030/25-29-69-21**), which sells high-quality reproductions of the ancient Greek, Roman, and Egyptian sculptures and jewelry sold in Berlin's museums, and **La Bottega de Mamma Ro** (✆ **030/25-29-63-68**), which specializes in Tuscan pottery, linens, table settings, and kitchenware, much of it in bright Mediterranean colors.

# 9 Berlin After Dark

In Berlin, nightlife runs around the clock, and there's plenty to do at any time. There are at least three magazines that list happenings in the city. The English-language monthly, ***Checkpoint Berlin,*** is available for free at hotel reception desks and tourist offices and sold at news kiosks. The German-language ***Berlin Programm*** is available at newsstands. The most detailed listings are found in ***zitty,*** a biweekly publication in German.

Berlin is famous not only for its opera, classical music, and theater, but also for its cabaret and nightclub entertainment. If you'd like to arrange tickets from America for shows and entertainment in Berlin, contact **Global Tickets,** (✆ **800/223-6108** or 212/398-0154; fax 212/302-4251; www.globaltickets.com). This company can mail actual tickets to your home in most cases or leave tickets at the box office for you. There's a 25% markup (more for opera and ballet) over the box office price, plus a U.S. handling charge of up to $8. Tickets are available for musicals, cabaret, opera, and dance.

## THE PERFORMING ARTS

### OPERA & CLASSICAL MUSIC

**Berliner Philharmonisches Orchester (Berlin Philharmonic Orchestra)** The Berlin Philharmonic, directed by Claudio Abbado, is one of the world's premier orchestras. Its home is the Philharmonie, noted for its excellent acoustics and unconventional interior design—the orchestra is in the middle of rising tiers of seats, and none of the 2,200 seats is more than 30m (100 ft.) from the podium. The box office is open Monday to Friday 3 to 6pm, Saturday and Sunday 11am to 2pm. You can't place orders by phone, but if you're staying in a first-class or deluxe hotel, the concierge can usually get seats for you. Herbert-von-Karajan-Strasse 1. ✆ **030/254-88-132.** Tickets 15.35€–51.10€ ($13.70–$45.65). S-Bahn: Potsdamer Platz.

### *Moments* The Love Parade

The **Love Parade** is the techno-rave street party to end all parties. During the second weekend of July, around 1 million (mostly) young people converge in the center of Berlin for 48 decidedly hedonistic hours. What began in 1988 as a DJ's birthday party with about 150 friends has grown into an immense corporate event that wreaks havoc on the rest of the city's usually impeccable organization (particularly the public transportation system).

The center of Berlin becomes awash with litter and good-natured debauchery. Because of the frenzied jiggling, gyrating, and very noisy good times, anyone wanting an even remotely peaceful weekend should follow the little old ladies and rock fans on the fast train out of town. The event starts off on Saturday afternoon, when a booming caravan of floats carries the best DJs in Europe from Ernst-Reuter-Platz to the Brandenburg Gate. If you want to see the procession, come early and grab as high a view as possible.

Everything imaginable is imbibed in high quantities, and every year serious worries are voiced over the deluge of urine in the Tiergarten, site of the evening celebrations. The entire city, in fact, transforms itself into a huge party. The BVG (public transport system) offers a 5.10€ ($4.55) "no limit" ticket to speed you from one rave to another. Traveling revelers should note that club prices skyrocket during the weekend.

Lots of fuss and bother or a really good time? It all depends on your point of view. This is a must for anybody with a love of synthesizers and a lot of steam to let off: The Love Parade has become an international fixture to rival Mardi Gras.

**Deutsche Oper Berlin** This opera company performs in Charlottenburg in one of the world's great opera houses, a notable example of modern theater architecture that seats 1,885. The company tackles Puccini favorites, Janácek rarities, or modern works, and has a complete Wagner repertoire. A ballet company performs once a week. Concerts, including Lieder evenings, are also presented on the opera stage. Bismarckstrasse 35. ✆ **030/3-43-84-01.** Tickets 15.35€–102.20€ ($13.70–$91.25). U-Bahn: Deutsche Oper and Bismarckstrasse.

**Deutsche Staatsoper (German State Opera)** The German State Opera performs in the Staatsoper Unter den Linden. This was for years the showcase of the opera scene of East Germany. Originally constructed in 1743 and destroyed in World War II, the house was rebuilt in the 1950s, reproducing as closely as possible the original designs of Georg Knobelsdorff. Some of the world's finest opera as well as concerts and ballet are presented here. The box office is open Monday to Friday 10am to 6pm, Saturday and Sunday noon to 6pm. The opera closes from mid-June to late August. Unter den Linden 7. ✆ **030/20-35-45-55.** Tickets, opera 11.25€–81.75€ ($10.05–$73); concerts 7.65€–61.30€ ($6.85–$54.75). U-Bahn: Französische Strasse. S-Bahn: Friedrichstrasse.

**Komische Oper Berlin** The Komische Oper has become one of the most highly regarded theater ensembles in Europe, presenting many avant-garde opera productions as well as ballet and musical theater. The box office is open Monday to Saturday 11am to 7pm. Behrensstrasse 55–57. ✆ **030/47-99-7400.** Tickets 8€–58€ ($7.15–$51.80). U-Bahn: Französische Strasse. S-Bahn: Friedrichstrasse or Unter den Linden.

**Konzerthaus Berlin** This 1821 building was created by Friedrich Schinkel. It offers two venues for classical concerts, the Grosser Konzertsaal for orchestra and the Kammermusiksaal for chamber music. Its organ recitals are considered the finest in Germany. Performances are often daring and innovative. The Deutsches Sinfonie-Orchester is also based here. In the Schauspielhaus, Gendarmenmarkt. ✆ **030/203-09-21-01.** Tickets 6€–80€ ($5.35–$71.45). U-Bahn: Französische Strasse.

### THEATER

Berlin has long been known for its theater. Even if you don't understand German, you may enjoy seeing a production of a familiar play or attending a musical.

Perhaps the most famous theater is the **Berliner Ensemble,** Am Bertolt-Brecht-Platz 1 (✆ **030/284-08-155;** U-Bahn/S-Bahn: Friedrichstrasse), founded by the late playwright Bertolt Brecht. His wife, Helene Weigel, played an important role in the theater's founding and was the ensemble's longtime director. Works by Brecht and other playwrights are presented here. Seats are reasonably priced.

The most important German-language theater in the country is **Schaubühne am Lehniner Platz,** Kurfürstendamm 153 (✆ **030/89-00-23;** U-Bahn: Adenauerplatz), at the east end of the Ku'damm, near Lehniner Platz. There are three different stages here.

Finally, **Theater des Westens,** located between the Berlin Zoo and the Ku'damm at Kantstrasse 12 (✆ **030/31-90-30;** U-Bahn/S-Bahn: Zoologischer Garten), specializes in plays, musical comedies, and the German equivalent of Broadway extravaganzas. The theater was built in 1896. Performances are held Tuesday to Saturday at 8pm and Sunday at 6pm. Ticket prices range from 16.35€–71.30€ ($14.60–$63.65).

## THE CLUB & MUSIC SCENE

### CABARET

Very popular among visitors to Berlin is the kind of nightspot depicted in the musical *Cabaret,* with floor-show patter and acts that make fun of the political and social scene.

**Die Stachelschweine** Since the beginning of the Cold War, the "Porcupine" has poked prickly fun at the German and American political scenes. The performance is delivered in rapid-fire German and evokes the legendary Berliner sense of satire, which can often be scathing in its humor. Although you need to understand German to really appreciate what goes on here, you'll still recognize some of the names (George W., Al Gore, and Hillary), and there's likely to be a deliberately corny selection of popular ditties ("Life is a cabaret, old chum") thrown in. Shows take place Tuesday to Friday at 7:30pm and Saturday at 6 and 9pm. The box office is open Tuesday to Friday 10am to 2pm and 3 to 7:30pm and Saturday 10am to 2pm and 3 to 8:45pm. It's closed in July. Tauentzienstrasse and Budapesterstrasse (in the basement of Europa Center). ✆ **030/2-61-47-95.** Cover 10.20€–20.45€ ($9.10–$18.25). U-Bahn: Kurfürstendamm.

**Wintergarten** The largest and most nostalgic Berlin cabaret, the Wintergarten offers a variety show every night, with magicians, clowns, jugglers, acrobats, and live music. The most expensive seats are on stage level, where tiny tables are available for simple suppers costing from 12.80€ to 24€

## Life Is a Cabaret in Berlin

Cabaret life in between-the-wars Berlin was a legend that inspired writers that included Christopher Isherwood, among many others. These emporiums of *schmaltz* have been reborn in the former East Berlin—though the satire might be a bit less biting than it was during the Weimar Republic. Today's cabaret shows might remind you of Broadway blockbusters, without much of the intimacy of the smoky and trenchant cellar revues of the 1930s. But for access to talent that includes multilingual comedians and singers, jugglers, acrobats, musicians, plenty of coyly expressed sexuality, and lots of costume changes, consider an evening at the **Friedrichstadt-Palast,** Friedrichstrasse 107 (✆ **030/23-26-23-26;** U-Bahn/S-Bahn: Friedrichstrasse). Although showtimes might vary with whatever revue is featured at the time of your visit, they tend to begin Tuesday to Saturday at 8pm, with additional performances every Saturday and Sunday at 4pm. The most visible and well-publicized competitor is **Winter Garten Variété,** Potsdamer Strasse 96 (✆ **030/230-88-230;** U-Bahn/S-Bahn: Potsdamer Platz). Shows, which are less high-tech than at the richly computerized Friedrichstadt-Palast, are usually presented Monday to Friday at 8pm, Saturday at 6 and 10pm, and Sunday at 6pm. Ticket prices are roughly equivalent at both venues, costing 30.15€ to 50.60€ ($26.90–$45.20), depending on the performance and the seat.

($11.45–$21.45). Balconies have conventional theater seats, but staff members pass frequently along the aisles selling drinks. Shows last around 2¼ hours each and begin Monday to Friday at 8pm, Sunday at 6pm, and Saturday at 6 and 10pm. Potsdamer Strasse 96. ✆ **030/23-08-82-30.** Cover Fri–Sat 30.15€–50.60€ ($26.90–$45.20), Sun–Thurs 17.90€–41.90€ ($16–$37.40) per person, depending on the seat. U-Bahn: Kurfürstenstrasse.

### DANCE CLUBS

**Big Eden** Everyone from Paul McCartney to Sylvester Stallone has danced here. This club accommodates some 1,000 dancers nightly on its huge dance floor, where top DJs play the latest international hits. The light effects and superstereo are impressive. There's a nightly happy hour. Kurfürstendamm 202. ✆ **030/8-82-61-20.** Cover 7€–10€ ($6.25–$8.95) Fri–Sat (includes 1 drink). Sun–Thurs 9pm–5am; Fri–Sat 9pm–6am. U-Bahn: Uhlandstrasse.

**Café Keese** This dance club caters to a more traditional clientele, most aged 35 to 40. Here women can ask the men to dance, and the management even reserves the right to kick out any male patron who turns down a request. The orchestra plays a lot of slow music, and the place is often jammed, especially on Saturday nights. The Keese sees itself as something of a matrimonial bureau and is always announcing statistics about the number of people who met on its premises and got married. Formal attire is requested. Open Tuesday to Thursday 8pm to3am, Friday to Saturday 8pm to 4am, Sunday to Monday 4pm to 1am. Bismarckstrasse 108. ✆ **030/3-12-91-11.** No cover, but a drink minimum of 5.10€ ($4.55) Fri and Sun, 7.15€ ($6.40) Sat. U-Bahn: Ernst-Reuther-Platz.

**Chip** Chip is an unusual and appealingly glossy dance club. It features a high-tech battery of accessories—laser-like lights, video clips, and a fog machine that adds a surreal mist to the crowded dance floor. Open Wednesday to Saturday 10pm to 4am. In the Berlin Hilton, Mohrenstrasse 30. ✆ **030/2-02-30.** Cover 8€ ($7.15). U-Bahn: Stadtmitte.

**Clärchen's Ballhaus** This place has been around since 1913, and it's schmaltzy enough to remind sentimental newcomers of the nostalgic old days. A renewed interest in ballroom dancing has kept it going. Live music from a dance band is the norm, with recorded music to fill in when the band takes a break. On Wednesday, women are encouraged to ask men to the dance floor. Open Tuesday, Wednesday, Friday, and Saturday 8:30pm to around 3am. Auguststrasse 24–25. ✆ **030/2-82-92-95.** Cover 5€ ($4.45). U-Bahn: Rosenthaler Platz. S-Bahn: Oranienburger Strasse.

**Far Out** Large and artfully drab, this industrial-looking disco plays danceable rock from the '70s to the '90s for hundreds of high-energy dancers. You'll see lots of students and artists, many dressed up in bizarre clothing. The place only really comes alive after midnight. Open Tuesday to Sunday 10pm to between 4 and 6am, depending on the crowd. Kurfürstendamm 156. ✆ **030/320-00-717.** Cover 5.10€–7.65€ ($4.55–$6.85). U-Bahn: Adenauerplatz.

**Metropole** On the outside, this club—originally built as a theater around 1906—boasts one of the great proto–Art Deco facades of Berlin. Inside, you'll find a replica of an ancient Egyptian temple, but with accessories that might have been designed for an early Hollywood stage set by Busby Berkeley. Most of the patrons are in their 20s, dancing the night away every Friday and Saturday 9pm until dawn. Don't confuse this place with the Kit Kat Club, an independent, more notorious venue that occupies the building's cellar (see "Gay & Lesbian Berlin," below). Nollendorfplatz 5, Schöneberg. ✆ **030/21-73-680.** Cover 7.65€ ($6.85). U-Bahn: Nollendorfplatz.

**SO36** The lines begin to form here about 30 minutes before the place even opens, but they move quickly as Berliner hipsters get into the spirit of one of the city's more witty and unconventional clubs. Its name derives from the postal code SO36 that applied to this district before World War II. Inside, you'll find two very large rooms, a stage, an ongoing rush of danceable music, and a scene that combines a senior prom in the high school gym with some of the more bizarre aspects of Berlin nightlife. Lots of women come here, both gay and straight, and there's a higher percentage of heterosexual men than you might have expected along this strip of bars in Kreuzberg. If you're lucky enough to be in town for the once-per-month Turkish drag night, you'll find one of the most amusing drag shows in Berlin, where Fatima the belly dancer is likely to be male, beguiling, and well-versed in the satirical aspects of life in a Turkish harem. The club is open most nights, based on an evolving schedule, 10:30pm to at least 4am. Oranienstrasse 190, Kreuzberg. ✆ **030/61-40-13-06.** Cover 5.10€–12.80€ ($4.55–$11.45). U-Bahn: Prinzenstrasse.

**Tresor Globus** One of Berlin's best techno venues, this club really packs them in. The building was once part of Globus Bank; downstairs there's a bunker-like atmosphere, with prison-type metal bars and harsh acoustics. The spacious dance floor upstairs has lighter house sounds. There's a bar in the back. In summer, tables are placed outside, and food is served. The club is open from 10pm Wednesday and from 11pm Friday to Sunday. Leipzigerstrasse 8. ✆ **030/2-29-06-11.** Cover 5.10€–12.80€ ($4.55–$11.45); 2.55€ ($2.30) on Wed only. U-Bahn: Mohrenstrasse.

## LIVE MUSIC

**A Trane** This small and smoky jazz house is an excellent choice for either beginning or ending an evening of bar-hopping in the neighborhood. It features musicians from all over the world. It's open Monday to Thursday 8pm to 4am, Friday and Saturday 9pm to 4am. Bleibtreustrasse 1. ✆ **030/3-13-25-50.** Cover 7.65€–15.35€ ($6.85–$13.70). Music begins around 10pm. S-Bahn: Savignyplatz.

**Knaack-Klub** This four-story club features a live-music venue, two floors of dancing, and a games floor. There are usually four live rock shows a week, with a fairly even split between German and international touring bands. Show days vary. There's dancing on Wednesday, Friday, and Saturday nights. Hours are Monday to Friday 10pm to 4am, Saturday and Sunday 10pm to 7am. Greifwalderstrasse 224. ✆ **030/4-42-70-60.** Cover 2.55€–5.10€ ($2.30–$4.55). S-Bahn: Alexanderplatz.

**Oxymoron** This is a good example of Berlin's newest crop of hyper-trendy, high-visibility hangouts where the food is served almost as an afterthought to an exhibitionistic/voyeuristic scene that can be a lot of fun and in some cases, intriguing. The setting is a high-ceilinged room with old-fashioned proportions and enough battered kitsch to remind you of a turn-of-the-century coffeehouse in Franz-Josef's Vienna. Local wits refer to it as a *Gesamtkunstwerk*—a self-obsessed, self-sustaining work of art that might have been appreciated by Wagner. Most nights after around 11pm, a slightly claustrophobic, much-used annex room—all black with ghostly flares of neon—opens for business as a disco, usually with a clientele that's about 75% hetero and 100% iconoclastic. If live bands appear at all, it will usually be on a Thursday. Open daily 11am to 3am. In the courtyard of the complex at Rosenthaler Strasse 40–41. ✆ **030/283-91-88-6.** Cover 5€–10€ ($4.45–$8.95). S-Bahn: Hackescher Markt.

**Quasimodo** This is the top Berlin jazz club. Although many different styles of music are offered here, including rock and Latin, jazz is the focus. Local acts are featured on Tuesday and Wednesday, when admission is free. Summer visitors should check out the "Jazz in July" festival. The club is open Tuesday to Saturday 9pm to 3am, with shows beginning at 10pm. Kantstrasse 12A. ✆ **030/3-12-80-86.** Cover 5€–20€ ($4.45–$17.85). U-Bahn: Zoologischer Garten.

**Wild at Heart** This club, with its kitschy knickknacks, colored lights, and wine-red walls, is dedicated to the rowdier side of rock. Hard-core punk, rock, and rockabilly bands from Germany and elsewhere are featured. Live performances take place Wednesday to Saturday nights. It's open Monday to Friday 8pm to 4am, Saturday and Sunday 8pm to 10am (yes, you may miss breakfast). Wienerstrasse 20. ✆ **030/6-11-70-10.** Cover 4€ ($3.55) for concerts only. U-Bahn: Görlitzer Bahnhof.

## DRAG SHOWS

**Chez Nous** The famous show at Chez Nous is played to an essentially straight crowd in a mock Louis XIV setting. Some of the world's best drag show acts appear here, from a sultry, boa-draped star from Rio de Janeiro to a drag queen who looks like a gun moll from the 1940s. Shows are nightly at 8:30 and 11pm. Marburgerstrasse 14. ✆ **030/2-13-18-10.** Cover 35€ ($31.25), which includes 1st drink. U-Bahn: Wittenbergplatz.

**La Vie en Rose** This club offers a highly polished, Vegas-style revue to a straight clientele, often businessmen. This is where "Barbra," "Dolly," and "Judy" are likely to appear. The box office is open daily 10am to 11pm. Shows start at 9pm Sunday to Thursday and at 10pm on Friday and Saturday. Europa Center. ✆ **030/3-23-60-06.** Cover 35€ ($31.25). U-Bahn: Zoologischer Garten.

## GAY & LESBIAN BERLIN

Traditionally, lesbian and gay life centered around the **Nollendorfplatz** (U-Bahn: Nollendorfplatz), the so-called "Pink Village." There is a history of homosexuality here at the **Schwules Museum,** Mehringdamm 61 (✆ **030/693-11-72**), open Wednesday to Monday from 2 to 6pm. Admission is 4€ ($3.55) adults, 2.10€ ($1.90) students. The **State-Supported Spinnboden-Lesbenarchiv,** Anklamerstrasse 38 (✆ **030/448-58-48**), caters to all sorts of lesbian cultural events. **Man-o-Meter,** Motzstrasse 5 (off Nollendorfplatz) (✆ **030/216-80-08**), is a gay information center.

Today, Motzstrasse is the location of many gay and lesbian bars. A trio of popular gay bars, **Tom's,** the **Prinz-Knecht,** and the **Knast Bar,** are sometimes referred to as "the Bermuda Triangle."

In the latter half of June, the **Lesbisch-Schwules Stadtfest** (Lesbian & Gay Men's Street Fair) takes place at Nollendorfplatz. This is topped in size, though not in exuberance, the last week in June by the **Christopher Street Day** parade, when 200,000 people congregate to have fun and drop inhibitions.

**Begine Café Bistro Bar Exklusiv für Frauen** This is a center for feminists and one of Berlin's best places for women to meet other women. It has a changing array of art exhibitions, and features poetry readings, German-language discussions, lectures, and other social events. Call in advance for the schedule. The premises are occasionally transformed into a disco. Potsdamerstrasse 139. ✆ **030/215-43-25.** No cover. Mon–Sat 5pm–1am. U-Bahn: Bulowstrasse.

**Connection Disco** Other discos occasionally challenge its entrenched grip on gay nightlife in Berlin, but somehow Connections continues to endure as an after-dark staple. It's very large, with two floors and a network of independently operated shops and specialty bars. Come here to dance to techno and trance music, but know in advance that this place is proud of the darkened labyrinth of cellar rooms it maintains for trysts—management cites them as the largest network of back rooms in Berlin. It's open Friday and Saturday from 11pm to 4am. Fuggerstrasse 31–33. ✆ **030/218-1432.** Cover 7€ ($6.25). U-Bahn: Wittenbergplatz.

**Kit Kat Klub** In Liza Minnelli's cinema version of *Cabaret,* Sally Bowles was an entertainer at the Kit Kat Club. Today's incarnation of that fictional club presents far more than dominatrix-style singers with hearts of gold. You'll check most of your clothes at the door (retain your shoes), and enter an ultra-permissive lounge, bar, and disco where Mr. or Ms. Right will probably show you all their charms on the first date. Tuesday, Wednesday, Friday, and Saturday, are for heterosexuals; Thursday and Sunday are all-gay and all-male. On those nights, clients must enter between 9 and 11pm, after which the doors are locked to newcomers, and the partying continues until much later. In the basement of the Metropole, Nollendorfplatz 5, Schöneberg. ✆ **030/21-73-680.** Cover 10€–14€ ($8.95–$12.50). U-Bahn: Nollendorfplatz.

**Kumpelnest 3000** Gay or straight, you're welcome here. All that's asked is that you enjoy a kinky good time in what used to be a brothel. This crowded and chaotic place is really a bar now, but there's also dancing to disco classics. Berliners often show up here for early morning fun after they've exhausted the action at the other hot spots. Open daily 5pm to 5am, even later on weekends. Lützowstrasse 23. ✆ **030/2-61-69-18.** U-Bahn: Kurfürstenstrasse.

**Lenz die Bar** It's convivial, it attracts lots of neighborhood acquaintances, and at its best, it can be a lot of fun. Caipirinas are one of the enduringly popular drinks. Priced at 7€ ($6.25) each, they bring a bit of Brazilian samba to foggy Berlin on a cold dark night. It's open nightly 8pm to 4am. Eisenacherstrasse 3. ✆ **030/217-7820.** No cover. U-Bahn: Viktoria-Luise-Platz.

**Prinzknecht** It's large, brick-lined, and mobbed with ordinary guys who just happen to be gay, and who just happen to be involved in computers, media, the building trades, and show business. The combination can be unpretentious and a lot of fun, especially when frothy pink Hemingways are bought by friends for friends, and when the stories start getting raunchy. If you want a place that manages to be both high class and earthy, within walking distance of lots of other gay options, this might be appropriate. It's open daily 3pm to 3am. Fuggerstrasse 33. ✆ **030/23-62-74-44.** No cover. U-Bahn: Viktoria-Luise-Platz.

**SchwuZ** If you hadn't been warned in advance, you might not even know that this was a nightclub, hidden as it is behind the conventional-looking facade of the Café Sundström. You'll descend into a battered-looking warren of basement rooms, outfitted in a surreal combination of glossy stainless steel that alternates with structural beams and cinderblock. The mostly gay, mostly male, and mostly under 35-year-old crowd comes to dance the night away, every day 11pm until around 4am. There are two separate dance floors, one with cutting edge, the other with more traditional dance music. Mehringdamm 61, Berlin-Kreuzberg. ✆ **030/693-70-25.** Cover 4€–6€ ($3.55–$5.35). U-Bahn: Mehringdamm.

**Tom's Bar** Tom's becomes crowded after 11pm with young gay men. Most of the clients show up here in rugged-looking T-shirts, flannel, jeans, and/or black leather, evocative of a Tom of Finland drawing. Upstairs, the porno action is merely on the screen; downstairs it's real. Monday nights feature two-for-one drinks. There's a cover charge for special occasions only. Motzstrasse 19. ✆ **030/2-13-45-70.** Daily 10pm–6am. U-Bahn: Nollendorfplatz.

## THE BAR & CAFE SCENE

### BEER GARDENS & WINE CELLARS

**Historischer Weinkeller** This squat and unpretentious inn might be the site of one of your more interesting evenings in Berlin. The setting is a highly atmospheric vaulted cellar. In winter the staff performs the medieval ceremony of "burning the punch," during which a sugar cone is lighted in your punch. As it burns, you're supposed to make a wish. The ritual takes place three times a week on Wednesday, Friday, and Saturday between 11 and midnight. The punch, a kind of hot spiced wine, costs 4€ ($3.55) per glass. You can also order beer or one of more than 100 German wines, as well as full meals that cost 12.80€ to 30.40€ ($11.45–$27.15). (If you plan to dine, make reservations in advance.) During summer months, an outdoor rustic beer garden is open. Open daily noon to midnight. Alt-Pichelsdorf 32 (about 1.5km/1mile west of the Olympia-Stadion). ✆ **030/3-61-80-56.** Reservations required. U-Bahn: Olympia-Stadion.

**Joe's Wirthaus zum Löwen** This cozy pub in the city center is attractively decorated with traditional Teutonic accessories. Even in winter, when you're snug and warm inside, you get the feeling you're sitting out under the chestnut trees. The kitchen offers good plain German food, including Bavarian specialties and some Italian dishes. Open daily 11am to 1am; the best time to come here is 7pm to midnight. Hardenbergstrasse 29 (opposite the Kaiser Wilhelm Memorial Church). ✆ **030/2-62-10-20.** U-Bahn: Zoologischer Garten.

**Loretta im Garten (Pupasch)** This surprisingly rustic indoor/outdoor beer garden is large, sometimes rowdy, and very German. It's outfitted with durable wooden banquettes, battered accessories, a large outdoor area, and a children's play area with its own Ferris wheel. Menu items include platters of sausage with sauerkraut and potatoes, spareribs, and stuffed baked potatoes. There's no live music; this a place for talk, gossip, and beer drinking. Many locals also come here for lunch. It's open April to early October only, daily 11am to 3am. Lietzenburgerstrasse 89. ✆ **030/8-82-33-54.** U-Bahn: Uhlandstrasse.

## THE BEST BARS

**Bar am Lützowplatz** Many hip locals cite this as their favorite bar, partly because it manages to be beautiful, chic, breezy, and artsy, and partly because it provides a concentrated kind of conviviality within a neighborhood that otherwise is prosperous but just a bit staid. Known as one the longest and narrowest bars in Berlin, it presents a flattering and almost reverential portrait of Mao-Tse-Tung as its visual focal point, the humor of which cannot be lost on the devoted capitalists and *bons vivants* who come here to see, be seen, and flirt. It's open daily 3pm until 4am. Lützowplatz 7. ✆ **030/26-26-807.** U-Bahn: Nollendorferplatz.

**Greenwich Bar—a.k.a. Cookie's** Its decor evokes the body of the Michelin Guide's animated tire, because of the foam-padded bands of florescent green Naugahyde that surround the room. That, along with built-in rows of bubbling aquariums and the refusal of management to post a sign identifying the location of this very in spot, create an iconoclastic setting where about 30% of the clients are openly gay and the remainder mysteriously undefined. It's open daily 6pm to 6am, serving stiff, party-colored drinks and martinis priced at from 5.10€ ($4.55) each. Recorded music plays, usually focusing on soul, drum and bass, and house music. Gipstrasse 5. No phone. U-Bahn: Weinmeisterstrasse.

**Harry's New York Bar** Harry's is an aggressively stylized bar with minimalist decor, pop art, and photographs of all the American presidents. It's modeled after the famous watering hole, Harry's New York Bar, in Paris. Its drink menu is a monument to the oral traditions of the IBF (International Bar Flies) Society, and includes such favorites as "Mizner's Dream" (created in 1962 for the Boca Raton Hotel Club in Florida) and the 1964 classic, "The Petrifier" (ingredients unlisted), for two. The menu lists almost 200 drinks, as well as a limited selection of food. Open 24 hours a day, 7 days a week. In the Grand Hotel Esplanade, Lützowufer 15. ✆ **030/25-47-88-21.** U-Bahn: Nollendorfplatz, Wittenbergplatz, or Kurfürstenstrasse.

**Kurvenstar** One of the most quirky and famous offbeat bars in Hackescher Höfe celebrates an artfully tacky decor that elevates the worst of the decorative and plasticized excesses of the 1970s into an art form of the highest degree of kitsch. Come here for ideas on how to recycle everything you might have stashed within your attic. Also visit for a drink, priced at around 6.15€ ($5.50), a dialogue, perhaps a snack, but not a full meal. 1 Grossepraesidentumstrasse. ✆ **030/28-59-97-10.** U-Bahn: Hackescher Markt.

**Lore Berlin** This is the bar most often cited by hipsters as a watering hole that combines cutting-edge design, fabulous dance music, and a stimulating mix of clients from all branches of Berlin society. The setting is a long and narrow, eerily backlit bar area where theatrical lighting makes almost everyone look attractive. Most clients remain at the bar, talking, flirting, and gossiping about the new Berlin, except for the high-energy danceaholics. These migrate to a blackened semicellar, where the hulking remains of what was originally built in the 19th century as a coal-fired heating station add visual interest. Even the washrooms and washbasins here are worth a comment, designed like poured-concrete reinterpretations of ancient Roman aqueducts. Neue Schönhauser Strasse 20. ✆ **030/28-04-51-34.** U-Bahn: Weinmeisterstrasse.

**Newton Bar** There have been more reviews about Berlin's Newton Bar than virtually any other watering hole in town. You might be rejected at the door by a bouncer who disapproves of your sense of style. Here's what you'll get if you're admitted: a high-ceilinged, well-proportioned room that evokes 1960s modernism at its best and a deeply ingrained sense of the well-heeled and socially conscious *bourgeoisie* looking for like-minded people. It's condemned for its sense of *chicki-miki* (self-conscious chic) by clients of counterculture bars in less expensive neighborhoods. But regardless of how you feel, you can't help but be intrigued by a huge black-and-white mural that sweeps an entire runway of naked fashion models across your field of vision, and service rituals inspired by Old Prussia. Love it or hate it, it's hard to ignore the Newton Bar. It's open daily 10am till at least 2am. Tharlogginstrasse 57. ✆ **030/20-61-29-99.** U-Bahn: Stadtmitte.

**Reingold** This bar is elegant and chic, stretching along the length of a long and narrow room. The overall effect has been called "Manet meeting Hopper." An aquarium seems *de rigueur* for Berlin bars, but the one here is modest. The beautiful people descend nightly to see and be seen. The truly beautiful ones show up after midnight. Novalisstrasse 11. ✆ **030/2838-7676.** U-Bahn: Friedrichstrasse.

**Roses** It might have been known 30 years ago as a storefront selling food supplies to the neighborhood's *Hausfrauen,* but it's very different from that today. You'll find a claustrophobic pair of rooms whose level of kitsch has been elevated to an art form; flickering candles, lavish graffiti, a Jamaican Gastarbeiter selling cookies reputed to have been baked with hashish, and gay and straight clients who seem very, very hip to whatever is happening in Berlin's *Nacht-szene.* It's open nightly 10pm until at least 5am. Oranienstrasse 187. Kreuzberg. ✆ **030/615-6570.** U-Bahn: Kottosser Tor.

**Times Bar** The cozy and intimate Times Bar has a quiet charm reminiscent of a wood-paneled private library in someone's home. The bar is dedicated to the *Times* (of London), whose latest edition is often displayed in the window. Guests sit in leather-upholstered chairs and read English-language newspapers. Menu items range from lobster soup to ice cream. Open daily 11am to 2am. In the Savoy Hotel, Fasanenstrasse 9–10. ✆ **030/31-10-30.** U-Bahn: Zoologischer Garten.

## FINDING A *KNEIPE*

A *Kneipe* is a cozy rendezvous place, the equivalent of a Londoner's local pub. The typical Berliner has a favorite Kneipe for relaxing after work and visiting with friends. There are hundreds in Berlin. Here's a handful to get you started.

**Gaststätte Hoeck (Wilhelm Hoeck)** The oldest Kneipe in Charlottenburg (1892) still sports original wood panels with inlaid glass on the walls. It also has a brightly illuminated facade jammed with local beer slogans. You (and half of the neighborhood) can have a drink in the very rowdy, sometimes raucous bar area, where (among other oddities) a clown may be playing the harmonica. The separate dining room serves traditional food. More than a dozen kinds of beer are offered (if in doubt, just ask for our favorite, Pilsner Urquell), as well as wine by the glass. Main courses cost 5.50€ to 14€ ($4.90–$12.50); hot food is served Monday to Saturday 11am to 10:30pm. Regular hours, however, are 8am to midnight. Wilmersdorferstrasse 149. ✆ **030/3-41-81-74.** U-Bahn: Bismarckstrasse.

**Lutter und Wegner 1811** This place was named after a gastronomic and social landmark, Lutter und Wegner, a hangout for actors in the 19th century. You can have a drink in the stand-up bar, or make reservations in advance to dine. Try the local specialty, Königsberger Klopse, with potatoes and a fresh salad. We also recommend the wiener schnitzel or pot roast with horseradish and sekt. The wide selection of drinks ranges from single-malt Scottish whiskies to Italian grappas. Main courses range from 14€ to 22€ ($12.50–$19.65). The restaurant is open daily 6pm to midnight; the bar is open daily 6pm to 1:30am or even later, depending on business. In summer, you can sit on a terrace and observe the passing parade. Schlüstrasse 55. ✆ **030/8-81-34-40.** S-Bahn: Savignyplatz.

## CAFE LIFE

At its mid–19th century zenith, Berlin was famous for its cafes. Max Krell, an editor, once wrote: "Cafes were our homeland. They were the stock exchange of ideas, site of intellectual transactions, futures' market of poetic and artistic glory and defeat." They've changed with the times, but cafes are still going strong in Berlin—particularly, these days, in what used to be East Berlin. In the heart of the old East German capital is a complex of about 100 bars, shops, and restaurants, called *Die Hackenschen Höfe* (S-Bahn: Hackescher Markt). This stylish minimall attracts hip counterculture denizens who wander between galleries, boutiques, and fashionable cafes. It has become one of the most prominent places in the city to go drinking.

**Cafe Aedes** Tucked away within what were once small 19th-century factories, this is a trendy and convivial cafe with a counterculture clientele that's very, very hip to the changing face of Berlin and its cultural scene. The decor includes lots of shimmering glass and free-form concrete, and the clientele includes a mixed collection of merchants, artists, performers, writers, and business people. Whisky with soda costs 7€ ($6.25), platters of simple food range from 6€ to 11€ ($5.35–$9.80). Beef consommé, salmon steaks with mango sauce, pasta with tuna and fresh tomatoes, and all vegetarian salads are what it's all about—that and ongoing dialogues. Open daily 10am to midnight. Rosenthaler Strasse 40–41. ✆ **030/285-82-75.** U-Bahn: Weinmeisterstrasse.

**Café/Bistro Leysieffer** This cafe opened in the early 1980s in what used to be the Chinese embassy. Some of the embassy's ornate moldings and lighting fixtures are still in place; a pair of gilded lions still guards the entrance. On the street level is a pastry and candy shop, but you can climb the flight of stairs to a marble-and-wood-sheathed cafe with a balcony overlooking the busy Ku'damm. The elegant breakfast menu here features Parma ham, smoked salmon, freshly baked baguettes, French butter, and, to round it off, champagne. Meals range from 9.20€ to 15.35€ ($8.20–$13.70). Open daily 10am to 7pm. Kurfürstendamm 218. ✆ **030/8-85-74-80.** U-Bahn: Kurfürstendamm.

**Café Silberstein** From the outside, this place looks like an art gallery, but once inside, you'll see that it's an artsy cafe, one of Berlin's trendiest, with sushi, ambient music, and an ultra-hip clientele. This is one of the best places to enjoy "new Berlin" in the formerly grim eastern sector. Open Monday to Friday 10am to 4am and Saturday and Sunday 10am to 5am. Oranienburger Strasse 27. ✆ **030/2-81-20-95.** S-Bahn: Oranienburger Tor.

**Cafe Wintergarten in Literaturhaus Berlin** Set within a Tuscan-style brick villa that was built in 1885 1 block south of the Ku'damm, a few steps from the Käthe-Kollwitz-Museum, this cafe is part of a private foundation that's devoted to the promotion—through lectures and research—of German literature. In addition to a prestigious and respectable bookshop that fills the building's basement, it contains lecture halls, offices that have links to Germany's academic community, and exhibition space for temporary exhibitions that cost from 2.55€ to 4.15€ ($2.30–$3.70) to see. The best way to unlock the secrets of this place is by heading for the cafe and restaurant, whose tables fill two old-fashioned Berliner-style rooms and spill into a much sought-after garden during clement weather. If you're hungry, the cheerful, old-Berliner-style staff will serve platters of noodles with cheese, rigatoni with beef strips, Argentinian steaks with herbs and parslied potatoes, and cucumber and tuna salads. Open daily 9:30am to 1am. Fasanenstrasse 23. ✆ **030/882-54-14.** U-Bahn: Hohenzollernplatz or Spichernstrasse.

**Dachgarten** This cafe is installed in the dome of Germany's Parliament, the Reichstag. Sad to say, the food is hardly the city's finest, although we find the setting and panorama so overpowering we recommended a visit if only for coffee and pastry. If you are a customer here, you can also avoid the long lines waiting to enter the dome. The cafe was stylishly redesigned by Sir Norman Foster, and it looks like a modern art museum. Even the Reichstag Küchenchef admits most diners come for the view and not the continental menu. A waiter recently confided to us, "Come back in the morning for breakfast. We get the least complaints about the food then."

Platz der Republik, Tiergarten. ✆ **030/2262-9933.** Main courses cost from 21€ to 30.65€ ($18.75–$27.35), with fixed-price menus going for 52€ to 61.30€ ($46.45–$54.75). Open daily 9am to 2pm and 6:30pm to midnight. U-Bahn: Unter den Linden.

## A CASINO

**Spielbank Berlin** It's brassy, it sparkles with lots of chrome, and the staff is about as jaded as any you'll find in a city that's legendary for its jaded citizens. The setting is a high-ceilinged, scarlet affair that might remind you of an airport. The basement is devoted to slot machines; the upper floors (Casino Royale) to a battery of more sophisticated gambling devices that include roulette and baccarat. Men must wear a necktie for access to the Casino Royale, but not to the basement-level slot machines. The cover charge of 5.10€ ($4.55) is refunded in the form of a casino chip. There are no maximum bets—the amount you lose, or can bet on any one play, depends on your credit rating with the casino. The slot machines are accessible daily 11:30am to 3am; the rest of the complex is available for bets daily 2pm to 3am. I.D. in the form of a passport is required to enter the casino. This is really the only casino in Berlin: Its only competition is a simple and rather small facility within the Forum Hotel, on Alexanderplatz. Marlene Dietrich Platz 1 (Potsdamer Platz). ✆ **030/255-990.** Cover 4€ ($3.55). U-Bahn: Potsdamer Platz.

## 10 A Side Trip: Potsdam & Its Palaces ★★★

24km (15 miles) SW of Berlin, 140km (87 miles) NE of Leipzig

The best day trip from Berlin is to the baroque town of Potsdam on the Havel River. It's often been called Germany's Versailles. World attention focused on Potsdam July 17 to August 2, 1945, when the Potsdam Conference helped shape postwar Europe. The town has many historic sights, and was beautifully planned, with large parks and a beautiful chain of lakes formed by the river. The palaces and gardens of **Sans Souci Park,** which lies to the west of Potsdam's historic core, are the major attractions here. A mile northwest of Sans Souci is the **Neuer Garten** on the Heiliger See, which contains the **Schloss Cecilienhof.**

## ESSENTIALS

**GETTING THERE** **By Train** **Potsdam Hauptbahnhof** is on the major Deutsche Bundesbahn rail lines, with 29 daily connections to the rail stations in Berlin (23 min. to Bahnhof Zoo and 54 min. to Ostbahnhof). There are also 14 trains daily to and from Hannover (3–3½ hr.), and 15 daily trains to and from Nürnberg (6–6½ hr.). For rail information and schedules, call ✆ **1805/996633.**

Potsdam can also be reached by S-Bahn Lines S3, S4, and S7 from Berlin, connecting at Wannsee station with Lines R1, R3, and R4. Travel time on these lines from Berlin to Potsdam is 30 minutes. For more information, call **BVG Berlin** (✆ **030/19-449**).

**By Bus** **Verkehrsverbund Potsdam** provides regional bus service with frequent connections between Berlin and Potsdam at Wannsee station (bus 133) in Berlin. For travel information and schedules, call **BVG Berlin** (✆ **030/19-449**).

**By Car** Access is via the E30 Autobahn east and west or the E53 north and south. Allow about 30 minutes to drive here from Berlin.

**VISITOR INFORMATION** Contact **Potsdam–Information,** Friedrich Strasse 5 (✆ **0331/27-55-80**), open April to October, Monday to Friday 9am to 7pm, Saturday 10am to 6pm, and Sunday 10am to 4pm; November to March, Monday to Friday 9am to 6pm and Saturday and Sunday 10am to 2pm.

**GETTING AROUND** **By Public Transportation** Ask at the tourist office about a **Potsdam Billet,** costing 4.35€ ($3.90) and good for 24 hours on the city's public transportation system. In Potsdam, **bus A1,** leaving from the rail station, will deliver you to the Potsdam palaces. Call ✆ **0331/2-80-03-09** for more information.

**By Boat** Because the area around Potsdam is surrounded by water, boat tours in fair weather are a popular diversion. Call **Weisse Flotte Potsdam** at ✆ **0331/275-92-10** for more information.

**By Bicycle** You can rent a bicycle from **City Rad Potsdam,** at the Potsdam Hauptbahnhof (✆ **0331/619052**), but you can't ride your bike on the grounds of Sans Souci Park. The rental shop is open May to October, Monday to Friday 9am to 7pm, Saturday and Sunday 9am to 8pm. Bicycles rent for 11€ ($9.80) per day.

## EXPLORING THE PARKS & PALACES

A British air raid on April 14, 1945, destroyed much of the old city center, but the major attraction, Sans Souci Park (www.spsg.de/e_htdoc/F_sanp.html) and its palaces, survived.

**Neuer Garten** On Heiliger See, or "Holy Lake," in the northern part of Potsdam, lies the Neuer Garten. The nephew and successor to Frederick the Great, Frederick William II, had these gardens laid out. Set between the park and the palace, this lovely baroque garden is well maintained, and it's a delight to take a walk into it, enjoying the flowerbeds, the well-trimmed hedges and arbors, and the fountains in decorated basins. The tract of land was walled in during the 18th century so that the king and his consort could walk in peace without "peeping Toms" intruding on their privacy.

On Heiliger See, about a mile northwest of Sans Souci. ✆ **0331/2-31-41.** Free admission. Same hours as Sans Souci (see below). Bus: 695.

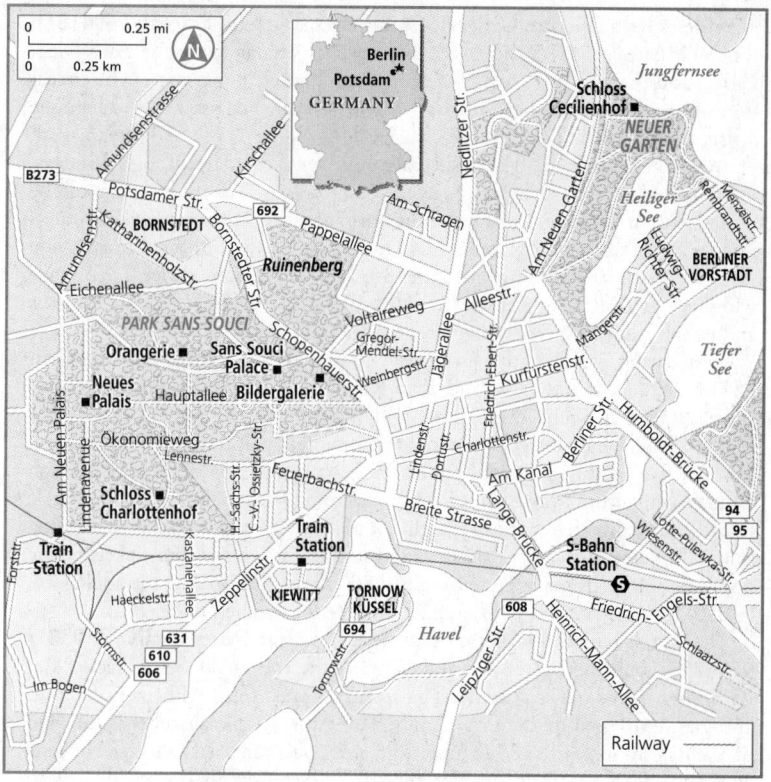


**Sans Souci Palace** ★★★ Sans Souci Park, with its palaces and gardens, was the work of many architects and sculptors. The park covers an area of about 1.6 km. sq. (1 square mile). Its premier attraction is the palace of Frederick I ("the Great"), **Sans Souci,** meaning "free from care." Frederick was one of the most liberal and farsighted of the Prussian monarchs. He was a great general, but he liked best to think of himself as an enlightened patron of the arts. Here he could get away from his duties, indulge his intellectual interests, and entertain his friend Voltaire. The style of the buildings he had constructed is called "Potsdam rococo," and is primarily the achievement of Georg Wenzeslaus von Knobelsdorff.

Sans Souci (or Sanssouci) Palace, with its terraces and gardens, was inaugurated in 1747. The long one-story building is crowned by a dome and flanked by two round pavilions. The elliptically shaped Marble Hall is the largest in the palace, but the music salon is the supreme example of the rococo style. A small bust of Voltaire commemorates Voltaire's sojourns here. Sans Souci Palace can only be visited with a guide. ***Be warned:*** it is best (especially in summer) to show up before noon to buy your tickets for the palace tour. At busy times, all the slots for the rest of the day can be completely filled by noon. The palace is open April to October, Tuesday to Sunday 9am to 5pm; November to March, Tuesday to Sunday 9am to 4pm; closed Mondays. Guided tours (in English) of the palace cost 8€ ($7.15) for adults; 5€ ($4.45) for children under 18 and students; free for children under 8.

**Bildergalerie (Picture Gallery),** Östlicher Lustgarden (✆ **0331/9694181**), was built between 1755 and 1763. Its facade is similar to that of Sans Souci Palace, and the interior is one of the most flamboyant in Germany. The collection of some 125 paintings features works by Italian Renaissance and baroque artists along with Dutch and Flemish masters. Concerts of the Potsdam Park Festival take place here. The Bildergalerie is open Tuesday through Sundays, only from May 15 to October 15, from 10am to 5pm. The Bildergalerie can be visited with or without a guide, and the crush of visitors here is nowhere near as intense as at Sans Souci Palace. Guided tours cost 3€ ($2.70) for adults; 2.50€ ($2.25) for students and people under 18; free for children under 8. Entrance without a guided tour costs 2€ ($1.80) for adults; 1.50€ ($1.35) for students and people under 18; free for children under 8.

West of the palace is the **Orangerie** (✆ **0331/969-4280**), built between 1851 and 1864. It was based on Italian Renaissance designs. Its purpose was to shelter southern plants during the cold months. In the central core is the Raphael Hall, which holds 47 copies of that master's paintings. In addition, you can visit five lavishly decorated salons. The Orangerie is open Tuesday through Sundays, only from May 15 to October 15, from 10am to 5pm. The Orangerie must be visited with a guide. Though not as severe a situation of overcrowding as you'll find at Sans Souci Palace, you should still try to get your tickets before noon, especially in midsummer. Guided tours cost 3€ ($2.70) for adults; 2€ ($1.80) for students and people under 18; free for children under 8.

The largest building in the park is the extravagant **Neues Palais** (✆ **0331/9694255**), built between 1763 and 1769, at the end of the Seven Years' War. Crowning the center is a dome. The rococo rooms, filled with paintings and antiques, were used by the royal family. The most notable chamber is the Hall of Shells, with its fossils and semiprecious stones. At the palace theater, concerts take place every year April to November. The Neues Palais is open April 1 to October 31, Saturday to Thursday from 9am to 5pm. During other months, it's open Saturday to Thursday from 9am to 4pm. It is always closed on Fridays. It charges 6€ ($5.35) for adults and 5€ ($4.45) for children (guided tour is included). The Neues Palais can be visited with or without a guide, and the crush of visitors isn't as intense as at Sans Souci. Showing up before noon here is not vital. Guided tours cost 6€ ($5.35) for adults; 5€ ($4.45) for students and people under 18; children under 8 enter free. Visits without tours cost 5€ ($4.45) for adults; 4€ ($3.55) for people under 18; children under 8 enter free.

***Note:*** During the summer months, when all four of the attractions are open, you can buy a combination ticket that incorporates guided access to all four of these monuments. It's valid for two days and costs 15€ ($13.40) for adults; 12€ ($10.70) for students and people under 18; free for children under 8.

Zur historischen Mühle. ✆ **0331/96-94-202.** Tues–Sun 9am–5pm. Tram: 94 or 96. Bus: 614, 631, or 632 to reach the sights in the park.

**Schloss Cecilienhof** This palace was completed in the style of an English country house. Kaiser Wilhelm II had it built between 1913 and 1917 for Crown Prince Wilhelm. The palace was occupied as a royal residence until March 1945, when the crown prince and his family fled to the West. In addition to the regular guided tour, offered in summer, there's a tour of the private rooms of Crown Prince Wilhelm and Princess Cecilie on the upper story. The tour takes place at 11am and 2pm and costs 1.55€ ($1.40) adults and 1€ (90¢) students and children. Note that you can lunch and spend the night here, if you wish.

Cecilienhof was the headquarters of the 1945 Potsdam Conference, attended by the heads of the allied powers, including Truman, Stalin, and Churchill. You can visit the studies of the various delegations and see the large round table, made in Moscow, where the actual agreement was signed.

In Neuer Garten. ✆ **0331/9-69-42-44.** Admission 8.20€ ($7.30) adults, 5.10€ ($4.55) students with guided tour (1€/90¢ less without); free for children under 6. Tues–Sun 9am–12:30pm and 5–7pm. Bus: 695.

**Schloss Charlottenhof** ★ This palace was built between 1826 and 1829 by Karl Friedrich Schinkel, Germany's greatest master of neoclassical architecture. He also designed most of the furniture inside. The nearby **Roman Baths** are on the north of the artificial lake known as *Maschinenteich* (Machine Pond). These baths, constructed between 1829 and 1835, were built strictly for the romantic love of antiquity and have no practical purpose. The schloss now closes in winter.

South of Okonomieweg. ✆ **0331/9-69-42-28.** Admission 5.10€ ($4.55) adults, 2.55€ ($2.30) children. Open year-round, Tues–Sun 10am–5pm. Tram: 96.

## WHERE TO STAY

**Astron Hotel Voltaire** ★★ This hotel, the best in Potsdam, is a radical renovation of the Brühlsche Palace, formerly a dour and crumbling relic built in 1732. Only the palace's baroque facade has been retained. The site belongs to the small Arkona chain. Rooms are scattered over three floors and, in almost every case, overlook the quiet, pleasant garden in back. Each unit comes with a small tiled bathroom with tub or shower. The rooms here are far better-furnished and more elegantly appointed than those within its closest rival, Schloss Cecilienhof (see below), although the latter has richer history. The décor is, in fact, so sophisticated here that the Astron accurately labels itself as "a designer hotel." Some of the accommodations are large enough to be used as a triple, with each guest having enough room to move about. Many families book into a suite here, although some of the regular rooms are large enough to accommodate an extra bed. The health club facilities are the best in Potsdam, and include a whirlpool, sauna, and solarium. An added feature is the roof terrace where you're treated to a panoramic view over Potsdam. The garden terrace is the venue for summer barbecues staged by the hotel.

Friedrich-Ebert-Strasse 88, 14467 Potsdam. ✆ **0331/2-31-70.** Fax 0331/2-31-71-00. www.astronhotels.com. 143 units. 121.26€ ($108.30) double; from 147€ ($131.25) suite. Rates include breakfast. AE, DC, MC, V. Parking 10.20€ ($9.10). Tram: 92. **Amenities:** Restaurant; lounge; bike rental; children's programs; room service; babysitting; laundry/dry cleaning. *In room:* A/C, TV, minibar, hair dryer, safe.

**relaxa Schlosshotel Cecileinhof** ★★ *Finds* Many visitors to Potsdam don't realize that they can stay in the palace where Truman and Churchill met the stone-faced Stalin during the 1945 Potsdam Conference. The hotel is better located than any other in Potsdam or Berlin for that matter, standing in the famous Neuer Garten, bordering a lake, lying about a 15-minute stroll from Sans Souci. The German government originally converted a residential wing of this former royal residence into one of the most charming country hotels and retreats in eastern Germany. Bedrooms are midsize to spacious and are traditionally furnished and well maintained, with immaculately-kept bathrooms, each with tub and shower combination. Residents can take their meals in the palace dining room, enjoying a first-class cuisine of both international and regional specialities.

Neuer Garten, Potsdam 14469. ✆ **0331/37050.** Fax 0331/292498. www.castle-cecilienhof.com/. 48 units. 150€–242€ ($133.95–$216.10) double; 282€–765€ ($251.85–$683.15) suite. AE, DC, MC, V. **Amenities:** Restaurant; bar; room service; dry-cleaning/laundry service; jogging track. *In room:* TV, minibar, hair dryer.

## WHERE TO DINE

**Juliette** ★ FRENCH (TRADITIONAL) At last, Potsdam has a world-class restaurant. The cozy and intimate Juliette lies in the center of the restored Holländisches Viertel (Dutch Quarter), 3 blocks north of the Altar Markt. You'll feel at home the moment you enter this restored old house, with its blazing fireplace, low ceilings, and tiny little windows. There is no more romantic choice in the city. Most of the excellent waiters are from France. Menu items include saddle of boar in cranberry sauce, fresh grilled fish, and some wonderful chicken dishes. All the desserts are freshly made on site.

Jägerstrasse 39. ✆ **0331/2701-791.** Reservations required. Main courses 19€–22€ ($16.95–$19.65). AE, MC, V. Daily noon–11pm. Tram 94 or 96.

**Villa Kellerman** ITALIAN One of the most talked-about restaurants in Potsdam is in an 1878 villa, once occupied by author Bernhardt Kellerman. The Italian cuisine here attracts a diverse clientele from finance and the arts. Your meal might include marinated carpaccio of sea wolf; ravioli stuffed with cheese, spinach, and herbs; John Dory in butter-and-caper sauce; or an array of veal and beef dishes. The wine list is mostly Italian.

Mangerstrasse 34–36. ✆ **0331/29-15-72.** Reservations recommended. Main courses 11€–21€ ($9.80–$18.75); fixed-price menu 42€ ($37.50). AE, DC, MC, V. Fri–Sun noon–midnight, Tues–Thurs 4–11pm. S-Bahn: Potsdam Stadt. Bus: 92 or 93.

# 5

# Saxony & Thuringia

Traveling in regions of the former East Germany today can still be an adventure. Once difficult to visit, famous cities are being restored and are inviting visitors from the west. These include: Dresden, destroyed during World War II and poignantly restored at least in part; Leipzig, where Johann Sebastian Bach spent most of his musical life as cantor (choirmaster) of St. Thomas Church; Meissen, famous for exquisite porcelain; and Weimar, still glowing from its designation at the millennium as European City of Culture. In addition, unspoiled scenery and medieval towns like Quedlinburg invite you to wander off the beaten track.

Since reunification, many visitors have come from around the world to explore the new political landscape and to honor the memory of the intellectual giants who once made East Germany their home—Goethe, Luther, Bach, Schiller, and Brecht, among others. Hotels are being built and tourist facilities developed. But the traveler should still take care in this rapidly changing terrain. The state of politics here is sometimes erratic and unpredictable, and the economy is weaker than in western Germany.

Eastern Germany today is a region in transition. Its long isolation also means that you'll find here some of Germany's most unspoiled countryside and untouched villages, where rural traditions that have disappeared from most of western Europe still linger. A visit can provide you with unforgettable new experiences and stories to tell your grandchildren.

Getting around eastern Germany is easier than ever. Some 1,600km (1,000 miles) of Autobahns and about 11,000km (7,000 miles) of secondary highways cut across the region. Train schedules are a bit smoother, because the German government has incorporated the former East German system into its vast national network.

## 1 Weimar ★★

260km (162 miles) SW of Berlin, 22km (14 miles) E of Erfurt

Weimar, a beautiful 1,000-year-old town on the edge of the Thuringian Forest, is an important destination for those interested in German history and culture. Unlike many cities in the former East Germany, Weimar still retains much of its old flavor: Many of its important historical monuments were spared from the bombings of World War II. Its atmospheric, narrow, winding streets, lined with houses with high-pitched gabled roofs, seem left over from the Middle Ages. A 19th-century writer called Weimar "one of the most walkable towns of Europe," and, today, it still fits into that category.

Weimar's history as a cultural center is centuries old. Lucas Cranach the Elder worked here in the 16th century. From 1708 to 1717, Bach was court organist. In 1775, the great Goethe came to reside at the court of Dowager Duchess Anna

**Impressions**

*Contrary to considered wisdom, Eastern Germany offers much more than just decaying housing blocks with tattooed boneheads scowling from the balconies.*

—Author Steenie Harvey

Amalia and her son, Charles Augustus II, and he attracted such notables as Herder and Schiller.

Later in the 19th century, Franz Liszt was musical director of the National Theater; under his auspices, Wagner's *Lohengrin* had its first performance. It was also in Weimar that the German national assembly met in February 1919, in the aftermath of World War I, to draw up the constitution for what was to be called the Weimar Republic.

## ESSENTIALS

**GETTING THERE** **By Train** **Weimar Hauptbahnhof** is on the major Deutsche Bundesbahn rail lines, which link Erfurt and Leipzig with Dresden. There are frequent daily connections in both directions. Trains from Berlin travel via Leipzig. For rail information and schedules, call ✆ **1805/996633.**

**By Bus** Regional buses to all parts of the city and the surrounding area are run by **Verkehrsgesellschaft Weimar** (✆ **03643/2-42-00**).

**By Car** Access is via the E40 Autobahn east and west.

**VISITOR INFORMATION** Head for Weimar's tourist agency, the **Tourist-Information Weimar,** Am Markt 10 (✆ **03643/2-40-00;** www.weimar.de). Year-round, the office is open Monday to Friday 10am to 6pm, Saturday 9:30am to 4pm, and Sunday 9:30am to 3pm.

## EXPLORING THE TOWN

Weimar enjoys a scenic location on the Ilm River, set against the backdrop of the Ettersberg and Vogtland hills. The city has many popular sights, but perhaps the best thing to do here is simply to wander about on foot. A walk at night through the old streets that once felt the footsteps of Goethe, Bach, Wagner, and Schiller is particularly rewarding.

The town's main square, called the **Marktplatz,** or market square, retains the old flavor of the city. Instead of breakfast at your hotel, visit one of the bakeries near the square and compose your own breakfast, the way many locals do. The daily produce market still takes place on the Marktplatz. The painter Lucas Cranach the Elder lived here during his last year, from 1552 to 1553. Today you can view the **Lucas Cranach the Elder House** from the outside, where it is richly decorated and bears a coat-of-arms of the Cranach family. There is a modern gallery inside the house but it is open only Thursday and Friday from noon to 8pm; Saturday 11am to 3pm.

For a midday break from sightseeing, we suggest a visit to Park an der Ilm or **Goethe Park,** flanking the river. Goethe himself actually landscaped this park. It sports numerous 18th-century pavilions and is the best place in Weimar for a picnic.

If you've had a little too much Schiller and Goethe, flee the inner city and escape to **Bauhaus Universität** on Marienstrasse, just across the footpath in

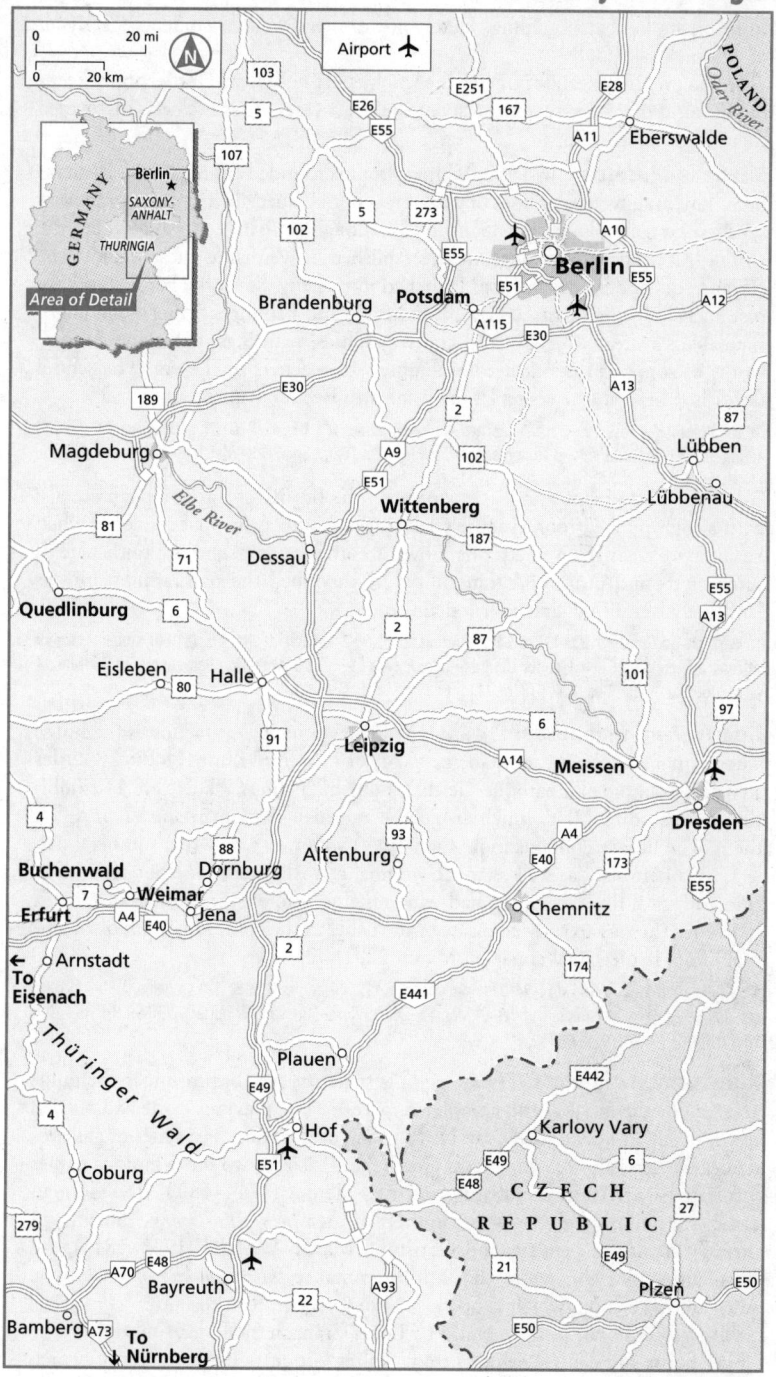
0 20 mi
0 20 km
N
Airport
GERMANY
Berlin
SAXONY-ANHALT
THURINGIA
Area of Detail
POLAND
Oder River
Eberswalde
Berlin
Brandenburg
Potsdam
Magdeburg
Elbe River
Wittenberg
Dessau
Lübben
Lübbenau
Quedlinburg
Eisleben
Halle
Leipzig
Meissen
Dresden
Buchenwald
Dornburg
Weimar
Erfurt
Jena
Altenburg
Chemnitz
Arnstadt
To Eisenach
Thüringer Wald
Plauen
Hof
Karlovy Vary
Coburg
CZECH REPUBLIC
Bayreuth
Plzeň
Bamberg
To Nürnberg

front of the Bauhaus building. Here you can meet Weimar students, nearly all of whom speak English.

In the evening, head for one of the smoky beer halls near **Herderplatz,** keeping in mind that Nietzsche, who spent the last 3 years of his life here, discovered them long before you.

**Bauhaus-Museum** In 1919, Walter Gropius founded his Staatliche Bauhaus here. This architectural school of design was noted especially for its program that synthesized technology, craftsmanship, and design aesthetics. It was to sweep the world. It is proper that a museum be established in Weimar as a testament to the elegance of Modernism that was launched in this city. From the Bauhaus school rose such towering artists as Klee, Kandinsky, and Feininger. The golden era of Bauhaus is recreated in arts and crafts, graphics, paintings, and representative works of some of the outstanding painters or teachers of the era. The school flourished here, in the center of town, next to Beethovenplatz, until 1925.

At Theaterplatz, across from the Deutsches Nationaltheater. ✆ **03643/546161.** Admission 3€ ($2.70) adults, 2€ ($1.80) children and students. Apr–Oct Tues–Sun 10am–6pm; Nov–Mar Tues–Sun 10am–4:30pm.

**Goethes Gartenhaus** ★★ In a park on the Ilm River stands a plain cottage with a high-pitched roof. Goethe selected this house as his first residence when he came to Weimar. Even after he moved to other quarters, he still came here in summer to find peace and tranquility. He described the park around him as "infinitely beautiful," and so it remains today.

Im Park an der Ilm. ✆ **03643/54-54-01.** Admission 2.50€ ($2.25) adults, 2€ ($1.80) students, senior citizens, and children 6–18. Free for children under 6. Mar 15–Oct 25 Wed–Mon 9am–6pm; Oct 26–Mar 14 Wed–Mon 9am–4pm. Bus: 1, 4, 6, 8, or 71.

**Goethe Nationalmuseum** ★★★ Weimar's principal attraction is the house where Johann Wolfgang von Goethe (1749–1832) lived from 1782 to 1832. It's a typical example of a baroque-German nobleman's house. There are 14 exhibition rooms, some pretty much as Goethe and his wife, Christiane Vulpius, left them. The library contains more than 5,000 volumes. The writer's mineral collection is here also, as well as much original art. Although Goethe's reputation rests today on his writing, he had wide-ranging interests, including an interest in science (he was an early advocate of the belief in the common origin of all animal life). He died in Weimar on March 22, 1832.

Am Frauenplan 1. ✆ **03643/54-54-01.** Admission 6€ ($5.35) adults, 4.50€ ($4) students, 1.50€ ($1.35) persons 6–18. Free for children under 6. Mar 15–Oct 25 Tues–Sun 9am–6pm; Oct 26–Mar 14 Tues–Sun 10am–4pm. Bus: 1, 4, 6, 8, or 71.

**Kunstsammlungen zu Weimar** This structure was begun under the guidance of Goethe in 1789 and completed in 1803. The previous castle had burned down in 1774; only a tower survived. In one of the wings is a series of galleries dedicated not only to Schiller and Goethe, but also to two other famous names associated with Weimar: Johann Gottfried Herder (1744–1803), the German critic and philosopher who was a pioneer of the *Sturm und Drang* ("Storm and Stress") literary movement, and Christoph Martin Wieland (1733–1813), the poet and critic who wrote the satirical romance *The Republic of Fools.* The museum has a shop, which is open April to October, 9am to 6pm.

The ground floor displays works by Lucas Cranach the Elder. On some of the upper floors you can see exhibits from Walter Gropius's Bauhaus school, which started in Weimar. The primary aim of this movement was to unify arts and crafts within the context of architecture. Its appeal derived from the changing

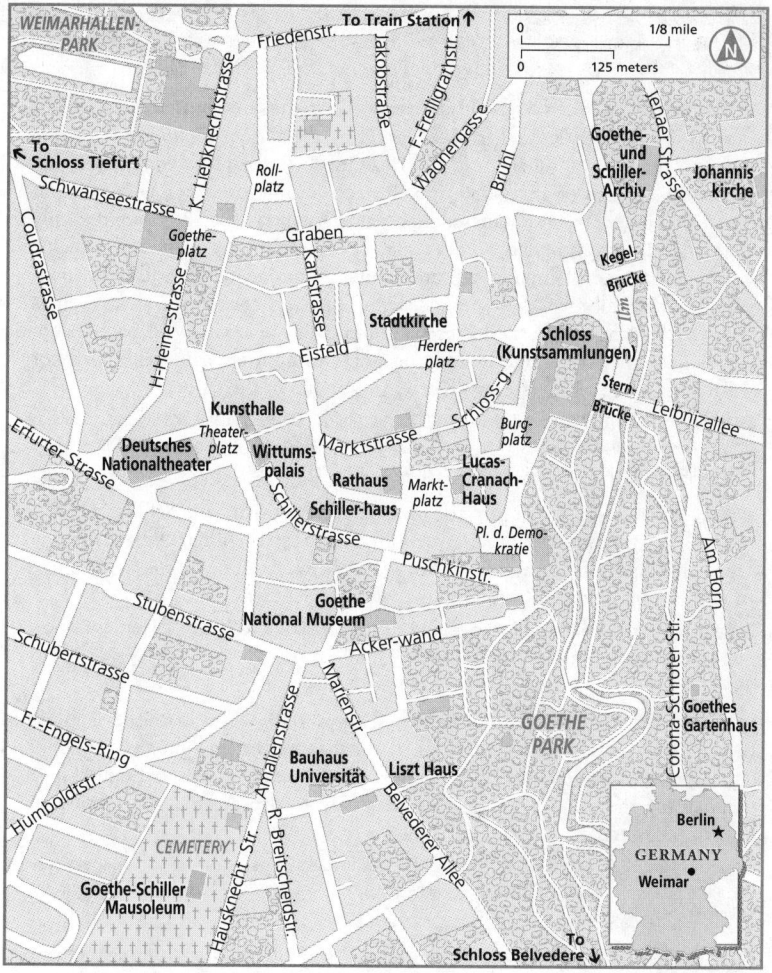


sensibilities of the Industrial Age, as well as from the need for inexpensive construction techniques in an era of rising costs and exploding demand for housing. Followers around the globe may have been impressed, but not the good people of Weimar. They "tolerated" Gropius's school until 1925, and then bombarded it in the press, until it finally moved to Dessau. There it stayed until the Nazis closed it in 1933, claiming it was a center of "Communist intellectualism."

Burgplatz 4. ✆ **03643/54-61-31.** Admission 2€ ($1.80) adults, 1.50€ ($1.35) children. Self-parking 1€ (90¢) hourly. Apr–Oct, Tues–Sun 9am–6pm; Nov–Mar, Tues–Sun 10am–4:30pm. Bus: 5.

**Liszt House** Franz Liszt (1811–86), the Hungarian composer and pianist, spent the last period of his life here. You'll find several mementos, both personal and musical, from the composer's life, including letters exchanged between Liszt and his son-in-law, as well as the piano at which he played and taught his pupils. The house was once the home for the royal gardeners of Weimar.

Marienstrasse 17. ✆ **03643/54-54-01.** Admission 2€ ($1.80) adults, 1.50€ ($1.35) students and children 6–18. Free for children under 6. May–Oct daily 9am–6pm; Nov–Apr daily 10am–4pm. Closed daily 1–2pm. Bus: 4, 6, 8, or 71.

**Neues Museum Weimar** This is eastern Germany's first museum devoted to modern art, an artistic field frowned upon by the former Communist regime with its more traditional (read 19th-century) tastes. The exhibitions are frequently changed or alternated, so you never know what you'll be viewing at any given time. The restored building was constructed in 1869 but radically overhauled to accommodate its new role. The museum was opened to coincide with the naming of Weimar as cultural capital of Europe in 1999. Its permanent exhibition includes works of American minimal and conceptual art as well as pieces by Italian painters and expressive works of the new "Wild painters" of Germany, as they are called. In addition, such major artists as Anselm Kiefer or Keith Haring are represented with extensive bodies of their work.

Weimarplatz 5. ✆ **03643/5460.** Admission 3€ ($2.70) adults, 2€ ($1.80) students and ages 17 and under. Apr–Oct Tues–Sun 10am–6pm, Dec–Mar Tues–Sun 10am–4:30pm. Located directly north of center, on the square adjoining Rathenauplatz. From the heart of town, Goetheplatz, walk north for ten minutes.

**Schillerhaus** ★★ After his friend Goethe, Friedrich von Schiller (1759–1805) is the greatest name in German literature. He lived here with his family from 1802 to 1805 and wrote his last works here, including *Wilhelm Tell.* The attic rooms have been furnished as they were in Schiller's day.

Schillerstrasse 9. ✆ **03643/54-54-01.** Admission 3.50€ ($3.15) adults, 2.50€ ($2.25) students and persons 6–18. Free for children under 6. Mid-Mar–October Wed–Mon 9am–6pm; Nov–mid-Mar Wed–Mon 9am–4pm. Bus: 1, 4, 6, 8, or 71.

**Schloss Belvedere (Château of Belvedere)** The baroque Schloss Belvedere was a favorite retreat of Anna Amalia and the "enlightened" Weimar set. It has an orangerie, along with the open-air theater and an English-style park. Inside the château are displays of dainty rococo art and a collection of historical coaches.

Belvederer Allee. ✆ **03643/54-61-31.** Admission 3€ ($2.70) adults, 2€ ($1.80) persons 6–18 and students; free for children under 6. Apr–Oct Tues–Sun 10am–6pm; closed Nov–Mar. Bus: 12. From Weimar, follow the Belvedereschlossallee south for 3km (2 miles).

**Schloss Tiefurt** This was formerly the site of another summer retreat of Duchess Anna Amalia. Guests today can wander through its pavilions and gardens. Coming here is a good excursion on a lovely day if you have extra time.

Schloss-Strasse, in Tiefurt.. ✆ **03643/54-54-01.** Admission 3.50€ ($3.15) adults, 2.50€ ($2.25) persons 6–18, students, and senior citizens. Free for children under 6. Mar 25–Oct 28 Tues–Sun 9am–6pm; off-season Tues–Sun 10am–4pm. Bus: 3 from Goetheplatz; Tiefurt is the last stop. Go east along Tiefurter Allee.

**Schlossmuseum** This is a special art museum that's often overlooked by the hurried visitor, but is appreciated by the art lover who cares to seek out its special treasures. Its collection of European art ranges from the Reformation period to the 20th century. The museum sprawls across three floors, with main works on the first floor, including paintings by Lucas Cranach. On the second floor is an exhibition of more German works, paintings done in the age of Goethe and various pieces of Romantic art. There is an exceptional collection of religious icons from the 19th and 20th centuries. In the graphic collection are exhibitions of the works of the great masters such as da Vinci, Dürer, or Rembrandt.

Burgplatz 4. ✆ **03643/546160.** Admission 4€ ($3.55) adults, 2.50€ ($2.25) students and persons under 18. Apr–Oct Tues–Sun 10am–6pm, Nov–Mar Tues–Sun 10am–4:30pm. From Markt, the market square in the town center, head east along Am Markt for 5 minutes.

### *Fun Fact* Goethe Gets a Touch-Up

The news out of Weimar is weird but true: Someone's been fiddling with Goethe's body. Around 30 years ago, the city's most famous corpse suffered the indignity of being dug up, loaded onto a cart, and pulled off to the nearby Goethe Museum. Why? Well, in the fall of 1970, shortly before the dirty deed was done, local authorities discovered that Goethe's sarcophagus had a broken lock. When they took a look inside, they saw that his corpse was in a bad state of decomposition. Weimar was an important weapon in East Germany's propaganda war against the cultural decadence of West Germany. Communist higher-ups decided that something had better be done soon or the great *Kulturstadt* (city of culture) would be shamed by its mistreatment of the great scribe's remains.

So the national poet and creator of Faust was removed from his comfortable resting place and brought to the museum, where the corpse's remaining fragments of flesh were removed by means of a process called "maceration." A special preserving agent was then applied to the bones to strengthen them. The laurel wreath around Goethe's head was likewise doused and strengthened.

Unfortunately, all did not run smoothly. The shroud Goethe was wearing was sent off for examination but, typically, got tangled up in bureaucratic red tape and didn't arrive back in Weimar in time for his reburial. It has since been kept hidden in the Schiller Museum (talk about dirty linen). The report outlining this skullduggery was only made public in 1999.

**Stadtkirche St. Peter und Paul** The origins of this church date from the founding of Weimar itself. The present building consists of three naves designed in a late Gothic style. Its most precious treasure is an altar painting begun by Lucas Cranach the Elder in the last year of his life and completed by his son.

Herderplatz 8 (follow Vorwerksgasse). ✆ **03643/85-15-18.** Free admission. Apr–Oct Mon–Sat 10am–noon and 2–4pm, Sun 11am–noon and 2–3pm; Nov–Mar Mon–Sat 11am–noon and 2–3pm, Sun 2–3pm. Bus: 1 or 7.

**Wittumspalais** If you follow Rittergasse to the end, you will come upon the 1767 Wittumspalais. This was once the residence of Dowager Duchess Anna Amalia, who presided over the German Enlightenment, which brought a stark rationalism to literature and the arts. The old ducal dower house is devoted to mementos of the movement.

Am Palais 3. ✆ **03643/ 54-54-01.** Admission 3.50€ ($3.15) adults, 2.50€ ($2.25) students, persons 6–18, and senior citizens, free for children under 6. Mar 15–Oct 25 Tues–Sun 9am–6pm; Oct 26–Mar 14 Tues–Sun 10am–4pm. Bus: 4, 6, or 8.

## MORE SIGHTS

In the **cemetery,** south of the town center, Am Posseckschen Garten, you can see the controversial **Denkmal der März Gefallenen,** a monument to the revolutionaries whose merciless and needless slaughter in 1919 (by government forces) so affected the ultra-liberal Gropius and his Bauhaus followers. But most interesting today is the **Goethe-Schiller Mausoleum,** once the family vault of the Weimar dynasty, where Goethe and Schiller, friends in life, lie side by side in death. It was built in 1825 through 1826 according to plans drawn up by Coudray, who consulted Goethe on the design and construction. Schiller was entombed here in 1827 and Goethe in 1832, both in oak coffins. Visiting hours are as follows: March to October Wednesday to Monday 9am to 1pm and 2 to 5pm; November through February, Wednesday to Monday 10am to 1pm and 2 to 4pm. Admission is free. A Russian-style **chapel** is on the south side of the mausoleum. It was built in 1859 for Maria Pavlovna, daughter-in-law of Duke Carl August.

**BUCHENWALD CONCENTRATION CAMP AND MEMORIAL SITE**

The Buchenwald bus (no. 6) from Weimar's Hauptbahnhof goes 6km (4 miles) northwest of Weimar to **Gedenkstätte Buchenwald** (✆ **03643/43-00;** www.buchenwald.de). It is estimated that a quarter of a million Jews, Slavs, gypsies, homosexuals, political opponents, prisoners of war, Jehovah's Witnesses, social misfits, criminals, and others were confined here from 1937 until the camp's liberation by the U.S. Army in 1945. Officially, Buchenwald was a work camp, so many fewer people were killed here than at other concentration camps.

Nonetheless, 56,000 people died in this camp; many, many thousands of others were sent on from here to other death camps; and a quarter of a million people, from more than 30 nations, suffered unspeakable pain as prisoners here. Furthermore, atrocities practiced in Buchenwald have made its very name synonymous with human perversity. Medical experiments on prisoners were common here, and prisoners did not, ironically, get nearly the amount of care and protection that animals in the SS men's zoo received. This is also the concentration camp from which famed author and Noble Peace Prize winner Elie Wiesel was liberated. (For more about his experiences at Buchenwald, read his bestselling book, *Night.*)

Buchenwald's sad history continued when Soviet occupation forces used the site as an internment camp from 1945 to 1950, where over 7,000 people died and were buried in mass graves.

Today, Buchenwald is a haunting sight. Only fragments of the camp have been preserved, as much of it has vanished by deliberate destruction and through the wear and tear of many years. The clock in the gate building reflects the time of the liberation by the U.S. Army in 1945. The gate has JEDEM DAS SEINE (to each his own) inscribed upon it: It is one of the only Nazi concentration camps whose gate was not inscribed with ARBEIT MACHT FREI (work will make you free). All but a few buildings have been replaced with eerie black rocks filling in the foundations (which you can still see) of old barracks and more. The storehouse (as well as some other buildings) still exists in its original form, and the museum inside reflects both the Soviet and the Nazi past of the camp.

A well-planned and -executed monument/memorial lies about 1km (.6 miles) from (closer to Weimar) the remnants of the camp itself, with its own parking lot. The monument has several facets (sculpture, bell tower, and so on) built over the graves of more than 3,000 Buchenwald victims.

You can visit Buchenwald May to September, Tuesday to Sunday 9:45am to 6pm; October to April, Tuesday to Sunday 8:45am to 5pm. Admission is free.

## SHOPPING

A visit to Weimar's antique stores offers a chance to buy porcelain, silver, crystal, and furniture that survived the devastation of World War II. The most interesting shops include **Antikitäten am Palais,** Schillerstrasse 22 (✆ **03643/59625**), and its immediate neighbor, **Kaiser Antikitäten,** Schillerstrasse 22 (same phone). Also appealing are **Antikitäten am Schloss,** Obereschlossgasse 2 (✆ **03643/51-29-93**), **Goethe-Antiquariat,** Marktstrasse 6 (✆ **03643/40-25-67**), selling books only; and **Thiersch Antikitäten,** Bräuhausgasse 15 (✆ **03643/40-25-40**).

## WHERE TO STAY

### EXPENSIVE

**Hilton Weimar** ★★★ Ironically, the credit for the excellence of this hotel's construction and the lavishness of its materials is due to the former East German government, which designed and built this hotel a few months before reunification. Now run by Hilton, it stands beside Goethe Park, a swath of greenery with posh residences and embassies left over from the Weimar Republic. The lobby is dramatic, with sun-flooded skylights and glass walls. Rooms are small but comfortable, and two are suitable for those with disabilities. The midsize to spacious bathrooms are the best in town, each with a tub-and-shower combination.

Belvederer Allee 25, 99425 Weimar. ✆ **800/445-8667** in the U.S. and Canada, or 03643/72-20. Fax 03643/72-27-41. www.hilton-weimar.de. 294 units. 125€–175€ ($111.65–$156.30) double; 350€–620€ ($312.55–$553.65) suite. AE, DC, MC, V. Parking 10€–12€ ($8.95–$10.70). Bus: 1. **Amenities:** 2 restaurants; bar; pool; health club; 2 saunas; room service; massage; babysitting; laundry. *In room:* A/C, TV, minibar, hair dryer, safe.

**Hotel Elephant, Weimar** ★★ The Elephant is Weimar's most famous hotel, although it's actually not quite as comfortable or well-accessorized as the Hilton (see above). Many celebrities have stayed at this hotel, including Tolstoy and Bach; the most notorious guest was Adolf Hitler. The Elephant became best known in Germany through Thomas Mann's novel *Lotte in Weimar* (published in English as *The Beloved Returns*). The elegant facade of this building (ca. 1696) is set off by a beautifully weathered terra-cotta roof, a series of elongated bay windows stretching from the second to the third floors, and, best of all, a frontage onto the old marketplace, which contains a dried-up fountain dedicated to Neptune. An Art Deco decor and bold color schemes make the rooms dramatically appealing. Bathrooms are small but neatly organized, mostly with a tub-and-shower combination.

Am Markt 19, 99423 Weimar. ✆ **03643/80-20.** Fax 03643/80-26-14. www.arabellasheraton.com. 102 units. 210€–250€ ($187.55–$223.25) double; 290€–435€ ($258.95–$388.45) suite. AE, DC, MC, V. Free parking. Bus: 10, 11 or 71. **Amenities:** 2 restaurants; lounge; room service; babysitting; laundry/dry cleaning. *In room:* TV, minibar, hair dryer, safe.

### MODERATE

**Christliches Hotel** *Value* Though not as roomy and comfortable as the choices previously endorsed, this is one of the most affordable. Originally built in 1826 as a private villa, it was enlarged in the early 1990s with a modern annex just across the street. Reception and breakfast facilities are in the older of the two buildings; if you're assigned a room in the annex, you'll be given a key to the annex's front door. Rooms in the annex are modern in their decor and styling, rooms in the hotel's original core are Beidermeier. The hotel has a convenient location, lying directly south of Goethe National Museum, within an easy walk of the town's historic core and major attractions. The breakfast buffet, the only meal served here, is decent.

Amalienstrasse 2, 99423 Weimar. ✆ **03643/54-90.** Fax 03643/54-91-10. www.weimar.de/amalienhof. 32 units. 95€–105€ ($84.85–$93.75) double; 155€ ($138.40) suite. Rates include buffet breakfast. AE, MC, V. Free parking. Bus: 1. **Amenities:** Breakfast room; lounge; room service. *In room:* A/C, hair dryer.

**Grand Hotel Russischer Hof** The Russischer Hof is a bit minimal, but well-maintained and reasonably comfortable. The hotel was built in 1805 by Russian aristocrats for their visits to the Weimar court. It sports a dark-green-and-white facade and opens onto an important square in the center of town. Inside, the pastel-colored public areas are elegant and intimate. Rooms are in a somewhat lackluster modern annex behind the hotel, each with a shower unit and a decor loosely based on 18th-century French motifs.

Goetheplatz 2, 99423 Weimar. ✆ **03643/77-40.** Fax 03643/77-48-40. www.deraghotels.de. 126 units. 169€–217€ ($150.90–$193.80) double, 215€–365€ ($192–$325.95) suites. Rates include buffet breakfast. AE, DC, MC, V. Parking 7€–10€ ($6.25–$8.95). Bus: 11 or 71. **Amenities:** Restaurant; bar; cafe; sauna; solarium; room service; babysitting; laundry. *In room:* A/C, TV, minibar, hair dryer, safe.

## INEXPENSIVE

**Thüringen** This affordable hotel in the center of town dates from 1897 but has been completely renovated and restored in modern style. The small rooms are clean and simply but adequately furnished, each with a compact shower bathroom. The focal point of the public areas is a glassed-in winter garden. The hotel is known for its *Gutbürgerlich* (home-style) cookery, which one reader described as "just like my Saxon mother used to cook."

Brennerstrasse 42, 99423 Weimar. ✆ **03643/903-675.** Fax 03643/903-676. www.hotel–thurningen-weimar.de. 36 units. 77€ ($68.75) double. Rates include buffet breakfast. AE, MC, V. Bus: 1 and 7. **Amenities:** Dining room; lounge; room service. *In room:* No phone.

## WHERE TO DINE

**Hotel Elephant, Weimar** GERMAN/INTERNATIONAL There are two restaurants in this previously recommended hotel. The more formal, **Anna Amalia,** is modern, sky-lit, and airy, with spacious tables, a garden terrace, and good service. Its German and international dishes are among the very best in the city. The chefs have an unerring sense of flavor and proportion as well as a fertile imagination. They use only the finest of ingredients available at the local markets. Filet Stroganoff, pork medallions, and sauerbraten are among the menu items. Goethe, Schiller, Bach, Liszt, and Wagner all wined and dined here.

You can reach the historic **Elephantenkeller** (Elephant Cellar) by a flight of stone steps at a separate entrance. It's decorated in a rustic style, with square travertine columns. An autumn specialty is *Zwiebelmarkt* salads, made from onions from the famous October onion market, a tradition dating from 1653.

Am Markt 19. ✆ **03643/80-26-39.** Reservations recommended. Main courses 21€–25€ ($18.75–$22.35); fixed-price lunch or dinner 56€ ($50). AE, DC, MC, V. Anna Amalia 6:30–10:30pm daily, also noon–3pm daily in summer, but on weekends only in winter. Elephantenkeller Mon–Sat noon–3pm and 6pm–midnight. Bus: 10, 11 or 71.

**Ratskeller** THURINGIAN A flight of stairs leads into a pair of dining rooms. The first is vaulted and white, the second more modern, paneled, and with a prominent bar. Everything is clean, correct, and proper. You might begin with goose liver on toast, followed with schnitzel, goulash with mixed salad, or pork cutlets prepared four different ways. These dishes aren't dazzling, but they're very satisfying. The venison, when in season, is excellent, and the wild boar and duck in red-wine sauce is reason enough for a meal here.

In the Rathaus, Markt 10. ✆ **03643/85-05-73.** Reservations recommended. Main courses 7.50€–13€ ($6.70–$11.60). AE, MC, V. Daily 11am–midnight. Bus: 7 or 71.

**Shakespeares** INTERNATIONAL Set in the town's center, a few steps from the Rathaus (Town Hall), this restaurant offers well-prepared food, a

### The Thuringian Forest ★★: Germany's Green Heart

"There is indeed no forest on all the earth as beautiful as the Thuringian," wrote the Danish novelist Martin Anderson Nexö in his tale "The Doll." Trekkers and nature lovers have long extolled the scenic beauties of this region, which has often been called "the green heart of Germany." The *Thüringer Wald* was the former stomping ground of such philosophers and artists as Goethe, Schiller, Martin Luther, Ludwig Bechstein, and Bach.

The mountains within the forest, though not nearly as tall as the German Alps, are geological highlights. The highest peaks, around 985m (3,230 ft.), are composed of gneiss, porphyry, and granite; the foothills are made of softer strata of sandstone and sedimentary limestone.

The scenic, 160km (100-mile), northwest-to-southeast ramble known as the "Thuringian High Road" was one of the most popular destinations anywhere for East German schoolchildren and campers before reunification. You can take a lowland driving version by following Route 88 between Eisenach and Ilmenau, a city that Goethe loved.

Just as attractive as the region's scenic beauty are the dozens of unspoiled, charming medieval villages that pepper the landscape. **Dornburg** has a series of three palaces, perched high above the Saale River. **Altenburg,** directly south of Leipzig, is the home of a hilltop castle. Finally, **Arnstadt,** founded in 704, is the oldest town in the Thuringian Forest. It lies just beyond Erfurt. Today, the town's medieval walkways and buildings are being restored to their former glory.

bar area, an angular modern decor, and big windows that overlook a garden strewn with tables for warm-weather dining. Menu items are well prepared and flavorful, and include salads, soups, risottos, fresh shellfish, and several kinds of grilled fish, some of them served with a Riesling sauce. Main courses might feature savory ragouts of chicken, lamb, or veal; noodles in cream sauce studded with ham and cheese; veal cutlets; and Wiener schnitzels. In addition to the street-level dining room, there's a small-scale auditorium (The Othello Theater) in the restaurant's cellar. Most of what's presented inside is scheduled for Friday and Saturday nights, with an occasional Sunday-afternoon jazz concert whose venue changes from week to week. Entrance to most concerts and plays costs around 12.50€ ($11.15) per person.

Windischenstrasse 4–6. ✆ **03643/901285.** Reservations recommended. Main courses 13€–16€ ($11.60–$14.30). No credit cards. Daily 11am–midnight.

## WEIMAR AFTER DARK

A good national theater, live music venues, and dance clubs provide a variety of choices for nightly entertainment. The city's bars and outdoor cafes are good places to drink and talk. Just walk down Schillerstrasse or along the Theaterplatz. All of the bars and cafes in this area carry free copies of *Schlagseite* and *Boulevard,* local entertainment papers. *Takt* is another good resource; you can save 2.55€ ($2.30) by picking it up in the tourist office (see "Visitor Information," earlier in this chapter), the only place where it's free.

Weimar's main performance venue, reopened in 1999, is the **Deutsches Nationaltheater,** Theaterplatz (✆ **03643/75-53-34**), where Franz Liszt and Richard Strauss once conducted. Call the box office or the tourist office for information about schedules. Tickets cost 8€ to 56€ ($7.15–$50).

**C-Keller Galerie,** Markt 21 (✆ **03643/50-27-55**), combines an art gallery with a cafe that serves beer, wine, tea, and light meals. It's a popular place to unwind. The art gallery has works for sale by local, national, and European artists. The cafe is open daily noon to 1:30am. The most popular and animated disco in Weimar isn't exactly cutting edge—it's more like Hannover than Hamburg or Berlin. But if you're interested in hearing a medley of disco favorites from the '70s and '80s, head for **Bistro Corona-Sthröter,** Goethe-Platz 5 (✆ **03643/515308**). It's open daily 9pm to midnight. Admission (Fri–Sat only) costs 3€ ($2.70) per person.

A three-story medieval tower, **Studentclub Kasseturm,** Goetheplatz (✆ **03643/ 904323**), has a beer hall on the first floor, live music on the second, and dancing on the third. As the name suggests, students flock to this place. Cover ranges from 3.05€ ($2.70) to as much as 13.50€ ($12.05), if there's a particularly well-known band. There's no cover on Monday, Tuesday, and Thursday. The club opens Monday to Saturday at 8pm, with no set closing time.

The most popular place in Weimar for punk and alternative rock is **Haus für Socio-Kultur,** Gerberstrasse 3 (✆ **03643/51-27-14**), a large, loud rock club (or a pub, depending on the evening) with a graffiti-art exterior. Hours are daily 8pm to 3am. There's no cover charge.

## SIDE TRIPS FROM WEIMAR

### ERFURT ★

The small, 1,254-year-old city of Erfurt, on the Gera River, is one of the most visited cities of eastern Germany, because it still exudes the spirit of a medieval market town. Erfurt is filled with historic houses, bridges, winding cobblestone alleys, and church spires reaching toward the skyline, as well as decorative and colorful Renaissance and baroque facades. The city emerged from World War II relatively unscathed and remains one of the best places to see what yesterday's Germany looked like. Nearly everything of interest is concentrated in the Altstadt (Old Town) area. It's well worth your time to take 2 or 3 hours to walk around this city of "flowers and towers."

Why flowers? Erfurt is a center of the German horticultural trade. It's also Europe's largest vegetable seed producer. One of Europe's biggest horticultural shows, the *Internationale Gartenbaustellung,* is held here in the Cyriaksburg Park every year from the end of March to September.

**GETTING THERE** You can reach Erfurt after a 24km (15-mile) train ride from the Weimar Hauptbahnhof; there are frequent connections. For rail information and schedules, call ✆ **1805/996633.** Access by car is via the E40 Autobahn and State Highway 4. The **Erfurt Tourist-Information** center is at Kräerbrücke (✆ **0361/6-66400;** www.erfurt.de). From April to October, it's open Monday to Friday 10am to 7pm (till 6pm Nov–Mar). Year-round, it's open Saturday and Sunday 10am to 4pm.

#### Exploring the City

Well-preserved patrician mansions built in both the Gothic and Renaissance styles are the town's dominant feature. Many of the narrow streets are lined with old half-timbered houses. One of Erfurt's curiosities is the **Krämerbrücke** (Shopkeepers' Bridge), which has spanned the Gera since the 14th century. It has houses on both sides, nearly three dozen in all, and is filled with bookstalls, cafes, and antiques shops. You'll certainly want to spend some time here browsing.

The ecclesiastical center is the **Domberg,** where two Catholic churches stand side by side, their 15th-century walls almost closing in on each other. The **Dom (cathedral)** (✆ **0361/6461-265**), on Domplatz, was begun in the 12th century and later rebuilt in the 14th century in the Gothic style. Its stained-glass windows above the choir date from 1370 to 1420 and are unusual in Germany because they depict scenes of everyday life. The interior of the cathedral is richly baroque, but it also has some notable works from 1160: a Romanesque altar of the Virgin and the statue-candelabra known as "the Wolfram." Note also the 13th-century tombstone of the count of Gleichen and his two wives. One version of a local legend says that the second woman wasn't his wife at all, but a Saracen beauty from the Holy Land who had saved his life under mysterious circumstances. The Dom is open May to October, Monday to Friday 9 to 11:30am and 12:30 to 5pm, Saturday 9 to 11:30am and 12:30 to 4:30pm, and Sunday 2 to 4pm; November to April, Monday to Saturday 10 to 11:30am and 12:30 to 4pm, and Sunday 2 to 4pm.

Its neighbor is the Gothic **Church of St. Severi** (✆ **0361/57-69-60**), a "hall type" church with five naves. Don't miss seeing its extraordinary font, a masterpiece of intricately carved sandstone, rising practically to the roof. You might also look for a notable sarcophagus of the saint (ca. 1365) in the southernmost aisle. St. Severi is linked to the Dom by a 70-step open staircase. It's open May to October, Monday to Friday 9am to 12:30pm and 1:30 to 5pm, Saturday 9 to 11:30am and 12:30 to 4:30pm, and Sunday 2 to 4pm; November to April, Tuesday to Friday 10am to 12:30pm and 1:30 to 4pm, and on Sunday 2 to 4pm. Admission is free. Closed January to February.

The most beautiful churches are the Romanesque **Peterskirche,** dating from the 12th and 14th centuries, and the 13th-century **Predigerkirche,** of the Order of Mendicant Friars. There are also three early Medieval churches: **Agidienkirche, Michaeliskirche,** and **Allerheiligengeistkirche.** The tourist office (see above) will give you a map pinpointing all these locations. Most can be reached on foot.

## Where to Stay & Dine

**Dorint Hotel Erfurt** Erfurt's newest hotel, in the heart of town, is also its best. It was built as a sophisticated enlargement of an inn (*Gasthaus*) from the 1300s. The medieval part—meticulously conserved and restored—faces onto a side street, the Futterstrasse. Otherwise, the hotel is modern, restrained, and tasteful. Most rooms correspond to middle-to-upscale chain-hotel standards. An additional 13 retain the wood paneling and architectural quirks of their original medieval construction and are more interesting. Each accommodation is equipped with a small but efficient private bathroom with shower stall.

Meienbergstrasse 26–27, 99084 Erfurt. ✆ **0361/5-94-90.** Fax 0361/5-94-91-00. www.dorint.de/erfurt. 142 units. 120€–200€ ($107.15–$178.60) double; 170€–260€ ($151.80–$232.20) suite. AE, DC, MC, V. Parking 9€ ($8.05). **Amenities:** Restaurant; bar; sauna; steam room; solarium; room service; laundry. *In room:* TV, minibar, hair dryer.

**Radisson SAS Hotel Erfurt** This is one of the town's better addresses. It hasn't fully escaped its East German Cold War boxy architectural quality, but the SAS group has poured tons of money into it to upgrade it and give it a lot more than a face-lift. Its modern rooms are comfortable but a bit cramped. Bathrooms are very compact, containing shower-tub combinations and inadequate shelf space. The location is halfway between the station and the town center.

Juri-Gagarin-Ring 127, 99084 Erfurt. ✆ **0361/5-51-00.** Fax 0361/551-02-10. www.radisson.com. 317 units. 110€–260€ ($98.25–$232.20) double; 165€–770€ ($147.35–$687.60) suite. Rates include buffet breakfast. AE, DC, MC, V. Parking 9€ ($8.05). **Amenities:** Restaurant; lounge; room service; laundry. *In room:* TV, minibar, hair dryer.

## EISENACH ★

This town lies on the northwestern slopes of the Thuringian Forest, at the confluence of the Nesse and Horsel rivers, 48km (30 miles) west of Erfurt. Eisenach, once a center of the East German auto industry, is not particularly charming, but it does have one of the region's finest castles, and a few sights associated with Luther and Bach, who was born here. Its ancient market square is ringed by half-timbered houses.

**GETTING THERE** Many trains from Erfurt (see above) arrive every day. For rail information and schedules, call ✆ **1805/996633.** Access by car is via the A4 Autobahn east and west. For tourist information, contact **Eisenach-Information,** Markt 3 (✆ **03691/79230**), open Monday 10am–6pm, Tuesday to Friday 9am to 6pm and Saturday and Sunday 10am to 2pm. Here you can pick up a map with the locations of all the tourist sites.

### Exploring the Town

Eisenach is best known as the site of **Schloss Wartburg** ★, Schlossberg 2 (✆ **03691/7-70-73;** bus: 3), reached only after a rigorous climb up a 180m (600-ft.) hill. Hitler called Wartburg Castle "the most German of German castles" and engaged in a battle with local authorities to take down its cross and replace it with a swastika. This ancient castle belonged to the landgraves of Thuringia and once hosted the medieval Minnesinger poets, immortalized by Wagner in *Tannhäuser.* This was also where Martin Luther hid upon his return from the Diet of Worms in 1521, so he could complete his translation of the Bible—he is said to have "fought the Devil with ink" at Wartburg. The castle has now been turned into a regional museum. It's open April to October daily 8:30am to 6pm, November to March daily 9am to 5:30pm. The last ticket is sold 1 hour prior to closing. Admission to the palace, museum, and the room within the castle where Luther lived and worked is 6€ ($5.35) for adults, 5€ ($4.45) senior citizens, and 3€ ($2.70) for students and persons aged 6 to 18. Admission is free for children under 6.

Eisenach is also the birthplace of Johann Sebastian Bach (1685–1750). **Bachhaus,** Am Frauenplan 21 (✆ **03691/79-340;** bus: 3, 7, 11, or 13), contains many mementos of the Bach family, along with a collection of musical instruments. It's open April to September, Monday noon to 6:45pm and Tuesday to Sunday 9am to 6:45pm; October to March, Monday 1 to 4:45pm and Tuesday to Sunday 9am to 4:45pm. Admission costs 2.50€ ($2.25) for adults, 2€ ($1.80) for students and persons 6–18. Children under 6 enter free.

If you're a diehard Luther fan, you can also visit the **Lutherhaus,** Lutherplatz 8 (✆ **03691/2-98-30;** bus: 1 or 5). Martin Luther stayed here as a schoolboy, and today it contains a series of exhibitions illustrating his life. It's open daily 9am to 5pm. Admission is 2.50€ ($2.25) for adults and 2€ ($1.80) for persons 6 to 18 and students. Children under 6 enter free.

### Where to Stay & Dine

**Best Western Hotel Kaiserhof** ★ Much of the elegance of the late 1800s is still evoked here in the lobby and in the dining room especially. Both are stellar role models of the stately-looking German Landhaus architecture. Rooms are generally spacious and tastefully renovated, each with comfortable furnishings and midsize bathrooms with a combination tub and shower.

Wartburger Allee 2, 99817 Eisenach. ✆ **03691/21-35-13.** Fax 03691/20-36-53. www.kaiserhof-eisenach.bestwestern.de. 64 units. 103€–145€ ($92–$129.50) double. Rates include buffet breakfast. AE, DC, MC, V. Free parking. Bus: 3. **Amenities:** Restaurant; lounge; room service. *In room:* TV, minibar, hair dryer.

**Steigenberger Hotel Thüringer Hof** We prefer the Kaiserhof (see below), but this is a desirable runner-up. This hotel was originally a very glamorous inn in the early 19th century. Today it's a part of the well-recommended Steigenberger chain. It boasts six floors of compact but recently renovated and well-designed rooms. Bathrooms are compact and contain showers. The hotel is located near almost every site of historic interest in town.

Near the railway station, Karlsplatz 11, 99817 Eisenach. ✆ **03691/280.** Fax 03691/281-900. www.thueringer-hof-eisenach.de. 127 units. 110€–123€ ($98.25–$109.85) double; 390€ ($348.25) suite. AE, DC, MC, V. Parking 10€ ($8.95). Bus: 3. **Amenities:** Restaurant; bar; room service; laundry. *In room:* TV, minibar, hair dryer.

## 2 Leipzig ★

164km (102 miles) SW of Berlin, 111km (68 miles) NW of Dresden, 126km (78 miles) NE of Erfurt

If you have limited time and have to choose between Dresden and Leipzig, make it Dresden. But if you can work Leipzig into your itinerary, you'll be richly rewarded.

More than any other city in former East Germany (except Berlin, of course), Leipzig brings you into the Germany of today. This once-dreary city is taking on a new life and vitality; a visit here can be absolutely invigorating. Glassy skyscrapers and glitzy nightlife add a cosmopolitan flavor you don't encounter in much of the rest of the region. The approximately 20,000 students who study in the area, as did Nietzsche, Goethe, and Leibniz, help add a spark. One resident put it this way: "Our grunge and metal bands are just as good as those of Berlin, and our cafes just as super-cool."

Leipzig is also famous for more traditional music. Johann Sebastian Bach is closely associated with Leipzig; Mozart and Mendelssohn performed here; and Wagner was born here in 1813.

Because of its strategic value as a rail center, both the RAF and the U.S. Air Force bombed the city heavily in World War II, but it's been rebuilt, more or less successfully. It still has some narrow streets and houses from the 16th and 17th centuries, as well as some Jugendstil (Art Nouveau) flair. And Leipzig is once again a major rail terminus. From its Hauptbahnhof—the largest in Europe, with 26 platforms—lines radiate to all the chief German cities and to the rest of the continent.

### ESSENTIALS

**GETTING THERE By Plane** The **Leipzig-Halle International Airport** lies 11km (7 miles) northwest of the city center. About 50 airlines link Leipzig with major German cities, such as Munich and Frankfurt, and also some continental destinations. For **Airport Information,** call ✆ **0341/2241155** or 0341/2240). A bus runs between the airport and the Leipzig Hauptbahnhof at 30 minutes intervals every day between 6:30am and 6pm; and at intervals of between 45 and 60 minutes the rest of the day and night. The fare costs 6.50€ ($5.80) each way for adults, and 3.50€ ($3.15) each way for persons 6 through

13. Children under 6 ride free. Taxis are also available, meeting all arriving planes, but the 25- to 30-minute ride to the city center will cost around 32€ ($28.60) each way for up to four passengers.

**By Train** The **Leipzig Hauptbahnhof,** Willy-Brandt-Platz, lies on the major Deutsche Bundesbahn rail line, with frequent connections to German cities. Seventeen trains arrive daily from Berlin (trip time: 2 hr. 10 min.–2 hr. 50 min.); 23 trains from Dresden (1 hr. 35 min.–2 hr.); and 15 trains from Frankfurt (3–4 hrs.). For information and schedules, call ✆ **1805/99-66-33.** The **Hauptbahnhof** has recently been restored and contains many cafes, shops, and restaurants; it's one of the most happening places in Leipzig.

**By Bus** Long-distance bus service to such cities as Berlin is provided by **Leipzieger Verkehrsbetriebe.** Buses depart from the east side of the main rail station. For information and schedules, call ✆ **0341/ 19449.**

**By Car** Access is via the Halle–Dresden Autobahn east and west or the E51 Autobahn north and south.

**VISITOR INFORMATION** Contact the **Tourist-Information** office at Richard Wagner Strasse 1 (✆ **0341/7104260;** www.leipzig.de), Monday to Friday 9am to 7pm; Saturday 9am to 4pm and Sunday 9am to 2pm. The office can supply a map pinpointing the major sights. This place becomes a beehive of activity at the time of the annual trade fairs.

**SPECIAL EVENTS** Upon arrival, be sure to drop in at the tourist office and see if any festivals are taking place. For a week every year, in September, for example, during the **Leipziger Jazztages,** the churches, the student clubs, and the opera house fill with jazz music. (For more information, click on www.jazzclub-leipzig.de.) During 1 weekend in late June, the city stages its official **Street Music Festival (Leipziger Strassen Musikfestival),** when musicians—some good, some surprisingly good, many awful—play in the area of the Markt, the parks, and other outdoor venues. Sometime between late May and early June, the **Leipziger Stadtfest** turns Sachsenplatz and Grimaische Strasse into one big carnival. For more on this and other events, contact the local tourist office.

**GETTING AROUND** A public transit system of trams, light railways, and buses provides frequent service to all parts of the city. An S-Bahn (light railway) serves the suburbs, arriving and leaving from the Hauptbahnhof in the center of Leipzig.

## EXPLORING THE CITY

Goethe, who was a student in Leipzig, called the city *klein Paris* (miniature Paris). We wouldn't go quite that far, but Leipzig definitely has its charms. One of the best things to do is to explore the handsomely restored Art Nouveau **Arkaden (arcades)** that thread through the historic core of the city center. "Mädler Mall" is Leipzig's finest arcade. This is the site of the famous **Auerbachs Keller** (see p. 172), the setting for one of the scenes of Goethe's *Faust.* A bronze group of characters from Faust, sculpted in 1913, beckon you down a stone staircase into the cellar restaurant. Nearby is a lovely Art Nouveau coffee shop called **Mephisto,** decorated appropriately in devilish reds and blacks. All through the Mädlerpassage you can find boutiques as chic and sophisticated as those in Berlin.

A gateway leads to **Nasch Markt,** which occupies the space behind the Altes Rathaus. If you walk around the front of the Altes Rathaus, you'll find yourself

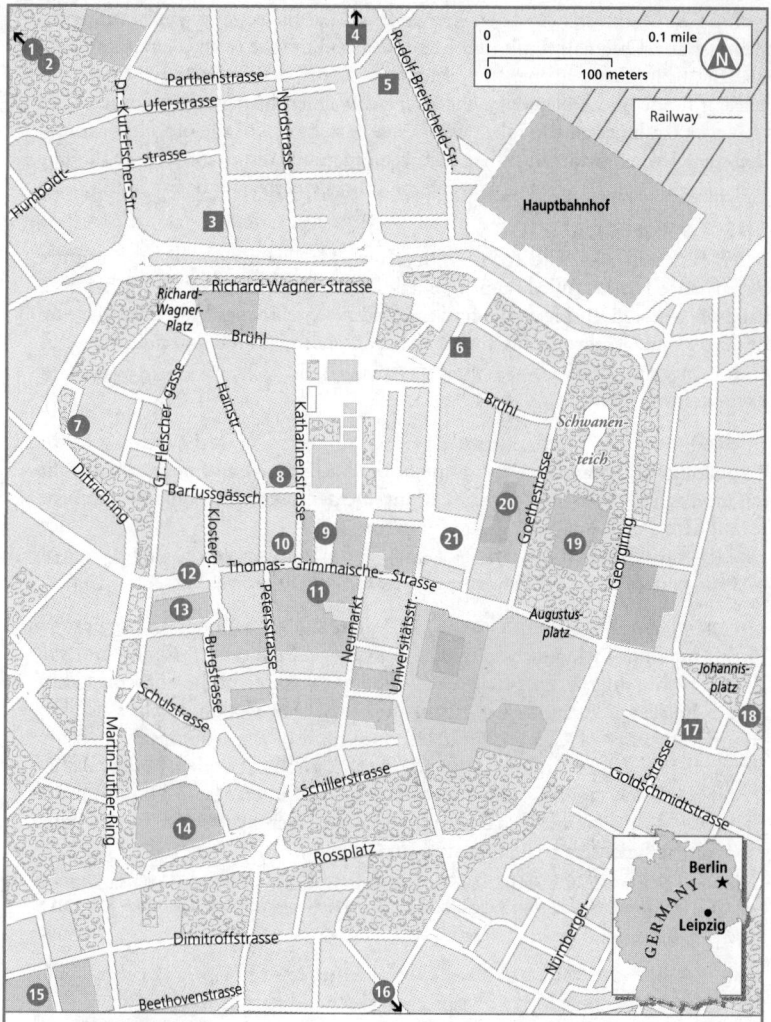


**ATTRACTIONS ●**

Altes Rathaus **8**
Auerbachs Keller **11**
Bach-Museum **12**
Bose Haus **12**
Deutsche Bücherei **16**
Königshaus **10**
Museum der Bildenden Künste **15**
Museum in der Runden Ecke **7**
Musikinstrumenten-Museum **18**
Nasch Markt **9**
Neues Rathaus **14**
Neues Opernhaus **19**
Nikolaikirche **21**
Schillerhaus **1**
Thomaskirche **13**
Universität Leipzig **20**
Zoologischer Garten Leipzig **2**

**ACCOMMODATIONS ■**

Holiday Inn Garden Court **5**
Hotel Fürstenhof **3**
Inter-Continental Leipzig **4**
Ringhotel Adagio Leipzig **17**
Seaside Park Hotel Leipzig **6**

within Am Markt, the city's best-known square, at the edge of which stands the **Königshaus.** Originally built in the late 1700s on the site of an even older building, the Königshaus at one time functioned as the city's official guesthouse for VIPs; it housed both Napoléon and Richard Wagner during their sojourns here.

**Neues Rathaus** on Burgplatz was erected on the site of the old Pleissenburg, the citadel where Martin Luther held a momentous disputation in 1519. The best place in Leipzig for people watching is on **Peterstrasse,** below Markt.

## THE TOP ATTRACTIONS

**Altes Rathaus** ★ The 16th-century Town Hall stands on the 12th-century Renaissance Markt. Allied bombs rained down on the building, but it has been carefully restored. Inside, you'll find the Stadtgeschichtliches Museum (Museum of City History), chronicling the city's history, both cultural and political.

Markt 1. ✆ **0341/96-51-30.** Admission 2.50€ ($2.25) adults, 1.50€ ($1.35) students and persons 6–18. Tues 2–8pm; Wed–Sun 10am–6pm. Tram: 4 or 6.

**Bach-Museum** The reconstructed Bose House stands in the shadow of the Thomaskirche. It was once the home of the Bach family and now contains the largest Bach archives in Germany. Many mementos of the composer are also found here.

Thomaskirchhof 15–16. ✆ **0341/91370.** Admission 3€ ($2.70) adults, 2€ ($1.80) students and persons 4–14. Free for children under 4. Daily 10am–5pm. Guided tours at 11am and 3pm. Tram: 21.

**Museum der Bildenden Künste** ★★ The 2,500 paintings and sculptures in this museum include works by Dürer, Rubens, Rembrandt, Rodin, and van Eyck. The building was constructed in 1888 as the home of the Supreme Court of the Reich and became a museum in 1952. One section displays exhibits relating the story of Georgi Dimitroff, once head of the Communist party in Bulgaria. Hitler accused Dimitroff and other Communist leaders of responsibility for the Reichstag fire. Hermann Göring himself interrogated Dimitroff, but the trial in Leipzig resulted in an acquittal. In the carefully preserved courtroom, tapes of the Reichstag trial are played (in German).

Grimmaische Strasse 1–7. ✆ **0341/21-69-90.** Admission 4€ ($3.55) adults, 2€ ($1.80) students and persons 4–14. Free for children under 4. Tues and Thurs–Sun 10am–6pm; Wed 1–9:30pm. Tram: 4, 8, 10, 11, 15, or 20.

**Museum in der Runden Ecke** This museum, one of Leipzig's newest, could hardly have been imagined 10 years ago. The building was the headquarters of the dreaded Stasi, the East German Ministry for State Security. Exhibits detail how Stasi operated within Eastern Germany through various methods, most interesting of which show the tools of espionage, such as hidden cameras and letter opening (and resealing) machines. Other exhibits show the extent of the massive spying, with entire floors devoted to handwriting samples from Leipzig's citizens, and extensive personal files on various members of the population. One exhibition, called "The Power and Banality of the East German Secret Police," documents the meticulous and paranoid methods by which the police monitored every exchange of information in the country. They constantly seized private letters and listened in on phone conversations—at times monitoring up to 2,000 calls at once. The exhibition also traces the steps local people took to throw off the Communist regime and end Stasi terror. On the nights of December 4 and 5, 1989, local citizens seized the building. Leipzig is called *Heldenstadt,* or "city of heroes," for its role in toppling the government of East Germany.

Dittrichring 24 (north of Thomaskirche). ✆ **0341/96-12-44-3.** www.runde-ecke-leipzig.de. Free admission. Daily 10am–6pm. Tram: 1, 3, 4, 7, 9, 12 14, or 15 to Goerderlerring or Thomaskirche.

**Musikinstrumenten-Museum (Museum of Musical Instruments)** This museum exhibits musical instruments, chiefly Italian, German, and French treasures of the 16th to the 19th centuries. Occasionally, performances are given, and then the historical instruments are played.

Thomaskirchhof 20. ✆ **0341/68-70-790.** Admission 3€ ($2.70) adults, 1.50€ ($1.35) students and persons 4–14. Tues–Sun 11am–5pm. Tram: 4, 6, 15, or 20.

**Schillerhaus** In this small farmhouse in Gohlis, a suburb about 20 minutes from the center of Leipzig, Friedrich von Schiller (1759–1805), the greatest name after Goethe in German literature, wrote his "Ode to Joy" in 1785. Beethoven incorporated the poem into the great final movement of his Ninth Symphony.

Menckestrasse 42, Gohlis. ✆ **0341/5-66-21-70.** Admission 2€ ($1.80) adults, 1.50€ ($1.35) students and persons 4–14, free for children under 4. Apr–Oct Tues–Sun 10am–6pm; Nov–Mar Wed–Sun 10am–4pm. Tram: 4 to Menckestrasse.

**Thomaskirche (St. Thomas Church)** ★ Leipzig's most famous resident, Johann Sebastian Bach (1685–1750), was cantor here from 1723 until his death. He spent his most creative years as choirmaster at this church and is buried just in front of the altar. Both Mozart and Mendelssohn performed in the Thomaskirche as well, and Richard Wagner was christened here in 1813. The church was built on the site of a 13th-century monastery and was heavily restored after World War II. Its high-pitched roof dates from 1496. When it's not touring, the city's Thomaner Choir (Thomaner Chor) presents concerts every Sunday morning and Friday evening.

Thomaskirchhof 18 (just off Marktplatz). ✆ **0341/9-60-28-55.** Free admission. Daily 9am–6pm. Tram: 4, 6, 8, 10, 11, or 13.

## Singing Through the Centuries: The St. Thomas Boys' Choir

In recent times while the Vienna Boys' Choir enjoyed worldwide fame, Leipzig's St. Thomas Choir (Thomasknasbenchor) languished in obscurity in the eastern zone. Now all that is changing. Any musical expert can tell you that the Leipzig choir has plenty of talent, and as it tours more widely in Europe, its fame will no doubt grow.

The choir has been here since the 13th century. The boys sang on every occasion in the Middle Ages—city celebrations, the installation of bishops, and even executions. Today, the setting for this venerable musical force is the **Thomaskirche (St. Thomas Church).** Choirboys still follow an almost medieval regime within a distinctive subculture that's a world unto itself. Each newcomer is assigned a "mentor" from among the trusted older members of the choir, and all members are required to eat, sleep, study, and rehearse according to a semi-monastic regimen. The most famous member was none other than Johann Sebastian Bach. He wrote his great cantatas for this choir and was cantor (choirmaster) for 27 years.

**Zoologischer Garten Leipzig** This zoo breeds animals to help conserve endangered species. It was founded in 1878 and is internationally known for the breeding of carnivores. The biggest aquarium in eastern Germany outside Berlin is also here.

Pfaffendorfer-Strasse 29. ✆ **0341/5-93-35-00.** Admission 7.50€ ($6.70) adults, 6€ ($5.35) students; 4€ ($3.55) children 4–14. Free for children under 4. Open daily as follows: Nov–[Mar 9am–5pm; April 9am–6pm; May–Oct 9am–7pm. Tram: 20 or 24.

## MORE SIGHTS & ACTIVITIES

The German Museum of Books and Scripts, the **Deutsche Bücherei,** Deutscher Platz 1 (✆ **0341/2-27-13-24;** tram 21), is the central archive of German literature. You can visit it for free from Monday to Saturday 9am to 4pm, but only with an advance phone call. The archive was established in 1912 to showcase the fine art of German printing and bookbinding. It's said to possess every item of German literature ever published. It also has a copy of *Iskra,* the Bolshevik newspaper that Lenin came here to print secretly in 1900.

Contrary to popular belief, Thomaskirche isn't the oldest church in Leipzig. That distinction belongs to **Nikolaikirche,** on Nikolaistrasse, erected in 1165. Many works by Bach, including the *St. John Passion,* were first performed here.

If the weather is fair, head for the **Leipzig University Tower,** near Nikolaikirche. This metal-and-glass tower overlooks street performers who take over on summer weekends. It's the greatest free show in Leipzig. (Well, not exactly free—the performers will pass the hat at the end of their acts.) Just beware of the skateboard warriors, who make walking about a bit perilous. The **Universität Leipzig,** founded in 1409, has contributed greatly to the cultural growth of the city. The East German government rechristened it Karl Marx University, but the old name was restored in 1990. **Augustusplatz** is the ideal center to rub elbows with the thousands of students who study here.

To escape the fumes and noise of the city, head for such "green lungs" as **Johannapark** on Karl-Tauchnitz-Strasse or one of the wildly overgrown cemeteries by the **Völkerschlachdenkmal.** On hot days, the fountains in **Sachensplatz** are popular for splashing about.

**SHOPPING** Leipzig has emerged as the art-buying capital of the former East Germany. Galleries hold rich inventories of paintings and sculpture by artists whose works were once unknown to western consumers. **Galerie für Zeitgenössiche Kunst,** Karl-Tauchnitz-Strasse 11 (✆ **0341/140-810**) is a privately-owned art gallery that displays international art, showing about 14 exhibitions a year. It charges 3€ ($2.70) for adults, 2€ ($1.80) for students and children 10 to 18 (free for those 10 and under). Other worthwhile art galleries include **ARTCO Galerie für Zeitgenössische Kunst,** Rosa-Luxemburg Strasse 19–21 (✆ **0341/960-38-51**).

If you're looking for examples of the antique furniture and art objects that many Leipziegers have dragged down from their attics since reunification, head for any of the dozen or so antiques dealers conducting business within the town's core. Antiques shops catering to walk-in clients include **Musik-Antiquariat,** Thomaskirchhof 15 (✆ **0341/960-48-63**), which is devoted entirely to musical instruments and **H. Beier,** Nikolaistrasse 55 (✆ **0341/980-6666**).

## WHERE TO STAY

**Hotel Fürstenhof** ★★★ This hotel, located in a historic 18th-century building, is the best in Leipzig. Its interior has been redecorated to reflect the building's original, almost-forgotten neoclassical theme. A corps of English and

Swedish designers has outfitted the rooms in a modern interpretation of neo-classical style. The rejuvenated bathrooms are the best in town, with deluxe toiletries and combination tub and shower. The ballroom (the Serpentinensaal) and a monumental staircase date from the 19th century.

Tröndlinring 8, 04105 Leipzig. ✆ **800/223-6800** or 0341/14-00. Fax 0341/1-40-37-00. www.arabellasheraton.com. 92 units. 215€–281€ ($192–$250.95) double; from 390€ ($348.25) suite. AE, DC, MC, V. Parking 19€ ($16.95). Tram: 15. **Amenities:** Restaurant; 2 bars, lounge; pool; health club; Jacuzzi; sauna; room service; babysitting; laundry/dry cleaning. *In room:* A/C, TV, minibar, hair dryer, safe.

**Inter-Continental Leipzig** ★★ Rising 27 floors, this is one of the tallest landmarks in "new" Leipzig and one of Eastern Germany's leading hotels. In this *luxe* category, we prefer the greater charm and comfort of the Fürstenhof (see above), although the Inter-Continental is fine in every way. Close to the railway station, this is the largest hotel in Leipzig, a businessperson's favorite, and also a popular venue for conventions. The hotel and its amenities are seemingly locked in a 1980s time capsule, with a honeycomb ceiling in the public lounge, an architectural detail beloved of the former rulers of East Germany. Don't expect lots of atmosphere or personal service here. All the bedrooms, ranging from small to spacious, are being renovated in stages, the work to be completed in 2003. Bathrooms are midsize, coming with tub and shower combinations. The hotel offers more diverse dining and drinking options than its competitors, everything from a Bierstube with Saxon cookery to a teppan-yaki grill with sushi and sashimi.

Gerberstrasse 15 (5 min. from Altes Rathaus), 04105 Leipzig. ✆ **800/327-0200** in the U.S. and Canada, or 0341/98-80. Fax 0341/9-88-12-29. www.hotel-interconti-leipzig.de. 447 units. 90€–170€ ($80.35–$151.80) double; from 240€ ($214.30) suite. Special offers on weekends. AE, DC, MC, V. Parking 11€ ($9.80). Tram: 4 or 6. **Amenities:** 2 restaurants; bar; cafe; pool; health club; sauna; 2 bowling lanes; car rental; salon; room service; massage; laundry. *In room:* TV, minibar, hair dryer, safe.

**Ringhotel Adagio Leipzig** *Kids* This is a restored and greatly refurbished late–19th century building in a tranquil location between the Neues Gewandhaus and the Grassimuseum. Each midsize bedroom is individually furnished with such themes as the Roaring 1920s. The hotel staff gives a special welcome to families traveling with children. Each room comes with a well-equipped modern bathroom, most often with tub and shower.

Seeburgstrasse 96, Leipzig 04103. ✆ **0341/21-66-99.** Fax 0341/9603078. www.hotel-adagio-leipzig.com. 26 units. 87€–143€ ($77.70–$127.70); 170€ ($151.80) suite. AE, DC, MC, V. **Amenities:** Restaurant; bar; room service; laundry/dry cleaning. *In room:* A/C, TV, minibar, hair dryer.

**Seaside Park Hotel Leipzig** Half a mile from the city center, this is the latest reincarnation of a hotel that opened in 1913 near the central rail depot. Back then it was hailed as the grandest first-class hotel in the city. Today the competition is too keen for it to reclaim its title, but the hotel has bounced back, lying behind a facade that its government protected as a historical monument. It caters mainly to the business traveler but welcomes vacationers with equal gusto to its well-furnished, midsize to spacious bedrooms, decorated in an Art Deco style with well-equipped bathrooms, mostly with tub-and-shower combination. Fine dining characterizes the kitchen here. Our favorite part of the hotel is a reconstruction of the famous Orient Express dining room.

Richard-Wagner Strasse 7, Leipzig D-04109. ✆ **0341/985-20.** Fax 0341/985-2750. www.seaside-hotel.de. 288 units. 98€–140€ ($87.50–$125) double; 170€–210€ ($151.80–$187.55) suite. AE, DC, MC, V. **Amenities:** 2 restaurants; bar; night club; health club; whirlpool; sauna; room service; massage; laundry/dry cleaning. *In room:* A/C, TV, minibar, hair dryer, safe.

## WHERE TO DINE

**Apels Garten** GERMAN Its name commemorates the site of a 400-year-old garden, no longer in existence. Today you'll find a modern mid-1980s building with a conservatively decorated street-level restaurant known for its home-style German food. Specialties include Leipzig-style onion soup or wild-duck soup with homemade noodles, roast goose with potatoes and vegetables, grilled wurst with potatoes and red cabbage, and sauerbraten with onions and red cabbage. The cuisine is more robust than refined, but it's very filling.

Kolonnadenstrasse 2. ✆ **0341/9-60-77-77.** Reservations recommended. Main courses 10€–15.50€ ($8.95–$13.85); fixed-price lunch 10€–15€ ($8.95–$13.40); fixed-price dinner 13€–25€ ($11.60–$22.35). AE, MC, V. Mon–Sat 11:30am–midnight; Sun 10am–3:30pm. Tram: 4, 6, 8, 10, 11, or 13.

**Auerbachs Keller** ★ GERMAN/INTERNATIONAL This is the famous restaurant and tavern where Goethe staged the debate between Faust and Mephistopheles in his play *Faust.* The cellar dates from 1530 and has a series of 16th-century murals representing the *Faust* legend. The chefs prepare mainly regional cuisine of Saxony, along with a selection of international dishes. Some of the most tempting offerings are filet of veal, beef, or saddle of lamb, prepared with special sauces and served with seasonal vegetables. The menu changes every 2 months. You can also order from a fine selection of wines and beers. Guests have a choice of the stately-looking Historic Rooms (dinner only) or the sprawling, Germanic-looking Big Room which has a different menu and whose paneling and high ceiling evokes an upscale beer tavern. Between 11:30am and 6pm, Monday to Saturday, visitors can see the Historic Rooms for a charge of 1€ (90¢).

Mädler Passage (off the market square, close to the Altes Rathaus), Grimmaischestrasse 2–4. ✆ **0341/21-61-00.** Reservations recommended. Historic Rooms, main courses 16€–21€ ($14.30–$18.75); fixed-price menus 34€–65€ ($30.35–$58.05). Big Room, main courses 11€–19€ ($9.80–$16.95). AE, MC, V. Historic Rooms Mon–Sat 6pm–midnight. Big Room daily 11:30am–midnight. Tram: 4 or 6.

**Paulaner Palais** GERMAN/BAVARIAN/AUSTRIAN This large restaurant (serving continental cuisine) is on the street level of a fine rococo 18th-century building. The largest section of this place is decorated like a typical Bavarian inn. Other areas, usually reserved for private functions, include rooms whose decors are themed around Meissen porcelain, the history of Leipzig, and the lavishly rococo palace of Sans Souci. More seats are in a summer courtyard. Although there's an excessive emphasis on boiled meats such as *Tafelspitz* (boiled beef with vegetables) and heavy sauces, the place remains an enduring local favorite. Wiener schnitzel and braised veal shank are two of the chef's other specialties. Foaming mugs of only one kind of beer are served: Paulaner Bier, brewed in Munich, the hometown of the owner.

Klostergasse 3–5. ✆ **0341/2-11-31-15.** Reservations recommended, especially Mon–Fri. Main courses 10€–20€ ($8.95–$17.85). AE, DC, MC, V. Daily 11am–midnight. Tram: 4 or 6.

## LEIPZIG AFTER DARK

Leipzig's active nightlife offers something for everyone. The area around the Markt is full of bars, cafes, and other entertainment options; it's a good place to kick off your search for a nightspot.

**THE PERFORMING ARTS** The **Leipzieger Oper** is one of Germany's most acclaimed opera companies. Its home is the **Neues Opernhaus** (it's sometimes referred to simply as "Oper Leipzig"), Augustusplatz 8 (✆ **0341/126-12-61;** tram: 4, 5, 12, 13, or 15), opposite Das Gewandhaus (see below). Part of its space is devoted to the **Kellertheater** (✆ **0341/12610**) a small-scale area that presents small ensemble progressive performances of all types. The box office for both the main opera house and the Kellertheater is open Monday to Friday 10am to 8pm, and Saturday 10am to 4pm. Tickets are 9.20€ to 30.65€ ($8.20–$27.35), with students getting up to one-third off, depending on the performance. Call the box office, or ask at the tourist office, for information. Tickets to the opera cost 15€ to 60€ ($13.40–$53.60); tickets to the Kellertheater cost 9€ to 35€ ($8.05–$31.25) depending on the performance.

The home of the famous **Gewandhaus Orchestra** ★ is a modern concert hall built in 1981, **Das Gewandhaus** (✆ **0341/1-27-02-80;** tram: 4, 5, 12, 13, or 15), which faces the Neues Opernhaus across Augustusplatz. Founded in 1781, the orchestra saw some of its greatest days under the baton of Felix Mendelssohn, who died in Leipzig in 1847. Other notable conductors have included Wilhelm Furtwängler, Bruno Walter, and Kurt Masur. Concerts, ballets, organ recitals, and other events are staged here. Tickets usually cost 10€ to 45€ ($8.95–$40.20), depending on the performance.

The main venue for theater in Leipzig is the **Schauspielhaus,** Bosestrasse 1 (✆ **0341/1268168;** tram 1, 2, 4, 6, 15, 17, 21, or 24), home to several arts companies that jointly stage an eclectic mix of theatrical and musical productions. Tickets cost from 10€ to 30€ ($8.95–$26.80) and are half price for students. The box office is open weekdays 10am to 6pm, Saturday 10am to 1pm, and 1 hour before show time.

**BARS** On the street level of the Auerbachskeller is the **Mephisto Bar,** Mädlerpassage (✆ **0341/216100;** tram: 4 or 6), which honors Goethe and the Faust legend. It also happens to be the hippest bar and cafe in Leipzig, and the best seat for people-watching in the historic core. Within a decor whose colors (black, red, orange, and green) emulate the fires of hell, you can sit at cramped tables, stand amid the crowd of trendies, and sip cocktails, beer, or wine, or order simple platters such as Camembert with grapes, soups, salads, or patés with toast. The most popular cocktail is the "Mephisto Feuer" (Satan's fire), made from a combination of schnapps, orange juice, and sekt. There's live piano music presented, without a cover charge, usually Thursday to Saturday, beginning around 8:30pm. Open daily 11am to 2am.

Another favorite Leipzig watering hole is the **Letterman Bar,** Gottsched Strasse 1 (✆ **0341/961-1293;** tram: 5 or 16), which is laid back and appealingly but discreetly permissive. Immediately adjacent to it, within the same building, is the young and hip and deceptively named **Milchbar,** Gottsched Strasse 1 (✆ **0341/9809594**), where virtually any kind of alcoholic drinks, including milk for anyone who wants it, is available.

**DANCE CLUBS** Two sites in Leipzig where you can go dancing include **Markt 1,** at Markt 1 (✆ **0341/960-3306**), where people ranging in age from their late 20s to their late 40s come to dance on a large floor, drink at one of two different bars, flirt, and unwind after a day at the office. Dress codes are a bit more formal, and tailored, than what you'll find in other dance clubs, and overall, there's a feeling somewhat like that of a private club. Entrance costs 5€ ($4.45) per person. It's open only Thursday to Saturday from 8:30pm till around 3am. Attracting a younger, more raffish crowd is **Spizz,** Marktplatz 9 (✆ **0341/960-8043**). Cramped, crowded, sweaty, hot, and usually convivial, they play boogey-woogie, reggae, pop, and disco music from the '80s and '90s. Entrance costs 3€ ($2.70) per person. It's open only Friday and Saturday nights from 9pm till around 3am.

**LIVE MUSIC** Built against the old city wall, **Moritzbastei,** Universitätsstrasse 9 (✆ **0341/702590;** tram: 4, 6, 15, or 20), is a raffish-looking, all-in-one entertainment complex that houses at least two stages for the presentation of concerts and cabarets, a labyrinthine pub with lots of different areas for drinking, carousing, and dancing, and a cafe. It's popular with students. Depending on the night of the week, and depending on the time of the night you show up, you'll find either live bands or DJs playing African, heavy metal, and rock mixed with contemporary dance music. Some aspect of this complex opens daily from 10am, but the nighttime energy only gets wound up Wednesday to Saturday from 8pm to 5am, when it charges a cover that ranges from 3€ to 12€ ($2.70–$10.70) depending on the night of the week and who's playing. Sometimes, films (foreign and German-language) are shown in one of the bar areas, costing around 3€ ($2.70) entrance fee.

For more blues, jazz, and the occasional presentation of German-language satire and cabaret, head to **Pfeffermühle,** Thomaskirchhof 16 (✆ **0341/960-2499;** tram: 4, 6, 8, 10, 11, or 13), on Monday night, when the bands start up at 10pm. Other nights, people gather to drink and talk. The courtyard here is very popular during warm weather.

**GAY BARS & CLUBS** The friendly, ultra-cool bar **RosaLinde,** Brühl 64–66 (✆ **0341/484-15-11),** a few steps from the main railway station, is the central focus of gay nightlife in Leipzig. It's open Sunday to Thursday as a bar from 7 to 11pm; Friday and Saturday, it functions as a cafe, bar, and disco from 5pm till 3am, with disco music beginning around 9pm. Come here for a drink and the chance to mingle with conventional, not-particularly fetishistic gay men (and to a lesser degree, lesbians) in their 20s and 30s. An equally worthy and popular gay hangout is **Blaue Trude,** Katharinenstrasse 17 (✆ **0341/212-6679;** tram: 1, 2, 3, 4, 6, 8, 15, 17, 21, 24, 27, or 31), which functions as a bar every night 8pm to 4am, and as a gay (mostly male) disco every Tuesday to Saturday from around 10pm to 5am. Admission is free.

**VARIETY** Recommended only for visitors who really understand fluent, and highly ironic, German-language nuances, **Schaubühne Lindenfels,** Karl-Heine-Strasse 50 (✆ **0341/484620;** tram: 1, 2, 4, 6, 15, 17, 21, or 24), offers alternative theater and cinema in a laid-back cafe-bar complex and is open daily 10am to 2am. Admission to movies, which are shown almost nightly, depending on that week's schedule, costs between 4€ and 7.50€ ($3.55–$6.70). Admission to theater productions, when they're scheduled, cost from 6€ to 12€ ($5.35–$10.70) per person. Depending on the seasonal lineup, they're presented Thursday to Saturday and sometimes Sunday. Call for information.

## SIDE TRIPS FROM LEIPZIG

### LUTHERSTADT WITTENBERG

This is the city associated with **Martin Luther** (1483–1546), leader of the German Reformation. It attracts pilgrims from all over the world. Wittenberg's other famous son was humanist Philipp Melanchthon (1497–1560), a Protestant reformer and scholar and a friend of Luther's and later of Calvin's. Both are honored with statues in front of the Rathaus. Wittenberg is a handsome enough city, but a stop here isn't a must unless you're particularly interested in Luther.

Wittenberg lies 68km (42 miles) northeast of Leipzig and 100km (62 miles) southwest of Berlin. Access by car is via the A9 Autobahn north and south, Route 187 east, and Highway 2 north and south. The Wittenberg Bahnhof is on the major Deutsche Bundesbahn rail line (Halle–Berlin), with frequent connections. It's an hour by train from Leipzig. For travel information, contact **Wittenberg-Information,** Schlossplatz 2 (✆ **03491/49-86-10**). November to February, it's open Monday to Friday from 10am to 4pm; Saturday from 10am to 2pm, and Sunday from 11am to 3pm. March to October, it's open Monday to Friday from 9am to 6pm, Saturday from 10am to 3pm, Sunday from 11am to 4pm.

Both Luther and Melanchthon are buried in the **Schlosskirche,** Friedrichstrasse 1a (✆ **03491/40-25-85**), which dates from the 15th century but was rebuilt in the 19th. It was on the Schlosskirche doors that Luther nailed his "Ninety-Five Theses" in 1517. The bronze doors were added in 1858 and bear the Latin text of the theses. The church is open November to April, Monday to Saturday 10am to 4pm, and Sunday 11:30am to 4pm; May to October, it's open Monday to Saturday 10am to 5pm, and Sunday 11:30am to 5pm. Services are held Sunday at 10am and Wednesday at noon. There's a 30-minute organ concert every Tuesday at 2:30pm. Admission to the church and to its concerts is free; a brief guided tour, conducted in either German or English, costs 1€ (90¢). For further information contact the tourist office at ✆ 03491/49-86-10.

Part of an Augustinian monastery in which Luther lived has been turned into the **Lutherhalle Wittenberg,** Collegienstrasse 54 (✆ **03491/420-311**). The parish church here, where Luther preached, dates from the 14th century. An oak tree marks the spot outside the Elster gate where Luther publicly burned his papal bull (edict) of excommunication in 1520. Hours are November to March, Tuesday to Sunday 10am to 5pm; April to October, Tuesday to Sunday 9am to 6pm. Admission costs 3.50€ ($3.15) for adults, 2€ ($1.80) for students people aged 7 to 18, and free for children 6 and under.

You can also visit the **Stadtkirche,** Judenstrasse 35 (✆ **03491/40-32-01**), where Luther did the majority of his preaching. It's called the "Mother Church of the Reformation." Sections date to the 13th century, making it the oldest structure in Wittenberg. The altar is by Lucas Cranach the Elder, who was once Bürgermeister of Wittenberg and a friend to Luther. It's open as follows: November to April, Monday to Saturday 10am to 4pm, Sunday 11:30am to 4pm; May to October, Monday to Saturday 9am to 5pm, Sunday 11:30am to 5pm. Admission is free.

### Where to Stay & Dine

**Park Plaza Wittenberg** Built in the early 1990s in a postmodern style that evokes a building that's at least a century older, this is the best hotel in town, located in the historic city center on a pedestrian mall. It's often filled in summer with pilgrims coming to pay their respects to Martin Luther. Rooms are comfortable but a bit lackluster, with modern furnishings and compact shower only bathrooms.

Neustrasse 7–10, 06886 Wittenberg. ✆ **03491/46-10.** Fax 03491/46-12-00. www.parkplazaww.com. 171 units. 85€–133€ ($75.90–$118.75) double. Rates include buffet breakfast. AE, DC, DISC, MC, V. Parking 8€ ($7.15). **Amenities:** Restaurant; bar; room service; laundry. *In room:* TV, minibar, hair dryer.

## QUEDLINBURG ★

In 1994, UNESCO cited Quedlinburg as "an extraordinary example of a medieval European city," and added it to its list of World Heritage Sites.

Quedlinburg, which survived World War II intact, is nestled at the foot of a rock pinnacle and crowned by a castle and an abbey church. It has origins going back to a Saxon settlement in the early 10th century. Here you'll see the church of St. Servatius, an architectural masterpiece, as well as a well-preserved castle and cobbled lanes with half-timbered houses dating from the 16th and 17th centuries. In fact, Quedlinburg has over 1,600 half-timbered buildings, which is more than any other town in the country.

There are three trains a day from Leipzig (travel time: 3 hr.). Call ✆ **1805/99-66-33** for information and schedules. Access by car is along B6. For tourist information, contact **Quedlinburg-Information,** Markt 2 (✆ **03946/90-56-24,** www.quedlinburg.de), open May to October, Monday to Friday 9am to 7pm, Saturday 10am to 4pm, and Sunday 10am to 3pm; November to April, it's open Monday to Friday 10am to 5:30pm and closed on Saturday and Sunday. Begin your tour in the **Altstadt (Old Town),** site of the **Markt (Marketplace).** The **Rathaus,** in the Renaissance style of the 1600s, was originally built in 1310. The statue (ca. 1420) on the left of the facade is of Roland, Charlemagne's knight. The buildings on the other three sides of the Markt are from the 1600s and 1700s. Branching off the square are small cobblestone lanes right out of the Middle Ages. The area around Breitstrasse has several colorful alleyways.

Take the ramp up to the castle to the broad terrace that offers a panoramic view of the medieval town. Here, on the site of the original 9th-century church, stands Quedlinburg's major attraction, the **Stiftskirche St. Servatius** ★★, Schlossberg 1 (✆ **03946/709-900**), one of the architectural masterpieces of the Romanesque era. The church was started in 1070 but wasn't consecrated until 1129. Craftsmen from northern Italy were imported to create the friezes and capitals above the central nave. Three aisles with diagonal rib vaulting divide the crypt beneath the chancel. The aisles are adorned with frescoes depicting scenes from the Bible.

The church is filled with treasures, including a treasury (Domschatz) with manuscripts from as far back as the 10th century. In 1990, a number of ecclesiastical artifacts that had disappeared after the war turned up in Texas, when the heirs of a U.S. Army officer tried to sell them. The purloined treasures have been returned and are now on permanent display. The church is open May to October, Tuesday to Saturday 10am to 6pm, Sunday noon to 6pm; off-season, Tuesday to Saturday 10am to 4pm and on Sunday noon to 4pm. Admission 3€ ($2.70) for adults 2€ ($1.80) for students and for persons aged 6 to 18. It's free for children under 6.

**Burgberg Schloss,** Schlossberg 1 (✆ **03946/27-30**) was once part of an abbey. A Saxon stronghold in the 10th century, the castle was expanded from the late 16th to the mid-17th centuries. The castle complex includes the Schlossmuseum, which displays 16th- and 17th-century Italian and Flemish paintings as well as exhibits on the history of the town. A Princes' Hall from the mid-1700s and the throne room can also be visited. The castle is open May to September, Tuesday to Sunday 10am to 6pm; off-season, Tuesday to Sunday 10am to 5pm. Admission is 2.50€ ($2.25) for adults, 1.50€ ($1.35) for children aged 6 to 18, and free for children under 6.

## Where to Stay

**Hotel Schlossmühle** ★★ Set in the medieval center, this government-rated four-star hotel has emerged as the finest in Quedlinburg. It combines a historic core with a modern addition. Ancient traditions and a modern ambience are perfectly wed here, creating a special atmosphere. Bedrooms are midsize to spacious and are completely up-to-date, each one tastefully furnished and comfortably decorated, with a midsize bathroom and a tub-and-shower combination. On site are two restaurants, offering a variety of regional and international dishes, the best in Quedlinburg. The hotel is also better-accessorized than its nearest competition, Romantik Hotel Am Brühl.

Kaiser-Otto-Strasse 28, 06484 Quedlinburg. ✆ **03946/7870.** Fax 03946/787419. 70 units. 180€–210€ ($160.75–$187.55) double; 230€–290€ ($205.40–$258.95) suite. AE, DC, MC, V. Parking 10€ ($8.95). **Amenities:** 2 restaurants; bar; library; fitness center. *In room:* TV, hair dryer.

**Romantik Hotel am Brühl** ★★ Romantic and tranquil, and set behind a richly historic brick and half-timbered facade, this hotel is run by the Schmidt family. Rooms come in a variety of shapes and sizes. All are well furnished with first-rate mattresses and fine linens; some open onto castle views. Virtually all major attractions are within walking distance.

Billungstrasse 11, 06484 Quedlinburg. ✆ **03946/9-61-80.** Fax 03946/9-61-82-46. www.hotelambruehl.de. 48 units. 100€–135€ ($89.30–$120.55) double; 130€–140€ ($116.10–$125) suite. Rates include buffet breakfast. AE, DC, V. Free parking. **Amenities:** Restaurant; lounge; sauna; solarium; room service; laundry. *In room:* TV, minibar, hair dryer.

**Romantik Hotel Theophano** ★★ Though not quite as tranquil or "Romantik" as the Am Brühl, this is a very close runner-up. Here, two old guild houses, each about 350 years old, were completely renovated and combined into one hotel. The small rooms are brightly furnished, individually decorated, and often outfitted with antiques. Some have canopied beds, and most of them come with a combination tub and shower. The location is central for sightseeing. In summer, guests can sit in the courtyard.

Markt 13–14 (on the marketplace), 06484 Quedlinburg. ✆ **03946/9-63-00.** Fax 03946/96-30-36. www.hoteltheophano.de. 22 units. 93€–120€ ($83.05–$107.15) double; 155€ ($138.40) suite. Rates include buffet breakfast. AE, MC, V. Free parking. **Amenities:** Restaurant; lounge; room service; laundry/dry cleaning. *In room:* TV, hair dryer.

**Zur Goldenen Sonne** This hotel, which dates from 1671, is a good traditional choice. It stands near the Mathildenbrunne, a landmark fountain. The building's wood-beam construction is typical of this part of Germany. The small rooms are cozily furnished in rustic style, and each is equipped with a small, shower-only bathroom. In summer, the garden is popular with locals and visitors alike for social gatherings.

Steinweg 11 (a 5-min. walk from the railway station), 06484 Quedlinburg. ✆ **03946/9-62-50.** Fax 03946/96-25-30. www.hotelzurgoldenensonne.de. 27 units. 67€–82€ ($59.85–$73.25) double. Rates include buffet breakfast. AE, MC, V. Parking free. **Amenities:** Restaurant; bar; lounge; room service; laundry. *In room:* TV, minibar, hair dryer.

### Where to Dine

**Ratskeller** GERMAN/INTERNATIONAL This longtime favorite is within walking distance of the railway station. Wine buffs should order the rare Saxon wine. The food is hearty and regional. Many of the meat and game specialties are served with wine sauerkraut and dumplings. In season, venison is likely to be on the menu.

Markt 1 (in the Rathaus). ✆ **03946/27-68.** Reservations recommended. Main courses 11€–20€ ($9.80–$17.85); fixed-price menu 17€ ($15.20). AE, DC, MC, V. Thurs–Tues 11:30am–10:30pm. Closed Jan.

## 3 Dresden ★★★

198km (123 miles) S of Berlin, 111km (69 miles) SE of Leipzig

Dresden, once known as "Florence on the Elbe," was celebrated throughout Europe for its architecture and art treasures. Then came the night of February 13, 1945, when Allied bombers rained down phosphorus and high-explosive bombs on the city, which had no military targets. By morning, the Dresden of legend was but a memory. No one knows for sure how many people died, but the number is certainly in the tens of thousands, and perhaps more. If you're interested in the subject, you might want to read Kurt Vonnegut's novel *Slaughterhouse Five.*

Today, Dresden is undergoing a rapid and dramatic restoration, and is once again a major sightseeing destination. For example, its once-fabled *Schloss* (castle), for decades only a few blackened walls, is scheduled to be completely rebuilt by late 2003. Dresden also boasts beautiful churches and palaces, as well as many world-class museums—among the finest in all of Germany.

City officials want the entire city rebuilt by the year 2006 in time for Dresden's 800th anniversary. Even though that dream is a long way from being realized, much has already been accomplished. Thankfully, the work has proceeded along sensible lines and has none of the unreal, theme-park feeling that some restorations produce. Wherever you go, you will not be allowed to forget the Allied bombings of February 1945, which destroyed about three-quarters of the Altstadt.

In August of 2002, the city of Dresden, battered by the rising floodwaters of the Elbe, battled furiously to save its cultural heritage (as well as its people, buildings, and even zoo animals). It more or less succeeded, and museum workers, the police, and even the German army were called out to rescue hundreds of paintings and other art treasures as the waters of the Elbe rose by the hour, threatening to destroy the works of such old masters as Rembrandt, Ruvens, and Raphael. Most of the city's major landmarks, including the Zwinger Palace, were under siege. The city was particularly saddened because it had been making gigantic efforts and, indeed, had realized impressive results, to restore itself to the glory it had achieved before Allied bombers virtually flattened it in 1945. City officials have promised to rekindle their restoration efforts and are promising visitors that they'll be as good as new again.

## ESSENTIALS

**GETTING THERE** **By Plane** The **Dresden-Klotsche** airport lies 10km (6 miles) north of the city center. The airport is served by Lufthansa and most international carriers, with regularly scheduled flights from 11 German cities and other major European cities. For flight information, call ✆ **0351/8813360.** A rail line that's linked to Dresden's U-bahn network stretches from the airport to the city's main railway station, requiring 20 minutes transit each way, and a one-way fare of 1.50€ ($1.35). To go from the airport to the center of Dresden by taxi costs about 18€ ($16.05).

**By Train** Dresden has two main rail stations, the **Hauptbahnhof,** on Wiener Platz, and the **Dresden-Neustadt,** at Schlesischer Park. Tram 11 connects the two. The city is served by the Deutsche Bundesbahn rail line, with frequent connections to major and regional cities. From Berlin, 15 trains arrive daily (trip time: 2–2½ hours); 12 trains pull in from Frankfurt (trip time: 5 hours). For rail information and schedules, call ✆ **1805/99-66-33.**

**By Car** Access is via the E50 Autobahn from the west or the E4 Autobahn from the north (Rostock, Berlin) or from the south.

**VISITOR INFORMATION** The **Information-Center,** Pragerstrasse 10 (✆ **0351/49-19-20**) is open year-round Monday to Friday 9am to 6pm; Saturday 9am to 4pm. It's closed on Sunday. Here you can book your accommodations and purchase a map of Dresden, get information booklets in English, and tickets for theater, opera, and concerts. The city has a second branch of its

**ATTRACTIONS ●**

Albertinum **17**
Altmarkt **5**
Altstadt **3**
Frauenkirche **18**
Gemäldegalerie Alte Meister (Zwinger) **7**
Grosser Garten **2**
Katholische Hofkirche **8**
Kreuzkirche **4**
Porcelain Museum (Zwinger) **7**
Rüstkammer (Zwinger) **7**
Semper Opera House **9**
Stadtmuseum Dresden **19**
Zwinger **7**

**ACCOMMODATIONS ■**

Art'otel **10**
Bülow Residenz **13**
Hilton Dresden **16**
Hotel am Terrassenufer **15**
Kempinski Hotel Taschenbergpalais **6**
Martha Hospiz **12**
Schlosshotel Dresden–Pillnitz **1**
Villa Emma **14**
Westin Bellevue **11**

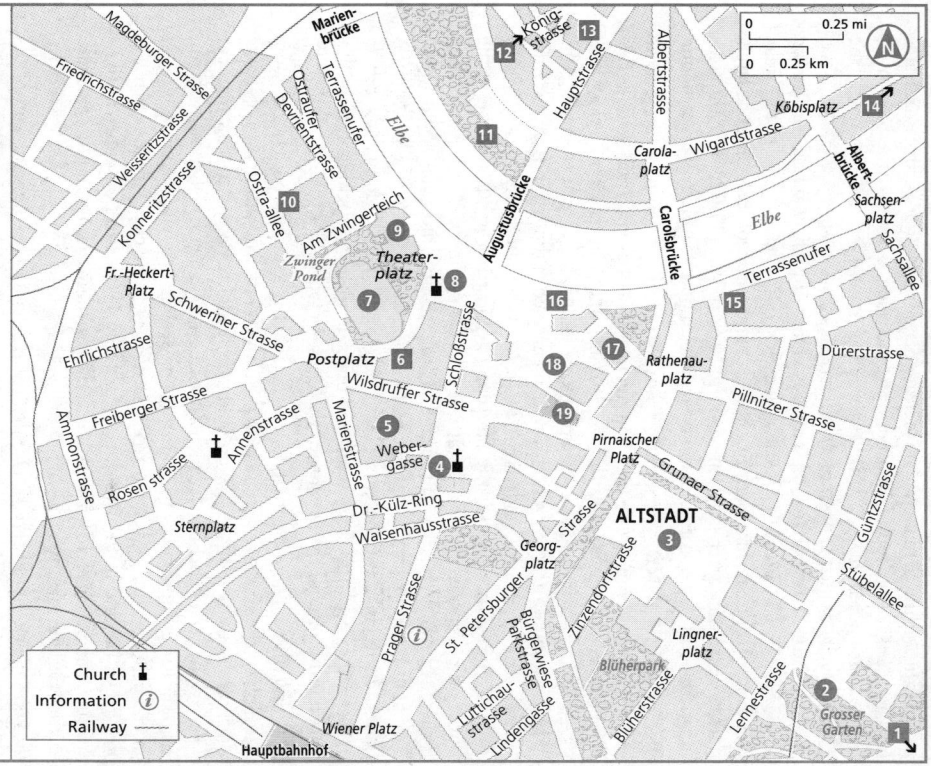

tourist office at the Schinkelwache, Theaterplatz (same phone), that maintains the same hours, year round, and performs the same services as the branch on Pragerstrasse noted above. Unlike the Pragerstrasse branch, however, the Schinkelwache branch is open on Sunday from 10am to 4pm.

The **Main Post Office,** Hauptpostamt, Königbrückerstrasse 21–29 (✆ **0351/819-13-70**), is in Dresden-Neustadt and is open Monday to Friday 8am to 6pm and Saturday 8am to noon. A branch post office, almost as large, that's closer to the center, is at Annenstrasse 10 (✆ 0341/439-0931), in the city's historic core. It's open Monday to Friday 8am to 6pm; Saturday 9am to noon.

**GETTING AROUND** **By Public Transportation** If you plan to see more than the historic core of Dresden, you might use the bus and tram lines. A ride of four stops or fewer costs 1.50€ ($1.35), or you can purchase a 24-hour pass for 4€ ($3.55). Maps and tickets are sold at automated dispensers outside the main rail station. After midnight, service is curtailed, although most major lines still operate every hour. Dresden's S-Bahn reaches the suburbs. Especially worthwhile to short-term visitors is the **Dresden City Card,** which is available at the tourist office. Priced at 16€ ($14.30), it provides 48 hours of transport on any of the city's trams or buses, entrance to 12 of the city's most important museums, plus discounts on city sightseeing tours. An adaptation of the same card is a **Dresden Regio-Card.** Priced at 25€ ($22.35), it offers 72 hours of access to an even wider network of city trams and buses, in this case reaching into the distant suburbs, plus all the benefits of the Dresden City Card.

**By Funicular** There are two funiculars in Dresden. The busier and more accessible of the two is the **Standseilbahn,** which links the suburb of Loschwitz to a hillside residential area, Weisser Hirsch. More remote, with less frequent runs, is the **Schwebebahn,** which links Loschwitz with Oberloschwitz on Saturday and Sunday only, carrying passengers to the viewing site at Loschwitzhöhe, which gives you an excellent view of the city. This funicular was the first of its kind in the world, built in 1898–1900. Fares on either of these funiculars costs 1.50€ ($1.35) each way. For operating hours and more details, contact the tourist office.

**By Ferry** Five ferries service Dresden, each operated by the same authorities that maintain the city's network of trams and buses. One is a vehicular ferry across the River Elbe between Dresden–Kleinzschachwitz and the Pillnitz Castle. To reach its departure point, take tram no. 1 from Postplatz. For more information, call ✆ **0351/857-1011.**

## SEEING THE SIGHTS

The amount of restoration going on here is tremendous. At present, and for years to come, expect to see some of the major sights of Dresden behind scaffolding. Despite the reconstruction, there are still many ruins of the war left, most notably the baroque **Frauenkirche (Church of Our Lady),** at Neumarkt (✆ **0351/498-1131**), built between 1726 and 1743 and once known throughout Europe for its cupola. The East German government deliberately let the blackened hulk remain, as a reminder of the horrors of modern warfare. But today the church is slowly being rebuilt. Guided English- and German-language tours of the massive construction site, which eerily combines a sense of both modern and medieval building techniques, are conducted at hourly intervals every day from 10am to 5pm. The cost of the tour is free, but donations for the continuing reconstruction of the church are appreciated.

The restored **Katholische Hofkirche (Catholic Court Church)** ★★, Schlossplatz (✆ **0351/484-4712**), is the biggest church in Saxony. It was built by the son of August the Strong, Frederick Augustus II, who ruled from 1733 to 1763. The church's facade has 38 biblical and historical figures in the high baroque style. Inside, you can see the crypt with the tombs of 49 rulers of Saxony and a box allegedly containing the heart of August the Strong. On the main floor you can see a beautiful stone pulpit by the royal sculptor, Balthasar Permoser (1651–1732), one of the leading sculptors of his time in Saxony. There's also an 18th-century church organ. Admission is free. This church, also known as the Cathedral of St. Trinitas, is open Monday to Friday 9am to 4:30pm, Saturday 10am to 4pm, and Sunday noon to 4pm. Guided tours, conducted only in German, and priced at 2.50€ ($2.25) per person, are conducted Monday to Thursday at 2pm and Saturday at 1 and 2pm.

The **Kreuzkirche (Church of the Cross)** ★ (✆ **0351/439-3920)** stands at the **Altmarkt,** or old market square. This church is the home of the *Kreuzchor,* the famous boys' choir of Dresden. Free concerts that showcase the boys' choir are conducted every Saturday at 5pm, unless the choir is traveling as part of its concert series. The church's architecture is a combination of baroque and Art Nouveau. The present building is from the late 18th century, although a church on this spot stood here as early as the 13th century. You can also view the reconstructed **Rathaus** (town hall) and the 18th-century **Landhaus** at the Altmarkt (✆ **0351/488-2347**). Most of the Rathaus' interior cannot be visited by casual visitors, but you can take an elevator to the Rathaus' tower for a fee of 2.50€ ($2.25) for adults, 1.25€ ($1.10) for students and persons 6 to 16. It's free for children under 6. The tower and its combination of stairs and elevator is open daily between April and October, from 10am to 6pm. (The last ticket is sold at 5:30pm.)

Of Dresden's many parks and gardens, the best and most popular is the **Grosser Garten,** to the southeast of the Altstadt. This park, which was mapped out in 1676, contains a zoo and a botanical garden. In the center is a minor *Lustschloss* (pleasure palace) built in 1670, that's most appealing from the outside, except for the occasional midsummer concerts conducted there. For more information, contact the tourist office.

## THE MAJOR MUSEUMS

**Albertinum** ★★★ This imposing imperial structure houses one of Germany's great galleries. It's named for the Saxon King Albert, who between 1884 and 1887 converted this former royal arsenal into a home for a vast collection of art and precious jewelry. The most famous exhibition is the extraordinary **Grünes Gewölbe (Green Vaults)** ★★★, a dazzling collection of 16th- to 18th-century treasures: rococo chests, ivory carvings, jewelry, intricately designed mirrors, and priceless porcelain. Many pieces were created by the craftspeople of local guilds; others were acquired from the far corners of the earth.

On the remaining two floors is the **Gemäldegalerie Neue Meister** ★★★, a collection of 19th- and 20th-century art, from Corot to Otto Dix. We are especially fond of the desolate and haunting landscapes of Caspar David Friedrich, the German Romantic artist. Impressionists and post-impressionists are well represented, including Gauguin, Degas, Manet, Monet, Corinth, Liebermann, Klimt, and van Gogh. Antifascist artists, whose works were either destroyed or banned in the Nazi era, are also on display.

Brühl Terrace. ✆ **0351/4-91-40.** Admission 3.60€ ($3.20) adults, 2.50€ ($2.25) children 6–18 and students. Free for children under 6. Fri–Wed 10am–6pm. Closed 2 weeks in Jan. Tram: 1, 3, 5, 7, or 8 to Rathenau Platz.

**Stadtmuseum Dresden** ★ This museum contains a rich display of Dresden's history. Especially fascinating are the photographs of the controversial 1945 Allied bombings. Most Germans view the air raids as pointless destruction; one British historian claims they were "Churchill's revenge for the Nazi bombing of Coventry."

Wilsdruffer Strasse 2. ✆ **0351/65-64-80.** Admission 3.60€ ($3.20) adults, 2.05€ ($1.85) persons 6–18 and students. Free for children under 6. Sat–Thurs 10am–6pm. Tram: 3 or 4.

**Zwinger** ★★★ Augustus the Strong, elector of Saxony (he was also king of Poland), built this baroque masterpiece, modeled after Versailles, in 1719. Here he staged tournaments and kept his dozens of concubines. His physique was called Herculean, his temperament Rabelaisian, but he also had a great love for the arts. Today, this artfully symmetrical complex of baroque buildings holds a collection of museums. The damage caused by the British air raid in 1945 was so devastating that some locals feared that the Zwinger would remain a ruin forever. However, it's been restored and it's back in business, welcoming new generations of art lovers.

The Zwinger was initially conceived by M. D. Pöppelmann (1662–1736) as the forecourt of the castle. In the center of the large quadrangle are formal gardens, fountains, and promenades, forming a deep curving bay enclosed by pavilions. Notable are the Wallpavilion in the center of the semicircular arched gallery in the west end, and the *Nyphenbad* (Bath of Nymphs) ★★ with its graceful fountains and mythological figures by Balthasar Permoser, who helped Pöppelmann in the construction of the Zwinger. On the northeast side is a Renaissance-style building, added in 1846 by Gottfried Semper (1803–79). Semper's two-story pavilions are linked by one-story galleries. The architectural critic Sir Nikolaus Pevsner once wrote: "What exultation in these rocking curves, and yet what grace! It is joyful but never vulgar; vigorous, boisterous perhaps, but never crude."

The most important museum in the complex is the **Gemäldegalerie Alte Meister** ★★★, which has its entrance at Theaterplatz 1. This gallery, one of the best on the continent, has as its showpiece Raphael's *Sistine Madonna.* You'll also find Giorgione's *Sleeping Venus,* Antonello da Messina's *The Martyrdom of St. Sebastian,* Titian's *Tribute Money,* and many famous works by Veronese, Tintoretto, Correggio, and Annibale Carracci. You'll also see Flemish, Dutch, and German paintings by van Dyck, Vermeer, Dürer, and Rembrandt, among others. The Rubens collection includes his spectacular *Neptune,* full of rearing horses, and an exquisite *St. Jerome.*

The **Rüstkammer (Historical Museum)** displays a vast collection of weaponry from the 15th to 18th centuries, including halberds, shields, cannons, and suits of armor for both men and horses. The Porzellansammlung displays the finery produced by the porcelain factories of Dresden during the 350 years since their founding.

Theaterplatz 1. ✆ **0351/4-91-46-19.** www.staatl-kunstsammlungen-dresden.de. Entrance to each individual museum costs 3.60€ ($3.20) for adults; 2.50€ ($2.25) for persons 6–18. Free for children under 6. Day ticket, valid 24 hours for entrance to 11 of Dresden's top museums and monuments, and available at any of the individual museums within the Zwinger costs 6.10€ ($5.45) for adults, 3.60€ ($3.20) for persons 6–18 and students. All 3 are open Tues–Sun 10am–6pm. All 3 closed for 2 weeks in Jan. Tram: 1, 2, 4, 7, 8, 11, 12, or 14. Bus: 82 and 94 to Postplatz.

## BUS TOURS

Responding to the flood of visitors coming to see the city's historic core, **Stadtrundfahrt Dresden,** Königstrasse 6 (✆ **0351/899-5650**), has organized

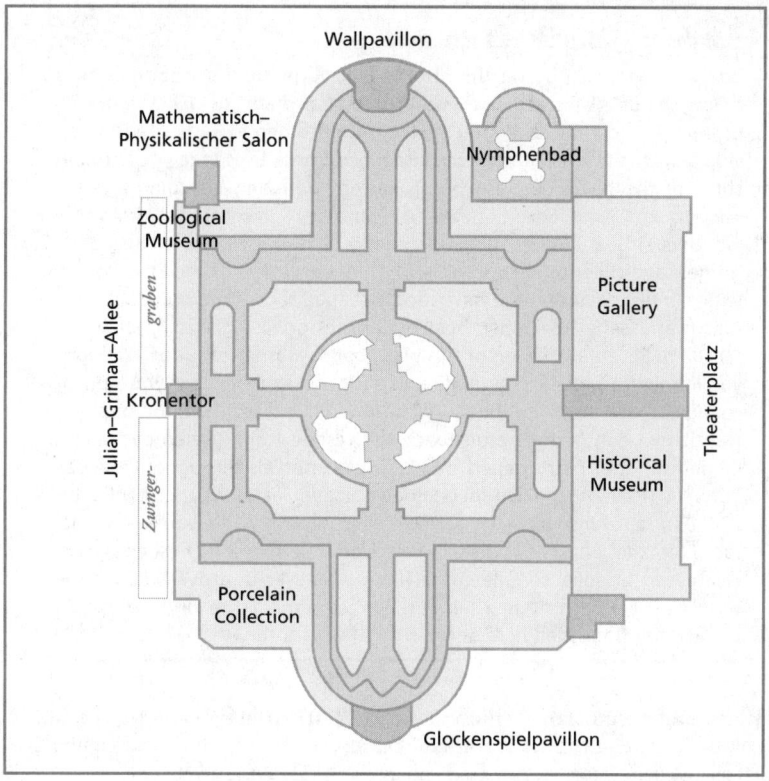


a flotilla of red and white buses that feature—via prerecorded descriptions and headsets—running commentary in eight languages. Every day April to early November 9:30am to 5pm, buses depart at 30-minute intervals, and early November to March at 60-minute intervals, for circular tours of the city that incorporate overviews of all the major monuments. Visitors can hop on or off the bus at any of 19 points along the way, and they can even postpone some of the stops until the following day. The point of origin of each tour begins at the Schlossplatz, adjacent to the Augustusbrücke. Additional stopovers include the Zwinger, the Grünes Gewölbe, the Frauenkirche, and many of the parks, gardens, and architectural highlights of the city. The price is 17€ ($15.20) per adult. There are no discounts for students, but it's free for children under 14 when they're accompanied by their guardians.

## SHOPPING

Perhaps because of Dresden's destruction in the final days of World War II, there's an emphasis here on collecting the high-quality antiques that remain. You'll find many antiques dealers in the city. Most of the inventory has been culled from homes and estate sales in the relatively unscathed surrounding hamlets. The most interesting shops in Dresden, and many of the most glamorous ones, line either side of the Königstrasse. Here, look for a roster of handcrafted goods and gift items. If you're seeking antiques and artwork, pay a visit to **Antikitäten und Kunst,** Obergraben 19 (✆ **0351/801-4331**), and its similarly named competitor,

### *Moments* A Cruise on the Elbe

You can take a cruise on the historic Elbe River from central moorings below the Brühl Terrace. **Sächsischer Dampfschiffahrt** (✆ **0351/86-60-90**) offers a 4½-hour cruise along the Elbe from Dresden to Rathen, a German village at the border of the Czech Republic. These trips take you through some of the finest river scenery in eastern Germany, including an area known as "Swiss Saxony," one of Germany's most popular natural wonders. It's a land of table-shaped outcrops, isolated pillars, deep gorges, and sheer sandstone cliffs. The upper reaches of the Elbe flow in wide curves through these fantastically shaped rock formations. Between March and early November, boat departures occur twice daily, at 9 and 10:30am. Because each leg of this waterborne journey requires 4½ hours, you'll have to block out an entire day for this experience if you opt for round-trip transport by boat. Alternatively, you can opt for one-way transit by boat, with a return back to Dresden from Rathen by train, a 40-minute ride. Trains depart at 30-minute intervals throughout the day between Rathen and Dresden. Boat passage, each way, costs 13.50€ ($12.05); rail transport, each way, costs 5€ ($4.45). While you're cruising, look for the *Blaues Wunder* (Blue Wonder), one of Dresden's most celebrated bridges, completed in 1893 and never destroyed during the wartime bombings. It is a beautiful expression of the bridge-building genius that flourished here at the turn of the century.

**Kunst und Antikitäten,** Görlitzerstrasse 39 (✆ **0351/804-5658**). An especially convenient antique gallery is **Antikitäten,** on the lobby level of the Kempinski Hotel Taschenbergpalais, Am Taschenberg (✆ **0351/490-14-79**).

The oldest manufacturer of porcelain in Dresden is **Wehsener Porzellan,** 5km (3 miles) southeast of the center at Donaustrasse 72 (✆ **0351/470-73-40;** bus: 72 or 76 from the main railway station). Its hand-painted objects are the most charming and interesting in Dresden. Anything you buy can be shipped.

And don't overlook the city's role as a purveyor of modern painting and sculpture. Two of the most interesting art galleries are **Galerie Gebrüder Lehmann,** Gorlitzerstrasse 16 (✆ **0351/801-1783**), and **Galerie am Blauen Wünder,** Pillnitzer Landstrasse 2 (✆ **0351/268-40-20**).

**Weihnachtsland am Zwinger,** Kleine Brüdergasse 5 (✆ **0351/862-1230**), is the best-stocked and most interesting gift shop in Dresden, with a year-round emphasis on Christmas, New Year's, and Easter ornaments that are handmade in the nearby Erzgebirge region. Look for pieces of delicate Plauener Spitze lace that's designed to hang on hooks affixed by suction cups to the glass of your windows—it's easy to transport, and some pieces of it can be acquired for less than 6€ ($5.35). There are also elaborately detailed Easter eggs, carved wooden figurines in the shape of either soldiers or angels, and framed still lifes and landscapes made from assemblages of dried flowers.

## WHERE TO STAY

Since reunification and the amazing increase in tourism, Dresden's hotel prices have soared, as has the demand for rooms. Even so-called "budget" hotels can command 130€ ($116.10) a night for a double.

## VERY EXPENSIVE

**Kempinski Hotel Taschenbergpalais** ★★★ Few hotels of post-reunification Germany have sparked as much pride among local citizens as this one. Its history dates from the early 18th century, when the elector of Saxony built a baroque castle for his favorite mistress, the Countess Cosel, who for mysterious reasons was later banished from his court. For 250 years, the palace was the pride of Dresden, a site visited almost as much as the Zwinger. Only the surreal remains of a massive marble staircase survived the bombs, but now the historic Taschenberg Palace is back better than ever.

In 1993, a Frankfurt-based real-estate developer spent $175 million on transforming the ruin into Dresden's finest hotel, restoring the five-story baroque, sculpture-dotted facade to its original opulence. Rooms are the most luxurious in town. Those on the west and north sides overlook the Zwinger or the Opera. Bathrooms are quite opulent as well, with heated floors, heated racks, robes, and both tubs and shower stalls. A tiny ruined portion of the structure has been artfully retained as a reminder of the bombs of 1945.

Taschenberg 3, 01067 Dresden. ✆ **0351/4-91-20.** Fax 0351/4-91-28-12. www.kempinski-dresden.de. 213 units. 280€–360€ ($250.05–$321.50) double; 430€–2,600€ ($384–$2,321.80) suite. AE, DC, MC, V. Parking 12.80€ ($11.45). Tram: 5 or 8. **Amenities:** Restaurant; bar; pool; health club; sauna; room service; massage; babysitting; laundry/dry cleaning. *In room:* A/C, TV, minibar, hair dryer, safe.

## EXPENSIVE

**Bülow Residenz** ★★★ Even more than the Hotel Taschenbergpalais, this is our preferred nest in Dresden, a boutique hotel of charm and grace and one of the most luxurious in eastern Germany. This hotel, with a restored facade from the 1700s, has been a success since its opening in the early '90s. The formal lounge, with its plush seating, sets the tone. A garden patio is the perfect place to be on a summer day. Individually decorated rooms are unusually spacious compared to most in Dresden. Oversize beds and contemporary redwood furnishings make for a restful ambience. Bathrooms have shower-tub combinations.

Rähnitzgasse 19 (near the Opera), 01097 Dresden. ✆ **0351/8-00-30.** Fax 0351/8-00-31-00. www.buelow-residenz.de. 30 units. 170€–210€ ($151.80–$187.55) double; 260€–380€ ($232.20–$339.35) suite. AE, DC, MC, V. Parking 8€ ($7.15). Tram: 3, 4., 8, or 11. **Amenities:** Restaurant; lounge; babysitting; laundry/dry cleaning. *In room:* TV, minibar, hair dryer, safe.

**Hilton Dresden** ★ This hotel is one of the best in the region, though lacking the romance and glamour of the Hotel Taschenbergpalais or the intimacy and charm of the Bülow (see above). Its conservative mansard-roofed facade blends harmoniously with the baroque buildings on the nearby Neumarkt. A glassed-in passageway connects the hotel to a 19th-century building, the Sekundogenitur, which contains two restaurants and an array of banqueting and conference rooms. Rooms are midsize, conservatively modern, and well maintained. Bathrooms are small and have shower-tub combinations. Double-glazed windows cut down on noise. The best rooms face the Frauenkirche.

An der Frauenkirche 5, 01067 Dresden. ✆ **800/445-8667** in the U.S. and Canada, or 0351/8-64-20. Fax 0351/8-64-27-25. www.hilton.com. 328 units. 150€–240€ ($133.95–$214.30) double; 280€–540€ ($250.05–$482.20) suite. AE, DC, MC, V. Parking 12€ ($10.70). Tram: 3, 5, 7, 8, or 12. **Amenities:** 6 restaurants; 4 bars; pool; fitness club; whirlpool; sauna; solarium; room service; babysitting; laundry. *In room:* TV, minibar, hair dryer, safe.

**Westin Bellevue** ★ The Bellevue, which we'd rank just under the Hilton, stands by the most attractive part of the Elbe. If you look out the hotel's windows or from its terraces to the opposite riverbank, you'll know you're in the spot where Canaletto painted his magnificent scenes. The ornate walls of a pair of courtyards that survived the 1945 bombings have been integrated into the structure and are now a protected monument. Some rooms overlook the courtyards; others are in modern wings that often open onto the Elbe. Whether you stay in the old part or in the new, you'll find well-appointed rooms. Bathrooms, however, are far from grand, with compact shower units. All rooms offer better views than those of the Hilton.

Grosse Meissner Strasse 15, 01097 Dresden. ✆ **0351/8050.** Fax 0351/8051609. www.westin.com. 339 units. 117€–260€ ($104.50–$232.20) double; 187€–560€ ($167–$500.10) suite. Breakfast 17€ ($15.20). AE, DC, MC, V. Parking 12€ ($10.70). Tram: 4 or 5. **Amenities:** 5 restaurants; bar; pool; health club; sauna; solarium; shopping arcade; room service; babysitting; laundry. *In room:* A/C, TV, minibar, hair dryer.

## MODERATE

**Art'otel** ★ *Finds* The six floors of this dramatic postmodern hotel are the most self-consciously "arty" of any hotel in Dresden. They were designed by Denis Santachiara, whose work has been heralded in Munich, Milan, New York, and Paris. One floor is an art gallery that focuses on striking contemporary paintings and sculpture by German artists. The stylish bedrooms are well furnished and most comfortable, each with a neat, efficiently organized private bathroom, mainly with combination tub and shower. The staff is very conscious of cutting-edge trends in German cities.

Ostra-Allee 33, 01067 Dresden. ✆ **0351/4-92-20.** Fax 0351/4-92-27-77. www.artotel.de. 174 units. 156€–180€ ($139.30–$160.75) double. Rates include buffet breakfast. AE, DC, MC, V. Parking 11.50€ ($10.25). Tram: 8, 9, 11, or 26. **Amenities:** Restaurant; bar; gym; sauna; room service. *In room:* TV, minibar, hair dryer.

**Hotel am Terrassenufer** Comfortable and reasonably priced, this hotel was built in the 1960s as a student dormitory. In the 1990s, it was renovated and enlarged into the streamlined 12-story hotel you see today. Set on the riverbank, a short walk from Dresden's historic core, it offers large, airy, big-windowed rooms with lots of sunlight and compact bathrooms with shower.

Terrassenufer 12, 01069 Dresden. ✆ **0351/440-95-00.** Fax 0351/440-96-00. www.hotel-terrassenufer.de. 196 units. 115€–175€ ($102.70–$156.30) double, 185€–260€ ($165.20–$232.20) suite. AE, DC, MC, V. Tram: 1, 3, or 5. **Amenities:** Restaurant; bar; room service; laundry. *In room:* TV, minibar, hair dryer.

**Rothenburger Hof** ★★ Beautifully renovated, this time-honored and traditional hotel, which first opened its doors in 1685, is once again claiming its regal position as a small luxury hotel. A family-run hotel, it is in Neustadt, the area rebuilt after a great fire in the late 1680s. It's within an easy walk of the historical monuments of the Old City. It's much more comfortable today than when it first opened, because so many modern improvements have been made, including the addition of a sauna, Turkish bath, and solarium. By the time of your visit, a swimming pool should have been added, an unusual luxury for a Dresden inner-city hotel. The midsize rooms are traditionally furnished and most comfortable, with freshly renovated, tiled bathrooms with tub and shower. Bedroom furnishings are tasteful reproductions of antiques.

In the hotel's restaurant, serving a good, though not spectacular cuisine, you feel as if you're dining with the Dresden elite a century and a half ago. Grace notes include a garden terrace and the installation of an elevator, which those 19th-century guests didn't get to enjoy.

Hauptstrasse 3, 01099 Dresden. ✆ **0351/81260.** Fax 0351/8126-222. 39 units 95€–135€ ($84.85–$120.55) double; 115€–145€ ($102.70–$129.50) suite. AE, MC, V. Free parking. Tram 11. **Amenities:** Restaurant; bar; room service; pool; sauna; Turkish bath; fitness center; solarium; laundry/dry cleaning; garden terrace. *In room:* TV, minibar, kitchen (in 13 units).

**Schlosshotel Dresden-Pillnitz** ★★ *Finds* Set within a few steps of Schloss Pillnitz (Pillnitz Castle), about 8km (5 miles) east of downtown Dresden, this historic building functioned as a restaurant as early as 1760, often feeding the courtiers and service personnel doing business with the castle. In 1999, the Zepp family poured time and money into its restoration. Today, the upper floors are devoted to clean, well-maintained, discreetly tasteful bedrooms, each with big windows, well-crafted furniture, and comfortable beds, plus tiled bathrooms with tub and shower. The lower floors contain a cafe, a reception hall, and a high-ceilinged restaurant with good food. Main courses at lunch focus on time-tested Teutonic specialities that include sauerbraten, wursts, salads, soups, and steaks. Dinners are more elaborate, more experimental, and more sophisticated. Specialties change regularly, but might include roasted pike with sautéed cabbage in Riesling sauce; filet of veal with goose liver, stuffed leeks, and duck-meat gnocchi; or filets of lamb served with a red onion and olive charlotte.

August-Böckelstiegel-Strasse 10, 01326 Dresden-Pillnitz. ✆ **0351/26-14-0.** Fax 0351/261-44-00. www.schlosshotel-pillnitz.de. 45 units. 100€–110€ ($89.30–$98.25) double; 180€–205€ ($160.75–$183.05) suite. Free parking. AE, MC, V. **Amenities:** Restaurant; cafe; laundry service. *In room:* TV, minibar.

## WHERE TO DINE

### EXPENSIVE

**Fischgalerie** ★ SEAFOOD This is the best seafood restaurant in town. Its culinary pizzazz stems directly from the chef's experience in upscale restaurants in Berlin and other cities. The interior, with its dramatic lighting, minimalist design, and blue-black color scheme, will remind you of a sophisticated enclave in Milan. There's a small aperitif bar near the entrance and a theatrical-looking open-view kitchen. Menus change every week, depending on the season, availability of ingredients, and the inspiration of the chef. Fresh seafood dishes might include salmon with fresh spinach and champagne sauce; tartare of herring with scrambled eggs, grilled filet of zander with red risotto; a combination of scampi with John Dory, served with tomato-flavored *spaghettini;* and crêpes stuffed with diced crabmeat. As an appetizer, you might try the fresh oysters from Brittany or marinated herring served with coarsely textured black bread.

Maxstrasse 2 (a 10-min. walk from both the Zwinger and the Kempinski Hotel). ✆ **0351/4-90-35-06.** Reservations recommended. Main courses 10€–25€ ($8.95–$22.35). AE, MC, V. Tues–Fri noon–3pm; Mon–Sat 6–11:30pm. Tram: 8, 9, or 26.

**Rossini** ★ ITALIAN Rossini offers Italian cuisine in a stylish setting, one floor above the lobby of the Dresden Hilton. Menu items might include chicken-liver paté in marsala wine, a buffet of Sicilian antipasti, carpaccio of swordfish marinated in marsala vinaigrette, Parma ham with coarse bread and a tapenade of olives; Sicilian-style fish soup, or grilled lamb with anchovy sauce. Dessert might be cassata made with ricotta cheese and candied fruit, or a *granita* (sorbet) of oranges and lemons floating on white wine.

In the Dresden Hilton, An der Frauenkirche 5. ✆ **0351/8-64-28-55.** Main courses 14€–26€ ($12.50–$23.20). AE, DC, MC, V. Daily noon–3pm and 6pm–midnight. Tram: 3, 5, 7, 8, or 12.

### MODERATE

**Brauhaus am Waldschlösschen** GERMAN This is a newly built replica of the old-fashioned beer halls and beer gardens that played such an important role in Dresden's past. Around 250 diners and drinkers can cram into a series of dining rooms, and another 800 can be accommodated within the sprawling garden (open Apr–Oct). Expect heaping platters of such time-tested Teutonic favorites as roast pork shank, sautéed fish with parsley and onions, schnitzels, soups, wursts, and roasts. Live music, usually from a jazzy pianist, is presented Monday to Saturday 8pm to midnight. Beer (Waldschlösschen) is brewed on the premises and comes in several degrees of darkness.

Am Brauhaus 8B (in the Neustadt district, 5km/3 miles northeast of the city center). ✆ **0351/811-990.** Reservations required. Main courses 4€–14€ ($3.55–$12.50). AE, DC, MC, V. Daily 11am–1am. Tram: 11 or 52. Bus: 91.

**Italianisches Dörfchen** ITALIAN/INTERNATIONAL Italianisches Dörfchen is a stately looking neoclassical building that was erected in 1911 on the site of the cluster of cottages ("the Italian Village") that once housed the mostly Italian crews of laborers building the nearby monuments of the Saxon kings. Today, it contains a quartet of restaurants, each of which has a different theme. The best way to decide which of them you'll patronize is to wander through the formal premises of the building and inspect them. Choices include the **Biersaal,** whose painted ceiling evokes the 18th century; the neoclassical **Weinzimmer,** a formal, rather uncomfortable and fussy-looking room outfitted in red; the **Bellotto,** an upscale Italian eatery on the top floor; and the **Café,** a graceful-looking antique room whose windows overlook the river. Prices in all four areas are about the same, although if you're interested just in coffee, tea, a drink, and/or pastries, you'd be best-advised to head directly for the cafe.

Theaterplatz 3. ✆ **0351/498160.** Reservations not necessary. Main courses 9€–18.50€ ($8.05–$16.50). AE, DC, MC, V. Daily 10am–midnight. Tram: 1, 2, 4, 7, 8, 11, 12, 14, or 17.

## INEXPENSIVE

**Ayers Rock** ★ *Finds* AUSTRALIAN The success of this likable Australian restaurant is proof of the growing sophistication of Dresden. It was named and modeled after the geological oddity in central Australia that deeply impressed the owner during one of his holidays. Lighthearted and breezy, the place serves almost 200 kinds of cocktails, as well as some brands of German and Aussie beer on tap. Menu items are inspired by what's cooking Down Under and include a savory version of lamb with green-bean stew; grilled veal shank; fresh asparagus with strips of chicken breast; and roebuck steak with mushrooms and glass noodles. After 8:30pm, the bar area gets crowded with those who are young at heart and available.

Münzgasse 8. ✆ **0351/490-1188.** Reservations not necessary. Main courses 8.50€–18€ ($7.60–$16.05). AE, DC, MC, V. Daily 11am–2am. Tram: 1, 2, 4, or 14.

**Bräuhaus Watzke** GERMAN One of Dresden's most famous and atmospheric beer halls lies 6.5km (4 miles) west of the city center, on a site overlooking the Elbe. Established in 1898, it proves the motto that governments in Germany rise and fall, but beer hall traditions remain intact. If the weather is clement, you can opt for a seat within the sprawling garden, where hardworking waitresses carry impossibly heavy loads of beer mugs and heaping platters to the long tables. Inside, the venue is appropriately woodsy-looking and *gemütlich* (cozy). Anything you drink here (including beers of the month) will have been brewed on the premises, within modern equipment that was installed in 1996. Regardless of which kind of beer you pick, a half liter costs 2.50€ ($2.25). It's never bottled in individual containers, only in kegs and it's almost never available anywhere except here and within a limited handful of other restaurants nearby. Menu items are appropriately hearty, and include a *Meltzer Schnitzel,* a filet of veal dredged in malt and fried; or a *Watzke bierfleische,* a ragout of beef stewed in dark aromatic beer. Salads, soups, and fish dishes are equally tasty.

Kötzschenbroder Strasse 1. ✆ **0351/85-29-20.** Reservations not necessary. Main courses 6.90€–11.90€ ($6.15–$10.65). AE, MC, V. Food daily 11am–midnight. Beer daily 11am–1:30am. Tram: 4 or 13.

**Café Schinkelwache** CONTINENTAL Designed like a miniature Ionic-style temple, this is one of the architectural gems of Dresden. This sandstone structure was built in 1832 by noted architect Karl Friedrich Schinkel to house soldiers and guards. In 1995, it was rebuilt and reconfigured into the cafe you see today. Its interior is more cozy and small-scale than you'd imagine from a view of its stately-looking facade. During clement weather, tables and parasols spill onto the terrace surrounding the building. Menu selections include pastries, meal-size salads, soups, cold platters, toasts, and at least two full-fledged dishes of the day. Wine, beer, and coffee are the preferred drinks.

Sophienstrasse am Theaterplatz. ✆ **0351/490-39-09.** Reservations recommended. Pastries 2.10€–2.90€ ($1.90–$2.60); platters 7€–15€ ($6.25–$13.40). AE, MC, V. Daily 10am–midnight. Tram: 1, 2, 4, 7, 8, 11, 12, 14, or 17.

**Sophienkeller im Taschenbergpalais** ★ *Finds* GERMAN The food here approximates the hearty medieval feasts you might have expected in the Royal Saxon Court, albeit in a more sanitized version. Your happiness in these deep but bustling cellars depends on where you happen to sit. Four distinct areas are available, but the ones we prefer, and the ones that are the most authentically historic, are the Grosses and Kleines Zunfi Gewölbe, where flickering candles, set beneath vaulted ceilings, provide most of the illumination. Waitresses in traditional dirndls haul steaming platters of grilled rabbit with thyme or perhaps filet of salmon in puff pastry with a white wine and shrimp sauce. A culinary specialty here is "August's Hunting Trophy," comprised of roasted medallions of venison, wild boar, and roebuck, served with asparagus and dumplings. It's a bit theme-ish, especially in its emphasis on 18th-century costumes, and at least part of its energies is devoted to the care and feeding of large tour groups, but the food is hearty and flavorful and the ambience can be very romantic.

Taschenberg 3. ✆ **0351/497-260.** Reservations recommended. Main courses 10€–20€ ($8.95–$17.85). AE, DC, MC, V. Daily 11am–1am. Tram: 5 or 8.

## DRESDEN AFTER DARK

Dresden is Saxony's cultural center. There's always a variety of options for nightlife here, whether you're looking for drama, classical concerts, punk-rock shows, dancing, or just a good place to drink.

**THE PERFORMING ARTS** Between the Elbe River and the Zwinger, on the western side of Theaterplatz, stands the **Semper Opera House,** Theaterplatz 2 (✆ **0351/491-17-05;** tram: 1, 2, 4, 7, 8, 11, 12, 14, or 17). Both Wagner and Weber conducted here. The building was designed by Gottfried Semper, the same architect who mapped out the famous picture gallery in the Zwinger. Restorers have brought the Renaissance-style two-tiered facade and the interior of the building back to life. Careful attention was paid to the replacement of Semper's original paintings and decorations. More importantly, the fine acoustics for which the opera house was known have been reestablished. Good seats can be had for 15€ to 70€ ($13.40–$62.50) The opera company takes a vacation mid-July to mid-August.

The **Dresden Philharmonic** appears at the **Kulturpalast,** in the Altmarkt (✆ **0351/48-66666;** tram: 3 or 5). Tickets cost 10€ to 30€ ($8.95–$26.80). Concerts, sometimes with accompaniment by ballet recitals, are also performed during June and August in the courtyards of the Zwinger. For more information about concerts in the courtyard of the Zwinger, contact the tourist office or call ✆ **0351/89540**).

For musical theater, come to the **Staats Operette,** Pirnaer Landstrasse 131, about 5km (3 miles) southeast of the city center (✆ **0351/207-99-29;** tram: 4), which mainly performs works from the 19th and early 20th centuries. The box office is open Sunday 1 hour before the show, Monday 11am to 4pm, Tuesday to Friday 11am to 7pm, and Saturday 4 to 7pm. Tickets cost 7€ to 20€ ($6.25–$17.85)

The classical stage for drama in the city is **Schauspielhaus,** Postplatz (✆ **0351/491-3555;** tram: 1, 2, 4, 7, 8, 11, 12, or 14), where dramas by Goethe, Schiller, and Shakespeare (in German) are performed. Performances usually start at 7:30pm. The box office is open Monday to Friday 10am to 6:30pm, and Saturday and Sunday 10am to 3pm. Tickets 10€ to 25€ ($8.95–$22.35). The Schauspielhaus box office also handles tickets and inquiries for the **Residenztheater im Schloss,** Schlossplatz (✆ **0351/49-13-50;** tram: 4 or 8), a small theater focusing on modern drama and small ensemble pieces. The cost is 10€ to 18€ ($8.95–$16.05). Both theaters are closed during August.

For a family theater experience, check out **Theater Junge Generation,** Meissner Landstrasse 4 (✆ **0351/42-91-20;** tram: 1; bus: 94), which interprets Shakespeare and fairy tales in a way that both kids and parents can enjoy. The box office is open Monday to Saturday 10am to 4pm, and 1 hour before performances. Ticket prices are 9€ to 22€ ($8.05–$19.65). In summer, some members of the troupe bring their acts outdoors, usually to the courtyard in front of the Staffhof, an imposing building originally intended as a stable.

Tickets for classical concerts, dance, and opera are available from the tourist office branch within the **Schinkelwache,** Theaterplatz (✆ **0351/49-11-705;** tram: 4 or 8), a historic building that was originally a guardhouse for the nearby castle.

**BARS** A small, low-key bar, **Café Hieronymous,** Louisenstrasse 10 (✆ **0351/801-17-39;** tram: 7 or 8), is the place to go if you don't want to deal with intrusive music or patrons. Open daily 7pm to 2am. **Die 100,** Alaunstrasse 100 (✆ **0351/801-3957;** tram: 7, 8, or 11), is a cheap and trendy drinking place, set in a cellar under a vaulted arch. It's popular with students and artists. Open daily 5pm to 3am.

At **Planwirtschaft,** Louisenstrasse 20 (✆ **0351/801-3187;** tram: 7 or 8), an upstairs cafe is open 9am to 1am, but at the downstairs bar, you can drink until 3am on weekends. It doesn't look like much, but **Raskolnikoff,** Böhmische Strasse 34 (✆ **0351/804-5706;** tram: 3, 5, 7, 8, or 11), is a hip dive with sand-covered floors. Artists, intellectuals, and wanna-bes tend to congregate here. Open daily 10am to 2am.

At **Kleine Busmann's Brazil,** Kleine Brüdergasse 5 (✆ **0351/498-9803;** tram: 1, 2, 4, or 11), you're likely to experience culture shock when you cross the street between the Zwinger and this Brazilian bar and restaurant where the music is hot and the food is spicy. Platters of food—roasted filet of pork is a specialty—are priced at 9€ to 16€ ($8.05–$14.30), although some specialty items, such as roasted rattlesnake, cost up to 40€ ($35.70). Most clients, however, just opt for a drink at the serpentine-shaped bar. Live music begins every night around 9pm. Open daily 11am to 2am.

At **Las Tapas,** Münzgasse 4 (✆ **0351/496-01-08;** tram: 1, 2, 4, or 14), within a stone-floored room modeled after an Iberian *tasca* (wine tavern), you'll find small tables and a stand-up bar area, where up to 40 kinds of Spanish-style marinated mushrooms, sausages, serrano hams, salted almonds, baked artichokes, and prawns in bacon are displayed behind glass. Priced at 1.10€ to 6.50€ ($1–$5.80), they go well with beer or the Spanish wines sold here. More substantial platters, priced at 12€ to 14€ ($10.70–$12.50) include lamb tenderloins with eggplant, and spits of marinated pork tenderloin served with sherry sauce. Open daily 11am to between 1 and 2am, depending on business.

A once run-down, recently gentrified nightlife destination that assembles about 20 different bars, art galleries, and restaurants into one historic site is **Kunsthof,** 70 Alaunstrasse (no phone), where a series of hip cafes, art galleries, and affordable restaurants line the edges of an interior courtyard. A particularly appealing bar, tapas bar, and restaurant within the complex is the Spain-inspired **El Perro** (✆ **0351/803-6723**). A few steps from the entrance to Kunsthof is the hip and popular **Frank's Bar,** 80 Alaunstrasse (✆ **0351/802-6727**), one of the busiest hangouts in the Neustadt area.

**CLUBS** Dance clubs that are known to virtually every 20-something resident of Dresden include **DownTown** (✆ **0351/804-6071**) and **Groove Station** (✆ **0351/810-5333**), set immediately adjacent to one another at Katherinenstrasse 11 and 13 (respectively; tram: 7 or 8). Clients can move freely from one to the other of this pair of cramped, sometimes convivial bars, where music rocks and rolls at high volumes and suds flow freely. Both are at their peak capacity on Friday and Saturday nights. Monday is gay and lesbian night, and on Sunday there's dinner and dancing. Both of them are open daily from 9pm "until everybody leaves." A single cover charge, ranging from 4€ to 8€ ($3.55–$7.15), depending on the night of the week, applies to both clubs.

**JAZZ** **Projekttheater Dresden,** Louisenstrasse 47 (✆ **0351/804-30-41;** tram: 7 or 8), a publicly funded organization, usually, but not always, gives a live jazz performance at 9pm Tuesday to Sunday and also maintains separate areas for the presentation of avant-garde films, lectures, and art exhibitions. Don't expect a nightclub-style cabaret, as no drinks are served. Tickets, available at the box office 1 hour before show time, cost 10€ ($8.95) each. Call to see if there is a performance scheduled.

All types of jazz bands hit the stage at the municipally-funded **Kultur Rathaus,** Königstrasse 15 (✆ **0351/488-8933**) every Friday and Saturday nights (the only nights when it's regularly open) when the music starts at 9pm. Check on other nights for infrequent shows. Entrance to the concerts here costs 8€ to 15€ ($7.15–$13.40). Tram 4 or 11.

**VARIETY** You'll find a wide variety of concert, theater, and dance performances in a setting that resembles an oversize pub with a stage at **Scheune,** Alaunstrasse 36 (✆ **0351/ 802-66-19;** tram: 7, 8, or 11), which also serves drinks and Indian food. It's open Monday to Friday 4pm to 2am, Saturday and Sunday 11am to 2am. Cover ranges from 5€ to 8€ ($4.45–$7.15), depending on the music and the night of the week. A busy and often aggressively promoted cultural complex, **Reisa Efau,** Adlergasse 14 (✆ **0351/866-02-11;** tram: 1), provides several options. It has two rooms where punk and other forms of electronic musical shows are held at 9pm for a 2.50€ ($2.25) cover. A movie theater on the premises charges 3€ ($2.70) for screenings held Thursday at 9pm in the summer and Sunday at 8pm in the winter. The bar on-site is open daily 5pm to 2am. There's also a space here devoted to the exhibition of one-artist shows; viewing hours change frequently, according to the exhibition on display at the time, but in most cases, hours tend to be Monday to Thursday 10am to 6pm, Friday 5 to 9pm, and Saturday 2 to 6pm.

For an insight into Germany's newest crop of political satirists, head for the irreverent premises of **Herkules Keule,** Sternplatz 1 (✆ **0351/492-5555;** tram: 1, 2, 4, 7, 8, or 11). Although it was well known during the heyday of the former DDR, its sometimes-scathing pronouncements have reached their sharpest and most shrill since reunification. Come here if your knowledge of German is extremely good and only if you're prepared for caustic, sometimes bitchy humor that touches on everything from politics to human sexuality. Shows are presented Monday to Friday at 7:30pm and Saturday at 6 and 9pm. Admission is 10€ to 15€ ($8.95–$13.40), depending on the night of the week.

**GAY BARS & CLUBS** Although limited, Dresden has its share of gay nightlife options. Foremost among them are **Roses,** Jordanstrasse 10 (✆ **0351/802-4264;** tram: 7 or 8); and **Queens,** Görlitzerstrasse 3 (✆ **0351/803-1650;** tram: 7 or 8), both of which cater to a youngish or young-at-heart crowd of gay men and to a lesser extent, women, from many miles around Dresden. The town's only leather bar, a labyrinth of dark corners, erotic movies, and cubbyholes, is **Bunker,** Priessnitzstrasse 51 (✆ **0351/441-2345;** tram 8).

## A SIDE TRIP TO THE SPREEWALD & SORB COUNTRY

A fascinating side trip, about an hour's drive north of Dresden, is to the history-rich Sorb country of Spreewald (Forest of the Spree), nearly 260 km sq. (100 sq. miles) of woodland, pastures, and canals. The flat, water-soaked landscape has an eerie beauty, and legends abound about spirits that inhabit the thick forests. Over a period of at least 1,000 years, the people of the region channeled the marshlands into a network of canals, streams, lakes, and irrigation channels, building their houses, barns, and chapels on the high points of otherwise swampy ground. Ethnologists consider this area a distinctive human adaptation to an unlikely landscape, and biologists appreciate the wide diversity of bird and animal life that flourishes in the lush and fertile terrain.

The area is inhabited by the Sorbs, descendants of Slavic tribes who settled here in the 6th century. They speak a language similar to Czech and Polish. The Sorbs were targeted by the Nazis, who outlawed their language and killed many of them. It's estimated that there are still 100,000 Sorbs living in Germany, 30,000 of whom inhabit the Spreewald. They grow vegetables and fruit in a protected landscape, using labor-intensive methods even today.

The Spreewald is at its most appealing in early spring and autumn, when the crowds of sightseers depart and a spooky chill descends with the fog over these primeval forests and shallow medieval canals. To get here from Dresden, take Autobahn 13 north until you come to either the first turnoff to Lübbenau, or the second turnoff, 10km (6 miles) farther, to Lübben. From either hamlet, drive toward the port (*Hafen*). From there, tour companies will take you through the canals via a shallow-draft boat propelled by a long pole, like a Venetian gondola. The guide is often a woman in traditional dress. Several waterside cafes along the canals serve food and drink.

Boat tours cost about 8€ ($7.15) per person for a 2½ hour excursion through the waterways of the Sorb Country. Few people speak English. The boat-tour companies operate only April to early October, with departures scheduled every day between 9am and 4pm. The companies include **Kahnfahrhafen Flottes Rudel,** Eisenbahnstrasse 3 (✆ **03546/8269**), in Lübben; and, in Lübbenau, **Kahn Fahr GmbH,** Dammstrasse (✆ **03542/2225**).

If you're interested in paddling around the Spreewald on your own, head for **Bootsverleih Gebauer,** Lindenstrasse, Lübben (✆ **03546/7194**), where canoes cost around 7.50€ ($6.70) for a 2-hour rental.

The tourist office in Lübben, the main point of departure for most Spreewald cruises, is on Ernst von Houwald Damm 16 (✆ **03546/3090**). The tourist office in Lübbenau, a secondary point of departure, is at Am Weg 15 (✆ **03542/3668**).

## 4 Meissen ★

23km (14 miles) NW of Dresden, 174km (108 miles) S of Berlin, 85km (53 miles) E of Leipzig

This "city of porcelain" is most often visited on a day trip from Dresden, although since reunification, it now has suitable accommodations for those who'd like to spend the night and get acquainted with the area.

Meissen lies on both banks of the Elbe, with the Altstadt on the left bank. It's a very old town, dating from A.D. 929. Since 1710, Meissen has been known around the world as the center for the manufacturing of Dresden china. The early makers of this so-called "white gold" were virtually held prisoner here, because the princes who ruled the city wanted to keep their secrets to themselves. Today, shoppers can find here the greatest selection of porcelain in all Germany. However, not wanting to undercut their distributors in such cities as Munich or Berlin, Meissen porcelain manufacturers keep their prices about the same as elsewhere.

### ESSENTIALS

**GETTING THERE** **By Train** **Meissen Bahnhof** is on the Deutsche Bundesbahn rail line, with connections departing for Dresden at 30- to 45-minute intervals throughout the day and evening. For rail information, call ✆ **1805/996633.**

**By Bus** Regional buses connecting Dresden with Meissen are operated by **Verkehrsgesellschaft Meissen.** Consult the tourist office in Meissen for a schedule of connections, or ask at the tourist office in Dresden.

**By Car** Access is via the E40 Autobahn from Dresden or the E49 from Leipzig.

**By Boat** If you're in Dresden in summer, you can go to Meissen by boat in about an hour and enjoy the scenery along the Elbe. The **Sächsischer Dampfschiffahrt** (✆ **0351/86-60-90**) leaves daily between May and late October at 9:15am from Dresden's Brühl Terrace, the fortified embankment on the other side of the Hofkirche. Boats arrive in Meissen 2 hours later. Waterborne returns to Dresden from Meissen depart at 3pm.

**VISITOR INFORMATION** Contact **Tourist-Information Meissen,** Markt 3 (✆ **03521/41-940**), November to March, Monday to Friday 10am to 5pm and Saturday 10am to 3pm (closed Sat in Jan); April to October, Monday to Friday 10am to 6pm, Saturday and Sunday 10am to 4pm.

### EXPLORING THE TOWN

Towering over the town is the Gothic-style **Dom** ★, Domplatz 7 (✆ **03521/45-24-90**), one of the smallest cathedrals in Germany, built between 1260 and 1450. Until the year 1400, the bishops of the diocese of Meissen had their seat next to the cathedral. Later, Saxon rulers were buried here, the first in 1428. Inside are works of art, including a painting by Lucas Cranach the Elder, along with rare Meissen porcelain. The cathedral has been Protestant since the 16th

### *Moments* Wine in Meissen

The terraces of the nearby vineyards in the Elbe Valley produce fine wines, for which Meissen has been known for 1,000 years. Look for the hard-to-obtain Meissner Domhert. The best selection of wines and the most romantic ambience is found at **Vincenz Richter** (reviewed below).

century. It's open daily 9am to 6pm. Admission costs 2€ ($1.80) per person. A 30-minute German-langued guided tour, departing at virtually any time you specify, costs 3€ ($2.70) per person

Sharing the castle quarter with the cathedral is **Albrechtsburg Castle** ★, Domplatz 1 (✆ **03521/47-070**), where the first Meissen porcelain was made. Construction of the castle began in 1471 and went on intermittently until 1525. From 1710 to 1864 it was the site of the Meissen Porcelain Manufactory. It's open daily 10am to 6pm; closed for 2 weeks in January. Admission is 3.50€ ($3.15) for adults, 2.50€ ($2.25) for children 6 to 16, and free for children 5 and under.

But the prime attraction in town is the **Porzellan-Manufaktur** ★, Talstrasse 9 (✆ **03521/46-87-00**). At this factory, you can see how the centuries-old process of making Meissen china is still carried on, using the same traditional designs. You can rent a prerecorded audio device, priced at 3.50€ ($3.15), that will direct you (in any of several languages) on a self-guided tour, that lasts between 30 and 60 minutes, depending on how fast you move through the premises. You can visit the on-site **Porcelain Museum,** with 3,000 pieces, plus the workshop. Other than the cost of the guided tour, admission is free. The factory, its museum, and the audio machines are available May to October, daily 9am to 6pm; November to April, daily 9am to 5pm.

The original factory was established back in 1710, not long after Johann Friedrich Böttger first succeeded in producing fine red stoneware in 1707 and then, in 1708, European white hard-paste porcelain. Böttger, then an apprentice pharmacist, had taken up alchemy and claimed to be able to make gold. When the Elector Augustus the Strong heard about this, he had Böttger put behind bars and ordered him to prove his claim. Böttger labored for many years, eventually producing "white gold," or porcelain. It wasn't long before Meissen porcelain was sought after in every great palace of Germany. The two most famous designers responsible for the classic Meissen motifs were Johann Gregorious Höroldt (1720–55), who produced the renowned blue onion pattern, and Johann Joachim Kändler (1706–75) who created figurines, giant animals, and elegant table services.

**SHOPPING** **Porzellan-Manufaktur** (see above), has recently crafted, hand-painted porcelain, which they'll ship home for you. However, don't expect prices to be much cheaper than in other German cities. The same organization also maintains a shop, with basically the same prices, in the center of Meissen at Burgstrasse 6 (✆ **03521/45-80-15**). If you're looking for (and can afford) 18th- or 19th-century porcelain or for antique furniture, bibelots, or artworks, head for **Meissener Antikitäten,** Holweg 4 (✆ **03521/45-37-52**).

## WHERE TO STAY

**Mercure Parkhotel Meissen** ★ This is the only first-rate hotel in town. For decades, Meissen didn't have a suitable hotel, but this Art Nouveau villa filled the void in the early '90s. You can request a room in the original villa, although most accommodations are in the more sterile modern annexes. A suite on the top floor under the eaves is perfect for romantic couples. Most rooms open onto panoramic vistas. Each comes with a well-organized bathroom, mainly with tub-and-shower combination.

Hafenstrasse 27–31 (on the Elbe, directly across the water from the castle), 01662 Meissen. ✆ **03521/7-22-50.** Fax 03521/72-29-04. www.mercure.de. 97 units. 112€–150€ ($100–$133.95) double; 170€–190€ ($151.80–$169.65) suite. Rates include buffet breakfast. AE, DC, MC, V. Parking 6€ ($5.35). **Amenities:** Restaurant; lounge; fitness center; whirlpool; sauna; solarium; babysitting; laundry. *In room:* TV, minibar, hair dryer.

## WHERE TO DINE

**Vincenz Richter** ★ SAXON This charming, hearty, and traditional restaurant is in a vine-sheathed 1523 building. It has a hardworking, devoted staff and a cozy setting of Germanic charm. The bar stocks an impressive inventory of local wines, and the kitchens serve ample portions of well-flavored Saxon food.

An der Frauenkirche 12 (uphill from Meissen's Marktplatz). ✆ **03521/45-32-85.** Reservations recommended. Main courses 9€–17.50€ ($8.05–$15.65). AE, DC, MC, V. Mon–Sat noon–11pm; Sun noon–6pm.

# 6

# Franconia & the German Danube

The Renaissance swept across all of Germany, but it concentrated its full force on that part of northern Bavaria that had once been a Frankish kingdom. Franconia today holds many of Germany's greatest medieval and Renaissance treasures. Its hillsides are still dotted with well-preserved medieval castles, monasteries, and churches. From the region's feudal cities sprang some of Germany's most significant artists—Albrecht Dürer, Lucas Cranach The Elder, Veit Stoss, Adam Krafft, and many others. Today, Franconia draws music lovers from all over the world to its annual **Mozart Festival** in Würzburg (see chapter 7) and **Wagner Festival** in Bayreuth.

Franconia owes much of its beauty to the limestone range along the southern edge of the province. Between these hills and the edge of the Bavarian Forest is the upper **Danube,** which begins about 30km (20 miles) from Regensburg. The Danube gradually builds force from the smaller streams flowing out of the Alps and Swabian Jura, and by the time it reaches the Austrian border, at Passau, it's large enough to carry commercial ships and barges. Although not as important to the German economy as the Rhine, the Danube was responsible for the growth of several influential towns.

Franconia's countryside is equally compelling, especially the forest called **Frankenwald.** This scenic region stretches from the Bohemian Forest on the border of the Czech Republic in the east to the fringes of Frankfurt in the west. The most beautiful part is called Frankisches Schweiz, the "Switzerland of Franconia." It's bounded by Bamberg on the west, Bayreuth in the east, and Kulmbach in the north.

## OUTDOORS IN FRANCONIA

The best **hiking** is found in the northern stretches of the province. Even the Germans themselves, who rush to the Bavarian Alps, often overlook hiking possibilities in this region. It's estimated that there are some 25,000 hiking trails in Franconia. Local tourist officials can provide details of the best hikes in their region. The most trails are found in the largest park in Germany, **Altmühltal Nature Park,** and in the Frankenwald. If you're a serious hiker, consider contacting **Fremdenver-kehrsverbund Franken,** Fürther Strasse 21, D-904 29 Nürnberg (✆ **0911/26-42-02**) for complete information about the hiking trails of Franconia.

Franconia can also be explored by **bike.** At all train stations in the area, you can rent a mountain bike for 9€ ($8.05) per day or for half-price if you have a valid train ticket. Local tourist offices can supply information on the best biking routes. The **Danube Bicycle Path** cuts right through Regensburg; cyclists can ride along its 650km (400 miles) from the river's source to Passau. The Regensburg tourist office (see the "Visitor Information" section under Regensburg, later in this chapter) is the most helpful source to contact to organize a biking trip. You can even go as far as Vienna. There's also the **Five Rivers Bicycle Path,** a circular route through the valleys of the Danube, Naab, and Vils that takes 3 to 5 days to complete. This path links Regensburg with Amberg and Nürnberg. Maps and further information about these cycling tours can be obtained from the local tourist information offices.

## 1 Bayreuth

230km (143 miles) N of Munich, 64km (40 miles) E of Bamberg, 92km (57 miles) NE of Nürnberg

Bayreuth lies in a wide valley on the upper basin of the Roter Main River. In the town's early years, the counts of Andechs-Meranien gave it the protection of a fortified castle. In the Middle Ages, Bayreuth became the property of the Hohenzollerns and grew into one of the leading centers of this part of Germany. It's now the capital of the district of upper Franconia.

Bayreuth is forever associated with the memory of **Richard Wagner** (1813–83). The town is worth a visit for its baroque and rococo architectural treasures even if you're not interested in its favorite son, but most people come here because it's the annual home of the Wagner opera festival, and the premier location for Wagnerian performance in the world. Bayreuth is Valhalla to Wagner enthusiasts.

Wagner's "endless melody" is said to pervade Bayreuth even to this day. The composer's early successes attracted the attention of Ludwig II, king of Bavaria. With the king's support, Wagner opened his first **Festspielhaus** in an old residence in Bayreuth in 1876; later he built and designed a new Festspielhaus, especially suited for his own operas. Wagner not only composed the music for his music dramas but also wrote the librettos and even designed the stage sets. *Tristan and Isolde* remains perhaps his most daring opera; his best known is the four-opera *Ring of the Niebelungs.*

### ESSENTIALS

**GETTING THERE** **By Plane** **Lufthansa** (✆ **800/645-3880**) offers three daily scheduled flights from Frankfurt Airport to Bayreuth.

**By Train** The **Bayreuth Hauptbahnhof** is on the main Nürnberg–Pegnitz–Bayreuth and the Bayreuth–Weiden rail lines, with good connections. Express trains arrive from Nürnberg every hour. For rail information and schedules, call ✆ **1-94-19.**

**By Bus** Long-distance bus service to Berlin and Munich is provided by **Bayern Express** and **P. Kuhn Berlin GmbH.** For information, call the **Deutsches Reisebüro** in Bayreuth (✆ **0921/88-50**). Local and regional buses in the area are run by **OVF Omnibusverkehr Franken GmbH** in Bayreuth (✆ **01805/996633**).

**By Car** Access by car is via the A9 Autobahn from the north and south.

**VISITOR INFORMATION** Contact **Tourist-Information,** Luitpoldplatz 9 (✆ **0921/885-88;** www.bayreuth.de), Monday to Friday 9am to 6pm and Saturday 9:30am to 1pm.

**GETTING AROUND** Many streets within the historic core of Bayreuth are exclusively reserved for pedestrians, and that, coupled with the city's small size, make walking between points of interest both easy and efficient. The centerpiece of the old town is the Marktplatz, from which buses 1, 7, 8, 9, and 16 make frequent runs to and from Bayreuth's modern neighborhoods around the Hauptbahnhof. One-way bus fare is 1.50€ ($1.35). Most able-bodied visitors opt to walk.

## THE BAYREUTHER FESTSPIELE

The town's claim to fame is that it's the site of the Richard Wagner opera festival, which takes place between mid-July and the end of August. If you arrive in Bayreuth then, you may think that the whole town has turned out to pay homage to the great composer, who built his opera house here, lived here, and was buried here following his death in Venice.

Visitors should know that tickets to the festival operas are almost impossible to obtain (there's a 5-year waiting list) but can sometimes be booked as part of a package tour (see chapter 3). Tickets cost €40.90 to €178.85, ($40–$175).

***Warning:*** During the 5 weeks of the festival, hoteliers raise their rates quite a bit. Always firmly establish the rate before booking a room, and make reservations far in advance.

## SEEING THE SIGHTS

**Altes Schloss Ermitage (Hermitage)** ★ The margraves of Bayreuth also had a pleasure palace outside the city, reached via a road lined with chestnut trees that were planted in honor of Frederick the Great. Georg Wilhelm built it in 1718 as a retreat. The structure looks as if it had been hewn out of a rock, but the interior felt the touch of Margravine Wilhelmine. Seek out the Japanese salon and the rococo music room. The castle is set in a park, full of formal as well as English-style gardens. In them, you can see the New Palace of the Hermitage, built around 1750. Its columns are covered with polychrome pebbles in mosaic style, a unique structural element in German architecture. A part of the palace becomes a cafe in summer and sometimes hosts painting exhibitions.

On Rte. 22, 5km (3 miles) northeast of Bayreuth toward Weiden. ✆ **0921/759-6937.** Gardens free; palace 3€ ($2.70) adults, free for children under 14. Gardens daily 24 hrs. Palace Apr–Sept Tues–Sun 9am–noon and 1–6pm. (until 8pm Thurs) Bus: 22 (runs every 20 min during the day).

**Festspielhaus** The operas of Wagner are dispensed like a musical Eucharist to Wagnerian pilgrims at the Festspielhaus, at the northern edge of town. The theater, designed by the composer himself, is not a beautiful building, but it's an ideal Wagnerian facility, with a huge stage capable of swallowing up Valhalla, and excellent, beautifully balanced acoustics throughout the auditorium. Because of the design, the orchestra never overwhelms the singers. The festival was opened here in 1876 with the epic *Ring* cycle. When the composer died in Venice, his wife, Cosima, took over. In the post–World War II era, Wagner's

### A Woman of Culture

The Margravine Wilhelmine (1709–58) was Frederick the Great's sister and a lifelong friend of Voltaire. She was also one of the most cultivated women of the 18th century. Wilhelmine was in line for the Prussian throne but instead married the Margrave Friedrich of Brandenburg-Bayreuth, although shortly thereafter decided he was rather dull. ("Margrave" and "Margravine" are titles of nobility similar to Marquis and Marquess.) She turned her attention to culture and ushered in the most brilliant period in Bayreuth's history, bringing in composers, decorators, writers, and artists. Wilhelmine personally spearheaded a movement that became known as "Bayreuth rococo." This style of architecture, characterized by garlands and flowers, differed markedly from the more rustic French rococo, which was in vogue at the time.

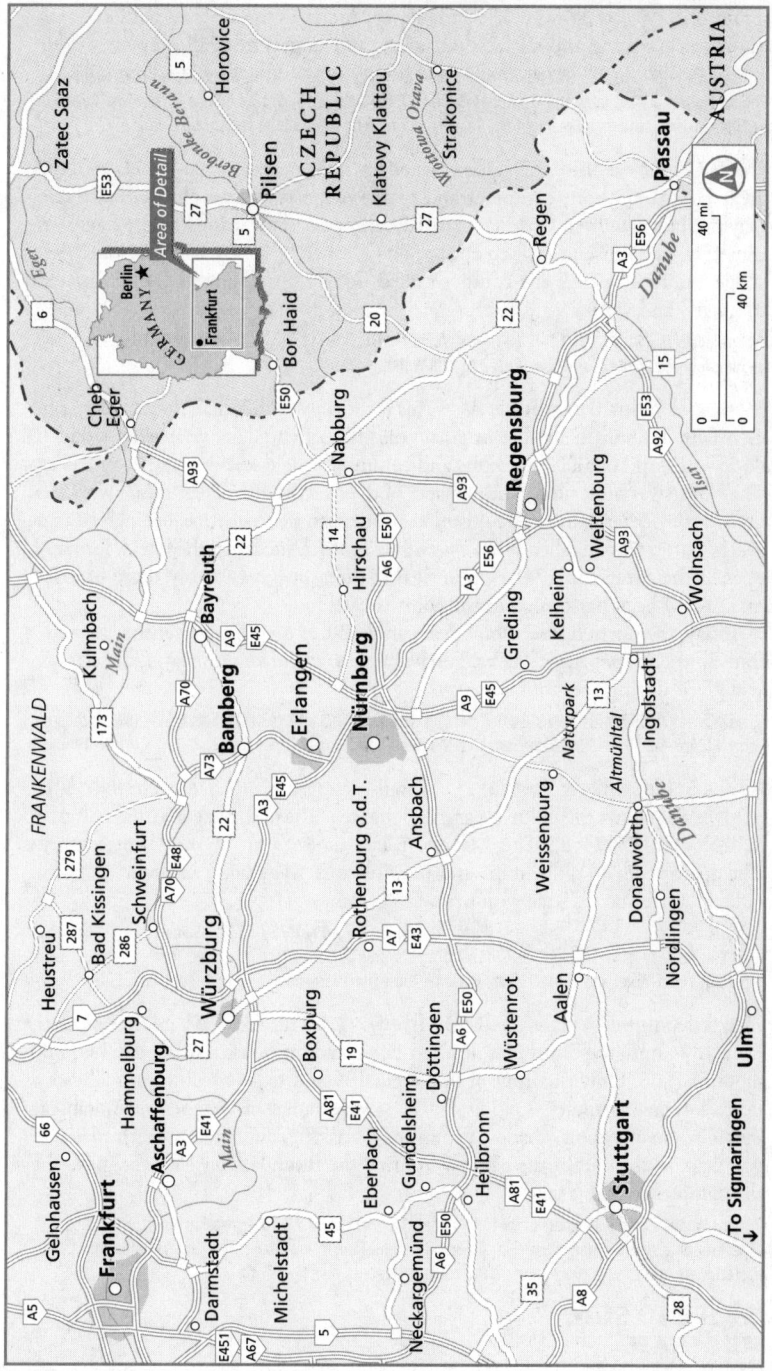
Zatec Saaz
Horovice
Berounka
Area of Detail
Berlin
GERMANY
Frankfurt
Pilsen
CZECH REPUBLIC
Klatovy Klattau
Otava
Vltava
Strakonice
Eger
Bor Haid
Cheb Eger
Nabburg
Regensburg
Regen
Passau
AUSTRIA
Danube
Isar
Wolnsach
Weltenburg
Kelheim
Greding
Hirschau
Nürnberg
Erlangen
Bayreuth
Bamberg
Kulmbach
Main
FRANKENWALD
Heustreu
Bad Kissingen
Schweinfurt
Würzburg
Rothenburg o.d.T.
Ansbach
Weissenburg
Naturpark
Altmühltal
Ingolstadt
Donauwörth
Nördlingen
Hammelburg
Aschaffenburg
Boxburg
Döttingen
Wüstenrot
Aalen
Gelnhausen
Frankfurt
Darmstadt
Michelstadt
Eberbach
Gundelsheim
Heilbronn
Neckargemünd
Stuttgart
To Sigmaringen
Ulm
40 mi
40 km

grandsons, Wolfgang and Wieland, have produced the operas, with exciting avant-garde staging and the best musicians and singers from all over the world.

Am Festspielhügel 2–3. ✆ **0921/7-87-80.** Guided tour only 1.30€ ($1.15). Tours offered in German only; English leaflets are available. Apr–Sept Tues–Sun at 10, 10:45am, 2:15, and 3pm; Oct and Dec–Mar Tues–Sun at 10:45am and 2:30pm. Tours might not be given during rehearsals and at festival time. Bus: 2.

**Franz-Liszt-Museum** Wagner's father-in-law was Franz Liszt (1811–86), the great Hungarian-born composer and piano virtuoso who revolutionized piano playing. His daughter, Cosima, married Wagner. Liszt is buried in the Bayreuth cemetery. The museum, which opened on October 22 (Liszt's birthday) in 1993, shows the room where the composer died. It also displays memorabilia related to his life and work.

Wahnfriedstrasse 9. ✆ **0921/5-5-16-64-88.** Admission 1.55€ ($1.35). Sept–June daily 10am–noon and 2–5pm; July–Aug daily 10am–5pm. Bus: 2 to Villa Wahnfried.

**Markgräfliches Opernhaus** ★ This is the only authentic baroque theater in Germany. It's still in its fine original condition. Behind its weathered wooden doors is a world of gilded canopies and columns, ornate sconces, and chandeliers. The house was built under the auspices of the Margravine Wilhelmine, who was known for her taste and her cultivation of the arts; her name has been given to a special baroque style called *Wilhelmian.* Her brother, Frederick the Great, formally opened the theater in 1748. Up until that time, operas (notably those of Telemann) had been performed in the court theater.

Today, the opera house, which seats only 520, is used for Bayreuth's "second" festival: the **Franconian Weeks' Festival,** usually held late in May. Concerts are also given during the summer.

Opernstrasse. ✆ **0921/759-6922.** Guided tours (in German only) 3.50€ ($3.15) adults, 2.50€ ($2.25) children under 14. Apr–Sept Tues–Sun 10am–5pm; Oct–Mar Tues–Sun 10am–3:30pm. Bus: 2.

**Neues Schloss (New Palace)** The well-preserved Neues Schloss in the center of town also shows the influence and enlightened taste of the talented and cultured Wilhelmine (1709–58). This baroque palace dates from the mid-18th century. The apartments of Wilhelmine and her husband, Margrave Friedrich, are decorated in a late-rococo style with period furnishings.

Ludwigstrasse (1 block from the Markgräfliches Opernhaus). ✆ **0921/759-69-21.** Guided tours (in German, with English leaflets available) 2.50€ ($2.25) adults, free for ages 17 and under. Tours given Apr–Sept Tues–Sun 10am–noon and 1:30–4:30pm; Oct–Mar Tues–Sun 10am–noon and 1:30–4pm. Bus: 2.

**Richard-Wagner-Museum (Wahnfried)** ★ This was Wagner's residence from 1874 until the time of his death in 1883, and the house remained in his family until 1966. Only the front of the original Wahnfried—which means "illusory peace"—remains intact. On display is a wide range of Wagner memorabilia, including manuscripts, pianos, furnishings, artifacts, and even a death mask. If you walk to the end of the garden, fronting the rotunda, you'll see the graves of the composer and his wife.

Richard-Wagner-Strasse 48 (south of the town center). ✆ **0921/7-57-28-16.** Admission 4€–4.50€ ($3.55–$4) at festival time. Apr–Oct daily 9am–5pm (to 8pm Tues and Thurs); Nov–Mar daily 10am–5pm (to 8pm Thurs). Bus: 2.

## WHERE TO STAY

### MODERATE

**Bayerischer Hof** Considering all the distinguished music lovers from around the world who descend on Bayreuth, the city needs a great old traditional and romantic inn. It doesn't really have one. Until that day comes along, the Bayerischer Hof remains a special favorite of Wagner fans, who find it the most convenient location for visitors arriving by rail. The hotel is well run and offers some of the best service in town. Bedrooms range from midsize to spacious and are furnished in both modern and traditional pieces, usually reproductions of antiques. Some of the furnishings are shipped in from France, whereas others are in the more functional Scandinavian modern style. Each bedroom comes with a tiled, compact, and well-organized private bathroom with shower only. The hotel dining facilities have even more charm and character than the hotel itself, and they're open to nonresidents, who enjoy both classical and modern dishes from an international and regional menu.

Bahnhofstrasse 14 (in front of the train station), 95444 Bayreuth. ✆ **0921/7-86-00.** Fax 0921/7-86-05-60. www.bayerischer-hof.de. 50 units. 110€–140€ ($98.25–$125) double; 250€ ($223.25) suite. Rates include buffet breakfast. AE, DC, MC, V. Parking 6.50€ ($5.80). **Amenities:** 3 restaurants; bar; pool; sauna; room service; babysitting; laundry. *In room:* TV, minibar, hair dryer.

**Goldener Anker** This inn is extremely popular locally and on the same comfort level as the Bayerischer Hof. It has hosted distinguished composers, singers, and conductors for more than 200 years. The framed photographs on the time-seasoned, oak-paneled walls are museum treasures. The guest book includes signatures of notables like Richard Strauss, Arturo Toscanini, Fritz Kreisler, Bruno Walter, William Saroyan, Lauritz Melchior, and Patrice Chereau. Furnishings include fine antiques and Oriental rugs. Rooms are individually designed, each with a small bathroom, most often with shower-tub combination.

Opernstrasse 6 (next door to the Markgräfliches Opernhaus), 95444 Bayreuth. ✆ **0921/6-50-51.** Fax 0921/6-55-00. www.anker-bayreuth.de. 35 units. 95€–155€ ($84.85–$138.40) double; from 195€ ($174.15) suite. Rates include continental breakfast. AE, DC, MC, V. Parking 7.65€ ($6.85). Closed Dec 20–Jan 10. Bus: 2. **Amenities:** Breakfast room; lounge; room service, babysitting; laundry. *In room:* Hair dryer.

### INEXPENSIVE

**Brauerei-Gasthof Goldener Löwe** ★ *Value* This is an unpretentious, well-managed inn—the town's best affordable choice. The facade is set off by window boxes loaded with flame-red geraniums. Rooms have a Bavarian theme, with checker-patterned down comforters and light-grained pinewood trim. Rooms and shower-only bathrooms are small but comfortable. The atmosphere is informal and home-like, and the staff is very hospitable.

Kulmbacher Strasse 30, 95445 Bayreuth. ✆ **0921/74-60-60.** Fax 0921/4-77-77. 13 units. 70€–95€ ($62.50–$84.85) double. Rates include continental breakfast. AE, DC, MC, V. Free parking. Bus: 2. **Amenities:** Dining room; bar; room service. *In room:* Hair dryer.

**Hotel-Gasthof Spiegelmühle** This high-ceilinged building, which dates from 1555 and was once a working mill, is now transformed into a modest and unassuming little hotel, kept clean and comfortable. In spite of its lack of pretensions, well-known conductors and singers often stay here during the festival. Many of the rooms are small but quite adequate, each with a compact, shower-only bathroom. Do not count on anybody speaking English.

Kulmbacher Strasse 28, 9445 Bayreuth. ✆ **0921/4-10-91.** Fax 0921/4-73-20. www.gasthof-spiegelmuhle.de. 13 units. 67€–74€ ($59.85–$66.10) double. Rates include continental breakfast. AE, DC, MC, V. Free parking. Bus: 6. **Amenities:** Breakfast room; bar; beer garden; room service. *In room:* TV, hair dryer.

## WHERE TO DINE

### EXPENSIVE

**Schloss Tiergarten** ★ CONTINENTAL No one makes a pilgrimage to Bayreuth for its restaurants, but this is a good one nonetheless. The building, which lies outside the center of town, was constructed as a private hunting lodge and has a hexagonal baroque tower. There are two dining rooms, the Kamin (meaning "fireplace") and the Venezianischersalon. The cuisine is in the culinary traditions of France, Italy, and Germany. Menu items might include lobster risotto with basil; stuffed halibut with caviar sauce and kohlrabi noodles; and terrine of sweetbreads. There's an impressive wine list.

The establishment is also a cozy hotel with eight large rooms boasting all the modern accoutrements. Doubles run 130€ to 170€ ($116.10–$151.80) including breakfast.

Oberthiergartener Strasse 36 (6km/4 miles south of Bayreuth center), 95406 Bayreuth. ✆ **09209/98-40.** Fax 09209/9-84-29. www.schloss-hotel-tiergarten.de. Reservations recommended. Main courses 18€–25€ ($16.05–$22.35). AE, DC, MC, V. Daily noon–2pmand 6–10pm. Bus: 11.

### MODERATE

**Gendarmerie** ★ FRENCH/FRANCONIAN Within the town center itself, the previously recommended Bayerischerhof contains the town's most intriguing dining choices. The hotel has a selection of restaurants offering both French and Franconian cooking. The Hans-Sachs-Stube, an air-conditioned replica of an old inn, has walls covered with pictures of famous opera singers who have performed in Bayreuth or dined here. You can also dine at the hotel's bistro, Spanische Stube. The best cuisine, however, is found at the Gendarmerie, the main a la carte restaurant. The food is superbly precise and refined here, combining inventive French dishes with the best of Franconian fare. Each dining room has a different decor, although the seasonally adjusted menu is the same in all three.

Bahnhofstrasse 14 (in front of the train station). ✆ **0921/7-86-00.** Reservations recommended. Main courses 12.50€–24€ ($11.15–$21.45). AE, DC, MC, V. Daily 7am–1am.

### INEXPENSIVE

**Braunbierhaus** FRANCONIAN The oldest house in Bayreuth, Braunbierhaus was built in 1430, with foundations that date from the 13th century. It offers inexpensive and down-to-earth food as well as its own beer. The specialty of the kitchen is a *Holzfäller* steak ("woodcutter's steak") served with hash-brown potatoes and a fresh salad. Portions are large, appetites are hearty, and the special house beer is consumed in mass quantities. No one puts on airs here.

Kanzleistrasse 15. ✆ **0921/6-96-77.** Main courses 6.70€–12€ ($6–$10.70). AE, DC, MC, V. Mon–Sat 10am–2pm and 5:30–10:30pm, Sun 11:30am–2pm. Bus: 3.

## 2 Bamberg ★★

238km (148 miles) NW of Munich, 61km (38 miles) NW of Nürnberg, 97km (60 miles) NE of Würzburg

This little city is one of the gems of Franconia, although visitors often pass it by. Bamberg is set in the rolling Franconian hills where the Regnitz River flows into the Main. It's loaded with attractions, including numerous architectural treasures, and suffered very little damage in World War II.

In the Middle Ages, Bamberg was a powerful ecclesiastical center. Originally, it was two towns divided by the river: the ecclesiastical town of the prince-bishopric, of which it was the capital for 800 years, and the secular town of the burghers. Bamberg's architecture reflects over 1,000 years of building, with styles ranging from Romanesque to Gothic, Renaissance to baroque, up to the eclecticism of the 19th century. There are narrow cobblestone streets, ornate mansions and palaces, and impressive churches.

Today, Bamberg and beer go together like barley and hops. The town has been called "a beer drinker's Eden" (there are more breweries here than in

Munich). The average Bamberger drinks 190 liters (50 gallons) of beer a year, making the rest of the German people look like teetotalers by comparison. Beer lovers come from afar for Rauchbier, a smoked beer first brewed in 1536.

## ESSENTIALS

**GETTING THERE** **By Train** The **Bamberg Bahnhof** is on the Stuttgart–Hof and the Berlin–Munich rail lines, with frequent connections in both directions. Most visitors arrive from Nürnberg (see "Nürnberg (Nuremberg)," later in this chapter) in just 1 hour. For information and schedules, call **✆ 01805/99-66-33.**

**By Bus** Bamberg has bus links with Bayreuth five times daily. The trip takes 1 hour 40 minutes and costs 6.80€ ($6.05) one-way. Contact **Omnibus Verkehr Franken** (**✆ 09561/749482**).

**By Car** Access by car is via the B22 from Würzburg or the A73 from Nürnberg.

**VISITOR INFORMATION** Contact the **Bamberg Tourist Information Office,** Geyerswöthstrasse 3 (**✆ 0951/87-11-61**). Office hours are Monday to Friday 9am to 6pm, Saturday to 3pm, and Sunday 10am to 2pm, May to October.

**GETTING AROUND** A well-run network of buses fan out from the Zentralomnibusbahnhof on Promenadestrasse, next to the railway station. A single ride costs 1.13€ ($1) and a five-ride ticket is 4€ ($3.55). For more information, head to I Punkt in the railway station, open Monday to Friday 7am to 7pm, and Saturday 9am to 2pm. Bus maps and tickets can be purchased at the station or from machines at stops along the route.

## EXPLORING THE CITY

The center square is dominated by the **Alte Hofhaltung,** the Renaissance imperial and episcopal palace, with a courtyard surrounded by late-Gothic framework buildings. Inside the palace are the remains of the original *Diet* (assembly) hall, built in the 11th century. Elaborately decorated and furnished, the palace is noted for its frescoed Kaisersaal and its Chinesisches Kabinet, the latter covered with walls of marquetry. Don't miss the rose garden.

Among other places of interest is the **Altes Rathaus** ★, the strangest town hall in Germany. Determined not to play favorites between the ecclesiastical and secular sections of the city, the town authorities built this Gothic structure on its own little island in the middle of the Regnitz River, halfway between the two factions—a true middle-of-the-road (or river) political stand. From the island, you get the best view of the old fishers' houses along the banks in the section called "Little Venice."

**Alte Hofhaltun** The former imperial and Episcopal palace lies on the north side of Bamberg's great cathedral. Although stripped of a lot of its former glory, it is still an impressive half-timbered pile in the Gothic style, with a spacious courtyard and Renaissance styling. Sometimes special events are staged in this courtyard. Ask at the tourist office for more information.

Inside the palace are the remains of the original Diet (Assembly) hall, built in the 11th century. The palace is noted for its lovely rooms, such as the frescoed Kaisersall, the main banqueting hall, or its Chinesisches Kabinet, the latter salon known for its walls of marquetry.

The building itself is more intriguing than its on-site Historisches Museum (Historical Museum), filled with artifacts, documents, and maps of the history of Bamberg. To fully appreciate this museum, you must either: be fluent in German; be writing a book on the history of Bamberg; and/or view the city as the place of origin of your ancestors.

Domplatz 8. ✆ **0951/871-142.** Admission 2€ ($1.80). May–Oct (only) Tues–Sun 9am–5pm.

**E. T. A. Hoffmann Haus** This was the home of the writer and poet from 1809 to 1813. The little narrow-fronted house is filled with mementos and memorabilia of the man whose strange tales formed the basis of Jacques Offenbach's famous opera *The Tales of Hoffmann.*

Schillerplatz 26. No phone. Admission 1.13€ ($1) adults, .50€ (45¢) children. May–Oct Tues–Fri 4–6pm; Sat–Sun 10am–noon. Bus: 10.

**Kaiserdom (Imperial Cathedral)** ★★ This cathedral on a hillside was begun in 1215 in Romanesque and early-Gothic style. It has a double chancel, the eastern one raised on a terrace to compensate for the slope. The massive towers at the four corners of the church dominate Bamberg's skyline. The interior contains some fine religious art. Best known is the 13th-century equestrian statue, the **Bamberger Reiter,** which represents the idealized Christian king of the Middle Ages. Among the many tombs is that of Emperor Heinrich II, who erected the original cathedral. Sculptor Tilman Riemenschneider labored more than a decade over this masterpiece of a tomb, as well as the one devoted to the emperor's wife, Kunigunde (who was suspected of adultery, commemorated in a scene on the tomb). In the west chancel is the only papal tomb north of the Alps, containing the remains of Pope Clement II, who died in 1047. The rich cathedral treasury may be seen in the adjoining **Diözesanmuseum.**

Domplatz. ✆ **0951/50-23-30.** Admission free. Apr–Oct daily 9am–6pm; Nov–Mar daily 9am–5pm. Diözesanmuseum 2€ ($1.80) adults, 1€ (90¢) students, .50€ (45¢) children ages 8–14, free children 7 and under. Diözesanmuseum Tues–Sun 9am–5pm. Bus 10.

**Neue Residenz** ★ Opposite the Alte Hofhaltung is the 17th-century Neue Residenz, the much larger palace of the prince-bishops, showing both Renaissance and baroque influences. This was the site of one of the most famous unsolved mysteries in Germany. In 1815, a corpse found beneath the windows of the palace turned out to be the body of Marshal Berthier, Napoléon's chief of staff, who retired here after Napoléon was exiled to Elba. No one knows if Berthier was murdered or committed suicide.

Upstairs, you can view works by German masters. On the second floor are the former **Imperial Apartments,** with Gobelin tapestries, baroque furnishings, and parquet floors. Notable is the **Emperors' Hall,** with portraits and frescoes.

Domplatz. ✆ **0951/563-51.** Admission 2.50€ ($2.25) adults, 2€ ($1.80) children. Apr–Oct Fri–Wed 9am–6pm, Thurs 9am–8pm; Nov–Mar daily 10am–4pm. Bus: 10.

**SHOPPING** The primary shopping district in Bamberg is around the cathedral, where you will find stores of all kinds, including more than a dozen antiques shops and numerous galleries. An antiques store that has it all, **Sebok,** Untere Königstrasse 21 (✆ **0951/20-25-93**), offers paintings, books, furniture, fine jewelry, silver, glass, toys, watches, clocks, and more. Auctions are held every 2 months, with the summer auction falling in July. **Manger,** Dominikanerstasse 7 (✆ **0951/2-34-54**), is a kitschy souvenir shop. If you're interested in local ceramics, go to **Topferladen,** Untere Brücke 1 (✆ **0951/5-69-13**), where you'll find ceramic candleholders, cups, dinnerware, vases, and garden statuary.

## WHERE TO STAY

### EXPENSIVE

**Bamberger Hof Bellevue** ★ This hotel plays a bit of second fiddle to the Residenzschloss Bamberg (see below), but the service and accommodations of both are roughly on a par. A great old palace of stone, crowned by a tower and facing a little park, it's the choice for soaking up the mellow atmosphere of yesteryear. Try to book one of the large rooms with sitting areas. Each unit is well furnished and attractively maintained, most often with a generous-size bathroom with tub-and-shower combination.

Schönleinsplatz 4, 96047 Bamberg. ✆ **0951/9-85-50.** Fax 0951/98-55-62. www.bambergerhof.de. 50 units. 130€–175€ ($116.10–$156.30) double; 450€ ($401.85) suite. Rates include buffet breakfast. AE, DC, MC, V. Parking 8€ ($7.15). Bus: 8 or 12. **Amenities:** Restaurant; lounge; room service; laundry/dry cleaning. *In room:* TV, minibar, hair dryer.

**Residenzschloss Bamberg** ★★ This elegant hotel is on a bank of the Regnitz, near the Altstadt and across from the Bamberg Symphony Orchestra building. This is the preferred choice in town, a blend of old and new. The building, with its ocher-colored baroque walls, was constructed by the local archbishop in 1787 as a hospital. Today, the original hospital chapel continues to host local weddings. A less-glamorous modern annex is connected to the main building by a glass-sided breezeway. Bathrooms are a bit small but tidily kept, most often with a tub and shower. The hotel is popular with conventioneers.

Untere Sandstrasse 32, 96049 Bamberg. ✆ **0951/6-09-10.** Fax 0951/6-09-17-01. www.hotel-residenzschloss.de. 184 units. 155€–175€ ($138.40–$156.30) double; 260€–310€ ($232.20–$276.85) suite. Rates include buffet breakfast. AE, DC, MC, V. Bus: 8. **Amenities:** Restaurant; lounge; gym; sauna; solarium; steam room; room service. *In room:* TV, minibar, hair dryer.

### MODERATE

**Barock Hotel am Dom** ★ *Value* Barock Hotel am Dom offers you some of the same style, tradition, and romance of the pacesetters above, but at a better price. The owners of this building have retained every detail of the original ornamented facade and renovated key areas of the interior. The result is a winning combination of baroque elements in a well-lit modernized building. Rooms are attractively furnished, although a bit cramped, as are the shower-only bathrooms. The comfort level and maintenance are high here. Reservations are important. The rates include a nourishing breakfast (the only meal available) of wurst and cheese, served in the most unusual breakfast room in Bamberg—the old cellar, where tables are set up under the plastered stone vaulting.

Vorderer Bach 4, 96049 Bamberg. ✆ **0951/5-40-31.** Fax 0951/5-40-21. 19 units. 82€–90€ ($73.25–$80.35) double. Rates include buffet breakfast. AE, DC, MC, V. Closed Feb 1–Mar 1. Bus: 8 or 12. **Amenities:** Breakfast room; lounge. *In room:* TV, minibar, hair dryer.

**Hotel Brudermühle** This is a traditional German city inn without pretense or glamour. Reasonable rates, good local cooking, and a hospitable, family-style welcome make this a worthwhile choice for those who like no-frills functionality. Rooms and shower-only bathrooms are tiny, but housekeeping is good. The functional modern furnishings are less interesting than the views of the old town from the windows. The building was constructed in 1314 as a mill powered by the Regnitz River. The hotel couldn't be more centrally located, within a few blocks of the cathedral.

Schranne 1, 96049 Bamberg. ✆ **0951/95-52-20.** Fax 0951/9-55-22-55. www.brudermuehle.de. 19 units. 123€ ($109.85) double; 110€–120€ ($98.25–$107.15) apartment. Rates include continental breakfast. DC, MC, V. Bus: 8 or 12. **Amenities:** Breakfast room; lounge; room service. *In room:* TV, hair dryer.

**Ring Hotel National** The National is still a favorite, though it no longer enjoys the renown it used to. Modernization has removed some of its quaint charm, and it lacks the style of the Romantik Hotel-Weinhaus Messerschmitt (see below), but the price is right, the food is good, and the rooms are first-rate, each with a tidily kept bathroom, most often with tub-and-shower combination. With its black mansard roof, iron balconies, baroque and classical detailing, and opulent public rooms, the hotel is attractive, if small. It has well-maintained and traditionally furnished rooms which tend to provide a comfortable stay.

Luitpoldstrasse 37, 96052 Bamberg. ✆ **0951/50-99-80.** Fax 0951/2-24-36. www.ringhotels.de. 41 units. 75€–90€ ($67–$80.35) double; 105€–115€ ($93.75–$102.70) suite. Rates include buffet breakfast. AE, DC, MC, V. Parking 5€ ($4.45). Bus: 5. **Amenities:** Restaurant; bar; room service; laundry/dry cleaning. *In room:* TV, minibar, hair dryer.

**Romantik Hotel-Weinhaus Messerschmitt** ★★ This old hotel, beloved by traditionalists, is Bamberg's most romantic choice. The building dates from 1422, making it one of the oldest in the area. The present exterior is 18th century, a gabled expanse of pale blue and yellow with baroque-style window frames. Inside, the mellow decor includes paneling, ceramic ovens, and antiques. Many of the beds have meticulously crafted headboards. Each accommodation comes with an old-fashioned though modernized private bathroom with tub-and-shower combination. The owner and his staff are very helpful.

Langestrasse 41, 96047 Bamberg. ✆ **0951/2-78-66.** Fax 0951/26-14-1. www.hotel-messerschmitt.de. 17 units. 112€–145€ ($100–$129.50) double; 165€ ($147.35) triple. Rates include buffet breakfast. AE, DC, MC, V. Parking 5€ ($4.45). Take any bus going to the Zentralomnibusbahnhof (Central Station). **Amenities:** Dining room; lounge; room service. *In room:* TV, minibar, hair dryer.

### INEXPENSIVE

**Hotel Garni Graupner** Much renovated, rebuilt, and overhauled over the years, this hotel continues a tradition started in the 14th century of accepting overnight guests. It's your best bet if you can't afford the properties outlined above. You can usually get a room here, perhaps with a view over the Altstadt, and it will be clean and decent, although short on charm. If the main hotel is full, guests are directed to the lackluster 1960s annex, about 8 blocks away across the canal. It offers 10 modern rooms for the same price charged in the main hotel, each with private shower-only bathroom. The same family also owns a rose-garden cafe a stone's throw from the cathedral.

Langestrasse 5, 96047 Bamberg. ✆ **0951/98-04-00.** Fax 0951/98-04-040. hotel-graupner@t-online.de. 30 units, 26 with bathroom. 49€ ($43.75) double without bathroom; 57€–67€ ($50.90–$59.85) double with bathroom; 77€–85€ ($68.75–$75.90) junior suite. Rates include continental breakfast. AE, MC, V. Parking €6.15, ($6). Bus: 1, 2, 4, 5, 8, or 16. **Amenities:** Breakfast room; cafe; lounge. *In room:* Hair dryer.

## WHERE TO DINE

**Historischer Brauereiausschank Schlenkerla** FRANCONIAN Diners congregate here much as they did in 1678, when the place was a brewery. The decor is rustic, with long wooden tables and smallish chairs. The price is right, and *gemütlich* (cozy) atmosphere is genuine. Wholesome and unpretentious Franconian fare is served here. You can sample such local dishes as *Bierbrauervesper* (smoked meat and sour-milk cheese) and *Rauchschinken* (smoked ham). Patrons wash down these dishes with a hearty malt, Rauchbier, which has an intense smoky aroma and flavor.

Dominikanerstrasse 6. ✆ **0951/5-60-60.** Main courses 6.15€–9.20€ ($5.50–$8.20). No credit cards. Wed–Mon 9:30am–11:30pm. Closed Jan 7–21. Bus: 8 or 12.

**Romantik Restaurant-Weinhaus Messerschmitt** ★ FRANCONIAN/INTERNATIONAL You can dine better here, and in a more refined atmosphere, than anywhere else in town. This pleasant restaurant is more than 160 years old. The cuisine is presented simply but is remarkably well made. Menu items vary depending on what ingredients are available. Freshwater fish are kept in an aquarium. Game is another specialty. Veal and lamb dishes are prepared with exquisite care. Some of the offerings, such as eels in dill sauce, may be a bit too regional for you, but the Franconian duck is an exquisite choice.

Langestrasse 41. ✆ **0951/2-78-66.** Main courses 13€–22€ ($11.60–$19.65). AE, DC, MC, V. Daily 11am–2pm and 6–10pm. Bus: 1 or 2.

## BAMBERG AFTER DARK

**Sinfonie an der Regnitz,** Mussstrasse 1 (✆ **0951/9-64-71-00**) is home to the Bamberg Symphony Orchestra from September 11 to July 17. From the last week in June to mid-July, there's a summer festival with weekend symphonic concerts. Tickets are 18€ to 34€ ($16.05–$30.35).

**Hofburg Repertory Theater** performs at the **E.T.A. Hoffman Theater,** Schillerplatz 5 (✆ **0951/87-14-33;** box office 0951/87-14-31). Its season runs from September through July. The productions range from 18th-, 19th-, and 20th-century classics to contemporary musicals. The box office is open daily 10am to 1pm and 1 hour prior to show time (also 4–6pm on Wed). In June and July, the company moves outdoors, performing a series of German-language drama within the courtyard of the Alte Hofhaltung (see above). Tickets for both indoor and outdoor performances are 12€ to 19€ ($10.70–$16.95), but students with a valid ID card pay half price. For more information about these and other cultural events in Bamberg, contact the Tourist Information Office (see "Visitor Information," above).

A young crowd gathers at **Jazzclub,** Obere Sandstrasse 18 (✆ **0951/5-37-40**), to listen to punk, gothic, and alternative music on Tuesday and Thursday nights from 9pm to 1am, when the cover is 2.55€ ($2.30) mid-September to April, the club opens its cellar for live jazz on Friday and Saturday 9pm to 2am, when the cover is 5.10€ to 12.80€ ($4.55–$11.45), depending on the group.

## 3 Nürnberg (Nuremberg) ★★

169km (105 miles) NW of Munich, 225km (140 miles) SE of Frankfurt, 204km (127 miles) NE of Stuttgart

When this city celebrated its 900th birthday in 1950, the scars of World War II were still fresh. Nürnberg was once the ideal of medieval splendor, but that legacy was lost in the ashes of war. With the exception of Dresden, no other German city suffered such devastation in a single air raid. On the night of January 2, 1945, 525 British Lancaster bombers rained fire and destruction on this city, the ideological center of the Third Reich.

Nürnberg today has regained its vitality and is now a symbol of postwar prosperity. Nürnberg is now swarming with people, both longtime residents and *Gastarbeiter* (foreign workers), who have flooded the city in recent years—many from the old Soviet Bloc countries to the east. For most of the year, the city is thronged with visitors, too. It's a notable industrial center, still associated with its traditional gingerbread products and handmade toys. The first pocket watches, the Nürnberg eggs, were made here in the 16th century.

Centuries of art and architecture made Nürnberg a treasure. During the 15th and 16th centuries, Nürnberg enjoyed a cultural flowering that made it the center of the **German Renaissance,** bringing together Italian Renaissance and German

Gothic traditions. In the artists' workshops were found such great talents as Veit Stoss, Peter Vischer, Adam Krafft, Michael Wolgemut, and above all, Albrecht Dürer. Koberger set up his printing press here, and Regiomontanus built an astronomical observatory. Here, too, flourished the guilds of the Meistersingers, composed of prosperous artisans; Wagner made their most famous member, Hans Sachs, the hero of his opera *Die Meistersinger von Nürnberg.*

Many of Nürnberg's most important buildings, including some of the finest churches in Germany, have been restored or reconstructed. The old part of the city, the **Altstadt,** lies mainly within a pedestrian zone. Today's visitors can see the ruins of the ramparts that once surrounded the city as well as more modern sites, such as the **Justice Palace,** where the War Crimes Tribunal sat in 1946.

Visitors can also see the **Zeppelinfeld arena,** the huge amphitheater where, from 1927 to 1935, Hitler staged those dramatic Nazi rallies that were immortalized by Leni Riefenstahl in *Triumph des Willens* (*Triumph of the Will*). Hitler's architect, Albert Speer, constructed what has been called a "concrete mecca," whose grounds today have been turned into a park with apartment blocks, a trade fair, and a concert hall. Speer's Congress Hall, larger than the Colosseum in Rome, has become a recording studio and warehouse.

## ESSENTIALS

**GETTING THERE** **By Plane** **Nürnberg Flughafen** is 6km (4 miles) north of the city center. Despite its relatively small size (it's only the ninth busiest in Germany), this airport is served by 14 airlines in scheduled flights to dozens of destinations throughout Europe. These are supplemented by charter flights. For information and schedules, call ✆ **01805/99-66-33.**

**By Train** The **Nürnberg Hauptbahnhof** lies on several major German rail lines, with frequent connections to big cities and many smaller regional towns. Travel time to Frankfurt is 2 hours 8 minutes; to Berlin, 6 hours; and to Munich, 1 hour 40 minutes. For information and schedules, call ✆ **01 805/99-66-33.**

**By Bus** Long-distance bus service from such cities as Munich and Frankfurt is provided by Europabus Lines 183 and 189E of Deutsche Touring GmbH, operating out of Frankfurt. For information in Nürnberg, call **Reisebüro Okyay** (✆ **0911/26-63-64**). Regional bus service with frequent connections to neighboring towns is offered by **OVF Omnibusverkehr Franken GmbH,** Kopernikusplatz 14 in Nürnberg (✆ **0911/4-39-06-66**).

**By Boat** The Main–Danube Canal links the Rhine, the Main, and the Danube. For information about riverboat connections, call the Hafenver-Waltung Nürnberg (✆ **0911/600-20-55**).

**By Car** From Munich, take the A9 Autobahn north; from Frankfurt, head southeast along the A3 Autobahn; from Berlin, take the A9 Autobahn south.

**VISITOR INFORMATION** Contact **Tourist Information,** in the Hauptbahnhof (✆ **0911/2-33-61-32**), Monday to Saturday 9am to 7pm. An additional branch in the **Rathaus** (✆ **0911/2-33-61-35**) is open Monday to Saturday 9am to 6pm and also Sundays in May 10am to 1pm and 2 to 4pm.

**GETTING AROUND** Nürnberg has its own subway system that consists of an east-west and a north-south line that intersects at the Hauptbahnhof. Depending on the distance you travel, one-way fares cost from 1.50€ to 2€ ($1.35–$1.80). Principal stops within Nürnberg's medieval core include Lorenzkirche and Weisser Turm. For more information, call ✆ **0911/27-07-99.** But walking between two points at opposite ends of the old town—the Hauptbahnhof (main railway station)

**ACCOMMODATIONS**
Atrium Hotel **1**
Burghotel-Grosses Haus **15**
City Hotel **8**
Deutscher Kaiser **7**
Drei Linden **19**
Dürer-Hotel **16**
Le Meridien **2**
Maritim **4**
Weinhaus Steichele **6**

**ATTRACTIONS**
Albrecht Dürer House **17**
Beautiful Fountain **12**
Germanisches Nationalmuseum **5**
Handwerkerhof **3**
Hauptmarkt **10**
Kaiserburg **18**
Lochgefängnis **11**
Rathaus **11**
St.-Lorenz-Kirche **9**
St.-Sebaldus-Kirche **13**
Spielzeugmuseum (Toy Museum) **14**

and the Kaiserburg (the base of the city's medieval castle)—will take you only about 30 minutes and will lead you through the heart of the city's medieval core and past most of its historic monuments. To summon a taxi, call ✆ **0911/1-94-10.**

## EXPLORING THE CITY

You can easily spend a full day here seeing the sights. Begin at the central market square, **Hauptmarkt,** the most colorful place in Nürnberg, filled with kiosks stacked tall with fresh produce brought in from the countryside. Nearly all the city's attractions lie nearby within the **medieval fortifications,** parts of which still remain. Between the main wall (which has rampart walks) and the secondary wall once ran the waters of a protective moat. Set at the "corners" of the Altstadt are the massive stone towers, still intact, of the city gates. The remains of dozens of other gateway towers still exist along the ramparts. Crowning the northern periphery of the Altstadt is the **Kaiserburg.**

The best example of Nürnberg's aesthetic passion is the **Beautiful Fountain** on Marktplatz. This stone pyramid, 18m (60-ft.) high, dates from 1396 and is adorned with 30 figures arranged in four tiers. Within it is enclosed the symbol of Nürnberg, the journeyman's ring.

At some point in your day, wander over to **Handwerkerhof,** near the main train station. In this mall, you can see artisans creating the products for which Nürnberg has been known since the Middle Ages: glassware, pewter (often in the form of beer mugs), intricate woodcarvings, and toys.

If you're interested in a famous landmark of World War II, visit the **Justizgebäude,** Fürtherstrasse 22 (U-Bahn: Bärenschanze), where the "Judgment of Nürnberg" took place. Here, in room 600, the surviving leaders of the Third Reich stood trial in October of 1946 for crimes against humanity. Afterward, 10 were hanged. The building still serves as a courthouse, and you'll have to ask the guard at the door if you can enter.

**Albrecht Dürer House** ★ The town's most popular shrine is the Albrecht Dürer House, just a short walk up the cobblestoned Bergstrasse from the Dürer Monument and St. Sebald Church. Typical of the half-timbered burghers' houses of the 15th century, the structure is the only completely preserved Gothic house in Nürnberg. The first floors are sandstone, surmounted by two half-timbered stories and a gabled roof with a view of the town below. Exhibits inside the house are devoted to Dürer's life and works. Many of the rooms are furnished with important historical pieces and contain original etchings and woodcuts, plus copies of Dürer's paintings.

Am Tiergartnertor, Albrecht-Dürer-Strasse 39. ✆ **0911/2-31-25-68.** Admission 4.50€ ($4) adults, 1.75€ ($1.55) students and children 6–15, free for children 5 and under. Tues–Sun 10am–5pm (Thurs until 8pm). Tram 4. Bus: 36.

## Albrecht Dürer & the German Renaissance

If Dürer's father had had his way, his son would have become a goldsmith. Fortunately, that didn't happen. Albrecht Dürer (1471–1528) began his artistic career as apprentice to Michael Wolgemut, then the leading artist in Nürnberg, in 1486. There he learned to excel in woodcutting and engraving. Almost everyone is familiar with the sketch he made of praying hands—it's been reproduced so often it's become a greeting-card cliché.

Dürer was not content to stay at home in Nürnberg. Beginning in 1490, he embarked on a series of travels that eventually took him to Italy, where he came into contact with the artists of the Renaissance. On his return to Nürnberg, he brought their ideas back with him. Dürer was thus largely responsible for pulling art north of the Alps out of the medieval world and into the new era.

A restless man, Dürer was always probing into the world about him; he produced several theoretical works on art, on architecture, and on the science of proportion. Even more interesting, at one point he invented a mechanical device for drawing a picture that was a first step toward the principle of the photographic camera.

Dürer was one of the first major world masters to paint an acknowledged self-portrait. In fact, he painted three of them, and his very first known drawing is a sketch of himself at the age of 13. These paintings show clearly how he saw the artist's role, and the importance of his own mission. The last self-portrait (in the Alte Pinokothek in Munich), shows Dürer in an almost Christ-like stance, representing the artist as an elevated figure concerned with the expression of universal ideas. Other important paintings of his include the portrait of *Charlemagne* at the Germanisches Nationalmuseum in Nürnberg, and his *Four Apostles,* commissioned for the Nürnberg Rathaus.

**Germanisches Nationalmuseum (Germanic National Museum)** ★★★ The largest museum of German art and culture is just inside the south section of the medieval city walls. It covers the entire spectrum of German craftsmanship and fine arts from their beginnings to the 20th century. The prehistoric and early historical section contains finds from the Stone Age and from the burial sites of the Merovingians. The extensive painting and sculpture sections include works by Albrecht Dürer and Veit Stoss, a sculptor and wood-carver known for his "nervous" angular forms and realism. The boundless variety and richness of German handcrafts is fully evident in this museum. There's also an important library and archive here.

Kartäusergasse 1 (near the Hauptbahnhof). ✆ **0911/1-33-10.** Admission 4€ ($3.55) adults, 2€ ($1.80) children. Tues and Thurs–Sun 10am–5pm; Wed 10am–9pm. U-Bahn: Opernhaus.

**Kaiserburg** ★ The Burg looms above the city from its hilltop at the northern edge of the Altstadt. From 1050 to 1571, it was the official residence of the German kings and emperors, including Frederick Barbarossa, the zealous crusader who entertained the emperor of Byzantium and the sultan of Tyre within its walls. The castle is divided into three complexes: the Kaiserburg (Imperial Castle), the Burgraves' Castle, and the Municipal Buildings of the Free City.

The oldest portion is the **Pentagonal Tower** (1050). It probably dates from the previous palace of the Salian kings, over which the Burgraves' Castle was constructed. Although the **Burgraves' Castle** has been in ruins since it was destroyed by fire in 1420, the remains offer the visitor an interesting look into the layout of a feudal castle. The watchmen and guards used the heavy ramparts with the parapet walks and secret passages to protect the burgraves and the emperors, who lived in the inner core of the castle complex.

The **Kaiserburg,** grouped around the inner court within the ramparts of the Burgraves' Castle, was the residence of the kings and emperors of Germany. Most of the buildings were constructed during the 12th century, centered around the once magnificent Palas built by Konrad III in 1138. The great Knights' Hall on the ground floor and the Imperial Hall on the floor above look much as they did when King Frederick III rebuilt them in the 15th century, with heavy oak beams and painted ceilings. The rooms are decorated with period Gothic furnishings. Adjoining the Palas is the Imperial Chapel—actually two chapels, one above the other in cross section but united at the center by an open bay. Thus, the emperor could worship with his court in the upper chapel to the same liturgy as the lesser members of his retinue in the lower chapel.

The third set of buildings, outside the Burgraves' Castle, was erected by the council of Nürnberg in the 14th and 15th centuries when it took over the responsibility of protecting the emperor. This section includes the imperial stables (now a youth hostel), the massive bastions of the fortress, the Tiefer Brunnen (Deep Well), and the castle gardens. Even more impressive than the fortress is the view of the roofs and towers of Nürnberg from its terraces.

The complex also includes the new **Kaiserburg Museum** (✆ **0911/20-09-540**), which contains antique weaponry, armor, and paintings, and explains the history of the castle.

Burgstrasse. ✆ **0911/22-57-26.** Admission (including all parts of the castle) 4.50€ ($4) adults, 3.50€ ($3.15) students; free for children 16 and under. Apr–Sept daily 9am–5pm; Oct–Mar daily 10am–4pm. Bus: 36 or 46.

**Lochgefängnis** Under the Altes Rathaus is a medieval prison with its original cells and torture chamber, a gruesome attraction. Opposite the torture chamber lie the remnants of a room that once hid the city council's treasures and important documents during wars and emergencies. An underground passage from the dungeons to the outside world existed from 1543 until 1945, when bombing rendered it impassable.

Rathausplatz. ✆ **0911/231-25-90.** Admission 2€ ($1.80) adults, 1€ (90¢) children. Tues–Sun 10am–4:30pm. Closed Jan–Mar, Oct–Nov, and on weekends. Bus: 36, 46, or 47.

**Spielzeugmuseum (Toy Museum)** Nürnberg is a major toy center, so it's only fitting that the city devote a museum to this industry. Toys, both hand- and machine-made, fill three floors. Some date from medieval times. The collection of old dollhouses is vastly amusing, as is a mechanical Ferris wheel. You'll often see adults here (even without children).

Karlstrasse 13–15. ✆ **0911/2-31-31-64.** Admission 4€ ($3.55) adults, 2€ ($1.80) children. Tues and Thurs–Sun 10am–5pm; Wed 10am–9pm. Bus: 36.

**St.-Lorenz-Kirche** ★ Across the Pegnitz River is the largest and stateliest church in Nürnberg. Begun in 1270, it took more than 200 years to complete, but the final result is one of Gothic purity, inside and out. The twin towers flank the west portal. The portal's sculptures depict the theme of redemption, from Adam and Eve through the Last Judgment. Upon entering the church, note the color and detail in the stained-glass rosette above the portal. Much of the church's stained and painted glass dates from the 15th century. The interior is marked by pillars that soar upward to become lost in the vaulting shafts above the nave. Each pillar is adorned with sculptures carrying on the theme introduced at the entrance. The oldest of these is *Mary with Child,* created around 1285. The continuing theme of the sculptures urges you toward the single east choir, the last portion of the church to be completed (1477). *The Angelic Salutation* (1519), carved in linden wood by Veit Stoss, is suspended from the roof of the church just behind the Madonna Chandelier. To the left of the altar is the Gothic Tabernacle, hewn from stone by Adam Krafft (1496), its upthrusting turret repeating the vertical emphasis of the church. Above the high altar is another masterpiece by Stoss, a carved crucifix. The painted panels at the beginning of the choir are by Michael Wolgemut, Dürer's teacher.

Lorenzer Platz 10. ✆ **0911/20-92-87.** Free admission. Mon–Sat 9am–5pm; Sun 1–4pm. U-Bahn: Lorenzkirche.

**St.-Sebaldus-Kirche** Consecrated in 1273, this church is a fine example of 13th-century transition from Romanesque to German Gothic styles. The nave and west choir are late Romanesque, with a narrow chancel containing a simple altar and an ancient bronze baptismal font. The larger east choir, consecrated in 1379, is pure Gothic and contains the church's most important treasures. Between the two east pillars is a huge 16th-century crucifixion group dominated by a life-size crucifix by Veit Stoss. Just behind the altar is the elaborate shrine of St. Sebald, whose remains are encased in a monument cast in brass by Peter Vischer in 1519. It's supported by an array of snails and dolphins and adorned with a host of statuettes. The nave of the church also holds several important **works of art** ★★, including 14th-century statues of St. Catherine and St. Sebald and the *Madonna with a Halo* (1440).

Sebalderplatz. ✆ **0911/214-2516.** Free admission. Mar–May daily 9:30am–6pm; June–Oct daily 9:30am–8pm; Nov–Feb daily 9am–4pm. Sun services at 8:30 and 10am. U-Bahn: Lorenzkirche.

## SHOPPING

Located near the railway station in the center of the city, **Handwerkerhof** (U-Bahn: Hauptbahnhof) is a crafts mall in a medieval castle setting, where Franconian artisans create and sell a wide range of handicrafts. It's open March 20 to

December 23, weekdays 10am to 6:30pm and Saturdays 10am to 4pm. In December, it opens Sundays 10am to 6:30pm.

**Obletter,** Königstrasse 2 (✆ **0911/2-14-99-90;** U-Bahn: Lorenzkirche), near the town center, has been the largest store for children's toys and playthings in Nürnberg for 20 years. Toys, many of them computerized, cover two floors (street level and cellar) of a building near the town center. For policy reasons, you'll find few of the war games that you'd expect in an equivalent stateside store, a credit to the establishment's enlightened management. Some of the devices, although intended for use by children and teens, might just appeal to adults.

**Hofman,** Rathaus Platz 7 (✆ **0911/20-48-48;** U-Bahn: Lorenzkirche), is devoted entirely to tin figures. The owner paints his historic soldiers, Christmas decorations, and other objects while manning the store.

At **Kistner,** Weinmarkt 6 (✆ **0911/20-34-82;** U-Bahn: Lorenzkirche), you can step back in time. This wonderful store is full of antique books, prints, and engravings, including some by Dürer, Rembrandt, and other masters. The owner, Herr Kistner, is an expert in the field.

**Villeroy & Boch,** Königstrasse 13 (✆ **911/22-31-82;** U-Bahn: Lorenzkirche), sells sets of china, crystal ware, and porcelain trinkets that make good souvenirs.

The largest department store in the city, **Karstadt,** Königstrasse 14 (✆ **0911/21-30;** U-Bahn: Lorenzkirche), carries clothing, housewares, and other home furnishings.

If you're hungry, stop by **Lebkuchen Frauenholz,** Bergstrasse 1 (✆ **0911/24-34-64;** U-Bahn: Lorenzkirche), a bakery that sells fresh gingerbread and honey packed in a container that looks like a half-timbered 18th-century German building.

Adding variety to prudence, **Condomi,** Ludwigstrasse 57 (✆ **0911/23-27-84;** U-Bahn: Weisser Turm), sells condoms in various colors, textures, flavors, and scents. It also has postcards and T-shirts.

## WHERE TO STAY

### EXPENSIVE

**Atrium Hotel** ★ The Atrium is not as grand as Le Meridien Grand Hotel or even the Maritim (see below), but it's close to the top of the heap. This hotel is one of the most modern in town; it looks like a four-story collection of concrete cubes set up on stilts. Inside, it's flooded with natural light, with many windows offering views of the landscaped park around it. For the most part, both the bedrooms and combination tub-and-shower bathrooms are roomy; the furnishings, though not terribly stylish, are comfortable and inviting. Three rooms are specially designed for travelers with disabilities. The hotel is directly connected to the Meistersingerhalle, where concerts and conventions take place.

Münchenerstrasse 25 (5-min. drive from the city center), 90478 Nürnberg. ✆ **0911/4-74-80.** Fax 0911/4-74-84-20. www.atrium-nurnberg.de. 200 units. 110€–290€ ($98.25–$258.95) double; from 200€ ($178.60) suite. Rates include buffet breakfast. Children under 12 stay free in parents' room. AE, DC, MC, V. Parking 10€ ($8.95). Tram: 9. Bus: 36. **Amenities:** 3 restaurants; bar; pool; room service; laundry/dry cleaning. *In room:* TV, minibar, hair dryer, safe.

**Le Meridien Grand Hotel** ★★★ This old-world palace is the best place to stay in Nürnberg. The Grand is a solid, six-story blockbuster built "when hotels were really hotels"—that is, before World War I. Rooms are the finest and most spacious in town. Furnishings are first-rate and stylish, and the roomy bathrooms are exceedingly well maintained with deluxe toiletries and tub-and-shower combinations. Many have a private sitting area.

Bahnhofstrasse 1–3 (across from the Hauptbahnhof), 90402 Nürnberg. ✆ **800/367-8340** in the U.S., or 0911/2-32-20. Fax 0911/2-32-24-44. www.grand-hotel.de. 186 units. 215€–345€ ($192–$308.10) double; from 415€ ($370.60) suite. AE, DC, MC, V. Parking 11€ ($9.80). U-Bahn: Hauptbahnhof. **Amenities:** Restaurant; bar; health club; sauna; solarium; room service; laundry/dry cleaning. *In room:* A/C, TV, minibar, hair dryer.

**Maritim** ★★ Maritim attracts those who prefer modern convenience to old-world charm. It used to be the city's most stylish hotel, until the Meridien chain upgraded the Grand. Rooms are good-size—although not as spacious as the Grand's—with large beds and many extras, such as good-size bathrooms with tub-and-shower combinations. Try an upper-floor room for a panoramic view over Nürnberg's medieval fortifications and busy traffic artery.

Frauentorgraben 11, 90443 Nürnberg. ✆ **0911/2-36-30.** Fax 0911/2-36-38-36. www.maritim.de. 315 units. 248€–274€ ($221.45–$244.70) double; 368€ ($328.60) suite. AE, DC, MC, V. Parking 12€ ($10.70). U-Bahn: Hauptbahnhof. **Amenities:** Restaurant; bar; pool; sauna; solarium; steam bath; room service; laundry/dry cleaning. *In room:* A/C, TV, minibar, hair dryer, safe.

## MODERATE

**Burghotel-Grosses Haus** *Value* This reliable hotel provides good solid comfort for the travel-weary. Sure, it's a ways down the pecking order among local hotels, but its limited facilities remain a good value. Bedrooms are compact and cozily furnished, but not without style. The functional bathrooms are tiled and come with shower units. Your door will practically open into one of the most historic parts of the old city—you're right next to Dürer 's house.

Lammsgasse 3, 90403 Nürnberg. ✆ **0911/20-44-14.** Fax 0911/22-38-82. www.altstadthotels-nuernberg.de. 46 units. 90€–156€ ($80.35–$139.30) double; 155€–185€ ($138.40–$165.20) suite. Rates include continental breakfast. AE, DC, MC, V. Parking 15€ ($13.40). Tram: Tiergärtnertor. Bus: 36. **Amenities:** Breakfast room; bar; lounge; pool; room service; laundry. *In room:* TV, minibar, hair dryer.

**Dürer Hotel** ★ The Dürer has steadily grown in prestige since it opened in the late '80s. It stands beside the birthplace of its namesake, right under the castle and near all the major sightseeing attractions. The ambience is one of cozy antique charm, combined with modern, well-furnished, midsize shower-only bathrooms. The only meal served is breakfast, but you're only a short walk from restaurants and cafes.

Neutormauer 32, 90403 Nürnberg. ✆ **0911/21-46-65-0.** Fax 0911/21-46-65-55-5. www.altstadthotelsnurnberg.de. 107 units. 120€–150€ ($107.15–$133.95) double. Rates include buffet breakfast. AE, DC, MC, V. Parking 9€ ($8.05). Tram: 4 or 9. Bus: 36 or 46. **Amenities:** Breakfast room; lounge; bar; fitness center; sauna; room service. *In room:* TV, minibar, hair dryer.

## INEXPENSIVE

**City Hotel** *Value* This serviceable if unspectacular hotel provides good value. It occupies the third, fourth, and fifth floors of an old-fashioned building, on a wide pedestrian thoroughfare. Take a small elevator upstairs to the third-floor reception area, where the efficient owner will show you one of her simple, cramped, but immaculate rooms. The tiny bathrooms have shower stalls.

Königstrasse 25–27 (near St.-Lorenz-Kirche), 90402 Nürnberg. ✆ **0911/22-56-38.** Fax 0911/20-39-99. 20 units. 92€ ($82.15) double. Rates include continental breakfast. AE, DC, MC, V. Parking 7€ ($6.25). Closed for 2 weeks after Christmas. U-Bahn: Lorenzkirche. **Amenities:** Breakfast room; lounge. *In room:* TV, hair dryer.

**Deutscher Kaiser** This attractive, gray-stone, 19th-century building, with steep gables and a high-pitched roof studded with dormers, stands at the top of a pedestrian mall. Three Romanesque-style arches lead into the main lobby. The general effect is one of comfort in immaculate surroundings. Rooms are small but have comfortable beds, and each comes with a compact, shower-only bathroom.

This hotel is crowded during December and February, when it's a popular off-season retreat for German visitors.

Königstrasse 55, 90402 Nürnberg. ✆ **0911/20-33-41.** Fax 0911/2-41-89-82. 51 units. 96€–145€ ($85.75–$129.50) double. AE, DC, MC, V. U-Bahn: Hauptbahnhof. **Amenities:** Restaurant; breakfast room; cafe; room service. *In room:* Hair dryer.

**Weinhaus Steichele** ★ This small and charming hotel retains its old-fashioned allure. It's located on a tranquil street but not far from the bustling activity of the train station, just outside the city wall. The building is a beautifully balanced and handcrafted structure of heavy stone blocks with a curved sloping roofline. Any overflow of guests spills into a modern annex next door that blends harmoniously with the older building. Rooms are decorated in a rustic Bavarian style, each with a small but efficiently organized shower-only bathroom.

Knorrstrasse 2–8 (near Jakobsplatz), 90402 Nürnberg. ✆ **0911/20-22-80.** Fax 0911/22-19-14. 58 units. 75€–125€ ($67–$111.65) double. Rates include buffet breakfast. AE, DC, MC, V. Parking 8€ ($7.15). U-Bahn: Weisser Turm. **Amenities:** Breakfast room; lounge. *In room:* TV, hair dryer.

## WHERE TO DINE

### EXPENSIVE

**Essigbrätlein** ★★★ FRENCH/CONTINENTAL This is now the outstanding dining choice of Nürnberg, dwarfing all other competition. The city's most ancient restaurant, dating from 1550, was originally a meeting place of wine merchants. Its upscale Franconian and continental cuisine is reason enough to go to the city in the first place. The cuisine is so inventive and refreshing, with many nouvelle recipes, that we'd view this as worth a detour. The chef firmly believes in market-fresh ingredients. Look for an ever-changing menu based on seasonal availability, but count on much care going into the preparation of each dish. The traditional specialty is roast loin of beef (what the name of the restaurant means in German).

Weinmarkt 3. ✆ **0911/22-51-31.** Reservations required. Main courses 18€–25€ ($16.05–$22.35); fixed-price lunch 35€ ($31.25) for 3 courses, 40€ ($35.70) for 4 courses; fixed-price dinner 62€ ($55.35) for 4 courses, 77€ ($68.75) for 6 courses. AE, DC, MC, V. Tues–Fri noon–1:30pm; Tues–Sat 7–9:30pm. Closed Jan 1–15 and 2 weeks in Aug (dates vary). U-Bahn: Karstadt.

**Goldenes Posthorn** ★ FRANCONIAN Goldenes Posthorn claims to be in the oldest house in Germany. Among its mementos are a drinking glass used by Albrecht Dürer and a playing card belonging to Hans Sachs from about 1560. Although the restaurant's glory days—it was once celebrated as among the finest in Germany—are long gone, no other place can match its antique atmosphere. Its modern Franconian cuisine features such old-fashioned but satisfying dishes as quail stuffed with goose liver and nuts; venison in red wine with plums; fresh carp (in winter); and wurst with a mixture of onions and vinegar. Two special fixed-price dinners are offered: a four-course house menu and a five-course Franconian menu. There are also fine wines dating from 1889.

Glöckleingasse 2. ✆ **0911/22-51-53.** Reservations required. Main courses 7.20€–20.50€ ($6.45–$18.30); fixed-price meals 15€ ($13.40) at lunch, 39€ ($34.85) at dinner. AE, DC, MC, V. Mon–Sat noon–2:30pm and 6–11:30pm. U-Bahn: Lorenzkirche.

### MODERATE

**Heilig-Geist-Spital** *Value* FRANCONIAN You wouldn't want to get much more Franconian than this. Heilig-Geist-Spital, Nürnberg's largest historical wine house, in business for 650 years, is entered through an arcade above the river. The main dishes are typical Franconian fare, hearty and filling. Carp is a specialty, as is pork knuckle—we're sure no one has altered this recipe since the days of Dürer himself. In season, you can order leg of venison with noodles and berries. The wine list is abundant and excellent, with more than 100 vintages.

Spitalgasse 16. ✆ **0911/22-17-61.** Main courses 6.90€–18€ ($6.15–$16.05). Daily 11:30am–midnight. Bus: 46 or 47.

**Weinhaus Steichele** ★ FRANCONIAN/BAVARIAN Steichele's walls are covered with polished copper pots, antique display cases lit from within, and hanging chandeliers carved into double-tailed sea monsters and other mythical beasts. The specialties here are a delight, and the wine list is superb. Try roast shoulder of pork with potato balls and sauerkraut; or paprika-coated baked ham in an onion sauce, served with french fries and a salad. Surely if former patron Hermann Hesse himself returned today, he would notice no major alteration in the cuisine. Amid all the change going on in Nürnberg, this place still respects older times.

Knorrstrasse 2. ✆ **0911/20-22-80.** Main courses 5.95€–18.90€ ($5.30–$16.90). AE, DC, MC, V. Mon–Sat 11am–midnight. U-Bahn: Weisser Turm.

### INEXPENSIVE

**Bratwurst-Häusle** FRANCONIAN This is the most famous bratwurst eatery in the city. You might make it a luncheon stopover as you explore historic Nürnberg. Prices are kept at a 1970s level, but portions are as large as ever. In winter, you'll find an open hearth to warm you; in summer, this is a refreshingly cool retreat from the heat. Fixed-price menus also include Franconian specialties; most diners, especially the large student clientele, prefer simply a platter of bratwurst and beer.

Rathausplatz 1 (opposite the Rathaus). ✆ **0911/22-76-95.** Main courses 5.50€–9.71€ ($4.90–$8.65). AE, MC, V. Mon–Sat 10am–10:30pm. U-Bahn: Lorenzkirche.

**Historische Bratwurst-Glöcklein** ★ *Kids* FRANCONIAN If you want to try bratwurst in all its variations, this place is for you. Nürnbergers refer to it as their Bratwurst-Lokale, and it's the only serious rival to Bratwurst-Häsle (see above). The kitchen prepares a bratwurst as a main course, with traditional side dishes, all served on tin plates. Because beer goes perfectly with wurst, you'll enjoy sampling some of the brews on tap while admiring the craftsmanship of the room, which dates from the Middle Ages. Ham hocks are a specialty. Be careful that you don't spend your entire afternoon on the sun terrace—it's that tempting.

Im Handwerkerhof. ✆ **0911/22-76-25.** Reservations recommended. Main courses 5€–7.35€ ($4.45–$6.55); fixed-price menu 11.75€–19.95€ ($10.50–$17.80). No credit cards. Mon–Sat 10:30am–9pm. U-Bahn: Hauptbahnhof.

## NÜRNBERG AFTER DARK

A theater complex offering quality productions of drama and opera, the **Städtische Bühnen,** Richard-Wagner-Platz 2–10 (✆ **0911/2-31-38-08;** U-Bahn: Opernhaus), houses the Kammerspiele, Opernhaus, and Schauspielhaus. The box office is open Monday to Friday 9am to 6pm; tickets are 5€ to 45.50€ ($4.45–$40.65). Students get 25% off, and the general public can check on discounted seats at the box office 1 hour before each performance.

Touring cabaret acts play at the **Loni-Ubler-Haus,** Marthastrasse 60 (✆ **0911/54-11-56;** U-Bahn: Hauptbahnhof), on Saturday and Sunday at 8pm. The box office is open Tuesday to Friday 9am to 10pm, and tickets are 8€ to 45€ ($7.15–$40.20). The city's premier outdoor venue, **St. Katarina,** is located in the ruins of the Katharinenkirche, Katherinenkloster 1 at Peter-Vischer-Strasse (U-Bahn: Lorenzkirche). It hosts concerts by an eclectic mix of international musical acts. Call the box office (✆ **0911/2-31-25-30**), Monday to Thursday

10am to 1pm and Friday 10am to noon, for recorded show listings and ticket information.

A garden house glowing in blue light marks the rear entrance to **Starclub,** Maxtorgraben 33 (✆ **0911/55-16-82;** U-Bahn: Rathenauplatz), the "House of 11 Beers." Brews start at 2.40€ ($2.15), accompanied by baguette sandwiches 3.80€ ($3.40) and other cheap snacks. Students come around for backgammon and darts or animated conversation on the patio out front. It's open daily 7am to 2am. An artists' hangout, **Triebhaus,** Karl-Griolenberger-Strasse 28 (✆ **0911/22-30-41;** U-Bahn: Weisser Turm), opens early for big breakfasts that run 3.50€ to 16.50€ ($3.15–$14.75), and offers soup, salad, and sandwich specials from 3€ to 3.70€ ($2.70–$3.30) throughout the day. At night it dims the lights and keeps serving drinks. It's open Monday to Friday 8am to 1am, and Saturday to Sunday 9am to 1am. Food is served until 10:30pm, and breakfast is served all day.

Another low-key arts scene, **Café Ruhestörung,** Tetzelgasse 21 (✆ **0911/22-19-21;** U-Bahn: Lorenzkirche or Rathenauplatz), offers some of the best people-watching in the city. Just sit on the patio and order a drink or a sandwich and watch the world waltz past. Draft beers are 2.50€ to 2.80€ ($2.25–$2.50). Open Monday to Friday 8:30am to 1am and Saturday and Sunday 9:30am to 1am.

At **Mach I,** Kaiserstrasse 1–9 (✆ **0911/203030;** U-Bahn: Lorenzkirche), Thursday and Friday move from disco to hip-hop, warming up for Saturday's big house party. Cover is 4.50€ ($4) on Thursday, 5.50€ ($4.90) on Friday, and 7.75€ ($6.90) on Saturday. It's open Thursday and Friday 10pm to 4am, and Saturday 10pm to 5am.

A popular gay bistro, **Cartoon,** An der Sparkgasse 6 (✆ **0911/22-71-70;** U-Bahn: Lorenzkirche), serves beer, wine, and light meals Monday to Saturday noon to midnight, and Sunday 2 to 11pm. For later hours, hit the dance clubs, all of which have both gay and straight clientele.

## 4 Regensburg ★★

122km (76 miles) NE of Munich, 100km (62 miles) SE of Nürnberg, 114km (71 miles) NW of Passau

Regensburg is one of Germany's best-preserved cities, relatively undamaged by World War II bombings. Despite this, it remains relatively obscure to many foreign visitors. Even if you don't have time to explore the city's museums or the interiors of its many historical monuments, try to take in the view of the Danube from one of its bridges, especially at sunset.

Regensburg started as a Celtic settlement called Radespona, around 500 B.C. The Romans later took it over, renamed it Castra Regina, and made it their center of power on the upper Danube. From the 7th century, the town was the center from which Christianity spread over southern Germany. The architecture of Regensburg testifies to its long history and past grandeur, which reached its peak by the beginning of the Gothic era. Its buildings and towers offer an unspoiled glimpse into history, and many of its ancient structures are still in active use today. The best example is the **Stone Bridge,** built in 1146 on 16 huge arches, in continuous service for more than 800 years.

### ESSENTIALS

**GETTING THERE** **By Train** The **Regensburg Hauptbahnhof** is on major rail lines, including Passau–Regensburg–Nürnberg and Munich–Landshut–Regensburg, with frequent connections in all directions. From Munich, 20 trains arrive daily (trip time: 1½ hr.), and from Frankfurt, 10 trains daily (trip time: 3¼ hr.). The trip from Nürnberg takes only an hour; from Passau (see "Passau," later in this chapter), 1½ hours. For rail information and schedules, call ✆ **01805/99-66-33.**

**By Bus** Regional buses service the nearby towns. Call ✆ **0941/601-2888** for information. For bus runs to such cities as Munich or Nürnberg, service is provided by **Firma Watzinger** in Bad Albach (✆ **0941/655-44** or 09405/95-940).

**By Car** Access by car is via the A3 Autobahn from east and west and the A93 from north and south.

**VISITOR INFORMATION** Contact **Tourist-Information,** Altes Rathaus (✆ **0941/5-07-44-10**). Hours are Monday to Friday 8:30am to 6pm, Saturday 9am to 4pm, and Sunday 9:30am to 2:30pm.

**GETTING AROUND** You can walk around the center of Regensburg covering the highlights. To get from the Hauptbahnhof to the town's medieval core (Altstadt) take any of the bright yellow ALTSTADT BUSES that line up along Maximilianstrasse, next to the station. One-way fare is .50€ (45¢). Buses run at 6-minute intervals every Monday to Friday 8:30am to 8:30pm. There's no service on Saturday and Sunday. If you wish to go farther afield, you'll find an adequate system of bus routes fanning out from the railway station. A single ride costs 1.50€ ($1.35), and buses run 6am to midnight daily. A list of bus routes is available at the railway station at the Presse & Buch kiosk.

## SEEING THE SIGHTS

Regensburg is a city of churches; it was once the focal point from which Christianity spread throughout Germany and even into Central Europe via the Danube. The most majestic of these churches is the towering **Dom St. Peter's** ★, Domplatz (✆ **0941/5-97-1002;** bus: 1, 2, or 3), which was begun in the 13th century on the site of an earlier Carolingian church. Because it was constructed with easily eroded limestone and green sandstone, this French Gothic edifice is constantly being restored. The massive spires of the two western towers, added in the mid-19th century, were almost completely replaced in 1955 with a more durable material. The well-preserved **stained-glass windows** ★★ in the choir (14th century) and south transept (13th century) are impressive. Most of the pillar sculptures in the aisles of the nave were made in the cathedral workshop in the mid-14th century. The two little sculptures in the niches on opposite sides of the main entrance are called *The Devil* and *The Devil's Grandmother* by the townsfolk. The cathedral is home to a famous boys' choir, the Dompatzen, which performs every Sunday morning at 9am mass. The performance is open to all. From May to October, the cathedral is open Monday to Saturday 8am to 6:30pm and Sunday noon to 6pm; November to April, Monday to Saturday 8am to 4pm and Sunday noon to 4pm. Admission is free.

You can also visit the cathedral treasures at the **Domschatzmuseum,** Krautermarkt 3 (✆ **0941/57-645;** bus: 1, 2, or 3), which displays goldsmiths' work and splendid textiles from the 11th to 20th centuries. Entrance is through a portal in the north aisle of the cathedral. It's open April to October, Tuesday to Saturday 10am to 5pm and Sunday noon to 5pm; December to March, generally only Friday and Saturday 10am to 4pm and Sunday noon to 4pm; closed in November. The charge is 2.50€ ($2.25) for adults and 1.55€ ($1.40) for children. You can also buy a combination ticket to the Domschatzmuseum and the Diozesanmuseum St. Ulrich (see below) that costs 2.55€ ($2.30) for adults and 3.60€ ($3.20) for a family. (Admission to the cloister isn't included with this ticket.)

### *Finds* A Side Trip to Walhalla

An interesting excursion is to **Walhalla** ★ (✆ **09403/96-16-80**), which lies on the steep northern bank of the Danube. This Greek-like temple was constructed between 1830 and 1842 on orders of Ludwig of Bavaria. It honors great Germans, most of them in the arts. The attraction itself isn't that spectacular—most visitors come for the view and the lovely ride down the river. Walhalla is open April to September daily 9am to 5:45pm, October daily 9am to 4:45pm, and November to March daily 10 to 11:45am and 1 to 4:45pm. There's a boat to Walhalla from Regensburg April to October daily at 10:30am and 2pm, with an additional departure May to September, Tuesday to Sunday at noon. The ride takes 45 minutes and costs 4.50€ ($4) each way for adults and 2.60€ ($2.30) for children. For information about departures, call **Regensburger Personen Schiffahrt,** Werftstrasse 8 (✆ **0941/553-59**).

The permanent collection of the **Diozesanmuseum St. Ulrich** is on exhibit in the former Church of St. Ulrich, an early Gothic building to the side of the cathedral, Domplatz 2 (✆ **941/595-322-530;** bus: 1, 2, 6, or 11). Sculptures, paintings, and goldsmiths' work form a representative selection of religious art in the diocese from the 11th to the 20th centuries. Of particular interest are various works on loan from the monastic foundations of the diocese. The museum is open April to October, Tuesday to Sunday 10am to 5pm. Admission costs 1.50€ ($1.35) for adults and 1.15€ ($1) for children, under 6 free.

Crossing the cathedral garden, you enter the **cloister** with its Romanesque All Saints' Chapel and St. Stephen's Church. The ancient frescoes on the walls of the chapel depict liturgical scenes from All Saints' Day. The 11th-century church of St. Stephen contains an altar made of a hollowed limestone rock with openings connecting to early Christian tombs. You can only visit the cloister and St. Stephen's Church on one of the guided tours, which are given (in English) from May to October, Monday to Saturday at 10, 11am, and 2pm, Sunday and holidays at noon and 2pm; November to April, Monday to Saturday at 11am and Sunday and holidays at noon. The charge is 2€ ($1.80) adults, 1.15€ ($1) students and children, free for children under 6.

Of all the remnants of Roman occupation of Regensburg, the ancient **Porta Praetoria** behind the cathedral is the most impressive, with its huge stones piled in the form of an arched gateway. Through the grille beside the eastern tower you can see the original level of the Roman street, nearly 3m (10 ft.) below—which is why you often have to step down into the churches of Regensburg.

Of the four **Museen de Stadt Regensburg,** the most important is **Kunst- und Kulturgeschichtliche Sammlungen,** Dachauplatz 2–4 (✆ **0941/5-07-24-48;** bus: 1, 2, or 3). This is not only the main museum of the city, but also one of the most notable in east Bavaria. Its displays show major developments in the history of the region from the earliest days up to the present. You'll see relics of the Roman period, such as a stone tablet marking the establishment of a garrison at Regensburg in the 2nd century. There's also a stone altar to the Roman god Mercury, as well as several Christian tombstones. The museum is open Tuesday to Sunday 10am to 4pm. Admission is 2€ ($1.80) for adults and 1.15€ ($1) for children.

No town hall in Germany has been preserved better than Regensburg's **Altes Rathaus** ★, Rathaus Platz (✆ **0941/5-07-44-11;** bus 1, 2, or 3). This Gothic structure, begun in the 13th century, contains a Reichssaal (Imperial Diet Hall), where the Perpetual Diet sat from 1663 to 1806. In the basement of the Rathaus are the dungeons, with the torture chamber preserved in its original setting. The Altes Rathaus is open daily. Guided tours in German are conducted Monday to Saturday every 30 minutes 9:30am to noon and 2 to 4pm; Sunday and holidays, every 30 minutes 10am to noon. The cost is 2.50€ ($2.25) for adults and 1.25€ ($1.10) for children.

## WHERE TO STAY

### EXPENSIVE

**Parkhotel Maximilian** ★ The next best thing to staying in one of Mad King Ludwig's palaces is to check into the Parkhotel Maximilian, an exquisitely renovated neorococo building. Its facade and public areas have been classified a public monument. The main salon, with a ceiling supported by columns of polished red stone, continues the theme of 18th-century opulence coupled with 20th-century convenience. Rooms are attractively furnished, and each comes with a roomy private bathroom with tub-and-shower combination.

Maximilianstrasse 28, 93047 Regensburg. ✆ **0941/56850.** Fax 0941/5-29-42. www.maximilian-hotel.de. 52 units. 142€–152€ ($126.80–$135.75) double; 400€ ($357.20) suite. Rates include breakfast. AE, DC, MC, V. Parking 9.50€ ($8.50). Bus: 1, 2, 3, or 6. **Amenities:** Restaurant; cafe; room service; laundry/dry cleaning. *In room:* TV, minibar, hair dryer.

### MODERATE

**Bischofshof am Dom** ★ This is a longtime favorite, appealing to traditionalists. This hotel was constructed as an ecclesiastical academy by the bishops of Regensburg in 1810. Today it blends 19th-century monastic with modern secular. Many of the units have hosted princes and even emperors. Rooms are attractively furnished, although the bathrooms with tub and shower are a bit small but well maintained. Part of the hotel takes in a piece of a Roman gateway. Behind the building is one of Regensburg's most popular sun terraces. Guests can also sit in the hotel's Weinstube, or in one of the 350 seats in the beer garden. The beer comes from a brewery dating from 1649.

Krautermarkt 3, 93047 Regensburg. ✆ **0941/5-84-60.** Fax 0941/584-61-46. www.hotel-bischofshof.de. 54 units. 119€–132€ ($106.25–$117.90) double; 175€ ($156.30) suite. Rates include breakfast. AE, DC, MC, V. Parking 8€ ($7.15). Bus: 1. **Amenities:** Restaurant; bar; room service; laundry. *In room:* TV, hair dryer.

**Karmeliten** In spite of its 130 years of tradition, the Karmeliten has a young, modern look. It's set on a square about 3 blocks from the river and a 4-minute walk from the Dom, reached via an open-air fruit-and-vegetable market. The whole place has a home-like atmosphere. Rooms and shower-only bathrooms are a bit small, but neatly organized, tidily kept, and functionally though comfortably furnished.

Dachauplatz 1, 93047 Regensburg. ✆ **0941/5-43-08.** Fax 0941/56-17-51. 80 units. 95€–115€ ($84.85–$102.70) double; from 120€ ($107.15) suite. Rates include buffet breakfast. AE, DC, MC, V. Parking 5.10€, ($5). Closed Dec 20–Jan 20. Bus: 1, 2, or 3. **Amenities:** Restaurant; lounge; room service. *In room:* TV, hair dryer.

### INEXPENSIVE

**Straubinger Hof** *Finds* This attractive, unpretentious hotel is little publicized, but bargain-hunters should seek it out. The small rooms are simple but satisfactory, with lots of sunlight. Bathrooms are tiny, containing a shower and rather thin towels.

Adolf-Schmetzer-Strasse 33 (a 15-min. walk east of the cathedral), 93055 Regensburg. ✆ **0941/60030.** Fax 0941/79-48-26. 60 units. 71€–92€ ($63.40–$82.15) double. Rates include breakfast. AE, DC, MC, V. Bus: 1. Free parking. **Amenities:** Dining room; lounge; room service. *In room:* TV, minibar, hair dryer.

## WHERE TO DINE

You can satisfy your sweet tooth by stopping by **Princess Konditorei,** Rathaus Platz 2 (✆ **0941/5-76-71;** bus: 1, 2, or 3), which has a tempting array of homemade pastries and candies.

**Ratskeller** *Value* BAVARIAN Traditional and unspoiled—that describes the Ratskeller. Here you'll get some of the best meals for your money in Regensburg. This comfortable establishment consists of two dining rooms with vaulted ceilings, paneled walls, and painted crests. The Germanic cuisine is good, with other internationally inspired offerings that add variety and flair. The best buy is the fixed-price luncheon. The Franconian soups are good and hearty. You can also try schnitzel cordon bleu or, for an exotic touch, an Indonesian *nasi-goreng* (the Indonesian version of fried rice).

Rathausplatz 1 (5 min. from the Dom). ✆ **0941/5-17-77.** Reservations recommended. Main courses 6.50€–16€ ($5.80–$14.30); fixed-price lunch 11.25€ ($10.05). AE, DC, MC V. Tues–Sun 10:30am–3pm; Tues–Sat 5:30pm–midnight. Bus: 1, 2, 3, or 6.

**Restaurant & Bistro Rosenpalais** INTERNATIONAL ★★ Positioned on the eastern fringe of Regensburg's historic core, this restaurant occupies a gracefully proportioned 18th-century baroque villa whose exterior is painted in tones of bright pink and cream. The use of this building has included stints as a private home as well as an upscale wine tavern (*Lustschloss*), a tradition it continues in two separate venues today. One floor above street level, you'll find the more formal venue, the restaurant, consisting of two high-ceilinged and somewhat restrained dining rooms, one of which is shaped like an octagon. Here, menu items are as posh and esoteric as you'll find anywhere in the area with seasonal variations that might include marinated calf's liver with tomato-and-basil vinaigrette; a very generously sized crayfish salad; cream of spinach soup garnished with braised mussels; caramelized goose liver with braised wild greens; a perfectly braised filet of tuna with mango-studded couscous and Chinese cabbage (pak choi); and venison cutlets with Bavarian herbs and seasonings.

Less expensive prices, and less formal and esoteric cuisine, is served in the somewhat more extroverted street-level bistro, where salads, pastas, and old-fashioned Teutonic and continental specialties include sole meuniere, wurst with sauerkraut; peppersteak with french fries, and French onion soup with a crusty top layer of Emmentaler cheese.

Minoritenweg 20. ✆ **0941/599-7579.** Reservations recommended. Restaurant main courses 24€–29€ ($21.45–$25.90); fixed-price menus in restaurant 38€–75€ ($33.95–$67); bistro main courses 13€–19€ ($11.60–$16.95). MC, V. Tues–Sat 11:30am–2pm and 6:30pm–1am.

**Zum Neuen Gänsbauer** ★ BAVARIAN/INTERNATIONAL For elegant dining, call for a table at Gänsbauer, one of the best restaurants in the city. The setting is mellow and old-fashioned, but the cuisine is strictly *neue Küche—cuisine moderne* with a continental influence. Well-known Bavarian dishes are given a lighter touch here, where only the freshest ingredients are used. Our recently sampled baby turbot in a Pernod sauce was superb in every way. The desserts are often exotic. The restaurant occupies a 500-year-old building with an open space where you can sit in fair weather. The street in front is a pedestrian zone, and there are tables here in summer.

Keplerstrasse 10. ✆ **0941/5-78-58.** Reservations recommended. Main courses 13€–22€ ($11.60–$19.65); fixed-price dinner from 32€–55€ ($28.60–$49.10). AE, DC, MC, V. Daily 6pm–1am. Bus: Fischmarkt.

## REGENSBURG AFTER DARK

The town's cultural center, **Alte Mälzerei,** Galgenberger Strasse 20 (✆ **0941/7-88-10 6**), hosts concerts and theater productions, as well as a run-down bar and beer garden that serves cheap drinks 2pm to 1am daily. In the same complex, **Cartoon,** Galgenberger Strasse 20 (✆ **0941/7-57-38;** bus: 6), has live reggae, blues, and rock bands on the main floor and a disco in the cellar. The club opens daily at 11am (2pm on weekends) and begins its entertainment at 8pm. Nighttime cover is 8€ to 19€ ($7.15–$16.95). Closing hours vary. The only late-night bar in town, **Wunderbar,** Keplerstrasse 11 (✆ **0941/5-31-30;** bus: Altstadtbus), serves drinks until 3am, 7 nights a week.

**Südhaus Dance Theatre,** Untere Bachgasse 8 (✆ **0941/5-19-46;** bus: Altstadtbus), is the best of the local dance clubs. Easy to spot, its entrance is marked by a statuary angel holding a lit bar sign. It's open Tuesday and Thursday 11pm to 3am, Friday and Saturday 11pm to 4am. On Thursday, it's the town's best lesbian and gay rendezvous. Admission is 3€ ($2.70) Tuesday and 3.50€ ($3.15) other nights. Somewhat more fashionable, and a bit more pretentious, is **Scala,** Gesandtenstrasse 6 (✆ **0941/5-22-93;** bus: Altstadtbus), where the dance floor is hemmed in by three bars. This club attracts an under-35 crowd. It's open Wednesday to Sunday 11pm to 3am (until 4am Fri and Sat). Admission is 1.50€ to 3.60€ ($1.35–$3.20).

If the weather's right when you reach Regensburg, head for the town's oldest inn, the **Goldene Ente,** Badstrasse 32 (✆ **0941/8-54-55;** bus: 12), which has a beer garden at the end of Eisernen Steg Brücke (along the Danube). Under the chestnut trees, you can sample spareribs, Würstchen, grilled schnitzel, and, of course, that famous brew. Beer prices range from 2.30€ to 4.40€ ($2.05–$3.95).

# 5 Passau ★★

191km (119 miles) E of Munich, 117km (73 miles) SE of Regensburg

For years, Passau languished in a lost corner of West Germany. But since reunification, the beauty and nostalgia of this old city has been appreciated more and more. With its romantic river setting and stately streets, Passau is a city of great harmony. It's located at the confluence of the Danube and two of its tributaries, the Ilz and Inn rivers. Passau's bustling port is worth a visit in itself.

## ESSENTIALS

**GETTING THERE** **By Train** Because Passau is a German border station, **Inter-City** trains stop here, with frequent daily arrivals from such cities as Nürnberg, Munich, and Vienna. The other major rail links include Frankfurt–Nürnberg–Passau–Vienna and Nürnberg–Regensburg–Passau, with frequent connections. Trip time from Nürnberg is 2 hours; from Frankfurt, 4½ hours; from Munich, 1 hour; from Regensburg, 1 hour; and from Vienna, 3¼ hours. For rail information and schedules, call ✆ **01805/99-66-33.**

**By Bus** There are no long-distance buses serving Passau. However, buses service the outskirts of the city. For a recorded list of schedules (in German), call ✆ **0851/756-370.**

**By Car** Access is by the A3 Autobahn from the north or south.

**VISITOR INFORMATION** For information, contact the **Tourist Information Office,** Rathausplatz 3 (✆ **0851/95-59-80**). Hours are April to October, Monday to Friday 9am to 6pm and Saturday and Sunday 10am to 2pm; November to March, Monday to Thursday 9am to 5pm and Friday 9am to 4pm.

**GETTING AROUND** A local bus, called **City-Bus,** runs through Passau from the Rathaus (Town Hall) to the Hauptbahnhof (train station) every 15 minutes. It connects all the places recommended below. Call the tourist office for schedule information.

## SEEING THE SIGHTS

The **Altstadt** is built on a rocky spur of land formed by the confluence of the Inn and the Danube. To best appreciate its setting, cross the Danube to the **Veste Oberhaus,** St. Georg Berg 125, a medieval episcopal fortress towering over the town and the river. Note how arches join many of the houses, giving them a unity of appearance. As you view the town, you can sense that the architecture here is more closely allied to northern Italy and the Tyrolean Alps than to cities to the north. The fortress houses a museum of regional history (✆ **0851/4933512**), going back to medieval times. It's open March to January, Monday to Friday 9am to 5pm, Saturday and Sunday 10am to 6pm. Admission is 4€ ($3.55) for adults and 2€ ($1.80) for children. Take the shuttle bus to the castle.

Dominating the town are the twin towers of the **Dom (St. Stephen's Cathedral),** Domplatz 9 (✆ **0851/39-33-74;** bus: City-Bus). The original Gothic plan is still obvious in spite of its 17th-century reconstruction in grand baroque style. Its most unusual feature is the octagonal dome over the intersection of the nave and transept. The interior of the cathedral is mainly Italian baroque—almost gaudy, with its many decorations and paintings. Of particular interest is

### *Moments* Cruising the Danube

One reason for visiting this Dreiflüssestadt (town of three rivers) on the Austrian frontier is to take one of the numerous boat tours along the Danube and its tributaries, the Inn and the Ilz. Trips range from a 45-minute three-river tour to a steamer cruise downriver to Vienna. The cruises depart from Fritz-Schäffer Promenade. Many passengers prefer to go by boat, then take a train back.

You might also be tempted to board one of the passenger ferries that makes runs (Apr–Oct only) every day from Passau downstream to the Austrian city of Linz. The trips take 5 hours each way, cost 21€ ($18.75) per person, and depart from the city's riverfront piers at 9am and at 1:10pm.

If you're interested in gaining even greater insights into life along the Danube, you can continue by train from Linz to Vienna, buying a ferryboat, train, and hotel package priced at a reasonable 229€ ($204.50) per person, which will include round-trip transit by boat and train to Vienna, via Linz, from Passau, and 1 night's stay at a four-star hotel in Vienna. For information about either the day trip to Linz or the overnight sojourn in Vienna, contact the **Donau-Schiffahrt Line** through its local representative, Würm & Koeck, Höllgasse 26, 94032 Passau (✆ **0851/929-292**).

the choir, which remains from the Gothic period. A newer addition is a huge organ, said to be the largest church organ in the world, built in 1928 and placed in an 18th-century casing. Concerts are given May to October Monday to Saturday at noon, costing 3€ ($2.70) for adults and 2€ ($1.80) for children and students, and also at 7:30pm on Thursday, costing 8€ ($7.15) for adults, 5€ ($4.45) for children. The Dom is open Monday to Saturday 8 to 11am and 12:30 to 6pm. Admission is free.

Below the cathedral, on the bank of the Danube, is the **Marktplatz** and the 13th-century **Rathaus,** with a facade decorated with painted murals depicting the history of the town. Inside, the huge knights' hall contains two large 19th-century frescoes illustrating incidents from the legend of the Niebelungen. The Town Hall has a Glockenspiel in its tower that plays at 10:30am, 2, and 7:25pm; on Saturday there's an additional performance at 3pm.

Next to the Rathaus, the **Glasmuseum (Glass Museum),** Rathausplatz (✆ **0851/ 3-50-71;** bus: City-Bus), features an impressive array of glassware from the 1700s to the 1930s, collected from Bavaria, Austria, Bohemia, and other parts of Europe. In all, there are 30,000 items on display, including the world's largest collection of Bohemian glass. The Biedermeier period of 1840 and the Jugendstil period of 1910 are particularly emphasized. The museum is open April to September, daily 10am to 4pm; October to March, daily 1 to 4pm. Admission is 4€ ($3.55) for adults, 2.50€ ($2.25) for students and older children, and free for children under 12.

## WHERE TO STAY

### EXPENSIVE

**Holiday Inn** ★ The Holiday Inn is rather sterile, but it's the best hotel in Passau. It's been integrated into the city's largest shopping center. Although the bedrooms are in a standard chain-hotel format, they are the most comfortable in town, each coming with a midsize bathroom with tub-and-shower combination.

Bahnhofstrasse 24 (across from the Hauptbahnhof), 94032 Passau. ✆ **0851/5-90-00.** Fax 0851/5-90-05-29. 129 units. www.passau.holiday-inn.com. 120€–180€ ($107.15–$160.75) double; 195€–230€ ($174.15–$205.40) suite. AE, DC, MC, V. Parking 5€ ($4.45). Bus: City-Bus. **Amenities:** Restaurant; bar; pool; health club; sauna; solarium; room service; laundry. *In room:* A/C, TV, hair dryer.

### MODERATE

**Passauer Wolf** ★ This hotel on the banks of the Danube lies behind an elegant baroque facade. It isn't as up-to-date as the Holiday Inn but has better food and more character. Rooms are modern and comfortable. Service is efficient.

The hotel's Passauer Wolf Restaurant is one of the most distinguished in town; you may want to dine here even if you're not a guest. It serves classic dishes and regional specialties.

Rindermarkt 6, 94032 Passau. ✆ **0851/9-31-51-10.** Fax 0851/9-31-51-50. 40 units. www.passauerwolf.de. 144€ ($128.60) double. Rates include breakfast. AE, DC, MC, V. Parking 10€ ($8.95). Bus: City-Bus. **Amenities:** Restaurant; lounge; room service; laundry/dry cleaning. *In room:* TV, minibar, hair dryer.

**Weisser Hase** *Value* This inn straddles the peninsula between the Danube and the Inn rivers, in the heart of Passau. Some prefer this hotel to the more highly rated Passauer Wolf, because it provides more value for your money. The bedrooms are midsize and neatly organized with functional furniture that is nonetheless comfortable; each comes with an average-size tiled bathroom with a modern shower unit. There's also a Weinstube (wine bar) with Bavarian-Austrian decor—carved wood and provincial chairs.

Ludwigstrasse 23 (off Ludwigsplatz, halfway between the Dom and the Hauptbahnhof), 94032 Passau. ✆ **0851/9-21-10.** Fax 0851/9-21-11-00. www.weisser-hase.de. 108 units. 105€–145€ ($93.75–$129.50) double. Rates include buffet breakfast. AE, DC, MC, V. Parking 9€ ($8.05). Bus: City-Bus. **Amenities:** Breakfast room; lounge; sauna. *In room:* TV, hair dryer.

### INEXPENSIVE

**Altstadt-Hotel Laubenwirt** ★ *Finds* The waters of the Danube, the Ilz, and the Inn converge at a point just a few steps from the foundations of this hotel. You'd stay here just for the view, but it's also a very well-run hotel for a good price. Many guests who could afford the Holiday Inn seek out this little charmer for its ambience. Rooms are comfortably furnished in traditional style; some overlook the confluence of the rivers. All the bedrooms come with an average-size and tidily kept bathroom with a modern shower. In summer, guests can enjoy breakfast or other meals on the terrace.

Bäugasse 23–29, 94032 Passau. ✆ **0851/33-70.** Fax 0851/33-71-00. www.alstadt-hotel.de. 57 units. 90€–135€ ($80.35–$120.55) double. Rates include buffet breakfast. AE, DC, MC, V. Parking 6€ ($5.35) in underground garage. Bus: City-Bus. **Amenities:** Restaurant; bar; room service. *In room:* TV, hair dryer.

**Hotel König** This hotel is located at the edge of a spit of land separating the Danube and Inn rivers. It stands behind massive stucco-covered buttresses and a salmon-colored facade. Despite its fortress-like appearance, it has an interior that's comfortably up-to-date. Each of the well-scrubbed rooms has pinewood accents. The best ones open onto views of the Danube or the Inn, although the location isn't as scenic as that of the Altstadt-Hotel Laubenwirt (see above). The private bathrooms are rather compact, each with some shelf space and a shower unit.

Untere Donaulande 1, 94032 Passau. ✆ **0851/38-50.** Fax 0851/38-54-60. www.hotel-koenig.de. 41 units. 82€–125€ ($73.25–$111.65) double. AE, MC, V. Parking 5.50€ ($4.90). Bus: City-Bus. **Amenities:** Lounge; sauna; solarium. *In room:* TV, hair dryer.

## WHERE TO DINE

For another dining option, head to the **Passauer Wolf** hotel (see above), which has one of the better restaurants in town.

**Heilig-Geist-Stift-Schenke** BAVARIAN/AUSTRIAN Each year we hope for the opening of a first-class restaurant in Passau, but until that great day comes, this little inn born in 1358 remains the top choice in town, with hearty, stick-to-your-ribs fare. In summer, you can sit in a beautiful wine garden under chestnut trees. Indoors, the dining room has an open fireplace, decorated with old tools used to press grapes. The restaurant has its own vineyard, and you can order its wines under the label "Grüner Veltliner." The ancient kitchen serves up many good, low-cost regional dishes, including boiled rump steak Austrian-style and roast suckling pig. *Passauer Schlosserbaum* is a dessert specialty (the waiter will explain). Bavarian, Austrian, and international dishes are featured.

Heiliggeistgasse. ✆ **0851/26-07.** Reservations recommended. Main courses 7.20€–14.80€ ($6.45–$13.20). MC, V. Thurs–Tues 11am–midnight. Closed Jan. Bus: City-Bus.

## PASSAU AFTER DARK

Combining quality drama with a dramatic setting, the **Stadttheater Company** is housed in the **Stadttheater Passau,** Gottfried-Schäfer-Strasse (✆ **0851/9-29-19-10**), a beautiful baroque opera house built by the local prince-bishops. Call for performance schedules and ticket prices. Summertime brings drama, pantomime, opera, jazz, and classical concerts to town, scheduled as part of the **Europäische Wochen (European Weeks) Festival,** which runs June to early August. Call ✆ **0851/ 560960** for information; for schedules, tickets, or reservations, contact the **Kartenzentrale der Europäischen Wochen Passau,** Dr.-Hans-Kapfinger-Strasse 22 (✆ **0851/752020;** fax 0851/7560207).

Home to Passau's popular cabaret company, **Theater im Schaarfrichter-Haus,** Milchgasse 2 (✆ **0851/3-59-00**), is open September to July. It also hosts a series of jazz concerts throughout the year. Contact the theater for schedules, prices, and ticket availability.

**Café Innsteg,** Innstrasse 15 (✆ **0851/5-12-57**), housed in a bungalow hanging over the Inn River, offers the town's most scenic setting in which to relax with a drink. Like every other cafe-bar in town, it's open from midmorning until 1am. **Café Kowalski,** Obere Sandstrasse 1 (✆ **0851/24-87**), is less dramatic but also has balcony views of the river. Underground, across the river, **Joe's Garage,** Lederergasse 38 (✆ **0851/3-19-99**), is a friendly student dive named after a Frank Zappa album.

## 6 Ulm ★★

97km (60 miles) SE of Stuttgart, 138km (86 miles) W of Munich

Visit Ulm for its architectural heritage and its history—not for great shopping, nightlife, or even an exciting local life. The city (situated at a strategic spot on the Danube) is a bit sleepy, smug, and satisfied with its monuments, especially its undeniably magnificent cathedral. Ulm's importance as a commercial river port has made it a prosperous city ever since the Middle Ages. Today, Ulm is a center of scientific and technological research, as befits the birthplace of Albert Einstein, who started life here in 1879. The old, narrow alleyways of the Altstadt lead to a modern city of riverbank promenades, beer gardens, spacious squares, and pedestrian zones.

### ESSENTIALS

**GETTING THERE** **By Train** The **Ulm Hauptbahnhof** is on several major and regional rail lines, with frequent connections in all directions. More than 40 trains per day arrive from Munich (trip time: 45 min.) and some 50 or more from Stuttgart (67 min.). Daily trains also arrive from Cologne (4 hr. 6 min.). From Frankfurt (2 hr. 20 min.), you can take an ICE (InterCity-Express), the fastest and most comfortable way to travel by rail. For rail information and schedules, call ✆ **01805/99-66-33.**

**By Bus** There are no buses from major cities; local buses service only satellite towns—mostly bedroom communities of Ulm.

**By Car** Access by car is via the A8 Autobahn east and west or the A7 north and south. It takes about 1½ hours to drive to Ulm from Munich and about 3 hours to drive from Frankfurt.

**VISITOR INFORMATION** **Tourist-Information,** Münsterplatz (✆ **0731/1-61-28-30**), is open Monday to Friday 9am to 5pm and Saturday 9am to 1pm.

**GETTING AROUND** Ulm's only tram line runs east-west, connecting the suburban convention center (Messe) with the main railway station (Hauptbahnhof) and Söflingen. Ulm's historic core (Altstadt) lies within an easy walk from the Hauptbahnhof. Buses 3, 7, and 8 radiate from the station to the suburbs. Buses and trams run at intervals of between 10 and 30 minutes, depending on the time of day and day of the week, and cost from 1.50€ to 2€ ($1.35–$1.80) depending on the distance you travel.

## SEEING THE SIGHTS

If you approach the town from the Stuttgart–Munich Autobahn, you'll miss the best view. So sometime during your visit, you should cross the Danube into Neu Ulm for a look at the gables and turrets of the Altstadt, which line the north bank of the river. Here is the **Fisher's Quarter,** with its little medieval houses and tree-shaded squares. Nearby are the elaborate Renaissance patrician houses and the Gothic Renaissance **Rathaus.**

**Rathaus** The Rathaus was built in 1370 as a warehouse but has served as the town hall since 1419. It contains some ornate murals dating from the mid-16th century. On the south gable hang coats of arms of cities and countries with which Ulm is linked by commerce. On the east gable is an astronomical clock from 1520. Above the interior staircase is a reproduction of the flying machine constructed by A. L. Berblinger, called "the tailor of Ulm." In 1811, he was one of the first people to make a serious attempt at flight.

Marktplatz 1. ✆ **0731/16-10.** Free admission. Tues–Fri 8am–6pm; Mon 8am–4pm. Bus: 4, 5, 6, or 9.

**Ulm Münster** ★★★ Before you even get close to the city, you'll see the towering Ulm Münster on the skyline. Its 162m (530-ft.) steeple is the tallest of any cathedral in the world, and the Ulm Münster itself is second only to Cologne Cathedral in size. Without the pews, the nave of the church could hold nearly 20,000 people, more than twice the population of Ulm at the time the cathedral was begun in 1377. When Ulm joined the Protestant movement in 1531, work on the building was suspended, not to be continued until 1844; it was completed in 1890. Miraculously, the cathedral escaped serious damage during World War II.

The exterior is almost pure German Gothic, even though bricks were often used in the walls along with the more typical stone blocks. The unusual feature of the Münster is that its architects placed as much emphasis on horizontal lines as on the vertical. Before entering, stop to admire the main porch whose three massive arches lead to two 15th-century doors. This section dates from the 14th and 15th centuries and contains a wealth of statues and reliefs.

The five aisles of the cathedral lead directly from the hall below the tower through the nave to the east chancel. The conspicuous absence of a transept heightens the emphasis on the chancel and also increases the length of the nave. Huge pillars towering into steep arches enclose each of the five aisles. The ceiling is swept into net-vaults so high that any of Germany's church steeples could sit comfortably beneath them. The nave is so large that, even with pews, it can accommodate more than 11,000 people at one service.

The most remarkable treasure of the cathedral is the **Chorgestühl** ★★★ or choir stalls, which are some of the finest examples in Germany of woodcarving. These were created between 1469 and 1474 by Jorg Syrliun the Elder. He depicted personages from the Bible facing those from the pagan era.

You can climb the tower as far as the third gallery (768 steps), where you can look out on the town and surrounding countryside over the Danube plain as far as the Alps.

Münsterplatz 1. ✆ **0731/967-50-23.** Münster free; tower 2.50€ ($2.25) adults, 1.50€ ($1.35) children. Buy tickets an hour before the climb. Nov–Feb daily 9am–4:45pm; Mar daily 9am–5:45pm; Apr–June and Sept daily 8am–6:45pm; July–Aug daily 8am–7:45pm; Oct daily 8am–5:45pm. Bus: 2, 7, or 9.

**Ulmer Museum** ★ The Ulm Museum contains an important collection of arts and crafts produced in Ulm and upper Swabia from medieval times onward. There are also successive exhibitions of both ancient and modern art and artifacts,

### *Finds* Farther up the Danube: Sigmaringen

**Schloss Sigmaringen** (✆ **07571/729-230;** www.hohenzollern.com/engl/frame.htm), one of the most impressive castles in Germany, lies about 97km (60 miles) southwest of Ulm, dramatically situated on a rock above the Danube. Inside, the rooms are filled with period furniture, porcelain objects, and works of art. The castle also holds displays of 15th- and 16th-century paintings and one of the biggest private collections of arms in Europe. Schloss Sigmaringen is open November and February to April daily 9:30am to 4:30pm; May to October daily 9am to 5pm; December and January only by private arrangements. To get to Sigmaringen from Ulm, take a train on the Ulm–frieberg line, or drive southwest on the B311 and then west on the B32. From the north, take the B313. There are also trains from Stuttgart.

ranging from the region's prehistory up to the 20th century, with works by Klee, Kandinsky, and Picasso.

Marktplatz 9 (near the cathedral). ✆ **0731/16-14-330.** Admission 2.50€ ($2.25) adults, 1.50€ ($1.35) students, free for children 14 and under. Tues–Wed and Fri–Sun 11am–5pm; Thurs 11am–8pm. Bus: 2, 5, or 6.

## WHERE TO STAY

**Maritime Hotel Ulm** ★★★ *Kids* A first-class hotel, this 16-story city center choice is the grandest hotel in and around Ulm, which up until the 1990s never had a first-rate hotel. All of its guest rooms are generous in size, furnished with first-rate pieces and deluxe mattresses as well as roomy bathrooms with both tub-and-shower combination. The hotel advertises itself as a home away from home, but few homes look like this palace, and even fewer have the facilities of this monument (see below). The hotel is also the most family-friendly in Ulm; the only one to offer rooms big enough for extra beds, babysitting services, and a pool.

Basteistrasse 40, 89073 Ulm. ✆ **0731/9230.** Fax 0731/9232001. www.maritim.de. 276 units. 140€–170€ ($125–$151.80) double; from 275€ ($245.60) suite. AE, DC, MC, V. **Amenities:** 2 restaurants; bar; indoor pool; room service; babysitting; laundry/dry cleaning. *In room:* A/C, TV, minibar, hair dryer, safe.

**Neu-Ulm Mövenpick Hotel** This hotel beside the Danube contains rather bland, but well-maintained, rooms. Many feature views of the river. Bedrooms are in a standard, chain format, but each is midsize and furnished comfortably. All the bedrooms contain a compact and well-organized bathroom in tiles, each with a shower-and-tub combination. The English-speaking staff is helpful.

Silcherstrasse 40, 89231 Neu Ulm. ✆ **0731/8-01-10.** Fax 0731/8-59-67. www.movenpick-neu-ulm.com. 135 units. 129€–149€ ($115.20–$133.05) double; 185€–205€ ($165.20–$183.05) suite. AE, DC, MC, V. Parking 6€ ($5.35). Bus: 2, 3, or 7. **Amenities:** Restaurant; bar; cafe; room service; laundry/dry cleaning. *In room:* TV, minibar, hair dryer.

**Ulmer Spatz** This is a corner stucco hotel, with most of its simply furnished rooms overlooking the cathedral tower. This is an exceedingly modest but clean and comfortable place. Its chief recommendation is its location in the center of Ulm. Rooms are a bit cramped, and each comes with a compact, shower-only bathroom.

Münsterplatz 27 (just beside the cathedral), 89073 Ulm. ✆ **0731/6-80-81.** Fax 0731/6-02-19-25. 35 units. 82€–87€ ($73.25–$77.70) double. Rates include continental buffet breakfast. AE, MC, V. Bus: 2, 3, or 4. **Amenities:** Restaurant; breakfast room; lounge; room service. *In room:* TV, hair dryer.

## WHERE TO DINE

**Zum Pflugmerzler** GERMAN/INTERNATIONAL This intimate restaurant is a winning choice for stick-to-your-ribs fare. Because it's open later than most restaurants in Ulm, it's a good place for a late-night supper in an old-world setting. The kitchen turns out home-style Swabian, Bavarian, and international meat and fish dishes. A specialty is Swabian *Fischmaultasche,* which looks like large ravioli, usually stuffed with a spinach-and-ricotta mixture. *Tafelspitz,* the famed boiled beef dish, is served with either a horseradish sauce or a green-herb sauce.

Pfluggasse 6. ✆ **0731/6-80-61.** Reservations recommended. Main courses 9.50€–19€ ($8.50–$16.95). No credit cards. Mon–Fri 11am–2pm and 6–11pm; Sat 11am–3pm. Closed last 2 weeks in July and 1st 2 weeks in Aug. Bus: 2, 3, or 4.

## ULM AFTER DARK

The best beer hall in town is **Barfusser,** Lautenberg 1 (✆ **0731/6021110**), a brewpub that also makes its own pretzels. If you'd like to go on a tavern crawl, you can walk **Neue Strasse** down to the river. But if you have a beer at every place, you may not even make it to the river.

# 7

# The Romantic Road

The aptly named Romantic Road, or *Romantische Strasse,* is one of Germany's most popular tourist routes. The road stretches for 290km (180 miles) between Würzburg in the north and Füssen in the foothills of the Bavarian Alps. Strung along the way is a series of medieval villages and 2,000-year-old towns. Frankfurt and Munich are convenient gateways for exploring the road by car, coach, or rail.

Another way to tour the route is by **bicycle.** Cyclists can begin at Würzburg and follow the bike path along the Main River. Tourist offices along the road provide cycling maps and other helpful information. Campgrounds are generally 10km to 20km (6–12 miles) apart. Bikes can be rented at any train station along the Romantic Road for 5€ to 8€ ($4.45–$7.15) per day with a valid train ticket.

The Romantic Road is more than just a scenic route—it's also a powerful marketing organization composed of 26 municipalities, each of which would love to welcome you for a visit. The Romantic Road Association will provide information on sights and attractions and mail information packs in English. Contact the **Romantische Strasse Arbeitsgemeinschaft,** Marktplatz, 91550 Dinkelsbühl (✆ **09851/9-02-71;** www.romantischestrasse.de).

**THE TOWNS OF THE ROMANTIC ROAD** Every town on the road has its special charms and attractions—and its drawbacks. **Rothenburg,** for example, is a perfect museum town but is overwhelmed with tourists. **Dinkelsbühl** is less perfect—it doesn't do as good a job of transporting you into the past—but at least it has an integrity of its own, independent of tourists. **Nördlingen** is less romantic even than Dinkelsbühl but is more real. **Augsburg** is Bavaria's third largest city (after Munich and Nürnberg) but still has a rich medieval past. **Würzburg,** traditionally the first town on the route, is the bustling center of the Franconian wine region and home to one of Germany's greatest palaces.

**BUS TOURS OF THE ROMANTIC ROAD** Green-and-white buses make three runs a day among all the member towns. April to October, a deluxe motor coach equipped with reclining seats and toilets departs from Frankfurt every morning at 8am, making stops on the main squares of 26 towns en route, eventually pulling into Füssen at 8:40pm. One-way transit between Frankfurt and Füssen costs 66€ ($58.95), but you can get off the bus and reboard it later at any town en route. Buses also run the other way, from Füssen to Frankfurt, following more or less the same schedule. Make advance reservations by phoning **Deutsche Touring GmbH** (✆ **069/790-350**), Am Römerhof 17, Frankfurt.

## 1 Würzburg ★★

280km (174 miles) NW of Munich, 119km (74 miles) SE of Frankfurt, 109km (68 miles) NW of Nürnberg

For Germans, the south begins at Würzburg, one of the loveliest baroque cities in the country. Würzburg is the best starting point for the Romantic Road. This

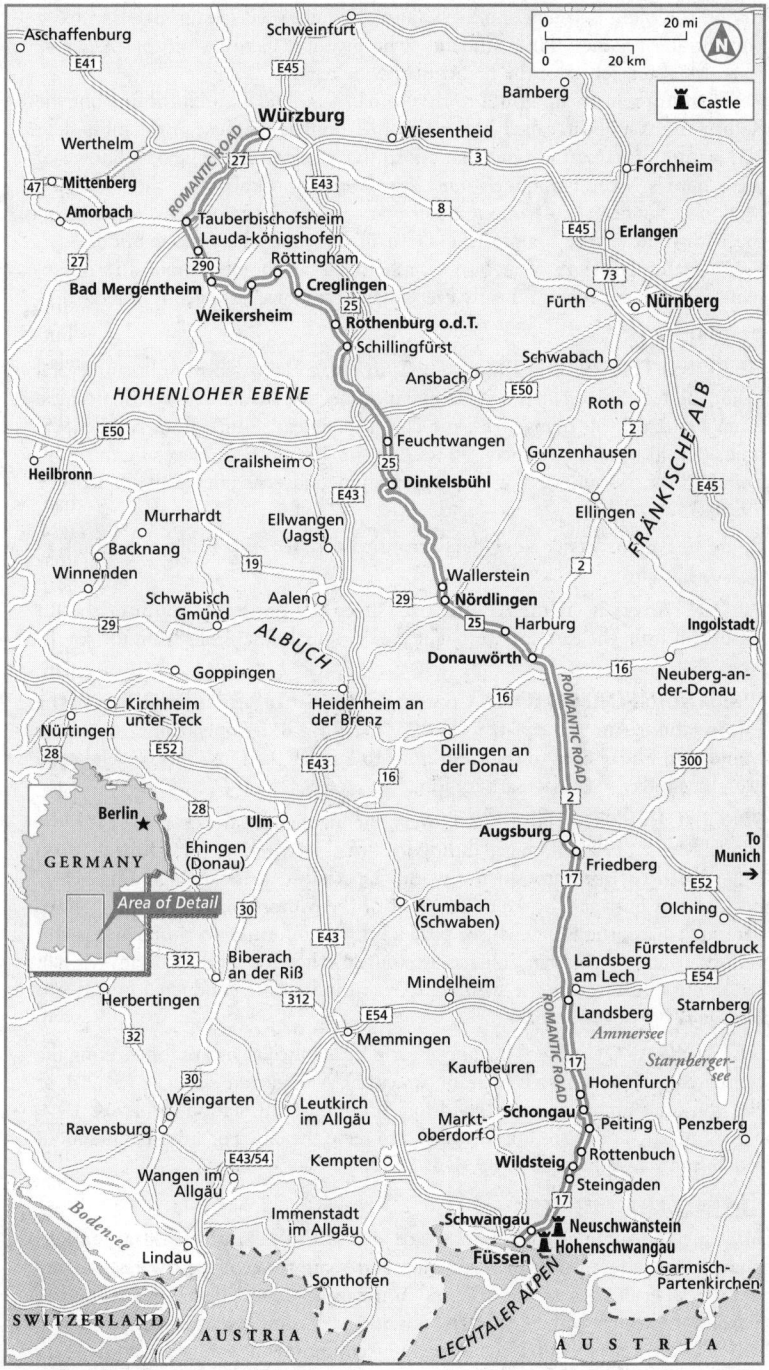
0 20 mi
0 20 km
N
Castle
Aschaffenburg
Schweinfurt
Bamberg
Würzburg
Wiesentheid
Werthelm
Forchheim
Mittenberg
Amorbach
Tauberbischofsheim
Lauda-königshofen
Röttingham
Erlangen
Bad Mergentheim
Creglingen
Weikersheim
Fürth
Nürnberg
Rothenburg o.d.T.
Schillingfürst
Schwabach
Ansbach
HOHENLOHER EBENE
Roth
FRÄNKISCHE ALB
Feuchtwangen
Gunzenhausen
Heilbronn
Crailsheim
Dinkelsbühl
Ellingen
Murrhardt
Ellwangen (Jagst)
Backnang
Winnenden
Wallerstein
Schwäbisch Gmünd
Aalen
Nördlingen
Harburg
Ingolstadt
ALBUCH
Donauwörth
Goppingen
Neuberg-an-der-Donau
Kirchheim unter Teck
Heidenheim an der Brenz
Nürtingen
Dillingen an der Donau
ROMANTIC ROAD
Berlin
Ulm
Augsburg
GERMANY
Ehingen (Donau)
Friedberg
To Munich
Area of Detail
Krumbach (Schwaben)
Olching
Fürstenfeldbruck
Biberach an der Riß
Landsberg am Lech
Mindelheim
Herbertingen
Landsberg
Starnberg
Ammersee
Memmingen
Starnberger-see
Kaufbeuren
Hohenfurch
Weingarten
Leutkirch im Allgäu
Schongau
Ravensburg
Markt-oberdorf
Peiting
Penzberg
Kempten
Wildsteig
Rottenbuch
Wangen im Allgäu
Steingaden
Bodensee
Immenstadt im Allgäu
Schwangau
Neuschwanstein
Hohenschwangau
Füssen
Lindau
Garmisch-Partenkirchen
Sonthofen
SWITZERLAND
AUSTRIA
LECHTALER ALPEN
AUSTRIA

city on the Main is young and lively (and often crowded in summer) and has a population of some 50,000 students, who give it a German version of *joie de vivre.* It's also a center of the Franconian wine region.

Würzburg remained faithful to the Roman Catholic Church throughout the Reformation. It's been called "the town of Madonnas" because of the more than 100 statues of its patron saint that adorn the house fronts. The best known of these statues is the baroque *Patrona Franconiae,* also known as the "Weeping Madonna," which stands among other Franconian saints along the buttresses of the 15th-century Alte Mainbrücke, Germany's second-oldest stone bridge.

On March 16, 1945, Würzburg was shattered by a bombing raid. In a miraculous rebuilding program, nearly every major structure has been restored.

## ESSENTIALS

**GETTING THERE** **By Train** The **Würzburg Hauptbahnhof** lies on several major and regional rail lines, with frequent connections to all major German cities. From Frankfurt, 30 trains arrive per day (trip time: 1½ hr.); from Munich, 20 trains (2½ hr.); from Nürnberg, 30 trains (1 hr. 10 min.); and several trains from Berlin (5 hr. 50 min.). For rail information and schedules, call ✆ **01805/99-66-33.**

**By Bus** For bus service along the Romantic Road, see "Bus Tours of the Romantic Road," above.

**By Car** Access is via the A7 Autobahn from the north and south or the A3 Autobahn from the east and west. The A81 Autobahn has links from the southwest.

**VISITOR INFORMATION** Contact the **Tourist Information Office,** in the Falcon House, Am Marktplatz 9 (✆ **0931/37-23-35**). It's open April to October Monday to Friday 8am to 6pm, Saturday to Sunday 9am to 2pm, November to March Monday to Friday 8am to 5pm.

**SPECIAL EVENTS** For Mozart lovers, the highlight of the cultural year is the annual **Mozart Festival,** staged during the first three weeks of June. Fans of Wolfgang Amadeus from around the world, especially Americans and Europeans, flock to this festival. The venue for most of the Mozart concerts is the glorious baroque palace, the Residenz (see page 234). For information about tickets and various concerts, you can contact the tourist office (see above). Many visitors book tours that feature the Mozart festival; the best are conducted by **Allegro Holidays** (✆ **800/838-6860**).

**GETTING AROUND** The quickest and most efficient means for covering the central core of Würzburg is by tram (streetcar). A single fare is 1.35€ ($1.20), or else you can purchase a ticket good for 24 hours at any station for 4.50€ ($4). The same fare applies to buses, which also serve the city. For information about routes and schedules, call ✆ **0931/361352.**

## SEEING THE SIGHTS

In spring and summer, the liveliest place in town is the **Markt (central marketplace).** Here street performers entertain and vendors hawk their wares, ranging from fresh fruit to souvenir trinkets. You can also stroll down the traffic-free **Schönbornstrasse,** with its modern boutiques and cafes. The wine merchants here will sell you a Bocksbeutel, the emerald-green, narrow-necked wine bottle that's native to the region. It's said that the shape came about because wine-drinking monks found it the easiest to hide under their robes.

**Dom St. Kilian** This cathedral, begun in 1045, is the fourth-largest Romanesque church in Germany. The interior was adorned with high-baroque stucco work done after 1700. The imposing row of bishops' tombs begins with that of Gottfried von Spitzenberg (ca. 1190), who was one of the first prince-bishops to rule over the town. Look for three sandstone tombstones by Riemenschneider, constructed between 1502 and 1506. The Dom is dedicated to St. Kilian, an Irish missionary to Franconia in the 7th century.

Domstrasse (at the end of Schönbornstrasse). ✆ **0931/321-183-0.** Free admission. Easter–Oct Mon–Sat 10am–5pm, Sun 1–6pm; Nov–Easter Mon[nd[Sat 10am–noon and 2–5pm, Sun 12:30–1:30pm and 2:30–6pm.

**Mainfränkisches Fortress (Festung Marienberg)** ★ Festung Marienberg (✆ **0931/4-30-16**), located across from the Altstadt, over the stone bridge, was the residence of the local prince-bishops from 1253 to 1720. Although portions of the stronghold have been restored, the combination of age and wartime destruction has taken a serious toll on its thick walls and once-impenetrable ramparts. But what remains is worth a visit. The 8th-century **Marienkirche,** one of the oldest churches in Germany, stands within its walls.

In the former arsenal and Echter bulwark, to the right of the first courtyard, is the **Mainfränkisches Museum** (✆ **0931/4-30-16**), housed here since 1946. It's the historical museum of the former Bishopric of Würzburg and Dukedom of Franconia as well as the provincial museum of lower Franconia. On display is a collection of important sculptures by the great flamboyant Gothic master, Tilman Riemenschneider (1460–1531), called "the master of Würzburg." The sculptor came to live here in 1483 and was the town's mayor in 1520 and 1521. Never a totally decorative artist, Riemenschneider concentrated on the reality of people's appearance, highlighting their hands, faces, and clothing. The museum also displays paintings by Tiepolo and sandstone figures from the rococo gardens of the prince-bishops' summer palace. A tribute to one of the few industries of the city, winemaking, is paid in the press house, which contains historic casks and carved cask bases and a large collection of glasses and goblets. Admission is 2.50€ ($2.25) adults, 1.50€ ($1.35) students; children 14 and under are free. Open Tuesday to Sunday 10am to 5pm.

**Fürstenbaumuseum** (✆ **0931/4-38-38**) is situated in the restored princes' wing of the fortress. Here the visitor gets a glimpse of the living quarters and living conditions of the prince-bishops up to 1718. The urban-history section offers a stroll through 1,200 eventful years of Würzburg's history, including an exhibit relating to the discovery of X-rays by Wilhelm Conrad Röntgen in 1895. A model of the town shows its appearance in 1525, and another shows the destruction after the bombing of 1945. Admission is free for the fortress. Admission for the Fürstenbaumuseum 3€ ($2.70) adults, free for children under 14. Apr–Oct Tues–Sun 10am–5pm; Nov–Mar Tues–Sun 10am–4pm. Bus: 9.

**Residenz (Schloss und Gartenverwaltung Würzburg)** ★★ The Residenz of Würzburg is the last and finest of a long line of baroque castles built in Bavaria in the 17th and 18th centuries. This great horseshoe-shaped edifice was begun in 1720 to satisfy Prince-Bishop Johann Philipp Franz von Schönborn's passion for elegance and splendor. Its design was the joint effort of the best Viennese, French, and German architects working under the leadership of an architect of genius, Balthasar Neumann (1687–1753). Both an architect and an engineer, Neumann was known for his technical virtuosity and the harmony of his compositions. This castle shows a unity of purpose and design unusual in structures of such size.

At the center of the castle is the masterful Treppenhaus (staircase). The high, rounded ceiling above is decorated with a huge fresco by Tiepolo. At its center, Apollo is seen ascending to the zenith of the vault. The surrounding themes represent the four corners of the world, the seasons, and signs of the zodiac. The painting appears to be overflowing onto the walls of the upper hall.

The other important attraction in the Residenz is the court chapel, in the southwest section. Neumann placed the window arches at oblique angles to coordinate the windows with the oval sections, thus creating a muted effect. The rectangular room is divided into five oval sections, three with domed ceilings. Colored marble columns define the sections, their gilded capitals enriching the ceiling frescoes by Johann Rudolf Byss. At the side altars, Tiepolo painted two important works: *The Fall of the Angels* on the left and *The Assumption of the Virgin* on the right.

During the summer, a **Mozart festival** is held in the upper halls. For information, call ✆ **0931/37-23-36.**

Residenzplatz 2, Tor B. ✆ **0931/355517-0.** Admission 4€ ($3.55) adults, 3€ ($2.70) students, free for children under 15 and seniors. Apr–Oct daily 9am–6pm; Nov–Mar daily 10am–4:30pm. Tram: 1 or 5.

## A DAY TRIP FROM WÜRZBURG

The most interesting excursion in the area is to the **Schloss Veitshöchheim** ★, Hofgarten 1 (✆ **0931/35-51-730**), about 8km (5 miles) away. You can take a Main River excursion (about 30 min.) to this delightful summer retreat of the 17th- and 18th-century prince-bishops. The palace here contains rococo and

Empire furniture. But it is the fantastic rococo park that makes the trip worthwhile. Take time to wander among the fine and sometimes comical statues along shaded walks and avenues bordered by lime trees. The park is open daily 7am to dusk. The palace can be visited April to October, Tuesday to Sunday 9am to noon and 1 to 6pm. Admission to the park is free, but a visit to the palace costs 4€ ($3.55) for adults, 2€ ($1.80) for children and seniors, free for children under 15.

## WHERE TO STAY

### EXPENSIVE

**Hotel Maritim** ★★★ Nothing in Würzburg matches this hotel for comfort and style, not even the closest contender, Hotel Rebstock (see below). The Maritim has views over the Main River and is linked to the city convention center. Its modern and imposing yellow facade is topped by a baroque-style mansard roof. Rooms are good-size and comfortable, each with a midsize, tiled bathroom with tub-and-shower combination.

Pleichertorstrasse 5, 97070 Würzburg. ✆ **0931/3-05-30.** Fax 0931/3-05-39-00. www.maritim.de. 275 units. 178€ ($158.95) double; 208€–250€ ($185.75–$223.25) suite. Rates include buffet breakfast. AE, DC, MC, V. Parking 8€ ($7.15). Tram: 1 or 5. **Amenities:** Restaurant; bar; cafe; pool; sauna; solarium; room service; laundry/dry cleaning. *In room:* A/C, TV, minibar, hair dryer, safe.

**Hotel Rebstock** ★★ The impressive Rebstock is housed in a palace that dates from 1408. It's not as stylish as the Maritim, but it appeals to those nostalgic for a taste of old Germany. Through a classical doorway, you enter a wide foyer with carved wooden doors and an old Spanish sea chest. The interior is tasteful. Rooms are equipped with bathrooms containing shower-tub combinations. A winter garden with a fountain and chimney replaces an old courtyard.

Neubaustrasse 7, 97070 Würzburg. ✆ **800/528-1234** in the U.S., or 0931/3-09-30. Fax 0931/3-09-31-00. www.rebstock.com. 72 units. 156€–190€ ($139.30–$169.65) double; 270€ ($241.10) suite. Rates include buffet breakfast. AE, DC, MC, V. Parking 8.50€ ($7.60). Closed Jan 4–25. Tram: 1, 3, or 5. **Amenities:** Restaurant; lounge; health club; car rental; room service; laundry/dry cleaning. *In room:* TV, minibar, hair dryer, safe.

**Walfisch** ★ From the windows of this inn's modernized rooms, you can gaze across the Main as far as Marienberg Castle, high on the opposite hill. Walfisch is a good third choice after the Maritim and Rebstock. Rooms range from small to medium in size. Furnishings are typically Franconian: heavy draperies, provincial cupboards, and flowery fabrics, and each unit comes with a good-size bathroom, mostly with tub-and-shower combination.

Am Pleidenturm 5, 97070 Würzburg. ✆ **0931/3-52-00.** Fax 0931/3-52-05-00. www.hotel-walfisch.com. 40 units. 126€–155€ ($112.50–$138.40) double. Rates include breakfast. AE, DC, MC, V. Parking 8€ ($7.15). Tram: 1, 3, or 5. **Amenities:** Restaurant; lounge; room service. *In room:* A/C, TV, minibar, hair dryer.

### MODERATE

**Franziskaner** *Value* For homespun cleanliness, this hotel is a winner—and the price is right, too. You'll receive a hearty welcome from the staff. The lobby has attractive black panels surrounded with natural wood; the breakfast room has fine large windows looking out to the greenery beyond. All of the rooms are well furnished, each with an immaculate bathroom, mostly with tub-and-shower combination. The hotel itself serves only breakfast.

Franziskanerplatz 2, 97070 Würzburg. ✆ **0931/3-56-30.** Fax 0931/3-56-33-33. hotel-franziskaner@t-online.de. 47 units. 97.10€–122.65€ ($95–$120) double. Rates include buffet breakfast. AE, DC, MC, V. Tram: 1. **Amenities:** Restaurant; breakfast room; room service. *In room:* TV, hair dryer.

**Hotel und Weinrestaurant Schloss Steinburg** ★ *Finds* This turreted castle and its outbuildings sprawl high on a hill overlooking Würzburg. The castle foundations date from the 13th century, but what you see was largely rebuilt around 1900. It's a good choice for motorists, offering a tranquil setting and reasonable rates. From the sun terrace, guests can view the Main River, the acres of vineyards surrounding the property, and the web of rail lines that carry cargo far into the distance. Rooms have a country nostalgia and come with small tiled bathrooms with showers.

Auf dem Steinberg, 97080 Würzburg. ✆ **0931/9-70-20.** Fax 0931/9-71-21. www.steinburg.com. 50 units. 120€–150€ ($107.15–$133.95) double. Rates include buffet breakfast. AE, DC, MC, V. Free outdoor parking; garage 5€ ($4.45). Take Rte. 27 3km (2 miles) toward Fulda. **Amenities:** Breakfast room; lounge; pool; sauna; room service. *In room:* TV, minibar, hair dryer.

### INEXPENSIVE

**Schönleber** You'll find this family hotel in the central part of historic Würzburg. The ground floor is rented to boutiques that monopolize the two enormous arched windows facing the sidewalk. The upper floors offer smallish but comfortable rooms. Bathrooms are very cramped and have showers. The staff is friendly and helpful.

Theaterstrasse 5, 97070 Würzburg. ✆ **0931/30-48-90-0.** Fax 0931/1-60-12. www.hotel-schonleber.de. 34 units, 27 with bathroom. 58€ ($51.80) double without bathroom; 64€–92€ ($57.15–$82.15) double with bathroom. Rates include buffet breakfast. AE, DC, MC, V. Parking 9€ ($8.05). Closed Dec 22–Jan 6. Tram: 1, 2, 3, or 5. **Amenities:** Breakfast room; lounge; room service. *In room:* TV, hair dryer.

**St. Josef** ★ St. Josef is the best inexpensive accommodation in the Altstadt. Its owner has been successful in bringing it up-to-date. Rooms, though small, are pleasantly furnished and well maintained, each equipped with an efficiently organized bathroom with shower unit. Breakfast is the only meal offered, but there are many Weinstuben and restaurants in the area. Fresh flowers add a personalized touch to this well-run establishment.

Semmelstrasse 28, 97070 Würzburg. ✆ **0931/30-86-80.** Fax 0931/3-08-68-60. 35 units. 80€–90€ ($71.45–$80.35) double. Rates include buffet breakfast. AE, DC, MC, V. Parking 8€ ($7.15). Tram: 1, 2, 3, or 5. **Amenities:** Breakfast room, lounge. *In room:* TV, minibar, hair dryer.

## WHERE TO DINE

Try the local specialty, *Zwiebelkuchen,* which is like a quiche Lorraine, and also look for another specialty, *Meerfischle* (a well-seasoned stew made from saltwater fish). White Franconian wine goes well with the local sausage.

**Backöfele** FRANCONIAN Because this place is a short walk from both the Residenz and the Rathaus, you'll probably eat here at least once while you're in Würzburg. Even the locals don't really know whether to call it a beer hall, a wine cellar, or a restaurant. Regardless, the place serves well-prepared traditional food in copious quantities.

Ursulinergasse 2. ✆ **0931/5-90-59.** Reservations recommended. Main courses 10.20€–21.50€ ($9.10–$19.20). AE, MC, V. Mon–Sat 11:30am–1am; Sun 11:30am–midnight. Tram: 1 or 4.

**Ratskeller Würzburg** *Value* FRANCONIAN/FRENCH This 500-year-old Ratskeller, part of the Rathaus, is not only an interesting place to visit, but also serves tasty Franconian fare at reasonable prices. Country cookery is an art here, as you'll discover if you order the boiled breast of beef with horseradish sauce and noodles. The English-speaking host will help you with menu selections. Game is featured in season. They also specialize in local beer and Franconian white wines.

Langgasse 1 (near the Alte Mainbrücke). ✆ **0931/1-30-21.** Reservations required Sat–Sun. Main courses 9.40€–14.30€ ($8.40–$12.75). AE, DC, MC, V. Daily 11:30am–2:30pm and 5:30pm–midnight. Tram: 1, 2, 3, or 5.

**Wein- und Fischhaus Schiffbäuerin** ★ *Finds* SEAFOOD One of the best dining spots in the region is this combined wine house/fish restaurant, across the river in an old half-timbered building on a narrow street, about 1 minute from the old bridge. The house specializes in freshwater fish, such as pike, carp, char, tench, trout, wels, and eel. Most of these dishes are priced per 100g (3.5 oz.). Soup specialties are fish, snail, lobster, and French onion.

Katzengasse 7. ✆ **0931/4-24-87.** Reservations recommended. Main courses 15€–24€ ($13.40–$21.45). No credit cards. Tues–Sun 11am–2:30pm; Tues–Sat 6–10pm. Closed Jan 1–8 and mid-July–mid-Aug. Tram: 3 or 4.

**Weinhaus Zum Stachel** ★ FRANCONIAN No other wine house in Würzburg is as old as this one, which dates to 1413. Seats and walls have been burnished by the homespun clothing of many hundreds of drinkers and diners during the past 500 years. The portions are generous. Try the veal cordon bleu, tender pepper steak aromatically flavored with cognac, or the more prosaic rump steak with onions. Some dishes, such as chateaubriand, are so elaborate that they're prepared only for two. The chef is proudest of his freshwater fish prepared according to old family recipes. In summer, you can dine in a vine-draped outdoor courtyard. Wines are from the restaurant's own vineyards.

Gressengasse 1. ✆ **0931/5-27-70.** Reservations required. Main courses 16€–21€ ($14.30–$18.75); fixed-price menu 38.50€ ($34.40). MC. Daily 11am–1am. Tram: 1, 3, 4, or 5.

**Weinstuben Juliusspital** FRANCONIAN One of the best known of Würzburg's Franconian wine taverns, the Juliusspital is decorated with traditional paneling and a beamed ceiling. It's distinguished by its wide range of regional dishes. The restaurant is a top address for wine connoisseurs, with an array of characteristic Franconian vintages.

Juliuspromenade 19. ✆ **0931/5-40-80.** Reservations required. Main courses 6€–15€ ($5.35–$13.40). No credit cards. Daily 10am–midnight. Tram 1, 3, or 5.

## WÜRZBURG AFTER DARK

Much of Würzburg's nightlife takes place in its numerous Weinstuben, many of which have an interesting character. For music and cultural happenings, scan the flyers posted in the *Studentenhaus* on Am Exerzierplatz at Münzstrasse.

A one-stop entertainment complex, **Autonomes Kulturzentrum Würzburg,** Frankfurter Strasse 87 (✆ **0931/41-78-00;** tram: 2 or 5), houses a bar and beer garden and offers a disco Thursday to Saturday with a cover charge of 2.55€ to 7.65€ ($2.30–$6.85). On Tuesday and Wednesday it hosts concerts, with tickets costing 14€ ($12.50). The complex is open Monday to Wednesday 6pm to 2am, Thursday to Saturday 6pm to 3am, Sunday 3pm to 1am. Call for listings and ticket information.

The city's oldest jazz cellar, **Omnibus,** Theaterstrasse 10 (✆ **0931/5-61-21;** bus: 14 or 20), has been packing it in for live acts for nearly 3 decades. This is also where people come to drink and play chess. It's open Monday to Thursday 8pm to 1am and Friday and Saturday 9pm to 2am. Cover for performances ranges from 8€ to 12€ ($7.15 to $10.70). A place for a cheap meal or a drink, **Standard,** Oberthurstrasse 11a (✆ **0931/5-11-40;** bus: 14 or 20), is open daily 9:30am to 1am. It occasionally has a live band on the weekend. **Kult Stattkneipe,** Landwehrstrasse 10 (✆ **0931/5-31-43;** tram: 1, 3, or 5), keeps the stereo cranking. It's open daily 11am to 2 am.

## 2 Miltenberg ★

29km (18 miles) S of Mespelbrunn, 71km (44 miles) W of Würzburg

This riverside town, along with Amorbach (see below), is located to the west of the traditional route of the Romantic Road, but it's very popular and well worth a visit. Miltenberg is sleepy, traditional, and full of half-timbered buildings. If you're looking for a medieval town, but want to avoid the tour-bus hordes that overrun places like Rothenburg (see "Rothenburg ob der Tauber," later in this chapter), Miltenberg is for you.

The town, which is still enclosed within walls and gate towers, is attractively situated under a steep wooded hill crowned by a castle. Its municipal charter dates from 1237, but the place was actually settled centuries earlier by the Romans. The best way to appreciate Miltenburg's charm is on a fast drive-through, with a pedestrian detour through its charming **Marktplatz** ★. Here, on steeply sloping terrain centered around a Renaissance-era red sandstone fountain and a wealth of flowers, you'll find a phalanx of half-timbered houses, and one of the oldest inns in Germany, the **Haus zum Reisen.**

### ESSENTIALS

**GETTING THERE** **By Train** Three or four trains per day arrive from Würzburg, 90 minutes away, and about a dozen come every day from the important railway junction of Aschaffenburg, 45 minutes away. For railway information, call ✆ **01805/99-66-33.**

**By Car** From the north, take Route B469 into town (it's signposted). From Würzburg, take the A3 west and then minor roads.

**VISITOR INFORMATION** The **tourist office,** Engelplatz 69 (✆ **09371/40-41-19**), offers pamphlets describing brief walking tours through the town. It's open Monday to Friday 9am to 5pm.

### SEEING THE SIGHTS

Park your car in the first convenient parking lot and walk into the center of town—don't attempt to drive. Other than the above-mentioned Marktplatz, the main attraction in town is **Schloss Miltenburg** ★. (Be warned in advance that this castle is sometimes identified simply as "Miltenburg.") Don't expect a rich tour of a medieval-looking interior, as all but a fraction of the castle's inside (a cafe) has been closed for a long-standing series of renovations. You can visit the courtyard, however, and climb to the top of a watchtower for a sweeping view over the surrounding forest. The courtyard, the tower, and the cafe that's associated with the site are open only April to October, Tuesday to Sunday 11am to 5:30pm. Admission costs 1.55€ ($1.40) adults and 1€ (90¢) for children under 12.

Beer-lovers might want to take a guided tour through one of the town's breweries, such as **Brauhaus Faust,** Hauptstrasse 219 (✆ **09371/97130**), or **Kalt-Loch Brauerei,** Hauptstrasse 201 (✆ **09371/2283**). These tours, given in German, take you through the full range of the hops-gathering and brewing processes and include several mugs' worth of tasting. The cost is 4€ ($3.55) per participant. If you like tasting more than touring, just sit down at any restaurant or pub in town—they all serve ample quantities of these breweries' products. A particularly good cafe is the **Café Bauer,** Hauptstrasse 41 (✆ **09371/2384**).

During your exploration of Miltenburg, don't overlook the oldest and most historic bar in town, a 500-year-old hangout that locals refer to simply as **Weinhaus,**

Marktplatz 185 (✆ **09371/5500**). Here, every evening between 5:30pm and midnight, you can order any of the local vintages, at a per-glass price of 3€ to 5€ ($2.70–$4.45).

## WHERE TO STAY & DINE

**Haus zum Riesen** ★ This awesomely historic hotel is permeated with a polite sense of modern management. Its origins date back to 1190, just before it hosted Frederick Barbarossa during his expeditions in this part of Germany. During the Thirty Years' War, it housed VIPs from both sides, depending on who was in control at the moment. Today, this hotel is the most evocative in town, graced with charmingly old-fashioned rooms, usually with beamed ceilings. Bathrooms range from midsize to spacious, most often with a tub-and-shower combination.

However, the place is more famous as a restaurant than as a hotel. Inside the old dining room, you can order such medieval-sounding dishes as roasted bear steak (the bear is imported from Russia), as well as a dish that we've seen in no other restaurant in Germany, *Ochsenfetzen* ("Torn-apart ox"). This delicacy, which has been the subject of many articles in culinary reviews and is based on authentic medieval scholarship, uses brisket of beef marinated for 2 weeks in marinades that change every 2 days. A hearty red wine is the best accompaniment for this age-old dish. Meals here cost about 20€ ($17.85).

Hauptstrasse 99. ✆ **09371/3644.** Fax 09371/67176. 14 units. 75€–105€ ($67–$93.75) double; 125€ ($111.65) suite. Rates include breakfast. No credit cards. **Amenities:** Restaurant; bar; lounge; room service. *In room:* TV, hair dryer.

**Hotel Altes Bannhaus** ★ This medieval hotel is set on the main street of town, behind a severely dignified stone facade that's graced with an elaborate iron bracket. It treads the fine line between authentically historical and merely dowdy. Overall, however, its vaulted stone cellars and massive masonry are charming. Rooms are more angular and modern looking than the authentically antique public areas. Each has functional furniture, small windows, and small shower-only bathrooms.

Hauptstrasse 211, 63897 Miltenberg. ✆ **09371/3061.** Fax 09371/68754. 10 units. 89€–95€ ($79.50–$84.85) double. Rates include breakfast. AE, MC, V. **Amenities:** Restaurant; lounge; room service. *In room:* TV, minibar, hair dryer.

# 3 Amorbach ★

11km (7 miles) S of Miltenberg, 92km (57 miles) SW of Würzburg

This little town shouldn't take up too much of your time, but it does offer a few rewarding sights, notably the Abtai Kirche of St. Maria, and it also contains one of the finest hotels in the region. As you wander about Amorbach's center, note the way that local homeowners have dotted many of the half-timbered facades with flower boxes.

## ESSENTIALS

**GETTING THERE** **By Train or Bus** Three or four trains arrive every day from Würzburg (trip time: 90 min.), and 12 arrive from Aschaffenburg (trip time: 45 min.). For railway information, call ✆ **01805/99-66-33.**

**BY CAR** From Miltenberg, follow route 469 south for 11km (7 miles).

**VISITOR INFORMATION** The Stadt Verkehrsarnt, at the Rathaus, Marktplatz 1 (✆ **09373/20940**), is open Monday to Friday 9am to 5:30pm.

## SEEING THE SIGHTS

Much of the fun of a visit to Amorbach lies simply in wandering through the streets of the old town, where half-timbered medieval buildings, some of them a bit artfully askew, still evoke old Germany.

The town's most important monument is the **Abtai Kirche St. Maria** ★, Kirchplatz (✆ **09373/971545**). This impressive church underwent at least a half-dozen enlargements and alterations between the 8th and the 18th centuries, but it still manages to retain a degree of charm and cohesiveness. The interior is a mass of ornate baroque stucco, centering around one of the most impressive baroque-era organs in Germany. Entrance is free, but a guided tour, conducted in German or English, costs 2.50€ ($2.25) per person. It's open Monday to Saturday 9:30am to noon and 1:30pm until sometime between 4 and 6pm, depending on the season and schedule of religious services and maintenance.

A small museum called **Sammlung Berger** (The Berger Collection), Wolkmannstrasse 2 (✆ **09373/99081**), holds around 17,000 teapots, many from the U.S. and Britain. Part of the funding of this museum comes from a local teapot manufacturer, whose wares are for sale in the museum shop. Entrance is 2.50€ ($2.25). It's open only April to October, Tuesday to Sunday 11am to 6pm.

The ruined remains of **Wildenberg Castle,** Odenwald (✆ **09373/20940**), lie 5km (3 miles) southeast of Amorbach. Originally built 1,000 years ago, it's now little more than a jumble of impressive medieval-looking rock piles. The restored watchtower, however, can be climbed every Sunday, 10am to 5pm. Admission to the castle and watchtower is free. The view over the Odenwald Forest is excellent.

## WHERE TO STAY & DINE

**Der Schafhof Amorbach** ★★★ The most romantic and carefully manicured hotel in the district lies within what was originally a Benedictine monastery (around 1450) and rebuilt in 1721 in a country-baroque style. The more historic rooms lie within the former abbey; more modern, better-equipped units are within a well-built modern annex. Our favorites lie under the eaves of the main building and are crisscrossed with a labyrinth of hand-hewn ceiling beams. All rooms are stylishly and comfortably outfitted in a plush but conservative style, each coming with a midsize tiled bathroom with tub-and-shower combination.

Odenwald. ✆ **09373/97330.** Fax 09373/4120. www.schafhof.de. 24 units. 124€–180€ ($110.75–$160.75) double; 200€–270€ ($178.60–$241.10) suite. Rates include breakfast. AE, DC, MC, V. From Amorbach, follow N47 (the Niebelungenstrasse) west for 5km (3 miles). **Amenities:** 2 restaurants; lounge; room service; laundry. *In room:* TV, minibar, hair dryer.

# 4 Bad Mergentheim ★

47km (29 miles) S of Würzburg, 106km (66 miles) NE of Stuttgart

Most of this spa town's fame derives from its role during and after the Renaissance as the home, beginning in 1525, of the Teutonic Knights, one of the most durable orders of feudal knights. From their base in Bad Mergentheim, they received tributes and pledges of allegiance from as far away as Lithuania. The knights' way of life ended abruptly in 1809, when Napoléon forcibly disbanded the order, consequently threatening the very existence of the town.

But Bad Mergentheim's fortunes were reversed in 1826, when a shepherd discovered rich mineral springs a short walk north of the town center during the time when Germany's spas were expanding at a rapid pace. The water turned out to be the strongest sodium-sulfate water in all of Europe; it was said to have health-giving properties, especially in the treatment of digestive disorders. With the knights gone, the little town had discovered the key to its future prosperity.

## ESSENTIALS

**GETTING THERE** **By Train or Bus** Access by train is easier and more convenient than by bus. From Würzburg, trains arrive almost every hour (trip time: 40 min.). From Stuttgart, they arrive at intervals of 90 to 120 minutes (trip time: 90 min.). For information about **railway schedules,** call ✆ **01805/99-66-33.** For bus service along the Romantic Road, see "Bus Tours of the Romantic Road," at the beginning of this chapter.

**By Car** From Würzburg, head south along Route 19.

**VISITOR INFORMATION** The Tourist Office, called **Kultur und Verkehrsamt,** is at Marktplatz 3 (✆ **07931/571-31**). It's open Monday to Friday 9am to 5pm, Saturday 10am to 4pm, Sunday 10am to 2pm.

## SEEING THE SIGHTS

The best way to see the town is to wander through its historically evocative streets, most of which radiate outward from the meticulously restored **Marktplatz.** Schloss Park leads to the spa establishments on the right bank of the Tauber. The Kursaal is a pump room with both a visitor center and bathing facilities.

The most impressive structure in town, noted for its relatively large size, is the somewhat sterile and barren-looking **Münster Kirche Sankt Johannes,** Ledermarkt 12 (✆ **07931/98600**), which was begun around 1250 and completed several centuries later. It's open daily 9am to dusk; entrance is free. More interesting is the medieval castle that once served as the Teutonic Knights' home base, the **Deutschordenschloss,** site of the **Deutschordensmuseum,** Schloss 16 (✆ **07931/52212**). Inside, you'll find a sweeping retrospective of chivalry's preconceptions and preoccupations, with all the requisite displays of suits of armor and weapons. Surprisingly, this medieval order of knights has been restored today and now serves as a religious and charitable organization. Note the corner towers in the inner courtyard, which are furnished with Renaissance spiral staircases. The building is open Tuesday to Sunday 10am to 5pm, charging an entrance of 4€ ($3.55), each entry includes a German-language guided tour.

A second-tier attraction that's a lot less worthwhile than a promenade through the town itself is the **Wildpark Bad** (Bad Mergentheim Game Preserve; ✆ **07931/41344**), 5km (3 miles) east of the town center. It contains wild animals both in cages and roaming within natural environments. Mid-March to October, it's open daily 9am to 6pm; November to mid-March, only Saturday and Sunday 10am to 5pm. Entrance costs 7€ ($6.25) for adults, 4.50€ ($4) for children.

## WHERE TO STAY & DINE

**Haus Bundschu** ★ *Finds* Though nowhere near as highly rated as the Victoria (see below), this is a cozy, affordable nest that we sometimes prefer to properties with more facilities. Inviting, understated, and cozy, this hotel was built about 15 years ago in a style that incorporated a masonry-covered courtyard, lots of exposed wood, and touches of Romantic Road nostalgia. It lies within a 5-minute walk of the town center. Rooms are sunny, thanks to big windows, and well maintained, each with a midsize bathroom with tub-and-shower combination.

Cronbergstrasse 15, 97980 Bad Mergentheim. ✆ **07931/9330.** Fax 07931/933-633. www.hotel-bundschu.de. 33 units. 90€–98€ ($80.35–$87.50). Rates include breakfast. AE, DC, MC, V. **Amenities:** Restaurant; lounge; room service. *In room:* TV, minibar, hair dryer.

**Hotel Victoria** ★★★ The best hotel in town occupies a stately, five-story, ocher-colored building. Inside, the color scheme is an oft-repeated and very pleasing combination of champagne, beige, yellow, and black. Rooms are modern and plush, with lots of concealed, very elegant lighting and supremely comfortable mattresses. All accommodations come with a roomy bathroom stylishly outfitted with deluxe fixtures, toiletries, and a tub-and-shower combination.

Poststrasse 2–4, 97980 Bad Mergentheim. ✆ **07931/593-0.** Fax 07931/593-500. www.victoria-hotel.de. 78 units. 50€–93€ ($44.65–$83.05) double; 132€–185€ ($117.90–$165.20) suite. Half board 24€ ($21.45) extra per person. Rates include breakfast. AE, DC, MC, V. Parking 9€ ($8.05) per day. **Amenities:** Restaurant; lounge; health spa; room service; massage. *In room:* TV, minibar, hair dryer.

## AN EXCURSION TO STUPPACH *Finds*

The agrarian village of **Stuppach** (pop. 500), located 11km (7 miles) southeast of Bad Mergentheim, is the site of one of the region's most important artistic treasures, the **Stuppacher Madonna** by Matthias Grünewald (ca. 1475–1528). This dark, brooding work is firmly opposed to the lighter motifs of such contemporaneous artists as Dürer. It's the artistic centerpiece of the village's only church, the **Fahrkirche Maria Krönung,** Kirchplatz (✆ **07931/2605**), which can be visited, without charge, daily 9am to dusk.

# 5 Weikersheim

10km (6 miles) E of Bad Mergentheim, 40km (25 miles) S of Würzburg

The architecture of this riverside town is consistently 18th century; it's one of the most stylistically unified towns on the Romantic Road. Weikersheim also boasts one of the mightiest castles on the Romantic Road.

## ESSENTIALS

**GETTING THERE** **By Train or Bus** Trains pull into Weikersheim from Würzburg at intervals of 60 to 120 minutes throughout the day (trip time: 40 min.). From Stuttgart, they arrive at intervals of 90 to 120 minutes (trip time: 90 min.). For information about railway schedules, call the station at ✆ **01805/99-66-33.** For bus service along the Romantic Road, see "Bus Tours of the Romantic Road," at the beginning of this chapter.

**By Car** Take the B232 from Bad Mergentheim.

**VISITOR INFORMATION** The **Tourist Office** at Marktplatz 7 (✆ **07934/10255**) is open Monday to Friday 9:30am to 5pm.

## SEEING THE SIGHTS

During its formative years, the very existence of the town was dependent on its castle, **Schloss Weikersheim,** Schlossstrasse (✆ **07934/8364**). It was begun in 1586 and completed a century later in a severely dignified style that had nothing to do with the baroque style then popular in other parts of Germany. When Count Ludwig II re-established Weikersheim as his family's main residence, he ordered that the old moated castle be replaced with a magnificent new Renaissance palace.

You can visit the castle's interior for 4€ ($3.55) per person, daily 10am to noon and 1 to 5pm. Its architectural and decorative highlight is the **Rittersaal (Knight's Hall)** ★★, which was completed in 1603 and shows the transition between the baroque and the earlier Renaissance style. This is the most sumptuous banqueting hall ever built in Germany. Note the bas reliefs of game animals lining the walls. The entrance doorway is carved with a scene of a battle against the Turks. The gigantic chimneypiece is adorned with an allegory illustrating the motto, "God gives luck." The castle contains one of the most remarkable collections of **antique furnishings** ★★ of any castle in Germany, a treasure trove stretching out for 2 centuries beginning in 1550. Also, allow some time to wander through the well-preserved **gardens.**

To one side of the castle is the **Marktplatz,** a semicircular market square that opens onto sweeping vistas. It was laid out in the early 18th century.

## WHERE TO STAY & DINE

**Flair Hotel Laurentius** ★ The most appealing hotel in town is an old-fashioned monument to the art of hospitality. It's an ideal stopover along the Romantic Road, either for a meal or an overnight stay. Its vaulted, street-level area is the site of a cozy restaurant and wine bar. Upstairs, a series of high-ceilinged rooms contain a pleasing, unpretentious mix of good reproductions and genuine antiques. Bathrooms are quirkily old-fashioned, but not without charm, each with a tub-and-shower combination.

Marktplatz 5, 97990 Weikersheim. ✆ **07934/91080.** Fax 07934/910818. www.hotel-laurentius.de. 11 units. 70€–95€ ($62.50–$84.85) double. AE, DC, MC, V. **Amenities:** Restaurant; bar; cafe; sauna; room service; laundry. *In room:* TV, hair dryer.

# 6 Creglingen

19km (12 miles) E of Weikersheim, 40km (25 miles) S of Würzburg

The history of Creglingen goes back more than 4,000 years. Originally, it was an important Celtic stronghold. Later on, around the year 1000, it was mentioned in written sources as a wine-growing site. By 1349, the town had gained the right to call itself a "city." Around the same time, Creglingen became an important pilgrimage site, thanks to the legend of a local farmer who claimed to have seen Jesus and a phalanx of angels plowing his fields.

Today, Creglingen is one of the quietest hamlets along the Romantic Road, with a tiny but colorful inner core of buildings that evoke Germany of long ago, and a charming but substandard set of accommodations, usually in local farmhouses. The surrounding countryside is called "The Lord God's Little Land"—locals believed that it resembled the Garden of Eden. You might think so, too, if you explore the local streams and lakes, where anglers fish for pike, carp, trout, eel, or perch.

## ESSENTIALS

**GETTING THERE** **By Train or Bus** Rail connections from Würzburg arrive about once every 2 hours, pulling into the hamlet of Steinach, about 19km (12 miles) from Creglingen. At the station, an employee will call a local taxi to carry you the rest of the way into Creglingen. For railway information, call the information service for the local train lines at ✆ **01805/99-66-33.** For bus service along the Romantic Road, see "Bus Tours of the Romantic Road," at the beginning of this chapter.

**By Car** Follow the signs west from Weikersheim.

**VISITOR INFORMATION** Tourist information is available at Bad Mergentheimer Strasse 14 (✆ **07933/631**), from Monday to Friday 9am to 5pm.

## SEEING THE SIGHTS

Creglingen is home of one of the most quirky museums in Germany, the **Fingerhutmuseum (Thimble Museum),** Herrgottstal (✆ **07933/370**), where the largest collection of thimbles in Europe have been accumulated. Some of them are bone rings dating from prehistoric times; others are made of brass that was smelted in Creglingen during the Middle Ages. It's open daily April to October 9am to 6pm; the rest of the year, Tuesday to Sunday 10am to noon and 1 to 4pm. Admission is 1.50€ ($1.35).

More stately is the **Feuerwehrmuseum (Fire-Brigade Museum),** in the Schloss Waldmannshofen, in the nearby hamlet of Waldmannshofen (for information, call either the tourist office or ✆ **09355/674**). Inside, you'll find a collection of implements and tools used since medieval times to fight fire. It's open only Easter to late October, daily 10am to noon and 2 to 4pm. Admission is 1€ (90¢).

The most important local attraction is the **Herrgottskirche (Chapel of Our Lord).** The chapel was built by the counts of Hohenlohe around 1525. Its enormous altarpiece, a 19m- (33-ft.-) tall structure showing the ascension of Mary, was decorated in the 16th century. All the artist's sensitivity is translated into the expression of the Virgin. The work is set in a filigree shrine specially constructed to catch the day's changing light effects. The chapel can be visited daily April to October, 9:15am to 5:30pm; November to March, 1 to 4pm. Admission is 1.50€ ($1.35). For more information, contact the tourist office (✆ **07933/508**), which is set 3km (2 miles) south of Creglingen within the Gerrgottstal Valley. It's clearly posted from the village center.

## WHERE TO STAY

Accommodations are not plentiful in Creglingen; most visitors are merely passing through. There are no restaurants here. However, there is one truly offbeat choice if you need to spend the night.

**Heuhotel Ferienbauernhof** *Finds* Don't expect plush comforts here; the allure of this place derives from its close links to nature and its age-old sense of Teutonic virtue. It lies within a solid-looking German farmhouse owned by the Stahl family. The six spartan rooms each have a thin but passably comfortable mattress and a stripped-down shower-bathroom. More folkloric is the establishment's barn, where a hayloft provides a soft, sweet-smelling bed for clients who enjoy as close a contact with nature as possible. Don't expect privacy, as the only barriers between the sleeping sites are burlap bags, sewn together and stretched on ropes as a kind of privacy screen. Your comfort here is enhanced by the warm welcome from the owners, not by amenities.

Weidenhof 1, 97993 Creglingen. ✆ **07933/378.** Fax 07933/7515. www.ferienbauernhof-heuhotel.de. 6 units with shower and toilet; 25 sleeping places in a hayloft with communal bathrooms. 42€ ($37.50) double, with breakfast included; 16€ ($14.30) per person for a sleeping site in the hayloft, with a cold supper included. No credit cards. From Creglingen, drive 10km (6 miles), following the signs to the hamlet of Weidenhof.

## 7 Rothenburg ob der Tauber ★★★

117km (73 miles) NE of Stuttgart, 51km (32 miles) SE of Würzburg

If you have time for only one town on the Romantic Road, make it Rothenburg. Admittedly, if you arrive at Rothenburg's Bahnhof, at the northeast corner of town, you may find it hard to believe that this is the best-preserved medieval city in Europe. Contemporary life and industry have made an impact, and as you leave the station, you'll first see factories and office buildings. But don't be discouraged. Inside those undamaged 13th-century city walls is a medieval town seemingly untouched by the passage of time.

The only drawback to this gem of a city is that it suffers from serious overcrowding, especially in summer. (The Rothenburg locals go so far as to put

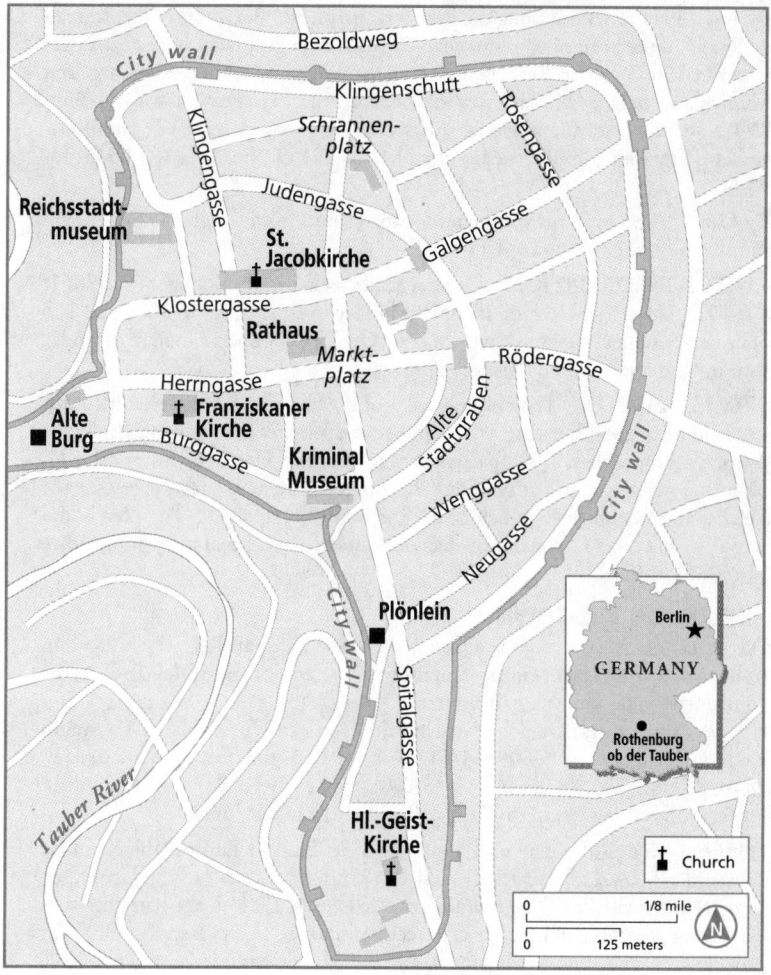


bumper stickers on their cars proclaiming in German, "I'm not a tourist—I actually live here.") Ironically, Rothenburg for centuries was impoverished and forgotten. It was first mentioned in written records in 804 as Rotinbure, a settlement above ("ob" in German) the Tauber River. The town grew to be a free imperial city, reaching its apex of prosperity under Burgermeister Heinrich Toppler in the 14th century.

## ESSENTIALS

**GETTING THERE** **By Plane** The nearest regional airport is Nürnberg (see chapter 6); from there it's a 2-hour train ride to Rothenburg.

**By Train** You can reach Rothenburg via a daily train from Frankfurt (trip time: 3 hr.), from Hamburg (trip time: 5½ hr.), or from Berlin (trip time: 7 hr.). Rothenburg lies on the Steinach–Rothenburg rail line, with frequent connections to all major German cities, including Nürnberg and Stuttgart. For information, call ✆ **01805/99-66-33.**

**By Bus** For bus service along the Romantic Road, see "Bus Tours of the Romantic Road," at the beginning of this chapter. Regular long-distance buses (Lines EH 190 and 190A) service Rothenburg from Frankfurt, Würzburg, Augsburg, and Munich, as well as Füssen. For information and reservations, call ✆ **069/79-03-50** in Frankfurt. Regional bus service is provided by **OVF Omnibusverkehr Franken GmbH,** Kopernikusplatz 5, 90159 Nürnberg (✆ **0911/43-90-60**).

**By Car** Access by car is via the minor road south from Creglingen, or the A7 Autobahn on the Würzburg-Ulm run.

**VISITOR INFORMATION** Contact **Stadt Verkehrsamt,** Rathaus (✆ **09861/4-04-92**). November to April, it's open Monday to Friday 9am to noon and 1 to 5pm and Saturday 10am to 1pm; May to October, it's open Monday to Friday 9am to 6pm and Saturday 10am to 3pm.

**SPECIAL EVENTS** The cultural event of the year is the **Meistertrunk festival,** held the second weekend of September; it celebrates the entire history of the town, with more than 1,000 participants in costume. Concerts, historical exhibitions, a parade, and a play about the Burgermeister Nusch's wager (see the Reichsstadtmuseum listing, below) are the festival's highlights. The play is also staged in July and October. For details, contact the visitor information office (✆ **09861/4-04-92**).

## EXPLORING THE TOWN

For an excellent view, take a walk on the **town ramparts** ★. The wall tour, from the massive 16th-century Spitaltor (at the end of the Spitalgasse) to the Klingentor, takes about a half hour.

If you want to escape the tourist hordes, you can rent a bike at **Hermann Kat's,** Galgengasse 33 (✆ **09861/6111**), or at **Rad und Tat,** Bensenstrasse 17 (✆ **09861/87984**), for about 11€ ($9.80) per day. Get a map from the tourist office and head out along the Tauber River with a picnic lunch.

**Kriminal Museum** The only museum of its kind in Europe, the Kriminal Museum is housed in a structure built in 1395 for the Order of the Johanniter, who cared for the sick. The building was redone in 1718 in the baroque style; it's the only example of baroque architecture in town. The museum's four floors provide an insight into the life, laws, and punishments of medieval days. You'll see chastity belts, shame masks, a shame flute for bad musicians, and a cage for bakers who baked bread too small or too light.

Burggasse 3. ✆ **09861/53-59.** Admission 3.05€ ($2.70) adults, 1.55€ ($1.40) children under 13. Apr–Oct daily 9:30am–6pm; Nov and Jan–Feb daily 2–4pm; Dec and Mar daily 10am–4pm.

**Rathaus** ★ Rothenburg's town hall consists of an older Gothic section from 1240 and a newer Renaissance structure facing the square. From the 50m (165-ft.) tower of the Gothic hall you get a great **view** ★ of the town below. The tower was first used as a sentry's lookout, but after a fire destroyed the Gothic hall's twin (where the Renaissance hall now stands) in 1501, it became a lookout for fire. Guards had to ring the bell every quarter hour to prove that they were awake and on the job.

The new Rathaus, built in 1572 to replace the portion destroyed in the fire, is decorated with intricate friezes, an oriel extending the building's full height, and a large stone portico opening onto the square. The octagonal tower at the center of the side facing the square contains a grand staircase leading to the upper hall. On the main floor is the large courtroom.

Marktplatz. ✆ **09861/40-40.** Rathaus free; tower 1€ (90¢) adults, .50€ (45¢) children. Rathaus Mon–Fri 8am–6pm. Tower Apr–Oct daily 9:30am–12:30pm and 1–5pm; Nov–Mar usually closed although occasionally open on weekends.

**Reichsstadtmuseum** The historical collection of Rothenburg is housed in this 13th-century Dominican nunnery. The cloisters are well-preserved, and you can visit the convent hall, kitchen, and apothecary. The museum collection includes period furniture and art from Rothenburg's more prosperous periods, including the original glazed elector's tankard, and a new section of archaeological objects from prehistoric times up to the Middle Ages. Among the artistic exhibits is the 1494 *Rothenburg Passion* series, 12 pictures by Martinus Schwartz that depict scenes from the suffering of Christ. You can also see the works of English painter Arthur Wasse (1854–1930), whose romantic pictures manage to capture the many moods of the city. Finally, there's a Jewish section, with gravestones from the Middle Ages and some cult objects.

But perhaps the most interesting object on display is an enormous tankard that holds 3½ liters—more than 6 pints. You'll find echoes of its story all over the city. In 1631, during the Thirty Years' War, the Protestant city of Rothenburg was captured by General Tilly, commander of the armies of the Catholic League. He promised to spare the town from destruction if one of the town burghers could drink down the huge tankard full of wine in one draught. Burgermeister Nusch accepted the challenge and succeeded, thus saving Rothenburg. Look for the clock on the Marktplatz with mechanical figures representing this event.

Klosterhof 5. ✆ **09861/93-90-43.** Admission 2.55€ ($2.30) adults, 1.55€ ($1.40) children and students. Apr–Oct daily 9:30am–5:30pm; Nov–Mar daily 1–4pm.

**St. Jakobskirche (Church of St. Jacob)** The choir of this Gothic church dates from 1336. In the west gallery is the **Altar of the Holy Blood** ★★, a masterpiece by the famous Würzburg sculptor Tilman Riemenschneider (ca. 1460–1531). The work was executed between 1499 and 1505, to provide a worthy setting for the Reliquary of the Holy Blood. This relic, venerated in the Middle Ages, is contained in a rock-crystal capsule set in the reliquary cross (ca. 1270) in the center of the shrine. The scene on the altar beneath *The Last Supper* immediately makes a strong impact on the viewer. Christ is giving Judas the morsel of bread, marking him as the traitor. The apostle John is leaning on Christ's bosom. The altar wings show the entry of Christ into Jerusalem (on the left) and Christ praying in the Garden of Gethsemane (on the right). The altar casing is the work of Erhard Harschner, Rothenburg's master craftsman. The fine painted-glass windows in the choir date from the late-Gothic period. To the left is the tabernacle (ca. 1400), which was a place of sanctuary for condemned criminals.

Klostergasse 15. ✆ **09861/7006-20.** Admission 1.50€ ($1.35) adults, .50€ (45¢) children. Apr–Oct Mon–Fri 9am–5:30pm, Sun 7:30am–5:30pm; Dec daily 9am–5pm; Nov and Jan–Mar daily 10am–noon and 2–4pm.

## SHOPPING

**Kunstwerke Friese,** Grüner Markt (✆ **09861/71-66**), specializes in cuckoo clocks and also carries Hummel figurines, pewter beer steins, music boxes, and dolls. It's Christmas every day at **Weihnachtsdorf (Christmas Village),** in the market square, which is filled with shops carrying everything from clothing and accessories to cuckoo clocks, but the real attractions are locally made toys and Christmas ornaments. If you collect teddy bears, you'll love **Teddyland,** Herrengasse 10 (✆ **09861/89-04**), which stocks more than 5,000 of them. Bear images are printed on everything from T-shirts to bags and watches.

## WHERE TO STAY

### EXPENSIVE

**Burg Hotel** ★ Although it ranks beneath the Eisenhut (see below), this inn is full of German charm. It lies at the end of a cul-de-sac in an old-fashioned timbered house that overlooks the Tauber Valley—just the kind of place Red Riding Hood might have visited to see Grandma. Parking is in the barn of a former Dominican monastery. Rooms are spread across three floors (no elevator). There are many extras, including spacious bathrooms with showers and large mirrors. Any room is likely to please, but for the best views, ask for number 7, 12, or 25. The inn also boasts state-of-the-art housekeeping.

Klostergasse 1–3, 91541 Rothenburg ob der Tauber. ✆ **09861/9-48-90.** Fax 09861/94-89-40. www.burghotel.rothenburg.de. 19 units. 100€–150€ ($89.30–$133.95) double; from 170€ ($151.80) suite. Rates include buffet breakfast. AE, DC, MC, V. Parking 7.50€ ($6.70). **Amenities:** Breakfast room; lounge; bike rental; room service. *In room:* TV, minibar, hair dryer, safe.

**Eisenhut (Iron Helmet)** ★★★ Eisenhut is the most celebrated inn on the Romantic Road and one of the finest small hotels in Germany. It's also rather expensive, but it's worth the money. Even though some other properties, such as the Goldener Hirsch (see below), have style and tradition, none can match the Eisenhut. If this hotel has a problem, it might be its popularity. The staff appears forever overworked. The hotel is composed of four medieval patrician houses joined together. Rooms range from medium to spacious, and all are unique. Yours may contain hand-carved and monumental pieces or a tufted satin headboard for a 1940s Hollywood touch. All are enhanced by bedside controls, spacious bathrooms with tub-and-shower combination, and ample closet space.

Herrengasse 3–5 (across from the Rathaus), 91541 Rothenburg ob der Tauber. ✆ **09861/70-50.** Fax 09861/7-05-45. www.eisenhut.com. 78 units. 154€–202€ ($137.50–$180.40) double; 280€–340€ ($250.05–$303.60) suite. AE, DC, MC, V. Parking 9€ ($8.05). **Amenities:** Restaurant; bar; beer garden; bike rental; babysitting; laundry/dry cleaning. *In room:* TV, minibar, hair dryer, safe.

**Goldener Hirsch** ★ This is one of the leading inns of Rothenburg, in the same class as the Burg (see above). It looks a bit more austere than some of the other inns and lacks a certain coziness. Nevertheless, it's extremely pleasant and well maintained. Because of its popularity, this hotel annexed another house across the street. In spite of the age of the building, the rooms are very modern, with built-in furniture, evoking Scandinavia more than Bavaria. Try for one of the older units, which are larger and furnished in a more Bavarian motif. Bathrooms are small to midsize, most with a tub-and-shower combination.

Untere Schmiedgasse 16–25 (off Wenggasse), 91541 Rothenburg ob der Tauber. ✆ **09861/70-80.** Fax 09861/70-81-00. www.goldenerhirsch.rothenburg.de. 72 units. 77€–164€ ($68.75–$146.45) double. Rates include breakfast. AE, DC, MC, V. Parking 2.60€ ($2.30). **Amenities:** Restaurant; bar; room service; babysitting. *In room:* Minibar, hair dryer.

**Romantik Hotel Markusturm** Markusturm is a part of the city's history. When it was built in 1264 next to St. Mark's Tower, it incorporated one of Rothenburg's defensive walls. Today that city wall is gone—except for the section that remains part of the hotel. Although the Markusturm cannot rival the splendor of the Eisenhut, it's a close competitor of the Burg Hotel. Its bold, masculine style may be a welcome relief from the many cute and cozily cluttered inns. Much of the hotel dates from 1988. Local art adds color and interest to the whitewashed walls, and Oriental rugs provide warm touches. Guest rooms have been modernized but are furnished in a traditional style with high-quality antique and rustic furniture. Some rooms have four-poster beds, and each comes with a tub-and-shower combination. Many tradition-minded guests request room 30, a cozy attic unit. The staff is one of the most helpful in town.

Rödergasse 1, 91541 Rothenburg ob der Tauber. ✆ **09861/94280.** Fax 09861/2692. www.romantikhotels.com/markusturm. 25 units. 115€–195€ ($102.70–$174.15). Rates include buffet breakfast. AE, DC, MC, V. Free parking. **Amenities:** Restaurant; bar; tennis court; room service; babysitting; dry cleaning/laundry. *In room:* TV, hair dryer.

### MODERATE

**Hotel Reichs-Küchenmeister** ★ We like this hotel a lot. It's one of the town's oldest structures and was salvaged from a World War II firestorm through a massive, thoroughly sensitive restoration. It's both stylish and well equipped. Rooms are furnished with regional wooden furniture; some contain minibars. Bathrooms are a bit small, but maintenance is tidy and each comes with a tiled shower. Seventeen rooms are also available in the less desirable annex across the street.

Kircheplatz 8 (near St. Jakobskirche), 91541 Rothenburg ob der Tauber. ✆ **09861/97-00.** Fax 09861/869-65/87-04-09. www.reichskuechenmeister.com. 53 units. 89€–108€ ($79.50–$96.45) double; 130€–215€ ($116.10–$192) suite. Rates include buffet breakfast. AE, DC, DISC, MC, V. Parking 5€ ($4.45) lot, 6.50€ ($5.80) garage. **Amenities:** Restaurant; lounge; whirlpool; sauna; solarium; room service. *In room:* TV, hair dryer.

### INEXPENSIVE

**Bayerischer Hof** This little B&B doesn't even try to compete with the grand inns of the town. The Bayerischer Hof stands midway between the Bahnhof and the medieval walled city. Petra and Harald Schellhaas welcome guests to their recently renovated, clean, and well-furnished accommodations. The exterior looks somewhat sterile, but the inside of the hotel is full of cozy Bavarian touches, like the traditional painted furniture. Rooms and shower-only bathrooms are small, but the housekeeping is excellent and the staff is most hospitable.

Ansbacherstrasse 21, 91541 Rothenburg ob der Tauber. ✆ **09861/60-63.** Fax 09861/8-65-61. www.bayerischerhof.com. 9 units. 64€–84€ ($57.15–$75) double. Rates include breakfast. MC, V. Free parking. Closed Jan. **Amenities:** Breakfast room; lounge; room service. *In room:* TV.

**Zum Greifen** Don't expect glamour and glitz here—just home-style warmth and comfort. Located in a patrician 1374 house, this hotel stands next door to the prestigious Baumeisterhaus restaurant (see "Where to Dine," below). Rooms are simple but cozy and comfortable, each with a little shower-only bathroom. The staff is willing to help in any way. You can order your morning coffee in the garden amid roses and geraniums.

Obere Schmiedgasse 5 (off Marktplatz), 91541 Rothenburg ob der Tauber. ✆ **09861/22-81.** Fax 09861/8-63-74. www.gasthof-greifen.rothenburg.de. 15 units. 77€ ($68.75) double. Rates include buffet breakfast. AE, MC, V. Closed Aug 22–Sept 2 and Dec 22–Feb 7. **Amenities:** Dining room; lounge; room service. *In room:* TV, no phone.

## WHERE TO DINE

### EXPENSIVE

**Romantik-Restaurant Louvre** ★★★ NEW GERMAN Chef Berhard Reiser is a man of multiple talents, and he has brought a lighter touch to the kitchens of Rothenburg with his *Neuer Küche* (new cuisine) style of cookery. While most Rothenburg chefs stick to the tried-and-true dishes, Herr Reiser is limited only by the availability of produce. His appetizers are dazzling, especially the goose-liver terrine with huckleberries and white port or his consommé of crayfish with ravioli. For a main course, try the perfectly cooked halibut with a potato sauce, or the roulade of guinea fowl with herb-infused cabbage and white-flour dumplings. The wine list, for the most part, is good and fairly priced.

Klingengasse 15. ✆ **09861/87809.** Reservations required. Main courses 19.95€–26.05€ ($17.80–$23.25); fixed-price menu 50.10€–74.10€ ($44.75–$66.15). AE, MC, V. Daily 6–11pm.

### MODERATE

**Baumeisterhaus** ★ FRANCONIAN The Baumeisterhaus is housed in an ancient patrician residence, built in 1596. It contains Rothenburg's most beautiful courtyard (which only guests can visit). The patio has colorful murals, serenely draped by vines. Frankly, although the menu is good, the romantic setting is the main attraction here. One of the chef's best dishes is sauerbraten (braised beef marinated in vinegar and served with *Spätzle,* small flour dumplings). The food, for the most part, is the rib-sticking fare beloved by Bavarians, including roast-suckling pig with potato dumplings or roast pork shoulder. Apple strudel is everybody's favorite dessert.

Obere Schmiedgasse 3 (right off Marktplatz). ✆ **09861/9-47-00.** Reservations required for courtyard tables. Main courses 7.65€–22.50€ ($6.85–$20.10). AE, DC, MC, V. Daily 9am–2pm and 6–9pm.

**Ratsstube** FRANCONIAN The Ratsstube enjoys a location right on the market square, one of the most photographed spots in Germany. It's a bustling center of activity throughout the day, beginning when practically every Rothenburger stops by for a cup of morning coffee. Inside, a true tavern atmosphere prevails, with hardwood chairs and tables, vaulted ceilings, and pierced copper lanterns. On the a la carte menu are many Franconian dishes, including sauerbraten and venison, both served with fresh vegetables and potatoes. For dessert, you can order homemade Italian ice cream and espresso. This place is a favorite of those who prefer Franconian cookery without a lot of fuss and bother.

Marktplatz 6. ✆ **09861/92411.** Reservations recommended. Main courses 9.20€–20.45€ ($8.20–$18.25). MC, V. Mon–Sat 9am–11pm; Sun 9am–6pm. Closed Jan 7–Mar 1.

**Reichs-Küchenmeister** FRANCONIAN The food served here is perfect for cold days. Liver-dumpling or goulash soup, sauerbraten, or pork tenderloin are typical dishes. We recently discovered that the chef makes one of the best Wiener schnitzels in town. White herring and boiled salmon are usually available. The restaurant has a typical Weinstube decor, along with a garden terrace and a Konditorei (cake shop). The service is warm and efficient.

Kircheplatz 8 (near St. Jakobskirche). ✆ **09861/97-00.** Reservations required. Main courses 7.55€–16.75€ ($6.75–$14.95). AE, MC, V. Daily 7am–9:30pm.

## ROTHENBURG AFTER DARK

Count Picasso is among those who have enjoyed the show at the **Figurentheater,** am Burgtor at Herrengasse 38 (✆ **09861/73-54** or 09861/33-33). Puppet shows are presented year-round Monday to Saturday at 8pm, and June 15 to September, also at 3pm. The evening shows cost 8€ ($7.15) for adults and 6€ ($5.35) for students. Matinee tickets are 6€ ($5.35) for adults, with student and children tickets costing 5€ ($4.45) and 4€ ($3.55), respectively.

The most idyllic place to go in the evening is **Unter den Linden** (✆ **09861/59-09**), at Detwang. This is a cafe-bar on the River Tauber. You reach it by going under the arch at St. Jakobskirche and following Klingengasse through the town gate, heading down a path to Detwang. The cafe is open April to October daily 10am to 10pm, but it reduces its hours in winter, depending on weather. If you'd like to sample some local wine, try **Zur Hölle,** Burggasse 8 (✆ **09861/42-29**), a mellow place in the town's oldest house. A wide assortment of wines is offered at 4€ ($3.55) and 5€ ($4.45) per glass.

## 8 Dinkelsbühl ★

93km (58 miles) SW of Nürnberg, 14km (71 miles) NE of Stuttgart, 105km (65 miles) SE of Würzburg

Still surrounded by its medieval walls and towers, Dinkelsbühl is straight out of a Brothers Grimm story, even down to the gingerbread, which is one of the town's main products. Behind the 10th-century walls, the town retains its quiet, provincial attitude in spite of the many visitors who come here. The cobblestone streets are lined with fine 16th-century houses, many with carvings and paintings depicting biblical and mythological themes.

### ESSENTIALS

**GETTING THERE** **By Train** The nearest train station is in Ansbach, which has several trains daily from Munich, Nürnberg, and Stuttgart. From Ansbach, Dinkelsbühl can be reached by bus. Train rides from Munich or Frankfurt take about 2½ to 3 hours, depending on the connection. For rail information, call ✆ **01805/99-66-33.**

**By Bus** For bus service along the Romantic Road, see "Bus Tours of the Romantic Road," at the beginning of this chapter. Regional buses link Dinkelsbühl with local towns. There are three to five buses a day to Rothenburg and five to six buses a day to Nördlingen.

**By Car** Access is via the A7 Autobahn or Route 25.

**VISITOR INFORMATION** Contact **Stadt Verkehrsamt,** Marktplatz (✆ **09851/9-02-40**), open Easter through October, Monday to Friday 9am to noon and 2 to 6pm, Saturday 10am to 1pm and 2 to 4pm, and Sunday and holidays 10am to 7pm; November to Easter, Monday to Friday 10am to noon and 2 to 5pm, and Saturday 10am to 1pm.

**SPECIAL EVENTS** This dreamy village awakens once a year for the **Kinderzeche (Children's Festival),** held from July 14 to 23. This festival commemorates the saving of the village by its children in 1632. According to the story, the children pleaded with conquering Swedish troops to leave their town without pillaging and destroying it—and got their wish. The pageant includes concerts given by the local boys' band dressed in historic military costumes.

### EXPLORING THE TOWN

Dinkelsbühl is a lively, wonderfully preserved medieval town, full of narrow, cobblestone streets. You might begin your explorations at the 14th-century gateway, **Rothenburger Tor,** and then head down the wide Martin Luther Strasse to the market square. Along the way you can take in the town's fine collection of early Renaissance burghers' houses. Dinkelbühl's main attraction is the late-Gothic **Georgenkirche,** on Marktplatz, built between 1448 and 1499. The church contains a carved Holy Cross Altar and pillar sculptures, many from the 15th century. The best evening activity here is to take a walk around the ramparts. There's a night watchman making the rounds about town, as in medieval times.

### WHERE TO STAY & DINE

**Blauer Hecht** ★ This inn, one of the best in town, is also a brewery tavern. In honor of its longtime role, beer is still brewed in its backyard. Now a chain hotel, it has been considerably modernized and updated. The elegant ochre building dates from the 17th century and has three hand-built stories of stucco, stone, and tile. Although it's centrally located, rooms are tranquil. Most are medium in size, although there are some small singles. Each unit contains a neatly kept and efficiently organized private bathroom with tiled shower.

Schweinemarkt 1, 91150 Dinkelsbühl. ✆ **09851/58-10.** Fax 09851/58-11-70. 44 units. 76.65€–102.20€ ($68.45–$91.25) double. Rates include continental breakfast. AE, DC, MC, V. Free parking. Closed Jan. **Amenities:** Restaurant; bar; room service. *In room:* TV.

**Deutsches Haus** ★ The facade of Deutsches Haus, which dates from 1440, is rich in painted designs and festive woodcarvings. Each room in this casually run hotel is different—you may find yourself in one with a ceramic stove or in another with a Biedermeier desk. For the tradition-minded, there are no finer rooms in town. Cozy comfort is the rule here. Each accommodation comes with a neatly tiled shower-only bathroom. Even if you don't stay here, you may want to dine in the **Altdeutsches Restaurant,** one of the finest in Dinkelsbühl. It's intimate and convivial, and serves Franconian and regional specialties.

Weinmarkt 3, 91550 Dinkelsbühl. ✆ **09851/60-58.** Fax 09851/79-11. www.deutsches/hausdkb.de. 9 units. 76.65€–104.30€ ($68.45–$93.15) double; from 127.75€ ($114.10) suite. Rates include continental breakfast. AE, DC, MC, V. Parking 8€ ($7.15). Closed Dec 23–Jan 6. **Amenities:** Restaurant. *In room:* TV, minibar; hair dryer.

**Eisenkrug** ★★ The sienna walls of this centrally located hotel were originally built in 1620. Today the Eisenkrug's forest-green shutters are familiar to everyone in town; many celebrate family occasions at the hotel restaurant. There's even a cafe with alfresco tables in warm weather. The stylish rooms are wallpapered with flowery prints and filled with engaging old furniture. An additional nine rooms are in an equally fine guesthouse nearby. All rooms in the newer wing are rather standardized and modern looking. The older rooms offer more charm, although some tend to be smaller. Some of the beds are canopied. Bathrooms range from small to spacious, mostly with shower-and-tub combination.

**Zum kleinen Obristen** serves a gourmet international cuisine. The chef takes an indigenous Franconian-Swabian approach, with many innovative touches. The superior wine cellar has some really unusual vintages.

Dr. Martin-Luther-Strasse 1, 91550 Dinkelsbühl. ✆ **09851/57700.** Fax 09851/577070. www.hotel/eisenkrug.de. 23 units. 86.85€–107.30€ ($77.55–$95.80) double. Rates include continental breakfast. MC, V. Parking is free. **Amenities:** Restaurant; cafe. *In room:* TV, minibar, hair dryer.

## 9 Nördlingen ★

130km (81 miles) NW of Munich, 95km (59 miles) SW of Nürnberg

Nördlingen is one of the most irresistible medieval towns along the Romantic Road. It's still encircled by well-preserved fortifications from the 14th and 15th centuries. Things are rather tranquil around Nördlingen today; nonetheless, the town still employs sentries to sound the reassuring message, *So G'sell so* (all is well), as they did in the Middle Ages.

The area wasn't always so peaceful. The town sits in a gigantic crater called the Ries. Once thought to be the crater of an extinct volcano, it is now known that the Ries was created by a meteorite at least half a mile in diameter. It struck the ground some 15 million years ago at more than 161,000 kph (100,000 mph). Debris was hurled as far as Slovakia, and all plant and animal life within a radius of 161km (100 miles) was destroyed. Today the Ries is the best-preserved and most scientifically researched meteorite crater on earth. The American astronauts from *Apollo 14* and *Apollo 17* did their field training in the Ries in 1970. Contact the **Rieskrater-Museum** (see below) for tours of the crater.

## ESSENTIALS

**GETTING THERE** **By Plane** The nearest major airport is in Nürnberg; from there you can make either bus or rail connections to Nördlingen.

**By Train** Nördlingen lies on the main Nördlingen-Aalen-Stuttgart line, with frequent connections in all directions. Call ✆ **0185/99-66-33** for schedules and more information. Nördlingen can be reached from Stuttgart in 2 hours, from Nürnberg in 2 hours, and from Augsburg in 1 hour.

**By Bus** For bus service along the Romantic Road, see "Bus Tours of the Romantic Road," at the beginning of this chapter.

**By Car** Access by car is via the A7 Autobahn north and south and Route 29 from the east. From Dinkelsbühl, take Route 25 south.

**VISITOR INFORMATION** Contact the **Verkehrsamt,** Marktplatz 2 (✆ **09081/43-80**), open Easter to October, Monday to Friday 9am to 5pm, and Saturday 9:30am to 1pm; November to Easter, Monday to Friday 9am to 5pm.

## EXPLORING THE TOWN

You can walk around the town on the covered parapet on top of the perfectly preserved walls. Along the way, you'll pass 11 towers and five fortified gates. At the center of the circular Altstadt, within the walls, is **Rübenmarkt.** If you stand in this square on market day, you'll be swept into a world of the past—the country people here have preserved many traditional customs and costumes, which, along with the ancient houses, evoke a living medieval city. Around the square stand a number of buildings, including the Gothic **Rathaus.** An antiquities collection is displayed in the **Stadtmuseum,** Vordere Gerbergasse 1 (✆ **09081/2738230**), open Tuesday to Sunday 1:30 to 4:30pm; closed November to February. Admission is 2.55€ ($2.30) for adults and 1.55€ ($1.40) for children, students, travelers with disabilities, and seniors.

**St. Georgskirche** ✪, on the square's northern side, is the town's most interesting sight and one of its oldest buildings. This Gothic Hall Church is from the 15th century. Plaques and epitaphs commemorating the town's more illustrious 16th- and 17th-century residents decorate the fan-vaulted interior. Although the original Gothic altarpiece by Friedrich Herlin (1462) is now in the Reichsstadtmuseum in Rothenburg, a portion of it, depicting the Crucifixion by Nikolaus Gerhart van Leydeu, remains in the church. Above the high altar today stands a more elaborate baroque altarpiece. The church's most prominent feature, however, is the 90m (295-ft.) French Gothic tower, called the "Daniel." At night, the town watchman calls out from the steeple, his voice ringing through the streets. The tower is accessible daily November to March 9am to 5pm and April to October 9am to 8pm. Admission to the tower is 1.55€ ($1.40) for adults and 1€ (90¢) for students and children. It's free to visit the church, which is open Easter to October, Monday to Friday 9:30am to 12:30pm and 2 to 5pm, and Saturday and Sunday 9:30am to 5pm.

**Rieskrater-Museum,** Eugene Shoemaker Platz 7 (✆ **09081/2738220**), documents the impact of the stone meteorite that crashed into the earth here on the Alb plateau, nearly 15 million years ago. Hours are Tuesday to Sunday 10am to noon and 1:30 to 4:30pm. Admission is 2.55€ ($2.30) for adults and 1.30€ ($1.15) for children over the age of 6 and students.

## WHERE TO STAY

**Astron Hotel Klösterle** ✪✪ The accommodations here are the best and most luxurious in town. This historic, white-sided, red-roofed building was originally constructed as a monastery in the 1200s. Since then, its ziggurat-shaped gables and steep roof have been an essential part of Nördlingen's medieval center. The hotel offers elevator access and a hardworking, polite staff. Guest rooms have dark-wood fixtures, lots of electronic extras, and larger-than-expected bathrooms with tub and shower.

Am Klösterle 1, 86720 Nördlingen. ✆ **09081/8-80-54.** www.astronhotelklosterle.de. 97 units. 130.80€–139.50€ ($116.80–$124.55) double. Rates include continental breakfast. AE, DC, MC, V. Parking 7.65€ ($6.85). **Amenities:** Restaurant; bar; fitness center; sauna; room service; laundry. *In room:* TV, minibar, hair dryer, safe.

**Kaiser Hotel Sonne** ★ The Sonne is in a bull's-eye position next to the cathedral and the Rathaus. It has a heady atmosphere from having entertained so many illustrious personalities since it opened as an inn in 1405. Among its guests have been emperors; kings; princes, including Frederick III, Maximilian I, and Charles V; the great poet Goethe; and, in more recent times, American astronauts. Many of the rooms contain hand-painted four-poster beds. Each is midsize to spacious and most tastefully and comfortably furnished, with excellent bathrooms, mostly with tub-and-shower combination.

Marktplatz 3, 86720 Nördlingen. ✆ **09081/50-67.** Fax 09081/2-39-99. 43 units (35 with bathrooms). 84.30€ ($75.30) double without bathroom, 97.10€ ($86.70) double with bathroom. Rates include breakfast. AE, DC, MC, V. Free parking. **Amenities:** Restaurant; lounge; room service; babysitting; laundry. *In room:* TV, minibar, hair dryer.

## WHERE TO DINE

**Meyers-Keller** ★ CONTINENTAL The conservative, modern decor here seems a suitable setting for the restrained Neuer Küche style of the talented chef and owner, Joachim Kaiser. The cuisine changes according to the availability of ingredients and the inspiration of the chef; typical selections are likely to include roulade of sea wolf, salmon with baby spinach and wild rice, and John Dory with champagne-flavored tomato sauce. There's also an impressive array of European wines, many reasonably priced.

Marienhöhe 8. ✆ **09081/44-93.** Reservations required. Main courses 15.35€–23€ ($13.70–$20.55); fixed-price menu 45.50€–56.20€ ($40.65–$50.20). AE, MC, V. Tues 6–10pm; Wed–Sun 11am–2pm and 6–10pm. Closed last 2 weeks of Feb. Local bus to Markplatz.

# 10 Donauwörth

40km (25 miles) N of Augsburg, 11km (7 miles) S of Harburg, 95km (59 miles) NW of Munich

Visitors come to Donauwörth for its architecture and sense of history, rather than for specific attractions. The town is located on what was the last navigable point on the Danube, which led to its becoming a key stop on the trade route between Augsburg and Nürnberg. Its attempted capture by the Imperial party in 1608 led directly to the division of Germany into warring Protestant and Catholic military alliances, leading to the Thirty Years' War.

The oldest part of town sits on an island in the middle of the stream, access to which is via the oldest surviving gate in town, the **Riederstor,** which funnels traffic along the island's most historic and evocative street, the **Reichsstrasse.** Donauwörth was badly damaged in World War II bombing raids in 1945, but it has been carefully restored. Part of the town's fortifications have survived.

## ESSENTIALS

**GETTING THERE** **By Train** Trains arrive from Augsburg at 30-minute intervals throughout the day (trip time: 35–45 min.). Trains also come hourly from Munich (trip time: 90 min.). For railway information call **01805/99-66-33.**

**By Bus** For bus service along the Romantic Road, see "Bus Tours of the Romantic Road," at the beginning of this chapter.

**By Car** From Augsburg, follow Route 2 north. From Nördlingen, take Route 25.

**VISITOR INFORMATION** Tourist-Information is at Rathausgasse 1 (✆ **0906/7891-51**), open Monday to Friday 9am to 5:30pm.

## EXPLORING THE TOWN

The town is dominated by the Heiligeskreuz or Holy Cross Church, a large 1720 baroque building with concave interior galleries. It's an outstanding example of the distinctive churches built and decorated by the craftsmen of Wessobrunn.

The site that draws the greatest numbers of visitors is the **Käthe-Kruse-Puppen-Museum,** Pflegstrasse 21A (✆ **0906/789185**). Inside, you'll find a small-scale collection of the dolls and dollhouses that were designed by master artisan Käthe-Kruse, whose most prolific period during the 1950s and 1960s has been called a high point in the history of doll making. May to September, it's open Tuesday to Sunday 11am to 5pm; October to April, Tuesday to Sunday 2 to 5pm. Entrance costs 2.55€ ($2.30) for adults, half price for children under 12.

## WHERE TO STAY & DINE

**Posthotel Traube** ★ This hotel's history goes back to the 1600s with a guest list that included Goethe and Mozart. Despite its modern conveniences, there's still the definite sense of old Mittel Europa here, thanks to a somewhat creaky staff and a no-nonsense approach to innkeeping. Rooms are nostalgically outfitted with engravings and prints of old-fashioned Germany. This is a comfortable choice with midsize to spacious bedrooms. Perhaps some of the furnishings show too much wear and tear, but tradition-minded guests like it here. Each bathroom is midsize to roomy, most often with a tub-and-shower combination. On the premises is a restaurant that serves cuisine prepared with first-rate ingredients. It is solid, reliable fare, not inventive in any way, but hearty and filling. Their recipes have been time-tested over a few generations.

Kapellstrasse 14–16, 86609 Donauwörth. ✆ **0906/706-440.** Fax 0906/706-5180. www.posthoteltraube.de. 42 units. 72€–80€ ($64.30–$71.45) double; 98€ ($87.50) suite. Rates include breakfast. AE, MC, V. **Amenities:** Restaurant; lounge; room service; laundry. *In room:* No phone.

# 11 Augsburg

68km (42 miles) NW of Munich, 80km (50 miles) E of Ulm, 160km (100 miles) SE of Stuttgart

Augsburg's 2,000 years of history have made it one of southern Germany's major sightseeing attractions. It's the Romantic Road's largest town and serves also as a gateway to the Alps and the south.

Augsburg was founded under Emperor Tiberius in 15 B.C., though little remains from the early Roman period. The wealth of art and architecture from the Renaissance, on the other hand, is staggering. Over the years, Augsburg has hosted many distinguished visitors and boasts an array of famous native sons, including painters Hans Holbein the Elder and the Younger and playwright Bertolt Brecht. In 1518, Martin Luther was summoned to Augsburg to recant his 95 theses before a papal emissary. Today, Augsburg, with a population of about 250,000, is an important industrial center and Bavaria's third largest city, after Munich and Nürnberg.

## ESSENTIALS

**GETTING THERE** **By Train** For railway information, call ✆ **01805/99-66-33.** Three to four trains arrive per hour from Munich (trip time: 45 minutes); two per hour from Stuttgart (trip time: 1¾ hours); and 2 per hour from Nürnberg (trip time: 1¾ hour). There is 1 train per hour from Würzberg (trip time: 2 hours).

**By Bus** For bus service along the Romantic Road, see "Bus Tours of the Romantic Road," at the beginning of this chapter.

**By Car** Access is via the A8 Autobahn east and west. From Donauwörth, take Route 2 south.

**VISITOR INFORMATION** Contact **Tourist-Information,** Bahnhafstrasse 7 (✆ **0821/50-20-70**), open October 15 to May, Monday to Friday 9am to 5pm and Saturday 10am to 1pm; May to October 14, Monday to Friday 9am to 6pm, Saturday 10am to 4pm, and Sunday 10am to 1pm.

**GETTING AROUND** The public transportation system in Augsburg consists of four tram lines and 31 bus lines. It operates from 5am to midnight daily and is provided by **Verkehr Gemeinschaft Augsburg VGA** (✆ **0821/3245888**). **Augsburger Verkehrsverbund AVV** (✆ **0821/15-70-07**) provides the service for transport outside the city.

## SEEING THE SIGHTS

Extending southward from the Rathaus is the wide **Maximilianstrasse** ★, lined with shops and old burghers' houses and studded with fountains by the Renaissance Dutch sculptor Adrien de Vries.

**Church of St. Ulrich and St. Afra** ★ Near the southern end of Maximilianstrasse is the Hercules Fountain, and behind it, the most attractive ecclesiastical compound in Augsburg. The churches of St. Ulrich and St. Afra were constructed between 1476 and 1500 on the site of a Roman temple. As a tribute to the 1555 Peace of Augsburg, which recognized two denominations, one Roman Catholic and the other Lutheran, these two separate churches—Catholic St. Afra and Protestant St. Ulrich—stand next to each other. The churches are mainly 15th-century Gothic with baroque overlays. St. Afra is the most elaborate, with a magnificent altar and finely carved baroque railings bordering the entrance. St. Ulrich is the former monastery assembly hall, taken over by the Lutherans. The shared crypt contains the tombs of the two namesake saints. The lance and saddle of St. Ulrich are displayed in the sacristy.

Ulrichplatz 15. ✆ **0821/34-55-60.** Free admission. Daily 9am–6pm. Tram: 1, 2, or 4.

**Dom St. Maria** The cathedral of Augsburg has the distinction of containing the oldest stained-glass windows in the world. These Romanesque windows, dating from the 12th century, are in the south transept and depict Old Testament prophets in a severe but colorful style. They are younger than the cathedral itself, which was begun in 944, and partially Gothicized in the 14th century. The 11th-century bronze doors, leading into the three-aisle nave, are adorned with bas reliefs of a mixture of biblical and mythological characters. The cathedral's interior, restored in 1934, contains side altars with altarpieces by Hans Holbein the Elder and Christoph Amberger. You'll find the ruins of the original basilica in the crypt beneath the west chancel.

Hoher Weg. ✆ **0821/31-66-353.** Free admission. Mon–Sat 7am–6pm; Sun 9:30am–6pm. Tram: 2.

**Fuggerei** ★ During the 15th and 16th centuries, Augsburg became one of Europe's wealthiest communities, mainly because of its textile industry and the political and financial clout of its two banking families, the Welsers and the Fuggers. The Welsers have long since faded away. But the founders of the powerful Fugger family have established themselves permanently by an unusual legacy, the

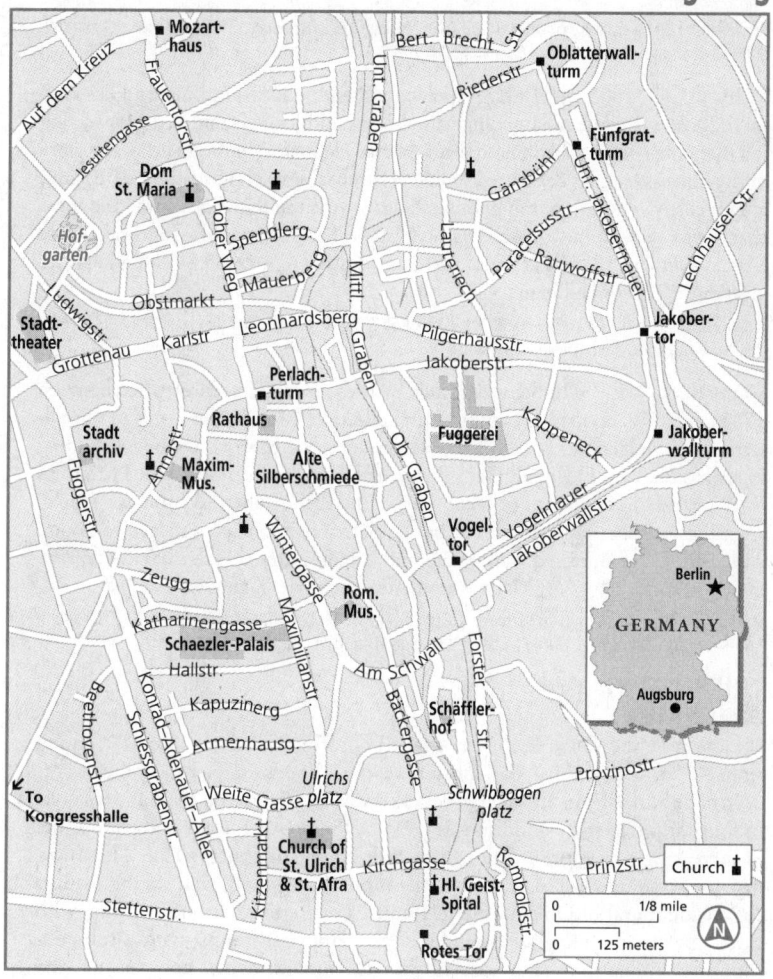


Fuggerei, set up in 1519 by Jakob Fugger the Rich to house poorer Augsburgers. It's Europe's oldest welfare housing.

The basic features, laid down in 1521, are still in force today. The nominal rent of 1€ (90¢) per annum (formerly one Rheinish guilder) has not changed in more than 450 years (the city council determines who gets the break—it's based on need). The only obligation is that tenants pray daily for the souls of their founders. The Fuggerei is a miniature, self-contained town with its own gates, which are shut from 10pm to 5am and guarded by a night watchman. Franz Mozart, a master mason fallen on hard times—and great-grandfather of Wolfgang Amadeus Mozart—once lived at Mittlere Gasse 14.

The Fugger Foundation owns the Fuggerei. A house at Mittlere Gasse 13, next to the one once occupied by Mozart's ancestor, is now the Fuggerei's museum. The rough 16th- and 17th-century furniture, wood-paneled ceilings and walls, and cast-iron stove, as well as other objects of everyday life, show what it was like to live here in earlier times.

At the end of Vorderer Lech. ✆ **0821/31-98-810.** Museum 1€ (90¢) adults, .50€ (45¢) students and children. Museum Mar–Dec daily 9am–6pm. Tram: 1.

**Rathaus** In 1805 and 1809, Napoléon visited the Rathaus, built by Elias Holl in 1620. Regrettably, the building was also visited by an air raid in 1944, leaving it a mere shell of what had once been a palatial eight-story monument to the glory of the Renaissance. Its celebrated "golden chamber" was left in shambles. But now, after a costly restoration, the public can again visit the Rathaus on walking tours that offer a view of the "golden chamber" as well as other rooms. Tours take place May to October 18 daily at 10am and 2pm, costing 6.50€ ($5.80) for adults and 4.60€ ($4.10) for children.

Am Rathausplatz 2. ✆ **0821/324-9180.** Admission 1.55€ ($1.40) adults, .75€ (65¢) children 7–14, free for children 6 and under. Daily 10am–6pm. Tram: 1 or 2.

**Schaezlerpalais** The Schaezlerpalais, a 60-room mansion constructed between 1765 and 1770, contains an amazing art collection. Most of the works in the collection are by German artists of the Renaissance and baroque periods, including Hans Holbein the Elder and Hans Burgkmair. One of the most famous paintings is Albrecht Dürer's portrait of Jakob Fugger the Rich. Rubens, Veronese, Tiepolo, and others are also represented. The palace-gallery also contains a rococo ballroom, with gilded and mirrored wall panels and a ceiling fresco, *The Four Continents.* Here, on April 28, 1770, Marie Antoinette danced the night away.

Maximilianstrasse 46 (facing the Hercules Fountain). ✆ **0821/3244102.** Admission 3€ ($2.70) adults, 1.50€ ($1.35) children over 10 and students. Wed–Sun 10am–5pm. Tram 1.

## WHERE TO STAY

### EXPENSIVE

**Steigenberger Drei Mohren** ★★ The original "Three Moors," dating from 1723, was one of the most renowned hotels in Germany before its destruction in a 1944 air raid. In 1956, it was reconstructed in a modern style in four- and five-story buildings. It remains the premier hotel in town in spite of increasing competition from Romantik Hotel Augsburger Hof. The drawing room contains a slatted natural-wood ceiling and wall, along with a roomwide mural of Old Augsburg. Rooms are comfortable and inviting, with thick carpets, double-glazed windows, and large bathrooms with a tub-and-shower combination. They vary in size and appointments, however, ranging from small economy specials to spacious and luxurious suites.

Maximilianstrasse 40, 86150 Augsburg. ✆ **800/223-5652** in the U.S. and Canada, or 0821/5-03-60. Fax 0821/15-78-64. www.steigenberger.de. 106 units. 135€–156€ ($120.55–$139.30) double; from 281€ ($250.95) suite. Rates include buffet breakfast. AE, DC, MC, V. Parking 11€ ($9.80). Tram: 1. **Amenities:** Dining room; lounge; room service; laundry/dry cleaning. *In room:* A/C, TV, minibar, hair dryer, trouser press.

### MODERATE

**Dom Hotel** *Value* The Dom Hotel lacks the decorative flair of its competitors, but it is a peaceful stay. That, combined with the moderate rates, makes this one of the most appealing choices in town. The 15th-century half-timbered structure rises imposingly beside Augsburg's famous cathedral. You don't get a lot of style here, but you do get comfort. Rooms on most floors are medium in size and nicely appointed, although we prefer the smaller attic accommodations, where you can rest under a beam ceiling and enjoy a panoramic sweep of the rooftops of the city. Each accommodation comes with a neatly tiled and efficiently organized compact bathroom with shower. Breakfast is the only meal served; during warm weather, it can be enjoyed in a garden beside the town's medieval fortifications.

Frauentorstrasse 8, 86152 Augsburg. ✆ **0821/34-39-30.** Fax 0821/34-39-32-00. www.domhotel-augsburg.de. 43 units. 85€–105€ ($75.90–$93.75) double. Rates include buffet breakfast. AE, DC, MC, V. Free parking in lot; 4.10€ ($3.65) garage. Tram: 2. **Amenities:** Breakfast room; lounge; pool; laundry. *In room:* TV, hair dryer.

**Romantik Hotel Augsburger Hof** ★ This is a favorite for its traditional and romantic atmosphere. This hotel was originally built in 1767 in a solid, thick-walled design with exposed beams and timbers. Rooms are completely up-to-date but not as romantic as the hotel's name suggests. They range from small to spacious. Some bathrooms seem crowded in as an afterthought, but each is beautifully maintained and contains a shower. Rooms overlooking the tranquil inner courtyard are more expensive than ones facing the street.

Auf dem Kreuz 2, 86152 Augsburg. ✆ **0821/34-30-50.** Fax 0821/3430555. www.romantikhotel-augsburger hof.de. 36 units. 75€–130€ ($67–$116.10) double. Rates include buffet breakfast. AE, DC, MC, V. Parking 6€ ($5.35). Tram: 2. **Amenities:** Restaurant; lounge; room service. *In room:* TV, minibar, hair dryer.

### INEXPENSIVE

**Hotel Garni Weinberger** *Value* The Weinberger is one of the best budget accommodations in the area. Rooms are small but well kept. The private shower-only bathrooms are rather cramped, but corridor bathrooms are adequate and tidy. Many of the patrons are Germans, who know a good bargain.

Bismarckstrasse 55 (about 3km/2 miles west of town center, along Augsburgerstrasse), 86391 Stadtbergen. ✆ **0821/24-39-10.** Fax 0821/43-88-31. 31 units. 76.65€ ($68.45) double. Rates include buffet breakfast. No credit cards. Free parking. Closed Aug 15–30. Tram: 2. **Amenities:** Cafe; lounge. *In room:* No phone.

## WHERE TO DINE

**Die Ecke** ★ FRENCH/SWABIAN This is the town's finest dining choice. This restaurant's guests have included Hans Holbein the Elder, Wolfgang Amadeus Mozart, and, in more contemporary times, Rudolf Diesel, of engine fame, and Bertolt Brecht. The Weinstube ambience belies the skilled cuisine of the chef—the elegant fare here is rivaled only by the Oblinger. Breast of duckling might be preceded by a paté or pheasant. The filet of sole in Riesling is a classic, and venison dishes in season, a specialty, are the best in town.

Elias-Holl-Platz 2. ✆ **0821/51-06-00.** Reservations required. Main courses 13.30€–28.10€ ($11.90–$25.10); fixed-price dinner 39.85€ ($35.60) for 4 courses, 58.75€ ($52.45) for 6 courses. AE, DC, MC, V. Daily 11am–2pm and 5:30pm–midnight. Tram: 2.

**Fuggerei Stube** GERMAN/SWABIAN This affordable restaurant can fit 60 persons at a time into its large, *gemütlich* dining room. Expect generous portions of well-prepared food such as sauerbraten, pork schnitzel, game, and fish dishes. The beer foaming out of the taps here is Storchenbräu; most visitors find that it goes wonderfully with the conservative German specialties that are this establishment's forte.

Jakoberstrasse 26. ✆ **0821/3-08-70.** Reservations recommended. Main courses 10.20€–17.90€ ($9.10–$16); fixed-price menu 20.45€ ($18.25). AE, MC, V. Tues–Sun 11:30am–2pm; Tues–Sat 5:30pm–1:30am. Tram: 1.

**Welser Kuche** SWABIAN Come to the Welser Kuche for a medieval feast on wooden tables. The traditional menu is served nightly by *Knechte* and *Mägde* (knaves and wenches) in 16th-century costumes. Fixed-price menus, called "Welser Feast," are eaten with a dagger and your fingers for cutlery. Stone walls, knotty-pine paneling, and stucco arches frame the wooden tables. Recipes here are from a cookbook, discovered in 1970, that belonged to Philippine Welser

(1527–1580), Baroness of Zinnenburg and wife of Habsburg archduke Ferdinand II. It takes about 3 hours to eat a meal here. Sometimes parties of two or four can be seated at the last minute, but reservations should be made as far in advance as possible. To reserve by phone, call ✆ **08231/9-61-10** or fax 08231/96-11-28. The reservations office is open Monday to Friday 8am to 6pm and Saturday 8am to noon.

Maximilianstrasse 83. ✆ **0821/961-10.** Reservations required. Feasts 32.65€ ($29.15) for 6 courses Thurs only; 39.35€ ($35.15) for 6 courses all other nights, 44.45€ ($39.70) for 8 courses, none of these prices include drinks. AE, DC, MC, V. Dinner seatings Mon–Sat at 8pm. Located close to the rail station. Tram: 2.

## AUGSBURG AFTER DARK

**Kongresshalle,** Güggingerstrasse 10 (✆ **0821/3-24-23-48;** information line 0821/5-86-86; tram: 1), presents concerts by the local ballet and opera companies and the chamber and symphony orchestras. Call for schedules, prices, and reservations. It's closed in August. The internationally renowned **Mozart Festival** is held in Augsburg every September. Contact the Tourist-Information office (see above) for details. In the courtyard of the Fugger Palace, the city hosts a **musical theater** production each June and July. Tickets run 12€ to 35€ ($10.70–$31.25). Information and reservations are available by calling ✆ **0821/33-44-900** Tuesday to Sunday 11:30am to 1pm and Tuesday to Friday 4:30 to 6pm.

Maximilianstrasse, the main shopping street, continues to be the focus of nightlife after the shops close, with its many cafes. **Brauereigasthaus Drei Königinnen,** Meister-Veits-Gässchen 32 (✆ **0821/15-84-05;** tram: 2 or 4), doubles as an art gallery, has a pleasant beer garden that's open 1:30 to 10pm, and has a main restaurant/bar that closes at 7am. Another garden/bar combo that keeps the same hours is **Thorbräu-Keller,** Heilig-Kreuz-Strasse 20 (✆ **0821/51-19-91;** tram: 2 or 4). **Liliom,** Unterer Graben 1 (✆ **0821/51-40-84;** tram: 2 or 4), is equipped with a good stereo system to go with drinks and conversation; here, too, local artwork is often available for purchase. The bar is open Monday to Thursday 7pm to 3am and Friday to Sunday 6pm to 1am.

# 12 Füssen ★

92km (57 miles) S of Augsburg, 119km (74 miles) SW of Munich

Füssen is situated in the foothills of the Bavarian Alps, at the end of the Romantic Road. The town is mainly a base for those going on to the castles at Neuschwanstein and Hohenschwangau, but it also has a number of attractive buildings, including a 15th-century castle once used by the bishops of Augsburg as a summer palace. In addition, Füssen is ideally located for excursions into the surrounding countryside.

## ESSENTIALS

**GETTING THERE** **By Plane** The nearest major airport is in Munich.

**By Train** Trains from Munich and Augsburg arrive frequently throughout the day. For information, call ✆ **01805/99-66-33.** Train time from Munich is 2½ hours; from Frankfurt, 6 to 7 hours.

**By Bus** For bus service along the Romantic Road, see "Bus Tours of the Romantic Road," at the beginning of this chapter. Regional service is provided by **RVA Regionalverkehr Schwäben Allgäu GmbH** in Füssen (✆ **08362/3-77-71**). This company runs at least 14 buses a day to the royal castles (see below). A one-way ticket costs from 1.50€ ($1.35).

**By Car** Access by car is via the A7 Autobahn from the north and also the B17 from Augsburg.

**VISITOR INFORMATION** Contact the **Kurverwaltung,** Kaiser-Maximilian-Platz 1 (✆ **08362/93-85-0**). Hours vary but are usually in summer Monday to Friday 8:30am to 6:30pm and Saturday 9am to 2:30pm; and in winter Monday to Friday 9am to 5pm and Saturday 10am to noon.

## EXPLORING THE TOWN

Füssen's main attraction is the **Hohes Schloss,** Magnusplatz (✆ **08362/90-31-64**), one of the finest late-Gothic castles in Bavaria. It was once the summer residence of the prince-bishops of Augsburg. Inside you can visit the Rittersaal or "Knight's Hall," known for its stunning coffered ceiling. There's also a collection of Swabian art work from the 1400s to the 1700s. The castle is open Tuesday to Sunday 11am to 4pm and charges 2.55€ ($2.30) for admission.

Immediately below the castle lies the 8th-century **St. Mangkirche** and its **abbey** (✆ **08362/48-44**), which was founded by the Benedictines and grew up on the site where St. Magnus died in 750. In the 18th century it was reconstructed in the baroque style, and in 1803 it was secularized. Free tours of the abbey are given July to September on Tuesday and Thursday at 4pm and on Saturday at 10:30am; May, June, and October on Tuesday at 4pm and Saturday at 9:30am; and January to April on Saturday at 10:30am.

Within the abbey complex, signs point the way to the **Chapel of St. Anne,** where you can view the macabre *Totentanz* or "dance of death," painted by an unknown local artist in the early 15th century. It has a certain bizarre fascination. The chapel is open April to October Tuesday to Sunday 9am to 6pm. Admission is free. Nearby is the **Museum of Füssen** (Heimatmuseum; ✆ **08362/90-31-45**), which displays artifacts relating to the history and culture of the region, including a collection of musical instruments. It keeps the same hours as the chapel and charges 2.55€ ($2.30) to enter.

The principal shopping spot in town is the **Reichenstrasse,** which was known in Roman times as the Via Claudia. This cobblestone street is flanked with houses from the Middle Ages, most of which have towering gables.

## A ROCOCO MASTERPIECE

From Füssen, you can take a fascinating side trip to the **Wieskirche** ★★ (✆ **08862/932930**), one of the most extravagant rococo buildings in the world, a masterpiece by Dominikus Zimmermann. The Wieskirche is a noted pilgrimage church, drawing visitors from all over the globe. It's located on the slopes of the Ammergau Alps between Ammer and Lech, in an alpine meadow just off the Romantic Road near Steingaden, where there is a visitor information office (✆ **08862/200**). The staff at the office can give you a map and confirm that the church is open.

With the help of his brother, Johann Baptist, Zimmermann worked on this church from 1746 to 1754. The ceiling is richly frescoed. It's amazing that so much decoration could be crowded into so small a place. The great Zimmermann was so enchanted with his creation that he constructed a small home in the vicinity and spent the last decade of his life here. A bus heading for the church leaves Füssen Monday to Friday twice per day (once per day on the weekend). Visitors should check the timetable at the station for bus information or ask at the Füssen tourist office (see above). The trip takes 1 hour and costs 5.50€ ($4.90) round-trip.

## WHERE TO STAY

**Fürstenhof** This hotel offers small but well-furnished and well-maintained rooms. Each accommodation comes with a small, shower-only bathroom. The ceilings are of massive exposed paneling, with full-grained beams set into modern stucco. Breakfast is the only meal served.

Kemptenerstrasse 23, 87629 Füssen. ✆ **08362/70-06.** Fax 08362/3-90-48. 15 units. 62€–70€ ($55.35–$62.50) double. Rates include continental buffet breakfast. AE, MC, V. Free parking. **Amenities:** Breakfast room; lounge. *In room:* TV, hair dryer.

**Hotel Christine** The Christine is one of the best local choices. The staff spends the long winter months refurbishing the rooms so they'll be fresh and sparkling for spring visitors. Breakfast, the only meal served, is presented on beautiful regional china as classical music plays in the background. A Bavarian charm pervades the hotel, and the small- to medium-size rooms are very cozy, though hardly fit for King Ludwig were he to return. Bathrooms are a bit cramped, each with shower.

Weidachstrasse 31 (5-min. ride from the train station), 87629 Füssen. ✆ **08362/72-29.** Fax 08362/94-05-54. 13 units. 92€–127.75€ ($82.15–$114.10) double. Rates include continental breakfast. No credit cards. Free parking. Closed Jan 15–Feb 15. **Amenities:** Breakfast room; lounge; room service. *In room:* TV, hair dryer.

**Seegasthof Weissensee** You get a real sense of living in Bavaria here. The paneled rooms at this hotel have sliding-glass doors opening onto a balcony overlooking the lake. Owners take extra care for the comfort of their guests. The rooms are small, but furnished with simple good taste, and designed for the comfort. Each accommodation comes with a small tiled bathroom with shower.

An der B-310 (6km/4 miles from central Füssen on B310), 87629 Füssen-Weissensee. ✆ **08362/9-17-80.** Fax 08362/91-78-88. 19 units. 64€–80€ ($57.15–$71.45) double. Rates include breakfast. No credit cards. Free parking. **Amenities:** Dining room; lounge; room service. *In room:* TV, minibar, hair dryer.

**Steig Mühle** *Value* Owners and hosts Gunter and Hedwig Buhmann like things to be cozy—their chalet-like guesthouse is almost a cliché of Bavarian charm. Rooms open onto a view of the lake or mountains, and many have their own balconies. They're furnished in a neat, functional style and kept immaculately clean. Each room comes with a tiny shower-only bathroom. There aren't a lot of frills here, but the place offers one of the best values in the area.

Alte Steige 3, 87629 Füssen-Weissensee. ✆ **08362/91-76-0.** www.steigmuehle.de. 13 units. 49€–62€ ($43.75–$55.35) double. Rates include buffet breakfast. No credit cards. Free outside parking; 2.50€ ($2.25) in garage. From Füssen, take Rte. 310 toward Kempten, a 5-min. drive. **Amenities:** Breakfast room; lounge. *In room:* TV, hair dryer.

## WHERE TO DINE

**Fischerhütte** ★ SEAFOOD This restaurant is at the edge of the lake, within sight of dramatic mountain scenery. There are four gracefully paneled, old-fashioned dining rooms, along with a terrace in summer. As its name (Fisherman's Cottage) suggests, the establishment specializes in seafood. Menu items read like an international atlas: one-half of an entire Alaskan salmon (for two); North Atlantic lobster; a garlicky version of French bouillabaisse; fresh alpine trout, prepared pan-fried or with aromatic herbs in the style of Provence; and grilled halibut. A limited array of meat dishes is also offered as well as a selection of succulent desserts. In summer, a beer garden serves simple Bavarian specialties.

Uferstrasse 16 (5km/3 miles northwest of Füssen), Hopfen am See. ✆ **08362/9-19-70.** Reservations recommended. Main courses 12.80€–23€ ($11.45–$20.55). AE, DC, MC, V. Daily 10am–2pm and 6–10:30pm.

**Zum Schwanen** SWABIAN/BAVARIAN A conservative yet flavorful blend of Swabian and Bavarian specialties is served to the loyal clients of this small, attractively old-fashioned restaurant. Specialties include homemade sausage, roast pork, lamb, and venison. Service is always helpful and attentive, and you get good value here, along with generous portions.

Brotmarkt 4. ✆ **08362/61-74.** Reservations required. Main courses 7€–16€ ($6.25–$14.30). V. Tues–Sat 11:30am–2pm and 6:30–10pm.

## 13 Neuschwanstein & Hohenschwangau

3km (2 miles) E of Füssen, 116km (72 miles) SW of Munich

Just east of Füssen are the two "Royal Castles" of Hohenschwangau and Neuschwanstein, among the finest in Germany. Hohenschwangau, the more sedate of the two, was built by Maximilian II in 1836; Neuschwanstein was the brainchild of his son, "Mad" King Ludwig II. The extravagant Ludwig was responsible for two other architectural flights of fancy besides Neuschwanstein: Linderhof, near Oberammergau, and Herrenchiemsee, on an island in Chiemsee (see chapter 9). Ludwig died under mysterious circumstances in 1886 (see box below).

After you've fought the crowds to get into these royal castles (in summer, the lines to get in can seem endless), you can spend the remaining time hiking around the surrounding alpine peaks and valleys for what might be some of the most memorable walks of your life. For one of the grandest panoramas in all of the Alps (in any country), hike up to the **Marienbrücke** (the trail is signposted), which spans the Pöllat Gorge behind Neuschwanstein Castle. If you're properly dressed and have stout boots, continue uphill from the gorge for another hour for the most splendid view possible of Mad King Ludwig's fantasy castle.

### ESSENTIALS

**GETTING THERE** **By Bus** Ten buses a day arrive from Füssen (see earlier in section).

**By Car** Head east from Füssen along the B17.

**VISITOR INFORMATION** Information about the castles and the region in general is available at the **Kurverwaltung,** Rathaus, Münchenerstrasse 2, in Schwangau (✆ **08362/8-19-80**), open Monday to Friday 8am to 5pm, Saturday 9am to noon.

### VISITING THE ROYAL CASTLES

Be prepared for very long lines (sometimes up to an incredible 4 or 5 hours) at the castles in the summer, especially in August. On some days, 25,000 people visit.

#### HOHENSCHWANGAU ★

Not as glamorous or spectacular as Neuschwanstein (see below), the neo-Gothic **Hohenschwangau Castle** nevertheless has a much richer history. The original structure dates from the days of the 12th-century knights of Schwangau. When the knights faded away, the castle began to fade, too, helped along by the Napoléonic Wars. When Ludwig II's father, Crown Prince Maximilian (later Maximilian II), saw the castle in 1832, he purchased it and in 4 years had it completely restored. Ludwig II spent the first 17 years of his life here and later received Richard Wagner in its chambers.

The rooms of Hohenschwangau are styled and furnished in a much heavier Gothic mode than those in Neuschwanstein. Many are typical of the halls of knights' castles of the Middle Ages in both England and Germany. There's no doubt that the style greatly influenced young Ludwig and encouraged the fanciful boyhood dreams that formed his later tastes and character. Hohenschwangau,

## The Fairy-Tale King

Ludwig II, often called "Mad" King Ludwig (although some Bavarians hate that label), was born in Munich in 1845, the son of Maximilian II. Only 18 years old when he was crowned king of Bavaria, handsome Ludwig initially attended to affairs of state, but he soon grew bored and turned to less subtle pursuits. Ludwig was a loner who never married. As time went on, he became more and more obsessed with acting out his extravagant fantasies.

At the baroque palace of **Nymphenburg** (see p. 302), the summer residence of the Bavarian rulers, you can still see in the Marstall Royal Stables the richly decorated coaches and sleighs in which young Ludwig loved to travel, often at night, with his spectacular entourage. His crown jewels can be admired in the treasury in the Königsbau wing of the **Residenz** palace, in the heart of Munich (see p. 300).

Ludwig had a long association with Richard Wagner and was both a great fan and a benefactor of the composer. The king had Wagner's operas performed for his own pleasure and watched them in royal and solitary splendor. At Linderhof, the first romantic palace that he built, he went so far as to reconstruct the Venus grotto from the Munich opera stage design for *Tannhäuser.*

Ludwig's architectural creations are legendary. To construct his own Versailles, he chose one of Germany's most beautiful lakes, Chiemsee. He called the palace **Herrenchiemsee** in homage to Louis XIV, the Sun King. Today, visitors can enjoy the castle's Versailles-style Hall of Mirrors and its exquisite gardens (see p. 337). **Linderhof,** in the Graswang Valley near Oberammergau, was a smaller creation but became his favorite castle; it was the only one completed by the time of his death (see p. 354).

Nestled in a crag high above the little town of Hohenswangen is the most famous of the royal designer's efforts, the multiturreted Disney-like **Neuschwanstein** (see below). From a distance, the castle appears more dream-like than real. It's the most photographed castle in Germany. The king's study, bedroom, and living room sport frescoes of scenes from Wagner's operas *Tristan and Isolde* and *Lohengrin.*

Finally, Ludwig's excesses became too much, and he was declared insane in 1886 when he was 41 years old. Three days later, he was found drowned in Lake Starnberg on the outskirts of Munich. He may have committed suicide, or he may have been murdered. A memorial chapel lies on the bank of the lake. Ludwig is buried along with other royals in the crypt beneath the choir of St. Michael's Church.

unlike Neuschwanstein, has a comfortable look about it, looking more like an actual home than just a museum.

Among the most attractive chambers is the **Hall of the Swan Knight,** named for the wall paintings depicting the saga of Lohengrin. Note the Gothic grillwork on the ceiling with the open spaces studded with stars.

Hohenschwangau, Alpseestrasse (✆ **08362/8-11-27**), is open March 15 to October 15, daily 8:30am to 5:30pm; October 16 to March 14, daily 10am to

4pm. Admission is 7.15€ ($6.40) for adults and 4.60€ ($4.10) for students and children 6 to 15; children 5 and under enter free. There are several parking lots that serve both castles.

## NEUSCHWANSTEIN ★★★

Neuschwanstein was King Ludwig II's fairy-tale castle. Construction lasted 17 years until the king's death, when all work stopped, leaving a part of the interior uncompleted. From 1884 to 1886, Ludwig lived in these rooms on and off for a total of only about 6 months.

The doorway off to the left side of the vestibule leads to the king's apartments. The **study,** like most of the rooms, is decorated with wall paintings showing scenes from Nordic legends. The theme of the study is the Tannhäuser saga. The only fabric in the room is hand-embroidered silk, used in curtains and chair coverings, all designed with the gold-and-silver Bavarian coat of arms.

From the vestibule, you enter the **throne room** through the doorway at the opposite end. This hall, designed in Byzantine style by J. Hofmann, was never completed. The floor is a mosaic design, depicting the animals of the world. The columns in the main hall are made of a deep-copper-red porphyry. The circular apse where the king's throne was to have stood is reached by a stairway of white Carrara marble. The walls and ceiling are decorated with paintings of Christ in heaven looking down on the 12 apostles and six canonized kings of Europe.

The **king's bedroom** is the most richly carved in the entire castle—it took 4½ years to complete this room alone. The walls are decorated with panels carved to look like Gothic windows, as well as with a mural depicting the legend of Tristan and Isolde. In the center is a large wooden pillar completely encircled with gilded brass sconces. The ornate bed is on a raised platform with an elaborately carved canopy. Through the balcony window you can see the 46m (150-ft.) waterfall in the Pöllat Gorge, with the mountains in the distance.

The fourth floor of the castle is almost entirely given over to the **Singer's Hall,** the pride of Ludwig II and all of Bavaria. Modeled after the hall at Wartburg, the Singer's Hall is decorated with marble columns and elaborately painted designs interspersed with frescoes depicting the life of Parsifal.

The castle, located at Neuschwansteinstrasse 20 (✆ **08362/8-10-35**), can be visited year-round. In September, visitors have the additional treat of hearing Wagnerian concerts along with other music in the Singer's Hall. For information and reservations, contact the tourist office, **Verkehrsamt,** at the Rathaus in Schwangau (✆ **08362/93-85-23**). Tickets go on sale in early June, and sell out rather quickly. The castle can only be visited on one of the guided tours (offered in English), which are given year-round, except November 1; December 24, 25, and 31; January 1; and Shrove Tuesday. April to October, tours are given 9am to 6pm; November to March, 10am to 4pm. Admission is 7.15€ ($6.40) for adults, 4.60€ ($4.10) for children and students, free for children 15 and under.

Reaching Neuschwanstein involves a steep ½-mile climb from the parking lot at Hohenschwangau Castle (see above). This can be a 25-minute walk for the athletic, an eternity for those less so. To cut down on the climb, you can take a bus to Marienbrücke, a bridge that crosses over the Pöllat Gorge at a height of 93m (305 ft.). From that vantage point, you, like Ludwig, can stand and meditate on the glories of the castle and its panoramic surroundings. If you want to photograph the castle, don't wait until you reach the top, where you'll be too close for a good shot. It costs 2.05€ ($1.85) for the bus ride up to the bridge or 1€ (90¢) if you'd like to take the bus back down the hill. From Marienbrücke, it's a 10-minute walk to Neuschwanstein castle. This footpath is very steep.

The most traditional way to reach Neuschwanstein is by horse-drawn carriage; this costs 5.10€ ($4.55) for the ascent and 2.55€ ($2.30) for the descent. Some readers have complained about the rides being overcrowded and not at all accessible for visitors with disabilities.

## WHERE TO STAY & DINE NEARBY

**Hotel Lisl and Jägerhaus** This graciously styled villa, with an annex across the street, provides views as well as comfort. Both houses sit in a narrow valley, surrounded by their own gardens. Most rooms have a view of at least one of the two royal castles; some superior rooms open onto views of both. We prefer the rooms in the main building to the more sterile annex. Each comes with a compact shower-only bathroom.

Neuschwansteinstrasse 1–3, 87645 Hohenschwangau. ✆ **08362/88-70.** Fax 08362/8-11-07. www.lisl.de. 51 units. 110€–160€ ($98.25–$142.90) double; 200€–360€ ($178.60–$321.50) suite. AE, DC, MC, V. Free parking. **Amenities:** 2 dining rooms; lounge; room service. *In room:* TV.

**Hotel Müller Hohenschwangau** The location of this hospitable inn, near the foundations of Neuschwanstein Castle, makes it alluring. Rooms are comfortable, inviting, and have a bit of Bavarian charm. Each is midsize and filled with tasteful, comfortable furnishings, along with small tiled bathrooms equipped with showers. Nature lovers especially enjoy hiking the short distance to nearby Hohenschwangau Castle.

Alpseestrasse 16, 87645 Hohenschwangau. ✆ **08362/8-19-90.** Fax 08362/81-99-13. www.hotel-mueller.de. 43 units. 120€–160€ ($107.15–$142.90) double; 190€–230€ ($169.65–$205.40) suite. Rates include buffet breakfast. AE, MC, V. Free parking. Closed Jan 1–Feb. Bus from Füssen stops here. **Amenities:** Restaurant; lounge; room service. *In room:* TV.

# 8

# Munich

The people of Munich never need much of a reason for celebrating. If you arrive here in late September, you'll find them in the middle of the **Oktoberfest,** which draws more than 7 million people every fall and lasts for 16 days, ending on the first Sunday in October. Although Oktoberfest, when beer flows as freely as water, is the most famous of Munich's festivals, the city is actually less inhibited during the more interesting pre-Lenten **Fasching** (see chapter 3). Even the most reserved Germans get caught up in this whirl of colorful parades, masked balls, and revelry.

Munich is a lively place all year long—fairs and holidays seem to follow one on top of the other. But this is no "oompah" town. Here you'll find an elegant and tasteful city with sophisticated clubs and restaurants, wonderful theaters, fine concert halls, and fabulous museums. According to various polls, it's also the Germans' first choice as a place to live.

## 1 Orientation

Munich is just slightly smaller than Berlin or Hamburg. You can explore the heart of Munich on foot, but many attractions are in the environs, so you'll have to rely on a car or public transportation.

### ARRIVING

**BY PLANE** About 29km (18 miles) northeast of central Munich at Erdinger Moos, the **Franz Josef Strauss International Airport** (✆ **089/97-52-13-13**), inaugurated in 1992, is among the most modern, best-equipped, and most efficient airports in the world. A second terminal was begun in 2000 and should be completed in 2003. The airport handles more than 400 flights a day, serving at least 65 cities worldwide. Passengers can fly nonstop from New York, Miami, Chicago, and Toronto, among other places.

**S-Bahn** (✆ **089/414-243-44**) trains connect the airport with the Hauptbahnhof (main railroad station) in downtown Munich. Departures are every 20 minutes for the 40-minute trip. The fare is 8€ ($7.15); Eurailpass holders ride free. A taxi into the center costs about 50€ ($44.65). Airport buses, such as those operated by Lufthansa, also run between the airport and the center.

**BY TRAIN** Munich's main rail station, the **Hauptbahnhof,** on Bahnhofplatz near the city center, is one of Europe's largest. It contains a hotel, restaurants, shopping, car parking, and banking facilities. All major German cities are connected to this station. Some 20 daily trains connect Munich to Frankfurt (trip time: 3¾ hr.), and 23 to Berlin (trip time: 6¾ hr.). For information about long-distance trains, call ✆ **01805/99-66-33.**

The rail station is connected with the **S-Bahn** rapid-transit system, a 418km (260-mile) network of tracks, providing service to various city districts and outlying suburbs. For S-Bahn information, call ✆ **089/4142-43-44.** The **U-Bahn**

# Munich Neighborhoods

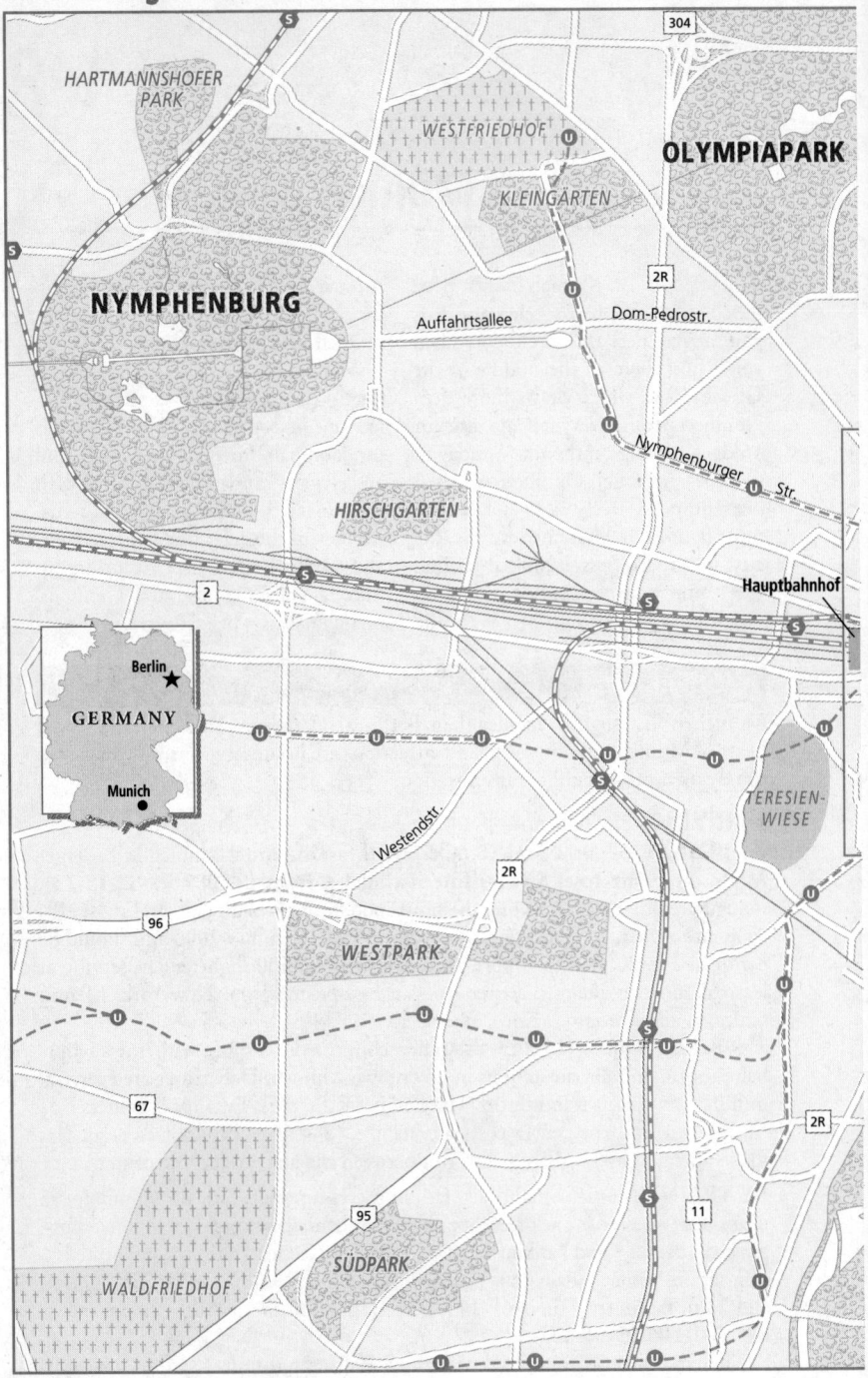

To Airport
NORD-FRIEDHOF
0 0.5 mi
0 0.5 km
N
Church
S-Bahn
U-Bahn
Railway
LUITPOLD-PARK
Leopoldstr.
ENGLISCHER GARTEN
Isar
Schleißheimerstr.
SCHWABING
See "Central Munich" maps
ARABELLAPARK
MUSEUM QUARTER
Königs-platz
Ludwigstr.
BOGENHAUSEN
Odeons-platz
HOFGARTEN
Prinzregentstr.
Residenz
Max-Joseph-Platz
Karlsplatz (Stachus)
Maximilianstr.
LEHEL
Marien-platz
ALTSTADT
PLATZL
Kaulingerstr.
Maximilians-brücke
Sendlinger Tor Platz
Isartor-platz
Gärtner-platz
Gasteig
Ludwigs-brücke
HAIDHAUSEN
Ostbahnhof
FRÜHLINGS-ANLAGEN
OST-FRIEDHOF
FLAUCHER
Hellabrun Tierpark (Zoo)

(subway) system serving Munich is also centered at the rail station. In addition, buses fan out in all directions.

**BY BUS** Munich has long-distance bus service from many German and European cities. Depending on their point of origin, buses depart from the section of the Hauptbahnhof called the West-Wing Starnberger Bahnhof, or from the Deutsche Touring Terminal on Arnulfstrasse 3, about a block away. For information about connections, tariffs, and schedules, call Deutsche Touring GmbH at ✆ **089/54-58-70-11.** Regional service to towns and villages within Bavaria can be arranged through Oberbayern Autobus, Heidemann-Strasse 220 (✆ **089/32-30-40**), or DER, Landshuher Allee (✆ **089/120-4242**).

## VISITOR INFORMATION

The main tourist office, **Fremdenverkehrsamt,** at the Hauptbahnhof, Bahnhofplatz 2 (✆ **089/2-33-03-00;** www.muenchen-tourist.de), is found at the south exit opening onto Bayerstrasse. It offers a free map of Munich and will also reserve rooms (see "Where to Stay," later in this chapter). Its hours are Monday to Saturday 9am to 8pm and Sunday 10am to 6pm.

## CITY LAYOUT

Munich's **Hauptbahnhof,** or rail station, lies just west of the town center and opens onto Bahnhofplatz. From there you can take Schützenstrasse to one of the major centers of Munich, **Karlsplatz** (nicknamed *Stachus*). Many tram lines converge on this square. From Karlsplatz, you can continue east along the pedestrians-only Neuhauserstrasse and Kaufingerstrasse until you reach **Marienplatz,** which is located deep in the **Altstadt (old town)** of Munich.

From Marienplatz you can head north on Dienerstrasse, which will lead you to Residenzstrasse and finally to **Max-Joseph-Platz,** a landmark square, with the Nationaltheater and the former royal palace, the Residenz. East of this square runs **Maximilianstrasse,** the most fashionable shopping and restaurant street of Munich, containing the prestigious Kempinski Hotel Vier Jahreszeiten München. Between Marienplatz and the Nationaltheater is the **Platzl** quarter, where you'll want to head for nighttime diversions; here you'll find some of the finest (and also some of the worst) restaurants in Munich, along with the landmark Hofbräuhaus, the most famous beer hall in Europe.

North of the old town is **Schwabing,** a former bohemian section whose main street is Leopoldstrasse. The large, sprawling municipal park grounds, the **Englischer Garten,** are due east of Schwabing.

**FINDING AN ADDRESS/MAPS** In the Altstadt, "hidden" squares may make finding an address difficult; therefore, you may need a detailed street map, not the more general maps handed out for free by the tourist office and many hotels. The best ones (containing a detailed street index) are published by Falk, and they're available at nearly all bookstores and at many newsstands.

## NEIGHBORHOODS IN BRIEF

**Altstadt** This is the historic part of Munich, the site of the original medieval city. The Altstadt is bounded by the Sendlinger Tor ("Tor" means gate) and Odeonsplatz to the north and the south, and by the Isar Tor and Karlstor to the east and west. The hub is **Marienplatz,** with its Rathaus (Town Hall) and its Glockenspiel performance. You can walk across the district in about 15 minutes.

**Schwabing** This is a large northern section of the city. After 1945, it became known as the bohemian district of Munich, similar to Greenwich Village in New York. **Leopoldstrasse** makes almost a straight axis through its center. The Englischer Garten forms its eastern border, the Studentenstadt is to its north, and Olympiapark and Josephplatz mark its western border.

**Olympiapark** Host to rock and pop concerts on weekends, this residential and recreational area was the site of the 1972 Olympics, which is remembered for the terrorist attack by the Arab "Black September" group against Israeli athletes. The 1972 Munich Olympic Games were meant to show the world the bold new face of a radically rebuilt Munich, showcasing the premises of the innovative Olympic City. The Black September Arab terrorists, however, had different plans. They managed to slip into the compound housing the athletes from Israel and, before the day was over, had slaughtered a total of 11 of Israel's finest athletes, each in place to compete in the Olympic games. A storm of protest was raised around the world. The games were virtually ruined, and Munich's bright new image was shattered (their police force seemed to make mistake after mistake), and dank memories of the Holocaust were revived at a time when Germany, and Munich specifically, was trying to forget its recent past and show the world that it had moved into a brighter and happier future. For more information, see p. 308.

**Museum Quarter** Between the Altstadt and Schwabing is the museum district, containing such great museums as the **Alte Pinakothek** (see "Seeing the Sights," later in this chapter). Bordered by Briennerstrasse and Theresienstrasse, it covers only 2 blocks, but it can take days to explore in depth if you visit all the wonderful state-owned museums.

**Nymphenburg** Take the U-Bahn to Rotkreuzplatz, then tram 12 to reach the Nymphenburg district, about 8km (5 miles) northwest of the city center, site of the summer palace of the Wittelsbach dynasty and the famous porcelain manufacturer (see "Seeing the Sights," later in this chapter).

## 2 Getting Around

The best way to explore Munich is by walking. In fact, because of the vast pedestrian zone in the center, many of the major attractions can only be reached on foot. Pick up a good map and set out.

### BY PUBLIC TRANSPORTATION

The city's underground rapid-transit system, the **U-Bahn** or Untergrundbahn network, is modern and relatively noise-free. The above-ground **S-Bahn,** or Stadtbahn, services suburban locations. At the transport hub, Marienplatz, U-Bahn and S-Bahn rails cross each other.

The same ticket entitles you to ride both the U-Bahn and the S-Bahn, as well as **trams** (streetcars) and **buses.** The U-Bahn is the system you will probably use most frequently. You're allowed to use your Eurailpass on S-Bahn journeys, as it's a state-owned railway. Otherwise, you must purchase a single-trip ticket or a strip ticket for several journeys at one of the blue vending machines positioned at the entryways to the stations.

If you're making only one trip, a **single ticket** will average 2€ ($1.80), although it can reach as high as 8€ ($7.15) to an outlying area. A more economical option is the **strip ticket,** called *Streifenkarte* in German. It's good for several rides and

# Munich U-Bahn & S-Bahn

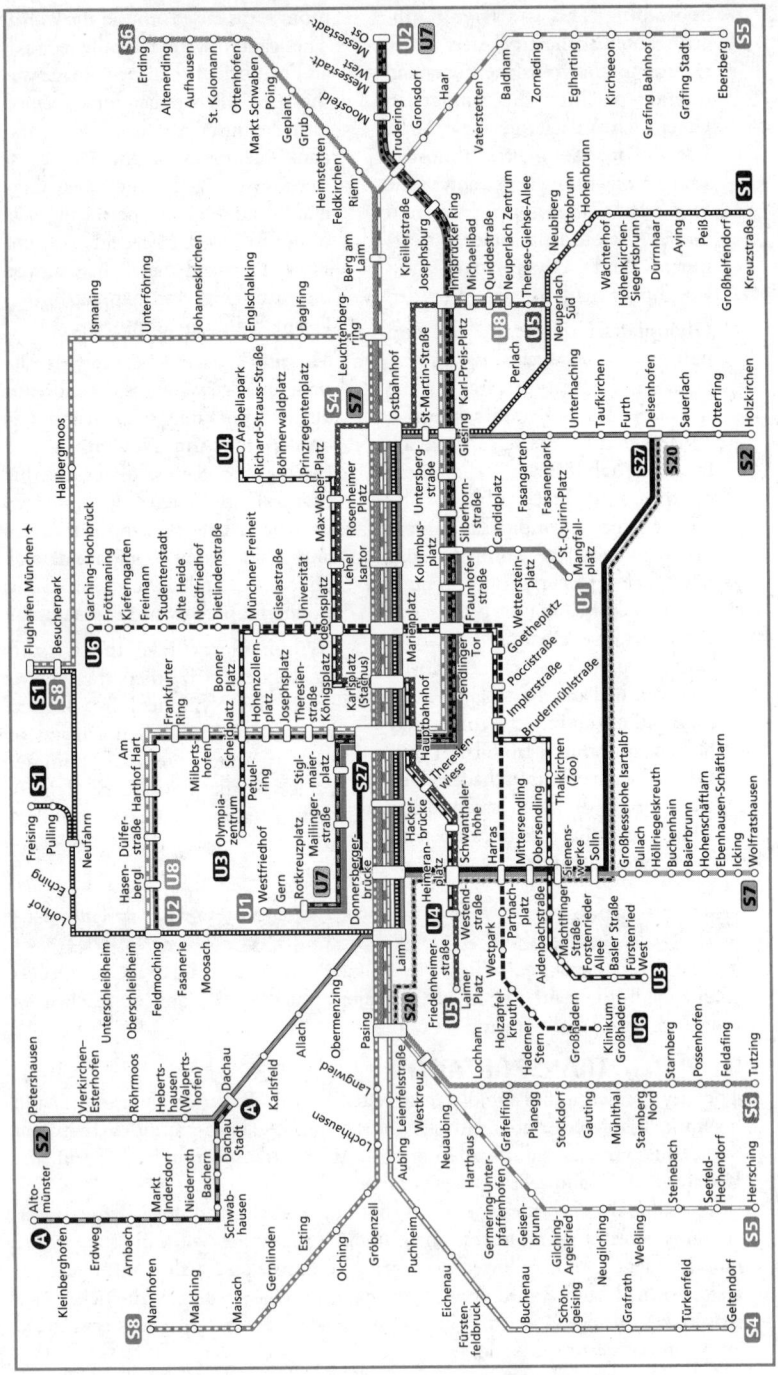

sells for 9€ ($8.05). A trip within the metropolitan area costs you two strips, which are valid for 2 hours. In that time, you may interrupt your trip and transfer as you like to any public transportation, as long as you travel in one continuous direction. When you reverse your direction, you must cancel two strips again. Children 6 to 14 use the red *Kinderstreifenkarte,* costing 3.50€ ($3.15) for five strips; for a trip within the metropolitan area, they cancel only one strip. Children over the age of 15 pay adult fares. A **day ticket** for 4.50€ ($4), called a *Tageskarte,* is also a good investment if you plan to stay within the city limits. If you'd like to branch out to Greater Munich—that is, within an 80km (50-mile) radius—you can purchase a day card for 10€ ($8.95). For public transport information, dial **✆ 089/21-03-30.**

## BY TAXI

Cabs begin at 2.50€ ($2.25), plus an additional 1.20€ ($1.05) per kilometer. Call **✆ 089/21-610** for a radio-dispatched taxi.

## BY CAR

It's usually cheaper to rent a car before leaving for Germany (see "Getting Around," in chapter 3), though you can also rent one here. Major car-rental companies have easy-to-spot offices at the airport.

If you're already in Munich and plan on making excursions into the Bavarian countryside, it's often more convenient to rent a car in the city center instead of trekking out to the airport. Car-rental companies are listed under *Autovermietung* in the Yellow Pages of the Munich phone book. Companies include **Avis,** Nymphenburger Strasse 61 (**✆ 089/12-60-00-20**), and **Sixt Autovermietung,** Einsteinstrasse 106 (**✆ 089/418-0050**), with another branch (**✆ 089/55-02-447**) at Munich's railway station.

Because of heavy traffic, don't attempt to see Munich itself by car. And beware if your hotel doesn't have parking. Parking garages tend to be expensive, often 13€ to 23€ ($11.60–$20.55) per night.

## BY BICYCLE

The tourist office sells a pamphlet for .50€ (45¢) called *Rad-Touren für unsere Gäste;* it outlines itineraries for touring Munich by bicycle. One of the most convenient places to rent a bike is **Aktiv-Rad,** Hans-Sachs-Strasse 7 (**✆ 089/26-65-06;** U-Bahn: Frauenhoferstrasse). It's open Monday to Friday 10am to 1pm and 2 to 6:30pm, Saturday 10am to 1pm. Depending on the bike, rentals cost from 11€ to 20€ ($9.80–$17.85) per 24-hour period.

## FAST FACTS: MUNICH

*American Express* American Express, Promenadeplatz 6 (**✆ 089/29-09-00;** tram: 19), is open for mail pickup and check cashing Monday to Friday 9am to 6pm and Saturday 9:30am to 12:30pm. There are no ATM machines at American Express, but across the street, at Deutsche Bank, Promenadeplatz 1, there are several available 24 hours.

*Bookstores* Try **Anglia English Bookshop,** Schellingstrasse 3 (**✆ 089/28-36-42;** U-bahn: Universität), in the Schwabing district, which sells English-language titles and travel books. It's open Monday to Friday 9:30am to 6:30pm and Saturday 9am to 1pm.

*Business Hours* Most **banks** are open Monday to Friday 8:30am to 12:30pm and 1:30 to 3:30pm (many stay open to 5:30pm on Thurs). Most **businesses** and **stores** are open Monday to Friday 9am to 6pm (many stay open to 8 or 9pm on Thurs) and Saturday 9am to 2pm. On *langer Samstag* (the 1st Sat of the month) stores remain open until 6pm.

*Consulates* See "Embassies & Consulates" in "Fast Facts: Germany," in chapter 3.

*Currency Exchange* You can usually get a better rate at a bank than at your hotel. On Saturday and Sunday or at night, you can exchange money at the rail-station exchange, in Bahnhofplatz; it's open daily 6am to 11:30pm.

*Dentists* For an English-speaking dentist, go to Klinik und Poliklinik für Kieferchirurgie der Universität München, Lindwurmstrasse 2A (✆ **089/51-60-29-11;** U-Bahn: Goetheplatz), the dental clinic for the university. It deals with emergency cases and is always open.

*Doctors* The American, British, and Canadian consulates as well as most hotels keep a list of recommended English-speaking physicians.

*Drugstores* For an international drugstore where English is spoken, try International Ludwig's Apotheke, Neuhauserstrasse 11 (✆ **089/2-60-30-21;** U-bahn/S-Bahn: Marienplatz), in the pedestrian shopping zone. It's open Monday to Friday 9am to 8pm, and Saturday 9am to 4pm.

*E-Mail* Head for the **Times Square Online Bistro** in the Hauptbahnhof, Bayerstrasse side (✆ **089/55-08-8000**). They have 16 computer workstations, a bistro, and bar, and are open daily 7am to 1am.

*Emergencies* For emergency **medical aid,** or for the police, call **110.** For the fire department, call **112.**

*Fax* Head for any of the many hole-in-the-wall kiosks labeled Deutsche Telecom. These include locations on the Marienplatz and in the Hauptbahnhof. Deutsche telecom phone cards are available in denominations of 6.50€ to 30€ ($5.80–$26.80). You can use these to operate self-service fax machines.

*Laundry/Dry Cleaning* A good dry-cleaning establishment is **Paradies Reiningung,** Octtingenstrasse 29 (✆ **089/22-34-65**). Look in the Yellow Pages under either *Wascherei* or *Waschsalon* for a coin-operated laundry near your hotel.

*Post Office* The **Postamt München** (main post office) is across from the Hauptbahnhof, at Bahnhofplatz 1 (✆ **089/599-0870**). If you want to have your mail sent to you, have it addressed Poste Restante, Postamt München, Bahnhofplatz 1, 80074 München, for general delivery. Take along your passport to reclaim any mail. The office is open Monday to Friday 7am to 8pm, Saturday 8am to 4pm, and Sunday 9am to 3pm. There are no fax, phone, or telex facilities available in the post office.

*Radio* Bayern 2 at 88.4 FM presents news in English, French, and Italian from Monday to Friday at 8:50am. You can also listen to the Voice of America at 1197 AM.

*Rest Rooms* Use the word *Toilette* (pronounced twa-*leht*-tah). Rest rooms may be labeled "WC", or "H" (for *Herren,* men) and "F" (for *Frauen,* women). The center of Munich has several clean, safe, and well-kept public facilities.

*Safety* Munich, like all big cities, has its share of crime, especially pickpocketing and purse- and camera-snatching. Most robberies occur in the much-frequented tourist areas, such as Marienplatz and the Hauptbahnhof, which is particularly dangerous at night. Many tourists also lose their valuables when they carelessly leave clothing unprotected as they join the nude sunbathers in the Englischer Garten.

*Television* There are two national TV channels, ARD (Channel 1) and ZDF (Channel 2). Sometimes these stations show films in the original language (most often English). The more expensive hotels often have cable TV, with such channels, in English, as CNN.

## 3 Where to Stay

There are many rooms available in Munich, though most are costly. Bargains are few and far between—but they do exist.

**Fremdenverkehrsamt** (main tourist office), Bahnhofplatz 2 at the Hauptbahnhof (✆ **0891/233-30-123**), open daily 9am to 5pm, is especially good if you arrive in Munich without a hotel reservation. Here, Bavarian personnel (most speak English), with some 35,000 listings in their files, will help you find a place to stay. Tell them what you can afford. They'll book you a room and even give you a map with instructions on how to reach it. Keep your receipt. If you don't like the room, go back to the tourist office, and they'll book you another at no extra charge. Reservations are free but a deposit equal to 10% of the total value of your stay will be collected in advance. For direct access to the hotel booking department, call ✆ **089/233-30-123** or fax 089/233-300-30.

### IN CENTRAL MUNICH

#### VERY EXPENSIVE

**Bayerischer Hof & Palais Montgelas** ★★★ The Bayerischer Hof hotel and the 17th-century Palais Montgelas combine to form a Bavarian version of New York's Waldorf-Astoria. This establishment has been the beneficiary of lavish sums of money's worth of improvements and is now better than ever, a rival even of the front-ranking Kempinski Hotel Vier Jahreszeiten (see below). It's been a favorite ever since King Ludwig I used to come here to take a bath (the royal palace didn't have bathtubs back then). Rooms range from medium to extremely spacious. The decor ranges from Bavarian provincial to British country house chintz. Many beds are four-posters. The large bathrooms have a private phone and plenty of shelf space, with a tub-and-shower combination. Palais Montgelas has 20 of the most upscale rooms as well as conference and banqueting rooms.

Promenadeplatz 2–6, 80333 München. ✆ **800/223-6800** in the U.S., or 089/2-12-00. Fax 089/2-12-09-06. www.bayerischerhof.de. 399 units. 271€–399€ ($242–$356.30) double; 1,089€ ($972.50) suite. AE, DC, MC, V. Parking 19€ ($16.95). Tram: 19. **Amenities:** Restaurant; bar; nightclub; pool; sauna; room service; massage; babysitting; laundry. *In room:* TV, minibar, hair dryer, safe.

**Hotel Palace** ★ It's tasteful, it's restrained, it's perfectly mannered, and it's very, very aware of how prestigious a stay here can really be. One of Munich's newest hotels, it's sought out by performers at the nearby theaters and concert halls as a peaceful and nurturing address in Bogenhausen, a stylish residential

# Central Munich Accommodations & Dining

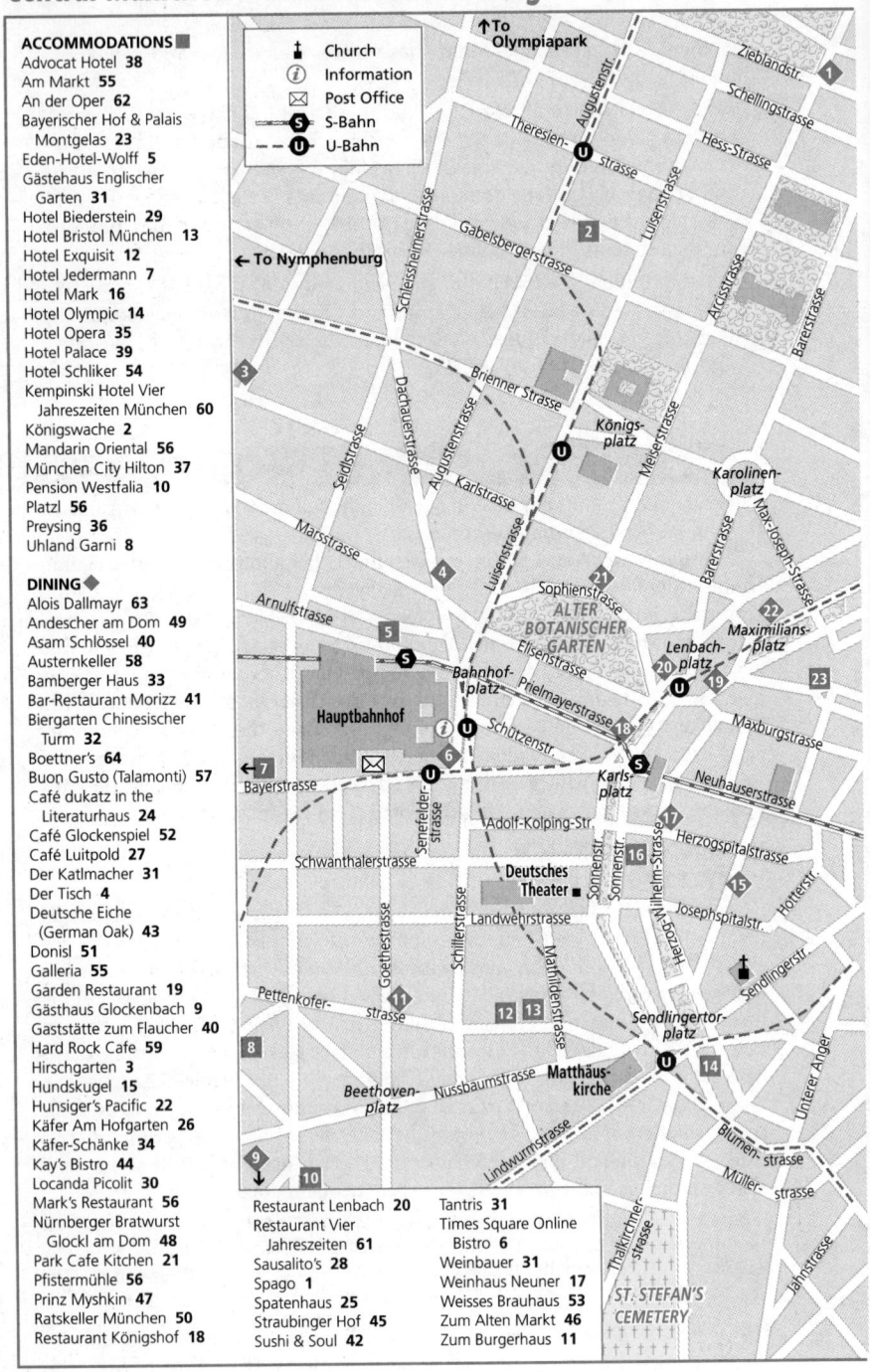


**ACCOMMODATIONS ■**

Advocat Hotel **38**
Am Markt **55**
An der Oper **62**
Bayerischer Hof & Palais Montgelas **23**
Eden-Hotel-Wolff **5**
Gästehaus Englischer Garten **31**
Hotel Biederstein **29**
Hotel Bristol München **13**
Hotel Exquisit **12**
Hotel Jedermann **7**
Hotel Mark **16**
Hotel Olympic **14**
Hotel Opera **35**
Hotel Palace **39**
Hotel Schliker **54**
Kempinski Hotel Vier Jahreszeiten München **60**
Königswache **2**
Mandarin Oriental **56**
München City Hilton **37**
Pension Westfalia **10**
Platzl **56**
Preysing **36**
Uhland Garni **8**

**DINING ◆**

Alois Dallmayr **63**
Andescher am Dom **49**
Asam Schlössel **40**
Austernkeller **58**
Bamberger Haus **33**
Bar-Restaurant Morizz **41**
Biergarten Chinesischer Turm **32**
Boettner's **64**
Buon Gusto (Talamonti) **57**
Café dukatz in the Literaturhaus **24**
Café Glockenspiel **52**
Café Luitpold **27**
Der Katlmacher **31**
Der Tisch **4**
Deutsche Eiche (German Oak) **43**
Donisl **51**
Galleria **55**
Garden Restaurant **19**
Gästhaus Glockenbach **9**
Gaststätte zum Flaucher **40**
Hard Rock Cafe **59**
Hirschgarten **3**
Hundskugel **15**
Hunsiger's Pacific **22**
Käfer Am Hofgarten **26**
Käfer-Schänke **34**
Kay's Bistro **44**
Locanda Picolit **30**
Mark's Restaurant **56**
Nürnberger Bratwurst Glockl am Dom **48**
Park Cafe Kitchen **21**
Pfistermühle **56**
Prinz Myshkin **47**
Ratskeller München **50**
Restaurant Königshof **18**
Restaurant Lenbach **20**
Restaurant Vier Jahreszeiten **61**
Sausalito's **28**
Spago **1**
Spatenhaus **25**
Straubinger Hof **45**
Sushi & Soul **42**
Tantris **31**
Times Square Online Bistro **6**
Weinbauer **31**
Weinhaus Neuner **17**
Weisses Brauhaus **53**
Zum Alten Markt **46**
Zum Burgerhaus **11**

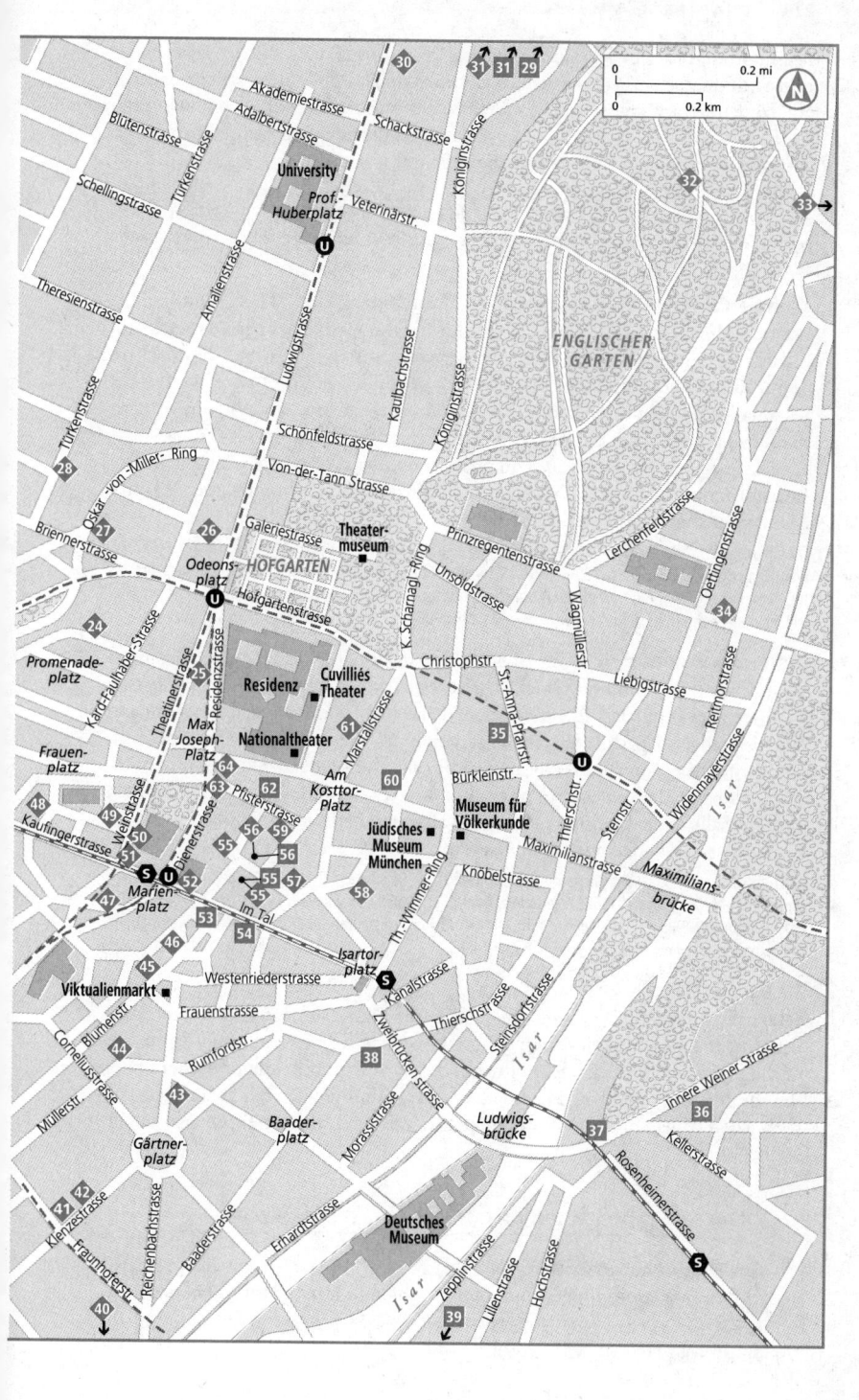
0
0.2 mi
0
0.2 km
N
Akademiestrasse
Adalbertstrasse
Schackstrasse
Königinstrasse
Blütenstrasse
Türkenstrasse
Schellingstrasse
University
Prof.-Huberplatz
Veterinärstr.
Theresienstrasse
Amalienstrasse
Ludwigstrasse
Kaulbachstrasse
ENGLISCHER GARTEN
Türkenstrasse
Schönfeldstrasse
Oskar-von-Miller-Ring
Von-der-Tann Strasse
Briennerstrasse
Galeriestrasse
Theater-museum
Prinzregentenstrasse
Lerchenfeldstrasse
Oettingenstrasse
Odeons-platz
HOFGARTEN
K.-Scharnagl-Ring
Unsöldstrasse
Hofgartenstrasse
Wagmüllerstr.
Kard.-Faulhaber-Strasse
Promenade-platz
Residenzstrasse
Residenz
Cuvilliés Theater
Christophstr.
St.-Anna-Pfarrstr.
Liebigstrasse
Reitmorstrasse
Theatinerstrasse
Max Joseph-Platz
Nationaltheater
Marstallstrasse
Frauen-platz
Am Kosttor-Platz
Bürkleinstr.
Widenmayerstrasse
Isar
Weinstrasse
Pfisterstrasse
Dienerstrasse
Museum für Völkerkunde
Thierschstr.
Sternstr.
Kaufingerstrasse
Jüdisches Museum München
Maximilianstrasse
Th.-Wimmer-Ring
Knöbelstrasse
Maximilians-brücke
Marien-platz
Im Tal
Isartor-platz
Westenniederstrasse
Kanalstrasse
Viktualienmarkt
Frauenstrasse
Thierschstrasse
Steinsdorfstrasse
Blumenstr.
Corneliusstrasse
Rumfordstr.
Zweibrückenstrasse
Innere Weiner Strasse
Müllerstr.
Morassistrasse
Ludwigs-brücke
Kellerstrasse
Baader-platz
Gärtner-platz
Rosenheimerstrasse
Klenzestrasse
Reichenbachstrasse
Baaderstrasse
Erhardtstrasse
Deutsches Museum
Fraunhoferstr.
Zeppelinstrasse
Lillienstrasse
Hochstrasse

neighborhood east of Munich's medieval core. Originally built in 1986 as an office building, it was later transformed into a hotel. Public areas are streamlined and contemporary, graced with elaborate hyper-modern balustrades on travertine-sheathed staircases. Rooms are immaculate and upscale, and each comes with a luxurious bathroom with tub-and-shower combination.

Trogerstrasse 21, D-81675 München. ✆ **089/41971-0.** Fax 089/41971-819. www.dpmu.de. 72 units. 260€–320€ ($232.20–$285.75) double; 340€–1,050€ ($303.60–$937.65) suite. AE, DC, MC, V. U-Bahn: Prinzregentumplatz. **Amenities:** Restaurant; bar; health club; sauna; steam room; room service; laundry. *In room:* A/C, TV, minibar, hair dryer, safe.

**Kempinski Hotel Vier Jahreszeiten München** ★★★ This grand hotel is not only the most elegant in Munich, but it's also Germany's most famous and distinctive, and among the finest in the world. Its tradition stretches back to 1858. Rooms and suites—which have hosted royalty, heads of state, and famed personalities from all over the world—combine the charm of days gone by with modern luxuries. The antique-style beds feature fine linen on sumptuous mattresses. The large bathrooms are equipped with all sorts of special treats, including luxurious robes and a tub-and-shower combination. The windows opening onto Maximilianstrasse are double-glazed.

Maximilianstrasse 17, 80539 München. ✆ **800/426-3135** in the U.S., or 089/2-12-50. Fax 089/21-25-27-77. www.kempinski.com. 316 units. 285€–385€ ($254.50–$343.80) double; from 590€ ($526.85) suite. AE, DC, MC, V. Parking 20€ ($17.85). Tram: 19. **Amenities:** Restaurant; bar; pool; sauna; solarium; 24-hr. room service; massage; babysitting; laundry/dry cleaning. *In room:* A/C, TV, dataport, minibar, hair dryer, safe.

**Mandarin Oriental** ★ One of Munich's smaller hotels is also one of its most posh. Only the Kempinski Hotel Vier Jahreszeiten München and the Bayerischer Hof (see above) outclass this sophisticated and luxurious winner. The stylish and elegant wedge-shaped 1880s building combines neo-Renaissance, neoclassical, and Biedermeier touches. It's located within sight of the Frauenkirche at Marienplatz. A marble staircase sweeps upward to the very comfortable, large rooms, each with specially crafted furniture or original antiques. Bathrooms are well appointed, each with a tub-and-shower combination.

Neuturmstrasse 1, 80331 München. ✆ **089/29-09-80.** Fax 089/22-25-39. www.mandarinoriental.com. 73 units. 330€–420€ ($294.70–$375.05) double; from 530€ ($473.30) suite. AE, DC, MC, V. Parking 19.50€ ($17.40). U-Bahn/S-Bahn: Marienplatz. Tram: 19. **Amenities:** 2 restaurants; bar; pool; room service; babysitting; laundry. *In room:* A/C, TV, minibar, hair dryer, safe.

## EXPENSIVE

**Eden-Hotel-Wolff** ★ If you must stay in the train station area, this is your best bet, despite the fact that it's often booked by groups. The austere stone-clad facade of the Eden-Hotel-Wolff does not reveal the warmth of the interior decoration or the comfort this hotel has. The interior is richly traditional, with chandeliers and dark-wood paneling. A few of the rooms are small, but most are spacious, and all

### *Kids* Family-Friendly Hotels

**Gästehaus Englischer Garten** (*see p. 282*) This ivy-covered villa oasis of calm and tranquility provides old-fashioned family atmosphere.

**Hotel Jedermann** (*see p. 281*) Families on a budget like this hotel, which supplies cribs or cots.

are tastefully furnished in a decor that runs the gamut from extremely modern to rustic. Bathrooms are large, each with a tub and shower. Some units are hypoallergenic, with special beds and a private ventilation system.

Arnulfstrasse 4–8 (opposite the train station), 80335 München. ✆ **089/55-11-50.** Fax 089/55-11-55-55. www.ehw.de. 210 units. 169€–289€ ($150.90–$258.10) double; 368€ ($328.60) suite. 1 child up to age 6 stays free in parents' room. Rates include buffet breakfast. AE, DC, MC, V. Parking 14€ ($12.50). U-Bahn/S-Bahn: Hauptbahnhof. **Amenities:** Restaurant; bar; car rental; laundry/dry cleaning. *In room:* TV, minibar, hair dryer.

**Hotel Opera** ★ *Finds* This charming little gem (not to be confused with the Hotel an der Opera) is a recent discovery of ours. It's filled with comfort and an authentic Bavarian atmosphere so lacking in many postwar Munich hotels. Each room is beautifully and individually decorated, often with antiques from the countryside. Those overlooking the courtyard contain French doors leading to small balconies. Those at the rear on the third and fourth floors are more tranquil, although they're slightly smaller than those fronting the street. Bathrooms are relatively small but well maintained, each with tub and shower. The location is desirable, too, only a 12-minute walk from the chic Maximilianstrasse, with some of the city's major attractions virtually at your doorstep.

St-Anna Strasse 10, 80538 München. ✆ **089/22-55-33.** Fax 089/21-04-09-77. www.hotel-opera.de. 25 units. 185€–210€ ($165.20–$187.55) double; 265€–295€ ($236.65–$263.45) suite. AE, MC, V. Parking 23€ ($20.55) nearby. U-Bahn: Lehel. **Amenities:** Breakfast room; bar; Jacuzzi; room service; laundry/dry cleaning; private garden. *In room:* TV, hair dryer.

## MODERATE

**Advokat Hotel** This hotel occupies a six-story apartment house originally constructed in the 1930s. Its stripped-down, streamlined interior borrows in discreet ways from Bauhaus and minimalist models. One Munich critic said the rooms look as if Philippe Starck had gone on a shopping binge at Ikea. The result is an aggressively simple, clean-lined, and artfully spartan hotel with few facilities, except each room comes with a well-equipped, compact bathroom, mainly with both tub and shower. The German government gives it three stars. The Advokat lies around the corner from its more upscale neighbor, the Hotel Admiral, with which it shares management, but whose rooms cost 30€ ($26.80) more, double occupancy, per category. There's no restaurant on the premises and no particular extras to speak of other than a cozy in-house bar and a delightful roof top breakfast. But the prices are reasonable, and the staff is helpful.

Baaderstrasse 1, 80469 München. ✆ **089/21-63-10.** Fax 089/21-63-190. www.hotel-advokat.de. 50 units. 165€–185€ ($147.35–$165.20) double; from 195€ ($174.15) suite. Rates include breakfast. S-Bahn: Isartor. **Amenities:** Breakfast room; bar. *In room:* TV, minibar.

**An der Oper** This five-floor hotel, built in 1969, is superbly located for sightseeing or shopping in the traffic-free malls, and it's just steps from the Bavarian National Theater. In spite of its basic decor, there are touches of elegance. Rooms, which range from small to medium, have double-glazed windows, a small sitting area with armchairs, and a table for those who want breakfast in their rooms. Bathrooms tend to be small, but are well organized and come mainly with just a shower.

Falkenturmstrasse 11 (just off Maximilianstrasse, near Marienplatz), 80331 München. ✆ **089/2-90-02-70.** Fax 089/29-00-27-29. www.hotelanderoper.com. 68 units. 145€–180€ ($129.50–$160.75) double. Rates include buffet breakfast. AE, MC, V. Parking 15€ ($13.40) nearby. Tram: 19. **Amenities:** Breakfast room; lounge; room service. *In room:* TV, minibar, hair dryer.

**Hotel Exquisit** ★ One of the most appealing hotels in the Sendlinger Tor neighborhood lies behind a wine-colored facade on a quiet residential street that seems far removed from the heavy traffic and bustle of the nearby theater district. Built in 1988, it has a paneled lobby whose focal point is a lounge that gets busy around 6 or 7pm. Staff is unusually pleasant, offering a genuine welcome and ushering you up to rooms that are spacious and comfortably furnished. About half overlook an ivy-draped garden, others look over the street. Bathrooms are efficient, with adequate shelf space and a tiled shower unit.

Pettenkoferstrasse 3, D-80336 München. ✆ **089/55-19-900.** Fax 089/55-199-499. www.augustiner-restaurant.com. 50 units. 120€–180€ ($107.15–$160.75) double, 185€ ($165.20) suite. Rates include breakfast. AE, DC, MC, V. U-Bahn: Sendlinger Tor. **Amenities:** Breakfast room; bar; sauna; solarium; room service; private garden. *In room:* TV, minibar, hair dryer.

**Hotel Mark** *Value* This hotel near the Hauptbahnhof's south exit is known for comfort and moderate prices. The rooms are functionally furnished, although a bit cramped, and mattresses were recently renewed, so you should sleep in peace. Bathrooms are small but tidily maintained, each with a shower unit. Breakfast is the only meal served.

Senefelderstrasse 12, D-80336 München. ✆ **089/55-98-20.** Fax 089/559-82-333. www.heh.de. 90 units. 112.40€–235.05€ ($110–$230) double. Rates include buffet breakfast. AE, DC, MC, V. Parking 7.65€ ($7.50). U-Bahn/S-Bahn: Hauptbahnhof. **Amenities:** Breakfast room. *In room:* TV, minibar.

**Hotel Olympic** ★ Built as a private villa around 1900, this hotel represents one of Munich's most appealing conversions of an antique building into a hip and attractive hotel. The lobby occupies a high-ceilinged, Victorian vestibule that retains many of the original details. Breakfast is served in a very large, graciously proportioned dining room where memories of the grand bourgeoisie of the Industrial Revolution still seem to permeate the woodwork. Rooms are minimalist and all white, much more modern than the ground-floor reception areas, but comfortable and well engineered. Most of the midsize bathrooms come with shower only. The hotel has earned an increasing number of gay clients recently, thanks to its location within a neighborhood that's loaded with gay bars and hangouts.

Hans Sachs Strasse 4, D-80469 München. ✆ **089/231-89-0.** Fax 089/231-89-199. www.hotel-olympic.de. 38 units. 130€ ($116.10) double; 150€ ($133.95) suite. Rates include breakfast. AE, DC, MC, V. U-Bahn: Sendlinger Tor. **Amenities:** Breakfast room; lounge; room service. *In room:* TV, minibar.

**Königswache** Built in 1962, the Königswache offers much to recommend it, in spite of its sterile facade. The location, about a 10-minute ride from the Hauptbahnhof and only 2 minutes from the technical university, is between Karlsplatz and Schwabing—a district safer at night than the railway-station area. The staff speaks English. Rooms are modern and comfortable, ranging from small to midsize, each coming with a compact tiled bathroom with a shower unit.

Steinheilstrasse 7, 80333 München. ✆ **089/5-42-75-70.** Fax 089/5-23-21-14. www.koenigswache.de. 39 units. 105€–176€ ($93.75–$157.15) double. Rates include buffet breakfast. AE, DC, MC, V. Parking garage (reservation required) 8€ ($7.15). U-Bahn: Theresienstrasse. **Amenities:** Breakfast room; bar; lounge; room service. *In room:* TV, minibar, hair dryer, safe.

## INEXPENSIVE

**Am Markt** This popular, though not luxurious, Bavarian hotel stands in the heart of the older section. Owner Harald Herrler has maintained a nostalgic decor in the lobby. Behind his reception desk is a wall of photographs of friends or former guests, including the late Viennese chanteuse Greta Keller. As Mr. Herrler points out, when you have breakfast here, you're likely to find yourself surrounded by opera and concert artists; the hotel is close to where they perform. Rooms are quite small, but modern and neat. Mattresses are well worn but comfortable. All units have sinks with hot and cold running water.

Heiliggeistrasse 6, 80331 München. ✆ **089/22-50-14.** Fax 089/22-40-17. 32 units, 12 with bathroom. 66€ ($58.95) double without bathroom; 87€–92€ ($77.70–$82.15) double with bathroom. Rates include continental breakfast. Parking 8€ ($7.15). S-Bahn: Marienplatz. **Amenities:** Breakfast room; lounge; room service. *In room:* TV.

**Hotel Biederstein** *Finds* Near the Englisher Garten, this B&B is a charmer and a new addition on the Munich hotel scene. Newly renovated, it is decorated with designer-style modern furnishings in the minimalistic style and is operated by the same people who run Gästehaus Englischer Garten, one of the most charming and heavily booked small inns of Munich. The hotel rents bikes to its guests to ride through the English Garden. Bedrooms are spacious and comfortable with neat tiled bathrooms with shower only. A first-rate breakfast is served on the terrace.

Keferstrasse 18, 80802 Munchen. ✆ **089/3899970.** Fax 089/389997389. 34 units. 95€–136€ ($84.85–$121.45) double, 132€–190€ ($117.90–$169.65) suite. V. Parking 8€ ($7.15). U-Bahn: Münchener Freiheit. **Amenties:** Breakfast terrace, room service for breakfast, laundry. *In room:* TV.

**Hotel Bristol München** Built around 1960, in a four-story format that includes a boxy-looking facade and a tiny reception area, this is an easy-to-live-in hotel with kindly management. Quieter rooms in back overlook a sheltered courtyard. Each has a tiny balcony and efficient but comfortable furnishings, plus a neatly organized and compact bathroom in tile containing a shower unit. There's no restaurant on-site, but the desk staff maintains good dialogues with several worthwhile restaurants within the neighborhood.

Pettenkoferstrasse 2, D-80336 München. ✆ **089/54-82-22-0.** Fax 089/59-14-51. www.bristol-muc.com. 57 units. 87€–97€ ($77.70–$86.60) double. Rates rise to 150€ ($133.95) during trade fairs. Rates include breakfast. AE, DC, MC, V. U-Bahn: Sendlinger Tor. **Amenities:** Breakfast room; lounge; room service. *In room:* TV, minibar, hair dryer.

**Hotel Jedermann** *Value* *Kids* Those in awe of the high prices of Munich hotels find comfort here. This pleasant, cozy spot has been deftly run by the Jenke family since 1961. Its central location and good value make it a desirable choice, especially for families (cribs and cots are available). The old-fashioned Bavarian rooms are generally small, but cozy and comfortable, each with a shower-only bathroom. A generous breakfast buffet is served in a charming room.

Bayerstrasse 95, 80335 München. ✆ **089/54-32-40.** Fax 089/54-32-4111. www.hotel-jedermann.de. 52 units, 47 with shower and toilet. 49€–74€ ($43.75–$66.10) double without bathroom; 67€–149€ ($59.85–$133.05) double with bathroom; 95€–160€ ($84.85–$142.90) triple with bathroom. Rates include buffet breakfast. MC, V. Parking 6.15€ ($6). 10-min. walk from Hauptbahnhof (turn right on Bayerstrasse from south exit). **Amenities:** Breakfast room; lounge; room service. *In room:* TV, safe.

**Hotel Schlicker** *Finds* In spite of its location between a McDonald's and a Burger King, this is a hotel of charm and tradition, with a pedigree going back to 1544. With a stay here you are in the heart of Munich, just steps away from the landmark Marienplatz and around the corner from our favorite food market in Germany, Viktualienmarkt. Only the breakfast room suggests that this place was once an ancient inn: The rest of the hotel is modernized. This friendly, inviting hotel is run by the Mayer family, a tradition since 1897. Bedrooms are comfortable and traditional, each midsize and come with a tiled, midsize bathroom with shower and tub.

Tal 74, 80331 München. ✆ **089/2428870.** Fax 089/296059. www.hotel-schlicker.de 69 units. 105€–156€ ($93.75–$139.30) double, 180€–215€ ($160.75–$192) suite. AE, DC, MC, V. Parking 10€ ($8.95). U-Bahn: Marienplatz. **Amenities:** Breakfast room, room service for breakfast. *In room:* TV.

**Pension Westfalia** ★ *Value* This four-story town house, originally built in 1895, near Goetheplatz is one of Munich's best pensions. It faces the meadow where the annual Oktoberfest takes place. Rooms are rather functional, and short on extras, but are well maintained, each with a small shower-only bathroom. Owner Peter Deiritz speaks English. Parking is free on the street when available.

Mozartstrasse 23, 80336 München. ✆ **089/53-03-77.** Fax 089/5-43-91-20. www.pension-westfalia.de. 19 units, 14 with bathroom. 52€ ($46.45) double without bathroom; 65€–75€ ($58.05–$67) double with bathroom. Rates include buffet breakfast. MC, V. U-Bahn: Goetheplatz. Bus: 58. **Amenities:** Breakfast room; lounge. *In room:* TV (only in 3 rooms).

**Uhland Garni** Located in a residential area, just a 10-minute walk from the Hauptbahnhof, the Uhland could easily become your home in Munich. The stately town mansion, built in Art Nouveau style, stands in its own small garden. The hotel offers friendly, personal service, and rooms are soundproof, snug, traditional, and cozy. Bathrooms contain showers. Only breakfast is served.

Uhlandstrasse 1, 80336 München. ✆ **089/54-33-50.** Fax 089/54-33-52-50. www.hotel-uhland.de. 25 units. 80€–160€ ($71.45–$142.90) double. Rates include buffet breakfast. AE, DC, MC, V. Free parking. Bus: 58. **Amenities:** Breakfast room; lounge; room service. *In room:* TV, minibar, hair dryer.

## IN SCHWABING

**Gästehaus Englischer Garten** ★★ *Kids* This oasis of charm and tranquility, close to the Englischer Garten, is one of our preferred stopovers in Munich. The decor of the small to medium rooms has been called "Bavarian grandmotherly"; furnishings include genuine antiques, old-fashioned but exceedingly comfortable beds, and Oriental rugs. Bathrooms with showers are small and not one of the hotel's stronger features, but their maintenance is first-rate. Fifteen units are across the street in an annex; these are small apartments, each with a bathroom and a tiny kitchenette. Try for room 10, 20, 30, or 90. In fair weather, breakfast is served in a rear garden.

Liebergesellstrasse 8, 80802 München-Schwabing. ✆ **089/3-83-94-10.** Fax 089/38-39-41-33. 25 units, 20 with bathroom. 68€–78€ ($60.70–$69.65) double without bathroom; 88€–109€ ($78.60–$97.35) double with bathroom. Breakfast 8.50€ ($7.60) extra. AE, MC, V. Parking 5.10€ ($5). U-Bahn: Münchener Freiheit. **Amenities:** Breakfast room; lounge; room service; private garden. *In room:* TV, minibar.

## IN HAIDHAUSEN

**München City Hilton** ★ The München City Hilton lies beside the Deutsches Museum and the performing arts center, Gasteig. This low-rise hotel, designed with red brick, shimmering glass, and geometric windows, is reminiscent of a Mondrian painting. Munich's historic center is an invigorating 25-minute walk across the river. Rooms contain modern adaptations of Biedermeier furniture and plush carpeting. The well-stocked bathrooms contain shower-tub combinations and luxurious robes.

Rosenheimerstrasse 15, 81667 München. ✆ **800/455-8667** in the U.S. and Canada, or 089/4-80-40. Fax 089/48-04-48-04. www.hilton.com. 481 units. 116€–395€ ($103.60–$352.75) double; from 495€ ($442.05) suite. AE, DC, MC, V. Parking 15€ ($13.40). S-Bahn: Rosenheimer Platz. **Amenities:** Restaurant; bar; cafe; room service; babysitting; laundry/dry cleaning. *In room:* A/C, TV, minibar, hair dryer.

**Preysing** ★ *Finds* If you want a quiet location and don't mind a hotel on the outskirts, consider the Preysing, located across the Isar near the Deutsches Museum. (A short tram ride will bring you into the center of the city.) When you first view the building, a seven-story modern structure, you may feel we've misled you. However, if you've gone this far, venture inside for a pleasant surprise. The hotel's style is agreeable, with dozens of little extras to provide home-like comfort.

Fresh flowers are everywhere, the furnishings have been carefully selected, and fresh fruit is supplied daily. The spacious bathrooms have shower-tub combinations and deluxe toiletries. The staff is also one of the most thoughtful in Munich.

Preysingstrasse 1, 81667 München. ✆ **089/45-84-50.** Fax 089/45-84-54-44. 76 units. 160€–212€ ($142.90–$189.30) double; 250€–390€ ($223.25–$348.25) suite. Rates include breakfast. AE, DC, MC, V. Parking 12€ ($10.70). Tram: 18. **Amenities:** Breakfast room; lounge; pool; whirlpool; sauna; solarium; babysitting; room service; laundry. *In room:* A/C, TV, minibar, hair dryer.

## 4 Where to Dine

Munich is one of the very few European cities that has more than one Michelin-rated "three-star" restaurant. This is the place to practice *Edelfresswelle* ("high-class gluttony"). The classic local dish, traditionally consumed before noon, is *Weisswurste,* herb-flavored white-veal sausages blanched in water. Sophisticated international cuisine is popular throughout the city, too.

### IN CENTRAL MUNICH

#### VERY EXPENSIVE

**Boettner's** ★★ INTERNATIONAL Long featured in this guide, Boettner's—in business since 1901 when it first opened as a tea and oyster shop—thrives at a new location where it has kept its old devotees but also gained new and younger fans. The restaurant today is housed in Orlandohaus, a Renaissance structure in the very heart of Munich. Culinary fans from yesterday will recognize its wood-paneled interior, which was dismantled and moved to the new site. If anything, the cookery seems better than ever—at least it's lighter and more refined. Try the lobster stew in a cream sauce and almost any dish with white truffles. Pike balls appear delectably in a Chablis herb sauce, and succulent lamb or venison also appears enticingly in a woodsy morel sauce. Desserts are as sumptuous as ever. The French influence is very evident, as are many traditional Bavarian recipes.

Pfisterstrasse 9. ✆ **089/22-12-10.** Reservations recommended. Main courses 25€–32€ ($22.35–$28.60). AE, DC, MC, V. Mon–Sat 11:30am–2:30pm and 6–9:30pm. U-Bahn: Marienplatz.

**Garden Restaurant** ★ MEDITERRANEAN/INTERNATIONAL This showcase restaurant within one of the showcase hotels of Munich looks like a miniature pastel-colored palace. It's set in a solemnly hushed room filled with blooming plants off the otherwise bustling hotel lobby. Upscale food is served to a cosmopolitan crowd. Menu items are about as cultivated and esoteric as you can find in Munich. Examples include thin noodles with strips of quail and mushroom sauce; a "land and sea" salad—a bouquet of greens accented with lobster meat and calves' liver; a soup of exotic mushrooms in puff pastry; and filet of beef stuffed with goose liver and fresh mushrooms. Despite the elaborate menu, one of the most sought-after dishes is filet of Dover sole in lemon-butter sauce, served simply but flavorfully with fresh spinach and boiled potatoes. Desserts are appropriately lavish, and wine choices are among the most varied in Munich.

In the Bayerischer Hof Hotel, Promenadeplatz 2–6. ✆ **089/21200.** Reservations recommended. Main courses 19€–30€ ($16.95–$26.80); fixed-price lunch 30€ ($26.80); fixed-price dinner 50€ ($44.65). AE, DC, MC, V. Daily noon–3pm and 6–11:30pm. Tram: 19.

**Restaurant Königshof** ★ INTERNATIONAL This still remains one of the grand hotel dining rooms of Munich. The Geisel family has made major renovations to the dining room, with its oyster-white panels of oak, polished bronze chandeliers, silver candelabra, and porcelain. The waiters are polite and skilled. The chefs here are highly inventive. They like extremely fresh ingredients, and the food here reflects this passion. If available, try the foie gras with sauternes, loin of lamb with fine herbs, curried breast of duck, lobster with vanilla butter, or sea bass supreme.

In the Hotel Königshof, Karlsplatz 25 (Am Stachus). ✆ **089/55-13-60.** Reservations required. Main courses 22€–35€ ($19.65–$31.25); fixed-price menu 75€–97€ ($67–$86.60). AE, DC, MC, V. Daily noon–2:30pm and 6:30–10pm. U-Bahn/S-Bahn: Karlsplatz/Stachus. Tram: 19.

**Restaurant Vier Jahreszeiten** ★ INTERNATIONAL Restaurant Vier Jahreszeiten is in a quiet and elegant location within walking distance of the opera house. The atmosphere is dignified and refined, the service extremely competent, and the food prepared along classic French lines with many imaginative variations, including Asian influences. The menu changes every 4 to 6 weeks, but appetizers are likely to include mushroom soufflé served with artichoke-cream sauce, freshly made vegetable soup flavored with pesto, or turbot encased in basil-flavored crust. For a main course, try breast of Bresse chicken with scampi, flavored with a ginger sauce; or roast medallions of venison with cherry-pepper sauce. Another specialty is blanquette of veal and lobster. Desserts include strawberries Walterspiel or, for two, tangerine soufflé served with foamy vanilla sauce.

> *Tips* **A Map Note**
>
> For the location of restaurants in this section, see the "Central Munich Accommodations & Dining" map on p. 276.

In the Kempinski Hotel Vier Jahreszeiten München, Maximilianstrasse 17. ✆ **089/2-12-50.** Reservations required. Main courses 22€–40€ ($19.65–$35.70); 3-course fixed-price menu 45€ ($40.20). AE, DC, MC, V. Daily noon–1:30am. Tram: 19.

## EXPENSIVE

**Austernkeller** ★ SEAFOOD This "oyster cellar" is a delight to both visitors and locals. You get the largest selection of oysters in town, from raw oysters to elaborate preparations such as oysters Rockefeller. A delectable dish to start is the shellfish platter with fresh oysters, mussels, clams, scampi, and sea snails. Or you might begin with a richly stocked fish soup or cold hors d'oeuvres. French meat specialties are also offered, but the focus is seafood—everything from lobster thermidor to shrimp grilled in the shell. The decor is elegant and refined, and the service is attentive.

Stollbergstrasse 11. ✆ **089/29-87-87.** Reservations required. Main courses 1€–30€ (90¢–$26.80). AE, DC, MC, V. Daily 5pm–1am. Closed Dec 23–26. U-Bahn: Isartor.

**Kay's Bistro** ★★ INTERNATIONAL It's fun, media-hip, and schmaltzy, with a clientele that's either blatantly gay or very, very tolerant. Every month or so, the decor is redefined, based on glittering themes that have included Carnival in Rio, Grace and the Grand Prix of Monaco, Chinatown, "Hooray for Hollywood," and—when we happened to drop in—New York City, when accessories included shopping bags from Bloomingdale's and plastic replicas of the Statue of Liberty. Even the background music is carefully calibrated to go with the theme of the moment. The place is fun, campy, and favored by celebrities who have included disco diva Gloria Gaynor. The cuisine changes frequently, but is light, urbane, and flavorful, and sometimes named after pop icons, such as Indian-style chicken breast "Diana Vreeland." Drinks include, among others, Louisiana milk punch and an almost psychedelic Velvet Underground.

Utzschneiderstrasse 1. ✆ **089/2-60-35-84.** Reservations required. Main courses 17.50€–20€ ($15.65–$17.85). AE, MC, V. Daily 7pm–3am. U-Bahn/S-Bahn: Marienplatz.

**La Galleria** ★ ITALIAN This is one of the most appealing of the several Italian restaurants in Munich's center and the one that takes the greatest risks with experimental Italian cuisine. It provides gracious service and a roster of dishes that change with the availability of ingredients and the inspiration of the chefs. Examples are poached sea wolf with fresh vegetables in fennel sauce; an aromatic guinea fowl scented with lavender; homemade spaghetti with white Italian truffles; herb-flavored risotto with chunks of lobster and braised radicchio (the best we've had in Munich); and roasted soft-shell crabs with a light onion sauce. Dessert might include a smooth zabaglione served with pears marinated in port wine.

Lederestrasse 2, at Sparkassenstrasse. ✆ **089/29-79-95.** Reservations recommended. Main courses 15€–22€ ($13.40–$19.65); fixed-price dinner 45€–50€ ($40.20–$44.65). AE, DC, MC, V. Mon–Sat noon–3pm and 6–11:30pm. Closed Aug 10–30. U-Bahn/S-Bahn: Marienplatz.

**Mark's Restaurant** ★ CONTINENTAL This restaurant, in the prestigious Mandarin Oriental, is appropriately elegant with an impeccably trained staff. Lunch is served in a small, cozy enclave off the lobby, Mark's Corner, and is usually limited to a fixed-price menu favored by businesspeople. Dinners are swankier and more elaborate; they're served one floor above street level in a formal dining room that overlooks a monumental staircase and the lobby below. On Sunday and Monday night only, the formal dining room is closed, and dinner is served in Mark's Corner. Menu items change according to the season and the inspiration of the chef. Many dishes are somewhat experimental but still succeed beautifully. Examples include filet of beef with a ragout of artichokes and potatoes and deep-fried baby garlic buds; sea wolf with green lentils, bacon, and goose liver; filet of pike-perch pan-fried in soy sauce and served with root vegetables; and filet of beef with horseradish, served with dumplings and Savoy cabbage.

In the Mandarin Oriental, Neuturmstrasse 1. ✆ **089/290980.** Reservations recommended. Fixed-price lunch in Mark's Corner 35€ ($31.25); fixed-price dinner in Mark's Restaurant 60€ ($53.60); main courses in Mark's Restaurant 21€–35€ ($18.75–$31.25). AE, DC, MC, V. Daily noon–2pm and 6:30–11pm. U-Bahn/S-Bahn: Marienplatz.

## MODERATE

**Alois Dallmayr** ★★ CONTINENTAL Alois Dallmayr, which traces its history back to 1700, is the most famous delicatessen in Germany. After looking at its tempting array of delicacies from around the globe, you'll think you're lost in a millionaire's supermarket—and in fact, Dallmayr has been a purveyor to many royal courts. Here you'll find Munich's most elegant consumers. The upstairs dining room serves a subtle German version of Continental cuisine, owing a heavy debt to France. The food array is dazzling, ranging from the best herring and sausages we've ever tasted to such rare treats as perfectly vine-ripened tomatoes flown in from Morocco and papayas from Brazil. The famous French poulet de Bresse (this Bresse chicken is identified throughout Europe as the most flavorful and tender chicken anywhere), beloved of gourmets, is also shipped in. The smoked fish is a taste sensation, and the soups are superbly flavored, especially the one made with shrimp. If you're dining alone, you might prefer to sit at the counter instead of a table. This bustling restaurant is crowded at lunchtime.

Dienerstrasse 14–15. ✆ **089/2-13-51-00.** Reservations required. Main courses 13€–35€ ($11.60–$31.25); fixed-price menus 30€ ($26.80) for 3 courses, 40€ ($35.70) for 4 courses. AE, DC, MC, V. Mon–Wed 9:30am–7pm; Thurs–Fri 9:30am–8pm; Sat 9am–4pm. Tram: 19.

**Buon Gusto (Talamonti)** ★ TUSCAN/ITALIAN Devotees claim that this is the finest Italian restaurant in Munich. Its interior features two dining areas: a simple, rustic-looking bistro overlooking an open kitchen and a more formal dining room. Menu items and prices are identical in both areas. Owned and managed by an extended family, the Talamontis, whose members are likely not to speak English, the site emphasizes fresh ingredients, strong and savory flavors, and food items inspired by the Italian provinces of the Marches and Tuscany. Delectable examples include ravioli stuffed with mushrooms and herbs, roasted lamb with potatoes, lots of different forms of scallopini, and fresh fish served simply, with oil or butter and lemon. The various risottos are especially flavorful. During Oktoberfest and trade fairs, the place is mobbed.

Hochbruckenstrasse 3. ✆ **089/296-383.** Reservations recommended. Main courses 12€–25€ ($10.70–$22.35). AE, DC, MC, V. Mon–Sat 11pm–midnight. U-Bahn/S-Bahn: Marienplatz.

**Der Tisch** ★★ INTERNATIONAL Its minimalist name, "the table," doesn't suggest the allure of this bistro, one of the best and most fashionable in Munich. Presented on a clipboard, the daily-changing menu at this 36-seat dining room is eclectic and well chosen, always created from market-fresh ingredients. The cookery is resolutely contemporary—start with the eggplant mousse with a perfectly balanced tomato vinaigrette or something simpler: tuna flavored with tomato sauce and accompanied by olives and capers. The main courses are always imaginative and satisfying, especially the pike-perch on a mound of cabbage, sprinkled with a beet-flavored pink sauce. In autumn, opt for venison in a red wine sauce.

Maxvorstadt, Nymphenburger Strasse 1. ✆ **089/557-154.** Reservations required. Main courses 10€–17€ ($8.95–$15.20). AE, DC, MC, V. Mon–Fri 11:30am–3pm and 6pm–midnight. U-Bahn: Stiglmeier Platz.

**Hunsinger's Pacific** ★ *Value* INTERNATIONAL/ASIAN This restaurant offers great value on excellent food. The menu is the creative statement of one of the city's most innovative young chefs, Werner Hunsinger. Fish is the premier item here—often flown in from Pacific waters just hours after it's caught. Preparation is based on classic French-inspired methods, but many of the innovative flavors come from Malaysia (coconut milk), Japan (wasabi), Thailand (lemongrass), and India (curry). You could begin with a tuna carpaccio with sliced plum, fresh ginger, and lime. Main courses include a succulent version of bouillabaisse with aïoli, which you might follow with cold melon soup garnished with a dollop of tarragon-flavored granita. Fried monkfish in the Malaysian style and turbot in chili and ginger sauce are evocative of Hawaii.

Maximiliansplatz 5 (entrance is on the Max-Joseph-Strasse). ✆ **089/5502-9741.** Main courses 21€–26€ ($18.75–$23.20); fixed-price 2-course lunch 15€ ($13.40). AE, MC, V. Mon–Sat noon–2:30pm; daily 6–10:30pm. U-Bahn/S-Bahn: Karlsplatz/Stachus.

**Käfer am Hofgarten** ITALIAN/FRENCH This likable and stylish bistro and bar is set midway between the imposing bulk of the Residenz and the Bavarian Ministry of Finance. It's a replica of something you might find in Paris or Lyon. There are outdoor terraces in front and back. Staff members are attentive and polite. A live pianist bashes out cabaret and jazz tunes every night. Tables are spaced close to one another, which enhances the sense of intimacy, though your conversation is likely to be overheard by your immediate neighbors. Menu items change daily according to the season and the inspiration of the chefs, but might include carpaccio of beef with olive oil and aromatic herbs; pressed filet of duck prepared with braised cabbage, apples, *rösti,* and noodles; pastas with seafood; succulent and very fresh salads; and rabbit braised with a medley of fresh root vegetables.

Odeonsplatz 6–7. ✆ **089/290-7530.** Reservations recommended. Main courses 12€–16€ ($10.70–$14.30). AE, MC, V. Daily 10am–1am. U-Bahn: Odeonsplatz.

### Kids Family-Friendly Restaurants

**Café Glockenspiel** (on the Marienplatz) Your kids can down delectable Bavarian pastries while enjoying the miniature "tournament" staged each day near the clock on the Rathaus facade.

**Nürnberger Bratwurst Glöckl am Dom** (Frauenplatz 9, facing the cathedral) Hot dogs will never taste the same again after your child has tried one of these delectable little sausages from Nürnberg.

**Tower Restaurant, Olympiapark** (See p. 307) For a panoramic view of the Alps as well as the Olympic grounds, take your kids here to dine and, later, out onto one of the observation platforms.

**Pfistermühle** BAVARIAN The country comes right into the heart of Munich at this authentic and old-fashioned place, a series of charmingly decorated dining rooms in a converted old mill. A warm welcome and a refreshing cuisine await you here. Many of the dishes would be familiar to your Bavarian grandmother, and portions are generous and most satisfying. Come here for some of the most perfectly prepared roasts in the city, always served with a selection of fresh vegetables. Instead of these meat courses, you can also opt for a fine array of fresh fish from the lakes and rivers of Bavaria, especially the delectable salmon trout or brown trout. Most fish dishes come with chive-flecked sour cream and a potato pancake. The fish is also simply prepared, such as pike-perch sautéed in butter. Finish with a pyramid of vanilla custard served with a fresh berry sauce followed by a glass of wild cherry schnapps.

In the Platz Hotel, Pfistermühle 4. ✆ **089/2370-3865.** Reservations recommended. Main courses 15€–22€ ($13.40–$19.65); fixed-price menus 30€–35€ ($26.80–$31.25). AE, DC, MC, V. Mon–Sat noon–2pm and 6–10pm. U-Bahn: Marienplatz.

**Ratskeller München** BAVARIAN Throughout Germany, you'll find Ratskellers, traditional cellar restaurants in Rathaus (city hall) basements, serving good inexpensive food and wine. Munich is proud of its Ratskeller. The decor is typical: dark wood and carved chairs. The most interesting tables are in the semi-private dining nooks in the rear, under the vaulted painted ceilings. Bavarian music adds to the ambience. The menu, generally a showcase of regional fare, also includes some international dishes, many of them vegetarian, which is unusual for a Ratskeller. Recently, the chef added an array of grilled food that's lighter than the usual heavy fare offered in many German Ratskellers.

Im Alte Rathaus, Marienplatz 8. ✆ **089/2-19-98-90.** Reservations required. Main courses 7.50€–18€ ($6.70–$16.05). AE, MC, V. Daily 10am–midnight. U-Bahn/S-Bahn: Marienplatz.

**Restaurant Lenbach** ★ EUROPEAN/MEDITERRANEAN One of the most appealing restaurants in Munich occupies the grandiose premises of a 19th-century palace (Bernheimerpalais am Lenbachplatz). The decorative theme revolves around the Seven Deadly Sins, albeit with a decidedly stylish, and highly permissive, twist. Adultery is represented by a provocative large-scale pre-Raphaelite painting behind the bar. The theme within the ultra-comfortable drinking lounge is Sloth. Even the toilet is accessorized with jailhouse bars and manacles, to represent Wrath. Other "sins" await your own discovery. Food items seem less important than the decor but are likely to include a "seven sins" platter that contains foie gras, lobster, carpaccio of beef, and mozzarella tarts; lamb loin "Lenbach-style" served with a gratin of potatoes and zucchini; salmon-trout *en papillote;* and heaping platters of sushi and fresh shellfish.

Ottostrasse 6. ✆ **089/549-1300.** Reservations recommended for dinner. In restaurant, main courses 15€–45€ ($13.40–$40.20); in cafe-bistro, main courses 8€–38€ ($7.15–$33.95). AE, DC, MC, V. Restaurant Mon–Sat 6pm–midnight; cafe-bistro daily 11am–midnight; bar Mon–Sat 3pm–3am. U-Bahn/S-Bahn: Karlsplatz/Stachus.

**Spatenhaus** BAVARIAN/INTERNATIONAL The Spatenhaus, one of Munich's best-known beer restaurants, offers wide windows overlooking the opera house on Max-Joseph-Platz. You can sit in an intimate, semiprivate dining nook or at a big table. Spatenhaus has old traditions, typical Bavarian food, and generous portions at reasonable prices. If you want to know what all this fabled Bavarian gluttony is all about, order the "Bavarian plate," which is loaded down with various meats, including pork and sausages. (After that, you'll have to go to a spa.) Of course, to be loyal, you should order the restaurant's own beer, Spaten-Franziskaner-Bier, with your meal.

Residenzstrasse 12. ✆ **089/2-90-70-60.** Reservations recommended. Main courses 12€–25€ ($10.70–$22.35). AE, MC, V. Daily noon–3pm and 5pm–midnight. U-Bahn: Odeonsplatz or Marienplatz.

**Weinhaus Neuner** BAVARIAN This is an *Ältestes Weinhaus Münchens,* one of the city's landmark taverns. It dates from the late 15th century and is the only building in Munich that has its original Tyrolean vaults. The place brims with warmth and charm. Once young priests were educated here, but after Napoléon brought secularization, it became a wine tavern and a rendezvous for artists, writers, and composers, including Richard Wagner. The casual Weinstube is the less-formal section and has lots of local atmosphere. The restaurant section is elegant, with candles and flowers. The chef happily marries nouvelle cuisine and regional specialties.

Herzogspitalstrasse 8. ✆ **089/2-60-39-54.** Reservations recommended. Main courses 14€–20€ ($12.50–$17.85); fixed-price lunch 14€ ($12.50); fixed-price dinner 39€ ($34.85). AE, MC, V. Mon–Sat noon–2pm and 6–10pm. U-Bahn/S-Bahn: Karlsplatz/Stachus.

**Zum Alten Markt** *Value* BAVARIAN/INTERNATIONAL Snug and cozy, Zum Alten Markt serves beautifully presented fresh cuisine at a good price. Located on a tiny square just off Munich's large outdoor food market, the restaurant has a mellow charm and a welcoming host, Josef Lehner. The interior decor, with its intricately coffered wooden ceiling, came from a 400-year-old Tyrolean castle. In summer, tables are set up outside. Fish and fresh vegetables come from the nearby market. You might begin with a tasty homemade soup, such as cream of carrot or perhaps black-truffle tortellini in cream sauce with young onions and tomatoes. The chef makes a great *Tafelspitz* (boiled beef). You can also order classic dishes such as roast duck with applesauce or a savory roast suckling pig.

Am Viktualienmarkt, Dreifaltigkeitsplatz 3. ✆ **089/29-99-95.** Reservations recommended. Main courses 10.50€–19.50€ ($9.40–$17.40). No credit cards. Mon–Sat 10am–midnight. U-Bahn/S-Bahn: Marienplatz. Bus: 52.

## INEXPENSIVE

**Andechser am Dom** GERMAN This restaurant and beer hall is set on two floors of a postwar building adjacent to the back side of the Frauenkirche. It serves beer brewed in a monastery near Munich (Andechser), as well as generous portions of German food. No one will mind if you order a snack, a full meal, or just a beer. Menu items are often accompanied with German-style potato salad and green salad and include such dishes as veal schnitzels, steaks, turkey croquettes, roasted lamb, fish, and several kinds of sausages that taste best with tangy mustard. In good weather, tables are set up both on the building's roof and on the sidewalk in front, both of which overlook the back of one of the city's finest churches.

Weinstrasse 7a. ✆ **089/29-84-81.** Reservations recommended. Main courses 9€–17.50€ ($8.05–$15.65). AE, DC, MC, V. Daily 10am–1am. U-Bahn/S-Bahn: Marienplatz.

**Bar-Restaurant Morizz** CONTINENTAL/THAI/INTERNATIONAL This is *the* hip gay restaurant of Munich. As estimated by the staff, it has a 70-percent gay-male clientele; lesbian women and gay-friendly straights make up the rest of the clients. Part of the space is devoted to a sprawling, attractive bar, where red leather chairs, mirrors, and an impeccably trained staff evoke a 1920s Paris hotel bar. You can enjoy at least 40 single-malt whiskies, a half-dozen single-barrel bourbons, and a wide array of unusual wines. The adjacent dining room offers an appealing combination of international and continental food, prepared by a central-European staff whose interpretation of Thai cuisine is especially enjoyable. Try the *Vorspeisen-Teller* of mixed Thai specialties; some fans find the lemongrass almost addictive. Other choices include veal preparations, fresh fish, pastas, and salads (including one garnished with strips of confit of duckling).

Klenzestrasse 43. ✆ **089/201-6776.** Reservations recommended. Main courses 8€–18€ ($7.15–$16.05). MC. Sun–Thurs 7pm–2am; Fri–Sat 7pm–3am. U-Bahn: Fraunhoferstrasse.

**Café Dukatz in the Literaturhaus** ★ INTERNATIONAL Our hangout in Munich is this cafe/restaurant that pays tribute to the writer Oskar Maria Graf (1894–1967) and is decorated with Graf memorabilia. Jenny Holzer, the New York artist, was called in to carry out the Graf theme. He took sentences from Graf's writings and inscribed them on the cafe's leather benches or on the plates you're served: You have to clean your plate to see what Graf had to say. A typical remark, "It must soon be that I am famous." Munich is the center of publishing in Germany, and writers, editors, and readers drop in throughout the day for coffee and cake. Management invites you to "drink books" and "eat pages." This is no mere coffeehouse, however. The restaurant serves a full-fledged freshly prepared cuisine using some the finest ingredients from the Bavarian countryside. At lunch, try one of the sandwiches such as a baquette with rabbit or the pastrami with sauerkraut. At our most recent dinner, we enjoyed baby roast lamb from Pauillac, which is a delicacy hard to come by even in France. The Blutwurst in pastry, with diced apples, was better than the typical boudin noir in a French bistro. For dessert, we took delight in the pear tart with almond cream. Newsweek recently named this cafe as one of "the world's top gathering places."

Salvatorplatz 1. ✆ **089/291-9600.** Reservations not needed. Main courses 12€–18€ ($10.70–$16.05). No credit cards. Daily 10am–1am. U-Bahn: Odeonsplatz.

**Deutsche Eiche (German Oak)** GERMAN The building was constructed in 1864, and there's been a restaurant with a mostly gay, or at least arts-oriented, clientele since its very debut. In the 1970s, Fassbinder, the noteworthy film director, hung out here a lot, usually dressed entirely in chains and leather. Late in the 1990s, the place was renovated into a less evocative, more streamlined-looking beerhall, still with a healthy percentage of gay clients, and with direct access to a 26-room hotel and one of the busiest gay saunas in Munich. Accommodations in the hotel are relatively affordable at 87€ to 98€ ($77.70–$87.50) for a double. Each has TV and telephone and an all-white, efficient-looking collection of furnishings. But we recommend the place as a restaurant and bar hangout. Simple beer-hall-style food includes chili with French bread; vegetarian strudel; roasted pork with potato dumplings; pork schnitzel with french fries; Wiener schnitzels; pork cordon bleu; and grilled turkey steak with fresh mushrooms.

Reichenbachstrasse 13. ✆ **089/231-1660.** Reservations not necessary. Main courses 5€–25€ ($4.45–$22.35). AE, MC, V. Daily 8am–midnight. U-Bahn: Fraunhoferstrasse.

**Donisl** BAVARIAN/INTERNATIONAL Donisl is Munich's oldest beer hall, dating from 1715. Readers have praised this Munich-style restaurant as *gemütlich,* with its relaxed and comfortable atmosphere, although the seating capacity is about 550. In summer, you can enjoy the hum and bustle of the Marienplatz by dining in the garden area out front. The restaurant has two levels, the second of which is a gallery. Most of the staff speaks English. The standard menu offers traditional Bavarian food as well as a weekly changing specials menu. A specialty is *Weisswürste,* the little white sausage that has been a decades-long tradition of this place. The chef also prepares a good duck. Select beers from Munich's own Hacker-Pschorr Brewery top the evening. A zither player at noon and an accordion player in the evening entertain diners.

Weinstrasse 1. ✆ **089/22-01-84.** Reservations recommended. Main courses 7€–12€ ($6.25–$10.70). DC, MC, V. Daily 9am–midnight. U-Bahn/S-Bahn: Marienplatz.

**Hundskugel** BAVARIAN The city's oldest tavern dates from 1440 and apparently serves the same food it did back then. Why mess with success? Perhaps half the residents of Munich at one time or another have made their way here. The cookery is honest Bavarian with no pretensions. Although the chef makes a specialty of *Spanferkel* (roast suckling pig with potato noodles), you might prefer *Tafelspitz* (boiled beef) in dill sauce or roast veal stuffed with goose liver. To begin, try one of the hearty soups, made fresh daily.

Hotterstrasse 18. ✆ **089/26-42-72.** Reservations required. Main courses 7€–18€ ($6.25–$16.05). No credit cards. Daily 10:30am–midnight. U-Bahn/S-Bahn: Marienplatz.

**Park-Café Kitchen** The darling of a media-hip crowd and sundry celebrities, this late-night eatery and disco is on the see-and-be-seen circuit. The food is not the best in the city, but it's invariably good, prepared with fresh ingredients. Try the *Tafelspitz* (boiled beef with vegetables), the favorite dish of the Emperor Josef Franz of neighboring Austria, as well as an array of other courses inspired by recipes from Asia or the Mediterranean. The vegetable stir-fries here are superb, served with various tomato and curry sauces. The potato gnocchi is another hearty, filling treat. An "all American" barbecue is often served in their Biergarten, and the chef also whips up a mean chili con carne. The lounge up front is in a vaguely minimalist sci-fi style, and the restaurant itself is more traditional with wooden tables and old bistro chairs.

Sophienstrasse 7. ✆ **089/598313.** Reservations recommended. Main courses 10€–20€ ($8.95–$17.85). AE, DC, MC, V. Daily 11am–11pm. U-Bahn: Hauptbahnhof.

**Prinz Myshkin** VEGETARIAN This popular vegetarian restaurant near the Marienplatz offers freshly made salads, some macrobiotic selections, Indian and Thai vegetarian dishes, as well as vegetarian *involtini* (stuffed roll ups) and casseroles, soups, and zesty pizzas, many of which are excellent. Wine and beer are sold as well. Smaller portions of many items are available for 5€ ($4.45).

Hackenstrasse 2. ✆ **089/26-55-96.** Reservations recommended. Main courses 7€–12.50€ ($6.25–$11.15). AE, MC, V. Daily 11am–12:30am. U-Bahn/S-Bahn: Marienplatz.

**Straubinger Hof** BAVARIAN Consistently crowded, this restaurant in the Altstadt is a well-managed, unpretentious, traditional place sponsored by the brewers of Paulaner beer. No one will mind if you stop in just for a brew in the morning and afternoon, although during peak lunch and dinner hours, it's good form to order at least a small plate of cheese or wurst or a steaming platter of *Tafelspitz* (boiled beef with horseradish) or roasted knuckle of pork. The food here caters to nostalgia—you may see the term *Grossmutter Art* ("in the style of grandmother") on the menu. The restaurant is close to the Viktualienmarkt, guaranteeing, at least in theory, ultra-fresh produce. Portions are ample and prices are reasonable. In summer, seating spills out onto the pavement. For a traditional Bavarian dessert, try the old-fashioned house specialty, *Apfelschmarrn.*

Blumenstrasse 5. ✆ **089/2-60-84-44.** Reservations recommended. Main courses 10€–15€ ($8.95–$13.40). No credit cards. Mon–Fri 9am–11pm; Sat 8am–4pm. U-Bahn/S-Bahn: Marienplatz.

**Sushi & Soul** JAPANESE Huge windows open onto a quiet residential street. Expect big airy spaces, candles, and a minimalist decor whose main ornamentation derives from a stylish crowd of good-looking singles and couples. The menu is based on sushi, salads, and hot Japanese food. Fresh ingredients go into the tasty fare, which is a refreshing change of pace from the typical Bavarian diet.

Klenzestrasse 71. ✆ **089/20-10-992.** Reservations recommended. Main courses 13€–18€ ($11.60–$16.05). V. Daily 6pm–1am. U-Bahn: Fraunhoferstrasse.

**Times Square Online Bistro** CONTINENTAL Food is well-prepared here, and its salads are especially humongous—very fresh medleys of exotic-looking greens loaded with vitamins. But the place has a gimmick that many computer-literate travelers especially appreciate: There are banks of online computers lining one side, which you can rent for 2.50€ ($2.25) per quarter hour. The setting is high-ceilinged, sunny, and very large; there's a bar in the middle, and a section for conventional (noncomputerized) dining, where you can order items that include Zürich-style pork cutlets; baked camembert; tagliatelle; and spinach strudel.

Bayerstrasse 10 A (in the Hauptbahnhof). ✆ **089/550-8800.** Reservations not necessary. Breakfasts 4€–10€ ($3.55–$8.95); snacks 3.25€–7€ ($2.90–$6.25); main courses 7€–15€ ($6.25–$13.40) AE, DC, MC, V. Sun–Thurs 6am–1am; Fri–Sat 6am–midnight. U-Bahn/S-Bahn: Hauptbahnhof.

**Weisses Bräuhaus** BAVARIAN/RHENISH Weisses Bräuhaus is big, bustling, and Bavarian with a vengeance. Not for the pretentious, this informal place does what it's been doing for centuries: serving home-brewed beer. At one time, the famous salt-trade route between Salzburg and Augsburg passed by its door, and salt traders were very thirsty. The front room, with smoke-blackened dark-wood paneling and stained glass, is for drinking and informal eating; the back room has white tablecloths and black-outfitted waiters. You can sample typical Bavarian dishes: smoked filet of trout; rich potato soup; roast pork with homemade potato dumplings and cabbage salad; or Viennese veal goulash with mushrooms and cream sauce. You'll have to share your table, but that's part of the fun.

Tal 7. ✆ **089/29-98-75.** Reservations recommended, especially for the back room. Main courses 10€–18€ ($8.95–$16.05). No credit cards. Daily noon–midnight. U-Bahn/S-Bahn: Marienplatz.

**Zum Burgerhaus** GERMAN Set behind Sendlingertorplatz, behind an antique, ocher-colored facade, this is a well-managed restaurant serving flavorful food to a loyal neighborhood clientele. Within several dining rooms outfitted with paneling and Bavarian memorabilia, you can order such good-tasting menu items as mixed whitefish with braised herbs; filet of pike-perch in olive oil with spinach and saffron sauce; and medallions of venison with juniperberries and noodles.

Pettenkoferstrasse 5. ✆ **089/59-79-09.** Reservations recommended. Main courses 15€–20€ ($13.40–$17.85). AE, MC, V. Mon–Sat 11am–2:30pm and 6–11pm. U-Bahn: Sendlinger Tor.

## NEAR THE SÜDBAHNHOF

**Gästhaus Glockenbach** ★★★ MODERN CONTINENTAL There's a good chance you'll be served one of your finest meals in Munich at this restaurant, should you choose to dine here. This unpretentious restaurant is capable of holding its own against more expensive, more *grand bourgeois* establishments, such as Tantris (see below). The setting is a 200-year-old building close to the Glockenbach, a tributary of the nearby Isar. The dignified country-baroque interior is accented with vivid modern paintings and the most elegant table settings in town. Cuisine changes with the season. You'll find imaginative preparations of venison and pheasant in autumn, lamb and veal dishes in springtime, and shellfish whenever in season. Ultra-fresh vegetables and exotica are imported from local farms and from sophisticated purveyors worldwide.

Kapuzinerstrasse 29, corner of Maistrasse. ✆ **089/53-40-43.** Reservations recommended. Main courses 23€–28€ ($20.55–$25); fixed-price lunch 26€ ($23.20), fixed-price dinner 75€ ($67). AE, MC, V. Tues–Sat noon–2pm (last order); and 7–10pm (last order). Closed 1 week at Christmas. U-Bahn: Goetheplatz.

## NEAR THE ISAR, SOUTH OF CENTER

**Asam Schlössl** BAVARIAN/INTERNATIONAL This Augustiner brewery restaurant offers a relaxed, relatively informal hideaway amid the congestion of Munich. The building was built as a private villa in 1724. Some of the original castle-like design remains, though the structure has been expanded and renovated over the years. All brews offered are products of Augustiner, including both pale and dark versions of Weissebier, beer fermented from wheat. Menu items include such typical Bavarian fare as *Böffla-mott* (beef braised in red wine) with *Semmelknödel* (bread dumplings), and a dish beloved by emperor Franz Josef of Austria, *gesottener Tafelspitz mit frischen Kren,* a savory form of the familiar boiled beef with horseradish.

Maria-Einsiedel-Strasse 45. ✆ **089/7-23-63-73.** Main courses 7€–23€ ($6.25–$20.55). AE, DC, MC, V. Daily 11am–1am. U-Bahn: Thalkirchen.

## IN SCHWABING

This district, which was called "bohemian" in the 1940s, overflows with restaurants. Many of them are awful, but there are several good ones, some of which attract a youthful clientele. The evening is the best time for a visit.

### VERY EXPENSIVE

**Tantris** ★★★ FRENCH/INTERNATIONAL Tantris serves Munich's finest cuisine. Chef Hans Haas was voted the top chef in Germany in 1994, and, if anything, he has refined and sharpened his culinary technique since. The setting is unlikely: a drab commercial area, with bare concrete walls and a garish decor. But once inside, you're transported by the fine service and excellent food that's a treat for the eye as well as the palate. The choice of dishes is wisely limited, and the cooking is subtle and original. You might begin with a terrine of smoked fish served with green cucumber sauce, then follow with classic roast duck on mustard-seed sauce, or perhaps a delightful concoction of lobster medallions on black noodles.

Johann-Fichte-Strasse 7, Schwabing. ✆ **089/36-19-59-0.** Reservations required. Fixed-price 5-course lunch 85€ ($75.90); fixed-price dinner 105€ ($93.75) for 5-courses, 123€ ($109.85) for 8 courses; special 5-course Tues–Thurs (including wine) 130€ ($116.10). AE, DC, MC, V. Tues–Sat noon–3pm and 6:30pm–1am. Closed public holidays and annual holidays in Jan and May. U-Bahn: Dietlindenstrasse.

### MODERATE

**Der Katzlmacher** ★ *Finds* ITALIAN Few Italian restaurants would have had the nerve to adopt as their name a pejorative German term referring to Italians.

This one did, however, and its sense of humor has helped make it beloved by loyal local fans. The setting is a postwar building near the university, whose dining rooms are evocative of an elegant and rustic mountain lodge high in the Italian Alps. Stylish and theatrical, and filled with well-dressed, prosperous-looking clients, it contains lavishly carved paneling, masses of artfully arranged flowers, and huge amounts of charm. The cooking is based on the culinary traditions of the Marches, Friuli, and Emilia-Romagna, all known for their fine cuisines and agrarian bounty. The owner is Claudio Zanuttigh, who supervises menu specialties that might include calzone stuffed with spinach and pine nuts, carpaccio of duck breast, a commendable grilled swordfish with red-wine vinaigrette, eel with champagne sauce, and a succulent version of *fritto misto del pesce* (mixed fried fish) based on whatever is in season.

Kaulbachstrasse 48. ✆ **089/348129.** Reservations recommended. Main courses 9€–11€ ($8.05–$9.80). MC, V. Mon–Fri noon–3pm and 6:30–11pm. U-Bahn: Universität.

**Locanda Picolit** ★ ITALIAN If you come here in the summer and sit on the outdoor terrace with a view over a garden, it's easy to believe that you've suddenly been transported to the Mediterranean world. The interior is full of streamlined furnishings and dramatic, oversize modern paintings. Menu items come from all over Italy, but the favorites are those from the owner's native Friuli, near Venice. There's a lavish use of in-season asparagus, arugula, shellfish, rabbit, wild mushrooms, and venison in such alluring preparations as ravioli stuffed with lobster, tagliatelle, rotini, linguini with braised radicchio and shellfish, and, when available, *saltimbocca* (veal with prosciutto).

Siegfriedstrasse 11. ✆ **089/396447.** Reservations recommended. Main courses 9€–14€ ($8.05–$12.50); fixed-price menu 34€ ($30.35). AE, DC, MC, V. Mon–Fri noon–2:30pm; daily 6–9:30pm. U-Bahn: Münchner Freiheit.

**Spago** ITALIAN Less self-conscious and self-promotional than its Los Angeles namesake, this amiable multilingual Italian restaurant still offers lots of Italian pizzazz as well as good, upscale Italian food. Some of the dishes are tagliatelle with porcini mushrooms; braised breast of chicken stuffed with herbs and spinach; ravioli with artichoke hearts or with potatoes and chanterelles; an especially delectable fish baked with herbs in a salt crust and wild mushrooms sautéed with herbs and arugula; a perfectly prepared suckling lamb with mint and balsamic vinegar; and an array of desserts as beautiful as they are tasty.

Neureutherstrasse 15 at Arcisstrasse. ✆ **089/271-2406.** Reservations recommended. Main courses 8.50€–20€ ($7.60–$17.85); fixed-price lunch 20€ ($17.85); fixed-price dinner 35€ ($31.25). AE, DC, MC, V. Mon–Sat 11:30am–2:30pm and 6–11pm. U-Bahn: Josephsplatz or Universität.

## INEXPENSIVE

**Sausalito's** MEXICAN Imagine a sprawling labyrinth of rooms whose layout and lighting suggests a German beer hall. Then imagine that instead of boozy, middle-aged clients swilling beer, it's loaded with young, nubile students from the nearby university. Add to that a heady blend of tequila-based parti-colored drinks and tacos, and you'll have the equivalent of Spring Break in Daytona Beach with a German accent. Come here to drink, dialogue, mingle, and to chow down on fajitas, enchiladas, quesadillas, steaks, burritos, and burgers.

Türkenstrasse 50. ✆ **089/28-15-94.** Reservations not necessary. Main courses 8.50€–13.50€ ($7.60–$12.05). AE, MC, V. Daily 5pm–1am. U-Bahn: Universität.

### Beer Gardens

If you're in Munich anytime between the first sunny spring day and the last fading light of a Bavarian-style autumn, you should head for one of the city's celebrated beer gardens (*Biergartens*). Traditionally, beer gardens were simply tables placed under chestnut trees planted above the storage cellars to keep beer cool in summer. (Lids on beer steins, incidentally, were meant to keep out flies.) It's estimated that today Munich has at least 400 beer gardens and cellars. Food, drink, and atmosphere are much the same in all of them.

**Bamberger Haus,** Brunnerstrasse 2 (✆ **089/3-08-89-66;** U-Bahn: Scheidplatz), located northwest of Schwabing at the edge of Luitpold Park, is named after a city noted for mass consumption of beer. The street-level restaurant serves Bavarian and international specialties: well-seasoned soups, grilled steak, veal, pork, and sausages. If you only want to drink, you might visit the rowdier and less-expensive beer hall in the cellar. Main courses in the restaurant range from 10€ to 22€ ($8.95–$19.65). A large beer costs 2.50€ ($2.25). The restaurant is open daily 11am to 10pm, the beer hall daily 10am to 1am. American Express, MasterCard, and Visa are accepted.

Englischer Garten, the park lying between the Isar River and Schwabing, is home to several beer gardens. Our favorite is **Biergarten Chinesischer Turm,** Englischer Garten 3 (✆ **089/3-83-87-20;** U-Bahn: Giselastrasse). It's the largest and most popular of its kind in Europe, taking its name from its location at the foot of an easy-to-find pagoda-like tower. Beer and Bavarian food, and plenty of it, are what you get here. A glass or mug of beer large enough to bathe in (ask for *ein mass Bier*) costs 5.50€ ($4.90). It will likely be slammed down, still foaming, by a server carrying 12 other tall steins. The food is cheap—a simple

## IN BOGENHAUSEN

**Käfer-Schänke** GERMAN/INTERNATIONAL This is a great spot for casual dining with elegant style, in a setting that evokes a chalet. It's located on the second floor of a famous gourmet shop called Käfer. The cuisine roams the world for inspiration—from Lombardy to Asia. You select your hors d'oeuvres from the most dazzling display in Munich. Often Käfer-Schänke devotes a week to a particular country's cuisine. On one visit, we enjoyed the classic soup of the French Riviera (sea bass with fennel). The salads have what one reviewer called "rococo splendor." From a cold table, you can choose smoked salmon or smoked eel. Venison, quail, and guinea hen are also regularly featured.

Prinzregentenstrasse 73. ✆ **089/4-168-247.** Reservations required. Main courses 16€–26€ ($14.30–$23.20); fixed-price lunch 28€ ($25). AE, DC, MC, V. Mon–Sat 11:30am–midnight. Closed holidays. U-Bahn: Prinzregentenplatz. Bus: 55.

## 5 Seeing the Sights

Munich is stocked with so many treasures that any visitor who plans to "do" the city in a day or two will not only miss out on many major sights but will also meal begins at 7€ ($6.25). Homemade dumplings are a specialty, as are all kinds of tasty sausages. You can also get a first-rate *Schweinbraten* (a braised loin of pork served with potato dumpling and rich brown gravy), which is Bavaria's answer to the better-known sauerbraten of the north. Huge baskets of pretzels are passed around, and they're eaten with *Radi,* the large, tasty white radishes famous from these parts. Oompah bands often play, adding to the festive atmosphere. The place is open every day May to October 11am to 1am, but November to April, its hours depend on the weather and the number of patrons.

If you're going to the zoo, you might want to stop at the nearby **Gaststätte zum Flaucher,** Isarauen 8 (✆ **089/7-23-26-77;** bus: 52), for fun and food. Gaststätte is mellow and traditional, with tables set in a tree-shaded garden overlooking the river. Here you can order the local specialty, *Leberkäse,* a large loaf of sausage eaten with freshly baked pretzels and plenty of mustard. Beer costs from 2.50€ ($2.25) for a half-liter mug. Main courses cost from 5.50€ to 10€ ($4.90–$8.95). May to October it's open daily 10am to midnight; November to April, only Friday, Saturday, and Sunday 10am to 9pm.

**Hirschgarten,** Hirschgartenstrasse 1, in Nymphenburg Park, near the palace (✆ **089/17-25-91;** S-Bahn: Laim; tram 17 to Romanplatz), is the largest open-air restaurant in Munich, capable of seating more than 8,000 beer drinkers and merrymakers. Full meals cost 6€ to 13.50€ ($5.35–$12.05). A 1-liter stein of Augustiner beer goes for 2.60€ ($2.30). It's open daily 9am to midnight. MasterCard and Visa are accepted. For information on Munich's other favorite drinking spots, beer halls, see "Munich After Dark," later in this chapter.

fail to grasp the city's spirit and absorb its special flavor. There are, however, a few vital highlights.

## THE TOP ATTRACTIONS

### THE CITY CENTER

**Marienplatz** ★ is the heart of the Altstadt, or Old City. On its north side is the **Neues Rathaus (New City Hall),** built in 19th-century Gothic style. Each day at 11am and also at noon and 5pm in the summer, the Glockenspiel on the facade performs a miniature tournament, with enameled copper figures moving in and out of the archways. You may wish to climb the 55 steps to the top of the Rauthaus's tower (an elevator is also available) for a good view of the city center. The **Altes Rathaus (Old City Hall),** with its plain Gothic tower, is to the right. It was reconstructed in the 15th century, after being destroyed by fire.

South of the square you can see the oldest church in Munich, **St. Peter's.** The **Viktualienmarkt,** just off Marienplatz and around the corner from St. Peter's church, has been a gathering place since 1807. Here, people gossip, browse, and snack, as well as buy fresh country produce, wines, meats, and cheese.

To the north lies **Odeonsplatz,** Munich's most beautiful square. The **Residenz (Royal Palace)** is just to the east, and the **Theatinerkirche** is to the south.

# Central Munich Attractions

Alte Pinakothek **2**
Altes Rathaus **16**
Antikensammlungen **6**
Asamkirche **10**
Bayerisches
  Nationalmuseum **32**
Cuvilliés Theater **22**
Deutsches Museum **34**
Deutsches Theater **9**
Englischer Garten **31**
Frauenkirche **18**
Glyptothek **4**
Hofgarten **23**
Isartor **33**
Karlstor **7**
Marienplatz **15**
Matthäuskirche **11**
Michaelskirche **8**
Münchner Stadtmuseum **12**
Nationaltheater **20**
Neue Pinakothek **1**
Neues Rathaus **17**
Peterskirche **14**
Propyläen **5**
Residenz **21**
Städtische Galerie
  im Lenbachhaus **3**
Theatinerkirche **19**
University **24**
Viktualienmarkt **13**

**NYMPHENBURG**
Amalienburg **29**
Badenburg Pavilion **30**
Magdalenenklause **26**
Marstallmuseum **28**
Pagodenburg **25**
Schloss **27**

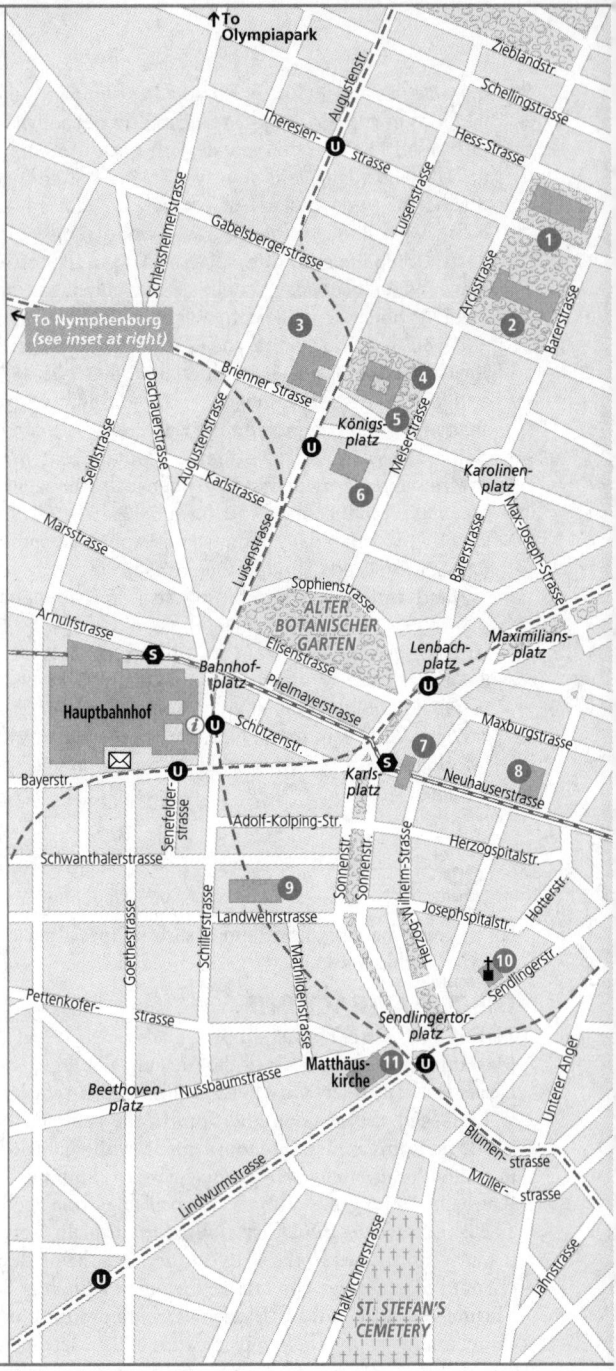


Church
Information
Post Office
S-Bahn
U-Bahn

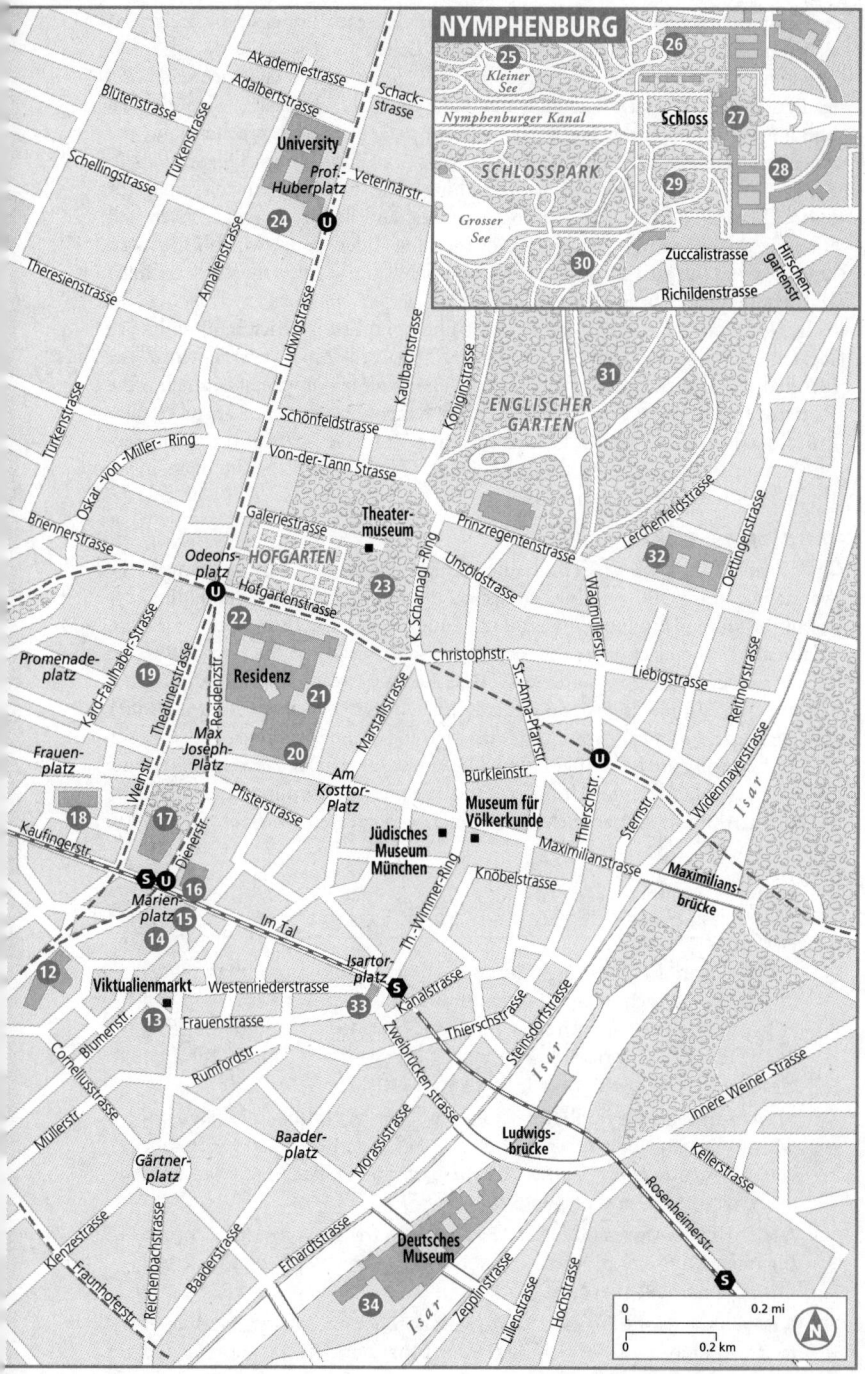
NYMPHENBURG
Kleiner See
Nymphenburger Kanal
Schloss
SCHLOSSPARK
Grosser See
Zuccalistrasse
Richildenstrasse
Hirschgartenstr.
ENGLISCHER GARTEN
Akademiestrasse
Adalbertstrasse
Schackstrasse
Blütenstrasse
Türkenstrasse
Schellingstrasse
University
Prof.-Huberplatz
Veterinärstr.
Amalienstrasse
Theresienstrasse
Ludwigstrasse
Kaulbachstrasse
Königinstrasse
Schönfeldstrasse
Von-der-Tann Strasse
Oskar-von-Miller-Ring
Galeriestrasse
Theatermuseum
Prinzregentenstrasse
Lerchenfeldstrasse
Oettingenstrasse
Briennerstrasse
Odeonsplatz
HOFGARTEN
Hofgartenstrasse
K.-Scharnagl-Ring
Unsöldstrasse
Wagmüllerstr.
Kaiserstrasse
Theatinerstrasse
Residenzstr.
Residenz
Christophstr.
St.-Anna-Pfarrstr.
Liebigstrasse
Reitmorstrasse
Promenadeplatz
Max-Joseph-Platz
Marstallstrasse
Frauenplatz
Weinstr.
Am Kosttor-Platz
Bürkleinstr.
Widenmayerstrasse
Isar
Pfisterstrasse
Museum für Völkerkunde
Thierschstr.
Sternstr.
Kaufingerstr.
Dienerstr.
Jüdisches Museum München
Maximilianstrasse
Maximiliansbrücke
Th.-Wimmer-Ring
Knöbelstrasse
Marienplatz
Im Tal
Isartorplatz
Kanalstrasse
Viktualienmarkt
Westenriederstrasse
Frauenstrasse
Thierschstrasse
Steinsdorfstrasse
Zweibrückenstrasse
Blumenstr.
Cornelius-strasse
Rumfordstr.
Innere Weiner Strasse
Müllerstr.
Morassistrasse
Ludwigsbrücke
Baaderplatz
Gärtnerplatz
Kellerstrasse
Rosenheimerstr.
Klenzestrasse
Reichenbachstrasse
Baaderstrasse
Erhardtstrasse
Deutsches Museum
Fraunhoferstr.
Zeppelinstrasse
Lilienstrasse
Hochstrasse
0 0.2 mi
0 0.2 km
N

Adjoining the Residenz is the restored **Nationaltheater,** home of the acclaimed Bavarian State Opera and Bavarian National Ballet.

Running west from Odeonsplatz is the wide shopping avenue, Briennerstrasse, leading to **Königsplatz.** Flanking this large Grecian square are three classical buildings constructed by Ludwig I—the **Propyläen,** the **Glyptothek,** and the **Antikensammlungen.** The busy Ludwigstrasse runs north from Odeonsplatz to the section of Munich known as **Schwabing.** This is the Greenwich Village or Latin Quarter of Munich, proud of its artistic and literary heritage. Ibsen and Rilke lived here, as well as members of the Blue Rider group, which influenced abstract art in the early 20th century. Today, Schwabing's sidewalk tables are filled with young people from all over the world.

**Isartor** (Isar Gate) is one of the most-photographed Munich landmarks. It's located east of Marienplatz at Isartorplatz. This is the only tower left from the fortified wall that once encircled Munich. The other major gate of Munich is the **Karlstor,** once known as Neuhauser Tor, lying northeast of Karlsplatz (also called Stachus) at the end of Neuhauserstrasse. It formed part of the town's second circuit of walls, dating from the 1500s. The Karlstor lost its main tower (built 1302) in an 1857 explosion.

## MUSEUMS & PALACES

**Alte Pinakothek** ★★★ This is one of the most significant art museums in the world. The nearly 900 paintings on display in this huge neoclassical building represent the greatest European artists of the 14th through the 18th centuries. Begun as a small court collection by the royal Wittelsbach family in the early 1500s, the artistic treasure trove grew and grew. There are only two floors with exhibits, but the museum is immense; we do not recommend that you try to cover it all in 1 day. Pick up a floorplan to guide you through the dozens of rooms.

The following are a few highlights. The landscape painter *par excellence* of the Danube school, Albrecht Altdorfer, is represented by six monumental works. Works of Albrecht Dürer include his final, and greatest, *Self-Portrait* (1500).

### Frommer's Favorite Munich Experiences

**A Morning at the Deutsches Museum** It would take a month to see all of the largest technological museum in the world, but a morning will at least whet your appetite. Everything is here: the first automobile by Benz (1886), the original V-2 rocket (Hitler's secret weapon), the first diesel engine, and plenty of buttons to push.

**An Afternoon at Nymphenburg Palace** The Wittelsbach family considered this the best place to be on a hot afternoon—and so might you. The grounds of Germany's largest baroque palace are filled with lakes, waterfalls, and pavilions.

**A Night at the Opera (Cuvilliés Theater)** It's the most beautiful rococo theater in the world: a small, elaborately gilded tier-boxed structure from the mid-18th century.

**A Day in the Beer Gardens** Münchners gather on weekends in summer to down high *masse* of beer and watch the world go by, especially at Chinesischer Turm in the Englischer Garten.

Here the artist has portrayed himself with almost Christ-like solemnity. Also displayed is Dürer's last great painting, a two-paneled work called *The Four Apostles* (1526). Works by Lucas Cranach the Elder include his *Venus.*

Several galleries are given over to Dutch and Flemish masters. There are more Rubens here than in any other museum in Europe. Roger van der Weyden's *St. Columbia Altarpiece* (1460–62) measures nearly 3m (10 ft.) across, a triumph of his subtle linear style. Rembrandts and Van Dycks are also displayed. French, Spanish, and Italian artists can be found in both the larger galleries and the small rooms lining the outer wall. Note Raphael's *Holy Family* and Leonardo da Vinci's *Madonna.*

Barerstrasse 27. ✆ **089/23-80-52-16.** Admission 5€ ($4.45) adults, 3.50€ ($3.15) students, free for children 14 and under. Tues–Sun 10am–5pm (until 10pm Thurs). U-Bahn: Königsplatz. Tram: 27. Bus: 53.

**Bayerisches Nationalmuseum (Bavarian National Museum)** ★★ In 1855, King Maximilian II began an institution to preserve Bavaria's historic and artistic treasures. The collection grew so rapidly that it had to be moved to larger quarters several times over the past 100 years. Its current building, near the Haus der Kunst, contains three vast floors of sculpture, painting, folk art, ceramics, furniture, and textiles, as well as clocks and scientific instruments.

After entering the museum, turn right into the first large gallery, the **Wessobrunn Room,** devoted to early church art from the 5th through the 13th centuries. Some of the museum's oldest and most valuable works are here, including ancient and medieval ivories. The most famous is the Munich ivory from about A.D. 400. At the crossing to the adjoining room is the stone figure, the *Virgin with the Rose Bush,* from Straubing (ca. 1300), one of the few old Bavarian pieces of church art influenced by the spirit of mysticism.

The **Riemenschneider Room** is devoted to the works of the great sculptor Tilman Riemenschneider (1460–1531) and his contemporaries. Characteristic of the sculptor's works is the natural, unpainted wood of his carvings and statuary. Note especially the *12 Apostles from the Marienkapelle in Würzburg* (1510), the central group of the high altar in the parish church of Münnerstadt (1490–92), and the figure of St. Sebastian (1490).

The second floor contains a fine collection of stained and painted glass—an art in which medieval Germany excelled. Other rooms include baroque ivory carvings, Meissen porcelain, and ceramics. Also on display are famous collections of 16th- to 18th-century arms and armor, and the collection of antique clocks, some dating from the 16th century.

Prinzregentenstrasse 3. ✆ **089/21-12-401.** Admission 3€ ($2.70) adults, 2€ ($1.80) students and seniors, free for children under 15, free for all Sun. Tues–Wed and Fri–Sun 10am–5pm; Thurs 10am–8pm. U-Bahn: Lehel. Tram: 17. Bus: 53.

**Deutsches Museum (German Museum of Masterpieces of Science and Technology)** ★★★ *Kids* This is the largest technological museum in the world. Its huge collection of priceless artifacts and historic originals includes the first electric dynamo (Siemens, 1866), the first automobile (Benz, 1886), the first diesel engine (1897), and the laboratory bench at which the atom was first split (Hahn, Strassmann, 1938). There are hundreds of buttons to push, levers to crank, and gears to turn, as well as a knowledgeable, English-speaking staff to answer questions and demonstrate how steam engines, pumps, or historical musical instruments work.

Among the most popular displays are those on mining, with a series of model coal, salt, and iron mines, as well as the electrical power hall, with high-voltage displays that actually produce lightning. There are also exhibits on transportation, printing, photography, and textiles, and halls devoted to air-and-space and high-tech themes. Activities include glassblowing and paper-making demonstrations. The astronomy exhibition is the largest in Europe. A good restaurant and a museum shop are on the premises.

Museumsinsel 1 (on an island in the Isar River). ✆ **089/21-791.** Admission 6€ ($5.35) adults, 4€ ($3.55) seniors, 2.50€ ($2.25) students, and children 6–12, free for children 5 and under. Daily 9am–5pm (closes at 2pm the 2nd Wed in Dec). Closed major holidays. S-Bahn: Isartor. Tram: 18.

**Pinakothek der Moderne** ★★ In 2002, one of the world's largest museums devoted to the visual arts of the 19th and 20th centuries opened in Munich, just minutes from the Alte and Neue Pinakothek. This is the vastest display of fine and applied arts in the country as, for the first time, four major collections came together under one roof. This is Munich's version of the Tate Gallery in London or the Pompidou in Paris.

Wander where your interest dictates: the **Staatsgalerie moderner Kunst** ★★★ (State Gallery of Modern Art) with paintings, sculpture, photography, and video; **Die Neue Sammlung,** which constitutes the national museum of applied art featuring design and craftwork; the **Architekturmuseum der Technischen Universität** (University of Architecture museum) with architectural drawings, photographs, and models; and the **Staatliche Grapische Sammlung,** with its outstanding collection of prints and drawings.

Whenever we visit, we spend most of our time in the modern art collection, lost in a world of our favorite artists such as Picasso, Magritte, Klee, Kandinsky, even Francis Bacon, de Kooning, and Warhol. The museum also owns 400,000 drawings and prints from Leonardo da Vinci to Cézanne up to contemporary artists. They are presented at alternating exhibits.

The architectural galleries hold the largest specialist collection of its kind in Germany, comprising some 350,000 drawings, 100,000 photographs, and 500 models. The applied arts section features more than 50,000 items. You're taken from the beginnings of the Industrial Revolution via Art Nouveau, up Bauhaus and today's computer culture.

Barerstrasse 40. ✆ **089/23805-118.** Admission: 10€ ($8.95) adults, 6€ ($5.35) students and ages 17 and under. Tues–Sun 10am–5pm. U-bahn: Odeonsplatz.

**Residenz** ★ When one of the Bavarian royals said that he was going to the castle, he could have meant any number of places, especially if he was Ludwig II. But if he said that he was going home, he could only be referring to the Residenz. This enormous palace, with a history almost as long as that of the Wittelsbach family, was the official residence of the rulers of Bavaria from 1385 to 1918. Added to and rebuilt over the centuries, the complex is a conglomerate of various styles. Depending on how you approach the Residenz, you might first see a German Renaissance hall (the western facade), a Palladian palace (on the north), or a Florentine Renaissance palace (on the south facing Max-Joseph-Platz).

The Residenz has been completely restored since its almost total destruction in World War II and now houses the Residenz Museum, a concert hall, the Cuvilliés Theater, and the Residenz Treasury. The **Residenz Museum** (✆ **089/29-06-71**) comprises the southwestern section of the palace, some 120 rooms of art and furnishings collected by centuries of Wittelsbachs.

The **Ancestral Gallery** is designed like a hall of mirrors, except that instead of mirrors, there are portraits of the Wittelsbach family, set into gilded, carved paneling. The largest room in the museum section is the **Antiquarium,** possibly

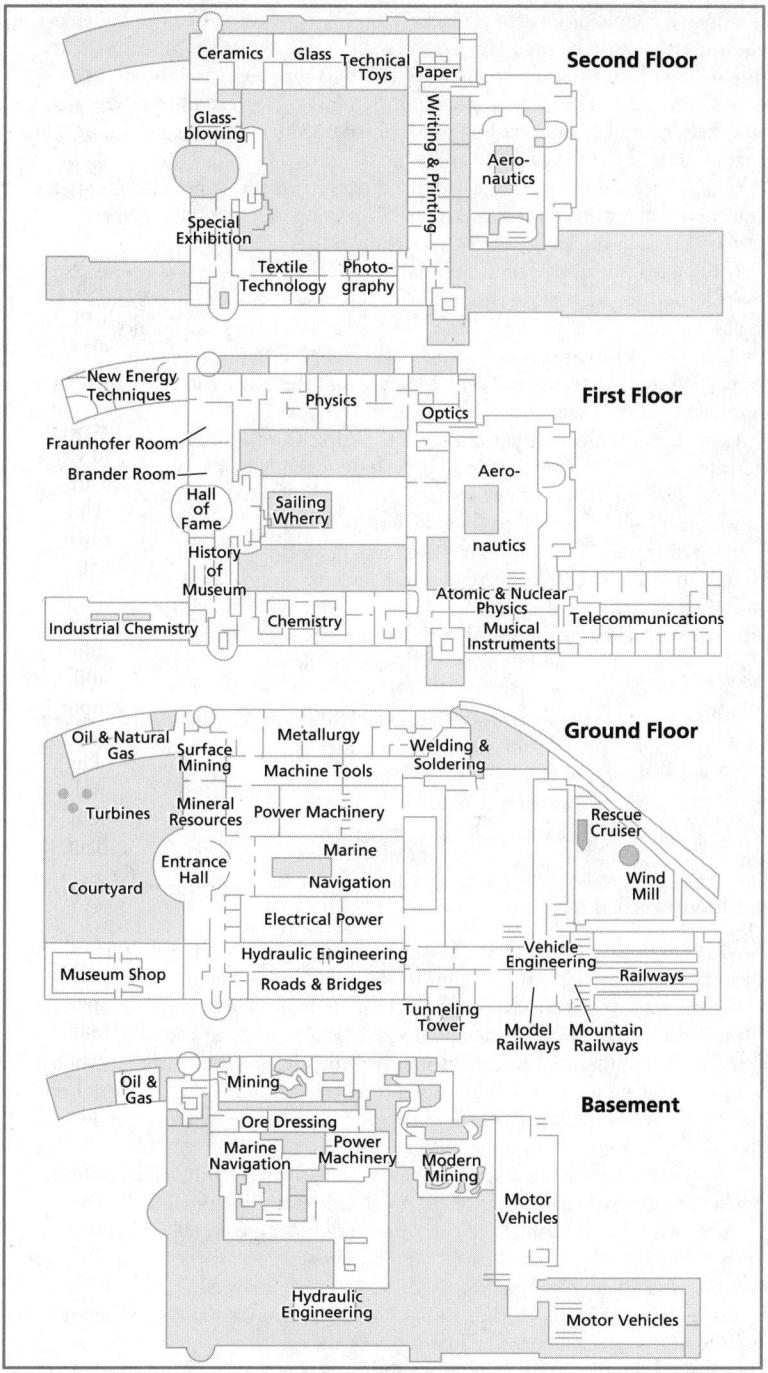
Second Floor
Ceramics
Glass
Technical Toys
Paper
Writing & Printing
Glass-blowing
Aero-nautics
Special Exhibition
Textile Technology
Photo-graphy
First Floor
New Energy Techniques
Physics
Optics
Fraunhofer Room
Brander Room
Aero-
Hall of Fame
Sailing Wherry
nautics
History of Museum
Atomic & Nuclear Physics
Telecommunications
Industrial Chemistry
Chemistry
Musical Instruments
Ground Floor
Oil & Natural Gas
Surface Mining
Metallurgy
Welding & Soldering
Machine Tools
Turbines
Mineral Resources
Power Machinery
Rescue Cruiser
Marine
Entrance Hall
Navigation
Wind Mill
Courtyard
Electrical Power
Hydraulic Engineering
Vehicle Engineering
Museum Shop
Roads & Bridges
Railways
Tunneling Tower
Model Railways
Mountain Railways
Basement
Oil & Gas
Mining
Ore Dressing
Marine Navigation
Power Machinery
Modern Mining
Motor Vehicles
Hydraulic Engineering
Motor Vehicles

the finest example of interior Renaissance secular styling in Germany. Frescoes adorn nearly every inch of space on the walls and ceilings. The room is broken into sections by pilasters and niches, each with its own bust of a Roman emperor or a Greek hero. The central attraction is the two-story chimneypiece of red stucco and marble, completed in 1600. It's adorned with Tuscan pillars and the coat of arms of the dukes of Bavaria.

On the second floor of the palace, directly over the Antiquarium, is an enormous collection of Far Eastern porcelain. Note also the fine assemblage of Oriental rugs in the long, narrow **Porcelain Gallery.**

If you have time to view only one item in the **Schatzkammer** ★★ (or treasury), make it the 16th-century Renaissance statue of *St. George Slaying the Dragon.* This equestrian statue is made of gold, but you can barely see the precious metal for the thousands of diamonds, rubies, emeralds, sapphires, and semiprecious stones embedded in it. Both the Residenz Museum and the Schatzkammer are entered from Max-Joseph-Platz on the south side of the palace.

From the Brunnenhof, you can visit the **Alte Residenztheater** or **Cuvilliés Theater** ★. This is Germany's most outstanding example of a rococo tier-boxed theater. Directly over the huge center box, where the royal family sat, is a crest in white and gold topped by a jewel-bedecked crown of Bavaria held in place by a group of cherubs in flight. Court architect François de Cuvilliés designed the theater in the mid-18th century (see box under "Munich After Dark," later in this chapter). During World War II, the interior was dismantled and stored. After the war, it was reassembled in the reconstructed building. In summer, this theater is the scene of frequent concerts and opera performances. Mozart's *Idomeneo* was first performed here in 1781.

To the north of the Residenz, the Italianate **Hofgarten,** or Court Garden, is one of the special "green lungs" of Munich. The garden was laid out between 1613 and 1617. It's enclosed on two sides by arcades; in the center is the Hofgarten temple, a 12-sided pavilion dating from 1615.

Max-Joseph-Platz 3. ✆ **089/29-06-71.** Museum and Treasury 4€ ($3.55) adults, 3€ ($2.70) students and seniors; Old Residenz Theater 3€ ($2.70) adults, 2€ ($1.80) students, free for children 15 and under. Combined ticket 7€ ($6.25) adults, 5€ ($4.45) students and children. Museum, Treasury, and Theatre daily 9am–6pm. U-Bahn: Odeonsplatz.

**Schloss Nymphenburg** ★★ In summer, the Wittelsbachs would pack up their bags and head for their country house, Schloss Nymphenburg. A more complete, more sophisticated palace than the Residenz, it was begun in 1664 by Elector Ferdinand Maria in Italian-villa style and took more than 150 years to complete. The final palace plan was created mainly by Elector Max Emanuel, who in 1702 decided to enlarge the villa by adding four large pavilions connected by arcaded passageways. Gradually the French style took over, and today the facade is a subdued baroque.

The palace interior is less subtle, however. Upon entering the main building, you're in the **great hall,** decorated in rococo colors and stuccos. The frescoes by Zimmermann (1756) depict incidents from mythology, especially those dealing with Flora, goddess of nymphs, for whom the palace was named. Concerts are still presented here in summer.

From the main building, turn left and head for the **arcaded gallery** connecting the northern pavilions. The first room in the arcade is the Great Gallery of Beauties, painted in 1710. More provocative, however, is Ludwig I's Gallery of Beauties in the south pavilion. Paintings by J. Stieler (1827–1850) include the

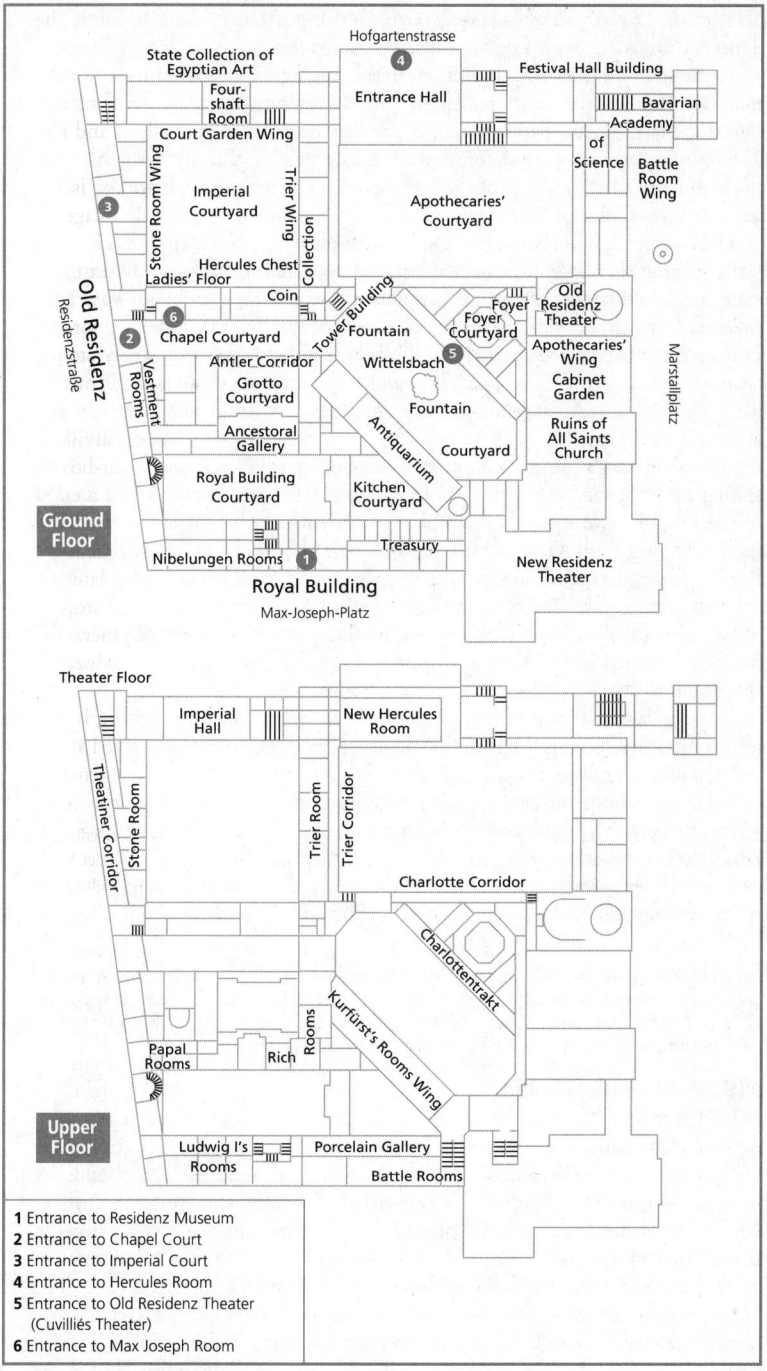
Hofgartenstrasse
State Collection of Egyptian Art
Four-shaft Room
Entrance Hall
Festival Hall Building
Bavarian Academy of Science
Battle Room Wing
Court Garden Wing
Stone Room Wing
Imperial Courtyard
Trier Wing
Collection
Apothecaries' Courtyard
Hercules Chest
Ladies' Floor
Coin
Old Residenz
Residenzstraße
Chapel Courtyard
Tower Building
Fountain
Foyer Courtyard
Foyer
Old Residenz Theater
Apothecaries' Wing
Antler Corridor
Wittelsbach
Cabinet Garden
Vestment Rooms
Grotto Courtyard
Fountain
Marstallplatz
Ancestoral Gallery
Antiquarium
Courtyard
Ruins of All Saints Church
Royal Building Courtyard
Kitchen Courtyard
Ground Floor
Treasury
Nibelungen Rooms
New Residenz Theater
Royal Building
Max-Joseph-Platz
Theater Floor
Imperial Hall
New Hercules Room
Theatiner Corridor
Stone Room
Trier Room
Trier Corridor
Charlotte Corridor
Charlottentrakt
Kurfürst's Rooms Wing
Rooms
Papal Rooms
Rich
Upper Floor
Ludwig I's Rooms
Porcelain Gallery
Battle Rooms
1 Entrance to Residenz Museum
2 Entrance to Chapel Court
3 Entrance to Imperial Court
4 Entrance to Hercules Room
5 Entrance to Old Residenz Theater (Cuvilliés Theater)
6 Entrance to Max Joseph Room

*Schöne Münchnerin* (*Lovely Munich Girl*) and a portrait of Lola Montez, the dancer whose affair with Ludwig caused a scandal.

To the south of the palace buildings, in the rectangular block of low structures that once housed the court stables, is the **Marstallmuseum.** In the first hall, look for the glass coronation coach of Elector Karl Albrecht, built in Paris in 1740. From the same period comes the hunting sleigh of Electress Amalia, with the statue of Diana, goddess of the hunt; even the sleigh's runners are decorated with shellwork and hunting trophies.

The coaches and sleighs of Ludwig II are displayed in the **third hall.** His constant longing for the grandeur of the past is reflected in his ornately designed state coach, which was meant for his marriage to Duchess Sophie of Bavaria, a royal wedding that never took place. The coach wasn't wasted, however, because Ludwig often used it to ride through the countryside to one of his many castles, creating quite a picture. The coach is completely gilded, inside and out. In winter the king would use his state sleigh (also on display), which is nearly as elaborate as the Cinderella coach.

**Nymphenburg's park** ★ stretches for 200ha (500 acres). A canal runs through it from the pool at the foot of the staircase to the cascade at the far end of the English-style gardens. A number of delightful pavilions are in the park: the Badenburg Pavilion, a bathing pavilion near the lake of the same name; the Pagodenburg, decorated in chinoiserie style; and the Magdalenenklause (Hermitage), meant to be a retreat for prayer and solitude.

Our favorite is the **Amalienburg** ★★ pavilion, whose plain exterior belies the rococo decoration inside. Built as a hunting lodge for Electress Amalia (in 1734), the pavilion carries the hunting theme through the first few rooms and then bursts into salons of flamboyant colors, rich carvings, and wall paintings. The most impressive room is the Hall of Mirrors, a symphony of silver ornaments on a faint blue background.

Other attractions include the **Porzellansammlung,** or museum of porcelain, which are above the stables of the Marstallmuseum. Some of the finest pieces of porcelain in the world, executed in the 18th century, are displayed here, along with an absolute gem—miniature copies in porcelain, done in extraordinary detail, of some of the grand masterpieces in the Old Pinakothek. Each was commissioned by Ludwig I.

Schloss Nymphenburg 1, 8km (5 miles) northwest of the city center. ✆ **089/17908-0.** Admission to castle 3.50€ ($3.15) free for children under 17. Admission to all attractions 7.50€ ($6.70), free for children under 17. Nov–Mar daily 10am–4pm; Apr–Oct daily 9am–6pm (Thurs until 8pm). Parking beside the Marstallmuseum. U-Bahn: Rotkreuzplatz, then tram 17 toward Amalienburgstrasse. Bus: 41.

## MORE ATTRACTIONS

### MUSEUMS

**Antikensammlungen (Museum of Antiquities)** ★ This collection grew around the vase collection of Ludwig I, who had fantasies of transforming Munich into a second Athens. It was originally called the Museum Antiker Kleinkunst (Museum of Small Works of Ancient Art). Many pieces are small in size but not in value or artistic significance.

The museum's five main-floor halls house more than 650 Greek vases. The oldest, the pre-Mycenaean "goddess from Aegina" (3000 B.C.), carved from a mussel shell, is in room I. The upper level of the Central Hall is devoted to large Greek vases discovered in Sicily and to Etruscan art. On the lower level is the collection of Greek, Roman, and Etruscan jewelry. (Note the similarities with today's design fashions.) Also on this level are rooms devoted to ancient colored glass, Etruscan bronzes, and Greek terra-cottas.

Königsplatz 1. ✆ **089/59-83-59.** Admission 3.50€ ($3.15) adults, 2€ ($1.80) students and seniors, free for children 14 and under. Joint ticket to the Museum of Antiquities and the Glyptothek 6€ ($5.35) adults, free for children under 14, fee for everyone on Sun. Tues and Thurs–Sun 10am–5pm; Wed 10am–8pm. U-Bahn: Königsplatz.

**Glyptothek** ★ The ideal neighbor for the Museum of Antiquities, the Glyptothek supplements the pottery and smaller pieces of the main museum with the country's largest collection of ancient Greek and Roman sculpture. Included are the famous pediments from the temple of Aegina, two marvelous statues of *kouroi* (youths) from the 6th century B.C., the colossal figure of a *Sleeping Satyr* from the Hellenistic period, and a splendid collection of Roman portraits.

Königsplatz 3. ✆ **089/28-61-00.** Admission 3€ ($2.70) adults, 2€ ($1.80) students and seniors, free for children 13 and under. Joint ticket to the Museum of Antiquities and the Glyptothek 6€ ($5.35) adults, free for children under 14. Tues–Wed and Fri–Sun 10am–5pm; Thurs 10am–8pm. U-Bahn: U2 to Königsplatz.

**Münchner Stadtmuseum (Municipal Museum)** ★ Munich's Municipal Museum offers insight into the city's history and people's daily lives. A wooden model shows Munich in 1572. Special exhibitions about popular arts and traditions are presented frequently. The museum's most important exhibit is its Moorish Dancers (*Moriskentanzer*) on the ground floor. These 10 figures, each 60cm (2 ft.) high, carved in wood, and painted in bright colors by Erasmus Grasser in 1480, are among the best examples of secular Gothic art in Germany. The second-floor photo museum traces the early history of the camera back to 1839. Daily at 6 and 9pm, the film museum shows two different films from its extensive archives. The historical collection of musical instruments on the fourth floor is one of the greatest of its kind in the world.

St. Jacobs-Platz 1. ✆ **089/233-22370.** Admission 2.50€ ($2.25) adults, 1.50€ ($1.35) students and children 6–15 (free 5 and under); Sun free for everyone. Tues–Sun 10am–6pm. U-Bahn/S-Bahn: Marienplatz.

**Neue Pinakothek** ★ This museum offers a survey of 18th- and 19th-century art, including paintings by Gainsborough, Goya, David, Manet, van Gogh, and Monet. Among the more popular German artists represented are Wilhelm Leibl and Gustav Klimt. Note particularly the genre works by Carl Spitzweg, whose paintings poke gentle fun at everyday life in Munich.

Barerstrasse 29 (across Theresienstrasse from the Alte Pinakothek). ✆ **089/23-80-51-95.** Admission 5€ ($4.45) adults, 3.50€ ($3.15) students, seniors, and children 14 and under. Wed–Mon 10am–5pm. U-Bahn: Königsplatz. Tram: 27. Bus: 53.

**Stadtische Galerie im Lenbachhaus** ★ This gallery is in the ancient gold-colored villa of portrait painter Franz von Lenbach (1836–1904). It's devoted both to his work and that of other artists. Enter through the gardens. You'll first be greeted by a large collection of early pieces by Paul Klee (1879–1940). There's also an outstanding group of works by Kandinsky, leader of the Blue Rider movement in the early 20th century, and many 19th- and 20th-century paintings throughout the villa. The enclosed patio is pleasant for a coffee break.

Luisenstrasse 33. ✆ **089/23-33-20-00.** Admission 5€ ($4.45) adults, 2.50€ ($2.25) students and children 6–12, free for children 5 and under. Tues–Sun 10am–6pm. U-Bahn: Königsplatz.

## CHURCHES

Munich has many beautiful churches in addition to those listed below. Visitors should not miss the **Asamkirche,** on Sendlinger Strasse (✆ **089/260-93-57;** U-Bahn/S-Bahn: Marienplatz), a beautiful rococo church built between 1733 and

1746 and dedicated to St. John of Nepomuk. The **Michaelskirche,** or St. Michael's Church, Neuhauserstrasse 52 (✆ **089/231-7060;** U-Bahn/S-Bahn: Marienplatz), is the largest Renaissance church north of the Alps. It was built by Duke William the Pious from 1583 to 1597. Lastly, the **Matthäuskirche,** or St. Matthew's Church, Nussbaumstrasse 1 (U-Bahn: Sendlinger Tor), is a modern Evangelical cathedral completed in 1955.

**Frauenkirche (Cathedral of Our Lady)** ★ When the smoke cleared from the 1945 bombings, only a fragile shell remained of Munich's largest church. Workmen and architects who restored the 15th-century Gothic cathedral used whatever remains they could find in the rubble, along with modern innovations. The overall effect of the rebuilt Frauenkirche is strikingly simple, yet dignified. The twin towers with their onion domes, which remained intact, have been the city's landmark since 1525. Instead of the typical flying buttresses, huge props on the inside, which separate the side chapels, support the edifice. Twenty-two simple octagonal pillars support the Gothic vaulting over the nave and chancel.

Entering the main doors, your first impression is that there are no windows (most of them are hidden by the enormous pillars). According to legend, the devil laughed at the notion of hidden windows and stamped in glee at the stupidity of the architect—you can still see the strange foot-like mark called "the devil's step" in the entrance hall. In the chapel directly behind the high altar is the cathedral's most interesting painting: Jan Polack's *The Protecting Cloak* (1510), showing the Virgin holding out her majestic robes to shelter all humankind. The collection of tiny figures beneath the cloak includes everyone from the Pope to peasants.

Frauenplatz 12. ✆ **089/29-00-82-0.** Free admission. Sat–Thurs 7am–7pm, Fri 7am–6pm. U-Bahn/S-Bahn: Marienplatz.

**Peterskirche (St. Peter's Church)** Munich's oldest church (1180), known locally as Old Peter, has turned over a new leaf, and it's a gold one at that. The white-and-gray interior has been decorated with gilded baroque accents and trompe l'oeil medallions. It contains a series of murals by Johann Baptist Zimmermann, but nothing tops the attraction of the bizarre relic in the second chapel on the left: the gilt-covered and gem-studded skeleton of St. Mundita. From its resting place on a cushion, it stares at you with two false eyes in its skull. Jewels cover the mouth of its rotten teeth, quite a contrast to the fresh roses usually kept in front of the black-and-silver coffin. The church also has a tall steeple, which you can climb, though it lacks an elevator. Colored circles on the lower platform tell you whether the climb is worthwhile: If the circle is white, you can see as far as the Alps.

Rindermarkt 1 (near the Rathaus). ✆ **089/2-60-48-28.** Church free; tower 1.50€ ($1.35) adults, 1€ ($ 90) students, .30€ (25¢) children. Mon–Sat 9am–7pm, Sun 10am–7pm. U-Bahn/S-Bahn: Marienplatz.

**Theatinerkirche** Named for a small group of Roman Catholic clergy (the Theatines), this church, dedicated to Saint Kajetan, is Munich's finest example of Italian baroque. Two Italian architects, Barelli and Zucalli, began building it in 1662. François de Cuvilliés the Elder added the facade a century later, and his son finally completed the structure in 1768. Fluted columns that line the center aisle support the arched ceiling of the nave. Above the transept, dividing the nave from the choir, the ceiling breaks into an open dome, with an ornate gallery decorated with large but graceful statues. Nothing detracts from the whiteness of the interior except the dark wooden pews and the canopied pulpit. Since 1954 the church has been under the care of the Dominican Friars.

Theatinerstrasse 22. ✆ **089/21-06-96-0.** Free admission. Church Mon–Fri 10am–1pm and 1:30–4:30pm; Sat 10am–3pm. U-Bahn: Odeonsplatz.

## PARKS & ZOOS

Munich's city park, the 18th-century **Englischer Garten** ★, borders Schwabing on the east and extends almost to the Isar River. This is one of the largest and most beautiful city parks in Germany. It was the brainchild of Sir Benjamin Thompson, the English scientist who spent most of his life in the service of the Bavarian government. You can wander for hours along the walks and among the trees, flowers, and sunbathers. Nude sunbathing is permitted in certain areas of the park (some claim these areas are Munich's most popular tourist attraction). For a break, stop for tea on the plaza near the Chinese pagoda, or have a beer at the nearby beer garden. You might also take along a picnic put together at the elegant shop of **Alois Dallmayr,** or less expensive fare from **Hertie,** across from the Hauptbahnhof, from **Kaufhof** at Marienplatz, or from Munich's famous open-air market, the **Viktualienmarkt.**

**Hellabrunn Zoo** stands in Tierpark Hellabrunn, about 6km (4 miles) south of the city center, at Tierparkstrasse 30 (✆ **089/62-50-80;** U-Bahn: Thalkirchen; bus: 52). It's one of the largest zoos in the world, with hundreds of animals roaming in a natural habitat. A walk through the attractive park is recommended even if you're not a zoo buff. There's a big children's zoo, as well as a large aviary. You can visit the zoo daily 8am to 6pm (in winter, 9am to 5pm); admission is 6€ ($5.35) for adults, 4.50€ ($4) for students and seniors, 3€ ($2.70) for children ages 4 to 14, and free for children 3 and under.

## THE OLYMPIC GROUNDS

**Olympiapark** (✆ **089/30-67-24-14;** U-Bahn: Olympiazentrum), site of the 1972 Olympic Games, occupies 300ha (740 acres) at the city's northern edge. More than 15,000 workers from 18 countries transformed the site into a park of nearly 5,000 trees, 43km (27 miles) of roads, 32 bridges, and a lake. Olympiapark has its own railway station, U-Bahn line, mayor, post office, churches, and elementary school. The planners even broke the city skyline by adding a 293m (960-ft.) television tower in the center of the park.

The area's showpiece is a huge stadium, capable of seating 69,300 spectators, and topped by the largest roof in the world—nearly 67,000 sq. m. (80,000 sq. yds.) of tinted acrylic glass. The supports for the stadium are anchored by two huge blocks, each capable of resisting about 3.6 million killograms (4,000 tons) under stress. The roof serves the additional purpose of collecting rainwater and draining it into the nearby Olympic lake.

**Olympia Tower,** Olympiapark (✆ **089/30-67-27-50**), is open daily 9am to midnight. A ticket for a ride up the tower (on the speediest elevator on the continent, no less) costs 3€ ($2.70) for adults and 1.50€ ($1.35) for children under 15. An exclusive dining spot in the tower is the **Tower Restaurant** (✆ **089/30668585**), which features a selection of international and German dishes. Food is served daily 11am to 5:30pm and 6:30pm to midnight. A complete dinner costs 35€ to 50€ ($31.25–$44.65). The food is good and fresh, but of secondary consideration—most come here for the extraordinary view, which reaches to the Alps. Four observation platforms look out over Olympiapark. The Tower Restaurant revolves around its axis in 60 minutes, giving guests who linger a changing vista of Munich. Diners Club, MasterCard, and Visa are accepted.

At the base of the tower is the **Restaurant Olympiasee,** Spiridon-Louis-Ring 7 (✆ **089/30-67-28-08**), serving genuine Bavarian specialties, with meals costing

## Black September for the Olympics

The 1972 Munich Olympics, the largest ever in history, was meant to celebrate peace among nations, and for the first ten days, they did. However, in the early morning hours of September 5, eight Palestinian terrorists, later claiming to be part of the "Black September," terrorist group, snuck into the Olympic Village. Within a few minutes of entering the quarters of the sleeping Israeli athletes, they had already killed two Israelis and taken nine of the others hostage.

As the ensuing siege was played out on TV sets around the world, the terrorists demanded the release of 200 Arab guerillas jailed in Israel, and safe passage for themselves and their hostages. Few novelists could have conceived the plot (and mistakes by German law enforcement) that ensued, as negotiations helplessly and hopelessly dragged on between the terrorists and the West German security officials. In Israel, Golda Meir firmly stood by her government's policy of "not dealing with terrorists." The job of dealing with the terrorists fell clearly upon the shoulders of the West Germans.

By 8:30pm on the day of the attack, the first of three helicopters landed at Olympic Village to fly the terrorists and their hostages out of West Germany via a Lufthanse 737 that was waiting at the military air base at Fürstenfeldbruck, 15 miles away. Blinded and tied close together, the Israeli athletes, along with their heavily armed captors, were placed into the helicopters and flown away, landing at Fürstenfeldbruck at 10:30pm.

The negotiations between the terrorists and West German security officials suddenly collapsed when a West German sharpshooter hidden in the darkness fired unexpectedly at the terrorists. The Palestinians quickly responded by unleashing automatic fire at the tied and bound Israelis; one tossed a hand grenade into a helicopter, killing all of the remaining hostages. In response, the West Germans unleashed their fire power, killing five of the terrorists, and eventually capturing the others.

Mark Spitz, an American Jew and winner of seven gold medals, was flown out of Germany for his own safety as the Olympic Games were suspended for the first time in their history. The world mourned, and in a controversial decision, the Germans continued the games 34 hours later, with mixed reactions from both the world at large and the participating athletes. The presiding officer of the games, Avery Brundage, issued a famous pronouncement, "The Games must go on!" and so they did.

For more on this tragic event, read or watch the book/documentary movie titled *One Day in September.*

8€ ($7.15) and up. Food is served daily 9:30am to 7pm (8:30pm in summer). The restaurant is popular in summer because of its terrace. No credit cards are accepted.

Near Olympiapark, you can visit the **BMW Museum,** Petuelring 130 (✆ **089/38-22-33-07;** U-Bahn: Petuelring or Olympiazentrum), where the history of the automobile is stunningly displayed in an atmosphere created by Oscar-winner Rolf Zehetbauer, a "film architect." The exhibition "Horizons in Time," housed in a demisphere of modern architecture, takes you into the future and back to the past. You can view 24 video films and 10 slide shows (an especially interesting one shows how people of yesterday imagined the future). Many of the exhibits are in English. The museum is open daily 9am to 4pm, charging 3€ ($2.70) for adults and 2€ ($1.80) for children. While here, you might also ask about BMW factory tours.

### ESPECIALLY FOR KIDS (Kids

Of all the museums in Munich, kids will like best the **Deutsches Museum,** Museumsinsel 1 (✆ **089/2-17-91;** S-Bahn: Isartor; tram: 18), which has many "hands-on" exhibits. For details, see "The Top Attractions," earlier in this chapter.

On the third floor of the **Münchner Stadtmuseum,** St. Jakobsplatz 1 (✆ **089/23-32-23-70;** U-Bahn/S-Bahn: Marienplatz), is an array of marionettes and hand puppets from around the world. Another special department is devoted to fairground art, including carousel animals, shooting galleries, roller-coaster models, and wax and museum figures. The main exhibit contains the oldest-known carousel horses, dating from 1820. For hours and admission fees, see "More Attractions," above.

**Spielzeugmuseum,** in the Altes Rathaus, Marienplatz 15 (✆ **089/29-40-01;** U-Bahn/S-Bahn: Marienplatz), is a historical toy collection. It's open daily 10am to 5pm. Admission is 3€ ($2.70) for adults, 1€ (90¢) for children, and 6€ ($5.35) for a family.

For a truly charming experience, go to the **Münchener Marionetten Theater,** Blumenstrasse 32 (✆ **089/26-57-12;** U-Bahn/S-Bahn: Marienplatz), which was established in 1858. It stages marionette productions of operas by Mozart and other composers every Wednesday, Thursday, Saturday, and Sunday at 3pm, and every Saturday at 8pm. At matinees, adults pay 5€ ($4.45) entrance; children 3€ ($2.70). At evening shows tickets for both adults and children go for 8€ ($7.15). Matinees tend to be more animated and crowded than evening shows, and are particularly well-suited for younger children ages 4 and up.

**Bavaria Film Studio,** Bavariafilmplatz 7, Geiselgasteig (✆ **089/64-99-23-04;** tram: 25 to Bavariafilmplatz), is Europe's largest filmmaking center—Munich's version of Hollywood. Visitors can watch such spine-tingling thrillers as *Adventure in the Devil's Mine* and *Cosmic Pinball.* The 30-minute Bavaria Action Show features a stunt team demonstrating fist fights and fire stunts, tumbling down staircases, and even taking a 28m- (92-ft.-) high plunge. Guided 1½-hour tours (book 4 weeks in advance for a tour in English) are given March to October, daily 9am to 4pm (off-season 10am–3pm). Admission is 10€ ($8.95) for adults, 9€ ($8.05) for students and senior citizens, 7€ ($6.25) for children ages 4 to 14, and free for children 3 and under.

**Hellabrunn Zoo** has a large children's zoo, where kids can pet the animals. For details, see "More Attractions," above.

## 6 Organized Tours

### BY BUS

Blue buses that give sightseeing tours in both German and English leave from the square in front of the Hauptbahnhof, at Hertie's, year-round. Tickets are sold on the bus; no advance booking is necessary. A 1-hour tour, costing 11€ ($9.80) for adults and 6€ ($5.35) for children 6 to 12, leaves daily every hour from 10am to 4pm.

A 2½-hour tour, including the Olympic Tower, costs 19€ ($16.95) for adults and 10€ ($8.95) for children. Departures are May to October at 10am and 2:30pm and November to April at 2:30pm.

A second 2½-hour tour, with roughly the same prices as the above, visits the famous Neue Pinakothek (painting gallery), the Frauenkirche, and the chiming clocks at Marienplatz. It departs Tuesday to Sunday at 10am.

A third 2½-hour tour, costing 21€ ($18.75) for adults and 10€ ($8.95) for children, visits Nymphenburg Palace and the Schatzkammer. It departs daily at 2:30pm.

If you'd like to go farther afield and visit major attractions in the environs (such as Berchtesgaden or Ludwig II's castles), contact **Panorama Tours.** The office is at Arnulfstrasse 8 (✆ **089/54-90-75-60**), to the north of the Hauptbahnhof. Hours are Monday to Friday 8am to 6pm, Saturday 8am to 2pm, and Sunday and holidays 8am to noon.

### BY BIKE

Pedal pushers will want to try Mike Lasher's popular **Mike's Bike Tour,** Hochbrückenstrasse (✆ **089/255-43-987**). His bike-rental services include maps, locks, child and infant seats, and helmets at no extra charge. English and bilingual tours of central Munich run from March through November at 12:30pm daily (call to confirm). Customers love Mike's charm. Participants meet under the tower of the old town hall, a gray building on the east end of Marienplatz. Mike, the consummate guide, will be here—whistle in mouth—letting everyone know who he is. The tour veers from the bike paths only long enough for a lunch stop at a beer garden. Fear not, fainthearted: the bikes are new, and the rides are easy, with plenty of time for historical explanations, photo opportunities, and question-and-answer sessions. Bike rentals for tours without a guide (Mike will supply a map) are 15€ ($13.40) for the day; full-day guided tours begin at 33€ ($29.45).

Some of the best bike and walking tours are offered by the aptly named **Bike & Walk Company** Tal 22 (✆ **089/589-589-33**). Tours are in English and given by experts. The most popular jaunt is the "infamous" beer-garden bike tour. You hit three beer gardens in 4 hours. The cost is 21€ ($18.75). A 3⅓ hour city bike tour takes in the most important landmarks and architecture at a cost of 16€ ($14.30).

### BY FOOT

One walk, costing 8€ ($7.15) takes you through the old town with visits to the Glockenspiel, the Frauenkircke, and the famous Hofbrauhaus, with stops at the Feldherrnhalle for some Third Reich history, and a call at Hofgarten with tales of a scandal. For another walk, the dark side of Munich's history is explored in a tour leaving only on Monday, Thursday, and Saturday at 2:30 and 5pm, costing 8€ ($7.15). It covers some of the landmarks that reveal Munich's role as the birthplace of Nazism. The tour (available in English) covers all the major sites that played a role in this black chapter in German history.

## 7 Sports & Outdoor Pursuits

### BEACHES, POOLS & WATER SPORTS

On hot weekends, much of Munich embarks for nearby lakes, the **Ammersee** and the **Starnbergersee,** where bathing facilities are clearly marked. You can also swim at **Maria-Einsiedel,** in the frigid, snow-fed waters of the Isar River. The city has several public swimming pools as well. The largest of these includes the giant competition-size pool in the Olympiapark, the **Olympia-Schwimmhalle** (✆ **089/30-67-22-90;** U-Bahn: Olympiazentrum). Admission is 7€ ($6.25). Information on both sailing and windsurfing is available from the **Bayerischer Segler-Verbund,** Georg-Brauchle-Ring 93 (✆ **089/15-70-23-66**).

### JOGGING

Regardless of the season, the most lushly landscaped place in Munich is the **Englischer Garten** (U-Bahn: Münchner Freiheit), which has a 11km (7-mile) circumference and an array of dirt and asphalt tracks. Also appropriate are the grounds of the **Olympiapark** (U-Bahn: Olympiazentrum) or the park surrounding **Schloss Nymphenburg** (U-Bahn: Rotkreuzplatz, then tram 17 toward Amalienburgstrasse; bus: 41.). More convenient to the center of the city's commercial district is a jog along the embankments of the Isar River.

### RAFTING

Raft trips on the Isar River are conducted between the town of Wolfratshausen and Munich early May to late September. Be advised that a raft may contain up to 60 other passengers. If you still want to try it, call **Franz and Sebastian Seitner,** Heideweg 9, 82515 Wolfratshausen (✆ **089/71/1-83-20**).

### ROWING

Rowboats add to the charm of the lakes in the **Englischer Garten.** There's a kiosk at the edge of the Kleinhesseloher See where you can rent them. There are also rowboat rentals on the southern bank of the **Olympiasee,** in the Olympiapark.

### SKIING

Because of the proximity of the Bavarian and Austrian Alps, many Munich residents are avid skiers. For information on resorts and getaway snow-related activities, contact the **Bayerischer Segler-Verbund,** Georg-Brauchle-Ring 93, 80992 München (✆ **089/15-70-23-66**).

### SPECTATOR SPORTS

Munich loves soccer and has one of Europe's outstanding teams, **Bayern München,** which plays at the Olympic Stadium in Olympiapark. If you want to attend a match, call ✆ **089/54-81-81-81.**

### TENNIS

At least 200 indoor and outdoor tennis courts are scattered around greater Munich. Many can be booked in advance by calling ✆ **089/54-81-81-81.** For information on Munich's many tennis tournaments and competitions, contact the **Bayerischer Tennis Verbund,** Georg-Brauchle-Ring 93, 80992 München (✆ **089/15-70-23-66**).

## 8 Shopping

The most interesting shops are concentrated on Munich's pedestrians-only street, between Karlsplatz and Marienplatz. Store hours in Munich are generally Monday to Friday 9 or 9:30am to 6pm and Saturday 9 or 9:30am to 1 or 2pm.

### ANTIQUES

**Philographikon Galerie Rauhut** This important gallery, set midway between the Hotel Vier Jahreszeiten and the National Opera House, represents one of the most celebrated success stories of Munich's art world. In 1978, Mr. Rauhut, a television producer, transformed his hobby of collecting rare engravings and manuscripts into a career by establishing this shop. Here you'll find one of the most comprehensive collections of antique art in Munich. Prices range from 30€ ($26.80) for a 19th-century steel engraving, to tens of thousands of euros for pre-Gutenberg illuminated manuscripts. Other curiosities include antique maps; English, French, and German botanical prints; and a series of rare prints by a Swiss-born engraver, Karl Bodmer, whose depictions in the 1820s of native American Indians are increasingly valuable on both sides of the Atlantic. Maximilianstrasse 15. ✆ **089/22-50-82.** U-Bahn/S-Bahn: Marienplatz.

**Squirrel** This unusual shop, established 20 years ago by its charming owners, Urban Geissel and his wife, Gisela, houses a collection of luggage made by English and French purveyors for the aristocrats of the Jazz Age. There are examples from such English makers as Finnegan's and Harrods. Although they tend to be heavy, they're still serviceable and richly imbued with the nostalgia of the great days of oceangoing travel. Schellingstrasse 54. ✆ **089/2-72-09-29.** U-Bahn: Universität.

## ART

**Galerie für Angewandte Kunst München** This is one of Germany's largest, most visible, and most historic art galleries, established in the 1840s as a showcase for local artists. The complex contains an upscale art gallery and a sales outlet, the Ladengeschäft, where attractive crafts are sold at prices that begin at 25€ ($22.35). Works by more than 400 artists are displayed and sold here. Examples include sculpture in all kinds of media, crafts, textiles, and woven objects. Pacellistrasse 8. ✆ **089/2-90-14-70.** U-Bahn: Karlsplatz.

## BOOKS

**Hugendubel** Not only is this Munich's biggest bookstore, but it also enjoys the most central location. It sells a number of English-language titles, both fiction and nonfiction, and also offers travel books and helpful maps. Marienplatz 22. ✆ **01803/484-484.** U-Bahn/S-Bahn: Marienplatz.

## CHINA, SILVER & GLASS

**Kunstring Meissen** During the coldest days of the Cold War, this was Munich's exclusive distributor of Meissen and Dresden china, manufactured behind the Iron Curtain in East Germany. With reunification, Kunstring's exclusive access became a thing of the past. Despite that, the shop still contains one of Munich's largest inventories of the elegant porcelain. Briennerstrasse 4. ✆ **089/28-15-32.** U-Bahn: Odeonsplatz.

**Rosenthal Studio-Hause** Rosenthal, established in 1879 in the Bavarian town of Selb near the Czech border, is one of the three or four most prestigious names in German porcelain. Much (though not all) of the line today focuses on contemporary design, an approach that separates it from the more traditional ways of Nymphenburg, Sevrès, or Limoges. The manufacturer pre-establishes prices for Rosenthal patterns and maintains them rigidly, so there are no price breaks at this factory outlet. You will, however, find the widest array of Rosenthal patterns available in Germany. In addition to porcelain, the line includes furniture, glass, and cutlery. Dienerstrasse 17. ✆ **089/22-26-17.** U-Bahn/S-Bahn: Marienplatz.

## CRAFTS

**Bayerischer Kunstgewerbeverein (Bavarian Association of Arts & Crafts)** At this showcase for Bavarian artisans, you'll find excellent handcrafts: ceramics, glasses, jewelry, woodcarvings, pewter, and seasonal Christmas decorations. Pacellistrasse 6–8. ✆ **089/2-90-14-70.** U-Bahn: Karlsplatz.

**Otto Kellnberger Holzhandlung** This small but choice emporium of traditional woodcarvings evokes remote alpine Bavaria. Its inventory features all the folkloric charm and much of the folkloric kitsch you might find in remote Oberammergau. Heiliggeistrasse 8. ✆ **089/22-64-79.** U-Bahn/S-Bahn: Marienplatz.

**Prinoth** *Finds* Most of the woodcarvings sold here are produced in small workshops in the folklore-rich Italian South Tyrol. The selection is wide-ranging, and because the shop is 6km (3½ miles) west of Munich's tourist zones, prices are reasonable compared to those of shops closer to the Marienplatz. Guido Schneblestrasse 9A. ✆ **089/56-03-78.** U-Bahn: Laimerplatz.

**Wallach** *Value* We consider Wallach the finest place in Germany for handcrafts, both new and antique, as well as folk art. Shop here for a memorable object to remind you of your trip. You'll find antique churns, old hand-painted wooden boxes and trays, milking stools, painted porcelain clocks, dirndls, leather pants, wooden wall clocks, doilies, napkins, towels, and more. Residenzstrasse 3. ✆ **089/22-08-71.** U-Bahn/S-Bahn: Marienplatz.

## DEPARTMENT STORES

**Hertie** This is our favorite department store in Munich, a sprawling four-story-plus basement emporium of all aspects of the German version of the good life. A fixture near the main railway station since the turn of the century, it has survived wars and revolutions with predictable mercantile style. Bahnhofplatz 7. ✆ **089/5-51-20.** U-Bahn/S-Bahn: Hauptbahnhof.

**Kaufhof** This is one of the largest department stores in town. You can wander freely among displays that are art forms in their own right. The inventory includes virtually everything, from men's, women's and children's clothing to housewares, and much more. Marienplatz. ✆ **089/23-18-51.** U-Bahn/S-Bahn: Marienplatz.

**Ludwig Beck am Rathauseck** Most merchandise here is intended for local residents; however, visitors will also be interested in this four-floor shopping bazaar, which sells handmade crafts from all over Germany, both old and new. Items include decorative pottery and dishes, etched-glass beer steins and vases, painted wall plaques, decorative flower arrangements, unusual kitchenware, fashions, textiles, and much more. Am Marienplatz 11. ✆ **089/23-69-10.** U-Bahn/S-Bahn: Marienplatz.

## ENGRAVINGS & POSTCARDS

**Philatelie und Ansichtskarten** *Finds* It doesn't really look like a shop at all, but rather like a dusty storeroom at a museum. It's the rendezvous for academics and collectors from throughout Germany, who phone in special requests for antique engravings and postcards that depict specific settings, personalities, and places. Merchandise, each piece carefully inventoried and stored in cardboard boxes arranged by subject, ranges from the sober to the schmaltzy. Bahnhofplatz 2. ✆ **089/59-67-57.** U-Bahn: Bahnhofplatz.

## FASHION

**Bogner Haus** Before you head for the slopes, shop here for the latest in ski clothing and styles. Willy Bogner, the filmmaker and Olympic downhill racer, sells this flamboyant attire. The store also sells more formal clothing for men and women. Residenzstrasse 15. ✆ **089/2-90-70-40.** U-Bahn/S-Bahn: Marienplatz.

**Dirndl-Ecke** One block up from the famed Hofbräuhaus, this shop gets our unreserved recommendation. It's a stylish place specializing in high-grade dirndls, feathered alpine hats, and all clothing associated with the alpine regions. Everything sold is of fine quality—there's no tourist junk. Other merchandise includes needlework hats, beaded belts, and pleated shirts for men. Be sure to see the stylish capes, the silver jewelry in old Bavarian style, the leather shoes, and the linen-and-cotton combinations, such as skirts with blouses and jackets.

Bavarian clothing for children is also available. Am Platzl 1/Sparkassenstrasse 10. ✆ **089/22-01-63.** U-Bahn/S-Bahn: Marienplatz.

**Frankonia** This store, established in 1907, has Munich's most prestigious collection of traditional Bavarian dress (called *Tracht*). If you see yourself dressed hunter style, or in traditional alpine garb, this place can outfit you well. There's a fine collection of wool cardigan jackets with silvery buttons. Maximiliansplatz 10. ✆ **089/2-90-00-20.** Tram: 19.

**Furore** If you're shopping for fashionable undergarments (brassieres, bustiers, or slips), and if you've been working out at the gym and look fabulous, this is the place for you. The designs are tasteful, in some cases filmy and subtly erotic, in silk, cotton, and synthetics. There's also a loungewear collection. Franz-Josef-Strasse 41. ✆ **089/34-39-71.** U-Bahn: Giselastrasse.

**Hirmer** In the pedestrian zone, this menswear shop has the best collection in town of German-made men's clothing. The staff here is especially helpful in outfitting you with something that looks good on you, the selection coming from such brand-names as Boss, Barbour, Rene Lezard, and van Laak. Both business and leisure suits are sold at middle to upper-bracket prices. They even cater to "big beer bellies." Kaufinger Strasse 28. ✆ **089/23683210.** U-Bahn: Marienplatz.

**Loden-Frey** You can see the twin domes of the Frauenkirche above the soaring glass-enclosed atrium of this shop's showroom. Go here for the world's largest selection of *Loden* clothing and traditional costumes, as well as for international fashions from top European designers such as Armani, Valentino, and Ungaro. Maffeistrasse 7–9. ✆ **089/21039-0.** U-Bahn/S-Bahn: Marienplatz.

**Maendler** This store is divided into a series of boutiques well known to virtually every well-dressed woman in Bavaria. You'll find the creative vision of Joop, New York New York, and Jil Sander here. Looking for that special something for your dinner with the mayor or the president of Germany? Ask to see formal eveningwear by Jean-Paul Gaultier. For something more experimental and daring, head for the branch called **Rosy Maendler,** Maximiliansplatz 12 (same phone; tram: 19), where you'll find a more youthful version of the same store. Theatinerstrasse 7. ✆ **089/2422-8850.** U-Bahn: Odeonsplatz.

**Red/Green of Scandinavia** This shop near the Marienplatz sells men's and women's relaxed, casual clothing, appropriate for wearing on a private yacht or the local golf links. Most of the inventory comes from Denmark, and because everything was designed to withstand the blustery winds and the clear sunlight of the Baltic, it's sturdy enough for any activity. Kaufingerstrasse 9. ✆ **089/2-60-64-89.** U-Bahn/S-Bahn: Marienplatz.

## FOOD

**Dallmayr** What Fortnum & Mason is to London, the venerable firm of Dallmayr is to Munich. Gastronomes as far away as Hamburg and Berlin telephone orders for exotica not readily available anywhere else. Dallmayr's list of prestigious clients reads like a who's who of German industry and letters. Wander freely among racks of foodstuffs, some of which are too delicate to survive shipment abroad, others of which can be shipped anywhere. Dienerstrasse 14–15. ✆ **089/2-13-50.** Tram: 19.

## JEWELRY & WATCHES

**Carl Jagemann's** Its reputation for quality and honesty goes back to 1864, as does some (but not all) of the merchandise it sells. It's one of the Altstadt's largest purveyors of new and antique timepieces of all types, from wristwatches to fine reproduction grandfather clocks. There's also a collection of new and antique jewelry. Residenzstrasse 3. ✆ **089/22-54-93.** U-Bahn/S-Bahn: Marienplatz.

**Hemmerle** This is *the* place for jewelry. The original founders of this conservative shop made their fortune designing bejeweled fantasies for the Royal Bavarian Court of Ludwig II. All pieces are limited editions, designed and made in-house by Bavarian craftspeople. The company also designs its own wristwatch, the Hemmerle. Maximilianstrasse 14. ✆ **089/24-22-60-0.** U-Bahn/S-Bahn: Marienplatz.

### PORCELAIN

**Porzellan-Manufaktur-Nymphenburg** At Nymphenburg, about 8km (5 miles) northwest of the heart of Munich, you'll find one of Germany's most famous porcelain factories, on the grounds of Schloss Nymphenburg. You can visit its exhibition and sales rooms, Monday to Friday 8:30am to 6:30pm, and Saturday 10am to 6pm. Shipments can be arranged if you make purchases. There's also a more central branch in Munich's center at Odeonsplatz 1 (✆ **089/28-24-28;** U-Bahn: Odeonsplatz). Nördliches Schlossrondell 8. ✆ **089/1-79-19-70.** Bus: 41.

### TOYS

**Münchner Poupenstuben und Zinnfiguren Kabinette** This is Germany's oldest miniature pewter foundry, dating from 1796. Many Germans visit Munich every December to purchase traditional Christmas decorations of a type once sold to Maximilian I, king of Bavaria. Managed by matriarchs of the same family, this store is one of the best sources in Germany for miniature houses, furniture, birdcages, and people, all cunningly crafted from pewter or carved wood. Some of the figures are made from 150-year-old molds that are collector's items in their own right. Anything in this place would make a great gift not only for a child but also for an adult with a nostalgic bent. Maxburgstrasse 4. ✆ **089/29-37-97.** U-Bahn: Karlsplatz.

**Obletter's** *Kids* Established in the 1880s, this is one of the largest emporiums of children's toys in Munich. The two floors of inventory contain everything from folkloric dolls to computer games. Karlsplatz 11. ✆ **089/55089510.** U-Bahn: Karlsplatz.

### WINE

**Geisel's Vinothek** Other than Dallmayr (see "Food," above), which has a much larger selection, this is the most sophisticated wine shop in Munich. Its inventory includes wines from Germany, Austria, Italy, and France, with bottles starting at 7.75€ ($6.90). The shop also doubles as a restaurant. Schützenstrasse 11. ✆ **089/55-13-71-40.** U-Bahn/S-Bahn: Hauptbahnhof.

## 9 Munich After Dark

To find out what's happening in the Bavarian capital, go to the tourist office on Platform 12 at the Hauptbanhof (✆ **089/2-33-03-00**) and request a copy of *Monatsprogramm* (a monthly program guide), costing 1.50€ ($1.35). It contains a complete cultural guide, telling you not only what's being presented—including concerts, opera, special exhibits, and museum hours—but also how to purchase tickets.

### THE PERFORMING ARTS

Nowhere else in Europe, other than London and Paris, will you find so many musical and theatrical events. And the good news is that seats don't cost a fortune—so count on indulging yourself and going to several performances. You'll get good tickets for anything from 10€ to 45€ ($8.95–$40.20).

If you speak German, you'll find at least 20 theaters offering plays of every description: classic, comic, experimental, contemporary—take your pick. The best way to find out what current productions might interest you is to go to a theater-ticket agency. Head for **WOM (World of Music),** Kaufingerstrasse 15 (✆ **089/2601-9100** or 089/235-05-720; S-Bahn: Marienplatz). WOM's leading competitors include **München Tickets** (✆ **089/54-81-81-81**) and **Hieber am Dom** (✆ **089/2900-8014**), both of which deal in tickets to basically the same cultural, entertainment, and sporting events within Bavaria, with access to the same computer database. Unfortunately, the use of a credit card for payment, both at WOM and at its competitors, carries a surcharge of at least 10€ ($8.95) per order. Be advised that for some sporting events (such as soccer) and musical events (including most of the operas subsidized by the city of Munich), where season tickets and long-term subscriptions reduce availability, you'll have to go to the venue's box office, as organizers tend not to cooperate with outside ticket agencies.

**Altes Residenztheater (Cuvilliés Theater)** An attraction in itself (see "Residenz" in "The Top Attractions," earlier in this chapter), this is also an important performance venue. The **Bavarian State Opera** (✆ **089/21-85-19-19**) and the **Bayerisches Staatsschauspiel** (✆ **089/2185-1920**), perform smaller works here, in keeping with the tiny theater's more intimate character. Box-office hours are the same as those for the Nationaltheater (see "Bayerischen Staatsoper," below). Residenzstrasse 1. ✆ **089/2185-1940,** or 089/21-85-19-20 for ticket information. Opera tickets 15€–150€ ($13.40–$133.95); play tickets 13€–55€ ($11.60–$49.10). U-Bahn: Odeonplatz.

**Bayerischen Staatsoper** The **Bavarian State Opera** is one of the world's great companies. The Bavarians give their hearts and souls to opera. Productions here are beautifully mounted and presented, and the company's roster includes some of the world's greatest singers. Hard-to-get tickets may be purchased at the box office Monday to Friday 10am to 6pm and Saturday 10am to 1pm, plus 1 hour before each performance. The Nationaltheater is also the home of the **Bavarian State Ballet.** Performing in the Nationaltheater, Max-Joseph-Platz 2. ✆ **089/2185-1920.** Tickets 8€–145€ ($7.15–$129.50), including standing room. U-Bahn/S-Bahn: Marienplatz.

**Bayerisches Staatsschauspiel (State Theater)** This repertory company is known for its performances of the classics: Shakespeare as well as Goethe and Schiller, and others. The box office, around the corner on Maximilianstrasse, is open Monday to Friday 10am to 6pm, Saturday 10am to 1pm, and 1 hour before performances. Max-Joseph-Platz. ✆ **089/21-85-19-40.** Tickets 12.50€–40€ ($11.15–$35.70). U-Bahn/S-Bahn: Marienplatz.

**Deutsches Theater** Musicals are popular here, but operettas, ballets, and international shows are performed as well. During Carnival in January and February, the theater becomes a ballroom—the costume balls and official black-tie festivities here are famous throughout Europe. Schwanthalerstrasse 13. ✆ **089/55-23-44-44.** Tickets 15.50€–85€ ($13.85–$75.90); higher for special events. U-Bahn/S-Bahn: Karlsplatz/Stachus or Hauptbahnhof.

**Münchner Kammerspiele** Contemporary plays as well as classics are performed here. The season runs early October to July. You can reserve tickets by phone Monday to Friday 10am to 6pm, but you must pick them up at least 2 days before a performance. The box office is open Monday to Friday 10am to 6pm and on Saturday 10am to 1pm, plus 1 hour before performances. There's also a second, smaller theater called **Werkraum,** Hildegardstrasse 1 (same phone as above), where new works are presented. Maximilianstrasse 26–28. ✆ **089/233-3700.** Tickets 8€–35€ ($7.15–$31.25). U-Bahn: Marienplatz. S-Bahn: Isartor. Tram: 19.

**Münchner Philharmoniker (Munich Philharmonic Orchestra)** This famous orchestra was founded in 1893. Its music director is James Levine, and its home is the Gasteig Cultural Center, where it performs in Philharmonic Hall. The center also shelters the Richard Strauss Conservatory and the Munich Municipal Library, and has five performance halls. You can purchase tickets at the ground-level Glashalle, Monday to Friday 10am to 8pm and Saturday 10am to 4pm. The Philharmonic season runs mid-September to July. Performing in the Gasteig Kulturzentrum in the Haidhausen district, Rosenheimerstrasse 5. ✆ **089/54-81-81-81.** Tickets 12€–60€ ($10.70–$53.60). S-Bahn: Rosenheimerplatz. Tram: 18 to Gasteig. Bus: 51.

## BEER HALLS

The Bierhalle is a traditional Munich institution, offering food, entertainment, and, of course, beer. It is said that Müncheners consume more beer than anyone else in Germany. Bernd Boehle once wrote: "If a man really belongs to Munich he drinks beer at all times of the day, at breakfast, at midday, at teatime; and in the evening, of course, he just never stops." A liter of beer will generally set you back about 5€ ($4.45). For information on outdoor beer gardens, see the "Beer Gardens" box earlier in this chapter.

### François Cuvilliés

In the 17th and 18th centuries, Bavaria's rulers were determined to rival Rome itself. They adorned their city with churches, abbeys, and monuments. In the cutthroat competition for commissions that followed, an unlikely candidate emerged for the role of Munich's most brilliant master of the rococo style.

François Cuvilliés (1695–1768) was a dwarf born in Belgium. Like many of his peers, he became first a pageboy and later court jester to Max Emanuel, elector of Bavaria. When the elector was exiled, François accompanied him, and in St-Cloud near Paris, he absorbed his patron's interest in the aesthetics of French baroque architecture. Ambitious and witty, he won Max Emanuel's friendship and support. When the elector was reinstated with pomp and ceremony as ruler of Bavaria, François became a draftsman for the court's chief architect.

Cuvilliés proved himself so talented that in 1720 Max Emanuel sent him for a 4-year apprenticeship to one of the leading architects of Paris, Jacques-François Blondel. After his return to Munich, his work soon eclipsed that of his master. By 1745, the former jester had been elevated to the title of chief architect to the Bavarian court.

His commissions between 1726 and his death in 1768 include some of southern Germany's most important rococo monuments, such as the interior of the **Amalienburg Pavilion** in the park of Nymphenburg Palace and the facade of the **Theatinerkirche.** His most famous creation is the remarkable **Altes Residenztheater,** familiarly called by his name. All his work is notable for a flamboyant sinuousness.

Cuvilliés' son, François Cuvilliés the Younger (1731–77), also became an architect, although he never achieved the greatness of his father. Most notably, he put the finishing touches on the facade of the **Theatinerkirche,** which his father had left unfinished at his death.

**Augustinerbräu** This beer hall's dark-wood panels and carved-plaster ceilings make the place look older than it is. It's been around for less than a century, but beer was first brewed on this spot in 1328 (or so they claim). The long menu changes daily, and the cuisine is not for dieters: It's hearty, heavy, and starchy, but that's what customers want. Open daily 9am to midnight. Neuhäuserstrasse 27. ✆ **089/23-18-32-57.** U-Bahn/S-Bahn: Karlsplatz/Stachus. Tram: 19.

**Hofbräuhaus am Platzl** ★ The state-owned Hofbräuhaus is the world's most famous beer hall. Visitors with only 1 night in Munich usually come here. The present Hofbräuhaus was built in 1897, but the tradition of a beer house on this spot dates from 1589. This one was the setting for the notorious meeting where Hitler took control of the tiny German Workers' Party in 1920. Fistfights erupted as the Nazis attacked their Bavarian enemies, right here in the beer palace.

Today, 4,500 beer drinkers can crowd in here. Several rooms, including a top-floor room for dancing, are spread over three floors. With its brass band (which starts playing at 11am), the ground-floor Schwemme is what you always expected of a beer hall—eternal Oktoberfest. In the second-floor restaurant, strolling musicians entertain, and dirndl-clad servers offer mugs of beer between sing-alongs. Every night the Hofbräuhaus presents a typical Bavarian show in its Fest-Hall 8pm to midnight. Admission is 5€ ($4.45). The hall is open daily 9am to midnight. Am Platzl 9. ✆ **089/22-16-76.** U-Bahn/S-Bahn: Marienplatz.

**Max Emanuel Brauerei** Löwenbräu turned this brewery into a beer hall in the 1920s. It still serves steins of beer and platters of filling German grub. On Wednesday and Friday, the second floor plays host to a popular salsa disco. Open daily 10am to 1am. Adalbertstrasse 33. ✆ **089/2-71-51-58.** Cover 6€ ($5.35), Wed, 7€ ($6.25) Fri–Sat. U-Bahn: Universität.

**Türkenhof** This beer hall is not the stereotypical schmaltzy old-Bavaria tourist trap. Here you'll find cosmopolitan cuisine made by a Greek co-owner and lively, intelligent conversation flowing among the student patrons. It's a big, fun bar created out of a 150-year-old butcher shop. There are five varieties of Augustiner beer available on tap. Open Sunday to Thursday 11am to 1am; Friday and Saturday 11am to 3am. Türkenstrasse 78. ✆ **089/2-80-02-35.** U-Bahn: Universität.

**Waldwirtschaft Grosshesselöhe** This popular summertime rendezvous, located above the Isar River near the zoo, has seats for some 2,000 drinkers. Music ranging from Dixieland to English jazz to Polish is played throughout the week. Entrance is free, and you bring your own food. Open daily 11am to 11pm (they have to close early because neighborhood residents complain). George-Kalb-Strasse 3. ✆ **089/74994030.** S-Bahn: Isartal Bahnhof. Tram: 7.

## NIGHTCLUBS

**Bayerischer Hof Night Club** Here in the extensive cellars of the Bayerischer Hof hotel (see "Where to Stay," earlier in the chapter), you'll find some of Munich's most sophisticated entertainment. Within one very large room is a piano bar where a musician plays every night 7 to 10pm. Behind a partition that disappears after 10pm is a bandstand for live orchestras, which play to a crowd of dancing patrons every night from 10pm to 3 or 4am, depending on business. Entrance to the piano bar is free, but there's a cover charge to the nightclub Friday and Saturday nights. Drinks begin at 7.50€ ($6.70). The club and bar are open daily 7pm to 3 or 4am. Daily happy hour is 7pm to 8:30pm, with drinks starting at 5€ ($4.45). In the Hotel Bayerischer Hof, Promenadeplatz 2–6. ✆ **089/2-12-09-94.** Cover 10€ ($8.95) Fri–Sat after 10pm; higher for special events. No cover for hotel guests. Tram: 19.

**Feierwerk** Whether it's independent theater or rock 'n' roll, the multiple stages inside this complex have hosted it. Entertainment ranges from the commercially viable to the truly underground. In the summer, this already-roomy complex expands outside into circus tents. Open daily 9pm to 4am. Hansastrasse 39–41. ✆ **089/743-1340.** Cover 5.50€–10€ ($4.90–$8.95). U-Bahn: Heimeranplatz.

**Kunstpark Ost** Set within the sprawling premises of what used to be a factory, this is Munich's newest complex of bars, restaurants, and dance clubs. People tend to move randomly from venue to venue, without any particular loyalty to one or the other. Your best bet is to show up sometime after 8pm, when all the bars will be functioning. The discos don't get going until at least 10:30pm. Grafingerstrasse 6. ✆ **089/49-00-27-30.** Cover 5€–7€ ($4.45–$6.25). S-Bahn: Ostbahnhof.

**Nachtwerk** This dance club in a huge factory warehouse also books bands. It's a festive place, not nearly as pretentious as other, more "exclusive" discos. Patrons even dance to rock music. The club is open Friday 10:30pm to 2:30am and Saturday 10:30pm to 5am. Landesbergerstrasse 185. ✆ **089/5-78-38-00.** Cover 5€–12€ ($4.45–$10.70). S-Bahn: Donnersbergerbrücke.

**Night Flight** *(Finds* This nightclub is located in the midst of enormous airfield hangars; it's designed to highlight the visual effect of airplane departures and arrivals. To get here, you'll have to drive 40km (25 miles) north of the city or take a 30-minute ride on the S-Bahn. There are three bars, a dance floor, and a restaurant. Frenetic dancing to techno music is the main attraction. In summer, dancers cool off and catch their breath on an outdoor terrace, where the main sport is watching the airport. Franz Josef Strauss Airport, Wartungsallee 9. ✆ **089/97-59-79-99.** Cover 4€ ($3.55) Tues–Thurs 9pm–2am, 5€–8€ ($4.45–$7.15) Fri–Sat. S-Bahn: Flughafen.

**Oklahoma** File under surreal. German and European bands decked out in cowboy hats and boots struggle with the nuances of an extremely foreign musical form. Even when the results are dead-on mimicry, there's something strange about watching German "cowboys" line dance or lean on the bar while guzzling Spaten. Cover is usually at the low end of the scale, rising when English and American acts hit the stage. Depending on your mood, this place can be a lot of fun. Pull on your jeans and come on in Tuesday to Saturday 7pm to 1am. Schäftlarnstrasse 156. ✆ **089/7-23-43-27.** Cover 7.50€–10€ ($6.70–$8.95). U-Bahn: Talkirchen.

**Parkcafé** Who'd ever guess this home to chic freaks was a Nazi hangout in the 1930s? The place contains five lively bars, two of them outfitted like the inside of a ship plus a strident color scheme using oranges and reds, among other colors. Many nights are themed, ranging from "Black Beat" music on Wednesdays to "gay Sundays." It's open Wednesday to Sunday 10pm to 4am. It's also open the first Tuesday of every month 11pm to 4am. Sophienstrasse 7. ✆ **089/59-83-13.** Cover 5€–8€ ($4.45–$7.15). U-Bahn: Lebachplatz.

**Rattlesnake Saloon** Same owner, same concept as Oklahoma (see above)—the difference is the rib-eye steaks, barbecued pork, chili, and other southern U.S. dishes available to hungry country-music fans. If you never learned line dancing at home, you can give it a chance here under the watchful eye of a Teutonic instructor. Open Wednesday to Sunday 7pm to 1am. The location is 5km (3 miles) north of the Marienplatz. Schneeglöckchenstrasse 91. ✆ **089/1-50-40-35.** Cover 5€–8€ ($4.45–$7.15). S-Bahn: Fasanerie.

## JAZZ

**Jazzclub Unterfahrt** This is Munich's leading jazz club, attracting artists from throughout Europe and North America. Reaching it requires wandering down a labyrinth of underground cement-sided corridors that might remind you of a bomb shelter during the Cold War. Once inside, the space opens to reveal flickering candles, a convivial bar, high ceilings, and clusters of smallish tables facing a stage and whatever singers and musicians happen to be emoting at the time. Off to one corner is an art gallery. The bar here opens daily at 7:30pm; live music is Monday through Thursday 9pm to midnight; Friday through Saturday 7:30pm to 3am. Einsteinstrasse 42. ✆ **089/448-2794.** Cover 8€–12€ ($7.15–$10.70). U-Bahn: Max-Weber-Platz

**Mister B's** This small, dark club hosts a slightly older, mellower crowd than the rock and dance clubs. Blues, jazz, and rhythm-and-blues combos take the stage Thursday to Saturday. Open Tuesday to Sunday 8pm to 3am. Herzog-Heinrichstrasse 38. ✆ **089/53-49-01.** Cover 4.50€–6€ ($4–$5.35). U-Bahn: Goetheplatz.

**Schwabinger Podium** This club offers varying nightly entertainment. Oldies and rock 'n' roll dominate some evenings. Open Sunday to Thursday 8pm to 1am and Friday and Saturday 8pm to 3am. Wagnerstrasse 1. ✆ **089/39-94-82.** Cover, but free until 10pm. U-Bahn: Münchner Freiheit.

## THE BAR & CAFE SCENE

See the review for Café Dukatz in the Literaturhaus on p. 320. Additionally, check out the below venues.

**Alter Simpl** Once a literary cafe, Alter Simpl takes its name from a satirical revue of 1903. Today it attracts a wide segment of locals. The real fun of the place occurs after 11pm, when the iconoclastic artistic ferment begins to resemble Berlin more than Bavaria. Open daily 10am to 4am, later on weekends. Türkenstrasse 57. ✆ **089/2-72-30-83.** Tram: 18. Bus: 53.

**Café Extrablatt** Owner Michael Grater is a prominent Munich newspaper columnist who has created a sprawling, smoke-filled sanctuary for writers, artists, and counterculture observers. Inside, it's decorated with celebrity photos and features a spacious well-designed bar, but the sidewalk tables are preferable during warm weather. Regulars convene here to converse and keep tabs on who's doing what, where. Open Monday to Thursday 8am to midnight, Friday and Saturday 9am to 1am, and Sunday 9am to midnight. Leopoldstrasse 7, Schwabing. ✆ **089/33-33-33.** U-Bahn: Universität.

**Café Puck** A dark-paneled retreat for students, artists, and workers, this cafe plays a variety of roles for its diverse crowd. It's a bar to students; a restaurant to the locals, who like the daily menu of German, American, Chinese, and Mexican dishes; and a hangover cure for artists and young people who creep in after midday for a big American breakfast. There's usually plenty of conversation and someone who wants to practice English, and there are always German- and English-language newspapers. Open daily 9am to 1am. Türkenstrasse 33. ✆ **089/2-80-22-80.** U-Bahn: Universität.

**Croccodrillo** In a cellar setting from around 1890, this bar is suddenly chic, drawing a hip crowd in their 20s to their early 40s who crowd in here nightly. It offers one of the longest bars in town, with modern lighting and excellent cocktails. A DJ plays disco and house on weekends, and live bands such as funk and rock often perform here during the week. Hours are daily from 7pm to 2am. Hohenzollernstrasse 11. ✆ **089/33-66-39.** U-Bahn: Muchnesfeiheit.

**Haus der 111 Biere** This unassuming corner bar is the type of small, dark place that adds character to any urban neighborhood. Among the beer selections is the strongest brew in the world: EKU Doppelbock Kulminator, a 22-proof oddity. Open Sunday to Thursday 8pm to 1am and Friday and Saturday 8pm to 3am. Franzstrasse 3. ✆ **089/33-12-48.** U-Bahn: Münchener Freiheit.

**Havana Club** This is not the spicy Cuban club you might expect. Employees may tell you about the bar's brush with fame, when Gloria Estefan made an appearance here, but its day-to-day function is as a lively singles bar fueled by rum-based cocktails. Open Sunday to Wednesday 6pm to 1am and Thursday to Saturday 6pm to 2am. Herrnstrasse 30. ✆ **089/29-18-84.** S-Bahn: Isartor.

**Master's Home** This is one of the historic core's most animated and convivial bars. It seems to attract a wider range of clients than most other watering holes in Munich. The setting is the ground floor of an imposing 19th-century building, within a large room outfitted with antiques and warm colors. The style evokes an Edwardian-era club in London. The premises also contain a restaurant, where fixed-price seven-course Italian-inspired meals cost 40€ ($35.70). Open nightly 6pm to 3am, with the last order accepted in the kitchen at 1am. Frauenstrasse 11 (close to the Marienplatz). ✆ **089/22-99-09.** S-Bahn: Marienplatz or Isartor.

**Nachtcafé** It hums, it thrives, and it captures everyone's nocturnal imagination. No other nightspot in Munich attracts such an array of soccer stars, film celebrities, literary figures, and, as one employee put it, "ordinary people, but only the most sympathetically crazy ones." Waves of patrons appear at different times of the evening: at 11pm, when live shows here begin; at 2am, when the restaurants close; and at 4am, when die-hard revelers seek a final drink in the predawn hours. There's no cover charge. The decor is updated 1950s; the music is jazz, blues, and soul. Open daily 9pm to 6am. Maximiliansplatz 5. ✆ **089/59-59-00.** Tram: 19.

**O'Reilly's Irish Pub** The all-Irish staff lends an air of authenticity to this pub, located in a historic vaulted cellar close to the Hotel Vier Jahreszeiten. Besides the obligatory Irish and German beers, you can also find good brews from England and the Czech Republic, as well as decent Irish stew, steaks, burgers, and mixed grills. Live Gaelic music is performed at irregular intervals throughout the month. Open Monday to Thursday 4pm to 1am, Friday to Sunday noon to 3am. Maximilianstrasse 29. ✆ **089/29-33-11.** U-Bahn/S-Bahn: Marienplatz.

**Pusser's New York Bar** This is the only European franchise of a small, well-run chain of restaurant-bars based in Tortola, British Virgin Islands. Its nostalgic decor celebrates the British navy of the 18th and 19th centuries. The specialties are Caribbean-inspired dishes and rum-based drinks. The cellar houses a piano bar. Open daily 5pm to 3am. Falkenturmstrasse 9. ✆ **089/22-05-00.** U-Bahn/S-Bahn: Marienplatz.

**Schultz** Schultz is a New York–style bar in Schwabing. It's popular with theater people, who crowd in as they do at Schumann's (see below) for smoke-filled chatter. The food is uncomplicated, and the decor, as they say here, is "unobvious and understated." Open daily 5pm to 1am. Barerstrasse 47. ✆ **089/2-71-47-11.** U-Bahn: Universität.

**Schumann's** Located on Munich's most desirable shopping street, Schumann's doesn't have to waste any money on decor. The local *beau monde* keep it fully fashionable. In cold weather, guests retreat inside, but in summer, they prefer the terrace that spills out onto the street. Schumann's is known as a "thinking man's bar." Author Charles Schumann wanted a bar that would be an artistic, literary, and communicative social focus. Popular with the film, advertising, and publishing worlds, his place is said to have contributed to a remarkable renaissance of bar culture in the city. Open Monday to Friday 5pm to 3am, Sunday 6pm to 3am. Oddly enough, it's closed on Saturday. Maximilianstrasse 36. ✆ **089/22-90-60.** Tram: 19.

**Shamrock** At this beer-lover's bar, you can compare the great brews of Germany with the best of the Irish exports. There's free entertainment every night at 9pm, when a mixed bag of Irish, rock, country, folk, funk, or blues musicians take to the stage. Located near the university, Shamrock gets a fair share of the student crowd. Open Monday to Thursday 5pm to 1am, Friday 5pm to 3am, and Saturday and Sunday 2pm to 3am. Trautenwolfstrasse 6. ✆ **089/33-10-81.** U-Bahn: Giselastrasse.

**Tomate Sports** Why is this bar named after a fruit? That's the only mystery about the place, which upon entrance, is immediately recognizable as a traditional sports bar, with a big-screen television broadcasting an overdose of athletics throughout the evening. Besides the soccer and rugby you might expect, the regulars also watch U.S. events, so stop in if you're a homesick American sports fan. The Paulaner brewery owns and operates this bar. Open Wednesday to Friday 7:30pm to 3am, Saturday 5:30pm to 3am, and Sunday to Tuesday 7:30pm to 1am. Siegesstrasse 19. ✆ **089/34-83-93.** U-Bahn: Münchener Freiheit.

## GAY CLUBS

Munich's gay and lesbian scene is centered around the blocks between the Viktualienmarkt and Gärtnerplatz, particularly on Hans-Sachs-Strasse.

**Bau** Macho and swaggering, this gay bar encourages leather, denim, and as many uniforms as can be crammed onto the bodies that surround its street-level bar. Dimly lit and international, it's not as scary as it might look at first. Don't be surprised if you spot several New York City cop uniforms on either level. It's open nightly 8pm to 3am. Müllerstrasse 41. ✆ **089/311-88-009.** U-Bahn: Sendlinger Tor.

**Moritzz** This is a stylish gay bar ringed with mirrors. Relax with drinks or food in red leather armchairs clustered around marble-topped tables. The eclectic menu includes well-prepared Thai dishes. Full meals, served until midnight, average 25€ ($22.35). Open Sunday to Thursday 7pm to 2am and Friday and Saturday 7pm to 3am. Klenzestrasse 43. ✆ **089/2-01-67-76.** U-Bahn: Frauenhoferstrasse.

**Nil** It's fun, it's convivial, and it has a clientele that's somewhat younger than the one at Teddy-Bar, just across the street (see below). In addition to fit and youthful German men hanging with one another at the octagon-shaped bar, you're likely to see faded stars (including Barbara Valentine, hailed during the 1960s as Germany's answer to Brigitte Bardot) from German stage and screen, sipping drinks with their men friends, reflecting on the glory days of their youth. Most of the clients come here to drink and mingle, but if you're hungry, platters of food are well-prepared and relatively inexpensive at 7€ to 12€ ($6.25–$10.70). Open daily 3pm to 3am. Hans-Sach-Strasse 2. ✆ **089/26-55-45.** U-Bahn: Sendlinger Tor.

**Ochsen Garten** Although it's a lot smaller and more cramped than most of its competitors, this is the leading leather bar in Munich, site of most of the city's leather S&M conventions and a hangout for regular guys who appreciate their sense of machismo. It's at its most crowded Thursday, Friday, and Saturday nights; on other nights it's likely to be virtually empty. It's open nightly 10pm to 3am. Müllerstrasse 47. ✆ **089/26-64-46.** U-Bahn: Sendlinger Tor.

**Teddy-Bar** Gay and neighborly, and ringed with varnished pine and a collection of teddy bears, this is a congenial bar patronized by gay men over 30. It's relatively easy to strike up a dialogue here, and if you're hungry, there are platters of Bavarian and German food. It's open nightly 6pm to 3am. October to April Sunday brunch at 11am. Hans-Sachs-Strasse 1. ✆ **089/260-33-59.** U-Bahn: Sendlinger Tor.

## 10 Side Trips from Munich

The **Bavarian Alps** are within easy reach (see chapter 9), or you can head for **Neuschwanstein** (see p. 263) to see Ludwig II's fairy-tale castle.

### DACHAU CONCENTRATION CAMP

In 1933, what had once been a quiet little artists' community just 16km (10 miles) from Munich became a tragic symbol of the Nazi era. Shortly after Hitler became chancellor, Himmler and the SS set up the first German concentration camp on the grounds of a former ammunition factory. The list of prisoners at the camp included enemies of the Third Reich, including everyone from communists and Social Democrats to Jews, homosexuals, gypsies, Jehovah's Witnesses, clergymen, political opponents, some trade union members, and others.

During its notorious history, between 1933 and 1945, more than 206,000 prisoners from 30 countries were imprisoned at Dachau, perhaps a lot more. Some were forced into slave labor, manufacturing Nazi armaments for the war and helping to build roads, etc. Others fell victim to SS doctors, who conducted grotesque medical experiments on them. And still others were killed after Dachau became a center for mass murder: Starvation, illness, beatings, and torture killed thousands who were not otherwise hanged, shot by firing squads, or lethally injected. The death toll was then compounded in December of 1944 when a typhus epidemic took thousands of lives within and around the camp, and forced marches in and out of the camp claimed thousands of others as well. At least 30,000 people were registered as dead while in Dachau between 1933 and 1945. However, there are many other thousands who were also murdered there, even if they weren't registered as dead.

The SS abandoned the camp on April 28, 1945, and the liberating U.S. Army moved in to take charge the following day. In all, a total of 67,000 living prisoners—all of them on the verge of death—were discovered at Dachau and its subsidiary camps.

Upon entering the camp, **KZ-Gedenkstätte Dachau,** Alte-Roemar-Strasse 75 (✆ **08131/17-41;** www.kz-gedenkstaette-dachau.de/english/index.html), you are faced by three memorial chapels—Catholic, Protestant, and Jewish—built in the early 1960s. Immediately behind the Catholic chapel is the "Lagerstrasse," the main camp road lined with poplar trees, once flanked by 32 barracks, each housing 208 prisoners. Two barracks have been rebuilt to give visitors insight into the conditions the prisoners endured.

The museum is housed in the large building that once contained the kitchen, laundry, and shower bathrooms. Photographs and documents show the rise of the Nazi regime and the SS; other exhibits show the persecution of Jews and other prisoners. Every effort has been made to present the facts. The tour of Dachau is a truly moving experience.

You can get to the camp by taking the frequent S-Bahn train S2 from the Hauptbahnhof to Dachau (direction: Petershausen), then bus 724 or 726 to the camp. The camp is open Tuesday to Sunday 9am to 5pm; admission is free. The English version of a 22-minute documentary film, *KZ-Dachau,* is shown at 11:30am and 3:30pm. All documents are translated in the catalog, which is available at the museum entrance.

# 9

# The Bavarian Alps

If you walk into a rustic alpine inn along the German-Austrian border and ask the innkeeper if he or she is German, you'll most likely get the indignant response, "Of course not! I'm Bavarian." Some older inhabitants of the region can still remember when Bavaria was a kingdom with its own prerogatives, even while a part of the German Reich (1871–1918).

The huge province of Bavaria includes not only the Alps but also Franconia, Lake Constance, and the capital city of Munich. This chapter explores the mountainous region along the Austrian border, a world unto itself. The hospitality of this area is famous, and the picture of the plump, rosy-cheeked innkeeper with a constant smile is no myth. Many travelers think of the Alps as a winter vacationland, but you'll find that nearly all the Bavarian resorts and villages boast year-round attractions.

**Munich** is the major driving gateway, with Autobahns leading directly to the Bavarian Alps. If you're beginning your tour in Garmisch-Partenkirchen in the west, you should fly into Munich. However, if your destination is Berchtesgaden in the eastern Alps, the nearest airport is Salzburg, Austria.

**OUTDOORS IN THE BAVARIAN ALPS** The Bavarian Alps are both a winter wonderland and a summer playground. The **skiing** here is the best in Germany. A regular winter snowfall in January and February usually measures from 30 to 50cm (12–20 in.). This leaves about 2m (6 ft.) of snow in the areas served by ski lifts. The great **Zugspitzplatt** snowfield can be reached in spring or autumn by a rack railway. The Zugspitze, at 2,960m (9,720 ft.) above sea level, is the tallest mountain peak in Germany. Ski slopes begin at a height of 2,650m (8,700 ft.).

The second great ski district in the Alps is **Berchtesgadener Land,** with alpine skiing centered on Jenner, Rossfeld, Götschen, and Hochschwarzeck. Snow conditions are consistently good until March. Visitors will find a cross-country skiing center, many miles of tracks kept in first-class condition, natural toboggan runs, one artificial ice run for toboggan and skibob (or snow-bike) runs, and artificial ice-skating and curling rinks.

In summer, **alpine hiking** is a major attraction—climbing mountains, enjoying nature, and watching animals in the forest. One of the best areas for hiking is the 1,240m (4,060-ft.) **Eckbauer,** lying on the southern fringe of Partenkirchen (the tourist office at Garmisch-Partenkirchen will supply maps and details). Many visitors come to the Alps in summer just to hike through **Berchtesgaden National Park,** bordering the Austrian province of Salzburg. The 2,466m (8,091-ft.) Watzmann Mountain, the Königssee (Germany's cleanest, clearest lake), and parts of the Jenner—the pride of Berchtesgaden's four ski areas—are within the boundaries of the park, which has well-mapped trails through protected areas, leading the hiker through spectacular natural beauty. For information about hiking in the park, contact **Nationalparkhaus,**

Franziskanerpl 7, 83471 Berchtesgaden (✆ **08652/64343**).

From Garmisch-Partenkirchen, serious hikers can embark on full-day or overnight alpine treks, following clearly marked footpaths and staying in isolated mountain huts. Some huts are staffed and serve meals. For the truly remote unsupervised huts, you'll be provided with information on how to gain access. For information, inquire at the local tourist office or write to the government-subsidized **German Alpine Association,** Von-Kaahr-Strasse 2–4, 80997 Munich (✆ **089/14-00-30;** fax 089/140-03-11) which will also direct you to a privately owned tour operator, the **Summit Club,** an outfit devoted to the organization of high-altitude expeditions throughout Europe and the world.

If you're a true outdoors-person, you'll briefly savor the somewhat touristy facilities of Garmisch-Partenkirchen, and then use it as a base for explorations of the rugged Berchtesgaden National Park. You can also stay at one of the inns in Mittenwald or Oberammergau and take advantage of a wide roster of outdoor diversions there. Any of the outfitters below will provide directions and link-ups with their sports programs from wherever you decide to stay. Street maps of Berchtesgaden and its environs are usually available for free from the **Kurdirektion** (tourist office), Königsseer Strasse, Berchtesgaden (✆ **08652/967-0**), and more intricately detailed maps of the surrounding alpine topography are available for a fee.

Another summer activity is **ballooning,** which, weather permitting, can be arranged through **Outdoor Club Berchtesgaden,** Ludwig-Ganghofer-Strasse 20½ (✆ **08652/50-01**).

Anglers will find plenty of **fishing** opportunities (especially salmon, pike-perch, and trout) at Lake Hintersee and the rivers Ramsauer Ache and Königsseer Ache. To acquire a fishing permit, contact the **Kurdirektion** (tourist office; see above) at Berchtesgaden, which will direct you to any of four different authorities, based on where you want to fish. For fishing specifically within the Hintersee, contact tourist officials in Ramsau at ✆ **08657/9889920.**

Despite the obvious dangers, **hang gliding** or **paragliding** from the vertiginous slopes of Mount Jenner can be thrilling. To arrange it, contact **Summit Club** (see above).

You can also practice your **kayaking** or **white-water rafting** techniques on one of the area's many rivers (water level permitting), such as the Ramsauer, Königisser, Bischofswiesener, and Berchtesgadener Aches. For information and options, contact the above-mentioned **Outdoor Club Berchtesgaden.**

If you would like to go **swimming** in an alpine lake—not to everyone's body temperature—there are many lidos found in the Bavarian Forest.

Of course, there's plenty to do outdoors during the winter as well, including some of the greatest **alpine** and **cross-country skiing** in all of Europe. Call the local "Snow-Telefon" at ✆ **08652/967-297** for current snow conditions. There's also skating between October and February at the world-class ice-skating rink in Berchtesgaden. Less reliable, but more picturesque, is skating on the surface of the Hintersee Lake, once it's sufficiently frozen. A particularly cozy way to spend an hour on a winter's night is to huddle with a companion in the back of a **horse-drawn sled.** Rides can be arranged in Garmisch through Bradntner, GMbH, at the Café Waldstein, Königseer Fussweg 17 (✆ **08652/2427**). The cost is around 46€ to 71.55€ ($41.10–$63.90) per hour.

## EXPLORING THE REGION BY CAR

Acclaimed as one of the most scenic drives in all of Europe, the **Deutsche Alpenstrasse (German Alpine Road)** ★ stretches for some 480km (300 miles) between Berchtesgaden in the east and Lindau on Lake Constance in the west (see chapter 10). The road goes through or past mountains, lakes, forests, and "castles in the sky." We prefer to take the drive in early spring or early autumn. In winter, mountain passes are often shut down, and even those highways that remain open can be dangerous.

**Day 1** After your stopover in Munich (see chapter 8), head south along Autobahn A8 (drive in the right lane if you want to avoid the hysterical speeders on the left). Turn south on Route B20 for **Berchtesgaden,** 158km (98 miles) southeast of Munich. After settling in and having lunch, take an afternoon excursion to **Obersalzberg** and **Kehlstein** (you can go by bus).

**Day 2** While still based in Berchtesgaden, explore the **Königssee,** to the south (about 2 hr. by boat). This long, narrow lake, famed for its steep banks and dark waters, is one of Europe's most dramatic and romantic sights. In the afternoon, drive west along the alpine road and then north on Route B20 some 20km (12 miles) to **Bad Reichenhall.** This is one of Germany's most famous spas. Return to Berchtesgaden for the night.

**Day 3** Get back on Autobahn A8 toward Munich but turn off at **Prien,** 85km (53 miles) southeast of Munich. The premier attraction here is the Neues Schloss, a fantastic castle begun by Ludwig II in 1878 on the island of Herrenchiemsee. You can find food and lodging at Prien.

**Day 4** Get back on the Autobahn to Munich, but take a cross-country route (472) toward Bad Tölz, which is one of Bavaria's leading spas, although it lacks any major attractions. Continue west from Bad Tölz along 472 to the town of Bichl, at which point you head south along Route 11 until you reach Benediktbeuern, a distance of 14km (9 miles) from Bad Tölz. Here you'll find **Benediktbeuern,** the most ancient Benedictine monastery in upper Bavaria. Records trace it back to the year 739. After a look, continue 6km (4 miles) south along Route 11 to **Kochel am See,** with its alpine vistas. Follow Route 11 south to the express highway, Route 2, which you then follow 32km (20 miles) to **Mittenwald** on the Austrian border. Plan an overnight stay.

**Day 5** You'll want to spend as much time as possible in **Mittenwald.** Goethe called it a "living picture book"—we think it looks like part of *The Sound of Music* film set. It's also a major center for violin making. Give it at least a morning before driving northwest for 20km (12 miles) on Route 2 to **Garmisch-Partenkirchen,** two towns combined. After checking in, head for the major attraction, the **Zugspitze,** the highest peak in German territory. Wear warm clothing. This could be the highlight of your trip to Bavaria.

**Day 6** Leaving Garmisch-Partenkirchen, head north on Route 2 for 20km (12 miles) toward **Oberammergau.** Along the way, you'll pass **Kloster Ettal,** founded in 1330. Its original 10-sided church is a stunning example of the Bavarian rococo style. Some 10km (6 miles) to the west is **Schloss Linderhof,** one of "Mad King" Ludwig's royal residences, built between 1874 and 1878 on the grounds of his hunting lodge. These two attractions will take up most of your day, but you'll still arrive in the little old wood-carver's village of Oberammergau, 11km (7 miles) northeast of Linderhof, in time to wander about. Later, enjoy a hearty Bavarian dinner before turning in to your alpine bed.

## 1 Berchtesgaden ★★

158km (98 miles) SE of Munich, 18km (11 miles) SE of Bad Reichenhall, 23km (14 miles) S of Salzburg

Ever since Ludwig I of Bavaria chose this resort as a favorite hideaway, the tourist business in Berchtesgaden has been booming. The village is situated below the many summits of Watzmann Mountain—2,713m (8,901 ft.) at its highest point. According to legend, the mountain peaks were once a royal family who were so evil that God punished them by turning them into rocks.

Berchtesgaden is a quiet old alpine village with ancient winding streets and a medieval marketplace and castle square. Its name is often linked with Hitler and the Nazi hierarchy, but this impression is erroneous. Hitler's playground was actually at Obersalzberg, on a wooded plateau about half a mile up the mountain.

### ESSENTIALS

**GETTING THERE By Air** The nearest airport is **Salzburg Airport** (✆ **0662/8580**). It has regularly scheduled air service to Frankfurt, Amsterdam, Brussels, Berlin, Dresden, Düsseldorf, Hamburg, London, Paris, and Zürich. Major airlines serving the Salzburg airport are **Austrian Airlines** (✆ 0662/85-45-11), **Lauda Air** (✆ 0662/85-45-11), **Air France** (✆ 0662/435-17-89), **Lufthansa** (✆ 0662/809-080), and **Tyrolean** (✆ 0662/85-45-33). From Salzburg you can take a 1-hour train ride to Berchtesgaden, although you'll have to change trains at Freilassing.

**By Train** The **Berchtesgaden Bahnhof** lies on the Munich–Freilassing rail line. Twelve trains a day arrive from Munich (trip time: 1½ hr.). For rail information and schedules, call ✆ **01805/99-66-33.** Berchtesgaden has three mountain rail lines—the Obersalzbergbahn, Jennerbahn, and Hirscheckbahn—going to the mountain plateaus around the resorts. For more information, contact **Berchtesgadener Bergbahn AG** (✆ **08652/9-58-10**) and **Obersalzbergbahn AG** (✆ **08652/ 25-61**).

**By Bus** Regional bus service to alpine villages and towns around Berchtesgaden is offered by **RVO Regionalverkehr Oberbayern** at Berchtesgaden (✆ **08022/ 3980** or 08022/86-03-20).

**By Car** Access by car is via the A8 Autobahn from Munich in the north or Route 20 from the south. The drive from Munich takes about 2 hours.

**VISITOR INFORMATION** Contact the **Kurdirektion,** Königsseerstrasse 2 (✆ **08652/967-0**). It's open Monday to Friday 8am to 5pm and Saturday 9am to noon.

### SEEING THE SIGHTS

**The Stiftskirche (Abbey Church),** dating from 1122, is adjacent to the Königliches Schloss Berchtesgaden. The church is mainly Romanesque, with Gothic additions. One of its ancient twin steeples was destroyed by lightning and rebuilt in 1866. The interior contains many fine works of art; the high altar has a painting by Zott dating from 1669. In the vestry is a small silver altar donated by Empress Maria Theresa of Austria.

**Schlossplatz** ★, partially enclosed by the castle and Stiftskirche, is the most attractive plaza in town. On the opposite side of the square from the church is a 16th-century arcade that leads to **Marktplatz,** with typical alpine houses and a wooden fountain from 1677 (restored by Ludwig I in 1860). Some of Berchtesgaden's oldest inns and houses border this square. Extending from Marktplatz is the **Nonntal,** lined with more old houses, some built into Lockstein Mountain, which towers above the town.

A minor but interesting museum, **Heimatmuseum,** Schloss Aldelsheim, Schroffen-Bergallee 6 (✆ **08652/44-10**), is devoted to alpine woodcarving. The craft here predates the more fabled woodcarving at Oberammergau. Some of the best examples in Germany are on display in this museum. Entry is allowed only as part of a guided tour offered Monday to Friday at 10am and again at 3pm for a charge of 2€ ($1.80).

**Königliches Schloss Berchtesgaden** In the Middle Ages, Berchtesgaden grew up around a powerful Augustinian monastery. Its monks introduced the art of woodcarving, for which the town is still noted. When the town became part of Bavaria in 1809, the abbey was secularized and eventually converted to a palace for the royal Wittelsbach family. Now it is a museum, mostly devoted to the royal collection of sacred art, including wood sculptures by the famed artists Veit Stoss and Tilman Riemenschneider. There's also a gallery of 19th-century art, a collection of Italian furniture from the 16th century, and a display of 17th- and 18th-century pistols and guns.

Schlossplatz 2. ✆ **08652/947-980.** Admission 7€ ($6.25) adults, 3€ ($2.70) children 6–17, free for children 5 and under. Easter–Sept Sun–Fri 10am–noon and 2–4pm; Oct–Easter Mon–Fri 11am–2pm. Bus: 9539.

**Salzbergwerk Berchtesgaden** These salt mines at the eastern edge of town were once owned by the Augustinian monastery. Operations began here in 1517. The deposits are more than 300m (990 ft.) thick and are still processed today from four galleries or "hills." Visitors are first given protective miner's clothing. Older children will especially enjoy the guided tours that begin with a ride into the mine on a small wagon-like train. After nearly a 1km (½-mile) journey, visitors leave the train and explore the rest of the mine, sliding down a miner's slide, and riding on the salt lake in a ferry. The highlight of the tour is the "chapel," a grotto containing unusually shaped salt formations illuminated for an eerie effect. The 1½-hour tour can be taken any time of the year, in any weather.

Bergwerkstrasse 83. ✆ **08652/600-20.** Admission 12€ ($10.70) adults, 6.50€ ($5.80) children. May 1–Oct 15 daily 9am–5pm; Oct 16–Apr 30 Mon–Sat 12:30–3:30pm. Bus: 9539.

## WHERE TO STAY

**Hotel Fischer** ★ Of a modest lot, this is the town's leading inn. This hotel, overlooking the town, was built in the late 1970s in the Bavarian style. Fronted with dark-stained wooden balconies against a cream-colored facade, it rambles pleasantly along the hillside. Rooms are cozy and traditional, each with a regional theme, and all bathrooms come equipped with showers.

Königsseerstrasse 51, 83471 Berchtesgaden, a short uphill walk from the railway station. ✆ **08652/95-50.** Fax 08652/6-48-73. www.hotel-fischer.de. 40 units. 98€–140€ ($87.50–$125) double. Rates include buffet breakfast. V. Closed Nov–mid-Dec. Parking 3.50€ ($3.15). **Amenities:** Restaurant; bar; pool; sauna; solarium; room service. *In room:* TV, hair dryer.

**Hotel Krone** *Value* One of the most appealing bargains in Berchtesgaden is this well-built chalet-inspired hotel. Operated by live-in managers, the Grafe family, and permeated with a sense of alpine thrift and good cheer, it offers cozy rooms sheathed with varnished pine. Each has a balcony or terrace, a comfortable mattress, and a compact bathroom containing a shower.

Am Rad 5, 83471 Berchtesgaden. ✆ **08652/94600.** Fax 08652/946010. 21 units. 64€–85€ ($57.15–$75.90) double; from 90€ ($80.35) suite; 10€ ($8.95) for half board. MC. Closed Nov 1–Dec 20. **Amenities:** Dining room; bar; lounge; room service. *In room:* TV, hair dryer.

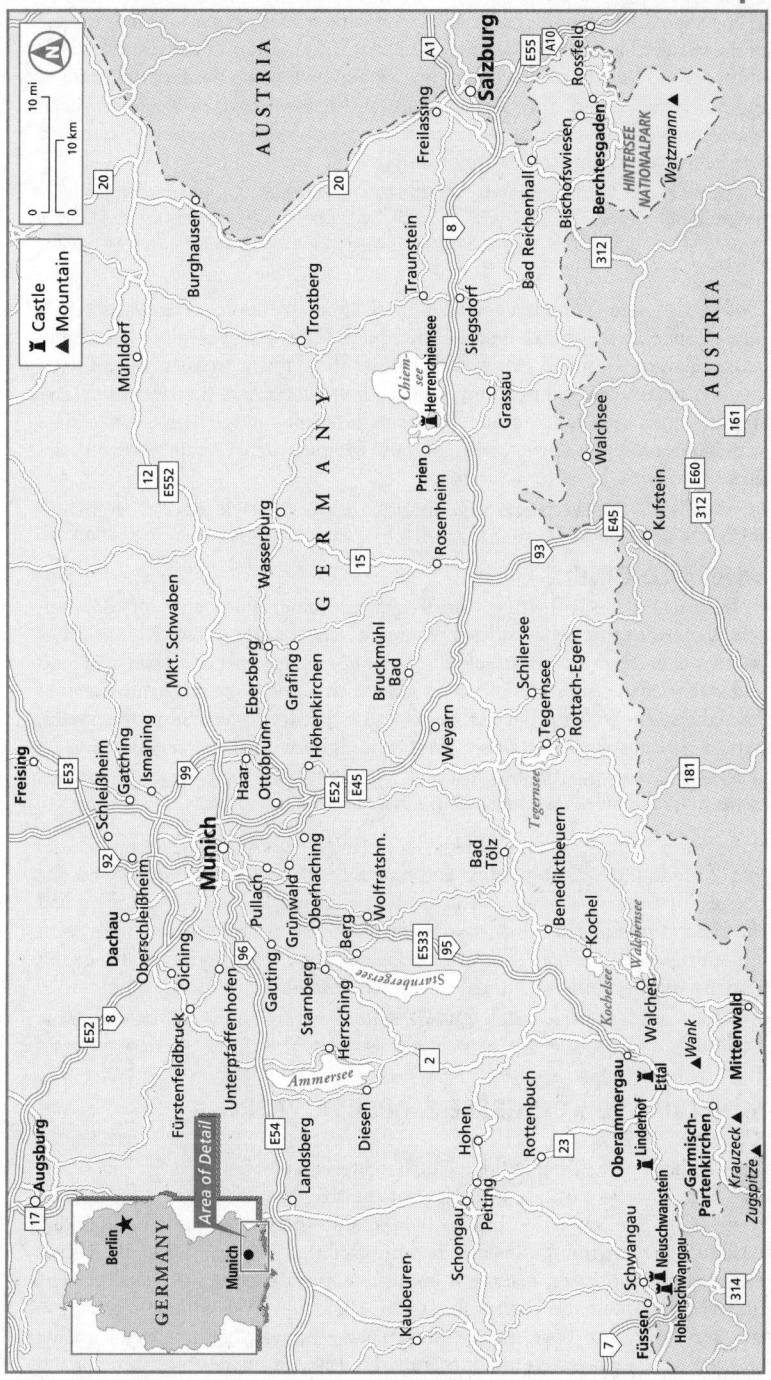
Castle
Mountain
0 10 km
0 10 mi
N
AUSTRIA
GERMANY
Salzburg
Freilassing
Traunstein
Siegsdorf
Bad Reichenhall
Bischofswiesen
Berchtesgaden
Rossfeld
HINTERSEE NATIONALPARK
Watzmann
Burghausen
Mühldorf
Trostberg
Chiemsee
Herrenchiemsee
Prien
Rosenheim
Grassau
Walchsee
Kufstein
Wasserburg
Mkt. Schwaben
Ebersberg
Grafing
Höhenkirchen
Bruckmühl
Bad Aibling
Weyarn
Schliersee
Tegernsee
Rottach-Egern
Bad Tölz
Benediktbeuern
Kochel
Walchensee
Tegernsee
Kochelsee
Walchensee
Freising
Schleißheim
Gatching
Ismaning
Munich
Haar
Ottobrunn
Pullach
Grünwald
Oberhaching
Wolfratshn.
Berg
Starnberg
Herrsching
Starnbergersee
Gauting
Unterpfaffenhofen
Oiching
Oberschleißheim
Dachau
Fürstenfeldbruck
Ammersee
Landsberg
Diesen
Augsburg
Kaubeuren
Schongau
Hohen Peiting
Rottenbuch
Oberammergau
Linderhof
Ettal
Walchen
Wank
Garmisch-Partenkirchen
Krauzeck
Zugspitze
Mittenwald
Schwangau
Füssen
Neuschwanstein
Hohenschwangau
Area of Detail
Berlin
Munich
GERMANY
17
E53
92
99
96
E52
8
E54
2
E533
95
E52
E45
12
E52
15
20
20
8
A1
E55
A10
312
93
E45
181
312
E60
161
7
314

**Vier Jahreszeiten** This is an old inn with modern extensions in the heart of the village. The inn has been remodeled and improved over the years and now offers a good level of comfort to its guests, almost rivaling the Fischer. Some of the newer units, with tiny sitting rooms and balconies, resemble suites. Each accommodation comes with a compact, tiled bathroom with shower. There's a terrace for your summer viewing pleasure.

Maximilianstrasse 20, 83471 Berchtesgaden. ✆ **08652/95-20.** Fax 08652/50-29. www.berchtesgaden.com/vier-jahreszeiten. 59 units. 77€–138€ ($68.75–$123.25) double. Rates include buffet breakfast. AE, DC, MC, V. Free outdoor parking; €5.10, ($5) in garage. **Amenities:** Restaurant; bar; lounge; pool; sauna; solarium. *In room:* TV, minibar, hair dryer.

**Watzmann** *Value* This is a good bet for an affordable choice. The Watzmann is located opposite the church on the main square. It has a large outdoor terrace and a cozy Bavarian-inspired decor, with turn-of-the-century artifacts, huge carved wooden pillars, oak ceilings, and wrought-iron chandeliers. Everyone seems to stop here for a beer, coffee, or lunch. Rooms are small but well maintained. Those with bathrooms have shower stalls; for those without, corridor bathrooms are adequate (you rarely have to wait in line).

Franziskanerplatz 2, 83471 Berchtesgaden. ✆ **08652/2055.** Fax 08652/5174. 38 units. 25€–39€ ($22.35–$34.85) double. AE, DC, MC, V. Free parking. Closed Nov 1–Dec 25. **Amenities:** Restaurant. *In room:* No phone.

## WHERE TO DINE

**Hubertusstube** GERMAN You'll get an undeniable sense of Bavarian *gemütlichkeit* in this richly paneled restaurant, where a trio of old-fashioned dining rooms, each with a century-old history of hospitality, offers well-prepared food and a view of the Alps. Menu items include rich servings of such game dishes as roasted venison with red wine sauce, as well as perfectly prepared pepper steaks, roasted pork shank, and salmon-trout. Service is traditional and very polite.

In the Hotel Vier Jahreszeiten, Maximilianstrasse 20. ✆ **08652/9520.** Reservations recommended. Main courses 7.50€–22€ ($6.70–$19.65). AE, DC, MC, V. Daily 11am–2pm and 6–10pm.

**Panorama Restaurant** GERMAN/INTERNATIONAL The decor includes lots of blond birchwood paneling and touches of pale blue, but virtually no one notices it because the windows encompass a sweeping view of Obersalzberg and the nearby mountains. Good-tasting menu items include braised trout with almonds; pepper steak; goulash or *Leberknoedelsuppe;* veal or pork schnitzels; and a savory version of the traditional rib-sticker, *Schweinshaxen* (pork shank).

In the Alpenhotel Kronprinz, Am Brandholz. ✆ **08652/60-70.** Reservations recommended. Lunch main courses 6€–18€ ($5.35–$16.05); dinner main courses 9€–18€ ($8.05–$16.05). AE, DC, MC, V. Daily noon–3pm and 6–9pm.

## SIDE TRIPS TO KÖNIGSSEE & OBERSALZBERG

### KÖNIGSSEE

This is the "jewel in the necklace" of Berchtesgaden. The waters of this scenic lake appear to be dark green because of the steep mountains that jut upward from its shores. Low-lying land on the lake's northern edge contains a parking lot and a few charming inns and bathing facilities, but the rest of the lake is enclosed by mountains, making it impossible to walk along the shoreline. The only way to explore the waters, unless you're like one of the mountain goats you may see above, is by boat. Electric motorboats—no noisy gas-powered launches allowed—carry passengers on tours around the lake throughout the summer and occasionally even in winter.

The favorite spot on Königssee is the tiny flat peninsula on the western bank, the site of a basilica as early as the 12th century. Today the Catholic **Chapel of St. Bartholomew** is still used for services (except in winter). The clergy must arrive by boat, because there's no other way to approach the peninsula. The adjacent buildings include a fisher's house and a restaurant, which was once a favored hunting lodge of the Bavarian kings. Here you can sample trout and salmon caught in the crisp, clean waters. At the southern end of the lake you come to the Salet-Alm, where the tour boats make a short stop near a thundering waterfall. If you follow the footpath up the hillside, you'll reach the summer pastures used by the cattle of Berchtesgaden. Just over the hill is **Lake Obersee,** part of Königssee until an avalanche separated them 8 centuries ago. If you prefer a shorter trip, you can take the boat as far as St. Bartholomew and back.

To reach Königssee from Berchtesgaden by car, follow the signs south from the town 5km (3 miles). It's also a pleasant hour's walk or a short ride by electric train or bus from the center of town.

For information about boat excursions, call **Schiffahrt Königssee** at ✆ **08652/96-36-18.** An entire tour of Königssee requires about 2 hours. There are boats in summer every 15 minutes, so getting off one boat and climbing aboard another is easy if you want to break up the tour. During the summer, the first boat departs every morning at 8:30am and the last boat leaves at 5:30pm. In winter, boats leave about every 45 minutes beginning at 9:45am. The important stops are at Salet and St. Batholomä. A round-trip fare for a lake tour is 13.80€ ($12.30) for adults and half fare for children.

## OBERSALZBERG ★★

The drive from Berchtesgaden to Obersalzberg at 1,000m (3,300 ft.) is one of Bavaria's most scenic routes. Obersalzberg was where Hitler settled down in a rented cottage after his prison term while he completed *Mein Kampf.* After he came to power in 1933, he bought Haus Wachenfeld and had it remodeled into his residence, the Berghof. Obersalzberg became the center for holiday living for Nazis such as Martin Bormann and Hermann Göring.

Today, you can walk around the ruins of Hitler's Berghof. This was where the famous 1938 meeting took place between Hitler and British Prime Minister Neville Chamberlain. The result was the Munich Agreement, which Chamberlain so mistakenly declared would bring "peace in our time." The Berghof was destroyed in 1945 by Bavarian government authorities at the request of the U.S. Army—the Americans did not want a monument to Hitler. One of the only fully remaining structures from the Nazi compound is a guesthouse called the General Walker Hotel that was used by U.S. troops stationed in Europe.

Hitler built the bunkers and air-raid shelter in 1943. Three thousand laborers completed the work in 9 months, connecting all the major buildings of the Obersalzberg area to the underground rooms. Many readers have expressed their disappointment when reaching this site, apparently thinking they would tour Hitler's sumptuously decorated private apartments. However, the only structures open to visitors are a part of Hitler's air-raid-shelter system and prison cells used by the Reichssicherheitsdienst (state security police), which were considered a last refuge for Hitler and other high officials. Wear good walking shoes, and be prepared to run into some VERBOTEN! signs.

A major point of interest is the **Kehlstein,** or **Eagle's Nest** ★★, which can be reached only by a thrilling bus ride up a 7km- (4½-mile-) long mountain road, blasted out of solid rock. This outstanding feat of engineering was begun in

## Springtime for Hitler

The big news blowing through the windswept Alps is that a luxury hotel is being built in Obersalzberg, the former site of Hitler's alpine command center. Over protests that the site would become a magnet for neo-Nazis, the Bavarian State Bank is moving ahead to create this alpine retreat, a project that is expected to take 3 years and one which will include a golf course on the site of the former holiday mansion of *Luftwaffe* commander Herman Göring.

Hitler's Berghof, where he lived with his mistress, Eva Braun, was destroyed in 1945, but this "Eagle's Nest" mountaintop retreat and bunker still exists. Once occupied by the U.S. Army, it was handed over to Bavaria in 1997. The American-based Intercontinental chain, which will operate the hotel, has committed itself to "not allowing any neo-Nazi tourism in the area." Vendors definitely won't be allowed to sell Third Reich souvenirs.

Jewish leaders weren't particularly enthusiastic about the plans, but their concerns have been eased somewhat since a Documentation Center was opened nearby in 1999. The center documents how the Nazi top brass commanded their forces from this mountain aerie and planned the destruction of the Jews and other minorities within Europe.

Already, the project is provoking satire in the press. In Munich, Reuters filed this bulletin: "Hilter's Hotel, anyone? Fancy a spot of golf at the alpine lair where *der Führer* planned the invasion of Poland? Or tennis, perhaps, where Eva Braun has the Görings in for tea?"

1937 under the leadership of Bormann, who intended it as a 50th-birthday gift for Hitler. The Eagle's Nest was not, as the name may suggest, a military installation. It was a site for relaxation and was not popular with Hitler, who rarely visited it.

To reach the spot, you must enter a tunnel and take a 120m (400-ft.) elevator ride through a shaft in the Kehlstein Mountain to its summit. The building, with solid granite walls and huge picture windows, houses a mountain restaurant, the Kehlsteinhaus, which is open mid-May to mid-October. You can enjoy the panoramic view and explore the rooms of the original teahouse, which include Eva Braun's living room. Below you'll have a view of the Obersalzberg area. Nearby is the site of Martin Bormann's house and the SS barracks. To the north you can see as far as Salzburg, Austria; below the mountain to the west is Berchtesgaden, with its rivers dwindling off into threads in the distance.

For information about trips to Obersalzberg and Kehlstein, call ✆ **08652/20-29.** Local RVO buses based in Berchtesgaden run from the Berchtesgaden Post Office to Obersalzberg-Hintereck. The round-trip journey costs 4€ ($3.55). Entrance to the bunker and prison cells is 3€ ($2.70); they're open daily 9am to 5pm. From Obersalzberg (the Hintereck parking lot), the Kehlstein line operates daily mid-May to mid-October; during that time full catering services are offered at Kehlsteinhaus. The bus to Kehlstein and elevator ride through the rock costs 11€ ($9.80). If you're up to it, instead of taking the elevator, you can walk the final stretch to the Eagle's Nest from the summit parking lot in about 30 minutes. The Kehlstein road is closed to private vehicles.

Guided tours in English are offered by the American-run **Berchtesgaden Mini Bus Tours,** Königsseerstrasse 2 (✆ **08652/6-49-71**). Tours, including Obersalzberg, Eagle's Nest, and the Bunker System as an afternoon history package, are conducted daily mid-May to mid-October, starting at the Berchtesgaden tourist office. The service also takes visitors to sights such as the Salt Mines and the Königssee. A 3½-hour tour costs 31€ ($27.70) adults, 8€ ($7.15) under 25, free 6 and under. There's a tour information and ticket booth at the Berchtesgaden tourist office, across the street from the train station. One of the most popular tours offered is the "Sound of Music" tour to nearby Salzburg.

### Where to Stay

For restaurants, go to the nearby town of Berchtesgaden (see above).

**Hotel zum Türken** The Hotel zum Türken, located in Obersalzberg, is legendary. It's designed in the alpine style and has terraces (for hotel guests only) with views. On its facade is a large painted sign of "The Turk"—legend has it that the first owner was a veteran of the Turkish war. In the 1930s, anti-Nazi remarks led to trouble for the proprietor, Herr Schuster, who was arrested. Afterward Bormann used the building as a Gestapo headquarters; it then fell victim to air raids and looting in April 1945. Herr Schuster's daughter, Therese Partner, was able to buy the ruin from the German government in 1949. The small- to medium-size rooms are well-maintained including neatly kept bathrooms with showers. They don't have private phones, but there is an international pay phone in the main hallway.

83471 Berchtesgaden-Obersalzberg. ✆ **08652/24-28.** Fax 08652/47-10. 17 units, 13 with shower or bathtub. 82€–98€ ($73.25–$87.50) double. Rates include continental breakfast. AE, DC, MC, V. Free parking. Obersalzberg bus from Berchtesgaden. **Amenities:** Breakfast room; bar; lounge. *In room:* No phone.

## 2 Bad Reichenhall ★

135km (84 miles) SE of Munich, 20km (12 miles) SE of Salzburg

The best German spas can call themselves *Staatsbad* (where the standards of maintenance and cleanliness, quality of the waters, and breadth of facilities are high enough for the government to recognize them as among the top-rated spas in the country), and Bad Reichenhall bears that title with pride. This town is the most important curative spa in the Bavarian Alps. Its brine springs, with a salt content as high as 24%, are the most powerful saline springs in Europe, and the town has been a source of salt for more than 2,400 years. The combination of the waters and the pure air has made Bad Reichenhall a recognized spa for centuries.

In 1848, King Maximilian of Bavaria stayed here, popularizing Bad Reichenhall as a fashionable resort. Today, visitors come from all over the world to take the waters, which supposedly treat asthma and other respiratory ailments. Treatment sessions take place almost exclusively in the morning at seven resort institutes, the therapy ranging from simply drinking the water to pneumatotherapy—even electronic lungs for the most serious cases.

### ESSENTIALS

**GETTING THERE** **By Air** The nearest airport is Salzburg (see "Berchtesgaden," earlier in this chapter for data about airport arrivals). From Salzburg, it's a 20-minute train ride into Bad Reichenhall, with trains leaving every hour throughout the day, with a change in Freilassing. There are also frequent bus and rail connections to and from Berchtesgaden, either trip taking about 45 minutes. Buses or trains leave every hour from Berchtesgaden heading for Bad Reichenhall.

**By Train** Bad Reichenhall is connected to the airport at Munich (see chapter 8) by frequent train service through Rosenheim. The trip takes about 2½ hours. For information and schedules, call ✆ **01805/99-66-33.**

**By Bus** Regional bus service to and from Bad Reichenhall is provided by Regionalverkehr Oberbayers Betrieb (✆ **08651/70-50** for information). From the spa, you can take a bus to various beautiful spots in the Bavarian Alps, including Berchtesgaden.

**By Car** Access is by the A8 Autobahn, from Munich in the north and Salzburg in the south. Exit on Federal Highway 21 into Bad Reichenhall.

**VISITOR INFORMATION** For tourist information, go to the Kur- und Verkehrsverein im Kurgastzentrum, Wittelsbacherstrasse 15 (✆ **08651/60-63-03**). It's open Monday to Friday 8am to 5pm and Saturday 9am to noon.

## SIGHTS & ACTIVITIES

The ideal climate permits a complete spectrum of outdoor events, from excursions into the mountains for skiing or hiking to tennis tournaments. Gardeners and botanists will enjoy the spa gardens; the sheltered location of the town amid the lofty Alps permits the growth of several varieties of tropical plants, giving the gardens a lush, exotic appearance. There's also a wide choice of indoor activities, from symphony concerts to folklore presentations to gambling in the casino.

The great fire of 1834 destroyed much of the town, but many impressive churches survived. An outstanding example is **St. Zeno,** a 12th-century Gothic church showing a later baroque influence. Its most remarkable feature is its painted interior, centering on the carved altarpiece of the *Coronation of the Virgin.*

**Bad Reichenhaller Saltmuseum,** Alte Saline Reichenhall (✆ **08651/700-21-46**), just a short walk from the Kurgarten, is the home of the ancient industry responsible for the growth and prosperity of Bad Reichenhall from Celtic times to the present. Parts of the old plant still stand today, but most of it was reconstructed in the mid-19th century by Ludwig I of Bavaria. The large pumps and huge marble caverns are impressive. Tours are offered May 1 to October 31, daily 10am to noon and 2 to 4pm; November to May 10, Tuesday and Thursday 1 to 4pm. Admission is 5€ ($4.45) for adults and 3€ ($2.70) for children; a combination ticket for the Saltmuseum and the Salzberwerk Berchtesgaden (see above) is 14€ ($12.50) adults and 7.50€ ($6.70) children.

## SHOPPING

Shops here are predictably upscale, rather limited in scope, and conservative. The town's only department store, **Kaufhaus Huhasz,** Ludwigstrasse 23 (✆ **08651/6-02-935**), stocks some traditional items. About 90% of the resort's shops are in a pedestrian-only zone, which is centered around the **Ludwigstrasse** and the **Salzburgerstrasse.** Since 1856, **Josef Mack Co.,** Anton-Winkler-Strasse 7 (✆ **08651/96-310**), has been the region's best place for medicinal herbs, many of which are grown in the Bavarian Alps.

## WHERE TO STAY

**Hotel Bayerischer Hof** *Value* This modern and inviting hotel is in the center of the spa on Main Street. It has a surprising number of facilities for a small place, although it's hardly in the same league as the Steigenberger or the Parkhotel Luisenbad (see below). Rooms are furnished in a well-maintained, functional modern style. Bathrooms are also well equipped with shower-tub combinations. The staff is well trained. The reception desk is helpful in arranging excursions to Obersalzberg, Berchtesgadener, and Salzburg.

Bahnhofplatz 14, 83426 Bad Reichenhall. ✆ **08651/60-90.** Fax 08651/60-91-11. 64 units. 129€–159€ ($115.20–$142) double. Rates include buffet breakfast. AE, DC, MC, V. Parking 4€ ($3.55). **Amenities:** Restaurant; bar; pool; sauna; solarium; bike rental; bowling alley; salon; room service; massage. *In room:* TV, minibar, hair dryer.

**Parkhotel Luisenbad** ★★ A world unto itself, Parkhotel Luisenbad is an 1860s hotel with a new wing in a garden setting. It's a good second choice to the Steigenberger, especially if you like traditional hotels. Rooms range from medium to spacious. The more modern ones are handsome, with bold colors and tasteful furnishings, but many guests prefer the older, more traditional rooms. Bathrooms are well-maintained, with shower-tub combinations and deluxe toiletries.

Ludwigstrasse 33, 83435 Bad Reichenhall. ✆ **08651/60-40.** Fax 08651/6-29-28. www.parkhotel.de. 89 units. 120€–180€ ($107.15–$160.75) double; 120€–200€ ($107.15–$178.60) suite. Rates include continental breakfast. DC, MC, V. Parking 5.50€ ($4.90). **Amenities:** Restaurant; lounge; pool; mud baths; sauna; room service; massage; laundry/dry cleaning. *In room:* TV, minibar, hair dryer.

**Salzburger Hof** *Value* This three-story hotel is one of the best buys in town. Its public areas are filled with old Bavarian charm. Best of all are the compact rooms, most of which contain streamlined sofas, beds with built-in headboards, and armchairs around a breakfast table; all open onto tiny balconies. All units contain bathrooms with showers. Price depends on the view.

Mozartstrasse 7, 83435 Bad Reichenhall. ✆ **08651/9-76-90.** Fax 08651/97-69-99. www.salzburgerhof.de. 25 units. 72€–87€ ($64.30–$77.70) double. Rates include continental breakfast. AE, MC, V. Parking 3€ ($2.70). **Amenities:** Breakfast room; lounge; room service. *In room:* TV, hair dryer.

**Steigenberger Axelmannstein** ★★★ This first-class hotel, set in its own 3ha (7½-acre) garden, is the best in town for traditional charm and spa conveniences, far superior to its closest rival, the Parkhotel Luisenbad. Public areas are traditionally furnished with antiques and reproductions. Rooms are well furnished and generally spacious. Many have views of the encircling Bavarian Alps. Bathrooms are medium in size and come with shower-tub combinations and deluxe toiletries.

Salzburger Strasse 2–6, 83435 Bad Reichenhall. ✆ **800/223-5652** in the U.S. and Canada, or 08651/77-70. Fax 08651/59-32. www.bad-reichenhall.steigenberger.de. 151 units. 200€–285€ ($178.60–$254.50) double; 310€ ($276.85) suite. Rates include buffet breakfast. AE, DC, V. Parking 5.10€, ($5). **Amenities:** 2 restaurants; bar; pool; tennis court; fitness center; sauna; solarium; room service; laundry/dry cleaning; hairdresser; cosmetic studio; cure department (spa). *In room:* TV, minibar, hair dryer.

## WHERE TO DINE

**Restaurant die Holzstube** GERMAN/ITALIAN/INTERNATIONAL The old-fashioned tradition and service here attract many regular patrons. This is a place where you can watch the flowers bloom and enjoy a world-class cuisine (with many diet-conscious selections). You might try one of the kitchen's own original recipes: for example, marinated and roasted medallions of venison Königin Luise, served with bacon, chanterelles, and whortleberries.

In the Parkhotel Luisenbad, Ludwigstrasse 33. ✆ **08651/60-40.** Reservations recommended. Main courses 13€–20€ ($11.60–$17.85). AE, DC, MC, V. Daily 11:30am–2pm and 6:30–9pm.

**Schweizer Stuben** ★ INTERNATIONAL No restaurant in Bad Reichenhall, even those in the luxury hotels, can hold a candle to this place for cuisine. It's located southwest of town in the center of the suburb of Kirchberg. The kitchen prepares light international dishes, along with specialties from Bavaria and the Berchtesgaden region. The decor is appropriately rustic. The chef seems to have a bent for updating contemporary classics. The fixed-price menu at lunch is an especially good value.

Kirchberg Schlössl, Thumseestrasse 11, Kirchberg. ✆ **08651/27-60.** Reservations required. Main courses 11€–22€ ($9.80–$19.65); fixed-price meals 19€ ($16.95) at lunch, 50€ ($44.65) at dinner. AE, DC, MC, V. Thurs–Tues 11am–3pm and 6pm–1am.

## BAD REICHENHALL AFTER DARK

Most guests on the nighttime circuit head for the **Bad Reichenhall Casino,** Wittelsbacherstrasse 17 (✆ **08651/95-800**), which offers roulette, American roulette, blackjack, and 50 types of slot machines. You must show your passport if you plan to do any gaming. It's open daily 3pm to 3am; admission is 5€ ($4.45). Men must wear jackets and ties. The **theater,** also located here at the Kurgastzentrum, site of the casino, is a setting for operas, operettas, plays, ballets, musicals, symphonies, folkloric evenings, and chamber-music recitals. The tourism office (see "Visitor Information," earlier in the chapter) keeps a complete list of events and ticket prices. When weather permits, performances are staged in an open-air pavilion. Tickets are 16€ to 35€ ($14.30–$31.25).

If you want to hang out with the locals, go to the **Axel Bar,** a woodsy bar in the Steigenberger Axelmannstein Hotel, Salzburgerstrasse 2–6 (✆ **08651/77-70**). Here you can dance to rather sedate disco music interspersed with folk tunes. There's also the **Tiffany Bar** at the Hotel Bayerischer Hof, Bahnhofplatz 14 (✆ **08651/24-80**), where folks sometimes dance to live music but mostly just drink. The Bayerischer Hof's nightclub hosts international acts. Good old-fashioned Bavarian suds is the order of the evening at everybody's favorite beer hall, **Burgerbräu,** Rathausplatz (✆ **08651/60-89**).

# 3 Chiemsee ★

Prien am Chiemsee: 85km (53 miles) SE of Munich, 22km (14 miles) E of Rosenheim, 64km (40 miles) W of Salzburg

Chiemsee, known as the "Bavarian Sea," is one of the most beautiful lakes in the Bavarian Alps. It's surrounded by a serene landscape. In the south, the mountains reach almost to the water. Resorts line the shores of this large lake, but the main attractions are its two islands, **Frauenchiemsee** and **Herrenchiemsee,** where Ludwig II built his palace, Neues Schloss.

## ESSENTIALS

**GETTING THERE By Train** Prien Bahnhof is on the major Munich–Rosenheim–Freilassing–Salzburg rail line, with frequent connections in all directions. Ten trains arrive daily from Munich (trip time: 1 hr.). For information, call ✆ **01805/99-66-33.**

**By Bus** Regional bus service in the area is offered by **RVO Regionalverkehr Oberbayern,** Betrieb Rosenheim (✆ **08061/70-86-30** for schedules and information).

**By Car** Access by car is via the A8 Autobahn from Munich.

**VISITOR INFORMATION** Contact the **Kur- und Verkehrsamt,** Alte Rathaus-Strasse 11, in Prien am Chiemsee (✆ **08051/6-90-50**). It's open Monday to Friday 9am to 7pm and Saturday 9am to 1pm.

**GETTING AROUND By Steamer** From the liveliest resort, Prien, on the lake's west shore, you can reach either Frauenchiemsee or Herrenchiemsee via lake steamers that make regular trips throughout the year. The round-trip fare to Herrenchiemsee is 6.50€ ($5.80) to Frauenchiemsee. The steamers, operated by **Chiemsee-Schiffahrt Ludwig Fessler** (✆ **08051/60-90**), make round-trips covering the entire lake. Connections can also be made from Gstadt, Seebruck, Chieming, Übersee/Feldwies, and Bernau/Felden. Large boats leave Prien/Stock for Herrenchiemsee May to September, daily, about every 20 minutes 9am to 5pm. The last return is at 7:25pm.

**By Bus** There's also bus service from the harbor to the DB station in Prien (Chiemsee-Schiffahrt) and around the lake by RVO.

## EXPLORING THE ISLANDS

### FRAUENCHIEMSEE

Frauenchiemsee (or Fraueninsel) is the smaller of the lake's two major islands. On its sandy shore stands a fishing village that holds an elaborate festival at Corpus Christi (usually in late May). Fishing boats are covered with flowers and streamers, fishers are outfitted in Bavarian garb, and young women of the village dress as brides. As the boats circle the island, they stop at each corner for the singing of the Gospels. The island is also the home of a Benedictine convent, Frauenchiemsee Abbey, founded in 782, which makes it the oldest in Germany. The convent is known for a liqueur called Kloster Likör—it's supposed to be an "agreeable stomach elixir."

You can walk around the island in about 30 minutes to enjoy panoramic views of the lake. **Torhalle** (✆ **08054/72-56**), a summer-only art gallery, is installed in the ancient hall that used to be the gatehouse of the Frauenwörth convent. Admission is 2€ ($1.80) for adults and 1.50€ ($1.35) for children.

### HERRENCHIEMSEE ★★

Herrenchiemsee (or Herreninsel) is home to the fantastic **Neues Schloss,** Herrenchiemsee 3 (✆ **08051/68-870**), begun by Ludwig II in 1878 (see "The Fairy-Tale King," in chapter 7). Never completed due to the king's death in 1886, the castle was to have been a replica of Versailles, which Ludwig admired. When work was halted in 1886, only the center of the enormous palace had been completed. Nonetheless, the palace and its formal gardens, surrounded by woodlands of beech and fir, remain one of the grandest and most fascinating of Ludwig's constructions.

The palace **entrance** is lit by a huge skylight over the sumptuously decorated staircase. Frescoes depicting the four states of existence alternate with Greek and Roman statues in niches on the staircase and in the gallery above. The vestibule is adorned with a pair of enameled peacocks, Louis XIV's favorite bird.

The **Great Hall of Mirrors** ★★ is unquestionably the most splendid room in the palace and the most authentic replica of Versailles. The 17 door panels contain enormous mirrors reflecting the 33 crystal chandeliers and the 44 gilded candelabra. The vaulted ceiling is covered with 25 paintings depicting the life of Louis XIV.

Practically every inch of the **state bedroom** ★ has been gilded. On the dais, instead of a throne, stands the richly decorated bed, its purple-velvet draperies weighing more than 135kg (300 lbs). Separating the dais from the rest of the room is a carved wooden balustrade covered with gold leaf. On the ceiling, a huge fresco depicts the descent of Apollo, surrounded by the other gods of Olympus. The sun god's features bear a strong resemblance to those of Louis XIV.

The **dining room** is a popular attraction for visitors because of the so-called "little table that sets itself." A mechanism in the floor permitted the table to go down to the room below to be cleared and re-laid between courses. Over the table hangs an exquisite chandelier of Meissen porcelain, the largest in the world and the single most valuable item in the palace.

You can visit Herrenchiemsee at any time of the year. April to September, tours are given daily 9am to 5pm; off-season, daily 10am to 4pm. Admission (in addition to the round-trip boat fare) is 5.50€ ($4.90) for adults, 4.50€ ($4) for students, and free for children under 16.

## WHERE TO STAY

**Bayerischer Hof** The rustic decor creates the illusion that this relatively severe modern hotel is older than it is. Of particular note is the painted ceiling in the dining room. The rest of the hotel is more streamlined—modern, efficient, and quite appealing, although the Yachthotel Chiemsee outside of town has more style and flair. Nonetheless, the rooms are very comfortable and bathrooms are well-equipped, with showers.

Bernauerstrasse 3, 83209 Prien am Chiemsee. ✆ **08051/60-30.** Fax 08051/6-29-17. www.bayerischerhof-prien.de. 46 units. 86€–89€ ($76.80–$79.50) double. Rates include buffet breakfast. AE, MC, V. Parking 6€ ($5.35). Closed Nov and last week of Jan. **Amenities:** Breakfast room; lounge; room service. *In room:* TV, hair dryer.

**Yachthotel Chiemsee** ★ The best place to stay on the lake is the Yachthotel Chiemsee, on the western shore of the "Bavarian Sea." This hotel offers attractively furnished rooms, all with balconies or terraces opening onto the water. Lakeside rooms are equipped with two double beds and a pull-out sofa for groups of four or more. Most rooms are fairly spacious, and all bathrooms contain shower-tub combinations.

Harrasser Strasse 49, 83209 Prien am Chiemsee. ✆ **08051/69-60.** Fax 08051/51-71. www.yachthotel.de. 102 units. 150€–170€ ($133.95–$151.80) double; 200€–270€ ($178.60–$241.10) suite. Rates include buffet breakfast. AE, DC, MC, V. Free parking. **Amenities:** Restaurants; bar; pool; squash court; health club & spa; whirlpool; sauna; solarium; yacht rental; room service; babysitting; laundry. *In room:* TV, minibar, hair dryer.

## WHERE TO DINE

**Restaurant Mühlberger** ★★ CONTINENTAL Set within a 2-minute drive (or a 5-min. walk) from the center of Prien, this is a cozy, relatively modern building whose exposed pine and coziness makes you think it might be older. The thoughtful and hospitable staff will present menu items that reflect the diversity of local culinary traditions, and although lots of imagination is shown in the kitchens, some of the recipes evoke strong memories of their childhoods in many of the patrons. Examples including *Saibling* (a local freshwater whitefish) served in herb sauce with new potatoes; filet of veal with exotic wild mushrooms and a sauce made from a local white wine, a tender form of veal-based *Tafelspitz* (the boiled-beef dish that's always associated with Vienna and its last emperor, Franz-Josef); many well-flavored versions of chicken; and such saltwater fish dishes as tuna steak with a curried tomato sauce; or turbot with béarnaise sauce. You might begin a meal here with a terrine of guinea-fowl with pearl onions; and end it with a house-made strudel that's layered with wild cherries, vanilla ice cream, and chocolate sauce.

Bernauerstrasse 40. ✆ **08051/966888.** Reservations recommended. Main courses 19€–24€ ($16.95–$21.45); lunch fixed-price menus 24€–61€ ($21.45–$54.45); dinner fixed-price menus 52€–61€ ($46.45–$54.45). MC, V. Thurs–Mon 12:30–2pm and Wed–Mon 6–10pm. Closed: 1 week in Feb and 1 week in Nov.

## 4 Bad Wiessee

53km (33 miles) S of Munich, 18km (11 miles) SE of Bad Tölz

If you've always believed that the best medicine is the worst tasting, you should feel right at home in Bad Wiessee—the mineral springs of this popular spa on the Tegernsee are saturated with iodine and sulfur. However, the other attractions of this small town more than make up for this healthful discomfort. The spa, with a huge lake at its feet and towering Alps rising behind it, is a year-round resort. In summer, swimming and boating are popular; in winter, you can ski on the slopes or skate on the lake. The springs are used for the treatment of many diseases, including rheumatism and heart and respiratory conditions. In spite of its tiny size, Bad Wiessee is advanced in its medicinal facilities, as well as in its accommodations and restaurants.

The main season begins in May and ends in October. During these busy times, you should definitely make a reservation. Many hotels close in winter, so be warned if you're an off-season visitor. In recent years, the town has become increasingly popular with vacationers from Munich.

From Bad Wiessee, a number of tours are possible, including visits to Munich, Chiemsee, and the castles of Neuschwanstein (see chapter 7), Herrenchiemsee, and Linderhof (covered later in this chapter). You can also visit Salzburg and Innsbruck in Austria. The tourism office (see below) will supply details.

### ESSENTIALS

**GETTING THERE By Train** Travelers arriving by train disembark at Gmund, 3km (2 miles) away. At the railway station there, a flotilla of buses (9–11 per day) meet every major train, with easy connections on to Bad Wiessee. For rail information, call ✆ **01805/99-66-33.**

**By Bus** Three to five buses depart every day for Bad Wiessee from Munich's Hauptbahnhof, with additional stops along the Zweibrückestrasse, adjacent to Munich's Deutsches Museum (trip time: 90 min.). Round-trip transport costs 13€ ($11.60) per person. For bus information, call ✆ **08022/19-412.**

**By Car** Access from either Munich or Salzburg is via the A8 Autobahn. Take the Holzkirchen exit heading toward Bad Wiessee and follow the signs.

**VISITOR INFORMATION** For information, go to the Kuramt, Adrian-Stoop-Strasse 20 (✆ **08022/19-412**). May to October, the tourism office's hours are Monday to Friday 8am to 5pm and Saturday and Sunday 9am to noon. In the off-season, hours are Monday to Friday 8am to noon and 2 to 5pm.

### SIGHTS & ACTIVITIES

Bad Wiesse offers plenty of activities, apart from its health treatments. In summer, there's sailing or windsurfing on the lake, or mountain biking and hiking. A drive up the **Wallberg Road** winds through the Moorsalm pasture to an altitude of 1,000m (3,300 ft.). There's also plenty of golf and tennis. In winter, experienced alpine skiers are drawn to the Wallberg, and there are many cross-country trails as well. Wintertime hiking is also a possibility, as about 100km (60 miles) of paths are cleared of snow. The less athletic can enjoy horse-drawn sleigh rides. Finally, you can also take a **mountain cable car,** which travels 1,550m (5,100 ft.) high.

The town of Bad Wiesse has an old-world charm. It's best explored via the old-fashioned steam train or by taking a carriage ride. During the annual lake festivals in summer, locals don traditional clothing and parade through the town. Worth the trip is the nearby **Tegernsee Ducal palace,** which contains the former monastery of St. Quinn, founded in A.D. 746.

## SHOPPING

You'll find traditional Bavarian souvenirs, loden coats, and lederhosen here. For a full selection of traditional Bavarian clothes, go to **Friedl Mandel,** Lindenplatz (✆ **08022/8-14-58**). If you want to acquire one-of-a-kind woodcarvings, either religious or secular, head for the studio of **Franz Trinkl,** Dr. Scheid Strasse 9A (✆ **08022/87-49**), where you'll find a charming and idiosyncratic collection of artfully carved figurines.

## WHERE TO STAY

### EXPENSIVE

**Hotel Lederer am See** ★ This spa and holiday hotel is the most distinguished choice in town. From the balcony of your room, you'll look out onto the Tegernsee and the Lower Bavarian Alps. The atmosphere is pleasant, with good service and attractive, well-maintained rooms, ranging in size from medium to spacious. Each unit comes with a midsize bathroom with tub-and-shower combination. The hotel stands in a large park.

Bodenschneidstrasse 9–11, 83707 Bad Wiessee. ✆ **08022/82-90.** Fax 08022/82-92-61. www.lederer.com. 114 units. 114€–196€ ($101.80–$175.05) double. AE, DC, MC, V. Closed Nov–Feb. Free parking. **Amenities:** Restaurant; lounge; nightclub; indoor pool; tennis courts; sauna; solarium; salon; room service; laundry/dry cleaning. *In room:* TV, hair dryer.

### MODERATE

**Hotel Rex** ★ A modern hotel with much charm and character, Kurhotel Rex is set against a backdrop of the Lower Bavarian Alps. It's an ideal choice for a vacation by the lake. The decorator tried to make the place as warm and inviting as possible. The well-maintained rooms are furnished in Bavarian style and contain bathrooms with shower-tub combinations.

Münchnerstrasse 25, 83707 Bad Wiessee. ✆ **08022/8-62-00.** Fax 08022/862-01-00. www.hotel-rex.de. 58 units. 94€–115€ ($83.95–$102.70) double; 135€ ($120.55) suite. No credit cards. Closed Nov 1–Apr 5. Free parking. **Amenities:** Restaurant; bar; lounge; room service; laundry. *In room:* TV, hair dryer.

**Landhaus am Stein** This typical Bavarian inn, with geranium-filled balconies and a roof overhang, is a real alpine resort, where people come to have a good time. It attracts scenery lovers in summer and skiers in winter. Rooms range from small to medium in size and are recently refurbished and completely modern; each has a balcony and a tiled shower-only bathroom.

Im Sapplfeld 8, 83707 Bad Wiessee. ✆ **08022/9-84-70.** Fax 08022/8-35-60. www.landhausamstein.de. 17 units. 100€–150€ ($89.30–$133.95) double. Rates include buffet breakfast. MC, V. Free parking. Garage 15€ ($13.40). **Amenities:** Breakfast room; lounge; sauna; room service; laundry/dry cleaning. *In room:* TV, hair dryer.

**Park Hotel Resi von der Post** *Value* This enduring favorite has been around much longer than many of its fast-rising competitors. It has been considerably modernized, and now has well-furnished, traditional rooms. Bathrooms, although a bit cramped, are well organized, neatly maintained, and are equipped with showers. Make reservations early; it's usually booked up for the year by summer.

Zilcherstrasse 14, 83707 Bad Wiessee. ✆ **08022/9-86-50.** Fax 08022/98-65-65. 30 units. 99€ ($88.40) double; from 105€ ($93.75) suite. Rates include buffet breakfast. AE, DC, MC, V. Free parking. **Amenities:** Restaurant; lounge; room service. *In room:* TV, hair dryer.

### INEXPENSIVE

**Kurhotel Edelweiss** This chalet/guesthouse is ornamented with wooden balconies and painted detailing. Rooms are functional and comfortably furnished. Additional but less-desirable units are available in the motel-like outbuildings beside the main structure. All rooms come with a small, tiled bathroom with shower stall. The modern public areas are suffused with a certain German kitsch.

Münchnerstrasse 21 (a .5km/¼ mile north of the center), 83707 Bad Wiessee. ✆ **08022/8-60-90.** Fax 08022/8-38-83. www.bad-wiessee.de/edelweiss. 40 units. 68€–82€ ($60.70–$73.25) double. Rates include continental breakfast. No credit cards. Free parking. **Amenities:** Restaurant; lounge; room service. *In room:* TV, hair dryer.

**Wiesseer Hof** This modern, but still traditional, four-story hotel looks like an overgrown chalet. Rooms are snug and cozy in the alpine tradition. Most have balconies, festooned in summer with boxes of geraniums, with views over a lawn dotted with greenery. The tiled bathrooms are small, each with a shower. The stuccoed wooden walls of the public areas create a *gemütlich* warmth.

Sanktjohanserstrasse 46, 83707 Bad Wiessee. ✆ **08022/86-70.** Fax 08022/86-71-65. www.wiesseerhof.com. 60 units. 76€–105€ ($67.85–$93.75) double. Rates include buffet breakfast. MC, V. Free parking. **Amenities:** Restaurant; lounge; room service. *In room:* TV, hair dryer, safe.

## WHERE TO DINE

At this resort, most guests dine at their hotels, since the spa is known for its hotels, not its restaurants. However, there is one (but only one) well-recommended restaurant here. See below.

**Freihaus Brenner** ★ CONTINENTAL This restaurant's setting is a cozy, steep-roofed farmhouse whose intricate murals and weathered balconies evoke the old-fashioned Teutonic world. The original version of this place was built in the early 1800s. Burnt to the ground around 1900, it was rebuilt nearby a few years later about 18 meters (20 yards) from the main location. Today, young and energetic proprietors keep the recipes fresh and international, and the service zippy, for clients who enjoy the *gemütlich* setting and the woodsy location overlooking the lake, about a 5-minute drive west from the center of Bad Wiessee. Menu items include selections from every country that borders Germany, including Italy, Switzerland, France, and Austria. The best examples of the local fare this place prepares with great zestiness include roasted duckling with red cabbage and potato salad and several different forms of wursts, sometimes served with braised celery and new potatoes.

Freihaushöhe. ✆ **08022/82004.** Reservations recommended. Main courses 9€–29€ ($8.05–$25.90). MC, V. Daily 9am–10pm. Warm food daily 11:30am–2pm and 6:30–10pm.

# 5 Mittenwald ★

106km (66 miles) S of Munich, 18km (11 miles) SE of Garmisch-Partenkirchen, 37km (23 miles) NW of Innsbruck

The year-round resort of Mittenwald, which lies in a pass in the Karwendel Range, seems straight out of *The Sound of Music.* Especially noteworthy and photogenic are the painted Bavarian houses with overhanging eaves. On the square stands a monument to Mathias Klotz, who introduced violin making to Mittenwald in 1684. The town is a major international center for this highly specialized craft.

## ESSENTIALS

**GETTING THERE** **By Train** Hourly train service runs on the express rail line between Munich and Innsbruck, Austria. From Munich, trip time is 1½ to 2 hours; from Frankfurt, 5 to 6 hours. Call ✆ **01805/99-66-33** for information.

**By Bus** Regional bus service from Garmisch-Partenkirchen and nearby towns is frequently provided by **RVO Regionalverkehr Oberbayern** at Garmisch (✆ **08821/94-82-74** for schedules and information).

**By Car** Access by car is via the A95 Autobahn from Munich.

**VISITOR INFORMATION** Contact the **Kurverwaltung und Verkehrsamt,** Dammkarstrasse 3 (✆ **08823/3-39-81**). It's open Monday to Friday 8am to noon and 1 to 5pm, and Saturday and Sunday 10am to noon.

## SIGHTS & ACTIVITIES

The town's museum, which contains a workshop, has exhibits that trace the history of violins and other stringed instruments from their invention through various stages of their evolution. The **Geigenbau- und Heimatmuseum,** Ballenhausgasse 3 (✆ **08823/25-11**), is open Tuesday to Friday 10am to 1pm and 3 to 6pm, and on Saturday and Sunday 10am to 1pm. Admission is 2.05€ ($1.85) for adults and 1€ (90¢) for students. The museum is closed November 1 to December 22.

In the surrounding countryside, the scenery of the Wetterstein and Karwendel ranges constantly changes. Some 130km (80 miles) of hiking paths wind up and down the mountains around the village. You can hike through the hills on your own, take part in mountain-climbing expeditions, or take horse-and-carriage trips and motor-coach tours to nearby villages. In the evening in the various inns, there's typical Bavarian entertainment, often consisting of folk dancing and singing, zither playing, and yodeling. Concerts during the summer are held in the music pavilion. Mittenwald also has good spa facilities, in large gardens landscaped with tree-lined streams and trout pools. In winter, the town is a skiing center.

## SHOPPING

The classical stringed instruments crafted here have been sought after by professional musicians for centuries. Prices may be steep for the amateur violinist, but a visit to **Geigenbau Leonhardt,** Mühlenweg 53A (✆ **08823/80-10**), is educational and interesting—even if you're just browsing.

If you've ever had the desire to traipse about in a dirndl, embroidered blouse, or lederhosen, head for **Trachtenstubön,** Obermarkt 35 (✆ **08823/85-55**).

## WHERE TO STAY

**Alpenrose** ★ *Value* This particularly inviting hotel is located in the village center at the foot of a rugged mountain. The facade is covered with decorative designs and window boxes. The inn's basic 14th-century structure was once part of a monastery. Rooms are divided between the Alpenrose (the former monastery) and its annex, the Bichlerhof. Try to stay in the main building, where rooms have a great deal of charm, with finely woven fabrics, old-fashioned farmhouse cupboards, and dark-wood paneling. Bathrooms in both buildings are a bit cramped, each equipped with shower. The tavern room, overlooking the street, has many ingratiating features, including handmade chairs, flagstone floors, and a square-tile stove in the center.

Obermarkt 1, 82481 Mittenwald. ✆ **08823/92700.** Fax 08823/3720. www.alpenrose.mittenwald.de. 18 units. 66€–85€ ($58.95–$75.90) double; 75€–97€ ($67–$86.60) suite. Rates include buffet breakfast. AE, DC, DISC, MC, V. Free parking. **Amenities:** Restaurant; bar; lounge; room service; laundry. *In room:* TV, minibar, hair dryer.

**Gästehaus Sonnenbichl** *Value* One of the more modest inns in town, this chalet nevertheless offers good value and comfort. It has a view of the village set against a backdrop of the Alps. The small but exceedingly well-kept rooms are freshly decorated in vivid natural colors and all contain neatly kept bathrooms with shower-tub combinations. Reserve well in advance.

Klausnerweg 32, 82481 Mittenwald. ✆ **08823/9-22-30.** Fax 08823/58-14. www.sonnenbichl.de. 20 units. 58€–89€ ($51.80–$79.50) double. Rates include buffet breakfast. No credit cards. Closed Nov 1–Dec 15. **Amenities:** Breakfast room; lounge; room service. *In room:* TV, minibar, hair dryer.

**Hotel Post** ★★ The Post provides Mittenwald's finest lodging. It's the most seasoned and established chalet hotel in the village, dating from 1632, when stagecoaches carrying mail and passengers across the Bavarian Alps stopped here to refuel. A delightful breakfast is served on the sun terrace, with a view of the Alps. Beds here are among the most comfortable in town, with duvets and beautiful linen. All the midsize bathrooms are efficiently organized, mostly with tub-and-shower combination. The maids are especially helpful.

Obermarkt 9, 82481 Mittenwald. ✆ **08823/938-2999.** Fax 08823/99-90. www.posthotel-mittenwald.de. 90 units. 86€–140€ ($76.80–$125) double; 116€–170€ ($103.60–$151.80) suite. Rates include buffet breakfast. MC, V. Parking free outside. **Amenities:** Restaurant; bar; lounge; pool; sauna; room service; massage. *In room:* TV, minibar, hair dryer, safe.

## WHERE TO DINE

**Restaurant Arnspitze** ★ BAVARIAN This traditionally decorated restaurant, housed in a modern chalet hotel on the outskirts of town, is the finest in Mittenwald. The cuisine is solid, satisfying, and wholesome. You might order sole with homemade noodles or veal steak in creamy smooth sauce, then finish with one of the freshly made desserts. There's also an excellent fixed-price lunch.

Innsbruckerstrasse 68. ✆ **08823/24-25.** Main courses 15.50€–19.80€ ($13.85–$17.70); fixed-price meal 22€ ($19.65) at lunch, 32.50€ ($29) at dinner. AE, MC, V. Wed 6–9pm; Thurs–Mon noon–2pm and 6–9pm.

# 6 Garmisch-Partenkirchen ★★★

97km (60 miles) SW of Munich, 117km (73 miles) SE of Augsburg, 60km (37 miles) NW of Innsbruck

The twin villages of Garmisch and Partenkirchen make up Germany's top alpine resort. In spite of their urban flair, the towns maintain the charm of an ancient village, especially Partenkirchen. Even today, you occasionally see country folk in traditional dress, and you may be held up in traffic while the cattle are led from their mountain-grazing grounds down through the streets of town.

## ESSENTIALS

**GETTING THERE** **By Train** The **Garmisch-Partenkirchen Bahnhof** lies on the major Munich–Weilheim–Garmisch–Mittenwald–Innsbruck rail line, with frequent connections in all directions. Twenty trains per day arrive from Munich (trip time: 1 hr. 22 min.). For information and schedules, call ✆ **01805/99-66-33.** Mountain rail service to several plateaus and the Zugspitze is offered by the **Bayerische Zugspitzbahn** at Garmisch (✆ **08821/79-70**).

**By Bus** Both long-distance and regional buses through the Bavarian Alps are provided by **RVO Regionalverkehr Oberbayern** in Garmisch-Partenkirchen (✆ **08821/ 94-82-74**).

**By Car** Access is via the A95 Autobahn from Munich; exit at Eschenlohe.

**VISITOR INFORMATION** Contact the **Verkehrsamt,** Richard-Strauss-Platz (✆ **08821/720-688**). It's open Monday to Saturday 8am to 6pm and Sunday and holidays 10am to noon.

### Hiking in the Bavarian Alps

Hiking is Bavaria's favorite pastime. Locals believe firmly in the emotional and spiritual benefits of walking and hill climbing and tend to hit the trails the moment the snows melt.

The tourist office in Garmisch-Partenkirchen will point you to hiking trails of varying degrees of difficulty, all clearly marked with signs. The office also offers a brochure outlining the half-dozen best trails. You don't have to be an Olympic athlete to enjoy them. Most hikes will take an energetic person 4 to 5 hours, but some of them are shorter and easy enough for children.

An easily accessibly destination is the 1,240m (4,060-ft.) **Eckbauer** peak that lies on the southern fringe of Partenkirchen. The easy trails on its lower slopes are recommended for first-time alpine hikers. You can even take a chairlift to the top, where, in the real Bavarian style, the Bergasthof (a guest house or café, usually in a high-altitude and rural location) will serve you a glass of buttermilk. In less than an hour, you can descend on relatively easy trails through a forest. The cable car stretching from Garmisch to the top of the Eckbauer departs year-round from the Eckbauerbahn (✆ **08821/3409**), adjacent to the ski stadium in Garmisch. Round-trip costs 11€ ($9.80) for adults, 8€ ($7.15) for children, and 25€ ($22.35) for two adults and a child.

More demanding are the slopes of the rugged **Alpspitz** ★ region, which begins about a mile southwest of Garmisch. The area is interlaced with wildflowers, unusual geology, alpine meadows, and a network of cable cars and hiking trails spread over a terrain ranging in altitude between 1,400m (4,600 ft.) and 1,920m (6,300 ft.). The highest trails are around the summit of the Alpspitz at 2,603m (8,541 ft.).

One of the most appealing ways to gain a high-altitude panorama over this region is to take a triangular trip up the Alpspitz. Begin your

**GETTING AROUND** An unnumbered municipal bus services the town, depositing passengers at Marienplatz or the Bahnhof, from which you can walk to all centrally located hotels. This free bus runs every 15 minutes.

## EXPLORING THE AREA

Garmisch-Partenkirchen is a center for winter sports, summer hiking, and mountain climbing. The symbol of the city's growth and modernity is the **Olympic Ice Stadium,** built for the 1936 Winter Olympics and capable of holding nearly 12,000 people. On the slopes at the edge of town is the **Ski Stadium,** with two ski jumps and a slalom course. In 1936, more than 100,000 people watched the events in this stadium. Today it's still an integral part of winter life in Garmisch—the World Cup Ski Jump is held here every New Year.

The town and its environs offer some of the most panoramic views and colorful buildings in Bavaria. The pilgrimage **Chapel of St. Anton,** on a pinewood path at the edge of Partenkirchen, is all pink and silver, inside and out. Its graceful lines are characteristic of the 18th century, when it was built. In the park surrounding the chapel, the **Philosopher's Walk** ★ is a delightful spot to wander, just to enjoy the views of the mountains around the low-lying town.

journey at the Kreuzeckbahn/Alpspitzbahn cable car terminus, a mile south of Garmisch. The cable car will carry you uphill along the Kreuzeckbahn for a 4-minute ride across a jagged landscape to the lowest station of the Hochalm cable car. Here the Hochalmbahn will carry you uphill for another 4 minutes to the top of the Osterfelderkopf, 1,920m (6,300 ft.) above sea level. Cable cars for both stages of this trip depart at 30-minute intervals daily 8:15am to 5:15pm. After your visit to the Osterfelderkopf summit, you can return to Garmisch via a different route, a direct downhill descent via the Alpspitzbahn, a 10-minute ride above jagged gorges, soaring cliffs, and grassy meadows. At the points where the cable car lines intersect, you might want to embark on short, high-altitude hikes to observe the unique alpine flora and fauna. Snacks are served at cafes and restaurants at major points on the itinerary.

Round-trip passage along this three-tiered alpine itinerary costs 33€ ($29.45) for adults and 20€ ($17.85) for children 5 to 16; it's free for children 4 and under. These fares and times of departure can fluctuate. For the latest details, call either the information service for the above-mentioned cable cars (✆ **08821/7970**) or check with the Garmisch **Verkehrsamt** (tourist office) on Richard-Strauss-Platz (✆ **08821/18-06**).

From Garmisch-Partenkirchen, many other peaks of the Witterstein range are accessible as well, via the 10 funiculars ascending from the borders of the town. From the top of the 1,780m (5,850-ft.) **Wank** to the east, you get the best view of the plateau on which the villages of Garmisch and Partenkirchen sit. This summit is also a favorite with the patrons of Garmisch's spa facilities because the plentiful sunshine makes it ideal for the *Liegekur* (deck-chair cure).

This area has always attracted German romantics, including "Mad" King Ludwig (see the box, "The Fairy-Tale King," on p. 264). Perhaps with Wagner's music ringing in his ears, the king ordered the construction of a hunting lodge here in the style of a Swiss chalet but commanded that the interior look like something out of *The Arabian Nights.* The lodge, **Jagdschloss Schachen,** is still here. It can only be reached after an arduous climb. The tourist office will supply details. Mid-June to mid-September, tours to the lodge usually leave from the Olympic Ski Stadium at 11am and 2pm, but check before you go.

## TO THE TOP OF THE ZUGSPITZE ★★★

From Garmisch-Partenkirchen, you can see the tallest mountain in Germany, the **Zugspitze,** 2,960m (9,720 ft.) above sea level. Ski slopes begin at a height of 2,650m (8,700 ft.). For a panoramic view of both the Bavarian and the Tyrolean (Austrian) Alps, go all the way to the summit. There are two different ways to reach the Zugspitze from the center of Garmisch. The first begins with a trip on the cog railway, the Zugspitzbahn, which departs from the back of Garmisch's main railway station daily every hour 8:35am to 2:35pm. The train travels uphill, past lichen-covered boulders and coursing streams, to a high-altitude plateau, the Zugspitzplatte, where views sweep out over all Bavaria. At the Zugspitzplatte, you'll transfer onto a cable car, the Gletscher Sielbahn, for a 4-minute ride uphill to the top of the Zugspitze. There, far-reaching panoramas, a cafe and restaurant, a gift shop, and many alpine trails await. Total travel time for this itinerary is about 55 minutes, but you may want to linger at the first stop, the Zugspitzplatte, before continuing up.

The other way to get to the summit is to take the Zugspitzbahn for a briefer trip, disembarking 14km (9 miles) southwest of Garmisch at the lower station of the Eibsee Sielbahn (Eibsee Cable Car), next to a clear alpine lake. The cable car will carry you from there directly to the summit of the Zugspitze, for a total transit time of about 38 minutes. The Eibsee Sielbahn makes its run at least every half hour 8:30am to 4:30pm (5:30pm in July and Aug).

Round-trip tickets allow you to ascend one way and descend the other, in order to enjoy the widest range of spectacular views. April to October, round-trip fares are 42€ ($37.50) for adults, 29€ ($25.90) for teenagers ages 16 and 17, and 25€ ($22.35) for children ages 6 to 15. Group fare for two adults and a child costs 74€ ($66.10). In winter, round-trip fares are reduced to 33€ ($29.45) for adults, 23€ ($20.55) for those ages 16 and 17, and 20€ ($17.85) for children ages 5 to 15. For more information, contact the Bayerische Zugspitzbahn, Olympiastrasse 27, Garmisch-Partenkirchen (✆ **08821/7-97-0**).

## SHOPPING

Your best bets are in the traffic-reduced Ludwigstrasse in Partenkirchen and in the almost traffic-free zone from Richard-Strauss-Platz to Marienplatz in Garmisch. A vast array of stores sell boots, boutique items, clothing, jewelry, art, antiques, and more. If you like traditional Bavarian dress but don't want to spend a lot of money, head for **Loisachtaler,** Burgstrasse 20 (✆ **08821/5-23-90**). Here,

### *Moments* A Dramatic Alpine Fantasy

Another interesting hike is through the **Partnachklamm Gorge** ★★, a canyon with a roaring stream at the bottom and sheer cliff walls rising on either side of the hiking trail. Take the Graseck Seilbahn from its departure point at the bottom of the gorge, less than a 1km (½ mile) south of Garmisch's ski stadium, and get off at the first station, which is adjacent to a cozy hotel, the **Forsthaus Graseck** (✆ **08821/5-40-06**). You might want to get a meal or drink here first. Afterward descend on foot along narrow paths by the sides of the stream, as it cascades downhill. The path crosses the gorge and returns you to the point where you entered. Many readers have found this one of their most memorable adventures in Bavaria. The experience of walking along a rocky ledge just above a rushing river and often behind small waterfalls, while looking up at 365m (1,200 ft.) of rocky cliffs, is truly awesome (and sometimes wet).

From its departure point to the Forsthaus, the 3-minute cable car ride costs 5€ ($4.45) per person each way. For information about the Seilbahn, contact Forsthaus Graseck (✆ **08821/5-40-06**). The cable car operates at 20-minute intervals 7am to 8pm, 11pm on weekends.

Petra Ostler has assembled the area's finest collection of secondhand clothing. Take your pick: a jaegermeister loden coat, an alpine hat with pheasant feathers, or a cast-off dirndl. They all look like new.

## WHERE TO STAY

### EXPENSIVE

**Grand Hotel Sonnenbichl** ★★ The most upscale hotel in the area is on the hillside overlooking Garmisch-Partenkirchen, 1.5km (1 mile) from the city center and 3km (2 miles) from the Bahnhof. It has excellent views of the Wetterstein mountain range and the Zugspitze (from front rooms only; rear rooms open onto a rock wall). Some of the spacious rooms are showing a bit of wear and tear; a few lack a complete bathtub. The decor is generally Art Nouveau.

Burgstrasse 97, 82467 Garmisch-Partenkirchen. ✆ **08821/70-20.** Fax 08821/70-21-31. www.sonnenbichl.de. 93 units. 135€–185€ ($120.55–$165.20) double; 360€ ($321.50) suite. Rates include buffet breakfast. AE, DC, MC, V. Free parking. Take Rte. 23 toward Oberammergau. **Amenities:** 2 restaurants; bar; pool; fitness center; sauna; solarium; room service; massage; laundry/dry cleaning. *In room:* TV, minibar, hair dryer.

### MODERATE

**Posthotel Partenkirchen** ★ The Posthotel Partenkirchen, which was founded in 1542, is one of the town's most prestigious hotels. In recent years, it has even surpassed its major rival, the Reindl's Partenkirchner Hof (see below). Here you'll experience old-world living and personalized service. The U-shaped rooms are stylish, with antiques and elaborately carved furnishings. The sunny balconies overlook a garden and offer a view of the Alps. Rooms are generally medium in size, though some are quite spacious, and each comes with a midsize bathroom with tub-and-shower combination.

Ludwigstrasse 49, 82467 Garmisch-Partenkirchen. ✆ **08821/93630.** Fax 08821/93-63-2222. www.posthotel.de. 57 units. 117.55€–143.10€ ($104.95–$127.80) double; 178.85€ ($159.70) suite. Rates include continental breakfast. AE, DC, MC, V. Free parking. **Amenities:** Restaurant; lounge; golf course; tennis courts; skiing; mountain climbing; room service; laundry. *In room:* TV, minibar, hair dryer.

**Reindl's Partenkirchner Hof** ★ Reindl's opened in 1911, and from the beginning it attracted a devoted following—and still does. Owners Bruni and Karl Reindl maintain a high level of luxury and hospitality in this special Bavarian retreat. The annexes, the Wetterstein and the House Alpspitz, have balconies, and the main four-story building has wraparound verandas, giving each room an unobstructed view of the mountains and town. Rooms are among the most attractive in town. The best are the suites opening onto panoramic views of mountains or the garden. Fine carpeting and rustic pine furniture add to the allure.

Bahnhofstrasse 15, 82467 Garmisch-Partenkirchen. ✆ **08821/5-80-25.** Fax 08821/73401. www.reindls.de. 63 units. 94€–202€ ($83.95–$180.40) double; 166€–368€ ($148.25–$328.60) suite. AE, DC, MC, V. Parking 8€ ($7.15). Closed Nov 10–Dec 15. **Amenities:** Restaurant; lounge; pool; health club; sauna; room service; laundry. *In room:* TV, minibar, hair dryer.

**Romantik-Hotel Clausing's Posthotel** ★ The history and identity of Garmisch are bound up in events that took place at this hotel in the heart of town. It began as a tavern in 1512. During the Thirty Years' War, it sheltered refugees from besieged Munich. In 1891, it was bought by the Berlin beer baron who invented Berliner Weissen, which quickly became one of the most popular brands in Garmisch. Nowadays, the upgraded hotel retains its sense of *gemütlichkeit.* Rooms range from spacious to rather small and cozy, successfully mingling Bavarian antique charm with modern comforts. Bathrooms are beautifully kept, containing shower-tub combinations.

Marienplatz 12, 82467 Garmisch-Partenkirchen. ✆ **08821/70-90.** Fax 08821/70-92-05. www.clausings-posthotel.de. 47 units. 102.20€–153.30€ ($91.25–$136.90) double. Rates include buffet breakfast. AE, DC, MC, V. **Amenities:** 2 restaurants; bar; room service. *In room:* TV, minibar, hair dryer.

### INEXPENSIVE

**Gasthof Fraundorfer** *(Finds* The family-owned Gasthof Fraundorfer is located on Partenkirchen's main street, just a 5-minute walk from the old church. Its original style has not been updated, so it retains the character of bygone days. There are three floors under a sloping roof, with a facade brightly decorated with murals depicting a family feast. You'll be in the midst of village-centered activities, near interesting shops and restaurants. Rooms are furnished with traditional alpine styling, some with four-poster beds, all with firm mattresses. Some larger units are virtual apartments, suitable for up to five guests. Bathrooms are compact with shower stalls. Owners Josef and Barbel Fraundorfer are proud of their country-style lodge. They also operate the Gästehaus Barbara in back, with 20 more beds, including a *Himmelbett* ("heaven bed"), which is loaded with soft, feather-stuffed pillows and comforters. A double in their new house costs 74€ ($66.10).

Ludwigstrasse 24, 82467 Garmisch-Partenkirchen. ✆ **08821/21-76.** Fax 08821/9-27-99. www.gasthof-fraundorfer.de. 30 units. 74€–186€ ($66.10–$166.10) double; 100€–180€ ($89.30–$160.75) family room for 2–5 people. Rates include buffet breakfast. MC, V. Free parking. **Amenities:** Dining room; lounge; room service. *In room:* TV, hair dryer.

**Haus Lilly** Many visitors appreciate this spotlessly clean guesthouse. It wins prizes for its copious breakfasts and the personality of its smiling owner, Maria Lechner, whose English is limited but whose hospitality is universal. Each small room comes with a comfortable bed fitted with a good mattress and includes free access to a kitchen, so in-house meal preparation is an option. Bathrooms are small and have shower stalls. Breakfast is a selection of cold cuts, rolls, cheese, eggs, pastries, and coffee, tea, or chocolate.

Zugspitzstrasse 20a (a 15-min. walk from the Bahnhof), 82467 Garmisch-Partenkirchen. ✆ **08821/5-26-00.** 8 units. 61€ ($54.45) double, triple, or quad. Rates include buffet breakfast. No credit cards. Free parking. **Amenities:** Breakfast room; lounge; room service. *In room:* TV.

**Hotel Hilleprandt** *(Value* This cozy, tranquil chalet is a good budget choice. Its wooden balconies, attractive garden, and backdrop of forest-covered mountains give the impression of an old-time alpine building. However, a complete renovation has brought streamlined modern comfort. Rooms are small but comfortable, each with a private balcony and tiled, shower-only bathroom.

Riffelstrasse 17 (near the Zugspitze Bahnhof and the Olympic Ice Stadium), 82467 Garmisch-Partenkirchen. ✆ **08821/28-61.** Fax 08821/7-45-48. www.hotel-hilleprandt.de. 18 units. 74€–96€ ($66.10–$85.75) double; 104€ ($92.85) suite. Rates include buffet breakfast. MC, V. Free parking. **Amenities:** Breakfast room; lounge; fitness center; sauna. *In room:* TV, hair dryer.

## WHERE TO DINE

### EXPENSIVE

**Posthotel Partenkirchen** ★ CONTINENTAL The restaurant at the Posthotel Partenkirchen is renowned for its distinguished continental cuisine—in fact, its reputation has spread throughout Bavaria. The interior dining rooms are rustic, with a mellow, old-fashioned atmosphere. You could imagine Dürer having a meal here. Everything seems comfortably subdued, including the diners. Perhaps your best choice is to order one of the fixed-price menus, which change daily. The a la carte menu is extensive, featuring game in the autumn. Other main dishes include schnitzel cordon bleu and mixed grill St. James. The Wiener schnitzel, served with a large salad, is the best of that dish we've had in this resort.

Ludwigstrasse 49, Partenkirchen. ✆ **08821/5-10-67.** Reservations required. Main courses 10.20€–28.10€ ($9.10–$25.10). AE, DC, MC, V. Daily noon–2pm and 6–10pm.

**Reindl's Restaurant** ★★ CONTINENTAL One of the best places to eat in Partenkirchen is Reindl's, a first-class restaurant in every sense of the word. The seasonal menu offers *cuisine moderne* as well as regional Bavarian dishes. As a good opening to a fine repast, we suggest the scampi salad Walterspiel with fresh peaches, lemon, and tarragon, or homemade goose-liver paté with Riesling jelly. For a main dish, try *coq au Riesling* (chicken in wine) with noodles, or veal roasted with *Steinpilzen,* a special mushroom from the Bavarian mountains. For dessert, try either the Grand Marnier sabayon with strawberry and vanilla ice cream or something more spectacular: a Salzburger Nockerl for two.

In the Partenkirchner Hof, Bahnhofstrasse 15. ✆ **08821/943-870.** Reservations required. Main courses 19€–25€ ($16.95–$22.35). AE, DC, MC, V. Daily noon–2:30pm and 6:30–11pm. Closed Nov 10–Dec 15.

### MODERATE

**Alpenhof** ★ *Value* BAVARIAN Alpenhof is widely regarded as the finest restaurant in Garmisch, along with the hotel dining rooms at the Posthotel Partenkirchen and Reindl's Partenkirchner Hof. The cuisine here is grounded in tradition. Renate and Josef Huber offer a variety of Bavarian specialties, as well as trout "any way you want," salmon grilled with mousseline sauce, and ragout of venison. For dessert, try a soufflé with exotic fruits. In summer, try for an outside table; in winter, retreat to the cozy interior, which is flooded with sunlight from a greenhouse.

Am Kurpark 10. ✆ **08821/5-90-55.** Reservations recommended. Main courses 8.60€–19.90€ ($7.70–$17.75). MC, V. Daily 11am–2pm and 5:30–11pm.

### INEXPENSIVE

**Flösserstuben** *Finds* INTERNATIONAL Regardless of the season, a bit of the Bavarian Alps always seems to flower in this intimate restaurant, close to the town center. On most evenings, the weathered beams above the dining tables reverberate with laughter and good cheer. You can select a seat at a colorful wooden table or on an ox-yoke-inspired stool in front of the spliced saplings that decorate the bar. Moussaka and souvlaki, Hungarian goulashes, sauerbraten, and all kinds of Bavarian dishes are abundantly available.

Schmiedstrasse 2. ✆ **08821/28-88.** Reservations recommended. Main courses 7.65€–15.35€ ($6.85–$13.70). MC. Daily 11:30am–3pm and 5–10:30pm (or as late as 1:30am, depending on business).

**Riessersee** BAVARIAN This cafe-restaurant is located on the shores of a small lake with emerald-green water. Stop in here after you explore the Zugspitze. It's the ideal place for a leisurely lunch or afternoon coffee with cakes, ice cream, and chocolates. You may like the place so much you'll stick around for one of the Bavarian dinner dishes. Caviar and lobster are available on occasion, and excellent veal dishes are served all the time.

Reiss 6 (3km/2 miles from the center of town). ✆ **08821/9-54-40.** Main courses 5€–21.90€ ($4.45–$19.55). Daily 8am–9pm. AE, MC, V.

## GARMISCH-PARTENKIRCHEN AFTER DARK

You can test your luck at the town's casino, **Spielbank Garmisch-Partenkirchen,** Am Kurpark 74 (✆ **08821/959-90**). Admission costs 2.50€ ($2.25) per person, and presentation of a passport is required. The casino is open daily 3pm to 2am. Beginning at 7pm, men must wear jackets and ties. Friday and Saturday, games of seven-card stud poker are arranged (book in advance).

If you'd like to meet the locals at night, head for one of the taverns for a beer. All major hotels have bars, but for a change of pace, go to the **Irish Pub,** Rathausplatz 8 (✆ **08821/39-38**), and order a Guinness. This pub, in the center of town, attracts one of the most convivial crowds in the area.

Many hotels have dance floors that keep the music pumping into the wee hours, but for dancing of a different sort, check out the summer program of **Bavarian folk music and dancing,** held every Saturday night mid-May to September in the Bayernhalle, Brauhausstrasse 19. During the same season Saturday to Thursday, **classical concerts** are held at the Garmisch park bandstand. On Friday, these live shows move to the Partenkirchen bandstand. Check with the local tourist office (see "Visitor Information," earlier in this chapter) for details about these programs as well as a 5-day **Johann Strauss Festival** held in June.

## 7 Oberammergau ★

95km (59 miles) SW of Munich, 20km (12 miles) N of Garmisch-Partenkirchen

In the summer of 2000, Oberammergau staged its famous Passion Play, which is performed only 1 year out of 10. Surely the world's longest-running show, it began in 1634 when the town's citizens took a vow to give dramatic thanks after they were spared from the devastating plague of 1633. The town is packed to the gills all summer for this major event. Attracting pilgrims from around the world, the Passion Play depicts the "suffering, death, and rebirth of Jesus Christ." In many ways, it's an authentic recreation of a medieval morality play. Though the theater and production methods are contemporary, the spirit of the play is highly traditional. The whole production is community-based. Locals do all the acting—the competition for the roles of Jesus and Mary can be fierce. Performances last all day, with a break for lunch. Viewing the production can alternate between tedious and highly dramatic—but in most cases, it's fascinating. Where else would you get to witness such a pocket of medievalism in the modern world?

However, a visit to Oberammergau is ideal at any time, even without the performance. The town is in a wide valley surrounded by forests, green meadows, and mountains. It offers first-class hotels and cozy inns, and has long been known for the skill of its wood-carvers. Numerous hiking trails lead through the nearby mountains to hikers' inns. You can also simply go up to the mountaintops on the Laber cable railway or the Kolben chairlift.

Oberammergau also offers opportunities for tennis buffs, minigolf players, cyclists, swimmers, hang-gliding enthusiasts, and canoeists. The recreation center, Wellenberg, with open-air pools, fountains, sauna, solarium, and restaurant, is one of the Alps' most beautiful. The surrounding Ammer Valley is a treasure trove for explorers. And Oberammergau is often used as a base for visiting Linderhof Castle, the Benedictine monastery at Ettal, or the fairy-tale Neuschwanstein and Hohenschwangau castles (see chapter 7).

### ESSENTIALS

**GETTING THERE** **By Train** The **Oberammergau Bahnhof** is on the Murnau–Bad Kohlgrum–Oberammergau rail line, with frequent connections in all directions. Through Murnau, all major German cities can be reached. Daily trains arrive from Munich in 2 hours and from Frankfurt in 7 hours. For rail information and schedules, call ✆ **01805/99-66-33.**

**By Bus** Regional bus service to nearby towns is offered by **RVO Regionalverkehr Oberbayern** in Garmisch-Partenkirchen (✆ **08821/94-82-74**). An unnumbered bus goes back and forth between Oberammergau and Garmisch-Partenkirchen.

**By Car** Many visitors drive here, the trip taking 1½ hours from Munich and 5½ hours from Frankfurt. Take the A95 Munich–Garmisch–Partenkirchen Autobahn and exit at Eschenlohe.

**VISITOR INFORMATION** Contact the **Verkehrsbüro,** Eugen-Papst-Strasse 9A (✆ **08822/9-23-10**). It's open Monday to Friday 8:30am to 6pm and on Saturday 8:30am to 1pm.

## EXPLORING THE TOWN

Oberammergau has much to offer. Consider taking an excursion to either the **Berg Laber,** which rises to the east of the town, or **Berg Kolber,** to the west. Berg Laber, slightly more dramatic, is accessible via a cable-gondola (✆ **08822/4770**) that operates year-round 9am to 11:30am and 1 to 5 or 5:30pm. The 10-minute ascent costs 10.50€ ($9.40) per person. The top of Berg Kolber is accessible via a two-passenger chairlift (✆ **08822/4760**) that operates year-round 9 to 11:45am and 1 to 4:30 or 4:45pm. The cost is 5.50€ ($4.90) round-trip.

Aside from the actors, Oberammergau's most respected citizens are **wood-carvers,** many of whom have been trained in the village wood-carver's school. In the **Pilatushaus,** Ludwig-Thoma-Strasse (✆ **08822/16-82**), you can watch local carvers, as well as painters, sculptors, and potters, as they work. May to October, their hours are Tuesday to Friday 1:30 to 6pm. You'll see many examples of their art throughout the town, on the painted cottages and inns and in the churchyard.

**Heimatmuseum,** Dorfstrasse 8 (✆ **08822/9-41-36**), has a notable collection of Christmas crèches, all hand carved and painted, from the 18th through the 20th century. It's open May 20 to October 15, Tuesday to Sunday 2 to 6pm; off-season, Saturday only 2 to 6pm. Admission is 2.05€ ($1.85) for adults, 1.55€ ($1.40) for students, and .75€ (65¢) for children under 14.

When strolling through the village, note the frescoed houses named after fairy-tale characters, such as the "Hansel and Gretel House" and "Little Red Riding Hood House." The citizens of Oberammergau have a long tradition of painting frescoes on their houses. Most often, these frescoes are based on scenes from fairy tales. The fresco artists seem to have been inspired most often by the characters of Hansel and Gretel, or else Little Red Riding Hood and the wicked witch. The most famous frescoes house is **Pilatushaus** on Ludwig-Thoma-Strasse (see above), which today is a home to artisans. The frescoes here are the most beautiful in town, the creation of Franz Seraph Zwinck, who was the greatest of the town's fresco artists. They were known as *Lüftmalerei* painters. Zwinck based his fresco not on a fairy tale, but on a depiction of Jesus Christ coming before Pilate—hence the name of the house, Pilatushaus.

## WHERE TO STAY & DINE

The cost of accommodation in Oberammergau includes a universally imposed *Kurtaxe* (special tax) of 1.30€ ($1.15). This entitles visitors to a card providing small discounts at local attractions.

### MODERATE

**Hotel Restaurant Böld** ★ This well-designed chalet hotel steadily improves in quality and now is among the town's premier choices, in a neck-to-neck race with Parkhotel Sonnenhof. It lies only a stone's throw from the river. Rooms are

## *Finds* Shopping for Woodcarvings

Oberammergau's woodcarvings are among the most sought-after in the Germanic world, and many an example has graced the mantelpieces and shelves of homes around the globe. Most subjects are religious, deriving directly from 14th-century originals; however, to cater to the demands of modern visitors, there's been an increased emphasis lately on secular subjects, such as drinking or hunting scenes. Competition is fierce for sales of these woodcarvings, many of which are made in hamlets and farmhouses throughout the region. Know before you buy that even some of the most expensive "handmade" pieces might have been roughed in by machine prior to being finished off by hand.

The **Holzschittschule (Woodcarving School)** has conditions of study that might remind you of the severity of the medieval guilds. Students who labor over a particular sculpture are required to turn it in to the school, where it's either placed on permanent exhibition or sold during the school's once-a-year sell-off, usually over a 2-day period in July.

**Josef Albl,** Devrientweg 1 (✆ **08822/64-33**), a taciturn but prestigious wood-carver, specializes in bas-reliefs, some of which are complicated and highly detailed. His subjects are both religious and secular, including hunting scenes. Some of the simple pieces sell for as little as 5€ ($4.45), but commissioned pieces can stretch into the tens of thousands of dollars.

**Tony Baur,** Dorfstrasse 27 (✆ **08822/8-21**), has the most sophisticated inventory of woodcarvings. The shop employs a small cadre of carvers who usually work from their homes to create works inspired by medieval originals. The outgoing and personable sales staff is quick to admit that the forms of many of the pieces are roughed in by machine, but most of the intricate work is completed by hand. Pieces are crafted from maple, pine, or linden (basswood). Prices start at 10€ ($8.95). Carvings are in their natural grain, stained, or poly-chromed (some of the most charming), and in some instances, are partially gilded.

**Peter Zwink,** Schnitzlergasse 4 (✆ **08822/8-57**), is the place to go for clocks. If you have your heart set on buying a cuckoo clock, you'll probably find one to your liking here, even though, as the staff will point out, the cuckoo clock belongs to the Schwarzwald region (see chapter 11). The more simple carved, handmade clocks are battery-run and cost 75€ ($67). More sophisticated clocks with mechanical movement and sound start at 310€ ($276.85). Look for mantel clocks and floor clocks carved in baroque designs. Some need to be wound only once a year, a tradition that some families carry out as part of their New Year's Day rituals.

well furnished; most have balconies. All of the accommodations are equipped with a midsize bathroom with tub-and-shower combination.

König-Ludwig-Strasse 10, 82487 Oberammergau. ✆ **08822/91-20.** Fax 08822/71-02. www.hotel-boeld.de. 57 units. 94€–119.55€ ($83.95–$106.75) double. Rates include buffet breakfast. AE, MC, V. Free outdoor parking; 5.10€ ($4.55) in garage. **Amenities:** Restaurant; bar; whirlpool; sauna; solarium; room service. *In room:* TV, minibar, hair dryer.

**Parkhotel Sonnenhof** ★ Short on charm and alpine rusticity, this modern hotel still has a lot going for it. It's placed far enough away from the summer crowds to offer guests peace and tranquility, but it's still within walking distance of the center. The hotel overlooks the Ammer River and a beautiful Pfarrkirche (parish church). Rooms are well-maintained, filled with first-class comforts, and have balconies with an alpine vista, often of Oberammergau's mountain, the Kobel. Each of the efficiently organized, midsize bathrooms come with tub-and-shower combination.

König-Ludwig-Strasse 12, 82487 Oberammergau. ✆ **08822/91-30.** Fax 08822/30-47. www.parkhotel-sonnenhof.de. 61 units. 94€–124€ ($83.95–$110.75) double; 110€–140€ ($98.25–$125) suite. Rates include half board. AE, DC, MC, V. **Amenities:** 2 restaurants; bar; pool; sauna; children's center; bowling alley; room service. *In room:* TV, hair dryer.

**Schlosshotel Linderhof** *Finds* This hotel is designed with gables, shutters, and half-timbering in the style of a Bavarian chalet. The famous palace (see "Side Trips from Oberammergau," below) is only about 350m (400 yds.) away. Rooms are dignified and high-ceilinged, with tasteful hints of 19th-century gentility but with modern conveniences, such as bathrooms with showers.

Linderhof 14 (near the palace), 82488 Ettal. ✆ **08822/7-90.** Fax 08822/43-47. www.schlosshotel-linderhof.com. 29 units. 98€ ($87.50) double. Rates include breakfast. AE, DC, MC, V. **Amenities:** Restaurant; lounge; room service. *In room:* TV, minibar, hair dryer.

**Turmwirt** A cozy Bavarian-style hotel, the Turmwirt offers small, snug rooms, many with private balconies opening onto mountain views. Each comes with a small but well-maintained private bathroom with shower. The present building was constructed in 1889 and has been altered and renovated many times. It's an intricately painted green-shuttered country house with a well-maintained home-like interior. The owners are three generations of the Glas family, who often present Bavarian folk evenings.

Ettalerstrasse 2 (5 min. from the town center), 82487 Oberammergau. ✆ **08822/9-26-00.** Fax 08822/14-37. 22 units. 80€–99€ ($71.45–$88.40) double. Rates include buffet breakfast. AE, DC, MC, V. Free parking. **Amenities:** Breakfast room; lounge; room service. *In room:* TV, minibar.

**Wolf Restaurant-Hotel** *Value* An overgrown Bavarian chalet, Wolf Restaurant-Hotel is at the heart of village life. Its facade, like others in the area, has an encircling balcony, heavy timbering, and window boxes spilling cascades of geraniums. Inside, it retains some local flavor, although concessions to modernity have been made, such as an elevator. Rooms range from small to medium, and five are singles. The small, tiled bathrooms with showers are spotless.

Dorfstrasse 1, 82487 Oberammergau. ✆ **08822/92330.** Fax 08822/92-3333. 32 units. 70€–80€ ($62.50–$71.45) double. Rates include buffet breakfast. AE, DC, MC, V. **Amenities:** Restaurant; lounge; outdoor pool; sauna; solarium; room service. *In room:* TV.

## INEXPENSIVE

**Alte Post** Alte Post is a provincial inn located in the village center, built in chalet style. It has a wide overhanging roof, green-shuttered windows painted with decorative trim, a large crucifix on the facade, and tables set on a sidewalk under a long awning. It's the village's social hub. The interior has a storybook charm, with a ceiling-high green ceramic stove, alpine chairs, and shelves of pewter plates. The rustic rooms range in size from cozy to spacious and have wood-beamed ceilings and wide beds with giant posts; most have views. All the small bathrooms are tiled, with shower units.

Dorfstrasse 19, 82487 Oberammergau. ✆ **08822/91-00.** Fax 08822/91-01-00. www.ogau.de. 32 units. 62€–81€ ($55.35–$72.35) double. Rates include continental breakfast. AE, DC, MC, V. Free parking. Closed Oct 25–Dec 19. **Amenities:** Restaurant; lounge; room service. *In room:* TV.

**Hotel Café-Restaurant Friedenshöhe** *Value* This villa enjoys a beautiful location. It's one of the town's best bargains, although for quality, it's not in the same league as the Böld or the Parkhotel Sonnenhof. It once hosted Thomas Mann. Rooms range from rather small singles to spacious doubles. They're furnished in tasteful modern style and are well maintained, each with a compact, tiled bathroom with shower unit. Opt for one of the corner rooms if possible (they're bigger). Bathrooms tend to be too small but do contain showers. There's an indoor terrace with a panoramic view.

König-Ludwig-Strasse 31, 82487 Oberammergau. ✆ **08822/35-98.** Fax 08822/43-45. www.friedenshoehe.com. 17 units. 61.30€–76.65€ ($54.75–$68.45) double. Rates include buffet breakfast. AE, DC, MC, V. Closed Nov–Dec 14. **Amenities:** Restaurant; 4 dining rooms; lounge. *In room:* TV.

**Hotel Der Schilcherhof** *Value* An enlarged chalet with surrounding gardens, the Schilcherhof offers a modern wing with snug, good-value rooms, all of which contain midsize, shower-only bathrooms. In summer, the terrace overflows with festive, beer-drinking patrons. Nearby is the Ammer River, which flows through the village. Although the house is built in the old style, with wooden front balconies and tiers of flower boxes, it has a fresh look.

Bahnhofstrasse 17, 82487 Oberammergau. ✆ **08822/47-40.** Fax 08822/37-93. 26 units. 59€–66€ ($52.70–$58.95) double. Rates include full breakfast. AE, MC, V. Free parking. Closed Nov 15–Christmas. **Amenities:** Breakfast room; lounge, room service. *In room:* No phone.

## SIDE TRIPS FROM OBERAMMERGAU

### SCHLOSS LINDERHOF ★★

Until the late 19th century, a modest hunting lodge, owned by the Bavarian royal family, stood on a large piece of land 13km (8 miles) west of the village. But in 1869, "Mad" King Ludwig struck again, this time creating a French rococo palace in the Ammergau Mountains. This is his most successful creation. Unlike his palace at Chiemsee (see "Chiemsee," earlier in this chapter), Schloss Linderhof was not meant to copy any other structure. And unlike the Neuschwanstein palace (p. 263), its concentration of fanciful projects and designs was not limited to the palace interior. In fact, the gardens and smaller buildings at Linderhof are, if anything, more elaborate than the two-story main structure.

The most interesting rooms are on the second floor, where ceilings are much higher because of the unusual roof plan. Ascending the winged staircase of Carrara marble, you'll find yourself at the **West Gobelin Room** (music room), with carved and gilded paneling and richly colored tapestries. This room leads directly into the **Hall of Mirrors,** where the mirrors are set in white-and-gold panels, decorated with gilded woodcarvings. The hall's ceiling is festooned with frescoes depicting mythological scenes.

The **king's bedchamber** is the largest room in the palace and overlooks the Fountain of Neptune and the cascades in the gardens. In the tradition of Louis XIV, who often received visitors in his bedchamber, the king's bed is closed off by a carved and gilded balustrade.

In the popular style of the previous century, Ludwig laid out the **gardens** ★★ in formal parterres with geometrical shapes, baroque sculptures, and elegant fountains. The front of the palace opens onto a large pool where, from a gilded statue in its center, a jet of water sprays 32m (105 ft.) into the air.

The park also contains several other small but exotic buildings, including a Moorish Kiosk where Ludwig could indulge his wildest Arabian nights fantasies. He would retreat here by himself for hours, smoking chibouk and dreaming of himself as an Oriental prince. He had ordered his agents to purchase this Moorish pavilion wholesale from the 1867 Paris Universal Exposition, where it had created quite a stir among the public. The pavilion is a mammoth artificial grotto that is amazingly realistic, although Ludwig ordered many changes made to its design. The magic grotto was created out of artificial rock that looks real, complete with stalagmites and stalactites. The cave-like grotto is divided into three separate chambers. The main chamber contains an artificially created lake which is illuminated from below. The king ordered the BASF Chemical Works, the major such company of its day, to develop a certain type of glass which would give the lake just the type of "blue lagoon" dreamlike hues so desired by Ludwig in his fantasy. When visiting the grotto, Ludwig would dress up like the legendary knight, Lohengrin, and order his servants to row him across the "lake" (actually a grotto pond) in a boat shaped like a swan. Instead of still water, he wanted the lake to have movement and currents. This was achieved by two dozen recently invented generators (called dynamo engines), which were a radically modern invention at the time. When he was in a festive mood, he would order performers to stage Wagner opera here for his amusement.

Schloss Linderhof, 82488 Ettal-Linderhof (✆ **08822/920-30**), is open to the public throughout the year, and makes a good day trip from Munich, as well as from Oberammergau. It's open April to September daily 9am to 5:30pm. From October to March, the grotto and Moorish Kiosk are closed, but the castle is open daily 9:30am to noon and 1 to 4pm. Admission in the summer is 5.50€ ($4.90) for adults, 4.50€ ($4) for students, and free for children 14 and under. In winter, admission is 4€ ($3.55) for adults, 3€ ($2.70) for students, and free for children 14 and under.

Buses run between Oberammergau and Schloss Linderhof seven times per day, beginning at 9am; the last bus leaves Linderhof at 5:35pm. Round-trip fare is 5€ ($4.45). Motorists from Oberammergau should follow the signs to Ettal, about 5km (3 miles) away, then go another 5km (3 miles) to Draswang, and from there follow the signs to Schloss Linderhof.

## KLOSTER ETTAL ★

Kloster Ettal, on Kaiser-Ludwig-Platz at Ettal (✆ **08822/7-40**), lies in a lovely valley sheltered by the steep hills of the Ammergau. This abbey was founded by Duke Ludwig the Bavarian in 1330. Monks, knights, and their ladies shared the honor of guarding its statue of the Virgin, attributed to Giovanni Pisano. In the 18th century, the golden age of the abbey, there were about 70,000 pilgrims here every year.

The church of Our Lady, within the abbey, is one of the finest examples of Bavarian rococo architecture in existence. The impressive baroque facade was built from a plan based on the designs of Enrico Zuccali. Around the polygonal core of the church is a two-story gallery. Visitors stand under a vast dome, admiring the fresco painted by John Jacob Zeiller in the summers of 1751 and 1752.

The abbey stands 3km (2 miles) south of Oberammergau, along the road to Garmisch-Partenkirchen. Admission is free, and it's open daily 8am to 8pm in summer, 6pm in winter. Buses from Oberammergau leave from the Rathaus and the Bahnhof once per hour during the day, with round-trip fare 3€ ($2.70). Call ✆ **8821/94-82-74** for information.

# 10

# Lake Constance (Bodensee)

Mild climate and plentiful sunshine make Lake Constance (*Bodensee* in German) a top vacation spot for lovers of sun and sand, as well as for sightseers and spa-hoppers. The hillsides that slope to the water's edge are covered with vineyards and orchards and are dotted with colorful hamlets and busy tourist centers. A network of cruise ships and ferries links every major center around the lake. Even though the 260km (162-mile) shoreline of Lake Constance is shared by three nations—Austria, Germany, and Switzerland—the area around the lake is united in a common cultural and historical heritage.

Lake Constance is actually divided into three lakes, although the name is frequently applied only to the largest of these, the Obersee. The western end of the Obersee separates into two distinct branches: One, the Überlingersee, is a long fjord; the other, the Untersee, is more irregular, jutting in and out of marshland and low-lying woodland. The two branches are connected by a narrow channel—which is actually the upper Rhine.

Lake Constance offers a wealth of **activities,** including swimming, sailing, windsurfing, diving, and rowing. Local tourist offices will connect you with various outfitters. You can swim either in the cold waters of the lake itself, or in one of the heated lakeside pools. The Eichwald Lido at Lindau boasts a 1km- (half-mile-) long "beach," with plenty of lawns for sunbathing German-style. The other popular place for lakeside swimming at a heated pool is the Jakob Lido at Constance.

One of the best ways to see the lake is to cycle around it. **Bicycles** ★ can be rented at all the major train stations, including Lindau and Konstanz. Car ferries allow bikes on board.

**Sailing** on Lake Constance is a major attraction. Some boatyards and sailing schools rent boats; you'll be asked to show some proof of proficiency (a certification from a sailing school, for example). On a more casual level, rowboats and motorboats can be rented at all major hotels along the lake.

From Munich, motorists should take the B12, via Landsberg and Kempten, to reach the lake. Drivers from Frankfurt head south along the A81 Autobahn to Memmingen, transferring to B18. The nearest international airport to Lake Constance is at Zürich, 79km (49 miles) southwest of the town of Konstanz. The Munich airport is about 225km (140 miles) north of the lake.

## 1 Lindau ★★

179km (111 miles) SW of Munich, 32km (20 miles) S of Ravensburg

Lindau dates from the end of the 9th century. It was a free imperial town of the Holy Roman Empire from the Middle Ages to 1804, when it became a part of Bavaria. For centuries, it was a center of trade between Bavaria and Switzerland.

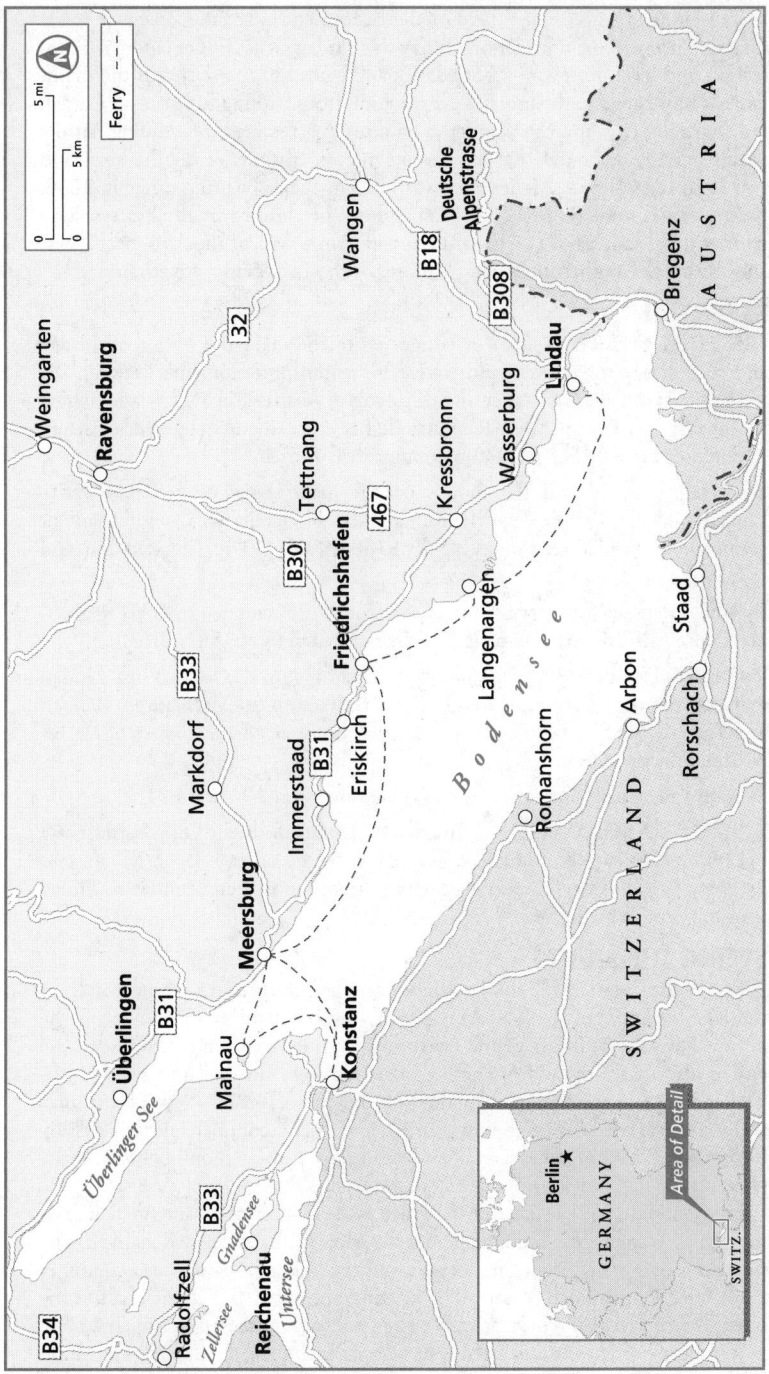
0
5 mi
0
5 km
Ferry
Weingarten
Ravensburg
32
Wangen
B18
Deutsche Alpenstrasse
B308
Bregenz
A U S T R I A
Lindau
Wasserburg
Kressbronn
467
Tettnang
B30
Friedrichshafen
Langenargen
Staad
Arbon
Rorschach
Romanshorn
B o d e n s e e
S W I T Z E R L A N D
Immerstaad
B31
Eriskirch
Markdorf
B33
Meersburg
Konstanz
Mainau
Überlingen
B31
Überlinger See
B33
Gnadensee
Reichenau
Untersee
Zellersee
Radolfzell
B34
Berlin
GERMANY
Area of Detail
SWITZ.

Its unique setting on an island at the eastern end of Lake Constance made Lindau a prime tourist attraction. Today this garden city is under landmark protection and has outgrown its boundaries and spread to the shores of the mainland. It now caters to the tourist's every whim, from bathing to baccarat. Lindau is a charming city. You can wander at will through the maze of winding narrow streets lined with houses that have stood the test of time. At the harbor stand two **lighthouses:** one, Mangturm, was built in the 1200s, the other in 1856. Each tower is some 37m (120 ft.) tall and can be climbed by the hearty, along narrow spiral staircases. The reward is a panoramic vista of the Alps, both Swiss and Austrian. Another interesting building is the 15th-century **Rathaus.**

## ESSENTIALS

**GETTING THERE** Lindau is connected to the mainland by a road bridge and a causeway for walkers and trains. It's a transportation link between the western part of Lake Constance and the towns of Austria and Switzerland, which lie directly across the water. Regional flights come in to the Friedrichshafen airport (see below). The nearest major airport is Zürich.

**By Train** The Lindau Bahnhof is on the major Basel–Singen–Radolfzell–Lindau and Lindau–Kissleg–Memmingen–Buchloe rail lines, with frequent connections in all directions. Call ✆ **01805/99-66-33** for information and schedules.

**By Bus** Regional bus service along Lake Constance is offered by **RAB Regionalverkehr Alb-Bodensee GmbH** in Friedrichshafen (✆ **07541/30130**).

**By Ferry** Five to seven ferries per day (depending on the season) link Lindau with Konstanz. Before reaching Lindau, boats stop at Meersburg, Mainau, and Friedrichshafen; the entire trip takes 3 hours. Call the tourist office for information and schedules.

**By Car** Access by car from Munich is via Autobahn A96 and B31.

**VISITOR INFORMATION** **Tourist-Information** is at Ludwigstrasse 68 (✆ **08382/26-00-30**). April 1 to September 5, the office is open Monday to Saturday 9am to 7pm; and Sunday 9am to noon; in winter, Monday to Friday 9am to noon and 2 to 5pm.

## SEEING THE SIGHTS

A tour of this *Ferieninsel* (Holiday Island) begins with the **old harbor,** seen from the lakeside promenade. The **Mangturm,** the old lighthouse, stands on the promenade as a reminder of the heavy fortifications that once surrounded the city. It also marks the point where Lindau was once divided into two islands. The entrance to the harbor is marked by the 33m (108-ft.) **New Lighthouse** and the **Bavarian Lion,** standing guard as yachts and commercial ships pass by below. From the promenade, you can gaze out past these monuments over the water to the Alps on the opposite side of the lake.

**Hauptstrasse,** in the center of the town, is the main street of the Altstadt. The most easily recognizable building here is the **Altes Rathaus,** erected in 1422. The stepped gables are typical of the period, but the building's facade also combines many later styles of architecture. The interior, once used as a council hall, is the town library. Frescoes represent scenes from a session of the 1496 Imperial Diet.

Just north of Hauptstrasse is the town's most familiar landmark, the round **Diebsturm (Thieves' Tower),** with its turreted roof. Next to it is the oldest building in Lindau, the 11th-century **St. Peter's Church,** which houses a war memorial chapel. In the church is a group of frescoes by Hans Holbein the Elder.

Returning to Hauptstrasse, which cuts through the exact center of the island, follow the street eastward to the **Haus zum Cavazzen,** Am Marktplatz (✆ **08382/94-40-73**), the handsomest patrician house on Lake Constance. It now houses the municipal art collection. Included are exhibits of sculpture and painting from the Gothic, Renaissance, and baroque periods. Some of the rooms are furnished with period pieces showing how wealthy citizens lived in the 18th and 19th centuries. Among the rarities is a collection of mechanical musical instruments. This attraction can be visited by guided tour only, April to October, Tuesday to Friday 11am to 5pm, and Saturday to Sunday noon to 5pm. Admission is 2.50€ ($2.25) adults, .50€ (45¢) students and children; children under 10 enter free.

Passing across Am Marktplatz and by the Collegiate Church and St. Stephen's Church, both baroque, you come to the strange pile of rocks known as **Heathen's Wall,** dating from Roman times. Beyond this is the **Stadtgarten (Town Garden),** which, although peaceful during the day, livens up at night when the wheels of the town's casino begin to spin.

## OUTDOOR PURSUITS

For 9.20€ ($8.20), you can rent a bike from the train station (✆ **08382/2-12-61**) and go cycling along the lake. Bikes can be rented Monday to Friday 9am to 1pm and 2 to 6pm, and Saturday 9:30am to 7pm. Lindenhofpark is the most scenic area (it's also ideal for a picnic).

The town has three lakeside beaches, all open in summer Monday to Friday 10:30am to 7:30pm and Saturday and Sunday 10am to 8pm. The biggest beach is **Eichwald,** about a ½-hour walk away along Uferweg (to the right if you're facing the harbor), or take bus 1 or 2 to Anheggerstrasse, then bus 3 to Karmelbuckel. Once here, admission is 2.55€ ($2.30) for adults, .55€ (49¢), for children. Another, smaller beach, attracting families, is **Römerbad;** it charges 2.55€ ($2.30) for adults or 1.30€ ($1.15) for children. To reach the final beach, **Lindenhofbad,** take bus 1 or 2 to Anheggerstrasse, then bus 4 to Alwind. Admission is 2€ ($1.80) for adults and 1.30€ ($1.15) for children.

You can rent windsurfers at **Kreitmeir,** In der Grub 17 (✆ **08382/23330**) for 10.50€ ($9.40) per hour. At the little dock next to Lindau's rail bridge, you can rent a paddleboat for 8€ ($7.15), a motorboat for 25€ ($22.35), or an electric boat from **Bootsvermietung Hodrius** (✆ **08382/29-77-71**).

## SHOPPING

Michael Zeller is known throughout Bavaria for staging a twice-yearly **Internationale-Bodensee-Kunstauktion** (art auction) here in the spring and fall (dates vary). There's a much smaller auction in December. His year-round store, **Michael Zeller,** 3 Bindergasse (✆ **08382/9-30-20**), offers Lindau's best selection of watercolors, engravings, and prints, along with jewelry and porcelain, and even some furniture. For the town's best selection of pottery, head for **Angelika Ochsenreiter,** Ludwigstrasse 29 (✆ **08382/2-38-67**), which has teapots, cups, dishes, and animal figures.

## WHERE TO STAY

### EXPENSIVE

**Hotel Bayerischer Hof** ★★★ This old-world hotel clearly outdistances all others in Lindau. It opens onto the lakeside promenade and looks almost like a hotel on the Mediterranean. The atmosphere and service here are first-rate. The large rooms are the finest in Lindau, each well-furnished with traditional styling, and the bathrooms contain shower-tub combinations. Most have good views; the less desirable units overlook a narrow thoroughfare.

Seepromenade, 88131 Lindau. ✆ **800/223-5652** in the U.S. and Canada, or 08382/91-50. Fax 08382/91-55-91. www.bayerischerhof-lindau.de. 100 units. 151€–225€ ($134.85–$200.95) double; 251€–405€ ($224.15–$361.65) suite. Accommodation free for children under 10. Rates include buffet breakfast. AE, DC, MC, V. Parking 6.50€–9.50€ ($5.80–$8.50). **Amenities:** Restaurant; bar; lounge; health club; sauna; room service; massage; laundry/dry cleaning. *In room:* TV, minibar, hair dryer, safe.

**Hotel Reutemann und Seegarten** ★★ Located next to its parent, the superior Bayerischer Hof, this hotel consists of two villas. The Reutemann has large rooms and bathrooms with showers and huge tubs. The Seegarten, built like a Bavarian villa, with little flower-filled balconies and trailing vines, has spacious and handsome rooms, especially those with lake views (which cost more, naturally). Both villas have their own waterfront gardens with furniture for sunbathing.

Seepromenade, 88131 Lindau. ✆ **08382/91-50.** Fax 08382/91-55-91. www.bayerischerhof-lindau.de. 64 units. 138€–195€ ($123.25–$174.15) double. Children under 10 free. Rates include buffet breakfast. AE, DC, MC, V. Parking 6.50€–9.50€ ($5.80–$8.50) depending on the size of the car and whether it's parked indoors or outdoors. **Amenities:** Restaurant; lounge; fitness center; sauna; room service; massage; babysitting; laundry/dry cleaning. *In room:* TV, minibar, hair dryer, safe.

### MODERATE

**Hotel-Garni Brugger** *Value* This modest, charming little hotel is the best affordable choice in Lindau. It's pleasingly proportioned, with a gabled attic and French doors that open onto the balconies in the back. The small rooms are up-to-date, furnished in a functional modern style, with lots of light, and each comes with a small, tiled bathroom with shower. The latest innovation is a winter garden filled with potted plants. The location is an easy walk from the lake and casino.

Bei der Heidenmauer 11, 88131 Lindau. ✆ **08382/9-34-10.** Fax 08382/41-33. www.hotel-garni.brugger.de. 23 units. 80€–88€ ($71.45–$78.60) double. Additional bed 26€ ($23.20) extra. Rates include continental breakfast. AE, DC, MC, V. Parking 7€ ($6.25). **Amenities:** Breakfast room; lounge. *In room:* TV, minibar.

**Insel-Hotel** Although not as stylish as its closest competitor (Hotel-Garni Brugger), the Insel is still a good buy for the area. Its small but comfortable rooms are furnished with modern pieces, and each comes with a small bathroom with shower unit. The breakfast room opens onto Maximilianstrasse, a pedestrian zone.

Maximilianstrasse 42 (a .5km/¼-mile from the lake), 88131 Lindau. ✆ **08382/260-160.** Fax 08382/260-1666. 28 units. 82€–112.50€ ($73.25–$100.45) double. Rates include continental breakfast. AE, DC, MC, V. Parking 8€ ($7.15). **Amenities:** 2 restaurants; lounge; room service. *In room:* TV, minibar.

## WHERE TO DINE

**Hoyerberg Schlüssle** ★★★ CONTINENTAL The Hoyerberg Schlüssle is the only restaurant on the lake that can rival the superb Seehotel Siber at Konstanz (see later in this chapter). The inner room is beautifully decorated, with a view of the mountains and lake. You can also dine on the two terraces. Continental delicacies include cream of scampi soup, Bodensee pike-perch stuffed with champagne-flavored herbs, and Allgäuer saddle of venison with small flour dumplings and French beans. Meals here are memorable; the chef has great flair and style, and doesn't over-sauce the food.

Hoyerbergstrasse 64, at Lindau-Aeschach. ✆ **08382/2-52-95.** Reservations required in the restaurant; not required in the cafe. Main courses 18€–30€ ($16.05–$26.80); fixed-price menu 54€ ($48.20). AE, DC, MC, V. Restaurant Tues–Sun noon–2pm and 6–10pm; cafe Tues–Sat 10am–5pm. Closed Feb.

**Villino** ★★ ITALIAN Set in the suburb of Hoyren, this hotel is better known for its excellent Italian restaurant than for its bedrooms. Only dinner is served, within a comfortable room decorated in high-tech Milanese style. The elegant menu items include pesto-laced spaghetti; Sicilian-style fish soup; a heaping platter of scampi served with stuffed squid and fresh tomatoes; anglerfish and lobster fried with cardamom; and a particularly succulent version of leg of lamb with garlic sauce.

If you're too stuffed to move on after your meal, the establishment maintains 10 rooms, priced at 140€ to 180€ ($125–$160.75) each, plus six suites at 230€ ($205.40) each. Each unit has a private balcony, minibar, TV, and telephone. Rates include breakfast, and parking is free.

Hoyren (a 1km/½-mile east of Lindau's center), Hoyerberg 34, 88131 Lindau. ✆ **08382/93-450.** Fax 08382/93-45-12. Reservations recommended. Main courses 31€–32€ ($27.70–$28.60); fixed-price 5-course menu 76€ ($67.85). MC, V. Tues–Sun 6–10:30pm.

**Zum Sünfzen** GERMAN/BAVARIAN Owned by the same family that runs the Insel-Hotel, this is an old, all-wood house/restaurant serving good food at reasonable prices. Dishes range from roast pork with vegetables to filet of venison. Fresh fish from Lake Constance is a specialty. The food is the type you might be served in a middle-class private home along the lake.

Maximilianstrasse 1. ✆ **08382/58-65.** Reservations recommended. Main dishes 9€–20€ ($8.05–$17.85). AE, DC, MC, V. Daily 10:30am–11pm.

## LINDAU AFTER DARK

Lindau's casino, Oskar-Groll-Anlage 6 (✆ **08382/27-740**), offers slot machines from noon to 2am and blackjack and roulette from 3pm to 2am. The bet ceiling is 6,000€ ($5,358) for roulette. Admission is 2.50€ ($2.25), and a passport is required as proof of age. Men should wear a jacket and tie.

## SIDE TRIPS FROM LINDAU

**WASSERBURG** The town of Wasserburg, which means "water castle," lies 6km (4 miles) west of Lindau. You can wander the traffic-free town's narrow streets, taking in the crooked little medieval houses. Its **fortress,** which stands on a promontory on a loop of the Inn River, is an enchanting discovery. It was sold to the Hapsburgs when its owner, the Fuggers of Augsburg, accumulated serious debts. Eventually the Bavarian government took over.

Head first for the center of the town, Marienplatz, where you can see the tall stepped gables of the **Rathaus** (town hall). Guided tours of the second floor Ratssaal are given Tuesday to Friday at 10 and 11am, and at 2, 3, and 4pm, and Saturday and Sunday at 10 and 11am. Tours cost 1.50€ ($1.35). The hall is richly adorned with painted panels and carved woodwork. The most interesting church, **St. Jakob,** can be seen on the Kirchplatz. The nave is a masterpiece by the Gothic architect Hans von Burghausen. In the 15th century, a chancel and tower were added. If the church is open, you can seek out its elaborate late Renaissance pulpit, another architectural masterpiece.

**LANGENARGEN** This town, which lies 8km (5 miles) west of Wasserburg, is celebrated for its **Montfort Castle,** Untere Seestrasse 5, named for its original founders, the counts of Montfort-Werdenberg. When King Wilhelm I of Württemberg took over, he reconstructed it in a faux-Moorish style. If you climb its tower, you'll be rewarded with a panoramic view of the lake. Hours are Easter to October only 10am to noon and 2:30 to 5pm; admission is 1.50€ ($1.35) adults, .50€ (45¢) children.

**Langenargen Stadtmuseum (City Museum),** Marktplatz 20 (✆ **07543-3410**), is worth a visit if you're interested in some of the slightly more obscure (but still talented) 20th-century painters. Notable is a series of works by Hans Purrmann (1880–1966), a great admirer of Henri Matisse. Purrmann lived at Langenargen from 1915 until 1935. The Nazis denounced his art as "decadent" and prevented it from being seen publicly in Germany. The museum is open April to October Tuesday to Sunday 10am to noon and 2:30 to 5pm. Admission is 1.50€ ($1.35).

## 2 Friedrichshafen

22km (13½ miles) W of Lindau, 20km (12 miles) S of Ravensburg

Friedrichshafen is set at the northeastern corner of the Bodensee, near the lake's widest point. This mostly modern city was almost completely rebuilt after the devastation of World War II. It's graced with one of the longest waterfront exposures of any town along the lake. Besides that, the town's highlights are two interesting museums and the dome-capped **Schlosskirche,** the premier reminder of Friedrichshafen's baroque past.

### ESSENTIALS

**GETTING THERE** **By Air** The **Friedrichshafen** airport (✆ **07541/28401**) lies 5km (3 miles) north of town. Flights come in from Zürich, Frankfurt, Düsseldorf, and Berlin. The nearest major airport is Zürich, 100km (62 miles) away.

**By Train** Friedrichshafen is the largest railway junction along the northern edge of the Bodensee and serves as a major transfer point for rail passengers going on to other cities and resorts along the lake. The town has two railway stations, the **Stadtbahnhof,** in the center, and the **Hafenbahnhof,** along the Seestrasse, about 1km (¾ mile) away. Both of these stations are interconnected by buses 1, 2, 3, 4, 5, 6, and 7. Trains arrive from Ulm and Stuttgart at intervals of 1 to 2 hours throughout the day. For information and schedules, call ✆ **01805/99-66-33.**

**By Bus** Regional bus service along Lake Constance is provided by **RAB Regionalverkehr Alb-Bodensee GmbH** in Friedrichshafen (✆ **07541/30130** for more information).

**By Car** Friedrichshafen is easily reached from both Stuttgart and Munich. From Stuttgart, follow Autobahn 8 east to the city of Ulm, then turn south onto Route 30 directly into Friedrichshafen. From Munich follow Autobahn 96 west/southwest to Lindau, then head west on Route 31 along Lake Constance to Friedrichshafen.

**By Boat** April to October, about eight lake steamers travel between Friedrichshafen and Lindau, Bregenz (Austria), and Konstanz. For departure times and details, call ✆ **07541/201389.** A ferry runs year-round between Friedrichshafen and Romanshorn, Switzerland (trip time: 40 min.) and costs 5.50€ ($4.90), for adults and 2.55€ ($2.30) for children.

**VISITOR INFORMATION** The city's **Tourist Information Office** is at Bahnhofplatz 2 (✆ **07541/30010**). May to September, it's open Monday to Friday 9am to 5pm, Saturday 10am to 2pm. October to April, it's open Monday to Thursday 9am to noon and 2 to 5pm, and Friday 9am to 1pm.

### Rebirth of the Zeppelin

The airship, Zeppelin, fell out of favor in 1937 when the *Hindenburg* crashed in New Jersey. But its post-millennium sibling is gliding peacefully over Lake Constance. Don't panic. The new Zeppelin is much smaller and rises with inert helium gas, not the explosive hydrogen used by the *Hindenburg*. The airship, named *Bodensee* (German for Lake Constance) can climb to 2,363m (7,875 ft.). The newer vessel carries 12 passengers and a crew of two, as opposed to the *Hindenburg*, which carried 100 aboard. Cruising at approximately 54 kmp (30 to 37 mph) scenically over the lake, it takes passengers on hour-long flights, costing 306€ ($278) Monday to Friday or 336€ ($305) on weekends. Flights are scheduled daily. For more information and takeoff points along the lake, call ✆ **49700/9377-2001;** www.zeppelin-nt.com.

## EXPLORING THE TOWN

The best thing to do in town is to stroll the lake-fronting **Seepromenade,** with its sweeping view that extends on clear days all the way to the Swiss Alps. Cycling along the broad Seestrasse is also a delight. A kiosk within the Stadtbahnhof rents bikes for 7€ to 9€ ($6.25–$8.05) a day. Contact the tourist office for details.

The town's architectural highlight is the 17th-century **Schlosskirche,** Schlossstrasse 33 (✆ **07541/21422**). The palatial ecclesiastical buildings that were once part of the church's monastery were converted in the 1800s into a palace for the kings of Württemberg. Today, they're privately owned and can't be entered, but the church itself is well worth a visit. It's open only Easter to October, daily 9am to 6pm.

**Zeppelin-Museum** (✆ **07541/38010**), in the Hafenbahnhof, Seestrasse 22, is a tribute to Count Ferdinand von Zeppelin. This native of Konstanz invented and tested the aircraft that bore his name around 1900. Within the museum's premises you'll find a re-creation of the giant and historic zeppelin *Hindenburg,* which exploded in a catastrophic fire in New Jersey in 1937, possibly due to sabotage. In addition to memorabilia associated with zeppelins and their inventor, the museum also contains a full-scale replica of the passenger cabins aboard the famous blimp. May to October, it's open Tuesday to Sunday 10am to 6pm; November to April, Tuesday to Sunday 10am to 5pm. Admission is 6.15€ ($5.50) for adults and 3€ ($2.70) for children 16 and under. There's a gift shop as well.

Of interest to students of educational techniques is Friederichshafen's **Schulemuseum,** Friedrichstrasse 14 (✆ **07541/32622**), which traces the development of education between 1850 (when classes were taught by monks and nuns) and 1930 (when education was the responsibility of the German state). The museum lies near the Schlosskirche in the historic heart of town. Look for the reconstructions of schoolrooms from various periods in the 19th and 20th centuries. April to October, the museum is open daily 10am to 5pm; November to March, Tuesday to Sunday 2 to 5pm. Admission costs 2€ ($1.80) for adults and 1€ (90¢) for children.

## WHERE TO STAY

**Hotel Buchhorner Hof** ★ This charming lakeside hotel provides a compromise between the luxurious, modern comfort of larger hotels and the traditional hospitality of smaller inns. It's housed in the oldest building in town. Rooms are well-furnished, and each comes with a midsize modern bathroom with tub-and-shower combination. The restaurant serves adequate fare at lunch and dinner, and the bar is a cozy retreat.

Friedrichstrasse 33, 88045 Friedrichshafen. ✆ **07541/20-50.** Fax 07541/3-26-63. www.buchornerhof.de. 98 units. 95€–139€ ($84.85–$124.15) double; 155€–180€ ($138.40–$160.75) suite. AE, DC, MC, V. Parking 8€ ($7.15). **Amenities:** Restaurant; bar; health spa; whirlpool; sauna; solarium; steam room; bike rental; room service; laundry/dry cleaning. *In room:* TV, minibar, hair dryer.

**Hotel City-Krone** This modern building in a lakeside setting isn't very traditional or charming, but it's comfortable and fun. Rooms are adequately furnished, each with small, shower-only bathrooms. Ask the hotel desk about excursions by bike, train, ship, or foot.

Schanzstrasse 7, 88045 Friedrichshafen. ✆ **07541/70-50.** Fax 07541/70-51-00. www.Hotel-City-Krone.de. 100 units. 120€–210€ ($107.15–$187.55) double. Rates include breakfast. AE, DC, MC, V. Free parking. **Amenities:** Restaurant; bar; pool; sauna; solarium; room service; laundry/dry cleaning. *In room:* TV, minibar, hair dryer.

**Hotel Goldenes-Rad** Located in the pedestrian center in the middle of town, this traditional hotel is a short walk from Lake Constance, the ferry, and the new Zeppelin Museum. Rooms are comfortable and modern, with showers and cosmetic mirrors. The location is not very car-friendly; however, the hotel does have its own parking lot nearby. The English-speaking staff is courteous and helpful.

Karlstrasse 43, 88045 Friedrichshafen. ✆ **800/528-1234** or 07541/28-50. Fax 07541/28-52-85. www.goldenes-rad.de. 70 units. 99€–130€ ($88.40–$116.10) double; 148€ ($132.15) suite. Rates include buffet breakfast. AE, DC, MC, V. Parking 4€ ($3.55). **Amenities:** Restaurant; lounge; health spa; sauna; solarium; bike rental; room service; massage; laundry/dry cleaning. *In room:* TV, minibar, hair dryer, safe.

**Seehotel Friedrichshafen** ★ *Finds* This is one of the newest and most appealing hotels in town. It's right beside the Seepromenade. The small rooms are sensibly, even stylishly, decorated. Some have air-conditioning; most have views of the water. All the bedrooms have midsize bathrooms, mostly with tub-and-shower combination. The staff is sensitive and well trained.

Bahnhofplatz 2 (near the railway station), 88045 Friedrichshafen. ✆ **07541/30-30.** Fax 07541/30-31-00. www.seehotelfn.de. 132 units. 126€–157€ ($112.50–$140.20) double; 172€ ($153.60) suite. Rates include buffet breakfast. AE, DC, MC, V. Parking free outside; 9€ ($8.05) inside. **Amenities:** Restaurant; bar; health spa; sauna; steam room; room service; laundry/dry cleaning. *In room:* A/C, TV, minibar, hair dryer, safe.

## WHERE TO DINE

**Hotel-Restaurant Maier** ★ *Finds* INTERNATIONAL/GERMAN Set at the center of the hamlet of Fischbach, at the edge of the lake, this establishment is best known for its restaurant. Local diners appreciate the generous, well-prepared portions, the attentive service, and the sweeping views over the lake. One dining room is contemporary and modern; the other a re-creation of a traditional *Stube* in the mountains. Menu items include marinated herring, venison in red wine sauce with mushrooms, salmon-trout or pike-perch from the nearby Bodensee, schnitzels, goulash soup, and elaborate pastries for dessert.

The establishment also contains 50 rooms, each with minibar, TV, and telephone. Doubles cost 100€ ($89.30) and include breakfast and free parking.

Poststrasse 1–3, Fischbach (6km/4 miles west of Friedrichshafen), 88048 Friedrichshafen. ✆ **07541/40-40.** Reservations recommended. Main courses 10€–20€ ($8.95–$17.85). AE, DC, MC, V. Daily 11am–2pm and 6–10pm.

**Restaurant Kurgarten** INTERNATIONAL Depending on the time of day, this place might look like a cafe, a bar, or a restaurant. It has a beautiful view over its own garden and the lake, and there's a wide range of tasty menu items. Vegetarian choices include mushrooms stuffed with spinach and zucchini stuffed with ratatouille. Other good options include an Argentine beefsteak with herb butter and grilled scampi on rice with slices of local vegetables and salad.

Olgastrasse 20. ✆ **07541/3-20-33.** Reservations not necessary. Main courses 10€–21€ ($8.95–$18.75). AE, MC, V. Daily 10am–midnight.

## 3 Meersburg ★

190km (118 miles) S of Stuttgart, 143km (89 miles) SE of Freiburg

Like the towns of Italy's lake district, this village on the northern shore of Lake Constance cascades in terraces down the hillside to the water. The heart of Meersburg is a pedestrian area. You can drive into town as far as the Neues Schloss; then you must leave your car and explore on foot. In the center, the streets become narrow promenades and steps wander up and down the hillside. From the dock, both large and small boats set out for trips on the water. Many water sports are offered here. One charming little feature of Meersburg is the presence of a town watchman who still makes nightly rounds, keeping alive an ancient tradition.

### ESSENTIALS

**GETTING THERE By Plane** Regional flights come in to the Friedrichshafen airport, 20km (12 miles) from Meersburg. The nearest international airport is at Zürich, 80km (49 miles) away.

**By Train** The nearest rail station is in **Überlingen,** 14km (9 miles) away, on the Basel–Singen–Radolfzell–Lindau rail line, with frequent connections in all directions. Call ✆ **01805/99-66-33** for more information. From Überlingen station, buses depart for Meersburg at 30-minute intervals every day 6:15am to 9:45pm, charging 3.60€ ($3.20) each way. Buses are marked either MEERSBURG or FRIEDRICHSHAFEN but always bear number 7395 on the front.

**By Bus** Buses arrive about every 30 minutes throughout the day from Friedrichshafen. Regional bus service along Lake Constance is provided by **RAB Regionalverkehr Alb-Bodensee GmbH** in Friedrichshafen (call ✆ **07541/30130** for information).

**By Ferry** Regular ferry service goes to the town of Konstanz.

**By Car** Access by car is via the A7 Autobahn from the north or Highways 31 and 33. You can drive from Munich in about 3 hours; from Frankfurt in about 4½ hours; and from Stuttgart in about 2 hours.

**VISITOR INFORMATION** For tourist information, contact the **Kur- und Verkehrsamt,** Kirchstrasse 4 (✆ **07532/43-11-11**). May to October, it's open Monday to Friday 8am to 6:30pm and Saturday 10am to 2pm. November to May, it's open Monday to Friday 9am to noon and 2:30 to 5pm.

**SPECIAL EVENTS** The surrounding vineyards produce excellent wine, and on the second weekend in September, winemakers around the lake come to Meersburg for the **Lake Constance Wine Festival.**

## EXPLORING THE TOWN

After you enter the town through the ancient **Obertor (Upper Gate),** you'll be on Marktplatz. Here lies the 16th-century **Rathaus,** which contains a typical German Ratskeller. Leading off from this is **Steigstrasse,** the most interesting artery, passing between rows of half-timbered houses whose arcades serve as covered walkways above the street.

Nearby, at Schlossplatz, is the **Altes Schloss** ★ (✆ **07532/80000**), which dates from 628 and is the oldest intact German castle. All the relics of a warring age are here—clubs, flails, armor, helmets, and axes—along with 30 fully furnished rooms, decorated with pieces from the various epochs. The bishops of Konstanz lived in this castle until the 18th century, when they moved to the Neues Schloss (see below). The baron of Lassberg, an admirer of medieval romance, then took over, and invited Annette von Droste-Hülshoff (1797–1848), his sister-in-law and Germany's leading female poet, to come as well. She had the castle turned into a setting for artists and writers. You can visit her luxuriously furnished chambers, as well as the murky dungeons and the castle museum with its medieval jousting equipment. The castle is open March to October, daily 9am to 6:30pm; November to February, daily 10am to 6pm. Admission is 5.50€ ($4.90) for adults, 4.40€ ($3.95) students, and 3€ ($2.70) for children. Next to the castle is the **Castle Mill** (1620), with a 9m (28-ft.) wooden waterwheel, the oldest of its kind in Germany.

You go from the medieval to the baroque when you enter the **Neues Schloss,** Schlossplatz (✆ **07532/414071**), which faces the Altes Schloss. The leading architect of the 18th century, Balthasar Neumann, was responsible for some of the castle's design. Ceiling paintings and frescoes were done by prominent artists and craftsmen. Elegant stucco moldings grace the ceilings and walls. The Spiegelsaal, or Hall of Mirrors, is the setting for an international music festival in summer. On the top floor is the **Dornier Museum,** which traces the history of Germany's aircraft and aerospace industries. Admission is 3€ ($2.70) for adults and 1€ (90¢) for children 12 and under. It's open March to November, daily 10am to 6pm.

On the promenade below stands the **Great House,** which dates from 1505. It now holds ticket offices for the railway and steamer lines on Lake Constance. Regular ferry service to Konstanz leaves from the dock on the outskirts of town.

## OUTDOOR PURSUITS

Rock-strewn beaches lie west of the town center; here you can go swimming or just soak up the sun for free. But you'll find the amenities better at the **Beheiztes Freibad,** Uferpromenade (✆ **07532/41-40-60**), east of the harbor. Here you can lie on the grass on a strip of sand adjacent to the lake, or immerse yourself in any of three outdoor swimming pools. There's also a sauna on the premises, plus refreshment stands. Entrance to the compound costs 3€ ($2.70) for adults, 2€ ($1.80) for students, 1.50€ ($1.35) for children; free for children under 4.

If you'd like to cycle along the lakefront promenades, head first to **Sport Pfan,** Unterstadtstrasse 7 (✆ **07532/48873**). You can rent one of the shop's 10 bicycles for 8.50€ ($7.60) a day. It is closed the month of January.

## WHERE TO STAY

**Gasthof zum Bären** ★ *Value* This picture-book hotel in the heart of town offers the best value in Meersburg. There's an ornately decorated corner tower, purple wisteria covers most of the facade, and window boxes overflow with red geraniums. The hotel was constructed in 1605 on the foundations of a building

### *Finds* A Taste of Honey

Just 10km (6 miles) from Meersburg is the famous **Wallfahrtskirche** (✆ **07556/9-20-30**) at Birnau, 5km (3 miles) southeast of Überlingen. This pilgrimage basilica, which dates from the mid-18th century, was built in rococo style, with rose, blue, and beige marble predominating. A celebrated statuette here is called the *Honigschlecker,* or "honey-taster"—it shows a baby sucking a finger as he's yanked out of a nest of bees. It's to the right of the St. Bernard altarpiece. The church is open daily 7am to 7pm. Admission is free.

from 1250 (the cellar of the original Bären is still here). The small rooms are attractive, snug, and cozily furnished. All contain bathrooms with shower-tub combinations. The innkeepers speak English.

Marktplatz 11, 88709 Meersburg. ✆ **07532/4-32-20.** Fax 07532/43-22-44. www.meersburg.de/baeren. 20 units. 74€–100€ ($66.10–$89.30) double. Rates include continental breakfast. No credit cards. Parking 5€ ($4.45). Closed mid-Nov–mid-Mar. **Amenities:** Restaurant; lounge; room service; laundry/dry cleaning. *In room:* TV, hair dryer.

**Seehotel zur Munz** *Value* If you're not looking for glamour or a romantic atmosphere and want to save some money, consider checking in here. Only a pedestrian walkway and an iron railing separate this hotel from the tree-lined lakefront. The ambience within lets you forget urban bustle. The rooms are neatly kept, all containing bathrooms with shower-tub combinations. The Seehotel zur Munz is the simplest of our recommendations, but it's clean, decent, and comfortable in every way.

Seestrasse 7, 88709 Meersburg. ✆ **07532/43590.** Fax 07532/77-85. 11 units. 82€–100€ ($73.25–$89.30) double. Rates include buffet breakfast. AE, MC, V. Parking 5€ ($4.45) covered; 3€ ($2.70) uncovered. **Amenities:** Breakfast room. *In room:* TV.

**Strandhotel Wilder Mann** This baroque country hotel is just beyond a stone embankment at the edge of the lake. The building's facade is the backdrop for a painted illustration of a traditional folk figure, called *der wilde Mann.* Here he's contemplating whether to have a stag or a unicorn for supper. The small rooms are comfortable and cozily furnished, containing bathrooms with shower-tub combinations. The hotel is open year-round.

Bismarckplatz 2, 88709 Meersburg. ✆ **07532/90-11.** Fax 07532/90-14. 33 units. 95€–140€ ($84.85–$125) double; 180€ ($160.75) suite. Rates include buffet breakfast. AE, MC, V. Parking 5€ ($4.45). **Amenities:** Restaurant; lounge; room service. *In room:* TV, hair dryer.

**Weinstube Löwen** ★ Weinstube Löwen is an old, charming inn on the market square. Its facade has green shutters, geranium-filled window boxes, and vines reaching the upper windows under the steep roof. The Fischer family has updated its interior while keeping a home-like ambience. All but a few rooms have been modernized in a streamlined functional style. They are, however, a bit cramped. All units contain bathrooms with shower-tub combinations.

Marktplatz 2, 88709 Meersburg. ✆ **07532/4-30-40.** Fax 07532/43-04-10. www.hotel-loewen-meersburg.de. 21 units. 80€–118€ ($71.45–$105.35) double. Rates include buffet breakfast. AE, MC, V. Parking 4.50€ ($4). **Amenities:** Restaurant; lounge; room service; laundry/dry cleaning. *In room:* TV.

## WHERE TO DINE

**Winzerstube zum Becher** ★ REGIONAL/GERMAN Year after year this little independently run restaurant manages to serve better food than any hotel in town. If you've come to Germany with images of a handcrafted Weinstube that radiates warmth, then you should dine here. A pea-green tile oven tucked away in a corner provides heat in winter. The chairs are not that comfortable, but the rest of the flowered, paneled, and happily cluttered room provide a cozy atmosphere. The specialty of the chef is onion-flavored Swabian *Rostbraten* with Spätzle, along with a host of other specialties, including fresh fish from Lake Constance. A superb fixed-price dinner cuts down on the cost. The restaurant also offers drinks (mostly wine) and snacks.

Höllgasse 4, near the Altes Schloss. ✆ **07532/90-09.** Reservations required. Main courses 11€–22.50€ ($9.80–$20.10); fixed-price lunch 22€–36.50€ ($19.65–$32.60), fixed-price dinner 35€–52.50€ ($31.25–$46.90). AE, DC, MC, V. Tues–Sun 10am–2pm and 5pm–midnight. Closed mid-Dec–mid-Jan.

## MEERSBURG AFTER DARK

**Spiegelsaal (Hall of Mirrors),** in the Neues Schloss at Schlossplatz, is the splendid backdrop for an annual international chamber-music festival. It takes place every Saturday from the last week in June to the first week in September. You might hear, for example, two baroque ensembles, a string quartet, and a pianist playing the works of Schumann. Tickets run from 5€ ($4.45). Call ✆ **07532/43-11-11** for information.

The **Konstanz Stadttheater,** the oldest theater in Germany, dating from 1609, moves to its summer theater in Meersburg during July and August. For more details about the Meersburg program offerings, call ✆ **07531/13-00-21.**

Other than the cultural offerings mentioned above, after dark in Meersburg means taking a romantic stroll along the Uferpromenade bordering the lake and visiting one of the bars or Bierhalles. The most charming and traditional place for a drink is at the previously recommended **Winzerstube zum Becher** (see above), which also is our preferred choice for dining as well, although you can visit just for drinks. On the Market Square, another fun place to go in the evening is the **Weinstube Löwen,** a delightful, centuries-old inn covered in vines. If you like your drinks enjoyed with a lakeview, head for the **Seehotel Off,** Uferpromenade (✆ **07532/43350**), fronting the Bodensee. It's especially romantic around here at night.

## 4 Konstanz (Constance) ★

179km (111 miles) S of Stuttgart, 76km (47 miles) NE of Zürich

Crowded against the shores of Lake Constance by the borders of Switzerland, the medieval town of Konstanz had nowhere to grow but northward across the river. Today this resort city lies on both banks of the Rhine, as the river begins its long journey to the North Sea. Its strategic position made Konstanz the most important city on the lake. Nowadays tourists come to enjoy the shops, the largest beach in the area, and the magical beauty of nearby **Mainau Island.**

Konstanz's history is long and distinguished. Early Celtic dwellings here were possibly fortified by the Romans under Claudius in A.D. 41. In the 3rd century, the fort was seized by the Germanic tribes, who later became Christianized and founded a bishop's see around A.D. 580. In the 12th century, Emperor Frederick I Barbarossa came here to make peace with the Lombard states. Many years later, after the defeat of the Protestant league, which it had supported, Konstanz was ceded to Austria. It remained part of Austria until 1805, when it was returned to Germany. Although Konstanz never regained the political status it had held in the early part of the 16th century, it is today still the economic and cultural center of the district.

## ESSENTIALS

**GETTING THERE** **By Train** Konstanz is on the main Konstanz–Singen–Villingen–Offenburg rail line, the Schwarzwaldbahn, with frequent connections to the major cities of Germany. For information, call ✆ **01805/99-66-33.**

**By Bus** Regional bus service around Konstanz is provided by **SBG Südbaden Bus GmbH** at Radolfzell (✆ **07732/9-94-70**). **RAB Friedrichshafen** (✆ **07541/2-20-77**) offers service along the lake going east.

**By Boat** Ferry service and lake cruises operate between Konstanz, Mainau Island, Meersburg, Lindau, and Bregenz. The operator is **Bodensee-Schiffsbetriebe,** Hafenstrasse 6 (✆ **07531/28-13-89** for schedules and information).

**By Car** Access by car is via the B33.

**VISITOR INFORMATION** Contact **Tourist-Information,** Bahnhofplatz 13 (✆ **07531/13-30-30**). April to July, the office is open Monday to Friday 9am to 6pm, Saturday 9am to 4pm, and Sunday 10am to 1pm; August to September, Monday to Friday 9am to 8pm and Saturday to Sunday 10am to 4pm; November to March, Monday to Friday 9am to noon and 2 to 6pm. It's also open the first 4 Saturdays of December 9am to 4pm.

## SEEING THE SIGHTS

The best way to see Konstanz is from the water. The **shoreline** ★ is fascinating, with little inlets that weave in and out around ancient buildings and city gardens. Several pleasure ships offer tours along the city shoreline and across the lake to Meersburg and several other destinations. Contact **Bodensee-Schiffsbetriebe,** Hafenstrasse 6 (✆ **07531/28-13-89**). Car ferries from Konstanz to Meersburg leave at the rate of two per hour from 8:30am to 11pm; then one per hour from 11pm to 8:30am. Saturdays, Sundays, and holidays, service may also be curtailed. For information, contact **Stadtwerke Konstanz** (✆ **07531/80-33-66**).

During the summer, outdoor concerts are presented in the **city gardens.** Below the gardens is the **Council Building,** where the Council of Constance met. The building was originally constructed as a storehouse in 1388 but came to be used for meetings during its early years. The hall was restored in 1911 and decorated with murals depicting the history of the town. On the harbor in front is an obelisk erected in memory of Count Ferdinand von Zeppelin, the citizen of Konstanz who invented the dirigible in the late 19th century.

The towers of the Romanesque **basilica** rise behind the city garden. Begun in 1052, this church took centuries to complete. The neo-Gothic spire was added only in 1856. During the Council of Constance, the members of the synod met here. From the top tower, a view opens onto the lake and the city.

**MAINAU ISLAND** ★★ The unusual, almost tropical island of Mainau, lies 6km (4 miles) north of Konstanz, in the arm of the Bodensee known as the Überlingersee. Here, palms and orange trees grow and fragrant flowers bloom year-round, practically in the shadow of the snow-covered Alps. In the center of this botanical oasis is an ancient castle, once a residence of the Knights of the Teutonic Order, now owned by Swedish Count Lennart Bernadotte. Only the island's gardens and parks can be visited by the public. They're open daily March to October 7am to 10pm; in winter, 9am to 5pm.

There are four restaurants on the island but no overnight accommodations. You can reach Mainau either by tour boat from Konstanz or by walking across the small footbridge connecting the island to the mainland, north of the city. Admission is 10€ ($8.95) for adults, 5€ ($4.45) for students, and 3€ ($2.70) for children. For more information, call ✆ **07531/3030** or visit www.mainau.de.

**OUTDOOR PURSUITS** **Strandbad Horn,** Eichhornstrasse 89 (✆ **07531/6-35-50**), at the tip of the peninsula, is the largest and most popular beach in the area. You can rent windsurfers for 6.50€ ($5.80) per hour. There's also a nude section. From the town center, bus 5 runs here about every 30 minutes.

If you'd like to go biking along the lake, visit **Velotours,** Mainaustrasse 34 (✆ **07531/9-82-80**), where rentals cost from 11€ ($9.80) per day. Open March to October daily 9am to 5:30pm. Rowboats and paddleboats can be rented at **Am Gondelhafen** (✆ **07531/13-30-30**); they cost 9€ to 11€ ($8.05–$9.80) per hour. Open May to October daily 10am to dusk.

## SHOPPING

The best way to explore the shopping options in this cosmopolitan town is to walk down the main commercial artery, **Hussenstrasse.** Among the best stores are **Jacqueline,** Hussenstrasse 29 (✆ **07531/2-29-90**), known for its stylish garments for women who seek a more mature look. Men can look for tuned-in fashion, both formal and sporty, at **Pierre,** Hussenstrasse 3 (✆ **07531/21-729**); and **Holzherr,** Rossgartenstrasse 32 (✆ **07531/128730**). For knit shirts, shorts, and tennis garb, try **La Coste,** Hussenpassage 5 (✆ **07531/2-77-02**).

## WHERE TO STAY

**Buchner Hof** Though located in Petershausen, this hotel is just a short walk from most points of interest. The pleasantly furnished rooms range from small to medium. Bathrooms are tiny, but do contain shower-tub combinations. The hotel is named after composer Hans Buchner, who became organist at the town cathedral in 1510 and was one of the first musicians to arrange and catalog the wealth of Gregorian chants found in the region.

Buchnerstrasse 6 (in Petershausen, across the Rhine from Konstanz), 78464 Konstanz. ✆ **07531/8-10-20.** Fax 07531/81-02-40. www.buchner-hof.de. 13 units. 85€–100€ ($75.90–$89.30) double; 110€ ($98.25) suite. Rates include continental breakfast. AE, DC, MC, V. Free outdoor parking; 10€ ($8.95) in garage. Closed Dec 23–Jan 7. **Amenities:** Breakfast room; lounge; sauna; solarium. *In room:* TV, minibar, hair dryer.

**Steigenberger Insel Hotel** ★★★ The Insel started life as a Dominican monastery in the 13th century; now it's the single finest place to stay along the German side of the lake. It has a prime location—on an island, with its own lakeside gardens and dock. The white step-gabled building holds an inner Romanesque cloister. Most of the spacious doubles have a living-room look, with sofas, armchairs, and tidy bathrooms with shower-tub combinations.

Auf der Insel 1, 78462 Konstanz. ✆ **800/223-5652** in the U.S. and Canada, or 07531/12-50. Fax 07531/2-64-02. www.steigenberger.de. 102 units. 230€–290€ ($205.40–$258.95) double; 260€–370€ ($232.20–$330.40) suite. Rates include buffet breakfast. AE, DC, MC, V. Parking 6.50€ ($5.80). **Amenities:** 2 restaurants; bar; health club; sauna; solarium; lake facilities; room service; babysitting; laundry/dry cleaning. *In room:* TV, minibar, hair dryer, safe.

## WHERE TO DINE

**Casino Restaurant am See** ★ INTERNATIONAL If you happen to lose at roulette on one of your casino outings in Konstanz, you can revive your spirits (and drink a few, too) on the lakeside terrace of this casino restaurant. The view is lovely, and the food first-rate. The restaurant offers a good choice of dishes; try the fresh fish or saddle of lamb. The food is backed up by a good wine cellar.

Seestrasse 21. ✆ **07531/81-57-65.** Reservations required. Jacket and tie required for men. Main courses 18€–27€ ($16.05–$24.10); fixed-price menu 32€ ($28.60). AE, DC, MC, V. Daily 6pm–midnight.

**Seehotel Siber** ★★★ CONTINENTAL This outstanding restaurant, in an Art Nouveau villa near the casino overlooking the lake, is the best not only in Konstanz but along the entire lake. Bertold Siber, one of the leading chefs in Germany, is in charge. The menu features a conservative version of *cuisine moderne.* Offerings change daily. Your meal might begin with lobster terrine with butter and red basil or freshly caught lake trout with an array of seasonings. Try either the roast Barbary goose with Beaujolais sauce or the stuffed turbot with lobster, if they're available. Most guests opt for one of two fixed-price dinners, although a la carte meals are also offered.

The Seehotel Siber is also a Relais & Châteaux hotel, renting handsomely furnished rooms in a building adjacent to the restaurant. The 11 double rooms cost 170€ to 214€ ($151.80–$191.10), and the one suite goes for 314€ ($280.40).

Seestrasse 25, 78464 Konstanz. ✆ **07531/6-30-44.** Fax 07531/6-48-13. www.integra.fr/relaischateaux/siber. Reservations required. Main courses 31€–42€ ($27.70–$37.50); fixed-price lunch 45€–82€ ($40.20–$73.25), fixed-price dinner 70€–105€ ($62.50–$93.75). AE, DC, MC, V. Daily noon–2pm and 6–10pm.

### NEARBY DINING

**Schwedenschenke** *Finds* REGIONAL/SWEDISH Visitors sometimes make a pilgrimage to Mainau Island in Lake Constance for a meal in this old-fashioned restaurant. The chef's specialty is assorted lake fish, including perch, pike-perch, and trout. You can also try Hungarian goulash, Swedish meatballs in cream sauce, and *Tafelspitz* (boiled beef with horseradish sauce). Pike-perch filets are served in a spicy sauce of tomatoes, capers, shallots, and mushrooms.

Mainau Island. ✆ **07531/30-31-56.** Reservations recommended. Main courses 8€–14.50€ ($7.15–$12.95) for lunch; 15.50€–20.50€ ($13.85–$18.30) for dinner. AE, DC, MC, V. Daily 11:30am–10pm. Bus: 4 from the center of Konstanz.

## KONSTANZ AFTER DARK

Classical music offerings throughout the year are numerous. The concert season of the **Bodensee Symphony Orchestra** (✆ **07531/90-08-10**) runs September to April, and a **summer music festival** is held mid-June to mid-July. There's also an **outdoor music festival** on the Island of Mainau for 3 days in July. Contact the visitor information office (see above) for tickets, schedules, and venues. In May, the **Bodensee Festival** (✆ **07541/72071**) offers a mix of classical concerts and theatrical productions, presented at various locations around the shores of the lake. Tickets are 8€ to 40€ ($7.15–$35.70).

Plays have been staged at the **Stadttheater Konstanz,** Konzilstrasse 11 (✆ **07531/130021**), Germany's oldest active theater, since 1609. It has its own repertory company. In July and August, the company moves to its summer theater in Meersburg (see "Meersburg," earlier in this chapter). Ticket prices depend on the production.

In the main room of the **Konstanz Casino,** Seestrasse 21 (✆ **07531/81-57-65**), you try your luck at blackjack, seven-card stud poker, or roulette. Slot machines are located in a side room. Entry into the casino requires a passport as proof of age, and there's a cover of 2.55€ ($2.30). Men are required to wear jackets and ties. The casino is open daily 2pm to 2am, and until 3am

Friday and Saturday. A restaurant on the premises (see "Where to Dine," above) offers continental cuisine from 6 to 11pm.

Those in the party mood should go next door to **Siber,** Seestrasse 25 (✆ **07531/6-30-46**), which offers drinking and dancing for 5€ ($4.45) 11pm to 5am Wednesday through Monday. On weekends, the DJs at **Theatercafé,** Konzilstrasse 3 (✆ **07531/2-02-43**), mix hip-hop and house late into the night. Latin beats play Monday, Friday, and Saturday nights at **Rheinterrasse,** Spanierstrasse 5 (✆ **07531/5-60-93**). Good Dixieland jazz and country are found at **Hafenhalle,** Hafenstrasse 10 (✆ **07531/2-11-26**), every Sunday. Call for details.

For a good pub, head to **Seekuh,** Konzilstrasse 1 (✆ **07531/2-72-32**), where they book winter shows to heat up the night. It's open 6pm to 1am weekdays and 7pm to 2am weekends. In the summer, the beer garden is a popular hangout.

Two **music festivals** featuring contemporary rock, jazz, and cabaret music are also held during the summer. An international menagerie of bands descends on the town June 23 to July 4th for a series of concerts held in huge tents. Ticket prices are 11€ to 30€ ($9.80–$26.80), but there are a few free shows, too. Throngs of revelers flood the town on September 1 for the annual **Rock Am See Festival,** where a 36€ ($32.15) ticket buys you admission to an all-day event that draws international stars. For schedules, call the festival office at ✆ **07531/9-08-80.**

## 5 Reichenau ★

10km (6½ miles) NW of Konstanz

Set within the more southerly of the two arms that stretch westward from the Bodensee, Reichenau is a small historic island that was only recently connected to the mainland by a causeway. By the end of the 800s, it was the site of three separate monasteries, the oldest of which had been established in 724. Later, Reichenau became a political force within the Holy Roman Empire. Today, much of the island is devoted to the cultivation of vegetables and salad greens, and consequently has a sedate aura, much prized by escapists looking for a quiet getaway.

### ESSENTIALS

**GETTING THERE** **By Train** Reichenau's railway station lies midway between the much larger railway junctions of Radolfzell (to the west) and Konstanz (to the east). Trains from throughout Germany and Switzerland make frequent stops at both those cities, from which passengers heading to Reichenau can transfer onto a small railway line that makes runs at hourly intervals on to Bahnhof Reichenau. Buses from Bahnhof Reichenau to Insel Reichenau (the city's historic core), take 10 minutes each way. For information call ✆ **01805/99-66-33.**

**By Bus** Bus service to Reichenau is limited and inconvenient. For information, call **SBG GmbH** (✆ **07732/19449**).

**By Car** From Konstanz, motorists should take Route 33 east to Reichenau.

**By Boat** For information about the ferryboats that ply the waters between Reichenau and the German lakeside hamlet of Allensbach, call ✆ **07533/6361.**

**VISITOR INFORMATION** The tourist office is the **Verkehrsbüro,** Mittelzell, Ergat 5 (✆ **07534/92070**). May to September, it's open Monday to

Friday 8:30am to noon and 2 to 6pm, Saturday 9am to noon; October and April, Monday to Friday 8:30am to noon and 2 to 5pm; November to March, Monday to Friday 8:30am to noon.

## EXPLORING THE TOWN

The island is divided into three separate villages (Oberzell, Mittelzell, and Niederzell), each of which is centered around the remains of a medieval monastery. The most impressive of these is the **Münster St. Maria and Markus,** Burgstrasse (✆ **07534/249**), in Mittelzell. Originally founded in 725, it became one of the most important centers of learning in the Carolingian era. It reached its peak around 1,000, when it was the home of about 700 monks. The structure is beautiful in its simplicity. Entrance is free, but a visit to the treasury costs 1.55€ ($1.40). The church is open daily, year-round, 9am to 6pm; its treasury is open only May to October, Monday to Saturday 11am to noon and 3 to 4pm. While you're in the vicinity, notice the **Krautergarten (Herb Garden),** in the shadow of the cathedral on the Hermann Contractus Strasse. It emulates the herb and vegetable gardens maintained by monks in the Middle Ages.

The hamlet of Niederzell is home to **Stiftskirche St. Peter and St. Paul,** Egino-Strasse (no phone). If it's not open at the time of your arrival, the tourist office will call someone to unlock the gates for you. In 1990, during restorations of the church's apse, a series of Romanesque frescoes were uncovered and are now on view.

The nearby hamlet of Oberzell is the site of the **Stiftskirche St. George,** Seestrasse (no phone). Rising abruptly from a cabbage field, it has a severely dignified, very simple facade, and a series of charmingly naive medieval frescoes inside. It's open daily 9am to 6pm. Admission is free.

A final site worth a stop is the **Heimatmuseum,** in the Stadthaus, Ergat 7, in Mittelzell (no phone). This is a showcase for the handcrafts and folklore that developed on Reichenau and the surrounding region. It's open May to October Tuesday to Sunday 3 to 5pm. Entrance costs 1.55€ ($1.40) adults, .50€ (45¢) children.

## SHOPPING

For a sampling of the many wines produced within the Bodensee region, head for **Winzer Vereins,** Munsterplatz (✆ **07534/293**), where you'll be able to see rack upon rack of local vintages. You can even get a single glass to decide if you want to buy a whole bottle.

## WHERE TO STAY

**Seehotel Seeschau** ★ This comfortable, well-maintained hotel is set directly beside the lake. It features good-size rooms with upscale reproductions of antique furniture and, in many cases, views over the lake. Bathrooms are neatly kept with shower-tub combinations. This hotel is especially appealing in the midsummer, when the flowers around its windows burst into bloom.

An der Schiffsländе, 78479 Reichenau. ✆ **07534/257.** Fax 07534/72-64. www.seeschau.mdo.de. 23 units. 128€–180€ ($114.30–$160.75) double; 230€ ($205.40) suite for 2. Rates include breakfast. AE, DC, MC, V. Free parking. **Amenities:** Restaurant; bar; room service; babysitting; laundry/dry cleaning. *In room:* TV, mini-bar, Jacuzzi, hair dryer, safe.

**Strandhotel Löchnerhaus** ★ This is a good, well-managed hotel, just a stone's throw from the lakefront. It's set within a pleasant garden and offers bathrooms with shower-tub combinations and well-maintained rooms, many of which have private verandas or terraces and lake views.

Schiffslände 12, 78478 Reichenau. ✆ **07534/80-30.** Fax 07534/582. www.strandhotel-reichenau.mdo.de. 42 units. 139€–150€ ($124.15–$133.95) double. Rates include breakfast. AE, DC, MC, V. Parking 8€ ($7.15). Closed Jan–Feb. **Amenities:** Restaurant; lounge; boat rental; room service; laundry/dry cleaning. *In room:* TV, minibar, hair dryer, safe.

## WHERE TO DINE

**Restaurant Strandhotel Löchnerhaus** GERMAN/INTERNATIONAL This restaurant, with its hardworking, kindly staff, is the traditional favorite of many locals. The 1950s-style dining room has lake views. Menu items include sea bass cooked either in Riesling sauce or in a potato crust, whitefish from the Bodensee, rack of lamb with horseradish and mint, grilled meats such as steak, and a savory version of goulash.

Schiffslände 12. ✆ **07534/80-30.** Reservations recommended. Main courses 19€–29€ ($16.95–$25.90). AE, DC, MC, V. Daily 11am–9pm. Closed Jan–Feb.

## REICHENAU AFTER DARK

Those seeking a "night on the town" often drive over to Constance (Konstanz) nearby. Life is considerably quieter in the more demure Reichenau after dark. Most visitors who come in summer prefer to sit out on one of the lakeside terraces—called ***Terrassen am See*** in German—enjoying the beer, the company, and mostly the romantic views of the town at night. The best of these is at the two previously recommended hotels, **Seehotel Seeschau** and **Standhotel Löchnerhaus.** When the weather is foul, the best place for drinking and having a good time is the **Kaminstube** at the Seehotel Seeschau.

# 6 Überlingen ★

40km (25 miles) N of Konstanz, 46km (28½ miles) E of Ravensburg, 24km (15 miles) W of Friedrichshafen

Locals call the town of Überlingen, founded in the 1200s, a German version of Nice because of its sunny weather and lakeside location. It's also one of the best-preserved medieval sites along the Bodensee.

## ESSENTIALS

**GETTING THERE** **By Train** Rail passengers are funneled through nearby Friedrichshafen, from where a smaller rail line goes through Überlingen to Radolfzell. Trains run in either direction along that line at hourly intervals throughout the day. Überlingen's railway station lies on the extreme western edge of town. For rail information call ✆ **01805/99-66-33.**

**By Bus** Regional bus service along Lake Constance is provided by **RAB Regionalverkehr Alb-Bodensee GmbH** in Friedrichshafen (call ✆ **07541/30130** for more information).

**By Car** Überlingen is off Route 31, just northwest of Konstanz. From Stuttgart via Ulm, take Route 30 south then Route 31 west at Friedrichshafen. From Munich, follow Autobahn 96 west/southwest to Lindau, then Route 31 west to Friedrichshafen and Überlingen.

**By Boat** April to October, 8 to 10 ferryboats a day carry passengers to Überlingen from Konstanz (trip time: 1 hr. 20 min.) for 7.50€ ($6.70) each way. For information call the **Weiss Flote,** an armada of lake steamers maintained by the Bodensee Schiffsbetriebe GmbH (✆ **07531/281398**). No cars are carried on any of these ferries.

**VISITOR INFORMATION** Tourist information is available at Ergat 5 (✆ **07534/9-20-70**). May to October, the office is open Monday to Friday

8:30am to 6pm, Saturday 9am to noon, and Sunday 2 to 5pm; November to April, Monday to Friday 8:30am to noon and 2 to 5pm.

## EXPLORING THE TOWN

The most important of the city monuments is the **Münster** ★, a surprisingly large medieval structure that required 200 years to build. The larger of its two towers functioned during war as a military watchtower and was later capped with an eight-sided Renaissance lantern. The severely dignified exterior is offset by an elaborate and intricate Gothic interior. Take special notice of the main altarpiece, carved in the early 1600s by Jorg Zurn. The cathedral is open daily 8am to 6pm.

On the opposite side of the square is Überlingen's **Rathaus** ★, built in the late 1400s. Most of its interior is devoted to municipal offices, except for the Ratsaal, whose vaulted ceiling and lavishly paneled walls make it the most beautiful public room in town. Notice the coats of arms representing various factions of the Holy Roman Empire. Open Monday to Friday 9am to noon and 2:30 to 5pm, Saturday 9am to noon. Entrance is free.

The city maintains a **Museum of Folklore (Heimatmuseum)** within one of its most prized buildings, the Reichlin-von-Meldlegg Haus, Krummeberggasse 30 (✆ **07551/991-079**). This building artfully emulates the style of the Florentine Renaissance. Inside you can also visit both a chapel and a lavishly ornate rococo ballroom. The building and its museum are open Tuesday to Saturday 9am to noon and 1:30 to 5pm, and Sunday 10am to 3pm. Admission is 2€ ($1.80) adults and 1€ (90¢) children.

Also look for the **Franziskanerkirche,** Spitalgasse. What is especially striking about this church is the contrast between its severely dignified exterior and its lavishly baroque interior. Open daily 8am to noon and 2 to 5pm.

The townspeople of Überlingen took great care to ornament the medieval fortifications that protected them from outside invaders. The best preserved of these walls is the **Stadtmauer,** which in recent times was landscaped into a graceful ramble lined with trees and shrubbery. It's part of the encircling walls that flank the north and east side of town.

Along Überlingen's waterfront promenade (Seepromenade), which offers a view of the faraway Swiss Alps, are two of the largest old buildings in town. One of these is the **Greth,** originally a market and storage vault for corn. Today it houses the city's tourist office. Immediately next door is the fanciful Gothic-era **Zeughaus,** Seepromenade (call tourist office to confirm that it's open). It contains a collection of medieval armor and weapons from the Middle Ages. This is a rather lackluster exhibition, and the sight could easily be missed without causing cultural deprivation to anyone. Of course, if you're writing a book on medieval weaponry, it might interest you. It's open only Easter to October, Monday to Saturday 10:30am to 1pm. Admission is 2.55€ ($2.30).

Überlingen is also the site of one of the best known medical clinics on the Bodensee. The **Buchinger Clinic,** Willhelmbeckstrasse 27 (✆ **07551/8070**) is expensive, aristocratic, and exclusive. Good spa treatments are available within two of the town's hotels, the Kur und Gasthaus Routher and the Gasthaus Seepark.

## WHERE TO STAY & DINE

**Landgasthof Adler** Set within the confines of a bucolic hamlet (Lippertsreute), this hotel and restaurant occupies two antique buildings, the older of which was built 300 years ago. Rooms are cozy, unpretentious, and appealingly (and artfully) rustic. All rooms contain bathrooms with shower-tub combinations.

The restaurant is well-known to locals. It serves heaping, well-prepared portions of time-tested Swabian dishes such as *Spanferkel* (roast suckling pig), *Zweibelrostbraten* (onion-flavored roast beef), and Bodensee whitefish prepared with white wine sauce.

Hauptstrasse 44, Lippertsreute (10km/6 miles north of the center), 88662 Überlingen. ✆ **07553/8-25-50.** Fax 07553/82-55-70. www.landgasthofzumadler.de. 16 units. 54€–84€ ($48.20–$75) double. Rates include breakfast. MC. Restaurant Fri–Tues 11:30am–2pm; Fri–Wed 5pm–midnight. Free parking. Closed Nov. **Amenities:** Restaurant; bar; room service; laundry/dry cleaning. *In room:* TV, hair dryer.

**Parkhotel St. Leonhard** ★★ Set on a hilltop, this hotel provides rest and recuperation to urban visitors. The woodsy-looking chalet is flanked by more angular, modern annexes. Rooms are good-size, modern, conservative, comfortable, and well-designed with bathrooms containing shower-tub combinations. The kitchen here serves both regional and international cuisine offered in a choice of two restaurants, and they succeed admirably. They are far from pretentious, serving wholesale, reliable, and good-tasting food prepared with market-fresh ingredients cooked according to traditional recipes. They are not gourmet or experimental, but the chefs will feed you very well.

Obere St. Leonhard-Strasse 71 (1.5km/1 mile north of the center), 8862 Überlingen. ✆ **07551/80-81-00.** Fax 07551/80-85-31. www.parkhotel-sankt-leonhard.de. 145 units. 145€–155€ ($129.50–$138.40) double; 195€–310€ ($174.15–$276.85) suite. Rates include breakfast. AE, MC, V. Restaurant open daily 11:30am–2pm and 5:30–11pm. Free parking. **Amenities:** 2 restaurants; bar; pool; health club; sauna; room service; babysitting; laundry/dry cleaning. *In room:* TV, minibar, hair dryer, safe.

## 7 Ravensburg

20km (12 miles) N of Friedrichshafen, 32km (20 miles) N of Lindau

Ravensburg isn't on Lake Constance, but it's nearby and makes a good side trip. The town boasts one of the most impeccably preserved medieval cores in the region. During the 1400s, the linen trade made Ravensburg into one of the richest towns in Germany, but economic stagnation set in during the 1600s as a result of the Thirty Years' War. Today, this quiet town is a tourist's delight.

### ESSENTIALS

**GETTING THERE** **By Train** Most passengers change trains in nearby Ulm. From there, trains depart at hourly intervals for Friedrichshafen, stopping en route in Ravensburg (trip time: 1 hr.). For information call ✆ **01805/99-66-33.**

**By Bus** Most bus routes into Ravensburg start at nearby villages and hamlets. For information, call **0751/2766.**

**By Car** From Stuttgart, follow Autobahn 8 east to the city of Ulm, then turn south onto Route 30 directly into Ravensburg. From along Lake Constance, you can take routes B33, B30, or 467 north to Ravensburg.

**VISITOR INFORMATION** Head to the **Stadtverkehrsamt,** Kirchestrasse 16 (✆ **0751/82324**). It's open Monday 8am to noon, Tuesday to Friday 8am to 5:30pm, and Saturday 9am to noon.

### EXPLORING THE TOWN

You'll appreciate that cars are banned from the narrow labyrinth of alleyways within Ravensburg's historic core. Two of the most evocative streets are **Untere Breite Strasse** and **Charlottenstrasse,** both of which lie near the town's central square. Lining the Marienplatz are the late-Gothic **Rathaus;** the 14th-century **Kornhaus,** once one of the largest corn exchanges in the region and now the town's library; and the **Waaghaus,** originally built in the 1400s as a warehouse for municipal supplies and now a bank. Look also for the old city **watchtower** and the Renaissance-era **Lederhaus,** the town's post office.

Also on the Marienplatz is the **Karmelitenklosterkirche.** It was originally a monastery in the 14th century and later housed a mercantile association devoted to the promotion of the linen trade. The complex's church can be visited every day 8am to 6pm. Nearby, at the corner of Kirkstrasse and the Herrenstrasse, is the **Liebfrauenkirche,** the parish church of Ravensburg. Deceptively simple on the outside, the 14th-century structure has been radically but authentically reconstructed on the inside. Look for remnants of original stained glass and a heavy sobriety reminiscent of the Middle Ages.

## WHERE TO STAY

**Hotel-Gasthof Obertor** *Value* This is the town's best choice for the frugal traveler. This hotel was built in the 12th century as a farmhouse and is almost as old as the town. It has a lovely garden terrace in front and a park in the back. Rooms vary greatly in size and in personality, so you may want to take a peek at a couple before deciding which to take. Turn-of-the-century antiques abound, mostly made of cherry wood—typical of the Bodensee area. All units contain neatly kept bathrooms with shower-tub combinations.

Markstrasse 67, 88212 Ravensburg. ✆ **0751/3-66-70.** Fax 0751/3-66-72-00. www.hotelobertor.de. 32 units. 94€–124€ ($83.95–$110.75) double. Rates include breakfast. AE, DC, MC, V. Free parking. **Amenities:** Restaurant; lounge; pool; health club; whirlpool; sauna; Jacuzzi; solarium; massage; room service; babysitting; laundry/dry cleaning. *In room:* TV, hair dryer.

**Romantikhotel Waldhorn** ★★ The most appealing hotel in Ravensburg occupies a late–18th century building and a more modern annex. Because both buildings lie within the town's all-pedestrian zone, it's easy to get a sense of the relaxed local lifestyle. Rooms are comfortable and cozy, and the staff is very charming. All the accommodations come with a midsize to large bathroom with tub-and-shower combination. The hotel is known for its two restaurants. The Rebleuterhaus, a simple and likable Weinstube, serves Swabian specialties such as large ravioli stuffed with meat and spinach, and Spätzle (dumplings).

### *Moments* Scaling the Ramparts

Part of Ravensburg's allure derives from its well-preserved network of medieval fortifications, studded with defensive towers. The most visible of these is the 52m (170-ft.) **Mehlsack Tower,** which has been adopted as the municipal symbol of Ravensburg itself. You can climb to its heights by means of 240 heavily worn, circular steps, but only on the third Sunday of every month mid-March to mid-October from 10am to noon. Entrance is free. Two other defensive towers can be spotted from the Marienplatz. These are the **Obertor,** the oldest gate in the city walls, accessible via Marktstrasse, and the **Grünerturm** (Green Tower), covered with moss-colored ceramic tiles, many of which date from the 14th century. Neither the Grünerturm nor the Obertor can be visited.

Ravensburg's only noteworthy museum is its **Heimatmuseum,** devoted to local folklore and handcrafts. It lies within the Folkshaus, Charlottenstrasse 36 (for information contact the tourist office) and is open Tuesday to Saturday 3 to 5pm. Admission is 1.55€ ($1.40).

Marienplatz 15, 88212 Ravensburg. ✆ **07151/36120.** Fax 07151/3612-100. www.waldhorn.de. 35 units. 124€–150€ ($110.75–$133.95) double; 160€–180€ ($142.90–$160.75) suite. Rates include breakfast. AE, DC, MC, V. Parking 8€ ($7.15). **Amenities:** 2 restaurants; lounge; room service; laundry/dry cleaning. *In room:* TV, minibar, hair dryer, safe.

## WHERE TO DINE

**Romantikhotel Waldhorn** ★ MODERN INTERNATIONAL This sophisticated restaurant is directed by celebrity chef Marcel Bouley. The stylish, gracefully antique dining room has massive ceiling beams. The Asian-influenced cuisine is among the most subtle, celebrated, and exotic in Germany. Menu items combine eastern and western culinary traditions with verve and zest, and change according to the seasons and the inspiration of the much-applauded chef. Your meal might include medallions of lamb with miso, lemon, and mint tempura or lobster ravioli with braised sweetbreads, brown butter sauce, caviar, and rosettes of zucchini.

Marienplatz 15. ✆ **0751/36120.** Reservations recommended. Main courses 21€–36€ ($18.75–$32.15); fixed-price menu 88€ ($78.60). AE, DC, MC, V. Tues–Sat 11:30am–2pm and 6–9:30pm.

## A SIDE TRIP TO WEINGARTEN

An important archaeological excavation is located within the agrarian hamlet of Weingarten, a sleepy village 5km (3 miles) north of Ravensburg. To reach the village, take bus 1 or 2 from Marienplatz. In the 1950s, teams of archaeologists discovered one of the richest troves of German graves in the country. Artifacts from the dig lay in the **Alamannen Museum,** located in Kornhaus, Karlstrasse 28 (✆ **0751/40-52-55**). It's open Wednesday, Saturday, and Sunday 3 to 5pm; closed February and November. Admission is 1.55€ ($1.40).

Weingarten is also home to the largest baroque church in Germany, the **Weingarten Basilica** (✆ **0751/56-12-70**), which rises to about 60m (200 ft.). It was established in 1056 by the wife of a prominent official in the Guelph dynasty. Inside is one of the holiest relics in Germany, a mystical vial, which, according to legend, contains several drops of Christ's blood. The relic was entrusted to the convent by the sister-in-law of William the Conqueror, the Guelph queen Juditha. Another highlight of the church is the organ—one of the largest in the country, its installation required 13 years, beginning in 1737. Also noteworthy are the ceiling frescoes by Cosmas Damian Asam, one of the leaders of the Baroque School. The church is open daily 8am to 6pm.

Finally, if you can manage to schedule your visit for the day after Ascension (the Thurs 40 days after Easter), you can witness a massive **procession** of pilgrims, at the head of which are more than 2,000 horsemen. The breeding of horses for this procession is a matter of quiet pride among local farmers.

For further information on Weingarten, call the **tourist office** at ✆ **0751/40-51-25.**

# 11

# The Black Forest (Schwarzwald)

The Black Forest covers a triangular section roughly 145km (90 miles) long and 40km (25 miles) wide in southwestern Germany. The pine- and birch-studded mountains here are alive with fairy-tale villages, well-equipped spas, and modern ski resorts. The peaks in the southern part of the forest reach as high as 1,525m (5,000 ft.) and are excellent for skiing in winter and hiking or mountain climbing in summer. The little lakes of Titisee and Schluchsee are popular for boating, swimming, and ice-skating. Fish abound in the streams and lakes.

**GETTING TO THE BLACK FOREST** International airports serving the area are located in Stuttgart (see chapter 12) and the Swiss city of Basel. Basel lies only 70km (44 miles) from Freiburg in Breisgau, the "capital" of the Black Forest. Trains run north and south through the Rhine Valley, with fast, frequent service to such Black Forest towns as Freiburg and Baden-Baden. Motorists should take the A5 Autobahn, which runs the length of the Schwarzwald. From Lake Constance (see chapter 10), continue along Route 13 for about 64km (40 miles) until you reach the Black Forest.

**EXPLORING THE REGION BY CAR** The roads through the forest are excellent, especially the **Schwarzwald Hochstrasse** (Black Forest High Road or Ridgeway, Route B500), which runs almost the entire length of the region, from Baden-Baden to Freudenstadt, then resumes at Triberg and goes on to Waldshut on the Rhine. While taking this scenic road, you'll have many opportunities to park your car and explore the countryside or to turn off on one of the side roads leading to hospitable villages, ancient castles, and rolling farmlands.

## 1 Freiburg im Breisgau ★★

208km (129 miles) SW of Stuttgart, 70km (44 miles) N of Basel (Switzerland), 280km (174 miles) S of Frankfurt

This scenic and interesting city, the largest in the Black Forest region, is often overlooked because of its out-of-the-way location. When approached from the Rhine plain on the west, Freiburg is silhouetted against towering mountain peaks, which are only an hour from the town by funicular or car.

Because of its remarkable climate, Freiburg is a year-round attraction and sports center. The city lies in the path of warm air currents that come up from the Mediterranean through the Burgundy Gap. In early spring, the town is usually bursting into bloom while the surrounding mountain peaks are still covered with snow. In the autumn, the smell of new wine fills the narrow streets even as snow is already falling on the nearby peaks.

## ESSENTIALS

**GETTING THERE** **By Train** Frequent trains connect Freiburg to major airports in Basel (Switzerland) and Stuttgart. Daily trains also go to Freiburg from Frankfurt (trip time: 2 hr.) and Hamburg (trip time: 8 hr.), as well as Berlin and Zürich, Switzerland. For information, call ✆ **01805/99-66-33.**

**By Bus** Long-distance bus service is provided by the **Südbaden Bus GmbH,** Central Bus Station, Freiburg (✆ **0761/3-61-72**), which has service from Freiburg to the EuroAirport Basel-Mulhouse, and **EuroRegioBus** (✆ **0761/3-61-72**), which has a bus between Freiburg and the French cities of Mulhouse and Colmar.

**By Car** Access by car is via the A5 Autobahn north and south.

**VISITOR INFORMATION** For tourist information, contact **Freiburg Information,** Rotteckring 14 (✆ **0761/3-88-18-80**). The office is open June to August, Monday to Saturday 9am to 8pm and Sunday 10am to noon; September to May, Monday to Friday 9:30am to 6pm and Saturday 9am to 2pm.

**GETTING AROUND** Freiburg is well-serviced by buses and trams, the latter running in the inner city. A one-way fare costs 2€ ($1.80), although you can buy a day pass for 5€ ($4.45), and two people can buy a day pass for 7€ ($6.25). For schedules and information, or to buy passes, go to Plus-Punkt, Salzstrasse 3 (✆ **0761/451-1500**) in the Altstadt. Hours are Monday to Friday 8am to 7pm and Saturday 8am to 2pm. Most of the city's public transportation network is shut down between 12:30 and 5:30am.

## SEEING THE SIGHTS

**Augustiner Museum** ★ The Augustiner Museum is housed in the former church and monastery of the Order of St. Augustine. It contains the town's finest collection of art, including religious art spanning more than 1,000 years. Among the treasures are some of the cathedral's original stained-glass windows, as well as the most important of its medieval gold and silver treasures, brought here for safekeeping. Among the best works in the collection are *The Snow Miracle* by Mathias Grünewald and works by Hans Baldung Grien, who was a pupil of Albrecht Dürer. There's also a rich collection of fine late-Gothic wooden sculpture, as well as Art Nouveau glass objects.

Augustinerplatz. ✆ **0761/2-01-25-31.** Admission 2€ ($1.80) adults, 1€ (90¢) students, free for children 17 and under. Tues–Sun 10am–5pm. Guided tours Wed at 12:30pm; Sun at 11am. Tram: 1.

**Freiburg Cathedral** ★★ This cathedral is one of the great masterpieces of Gothic art in Germany. Its unique spire is of filigree stonework; the steeple sits on an octagonal belfry, which holds a historic 5-ton (4,500 kg) bell dating from 1258. Although begun in 1200 in the Romanesque style, by the time it was completed in 1620, the builders had incorporated various Gothic styles.

Upon entering by the south door, you'll be in the transept facing an early 16th-century sculpture of the adoration of the Christ child by the Magi. If you turn left into the nave, you'll see at the far end of the aisle, by the entrance to the tower, a fine 13th-century statue of the Virgin flanked by two adoring angels. The high altar has an altarpiece built between 1512 and 1516 by Hans Baldung Grien. Resting against one of the Renaissance pillars along the aisle is a carved 16th-century pulpit, with stairs winding around the curve of the column. The figures below the stairs are likenesses of the townspeople, including the sculptor.

In the aisles are 14th-century stained-glass windows. The oldest stained glass, dating from the 13th century, is in the small round windows of the south

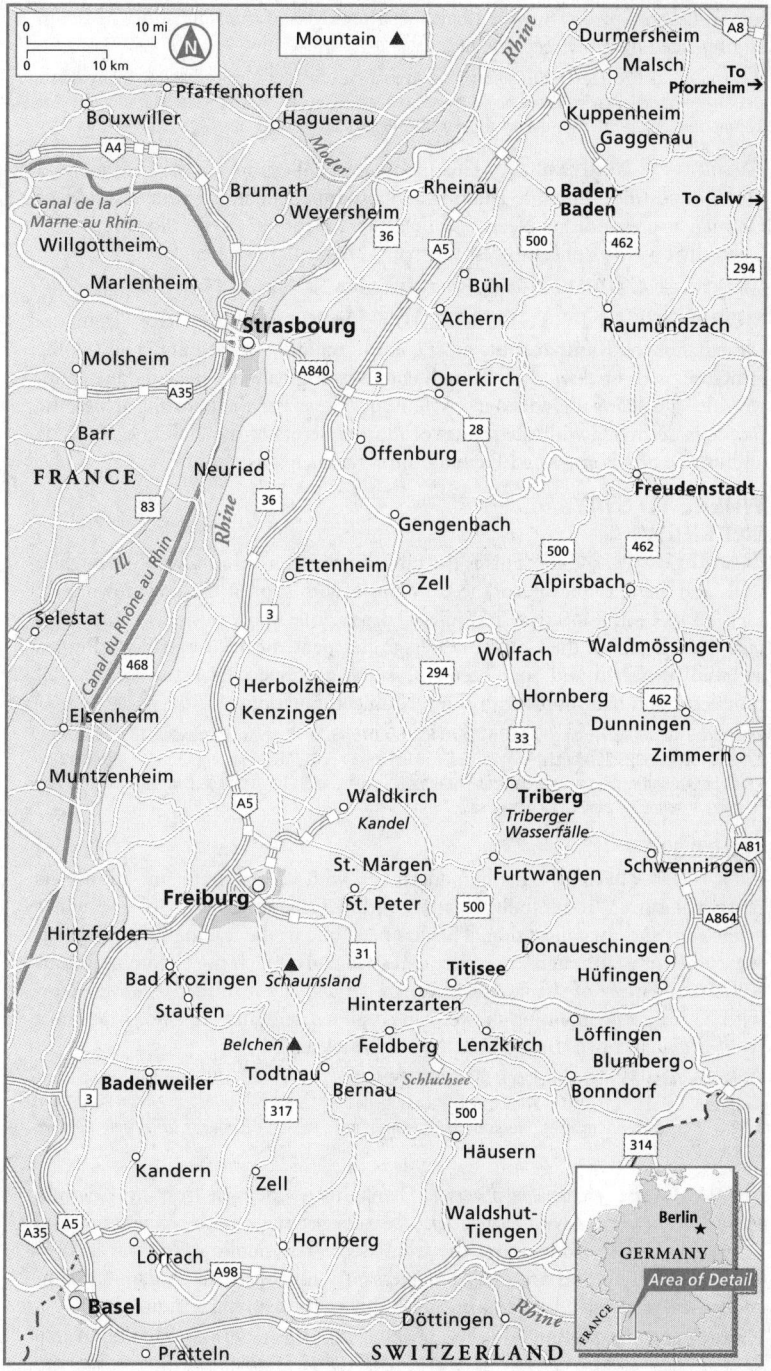
0 10 mi
0 10 km
N
Mountain ▲
Rhine
Durmersheim
A8
Malsch
To Pforzheim →
Pfaffenhoffen
Bouxwiller
Haguenau
Kuppenheim
Gaggenau
A4
Moder
Canal de la Marne au Rhin
Brumath
Weyersheim
Rheinau
Baden-Baden
To Calw →
36
A5
500
462
294
Willgottheim
Marlenheim
Bühl
Achern
Raumündzach
Strasbourg
Molsheim
A840
3
Oberkirch
A35
28
Barr
Offenburg
FRANCE
Neuried
Freudenstadt
83
36
Gengenbach
Rhine
500
462
Ill
Canal du Rhône au Rhin
Ettenheim
Zell
Alpirsbach
Selestat
3
Wolfach
Waldmössingen
468
294
Herbolzheim
Hornberg
462
Elsenheim
Kenzingen
Dunningen
33
Zimmern
Muntzenheim
A5
Waldkirch
Triberg
Kandel
Triberger Wasserfälle
A81
St. Märgen
Furtwangen
Schwenningen
Freiburg
St. Peter
500
A864
Hirtzfelden
31
Donaueschingen
Titisee
Hüfingen
Bad Krozingen
Schaunsland
Hinterzarten
Staufen
Löffingen
Belchen ▲
Feldberg
Lenzkirch
Blumberg
Badenweiler
Todtnau
Bernau
Schluchsee
Bonndorf
3
317
500
314
Häusern
Kandern
Zell
Waldshut-Tiengen
A35
A5
Hornberg
Lörrach
A98
Basel
Döttingen
Rhine
Pratteln
SWITZERLAND
Berlin
GERMANY
Area of Detail
FRANCE

transept. Some pieces, however, have been removed to the Augustiner Museum and replaced by more recent panels.

Münsterplatz. ✆ **0761/20-27-90.** Cathedral free; to climb the tower 2€ ($1.80) adults, 1€ ($.90) children, and free for children under 15. Cathedral Mon–Sat 10am–6pm; Sun 1–6pm. Tower May–Oct Mon–Sat 9:30am–5pm, Sun 1–5pm; Nov–Apr, Wed–Sat 9:30am–5pm. Tram: 4, 5, or 6.

**Museum für Neue Kunst** This modern art collection was formerly housed in the Augustiner Museum. Painting and sculpture, beginning with examples of German expressionism, Neue Sachlichkeit, and other classic modern works, especially by artists of southwest Germany, are displayed here.

Marienstrasse 10A. ✆ **0761/2-01-25-81.** Free admission. Tues–Sun 10am–5pm. Tram: 1, 4, 5, or 6.

**MORE SIGHTS IN THE ALTSTADT** In Münsterplatz, across from the cathedral, is the **Kaufhaus,** the most colorful building in Freiburg. This Gothic structure, with oriel windows at each end, was originally an ancient emporium, to which a balcony was added in 1550. Above the massive supporting arches, the facade is decorated with the statues of four emperors of the Habsburg dynasty, all but one of whom visited Freiburg during their reigns.

## WHERE TO STAY

### EXPENSIVE

**Colombi Hotel** ★★★ This is the most luxurious hotel in town. Snow-white walls and angular lines make the Colombi easy to spot in the downtown area. Despite its central location, it's quiet and peaceful. Many business conferences take place here, but the Colombi caters to independent travelers as well. Rooms are well furnished and appointed; the suites are especially luxurious, and all rooms contain bathrooms with shower-tub combinations.

Rotteckring 16, 79098 Freiburg. ✆ **0761/2-10-60.** Fax 0761/3-14-10. www.colombi.de. 118 units. 220€–250€ ($196.45–$223.25) double; from 290€ ($258.95) suite. AE, DC, MC, V. Parking 13€ ($11.60). Tram: 10, 11, or 12. **Amenities:** Restaurant; bar; pool; health club; sauna; salon; room service; babysitting; laundry/dry cleaning. *In room:* TV, minibar, hair dryer, safe.

### MODERATE

**Park Hotel Post** ★ This baroque hotel, with an elaborate zinc cap on its octagonal turret, is centrally located, within walking distance of the major attractions and the rail station. This has been one of the leading hotels in town for a long time, although its services and style don't match the Colombi. Rooms come in a variety of shapes and sizes, are attractively furnished, are well kept, with bathrooms containing shower-tub combinations, and are among the most comfortable in town. Breakfast is the only meal served.

Eisenbahnstrasse 35, 79098 Freiburg. ✆ **0761/38-54-80.** Fax 0761/3-16-80. www.park-hotel-post.de. 45 units. 139€–159€ ($124.15–$142) double. Rates include buffet breakfast. AE, MC, V. Parking 8€ ($7.15). Tram: 10, 11, or 12. **Amenities:** Breakfast room; lounge; room service; babysitting; laundry/dry cleaning. *In room:* TV, minibar.

**Victoria** The Victoria is peaceful, thanks to its location fronting Colombi Park. The facade is a symmetrical 19th-century rectangle, with big windows and a wrought-iron balcony above the front door. The public rooms are lavishly paneled. Guest rooms are small but pleasantly furnished, all containing bathrooms with shower-tub combinations. Many rooms contain antiques.

Eisenbahnstrasse 54 (135m/450 ft. from the Hauptbahnhof), 79098 Freiburg. ✆ **0761/ 20-73-40.** Fax 0761/ 20-73-44-44. www.hotel-victoria.de. 63 units. 110€–145€ ($98.25–$129.50) double. Rates include buffet breakfast. AE, DC, MC, V. Parking 3€–9€ ($2.70–$8.05). **Amenities:** Restaurant; bar; cafe; room service; laundry/dry cleaning. *In room:* TV, minibar, hair dryer.

### *Moments* An Excursion to the Upper Black Forest ★★★

From Freiburg you can make a 145km (90-mile) 1-day circuit through one of the most scenic parts of the Black Forest, returning in time for dinner. Along the way, you'll pass a trio of the highest summits in the Black Forest and two of the region's most beautiful lakes.

Head immediately south to **Schauinsland** along Route 317, a narrow twisting road. At the car park you can climb some 100 steps to the belvedere tower for a panoramic view of the area.

Continuing south, you reach **Belchen** mountain, which rises to a height of 1,115m (4,640 ft.). From where the road ends, you can walk to the summit in about 20 minutes. On a clear day, you can look out from the observation platform here and take in a panoramic sweep of the Rhine plain, plus a view of the Alps from Säntis to Mont Blanc.

Upon leaving, continue east to the hamlet of Todtnau, where visitors can walk up a footpath to **The Falls of Todtnau,** about a mile away. Back at Todtnau, continue east along Route 317 to Feldberg. Here a chairlift takes visitors to the 1,450m (4,750-ft.) **Seebuck** peak, which is crowned by the Bismarck monument and offers another sweeping panoramic view of the Black Forest.

Back on the road again, follow Route 317 east until it becomes Route 500 heading south to **Schluchsee,** one of the loveliest lakes of the area and the most important body of water in the Black Forest.

After a visit here, head north along Route 500 to the hamlet of **Lenzkirch,** from which you'll have a view of Lake Titisee. The road then continues to the resort of **Titisee** itself (see later section of this chapter). After a visit you can return to Freiburg by heading west along Route 31.

**Zum Roten Bären** ★ This is one of the oldest buildings in Freiburg, with parts dating from 1120. It's also said to be the oldest inn in Germany. A modern wing blends in pleasantly. The interior is delightfully decorated, emphasizing original construction elements along with scattered pieces of antique furniture. Rooms are well styled and furnished, all with bathrooms containing shower-tub combinations. Try for one in the older section; they have more tradition and atmosphere.

Oberlinden 12, 79098 Freiburg. ✆ **0761/38-78-70.** Fax 0761/3-87-87-17. www.roter-baeren.de. 25 units. 133€–180€ ($118.75–$160.75) double. Rates include buffet breakfast. AE, DC, MC, V. Parking 8€ ($7.15). Tram: 1. **Amenities:** Restaurant; bar; health club; room service; laundry/dry cleaning. *In room:* TV, minibar, hair dryer, safe.

## INEXPENSIVE

**Rappen** *Finds* This charming inn in the pedestrians-only Altstadt has a lot more cozy Black Forest ambience than such nearby competitors. It's marked with a wrought-iron hanging sign, little dormer windows in its steep roof, window boxes, and shutters. Rooms are small and simply but comfortably furnished; the most desirable have views of the cathedral.

Münsterplatz 13, 79098 Freiburg. ✆ **0761/3-13-53.** Fax 0761/38-22-52. www.hotelrappen.de. 18 units, 13 with bathroom. 70€–80€ ($62.50–$71.45) double without bathroom 110€ ($98.25) with bathroom.

Rates include buffet breakfast. AE, MC, V. All trams stop 18m (60 ft.) behind the hotel. **Amenities:** Restaurant; bar; lounge; room service; laundry/dry cleaning. *In room:* TV, hair dryer.

## WHERE TO DINE

### EXPENSIVE

**Eichhalde** ★★ FRENCH/GERMAN This notable French bistro lies in the Herden district, a 20-minute walk from the center. It gets a lot of neighborhood patronage. Fixed-price lunches and dinners are available. The bill of fare is likely to include goose-liver terrine with port aspic, sea bass in thyme sauce, and turbot salad with mustard sauce. The chef has steadily built up a good local reputation, and the food here is always reliable and well prepared.

Stadtstrasse 91. ✆ **0761/5-48-17.** Reservations required. Main courses 22€–29€ ($19.65–$25.90); fixed-price menu 26€ ($23.20) for 3 courses, 49€–65€ ($43.75–$58.05) for 4 and 5 courses. MC. Sun–Mon and Wed–Fri noon–2pm; Wed–Mon 6:30–10pm. Tram: 14.

**Hans-Thoma-Stube/Colombi Restaurant** ★★ REGIONAL/FRENCH This is justifiably the most acclaimed restaurant in the area. Gracious and skillful service, along with a sumptuous setting, ensure a memorable meal. Choice ingredients, masterly preparation, and creative presentation delight both the eye and the palate. The chef prepares a light modern cuisine, although many regional dishes are also offered. The menu is ever changing, based on the seasons, but might include a terrine of turbot, chanterelles over filet of venison, or an array of Atlantic fish dishes perfectly prepared and impeccably served. There are two 18th-century-style dining rooms.

In the Colombi Hotel, Rotteckring 16. ✆ **0761/2-10-60.** Reservations required. Main courses 27€–30€ ($24.10–$26.80); 3-course business lunch 23€–28€ ($20.55–$25); fixed-price dinner 62€ ($55.35) for 4 courses, 102€ ($91.10) for 7 courses. AE, DC, MC, V. Daily noon–3pm and 7–11pm. Tram: 10, 11, or 12.

**Weinstube zur Traube** ★ FRENCH/SWABIAN This 600-year-old Weinstube is the coziest choice in town for tavern dining. The pewter and earthenware dinner services decorating the walls are art objects in their own right, and the ceramic stove is more than 300 years old. The food here is regional and well prepared, emphasizing game, meat, and fish. Try the pike roulade with crab sauce. Fresh ingredients get a lot of respect around here and are deftly handled by the kitchen staff. There's also a fine wine list.

Schusterstrasse 17. ✆ **0761/3-21-90.** Reservations required. Main courses 17€–27€ ($15.20–$24.10); fixed-price menus 28.50€–80€ ($25.45–$71.45). AE, MC, V. Tues–Sat noon–3pm and 6–10pm. Closed last 2 weeks in Aug. Tram: 10, 11, or 12.

### MODERATE

**Oberkirchs Weinstuben** *Value* GERMAN The innkeeper provides excellent regional cooking and comfortable rooms in this traditional Freiburg establishment. The setting, on a colorful square, is pure picture-postcard. The main Weinstube is old, with a monumental ceiling-high ceramic stove made with ornate decorative tiles. You get good old-fashioned food here—tasty soups, meat dishes, and poultry—and plenty of everything. In season, you might try young pheasant. In the rear is a modern complex fronting an open patio with a fish pond.

The Weinstube also has 25 excellent rooms, all with private bathrooms or showers. Doubles cost 118.50€ to 155€ ($105.80–$138.40), with continental breakfast included.

Münsterplatz 22, 79098 Freiburg. ✆ **0761/202-68-68.** Fax 0761/202-68-69. Reservations recommended. Main courses 8€–22€ ($7.15–$19.65). AE, MC, V. Mon–Sat noon–2pm and 6:30–9:15pm. Closed Jan. Tram: 1, 4, or 5.

**Wolfshöhle** ★ ITALIAN Wolfshöhle's warmly paneled ambience might remind you of a cozy inn high in the mountains on the border between Italy and the German-speaking world. The cuisine is sophisticated but fortifying. Choices include veal scaloppini with lemon, delicately seasoned filet of veal, well-prepared lamb dishes, and calves' liver. You might begin with a hearty soup or select an appetizer such as veal with tuna, the antipasto of the day, or two different versions of carpaccio.

Konviktstrasse 8. ✆ **0761/3-03-03.** Reservations recommended. Main courses 15.10€–20.95€ ($13.50–$18.70); fixed-price menus 20.50€–41.95€ ($18.30–$37.45). AE, DC, MC, V. Summer, Mon–Sat 11am–midnight; off-season, Mon–Sat noon–2pm and 6pm–midnight. Tram: 10, 11, or 12.

## FREIBURG AFTER DARK

An impressive entertainment complex, the **Konzerthaus** hosts a variety of events, ranging from classic music to theater to pop concerts. In June and July, huge tents are raised to house the annual **Zeltmusik festival,** which emphasizes jazz but includes other musical styles as well. Summer also brings a series of **chamber-music concerts** to the Kaufhaus, in Münsterplatz, and a program of **organ recitals** to the Freiburg Cathedral. Information about all venues and events listed above, including program schedules and ticket sales, is available from **Freiburg Information** (see earlier in this chapter).

The city also has a thriving bar and club scene that goes on into the wee hours. Two clubs in one, **Crash,** Schnewlinstrasse 3 (✆ **0761/3-24-75;** tram: 1, 4, 5, or 6), serves drinks and plays punk, house, and funk as background music to the lively banter of patrons; in the basement, **Drifler's Club** plays house and techno for dancers. Crash is open Wednesday to Saturday 10pm until 3:30am, and Drifler's Thursday to Saturday midnight to 4am. There is no cover at either club.

**Jazz Haus,** Schnewlinstrasse 2 (✆ **0761/3-49-73;** tram: 1, 4, 5, or 6), hosts pop, folk, blues, and jazz shows by international, regional, and local bands. The club is open nightly 7pm until 1am, with a cover of 2.50€ to 25.50€ ($2.25–$22.75). Occasionally, bands play jazz or rock at **Le Cher,** Niemensstrasse 8 (✆ **0761/3-28-00;** tram: 1, 4, 5, or 6), but usually it's a place just to drink and talk. It's open Monday to Saturday 10am to 1am and Sunday noon to 1am. Until 8pm, the **Café Atlantik,** Schwabentorring 7 (✆ **0761/3-30-33;** tram: 1), serves up spaghetti platters for 5.50€ ($4.90), but later on, it's mainly a place to drink and listen to the occasional band. Open daily 11am to 1am.

**Hausbräuerei Feierling,** Gerberau 46 (✆ **0761/2-66-78;** tram: 1 or 2), is a brewery-pub, with a beer garden across the street. It's open daily 11am to midnight. Those who want a darker, smoky bar should head to the local Irish pub, the **Isle of Innisfree,** Augustinerplatz 2 (✆ **0761/22984;** tram: 1, 4, 5, or 6), which sometimes has live music. **Cafe Brasil,** Wannerstrasse 21 (✆ **0761/28-98-88;** tram: 1, 5, or 6) has a tropical feel. It's open daily 10am to 1am.

## 2 Badenweiler ★

35km (22 miles) S of Freiburg, 240km (150 miles) W of Stuttgart

Badenweiler is one of the smallest, and one of the most charming, spa towns in the Black Forest. It's also known as the site of the best-preserved Roman baths north of the Alps. Town authorities here are intent on keeping their community spotless, squeaky-clean, and steeped in Black Forest myth and legend. Badenweiler is located halfway between Freiburg and Basel, near the Swiss border.

## ESSENTIALS

**GETTING THERE** **By Train** There's no railway station in Badenweiler, so rail passengers should first go to Freiburg, then switch onto any of the dozen-or-so daily trains that carry them to the town of Müllheim. From there, it's easiest to take any of the taxis lined up at the railway station for the 4km (2½-mile) eastward trip to Badenweiler. There's also a bus (marked "Badenweiler") from Müllheim; it's timed to coincide with the arrival of trains. Taxis line up at the Müllheim railway station, and they make special efforts to time their being there to the arrival of trains from anywhere. A taxi will charge, each way, between 11€–15€ ($9.80–$13.40) to anywhere in Badenweiler, a distance of 4km (2½ miles). If, by any chance, there are no taxis in line, a traveler can call for one at **✆ 07632/455.**

There are also buses lined up at Müllheim's railway station, charging 1.75€ ($1.55) for the short ride on to Badenweiler. Bus no. 111 is the one that heads to Badenweiler and beyond, with departures scheduled every 40 to 65 minutes, depending on the time of the day or evening.

**By Bus** Unless you're coming into Badenweiler from one of the nearby communities, bus travel is not convenient.

**By Car** From the A5 Autobahn, which runs north to south between Karlsruhe and Basel, exit at the Müllheim/Badenweiler exit, then follow the signs to Badenweiler.

**VISITOR INFORMATION** Head for **Kur-Touristik,** Ernst-Eisenlohr-Strasse 4 (**✆ 07632/7-99-00**), which is open Monday to Friday 8:30am to noon and 3 to 5pm and Saturday 8:30am to noon.

## EXPLORING THE AREA

The town offers a wide range of hiking trails through the Black Forest, the most interesting of which is a trek to the **Schloss Bürgeln,** 7846 Schliengen (**✆ 07626/237**), 20km (12 miles) south of Badenweiler. It's also accessible by car (follow the signs from Badenweiler's center). Schloss Bürgeln was built in 1764 by order of the abbot of St. Blasein. It offers a commanding view of the surrounding countryside; on a clear day, you can see Basel, the Vosges of France, and the bend in the Rhine as it flows into Switzerland. Especially noteworthy

### *Moments* Bathing as the Romans Did

The springs that pour water into the spa facilities here are very little changed since Roman days, a fact that the local resort, the **Cassiopeia Therme,** Kurpark (**✆ 07632/7990**), won't let you forget. It offers mud packs, massage, sauna, and steam bath treatments. The well-preserved Roman baths, originally built in A.D. 75, still stand today within the Kurpark, or spa gardens. Tours of the ancient Roman baths, complete with descriptions of how the Romans actually bathed, are given Tuesday at 5pm and Sunday at 11:15am. Tours cost 1€ (90¢). For information, contact the spa directly. The baths are open daily 9am to 10pm. The cost is Monday to Friday 10€ ($8.95) adults, 6.50€ ($5.80) children; Saturday, Sunday, and holidays 9€ ($8.05) adults, 5.50€ ($4.90) children; 20€ ($17.85) for two adults and up to three children under age 18; an evening card for Monday to Friday after 7pm is 5.50€ ($4.90) for everyone.

are the verdant gardens around the castle. The castle can only be visited March to November on guided tours given every day except Tuesday at 11am and 2, 3, 4, and 5pm. If there are classical concerts, there is no 5pm tour. Adults pay 3€ ($2.70), children under 12, 1.50€ ($1.35).

One of the highlights of Badenweiler's cultural scene is the four-times-per-year concert series conducted inside the town's most prestigious hotel, the Römerbad (see below), in March, June, September, and November. All tickets cost 29€ to 35€ ($25.90–$31.25) and are sold exclusively by the hotel itself, often as part of overnight packages.

## WHERE TO STAY

**Hotel Ritter** ★ Informal and personal, this hotel is composed of a trio of buildings. The oldest and most traditional looking is a 150-year-old chalet that contains the cheapest of the accommodations. Newer and somewhat more comfortable lodgings lie within a pair of relatively new annexes. Rooms are cozy simple, and modern, with clean bathrooms containing shower-tub combinations.

Friedrichstrasse 2 (a 10-min. walk west from the center), 79410 Badenweiler. ✆ **07632/83-10.** Fax 07632/831299. www.hotelritter.de. 75 units. 150€–230€ ($133.95–$205.40) double; 195€–232€ ($174.15–$207.20) suite. Rates include breakfast. Half board is included for 2 or more nights; otherwise it costs 13€ ($11.60) per person. AE, MC, V. **Amenities:** Restaurant; bar; pool; health club; spa; sauna; massage; room service; babysitting; laundry/dry cleaning. *In room:* TV, minibar, hair dryer.

**Hotel Römerbad** ★★★ This is the best, most elaborate, and most historic spa and hotel in town, attracting urbanites in need of R&R from throughout Germany. The staff is steeped in an old-world sense of courtliness. The clientele has included Nietzsche, Thomas Mann, and Andy Warhol. The domes, mansard roofs, and balconies of this bone-white structure inspire a comparison to an elaborate wedding cake. Inside, the hotel combines an opera-house grandeur with antiques, ornate ceiling medallions, and touches of gilt. Rooms are traditionally furnished, often spacious, and beautifully maintained, with sumptuous beds and bathrooms containing shower-tub combinations.

The Römerbad is also known for its seasonal presentations of concerts. The hotel's concert hall, built in the early 1800s as a shelter for horses and carriages, is sought out by music lovers throughout the country. A series of classical or jazz concerts, each performed over a period of about 4 days, is presented three or four times a year. For information, contact the hotel directly.

Schlossplatz 1, 79410 Badenweiler. ✆ **07632/700.** Fax 07632/70200. www.hotel-roemerbad.de. 82 units. 185€–250€ ($165.20–$223.25) double; from 290€ ($258.95) suite. Rates include breakfast. AE, DC, MC, V. Parking 5€ ($4.45). **Amenities:** Restaurant; bar; 2 pools; 2 tennis courts; health club; room service; massage; babysitting; laundry/dry cleaning. *In room:* TV, minibar, hair dryer, safe.

**Hotel Schwarzmatt** ★★ Although it ranks behind the Römerbad (see above), this hotel is a consistently popular choice, thanks to its lack of pretension and hardworking, English-speaking staff. The modern, three-story building is adorned with flower boxes along its balconies and flanked by verdant evergreens. The comfortable rooms range from medium to large; all have elegant beds and immaculate bathrooms, with shower-tub combinations.

Schwarzmattstrasse 6 (a short walk east of the town center), 79410 Badenweiler. ✆ **07632/8-20-10.** Fax 07632/820120. 41 units. 224€–304€ ($200.05–$271.45) double; 334€ ($298.25) suite. Rates include breakfast. AE, MC, V. Indoor parking 6.15€ ($5.50); outdoor parking free. **Amenities:** Restaurant; bar; lounge; pool; health club; room service; laundry/dry cleaning. *In room:* TV, hair dryer, safe.

**Romantik Hotel zur Sonne** ★ Comfortable and cozy, this hotel occupies a rambling chalet that was built in stages beginning around 350 years ago. Rooms come in a variety of shapes and sizes and are attractively furnished, with traditional Black Forest motifs and the views of a quiet street near the center of the resort. All are exceedingly comfortable and well maintained with bathrooms containing shower-tub combinations.

Moltkestrasse 4, 79410 Badenweiler. ✆ **07632/75-08-0.** Fax 07632/75-08-65. www.romantik-hotel-zur-sonne.de. 55 units. 105€–120€ ($93.75–$107.15) double. Rates include breakfast. Half board 8€ ($7.15) per person. AE, DC, MC, V. Parking 5€ ($4.45) for garage. **Amenities:** Restaurant; lounge; room service; laundry/dry cleaning. *In room:* TV, minibar, hair dryer.

## WHERE TO DINE

**Romantik Hotel zur Sonne** ITALIAN/GERMAN This hotel is more famous among locals for its cuisine than for its rooms. The Weinstube decor includes old paneling and timbers. Menu items feature a savory mixture of German and Italian cuisine, including braised guinea fowl with arugula; carpaccio of veal with arugula and shaved Parmesan cheese; lobster cocktail; and ravioli stuffed either with lobster and sage, or with ham and ricotta, according to your tastes. In springtime, an entire menu category is devoted exclusively to variations on asparagus.

Moltkestrasse 4. ✆ **07632/75-08-0.** Reservations recommended. Main courses 11€–25€ ($9.80–$22.35) fixed-price menu 35€–58€ ($31.25–$51.80). AE, DC, MC, V. Daily noon–2pm and 6–9pm.

**Schwarzmatt** REGIONAL/INTERNATIONAL There's nothing about this restaurant that's homey or traditional. Instead, you'll find an airy, high-ceilinged, modern decor with views out over the garden. The well-prepared food consists of specialties of the Black Forest, as well as such international dishes as steaks, pastas, salads, and casseroles. The menu is ever changing but always good. The kitchen staff is skillful, and the service professional. Every afternoon from 3 to 5pm, there's a buffet with an impressive assortment of regional and international cakes and other treats served with coffee.

In the Hotel Schwarzmatt, Schwarzmattstrasse 6. ✆ **07632/8-20-10.** Main courses 17.90€–28.10€ ($16–$25.10); fixed-price menu 45€–54€ ($40.20–$48.20). AE, MC, V. Daily noon–2pm and 7–10pm.

# 3 Titisee ★

53km (33 miles) E of Freiburg, 160km (99 miles) W of Stuttgart

Titisee is the quintessential German retreat, favored by thousands for its ability to soothe, relax, and refresh the spirit and body. This small lakeside resort, which can be traversed on foot within about 12 minutes, offers access to all the natural bounty of the Schwarzwald. Well-marked hiking trails lead up the hillsides. Motorized vehicles are forbidden on the lake, for the sake of swimmers and general tranquility. Nearby rises the Feldberg, at 1,525m (5,000 ft.), the highest point in the Black Forest.

Titisee has a year-round population of 2,000, although on busy summer days when visitors come in from nearby cities such as Freiburg, the population can easily swell to three times that amount. More facilities are available at the more workaday community of Neustadt, about 6km (4 miles) away.

## ESSENTIALS

**GETTING THERE** **By Train** From Freiburg, trains arrive at intervals of every 30 minutes (trip time: 45 min.). The Titisee rail station is on Parkstrasse (✆ **07651/8298**). For information call ✆ **01805/99-66-33.**

**By Bus** Bus connections into Titisee are mostly limited to rural hamlets within the surrounding Schwarzwald. For information, call the local bus company, **Südbaden Bus GmbH,** at ✆ **07651/5120.**

**By Car** Titisee is set near the junction of highway B31 and B317. It's clearly marked from each of the larger towns that surround it. Driving time from Freiburg is 45 to 60 minutes, depending on traffic; from Stuttgart the trip takes 90 minutes.

**VISITOR INFORMATION** Contact the tourist office at Strandbadstrasse 4 (✆ **07651/98040**). May to October, it's open Monday to Friday 8am to noon and 1:30 to 5:30pm, Saturday 10am to noon and 3 to 5pm, and Sunday 10am to noon. November to April, it's open Monday to Friday only, from 8am to noon and 1:30 to 5:30pm. There's another tourist office in nearby Neustadt, at Sebastian-Kneipp-Anlage (✆ **07651/20-62-50**), maintaining the same hours.

## EXPLORING THE AREA

The cold, clear waters of Lake Titisee are among the most sought after in the region. The town's premier bathing spot is **Schwimmbad Titisee,** Strandbadstrasse (✆ **07651/8272**), which combines the chlorinated waters of the town's largest swimming pool with immediate access to a sandy beach adjacent to the lake, complete with cabanas, showers, and refreshment stands. Entrance to the complex costs 3€ ($2.70) adults, 1.50€ ($1.35) children and students. It's open April to May, Monday to Friday 4 to 9:30pm, Saturday 2 to 7pm; open daily June to September 15, 9am to 8pm.

Except for a handful of medium-size steamers that slowly circumnavigate the lake (see below), local ordinances allow only rowboats, foot-operated paddleboats, and electric (not gas-operated) motorboats on the water's surface, a rule that keeps noise, pollution, and rowdiness to a minimum. You can rent rowboats and paddleboats for 5€ to 8€ ($4.45–$7.15) per ½ hour. About a half-dozen purveyors of these rental craft line the edges of the Seestrasse, the town's main lakefront promenade; the two best are **Drubba** (✆ **07651/981200**), and **Schweizer-Winterhalder** (✆ **07651/8214**).

Schweizer-Winterhalder also operates **lake steamers,** which provide a more comfortable excursion. June to September, they depart during the day at hourly intervals from the company's pier. Trips last about 40 minutes and are priced at 3€ ($2.70) per person. Don't expect museums or monuments at this outdoorsy resort. Spa clients within Titisee head for the facilities within the **Hotel Brügger,** Am See, Strandbadstrasse 14 (✆ **07651/8010**), which are open to residents of other hotels. In nearby Neustadt, the **Kneipp-Kur,** in the Kurkpark (✆ **07651/1270**), offers an equivalent spa facility, which offers treatments for cardiac and vascular disorders, rheumatism, and intestinal diseases.

Shoppers and boaters head to the stores that line the lakefront **Seestrasse.** In the early evening, a Bavarian-style marching band promenades along the lakefront, its members stopping at various hotels en route.

## WHERE TO STAY

**Brugger am See** *Value* This is one of the most affordable spa hotels around the waterfront. Its allure lies in its relaxation and beauty treatments. The building is a modified chalet, with balconies and an all-window dining room. Rooms are contemporary and mostly good size, with exceedingly comfortable furnishings and bathrooms containing shower-tub combinations.

Strandbadstrasse 14, 79822 Titisee. ✆ **07651/80-10.** Fax 07651/82-38. www.hotel-brugger.de. 65 units. 125€–155€ ($111.65–$138.40) double. Rates include breakfast. Half board 23.50€ ($21) per person. MC, V. Free parking. **Amenities:** Restaurant; lounge; pool; health spa; salon; room service; massage; laundry/dry cleaning. *In room:* TV, hair dryer.

**Parkhotel Waldeck** ★ *Value* This hotel is extremely popular, and for good reason—it offers tremendous value and numerous luxuries. A richly decorated interior with Oriental rugs, hexagonal floor tiles, and a beamed and paneled wooden ceiling greets you, along with the bright faces of the helpful staff. The exterior is sheltered against a pine-covered hillock. The small rooms are colorful and comfortable. All bathrooms contain shower-tub combinations.

Parkstrasse 6, 78922 Titisee. ✆ **07651/80-90.** Fax 07651/8-09-99. www.parkhotelwaldeck.de. 53 units. 86€–130€ ($76.80–$116.10) double; 184€ ($164.30) suite for 2. Rates include buffet breakfast. AE, DC, MC, V. Parking in garage 5€ ($4.45). **Amenities:** 2 restaurants; bar; lounge; 2 pools; health club; sauna; solarium; room service; laundry/dry cleaning. *In room:* TV, minibar, hair dryer, safe.

**Trescher's Schwarzwaldhotel am See** ★★ This sprawling hotel, right in the center of the resort, is the most comprehensive in Titisee. It's composed of three massive annexes, each bordering a flower-filled courtyard constructed on a platform built directly into the waters of the lake. The spacious rooms are graceful and conservatively decorated, all containing bathrooms with shower-tub combinations.

Seestrasse 10, 79822 Titisee-Neustadt. ✆ **07651/805-0.** Fax 07651/8116. www.schwarzwaldhotel-trescher.de. 101 units. 128€–200€ ($114.30–$178.60) double; 215€–306€ ($192–$273.25) suite. AE, DC, MC, V. Parking 11€ ($9.80). Closed Nov 1–Dec 15. **Amenities:** Restaurant; bar; pool; health club; room service; babysitting; laundry/dry cleaning. *In room:* TV, minibar, hair dryer, safe.

## WHERE TO DINE

**Trescher's Schwarzwaldhotel am See** ★ INTERNATIONAL/BLACK FOREST The formal dining room in this hotel (recommended above), with picture windows opening onto the lake, is the finest choice for cuisine at Titisee. Diners here enjoy refined service and sublime cuisine. Many of the chef's specialties are regional. Appetizers include melon with Black Forest ham and carpaccio of beef with Parmesan. As for main courses, the Black Forest trout is delectably broiled and served with parsley potatoes, and there's also a hunter's plate, Black Forest style, with Spätzle (dumplings). A good authentic regional choice is the boiled calf's head and tongue, served in an onion-red wine sauce. For dessert, try the Black Forest cherry bombé.

Seestrasse 10. ✆ **07651/805-0.** Reservations required. Main courses 17.40€–27.10€ ($15.55–$24.20); fixed-price lunch 30€ ($26.80). AE, DC, MC, V. Daily 7am–11pm. Closed Nov 7–Dec 20.

## NEARBY PLACES TO STAY & DINE

Just 5km (3 miles) west of Titisee, or 32km (20 miles) east of Freiburg, lies **Hinterzarten,** one of the major pockets of posh within the Black Forest. You may want to retreat here instead of Titisee itself, as Hinterzarten is more tranquil and luxurious. In the center of town stands St. Oswald's, a church constructed in 1146.

**Hotel Reppert** ★ Although not rated as highly as the Park Hotel Adler (see below), this is a good second choice, a luxurious and traditional hotel in a sunny and central location in a church meadow fronting the village pond. Its many rooms open onto balconies, each shaded by an umbrella. All units come with shower-tub combination bathrooms. A rich, warm ambience inhabits the comfortable, well-furnished rooms. The traditional lobby is filled with antiques.

Adlerweg 21–23, 79856 Hinterzarten. ✆ **07652/1208-0.** Fax 07652/1208-11. www.reppert.de. 43 units. 156€–216€ ($139.30–$192.90) double; 216€–336€ ($192.90–$300.05) suite. Rates include buffet breakfast. Half board 13€–27€ ($11.60–$24.10) per person. AE, DC, MC, V. Garage parking 8€ ($7.15). Closed Nov 24–Dec 12. **Amenities:** Restaurant; lounge; 3 pools; tennis courts; health club; 2 Jacuzzis; steam room; room service; babysitting; laundry/dry cleaning. *In room:* TV, minibar, hair dryer.

**Park Hotel Adler** ★★★ This is one of the great inns of the Black Forest. Chic and country estate-ish, the inn suggests luxury at every turn, with a wealth of leisure facilities. It's located in the middle of a lovely 4ha (10-acre) park. Rooms are sumptuously appointed and beautifully maintained, and many are quite spacious. Beds are so comfortable you won't want to get out of them, and the beautiful bathrooms are equipped with shower-tub combinations. The hotel's family ownership dates from 1446.

Adlerplatz 3, 79856 Hinterzarten. ✆ **07652/1270.** Fax 07652/127-717. www.parkhoteladler.de. 90 units. 180€–230€ ($160.75–$205.40) double; 250€–360€ ($223.25–$321.50) junior suite; 297€–530€ ($265.20–$473.30)suite. Rates include buffet breakfast. AE, DC, MC, V. Parking 8€ ($7.15). **Amenities:** 3 restaurants; bar; pool; driving range; tennis courts; health spa; Jacuzzi; sauna; salon; room service; babysitting; laundry/dry cleaning. *In room:* TV, minibar, hair dryer, safe.

## 4 Triberg ★

138km (86 miles) SW of Stuttgart, 48km (30 miles) NE of Freiburg

Triberg, deep in the heart of the Black Forest, is home to the highest waterfall in the country. It also claims to be the birthplace of the cuckoo clock. If you're looking for an interesting traditional timepiece, this is the place to find it. You'll also find many little shops selling woodcarvings, music boxes, and other traditional crafts. ***Warning:*** Because there is a certain enchantment here, Triberg is virtually overrun with tour buses in summer, and the traffic tie-ups on the road to Triberg can be horrendous.

### ESSENTIALS

**GETTING THERE** **By Plane** The nearest major airport is at Stuttgart, 2½ hours away by train.

**By Train** Trains arrive daily from Munich (trip time: 4½ hr.) and from Frankfurt (trip time: 3 hr.). The **Triberg Bahnhof** is on the Konstanz–Singen–Villingen–Offenburg Schwarzwaldbahn rail line, with frequent connections in all directions. Call ✆ **01805/99-66-33** for schedules and information.

**By Bus** Regional bus service in the Black Forest area is provided by **SBG Südbaden Bus GmbH** in Villingen (✆ **07721/9-28-521**).

**By Car** Access is via the A5 Autobahn north and south; exit at Offenburg and then follow the signs along Route 33 south.

**VISITOR INFORMATION** For tourist information, contact the **Kurverwaltung,** Kurhaus (✆ **07722/95-32-30**), open year-round Monday to Friday 9am to 5pm and May to October also Saturday 10am to noon.

### EXPLORING THE AREA

The waterfall, called the **Gutach Falls** ★, is exceptional, but be prepared to walk an hour or so to reach it. The falls drop some 160m (530 ft.), spilling down in seven stages. To get there, you park your car in a designated area near the Gutach Bridge (in the town center) and then walk along a marked trail. It's open daily 9am to 6pm in summer and costs 1.20€ ($1.05) adults, .50€ (45¢) children. At the bottom of the falls is a year-round cafe/restaurant serving the famed Black Forest cake for which, by then, you'll have worked up an appetite.

**Schwarzwald-Museum of Triberg,** Wallfahrstrasse 4 (✆ **07722/44-34**), brings the olden days of the Black Forest vividly to life, with displays of dresses, handcrafts, furnishings, bird music boxes, and, of course, clocks and clockmaking. You can also see the famed Schwarzwaldbahn railway, which really works, a mineral exhibit of the area, and Europe's largest barrel organ collection. The museum is open May to October, daily 10am to 6pm; November to April, daily 10am to 5pm. Admission is 3€ ($2.70) adults, 2€ ($1.80) students, and 1.50€ ($1.35) for children.

One of the most beautiful churches in the Black Forest, the **Wallfahrtkirche Maria in der Tannen (Church of Our Lady of the Fir Trees),** is within easy reach. Built in the early 18th century, it has superb baroque furnishings, including a remarkable pulpit.

After a visit to the church, drive to the **Freilichtmuseum Schwarzwälder** in Gutach (✆ **0783/935-60**), which contains original Black Forest homes as many as 4 centuries old. In summer, guides demonstrate weaving on some of the looms. The museum is open April to October, daily 10am to 5pm. Admission is 4.50€ ($4) for adults and 3€ ($2.70) for children and students. From the A5, turn off at the Offenburg exit and follow B33 toward Gengenbach, Hausach, and Triberg; at Hausach, turn right to Gutach.

A 16km (10-mile) drive south of Triberg is the **Deutsches Uhrenmuseum (German Clock Museum),** Gerwigstrasse 11, in Furtwangen (✆ **07723/92-01-17**). It's open daily November to April 10am to 5pm and May to October 9am to 6pm. Admission is 3€ ($2.70) for adults and 2€ ($1.80) for children. This museum presents a history of timepieces, including displays of a wide variety of Black Forest clocks, some from the early 18th century. Many are elaborate and complicated. Look for the mechanical music automata and the cuckoo clocks.

## WHERE TO STAY

**Romantik Parkhotel Wehrle** ★★ This is the finest and most traditional inn in the area. Built in the early 1600s, Parkhotel Wehrle was acquired around 1730 by the family that has owned it ever since. Its lemon-yellow walls and gabled mansard roof occupy one of the most prominent street corners in town. The main house offers an old-world atmosphere, but forest-loving vacationers often request accommodation near the woods in a separate chalet, where a pool and breeze-filled balconies create a modern sylvan retreat. The good-size rooms are beautifully furnished and individually decorated, sometimes with antiques. All bathrooms are neatly kept with shower-tub combinations.

Gartenstrasse 24 (1.5km/1 mile from the train station), 78098 Triberg. ✆ **07722/86-02-0.** Fax 07722/86-02-90. www.parkhotel-wehrle.de. 52 units. 130€–210€ ($116.10–$187.55) double; from 245€ ($218.80) suite. Rates include buffet breakfast. AE, DC, MC, V. Free parking outdoors; 7.50€ ($6.70) in garage. **Amenities:** 3 restaurants; bar; 2 pools; health club; sauna; room service; babysitting; laundry/dry cleaning. *In room:* TV, dataport, minibar, hair dryer, safe.

---

### *Finds* Stop for Clocks

You may want to make a stop along the B33 between Triberg and Hornberg at the **Haus der 1000 Uhren (House of 1,000 Clocks),** An der Bundesstrasse 33, 78098 Triberg-Gemmelsbach (✆ **07722/96300**). You'll recognize the shop immediately because of the giant cuckoo clock and waterwheel in front. A painter of clock faces, Josef Weisser, launched the business in 1824; today his great-great-grandson owns the place. The shop is open Monday to Saturday 9am to 5pm. It ships to the United States and Canada and takes all major credit cards. There's another branch in the center of Triberg, near the entrance to the waterfall.

---

### *Moments* Wunderhiking in the Black Forest

You can see the loveliest parts of the Black Forest by hiking the ancient trail of the cuckoo-clock traders. Really. The market trail follows the route of the traders who, centuries ago, carried the famous Black Forest clocks across Europe. Along the village-to-village journey, you'll pass through deep, fragrant pinewoods and sunny pastures where farmhouses are set scenically on hillsides.

The circle trail starts at Triberg, with its waterfalls. An arrangement with a series of hotels along the trail, beginning with the **Parkhotel Wehrle** (see below), allows you to hike with only a small rucksack; vans haul your luggage on to the next hotel. You can hike anywhere from 1 to 2 to 10 days and more if you have the time (but most hikers have their fill long before this). Distances for a day's hike between hotels can be anywhere from 20km to 27km (12–17 miles).

Clearly marked signs guide you across this easy trail, and the Parkhotel Wehrle provides detailed road descriptions and a road map, with instructions in English, to set you on your way. Restaurants and farmhouses offering food and refreshment are not far apart, and the area is quite safe, even for a woman walking alone.

**Römischer Kaiser** *Value* You get old-style charm here and old-style prices, too. This comfortable, charmingly preserved hotel has been owned by several generations of the same family since 1840. The exterior has lots of exposed wood. Rooms come in a wide range of shapes and sizes, but all are pleasant and well maintained. Bathrooms are roomy with shower-tub combinations.

Sommerauerstrasse 35 (just over 1.5km/1 mile outside Triberg), 78098 Triberg-Nussbach. ✆ **07722/9-69-40.** Fax 07722/96-94-29. www.roemischer-kaiser.com. 26 units. 63€–68€ ($56.25–$60.70) double. Rates include buffet breakfast. AE, DC, MC, V. Free parking. Closed Nov 15–Dec 7. **Amenities:** Restaurant; lounge; room service. *In room:* TV, hair dryer.

## WHERE TO DINE

**Parkhotel Wehrle** ★ CONTINENTAL People come from great distances to eat at this fine, famous restaurant. Meals here are accompanied by the ticking of a stately grandfather clock; meanwhile, the clientele relaxes in the comfort of cane-bottomed French-style armchairs. The cuisine is intelligent and imaginative, with a focus on natural flavors. Even simple dishes have a certain flair. Try the trout or saddle of venison with juniperberry cream sauce and Spätzle. A traditional dessert is apples baked with pine honey and flambéed with Kirschwasser. Some of the game specialties are prepared for two.

Marktplatz. ✆ **07722/8-60-20.** Reservations required. Main courses 16.40€–28.90€ ($14.65–$25.80); fixed-price lunch 32.70€ ($29.20); fixed-price dinner 36.80€–43.50€ ($32.85–$38.85). AE, DC, MC, V. Daily noon–2pm and 6–10pm.

## 5 Freudenstadt

92km (57 miles) N of Freiburg

One of the most important transportation hubs in the northern tier of the Black Forest is Freudenstadt, a riverside town known for clear air, streaming sunshine, and a sense of cleanliness and conservatism. Originally founded in 1599 by Duke Friedrich I of Württemberg, Freudenstadt provided a home at the time for Protestants fleeing religious persecution within Carinthia, in southern Austria. French troops set most of the town ablaze in the closing days of World War II, but it was completely rebuilt, more or less to the original plans, before 1950.

## ESSENTIALS

**GETTING THERE** **By Train** Trains from Frankfurt arrive at hourly intervals throughout the day (trip time: 3½ hours). There are also 10 trains per day from Munich (trip time: 4½ hours). Freudenstadt has two railway stations, the **Stadtbahnhof** (✆ **07441/4554** for information), in the center of town, and the **Hauptbahnhof** (✆ **07441/2015** for information), about a mile south of the center. Most trains stop at both. For information, call ✆ **01805/99-66-33.**

**By Bus** Bus travel tends to be convenient only for those coming from surrounding hamlets. Buses stop at both the Bahnhofplatz and the Marktplatz. For information, call ✆ **07441/860-130.**

**By Car** Driving from Stuttgart, following the B28, takes about a ¼ hour; from Karlsruhe via the B462, about a ½ hour.

**VISITOR INFORMATION** The **Tourist Information Office** is at Am Promenadeplatz 1 (✆ **07441/86-47-10**). It's open year-round Monday to Friday 9am to 6pm, Saturday 10am to 1pm.

## EXPLORING THE TOWN

Freudenstadt's appeal lies not so much in the town itself, as in its ideal location in the midst of the best hiking and camping country in the Black Forest. Trails wind for hundreds of miles through the nearby hills. In winter, the snow-covered paths are great for skiing.

Unlike many German towns, Freudenstadt has no castle overshadowing it, but it certainly does have an enormous castle square. This plot of land, the largest marketplace or **Marktplatz** ★ in Germany, was laid out in the 16th century for a castle that was never built. History's loss is today's gain. The market square that greets the visitor to Freudenstadt is a maze of lawns and concrete, broken by patches of flowers and kiosks. The buildings surrounding the square are mainly postwar, because the air raids and fires of World War II almost completely destroyed the city. A few of the old Renaissance structures on the square have been reconstructed, up to their neat little archways and gabled roofs.

The town takes pride in its **Stadtkirche,** Marktplatz (✆ **07441/6554**), dating from the 17th century. The unusual L-shaped architecture of the church brings the two main aisles together at right angles. Over the entrance stand identical towers, topped with rounded domes and narrow spires. The church's most important treasure is the 12th-century reading desk, supported by carved and painted likenesses of the Evangelists. The church is open daily 9am to 5pm. Entrance is free.

Regrettably, Freudenstadt doesn't have any other museums or attractions worth mentioning, with the exception of a small regional folk and crafts museum, the **Heimatmuseum,** in the Stadthaus, Marktplatz (✆ **07441/6177**). It's open Monday 3 to 6pm, Tuesday and Wednesday 9 to 11am and 3 to 6pm, Thursday 9 to 11am and 3 to 7pm, Friday 3 to 6pm, and Sunday 10am to noon; closed on Saturday. Entrance is free.

## WHERE TO STAY

**Hotel Bären** This establishment is best known for its well-managed restaurant (see "Where to Dine," below), but it's also an eminently respectable hotel.

The cozy interior, lined with old panels and capped with heavy ceiling beams, might remind you of the inside of a prosperous local farmhouse. Rooms are cozy, traditionally decorated, and well-maintained, containing shower-tub combinations. The staff is charming and polite, managing to convey a nostalgic sense of traditional Germany.

33 Langestrasse (near the Marktplatz), 72250 Freudenstadt. ✆ **07441/27-29.** Fax 07441/2887. 24 units. 80€–87€ ($71.45–$77.70) double. MC, V. Free parking. **Amenities:** Restaurant; lounge; room service; laundry/dry cleaning. *In room:* TV, hair dryer.

**Hotel Hohenried im Rosengarten** ★ This three-story hotel is designed like a modern version of an alpine chalet. The garden contains more than 2,000 well-tended rose bushes. Views from the windows of the comfortable and contemporary-looking rooms overlook a golf course and stately trees. In summertime, the balconies are adorned with geranium-filled flower boxes. All the accommodations come with neatly tiled bathrooms with shower units. The staff is polite and speaks English.

Zeppelinstrasse 5 (about 1.5km/1 mile south of Freudenstadt's center), 72250 Freudenstadt. ✆ **07441/24-14.** Fax 07441/25-59. hotelhohenried@gmx.de. 27 units. 98€–105€ ($87.50–$93.75) double; 115€ ($102.70) suite. AE, DC, MC, V. Bus 14. **Amenities:** Restaurant; bar; lounge; pool; health club; sauna; room service; laundry/dry cleaning. *In room:* TV, hair dryer.

**Luz Posthotel** This is a solidly reliable and dependable choice. This hotel, built in 1809, was almost demolished during World War II and then was reconstructed along more modern lines shortly thereafter. Since then, strands of climbing ivy have added to a more antique-looking appearance. Today, this comfortable, contemporary, four-story hotel combines touches of Black Forest nostalgia with a smooth, conservatively modern decor. Rooms are medium-size, clean, tastefully modern, and comfortable, all of which contain bathrooms and shower-tub combinations.

Stuttgarterstrasse 5, 72250 Freudenstadt. ✆ **07441/8970.** Fax 07441/84533. 52 units. 76€–97€ ($67.85–$86.60) double; 97€ ($86.60) suite. Rates include breakfast. AE, DC, MC, V. Free parking. **Amenities:** 2 restaurants; bar; room service; laundry/dry cleaning. *In room:* TV.

## WHERE TO DINE

**Hotel Bären** *Value* SWABIAN/GERMAN This is an attractive, 200-year-old inn. The warmly decorated, richly beamed and paneled interior will soothe urban hearts. The well-prepared cuisine emphasizes fresh Atlantic and Mediterranean fish. Look for filet of monkfish with garlic and parsley, filets of sole with a Riesling sauce, spicy fish soup redolent with saffron and garlic, savory game dishes, and beer and wine from every part of Germany.

33 Langestrasse. ✆ **07441/27-29.** Reservations recommended. Main courses 9€–20€ ($8.05–$17.85); fixed-menu 16€–24€ ($14.30–$21.45). MC, V. Sun–Thurs 11am–3:30pm and 6–10pm; Fri 11am–3:30pm.

**Jägerstüble** SWABIAN/GERMAN Like most of the buildings around it, this is an excellent re-creation of a medieval house that was severely damaged during World War II. Inside, foaming mugs of beer and hardworking waitresses in folkloric costumes contribute to an unpretentious re-creation of the Germany of another era. The hearty and savory dishes include *Eisbein* (veal shank) with sauerkraut, farmer's omelets, venison steak prepared with garlic and red wine, and goulash of venison.

Marktplatz 12. ✆ **07441/23-87.** Reservations recommended. Main courses 16€–25€ ($14.30–$22.35). MC, V. Tues–Sat 11am–2pm and Tues–Sun 7–9pm.

## WHERE TO STAY NEARBY

If you want to experience the Schwarzwald at its most isolated and remote, consider a stay at either of the following two hotels, which are positioned south and north of the hamlet of Baiersbronn, respectively. Baiersbronn lies 6km (4 miles) northwest of Freudenstadt. Trains arrive in Baiersbronn about once an hour from Stuttgart and Karlsruhe, stopping in Baiersbronn before continuing south for another 6km (4 miles) to Freudenstadt. Local buses (marked "Baiersbronn") depart from the Marktplatz in Freudenstadt for Baiersbronn, but there are only about four a day, and they won't take you anywhere near either of the two hotels. For the short distance involved, it's a lot more convenient to take any of the taxis lined up in Freudenstadt's Marktplatz.

**Hotel Bareiss** ★★ This deluxe resort hotel is equivalent in most ways to the Hotel Traube Tonbach (see below), but it's a bit less formal and a lot less stiff. It provides a soothing, carefully orchestrated, well-manicured environment, where peace, quiet, and access to the surrounding forest are fiercely guarded. You'll find lots of urban refugees on-site, recuperating from stressful careers. Rooms are spacious, carefully maintained, conservatively modern, and very comfortable. All have views over the forest and have bathrooms with shower-tub combinations.

Gärtenbühlweg 14, 072270 Baiersbronn/Mitteltal. ✆ **07442/470.** Fax 07442/47320. www.bareiss.com/engl/philo/index.htm. 100 units. 130€–160€ ($116.10–$142.90) double; 160€–190€ ($142.90–$169.65) apartment; from 200€ ($178.60) suite. Rates include breakfast. AE, DC, MC, V. Garage parking 6€ ($5.35). From the center of Baiersbronn, follow signs pointing to Hotel Bareiss for 10km (6 miles), heading south. **Amenities:** 4 restaurants; bar; 2 pools; tennis court; health club; sauna; bike rental; salon; room service; massage; babysitting; laundry/dry cleaning. *In room:* TV, minibar, hair dryer, safe.

**Hotel Traube Tonbach** ★★★ This is the grande dame of Black Forest resorts. In 1957, this establishment was massively enlarged into the stately looking, many-balconied resort you see today, and immediately attracted one of the grandest resort clienteles in Germany. Set closer to Baiersbronn (only about a mile north of town) than its competitor, the Bareiss (see above), the Traube Tonbach prides itself on its conservatism, its strictly enforced sense of peace and quiet, and the glamour of its very upscale clientele. Rooms are good-size, solid, well built, quiet, and very, very comfortable. All bathrooms are neatly appointed with shower-tub combinations. Ask the staff for advice on nearby hiking trails.

Ortsteil Tonbach, Tonbachstrasse 237, 72270 Baiersbronn. ✆ **07442/4920.** Fax 07442/492-692. www.traube-tonbach.de. 175 units. 210€–278€ ($187.55–$248.25) double; 476€–510€ ($425.05–$455.45) suite. Rates include breakfast and parking. Half board 16€ ($14.30) per person. AE, DC, MC, V. Parking 4€ ($3.55). **Amenities:** 3 restaurants; bar; lounge; 4 pools; tennis courts; health club; whirlpool; sauna; steam room; bowling alley; room service; massage; babysitting; laundry/dry cleaning. *In room:* TV, minibar, hair dryer, safe.

# 6 Calw

20km (12½ miles) S of Pforzheim, 66km (41 miles) N of Freudenstadt

Many residents of other parts of Germany call Calw the most appealingly folkloric town in the Black Forest. Hermann Hesse, who was born here in 1877, described Calw as "the most beautiful place I know."

## ESSENTIALS

**GETTING THERE** **By Train** Trains arrive at Calw's Bahnhof at hourly intervals from both Stuttgart and Karlsruhe. Both cities are about an hour away. For railway information, call ✆ **01805/99-66-33.**

**By Bus** Buses that travel between Horb, Nagold, and Pforzheim make stops at Calw's Bahnhofplatz. For information, call ✆ **07051/968850.**

**By Car** Calw lies midway between Pforzheim and Nagold, along Highway B463. From the A8 Autobahn, exit at the signs indicating Calw.

**VISITOR INFORMATION** The **Tourist Information office** in Calw is at Marktbrücke 7 (✆ **07051/96-88-10**). It's open Monday to Friday 9am to 12:30pm and 2 to 5pm (to 6:30pm Thurs), and also Saturday April to October 9:30am to 12:30pm.

## EXPLORING THE TOWN

Calw's allure derives from its impressive and meticulously maintained roster of late–17th and early–18th century houses, whose half-timbered facades add an undeniable charm to such sites as the Marktplatz. The town's most prominent bridge, the 14th-century **Nikolausbrücke,** in the center, merits a stroll in admiration of its carefully chiseled masonry.

The birthplace of Herman Hesse, the **Hesse Haus,** Marktplatz 30 (✆ **07051/7522**), is a literary shrine for scholars and fans. Entrance is 2.50€ ($2.25) adults, 1.50€ ($1.35) children and students. The only other formal attraction in town is a free small-scale folklore museum called **Palais Vischer,** Bischofsstrasse 10 (same phone as Hesse Haus).

## WHERE TO STAY

**Hotel Kloster Hirsau** The best place for overnighting lies right outside of town 2km (1¼ miles) to the north in the direction of Hirsau. Parts of the foundation of this historic hotel date from 1092, when the site functioned as a monastery that was noted for housing overnight visitors. Today, the establishment retains its medieval touches and antique charm. The good-size rooms have lots of Schwarzwald-inspired features, including pinewood trim and reproductions of traditional furniture. Bathrooms are tidily kept with shower-tub combinations. The oldest are numbers 114 to 235.

Ortsteil Hirsau, Wildbacher Strasse 2, 75365 Calw. ✆ **07051/9-67-40.** Fax 07051/967-469. www.hotel-kloster-hirsau.de. 43 units. 80€–100€ ($71.45–$89.30) double. Rates include breakfast. Half board 18€ ($16.05) per person. AE, MC, V. Free parking; parking in garage 3€ ($2.70). **Amenities:** Restaurant; lounge; pool; tennis court; health club; sauna; salon; room service; laundry/dry cleaning. *In room:* TV, minibar, hair dryer.

## WHERE TO DINE

**Ratstube** SWABIAN/INTERNATIONAL This is the most popular and reliable restaurant in town. The interior is a labyrinth of masonry-sided rooms.

### *Moments* Off-the-Beaten Trail

The environs of Calw also merit some attention if you have the time. Of exceptional interest is the hamlet of **Zavelstein,** which is signposted in Calw. Follow the road south for 5km (3 miles). A drive to this little hamlet is especially interesting in late March and April, when the meadows blossom with edelweiss and crocuses. You might want to continue south in the direction of Talmühle-Seitzental, where you'll see a sign pointing along a twisting road leading to **Neubulach** (✆ **07053/969-51-0**). Until it closed in the mid-1920s, this was one of the most active silver mines in the Black Forest. Long after it was abandoned, the medical profession learned that its dust-free interior was beneficial in the treatment of asthma. A therapy center is now located inside. The mine's ancient shafts can be visited on guided tours given daily April to November 10am to noon and 2 to 4pm, costing 2€ ($1.80) for adults and 1€ (90¢) for children.

The well-prepared, but not particularly innovative dishes include *Zwiebelrostbraten* (filet of sole in wine sauce); stingray in black butter sauce; trout with almonds or meunière-style; and an array of sausages served with cabbage and roasted potatoes. Service is competent.

The inn also rents the best rooms within the town center.

Marktplatz 12, 75365 Calw. ✆ **07051/9-20-50.** Reservations recommended. Main courses 9€–14€ ($8.05–$12.50). AE, DC, MC, V. Daily 11:30am–2:30pm and 5:30–10pm.

**Restaurant Klosterschanke** SWABIAN/INTERNATIONAL Cozy and historically authentic, this restaurant occupies a trio of dining rooms whose beamed and/or vaulted ceilings in some cases are hundreds of years old. Menu items include fresh house-marinated sardines; rack of lamb with white beans; *Zwiebelrostbraten* (onion-flavored roast beef); monkfish braised in olive oil with herbs; and several kinds of schnitzel. Although cuisine here never reaches the sublime, it's always fresh and competently prepared.

Wildbader Strasse 2. ✆ **07051/96740.** Reservations recommended. Main courses 10€–21.95€ ($8.95–$19.60); fixed-price menu 28.50€–51€ ($25.45–$45.55). DC, V. Lunch noon–2pm; Kafe mit Kuchen (coffee and cakes) 2–5pm; dinner 6–11pm.

## FREUDENSTADT AFTER DARK

In lieu of any real nightlife, locals head for one of the local stubs or beer halls for a "night on the town." Most of these drinking places are within hotels, and two of the best are at the previously recommended Hotel Bären or the Jägerstüble (see above), the latter serving the largest mugs of beer in town. In winter, you can find beer drinkers gathered around the old tile stove of the **Ratskeller,** Marktplatz 8 (✆ **07441/2693**). If you like the place, you can stick around to feast on traditional Swabian dishes such as onion-flavored roast beef served with sauerkraut.

# 7 Pforzheim

35km (22 miles) S of Karlsruhe, 53km (33 miles) SW of Stuttgart

Set at the northern edge of the Black Forest, at the junction of three rivers (the Würm, the Enz, and the Nagold), Pforzheim is one of the Schwarzwald's largest settlements. It was founded by the Romans as a fortified camp, and developed into an important mercantile center during the Middle Ages. Key industries have traditionally included the crafting of jewelry and clock making. Although it was severely damaged by bombs during World War II, Pforzheim is a worthwhile site for an overnight stay between forays into the Black Forest.

## ESSENTIALS

**GETTING THERE** **By Train** Trains pull into Pforzheim at least once an hour from Munich (trip time: 3 hours), Frankfurt (trip time: 2 hours), and Stuttgart (trip time: 1½ hours). The railway station lies within an 8-minute walk of the center. For information, call ✆ **01805/99-66-33.**

**By Bus** Bus travel to Pforzheim is a lot less practical than rail travel. The bus stop is at Leopoldsplatz, in the town center.

**By Car** Pforzheim lies beside the high-speed A-8 Autobahn that stretches between Munich and Karlsruhe. Transit from Stuttgart takes between 75 and 90 minutes; from Munich, around 2½ hours; and from Frankfurt, around 2 hours.

**VISITOR INFORMATION** Head to **Stadinformation,** Marktplatz 1 (✆ **07231/1454560**), open Monday to Friday 9am to 6pm and Saturday 10am to 1pm.

### *Finds* Medieval Excursion from Pforzheim

One of the Schwarzwald's most evocative sights lies 18km (11 miles) to the northeast of Pforzheim, within the agrarian hamlet of Maulbronn. **Kloster Maulbronn** (✆ **07043/92-66-10**) has been called the best-preserved medieval monastery north of the Alps. Most of its more than 30 stone-sided buildings were constructed between 1150 and 1390, within an encircling wall that protected the monks and their allies from outside attackers. The most visible of the buildings is the compound's church, which combines aspects of Romanesque and Gothic architecture, and which influenced the design of later structures throughout central and northern Europe. Look for the complicated irrigation system, still intact, which distributed water to key elements within the compound. Most visitors arrive by car or taxi from the center of Pforzheim, although there's also a bus that departs for Maulbronn from Pforzheim's Leopoldplatz at 50-minute intervals throughout the day. The monastery is open March to October, daily 9am to 5:30pm; November to February, Tuesday to Sunday 9:30am to 5pm. Admission is 4€ ($3.55) adults, 2€ ($1.80) children and students.

## EXPLORING THE TOWN

Much of Pforzheim was demolished by Allied bombs during World War II. Of the limited number of buildings that have been restored to their former grandeur, **Sankt Michaelerskirche (St. Michael's Church),** Schlossberg 10 (✆ **07231/102484**), is the most dramatic. It was built in stages between the 1200s and 1400s and combines aspects of both Romanesque and Gothic architecture. It's open daily 8:30am to 6pm. A fine example of a more modern church is the **Stadtkirche,** on Melanchthonstrasse (no phone), in the town center across from the Parkhotel. Rebuilt from the town's rubble during the 1950s, this is a symbol of Pforzheim's rebirth from the devastation of World War II.

For insights into the role that clock making has always played in Pforzheim, head for the city's **Technisches Museum,** Bleichstrasse 81 (✆ **07231/392869**), where souvenirs and mementos of the clock-making trade commemorate humankind's painstaking efforts to organize time. On the premises is a reconstruction of a clock-making studio from the early 1800s. The museum is open every Wednesday 9am to noon and 3 to 6pm, and every 2nd and 4th Sunday 10am to 5pm. Admission is free, although donations are appreciated.

The equally nostalgic **Schmuckmuseum,** Jahnstrasse 42 (✆ **07231/392-126**), is devoted to Pforzheim's jewelry-making trade. Its collection includes ornaments from the 3rd century B.C. to modern times. The museum is open Tuesday to Sunday 10am to 5pm. Admission is 2.50€ ($2.25).

If you're passionate about botany or gardening, you might enjoy a visit to the **Alpengarten (Alpine Garden),** Auf dem Berg 6 (✆ **07231/70590**), in which about 100,000 varieties of high-altitude plants are grown in a natural-looking milieu. It's set adjacent to the banks of the Würm River, about 3km (2 miles) south of Pforzheim's center, and is open April to November, daily 8am to 7pm. Admission costs 2.50€ ($2.25). To reach it from Pforzheim, follow the signs pointing to Würm.

## WHERE TO STAY

**Hotel Royal** Equivalent in most ways to the Parkhotel (see below), the Royal's only drawback is its location on the outskirts of town. It was built in 1995 in a two-story, modern format. Rooms are small to medium-size, contemporary, sunny, comfortable, clean, and utterly without pretension. All bathrooms contain shower-tub combinations. The staff is polite and well trained.

Wilhelmbeckerstrasse 3A (less than 1.5km/1 mile north of the center), 75179 Pforzheim. ✆ **07231/14250.** Fax 07231/142599. 43 units. 95€–100€ ($84.85–$89.30) double. Rates include breakfast and free parking. AE, DC, V. Bus: 29. **Amenities:** Restaurant; bar; room service; laundry/dry cleaning. *In room:* TV, minibar, hair dryer.

**Parkhotel** ★ Set in the center of town, the four-story, contemporary Parkhotel is the meeting place for most of the civic and charitable organizations in Pforzheim. Inside, you'll find a streamlined, tasteful decor with lots of exposed wood and stone. Rooms are good size, airy, and comfortable with bathrooms containing shower-tub combinations.

Deimlingerstrasse 36, 75175 Pforzheim. ✆ **07231/1610.** Fax 07231/161690. www.parkhotelpforzheim.de. 144 units. 143€–290€ ($127.70–$258.95) double. Rates include breakfast. AE, DC, DISC, MC, V. **Amenities:** 2 restaurants; bar; health club; Jacuzzi; sauna; room service; babysitting; laundry/dry cleaning. *In room:* TV, minibar, hair dryer, safe.

## WHERE TO DINE

**Parkrestaurant** GERMAN This well-managed restaurant offers solid home-style cuisine, a view over the Stadt Theater and the banks of the Enz River, and a polite, well-trained staff. We prefer this place to the Galarestaurant, its more upscale sibling within the same hotel. Menu items include schnitzels, stews, roulades and grills, soups, salads, and hearty, regional desserts layered with chocolate and whipped cream.

In the Parkhotel, Deimlingerstrasse 36. ✆ **07231/1610.** Reservations not necessary. Main courses 20€–42€ ($17.85–$37.50); fixed-price menu 28€–42€ ($25–$37.50). AE, DC, DISC, MC, V. Open daily noon–3pm and 6–11:30pm.

# 8 Baden-Baden ★★

111km (69 miles) W of Stuttgart, 111km (69 miles) NE of Freiburg, 174km (108 miles) S of Frankfurt

Baden-Baden, where the bath-conscious Roman emperor Caracalla once came to ease his arthritic aches, was rediscovered in the 19th century by the nobility of Europe. Swanky clients such as Queen Victoria, Kaiser Wilhelm I, Napoléon III, Berlioz, Brahms, and Dostoyevsky helped make Baden-Baden the most elegant and sophisticated playground in Germany. Tolstoy set a scene in *Anna Karenina* here, though he gave the town a different name. Today, the clientele may have changed, but Baden-Baden still evokes an aura of 19th-century privilege, combined with the most up-to-date facilities. More recent clients have included everybody from Barbra Streisand to Yasser Arafat.

Baden-Baden is the ideal choice for sports and outdoor enthusiasts. Golf, tennis, and horseback riding are all popular here. Lovers of horse racing will enjoy the international racing season each August at Iffezheim Track. The surrounding countryside is good for hiking and mountain climbing. During the winter, Baden-Baden is a convenient center for skiing: After a day on the slopes, you can return to a soothing swim in a thermal pool and a night out at the casino.

## ESSENTIALS

**GETTING THERE** **By Train** Baden-Baden is on major rail lines connecting Frankfurt and Basel, and Stuttgart and Munich. There are 20 trains daily from Stuttgart (trip time: 1 hr. 15 min.); 25 from Munich (trip time: 4 hr. 10 min.), and 45 from Frankfurt (trip time: 3 hr.). For information, call ✆ **01805/99-66-33.** The railway station is at Baden-Oos, north of town; regrettably, it's an expensive 20-minute taxi ride from the town center.

**By Bus** Long-distance bus service is provided to Freudenstadt and Tübingen (Line 1070), operated by **Deutsche Touring GmbH** (✆ **0721/30804** for information).

**By Car** Access to Baden-Baden is via the A5 Autobahn north and south or the A8 Autobahn east and west. The drive south from Frankfurt takes 2 hours; from Munich, about 4 hours.

**VISITOR INFORMATION** For information, contact **Tourist-Information,** Schwarzwaldstrasse 7 (✆ **07221/27-52-00**), daily 9am to 7pm. Also, see www.baden-baden.de/en/index.html.

**GETTING AROUND** Baden-Baden is serviced by a network of buses whose routes coincide at the Leopoldplatz, in the center. Bus 201, which runs at 10-minute intervals, interconnects most of the important sites with the railway station, about 5km (3 miles) from the center. One-way fare is 2€ ($1.80), and a day pass, good for 24 hours of unlimited public transport for two adults and two children, costs 4.75€ ($4.25).

## EXPLORING THE TOWN

**Caracalla-Therme** These baths have been made more pleasing visually by the addition of a round colonnaded extension with splashing and cascading pools. You can decide on your own bath system here. Medicinal treatment includes mud baths, massages, and whirlpools. The slightly radioactive water, rich in sodium chloride, comes from artesian wells 1,800m (6,000 ft.) under the Florentiner Mountain. Its temperature is around 70°C (160°F). Bathers usually begin in cooler pools, working up to the warm water. The baths also have a sauna area, with foot baths and sun baths; sauna temperatures go from 85°C to 90°C (185°F–200°F). You must wear bathing suits in the pools, but everyone goes nude in the saunas.

Römerplatz 1. ✆ **07221/27-59-40.** Admission 13€ ($11.60) for 3 hr., 15€ ($13.40) for 4 hr. Daily 8am–10pm. Bus: 1.

### *Moments* The Town's Preoccupation: Ambling on the 'Ohs'

The center of Baden-Baden activity is **Lichtentaler Allee** ★★, the park promenade along the bank of the Oosbach River (affectionately called the Oos—pronounced *ohs*), which runs through the center of town. As you stroll along this walk, you'll be amazed at the variety not only of exotic shrubs and trees but also of the rhododendrons, azaleas, and roses. At the north end of the park, on the banks of the stream, are the buildings of the **Kurgarten,** including the classical Kurhaus, used as an entertainment complex.

Your hotel can give you full information on the facilities available at both the Friedrichsbad and the Caracalla, which are in the heart of the Altstadt.

**Friedrichsbad** Friedrichsbad, also known as the Old Baths, was built from 1869 to 1877 at the behest of Grand Duke Friedrich von Baden. Following the Roman-Irish method, it takes about 2 hours to have the complete program, which involves a shower, two saunas 55°C to 70°C (130°F–160°F), a brush massage soaping, thermal steam baths, and three freshwater baths ranging from warm to 15°C (60°F). After a 30-minute period of rest and relaxation, you're supposed to feel rejuvenated. Other types of therapy, including massage, electrotherapy, and hydrotherapy, are also offered. Massages are 20.40€ ($18.20) for 20 minutes and 40.50€ ($36.15) for 40 minutes.

Römerplatz 1. ✆ **07221/27-59-20.** Admission 21€ ($18.75) without soap-brush massage, 29€ ($25.90) with soap-brush massage. Mon–Sat noon–10pm; Sun 9am–8pm (last admission 8pm Mon–Sat; 6pm on Sun).

**Trinkhalle (Pump Room)** The spa gardens contain the Pump Room (*Trinkhalle*), where visitors can sip the water. The loggia of the hall is decorated with frescoes depicting Black Forest legends. The springs of Baden-Baden have been recognized for more than 2,000 years, and their composition is almost the same today as when the Romans built their baths here in the 3rd century.

Kaiserallee 3. ✆ **07221/2752-0017.** Free admission. Apr–Oct daily 10am–5:30pm. Bus: 201.

## THE CASINO

**Spielbank** Open year-round, this is the oldest casino in Germany, popular for more than 200 years. Dostoyevsky is said to have written *The Gambler* after he lost his shirt, and almost his mind, at the tables here. The various casino rooms were designed in the style of an elegant French château. Jackets and ties for men are mandatory, as is eveningwear for women. To enter the casino during gambling hours, you must possess a valid passport or identification card and be at least 21 years old.

The historic gaming rooms may be viewed daily 9:30am to noon on a tour costing 4€ ($3.55). For those who want to gamble later, a full day's ticket is available for 6€ ($5.35). The minimum stake is 5€ ($4.45), but visitors are not obligated to play. Hours are daily 2pm to 2am (until 3am on Fri and Sat). Admission is 3€ ($2.70).

Kaiserallee 1. ✆ **07221/2-10-60.** Bus: 1.

## SPORTS & OUTDOOR PURSUITS

For an entirely new perspective on the area, go hot-air ballooning. **Balloon 2000** offers rides between the Black Forest and the Vosges. Contact pilot Jean-Marc Culas (✆ **07223/6-00-02**) for details. A 2-hour, champagne breakfast trip over the Rhine Valley goes for 253€ ($225.95) per person.

For a more up-close and personal experience, rock climbing at all levels and altitudes can be enjoyed on the Battert rocks directly over the city. For a climber's guide, contact the **German Alpine Club,** Rathausplatz 7 (✆ **07221/1-72-00**). You can also walk the 8km (5-mile) nature trail from the Strouzda chapel via Friesenberg to Fremersberg.

Horse races are another diversion here. **The International Club,** Lichtentaler Allee 8 (✆ **07221/2-11-20**), invites all comers to "Spring Meeting" May 25 to June 2 and to "Grand Week" August 23 to September 1. Those not content to watch can ride on a 1km (½-mile) track, provided by **Equestrian Hall,** Gunzenbachstrasse 4A (✆ **07221/949625**) for from 14€ ($12.50) per hour. Instruction is also available.

Many other outdoor sports are offered as well. The local 18-hole course in Fremersberg is one of the most scenic in Europe; contact the **Baden-Baden Golf**

**Club** at ✆ **07221/2-35-79.** For tennis, contact either **TH 365,** Rheinstrasse (✆ **07221/6-78-08**), which serves up two indoor courts under a retractable roof or **Red-White Tennis Club** at Lichtentaler Allee 5 (✆ **07221/2-41-41**), which offers 10 outdoor courts. Swimmers can take a dip in the indoor and outdoor **swimming pools** in Bertholdbad at Ludwig-Wilhelm-Strasse 24 (✆ **07221/93-26-11**), at a cost of 2.60€ ($2.30) for adults and 1.70€ ($1.50) for students per day.

## SHOPPING

A flower-flanked pedestrian zone includes **Sophienstrasse** and **Gernsbacher Strasse.** These streets are lined with upscale boutiques, among the most expensive in Germany. Women's clothing by one of Germany's most emulated designers is available at **Escada Boutique,** Sophienstrasse 18 (✆ **07221/39-04-48**). Another shop, **Münchner Moden,** Lichtentalerstrasse 13 (✆ **07221/3-10-90**), carries women's designs in loden-colored wool during autumn and winter and offers Austrian and Bavarian silks, linens, and cottons during warmer months. The best men's store, **Herrenkommode,** Sophienstrasse 16 (✆ **07221/2-92-92**), is a bit more international, focusing on Giorgio Armani and Renee Lazard.

Leather goods by Gold Pfiel and other manufacturers are sold at **Inka,** Sophienstrasse 26 (✆ **07221/2-39-55**), where the inventory includes luggage, wallets, and handbags. Cuckoo clocks, puppets, and other locally produced items can be found at **Boulevard,** Lichtentaler Strasse 21 (✆ **07221/2-44-95**).

Among the beeswax- and honey-based products available at **Schwarzwald Bienen-Honig-Haus,** Langestrasse 38 (✆ **07221/3-14-53**), are candles, cosmetics, candies, schnapps, and wine. Several varieties of bottled honey are sold as well. A 400-year-old wine tavern and shop, **Nägelsförster Hof,** Nägelsförst 1 (✆ **07221/3-55-50**), conducts daily wine tastings of the vintages available for purchase.

## WHERE TO STAY

### VERY EXPENSIVE

**Brenner's Park Hotel & Spa** ★★★ This sumptuously furnished hotel is one of the finest in the world, far outdistancing the two Steigenberger properties (see below). It lies in a large private park facing the River Oos and Lichtentaler Allee. The spa facilities here, Baden-Baden's best, are a major draw. Some of its international habitués wouldn't dare let a year go by without making an appearance at this glamorous place. Rooms and suites are the last word in luxurious appointments. Beds are sumptuous, and bathrooms are state-of-the-art.

Schillerstrasse 4–6, 76530 Baden-Baden. ✆ **07221/90-00.** Fax 07221/3-87-72. www.brenners-park.com. 100 units. 670€–1,180€ ($598.30–$1,053.75) suite. AE, DC, MC, V. Parking 15.35€ ($15). Bus: 1. **Amenities:** 2 restaurants; bar; lounge; pool; fitness center; sauna; solarium; salon; room service; massage; babysitting; laundry/dry cleaning. *In room:* TV, minibar, hair dryer, safe.

### EXPENSIVE

**Der Kleine Prinz (The Little Prince)** ★ *Finds* This small hotel is located in a century-old baroque building in the central pedestrian zone, a short walk from the casino and the thermal baths. Two elegant city mansions were combined to form the most personalized, cozy, and intimate nest at the spa. Norbert Rademacher, who owns the hotel with his wife, has had 25 years experience in the United States as director at the Waldorf-Astoria and the New York Hilton. He and his wife have totally renovated and upgraded the hotel. Each of the good-size rooms has its own special feature: an open fireplace, a tower, a balcony, or a whirlpool bathtub. All have neatly kept bathrooms with shower-tub combinations. Personalized service adds to the attractiveness of this intimate, immaculate hotel.

Lichtentalerstrasse 36, 76530 Baden-Baden. ✆ **07221/34-66-00.** Fax 07221/34-660-59. www.derkleineprinz.de. 40 units. 150€–250€ ($133.95–$223.25) double; 275€–350€ ($245.60–$312.55) suite. Rates include buffet breakfast. AE, MC, V. Parking 8€ ($7.15). **Amenities:** Restaurant; bar; tennis courts; health club; Jacuzzi; sauna; room service; message; babysitting; laundry/dry cleaning. *In room:* A/C, TV, minibar, hair dryer, safe.

**Hotel Belle Epoque** ★★ This is one of the newest, and also the most charming, hotels in Baden-Baden, and it's operated by the same people who run the romantic Der Kleine Prinz (see above). Constructed as a private home in 1870, this gem lives up to its namesake. Each room is different, medium in size, and luxuriously furnished with swag draperies, lace curtains, and either antiques or reproductions. All bathrooms come equipped with shower-tub combinations. The owners will, if possible, give you the style of furnishings you request—Empire, Louis XV, Louis XVI, Biedermeier, Victorian, or Louis Philippe.

Maria-Viktoria-Strasse 2b, 76530 Baden-Baden. ✆ **07221/300-66-0.** Fax 07221/300-66-6. www.hotelbelleepoque.de. 16 units. 175€–250€ ($156.30–$223.25) double; 275€–350€ ($245.60–$312.55) suite. Rates include buffet breakfast. AE, DC, MC, V. Bus: 201. **Amenities:** Restaurant; lounge; health club; sauna; room service; laundry/dry cleaning. *In room:* A/C, hair dryer.

**Privahotel Quisisana** ★★ Although Brenner's Park Hotel and even the Steigenberger properties are far superior (see above and below), this runner-up is more tranquil. It's set in a spacious park, 8 minutes away from the town center on foot. Some of the most up-to-date health facilities in the Black Forest are here. You can spend an early morning in group calisthenics, for example, followed by treatments with any one of a dozen skin- and muscle-toning techniques. One of the more unusual facilities is the tepidarium, where a room is warmed to body temperature as you sit and listen to meditation music. Rooms are beautiful, well-kept, spacious, and well-appointed, furnished with both traditional and modern styling and with bathrooms containing shower-tub combinations.

Bismarckstrasse 21 (an 8-min. walk from the town center), 76530 Baden-Baden. ✆ **07221/36-90.** Fax 07221/36-92-69. 69 units. 180€–230€ ($160.75–$205.40) double; 235€–275€ ($209.85–$245.60) suite. Rates include continental breakfast. AE, MC, V. Free parking. Bus: 216. **Amenities:** Restaurant; bar; pool; health club; small spa; sauna; room service; babysitting; laundry/dry cleaning. *In room:* TV, hair dryer, safe.

**Steigenberger Badischer Hof** ★★ A Baden-Baden landmark, this famed traditional hotel isn't quite as highly rated as Brenner's, but it's neck-and-neck with its sibling, the Europäischer Hof (see below). Badischer Hof is on a busy street in the center of town, but in the back you'll find an elegant garden with a wide balustraded terrace, flowerbeds, and a lawn around a stone fountain. The hotel began its career in 1809 as a social center for famous personalities, who came here for "the season." The four-story-high colonnaded hallway, with its great staircase and encircling balustraded balconies, is the hotel's most distinguishing feature. The well-furnished rooms are priced according to size and view. Many have private balconies, and all have bathrooms with shower-tub combinations. Each is elegantly appointed with tasteful fabrics and comfortable beds. Those in the monastery building have thermal water piped into the bathrooms.

Langestrasse 47, 76530 Baden-Baden. ✆ **800/223-5652** in the U.S. and Canada, or 07221/93-40. Fax 07221/93-44-70. www.steigenberger.de. 139 units. 166€–248€ ($148.25–$221.45) double; 302€ ($269.70) suite. Rates include buffet breakfast. AE, DC, MC, V. Parking 11.50€ ($10.25). Bus: 201. **Amenities:**

Restaurant; bar; lounge; 2 pools; health club; Jacuzzi; sauna; beauty farm; room service; babysitting; laundry/dry cleaning. *In room:* TV, minibar, hair dryer, safe.

**Steigenberger Europäischer Hof** ★★ This is the liveliest and most social of the centrally located hotels, with a far more bustling atmosphere than Brenner's or the other Steigenberger (see above). The elegant Europäischer Hof is adjacent to the Oos River, which runs at the edge of the Kurpark. The hotel consists of a pair of joined structures that were built back when spacious living facilities were more affordable. Its colonnaded central hallway is stunning. Many suites and rooms open onto balconies, and all rooms contain bathrooms with shower-tub combinations. The staff is a bit too formal for our tastes but highly efficient.

Kaiserallee 2 (opposite the Kurgarten and the casino), 76530 Baden-Baden. ✆ **800/223-5652** in the U.S. and Canada, or 07221/93-30. Fax 07221/93-37-12. 145 units. 174€–241€ ($155.40–$215.20) double; 329€–979€ ($293.80–$874.25) suite. Rates include buffet breakfast. AE, DC, MC, V. Parking 16€ ($14.30). Bus: 201. **Amenities:** Restaurant; bar; fitness center; salon; room service; babysitting; laundry/dry cleaning. *In room:* TV, minibar, hair dryer, safe.

## MODERATE

**Bad-Hotel zum Hirsch** ★ This beautiful old-fashioned hotel is a tranquil compound of several buildings. Its antique furnishings make it a living museum of fine period pieces. The formal dining room is dominated by crystal chandeliers and paneled walls; the Blauer Salon is equally attractive, with blue-velvet provincial armchairs and classic draperies. The interesting old-style rooms are individually furnished, as if in a country home. All have piped-in thermal water and shower-tub combinations.

Hirschstrasse 1, 76530 Baden-Baden. ✆ **800/223-5652** in the U.S. and Canada, or 07221/93-90. Fax 07221/3-81-48. 58 units. 135€–150€ ($120.55–$133.95) double. Rates include buffet breakfast. AE, DC, DISC, MC, V. Parking 12€ ($10.70). Bus: 201. **Amenities:** Breakfast room; lounge; health club; sauna; laundry/dry cleaning. *In room:* TV, minibar, hair dryer, safe.

**Haus Reichert** The five-floor 19th-century Haus Reichert is an inviting place to stay in a central location, not far from the casino. Rooms are good size, high-ceilinged, and comfortable, although little of the original furniture or detailing has survived the many renovations. All of the neatly kept bathrooms contain shower-tub combinations. Most are priced at the lower end of the scale given below.

Sophienstrasse 4, 76530 Baden-Baden. ✆ **07221/2-41-91.** Fax 07221/2-95-34. www.hotelhausreichert.de. 30 units. 90€–160€ ($80.35–$142.90) double. Rates include continental breakfast. AE, DC, MC, V. Parking 5€ ($4.45). Bus: 201. **Amenities:** Breakfast room; lounge; pool; fitness center; sauna; room service; laundry/dry cleaning. *In room:* TV, minibar, hair dryer.

## INEXPENSIVE

**Hotel am Markt** On the old marketplace, this hotel is far removed from the grander social life of Baden-Baden and its deluxe palace hotels. But though it may be at the bottom of the pecking order, it's number one in town for economy. The location is first-rate, with the quiet interrupted only by chimes from the church across the square. A tiny terrace cafe in front has petunia-filled window boxes. Innkeeper Herr Bogner offers small, simply furnished, comfortable rooms.

Marktplatz 18, 76530 Baden-Baden. ✆ **07221/27-04-0.** Fax 07221/27-04-44. 27 units, 12 with bathroom or shower. 62€ ($55.35) double without bathroom or shower; 80€ ($71.45) double with bathroom or shower. Rates include continental breakfast. AE, MC, V. Bus: 201. **Amenities:** Breakfast room; bar; laundry/dry cleaning. *In room:* TV.

## WHERE TO DINE

**Le Jardin de France** ★★★ MODERN/FRENCH Set nearly adjacent to the Baths of Caracalla, within a 5-minute drive northeast of the center of Baden-Baden, this Alsatian-owned restaurant defines itself as a "small corner of France set within Germany." The setting, suitable for only 35 diners at a time, is modern, warm-toned, uncluttered, and cozy, a feeling that's enhanced by the creative cuisine of Stephan and Sophie Bernhard. There is no more finely honed cuisine served at the spa. The chef regales you with his braised goose liver with rhubarb apple salad, laced with balsamic vinegar and wins your heart with his crayfish with fresh chanterelles. One blistery winter day we arrived to find an astonishingly good version of roast duck with raisins, nuts, and figs. Among the seafood dishes, our party found a star culinary attraction in the curried ragout of lobster and turbot. Service is among the most attentive and finely tuned in Baden-Baden.

Rotenbachtalstrasse 10. ✆ **07721/300-7860.** Reservations required. Main courses 15€–29€ ($13.40–$25.90); fixed-price menu 42€–69€ ($37.50–$61.60). AE, DC, MC, V. Wed–Thurs, Sat–Sun noon–2pm and Tues–Sun 6:45–9:30pm. Closed 2 weeks in Aug.

**Münchner Löwenbräu** GERMAN/BAVARIAN Baden-Baden has many fine restaurants dispensing haute cuisine, but this isn't one of them—the food here is simple and affordable. The terrace is beneath a copse of clipped and pruned linden trees, and the indoor dining room, with its curved glass walls, is up a flight of stone steps at the rear. Many kinds of German sausage are offered, along with Bavarian specialties and a wide selection of cheeses. Regional devotees order pork knuckles fresh from "the pork-knuckle grill." Regulars often ask for the "Löwenbräu platter of bites," which is a hearty plate with everything from black pudding to sliced pork. For dessert, we'd suggest the apple fritters. The restaurant also has a popular beer garden.

Gernsbacher Strasse 9 (in the Altstadt). ✆ **07221/2-23-11.** Main courses 12€–28€ ($10.70–$25). AE, DC, V. Daily 10am–11:30pm. Bus: 201.

**Park-Restaurant** ★ INTERNATIONAL/RHINELAND Park-Restaurant serves the best food in the center of Baden-Baden, although its cuisine is not quite as refined as that of Zum Alde Gott (see below) on the outskirts. This is one of the renowned spa dining rooms of Europe, and the cuisine and service are definitely worth the high price. The emphasis is on French (Alsatian) dishes, along with regional Badish and Rhine Valley foods. Specialties include paté of quail and goose liver and roast saddle of venison or lamb noisettes with tarragon sauce. For dessert, try an ice-cream soufflé.

In Brenner's Park Hotel, Schillerstrasse 6 (at the corner of Lichtentaler Allee). ✆ **07221/90-00.** Reservations required. Main courses 32€–37€ ($28.60–$33.05). AE, DC, MC, V. Daily 6:30–9:30pm. Bus: 201.

**Stahlbad** ★ CONTINENTAL Stahlbad is a luxury restaurant with an elegant decor. Although its food may not be as good as Park-Restaurant's (see above), it's the most tranquil and charming choice in the center of town, mainly because of its garden terrace. The owner, Frau Uschi Mönch, welcomes you in the dining room. The decor and atmosphere evoke a tavern, with prints, copper vessels, antique pewter plates, mugs, and engravings. Continental specialties are pepper steak and venison steak (in hunting season), fresh fish, and lobster thermidor (very expensive). The homemade fettuccine Alfredo with white truffles (in season) is as good as any you'll have in Rome.

Augustaplatz 2. ✆ **07221/2-45-69.** Reservations required. Main courses 15€–28.50€ ($13.40–$25.45). AE, DC, MC, V. Tues–Sun noon–2pm and 6–10pm. Bus: 201.

## DINING AT NEUWEIER

It's traditional for Baden-Baden's visitors to dine at the satellite resort of Neuweier, 10km (6 miles) southwest via Fremersbergstrasse. Here are two suggestions:

**Schloss Neuweier** INTERNATIONAL Schloss Neuweier is a small 12th-century castle entirely surrounded by defensive water fortifications and vineyards belonging to the estate. Its restaurant is not large but offers impeccable service in a decor of tile walls hung with portraits of former inhabitants. The house practices international cookery with flair. Try the brisket with horseradish sauce or the baked ray. The kitchen is consistent, and dishes are well prepared.

Mauberbergstrasse 21. ✆ **07223/96-14-99.** Reservations required. Main courses 21€–29€ ($18.75–$25.90); 3-course fixed-price lunch 44€ ($39.30); 3- or 4-course fixed-price gourmet dinner menu 39€ ($34.85), 5-course menu 64€ ($57.15) AE, MC. Wed–Mon noon–2pm and 6–9:30pm. Bus: 6.

**Zum Alde Gott** ★★ BADISCHE Here's where the true gourmet comes to dine. In this attractive and very old wine cellar, Wilfried Serr, the most distinguished chef in the Baden-Baden area, mixes his palette of flavors with astounding skill and imagination. Wild game in season is a fine art here. Try also the Black Forest trout or the sea bass. There are only 12 tables, and the ambience is bright and cheerful. An added bonus is an open-air terrace.

Weinstrasse 10. ✆ **07223/55-13.** Reservations required. Main courses 23€–29€ ($20.55–$25.90). AE, DC, MC, V. Fri–Wed noon–3pm and 7:30pm–midnight. Bus: 6.

## BADEN-BADEN AFTER DARK

A busy annual schedule of concert, dance, and dramatic performances entertains Baden-Baden locals and visitors alike. The centerpiece for most of the resort's cultural activities is the oft-photographed **Kurhaus,** Kaiserallee 1 (✆ **07221/353207**). Originally built in the 1870s as the focal point of the resort, the Kurhaus does not, as its name implies, contain spa facilities, but is rather a catch-all entertainment complex. In the same building is Baden-Baden's casino, the **Spielbank** (see "The Casino," earlier in this chapter).

The **Theater am Goetheplatz,** Goetheplatz (✆ **07221/93-27-00**), is a well-maintained and beautiful baroque-style theater that presents opera, ballet, and drama productions. It opened auspiciously with the world premiere of the Berlioz opera *Beatrice et Benedict* in 1862. A month-long celebration of music is held during the summer, when the **Musikalischer Sommer Festival** brings a series of concerts to venues scattered throughout the town. For dates, schedule, and ticket information, contact the **Philharmonic Orchestra of Baden-Baden** at Schloss Solms, 76530 Baden-Baden (✆ **07221/93-27-00**), or the tourist information office (see "Visitor Information," earlier in this chapter).

Bars in the resort hotels often have low-key entertainment. Try the **Jockey Bar,** in the lobby of the Steigenberger Badischer Hof (✆ **07221/93-40**) or the **Oleander Bar** in Brenner's Park Hotel, Lichtentaler Allee (✆ **07221/9000**).

# 12

# Heidelberg, Stuttgart & the Neckar Valley

Ancient castle ruins in the midst of thick woodlands, quiet university towns, busy manufacturing centers—you'll find all these in the countryside of southwestern Germany. The area extends along the Neckar River from Heidelberg past medieval towns and modern cities as far as Tübingen. The Neckar flows between the Black Forest and the Schwäbische Alb region. Although the river is open to commercial shipping vessels as far as Stuttgart, much of the valley has remained unspoiled. The castles that rise around every bend in the river were once home to the German royal families of Hohenstaufen and Hohenzollern. Some of these ruins were the summer palaces of kings and emperors. Today, castles and country palaces sometimes offer bed and board to travelers.

## 1 Heidelberg ★★★

120km (75 miles) NW of Stuttgart, 20km (12 miles) SE of Mannheim, 88km (55 miles) S of Frankfurt

Summertime in Heidelberg, according to the song from *The Student Prince,* is a time for music and romance. Today, it's also a time when droves of visitors invade this beautiful city. Heidelberg is one of the few German cities that was not leveled by air raids in World War II, and therefore still has original buildings from the later Middle Ages and early Renaissance. Modern Heidelberg is centered around Bismarckplatz at the foot of the Theodore-Heuss-Brücke; in this part of the city, you'll find many of the best hotels and restaurants. The tall buildings and shopping plazas here contrast with the Altstadt nearby. Across the Neckar are sports grounds, a zoo, and a large botanical garden.

Heidelberg is, above all, a university town and has been since 1386. Students make up much of the population. The colorful atmosphere that university life imparts to the town is felt especially in the old student quarter, with its narrow streets and lively inns. This oldest university in Germany is officially named **Ruprecht-Karl-University,** honoring both its founder, Elector Ruprecht I of the Palatinate, as well as the man who, in 1803, made it the leading university in the state of Baden, Margrave Karl Friedrich. The school was founded after the Great Schism of 1378, when conflicting claims to the papacy created unrest, and German teachers and students fled the Sorbonne in Paris.

The university grew rapidly. At first monastic in character, it changed in the 16th century with the appointment of a married rector. The so-called Old University was built in the early-18th century; the New University was constructed nearby from 1930 to 1932. Funds for this structure came from American sources, including Henry Ford. Today, lecture halls, institutes, seminar buildings, and clinics are scattered all over town, but a new university quarter has

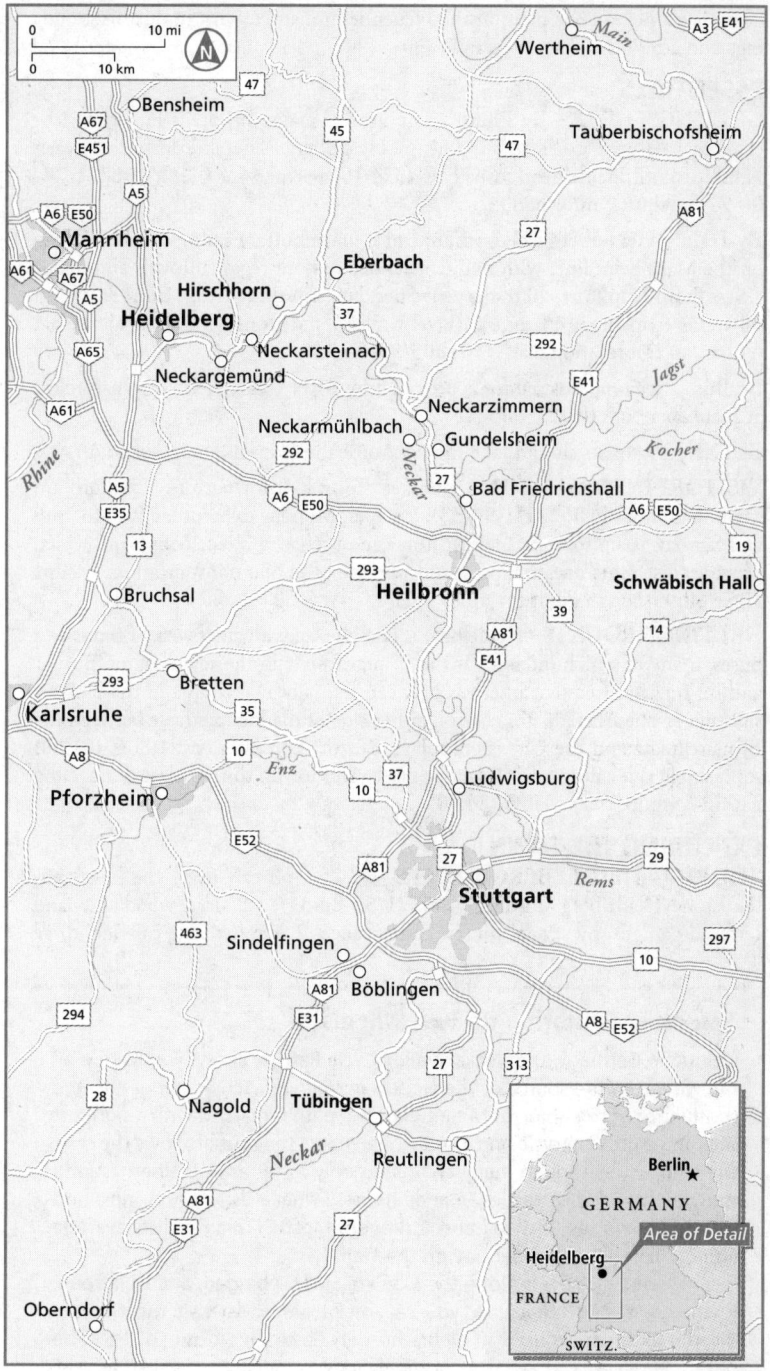
0 10 mi
0 10 km
N
Wertheim
Main
A3
E41
47
Bensheim
A67
E451
45
47
Tauberbischofsheim
A5
A6
E50
A81
27
Mannheim
Eberbach
A61
A67
A5
Hirschhorn
37
Heidelberg
292
A65
Neckarsteinach
Neckargemünd
E41
Jagst
A61
Neckarzimmern
Neckarmühlbach
Gundelsheim
292
Kocher
Rhine
Neckar
27
A5
Bad Friedrichshall
E35
A6
E50
A6
E50
13
19
293
Heilbronn
Schwäbisch Hall
Bruchsal
39
A81
14
E41
293
Bretten
Karlsruhe
35
A8
10
Enz
37
Ludwigsburg
Pforzheim
10
E52
A81
27
29
Rems
Stuttgart
463
Sindelfingen
297
10
A81
Böblingen
294
E31
A8
E52
27
313
28
Nagold
Tübingen
Neckar
Reutlingen
A81
E31
27
Oberndorf
Berlin
GERMANY
Area of Detail
Heidelberg
FRANCE
SWITZ.

been developed on the plain in the Neuenheim district, with multistory buildings and a modern cancer-research center.

## ESSENTIALS

**GETTING THERE** **By Plane** The nearest major airport is Frankfurt (see chapter 13), with a direct bus link to Heidelberg. The shuttle bus between Frankfurt and Heidelberg costs 27€ ($24.10) per person. Call ✆ **06221/77-00-77** for shuttle information.

**By Train** **Heidelberg's Hauptbahnhof** is an important railroad station, lying on the Mannheim line, with frequent service to both regional towns and major cities. From Frankfurt, 40 trains arrive per day (trip time: 1 hr.); from Stuttgart, 30 trains (trip time: 45 min.). Travel time to and from Munich is about 3½ hours. For information, call ✆ **01805/99-66-33.**

**By Bus** Regional bus service is provided by **BRN Busverkehr Rhein-Neckar** at Heidelberg (✆ **06221/606220**).

**By Car** Motorists should take the A5 Autobahn from the north or south.

**VISITOR INFORMATION** Contact **Tourist-Information,** Pavillon am Hauptbahnhof (✆ **06221/1-94-33**). It's open Monday to Saturday 9am to 7pm and Sunday 10am to 6pm. Here visitors can purchase a Heidelberg Card, which provides discounts on attractions and free use of public transportation. It costs 10€ ($8.95) for an adult for up to 2 days.

**GETTING AROUND** Heidelberg is crisscrossed with a network of trams and buses, many of which intersect at the Bismarckplatz in the town center. Bus 41 and 42 travel at frequent intervals between the railway station and the Universitätsplatz. The Altstadt stretches on either side of the Hauptstrasse between the Bismarckplatz and the Universitätsplatz. Bus or tram fares cost 1.80€ ($1.60) for a single ride, although a 24-hour pass, valid for up to five persons traveling within a group, costs 5.50€ ($4.90).

## EXPLORING THE TOWN

**TOURING HEIDELBERG CASTLE** ★★★ You can reach the huge red-sandstone Heidelberg Castle (✆ **06221/53-84-31**), set amid woodlands and terraced gardens, by several routes. Either take a 2-minute cable-car ride, drive

---

### *Moments* Exploring on Two Wheels

Unique in Germany, the **Neckar Valley Cycle Path** ★ allows you to ride all the way from the source of the Neckar in Villingen-Schwenningen to the confluence of the Rhine at Mannheim. The path is marked with a signpost showing a green bicycle and a red wheel mark. The route follows the river the whole way, though many cyclists go only as far as Heidelberg. Along the way, you'll pass castles, manor houses, vineyards, country inns, and such old towns as Rottweil and Esslingen. Most German cyclists average about 48km (30 miles) per day on the trail.

Suggested stopovers along the way are Sulz, Tübingen, and Heilbronn. In the town of Neckarsulm, you can make a stop to visit the **German Bicycle Museum,** housed in Deutschorden Castle. It's close to the cycle path. Here you can see the original "dandy horse," the first bicycle, invented in 1819.

---

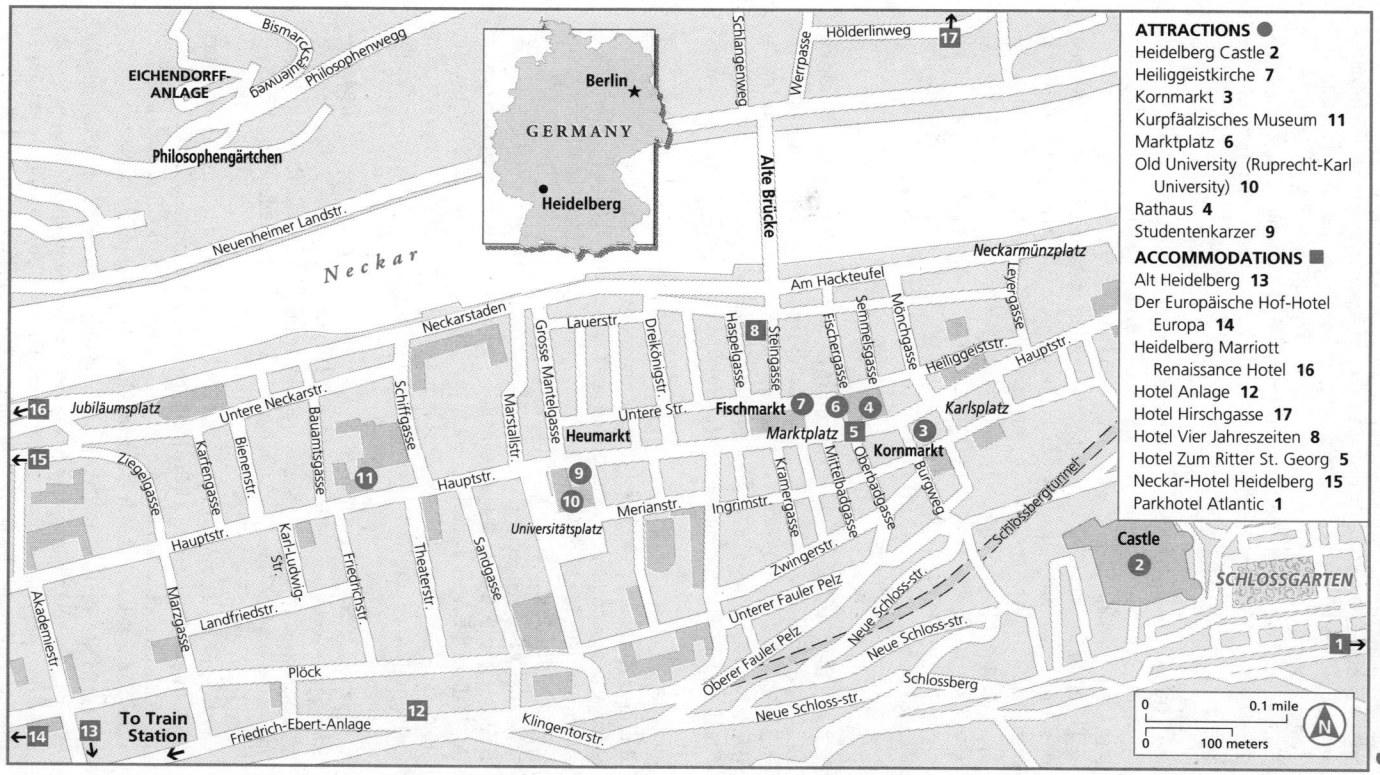
ATTRACTIONS
Heidelberg Castle 2
Heiliggeistkirche 7
Kornmarkt 3
Kurpfäalzisches Museum 11
Marktplatz 6
Old University (Ruprecht-Karl University) 10
Rathaus 4
Studentenkarzer 9
ACCOMMODATIONS
Alt Heidelberg 13
Der Europäische Hof-Hotel Europa 14
Heidelberg Marriott Renaissance Hotel 16
Hotel Anlage 12
Hotel Hirschgasse 17
Hotel Vier Jahreszeiten 8
Hotel Zum Ritter St. Georg 5
Neckar-Hotel Heidelberg 15
Parkhotel Atlantic 1
Berlin
GERMANY
Heidelberg
Neckar
EICHENDORFF-ANLAGE
Bismarckweg
Philosophenwegg
Philosophengärtchen
Neuenheimer Landstr.
Schlangenweg
Werrpasse
Hölderlinweg
Alte Brücke
Neckarmünzplatz
Am Hackteufel
Neckarstaden
Lauerstr.
Grosse Mantelgasse
Dreikönigstr.
Haspelgasse
Steingasse
Fischergasse
Semmelsgasse
Mönchgasse
Leyergasse
Heiliggeiststr.
Hauptstr.
Jubiläumsplatz
Untere Neckarstr.
Bauamtsgasse
Schiffgasse
Marstallstr.
Untere Str.
Fischmarkt
Karlsplatz
Heumarkt
Marktplatz
Kornmarkt
Ziegelgasse
Karfengasse
Bienenstr.
Hauptstr.
Meriantstr.
Ingrimstr.
Kramergasse
Mittelbadgasse
Oberbadgasse
Burgweg
Schlossbergtunnel
Universitätsplatz
Karl-Ludwig-Str.
Friedrichstr.
Theaterstr.
Sandgasse
Zwingerstr.
Castle
SCHLOSSGARTEN
Akademiestr.
Marzgasse
Landfriedstr.
Unterer Fauler Pelz
Neue Schloss-str.
Oberer Fauler Pelz
Plöck
Schlossberg
To Train Station
Friedrich-Ebert-Anlage
Klingentorstr.
0 0.1 mile
0 100 meters
N

# Heidelberg

up the winding Neue Schlosstrasse past the old houses perched on the hillside, or walk. Walking is the most rewarding approach because of the constantly changing scenic view of the town and surrounding countryside. You can take the more gradual slope from the Klingentor, or make the shorter walk up the steep Burgweg from Kornmarkt. The cable car leaves from the platform near the Kornmarkt and costs round-trip 3€ ($2.70) for adults and 2€ ($1.80) for children. The Klingentor, the much easier walk, takes about 20 minutes. The steep Burgweg walk, from Kornmarkt in the center of town, can take a good 30 or 40 minutes, depending on your stamina. Our suggestion is to take the cable-car ride up to the top, then walk back down to take in the view.

The castle is a dignified ruin today, but even in its deteriorated state, it's one of the finest Gothic-Renaissance castles in Germany. Entering the walls at the main gate, you first come upon the huge **Gun Park** to your left, from which you can gaze down upon Heidelberg and the Neckar Valley. Straight ahead is the **Thick Tower,** or what remains of it after its 8m (25-ft.) walls were blown up by the French in the late 17th century. Leaving the Gun Park via Elizabeth's Gate (erected by Friedrich V in 1615 for his Scottish wife, the daughter of James I), you come to the Bridge House and the bridge crossing the site of the former moat.

Along the north side of the courtyard stretches the stern **palace of Friedrich IV** ★★, erected 1601 to 1607. The palace is less damaged than other parts of the castle, and its rooms have been almost completely restored, including the gallery of princes and kings of the German empire from the time of Charlemagne. The ancient bell tower, at the northeast end of the Altan, dates from the early 1500s.

At the west end of the terrace, in the cellars of the castle, is the **Wine Vat Building** ★, built in the late 16th century and worth a visit for a look at the Great Cask, symbol of the abundant and exuberant life of the Rhineland-Palatinate. This huge barrel-like monstrosity, built in 1751, is capable of holding more than 208,000 liters (55,000 gal.) of wine.

To the east, connecting the palace of Friedrich IV to the **Ottheinrich Building,** itself an outstanding example of German Renaissance architecture, is the **Hall of Mirrors Building,** constructed in 1549—a Renaissance masterpiece. Only the shell of the original building remains, enough to give you an idea of its former glory, with its arcades and steep gables decorated with cherubs and sirens.

Next to Ottheinrich's palace is the Chemist's Tower, housing the **Pharmaceutical Museum** ★ (✆ **06221/25880**). This museum shows a chemist's shop with utensils and laboratory equipment from the 18th and 19th centuries. It's open daily 10am to 5pm, and admission is 2€ ($1.80) for adults and 1€ (90¢) for children.

A 1-hour guided tour of the castle costs 3€ ($2.70) for adults and 1.50€ ($1.35) for children. Tours are frequent, especially in summer. Admission to the grounds is free; admission to the entrance courtyard and Great Cask is 2.05€ ($2) for adults, 1€ (90¢) for children. Open daily 8am to 6pm.

**EXPLORING THE ALTSTADT** All the important sights of Heidelberg lie on or near the south bank of the Neckar. However, you should cross to the north side of the river (via the 18th-century Karl Theodore Bridge) for the best overall view. **Philosophenweg (Philosopher's Way),** halfway up the hill on the north bank, offers an especially good vista.

### *Moments* Boating in the Neckar

Heidelberg is a good point from which to explore the romantic Neckar Valley. From April to early October, you can take a boat tour along the river as far as Neckarsteinach and back. There are usually four or five round-trips daily, and you need not return on the same boat. Boats are operated by the **Rhein-Neckar-Fahrgastschiffahrt GmbH,** Stadthalle, Heidelberg (✆ **06221/2-01-81**). Trips between Heidelberg and Neckarsteinach cost 9.50€ ($8.50) round-trip, and those between Heidelberg and Hirschhorn (which operate June 17–Sept 30) cost 12.50€ ($11.15) round-trip. You can order drinks or snacks on the boat. Some of the people operating the boats are descended from the Neckar fishers who helped Mark Twain when he rafted down from Hirschhorn. The same families have been working the Neckar since the early 1600s.

In the town itself, a tour of the main attractions begins with **Marktplatz** in front of the Rathaus. On market days, the square is filled with stalls of fresh flowers, fish, and vegetables. At the opposite end of the square is the late-Gothic **Heiliggeistkirche,** built around 1400, the largest Gothic church in the Palatinate. For nearly 300 years, the church was the burial place of the electors, but most of the graves were destroyed in the French invasion late in the 17th century. Around the corner is the famous old mansion **Zum Ritter,** recommended in the hotel listings below.

**Kurpfälzisches Museum (Museum of the Palatinate)** ★ This museum is housed in a baroque palace. It contains a large collection of painting and sculpture from 6 centuries. Notable is the Riemenschneider Altar from Windsheim (1509), showing Christ and the 12 Apostles. There's also an archaeological collection with a cast of the jawbone of the 500,000-year-old Heidelberg Man and a section on the history of the Palatinate. The restaurant is a good lunch stop (see "Where to Dine," below).

Hauptstrasse 97. ✆ **06221/58-34-02.** Admission 2.50€ ($2.25) adults, 1.50€ ($1.35) students, .75€ (65¢) children 17 and under. Tues and Thurs–Sun 9am–5pm; Wed 10am–8pm. Bus: 11,12, 35, or 42.

**Studentenkarzer (Student Jail)** The walls and even the ceilings of the prison are covered with graffiti and drawings, including portraits and silhouettes. The last prisoners (unruly and drunken students) were held here in 1914. Ring the caretaker's bell for admission.

Augustinergasse 2. ✆ **06221/54-35-34.** Admission 2.50€ ($2.25) adults, .50€ (45¢) students and children 14 and under. Apr–Oct Tues–Sat 10am–4pm. Bus: 10, 12, or 35.

## SHOPPING

The main shopping street is the traffic-free **Hauptstrasse,** which is filled with stores selling glass, crystal, handcrafts, and other items. Heidelberg is also known for its markets, including the one held on Wednesday and Sunday mornings at Marktplatz and another held Tuesday and Friday mornings at Friedrich-Ebert-Platz. A giant flea market sprawls along Guteramtsstrasse near the Customs office one Saturday a month, but there isn't a designated week within which it falls.

In a city of this size, there are lots of stores to choose from. **Michael Kienscherff,** Hauptstrasse 177 (✆ **06221/2-42-55;** tram: 1 or 5), offers a wide assortment of handcrafts from all over Germany: music boxes, nativity scenes, nutcrackers, and glass and crystal ornaments. The two branches of **Gätschenberger,** Hauptstrasse 6 and 42 (✆ **06221/1-44-80;** tram: 1 or 5), share a telephone, but no. 42 is known for its array of fine linens and embroideries for bed, bathroom, and table, whereas no. 6 sells men's and women's undergarments. A toy store, **Muckels Maus,** Plöck 71 (✆ **06221/2-38-86;** tram: 1 or 5), is the place to find beautifully handcrafted puppets, including replicas of characters from the operas of Mozart, antique-looking and ultra-modern dolls, and wooden blocks and figures.

Other shops of interest include **Unholtz,** Hauptstrasse 160 (✆ **06221/2-09-64;** tram: 1 or 5), which carries Solingen cutlery, tableware, and scissors; and **Spiess & Walther,** Friedrich-Ebert-Anlage 23a (✆ **06221/2-22-33;** bus: 11 or 33), which features exclusive designs in contemporary furniture, antiques, and textiles. For all things leather, stop by **Leder-Meid,** Hauptstrasse 88 (✆ **06221/2-25-70;** tram: 1 or 5), which sells the crafts of German and other manufacturers. **Tischer,** Hauptstrasse 73 (✆ **06221/1-48-00;** tram: 1 or 5), carries high-quality cooking items.

If you want more variety under one roof, go to either branch of Heidelberg's best department store, **Kaufhof,** Hauptstrasse 22–32 (✆ **06221/50-40;** tram: 1 or 5), or Bergheimerstrasse 7 (✆ **06221/91-60;** tram: 1 or 5).

## WHERE TO STAY

### EXPENSIVE

**Der Europäische Hof-Hotel Europa** ★★★ This glamour hotel is by far the best in Heidelberg. It fronts the city park in the heart of town, within walking distance of the castle and the university. Its interior is like that of a gracious home, with antiques, crystal chandeliers, and Oriental rugs. Some rooms and several suites face a quiet inside garden; front rooms in the oldest section tend to be noisy (from traffic). Nineteen have whirlpool tubs.

Friedrich-Ebert-Anlage 1, 69117 Heidelberg. ✆ **800/223-4541,** 800/223-6800 in the U.S. and Canada, or 06221/5150. Fax 06221/51-55-06. www.europaeischerhof.com. 118 units. 220€–324€ ($196.45–$289.35) double; 282€–525€ ($251.85–$468.85) suite. AE, DC, MC, V. Parking 15.90€ ($14.20). Tram: Bismarckplatz. **Amenities:** 2 restaurants; bar; Jacuzzi; room service; babysitting; laundry/dry cleaning. *In room:* A/C, TV, minibar, hair dryer, safe.

**Hotel Hirschgasse** ★★ This historic country-home-style hotel, nestled on the hillside of a historic lane adjoining Philosopher's Way, is tops in Heidelberg for its tranquil and romantic setting. It dates from 1472 and has lodged such impressive figures as Mark Twain and Bismarck. Rooms are all suites decorated in Laura Ashley designs, and all come equipped with shower-tub combinations.

Hirschgasse 3, 69120 Heidelberg. ✆ **06221/45-40.** Fax 06221/45-41-11. www.hirschgasse.de. 20 units. 50€ ($44.65) junior suite for 2; 195€–245€ ($174.15–$218.80) senior suite for 2; 285€–335€ ($254.50–$299.15) salon suite for 2. AE, DC, MC, V. Free parking. Bus: 34. **Amenities:** 2 restaurants; bar; room service; babysitting; laundry/dry cleaning. *In room:* TV, minibar, hair dryer, safe, Jacuzzi.

**Hotel Zum Ritter St. Georg** ★ A glorious old inn right out of the German Renaissance, the Zum Ritter is a well-preserved rarity, although it's inferior to the Hirschgasse (see above) in comfort and antique charm. Built in 1592 by Frenchman Charles Bèlier, it's now listed among the major sightseeing attractions of this university town. There are no public lounges. Many rooms are somewhat cramped, but beds are most comfortable and the bathrooms have been renewed. All units contain bathrooms with shower-tub combinations.

Hauptstrasse 178, 69117 Heidelberg. ✆ **06221/13-50.** Fax 06221/13-52-30. www.ritter-heidelberg.de. 40 units. 160€–220€ ($142.90–$196.45) double; 260€ ($232.20) suite. Rates include buffet breakfast. AE,

DC, MC, V. Bus: 10, 11, or 12. **Amenities:** Restaurant; room service; laundry/dry cleaning. *In room:* TV, minibar, hair dryer.

## MODERATE

**Heidelberg Marriott Renaissance Hotel** This hotel sits on the banks of the Neckar, just a few minutes from the Altstadt and the main train station. Although it doesn't have the flair and traditional style of Der Europäische Hof (see above), it's far superior to its nearest rival, Holiday Inn Crowne Plaza at Kurfürstenanlage 1. The exit from the Autobahn is only minutes away, making it convenient for motorists. Rooms are comfortably furnished and newly renovated, many with views over the river or the hills beyond. All rooms have bathrooms with shower-tub combinations. As a special service, the hotel operates a shuttle service to and from Frankfort International Airport.

Vanerowstrasse 16, 69115 Heidelberg. ✆ **06221/90-80.** Fax 06221/90-86-08. www.marriott.com. 248 units. 99€–175€ ($88.40–$156.30) double; 205€ ($183.05) junior suite; 360€ ($321.50) suite. AE, DC, MC, V. Parking 14€ ($12.50). Tram: 1, 4, or 5. **Amenities:** Restaurant; bar; lounge; pool; health club; sauna; solarium; room service; massage; laundry/dry cleaning. *In room:* A/C, TV, minibar, hair dryer, safe.

**Parkhotel Atlantic** ★ *Finds* This grand hotel on the wooded outskirts of Heidelberg, near the castle, offers modern comfort in annexes built around the core of an older villa. Visitors are assured calm and comfort and can take advantage of the many woodland trails extending through the Neckar Valley. This hotel's setting makes it the best in its price range; hotels in the city center, unless soundproofed, get a lot of traffic noise. Rooms are decorated in 1965-ish modern style but are quite comfortable, and all contain bathrooms with shower-tub combinations.

Schloss-Wolfsbrunnen-Weg 23, 69117 Heidelberg. ✆ **06221/60-42-0.** Fax 06221/60-42-60. 24 units. 95€–145€ ($84.85–$129.50) double. Rates include buffet breakfast. AE, DC, MC, V. Free parking. Bus: 11, 12, or 33. Head east from the Hauptbahnhof, along Kurfürstenanlage going through the tunnel, and take the 2nd right, bringing you to Heidelberg Castle; continue straight beyond the castle to the hotel. **Amenities:** Breakfast room; lounge; room service; laundry. *In room:* TV, minibar.

## INEXPENSIVE

**Hotel Anlage** *Value* This is one of Heidelberg's best affordable hotels, located in the heart of the city, on the street leading up to the castle. It occupies one wing of a lavishly built, late–19th century palace. Rooms are cozy and have bathrooms containing shower-tub combinations.

Friedrich-Ebert-Anlage 32, 69117 Heidelberg. ✆ **06221/58-50-96-0.** Fax 06221/58-50-96-130. www.hotel-anlage.de. 19 units. 95€–101€ ($84.85–$90.20) double. Rates include continental breakfast. AE, DC, MC, V. Parking 5€ ($4.45). Bus: 11, 12, or 33. **Amenities:** Restaurant; lounge; room service; laundry/dry cleaning. *In room:* TV.

**Hotel Vier Jahreszeiten** This hotel is a worthy choice for any of the "four seasons." It's located near the starting point for many interesting walks. Several famous student inns (drinking taverns patronized mainly by students of the university at Heidelberg, although open to all) and the castle are also nearby. The hotel has been improved over the years; the newly renovated rooms are comfortable, with bathrooms equipped with shower-tub combinations. The price and the location here are hard to beat.

Haspelgasse 2 (near the Alte Brücke), 69117 Heidelberg. ✆ **06221/2-41-64.** Fax 06221/16-31-10. www.jahreszeiten.de. 22 units. 110€–115€ ($98.25–$102.70) double. Rates include continental breakfast. AE, DC, MC, V. Parking 8€ ($7.15). Closed Dec 24–Jan 10. Bus: 33, 34. **Amenities:** Breakfast room; lounge. *In room:* TV.

## WHERE TO DINE

### EXPENSIVE

**Kurfürstenstube** ★★ FRENCH The best dining spot in Heidelberg is in the ground-floor wing of this deluxe hotel. The wood-paneled grillroom is attractively decorated with provincial furnishings. The menu is in English, but the cuisine is mainly French, with both fixed-price and a la carte meals. Only the highest quality seasonal ingredients are used. Perhaps the menu will feature roast John Dory with garlic-flavored cream sauce and braised peppers and tomatoes, or saddle of Limousin lamb with a coating of herbs, essence of basil, green beans, and pesto-flavored polenta. The chef never over-sauces or over-seasons. For a spectacular finish, try the crêpes flambé with bananas and maple sauce. The wine list is the most impressive in town.

In Der Europäische Hof-Hotel Europa, Friedrich-Ebert-Anlage 1. ✆ **06221/51-50.** Reservations required. Main courses 29€–32€ ($25.90–$28.60); fixed-price meals from 45€ ($40.20). AE, DC, MC, V. Daily noon–3:30pm and 6:30–11:30pm. Tram: Bismarckplatz.

**Simplicissimus** ★★ FRENCH This elegant spot is ideal for a gourmet rendezvous. Johann Lummer, one of the finest chefs in Heidelberg, prepares a *cuisine moderne* with consummate skill. *Gourmet* magazine said that Herr Lummer "paints with food," and we agree. Not only are his dishes delectable to the taste buds, but their presentation is equally pleasing. The menu varies but is likely to include fresh mushrooms in cream sauce with homemade noodles, or crayfish with fresh melon and herb-flavored cream sauce.

Ingrimstrasse 16. ✆ **06221/18-33-36.** Reservations required. Main courses 20€–24€ ($17.85–$21.45); fixed-price menu 53€ ($47.35). AE, MC, V. Wed–Mon 6–11pm. Closed 1 week in Mar and 1st 3 weeks in Aug. Bus: 11, 12, 33, 35, or 41.

**Zum Ritter St. Georg** ★ GERMAN/INTERNATIONAL This restaurant (located in one of Heidelberg's most famous Renaissance buildings) is popular with both students and professors, who know that they can get not only good German cooking here but also the wonderful Dortmunder Actien-Bräuerei beer. You dine either in the first-class Great Hall (the Rittersaal) or in the smaller Councillors' Chamber. We like the elegant larger room, with its sepia ceilings, wainscoting, and Oriental rugs. The house specialty is saddle of Odenwald venison for two (in season); when this dish is offered, locals flock here. A good beginning might be game soup St. Hubertus with brandy foam, and crêpes suzette is a fine dessert.

Hauptstrasse 178. ✆ **06221/1-35-0.** Reservations recommended. Main courses 10.50€–21.50€ ($9.40–$19.20); fixed-price menu 14€–35€ ($12.50–$31.25). AE, DC, MC, V. Daily noon–2pm and 6–10pm. Bus: 10, 11, or 12.

**Zur Herrenmühle** ★ FRENCH/INTERNATIONAL This family-owned restaurant is in a 17th-century house, with thick walls and antique paneling. The sophisticated maître d' adds both glamour and an appropriate theatricality. The succulent classical cuisine is based on fresh ingredients. Try the rack of lamb with herbs and homemade green noodles, or the roast roebuck with a vinegar-and-honey sauce. The desserts make better use of fresh fruit than any other place in town; try the sorbet flavored with blood oranges and served with a parfait of mandarin oranges. The service here is equaled only at the Kurfürstenstube (see above).

Hauptstrasse 237–239. ✆ **06221/60-29-09.** Reservations recommended. Main courses 20€–28€ ($17.85–$25); fixed-price menu 48€–56€ ($42.85–$50). AE, DC, MC, V. Mon–Sat 5:30pm–midnight. Bus: 33.

### MODERATE

**Kurpfälzisches Museum Restaurant** GERMAN This quiet culinary oasis at the museum makes an interesting stopover for lunch. The baroque palace setting is sometimes more interesting than the food. You can order such dishes as rump steak Madagascar with green pepper while you enjoy the view of the little garden and splashing fountain. The food is satisfying, though hardly a challenge to the chefs at Kurfürstenstube or Simplicissimus (see above).

Hauptstrasse 97. ✆ **06221/2-40-50.** Reservations required. Main courses 9€–20€ ($8.05–$17.85). AE, DC, MC, V. Daily noon–2:30pm and 6–10pm. Bus: 1, 35, or 97.

**Mensurstube** ★ GERMAN/REGIONAL No other place in Heidelberg captures bygone days quite like this one. In this rustic and cozy spot, you sit at tables more than 2 centuries old—you can still see where Bismarck and many others carved their names. Swords hang from the ceiling—in the past, when dueling was the regular sport of the student fraternities, many duels were fought in what is now the dining room. Traditional recipes are served; the menu is limited but all the ingredients are fresh. Potato soup is a good starter, followed by homemade noodles, oxtail, or lamb shank. *Rinderfilet* (filet of beef) is often served with bone marrow and a red-wine sauce with potatoes gratin.

In the Hotel Hirschgasse, Hirschgasse 3. ✆ **06221/454165.** Reservations recommended. Main courses 17€–19€ ($15.20–$16.95). AE, DC, MC, V. Tues–Sat 6–10pm. Bus: 34.

### INEXPENSIVE

**Konditorei-Café Schafheutle** PASTRIES/GERMAN Rain need never ruin your summer outing in this partially roofed cafe garden. You can order light meals or choose from the large selection of pastries. Service is attentive. This is a good choice for afternoon coffee or for a quick bite as you're dashing up to the castle.

Hauptstrasse 94. ✆ **06221/1-46-80.** Main courses 9€–12€ ($8.05–$10.70). Credit cards not accepted. Mon–Fri 9:30am–7pm; Sat 9am–6pm. Closed holidays. Bus: 10 or 12.

## HEIDELBERG AFTER DARK

Nights here are alive with the youthful enthusiasm of Heidelberg's students. Early evenings often start in the bars along Hauptstrasse; then late nights get rolling in the clubs around Marktplatz.

**THE PERFORMING ARTS** The main performance stage is **Theater der Stadt,** Friedrichstrasse 5 (✆ **06221/58-35-02;** bus: 41 or 42), where nightly entertainment includes plays, opera, and dance productions. For 5 weeks beginning in late July, the **Schlossfest-Spiele** festival brings opera, classical music, jazz, and theater to venues around the area, including Heidelberg Castle. Contact ✆ **06274/-582-000** for tickets.

**HISTORIC STUDENT DRINKING CLUBS** Heidelberg's most famous and revered student tavern, **Zum Roten Ochsen (Red Ox Inn)** ★, Hauptstrasse 217 (✆ **06221/2-09-77;** bus: 33), opened in 1703. For six generations it has been in the Spengel family, and they have welcomed everybody from Bismarck to Mark Twain. It seems that every student who has attended the university has left his or her mark (or initials) on the walls. The series of rooms, where revelers sit at long oak tables under smoke-blackened ceilings, is arranged in horseshoe fashion; the U part has a pianist who sets the musical pace. As the evening progresses, the songs become louder and louder. Motherly looking waitresses bring in huge steins of beer and plates of food. A mug of beer costs 2.40€ ($2.15) and up. Meals go from 8.90€ to 18€ ($7.95–$16.05). The tavern is open Monday through Saturday from 11:30am to 2pm and 5 to 11:30pm (sometimes to midnight). Closed mid-December to mid-January.

Next door is **Zum Sepp'l,** open since 1634, Hauptstrasse 213 (✆ **06221/2-30-85;** bus: 41 or 42), the second most famous drinking club in Heidelberg. It's also filled with photographs and carved initials of former students, along with memorabilia that range from old Berlin street signs to Alabama license plates. The building itself dates from 1634. Meals cost 5.80€ to 12.50€ ($5.20–$11.15) A mug of beer goes for 2.90€ ($2.60). There's live piano music daily from 8pm to midnight. When the university is closed, the activity here dies down considerably. It's open daily from noon to 1am. Students also like to drink beer at **Reichsapfel,** Unterestrasse 35 (✆ **06221/2-79-50;** bus: 41 or 42), a popular hangout for more than 300 years. It sells nothing but beer. Open daily 5pm to 1am.

**BARS & CAFES** **Max Bar,** Marktplatz 5 (✆ **06221/2-44-19;** bus: 11 or 33), is a beer-drinker's bar, but you can also get a baguette or croissant to soak up some of the alcohol. There's indoor and patio seating. Open daily 8am to 1am. When you tire of beer and want a more spirited drink, wander over to **Sonder Bar,** Unterestrasse 13 (✆ **06221/2-52-00;** bus: 41 or 42), which stocks more than 150 brands of whisky, 10 kinds of vodka, and sundry other potions, besides its 11 types of beers. Open daily 7pm to 1am.

Catch up on the latest news and trends at **Café Journal,** Hauptstrasse 162 (✆ **06221/16-17-12;** bus: 41 or 42), where drinkers linger over beer while scanning newspapers and magazines from all over Europe and the United States. Open daily 8am to 1am. **Hard Rock Cafe,** Hauptstrasse 142 (✆ **06221/2-28-19;** bus: 41 or 42), has a branch here, open 10am to 1am. A popular bar with a mixed gay crowd, **Mata Hari,** Oberbadgasse 10 (✆ **06221/18-18-08;** bus: 11 or 33), is a mellow place to meet and drink. Open 8pm to 3am nightly.

**LIVE MUSIC & CLUBS** The **Schwimmbad Musik Club,** Tiergartenstrasse 13 (✆ **06221/47-02-01;** bus: 33), which features trend-setting local and international bands, is open Wednesday and Thursday 8pm to 3am, Friday and Saturday 8pm to 4am. Cover is 1.50€ to 11€ ($1.35–$9.80) depending on the act. At **Dr. Flotte,** Hauptstrasse 130 (✆ **06221/2-05-69;** bus: 41 or 42), jazz bands appear on Sundays from September to May, 4 to 7pm. A variety of music is featured at other times. Open daily 11am to 1am (Fri–Sat to 3am).

Named after a barbecue sauce from Texas, **Ziegler-Bräu/Billy Blue's,** Bergheimer Strasse 1B (✆ **06221/2-53-33;** tram: 1 or 5), serves up barbecue in the front room while local and international bands play soul, funk, and blues in the back Wednesday to Saturday nights. Open daily 5pm to 3am; cover is 4€ ($3.55) on Wednesday or 2€ to 5€ ($1.80–$4.45) on weekends (otherwise free).

Known as one of the oldest jazz clubs in Germany, **Cave 54** Krämergasse 2 (✆ **06221/278-40;** bus: 11 or 33), is a perennial favorite. It offers live jazz every Sunday, with other nights devoted to soul, funk, and reggae. Open daily 9pm to 3am, cover is 3€ ($2.70) Tuesday night and 6.50€ ($5.80) on Sunday (otherwise free).

## 2 Hirschhorn, Eberbach & Heilbrunn

From April to early October, you can take a boat tour in the Neckar Valley as far as Neckarsteinach and back (see "Boating in the Neckar" earlier in this chapter). You can also see the many attractions along the banks of the Neckar by car, driving eastward along the right bank of the river.

## HIRSCHHORN

This medieval town, 26km (16 miles) east of Heidelberg, is known as the gem of the Neckar Valley. Overlooking the town and the river from a fortified promontory is the 18th-century **Hirschhorn Castle.** The castle defenses are from the 14th century, and wall paintings from that period can be seen in the chapel. The castle is now a hotel and restaurant (see below). For a view of the sharp bend of the Neckar below the town, climb to the top of the tower.

**GETTING THERE** Access by car is via Route 45 east from Heidelberg. Hirschhorn lies on the Neckarelz–Heidelberg rail line with frequent local service between the two towns. For information, call ✆ **01805/99-66-33.**

### WHERE TO STAY & DINE

**Schloss-Hotel** This hotel offers rooms in a hilltop castle looming over the center of town. Rooms have river views and collections of good antiques. Some are in a guesthouse annex, but those in the castle have more space, style, and tradition. Central heating and an elevator have been installed. Bathrooms are neatly kept with shower-tub combinations. The restaurant serves traditional dishes to nonresidents, but you have to phone in advance. Specialties include various kinds of game, smoked trout, and home-baked bread.

Auf Burg Hirschhorn (on Route B37), 69434 Hirschhorn. ✆ **06272/92-09-0.** Fax 06272/32-67. www.german-castles-road.com/schlosshotel-hirschhorn/. 25 units. 110€–124€ ($98.25–$110.75) double; 132€ ($117.90) suite. Rates include continental breakfast. AE, MC, V. Free parking. Closed mid-Dec–Jan. **Amenities:** Restaurant; lounge; room service. *In room:* TV, minibar, safe.

## EBERBACH

The Imperial City of Eberbach, established in 1227, is 11km (7 miles) farther along the Neckar, at a point where the river twists to make a wide bend to the south. Its castle, which dates all the way from 1190, was mostly destroyed in the 15th century, but its ivy-covered ruins attract many visitors today. The old Pfarrhof, the medieval center of the town, is within the city walls. Eberbach is proud to be the city where Queen Victoria was conceived; the event is commemorated by a plaque outside her parents' home, Haus Thalheim.

Eberbach was once heavily fortified, and the remains of three castles (all of them in ruins) once stood here. Today you can walk along its ancient streets and take in views of the facades of its historic houses.

Begin your tour at the **Alter Markt,** or old market square. The most colorful façade here is the frescoed **Hotel Karpften,** Alter Market 1. Many visitors can be seen photographing what the Germans called its *sgraffito* (frescoed) façade.

You can visit the tourist office in the historic **Haus Thalheim,** Kellereistrasse 36 (✆ **06271/4899**). This is the house, or so it is believed, where Great Britain's future Queen Victoria was conceived. Victoria's parents were on an extended holiday, living in Haus Thalheim, nine months prior to her birth. In a controversial claim, some local historians assert that Victoria was actually born aboard the family's yacht moored in the Neckar. The same historians also claim, for reasons having to do with public relations and anti-German sentiment among the British at the time, that soon thereafter, the family took their newborn daughter to England and announced that Victoria had actually been born on British soil. The debate continues, quietly, today in Eberbach.

Upstairs, above the tourist office, is the headquarters of the **Naturpark Informationszentrum,** the organization that dispenses maps and advice about hiking or walking through the enveloping Odenwald forest. They'll tell you about overnight shelters, give you a list of guesthouses, and outline the carefully marked footpaths leading through the forest. These offices are open Monday to Friday 8am to noon and 2 to 5:30pm. From May to October, they're also open on Saturday morning from 10am to noon, and on Sunday afternoon from 2 to 4pm.

Every Saturday from May to October, beginning at 10:30am, departing from the tourist office, there's a one-hour guided walking tour, in English and German, of Eberbach's old town. The cost, per person, adult or child, is usually 1€ (90¢), but for anyone who shows that he or she is staying in any of Eberbach's hotels, the tour is free.

**Eberbach Castle (Burg Eberbach)** lies two-thirds of a mile (a steep uphill 30-minute climb) northeast of the town center. It is only a ruin, a jumble of once-fortified walls and arches, that visitors can wander through without charge, at any hour of the day or night. Views from the base of the ruin are panoramic.

From **Burg Eberbach,** signs point to a forest path that leads, after an additional 90-minute relatively flat walk, to **Katzenbuckl.** Here, you'll see the **Turm (Tower) Katzenbuckl,** a tower built during the Victorian age of the "Grand Tour" that marks the highest point in the Odenwald Forest. The stone-sided tower (a 19th-century mock-medieval folly) is open without charge day and night. Views are also panoramic. From Eberbach to Katzenbuckl requires a total walk of two hours, a distance of about 6km (3½ miles).

**GETTING THERE** Routes 37 and 45 connect to the A5 Autobahn heading north and south or the A6 going east and west. From Heidelberg, head east along Route 37. Eberbach lies on the Neckarelz–Heidelberg rail line, with frequent service. Call ✆ **01805/99-66-33** for information.

**VISITOR INFORMATION** Contact the **Kurverwaltung,** Im Kuzentrum, Kellerei-Strasse 32 (✆ **06271/48-99**), Monday to Friday 8am to noon and 2 to 5:30pm; May 15 to October 15, also Saturday 8:30am to noon.

### WHERE TO STAY & DINE

**Hotel zum Karpfen** ★ This is the best and most colorful hotel in town. On its facade are authentic *sgraffiti* (scratched-on paintings) depicting the story of Eberbach. The building is more than 2 centuries old. Each room contains a bathroom with shower-tub combinations. The old-world restaurant serves well-prepared meals.

Am Alten Markt 1–4, 69412 Eberbach. ✆ **06271/7-10-15.** Fax 06271/71010. 68 units. 75€–90€ ($67–$80.35) double; 120€ ($107.15) suite. Rates include buffet breakfast. AE, MC, V. Free parking. **Amenities:** Restaurant; lounge; room service. *In room:* TV, hair dryer.

## HEILBRONN

Heilbronn is a major commercial and cultural center. It was made an Imperial City by Emperor Karl IV in 1371; however, documents show that a Villa Heilbrunna existed here in A.D. 741. The town owes its name to a holy spring (Heiligbronn) that bubbled up from beneath the high altar at **St. Killian's Church,** the city's most important monument. The old city was largely destroyed in World War II, but the church has been rebuilt in its original Gothic and High Renaissance style. The church's 64m (210-ft.) tower is the earliest example of Renaissance architecture in Germany. Inside are excellent original woodcarvings, preserved during the war, including an elaborate choir and altar.

Opposite the church is the **Rathaus,** also reconstructed, a combination of Gothic and Renaissance architecture. On its balcony is an astronomical clock dating back to 1580. It was designed by the best-known horologist of the time, Isaak Habrecht, who created the famous clock inside the cathedral at Strasbourg, France.

Some 4,000ha (10,000 acres) of wooded parkland surround the city, accessible by footpaths and nature trails.

**GETTING THERE** Access by car is via the A6 Autobahn east and west and the A81 north and south. From Heidelberg, drive south along Route 45, then take A6 east. Heilbronn lies on the major Stuttgart–Würzburg rail line with frequent service. Call ✆ **01805/99-66-33** for information. Bus service to Stuttgart is provided by **Regional Bus Stuttgart GmbH** at Heilbronn (✆ **07131/6-24-50** for more information). For local transport information, call Heilbronner Verkehrbund at ✆ **07131/78560.**

**TOURIST INFORMATION** Contact the **Stadtisches Verkehrsamt,** Rathaus, Marktplatz 7 (✆ **07131/56-22-70**), Monday to Friday 9am to 6pm and Saturday 9am to 1pm.

## WHERE TO STAY

**Insel-Hotel** ★ The leading first-class choice in town and the finest hotel in the area, Insel stands on an island (*Insel* in German) in the river, right in the heart of Heilbronn. It's superior in style to the Hotel Götz, and its midsize to spacious bedrooms are better-furnished, each coming with a good-sized tiled bathroom with tub and shower combination. Many of the bedrooms have private balconies opening onto a view of the weeping willows in the hotel's private park. The hotel's recreational facilities are also the finest in town, complete with an indoor pool.

The front terrace of the hotel is the virtual nerve center of town, with locals stopping in to order a beer and catch up on all the gossip. The in-house restaurant is also an excellent choice, even if you're a non-guest. The chefs specialize in Swabian dishes that include onion-flavored roast beef and homemade Spätzle.

Friedrich-Ebert-Brücke, 74072 Heilbronn. ✆ **07131/6300.** Fax 07131/626060. insel@insel-hotel.de. 120 units. 125€–145€ ($111.65–$129.50) double, 195€–245€ ($174.15–$218.80) suite. AE, DC, MC, V. **Amenities:** Restaurant; bar; pool; sauna; solarium; room service; babysitting . *In room:* TV, hair dryer.

## WHERE TO DINE

**Ratskeller** GERMAN/SWABIAN This is your best bet for dining in Heilbronn. It's an authentic Ratskeller, unlike so many others, but it's been given the modern treatment, with upholstered banquettes and wrought-iron grillwork. The rib-sticking fare here is solid and reliable. Main dishes include goulash, pepper steak with french fries and salad, and grilled sole. Fish specialties and vegetarian meals are also featured. There's an impressive wine list, although many diners consider the "wine of the cellar" (house wine) perfectly adequate.

Im Rathaus, Marktplatz 7. ✆ **07131/8-46-28.** Reservations recommended. Main courses 8€–19.40€ ($7.15–$17.30). AE, MC, V. Mon–Sat 11am–1am. Closed 10 days in Sept.

---

### *Moments* A Tribute to Bacchus

Heilbronn is the largest producer of wine in the Neckar Valley, growing mainly Trollinger and Riesling grapes. The 220ha (550 acres) of vineyards around the town yield about 5 million liters (about 1.3 million gallons) of wine annually. Every September, a large arena around the Rathaus is converted into a **"wine village."** At various booths, you can sample the vintage, often at bargain prices. Merriment and music fill the air. Local food is sold as well, including *Zwiebelkuchen* (onion cake) and *Dicker Hund,* which has been compared to a "pork hamburger" (don't order it rare).

## 3 Stuttgart ★

203km (126 miles) SE of Frankfurt, 222km (138 miles) NW of Munich, 126km (78 miles) SE of Heidelberg

Unlike many large, prosperous industrial centers, Stuttgart is not a city of concrete—on the contrary, two-thirds of the land inside the city limits is devoted to parks, gardens, and woodland. Yet Stuttgart is one of Germany's largest manufacturing cities, the home of Mercedes and Porsche, Zeiss optical equipment, and many other industrial concerns. It's also the site of international trade fairs and congresses.

As a cultural center, it's without peer in southwestern Germany. The Stuttgart Ballet is known throughout the world; its State Opera and Philharmonic Orchestra are also highly regarded. In addition, Stuttgart boasts an abundance of theater groups, cultural festivals, and museums, and is also the largest wine-growing city in Germany.

The name "Stuttgart" comes from a stud farm owned by one of the dukes of Swabia, son of Emperor Otto the Great; a horse can be seen today in the city's coat of arms. By 1427, Stuttgart had become the capital and residence of the counts of Württemberg. The city grew and prospered under the reign of Kaiser Wilhelm I (1816–64). At the turn of the 20th century, it had a population of 175,000. By the beginning of World War I, Stuttgart had reached out to embrace several districts, notably ancient Cannstatt, so that its landmass extended as far as the Neckar River.

In World War II, 53 bombing attacks leveled 60% of Stuttgart's buildings. Not one of its landmarks or historic structures came through intact. After the war, Stuttgart became the capital of the newly formed state of Baden-Württemberg (many still prefer to call it "Swabia"). Stuttgart's population today is about 580,000.

### ESSENTIALS

**GETTING THERE** **By Plane** The **Stuttgart Echterdingen Airport** (✆ **0711/948-33-88**) is 14km (9 miles) south of the city near Echterdingen. The airport has connections with most major German and European cities. Trip time from Frankfurt is 50 minutes; from Hamburg or Berlin, 1¼ hours. The commuter train to Stuttgart's main rail station leaves from below the arrival level of Terminal 1. Trains depart every 20 minutes, taking 27 minutes to reach the heart of Stuttgart. A one-way fare is 3€ ($2.70). A taxi to the center of the city costs from 25€ ($22.35).

**By Train** Stuttgart has rail links to all major German cities, with frequent connections. The train station is directly north of the historic area. Forty-five daily trains run from Munich (trip time: 2–3 hr.), and 30 trains run from Frankfurt (trip time: 1½–2 hr.). For information, call ✆ **01805/99-66-33.**

**By Bus** Long-distance bus service from several major German cities, including Frankfurt, is provided by Europabus Line 1012. Call **Deutsche Touring GmbH** in Stuttgart (✆ **0711/2265881**) or in Frankfurt (✆ **069/7-90-35-0**) for information.

**By Car** Access by car is via the A8 Autobahn east and west or the A81 north and south.

**VISITOR INFORMATION** Information about transportation, sightseeing, and hotels is available at the **Touristik-Zentrum,** Königstrasse 1A (✆ **0711/2-22-82-40**), which is open Monday to Friday 9:30am to 8:30pm and Saturday

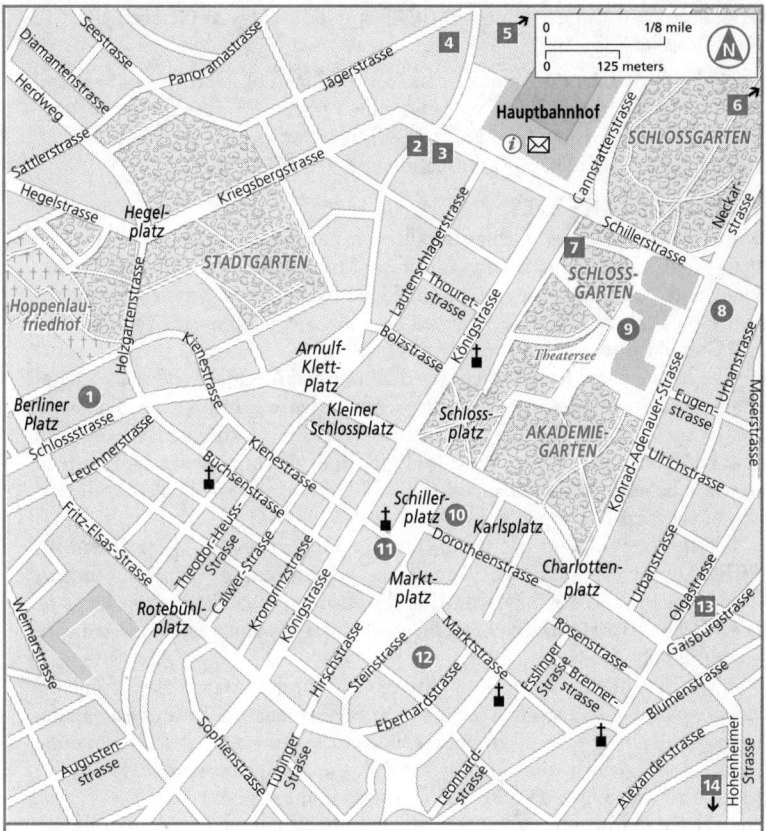

**ATTRACTIONS ●**

Altes Schloss and Württembergisches Landesmuseum **10**
Liederhalle **1**
Neues Schloss **11**
Rathaus **12**
Staatsgalerie (State Gallery of Stuttgart) **8**
Staatstheater **9**

**ACCOMMODATIONS ■**

City Hotel **13**
Hotel Ruff **5**
Hotel am Schlossgarten **7**
Hotel Wörtz-Zur Weinsteige **14**
Mack und Pflieger **4**
Parkhotel am Rundfunk **6**
Rieker **2**
Steigenberger Hotel Graf Zeppelin **3**

Church ✝
Information ⓘ
Post Office ✉

9:30am to 6pm. Sunday hours are 10:30am to 6pm, May to October, and 1 to 6pm, November to April.

**GETTING AROUND** Stuttgart has a streamlined bus and streetcar system, as well as a modern U-Bahn, with more lines planned for the future. A 3-day pass, called a *Tageskarte,* costs 11€ ($9.80). It allows visitors to travel on all city transportation facilities. For information, call ✆ **0711/19449.**

## EXPLORING THE CITY

Many of the most remarkable structures in today's Stuttgart are of advanced design, created by such architects as Ludwig Mies van der Rohe, Walter Gropius, Hans Scharoun, and Le Corbusier. The **Liederhalle,** Schloss-Strasse, constructed in 1956 of concrete, glass, and glazed brick, is fascinating inside and out. The hall contains three auditoriums.

The town's older section is clustered around **Schillerplatz** and the statue of the great German poet and dramatist, Schiller. **Neues Schloss,** on Schlossplatz, can be visited only by group tour. It was originally constructed between 1746 and 1807 and rebuilt beginning in 1958. Today it houses state government rooms. The modern **Rathaus** faces the old Marktplatz, where flowers, fruit, and vegetables are sold in open stalls.

For the best view of Stuttgart, climb to the top of the 512m (1,680-ft.) **Birkenkopf,** west of the city. The hill was created from the debris of Stuttgart dumped here after World War II. After the 20-minute walk to the top, you'll be rewarded by a view of the city and the surrounding Swabian Hills, covered with vineyards and woods.

A free organized walking tour through historical Stuttgart leaves from the inner courtyard of the Altes Schloss on Schillerplatz on Saturday at 10am, lasting until about 5pm. There's also a bus tour, starting at 1pm and continuing until 3:30pm, which winds its way through the city. The cost is 14€ ($12.50) for adults and 8.50€ ($7.60) for children, if they need a seat. For tickets, contact the tourist office (✆ **0711/2-22-82-40**).

**Altes Schloss and Württembergisches Landesmuseum (Old Castle and Württemberg Regional Museum)** ★ One of Stuttgart's oldest standing structures, this huge ducal palace was originally a moated castle built in the 13th century and was later redone in the 16th century in Renaissance style. Now it houses the Württembergisches Landesmuseum, which traces the art and culture of Swabia from the Stone Age to the present. The most valuable items include a survey of European glass through the ages, the ducal art chamber, and the crown jewels. The museum also houses a large collection of Swabian sculptures; an exhibition of clocks, coins, and musical instruments; the famous treasures of the tomb of the Celtic prince of Hochdorf (ca. A.D. 530); and a large collection from the Merovingian period in the early Middle Ages.

Schillerplatz 6. ✆ **0711/2-79-34-00.** Admission 2.60€ ($2.30) adults, 1.50€ ($1.35) students. Tues 10am–1pm; Wed–Sun 10am–5pm. U-Bahn: Schlossplatz.

**Fernsehturm (Television Tower)** This 217m (712-ft.) tower, capped with a red-and-white transmitter, soars above a forested hillock south of Stuttgart. It was designed and built in 1956 using radically innovative applications of aluminum and prestressed reinforced concrete, and served as a prototype for larger towers in Toronto and Moscow. You'll find a restaurant at the tower's base, and a cafe, bar, restaurant, observation platform, and information about the tower's construction at the top of a 150m (492-ft.) elevator. Food is served daily

10am to 8pm. Look outside for the mobile platforms used by window washers. Views from the top are panoramic.

Jahnstrasse 120, Stuttgart-Degerloch, south of the city, just off B3. ✆ **0711/232597.** Admission 3€ ($2.70) adults, 2€ ($1.80) children. Daily 9am–10:30pm. Tram: 15.

**Mercedes-Benz Museum** ★ This museum honors the oldest automobile factory in the world and the invention of the motorcar by Carl Benz and Gottlieb Daimler. Nearly 75 historical vehicles are shown, including a Daimler Reitwagen from 1885, the first motor bicycle. You can also see the Daimler company's first Mercedes of 1902. Racecars on display date from 1899, and include the Blitzen-Benz, the Silver Arrow, the Sauber Mercedes, the Indy car, and some vehicles built especially to achieve speed records.

Mercedesstrasse 136, Stuttgart-Cannstatt. ✆ **0711/1-72-25-78.** Free admission. Tues–Sun 9am–5pm. S-Bahn: 1 to Gottlieb-Daimler-Stadion; then walk to the entrance of the plant, where you'll be taken on a special bus to the museum.

**Staatsgalerie (State Gallery of Stuttgart)** ★ The city's finest art museum exhibits works spanning some 550 years. However, the best collection is from the 19th and 20th centuries, especially the works of the German expressionists—Kirchner, Barlach, and Beckmann—as well as representatives of the Bauhaus school and Blue Rider group, such as Klee and Feininger. There are also good examples of French art of the 19th and 20th centuries and of the European and American postwar avant-garde.

Konrad-Adenauer-Strasse 30–32. ✆ **0711/2-12-40-50.** Admission 4.50€ ($4) adults, 2.50€ ($2.25) students, free for children 13 and under. Tues–Wed and Fri–Sun 10am–6pm; Thurs 10am–9pm. Open to midnight the 1st Sat of each month. U-Bahn: Staatsgalerie.

## SHOPPING

Home to clothing designers Hugo Boss and Ulli Knecht, Stuttgart has its fair share of boutiques that range from interesting to elegant. **Klett Passage,** located across from the train station, is an underground mall full of upscale shops. If you follow the Königstrasse from the station for about half a mile, you'll likely find anything you want in one of the retail stores that line the street. There are boutiques along the Calwer Strasse, especially in the gleaming chrome-and-glass arcade, **Calwer Passage.** Bargains galore can be found at the Saturday morning **flea market** held on the Karlsplatz between the old castle and the new palace, where clothes, books, furniture, household items, art, and just about anything else is likely to turn up.

The latest styles for men can be found at **Holy's,** Königstrasse 54A (✆ **0711/22-29-44-4;** S-Bahn: Hauptbahnhof), which carries the work of local heroes Boss and Knecht as well as other leading international designers, from Prada to Dolce Gabbana. North of the city, **Salamander,** Stammheimerstrasse 10, Kornwestheim (✆ **07154/1-50**), has a factory outlet selling shoes for the whole family in styles ranging from fun and functional to the more conservative.

**Gunter Krauss,** Kronprinzstrasse 21 (✆ **0711/29-73-95;** S-Bahn: Stadtmitte), has won numerous design awards for its interior of white marble, mirrors, and gilded fixtures; it houses an impressive array of designer jewelry. In business since 1723, **Tritschler,** Am Marktplatz (✆ **0711/29-15-82;** U-Bahn: Charlottenplatz), stocks glass, porcelain, and fine china as well as cutlery and decorative housewares. **Pavillon,** Eberhardstrasse 31–33 (✆ **0711/24-31-34;** U-Bahn: Rathaus), specializes in silver from the 19th and 20th centuries, and also sells glass, crystal, Meissen porcelain, and a few paintings.

**Kurtz,** Am Marktplatz 10 (✆ **0711/23-85-20;** U-Bahn: Charlottenplatz), sells puzzles, games, dolls, and toys for children of all ages. The city's largest bookstore, **Wittwer,** Königstrasse 30 (✆ **0711/2-50-70;** S-Bahn: Hauptbahnhof), carries many books in English and has tables placed throughout the store so you can comfortably scan potential purchases. For a bit of everything, head to the city's largest department store, **Breuninger,** Marktstrasse 3 (✆ **0711/21-10;** U-Bahn: Charlottenplatz), where glass elevators whisk you through several floors of housewares, furnishings, and fashion. Take a break for chocolate or gingerbread at **Susi,** Königstrasse 1 (✆ **0711/2-26-41-15;** S-Bahn: Hauptbahnhof), and you'll feel well-rewarded no matter how the shopping is going.

## WHERE TO STAY

No matter when you come to Stuttgart, you'll probably find an international trade fair in progress, from the January glass-and-ceramics exposition to the December book exhibition. (Stuttgart is also southern Germany's most important publishing center.) Good accommodations may be difficult to find at almost any time, so you should always reserve in advance.

### EXPENSIVE

**Hotel am Schlossgarten** ★ This tasteful 10-floor hotel isn't splashy, but it offers very good conveniences and comfort. Rooms are good-size and well furnished, with feather comforters and bathrooms containing shower-tub combinations.

Schillerstrasse 23 (on the Hauptbahnhof square), 70173 Stuttgart. ✆ **0711/2-02-60.** Fax 0711/2-02-68-88. www.hotelschlossgarten.com. 116 units. 230€–270€ ($205.40–$241.10) double; from 276€ ($246.45) suite. AE, DC, MC, V. Parking 12€ ($10.70). U-Bahn: Hauptbahnhof. **Amenities:** 2 restaurants; bar; fitness center; Jacuzzi; sauna; room service; massage; babysitting; laundry/dry cleaning. *In room:* TV, minibar, hair dryer.

**Steigenberger Hotel Graf Zeppelin** ★★ This is the best hotel for those who come to wheel and deal with Stuttgart businesspeople. Although situated right at the train station, it's not only attractive but also dignified and stylish, once you get by its plain postwar exterior. The spacious soundproof rooms are colorfully decorated, all with tidily kept bathrooms with shower-tub combinations.

Arnulf-Klett-Platz 7, 70173 Stuttgart. ✆ **800/223-5652** in the U.S. and Canada, or 0711/2-04-80. Fax 0711/2-04-85-42. www.steigenberger.com. 195 units. 220€–240€ ($196.45–$214.30) double; 312€–348€ ($278.60–$310.75) suite. AE, DC, MC, V. Parking 16€ ($14.30). U-Bahn: Hauptbahnhof. **Amenities:** 3 restaurants; 2 bars; pool; fitness center; Jacuzzi; sauna; room service; babysitting; laundry/dry cleaning. *In room:* A/C, TV, minibar, hair dryer, safe.

### MODERATE

**City Hotel** *Finds* The City is a renovated bed-and-breakfast-type hotel, within walking distance of the sights in the city center. It offers pleasantly furnished but hardly spectacular rooms equipped with private showers (no tubs) and direct-dial telephones. The generous breakfast buffet, the only meal served, is offered in a sunny winter garden.

Uhlandstrasse 18 (directly west of Charlottenplatz), 70182 Stuttgart. ✆ **0711/21-08-10.** Fax 0711/2-36-97-72. 31 units. 95€–115€ ($84.85–$102.70) double. Rates include buffet breakfast. AE, DC, MC, V. Free parking. U-Bahn: Olgaeck. **Amenities:** Breakfast room; lounge; room service. *In room:* TV, minibar, hair dryer.

**Hotel Ruff** ★ This hotel, although not as centrally located as the City Hotel, offers a lot more style and better rooms. Other side benefits are an attractively tiled indoor pool with a sauna and a manicured garden where a waiter will take your drink order. Rooms are well maintained, inviting, and a good value for the price. Most are medium in size, although some are quite small. All contain showers.

Friedhofstrasse 21, 70191 Stuttgart. ✆ **0711/2-58-70.** Fax 0711/2-58-87-404. rema-ruff@T-online.de. 90 units. 108€–220€ ($96.45–$196.45) double. Rates include buffet breakfast. AE, DC, MC, V. Parking 10€ ($8.95). U-Bahn: Turlenstrasse/Burgerhospital. **Amenities:** Restaurant; lounge; room service. *In room:* TV, minibar, hair dryer.

**Parkhotel am Rundfunk** If you're looking for a first-class accommodation in a secluded and quiet area, this is your place. It's outside the center in the gardens of the Villa Berg, within walking distance of a mineral-water pool surrounded by a park. Rooms are good-size, well designed, and have a decidedly personal air, all with bathrooms containing a shower-tub combination.

Villastrasse 21, 70190 Stuttgart. ✆ **0711/2-80-10.** Fax 0711/2-86-43-53. www.parkhotel-stuttgart.de. 69 units. 113€ ($100.90) double. Rates include buffet breakfast. AE, DC, MC, V. Parking 7€ ($6.25). Tram: 1, 2, or 14. **Amenities:** 2 restaurants; lounge; room service; babysitting; laundry/dry cleaning. *In room:* TV, minibar, hair dryer.

## INEXPENSIVE

**Hotel Wörtz-Zur Weinsteige** *Value* The amber lights of a Weinstube welcome visitors to this local favorite in Stuttgart, which has the best rooms and the best food of all local hotels in this price range. The small rooms are paneled and sometimes have massive hand-carved armoires; all are soundproof. The Weinstube evokes the feeling of a remote corner of Swabia—it's perfect for relaxing after a long trip. The hotel is known for its garden terrace.

Hohenheimerstrasse 28–30, 70184 Stuttgart. ✆ **0711/2-36-70-00.** Fax 0711/2-36-70-07. www.hotel-woertz.de. 25 units, 22 with bath or shower. 75€ ($67) double without bath or shower; 100€–135€ ($89.30–$120.55) double with bath or shower. Rates include buffet breakfast. AE, DC, MC, V. Parking 6€ ($5.35). S-Bahn: Dobelstrasse. **Amenities:** Restaurant; lounge; room service. *In room:* TV, hair dryer.

**Mack und Pflieger** This hotel, behind an uninspired modern facade, is actually two in one. Hotel Mack and Hotel Pflieger stand close to each other and are under the same management. Check in at the Mack, because there's always someone there at the reception desk. Home-like and cozy, the hotel offers up-to-date rooms that are small and basic but still quite adequate. The rooms all come with either a bath or shower.

Kriegerstrasse 7–11 (an 8-min. walk from the Hauptbahnhof), 70191 Stuttgart. ✆ **0711/29-19-27.** Fax 0711/29-34-89. www.hotel-mack-pflieger.de. 40 units, 25 with tub or shower. 67€–120€ ($59.85–$107.15) double. Rates include buffet breakfast. AE, DC, MC, V. Free parking. U-Bahn: Hauptbahnhof. **Amenities:** Breakfast room; lounge. *In room:* TV.

**Rieker** This well-furnished hotel offers a convenient location and a certain charm. Its public areas have lots of comfortably upholstered armchairs and Oriental rugs scattered over parquet or terrazzo floors. Some of the virtually soundproof rooms are designed with sleeping alcoves and draw curtains. All rooms contain a neatly kept bathroom with a shower-tub combination. It's only a 1-minute walk from Stuttgart's Municipal Air Terminal, where buses leave frequently for Echterdingen Airport.

Friedrichstrasse 3, 70174 Stuttgart. ✆ **0711/22-13-11.** Fax 0711/29-38-94. www.hotel-rieker.de. 63 units. 96€–136€ ($85.75–$121.45) double. Rates include breakfast. AE, DC, MC, V. Parking 8€ ($7.15). U-Bahn: Hauptbahnhof. **Amenities:** Breakfast room; lounge; room service; babysitting; laundry/dry cleaning. *In room:* TV, hair dryer.

## WHERE TO DINE

### EXPENSIVE

**Délice** ★★ AUSTRIAN/INTERNATIONAL A 200-year-old vaulted ceiling arches over the tables of this sophisticated cellar-level restaurant. This icon of *neue Küche* (modern cuisine) is a showcase for the cuisine of Vienna-born Friedrich Gutscher, whose alchemy in the kitchen can be observed from some of the tables. The menu changes virtually every week. Starters might include cream of cucumber soup in summer, or consommé of pigeon with truffles in winter. A succulent main course might be a filet of Brittany sea wolf marinated in lemon juice and olive oil and served with a salad of warm asparagus and exotic mushrooms. A nougat truffle, or a traditional Austrian treat called *Topfenknoedel* (a cottage cheese dumpling) are excellent desserts. The wine list is almost overwhelming, with selections from virtually every wine-producing region in Europe.

Hauptstätter Strasse 61. ✆ **0711/6-40-32-22.** Reservations recommended. Main courses 25€–29€ ($22.35–$25.90); fixed-price menu 70€ ($62.50). Mon–Fri 6:30pm–midnight. No credit cards. Closed 2 weeks in June. U-Bahn: Österreichischer Platz.

### MODERATE

**Alte Kanzlei** SWABIAN/INTERNATIONAL This popular folkloric restaurant is in the section of the old castle (Altes Schloss) originally built in 1533. One of the most popular Swabian specialties is *Maultaschen,* the Stuttgart version of ravioli, stuffed with ham or spinach. Equally popular is *Stuttgarter Ratsherrenteller,* filet of pork and beef served with *Spätzle* (dumplings), fresh vegetables, and mushroom gravy. To accompany your meal, ask for the local Pils beer or some of the region's fine wines, such as Tuniberg, a pale rosé, or one of the full-bodied red wines made from the Trollinger grape.

Schillerplatz 5A. ✆ **0711/29-44-57.** Reservations recommended. Main courses 11.50€–17€ ($10.25–$15.20). AE, DC, MC, V. Daily 11am–11pm. U-Bahn: Schlossplatz.

**Zeppelin-Stüble** SWABIAN In this elegantly appointed restaurant furnished with Swabian antiques, each dish is individually prepared from fresh ingredients, according to the season. Swabian specialties like *Rostbraten* (roast beef) and *Maultaschen* (Stuttgart's version of ravioli, stuffed with ham or spinach) are offered. Although many restaurants in Stuttgart have abandoned true Swabian cuisine for more international fare, the chefs here still turn out the old-fashioned specialties preferred by locals. The kitchen does an excellent *Schwäbischer* sauerbraten (a Swabian version of marinated beef) with Spätzle and salad.

In the Steigenberger Hotel Graf Zeppelin, Arnulf-Klett-Platz 7. ✆ **0711/20-48-184.** Fax 0711/2048-542. Reservations recommended. Main courses 9€–18€ ($8.05–$16.05); fixed-price menu 8.50€–40€ ($7.60–$35.70). AE, DC, MC, V. Mon–Sat 11:30am–2:30pm and 6–10:30pm; Sun 11am–2:30pm. U-Bahn: Hauptbahnhof.

**Zur Weinsteige** ★ INTERNATIONAL The interior of this place is a celebration of German handcrafts. Everything looks handmade, from the hand-blown leaded glass in the small-paned windows to the carved columns and tables and chairs. International cuisine, with numerous Swabian specialties, is offered. In summer, you'll be tempted to sit among the grapevines stretching over the sun terrace. Also worth seeing is the wine cellar, well stocked with the best regional wines and a good selection of German and international wines. You can even buy wine directly from the hotel's vineyards. Next to the cellar is a room for sitting and tasting. The Hotel Wörtz also has 32 well-furnished but small rooms, each with minibar and TV. Doubles cost 130€–135€ ($116.10–$120.55) with suites going for 300€ ($267.90), including breakfast. The hotel's original core was built in 1955 and still carries a 1950s aura about it, albeit with softening touches from lots of antique artifacts hauled in from since-demolished buildings. A new and more comfortable annex was built in 2002 with better accommodations. The website is www.hotel-woertz.de.

In the Hotel Wörtz, Hohenheimerstrasse 30. ✆ **0711/2-36-70-00.** Fax 0711/2-36-70-07. Reservations recommended. Main courses 8€–25€ ($7.15–$22.35); fixed-price lunch 10€ ($8.95); fixed-price menu 25€–60€ ($22.35–$53.60). AE, DC, MC, V. Tues–Sat noon–2pm and 6–10pm. Closed holidays, 3 weeks in Jan, and 3 weeks in Aug. S-Bahn: Dobelstrasse.

## STUTTGART AFTER DARK

Listings of the various cultural events, as well as tickets, are available from the tourist office (see earlier in this section). The magazine *Lift,* available at newsstands, lists all the happenings around Stuttgart.

**THE PERFORMING ARTS** **Staatstheater,** Oberer Schlossgarten (✆ **0711/20-20-90;** S-Bahn: Hauptbahnhof), is the leading cultural venue in Stuttgart. The theater consists of a Grosses Haus for opera and ballet, a Kleines Haus for theater, and the Kammer-Theater, which puts on experimental works. This is home to the world-class **Stuttgart Ballet,** established by the American choreographer John Cranko in the 1960s, and now led by Reid Anderson. It also houses the respected **Staatsoper (State Opera).** Tickets are 9€ to 75€ ($8.05–$67) and can be purchased at the Staatstheater box office. Closed August and September.

Classical and other concerts may be heard in the three halls of the **Liederhalle,** Schloss-Strasse (✆ **0711/2167110;** U-Bahn: Liederhalle/Berlinerplatz), which is home to the **Stuttgarter Philharmoniker,** under the baton of Jörg Peter Weigle, and the **Radio Symphony Orchestra.** Tickets for all concerts are on sale at **SKS Russ,** Charlottenplatz 17 (✆ **0711/1635321;** U-Bahn: Charlottenplatz). Prices are 8€ to 25€ ($7.15–$22.35).

**THE BAR, CAFE & CLUB SCENE** You might start your evening with a drink at **Amadeus,** Charlottenplatz 17 (✆ **0711/29-26-78;** U-Bahn: Charlottenplatz), where students and locals gather. It's open 11am to 2am Monday and Tuesday, 11am to 3am Wednesday and Thursday, and 11am to 4am Friday and Saturday. For a trendier locale, head to **Palast der Republik,** Friedrichstrasse 27 (✆ **0711/2-26-48-87;** U-Bahn: Keplerstrasse), a 100-year-old bar that attracts an artsier crowd. DJs play funk and soul. It's open Monday to Wednesday 11am to 2am and Thursday to Saturday 11am to 3am.

**Café Stella,** Hauptstätter Strasse 57 (✆ **0711/6-40-25-83;** U-Bahn: Österreichischerplatz), hosts local jazz bands on the first Monday of the month. It's open daily 9am until 1am.

Gay men dance at **King's Club,** Calverstrasse 21 (✆ **0711/2-26-45-58;** S-Bahn: Stadtmitte), until Sunday, when they're booted for a women-only night. The club is open Wednesday to Sunday 10pm to 6am, with a 10€ ($8.95) cover Friday and Saturday, which includes two drinks. **Laura's Club,** Friedrichstrasse 7 (✆ **0711/29-01-60;** S-Bahn: Stadtmitte), is a lesbian and gay bar with a dance floor. It's open Thursday to Saturday 10pm to 5am. There's no cover.

## 4 Tübingen ★★

47km (29 miles) S of Stuttgart, 153km (95 miles) NE of Freiburg

Though it's often compared to Heidelberg, this quiet old university town on the upper Neckar has a look and personality all its own. Gabled medieval houses are crowded against the ancient town wall at the bank of the river. In summer, students pole gondola-like boats up and down the river. This far upstream, the Neckar is too shallow for commercial vessels, so Tübingen has been spared the industrial look of a trading community.

Progress has not passed the city by, however. In spite of its medieval aspect, it has a new residential and science suburb in the shadow of the Schoenbuch Forest north of the city, with medical facilities, research institutes, and lecture halls affiliated with the university. The buildings of the old university, founded in 1477, are located north of the botanical gardens. The humanist Melanchthon taught here in the 16th century, and later on Schiller, Hegel, and Hölderlin were students.

### ESSENTIALS

**GETTING THERE** **By Air** The nearest major airport, at Stuttgart (see earlier in this chapter), has good connections to Tübingen, including a direct bus link.

**By Train** The Stuttgart–Tübingen rail line offers frequent service. Tübingen also has good rail ties to other major cities in Germany, including Frankfurt (trip time: 3½ hr.), Berlin (trip time: 11 hr.), and Hamburg (trip time: 8½ hr.). For information, call ✆ **01805/99-66-33.**

**By Bus** Long-distance buses link Tübingen with major German cities, like Stuttgart. For information, call **Deutsche Touring GmbH** in Frankfurt (✆ **069/23-07-35**) or in Stuttgart (✆ **0711/226588**).

**By Car** Access is via Route 27 west from the A8 Autobahn running east and west or Route 28 east from the A81 Autobahn running north and south.

**VISITOR INFORMATION** Contact the **Verkehrsverein,** An der Eberhardsbrücke (✆ **07071/9-13-60**), open Monday to Friday 9am to 5pm and Saturday 9am to 3pm.

### SEEING THE SIGHTS

The Neckar River runs through Tübingen. With landfill, the city created a long and narrow island in the river's center. This artificially created island is reached by walking across a wide bridge called Eberhardesbrücke. Locals like to cross the bridge to this island for summer promenades. The tree-shaded promenade where they like to walk is called **Platanenallee** ★★, which in fair weather, in summer, is filled with strollers. From there, you get a panoramic view of the town, with its willows and houses reflected in the river. Towering above the other buildings is the Renaissance castle, which is now used by the university. It's worth climbing up to the castle for the dramatic view from the terraces.

The narrow streets of the Altstadt wind up and down the hillside, but they all seem to lead to **Marktplatz** ★, where festive markets are held on Monday, Wednesday, and Friday. You'll feel as if you're stepping into the past when you come upon country people selling fruit and vegetables in the open square. Facing the square is the **Rathaus** ★, which dates from the 15th century but also has more recent additions, including the 19th-century painted designs on the facade.

On a hillside above Marktplatz is **Stiftskirche,** Holzmarkt, the former church of the Stift, an Augustinian monastery. The monastery became a Protestant seminary in 1548, and its church became the Collegiate Church. Worth seeing inside are the tombs of the dukes of Württemberg in the chancel and the 15th-century French Gothic pulpit and rood screen. The church is open daily 9am to 5pm. You can climb the **tower** (enter on the left of the chancel) for a panoramic view. The chancel and tower are open April to November daily 10:30am to 5pm. Admission to the tower is 1.55€ ($1.40) for adults and 1€ (90¢) for children.

**Hölderlinturm,** Bursagasse 6 (✆ **07071/2-20-40**), lies at the end of a walk by the Neckar River. This was the home of the lyric poet, Friedrich Hölderlin, who resided here with the Zimmer family from the onset of his mental illness at age 36 until his death in 1843. Hölderlin is not well-known outside Germany, but we highly recommend that you read a few of his poems in translation. Most tours of the museum are in German, but you can request one in English; otherwise you won't understand many of the exhibits. The house is open Tuesday to Friday 10am to noon and 3 to 5pm; Saturday and Sunday 2 to 5pm. Admission is 1.55€ ($1.40) adults, 1€ (90¢) children and students.

## WHERE TO STAY

**Hotel am Bad** *Value* This hotel, located in the center of one of Tübingen's well-maintained public parks, offers woodland calm not far from the city center. Its rambling rose-colored exterior complements the masses of red flowers on the sun terrace. Rooms are modest and a bit small but still comfortable, all containing bathrooms with shower-tub combinations.

Am Freibad 2, 72072 Tübingen. ✆ **07071/79740.** Fax 07071/7-53-36. 35 units. 83€–95€ ($74.10–$84.85) double. Rates include buffet breakfast. AE, MC, V. Free outdoor parking; 6€ ($5.35) in garage. Closed Dec 10–Jan 10. **Amenities:** Breakfast room; bar; pool; fitness center; sauna; room service; babysitting; laundry/dry cleaning. *In room:* TV, minibar, hair dryer.

**Krone Hotel** ★ The town's most prestigious hotel is located right off the river, in the heart of Tübingen. It's traditional and conservative, with a home-like atmosphere. The decor includes a liberal use of antiques or good reproductions. Rooms are personalized; many are decoratively tiled, and all contain bathrooms with shower-tub combinations.

Uhlandstrasse, 72072 Tübingen. ✆ **07071/1-33-10.** Fax 07071/13-31-32. www.krone-tuebingen.de. 50 units. 123€–153€ ($109.85–$136.65) double; from 163€–193€ ($145.55–$172.35) suite. Rates include buffet breakfast. AE, DC, MC, V. Free parking. Closed Dec 23–31. **Amenities:** Restaurant; lounge; room service; laundry/dry cleaning. *In room:* TV, hair dryer.

## WHERE TO DINE

In addition to the restaurants below, the **Krone Hotel** (see above) is a good dining spot.

**Restaurant Museum** ★ *Value* INTERNATIONAL/SWABIAN This is one of Tübingen's foremost restaurants. It's a pleasant place to dine on international specialties, such as Marseille snail soup, or regional dishes, such as Swabian medallions of veal. The lunches here are considered by many locals (including students) to be not only the best in town but also the best value.

Wilhelmstrasse. ✆ **07071/2-28-28.** Reservations recommended. Main courses 15€–22€ ($13.40–$19.65). AE, MC, V. Daily 11:30am–2:30pm; Tues–Sun 6:30–11:30pm.

**Restaurant Rosenau** ★★ GERMAN/SWABIAN This restaurant, near the botanical gardens, offers the finest food in the town center, though it's not as good as at the Gasthof Waldhorn (see below), on the outskirts. Landgasthof

Rosenau is like a roadhouse with a cafe annex. The owner serves superb Swabian specialties along with modern cuisine. The typical regional fare is listed under the gutbürgerlich selections. Try the tasty and filling Swabian hot pot with Spätzle (dumplings) and fresh mushrooms. From the section of the menu "reserved for gourmets," you might choose a delectable veal steak with morels. Desserts are often elaborate concoctions. In fair weather, guests can order drinks out in the sun.

Beim Neuen Botanischen Garten. ✆ **07071/6-88-66.** Reservations recommended. Main courses 13€–22€ ($11.60–$19.65). AE, DC, MC, V. Tues–Sun 11am–midnight.

### NEARBY DINING

**Gasthof Waldhorn** ★★★ GERMAN/FRENCH The finest restaurant in the area is not in Tübingen but on its outskirts, at Tübingen-Bebenhausen. It's decorated like a farmhouse. Herr and Frau Schilling offer a light German and French cuisine based on regional ingredients, backed up by an impressive wine list (with many half bottles). This restaurant truly deserves its stars. The chef combines inventiveness with a solid technique. The menu changes daily but is likely to include trout terrine and wild venison with forest mushrooms, along with whatever vegetable is in season. The dessert specialty is a soft cream concoction flavored with rose hips. Behind the house is a garden with five tables for summer dining.

Schönbuchstrasse 49 (6km/4 miles from the town center). ✆ **07071/6-12-70.** Reservations required. Main courses 18€–33€ ($16.05–$29.45); fixed-price lunch 55€ ($49.10); fixed-price dinner 40€–90€ ($35.70–$80.35). AE. Wed–Sun noon–2:30pm and 6:30pm–midnight. Closed Aug 18–30.

## TÜBINGEN AFTER DARK

Student-inspired nightlife makes this old town very young at heart. Just head into the Marktplatz at night and follow the sound of revelry. You can order a beer and read the comics hanging on the walls of **Marktschenke,** Am Markt 11 (✆ **07071/2-20-35**), then join the students spilling outside into the square. Daily hours are 9am to 1am. Or you might start your evening in the ancient **Boulanger,** Collegiumsgasse 2 (✆ **07071/2-33-45**), where you could offer to pick up Hegel's bar tab, which has gone unpaid for more than 200 years. A riverside retreat, **Neckarmüller,** Gartenstrasse 4 (✆ **07071/2-78-48**), has a barroom, but more inviting in nice weather are the picnic tables on the banks of the river. It's open daily 10am to 1am. Also on the Neckar, **Ammerschlag,** Ammergasse 13 (✆ **07071/5-15-91**), has live music one Sunday a month, ranging from blues to rap. Hours are daily 3pm until 1am.

Located next to the Stiftskirche steps, **Tangente-Night** (✆ **07071/2-30-07**) is a place to dance to techno, acid jazz, and house at night. It's open daily 11am until 3am. Dancing is also top priority at **Zentrum Zoo,** Schleifmuhleweg 86 (✆ **07071/9-44-80**), open Tuesday and Thursday to Saturday 9pm until 2am; Sunday 8:30pm to 1am. Cover is 3€ ($2.70).

## 5 Schwäbisch Hall ★★

97km (60 miles) NE of Stuttgart, 138km (86 miles) W of Nürnberg

Technically, this medieval town is not in the Neckar Valley; however, if you skip it in your travels through this region, you'll have missed one of the treasures of southwestern Germany. Schwäbisch Hall is located in the heart of the forests of the Schwäbische Alb, where it clings to the steep banks of the Kocher River, a tributary of the Neckar. The houses of the Altstadt are set on terraces built into the hillside; from the opposite bank they appear to be arranged in steps, overlooking the old wooden river bridges.

## ESSENTIALS

**GETTING THERE** **By Train** Trains run daily from Stuttgart and Nürnberg into the Bahnhof Schwäbisch Hall. For information call ✆ **01805/99-66-33.**

**By Bus** Regional bus service in the area is offered by **Stuttgart GmbH. Call** (✆ **07131/6-24-50**) for schedules and information.

**By Car** Access is via the A6 Autobahn running east and west, or Route 14 from the east and Route 19 from the north.

**VISITOR INFORMATION** The **Verkehrsverein** is at Am Markt 9 (✆ **0791/75-12-46**). Open October to April, Monday to Friday 9am to 5pm; May to September, Monday to Friday 9am to 6pm and Saturday 10am to 3pm.

## SEEING THE SIGHTS

Schwabisch's **Marktplatz** ★★ is the most attractive market square in all of Germany. Flanking the sloping square are fine half-timbered patrician houses and at the lower end stands the baroque Rathaus. In the center of the square is a 16th-century Gothic fountain adorned with statues of St. Michael with St. George and Samson. The Marktplatz is the scene of festive occasions, such as the annual Kuchenfest, celebrating the ancient salt industry that grew around the salt springs in Schwäbisch Hall.

On the north side of Marktplatz, facing the Rathaus, are 54 large, imposing, delicately curved stone steps leading to **Michaelskirche.** This cathedral is a 15th-century Gothic Hallenkirche with a 12th-century tower. Many pews date from the 15th century, as does St. Michael's altarpiece in the side chapel. The church is open Monday 2 to 5pm, Tuesday to Saturday 9am to noon and 2 to 5pm, and Sunday 11am to noon and 2 to 5pm.

## WHERE TO STAY & DINE

**Der Adelshof** ★ The Adelshof is in an attractive stone building, much of it dating from 1400. Its advantage is its location, right in the center of town. Rooms are clean and comfortable, if a bit small, all equipped with bathrooms containing shower-tub combinations. Downstairs, the restaurant serves some of the best food in town. The recently refurbished, 500-year-old Kellerbar has become one of the town's most popular bars.

Am Markt 12 (on Marktplatz), 74523 Schwäbisch Hall. ✆ **0791/7-58-90.** Fax 0791/60-36. www.hotel-adelshof.de. 47 units. 125€ ($111.65) double; 245€ ($218.80) suite. Rates include breakfast. AE, DC, MC, V. Free parking. **Amenities:** Restaurant; bar; fitness center; sauna; solarium; room service; laundry/dry cleaning. *In room:* TV, hair dryer.

**Hotel Hohenlohe** ★★ The Hohenlohe is on the left bank of the Kocher River, in the historic Freie Reichsstadt district opposite the town center. Rooms are pleasant and compact, with bright color accents. Most of the accommodations open onto scenic views, and all of them have a combination tub and shower. Breakfast is served on an open-view roof deck. The restaurant offers regional meals; a cafeteria and a bar are also on the premises.

Am Weilertor 14, 74523 Schwäbisch Hall. ✆ **0791/7-58-70.** Fax 0791/75-87-84. www.ringhotels.de. 130 units. 117€–144€ ($104.50–$128.60) double; 204€–229€ ($182.15–$204.50) suite. Rates include buffet breakfast. AE, DC, MC, V. Parking 5€ ($4.45) inside and free outside. **Amenities:** Restaurant; cafeteria; bar; 3 pools; fitness center; sauna; solarium; bowling alley; room service; massage. *In room:* TV, minibar, hair dryer.

# 13

# Frankfurt

The thriving industrial metropolis of Frankfurt, Germany's fifth-largest city and Goethe's hometown, may well be your first glimpse of Germany.

Most international flights land here at Frankfurt's huge airport, and its massive 19th-century railway station is the busiest in Europe. Frankfurt is a heavily industrial city, with more than 2,450 factories operating around the ford (Furt) on the Main River, where the Frankish tribes once settled. As the home of the Bundesbank, Germany's central bank, Frankfurt is also the country's financial center. It's been a major banking city ever since the Rothschilds opened their first bank here in 1798. Frankfurt also has a leading stock exchange.

Frankfurt's international trade fairs in spring and autumn bring some 1.5 million visitors to the city and its *Messe Frankfurt* (fairgrounds), often causing a logjam at hotels. Fairs include the Motor Show, the Textile Fair, the Chemical Industries Fair, and the Cookery Fair. But the best known is the International Book Fair, which draws some 5,500 publishers from nearly 100 countries and is the most important meeting place in the world for the acquisition and sale of book rights and translations.

If all roads used to lead to Rome, today they seem to converge on Frankfurt, making it the hub of a great network of European traffic routes. Frankfurt today is both a much visited business center and a worthy tourist destination with a distinct personality.

## 1 Orientation

### GETTING THERE

**BY PLANE** **Flughafen Frankfurt/Main** (✆ **069/69-00;** www.frankfurt-airport.de), lies 11km (7 miles) from the city center at the Frankfurter Kreuz, the intersection of two major expressways, A3 and A5. This airport, continental Europe's busiest, serves more than 240 destinations in about 110 countries worldwide. It's also Germany's major international gateway. From here, all important German airports can be reached via Frankfurt. Flying time from Frankfurt to Berlin and Hamburg is 70 minutes, and to Munich, 60 minutes.

At the **Airport Train Station** beneath Terminal 1, you can connect to German InterCity trains and S-Bahn commuter trains to Frankfurt and nearby cities. Terminal 2 is linked to Terminal 1 by a people-mover system, Sky Line, which provides quick transfers (the airport's standard connection time is 45 min. maximum).

Train information is available at the **German DB Travel Center** (✆ **01805/99-66-33**). **S-Bahn** line S-8 between the airport and Frankfurt center runs every 10 minutes and deposits passengers at the main rail station in 11 to 15 minutes. A one-way ticket costs 1€ (90¢). Tickets should be purchased before boarding.

**BY TRAIN** Frankfurt's main rail station, the **Hauptbahnhof,** the busiest in Europe, is the arrival point for some 1,600 trains per day carrying about 255,000 passengers. A train arrives from most major cities of Germany every hour until 8pm. Many other European cities also have direct rail links with Frankfurt. For travel information, ticket reservations, and seat information, call **Deutsche Bahn** (✆ **01805/99-66-33** or visit www.bahn.de/ and click on "International Guests").

**BY BUS** Frankfurt has long-distance bus service to about 800 German and European cities. Buses depart from the south side of the Hauptbahnhof. For information, contact **Deutsche Touring,** Am Römerhof 17 (✆ **069/230735**).

**BY CAR** The A3 and A5 Autobahns intersect at Frankfurt. The A3 comes in from the Netherlands, Cologne, and Bonn, and continues east and south to Würzburg, Nürnberg, and Munich. The A5 comes from the northeast (Hannover and Bad Hersfeld) and continues south to Heidelberg, Mannheim, and Basel (Switzerland). From the west, the A60 connects with the A66, which leads to Frankfurt and the inner city, hooking up with the A3. Road signs and directions are frequently posted.

## VISITOR INFORMATION

The **tourist office** is in two locations: At the Hauptbahnhof, opposite the main entrance (✆ **069/21-23-88-49;** www.frankfurt-tourismus.de), open Monday to Friday 8am to 9pm, Saturday and Sunday 9am to 6pm and the other is in Römer (✆ **069/21-23-87-08**) and is open Monday to Friday 8am to 5pm, Saturday and Sunday 9am to 4pm, closing 1 hour later in the summer months. **Amerika Haus** is an American cultural Institute at Staufenstrasse 1 (✆ **069/9-71-44-80;** www.usembassy.de/frankfurt/amerikahaus/).

## CITY LAYOUT

Most of Frankfurt's sights, nightlife, restaurants, and hotels lie in the **Stadmitte** or center of town. However, chances are you'll cross the Main River to visit the apple-wine taverns in the **Sachsenhausen** area as well. It is also possible that you'll seek out both restaurants and hotels in the increasingly fashionable **Westend.** Most of the other areas of Frankfurt probably will not concern you unless you're hunting for intriguing restaurants in the **Nordend** or even in the **Ostend** or "east end."

Most of the heart of Frankfurt can be covered on foot. Nearly all the main sights lay within the boundaries of the old town walls, which today form a stretch of narrow parkland, almost a perfect half moon around the Alstadt or old city.

A good place to start exploring Frankfurt is at the **Römerberg,** or historical core of the city. This is actually the site where Charlemagne erected his fort. In medieval times, the Römerberg was the marketplace of Frankfurt.

Once one of the great old towns of Europe, the Altstadt was blasted in two horrendous air raids in 1944. Some of its buildings have been sympathetically reconstructed in the old style.

The most important building in the Stadmitte is the red-sandstone church of **St. Bartholomäus,** often called "the Dom" although it isn't a cathedral. It was the venue for the coronation of the Holy Roman Emperors even though it didn't have cathedral status.

Directly to the east of Römerplatz stands the glaring modern building, **Kultur-Schirn,** a cultural center where various exhibitions are held. It is a

# Frankfurt

Berlin
GERMANY
Frankfurt
MIQ./ADICKESALLEE
Adickes allee
Miquel allee
Hansa Allee
Eyssenecksstrasse
Cron-stettenstr.
Bremer Strasse
Holzhausenstr.
HOLZHAUSENSTRASSE
GRÜNEBURG PARK
Franz Rücker allee
Falkstrasse
Leipziger Str.
Miquel allee
Wolfgangstr.
Furstenbergerstr.
Grüneburgweg
Wolfgangstr.
Baustrasse
GRÜNEBURGWEG
Siesmayer str.
Feldburgstr.
Freidburgstr.
Grüneburgweg
WESTEND
Bockenheimer Landstrasse
Staufenstr.
Gärtnerweg
ESCHENHEIMER TOR
Rothschild's Park
Bockenheimer Anl.
University
Senckenberganl
Schumannstr.
Beethovenstr.
Mendelssohnstr.
Arndtstr.
Lindenstr.
Bockenheimer Hochstr.
Guiollett str.
Gr. Bockenheimerstr.
HAUPTWACHE
TAUNUSANLAGE
Junghof Str.
Neue Mainzer
Haupt-Güterbahnhof
Westendstrasse
Berliner str.
THEATERPLATZ
HAUPTBAHNHOF
Taunus str.
Kaiserstr.
Munchener Str.
Untermainbr.
Mainzer Land str.
Leuschner str.
Untermain kai
Main
Schaumainkai
Schweizer Pl.
GUTLEUTVIERTEL
Gutleut strasse
Friedensbrücke
Kennedy allee
Oppenheimer
Güterbahnhof
S-Bahn
U-Bahn Station

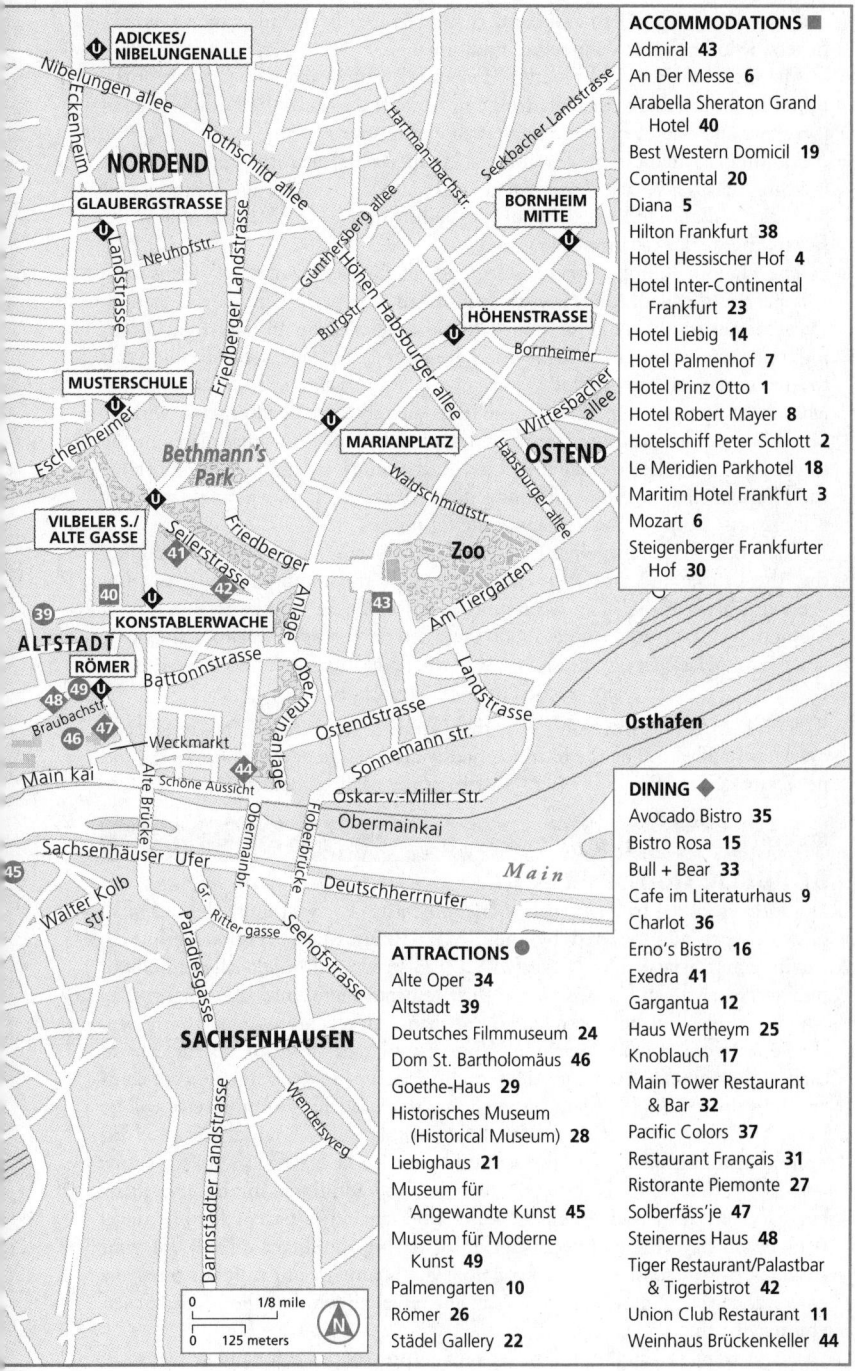


**ACCOMMODATIONS ■**

- Admiral **43**
- An Der Messe **6**
- Arabella Sheraton Grand Hotel **40**
- Best Western Domicil **19**
- Continental **20**
- Diana **5**
- Hilton Frankfurt **38**
- Hotel Hessischer Hof **4**
- Hotel Inter-Continental Frankfurt **23**
- Hotel Liebig **14**
- Hotel Palmenhof **7**
- Hotel Prinz Otto **1**
- Hotel Robert Mayer **8**
- Hotelschiff Peter Schlott **2**
- Le Meridien Parkhotel **18**
- Maritim Hotel Frankfurt **3**
- Mozart **6**
- Steigenberger Frankfurter Hof **30**

**DINING ◆**

- Avocado Bistro **35**
- Bistro Rosa **15**
- Bull + Bear **33**
- Cafe im Literaturhaus **9**
- Charlot **36**
- Erno's Bistro **16**
- Exedra **41**
- Gargantua **12**
- Haus Wertheym **25**
- Knoblauch **17**
- Main Tower Restaurant & Bar **32**
- Pacific Colors **37**
- Restaurant Français **31**
- Ristorante Piemonte **27**
- Solberfäss'je **47**
- Steinernes Haus **48**
- Tiger Restaurant/Palastbar & Tigerbistrot **42**
- Union Club Restaurant **11**
- Weinhaus Brückenkeller **44**

**ATTRACTIONS ●**

- Alte Oper **34**
- Altstadt **39**
- Deutsches Filmmuseum **24**
- Dom St. Bartholomäus **46**
- Goethe-Haus **29**
- Historisches Museum (Historical Museum) **28**
- Liebighaus **21**
- Museum für Angewandte Kunst **45**
- Museum für Moderne Kunst **49**
- Palmengarten **10**
- Römer **26**
- Städel Gallery **22**

controversial postmodern structure that meets with ridicule among Frankfurters, who like their architecture traditional.

The **Goethe-Haus** and **Goethe-Museum** lie only a short walk north of the center in the northern Altstadt. To the north of this is **Zeil,** the Fifth Avenue of Germany and one of Europe's greatest shopping streets.

Another landmark of the Stadmitte is **Hauptwache,** an 18th-century baroque building that is a virtual Times Square of Frankfurt, as it lies at the junction of both the U-Bahn and the S-Bahn lines. Northwest of the Hauptwache is the **Börse,** the stock exchange of Frankfurt.

The Hauptbahnhof, at the western edge of the center of town, opens onto a large street called **Am Hauptbahnhof.** As you walk out of the station, Düsseldorferstrasse will be on your left and Baselerstrasse on your right, heading south toward the Main River. You have a choice of three streets heading east to the center of the **Altstadt** (old town): Taunusstrasse, Kaiserstrasse, and Münchner Strasse. Münchner Strasse leads directly into **Theaterplatz,** with its opera house. Taunusstrasse goes to three of the major Altstadt squares in the southern part of the city: **Goetheplatz, Rathenauplatz,** and (most important) the **Hauptwache,** with its rail connections. In this section of Frankfurt, along Kaiserstrasse, some of the best shops are found.

The **Main River** flows slightly south of the Altstadt. Many bridges, including the Alte Brücke and the Obermainbrücke, cross this important waterway. On the south bank of the Main is a popular district, **Alt-Sachsenhausen,** center of the apple-wine taverns (more about them later). For other major attractions, you'll have to branch out, heading east to the Frankfurt Zoo or northwest to the Palmengarten (both easily reached by public transportation).

**STREET MAPS** Arm yourself with a detailed street map, not the general overview handed out by the tourist office. Maps are sold at most bookstores and news kiosks. See "Bookstores" in "Fast Facts: Frankfurt," below.

## 2 Getting Around

### BY PUBLIC TRANSPORTATION

Frankfurt is linked by a network of fast, modern subways, trams, and buses, all of which are administered by the **RMV (Rhein-Main Verkehrsverbund),** Mannheimer Strasse 15 (✆ **069/213-22-23-5;** www.rmv.de). All methods of public transport can be used within their respective fare zones at a single price, which includes transfers between any of them. Tickets are purchased at green, coin-operated automatic machines (*Fahrscheine*) that are lined up adjacent to each of the points of departure. The machines accept all denominations of coins and bills up to 20€ ($17.85), but be aware that any change you receive will be in coins, so try to use the smallest bills possible. A 24-hour ticket, good for unlimited travel inside Frankfurt's central zone, costs 4.35€ ($3.90) for adults and 2.65€ ($2.35) for children. Zone charts and additional information in six languages are displayed on all the automatic machines. Except for bus travel (where you have the additional option of paying the driver directly for your passage), be sure to buy your ticket before you board any of the public transport conveyances of Frankfurt. If you're caught traveling without the proper ticket, you may be fined 30€ ($26.80).

If you want to simplify the ticket-buying process, both for public transport and museum admissions within Frankfurt, consider the purchase of a **Frankfurter Tageskarte (Frankfurt Card)** from either of the city's tourist offices. These cards allow unlimited travel anywhere within the greater Frankfurt area, plus transport on the shuttle bus going to and from the airport, plus half-price admission to any of the city's museums. The cost is 6.65€ ($5.95) for a 1-day card and 11€ ($9.80) for a 2-day card. For more information, contact the tourist office.

For more information about Frankfurt's public transportation system, call **RMV,** the city transport office, at ✆ **069/25-771** or visit www.rmv.de and look for the information listed in English.

## BY TAXI

There's no surcharge for calling for a taxi; dial ✆ **069/23-00-01,** 069/23-00-33, or 069/25-00-01. Otherwise, you can get a cab either by standing at any of the city's hundreds of clearly designated taxi stands or by hailing one with an illuminated dome light. Taxis charge by the trip and by the carload, without surcharge for pieces of luggage. Some are suitable for carrying up to six passengers, others for a maximum of only four. Regardless of their size, the initial fee you'll pay for a Frankfurt taxi is 2.60€ ($2.30); additional kilometers cost 1.50€ to 1.75€ ($1.35–$1.55) each, depending on the time of day. The most expensive rates are charged on holidays between the hours of 10pm and 6am; the least expensive are charged between 10am and 4pm.

## BY RENTAL CAR

The big rental companies each maintain offices at the airport and at central locations throughout Frankfurt. The most reliable are **Avis,** whose downtown branch is at Schmidtstrasse 39 or inside the Hauptbahnhof (✆ **069/27-99-7010;** www.avis.de), and **Hertz,** whose offices are in the Hauptbahnhof (✆ **069/23-04-84;** www.hertz.de), and on the Hanauer Landstrasse 117 (✆ **069/44-90-90**). Also recommended is **Europcar,** which maintains offices at the Hauptbahnhof (✆ **069/242-9810;** www.europcar.com) and downtown at Am Industriehof 3–5 (✆ **069/970-6410**).

### *FAST FACTS:* Frankfurt

*American Express* Centrally located at Kaiserstrasse 8 (✆ **069/2-10-50;** U-Bahn/S-Bahn: Hauptwache), the American Express offices are open Monday to Friday 9:30am to 6pm and Saturday 10am to 2:30pm. Unless you have an American Express card or traveler's checks, you'll be charged 1€ (90¢) for using their mail service.

*Bookstores* The best English-language bookstore is **British Bookshop,** Börsenstrasse 17 (✆ **069/28-04-92;** U-Bahn/S-Bahn: Hauptwache). It's open Monday to Friday 9:30am to 7pm and Saturday 9:30am to 4pm. Many English-language editions are also for sale at **Sussmann's Presse und Buch,** Zeil 127 (✆ **069/1-31-07-51;** U-Bahn/S-Bahn: Hauptwache), open Monday to Wednesday and Friday 9am to 7pm, Thursday 9am to 8pm, and Saturday 9am to 4pm.

*Currency Exchange* Go to the Hauptbahnhof's **Reise-Bank AG** kiosk (✆ **069/24-27-85-91** or **069/24-27-85-92**), which is open daily 7:30am to 10pm. The same bank maintains two separate branches within the Frankfurt airport. The smaller branch (✆ **069/69-07-20-71**) is open daily 7am to 7pm; the larger (✆ **069/69-03-50-61**) is open daily 6am to 11pm.

*Dentists and Doctors* For an English-speaking dentist or doctor, call ✆ **069/19292** to arrange an appointment.

*Drugstores* For information about pharmacies open near you, call (✆ **069/19292**). Otherwise you can go to Kissel-Apotheke, Mörfelder Landstrasse 235 (✆ **069/63-11-522**).

*Emergencies* Dial ✆ **110** for the police; ✆ **112** for a fire, first aid, and ambulance; ✆ **069/1-92-92** for emergency medical service; and ✆ **069/660-72-71** for emergency dental service.

*Internet Access* Head for **CyberRyder,** Tongegasse 31 (✆ **069/913-96-754;** www.cyberyder.de), open Monday to Thursday 9am to 11pm, Friday and Saturday 9am to 1am, and Sunday 2 to 11pm.

*Laundry* Try **SB Wasch Center,** Grosse Seestrasse 46 (✆ **069/70-74-618**), U-Bahn: Leipziger Strasse, open daily 6:30am to 10pm.

*Luggage Storage/Lockers* Lockers can be rented and luggage stored at the Hauptbahnhof.

*Post Office* There's a post office at the Hauptbahnhof 60036 Frankfurt (✆ **069/26990**), open Monday to Friday 6:30am to 9pm, Saturday 8am to 6pm, and Sunday and holidays 11am to 6pm.

*Restrooms* There are many decent public facilities in central Frankfurt, especially in the Altstadt. A restroom is called a *Toilette* and is often labeled WC, with either F (for *Frauen*, women) or H (for *Herren*, men).

*Safety* Frankfurt is a relatively safe city, but you should still stay alert at all times. Stay out of the area around the Hauptbahnhof at night, as muggings are frequent.

## 3 Where to Stay

Frankfurt is notorious for room shortages during busy trade fairs. If you have the bad luck to arrive when one of them is scheduled, you might find all the more central hotels fully booked. To find an available room, head to one of the tourist offices. Either branch will charge you 2.55€ ($2.30) for a room-finding service.

Even without the fairs, Frankfurt is one of the world's great commercial hubs, so business people pour into the city at all times of the year. Hotels, for the most part, are expensive. However, you can sometimes negotiate a rate decrease on weekends when the business clients don't predominate. Hotels also tend to be booked well in advance, so reservations are important.

Nearly all the major hotels in the city center are convenient for the train station, the business district, and the fair grounds. Of course, you can take a taxi, but walking time is often no more than 20 minutes to where you're going.

### IN THE CENTER

#### VERY EXPENSIVE

**Hotel Hessischer Hof** ★★★ Frankfurt doesn't get much better than this. Only the Steigenberger Hotel Frankfurter Hof knocks it from the top-ranking hotel in the city. A private and traditional place with an elegant atmosphere, this boxy, nine-story hotel has *luxe* style and amenities all the way. The hotel is located opposite the trade-fair building. The relatively modest postwar exterior doesn't prepare you for the spacious and glamorous interior. Many of the bedrooms are furnished with antiques. The bathrooms are equipped with tub-and-shower combos and thoughtful little extras such as perfumed soap and luxurious bathrobes. In the older building in front, accommodations are traditionally furnished with chandeliers strung from high ceilings, antique furnishings, and 19th-century lithographs, and not quite as elegant as rooms at the Frankfurter Hof and Meridien. But in the newer wing, call *Nordflugel*, the bedrooms outrank even the stiffest Frankfurt competitors. The hotel staff follows the old European custom of having guests leave their shoes outside the bedroom door at night, to be returned shined the next morning.

Friedrich-Ebert-Anlage 40, 60325 Frankfurt am Main. ✆ **800/223-6800** in the U.S. and Canada, or 069/7-54-00. Fax 069/75-40-29-24. www.hessischer-hof.de. 117 units. 256€–342€ ($228.60–$305.40) double; from 300€ ($267.90) suite. Children 12 and under stay free in parents' room. AE, DC, MC, V. Parking 16€ ($14.30). S-Bahn: Platz der Republik. **Amenities:** Restaurant; bar; fitness equipment; room service; babysitting; laundry/dry cleaning. *In room:* A/C, TV, dataport, minibar, hair dryer, safe.

**Hotel Inter-Continental Frankfurt** ★★★ This blockbuster-modern hotel occupies a pair of tall buildings (20 and 21 floors) set across the street from one another, a short walk south of the railway station and the red-light district. Both buildings have separate reception areas (although you can register in either for accommodations in either), lots of beige marble and mahogany or walnut paneling, a uniformed and highly competent staff, and a sense of cosmopolitan sophistication. The more expensive, and more-plush, rooms lie in the "Main" (referring to the river, in this case) building. Each has deep upholsteries, heavy curtains, and impeccable good taste. Somewhat less glamorous and slightly smaller rooms are across the street, in what's referred to as "the City Wing."

Wilhelm-Leuschner Strasse 43, 60329 Frankfurt am Main. ✆ **800/327-0200** in the U.S., or 069/2605-0. Fax 069/252467. www.interconti.com. 770 units. 240€–425€ ($214.30–$379.55) double; from 510€ ($455.45) suite. Extra bed 31€ ($27.70). Rates include breakfast. Parking 21€ ($18.75). AE, DC, MC, V. U-Bahn: Hauptbahnhof. **Amenities:** 2 restaurants; bar; piano bar; nightclub; Frankfurt's largest hotel pool; fitness center; whirlpool; sauna; solarium; business center; 24-hr. room service. *In room:* A/C, TV, minibar, hair dryer.

**Le Meridien Parkhotel** ★★ *Kids* We prefer this hotel over its bigger, more impersonal competitors: the Frankfurt Intercontinental at Wilhelm-Leuschner-Strasse 43 and the Frankfurt Marriott Hotel at Hamburger Allee 2. Le Meridien Parkhotel provides warmth and personal attention for its guests, mainly from the world of commerce, who can walk over in a few minutes to the fair grounds. It opens onto a verdant, park-like square. The hotel has been built in two sections—an ornately decorated, recently renovated 1905 palace and a sleek but duller 1970s boxy wing. We prefer the older, more traditional rooms in the *palais*, although they are more expensive than those in the annex. Palais accommodations have a luxurious atmosphere and are individually designed. Annex units are larger, however, with high ceilings and built-in furnishings. Each unit comes with tub-and-shower combos, robes, and deluxe vanity items. For families who travel upmarket, this is a favorite because of its gracious welcome and helpful staff.

Wiesenhüttenplatz 28–38 (near the Hauptbahnhof), 60329 Frankfurt am Main. ✆ **800/225-5843** in the U.S. and Canada, or 069/2-69-70. Fax 069/2-69-78-84. www.forte-hotels.com. 297 units. 275€–415€ ($245.60–$370.60) double; 355€–595€ ($317–$531.35) suite. AE, DC, MC, V. Parking 20€ ($17.85). S-Bahn: 8. **Amenities:** Restaurant; bar; sauna; solarium; business center; room service; babysitting; laundry/dry cleaning. *In room:* A/C, TV, minibar, hair dryer.

**Maritim Hotel Frankfurt** ★★ This is one of the largest hotels in Germany, with a layout that almost defines it as a small town within a city. Set behind a curved, mostly glass eight-story facade, it's the only hotel in Frankfurt with direct access, via a covered walkway, to the trade fairgrounds. As such, its goal involves servicing the needs of the exhibitors, salespersons, and buyers who pour in and out of its low-ceilinged, marble-sheathed lobby. Expect well-orchestrated, but somewhat anonymous, comforts at this Bauhaus-industrial behemoth, and a location that requires a bit of a hike, or a taxi ride, to more scenic and historic neighborhoods of Frankfurt. Bedrooms may be neutral in their cultural references, but they are very comfortable (writing desks are big if you need to set up a small office) and are more stylish than those at the Marriott across the street. Bathrooms are well equipped, containing deluxe toiletries and shower-and-tub combinations. This is commercialized Germany at its most unapologetic, but considering the many facilities at your fingertips, plus the convenience to the fairgrounds, the convenience of a stay here is worth it.

Theodor-Heuss-Allee 3, 60486 Frankfurt am Main. ✆ **069/75-78-0.** Fax 069/75-78-10-00. www.maritim-hotels.de. 543 units. 275€–480€ ($245.60–$428.65) double; 330€–950€ ($294.70–$848.35) suite. Parking 20€ ($17.85). AE, DC, MC, V. U-Bahn: Messe Frankfurt. **Amenities:** 2 restaurants; 2 bars; pool; fitness club; sauna; solarium; 24-hr. room service; massage. *In room:* A/C, TV, minibar, hair dryer, safe.

**Steigenberger Frankfurter Hof** ★★★ This is the most famous, most prestigious, and most legendary hotel in Frankfurt, with service and a historic setting that's unmatched anywhere else in town. The only hotel in Frankfurt that really matches it is our favorite, the Hessischer Hof, but dining is better at the Steigenberger. The highly visible five-story flagship of one of Germany's most elegant hotel chains; it was established in 1872 behind a landmark stone facade that's very central, very prominent, and very grand. Its rooms are hotly contested by visiting dignitaries, especially during the Book Fair, when guests as prominent as the former King of Greece have been denied a room. Public areas are discreet and plush; bedrooms high-ceilinged, sun-flooded, and gracefully furnished. The rooms have some of the largest and most up-to-date full bathrooms in Frankfurt. Some of the more traditional rooms have valuable antiques, but those in the Bethmann Wing have a 1970s aura with bland blond wood furnishings. Its art collection, including Gobelin tapestries, French antiques, and 18th-century portraits, is noteworthy.

Am Kaiserplatz, 60311 Frankfurt am Main. ✆ **800/223-5652** in the U.S. and Canada, or 069/2-15-02. Fax 069/215-900. www.frankfurter-hof.steigenberger.de. 332 units. Mon–Thurs 385€–435€ ($343.80–$388.45) double; Fri–Sun 210€–235€ ($187.55–$209.85) double. Weekend rates include breakfast, but weekday rates do not. 540€–1,165€ ($482.20–$1,040.35) suites weeklong, without breakfast. Parking 18€ ($16.05). AE, DC, MC, V. U-Bahn: Willy-Brandt-Platz. **Amenities:** 2 restaurants (1, Restaurant Français; see p. 445); bar; health club; sauna; solarium; business center; 24-hr. room service; babysitting; valet/laundry. *In room:* A/C, TV, minibar, hair dryer, safe.

## EXPENSIVE

**An Der Messe** ★ This quiet charmer is the choice of seasoned and discriminating visitors to Frankfurt. It's just a 5-minute walk from the university, the Hauptbahnhof, the banking district, and the fairgrounds. The staff does much to make guests feel comfortable. Rooms are large and stylishly furnished; many have an Asian motif. The bathrooms are luxurious and have tub-and-shower combos. A half-dozen singles are rented, but they're hard to come by unless you reserve well in advance.

Westendstrasse 104, 60325 Frankfurt am Main. ✆ **800/221-6509** in the U.S., or 069/74-79-79. Fax 069/74-83-49. 46 units. 123€–290€ ($109.85–$258.95) double. Rates include breakfast. AE, DC, MC, V. Underground garage parking 11€ ($9.80). Tram: 16 or 19. **Amenities:** Breakfast dining room; room service; babysitting; laundry/dry cleaning. *In room:* TV, minibar, hair dryer.

**Best Western Hotel Domicil** ★ *Value* Rooms at this hotel are more compact than at some of its nearby competitors, but they're well-organized, well-scrubbed, and attractively furnished with wood-veneer furniture, some of it built-in. Bathrooms are genuinely tiny, with showers ringed with plastic curtains and absolutely no extra space for primping. But to its advantage, it's considered relatively affordable for the neighborhood, and as such, it attracts a regular repeat clientele who feel lucky to secure rooms during the height of the trade fairs. It lies within a 3-minute walk of the railway station, behind an ochre-colored, boxy-looking facade that's trimmed in stone.

Karlstrasse 14, 60329 Frankfurt am Main. ✆ **800/528-1234** in the U.S., or 069/27-11-10. Fax 069/25-32-66 www.domicil-frankfurt.bestwestern.de. 67 units. 128€–165€ ($114.30–$147.35) double. Rates include breakfast. Free parking. AE, DC, MC, V. U-Bahn: Hauptbahnhof. **Amenities:** Breakfast buffet. *In room:* TV, minibar, hair dryer.

**Hilton Frankfurt** ★★ Nearly every European city boasts a spectacularly modern hotel dripping with a sense of postmodern architectural daring and imagination. In Frankfurt, that hotel is the Hilton, whose soaring 12-story atrium and vast expanses of glass have won architectural awards since it opened late in 1998. The Inter-Continental knocks it off its pedestal, but the Hilton is better than Maritim and Marriott. Come here for a sense of design-related theatricality, a cooperative and well-trained staff, and very comfortable bedrooms, each with a definite sense of hipster style and whimsy. They come in different degrees of luxury, with varying prices depending on amenities, size, and view. Classic rooms overlook the hotel's central atrium and are the least expensive. Park rooms are the same size but have outside views. Deluxe rooms are somewhat bigger, with very comfortable furnishings and small-scale niceties. Executive rooms are best-accessorized of all, with access to a private concierge and a private bar.

Hochstrasse 4, 60313 Frankfurt/Main. ✆ **800/445-8667** in the U.S., or 069/1338-000. Fax 069/1338-1338. 342 units. 299€–399€ ($267–$356.30) double; from 460€ ($410.80) suite. Parking 20€ ($17.85). AE, DC, MC, V. U-Bahn: Eschenheimer Tor. **Amenities:** 2 restaurants; 2 bars; pool; health club; room service; babysitting; laundry/dry cleaning. *In room:* A/C, TV, minibar, hair dryer, safe.

## MODERATE

**Continental** The choice of many businesspeople, this hotel is a leader among middle-bracket hotels near the Hauptbahnhof. Founded in 1889, it enjoyed its heyday in the Belle Epoque era. The rooms are modern and comfortable, though the shower bathrooms are small. Around the corner are lively bars, but serenity prevails inside. The windows have been soundproofed to keep out traffic noise.

Baselerstrasse 56, 60329 Frankfurt am Main. ✆ **069/23-03-41.** Fax 069/23-29-14. www.hotelconti-aol.com. 85 units. 110€–204€ ($98.25–$182.15) double. Rates include buffet breakfast. AE, DC, MC, V. Parking 15€ ($13.40). U-Bahn/S-Bahn: Hauptbahnhof. **Amenities:** Restaurant. *In room:* TV.

**Hotel Prinz Otto** Other than the fact that it has a brick neoclassical facade that's a lot more historic looking than many of its neighbors, there's very little that's particularly distinctive about this small-scale and completely unpretentious hotel. Rooms tend to be fully booked during trade fairs, however, because of their relatively low rates, their cleanliness, and a simplicity that might remind you of one of the simple bedrooms you might have occupied during college. Each unit comes with a very small tiled bathroom with a shower stall. Accommodations are scattered over four floors of this place (there's no elevator), which was very obviously built during the 19th century as a private home.

Ottostrasse 5, 60329 Frankfurt/Main. ✆ **069/25-30-30.** Fax 069/25-26-04. www.hotel-prinz-otto.de. 23 units. 65€–220€ ($58.05–$196.45) double; 80€–280€ ($71.45–$250.05) triple. Rates include breakfast. Parking 10€ ($8.95). AE, DC, MC, V. U-Bahn: Hauptbahnhof. **Amenities:** Breakfast room. *In room:* TV.

### INEXPENSIVE

**Admiral** *Kids* This hotel is a favorite with families, who like its location near the zoo, a short haul from the center of Frankfurt. The rooms are plainly but comfortably furnished with a natural-wood, Scandinavian-style decor. The bathrooms are small but adequate, each with a shower stall. Only breakfast is served.

Hölderlinstrasse 25, 60136 Frankfurt am Main. ✆ **069/44-80-21.** Fax 069/43-94-02. 59 units. 78€–150€ ($69.65–$133.95) double. Rates include breakfast. AE, DC, MC, V. Parking 6€ ($5.35). U-Bahn: Zoologischer Garten (Zoo). **Amenities:** Breakfast room. *In room:* TV, minibar.

**Hotelschiff Peter Schlott** ★ *Finds* This 1950s riverboat, now permanently moored at the Frankfurt suburb of Höchst, has some of the smallest, but most evocative, hotel rooms in the area. The style evokes life at sea: Everything is tiny and cramped, and mattresses are a bit thin. But the unusual nature of the accommodations helps soften any disagreeability, and the waters of the Main lap soothingly beneath your portholes. You'll have to exercise caution on this ship's narrow and steep staircases. If you have enormous amounts of luggage, consider a stay in a more conventional hotel.

Mainberg, 65929 Frankfurt. ✆ **069/300-4643.** Fax 069/307-671. www.hotel-schiff-schlott.de. 19 units (all with washbasins, 11 with showers, none with toilets). 63€–68€ ($56.25–$60.70) double without shower; 66€–88€ ($58.95–$78.60) double with shower. Rates include breakfast. AE, DC, MC, V. S-Bahn: Höchst. **Amenities:** Restaurant. *In room:* No phone.

## THE WESTEND

### EXPENSIVE

**Hotel Liebig** ★ *Finds* The aura within this upscale B&B is small-scale, intimate, and luxurious, with an intensely "decorated" look that might have been lifted directly from the pages of a Laura Ashley (or Versace) catalogue. As such, it presents a welcome change for business travelers looking for something more personalized and less anonymous than what's available within one of the blockbuster hotels closer to the fairgrounds. The town house that contains it was built in 1905 and still retains its ornate maroon sandstone facade, its curving interior staircase, and proportions that hint at its origins as an upscale private home. The full bathrooms are handsomely decorated and spotlessly maintained.

Liebigstrasse 45, 60323 Frankfurt am Main. ✆ **069/72-75-51.** Fax 069/72-75-55. 20 units. 114€–195€ ($101.80–$174.15) double. Breakfast 10.50€ ($9.40) extra. Parking 10.50€ ($9.40). AE, DC, MC, V. U-Bahn: Westend. **Amenities:** Breakfast room; garden. *In room:* TV, minibar.

**Hotel Palmenhof** ★ A short walk from the Botanical Gardens, this is a five-story Art Nouveau building. Some of the original architectural features have been preserved. The facade is very grand, a reddish sandstone romantic-era pile from the 1890s. It stands across from the Cafe im Literaturhaus, which factors visibly as a wining and drinking spot as authors are seduced during book fairs. The interior has such architectural features as skylights beaming light down onto a Belle Epoque set of furnishings. Rooms have somewhat fussy furnishings but are well kept and often contain high ceilings. Each comes with a well-maintained private bathroom with tub and shower.

Bockenheimer Landstrasse 89–91, 60325 Frankfurt am Main. ✆ **069/753-0060.** Fax 069/753-00666. www.palmenhof.com. 42 units. Mon–Thurs 155€–165€ ($138.40–$147.35) double; 222€–255€ ($198.25–$227.70) suite. Fri–Sun 95€ ($84.85) double; 185€–200€ ($165.20–$178.60) suite. Rates include breakfast. Parking 18€ ($16.05). AE, DC, MC, V. U-Bahn: Westend. **Amenities:** Restaurant; room service; laundry/dry cleaning. *In room:* TV, minibar, hair dryer.

**Hotel Robert Mayer** ★ *Finds* This is one of the most artfully decorated hotels in town. It's within walking distance of Frankfurt's trade fair complex.

Though the building dates from 1905, the rooms date from 1994, when the manager hired 11 lesser-known artists each to impose his or her vision on one of the bedrooms. You might find a thought-provoking jumble of furniture inspired by Frank Lloyd Wright or an anonymous Milanese postmodernist piece set adjacent to pop art. Creature comforts, however, remain high. There's no restaurant on the premises, but many dining options lie within a short walk.

Robert-Mayer-Strasse 44, 60486 Frankfurt. ✆ **069/970910.** Fax 069/97091010. www.art-hotel-robert-mayer.de. 11 units. 122€–178€ ($108.95–$158.95) double. Rates include breakfast. AE, DC, MC, V. U-Bahn: Bockenheimer Warte. *In room:* TV.

### INEXPENSIVE

**Diana** *Value* Spotless and homey, the Diana is a bargain. It's a copy of a private villa, with a drawing room and an intimate breakfast salon. It's located in the Westend district on a pleasant residential street. The small bedrooms are rather lackluster, but comfortable and clean, each with a neat little bathroom with a shower stall.

Westendstrasse 83, 60325 Frankfurt am Main. ✆ **069/74-70-07.** Fax 069/74-70-79. 25 units. 90€ ($80.35) double; 115€ ($102.70) triple. Rates include continental breakfast. AE, DC, MC, V. Parking 5€ ($4.45). U-Bahn: Westend. Bus: 17. **Amenities:** Breakfast room. *In room:* TV.

**Mozart** ★ *Value* Perhaps the best small hotel in Frankfurt, the Mozart stands on the periphery of the Palmengarten, right off the busy Fürstenbergerstrasse. Everything inside—walls, furniture, and bed coverings—is white or pink. Rooms are small but comfortable, each with a tidily kept shower-only bathroom. The breakfast room, with its crystal chandeliers and Louis XV–style chairs, could pass for an 18th-century salon. The staff is polite and helpful.

Parkstrasse 17 (near the Alte Oper), 60322 Frankfurt am Main. ✆ **069/55-08-31.** Fax 069/1568061. 35 units. 115€ ($102.70) double; 150€ ($133.95) during trade fairs. Rates include buffet breakfast. AE, DC, MC, V. Closed Dec 24–Jan 1. U-Bahn: Holzhausenstrasse. Bus: 36. **Amenities:** Breakfast room; lounge; laundry/dry cleaning service. *In room:* TV, minibar.

## 4 Where to Dine

Almost overnight, without much of the world being aware, the city of Frankfurt has become one of Europe's great dining capitals. Everybody knows it for its banking and business, but serious gourmets also descend on the city, which offers one of Europe's most varied cuisines. It still doesn't have as eclectic a mixture of cuisine as New York (which has virtually every cuisine served on earth), but Frankfurt is getting there.

For years, visitors to the famous Book Fair always came home to tell visitors, "You can't get a decent meal in Frankfurt." That wasn't even true way back then, and it's gross libel today. Still fighting to overcome a terrible culinary reputation, Frankfurt now ranks up there with Berlin and Munich as a dining mecca.

See the map on p. 437 for restaurant locations.

### IN THE CENTER

#### VERY EXPENSIVE

**Restaurant Français** ★★★ FRENCH This restaurant is very stylish and very conscious of maintaining the top-notch standards that you might expect from an upscale hotel restaurant in Paris. It occupies a duet of stately rooms outfitted in tones of imperial blue and gold, on the lobby level of Frankfurt's most prestigious hotel. Don't think you can go slumming if you drop in for a bite here. Jackets and (preferably) ties are recommended for gentlemen. Menu items are cultivated, posh, and beautifully prepared and presented. The menu will have you salivating before you take a bite. The offerings fairly crackle with brilliant inventions such as a goose-liver terrine with a kumquat compote, or beetroot tart with caviar. Two of the most imaginative soups we enjoyed on our last visit to Frankfurt were the cream soup of sea urchin flavored with lobster and port, and the quail consommé with truffle-stuffed tortellini. An exciting main course selection is saltwater crayfish with marinated duck's tongue, served with a vegetable couscous and honey-coriander *jus.* We were also impressed with the saddle of suckling pig and pig's foot served with stuffed vegetables, caramelized garlic, and purple mustard sauce.

In the Steigenberger Frankfurter Hof, Am Kaiserplatz. ✆ **069/2-15-02.** Reservations required. Main courses 30€–38€ ($26.80–$33.95); 2-course fixed-price lunch 38€ ($33.95). AE, DC, MC, V. Daily noon–2pm and 6:30–10 pm. U-Bahn: Willy-Brandt-Platz.

**Tiger Restaurant/Palastbar & Tigerbistrot** ★★★ INTERNATIONAL This restaurant offers Frankfurt's finest dining. No one had expected a restaurant associated with a cabaret to be as good as this. It's contained within a basement-level dining room that's immediately adjacent to a cabaret theater (Tigerpalast) that's separately recommended in "Frankfurt After Dark" later in this chapter. Whimsical murals cover the walls of a dining room that has witnessed the arrival and departure of Joan Collins, magicians Siegfried & Roy, lots of CEOs of local corporations, and most of the high-ranking ministers of the local government. Menu items are impeccably presented and may include sautéed foie gras with glazed figs and truffle sauce; a strudel of sole and scallops with spinach and Noilly Prat sauce; lasagne of lobster with truffled leeks and shellfish sauce; or pan-seared red mullet with sautéed arugula, served with a creamy artichoke risotto drizzeled with a paste of anchovy, black olives, and red wine. Meals in the Palastbar & Bistro are less elaborate and less expensive, served under the vaulted brick ceiling of what was built as a warehouse about a century ago. Examples include vegetarian paella in saffron sauce; and breast of chicken stuffed with tomato, sage, and Parma ham, served with an eggplant mousse and potato gnocchi.

Heiligkreuzgasse 16–20. ✆ **069/92-00-22-50.** Reservations required. Main courses in Restaurant 20€–31€ ($17.85–$27.70). Main courses in Palastbar & Tigerbistrot 20€–22€ ($17.85–$19.65); fixed-price menu in Palastbar & Bistro 27€ ($24.10) for 2 courses, 34€ ($30.35) for 3 courses, 41€ ($36.60) for 4 courses. AE, MC, V. Restaurant Tues–Sat 5:30–11pm. Palastbar & Tigerbistrot Tues–Sun 5pm–1:30am. U-Bahn: Konstablerwache.

## EXPENSIVE

**Avocado Bistro** ★★★ FRENCH/GERMAN Chic, upscale, and soothing, this bistro has lots of fresh flowers, a turquoise-and-peach-toned color scheme, and an atmosphere that manages to be both grandly bourgeois and artsy at the same time. It's the kind of place where you might expect to hear champagne corks popping, and frequently do, within what's a suitable venue for either a seduction or a sales pitch. Menu items change with the seasons. Food selections on any given night are wisely limited, but you're almost assured that every item is fresh and carefully chosen by the chef. Inventiveness and solid technique go hand in hand here. On our last meal we launched ourselves with a confit of quails sprinkled with truffle oil. Next a saddle of turbot cooked in saffron broth and filled with poached baby vegetables was resting on our plate. The dish was made celestial with an accompanying champagne mousse. Another member of our party feasted on saddle of rabbit roasted with black salsify julienne and served with plums in a coat of bacon on a mousse of beetroots. Finish with one of the divine desserts, especially the chestnut mousse with chocolate truffles on rose pear coulis.

Hochstrasse 27. ✆ **069/292-867.** Reservations required. Fixed-price 3-course lunch 29.50€ ($26.35), 5-course fixed-price dinner 57€ ($50.90); main courses 23.50€–27€ ($21–$24.10). AE, DC, MC, V. Mon–Sat noon–2:30pm and 6–11:30pm. U-Bahn: Opernplatz.

**Weinhaus Brückenkeller** ★ GERMAN/INTERNATIONAL In the heart of the Altstadt, this is one of Frankfurt's leading restaurants and a favorite spot of well-heeled North American visitors. Tables are candlelit, and strolling musicians encourage singing. Here the age of Bismarck lives again. Franconian carvings adorn the alcoves, and huge wooden barrels are decorated with scenes from Goethe's *Faust.* The food is light and subtle. A typical meal might begin with cream of sorrel soup or more substantial roast goose liver with green beans, followed by a tender and perfectly flavored saddle of venison or young lamb. The *Tafelspitz* (boiled beef) is the best in town, and it comes with a side of vegetables. For a perfect finish, you might order a soufflé of strawberries with vanilla sauce. The evening meal includes homemade sourdough bread. The wine cellar holds an excellent collection of German wines, including the best from the Rhineland. Personal attention and efficient service are hallmarks.

Schützenstrasse 6. ✆ **069/29-80-07-0.** Reservations required. Main courses 23€–34€ ($20.55–$30.35). AE, DC, MC, V. Mon–Sat 7–11pm. Closed Dec 20–Jan 8. U-Bahn Konstablerwache.

## MODERATE

**Charlot** CONTINENTAL Few other restaurants evoke the Belle Epoque era as effectively as this one. A bit grander and more formal than its also-recommended neighbor, Brasserie an den Alte Oper, it has an elaborate *Jugendstil* decor, a uniformed, mostly Italian staff that maneuvers effectively in the narrow spaces between tables, and a savory blend of cuisines from Italy, Germany, and France. Menu items change with the seasons but might include carpaccio of tuna with herbs and fresh balsamic vinegar; pastas garnished with whatever seasonal vegetable is available at the time; braised filet of sole in the Provençal style; quail braised "in the Tuscan style"; and roasted rack of lamb with black peppercorn sauce. These dishes, more than those at any other cafe in Central Frankfurt, evoke "cafe dining." Everything is dependably good, if not particularly original. Tables expand onto the pavement in front during clement weather.

Opernplatz 10. ✆ **069/28-70-07.** Reservations recommended. Main 19.50€–30€ ($17.40–$26.80). AE, DC, MC, V. Mon–Sat noon–3pm and 6pm–midnight; Sun 6–11:30pm. U-Bahn: Alte Oper.

**Exedra** ★ GREEK/MACEDONIAN Our favorite Greek restaurant in Frankfurt, Exedra lies behind a grand and ornate 19th-century facade, but once you're inside, you'll find a large and relatively undecorated *taverna* with big windows overlooking the street. Several dishes merit special mention, especially the grilled lamb filet with feta cheese sauce and grilled sweet peppers. The cuisine is solidly reliable, as you'll agree if you dig into the grilled octopus in an oregano-flavored butter sauce. Pan-fried veal with a white wine and lemon sauce takes you back to the Greek Isles. For something imaginative, try the leg of rabbit braised in shallots, cinnamon, and red wine. In the mornings and throughout the afternoon, Exedra functions as a neighborhood bar and cafe.

Heiligkreuzgasse 29. ✆ **069/28-73-97.** Reservations recommended. Main courses 10.50€–16€ ($9.40–$14.30). AE, DC, MC, V. Mon–Thurs 8:30am–1am; Fri–Sat 8am–2am; Sun 4pm–1am. U-Bahn: Konstablerwache.

**Main Tower Restaurant & Bar** ★ CONTINENTAL/ASIAN Architecturally, this is the most unusual restaurant in Frankfurt, with a long line of diners (the clientele is diverse) who ascend every day for lunch, dinner, and after-work cocktails. Set on the circular 53rd floor of one of the tallest buildings in Frankfurt, it offers a starkly postmodern environment (steel tables and minimalist chairs), whose main aesthetic intrigue lies in views that extend for miles in all directions. The chefs don't try to get by on the view alone. Their cuisine is hardly the most imaginative in the city, but it is solid and reliable, prepared with fresh ingredients. For appetizers, the range is from a smoked salmon with a pesto sauce to a carpaccio of beef with eggplant. A first for many diners is the spaghetti in a campari-orange cream sauce with walnuts and fresh mint. It's an acquired taste. Many dishes are "from the wok," including chicken cut in strips in a red Thai curry. The grilled pike-perch filet is a flavor-filled delight, served on black tagliatelli with a glazed yellow pepper purée.

In the Landesbank Hessen-Thüringen Building, Neue Mainzer Strasse 52–58. ✆ **069/36-50-47-77.** Reservations recommended. Fixed-price lunch 13€ ($11.60) 2 courses, 15€ ($13.40) 3 courses; main courses 14€–20€ ($12.50–$17.85). AE, DC, MC, V. Sun–Thurs 10am–1am; Fri–Sat 10am–2am. U-Bahn: Willy-Brandt-Platz.

**Pacific Colors** ★ CALIFORNIAN You'll get the sense that the most avant-garde hotel in Frankfurt (the Hilton) made special efforts to attract an avant-garde cuisine into its signature restaurant, and that's exactly what happened in this intensely dramatic lobby-level restaurant. It boasts a New Age design in (what else?) Pacific tones of sea green and blue, with big-windowed views over the trees and walkways of the Friedberger Anlage park. The food is what keeps gastronomes coming back, however—the restaurant serves a Mediterranean-inspired cuisine that manages to be both airy and earthy, and which has been referred to as the New World's most successful re-invention of Mediterranean cuisine. As conceived by culinary artist Maik Templin, the exact composition of the menu changes about every 3 months, but the best examples include mussels in a Chardonnay marinade, apple and celery soup, and arugula salad with pecorino cheese and grilled prawns. Especially full of flavor is a platter with both carpaccio of tuna and grilled medallions of tuna, both of them served in a lime and truffle marinade. Breast of chicken is perfectly married to a black-bean ragout and green paprika sauce; and a filet of blue marlin served on a bed of papaya with saffron sauce made us want to return.

In the lobby of the Hilton Hotel, Hochstrasse 4. ✆ **069/1338-000.** Reservations recommended. Main courses 17.50€–28€ ($15.65–$25). AE, DC, MC, V. Daily noon–3pm and 6–11:30pm. U-Bahn: Eschenheimer Tor.

**Ristorante Piemonte** ★ NORTHERN ITALIAN This is one of the best bets for casual Italian dining in Frankfurt. This restaurant isn't particularly "decorated," featuring a much-used and not particularly imaginative ensemble of furniture that might have originally been installed sometime in the 1970s. The ambience that's created, however, in a postwar ensemble of buildings just behind the Römer, is warm and nurturing, with well-prepared food that's evocative of the mountainous region of northwestern Italy. For appetizers, the chef specializes in carpaccio, our favorite being one made with three types of fish. There's also a delectable carpaccio of herb-flavored raw salmon. All those soups from mamma mia's kitchen are here, including a truly excellent Italian minestrone. The pastas reign supreme on the menu, with that old favorite *rigatoni ai quattro formaggi* (with four different kinds of cheese) winning new fans. Many of the pasta dishes are homemade, including ravioli served plain with butter and fresh sage. There's a special emphasis on a wood-fired grill, so the aromas of beef, Italian sausage, and other meats perfume the air. The chef is also known for classic veal dishes including medallions in a lemon sauce.

Alte Mainzer Gasse 15. ✆ **069/2199-5754.** Reservations recommended. Main courses 14.50€–21.50€ ($12.95–$19.20). AE, MC, V. Sun–Fri noon–3pm and 6–11:30pm. U-Bahn: Römer.

## INEXPENSIVE

**Bull + Bear** INTERNATIONAL The decor here might remind you of life inside a glass-sided cube, thanks to soaring ceilings and a glittery, metallic look that evokes the waiting room of an international airport. The room's focal point is a shimmering circular bar that's illuminated with pin lights and spotlights, perhaps a high-tech version of a pagan temple. Well-prepared menu items include club sandwiches, tortellini stuffed with ricotta and spinach, saddle of lamb with Provençal vegetables, and a wide selection of grilled Angus steaks. The clientele is as interesting as the food. Don't overlook this place as a singles bar and a late-night dance fest. In the basement, there's a dance floor that's usually mobbed, especially on Thursdays, when it's the site of a well-attended after-work party. Drinks cost 4.50€ ($4) each during happy hour, daily from 4:30 to 7pm.

Am Börsenplatz, Schillerstrasse 11. ✆ **069/133-887-33.** Reservations recommended for parties of 6 or more. Lunch salads, sandwiches, and platters 9€–12€ ($8.05–$10.70); dinner main courses 15€–18€ ($13.40–$16.05). AE, DC, MC, V. Mon–Thurs 9am–1am; Fri–Sat 9am–3am; Sun 10am–1am. U-Bahn/S-Bahn: Hauptwache.

**Haus Wertheym** GERMAN/HESSIAN Few other restaurants evoke Old Frankfurt as authentically as this half-timbered house that sits a half block from the Main, on a cobble-covered street near the Nicolaikirche. Originally built in 1479, then reconstructed in the same style after the 1944 bombings, it has a somewhat claustrophobic interior loaded with wood paneling, antique accessories, and cheerfully brusque waiters. Don't expect grand cuisine or any sense of internationalism; this is a deeply entrenched monument featuring cuisine that hasn't changed very much in the past 50 years. Examples include pork schnitzels with french fries, pork schnitzels in green sauce, *Frankfurter Hacksteak* (chopped steak), and a fine version of *Tafelspitz,* the boiled beef specialty beloved by the Austrians. Virtually everything here, unless you specify differently, is served with the restaurant's trademark green sauce and in most cases, parslied potatoes.

Fahrtor 1. ✆ **069/28-14-32.** Reservations recommended. Main courses 8.50€–22€ ($7.60–$19.65). No credit cards. Wed–Mon 11am–midnight. U-Bahn: Römer.

**Solberfäss'je** ★ *Finds* HESSIAN Cramped, old-fashioned, and gregarious, this restaurant is firmly committed to maintaining its role as the kind of beer bar and working-class restaurant that thrived in this neighborhood a century ago. Food items focus on schnitzels, sauerbratens, *rouladens* of beef, and the kinds of roasted knuckles and joints that dyed-in-the-wool beer lovers savor and which have been associated with Bierkellers since anyone can remember. They include roasted shanks of lamb, veal, pork, beef, and turkey, each of which emerges savory and crackling from the ovens. A smoked version of *Eisbein* is particularly popular. The restaurant's name, in Hessian dialect, refers to a medieval technique of preserving meat in barrels filled with salt.

Grosse Friedberger Strasse 8. ✆ **069/29-67-67.** Reservations recommended. Main courses 6€–16€ ($5.35–$14.30). AE, DC, MC, V. Mon–Sat 9am–1am. U-Bahn: Konstabler Hauptwache.

**Steinernes Haus** GERMAN The 500-year-old Steinernes Haus, in the historic heart of Frankfurt, was restored simply and unpretentiously after the war.

Locals come here for good German beer and hearty rib-sticking fare. This is the type of food Germans enjoyed "between the wars." Nouvelle here translates as anything that came after Bismarck. The daily main-dish specialty includes salad and potatoes. Other choices include a selection of sausages, beef filet, and such popular German dishes as *Zigeunerhackbraten* (spicy meat loaf) and *Frankfurter Rippchen* (smoked pork). The best choice is a filet steak cooked on a hot plate right at your table.

Braubachstrasse 35 (around the corner from the Rathaus). ✆ **069/28-34-91.** Main courses 11€–26€ ($9.80–$23.20); daily platters 7.65€–10.25€ ($6.85–$9.15). MC, V. Daily 11:30am–11pm. Tram: 11.

## IN WESTEND

### VERY EXPENSIVE

**Erno's Bistro** ★★★ FRENCH/INTERNATIONAL A chic midtown rendezvous, Erno's draws everybody from visiting film stars to bank executives. This cramped, claustrophobic place with an English-speaking staff offers fine service, plus a commendable cuisine that seems to improve year after year. Under its former chef and namesake, Erno Schmitt, this restaurant became the first in Frankfurt to earn a Michelin star. He's gone, but Valéry Mathis carries on in a grand tradition. Actually we like this bistro better than before. Frankfurt foodies recommend the place for its great cuisine, people-watching, and sense of theatrical flair. The kitchen serves fish brought fresh by air from European waters. The chef offers both *cuisine moderne* and what is known as *cuisine formidable.* The most exciting (and expensive) appetizer is artichokes in puff pastry with sautéed potatoes and foie gras. For a main course, we'd suggest the grilled brill, whose flesh is very delicate and light, served with a rare type of mushroom. Another excellent choice is filet of venison coated with truffles and served with a smooth and creamy savoy cabbage. A recent main course was a braised leg of rabbit so tender it fell off the bone. It was served on a bed of lentils and diced carrots infused with a soupçon of curry. The chef also regales you with braised rack of lamb served with haricots verts and caramelized carrots.

Liebigstrasse 15 (between the Alte Oper and the Palmengarten). ✆ **069/72-19-97.** Reservations required. Main courses 28€–38€ ($25–$33.95); business menu 31€–41€ ($27.70–$36.60); fixed-price menu 80€ ($71.45). AE, DC, MC, V. Mon–Fri noon–2pm and 7–10pm. Closed mid-June–mid-July. U-Bahn: Westend.

**Gargantua** ★★★ CONTINENTAL One of the Westend's genuinely stylish restaurants, Gargantua evokes an upscale and somewhat snobbish 1920s-era bistro in Paris. Set on a verdant street corner with outdoor tables, it's outfitted in tones of green and white, and named after the hearty gourmand (Gargantua) that was created during the French Renaissance by Rabelais. The guiding force behind the cuisine here is a local food writer and columnist, Klaus Trebes, who with his wife, Monika, is usually directing the restaurant in a discreet, well-versed way that includes a sophisticated knowledge of German wines. Patrons come here expecting a near-perfect dining experience, and that's what they get. Flavors, textures, and colors combine to delight in such dishes as a creamy soup with black sausage and Périgord truffles, or a zesty risotto with radicchio, squid, and spicy chorizo sausage. The chef goes international with a platter of salmon and tuna in an herb-flavored crust. It's cooked pink and served in a Thai-style curry sauce. Deliciously aromatic in its *jus* is a supreme of chicken with chicory, cardamon, and orange sauce.

Liebigstrasse 47. ✆ **069/72-07-18.** Reservations required. Main courses 27€–73€ ($24.10–$65.20); fixed-price dinner 50€ ($44.65) for 4 courses, 65€ ($58.05) for 6 courses. AE, DC, MC, V. Mon–Fri noon–3pm and Mon–Sat 6–10pm. U-Bahn: Westend.

**Union Club Restaurant** ★★★ CONTINENTAL/INTERNATIONAL Some of the most exquisite food in Frankfurt is served here, filled with zesty flavors and a lot of creative imagination. Only the Tiger Restaurant is better. The French neoclassical villa that contains this restaurant was built in 1925 by a wealthy metallurgist and industrialist, Richard Merton. Today, in an upscale neighborhood west of the Palmengarten, it's the headquarters of a private club that includes many of the diplomats and bankers of Frankfurt. On weekends it's reserved only for the use of its members. Monday to Friday, however, you can visit. Be warned in advance that this place does not resemble a conventional restaurant, and on some nights, especially Monday to Wednesday, it can appear somber and anything but cutting-edge. Lunchtime, however, attracts many of the diplomats from the many nearby consulates, and can get very busy. The cuisine is superb, well worth the trek from central Frankfurt. Menu items change with the seasons. We went here with the mayor's party. His Royal Highness demanded that we try the cream of black salsify with truffles. We were so pleased we told him when he retired as mayor he could hire out as a food critic. Following his advice, we also tried the breast of Barbary duck with an apple and pine-nut cabbage with potato strudel. What a treat. We got merely a tasting of the ravioli of Norwegian lobster on pea pudding, but it was so superb we wanted to come back the next day to have more. Another hit of the evening was filet of turbot and lobster cooked delectably with a fennel and saffron sauce. We were invited back in the autumn for their venison ragout with fresh chanterelles.

Am Leonhardsbrunn 16. ✆ **069/70-30-33.** Reservations required. Main courses 23€–28€ ($20.55–$25); fixed-price lunch 26€ ($23.20). AE, DC, MC, V. Mon–Fri 11am–3pm; Sat–Sun 6–10:30pm. U-Bahn: Leipziger Strasse or Bockenheimer Warte.

## EXPENSIVE

**Cafe im Literaturhaus** ★ INTERNATIONAL This is the literary focal point of Frankfurt, a city whose self-image is firmly entrenched as the site of the largest literary marketplace in the world. It's housed within what was built as a distinguished private villa in 1912 and which was acquired as a headquarters for a privately endowed literary organization in 1991. Today, it is the site of lectures and book signings by recognized critics, academics, and authors, many of whose works are available only in German. The dining room is a high-ceilinged but sparsely furnished room that's patterned on the literary cafes of Vienna during the late 19th century. During the Book Fair, large blocks of the site are commandeered by some of Europe's biggest publishers, and the restaurant is likely to be either reserved for private dinners or mobbed to the point where tables are simply not available. At other times, however, you'll be able to sit on one of the notoriously uncomfortable bentwood chairs, either in the spartan-looking inside or on the garden terrace, soaking up the auras of the literati. Sample dishes include risotto with Parmesan and vegetables, tagliatelle with a ragout of fish, ravioli with sage-flavored butter, Provençal-style fish soup, pork filet with apple-calvados sauce, and chicken tikka with eggplant salad. Although these dishes are quite tasty, the food seems a mere afterthought here.

Bockenheimer Landstrasse 102. ✆ **069/75-61-840.** Reservations recommended. Main courses 15€–18€ ($13.40–$16.05); fixed-price menu 25€ ($22.35) for 3 courses, 35€ ($31.25) for 4 courses. AE, MC, V. Sun–Fri 10am–midnight. U-Bahn: Westend.

## MODERATE

**Bistro Rosa** CONTINENTAL From the outside, the gingham curtains and brass rails of this place evoke a saloon. From the inside, the venue resembles a

French bistro, complete with caricatures of pigs that bear vague resemblances to Toulouse-Lautrec, Goethe, and some of Germany's politicians, each of them satirically transmuted into more hoggish forms. Although pork occasionally appears on the menu, for example, in the form of strips of filet of pork in a mustard-flavored cream sauce, a more likely bet might include duck breast with orange sauce. You don't have to wait for the holiday season to enjoy that old-time German favorite, roast goose with red cabbage and chestnuts. A dish unlikely to be found anywhere else is their breast of pheasant, a real delicacy, served with pineapple. In summer, a narrow terrace, separated from a parking lot with ivy-covered lattices, provides outdoor seating.

Grünebergweg 25. ✆ **069/72-13-80.** Reservations recommended. Main courses 20€–24€ ($17.85–$21.45). Mon–Sat 6pm–midnight. MC, V. U-Bahn: Westend.

**Knoblauch** INTERNATIONAL/FRENCH This is a less pretentious and less expensive version of the grander and more expensively decorated restaurant, Erno's, which sits virtually across the street. Don't judge the place by its decor—it might remind you of a battered trucker's bar in central France, thanks to a rather artless collection of paintings and vertical-plank paneling that hasn't been upgraded since the 1960s. Cuisine, however, draws a loyal clientele back to the dining rooms for tastes of such seasonal dishes as wild greens with asparagus, salmon in herb sauce, quail in port wine sauce, and stuffed breast of chicken with saffron sauce. An uncompromising Teutonic staple that's almost constantly available is Tafelspitz, a boiled beef main course, served with horseradish that was the preferred dish of Austrian emperor Franz Josef. The restaurant contains only 10 tables, some of which might be occupied by families with young children.

Staufenstrasse 39. ✆ **069/72-28-28.** Reservations recommended. Main courses 12.15€–21€ ($10.85–$18.75). No credit cards. Mon–Fri noon–2pm and 6:30pm–1am. U-Bahn: Westend.

## 5 Seeing the Sights

When bombs rained on Frankfurt in 1944, nearly all the old half-timbered buildings were leveled. In what might have been a record reconstruction, however, residents of Frankfurt rebuilt their city into a fine melange of modern and traditional architecture and faithfully restored some of their most prized old buildings as well.

Although Frankfurt doesn't have the monuments or museums to equal Munich or Berlin, its museums and exhibition halls still lure some 2 million annual visitors. As the cultural director of the city of Frankfurt, Dr. Hans Bernhard Nordhoff told us, "We offer you everything from Goethe to Andy Warhol, from *Tyrannosaurus Rex* to the female ideal of Botticelli."

Many of the grandest museums lie along the Main on the south bank—often called "Museum Embankment," in itself a dazzling array of contemporary architecture even before you go inside to look at the exhibits.

See the map on p. 437 for the location of Frankfurt's major attractions.

### THE TOP ATTRACTIONS

#### ALTSTADT ★★

Allow about half a day to explore the attractions of the old town, which was once one of the greatest and most historic in Germany before World War II bombing raids turned it to dust. It has been sensitively restored. Its specific attractions include the Goethe House, which was the birthplace of Germany's greatest writer in 1749. He spent his early life wandering around the Alstadt, and you can follow in his footsteps.

Among the more intriguing sights is the Dom (detailed below), which was consecrated in 1239. This cathedral was chosen to serve as the electoral site for the kings of the Holy Roman Empire in 1356. Ten imperial coronations took place here between 1562 and 1792.

Among other attractions are the Römer, an interconnected trio of medieval patrician's houses, which functioned as the city hall of Frankfurt as early as 1405. Today it is still the official seat of Frankfurt's Lord Mayor. The Römerberg is the historic core of the old Altstadt, famous for its magnificent half-timbered houses reconstructed after bombings, according to their original plans.

At the northern edge of the Altstadt is **An der Hauptwache,** named for the old guardhouse (Hauptwache), which stands upon it. This square is the heart of modern Frankfurt. Underneath is the Hauptwache U-Bahn station with a modern shopping promenade.

**Goethe-Haus** ★ This house, where Johann Wolfgang von Goethe (1749–1832) was born, has been a shrine for Goethe enthusiasts since it opened to the public in 1863. One observer wrote that the postwar restoration was carried out "with loving care and damn-the-expense craftsmanship." The house is decorated in various styles, all reflecting the fashion trends of the 18th century: neoclassical, baroque, and rococo. You can view the library, where Goethe's father worked and often watched the street for the return of his son. A portrait of the severe-looking gentleman hangs behind the door of his wife's room.

On the second floor is an unusual astronomical clock built around 1749 and repaired in 1949 to run for another 200 years. The picture gallery contains paintings collected by Goethe's father. These works, mainly by contemporary Frankfurt artists, influenced Goethe's artistic views for a great part of his life. You can also see one of Goethe's most important childhood possessions, a puppet theater, which played a significant role in his novel *Wilhelm Meister.*

Annexed to the house is the **Frankfurter Goethe-Museum.** This museum contains a library of 120,000 volumes and a collection of about 30,000 manuscripts, as well as 16,000 graphic artworks and 400 paintings associated with Goethe and his works.

Grosser Hirschgraben 23–25. ✆ **069/13-88-00.** Admission 5€ ($4.45) adults, 2.50€ ($2.25) students, 1.50€ ($1.35) children. Free 6 and under. Apr–Sept Mon–Fri 9am–6pm; Sat–Sun and holidays 10am–4pm; Oct–Mar Mon–Fri 9am–4pm; Sat–Sun and holidays 10am–4pm. U-Bahn/S-Bahn: Hauptwache.

**Liebighaus** ★★★ This sculpture museum stands alongside the Bargello in Florence as one of the most important in Europe. The building is an 1896 villa. Its collection includes objects from ancient Egypt, classical Greece and Rome, and medieval and Renaissance Europe. Highlights include a small 8th-century B.C. bronze horse and Roman copies of the *Torso* of Polycletus, Praxiteles's *Satyr,* and Myron's *Athena.* Although the most ancient artifacts generate the most excitement, the medieval section is also fascinating. Look for the *Virgin and Child* created in Trier in the 11th century, the head of Barbel von Ottenheim (attributed to van Leyden in 1462), the Riemenschneider *Madonna,* Andrea della Robbia's altarpiece of the Assumption, and the 16th-century *Black Venus with Mirror.*

Schaumainkai 71. ✆ **069/212-368-15.** Admission 4.50€ ($4) adults, 1.50€ ($1.35) seniors, students, and children. Tues and Thurs–Sun 10am–5pm; Wed 10am–8pm. Tram: 15 or 16 to Otto-Hahn-Platz.

**Städel Gallery** ★★★ This is Frankfurt's most important art gallery, containing a fine collection of most European schools of painting. The first floor features French impressionists such as Renoir and Monet, along with German painters of the 19th and 20th centuries. Note in particular Kirchner's *Nude Woman with Hat.* Also on the first floor is Tischbein's *Portrait of Goethe in the Campagna in Italy.* But if you're short on time, go directly to the second floor to view the outstanding collection of Flemish primitives, 17th-century Dutch artists, and 16th-century German masters such as Dürer, Grünewald, Memling, Elsheimer, and many others. One of the most impressive paintings is Jan van Eyck's *Madonna* (1433). Lucas Cranach The Elder is represented by a large winged altarpiece and his rather impish nude Venus. Recent acquisitions include Jean Antoine Watteau's *L'Ile de Cythère* (1709). In the Department of Modern Art are works by Bacon, Dubuffet, Tapies, and Yves Klein.

Schaumainkai 63 (on the south bank of the Main). ✆ **069/60-50-98-0.** Admission 5€ ($4.45) adults, 4€ ($3.55) children 9–16. Free ages 8 and under; Tues free for everyone. Tues and Thurs–Sun 10am–5pm; Wed 10am–8pm. U-Bahn: Schweizer Platz.

## RÖMERBERG ★

The Altstadt (U-Bahn/S-Bahn: Hauptwache) centers around three Gothic buildings with stepped gables, known collectively as the **Römer,** Römerberg (✆ **069/21-23-48-14**). These houses were originally built between 1288 and 1305 and bought by the city a century later for use as the Rathaus. The second floor of the center house is the **Imperial Hall (Kaisersaal),** lined with the romanticized 19th century portraits of 52 emperors; 13 of them celebrated their coronation banquets here. You can visit this hall daily 10am to 1pm and 2 to 5pm. An hourly tour costing 2€ ($1.80) is obligatory. Tickets can be purchased at the entrance to the Römer.

The elaborate facade of the Römer, with its ornate balcony and statues of four emperors, overlooks **Römerberg Square.** On festive occasions in days gone by, the square was the scene of oxen roasts that featured flowing wine. Today, unfortunately, the Fountain of Justitia pours forth only water, but oxen are still roasted on special occasions.

## DOM ★

The dominant feature of the Altstadt is the 15th-century, red-sandstone tower of the **Dom St. Bartholomäus** in whose chapels the emperors of the Holy Roman Empire were elected and crowned for nearly 300 years. The church was constructed between the 13th and 15th centuries on the site of a Carolingian building. It is most noted for its **west tower** ★★ or Westturm, which is greatly ornamented and crowned by a polygonal gable. It's topped by both a lantern and a dome. Surprisingly, the cathedral was not completed until 1877, but it was based on plans created by the Dom's original architect, Madern Gerthener. Destroyed by Allied bombs in 1944, it was rebuilt in 1953. One of its chief treasures is its **choir stalls** ★, which represent brilliant Upper Rhine craftsmanship, dating from around the mid-14th century. In the north chancel look for ***Maria Schlaf,*** the Altar of Mary Sleeping, dating from 1434. It is the only alter remaining from the church's original interior.

In the cloister of the church is the **Dom Museum** (✆ **069/28-92-29**), which exhibits robes of the imperial electors, among other exhibits. These robes, which are still quite sumptuous, were worn at coronation ceremonies. The oldest vestments date from the 1400s. If you walk west of the cathedral you'll discover a little **Historischer Garten,** or archaeological garden, with ruins of both

Roman and Carolingian fortifications. The Dom Museum is open Tuesday to Friday 10am to 5pm and Saturday and Sunday 11am to 5pm. Admission is 2.50€ ($2.25) for adults and .50€ (45¢) for children.

Domplatz. ✆ **069/29-70-32-36.** Free admission. Daily 9am–noon and 2–6pm. U-Bahn or S-Bahn: Hauptwache.

## OTHER TOP MUSEUMS

**Deutsches Filmmuseum (German Film Museum)** ★ This is the finest film museum in Germany. Old films from the collection are shown continuously on the second floor. The rooms downstairs chronicle the history of the filmmaking industry. Exhibits include Emile Reynaud's 1882 Praxinoscope, Edison's Kinetoscope from 1889, and a copy of the Lumière brothers' Cinematograph from 1895. There are also models illustrating how special effects are shot, including those in *King Kong.*

Schaumainkai 41, at the corner of Schweizerstrasse. ✆ **069/212-388-30.** Admission 2.50€ ($2.25) adults, 1.30€ ($1.15) students and children; film screenings 4.60€ ($4.10) adults, 3.60€ ($3.20) students and children. Tues–Thurs 2–8pm; Fri–Sun 10am–5pm. U-Bahn: Schweizer Platz.

**Historisches Museum (Historical Museum)** ★ Since it was established in a stately looking building near Town Hall in 1878, curators of this dignified museum have systematically added exhibits that showcase the history and culture of Frankfurt. Collections include examples of gold and silver plateware and jewelry; pottery and porcelain; paintings, lithographs, and photographs; and scaled-down models of the Altstadt at various periods of its development.

Saalgasse 19. ✆ **069/212-355-99.** Admission 4€ ($3.55) adults, 2€ ($1.80) for children 6–18. Free for children under 6. Tues–Sun 10am–5pm Wed 10am–8pm. U-bahn: Römer.

**Museum für Angewandte Kunst (Museum of Applied Arts)** ★ More than 30,000 objects, ranging across Europe and Asia, are exhibited at the Museum of Applied Arts. Two buildings house the collection: a 19th-century villa and 1985 structure designed by New York architect Richard Meier. The museum has an outstanding collection of German rococo furnishings (called *Mainzer Meistermobel*) created in Mainz. The glassware is a highlight, with some Venetian pieces from the 15th century. On the second floor, the Far East and Islamic department has a rich collection of Persian carpets and faience dating from the 9th century. One of Germany's finest porcelain collections is here as well.

Schaumainkai 17. ✆ **069/21-23-40-37.** Admission 5€ ($4.45) adults, 2.50€ ($2.25) students and children over 5. Tues and Thurs–Sun 10am–5pm; Wed 10am–8pm. U-Bahn: Schweizer Platz.

**Museum für Moderne Kunst (Museum of Modern Art)** This museum opened in 1991 in a building created by Hans Holbein, the Viennese architect. The structure is designed like a boat, but in spite of its somewhat bizarre shape, the gallery has a bright, spacious air. (Some unkind critics have claimed that the dazzling architecture is more interesting than the exhibits.) Major artists since the 1950s are displayed here, including Roy Liechtenstein (see his *Brush-Stroke*), Andy Warhol, and George Segal, with his *Jazz Combo.* Modern German artists include George Flintzer, Inge Rambow, August Sambe, Gerhard Richter, and others.

Domstrasse 10 (in the center of the Innenstadt, near Römerberg). ✆ **069/21-23-04-47.** Admission 5€ ($4.45) adults, 2.50€ ($2.25) students. Free for children under 6. No admission charged on Wed. Tues and Thurs–Sun 10am–5pm; Wed 10am–8pm. U-Bahn: Römer. Tram: 11 to Domstrasse.

### PARKS

The **Palmengarten** ★, Siesmayerstrasse 61 (✆ **069/21-23-39-39;** U-Bahn: Westend; bus: 36), is a park and a botanical garden. During the last decade, the gardens have been renewed and the conservatories and historic greenhouses completely reconstructed. You can admire a perennial garden, an expanded rock garden, and a beautiful rose garden. In recent years, new conservatories have been added: The Tropicarium is a complex for tropical vegetation; the Sub-Antarctic House displays plants from southern Chile, Argentina, and New Zealand; and the Entrance Conservatory houses insectivorous plants and bromeliads. Collections of orchids, palms, succulents, water lilies, and many others are also on display.

Admission to the botanical garden is 3.50€ ($3.15) for adults and 1.50€ ($1.35) for children, or 7.50€ ($6.70) for a family ticket. It's open daily March to September 9am to 8pm, October and February 9am to 6pm, and November to January 9am to 4pm. In the park area, there's a small lake where people can row boats. In summer, concerts are given in the band shell; evening events include open-air dancing, jazz, and an illuminated fountain. There are some facilities for food.

Frankfurt has a lot of parkland. Locals like to point out that the city has no Central Park as in New York. The city is a central park in itself, they say. The enclosing city walls of old Frankfurt have been replaced by a botanic city ring. Along the Main is a park landscape where you'll see bankers taking their lunch break beneath statues of heroes from the past. **Bethmann Park,** with its Chinese gardens, is one of the city's most interesting parks. It lies immediately to the northeast of Stadmitte and is reached by bus 30 or tram 12.

## 6 Sports & Outdoor Pursuits

### GOLF

**Golf Anlage im Frankfurter Waldstadion,** Morfelder Landstrasse 362, 60528 Frankfurt (✆ **069/67-80-4114**), located within the city limits, is open to all. This course has nine holes, plus a floodlit driving range. Greens fees are 15€ ($13.40) for 12 holes. Open daily 10am to 9pm.

### JOGGING

A good jogging route is along the quays of the River Main, using both sides of the river and the bridges to create a loop. Another choice is the centrally located Gruneberg Park, whose walkways are suitable for jogging.

### TENNIS

Few of the tennis courts in Frankfurt allow nonmembers to play. A noteworthy exception is the **Tennisplatz Eissporthall,** Am Bornheimer hang, 60486 Frankfurt (✆ **069/21-23-08-25** or 069/212-39-30-81; U-Bahn/S-Bahn: Eissporthalle), which has a half-dozen courts. They're open May to October daily 7am to sundown. The cost is 11€ ($9.80) per hour.

## 7 Shopping

When it comes to shopping, Frankfurt has everything. The specialty shops here are so much like those in the United States that most visitors from America will feel right at home. Shops in the central area are open Monday to Friday 9am to 6:30pm and Saturday 9am to 2pm (to 4 or 6pm on the first Sat of the month).

In Frankfurt, the shopping scene is divided into different regions. On "The Golden Mile," the **Zeil,** a pedestrian zone between the Hauptwache and Konstablerwache, you'll find department stores, clothing shops, shoe stores, and furniture outlets. Once one of the most famous shopping streets on the Continent, the Zeil was destroyed in the war and hasn't regained all of its former prestige, though it still has the highest sales of any shopping area in Germany. Zeil remains as the Fifth Avenue of Germany and as one of Europe's greatest shopping streets, but the shopping has become too diversified and there is too much competition for the Zeil to enjoy the prestige it once had. In the 14th century, it was a cattle market. Nearby is the **Kleinmarkthalle,** a covered market with international grocery products.

The **Hauptwache,** in the center of Frankfurt, has two shopping areas, one above and one below ground. Groceries, book dealers, flowers, clothing, tobacco, photo supplies, recordings, and sporting equipment abound. In the Hauptwache-Passage are restaurants, travel agencies, and banks.

**Schillerstrasse,** another pedestrian zone, lies between Hauptwache and Eschenheimer Turm, near the stock exchange. Walking from Schillerstrasse northeast toward Eschenheimer Tor, you'll pass many elegant boutiques and specialty shops.

Southwest of the Hauptwache is the Alte Oper. You can reach it by taking either the **Goethestrasse,** with exclusive stores evocative of Paris or Milan, or the parallel **Grosse Bockenheimerstrasse,** traditionally nicknamed Fressgasse or "Pig-Out Alley." Most wine dealers, delis, and butcher shops here look back on a long and venerable past. At **Opernplatz** you'll find a variety of restaurants and cafes.

West of the Hauptwache is Rossmarkt, leading to **Kaiserstrasse.** It passes the BFG skyscraper, which has three floors of exclusive retail stores, boutiques, and restaurants and directly connects the downtown area to the Hauptbahnhof. Kaiserstrasse is also known for its large selection of stores selling clothing, audio and photography equipment, and stainless-steel ware. The heart of the fur trade in Frankfurt is **Düsseldorfer Strasse,** opposite the Hauptbahnhof. Most book dealers are located around the Hauptwache and **Goetheplatz.** Antiques, old books, etchings, and paintings on **Braubachstrasse** can be found near the Römer, at the Dom, and on Fahrgasse.

Art and antiques are the domain of **Alt-Sachsenhausen,** an appealing and original neighborhood. The famous **Frankfurt Flea Market** takes place here every Saturday 8am to 2pm along the Main River on the Sachsenhausen side. To get there, walk from the Römer toward the river and cross the Eisener Steg bridge.

## DEPARTMENT STORES

**Hertie** A Frankfurt shopping tradition along "The Golden Mile," this vast store offers clothes and shoes for every mood. It also caters to a wide range of budgets. Families with small children may want to check out the selection of toys, and foodies take delight in the food hall in the basement, with tidbits from all over the globe. On the ground floor is a selection of jewelry and cosmetics, among other items. Zeil 90. ✆ **069/92-90-50.** U-Bahn: Konstablerwache.

**Kaufhof** Hertie's main competitor, this department store accurately touts itself for one-stop shopping. On its seven floors, it's got about everything, including a food hall in the basement, although we think Hertie excels in this. Nonetheless, Kaufhof has enough merchandise to dazzle—porcelain, accessories to clothes, jewelry, and glassware. Tired of shopping? Retreat to the top-floor restaurant, which has one of the most panoramic views of Frankfurt. Zeil 116–126. ✆ **069/21910.** U-Bahn: Hauptwache.

## FASHION

For routine wear, check out the vast array of clothing at the previously recommended department stores. The following stores primarily carry women's fashions but have some men's clothing as well.

**Caos 2** For funky shopping, Caos is the place to go, deliberately leaving the "H" out of its name. Cluttered and a bit messy, the shop often has hidden gems, but you'll have to fight your way through the stacks of clothing, including evening wear and accessories. Adalbertrasse 27. ✆ **069/77-44-36.** U-Bahn: Bockenheimer Warte.

**Chris Bittong** For opulent luxury, the shop of this designer is classic and elegant. In addition to the perfectly tailored look, Chris Bittong also stocks an array of matching accessories. The clothing is created in-house. Oppenheimer Landstrasse 19. ✆ **069/62-84-64.** U-Bahn: Schweizer Platz.

**Kleidoskop** You won't really feel like Secondhand Rose here even though the shop specializes in secondhand clothing. In spite of that, it has designer fashions in the medium-price range, and much of the clothing appears to be new. For those who like designer labels, there is an array of Gucci, Armani, Prada, and other big names—all up for grabs at cut-rate prices. Oeder Weg 56. ✆ **069/55-08-37.** U-Bahn: Eschenheimer Tor.

## GIFTS

**Mercedes Benz Giftshop** This is the only store of its kind in Germany, selling memorabilia associated with one of Germany's most famous auto manufacturers. Inside, in a more upscale version of what you might see at a Harley-Davidson store, you'll find jackets, vests, baseball caps, and key rings commemorating the Mercedes' lore and mystique. There's even luggage, one piece of which was specifically designed to fit snugly into the trunk of one of Mercedes' most experimental, and most expensive, limited edition sports cars. Kaiserstrasse 19–21. ✆ **069/973-55-490.** U-Bahn: Willy-Brandt-Platz.

## JEWELRY

**Christ Juweliere & Ohrmacher** This is the largest jewelry and watch retail store in Europe. On two floors there is an array of almost any goodie you'd like to adorn yourself with, including sparkling studs, rings, and bracelets, along with necklaces and even dashing wrist and pocket watches. All items can be altered to fit. Check out the top-quality selection of pearls from the South Pacific. Kaiserstrasse 1. ✆ **069/13-88-20.** U-Bahn: Hauptwache.

**House of Silver** This little shop set in the midst of the apple-wine taverns of Sachsenhausen is a discovery. Savvy Frankfurter collectors go here to indulge their taste in silver jewelry. The store is small, but the range is wide, going from classic motifs to jewelry along more modern lines. Schweizer Strasse 73. ✆ **069/62-76-81.** U-Bahn: Schweizer Platz.

## PORCELAIN

**Höchster Porzellan Manufacture GmbH** This gilt and blue-painted showroom contains one of Germany's largest inventories of what's been created by Hochst Porcelain for more than 150 years. Quality of the "white gold" is almost flawless, and the prestige level of virtually anything associated with this outfit is about as good as it gets in Frankfurt today. (Even Goethe's mother collected the stuff, praising its virtues to her impressionable and articulate young son.) Unless the object of your desire lies on the sale table, where they might be marked up to 40% off retail prices, expect to pay around 155€ ($138.40) for a teacup. You can request particular color schemes for whatever object you select, as long as it's within the historical/aesthetic framework of the era when the original item was produced. Look in particular for illustrated platters inspired by the Struwwelpeter legends, beloved by children in *Mitteleuropa* for generations. Am Kornmarkt/Berliner Strasse 60. ✆ **069/29-52-99.** U-Bahn: Römer.

**Mitsukoshi** The more frequently visited half of this shop is devoted to one of the most complete inventories of Meissen porcelain in Frankfurt. The other half contains a relentlessly upscale assortment of luxury goods made by, among others, Gucci. Widely publicized by journalists in Tokyo and Osaka, this shop is an essential stop for most of the Japanese travelers visiting Frankfurt. As such, most of the staff members speak fluent Japanese, and when tour buses arrive, there are likely to be mobs of Asian clients. Part of the second floor contains a "museum" with copies of antique Meissen candelabra and tureens, any of which can be duplicated if you have enough money and time to wait for their eventual delivery. Kaiserstrasse 13. ✆ **069/92-18-87-0.** U-Bahn: Willy-Brandt-Platz.

## 8 Frankfurt After Dark

For details of what's happening in Frankfurt, you can pick up copies of *Journal Frankfurt* at newsstands throughout the city. Also listing events are *Fritz* and *Strandgut,* both free and available at the tourist office.

To purchase tickets for many major cultural events, go to the tourist office at the Hauptbahnhof. The department store **Hertie,** Zeil 90 (✆ **069/294848**), also has a theater ticket office, which is open during regular store hours.

Of course, one of the greatest ways to spend an evening in Frankfurt is at one of the apple-wine (*Apfelwein*) taverns across the south bank of the Main in the district of Sachsenhausen.

### THE PERFORMING ARTS

**Theater der Stadt Frankfurt,** Untermainanlage 11 (✆ **069/21237999;** U-Bahn: Willy-Brandt-Platz), has three stages. One belongs to the **Frankfurt Municipal Opera,** whose productions have received worldwide recognition in recent years. Two stages are devoted to drama. If your German is adequate, you might want to see a performance at **Städtische Bühnen/Schauspiel** (✆ **069/13-40-400**), a forum for classic German plays as well as modern drama. A variety theater, **Kunstlerhaus Mouson Turm,** Waldschmidtstrasse 4 (✆ **069/4058-9520;** U-Bahn/S-Bahn: Merianplatz), hosts plays, classical music concerts, and dance programs almost every night of the week. Tickets run 12€ to 18€ ($10.70–$16.05).

**Alte Oper** The old opera house is still the pride of Frankfurt, even though opera is no longer presented here. This building was reopened in 1981, following its reconstruction after World War II bombings. The original structure had been officially opened in 1880 by Kaiser Wilhelm I. At that time it was hailed as one of the most beautiful theaters in Europe. Today the Alte Oper is the site of frequent symphonic and choral concerts. Opernplatz. ✆ **069/1-34-04-00.** www.alteroper.de. Tickets 17€–80€ ($15.20–$71.45). Box office Mon–Fri 8:30am–8:30pm, Sat 9:30am–2pm. U-Bahn: Alte Oper.

**English Theater** This English-language theater was founded by the actress Judith Rosenbauer, who is still its artistic director. It began in a Sachsenhausen backyard but was later moved to this location, compliments of the city of Frankfurt. The Art Deco auditorium, which seats 230, has an adjoining cafe. Musicals, comedies, dramas, and thrillers are produced. During the season (Sept–July), performances are Tuesday to Saturday at 8pm and Sunday and Wednesday at 6pm. Kaiserstrasse 52 (near the Hauptbahnhof). ✆ **069/24-23-16-20.** Plays 22.95€–29€ ($20.50–$25.90); reduced student price 11€–14€ ($9.80–$12.50); musicals 34€ ($30.35); reduced student price 21€ ($18.75). Tues and Sun, prices are 4€ ($3.55) less. Box office daily 10am–7pm. S-Bahn: Hauptbahnhof.

**Oper Frankfurt/Ballet Frankfurt** This is Frankfurt's premier showcase for world-class opera and ballet. Acclaimed for its dramatic artistry, the **Frankfurt Opera** is under the charge of conductor Sylvain Cambreling. The world-renowned **Frankfurt Ballet** is directed by William Forsythe. Willy-Brandt-Platz (between the Hauptbahnhof and the Innenstadt). ✆ **069/134-04-00.** Opera and ballet 11€–110€ ($9.80–$98.25). Box office Mon–Fri 8am–8pm; Sat 8am–6pm. U-Bahn: Willy-Brandt-Platz.

## THE CLUB & MUSIC SCENE

### CABARET

**Tigerpalast** This is the most famous and sought-after cabaret in Frankfurt. Shows are presented in a not-very-large blue and black theater, where guests that have included Joan Collins sit at tiny tables to see about eight different artists per show. The acts usually include four Italian acrobats, three Russians who jump into one another's arms from dizzying heights, an East Indian shadow puppeteer who imitates famous German and U.S. politicians, a Mexican juggler, and a Ukrainian ballet artist who dances to the melodies of Edith Piaf. A tiger, a panther, and a sea lion all make carefully choreographed appearances as well, each presented with an emphasis on razzmatazz, nostalgia, and the schmaltziness of show biz. Each show lasts 2 hours with breaks for drinks and snacks, and each is presented as child-approved family-style entertainment without nudity. Two well-recommended restaurants are associated with this cabaret (see "Where to Dine" earlier in this chapter). Heiligkreuzgasse 16–20. ✆ **069/92-00-22-50.** Tickets 45€ ($40.20); half price for children under 12. Drinks extra from 6€ ($5.35). Shows Tues–Thurs 7pm; Fri–Sat 8 and 11pm; Sun 5 and 9pm.

### DANCE CLUBS

In a 16-square-block area in front of the Hauptbahnhof, you'll find a rowdy kind of entertainment: what the Germans call *erotische Spiele.* Doormen will practically pull you inside to view porno movies, sex shows, sex shops, and discos teeming with prostitutes. ***Warning:*** This area can be dangerous—don't come here alone. For less lurid activities in a safer environment, head to the live-music clubs, discos, bars, and cafes across the Main River in the **Sachsenhausen** district. Most gay bars and clubs are located in a small area between Bleichstrasse and Zeil.

**Cooky's** Tuesday to Sunday, DJs at Cooky's mix a dance soundtrack of hip-hop and house music. Hours are Tuesday, Thursday, and Sunday 11pm to 4am, Friday and Saturday 10pm to 6am. Am Salzhaus 4. ✆ **069/28-76-62.** Cover Sun and Tues–Thurs 6€ ($5.35), Fri–Sat 8€ ($7.15). U-Bahn/S-Bahn: Hauptwache.

**Nacht Leben** This club has a cafe-bar upstairs and a disco downstairs. Here you can either have drinks and conversation or dance to the throbbing beat of hip-hop, funk, soul, and house. The club occasionally books a live band. Open

Monday to Wednesday 11:30am to 2am, Thursday to Saturday 11:30am to 4am. Kurt-Schumacher-Strasse 45. ✆ **069/2-06-50.** Cover 4€–10€ ($3.55–$8.95). U-Bahn/S-Bahn: Konstablerwache.

## LIVE MUSIC

**An Sibin** This Irish cellar pub is decorated with pushcarts, wagons, and antique instruments. There's a band on most nights; the music is Irish-only on Tuesday. You'll find Guinness on tap, English and Irish pub grub, and a friendly barkeep who'll teach you a few phrases in Gaelic. Open Monday to Thursday 7pm to 1:30am, Friday to Sunday 7pm to 3am. Wallstrasse 9. ✆ **069/6-03-21-59.** U-Bahn/S-Bahn: Hauptwache.

**Der Jazzkeller** This basement club, established in 1952, is one of the most famous and atmospheric jazz clubs in Germany. Its reputation is as solid as the 200-year-old redbrick walls that surround it. The place has played host to such jazz luminaries as Louis Armstrong, Dizzy Gillespie, and Gerry Mulligan. Wednesday and Friday, patrons dance to the club's "Cool Music Mix." Thursday and Saturday, live music is presented. Open Tuesday to Sunday 9pm to 3am. Kleine Bockenheimer 18A, near Goethestrasse. ✆ **069/28-85-37.** Concerts 6€–22€ ($5.35–$19.65), disco 6€–11€ ($5.35–$9.80). U-Bahn/S-Bahn: Alte Oper.

**Dreikönigskeller** This tiny place features live performances of any and every pop musical style from the 1940s through the contemporary music scene. It opens daily at 9pm. Färberstrasse 71. ✆ **069/62-92-73.** Cover 3€–6€ ($2.70–$5.35) when there's a concert. U-Bahn/S-Bahn: Schweizerplatz.

**One Ninety East** Of the many nightclubs in Frankfurt, this one pays more homage to New York City–style house music than any other in town. Part of this derives from its ownership by a German-American team of DJs, one of whom makes frequent pilgrimages to New York and L.A., returning with suitcases full of whatever CDs are hot at the time. Originally a pair of underground storage rooms for a brewery, it contains two bars, an industrial-looking decor of blue lights and brushed steel, and a clientele that's about 30% gay, 60% straight, and 10% unidentifiable. Don't be surprised if you don't see the entrance from the busy Hanauer Landstrasse: You'll have to navigate your way into a 19th-century brick courtyard, (the *Uniongelände Complex)* that's the headquarters of a local labor union. Open Wednesday through Saturday from 9pm to 4am. Hanauer Landstrasse 190. No phone. Cover 5€ ($4.45) Fri–Sat only. Tram: 11 or 14.

**Sinkkasten** At this live-music institution, regulars show up regardless of who's playing. Rock, reggae, blues, pop, jazz, and African music bands might be found here, except on Thursday, Saturday, and late Friday, when the club turns disco. Come early to beat the crowd or risk being turned away. Open Sunday to Thursday 9pm to 2am, Friday and Saturday 9pm to 3am. Brönnerstrasse 9. ✆ **069/28-03-85.** Disco 4€–6€ ($3.55–$5.35), concerts 6€–20€ ($5.35–$17.85). U-Bahn/S-Bahn: Konstablerwache.

## GAY & LESBIAN FRANKFURT

**Blue Angel** This club was named after gay icon Marlene Dietrich's first movie hit. The DJs keep you guessing by mixing dance styles. The revelry often picks up steam late in the night, so hours generally extend into the early morning (club opens at 10pm). Bronnerstrasse 17. ✆ **069/28-27-72.** Cover 5€–8€ ($4.45–$7.15). U-Bahn/S-Bahn: Konstablerwache.

**Harvey's Cafe Bar** This indoor/outdoor bistro sometimes has live disco bands on the weekend. It's a popular place for a gay date. It's open daily 10am to 1am (to 2am Fri–Sat). Bornheimer Landstrasse 64. ✆ **069/49-73-03.** U-Bahn/S-Bahn: Hauptwache.

**La Gata** This is the most crowded, most visible, most proud, and most notorious lesbian bar in Frankfurt, with a frequently reinforced reputation for refusing entrance to most men, especially if they're heterosexual. The decor evokes a somewhat macho-looking English pub, with white walls, lots of dark-stained bar fixtures, and bulletin boards plastered with photos of some of the bar's regular clients, usually during their holidays. Soups and snacks are available for between 2.50€ and 3.50€ ($2.25–$3.15) each, daily 9pm to 1am. Seehofstrasse 3. ✆ **069/614-581.** U-Bahn: Südbahnhof.

**Lucky's Manhattan** Best described as a gay cafe and bar wrapped into one, Lucky's also has aspects of a conservative tearoom. Most folks come here to drink beer or apple wine, or perhaps to nibble on a limited array of toasts and crêpes. It's a worthwhile place to begin, but not to end, an evening on the town. Open daily noon to 1am (until 2am Fri–Satu). Schäfergasse 27. ✆ **069/28-49-19.** U-Bahn/S-Bahn: Konstablerwache.

**Mr. Dorian's Club** New management, as of early 2001, breathed new life into this gay bar, where men in their 40s and 50s meet somewhat provocative younger partners (some of whom expect to be paid for their company). There's dancing to recorded house and garage music Friday and Saturday nights after 10pm, but usually the place functions just as a bar where even the most unlikely-looking patron can find male companionship. Alte Gasse 34. ✆ **069/92-88-29-66.** U-Bahn: Konstablerwache.

**Pulse** This is a cafe with an active bar trade; a clientele that's mostly fashionable, male, and gay; and a throbbing Valentine-colored decor of red, black, and gray. Come here for salads, sandwiches, and late-night platters that include miniquiches. Menu items cost from 8€ to 13€ ($7.15–$11.60), mixed drinks from 5€ to 9€ ($4.45–$8.05), unless they're alcohol-free (an example is a "safe sex on the beach"), when they go for 4€ ($3.55). Some nights, house and garage music begins after around 10pm, transforming the place into something that you might define as a disco with food service. Open Monday to Saturday 11am to 1am (until 3 or 4am Sat), Sunday 9:30am to 1am. Bleichstrasse 38A. ✆ **069/13-88-68-02.** U-Bahn: Konstablerwache.

## BARS & CAFES

**Balalaika** For one of your most charming evenings in Frankfurt, head across the Main to Sachsenhausen—not for an *Apfelwein* tavern, but to visit this shoebox-size club. It is the domain of Anita Honis, an American from Harlem who imbues the club with her personal charm and her music. Several times a night she'll bring out her guitar and entertain guests while perched on a wooden bar stool. Open Sunday to Thursday 8pm to 2am, Friday and Saturday 8pm to 3am. Dreikönigstrasse 30. ✆ **069/61-22-26.** Bus: 30 or 36.

**Café Karin** The mayor of Frankfurt first steered us to this place. He claimed that "the real Frankfurter" patronizes this cafe and told us to "come here for a preview of German culture." Inside you'll find art-filled walls, old wooden tables, daily newspapers (which some patrons read for hours), and cafe food. It's a place to relax and linger. Perhaps every hour or so a waiter might come over, but don't count on it. We like to hit this place for breakfast and then later stop off for a nightcap around midnight. It's open Monday to Thursday 9am to 1am,

Friday and Saturday 9am to 2pm, and Sunday 10am to 7pm. Grosser Hirschgraben 28. ✆ **069/29-52-17.** U-Bahn: Hauptwache.

**Café Laumer** If you're nostalgic for the last days of the Austro-Hungarian empire, you can waltz into this place. It's a classic German *Kaffeehaus* with a large garden, attracting a middle-aged crowd. Back in the old days, it was known as the favorite retreat of Frankfurt philosophers. Today it serves some of the best pastries in town. Just wait until you try the chef's gigantic raspberry schorle. Open Monday to Saturday 7:30am to 9pm, Sunday 10am to 7pm. Bockenheimer Landstrasse 67. ✆ **069/72-79-12.** U-Bahn: Westend.

**Café-Restaurant in der Schirn** No other bar in Frankfurt's medieval core conveys such a sense of trimmed-down postmodernism, and few others are as big-league stylish. Some aspects of its high-ceilinged, steel, glass, and granite premises were designed by Philippe Starcke, a fact that adds enormously to its cachet with hip patrons who tend to dress mostly in black. Faced with the predominance of the bar here, tables (which spill out onto the pavement in summer) seem almost like an afterthought, but if you want to dine, a limited menu is available. The restaurant is open Tuesday to Friday noon to 3pm and 6 to 10:30pm; Saturday and Sunday noon to 10:30pm. The bar is open Tuesday to Sunday noon to midnight. Römerberg 6A. ✆ **069/29-17-32.** U-Bahn: Römer.

**Jimmy's Bar** To impress that really big client, take him or her to Frankfurt's most elegant bar in its most elegant hotel, Hessischer Hof. Against a backdrop of gently playing piano music, you can drink your Tom Collins in style with the city's smoothest service. Evocative of Cuba, the *mojito* (a rum-and-citrus drink), so beloved by Hemingway, has made it to Frankfurt and is the drink of the hour. The bartenders seem to know how to fill all requests, regardless of how unusual. Open daily 8pm to 4am. In the Hessischer Hof, Friedrich-Ebert-Anlage 40. ✆ **069/7-54-00.** Bus: 32 or 33. S-Bahn: Platz der Republik.

**Luna** This is a hip straight bar that's always packed. With cool jazz playing in the background, this bar attracts the young professionals of Frankfurt who go here for cocktails. The bartenders, some of whom evoke Tom Cruise in his flop movie, *Cocktail,* perform gymnastics in making such drinks as Grasshoppers, juleps, champagne fizzes, and tropical coladas. The place is packed on weekends. Open Sunday to Thursday 7pm to 2am, Friday and Saturday 7pm to 3am. Stiftstrasse 6. ✆ **069/29-47-74.** U-Bahn: Hauptwache.

## 9 Side Trips from Frankfurt

Picturesque Aschaffenburg and some of the leading spas of Germany lie on Frankfurt's doorstep. Another good side trip is to Mainz (see chapter 14).

### ASCHAFFENBURG

40km (25 miles) SE of Frankfurt, 77km (48 miles) NW of Würzburg

Aschaffenburg was originally a Roman settlement on the right bank of the Main River and later became an important town in the Middle Ages. In recent years, it's grown industrially, but even with 250 garment manufacturers, the town has remained peaceful and provincial. Its many parks and shady lanes make it a fitting gateway to the streams and woodlands of the Spessart Hills. Weekly fairs are held on the square, where fishers along the banks of the Main sell seafood straight from their buckets. Many traditional shops are in a pedestrian zone, with lamps, fountains, and flowers.

## ESSENTIALS

**GETTING THERE** **By Train** The **Aschaffenburg Bahnhof** is on the major Nürnberg–Würzburg–Frankfurt line and on the regional Maintal Aschaffenburg–Mittenburg–Wertheim line, with frequent connections in all directions. From Frankfurt, 45 trains arrive daily (trip time: 30–45 min.). For information, call ✆ **01805/99-66-33.**

**By Bus** There is no direct bus service between Frankfurt and Aschaffenburg.

**By Car** Access by car is via the A3 Autobahn east and west.

**VISITOR INFORMATION** Contact **Tourist-Information,** Schlossplatz 1 (✆ **06021/39-58-00;** www.info-aschaffenburg.de). It's open Monday to Friday 9am to 5pm and Saturday 10am to 1pm.

**GETTING AROUND** Aschaffenburg and the immediate region around it are served by a network of green-painted buses whose junction point is the city's main railway station (*Hauptbahnhof*). Because many of the streets within the city's historic core are reserved for pedestrians, many sightseers take bus 1, 4, 5, or 8 between the Hauptbahnhof and the Stadthalle (town hall), immediately adjacent to the *Altstadt.* Buses run daily 5:30am to 9pm. Rides within the central zone cost 1€ (90¢) per person each way. An all-day ticket goes for 2€ ($1.80). For information, call the city tourist office (✆ **06021/39-58-00**).

## SEEING THE SIGHTS

The best park in Aschaffenburg is **Schönbusch Park,** Kleine Schönbuschallee 1 (✆ **06021/873-08;** bus: 4), located 3km (2 miles) across the Main. It's a marvel of planning, using the natural surroundings as a setting for formal 18th-century gardens, shady lanes, temples, and gazebos. At the edge of the mirror-smooth lake is a small neoclassical castle, really a country house, once used by the electors of Mainz. The house is open April to October, Tuesday to Sunday 10am to 12:30pm and 2:30 to 6pm. Admission is 2.50€ ($2.25) for adults, 2€ ($1.80) for students, and free for children under 15. In summer, it's possible to rent a small boat to go on the lake. There's also a cafe-restaurant open daily 8am to 8pm.

The most impressive castle in Aschaffenburg is the huge Renaissance **Schloss Johannisburg** ★, Schlossplatz 4 (✆ **06021/386-570;** bus: 1, 2, or 8), reflected in the waters of the Main. Erected from 1605 to 1614, it became the residence of the rulers of the town, the prince-electors of Mainz. The red-sandstone castle is almost perfectly symmetrical, with four massive lantern towers surrounding an inner courtyard. April to October, the castle is open 9am to noon and 1 to 6pm, Tuesday to Sunday; off-season, Tuesday to Sunday 10am to 4pm. Admission is 2.50€ ($2.25) for adults and 2€ ($1.80) for children 14 and under. While here you might visit the Schlossweinstuben (see "Where to Stay & Dine," below). From the castle gardens you can reach the **Pompeianum,** built by Bavaria's King Ludwig I as a replica of the Castor and Pollux palace discovered among the ruins of Pompeii. The Pompeianum is open mid-March to mid-October, Tuesday to Sunday 10am to noon and 2:30 to 6pm. Admission is 2€ ($1.80) for adults, 1.50€ ($1.35) for students, and free for children.

**Stiftskirche St. Peter and St. Alexander,** Stiftsgasse 5 (✆ **06021/2-24-20;** bus: 1, 4, or 10), has stood on its hill overlooking the town for 1,000 years. Its architecture has changed over the centuries, however, with remodeling and reconstruction, and today it stands as a combination of Romanesque, Gothic, and baroque. Its most precious treasure is the painted retable *The Lamentation* *of Christ,* by Mathias Grünewald. The interior is decorated with several paintings of the school of Lucas Cranach, as well as a marble-alabaster pulpit by Hans Juncker. One of the oldest pieces is a Roman-style crucifix from A.D. 980. Adjacent to the north side of the church is a Romanesque cloister from the 13th century. The church is open Wednesday to Monday 10am to 1pm and 2 to 5pm. Admission is free, but a tour costs 1.50€ ($1.35) adults and 1€ (90¢) children and students.

### WHERE TO STAY & DINE

**Hotel Dalberg** Newly built in 1994, this hotel occupies a prominent site that's within a 5-minute walk from Aschaffenburg's historic core and its pedestrian zone. Rising behind an all-white, four-story facade, it offers cozy, well-designed rooms, each with a tiled shower. On the premises you'll find a rustic-looking Weinstube serving regional cuisine and drinks from a bar.

Pfaffengasse 12–14. D-63739 Aschaffenburg. ✆ **06021/3560.** Fax 06021/21-98-94. www.hotel-dalberg.de. 26 units. 89€–95€ ($79.50–$84.85) double. Rates include breakfast. AE, MC, V. Bus: 1 or 4. **Amenities:** Restaurant; bar; room service. *In room:* TV, minibar.

**Hotel Post** This is the town's premier hotel, offering greater comfort than its rivals. Close to the heart of town, it was built in 1919 and completely renovated in 2000. Rooms are well maintained and decorated in traditional style. Some units come with a tub and shower, others only a shower. The dining room is a stylized version of an old posting inn; it includes an original mail coach, timbered walls and ceiling, and lead-glass windows. Reasonably priced and very good Franconian meals are served here.

Goldbacherstrasse 19, 63739 Aschaffenburg. ✆ **06021/33-40.** Fax 06021/1-34-83. www.post-ab.de. 69 units. 102€–114€ ($91.10–$101.80) double. Rates include breakfast. AE, DC, MC, V. Parking 8€ ($7.15). Bus: 1, 3, 4, 6, or 10. **Amenities:** Restaurant; indoor swimming pool; sauna; solarium; laundry. *In room:* TV, minibar.

**Schlossweinstuben** FRANCONIAN/BAVARIAN One of the most alluring corners of this historic castle is its popular wine cellar. Here you'll find a wide variety of German wines to complement the conservative but well-prepared menu items. A meal might begin with liver-dumpling soup, then follow with a game specialty (depending on the season). The selection of very fresh fish is likely to include trout and pike. There is no pretension to this cuisine—it's just good, hearty, rib-sticking fare.

Schloss Johannisburg. ✆ **06021/1-24-40.** Reservations recommended. Main courses 10.80€–29.80€ ($9.65–$26.60). No credit cards. Tues–Sun 10am–midnight. Bus: 1, 3, or 4.

**Syndikus** An unpretentious three-story facade greets visitors to this hotel. The bar area is rustically decorated with timbered ceilings and wheel chandeliers. All rooms are well maintained and have up-to-date furnishings, each with a shower. Although the hotel is open year-round, its restaurant is closed in August.

Löherstrasse 35, 63739 Aschaffenburg (a few blocks from the cathedral). ✆ **06021/44-9990.** Fax 06021/44-99944. 20 units. 73€–84€ ($65.20–$75) double; 93€–140€ ($83.05–$125) suite. Rates include breakfast. MC, V. Parking 3.50€ ($3.15). Bus: 3 or 6. **Amenities:** Restaurant. *In room:* TV.

## WIESBADEN

40km (25 miles) W of Frankfurt, 151km (94 miles) SE of Bonn

This sheltered valley, between the Rhine and the Taunus Mountains, has held a spa since Roman times. Today Wiesbaden competes with Baden-Baden for the title of Germany's most fashionable resort. Its success is based partly on its 26 hot springs, with temperatures of 47°C to 66°C (117°F–150°F), and partly on its proximity to Frankfurt's transportation centers, which gives the spa a distinctly international flavor.

Wiesbaden is also a major cultural center. Every spring it plays host to the International May Festival of music, dance, and drama. The major concert halls are in the **Kurhaus,** a lively, multiroomed structure centered around a cupola-crowned hall. In addition to concerts, the complex hosts plays and ballets, plus a variety of social gatherings, such as international conferences, congresses, exhibitions, and trade fairs. It also holds a casino, a lively restaurant, and an outdoor cafe.

For the more active visitors, Wiesbaden offers horseback riding, a golf course, swimming, tennis, and hiking. The streets of the city are enjoyable for strolling, as is the **Kurpark,** which has a lake surrounded by old shade trees. It's especially beautiful at night, when the lights of the spa are reflected in the water and the huge fountains are lit. The park stretches for half a mile northward along the Kuranlagen, ending in a fancy residential quarter, the Sonnenberg.

## ESSENTIALS

**GETTING THERE** **By Train** Trains run between Frankfurt airport and Wiesbaden about every hour, leaving from the airport's lower level (trip time: 30 min.). Tickets can be purchased at machines in the station area or at the airport's railway ticket counter. There's also frequent train service from the center of Frankfurt on S-Bahn S-1 and S-9 (trip time: 30–40 min.). For information, call ✆ **01805/99-66-33.**

**By Bus** **Deutsche Touring GmbH** in Frankfurt (✆ **069/7903261**) operates frequent service to Wiesbaden (Line T81 or T82).

**By Car** Wiesbaden lies at a major crossroads, with access via the A3 Autobahn from the north and south, connecting with the A66 Autobahn from the west and east. Travel time by car from Frankfurt (Route 66) is about 20 to 30 minutes, depending on traffic. From the Frankfurt airport to Wiesbaden by car is about 20 minutes.

**VISITOR INFORMATION** The **Verkehrsbüro,** Marktstrasse 6 (✆ **0611/1-72-97-80;** www.wiesbaden.de), is open Monday to Friday 9am to 6pm and Saturday 9am to 3pm. Closed on Sundays.

**GETTING AROUND** The Hauptbahnhof is the junction point for most of the city's bus lines. Buses are blue-sided and charge 1.40€ to 1.80€ ($1.25–$1.60) for rides to most points in town, depending on distance. Buses run daily 5am to midnight. Kirchgasse is one of the most prominent streets in the pedestrian zone, but the closest point to catch a bus is in front of the Stadtteater.

**SHOPPING** The shopping scene here is prosperous, squeaky-clean, and in the eyes of some, a bit smug. The resort's major shopping artery is **Wilhelmstrasse.** Wiesbaden is also a center for antiques, although we find them too pricey. **Taunusstrasse** is lined with antique shops.

## WHERE TO STAY

### Very Expensive

**Hotel Nassauer Hof** ★★★ The super-luxurious Nassauer Hof, often referred to as the "grande dame" of Wiesbaden, is among the most appealing in town. It's an old favorite with up-to-date conveniences. The spacious rooms feature soundproof windows and elegant furnishings; some have air-conditioning. Bathrooms contain deluxe beauty products and robes. The hotel stands in the city center, within walking distance of the Kurhaus, Spielbank, theaters, and the shopping area.

Kaiser-Friedrich-Platz 3–4, 65183 Wiesbaden. ✆ **800/223-6800** in the U.S., or 0611/13-30. Fax 0611/13-36-32. www.nassauer-hof.de. 186 units. 260€–308€ ($232.20–$275.05) double; 370€–1,380€ ($330.40–$1,232.35) suite. AE, DC, MC, V. Parking 17€ ($15.20). Bus: 5, 18, or 25. **Amenities:** 2 restaurants; bar; pool; fitness center; beauty spa; sauna; solarium; 24-hr. room service; babysitting; laundry/dry cleaning. *In room:* A/C, TV, minibar, hair dryer, safe.

## Expensive

**Hotel Klee am Park** ★★ *Value* This hotel is highly recommended for those who might find the older, more luxurious Nassauer Hof a bit too monumental. Klee am Park is a square, modern hotel in a tranquil setting, surrounded by its own informal gardens. The theater, casino, and shopping area are nearby. Rooms have French doors opening onto balconies.

Parkstrasse 4, 65189 Wiesbaden. ✆ **0611/9-00-10.** Fax 0611/9-00-1310. www.klee-am-park.de. 54 units. 138€–183€ ($123.25–$163.40) double. AE, DC, MC, V. Free parking. Bus: 2 or 8. **Amenities:** Cafe/restaurant; bar; terrace; room service; babysitting; laundry/dry cleaning. *In room:* TV, minibar, hair dryer.

**Ramada Hotel Wiesbaden** ★ Lots of businesspeople stay at the Ramada instead of staying in Frankfurt, as it's only 20 minutes from the Frankfurt airport. It's also a good center for visitors to Wiesbaden, within a 5-minute walk of the Kurhaus and the elegant boutiques and old cafes of the pedestrian zone. Rooms are modern and comfortably furnished. The small bathrooms are well maintained, each with a tub and shower.

Abraham–Lincoln-Strasse 17, 65189 Wiesbaden. ✆ **800/854-7854** in the U.S. and Canada, or 0611/79-70. Fax 0611/76-13-72. www.ramadahotels.com. 205 units. Mon–Thurs 111€–121€ ($99.10–$108.05) double; Fri–Sun 95€ ($84.85) double (rate includes breakfast); 200€–240€ ($178.60–$214.30) suite. AE, DC, MC, V. Free parking. Bus: 5, 18, or 25. **Amenities:** Restaurant; bar; pool; fitness center; sauna; solarium; babysitting; laundry/dry cleaning. *In room:* A/C, TV, minibar, hair dryer.

## Moderate

**Admiral Hotel** *Value* The centrally located Admiral is a favorite of traditionalists and one of the best values in Wiesbaden. Readers constantly praise the owners for their hospitality. Rooms are furnished in a charmingly old-fashioned way, often with brass beds. Bathrooms are small but clean, and contain showers. The hotel offers health food. The owners are a retired U.S. Army officer and his German-born wife.

Geisbergstrasse 8, 65193 Wiesbaden (a 5-min. walk from the Kurhaus). ✆ **0611/5-86-60.** Fax 0611/52-10-53. www.admiral-hotel.de. 28 units. 110€–118€ ($98.25–$105.35) double. Rates include buffet breakfast. AE, DC, MC, V. Parking 7.80€ ($6.95). Bus: 1 or 8. *In room:* TV, hair dryer.

**Hotel am Landeschaus** This hotel in central Wiesbaden is one of the spa's best reasonably priced hotels. It's completely modern but also warm, cozy, and inviting. Rooms are well kept, with small, shower-only bathrooms. Guests can enjoy drinks in a rustic ale tavern.

Mortitzstrasse 51, (within walking distance of the railroad station) 65185 Wiesbaden. ✆ **0611/99-66-60.** Fax 0611/99-66-66. 20 units. 92€ ($82.15) double. Rates include buffet breakfast. MC, V. Parking 6€ ($5.35). Bus: 10, 14, or 16. **Amenities:** Breakfast room; bar. *In room:* TV.

## Inexpensive

**Zur Rose** (see "Where to Dine," below) also rents inexpensive rooms.

**Hotel Klemm** This hotel occupies a late–19th century Jugendstil villa with solid stone walls. Although the setting is well scrubbed and respectable, it has touches of genteel shabbiness that seem to go well with the nostalgia that permeates this part of Wiesbaden. This place enjoys many repeat visitors. Rooms are simple, but comfortable and well kept with shower-only bathrooms. Only breakfast is served.

Kapellenstrasse 9, 65193 Wiesbaden (near the Kurhaus). ✆ **0611/58-20.** Fax 0611/58-22-22. www.info-wiesbaden.de. 65 units. 80€–110€ ($71.45–$98.25) double. Rates include breakfast. AE, DC, MC, V. Bus: 1, 2, or 8. *In room:* TV.

## WHERE TO DINE

**Ente Restaurant** ★★★ CONTINENTAL This restaurant serves the best food in town. The innovative chef makes sure the meals are as pleasing to the eye as they are to the palate. Cuisine is light and modern. Specialties change from week to week. Typical offerings include parfait of duck livers, a whole roast duck for two, roast medallions of venison with chanterelles, and clams in puff pastry. Desserts alone are reason to visit, especially the lemon soufflé with strawberries and the mountain-honey ice cream. Ente also has one of the best wine lists in Europe. Many are moderate in price. A boutique, delicatessen, wine cellar, and bistro are attached.

In the Hotel Nassauer Hof, Kaiser-Friedrich-Platz 3–4. ✆ **0611/133666.** Reservations required. Main courses 24€–32€ ($21.45–$28.60); fixed-price dinner 69€–95€ ($61.60–$84.85). AE, DC, MC, V. Restaurant and bistro daily noon–2:30pm and 6pm–midnight. Bus: 5, 18, or 25.

**Käfer's** INTERNATIONAL Käfer's directs two restaurants within one of the stately and prestigious Kurhaus. The more appealing of the two is Käfer's Bistro, a replica of the kind of bustling, upscale, well-run bistro you might find in Lyon or Paris. In an adjoining room is the airier, quieter, and more self-consciously formal Casino Restaurant. The menu and prices are the same as in the bistro, but the atmosphere is calmer and frankly a bit more stuffy. Men are required to wear a jacket and tie. Menu items change every 2 weeks. Examples might include smoked salmon served with a *rösti* pancake, crème fraîche, and chives; Canadian lobster with yogurt-flavored cocktail sauce and lemon; penne pasta with pesto sauce and grilled giant prawns; vegetarian dishes; and in springtime, asparagus with filet mignon, bacon, or salmon steak. Dessert might be a mousse flavored with three kinds of chocolate.

In the Kurhaus, Kurhausplatz 1. ✆ **0611/53-62-00.** Reservations recommended. Main courses 16.50€–24€ ($14.75–$21.45). AE, MC, V. Daily 11:30am–2am. Bus: 1, 2, or 8.

**Zur Rose** FRENCH/GERMAN This nearly 200-year-old restaurant, located in a half-timbered building, offers cozy, nostalgic decor, with a ceramic-tile oven, rose-colored lace tablecloths, and candlelight. You can enjoy freshly baked rolls as you peruse the menu. Begin with cucumber-cream soup with dill-flavored shrimp, then try the Barbary duck breast with goose-liver sauce. Smoked salmon, trout, other fresh fish, and shrimp are also regularly featured. For dessert, try puff pastry filled with fresh fruit or poppy-seed mousse with rum-marinated fruit.

Zur Rose also rents 10 rooms, each with shower, TV, and phone. The charge for a double is 80€ ($71.45), including breakfast.

Bremthaler Strasse 1 (east of the town center), 65207 Naurod. ✆ **06127/40-06-06.** Reservations recommended. Main courses 20€–25€ ($17.85–$22.35); fixed-price menu 28€–40€ ($25–$35.70). AE, DC, MC, V. Apr–Oct daily 11am–3pm and 6pm–midnight; off-season Mon–Sat 6–11pm, Sun 11am–2pm. Bus: 21, 22, or 23.

## WIESBADEN AFTER DARK

*"Rien ne va plus"* (All bets are now finished) is the call when the ball starts to roll on the gaming tables at the **Spielbank Wiesbaden,** Im Kurhaus, Kurhausplatz 1 (✆ **0611/53-61-00;** bus: 1, 8, or 16). The casino is open daily 3pm to 3am and admission is 2.50€ ($2.25). Roulette, blackjack, and poker are the featured games. It's located at the end of Wilhelmstrasse, one of the most famous streets in Wiesbaden. To enter, you must present a passport or an identification card. Men must wear jackets and ties.

**Music** and **theater** flourish in Wiesbaden throughout the year. For information on performances during your visit, check at the Wiesbaden tourist office (see "Visitor Information," above). For information about any of the conference and cultural facilities in the **Kurhaus** compound, Kurhaus Platz 1, including the casino and theater, call ✆ **0611/1729910.**

**Hessisches Staatstheater,** Christian-Zais-Strasse (✆ **0611/13-23-25;** bus: 1), built in 1894 by Emperor Wilhelm II, is one of the most beautiful theaters in Germany. It presents a program of operettas, musicals, ballets, and plays. The season lasts September 15 to June 30; tickets are 5€ to 40€ ($4.45–$35.70).

The **International May Festival** features concerts, classical in-house drama productions, and a wide selection of guest performances by internationally renowned theaters. For information and tickets, call ✆ **0611/132325.**

The **Prak Café,** Wilhelmstrasse 36 (✆ **0611/3-93-21;** bus: 1), incorporates a cafe, brasserie, and disco. It's sprawling and often very busy. The cover ranges from 5€ to 10€ ($4.45–$8.95), and it's open daily 9pm to 4am. Much louder is **The Big Apple,** Kirchgasse 66 (✆ **0611/37-40-33;** bus: 4, 5, 14, or 15), where music that will remind you of New York City and Los Angeles is played to a crowd of enthusiastic dancers, mostly in their early 20s. The cover ranges from 5€ to 15€ ($4.45–$13.40), and it's open daily 9pm to 3am. For beer in an appealingly old-fashioned atmosphere, head for the **Ratskeller,** also known as the **Rathsbräu Keller,** Schlossplatz (✆ **0611/200023;** bus: 4). Open Monday to Saturday 11am to 1am.

## BAD HOMBURG ★

16km (10 miles) N of Frankfurt, 45km (28 miles) NE of Wiesbaden

Bad Homburg is one of Germany's most attractive spas, still basking in the grandeur left over from turn-of-the-20th-century Europe. The spa's saline springs are used to treat various disorders, especially heart and circulatory diseases. The town has been a popular watering spot since Roman times. Royalty from all over the world have visited. King Chulalongkorn of Siam (Thailand) was so impressed that he built a Buddhist temple in the Kurpark. Czar Nicholas I erected an onion-domed Russian chapel nearby. The name of the town was popularized by England's Edward VII when, as Prince of Wales, he visited the spa and introduced a new hat style, which he called the "homburg." The town became the gaming capital of Europe when the Blanc brothers opened the casino in 1841.

The **Spa Park** ★ is a verdant, carefully landscaped oasis in the middle of an otherwise rather commercial-looking town. The actual spa facilities are in the **Kaiser Wilhelms Bad,** Im Kurpark (✆ **0611/17290**). They're open Monday 10am to 8pm; Tuesday to Friday 7:30am to 10pm; Saturday 10am to noon. It costs 17.50€ ($15.65) for use of the sauna and pool. The immaculately tended gardens in the surrounding Kurpark are filled with brooks, ponds, arbors, and seasonal flowers. The town center has a sprawling pedestrian-only district that offers many shops, restaurants, and cafes.

## ESSENTIALS

**GETTING THERE** **By Train** Visitors from Frankfurt usually opt to take the S-5 train, which runs from Frankfurt's main railway station to Bad Homburg for a cost of 3.10€ ($3.05) each way. The trip takes about 20 minutes. Call ✆ **01805/99-66-33** for information.

**By Bus** The **Alpina-Airport-Express** is Bad Homburg's hourly, nonstop shuttle service to and from the Frankfurt airport (trip time: 30 min.).

**By Car** Access by car from the north or south is via the A5 Autobahn, exiting at Bad Homburg.

**VISITOR INFORMATION** For information, go to the **Verkehrsamt im Kurhaus,** Louisenstrasse 58 (✆ **06172/1780;** www.bad-homburg.de). It's open Monday to Friday 8:30am to 6:30pm and Saturday 9am to 1pm.

**GETTING AROUND** Public transport in Bad Homburg is provided by a network of green and white buses, whose main junction points are the Hauptbahnhof, a 10-minute walk southwest of the city center, and in front of the Kurhaus, in the city center. Buses, which run daily 5am to midnight, charge 1.20€ ($1.05) per ride.

## SIGHTS & ACTIVITIES

**Bad Homburg Palace** This palace was the residence of the landgraves of Hesse-Homburg from its construction in 1680 until the mid-19th century. Its builder, Prince Frederick II von Homburg, preserved the White Tower from the medieval castle that stood on the site. In the late 19th century, the palace became a summer residence for Prussian kings and, later, German emperors. After World War I, the state assumed ownership. The interior contains 18th-century furniture and paintings, including a bust of Prince Frederick II by Andreas Schlüter, Germany's greatest baroque sculptor. The former "telephone room of the empress" includes *Cleopatra* by Pellegrini.

Schlossverwaltung (a few blocks from the spa gardens). ✆ **06172/926-200.** Admission 3.50€ ($3.15) adults, 2.50€ ($2.25) children. Palace and formal gardens Tues–Sun 10am–4pm. Bus: 1, 4, or 11.

**Taunus Therme** A large recreation area, Taunus Therme boasts several pools, a sauna, a solarium, and a health center, plus TVs, cinemas, and two restaurants.

Seedammweg. ✆ **06172/4-06-40.** Admission Mon–Fri, 12€ ($10.70) for 2 hr., 16€ ($14.30) for 4 hr., 24€ ($21.45) for all day; Sat–Sun and holidays, 14€ ($12.50) for 2 hr., 18€ ($16.05) for all day; daily, free for children 3 and under. Sun–Tues 9am–11pm; Wed and Fri–Sat 9am–midnight. Bus: 6.

## WHERE TO STAY

### Expensive

**Maritim Kurhaus-Hotel** ★ This hotel near the spa facilities offers visitors plush rooms, many with tall bay windows. As sleek and up-to-date as this hotel is, it's still far outclassed by the Steigenberger Bad Homburg. Double rooms feature king-size beds; singles have queen-size beds. All contain computer outlets. Some rooms have balconies or terraces, permitting wide-angle views over the greenery of the surrounding park. The luxurious bathrooms contain a combination tub and shower. Both international and regional fare are served at the Bürgerstube, which is open daily.

Kurpark, Ludwigstrasse, 61348 Bad Homburg. ✆ **06172/66-00.** Fax 06172/66-01-00. www.maritimhom.de. 148 units. 125€–179€ ($111.65–$159.85) double; 151€–205€ ($134.85–$183.05) suite. AE, DC, MC, V.

Parking 10€ ($8.95). Bus: 1, 2, 3, 4, 11, or 12. **Amenities:** Restaurant; bar; indoor pool; sauna; room service; babysitting; laundry/dry cleaning. *In room:* TV, dataport, minibar, hair dryer, safe.

**Steigenberger Bad Homburg** ★★★ This is the resort's best and most prestigious hotel. Europe's high society used to stroll here in days of yore, and an ambience of luxury still prevails. Rooms are beautifully furnished, each with individually adjustable air-conditioning and extra-long beds. The spacious bathrooms contain deluxe luxury items, sumptuous robes, and combination tub and showers. The elegant Parkside Restaurant offers creative contemporary cuisine. There's also the French-style Charly's Bistro.

Kaiser-Friedrich-Promenade 69–75 (opposite the spa gardens and casino), 61345 Bad Homburg. ✆ **800/223-5652** in the U.S. and Canada, or 06172/18-10. Fax 06172/18-16-30. www.steigenberger.de. 169 units. 174€–214€ ($155.40–$191.10) double; 355€ ($317) suite. AE, DC, MC, V. Parking 12€ ($10.70). Bus: 1, 2, 3, 4, 11, or 12. **Amenities:** Restaurant; bistro; bar; sauna; solarium; steam bath; beauty center; room service; babysitting; laundry/dry cleaning. *In room:* A/C, TV, minibar, hair dryer, safe.

## Moderate

**Hardtwald Hotel** ★ This hotel, which resembles a chalet set in a forest, is an ideal retreat near the spa gardens. In spring, flowers overflow from its window boxes. Its rooms overlook the forest. Each is comfortably furnished and well maintained, coming with a compact tiled bathroom with tub and shower or only shower. The chef in the excellent, flower-filled dining room uses only the freshest of ingredients to prepare his well-known international and German dishes. In summer, tables are set on the large patio. Next to the hotel is a stable where you can rent horses.

Philosophenweg 31 (a 20-min. walk from the center of town), 61350 Bad Homburg. ✆ **06172/98-80.** Fax 06172/898-560. 42 units. 80€–190€ ($71.45–$169.65) double. Rates include buffet breakfast. AE, DC, MC, V. Parking 7.65€ ($7.50). Bus: 3. **Amenities:** Restaurant; bar; room service; laundry. *In room:* TV, minibar.

**Parkhotel Bad Homburg** *Value* This is your best bet for a moderately priced spa vacation. This hotel has an enviable location in the middle of the Kurpark's well-maintained gardens, near the thermal springs. Although its design is modern and angular, its edges are softened with window boxes. Rooms are conservatively furnished. Bathrooms are well kept and contain a combination tub and shower. On the premises are a bar and a sunroom. The hotel restaurant serves Chinese cuisine.

Kaiser-Friedrich-Promenade 53–55, Am Kurpark, 61348 Bad Homburg. ✆ **06172/80-10.** Fax 06172/80-14-00. 120 units. 140€–198€ ($125–$176.80) double; 158€–218€ ($141.10–$194.65) suite. Rates include buffet breakfast. AE, DC, MC, V. Parking 9€ ($8.05). Tram: 5. **Amenities:** Restaurant; bar; health club; sauna; solarium; room service; laundry. *In room:* TV, minibar.

## Inexpensive

**Haus Daheim** *Value* When you're trying to save, head here. This hotel, in a light-blue corner building, is one of the finest small hotels in the town. The comfortable rooms have good beds with firm mattresses, plus tiled bathrooms with shower. This is an admittedly modest choice after the hotels reviewed above, but for value, it's hard to beat.

Elisabethenstrasse 42 (a short walk from the Kurhaus), 61348 Bad Homburg. ✆ **06172/67-73-50.** Fax 06172/677-35-500. www.bad-homburg.de/hausdaheim. 19 units. 107€–157€ ($95.55–$140.20) double. Rates include buffet breakfast. AE, DC, MC, V. Parking 8€ ($7.15). Tram: 5. **Amenities:** Breakfast salon.

## WHERE TO DINE

**Casino-Restaurant** FRENCH/GERMAN At this site, you can gamble and dine at the same time. Until a few years ago, this was the only restaurant in Germany that directly adjoined the gaming tables of a casino. It's one of the finest in town, although not in the same class as Sängers (see below). The dining room is decorated in a formal, vaguely English style. It offers attentive service and a winning combination of light French and German cuisine. The frequently changing menu features seasonal specialties with the freshest of ingredients—head chef Gunther Schwanitz begins each workday at the local markets. Lobster is a universal favorite here, attracting diners from as far away as Frankfurt. Although the main kitchen service stops at 10:30pm, there's a reduced menu until 12:30am.

Im Kurpark. ✆ **06172/1-70-170.** Reservations required. Jacket and tie required for men. Main courses 10€–20€ ($8.95–$17.85); fixed-price menu 25€ ($22.35). AE, DC, V. Daily 6–10:30pm. Tram: 5.

**Sängers Restaurant** ★★★ FRENCH Local food lovers and spa devotees crowd this restaurant to enjoy the highly personal and inventive cuisine, the best in the spa. The two elegant dining rooms are outfitted in the style of Louis XIV. Menu items might include carpaccio of turbot with Iranian caviar; goose-liver terrine served with brioche and gelatin of wild berries; a foam-capped celery soup with quail eggs; roast breast of duck on a bed of rhubarb; and a succulent array of desserts.

Kaiser-Friedrich-Promenade 85 (next to the Steigenberger Bad Homburg). ✆ **06172/92-88-39.** Reservations required. Main courses 23€–29€ ($20.55–$25.90); fixed-price dinner 50€–85€ ($44.65–$75.90). AE, MC, V. Tues–Fri noon–2pm; Mon–Sat 7–11pm. Closed the 1st week of Jan. Bus: 1, 4, 11, or 12.

### BAD HOMBURG AFTER DARK

**Spielbank Im Kurpark** (✆ **06172/1-70-10;** tram: 5), called the "Mother of Monte Carlo," is the spa's major attraction. This casino opened way back in 1841 and helped make Bad Homburg famous. Roulette, blackjack, and baccarat are the games here. Passports are required for entrance, and men must wear jackets and ties. Admission is 2.50€ ($2.25) hours are daily 2:30pm to 3am.

The most active disco in town is the **Tennis Bar,** Kisseleffstrasse 20 (✆ **06172/2-60-41;** bus: 6), named for the municipal tennis courts in the nearby Kurpark. It offers both recorded and live rock music. If you thought you were too old to hang out in a disco, think again, as this one attracts clients ages 25 and over. It's open from 9pm Tuesday to Saturday, with a varying cover. More traditional is the town's favorite beer hall and Weinstube, **Zum Wasser Weibehen,** Am Mühlberg 57 (✆ **06172/2-98-78;** bus: 1, 4, or 11). About 1.5km (1 mile) east of the town center, you'll find another folkloric place, **Zum Ruppe Karl,** Hamburgerstrasse 6 (✆ **06172/4-24-84;** bus: 2 or 12), whose home-style cuisine is enhanced with the establishment's homemade apple wine. The **Kurhaus** also contains a handful of bars, cafes, and shops that usually stay open late.

## BAD NAUHEIM ★

35km (22 miles) N of Frankfurt, 64km (40 miles) NE of Wiesbaden

Like many spas throughout Germany, Bad Nauheim became popular in the early part of the 20th century, when the railroad became a convenient and inexpensive means of transportation. Still going strong today, this resort at the northern edge of the Taunus Mountains is a center for golf, tennis, and ice-skating, as well as the starting point for hiking up the 236m (773-ft.) Joannisberg, which towers over the town.

The warm carbonic-acid springs of the spa are used to treat heart and circulatory disorders and rheumatic diseases. The Kurpark is attractive, well maintained, and filled with promenaders all summer long. The impressive bathhouse

### *Fun Fact* Elvis in Bad Nauheim

Many famous guests have visited this spa, including Otto von Bismarck (1859) and Richard Strauss (1927). Franklin D. Roosevelt spent about 2 years here with his family when he was a small child. Locals believe that Bad Nauheim was spared destruction during World War II, even though a Nazi radio transmitter was installed here, because President Roosevelt had fond memories of the place.

Real fame came to the spa when a private named Elvis Presley arrived and found a home off-base, right next to the Kurhaus. The singer was stationed in nearby Friedberg/Hessen at Ray Barracks Kaserne from October 1958 to March 1960, and his presence had an electrifying effect on the German youth scene. It was here that Elvis fell in love with Priscilla. She was 14 at the time, and when she first arrived at the plain, old-fashioned villa where he lived, the street was full of German girls, waiting by the sign AUTOGRAPHS BETWEEN 7 AND 8PM ONLY. After that first meeting, she saw him once more, and when he returned to the States, he vowed to send for her.

Elvis wasn't the only famous American to visit. It was the habit of newspaper magnate William Randolph Hearst to come here every year with his mistress, Marion Davies, and a dozen or so of her women friends—Hearst would have the women chauffeured around the countryside in style. He firmly believed Bad Nauheim's physicians were the answer to his minor heart problem. Here he had his notorious meeting with Mussolini in 1931 ("a marvelous man"), and from here he flew to Berlin to meet Hitler in 1934. He claimed that he had done "much good" in advising Hitler to drop his persecution of the Jews, but afterwards he spent most of his life trying to live down his image as a supporter of the Nazi cause.

is the single largest complex of Jugendstil architecture in Germany. The Sprudelhof (fountain court), at the center, stretches from the Hauptbahnhof to the Kurpark and all the way to the Kurhaus. All the important sights, including the bathhouse complex, can be visited in half a day. The resort has a busy activity calendar, with concerts twice daily, along with operas, plays, dances, and fashion shows.

## ESSENTIALS

**GETTING THERE** **By Train** Bad Nauheim can easily be reached from Frankfurt. Trains arrive at least once per hour (every 30 min. during rush hours) during the day (trip time: 30 min.). Service is on the Weatherman line between Frankfurt and Giessen. For information call ✆ **01805/99-66-33.**

**By Car** Access is via the A5 Autobahn from the north and the south. Driving time from Frankfurt is about half an hour.

**VISITOR INFORMATION** For information, go to the **Verkehrsverein,** Neue Kurolonnade (✆ **06032/92-99-22;** www.bad-auheim.de). It's open Monday to Friday 9am to noon and 2 to 5pm, Saturday 9am to noon and 2 to 4pm, and Sunday 10am to noon.

## WHERE TO STAY

**Advena Hotel Rosenau** This is one of the better choices at the resort, though it's not nearly as good as the Parkhotel am Kurhaus. The Rosenau is an updated version of a German manor house, with white walls and a red-tiled hip roof. Inside, the decor is one of light-toned wood and pastel colors. Rooms are modern and attractive, with combination tub and shower. On the premises there's a good bistro and the fine Rosengarten restaurant (see "Where to Dine," below).

Steinfurther Strasse 1, (west of Grosser Teich, the town lake) 61231 Bad Nauheim. ✆ **06032/9-64-60.** Fax 06032/964-6666. 54 units. 97€–107€ ($86.60–$95.55) double. Rates include continental breakfast. AE, DC, MC, V. Free parking. Closed Dec 27–Jan 8. **Amenities:** 2 restaurants, bar, pool, room service, laundry/dry cleaning. *In room:* A/C, TV, minibar, hair dryer.

**Hotel Gaudesberger** This centrally located hotel is known mainly for its restaurant (see "Where to Dine," below). Rooms are simply furnished, each coming with a small bathroom with shower. Except for a phone, there are no in-room amenities. The place is plain and decent, not grand in any way. The staff speaks no English.

Hauptstrasse 6, 61231 Bad Nauheim. ✆ and fax **06032/25-08.** 8 units, none with bathroom. 48€ ($42.85) double. Rates include continental breakfast. AE, DC, MC, V. Closed Jan 15–Feb 15. **Amenities:** Restaurant.

**Parkhotel am Kurhaus** ★★ This modern hotel is the finest in town, with better amenities than the Rosenau. It's located in the middle of the park that rings the resort's thermal springs. Its public areas are filled with green plants and arching windows. Rooms, with big sliding glass windows and balconies, provide calm, quiet, and conservative comfort. Bathrooms are luxurious and contain deluxe luxury items and combination tubs and showers. Special diets and vegetarian menus are offered.

Nordlicher Park 16, 61231 Bad Nauheim. ✆ **06032/30-30.** Fax 06032/30-34-19. www.bestwestern.de/badnauheim. 158 units. 138€–148€ ($123.25–$132.15) double; 183€–186€ ($163.40–$166.10) suite. Rates include continental breakfast. AE, DC, MC, V. Parking 4€ ($3.55). **Amenities:** 2 restaurants; cafe; beer tavern; wine tavern; bar; room service; babysitting; laundry/dry cleaning. *In room:* TV, minibar, hair dryer, safe.

## WHERE TO DINE

**Restaurant Gaudesberger** INTERNATIONAL A large menu of well-prepared dishes is offered here in comfortable but simple surroundings. You can stick to the tried-and-true choices, such as chateaubriand with béarnaise sauce or herring filet in dill sauce, or you can dip into the other specialties, such as pork in curry-cream sauce, ox tongue in Madeira sauce, or trout and salmon prepared in at least four different ways. Ingredients are fresh, and everything is prepared home-style. The staff is cooperative and courteous.

In the Hotel Gaudesberger, Hauptstrasse 6. ✆ **06032/25-08.** Reservations recommended. Main courses 8€–16€ ($7.15–$14.30). AE, DC, MC, V. Thurs–Tues 11:30am–2pm and 5:30–9pm.

**Rosengarten** INTERNATIONAL This restaurant is known as one of the best in town. It serves a fixed-price lunch plus a la carte evening meals. The flavorful dishes might include cream of tomato and young-vegetable soup, roast breast of young hen, and filet of salmon with fresh herbs, plus several different pork and game dishes, depending on the season. The cookery is not innovative, but we were impressed with its honesty and freshness. There are no pretensions here.

In the Hotel Rosenau, Steinfurther Strasse 1. ✆ **06032/9-64-60.** Main courses 13.50€–16€ ($12.05–$14.30); fixed-price buffet lunch 15.50€ ($13.85). AE, DC, MC, V. Tues–Sun noon–2pm and 6–10pm. Closed Dec 27–Jan 30.

# 14

# The Rhineland

Few rivers of the world can claim such an important role in the growth of a nation as the Rhine. The Rhine rises in Switzerland and ultimately flows through the Netherlands in its progress to the sea, but most of its 1,370km (850 miles) snake through the mountains and plains of Germany. For more than 2,000 years, it has been a chief trade route, its deep waters enabling modern seagoing vessels to travel downstream from the North Sea as far as Cologne.

From its earliest times, the Rhine has also been a main road for religious, intellectual, and artistic ideas. It has been called a "triumphal avenue of the muses," and a trip along its banks today reveals endless treasures. Legend and history wait around every bend of the river.

From Mainz north to Koblenz, the winding river cuts through steep vine-covered hillsides dotted with towns whose names are synonymous with fine German wine. Here you'll find the dramatic Lorelei, the legendary rock from which a siren lured men to their doom. The saga of *The Nibelungenlied,* the best known of the Rhine legends, is associated with the topography from the Siebengebirge (the Seven Mountains) near Bonn, where Siegfried slew the dragon, to the city of Worms, where Brünnhilde plotted against the dragon-slayer.

The Rhine is also the home of many of Germany's largest and most modern cities. **Cologne** (Köln) and **Düsseldorf** vie for trade and tourism. Cologne is also a common starting point for boat tours of the river.

Roadways along the Rhine tend to be heavily trafficked, so allow adequate time. Main roads hug both the left and right banks of the river, and at many points you'll come across car-ferries that can take you across. The most scenic stretch for driving is the mid-Rhine, between Koblenz and Mainz. EuroCity and InterCity trains connect all the major cities, including Cologne, Düsseldorf, Bonn, and Mainz. Rail service also extends as far north as Hamburg and as far south as Munich.

## 1 Speyer

93km (58 miles) S of Mainz, 21km (13 miles) SW of Heidelberg

One of the oldest Rhine cities, Speyer celebrated its 2,000th jubilee in 1990. It became a significant religious center early on when the Diet of Speyer, in 1529, united the followers of Luther in a protest against the Church of Rome.

### ESSENTIALS

**GETTING THERE** **By Train** Trains reach Speyer only by connections at Heidelberg and Mannheim. The trip from Frankfurt takes 2 hours; from Munich, 5 to 6 hours. Call ✆ **01805/99-66-33** for schedules.

**By Bus** About one bus per hour arrives from Heidelberg. Regional service is provided by **BRN Busverkehr Rhein-Neckar GmbH** at Ludwigshafen (✆ **06231/51-21-22;** www.brn.de).

**By Car** You can drive from Frankfurt in about an hour, from Munich in about 4 hours. Access is by the A61 Autobahn east and west connecting with Route 9 south.

**VISITOR INFORMATION** For information, go to the **Verkehrsamt,** Maximilianstrasse 11 (✆ **06232/14-23-92;** www.speyer.de). Open year-round Monday to Friday 9am to 5pm; May to October, also open Saturday 10am to 4pm and Sunday 11am to 3pm; in the off-season, also open Saturday 10am to noon.

**GETTING AROUND** A blue-and-white "City Shuttle" (bus) runs from the Speyer Hauptbahnhof through the town to Festplatz near the cathedral, east of the Altstadt. It connects most major hotels and restaurants. The bus comes every 10 minutes, and the service runs daily 7am to 7pm. The trip costs .70€ (65¢).

## THE IMPERIAL CATHEDRAL

Nothing brings back the medieval German empire as much as the **Kaiserdom (Imperial Cathedral)** ★★ in Speyer (✆ **06232/10-22-98**), the greatest building of its time. This cathedral, consecrated in the early 11th century, is the largest Romanesque edifice in Germany. Having weathered damage by fires, wars, and restorations, the cathedral was finally restored to its original shape from 1957 to 1961. When you enter the church through the single west door set in a stepped arch, you're immediately caught up in the vastness of its proportions; the whole length of the nave and east chancel opens up before you, lit by the muted daylight from above. The church contains the royal tombs of four emperors, three empresses, and four German kings, as well as a row of bishops' tombs. Open April to October, Monday to Friday 9am to 7pm, Saturday 9am to 6pm, and Sunday 1:30 to 6pm; off season daily from 9am to 5pm.

Other attractions include **Historisches Museum der Pfalz** (Palatinate Historical Museum), whose main attraction is the Domschatz or Cathedral treasury. Inaugurated in 1910, this museum is housed in a castle with four wings and lies directly next to the catheral. In all, there are 300,000 artifacts here related to the history of the Palatinate and the city of Speyer. Relics go back to prehistorical times, with a strong emphasis on the Roman and medieval eras.

On site is a Wine Museum with exhibits showing how the Romans produced their *vino*. The world's oldest bottle of wine (circa 300 A.D.) is also exhibited. Objects found in tombs of former emperors under the Dom are exhibited in the treasury. The most celebrated exhibit is the Bronze Age *Golden Hat of Schifferstadt*. This is a golden, cone-shaped object used in religious celebrations in ancient times. The entrance to the museum (✆ **06232/13250**), is on Domplatz. Hours are Tuesday to Sunday 10am to 6pm, Wednesday 10am to 7pm. Entrance is 4€ ($3.55).

In a former aircraft hanger from 1913 lies the **Technik-Museum** (Museum of Technology), Geibstrasse 2 (✆ **06232/67080**). Here you can view a vast array of airplanes, locomotives, vintage automobiles, fire engines, and even automatic musical instruments. For us, the biggest thrill is going inside a 20-ton U-boat once used to terrorize Allied shipping in the Atlantic.

Annexed to the museum is the Marine Museum, displaying a rich collection of historical model ships. Part of the attraction is a monumental 3-D IMAX cinema.

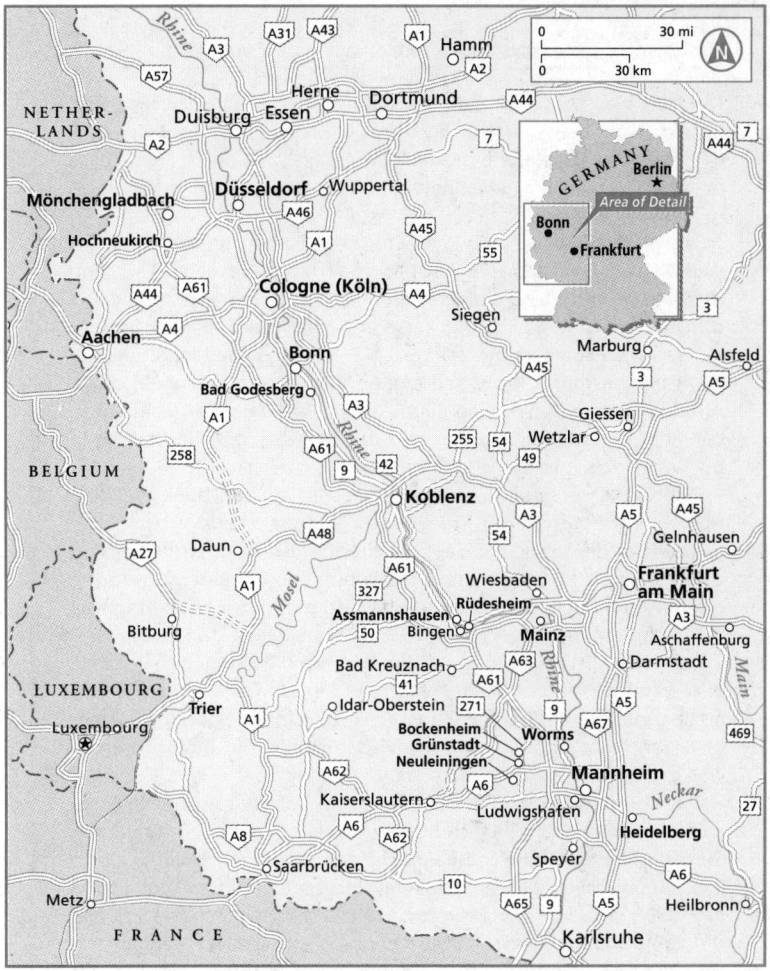


**Dreifaltigkeitskirke** (Trinity Church) on Groose Himmelsgasse, dates from 1701 to 1717 when it was constructed in an elaborate baroque style. The Interior is one of the most richly adorned and decorated churches along the Rhine, containing a two-story gallery with a splendid balustrade of wooden capped vaulting which was also painted by artisans. This is the only church in this elaborate baroque style which still exists in the Rhine-Main-Neckar region. It was designed by Johann Peter Grabner, architect to the court of Palatinate. When you get to Speyer, check with the tourist office to se if this historic church is open on the day of your visit.

Once Speyer was one of the most important centers of Jewish culture along the Rhine, although precious little of that settlement remains today. However, some ruins from the old **Jewish quarter** can still be seen behind the Palatinate Historical Museum.

Enter the ruins from Judengasse (✆ **06232/291971**). The east wall of the ancient Synagogue is the Judenbad (called *Mikwe* in Hebrew), a 12th-century

### *Moments* Cruising the Rhine

The best way to get a really intimate look at the river valley that helped shape the history of Europe is to travel its waters by ship. A wide range of **cruises** ★ is available from several shipping lines. These range from an 800km (500-mile) tour on a luxury yacht to 1-day cruises to historical and artistic sites.

The premier carrier is **KD River Cruises of Europe,** Frankenwerft 15, 50667 Cologne (✆ **0221/25-83-01-1;** www.rivercruises.com). This company has been running cruises since early in the 19th century; today it owns a fleet of more than 25 vessels. Its river tours, elegant but not glitzy, are on compact but comfortable ships equipped with open-air pools, dining rooms, bars, and highly competent multilingual staffs. Although a traditional band might play over dinner, the main entertainment comes from chatting with fellow passengers and taking in the sweeping views of the landscape.

Depending on your tastes and schedule, you can book anything from a short day tour from Cologne to a leisurely weeklong cruise. Our favorite excursion is a 5-day trip from Düsseldorf with stops at Cologne, Koblenz, Speyer, and a final destination of Basel. This tour is offered April to October every Tuesday afternoon. The round-trip fare ranges from 735€ to 1,065€ ($656.35-$951.05).

A longer option is a 6-day cruise between Amsterdam and Basel, priced at 1,055€ to 1,565€ ($942.10-$1,397.55) per person, double occupancy, all-inclusive. The longer river tours include docking at cities of historical or cultural interest and participation in motor-coach or walking tours of the city where you're docking.

Day cruises don't stop for very long, but passengers can still often embark or disembark at such historic towns as Bonn, Linz, Bräubach, St. Goarshausen, and Rüdesheim. On day excursions, children up to age 4 and holders of Eurailpasses travel free, and children ages 4 to 13 pay 2.50€ ($2.25). Tickets for day excursions cannot be reserved and should be bought directly on the pier before departure. Arrangements for cruises of 2 nights or more can be booked through the company's U.S.-based sales representative. For more information in the U.S., contact **KD River Cruises of Europe** (represented in North America by JFO Cruise Service), 2500 Westchester Ave., Purchase, NY 10577 (✆ **800/346-6525**); or 323 Geary St., San Francisco, CA 94102 (✆ **800/858-8587**); or visit the company's website at www.rivercruises.com.

ritual bathhouse for women. The masons who constructed the Dom also built this bathhouse, which is the oldest and best preserved relic of its kind in the country and a poignant, nostalgic reminder of a vanished culture. The site is open April to October Monday to Friday 10am to 1pm and 2 to 5pm, and on Saturday and Sunday from 10am to 5pm, costing 1€ (90¢) admission.

## WHERE TO STAY

**Goldener Engel** This is the most atmospheric choice in town, adjoining one of Speyer's finest restaurants, Wirtschaft Zum Alten Engel (see below). The centrally located inn lies near the Gothic town gate at Maximilianstrasse. It is imbued with lots of character in the spirit of old Rhinelander hotels, complete with many traditional touches and antiques such as baroque free-standing clothes closets. In contrast, the midsize bedrooms are completely modern and up-to-date, with well-maintained private bathrooms with showers and tubs.

Mühlturmstrasse 5–7, 67346 Speyer. ✆ **06232/13260.** Fax 06232/132695. 46 units. 75€–110€ ($67–$98.25). AE, DC, MC, V. **Amenities:** Restaurant next door; bikes for guests. *In room:* TV.

**Rhein-Hotel Luxhof** This hotel is imbued with an unusual character. It's modern in style, but somehow the spirit of a rambling country inn has been retained. The blandly decorated rooms are well designed and compact, often featuring small sitting areas that open onto tiny balconies. All come equipped with bathrooms containing shower-tub combinations.

At the Rhine Bridge, just outside the town, 68766 Hockenheim. ✆ **06205/30-30.** Fax 06205/3-03-25. www.luxhof.de. 45 units. 87€–100€ ($77.70–$89.30) double. Rates include buffet breakfast. AE, DC, MC, V. Free parking. **Amenities:** Dining room; lounge; health club; sauna; solarium. *In room:* TV.

## WHERE TO DINE

**Backmulde** ★ *Finds* FRENCH/SEAFOOD Backmulde is owned by Gunter Schmidt, who has researched the centuries-old recipes of the Rhineland-Palatinate, added a modern touch, and come up with a combination that has made this Speyer's best restaurant. You can savor such unusual delicacies as gratiné of oysters in champagne sabayon, quail stuffed with well-seasoned sweetbreads, or a meltingly tender roast lamb with freshly picked spinach.

Karmeliterstrasse 11–13. ✆ **06232/7-15-77.** Reservations required. Main courses 18€–25€ ($16.05–$22.35). AE, DC, MC, V. Tues–Sat 11am–1:30pm and 7pm–midnight. Closed 3 weeks from the end of Aug–mid-Sept.

**Wirtschaft zum Alten Engel** *Value* RHINELANDER To reach this place, one of the finest restaurants in Speyer, you'll descend a flight of antique masonry steps to a century-old brick-vaulted cellar, flickering with candles and awash with German antiques. Much in demand among locals, and set in Speyer's historic core, it specializes in hearty regional cuisine that's accompanied with one of the more than 180 kinds of wine from around Germany and the world. Menu items usually include hearty *gutbürgerlich* fare of the kind many locals remember from their childhoods. The best examples of this old-fashioned "home-and-hearth" cookery include fried sausages, liver dumplings, a Rhenish version of sauerbraten, pepper steak, veal cutlets, and at least two different preparations of lamb. This place is animated, loud, convivial, and extremely sought after.

Mühlturmstrasse 7. ✆ **06232/70914.** Reservations required. Main courses 7€–20€ ($6.25–$17.85); fixed-price menu 18€ ($16.05). MC, V. Mon–Sat 6pm–midnight, Sun 5pm–midnight. Closed: 2 weeks in July or Aug.

# 2 Worms ★

45km (28 miles) S of Mainz, 43km (27 miles) SW of Darmstadt

This ancient city traces its beginnings from the earliest civilizations. Before the Romans settled here, Germanic peoples had made Worms their capital. Here, Siegfried began his legendary adventures, recorded in *The Nibelungenlied.* Later on, the town's most famous visitor, Martin Luther, arrived under less than desirable circumstances. He was "invited" to appear before the Imperial Diet at Worms, and after refusing to retract his grievances against the Church of Rome, Holy Roman Emperor Charles V declared him an outlaw. Now that Worms is mainly Protestant, a huge monument to Luther and other giants of the Reformation has been erected.

Worms also makes an excellent base for a tour of the Deutsche Weinstrasse, an 80km (50-mile) route through local wine towns (see the "A Driving Tour of the German Wine Road" section, below).

## ESSENTIALS

**GETTING THERE** **By Plane** The nearest airport is at Frankfurt (see chapter 13), 69km (43 miles) away.

From Frankfurt, you can drive to Speyer in a rented car. Trains heading south go through the industrial city of Mannheim (very frequent service). At Mannheim, one train per hour runs south in to Speyer (trip time: 30 minutes).

**By Train** Worms enjoys good rail connections to major German cities. It lies on the main Mainz–Mannheim line, with frequent service. For rail information and schedules, call ✆ **01805/996633.**

**By Bus** Regional bus service for the area is provided by **BRN Busverkehr Rhein-Neckar GmbH** (✆ **06241/1077028**) in Worms.

**By Car** From Mainz (see section 3, later in this chapter), continue south along Route 9.

**VISITOR INFORMATION** For tourist information, go to the **Verkehrsverein,** Neumarkt 14 (✆ **06241/2-50-45;** www.worms-tourist info.de). It's open year-round Monday to Friday 9am to 6pm; from April to October, it's also open Saturday 10am to 3pm.

**GETTING AROUND** A network of cream-colored buses traverse most neighborhoods of the town and its suburbs. The city's main junction point is the Hauptbahnhof. Buses run 6am to midnight and charge 1.50€ ($1.35) and 2.50€ ($2.25) depending on how far you go, paid directly to the driver.

## SEEING THE SIGHTS

Towering physically and historically above all the other ancient buildings of the city is the majestic **Dom St. Peter** ★★, Lutherring 9 (✆ **06241/61-15;** bus: 2). This basilica is a fine example of High Romanesque style. The east choir, with a flat facade and semicircular interior, is the oldest section, dating from 1132. It was designed as the sanctuary, where the clergy performed the rites of divine service. The chancel glows with the gold and marble of the pillared enclosure of the baroque high altar by the famous 18th-century architect Balthasar Neumann. This opulent work was so large that there was no place for a proper transept. In Gothic times the choir stalls stood in the apse, but later they were built into the transept. The interior has a quiet elegance, with little decoration other than the rosette window and several memorial slabs and monuments. Well worth seeing is the highly decorated 14th-century side chapel of St. Nicholas, with its Gothic baptismal font and new stained-glass windows. This was the setting of history's famous Diet of Worms, an assembly of august figures of the catholic hierarchy, an imperial court that banished Martin Luther into exile when he refused to renounce his so-called "heretical doctrine." (Luther adamantly maintained that religious truth exists in scripture, not in papal power or edicts.) The cathedral is open for visitors daily 9am to 6pm.

North of the Altstadt is the restored **old Jewish quarter** (bus: 2). Before World War II, Worms had one of the oldest Jewish communities in Germany. The still-functioning **synagogue,** Hintere Judengasse 6 (✆ **06241/853-4701**), which dated from the 11th century, was destroyed in 1938. It has since been rebuilt, using some of the original masonry. Inside, you'll find the **Raschi-Haus Museum** (same phone; http://www.worms.de/kultur/museen/raschihaus englisch.html), containing memorabilia from the original synagogue and references to the Holocaust. Both the synagogue and its museum are open daily May to October, 10am to noon and 2 to 6pm; November to April, 10am to 12:30pm and 1:30 to 5pm. Admission is 1.55€ ($1.40). A staff member inside will point you in the direction of the **Judenfriedhof (Jewish cemetery)** ★, off the Lutherring, one of the oldest and largest in Europe, with hundreds of tombstones, some of them more than 900 years old.

## WHERE TO STAY

**Central Hotel Worms** *Value* This is one of the best small hotels in the city, although it's a modest and unassuming choice. Innkeeper Alexandra Hill rents comfortably furnished but rather small rooms. All contain bathrooms with shower-tub combinations. The reception staff speaks English, and the hotel has an ideal central location, within walking distance of all major historic monuments.

Kämmererstrasse 5, 67547 Worms. ✆ **06241/6-45-70.** Fax 06241/2-74-39. www.centralhotel-worms.de. 19 units. 70€–80€ ($62.50–$71.45) double. Rates include buffet breakfast. AE, DC, DISC, MC, V. Parking 5€ ($4.45). Closed Dec 22–Jan 22. Bus: 2 or 4. **Amenities:** Breakfast room; lounge. *In room:* TV.

**Dom-Hotel** This is an ideal choice for the in-and-out traveler. Recently renovated, the all-purpose hotel is a postwar structure built in a complex of shops and boutiques. Rooms are a little boxy and functionally furnished, but all are well maintained and contain bathrooms with shower-tub combinations.

Am Obermarkt 10 (about a block from the cathedral), 67547 Worms. ✆ **06241/90-70.** Fax 06241/2-35-15. www.dom-hotel.de. 55 units. 92€–110€ ($82.15–$98.25) double; 128€ ($114.30) suite. Rates include buffet breakfast. AE, DC, MC, V. Free parking. Bus: 2. **Amenities:** Restaurant; lounge; room service; laundry/dry cleaning. *In room:* TV, minibar, hair dryer.

**Hotel Nibelungen** ★ The most modern place to stay in Worms is the Nibelungen, in the center of town. It offers up-to-date comfort behind a rather sterile facade. The well-furnished rooms are the best in town and are generally spacious, although devoid of any particular Rhinelander flavor. All rooms contain shower-tub combinations. Breakfast is the only meal served.

Martinsgasse 16, 67547 Worms. ✆ **06241/92-02-50.** Fax 06241/92-02-55-05. www.nibelungen-hotel.de. 46 units. 77€–124€ ($68.75–$110.75) double. Rates include buffet breakfast. AE, MC, V. Parking 4€ ($3.55). Bus: 2. **Amenities:** Breakfast room; lounge. *In room:* TV, minibar, hair dryer.

## WHERE TO DINE

**Le Bistro Léger** RHINELAND The nostalgically decorated Le Bistro Léger offers regional cuisine at reasonable prices. An outdoor terrace is a favorite in warm weather. Fresh ingredients go into the food. You might try veal cutlets prepared in the style of the Rhineland, fish filet, or oysters (in season). The well-chosen wine list is mostly German.

Siegfriedstrasse 2. ✆ **06241/4-62-77.** Reservations recommended. Main courses 10€–20€ ($8.95–$17.85). MC. Mon–Sat noon–2pm and 6–11pm. Bus: 2.

**Rôtisserie Dubs** ★ CONTINENTAL The prices are a bit steep for the area, but you're paying for imaginative cookery and quality ingredients. Despite rustic ceiling beams and the massive stonework of the fireplace, Rôtisserie Dubs has a feeling of elegant airiness. The light Continental cuisine adds to that impression. Owner Wolfgang Dubs features such French-inspired dishes as salmon in champagne marinade and delicately seasoned pike-and-cabbage soup. His steak in snail sauce is worth the trip outside of town (it may not sound appealing but it's quite sublime). Regrettably, at this writing, this restaurant is open only 2 days a week for lunch and only 4 days a week for dinner.

Kirchstrasse 6 (at Rheindurkheim, take Rte. 9 north for 8km/5 miles). ✆ **06242/20-23.** Reservations required. Main courses 19€–25€ ($16.95–$22.35); fixed-price menu 34€–64€ ($30.35–$57.15). No credit cards. Fri–Mon 6–10pm; Sun–Mon 11:30am–2pm.

## WORMS AFTER DARK

The city's most important showcase for music, classical drama (in German only), and opera is the **Städtisches Spiel und Festhaus** (ca. 1962), Rathenaustrasse 4 (✆ **06241/22525;** bus: 2). For information about coming events, either contact the theater directly or call **Theater-Kasse,** Rathenaustrasse 4 (✆ **06241/225-25**), for a list of upcoming events and ticket availability.

Don't expect raucous nightlife in Worms. Our best advice, if you want a drink in the town center, is to head for the **Judengasse** (bus: 2), a street with a denser collection of nightlife options than any other in town. One of the most appealing is the **Altstadt Bar,** Judengasse 17 (✆ **06241/222-16**), which opens for business every day at 3pm, carrying on into the wee hours.

## A DRIVING TOUR OF THE GERMAN WINE ROAD ★★

Germany's oldest designated tourist route, the **Deutsche Weinstrasse,** runs south for 80km (50 miles) from Bockenheim, a small town 14km (8½ miles) west of Worms, to Schweigen-Rechtenbach on the frontier with France. This is a land of old castles (most in ruins) and venerable vineyards. Most of the wines produced here are whites, with special emphasis on clear, aromatic Rieslings and Weissburgunders. The area also abounds in old Rhineland-Palatinate inns and wine taverns, serving hearty local specialties such as "white cheese."

Armed with a good map, available at the Worms tourist office, you can set out to explore the area beginning in the north at **Bockenheim.** From Bockenheim, follow Route 271 directly south to Grünstadt, where signs point the way to the village of **Neuleiningen,** 10km (6 miles) away. The locals here are known rather unflatteringly as *Geesbocke* or "billy goats," a reference to their longtime poverty—goats (supposedly) were the only livestock they could afford. Today they bear the label with a certain pride. While here, sample the local fare at **Alte Pfarrey,** Untergasse 54, Oberstadt (✆ **06359/86066**), where fixed-price menus cost 25€ ($22.35) at lunch or 75€ ($67) at dinner. Closed Monday and Tuesday for lunch but open for dinner.

From here, Highway 271 leads south to Kallstadt, a distance of 10km (6 miles), where our next stopover at **Bad Dürkheim** is signposted. Here you can view the remains of the **Monastery of Limburg,** once one of the most significant Romanesque structures in the country. The best restaurant is **Weinrefugium,** Schlachthausstrasse 1A (✆ **06322/6-89-74**), which charges 20€ to 34€ ($17.85–$30.35) for a fixed-price menu of regional food. Closed Monday.

Route A37 en route to Kaiserslautern, west of Bad Dürkheim, leads to **Frankenstein Schloss,** a castle from the Middle Ages (now in ruins). Local legend claims it was this Schloss that inspired Mary Shelley's classic monster.

A journey 8km (5 miles) south along 271 leads to the **Deidesheim,** the medieval seat of the bishops of Speyer. The grounds that surround their former Schloss, now a picturesque ruin, have been turned into a lovely park. Some of the wine road's most charming half-timbered buildings are found on the main square, Marktplatz.

The most elegant hotel in the neighborhood is the very stylish **Deidesheimer Hof,** Am Marktplatz 1 (✆ **06326/96870;** www.deidesheimerhof.de), where doubles cost 135€ to 202€ ($120.55–$180.40). Inside are two restaurants, the **Schwarzer Hahn,** where fixed-price menus go from 49€ to 102€ ($43.75–$91.10), and the more artfully rustic **St.-Urban,** which charges 33€ to 49€ ($29.45–$43.75) for fixed-price menus.

From Deidesheim, continue along Route 271 for another 15 minutes, following the signs to **Neustadt-an-der-Weinstrasse,** the largest town on the Weinstrasse, lying at the foot of the Haardt hills. Pass quickly through its ugly suburbs to reach the heart of the old town, with its narrow, often-crooked streets. There are some 2,000ha (5,000 acres) of vineyards within the town limits, and the main streets are lined with taverns and wine shops. The most appealing restaurant in town is **Brezel,** Rathaustrasse 32 (✆ **06321/481971**), an elegant restaurant whose menu is a showcase of the finest of regional fare, with fixed-price menus costing from 28€ ($25).

From Neustadt, you can drive 5km (3 miles) south to historic **Schloss Hambach** (✆ **06321/30-881**), half a mile outside the village of Hambach. It's open March to November daily 10am to 6pm; admission is 4.50€ ($4).

A 8km (5-mile) drive south takes you into the sleepy hamlet of St. Martin, which for our money is the loveliest village along the wine road, filled with antique houses draped with flowering vines. A castle here, whose nostalgic ruins still tower over St. Martin, happens to have the best food and lodging along the wine road. Its name is **St. Martiner Castell,** Maikammer Strasse 2 (✆ **06323/95-10;** www.hotelcastell.de), and each of its 26 rooms rent for around 86€ ($76.80) double occupancy, with breakfast included. In its restaurant, fixed-price menus are 33.50€ to 43€ ($29.90–$38.40).

Yet another 5km (3 miles) south (the road is signposted) takes you to **Gleisweiler,** a wine-producing hamlet known as the warmest village in Germany. Fig trees flourish in its rich soil and almost subtropical climate.

From Gleisweiler, it's 13km (8 miles) south along Route B38 to **Annweiler,** site of **Burg Trifels,** the Rhineland's most fabled castle, set imperiously on a jagged crag. In 1193, Richard the Lionhearted was captured and imprisoned here until he was bailed out with a huge ransom. From the panoramic peak, you can also view the ruins of Scharfenberg Castle and Anebos Castle to the south. Burg Trifels (✆ **06346/8470**) is open daily January to March and October to November 9am to 5pm; April to September 9am to 6pm; closed in December.

In Annweiler, if you opt to stay the night, check out the facilities at **Zum Goldenen Lamm,** Ramberg, 7697 Annweiler (✆ **06345/8286**). Rooms cost 48€ ($42.85) each, with breakfast included. On the premises is a loud and sometimes rowdy, but very good, restaurant, which charges 23€ ($20.55) for a fixed-price meal.

The B38 leads next to **Klingenmünster,** a journey of only 8km (5 miles) south. From here, a sign points the way to the ruins of **Burg Landeck,** reached after a 30- to 40-minute stroll through a chestnut tree forest. At the end, the castle ruins stand at one of the most scenic spots along the wine road, with views extending as far as the Black Forest.

From here, B38 goes yet another 8km (5 miles) to reach **Bad Bergzabern,** an old spa, without equal for its old half-timbered houses.

From Bad Bergzabern, a 10km (6-mile) drive along Highway B38 (the final lap of your journey) will deliver you to **Schweigen-Rechtenbach,** a village at the French frontier. In the summer of 1935, local vintners constructed a gargantuan stone arch, the **German Wine Gate (Deutsches Weintor),** marking the southern end of this oft-traveled tourist route. From a gallery atop the gate, you can view miles of vineyards and even see a panorama of the Vosges in France. Visitors can cross the border, some 230m (250 yd.) from the arch, to sample the vintages on the French side as well, as there are no border formalities here. You can follow a trail known as the *Weinlehrpfad* (wine inspection path), going on for a mile until you reach the vineyards at the hamlet of Sonenberg. This is one of the most rewarding walks along the wine route.

In Schweigen-Rechtenbach, one of the best values for lodging is found in the town center at **Am Deutschen Weintor,** Bacchusstrasse 1 (✆ **06342/7335**), which charges 47€ to 68€ ($41.95–$60.70) for a double room, breakfast included. We suggest getting a meal at the **Hotel Schweigenhof,** Hauptstrasse 2, 76889 Schweigen-Rechtenbach (✆ **06342/244**), which charges 14€ to 48€ ($12.50–$42.85) for a fixed-price lunch or dinner (wine is extra).

## 3 Mainz ★

13km (8 miles) S of Wiesbaden, 82km (51 miles) NW of Mannheim, 40km (25 miles) SW of Frankfurt

Mainz is located on the left bank of the Rhine, across from the Rhine's intersection with the Main River. It is thought that there may have been wine-producing vines in the area even before the coming of the Romans in 38 B.C., although it was from that time that the regions of the Rheingau and Rheinhessen became widely known for fine viticulture.

At the beginning of the Christian era, the settlement on the Rhine's left bank and the Roman fortifications opposite were connected by a bridge. In the 8th century, the town became a primary archbishopric. Over the centuries, church politics and a series of wars shuffled control of the city back and forth between the French (who called it "Mayence") and various German factions. Mainz never became the great commerce center that its location would seem to merit. However, today it's a bustling city, with a prosperous trade in wine and other businesses.

Most visitors will be interested in the relatively compact **Altstadt,** which has been restored with taste and care. The heart of the old town is the Marktplatz, which is dominated by the cathedral.

### ESSENTIALS

**GETTING THERE** **By Plane** The nearest airport is at Frankfurt (see chapter 13). There is direct rail service from the airport (S-14 train) via Wiesbaden to Mainz. For information, call the Mainz Railway Station at ✆ **06131/15107553.**

**By Train** From Frankfurt, an express train takes 25 minutes to reach Mainz, while the S-Bahn arrives in 40 minutes. There are also trains leaving Mainz for Heidelberg and Koblenz (trip time: 1 hr.) or Cologne (trip time: 2 hr.). Daily trains to and from Munich take about 4½ hours. For more rail information, call ✆ **01805/99-66-33.**

**By Bus** Regional bus service is provided by **ORN Omnibusverkehr Rhein-Nahe GmbH,** at Mainz (✆ **06131/12-76-88;** www.orn-online.de).

**By Car** Access by car to Mainz is via the A60 east and west, and the A63 south and A643 north.

**VISITOR INFORMATION** Go to **Touristik Centrale,** Brückenturm am Rathaus (✆ **06131/28-62-10**). Open Monday to Friday 9am to 6pm and Saturday 9am to 1pm.

**GETTING AROUND** Trams and buses fan out across the city from the Hauptbahnhof from 5am until around midnight. Fares are 1.20€ to 2€ ($1.05–$1.80) depending on how far you go.

**SPECIAL EVENTS** The most celebrated merrymaking in festive Mainz is the All Fools capers at **Carnival** each spring, on the Monday before Ash Wednesday, where merrymakers act like fools, jesters, and clowns. This festival is broadcast throughout Germany like the Macy's parade is throughout the U.S. Each year in June, the **Gutenberg Festival** sponsors a cultural season as a living memorial to the city's favorite son, the inventor of the movable-type printing press. There's also an annual **Wine Fair** in August and September. For information, contact the tourist office at ✆ **06131/286210.**

## EXPLORING THE TOWN

### Dom und Diözesan Museum (Cathedral and Dionxsian Museum) ★

Above the roofs of the half-timbered houses in the Altstadt rise the six towers of St. Martin's Cathedral, the most important Catholic cathedral in the country after Cologne's. It dates from A.D. 975 but was continually rebuilt and restored, reaching its present form mainly in the 13th and 14th centuries. Below the largest dome, a combination of Romanesque and baroque styles, is the transept, separating the west chancel from the nave and smaller east chancel. Many of the supporting pillars along the aisles of the nave are decorated with carved and painted statues of French and German saints.

A collection of religious art is housed in the cathedral's Diocesan Museum. In it are exhibitions of reliquaries and medieval sculpture, including works by the Master of Naumburg. In the 1,000-year-old cathedral crypt is a contemporary gold reliquary of the saints of Mainz. Among the most impressive furnishings in the sanctuary are rococo choir stalls and an early 14th-century pewter baptismal font.

Domstrasse 3. ✆ **06131/223727** or 06131/253344. Cathedral free; Diocesan Museum 2.55€ ($2.30) adults, 1.55€ ($1.40) children (charge applies to special exhibitions only). Cathedral: Apr–Sept Mon–Fri 9am–6:30pm, Sat 10am–4pm, Sun 12:45–3pm; Oct–Mar Mon–Fri 9am–5pm, Sat 10am–3:30pm, Sun 12:45–3pm. Museum: Mon–Wed and Fri 10am–4pm; Thurs 10am–5pm; Sat 10am–2pm. Bus: 1, 7, 13, 17, or 23.

### Gutenberg Museum ★★

This museum is a unique memorial to the city's most famous son. In the rebuilt Gutenberg workshop, visitors can trace the history of printing, beginning with Johannes Gutenberg's hand press, on which he printed his 42-line-per-page Bible from 1452 to 1455. The collections cover the entire spectrum of the graphic arts in all countries, past and present, as well as printing, illustration, and binding. Two Gutenberg Bibles are the most popular exhibits.

Liebfrauenplatz 5 (opposite the east towers of the cathedral). ✆ **06131/1226-40-44.** Admission 3€ ($2.70) adults; 1.50€ ($1.35) children 6–18, seniors, and students; free for children 5 and under. Free admission Sun and holidays. Tues–Sat 9am–5pm; Sun 10am–1pm. Closed Jan. Bus: 1, 7, 13, 17, or 19.

### Landesmuseum Mainz (Provincial Museum of the Central Rhineland) ★

It's worth a visit here to get a pictorial history of Mainz and the middle Rhineland ranging from prehistoric times to the present. The **Lapidarium** shows one of the most important collections of Roman monuments in Europe. The most impressive exhibits are the Roman tombstones of soldiers and civilians of the 1st century A.D. and the towering Column of Jupiter, erected in Mainz at the time of Nero, around A.D. 65 to 68. There's a true-to-life replica of the column in front of the Parliament building.

Grosse Bleiche 49–51. ✆ **06131/285-70.** Admission 5€ ($4.45) adults, 3€ ($2.70) children under 18 and students; free admission Sat. Mon–Tues 10am–8pm, Wed–Sun 10am–5pm. Bus: 6, 15, or 23.

## SHOPPING

The city's most active shopping area is **Am Brand,** a short boulevard near the cathedral that's lined with shops on either side (bus: 1 or 54). One of the town's best clothing emporiums is **Peek & Kloppenburg,** Brand 38 (✆ **06131/66-92-00**), which sells clothing for men, women, and children, in styles ranging from very formal to chic and casual. For German designer fashions, head to **Sinn,** Am Brand 41 (✆ **06131/27-30**), which carries men's and women's clothing, and **Leininger,** Ludwigstrasse 11 (✆ **06131/28-88-20;** bus: 54), which sells outfits for women and children.

Whatever you can't find along the Am Brand will almost certainly be available among the vast inventories of Mainz's most visible department store, **Kaufhof,** Schusterstrasse 41 (✆ **06131/2541;** bus: 54). To find a treasure trove of secondhand goods, shop the **Krempelmarkt flea market,** held along the banks of the Rhine on the first Saturday of each month, February to October (Bus: 54).

Many of Mainz's hotels, restaurants, and banks take an interest in modern art. You might also want to visit the city's most prestigious modern art gallery, **Galerie H. G. Lautner,** Augustinerstrasse 52 (✆ **06131/22-57-36;** bus: 54). Another place rich with middle Europe's contemporary art is **Atelier 9,** Heidelberger Fassgasse 18 (✆ **06131/23-26-42;** bus: 9).

## WHERE TO STAY

### EXPENSIVE

**Hilton International** ★★ The Hilton, renovated in 1998, is one of the most imaginatively designed and strikingly modern hotels along the Rhine Valley. It occupies two desirable plots of land near the center of town. Its twin sections are sheathed in reflective mirrors and soaring spans of steel, and are connected by a glass-sided, covered walkway above the traffic below. The labyrinthine interior has sun-flooded atriums with live plants and acres of marble flooring. The spacious rooms are the most artfully decorated in the region. Bathrooms are also roomy, all with shower-tub combinations.

Rheinstrasse 68 (a 5-min. walk from the cathedral), 55116 Mainz. ✆ **800/445-8667** in the U.S. and Canada, or 06131/24-50. Fax 06131/24-55-89. www.hilton.com. 433 units. 124€–250€ ($110.75–$223.25) double; from 350€ ($312.55) suite. AE, DC, MC, V. Parking 15€ ($13.40). Bus: 7, 13, 17, 34, or 37. **Amenities:** 4 restaurants; 2 bars; health club; sauna; hairdresser; room service; babysitting; laundry/dry cleaning. *In room:* A/C, TV, minibar, hair dryer.

**Hyatt Regency Mainz** ★★ Opening onto the Rhine, this deluxe palace has eclipsed the two Hiltons and now reigns supreme. Sparkling new, it is the best hotel south of Cologne, done in a strikingly modern architectural style. A glittering 21st-century aura prevails in the public rooms, restaurants, and guest accommodations. The room furnishings are tasteful and sleekly sophisticated, with modern art decorating the walls. Fabrics are expensively elegant, and the spacious bathrooms contain deluxe toiletries and tub-and-shower combinations. The more desirable units open onto the Rhine, and these have even more generous-size bathrooms. The public facilities are among the best in this part of Germany, with a wine bar and the Bellpepper restaurant featuring a grand river terrace along the Rhine. In summer a beer garden goes full blast.

Malakoff-Terrasse 1, 55116 Mainz. ✆ **06131/73-12-34.** Fax 06131/731235. www.main.hyatt.com. 265 units. 185€–330€ ($165.20–$294.70) double; from 250€ ($223.25) suite. AE, DC, MC, V. **Amenities:** Restaurant; bar; wine bar; beer garden; room service; babysitting; laundry/dry cleaning. *In room:* A/C, TV, dataport, minibar, hair dryer, safe.

**Mainz City Hilton** ★★ This city on the Rhine is blessed with two Hiltons (see above), although the newer Hyatt has stolen the thunder. In the historic zone of Mainz, about a 3-block walk from the rail terminus, this hotel is a bit livelier than its sibling, but the rooms in both hotels are of equal appeal, so it won't matter much which you are booked in, as you get comfort in either. We prefer this one only because it doesn't have quite the hustle-bustle of the other one, and somehow the staff seems more personal in its service. We also like architectural touches here, including an ancient wall discovered during reconstruction. The wall was preserved and now frames the courtyard terrace. Rooms are a bit on the cookie-cutter side, but are tasteful and spacious, each coming with a deluxe bathroom with shower stalls and deep tubs. Rooms are priced according to view and location, those on the top costing the most money because of their panoramic views and balconies. The least desirable are on the lower floors, facing a park.

Munsterstrasse 11, 55116 Mainz. ✆ **06131/2780.** Fax 06131/278567. www.hilton.com. 126 units. 125€–270€ ($111.65–$241.10) double; 250€–550€ ($223.25–$491.15) suite. AE, DC, MC, V. **Amenities:** Restaurant; 2 bars; cabaret theater; room service; babysitting; laundry/dry cleaning. *In room:* A/C, TV, minibar, hair dryer, safe.

### MODERATE

**Hotel Mainzer Hof** ★ Mainzer Hof is six floors of modernity directly on the Rhine, almost at the point where some of the boats dock. This hotel is a clean-cut, convenient stopover. The medium-size rooms are well furnished and well maintained and have bathrooms with shower-tub combinations.

Kaiserstrasse 98 (a 10-min. walk from the Hauptbahnhof), 55116 Mainz. ✆ **06131/28-89-90.** Fax 06131/22-82-55. 93 units. 105€–155€ ($93.75–$138.40) double. Rates include buffet breakfast. AE, DC, MC, V. Parking 5.50€ ($4.90). Bus: 9. **Amenities:** 2 restaurants; lounge; room service; laundry/dry cleaning. *In room:* TV, minibar, hair dryer, safe.

## WHERE TO DINE

Palatinate is the regional cuisine of the area in which Mainz is located. Every province has its own cuisine. Palatinate is basic German fare with many regional subtleties based on the availability of local ingredients.

**Geberts Weinstuben** *Finds* PALATINATE This traditional Weinstube is housed in one of the oldest buildings in Mainz, with a decor that's almost spartan. But decor is not the reason people come here, and they come in great numbers. Once seated, you're treated to a traditional meal of game, fish, or regional specialties such as goose a l'orange. The menu is robust Palatinate fare.

Frauenlobstrasse 94. ✆ **06131/61-16-19.** Reservations required. Main courses 17€–27€ ($15.20–$24.10). AE, DC, MC, V. Mon–Fri 11:30am–2pm; Mon–Fri and Sun 6–10pm. Closed mid-July–mid-Aug. Bus: 7 or 21.

**Haus des Weines** GERMAN Set in Mainz's historic core, immediately adjacent to the Stadt Theater, this modern, contemporary-looking restaurant focuses on a savory combination of German food and mostly German wines. Wines run the complete gamut of virtually every vintage produced within Germany, and a staff member is well-versed in their compatibility with menu items that include, but are not limited to, fresh or marinated salmon, all kinds of venison (available year-round); a savory version of rumpsteak, and perfectly grilled fish. Expect lots of emphasis on whatever vegetable is in season at the moment of your arrival, including, among others, asparagus. In April or May, asparagus' arrival is celebrated like a rite of spring, with at least a dozen variations that are served either as starters or as main courses. No one will object here if you order just wine and a small platter of food; examples include *Spundekäse,* an age-old recipe that mingles local cheese whipped with onions and cream into a soft paste. It's best served with rough-textured bread and, naturally, wine.

Gutenbergplatz 3. ✆ **06131/22-13-00.** Reservations recommended. Main courses 11.30€–15€ ($10.10–$13.40). AE, MC, V. Daily noon–10pm.

**Langolo** ITALIAN This informal Italian-inspired trattoria is known for its congenial staff and its excellent pizza and pasta. You can also order freshly made salads, with shrimp or prosciutto, and meat dishes consisting of escalopes of either pork or veal. Reasonable prices and a full bar generally keep this place packed.

Augustinerstrasse 8. ✆ **06131/23-17-37.** Pizzas and pastas 6€–10€ ($5.35–$8.95); meat platters 10€–14€ ($8.95–$12.50). No credit cards. Daily 11am–midnight. Bus: 6, 15, or 23.

**Weinstube Lösch** *Value* RHINELAND This old-fashioned Weinstube in the heart of the Altstadt has been popular for generations and is rich in tradition. Meals feature both hot and cold dishes, plus lots of Rhine wine. The menu offers regional dishes and interesting salads. The pork schnitzel with mushrooms is particularly savory. There are only 12 tables, but they seat 85 guests. Six additional tables are placed out front in summer on the pedestrian mall.

Jakobsbergstrasse 9. ✆ **06131/22-03-83.** Reservations recommended. Main courses 7€–15.50€ ($6.25–$13.85). No credit cards. Daily 5:30pm–1am. Bus: 6 or 23.

## MAINZ AFTER DARK

The cultural center of the city is **Frankfurter Hof,** Augustinerstrasse 55 (✆ **06131/22-04-38;** bus: 54), which stages concerts of classical music, jazz, folk, and pop. The center also hosts an annual tent festival featuring an eclectic mix of international performers. Tickets to all events cost between 6€ to 37€ ($5.35–$33.05). Call for scheduled shows, festival dates and performers, and ticket information.

Although you can buy tickets at the offices of any of the theaters and entertainment venues in Mainz, a more convenient way is to contact the **Ticket Service,** which is a division of the town's tourist office at Brückenturm am Rathaus, 55116 Mainz (✆ **06131/28-62-10;** bus: 54). A privately funded competitor of the city's Ticket Service is **Kartenhaus,** Schillerstrasse 11 (✆ **06131/22-87-29;** bus: 54).

In terms of its nightlife, Mainz is sleepy enough to compel many residents to head to Cologne or Düsseldorf after dark. But if you don't want to get too quickly out of town, consider dancing the night away at the **Disco Kuz,** Winterhaven 12 (✆ **06131/28-68-60;** bus: 61), where you'll find good music and attractive people drinking, dancing, and talking. It's open nightly 10pm until at least 2am, charges a 4.60€ to 6€ ($4.10–$5.35) cover, and attracts a crowd aged 20 to around 35. The hottest new address in town is **RED CAT,** Emmerich-Josef-Strasse 13 (✆ **06131/225656**), in the heart of town, lying right off the landmark Schillerplatz. The club is tiny, as is its dance floor, but hip young Mainzers pack the joint anyway. **Chapeau Claque,** Kleine Landgasse 4 (✆ **06131/223-111;** bus: 9), is a gay bar that's open nightly 6pm to 4am.

## 4 The Rheingau ★★★

Legend says that when God was looking for a place to set up Paradise, the sunny slopes between the Taunus Mountains and the Rhine nearly won the prize. Today the Rheingau is the kingdom of another god: Bacchus. Nearly every town and village from Wiesbaden to Assmannshausen, no matter how small, is a major wine producer. The names suddenly seem familiar—Bingen, Johannisberg, Rüdesheim, Oestrich—because they're featured on the labels of many wines.

The Rheingau is also rich in old churches and castles, as well as landmarks. The **Niederwald Monument,** on a hill halfway between Rüdesheim and Assmannshausen—it can be reached by cable car from either town—is a huge statue of Germania, erected by Bismarck in 1883 to commemorate the unification of Germany. Below it, on a small island at the bend of the Rhine, is the **Mäuseturm (Mouse Tower),** where, according to legend, the greedy archbishop of Mainz was devoured by a swarm of hungry mice. But the real attraction of the Rheingau is the cheerful character of the wine villages and their people. Rüdesheim and Assmannshausen are the most visited towns. Assmannshausen is actually part of Rüdesheim—its center lies 5km (3 miles) to the northwest of Rüdesheim's center on the Rhine River.

### ESSENTIALS

**GETTING THERE** **By Plane** The nearest airport is at Frankfurt (see chapter 13), 48km (30 miles) away.

From the airport, you can rent a car. Otherwise, take the train or bus from Wiesbaden (see the "By Train" or "By Bus" sections below). There are bus links from the Frankfurt airport to Weisbaden's bus and train transport hubs.

**By Train** The main rail station at Rüdesheim is on the Wiesbaden–Koblenz line, with frequent service to regional towns and connections to all major cities. For rail information and schedules, call ✆ **01805/99-66-33.** Train service from Frankfurt is via Wiesbaden and takes 1 hour.

**By Bus** Bus service for the region is provided by **ORN Omnibusverkehr Rhein-Nahe GmbH,** in Wiesbaden (✆ **0611/97-75-822;** www.orn-online.de).

**By Car** Access by car is via the A61 Autobahn from the north and highway 42 connecting with the A671 from the west. From Frankfurt, motorists can take the A66 until they reach the junction with Route B42, which will be signposted and lead them right to Rüdesheim. Motorists heading from Koblenz on the west bank of the Rhine can use the A61 to Bingen, then follow the signs for the ferryboats that cross the river to Rüdesheim. For information on the ferry service, call ✆ **06721/1-41-40.** From Koblenz, you can also take B42 along the east bank of the river, which will lead directly into Rüdesheim. Route B42 links Rüdesheim with Assmannshausen.

**VISITOR INFORMATION** For information about Rüdesheim and Assmannshausen (see below), go to the **Stadt Verkehrsamt,** Rheinstrasse 16 in Rüdesheim (✆ **06722/19433**). It's open year-round Monday to Friday 9am to 6pm, and May to October also Saturday 10:30am to 4pm and Sunday 11:30am to 3:30pm.

### RÜDESHEIM ★

With its old courtyards and winding alleyways lined with timbered houses, Rüdesheim is the epitome of a Rhine wine town. The vineyards around the village date back to the Roman emperor Probus. The full-bodied Riesling is produced here, as well as brandy and champagne (*Sekt*). Rüdesheim is also the scene of the annual August wine festival, when the old taverns on the narrow and very touristy **Drosselgasse** are crowded with visitors from all over the world. Drosselgasse has been called "the smallest but the happiest street in the world." From April to November, you can listen to music and dance in these taverns daily noon to 1am.

To prove how seriously Rüdesheimers take their wine, they have opened a wine museum in Bromserburg Castle. The **Rheingau- und Weinmuseum,** Rheinstrasse 2 (✆ **06722/23-48**), charges 3€ ($2.70) for adults and 1.50€ ($1.35) for children under 12, and is open mid-March to October daily 9am to 6pm. It traces the history of the grape and has an exhibition of wine presses, glasses, goblets, and drinking utensils from Roman times to the present.

## WHERE TO STAY & DINE

### Moderate

**Breuer's Rüdesheimer Schloss** ★★ This hotel is the first choice for staying and dining in town. The wine cellar dates from 1729. The Breuer family is noted for its wine cellars and plentiful food and drink. The mostly medium-size rooms are immaculately kept, and a few are even quite spacious, all with bathrooms equipped with shower-tub combinations. The hotel staff will help you prepare a tailor-made package of excursions or perhaps a "gastronomic feast" and a musical evening on their premises.

Steingasse 10, 65385 Rüdesheim. ✆ **06722/9-05-00.** Fax 06722/4-79-60. www.ruedesheimer-schloss.com. 21 units. 105€–135€ ($93.75–$120.55) double. Rates include buffet and local champagne. AE, DC, MC, V. Free outdoor parking; 8€ ($7.15) in garage. Closed Dec 22–Jan 5. **Amenities:** Restaurant; lounge; room service; massage; babysitting; laundry/dry cleaning. *In room:* TV, minibar, hair dryer, safe.

**Hotel und Weinhaus Felsenkeller** The beautifully carved timbers on the facade of this 1613 building suggest the traditional aura you'll find inside. A sampling of Rhine wine can be enjoyed in a room with vaulted ceilings and murals with vine leaves and pithy pieces of folk wisdom. In fair weather, guests can eat on the terrace. The small, attractively modern and freshly painted rooms open onto views of the vineyards surrounding the house. Each comes with a small and tidily kept bathroom with tub-and-shower combination.

Oberstrasse 39–41 (in the center of the old town), 65385 Rüdesheim. ✆ **06722/9-42-50.** Fax 06722/4-72-02. www.ruedesheim-rhein.com. 60 units. 75€–110€ ($67–$98.25) double; 97€–130€ ($86.60–$116.10) triple. Rates include buffet breakfast. AE, MC, V. Garage parking 5€ ($4.45). Closed Nov–Easter. **Amenities:** Restaurant; lounge; private garden. *In room:* TV, minibar.

**Rüdesheimer Hof** *Value* This village inn, set back from the Rhine, boasts a side garden and terrace where wine tasters gather at rustic tables. Most of the units are roomy and comfortably furnished, all with bathrooms containing shower-tub combinations. The atmosphere is informal. If you stay here, you can sample the lifestyle of a Rhine village by mingling with the townspeople, eating the regional food, and drinking the Rheingau wines. Guests dine at cafe tables placed under a willow tree. Food is served daily 11:30am to 9:30pm.

Geisenheimerstrasse 1 (a 10-min. walk from the Bahnhof), 65385 Rüdesheim. ✆ **06722/91-19-0.** Fax 06722/4-81-94. www.ruedesheimer-hof.de. 38 units. 70€–87€ ($62.50–$77.70) double. Rates include buffet breakfast. AE, DC, MC, V. Free parking. Closed Dec–mid-Feb. **Amenities:** Restaurant; lounge. *In room:* TV.

### Inexpensive

**Gasthof Krancher** *Finds* This is a home-and hearth choice. Gasthof Krancher has been in the Krancher family for four generations. It's located next to the inn's own vineyards. Naturally, the Kranchers make their own wines, and they'll gladly show you the cellar where they store bottles that have won gold and silver medals. Everything is decorated in a regional motif. Rooms are a bit cramped but are reasonably comfortable. All units contain private bathrooms with showers. From your window you can look out on the vineyards. The cuisine is first-class, as are the wines.

Eibinger-Oberstrasse 4 (a 10-min. hike uphill from the town center), 65385 Rüdesheim. ✆ **06722/27-62.** www.gasthof-krancher.de. Fax 06722/4-78-70. 62 units. 53€–68€ ($47.35–$60.70) double. Rates include buffet breakfast. V. Free parking. **Amenities:** Restaurant; lounge. *In room:* TV.

**Hotel Rheinstein** The Rheinstein's elongated terrace facing the street is one of the most popular gathering places in Rüdesheim. Many locals drop in during the afternoon to enjoy the excellent cakes, all baked on the premises. Irene Gehrig offers small and well-kept rooms furnished with modern styling. Each unit is rented with a small bathroom containing a shower.

Rheinstrasse 20 (across from the riverside landing stage of the Cologne–Düsseldorf Anlegestelle), 65385 Rüdesheim. ✆ **06722/20-04.** Fax 06722/4-76-88. www.hotel-rudesheim.info. 40 units. 50€ ($44.65) double with shower; 75€ ($67) double with bath. Half board 35€–40€ ($31.25–$35.70) per person. Rates include buffet breakfast. AE, DC, MC, V. Closed Dec–Mar. **Amenities:** Restaurant; lounge. *In room:* TV.

## ASSMANNSHAUSEN

This old village at the northern edge of the Rheingau is built on the slopes of the east bank of the Rhine. Its half-timbered houses and vineyards seem precariously perched on the steep hillsides, and the view of the Rhine Valley from here is awe-inspiring. Assmannshausen is known for its fine Burgundy-style wine. It lies 5km (3 miles) northwest of Rüdesheim and 60km (37 miles) west of Frankfurt.

### WHERE TO STAY & DINE

**Alte Bauernschanke-Nassauer Hof** ★ The wine-grower owners have turned two of the oldest mansions in town into a hotel and restaurant. The interior decor is luxurious, the comfort fine, and the welcome hearty. Rooms are beautifully furnished in traditional style. All units have bathrooms with shower-tub combinations. The restaurant has live folk music every night. Try goulash soup, pepper steak with fresh green beans and french fries, and a bottle of the growers' red wine.

Niederwaldstrasse 23 (near the church, about .5km/¼ mile from the Rhine), 65385 Rüdesheim-Assmannshausen. ✆ **06722-4999-0.** Fax 06722/4-79-12. www.altebauernschaenke.de. 53 units. 77€–103€ ($68.75–$92) double; 130€ ($116.10) suite. Rates include buffet breakfast. AE, MC, V. Closed Dec–Mar. **Amenities:** Restaurant; lounge; room service. *In room:* TV, hair dryer.

**Ewige Lampe und Haus Resi** This hotel is within a few miles of historic vineyards, plus some woodland trails through Rhenish forest. You'll find a lot to do in this wine-producing center. Hosts Engelbert and Renate Uri will welcome you to their cozy, tastefully furnished guesthouse. Many of the medium-size rooms have wooden ceilings, some have colorfully tiled bathrooms, all are impeccably clean with shower-tub combinations. The fortifying breakfast is often served on a sun terrace under parasols.

Niederwaldstrasse 14, 65385 Rüdesheim-Assmannshausen. ✆ **06722/24-17.** Fax 06722/4-84-59. 24 units. 60€–95€ ($53.60–$84.85). Rates include continental breakfast. No credit cards. Free parking. Closed Jan 6–Feb 6. **Amenities:** Restaurant; lounge. *In room:* TV.

**Krone Assmannshausen** ★★★ This distinguished hotel offers the most luxurious accommodations in the entire Rüdesheim am Rhein district. It's on the banks of the Rhine, surrounded by lawns, gardens, and a pool. Its origins can be traced back 400 years. The inn is a great big gingerbread fantasy. A small second-floor lounge is virtually a museum, with framed letters and manuscripts of some of the famous people who have stayed here—Goethe, for one. There's a stack of about 40 autograph books dating from 1893 signed by writers, painters, diplomats, and composers. You may stay in a medieval, a Renaissance, or a post-war building. The spacious rooms have an old-inn character, with traditional furnishings and compact bathrooms containing shower-tub combinations.

Rheinuferstrasse 10, 65385 Rüdesheim-Assmannshausen. ✆ **06722/40-30.** Fax 06772/30-49. www.hotel-krone.com. 65 units. 130€–180€ ($116.10–$160.75) double; 210€ ($187.55) junior suite; 350€–450€ ($312.55–$401.85) suite. AE, DC, MC, V. Free parking. **Amenities:** Restaurant; pool; fitness center; sauna; room service; babysitting; laundry/dry cleaning. *In room:* TV, minibar, hair dryer.

## 5 Koblenz ★

88km (55 miles) SE of Cologne, 63km (39 miles) SE of Bonn, 100km (62 miles) NW of Frankfurt

Koblenz has stood at the confluence of the Rhine and the Mosel for more than 2,000 years. Its strategic location in the mid-Rhine region has made the city a vital link in the international river trade routes of Europe. The city is surrounded by vine-covered hills dotted with castles and fortresses. Koblenz is also the place where many cruises through the Rhine begin or end.

### ESSENTIALS

**GETTING THERE** **By Plane** The nearest airports to Koblenz are Frankfurt (see chapter 13) and Cologne (see section 9 later in this chapter).

From there, you can rent a car or go by train. See below for train information.

**By Train** The **Koblenz Hauptbahnhof** lies on a major rail line, with frequent connections to important German cities. For train information, prices, and schedules, call ✆ **01805/99-66-33.** Thirty trains per day arrive from Frankfurt (trip time: 2 hr.) and 16 from Berlin (trip time: 8½ hr.). Trains also arrive every 30 minutes from Cologne (trip time: 45 min.–1 hr.).

**By Bus** Rail is by far the best way to get to Koblenz, but information on bus service is available by calling ✆ **0261/303-88-23.**

**By Car** Access by car to Koblenz is via the A48 Autobahn east and west, connecting with the A3 north to south.

**VISITOR INFORMATION** For information about tours, boat trips on the Rhine, and bus and train connections, contact the **Koblenz Tourist Office,** Löhrstrasse 141 (✆ **0261/3-13-04**). It's open May to September Monday to Friday 9am to 8pm, Saturday and Sunday 10am to 8pm; October and April Monday to Friday 9am to 6pm, Saturday and Sunday 10am to 5pm; November to March Monday to Friday 9am to 5pm.

**GETTING AROUND** The city is served by 10 main bus lines. Fare is 1.40€ to 2.60€ ($1.25–$2.30) depending on how far you go, paid on the bus (the bus driver will help you get the proper ticket, though most tourists will stay in the central zone and pay the cheaper fare). A day pass, sold at the tourist office, costs 4.60€ ($4.50).

### SEEING THE SIGHTS

Koblenz was heavily bombed during World War II, but many of the historic buildings have been restored.

### *Moments* A Lofty Look at the Corner of Germany

For the most panoramic view of Koblenz, go to the point where the two rivers meet. It is called *Deutsches Eck* or the "corner of Germany." From the top of the base where a huge statue of Wilhelm I once stood, you can see the Altstadt and across the Rhine to the Festung Ehrenbreitstein.

The focal point of the Altstadt is the **Liebfrauenkirche (Church of Our Lady),** a 13th-century Gothic basilica built on a Romanesque foundation, with twin towers topped by onion-shaped spires. The early 18th-century **Rathaus** was formerly a Jesuit college. In the courtyard behind the hall is a fountain dedicated to the youth of Koblenz called *Das Schängelchen* (*The Spitting Boy*), and that's just what he does. At the edge of the old town, near the Deutsches Eck, is Koblenz's oldest and most attractive church, **St. Castor's,** originally built in 836, though in its present form it dates mostly from the 12th century.

**Festung Ehrenbreitstein** (✆ **0261/970-30**), across the Rhine from Koblenz, can be reached by chairlift. You can also drive there via the Pfaffendorfer Bridge just south of the Altstadt or take bus 8, 9, or 10 from the rail station. The fortress was constructed on a rock and towers 122m (400 ft.) above the Rhine. The present walls were built in the 19th century. From the stone terrace, you get one of the best views along the Rhine; the panoramic vista includes not only Koblenz but also several castles on the river and many terraced vineyards. To reach the fortress, make the 1€ (90¢) one-way passage across the river from the main Rhine dock. Ferries operate mid-April to late November, daily 9am to 5:15pm. The chairlift (*Sesselbahn*) operates May to September daily 9:30am to 6pm. Round-trip tickets cost 5.10€ ($5) for adults, 3.05€ ($3) for children under 14.

## WHERE TO STAY

### EXPENSIVE

**Mercure** ★★ Glittering and stylish, the Mercure is easily the best hotel in town. It's perched on a hillock at the edge of the Rhine. Its streamlined architecture contrasts with the century-old trees and ancient stones of the medieval town surrounding it. Rooms are well insulated against sound from the street and neighboring rooms; each has a neatly kept bathroom with a shower-tub combination. One of the city's loveliest riverside promenades lies just a short walk away.

Julius-Wegeler-Strasse 6, 56068 Koblenz. ✆ **0261/13-60.** Fax 0261/1-36-11-99. www.mercure.com. 168 units. 141€ ($125.90) double; 250€ ($223.25) suite. Rates include buffet breakfast. AE, DC, MC, V. Parking 10€ ($8.95). Bus: 9 or 10. **Amenities:** Restaurant; lounge; pool; whirlpool; sauna; solarium; room service; babysitting; laundry/dry cleaning. *In room:* TV, minibar, hair dryer, safe.

### MODERATE

**Hotel Brenner** ★ This hotel is your best bet if you're seeking a good moderately priced choice. The small- to medium-size rooms are spotlessly maintained. Each bathroom has a shower-tub combination. The garden retreat is a good spot for getting back to nature.

Rizzastrasse 20–22 (near the Kurfürstl Schloss), 56068 Koblenz. ✆ **0261/91-57-80.** Fax 0261/3-62-78. www.hotel-brenner.de. 24 units. 80€–150€ ($71.45–$133.95) double. Rates include buffet breakfast. AE, DC, MC, V. Parking 6€–7.50€ ($5.35–$6.70). Bus: 1 or 5 to Christuskirche. **Amenities:** Breakfast room; lounge. *In room:* TV, minibar, hair dryer.

**Kleiner Riesen** This is one of the few hotels in central Koblenz that sits directly on the banks of the Rhine. Its rooms are close enough to view the boats as they go by. Within the city proper, only the Mercure is better. The Kleiner Riesen is a large, overgrown, informal chalet, with several lounges and comfortable rooms. All units come equipped with neatly kept bathrooms with shower-tub combinations. It's away from town traffic, so it has a peaceful small-town quiet.

Kaiserin-Augusta-Anlagen 18, 56068 Koblenz. ✆ **0261/3-20-77.** Fax 0261/16-07-25. 27 units. 93€–103€ ($83.05–$92) double. Rates include buffet breakfast. AE, DC, MC, V. Parking 8€ ($7.15). **Amenities:** Restaurant; lounge; room service. *In room:* TV.

### INEXPENSIVE

**Hotel Scholz** Scholz is a personally run family hotel. It offers sparsely furnished units that make for a reasonably priced overnight stopover. Rooms are small, but the beds are comfortable, the bathrooms contain shower-tub combinations, and the maintenance is good.

Moselweisserstrasse 121 (a 5-min. bus ride from the town center), 56073 Koblenz. ✆ **0261/94260.** Fax 0261/94-26-26. www.hotel-scholz.de. 66 units. 70€–82€ ($62.50–$73.25) double. Rates include buffet breakfast. AE, DC, MC, V. Free parking. Bus: 6. Closed Dec 20–Jan 7. **Amenities:** Restaurant; lounge. *In room:* TV.

## WHERE TO DINE

**Gillstuga** RHINELANDER/INTERNATIONAL Elegantly modern in both design and flavor, Gillstuga is one of the leading restaurants of Koblenz, though that's not saying much—Koblenz is a notoriously bad-restaurant town. In summer here, you dine on a wide flower-trimmed terrace with a partial view of the river. Otherwise you dine inside in an ambience of pastel and polished wood. Dishes are well prepared, although rarely exciting. Start with smoked salmon in a mustard dill sauce or perhaps a smooth consommé of pink mushrooms. Fish dishes are excellent, especially the fried catfish with a lime sauce or perch Strindberg with onions and mustard. Strips of veal appear in a mushroom cream sauce with potato *rösti* and a salad from the buffet.

In the Mercure, Julius-Wegeler-Strasse 6. ✆ **0261/13-60.** Reservations recommended. Main courses 12.50€–23€ ($11.15–$20.55). AE, DC, MC, V. Daily 11am–midnight. Bus: 1 or 5.

**Weinhaus Hubertus** GERMAN Weinhaus Hubertus looks like a timbered country inn. It's the oldest wine tavern in town, dating from 1696. The place offers German wines accompanied by a choice of homemade dishes—soups, sandwiches, and light platters, all designed to go well with the wines offered. The furnishings and the decor are family style, providing a home-like atmosphere. There's a choice here of 100 wines from all over Germany, 30 of these by the glass. In summer, you can enjoy the view of the Altstadt from the terrace.

Florinsmarkt 6 (across from the Old Rathaus). ✆ **0261/3-11-77.** Reservations recommended. Menus 8€–17€ ($7.15–$15.20); glass of wine 2.30€–4.50€ ($2.05–$4). MC, V. Wed–Mon 4pm–midnight. Bus: 1.

## KOBLENZ AFTER DARK

**THE PERFORMING ARTS** The **Rheinische Philharmonie Orchestra** performs in the **Rhein-Mosel-Halle,** Julius-Wegeler-Strasse (✆ **0261/129-1652;** bus: 9 or 10), which also hosts other performances. The symphony's season is September to June, and tickets cost 11€ to 54€ ($9.80–$48.20). Call for listings, dates, and prices of other performances. The **Stadtheater (City Theater),** housed in the **Grossehaus,** Dinehartplatz (✆ **0261/1292840;** bus: 9 or 10), stages dramas, comedies, and musicals (in German) September to June. The box office is open daily 9am to noon and 1 to 4:30pm. Tickets are 18€ to 45€ ($16.05–$40.20).

**BARS** Three of our favorite bars in Koblenz are devoted to individual themes that local residents embrace with relish. The first is the arts-conscious (and devilish) **Mephisto,** Eltzerhofstrasse 3 (✆ **0261/31735;** bus: 1), the walls of which are covered with photographs of famous German actors dressed for the part of Mephistopheles in various productions of *Faust.* Open Sunday to Friday 7pm to 2am, and Saturday until 4am. Nearby is another establishment with an almost equivalent theme, the **Faustus Bar,** Eltzerhofstrasse 11 (✆ **0261/17991;** bus: 1), open 11am to 3am.

For a laugh or two as you drink, head for the **Blauer Biwel,** Entenpfuhl 9 (✆ **0261/35577;** bus: 1), a bar where local stand-up comics sometime perform. Even if your German isn't up to the challenge, you might like the disco music they sometimes play.

A pub-oriented crowd, mostly under 40, hangs out late at night at **Café Balthazar,** Firmungstrasse 2, Am Görresplaz (✆ **0261/100-5833**), before heading for one of the many pubs on Florinsmarkt for night caps.

**LIVE MUSIC** **Pflaumenbaum,** Friedrich-Ebert-Ring 32 (✆ **0261/30-90-70;** bus: 9 or 10), is a smoke-filled, woodsy pub enhanced with live jazz, pop, and other types of music. It's open daily 5pm to 4am. At **Irish Pub Koblenz,** Burgstrasse 7 (✆ **0261/17377;** bus: 1), copious amounts of Guinness, Kilkenny, hard cider, and German beers are served as accompaniment to live music, everything from traditional Gaelic songs to progressive rock 'n' roll. Open Sunday to Thursday 1pm to 1am and Friday and Saturday 1pm to 2am.

**DANCE CLUBS** Koblenz's largest nightlife complex, **Extra,** lies 4km (2½ miles) north of the town center at August-Horch-Strasse 2 (✆ **0261/809-050;** bus: 6045). It includes a half-dozen movie theaters and a scattering of bars and dance clubs that play everything from old-time mountain-style evergreen music to cutting-edge tunes. The best way to experience the complex is to wander through its hallways, popping into whatever place suits your fancy. Entrance to most of the bars is free; cover charge to some of the dance emporiums runs 3€ to 8€ ($2.70–$7.15).

## 6 Bonn ★

72km (45 miles) S of Düsseldorf, 27km (17 miles) S of Cologne, 174km (108 miles) NW of Frankfurt

Until 1949, Bonn was a sleepy little university town, basking in its 2,000 years of history. Then suddenly it was shaken out of this quiet life and made capital of the Federal Republic of Germany. But in 1991, after the reunification of Germany, Berlin again became the official capital.

Although Bonn will continue to function as a smaller "second capital," no other cities stand to lose as much, especially in terms of prestige and political influence. Six of the major 15 departments of the German government, including the Defense Ministry, will remain here, although they will also have smaller offices in Berlin.

From the 13th through the 18th centuries, Bonn was the capital of the prince-electors of Cologne, who had the right to participate in the election of the emperor of the Holy Roman Empire. The city is also proud of its intellectual and musical history—Beethoven was born here; composer Robert Schumann and his wife, pianist Clara Schumann, lived here; and Karl Marx and

Heinrich Heine studied in Bonn's university. Bonn's latest cultural addition is the "Museum Mile," which includes the **Bundeskunsthalle (Federal Art and Exhibition Hall)** and the **Kunstmuseum (Art Museum).**

Bonn is also within sight of the **Siebenbirge (Seven Mountains),** a volcanic mountain range rising up on the eastern bank of the Rhine. The entire range is today a national park. The local wine produced on these slopes is known as Drachenblut (Dragon's Blood), and is better than most German reds.

## ESSENTIALS

**GETTING THERE By Plane** The nearest airport is **Flughafen Köln/Bonn** (see section 9, "Cologne," later in this chapter). Buses from the airport to Bonn's main rail station run every 30 minutes daily 6am to 10:30pm.

**By Train** The **Bonn Hauptbahnhof** is on a major rail line, with connections to most German cities. There are 12 trains daily to Berlin (trip time: 7 hr.), more than 30 trains to Frankfurt (trip time: 2 hr.), and service to Cologne every 15 minutes (trip time: 20 min.). For information, call ✆ **01805/99-66- 33.**

**By Bus** Long-distance bus service goes to such cities as Munich, Stuttgart, Aachen, Brussels, and London. For information, call **Deutsches Touring GmbH** in Frankfurt (✆ **069/7-90-35-0**). Regional bus service to Bad Godesberg and nearby towns is provided by **Regionalverkehr Köln GmbH at Meckenheim** (✆ **0228/7111**).

**By Car** Access is by the A565 Autobahn connecting with the A3 Autobahn from the north or south.

**VISITOR INFORMATION** Go to the **Bonn Tourist Office,** Cassius-Passage, Münsterstrasse 20 (✆ **0228/19433**), open Monday to Friday 9am to 6:30pm, Saturday 9am to 4pm, and Sunday 10am to 2pm.

**GETTING AROUND** If you visit the Reisenzentrum under the Bonn railway station, you can pick up a free map outlining the city's transportation network. The office is open Monday to Saturday 5:30am to 10pm and Sunday 6:30am to 10pm. Bus or underground tickets cost 1.25€ to 7.50€ ($1.10–$6.70). From Automaten (ticket dispensers) you can purchase 4-ride tickets for 4.30€ to 6.85€ ($3.85–$6.10), or day tickets for 5.40€ to 18.50€ ($4.80–$16.50).

## EXPLORING THE TOWN

Residents and tourist officials within Bonn show an extraordinary degree of civic and cultural pride whenever they discuss their city. Part of this manifests itself in walking tours that stress the 2,000 years of Bonn's history, with an emphasis on its role as a city of culture during the 19th century, and its changing role within Germany since reunification. April to October, 2-hour walking tours of Bonn are offered Saturday at 10:30am and 2pm and Sunday at 10am. Between November and March, there's only one tour a week: Saturday at 2pm. Tours cost 13€ ($11.60) for adults and 6.50€ ($5.80) for students and children under 16. The meeting point for these tours is the Bonn Tourist Office (see above). Call ✆ **0228/19433** for reservations and advance confirmation.

The **government quarter,** along the west bank of the Rhine, is a complex of modern, rather nondescript white buildings. The two most impressive, both along Koblenzerstrasse, are the former residences of the president and chancellor. These empire-style villas are reminiscent of the older Bonn, before it became an international center of diplomatic activity. They are not open to the public.

Running north along the Rhine from the government buildings is a tree- and flower-lined promenade, which ends at the **Alter Zoll.** This ruined ancient fortress makes a good viewing point from which visitors can see across the Rhine to the Siebengebirge and the old village of Beuel. These grounds have, in essence, become a city park.

**Beethoven House** Beethoven House is Bonn's pride and joy. Beethoven was born in 1770 in the small house in back, which opens onto a little garden. On its second floor is the room where he was born, decorated only with a simple marble bust of the composer. Many of Beethoven's personal possessions are in the house, including manuscripts and musical instruments. In the Vienna Room, in the front of the house overlooking the street, is Beethoven's last piano. The instrument was custom-made, with a special sounding board to amplify sound for the hearing-impaired composer.

Bonngasse 20 (in the old section of town, just north of the marketplace). ✆ **0228/9-81-75-25.** www.issay.com/bonn-beethoven-house. Admission 4€ ($3.55) adults, 3€ ($2.70) students and children. Guided tours by prior arrangement 8€ ($7.15). Apr–Sept Mon–Sat 10am–5pm, Sun 11am–4pm; Nov–Mar Mon–Sat 10am–6pm, Sun 11am–4pm. Tram: 61 or 62.

**Haus der Geschichte der Bundesrepublik Deutschland (House of History of the German Republic** All the sweep and drama of Germany's modern history is brought to life in this museum, in artifacts, photographs, and other displays. Exhibits trace the history of Germany after 1945, up to the breakdown of law and order in the eastern sector that led to reunification. The museum made headlines in 2001 when Emilie Schindler, the 93-year-old widow of Oskar Schindler, donated some of her famous husband's documents to the museum. Oskar Schindler was the subject of Steven Spielberg's film *Schindler's List,* one of the most famous movies ever made of the Holocaust. The bequest includes excerpts from the diary of one of hundreds of Jews that Schindler, a German industrialist, saved from the Nazi death camps. The donation also includes a photo album of the making of the Spielberg movie and a congratulatory letter from then American President Clinton.

Willy-Brandt-Allee 14. ✆ **0228/9-16-50.** www.hdg.de. Free admission. Tues–Sun 9am–7pm. U-Bahn: Heussallee.

**Kunstmuseum Bonn** One of the major buildings along the new "Museum Mile," this triangular structure, flooded with light, contains one of the most important art collections along the Rhine. The highlight is 20th-century art, including works by Rhenish expressionists, most notably August Macke. There are also works by Kirchner, Schmidt-Rottluff, Campen-Donk, Ernst, Seehaus, and Thuar.

Friedrich-Ebert-Allee 2. ✆ **0228/77-62-60.** Admission 5€ ($4.45) adults, 2.50€ ($2.25) children. Tues–Sun 10am–6pm; Wed 10am–9pm. U-Bahn: Heussallee.

## SHOPPING

Not surprisingly, you'll find lots of shops in town specializing in garments suitable for diplomacy and business. Most of the best are on the **Sternstrasse** (S-Bahn: Hauptbahnhof), partly a pedestrian-only street for certain times of day. Fanning out from here, you'll find women's clothing at **Beatrix Moden,** Münsterplatz 26 (✆ **0228/63-46-96**) and **La Belle,** Friedrichstrasse 51 (✆ **0228/63-74-75**).

Eighteenth-century German and French furniture as well as Biedermeier is found at **Paul Schweitzer,** Loebestrasse 1 (✆ **0228/36-26-59;** S-Bahn:

Godesberger Bahnhof), which also handles Oriental carpets, silver, French glass, and estate jewelry. A market called the **Flohmarkt,** at Rheinaue, Ludwig-Erhard-Strasse (Tram: 66), is where you'll find all manner of secondhand goods and collectibles. It's held the third Saturday of each month April to October. A weekly market, **Wochenmarkt,** on the square of the same name is held Monday to Saturday. You can enjoy a good lunch here, buying cooked food as you walk along inspecting the produce and various flea market items.

## WHERE TO STAY

### VERY EXPENSIVE

**Günnewig Bristol Hotel** ★★ This somewhat sterile, Cold War–era concrete and glass tower is still the best address in town. The good-size rooms are the best in Bonn, with such extras as trouser presses and double-glazing on the windows, along with fashionable and well-equipped bathrooms with shower-tub combinations and robes. The staff is also the finest in town.

Prinz-Albert-Strasse 2 (near Poppelsdorf Castle), 53113 Bonn. ✆ **0228/2-69-80.** Fax 0228/2-69-82-22. www.guennewig.de. 116 units. 180€–215€ ($160.75–$192) double; 320€ ($285.75) suite. Rates include American breakfast. AE, DC, MC, V. Parking 12€ ($10.70). Tram: 61 or 62. **Amenities:** 3 restaurants; bar; lounge; pool; sauna; solarium; room service; babysitting; laundry/dry cleaning. *In room:* A/C, TV, minibar, hair dryer, safe.

### EXPENSIVE

**Dorint Hotel Venusberg** ★ The elegant and intimate hotel, built in a style evocative of a French country home, is surrounded by the beauty of the Venusberg nature reserve, part of the larger Kottenforst. About half the units offer private balconies overlooking the hills. Bathrooms are well accessorized, all equipped with shower-tub combinations.

An der Casselsruhe 1 (2.5km/1½ miles southwest of Bonn, via Trierer Strasse), 53127 Bonn. ✆ **0228/28-80.** Fax 0228/28-82-88. www.dorint.com. 85 units. 165€–255€ ($147.35–$227.70) double; 280€–380€ ($250.05–$339.35) suite. Rates include continental breakfast. AE, DC, MC, V. Parking 8.50€ ($7.60). **Amenities:** Restaurant; lounge; health club; sauna; room service; massage; babysitting; laundry/dry cleaning. *In room:* TV, minibar, hair dryer, safe.

**Hotel Domicil** ★★ This modern and convenient hotel, like the Kaiser Karl (see below), is an oasis of charm and grace amid the rather sterile environment of Bonn. It's like an exclusive London town house and provides a viable alternative to the Günnewig Bristol. In the front, a glass-and-steel portico stretches over the sidewalk. The interior is one of the most elegant in the capital. The handsomely designed and spacious rooms range in style from Belle Epoque to Italian modern. All units contain neatly kept bathrooms with shower-tub combinations.

Thomas-Mann-Strasse 24–26 (4 blocks north of the cathedral, near the Hauptbahnhof), 53111 Bonn. ✆ **800/528-1234** in the U.S., or 0228/72-90-90. Fax 0228/69-12-07. www.bestwestern.de. 44 units. 159€–194€ ($142–$173.25) double; 220€ ($196.45) suite. AE, DC, MC, V. Free parking. S-Bahn: Hauptbahnhof. **Amenities:** Restaurant; 2 bars; sauna; car rental; room service; babysitting; laundry/dry cleaning. *In room:* TV, minibar, hair dryer.

**Kaiser Karl** ★★ *Finds* Kaiser Karl is one of Bonn's gems. Like the Domicil (see above), it has more style and atmosphere than other luxury leaders. Constructed in 1905 as a private town house, it was converted in 1983 into a stylish four-story hotel. The attractive decor includes lacquered Japanese screens, English antiques, Oriental carpets, Venetian mirrors, and Edwardian potted palms. Each beautifully furnished room has a bathroom with shower-tub combination.

Vorgebirgstrasse 56, 53119 Bonn. ✆ **0228/98-55-70.** Fax 0228/98-55-777. 42 units. 70€–215€ ($62.50–$192) double; 250€–400€ ($223.25–$357.20) suite. AE, DC, MC, V. Parking 12€ ($10.70). Bus: 624 or 634. **Amenities:** Breakfast room; lounge; room service; laundry/dry cleaning. *In room:* TV, minibar, hair dryer, safe.

### MODERATE

**Sternhotel** This is one of the best of Bonn's moderately priced hotels. It offers an informal, cozy atmosphere. Rooms are home-like, all with comfortable furnishings and bathrooms equipped with shower-tub combinations.

Markt 8 (next to the Rathaus), 53111 Bonn. ✆ **0228/7-26-70.** Fax 0228/7-26-71-25. www.sternhotel-bonn.de. 80 units. 85€–135€ ($75.90–$120.55) double. Rates include buffet breakfast. AE, DC, MC, V. Parking 15€ ($13.40) garage. U-Bahn: Uni-Markt. Bus: 624, 625, or 626. **Amenities:** 2 restaurants; lounge; room service. *In room:* TV, minibar.

### INEXPENSIVE

**Haus Hofgarten** *Value* A hard-working couple presides over this unique establishment, which offers the charm of another era. It's an excellent value for Bonn. A wide mahogany staircase leads to the cozy rooms, which are simply but comfortably furnished and very well kept. Each comes with a compact, tiled bathroom with shower.

Fritz-Tillmann-Strasse 7 (a 5-min. walk from the Hauptbahnhof), 53113 Bonn. ✆ **0228/22-34-72.** Fax 0228/21-39-02. 15 units. 66€ ($58.95) double without bathroom; 97€ ($86.60) double with bathroom. Rates include buffet breakfast. AE, DC, MC, V. Parking 6€ ($5.35). Tram: 61 or 62. **Amenities:** Breakfast room: lounge. *In room:* TV.

**Hotel Beethoven** One of the Beethoven's wings faces the Rhine. The hotel's main attraction is a panoramic view of the river traffic from the high-ceilinged dining room, where first-class meals are served, supervised by the owner. Double-glazed windows prevent urban noises from disturbing the calm in the well-furnished rooms, which range from small to medium. All units contain bathrooms containing shower-tub combinations.

Rheingasse 24–26 (across the street from the Stadttheater, a 10-min. walk from the Hauptbahnhof), 53113 Bonn. ✆ **0228/63-14-11.** Fax 0228/69-16-29. www.hotel-beethoven-bonn.com. 59 units. 78€–97€ ($69.65–$86.60) double. Rates include buffet breakfast. AE, DC, MC, V. Free parking. Tram: 62. Bus 638. **Amenities:** Restaurant; lounge; room service. *In room:* TV, hair dryer.

## WHERE TO DINE

### EXPENSIVE

**Le Petit Poisson** ★ FRENCH/SEAFOOD The food here is the finest in the center of Bonn. All ingredients are fresh, and many dishes are temptingly light and contemporary. Try the cream of fish and mushroom soup. Savory meat and game dishes include venison in vermouth sauce. Many diplomats dine here.

Wilhelmstrasse 23A. ✆ **0228/63-38-83.** Reservations recommended. Main courses 22€–30€ ($19.65–$26.80); fixed-price dinner 38€–61€ ($33.95–$54.45). AE, DC, MC, V. Tues–Sat 6pm–midnight. Tram: 61 or 62.

**Ristorante Grand'Italia** ★ ITALIAN/INTERNATIONAL This is one of the most appealing Italian restaurants along the Rhine. Main courses might include a *filletto della casa* (filet of beef prepared in a "special sauce" whose composition the chefs won't discuss); tagliorini with white truffles; and an autumnal version of roast pheasant. Also look for Roman-style *osso buco* (veal shank layered with prosciutto), a succulent risotto Milanese, and such desserts as a velvety version of zabaglione.

Bischofsplatz 1 (adjacent to the old market square). ✆ **0228/63-83-33.** Reservations recommended. Main courses 12.25€–19.85€ ($10.95–$17.75); fixed-price menu 22€–39.10€ ($19.65–$34.90). AE, DC, MC, V. Daily noon–3pm and 6–11:30pm. Tram: 62 or 66.

### MODERATE

**Zur Lese** GERMAN This restaurant's polite service and outdoor terrace with a sweeping view over the Rhine attract many local residents, especially in the afternoon, when visitors drop in for coffee, cakes, and glasses of wine after strolling in the nearby Hofgarten. Elegant, well-prepared lunches are also offered. Dinner is served in the cafe. A menu of German specialties (with English translations) includes pork with curry sauce and the chef's superb *Gulasch Lese* (goulash). You can also choose rainbow trout or lobster from the terrace aquarium. The food is home-style and hearty, with no pretense.

Adenauerallee 37. ✆ **0228/22-33-22.** Reservations recommended. Main courses 13€–22€ ($11.60–$19.65); fixed-price dinner 27€–32€ ($24.10–$28.60); fixed-price 3-course lunch 21€ ($18.75). AE, DC, MC, V. Restaurant Tues–Sun 11am–11pm; cafe Tues–Sun 10am–11pm.

### INEXPENSIVE

**Em Höttche** *Value* GERMAN Em Höttche enjoys a long and colorful history, stretching all the way from 1389. It's fed thousands over the centuries with its rib-sticking fare—perhaps changing the recipes every 100 years or so. The interior has been restored, with carved-wood paneling, natural brick, old beamed ceilings, decoratively painted plaster, and curlicue chandeliers. Favorite dining spots are tables set inside the walk-in fireplace. On the a la carte list, you'll find specialties for two, including entrecôte. Fresh salmon is often available. Complement your meal with a carafe of local wine—the best buy in the house.

Markt 4 (next to the Rathaus). ✆ **0228/69-00-09.** Reservations not accepted. Main courses 8.70€–15.40€ ($7.75–$13.75). No credit cards. Daily 11am–1am. Tram: 47. Bus: 618.

**Im Bären** GERMAN The name of this historic inn appears in documents dating from 1385. Today it occupies a prominent position in Bonn's pedestrian zone and is one of the best-known restaurants in town. Most diners head for tables on the street level, although there's a large additional room on the second floor. The food is hearty Rhinelander cuisine, including everything from simple wursts with potatoes to more elaborate steaks with béarnaise sauce and salad. Service is bustling, matter-of-fact, and efficient.

Acherstrasse 1–3 (5 min. from the Hauptbahnhof). ✆ **0228/63-32-00.** Reservations recommended. Main courses 7.90€–18€ ($7.05–$16.05). No credit cards. Daily 9am–midnight. Tram: 61, 62, or 63.

**Im Stiefel** RHINELAND This atmospheric restaurant is a local favorite. You dine at bare bleached tables in rooms with wood paneling and stained glass. There's a stand-up bar for mugs of beer. The short menu features down-home Rhineland dishes, including a local dish, *Hämmchen* (pork trotters), served with sauerkraut and mashed potatoes. A specialty is braised beef marinated in almond-raisin sauce.

Bonngasse 30 (a few doors down from the Beethoven House). ✆ **0228/630805.** Reservations recommended. Main courses 7.50€–18€ ($6.70–$16.05); fixed-price menus 14€–31€ ($12.50–$27.70). AE, DC, MC, V. Mon–Sat 11am–1am. Tram: 61 or 62.

## BONN AFTER DARK

Once considered a dismal place to go out on the town, Bonn now has a thriving fine-arts community and a brisk nightlife. If you're in the area around the first Saturday in May, don't miss the spectacular annual fireworks display, visible for a distance of 26km (16 miles) south of the city.

**THE PERFORMING ARTS** Bonn has always struggled with the perception that it can't compete with the larger arts communities in Hamburg and Berlin, and consequently it has compensated (or overcompensated) with an impressive roster of cultural events. One of the most visible is "La Scala of the Rhineland," the **Oper der Stadt Bonn,** Am Boselagerhof 1 (✆ **0228/77-36-67;** S-Bahn: Hauptbahnhof), where ballet and opera are performed at regular intervals mid-August to June. Box office hours are Monday to Friday 8:30am to 6pm, Saturday 9am to 4pm, and Sunday 10am to 2pm. Tickets are 12€ to 95€ ($10.70–$84.85) each, depending on the event.

The **Bonn Symphony Orchestra** performs in Beethovenhalle, Wachsbleiche 26 (✆ **0228/7222100;** S-Bahn: Hauptbahnhof), September to June, with occasional free concerts given on Sunday mornings. Otherwise, tickets cost 11€ to 57€ ($9.80–$50.90). On a more intimate scale, chamber music is sometimes presented within a small but charming concert hall within the **Beethoven House** (✆ **0228/981-7525** for details).

During the Bonner Summer Festival, mid-May to August, an international selection of dance and music groups perform, mostly for free, in open-air locations around the city. Contact ✆ **0228/19433** or 0228/774400 for details. In addition, the **Beethoven Festival,** a rekindling of both the nostalgia and the music associated with Bonn's greatest musical genius, takes place in September. Contact the visitor information center (see "Visitor Information" under "Essentials," earlier in this section) for information.

Bonn's **Theater-Kasse,** Mühlheimerplatz 1 (✆ **0228/773-6667;** S-Bahn: Hauptbahnhof), is a well-known and highly resourceful ticket agency associated with the city's tourist office. It has access to tickets for virtually every sporting, entertainment, and cultural venue in Bonn. Also call for information on performers, schedules, and prices.

**DANCE CLUBS** A weekend-only club, **Sharon,** Oxfordstrasse 20–21 (no phone; S-Bahn: Hauptbahnhof), is straight out of the 1970s, with dancing to soul and funk under a spinning mirror ball and strobe lights. It's open 10pm to 5am, with a 5.10€ to 7.65€ ($5–$7.50) cover.

**LIVE MUSIC & CABARET** Live jazz is featured Friday and Saturday 8pm to around 4am at **The Jazz Galerie,** Oxfordstrasse 24 (✆ **0228/63-93-24;** S-Bahn: Hauptbahnhof). Cover is 6€ to 15€ ($5.35–$13.40), depending on the band. The **Pantheon Theater,** Bundeskanzlerplatz (✆ **0228/21-25-21;** bus: 610), stages jazz and pop concerts, comedy shows, and political cabaret. Nearly every weekday there is a performance of some sort. Friday and Saturday, the facility becomes a disco. The box office is open Monday to Friday noon to 6:30pm.

**BARS** **Pawlow,** Heerstrasse 64 (✆ **0228/65-36-03;** S-Bahn: Tanninbusche Sud), has an alfresco terrace. While here, don't let appearances intimidate you—a sometimes fierce-looking crowd with tattoos and body piercings is actually a bored intelligentsia at heart. Open daily 11am to 1am.

**GAY BARS** The most crowded gay bar is **Boba's Bar,** Josefstrasse 17 (✆ **0228/65-06-85;** S-Bahn: Hauptbahnhof), near the railway station, adjacent to the Rhine. It welcomes a drinking (but not dancing) crowd in their 20s and 30s. It's open Sunday to Tuesday 8pm to 3am and Friday and Saturday 9pm to 5am. Another gay bar is **Charley,** Kölnstrasse at Theaterstrasse (✆ **0228/69-07-61;** S-Bahn: Hauptbahnhof), open Sunday to Thursday 9pm to 3am and Friday and Saturday 9pm to 5am. There's also **Le Copain,** Tomasmannstrasse 3A (✆ **0228/63-99-35;** S-Bahn: Hauptbahnhof), which attracts a somewhat older clientele and is open 9pm to 2 or 3am.

## 7 Bad Godesberg

6km (4 miles) S of central Bonn

Part of greater Bonn, Bad Godesberg is one of the Rhine's oldest spa towns. It's located just opposite the legendary Siebengebirge (Seven Mountains), with a view of the crag, Drachenfels (Dragon's Rock), where according to legend, Siegfried slew the dragon. Dragons are no longer found on the Rhine, but you can still see some ancient castle ruins on the hills. The most interesting is **Godesberg Castle,** built in the 13th century by the electors of Cologne (its ruins have been incorporated into a hotel, described below). From the promenade along the Rhine, you can watch a flow of boats and barges wending their way up and down the river.

Most of the spa's activities center around the small but elegant 18th-century **Redoute Palace.** Although the town is mainly a residential center, there is seemingly no end to the entertainment and cultural facilities here. Theaters, concerts, and social functions offer a constant whirl of events. Since these events are not permanent, check with the tourist office, which publishes a weekly list of current events happening at the time of your visit.

**GETTING THERE** You can reach Bad Godesberg from Bonn by taking tram 16 or 63 from Bonn's central rail station (trip time: 20 min.). If you're driving from the center of Bonn, take the B9 (driving time: 20 min.). For information about the town, consult the Bonn Tourist Office (see "Visitor Information" under section 6, "Bonn," earlier in this chapter).

### WHERE TO STAY

**Günnewig Godesberg Castlehotel** ★ A winding road leads up to this hilltop castle ruin, now converted to a hotel that we highly recommend. Its tall tower and many of its rugged stone walls were erected in 1210 by the archbishop of Cologne and are still intact. A lounge built against one of the stone walls provides a sunny perch with a view of the river. There's also a roof terrace, with tables for drinks. The small rooms are traditionally furnished and well maintained and have picture windows. Each comes with a small bathroom with a shower unit.

Auf dem Godesberg 5, 53177 Bonn-Bad Godesberg. ✆ **0228/31-60-71.** Fax 0228/31-12-18. 13 units. 81€–94€ ($72.35–$83.95) double. Rates include continental breakfast. AE, DC, MC, V. Free parking. Tram: 16 or 63 from Bonn. **Amenities:** Restaurant; bar; lounge; room service. *In room:* TV.

### WHERE TO DINE

**Halbedel's Gasthaus** ★★★ CONTINENTAL Here, amid many nostalgic souvenirs and antique tables and chairs, the courtly owners will welcome you to their turn-of-the-century villa. The kitchen prides itself on using mostly German-grown produce. The chefs are true artists, using ingredients of superlative quality to create harmonious flavors and textures. Some of the dishes will be familiar; others are imaginative inventions. Menu choices might include wild mushroom soup, rack of lamb prepared French style, and a salad of dandelion greens and wild lettuce, followed by flavor-filled desserts.

Rheinallee 47. ✆ **0228/35-42-53.** Reservations recommended. Main courses 25€–29€ ($22.35–$25.90); fixed-price menu 60€–69€ ($53.60–$61.60). AE, MC, V. Tues–Sun 5:30–10:30pm. Closed mid-July–mid-Aug. Tram: 16 or 610 from Bonn.

**Zur Korkeiche** CONTINENTAL Zur Korkeiche is a wine-and-sherry house. It's located in a well-maintained, 150-year-old half-timbered building.

There are two stories of cozy comfort and tradition. The decor is rustic in a country-elegant way. The head chef prepares a light cuisine. Menu choices include a delicately seasoned smoked salmon in champagne sauce.

Lyngsbergstrasse 104 (1km/½ mile south of Bad Godesberg in the village of Lannesdorf). ✆ **0228/34-78-97.** Reservations recommended. Main courses 18€–20€ ($16.05–$17.85). MC, V. Tues–Sun 6–11:30pm. Closed 2 weeks in Oct and 2 weeks in Apr (dates vary). Bus: 14.

## 8 Aachen (Aix-la-Chapelle) ★

64km (40 miles) W of Cologne, 80km (50 miles) SW of Düsseldorf

The ancient Imperial City of Aachen (Aix-la-Chapelle), at the frontier where Germany, Belgium, and the Netherlands meet, is inseparably connected with Charlemagne. He selected this spot as the center of his vast Frankish empire. History is important at this spa town, but today there's also a youthful *joie de vivre* that attracts young people from all over the world. Visitors also come for the sulfurous hot springs or the magnificent cathedral, or to use Aachen as a launching pad for exploring the Benelux nations.

Aachen has an even longer history as a spa than as an imperial city. Roman legionnaires established a military bath here in the 1st century A.D. By the end of the 17th century, Aachen was known as the "Spa of Kings" because royalty from all over Europe came here to take the cure. In 1742 Frederick the Great visited, and in 1818 the "Congress of Monarchs" brought Czar Alexander from Russia. After World War II, the spa was rebuilt and today enjoys a reputation as a remedial center. Its springs are among the hottest in Europe. The treatment includes baths and the *Trinkkur* (drinking the water). The spa gardens are the center of resort activity, with attractive ponds, fountains, and shade trees.

Aachen can be visited as a sightseeing day trip from Cologne. However, those interested in using the spa facilities should stay at one of the hotels described below.

### ESSENTIALS

**GETTING THERE** **By Train** The Hauptbahnhof at Aachen receives some 200 trains a day from all parts of Germany and from Paris, with easy connections from most major cities as well as nearby Cologne (trip time: 45 min.). Frankfurt is 3½ hours away, and Munich, 7 hours. For information, call ✆ **01805/99-66-33.**

**By Bus** It's best to take the train, but once you arrive in Aachen, regional bus service is provided by **BVR Busverkehr Rheinland GmbH** at Simmerath (✆ **02473/66-46** or 01803/044-044 for schedules and information).

**By Car** Access is by the A4 Autobahn east and west or the A44 north or south. Driving time from Cologne is 50 to 60 minutes, depending on traffic. Frankfurt is 3½ hours away by car; Munich, 6½ hours.

**VISITOR INFORMATION** You'll find the **Tourist Office Aachen** on Friedrich-Wilhelm-Platz (✆ **0241/19433**). Office hours are Monday to Friday 9am to 6pm and Saturday 9am to 2pm.

**GETTING AROUND** Buses pull into the main railway station in the center of town at Peterskirchhof and Peterstrasse. Tickets are 1.40€ to 5.10€ ($1.25–$4.55). A 24-hour pass, available at the bus station, offers unlimited travel within Aachen for 4.10€ ($4)

## SEEING THE SIGHTS

Aachen's Altstadt is small enough to be covered on foot. Marktplatz, in the heart of town, is overshadowed by the Gothic Rathaus, which contains the city archives. From here, you can head down one of the most popular and busiest pedestrian precincts in the city, Krämerstrasse, which will lead to **Münsterplatz (Cathedral Square)** and the famous cathedral (see below), one of the masterpieces of architecture in the Western world. Past the cathedral you reach the Elisengarten, bordered on the south by the symbol of Bad Aachen, the Elisenbrunnen, a rotunda with a thermal drinking fountain. From Münsterplatz you can go through the great iron gate to the Fischmarkt, with old merchants' houses and the Fischpuddelchen fountain with spouting fish.

The **Wingerstberg Kurgarten** and the **Stadtgarten,** with its thermal bath and casino, lie to the northeast of town, and the **Hauptbahnhof** is on the southern ring, opening onto Römerstrasse.

**Couven Museum** ★ This gracefully designed villa gives you an insight into the decorative traditions of the late 18th and 19th centuries. It has one of the best collections of antique furnishings of any museum in the region. On the ground floor is a reproduction of a small-scale chocolate factory. You'll find treasures, some of them low-key and discreet, virtually everywhere you look.

Huhnermarkt 17. ✆ **0241/4-32-44-21.** Admission 1.50€ ($1.35) adults, 1€ (90¢) children. Tues–Wed and Fri–Sun 10am–5pm; Thurs 10am–1pm. Bus: 1, 11, or 21.

**Dom (Cathedral)** ★★ About A.D. 800, the emperor Charlemagne built the "octagon," the core of the Imperial Cathedral. Within stands the marble *Königsstuhl,* Charlemagne's throne, one of the most venerable monuments in Germany. (Visitors to the cathedral can view the throne of Charlemagne only with a guide; request one at the treasury or call ahead.) From 936 to 1531 the Holy Roman emperors were crowned here, until Frankfurt became the coronation city.

The cathedral is an unusual mixture of Carolingian (the well-preserved dome), Gothic (the choir, completed in 1414), and baroque (the Hungarian chapel), all united into a magnificent upward sweep of architecture. The **treasury** ★★★, in the adjoining house (entry: Klostergasse), is the most valuable and celebrated ecclesiastical treasure trove north of the Alps. But the cathedral itself holds its own share of wealth. The elaborate gold shrine (1215) in the chancel contains the **relics of Charlemagne** ★★★. The **pulpit** ★★★ of Henry II (ca. 1002) is copper studded with precious gems.

Klosterplatz 2. ✆ **0241/47-70-91-27.** www.aachendom.de. Cathedral free; treasury 2.50€ ($2.25) adults, 1.50€ ($1.35) children and students. Mon 10am–12:30pm; Tues and Thurs–Sat 10am–5:30pm; Wed 10am–8:30pm; Sun 10am–5pm. Bus: 1, 11, or 21.

**Rathaus** The 14th-century Rathaus was built on the original site of Charlemagne's palace. Part of the ancient palace structure can still be seen in the so-called Granus Tower at the east side of the hall. The richly decorated facade, facing the marketplace, is adorned with the statues of 50 German rulers, 31 of them crowned in Aachen. In the center, standing in relief, are the "Majestas Domini," the two most important men of their time in the Holy Roman Empire, Charlemagne and Pope Leo III.

On the second floor of the Rathaus is the double-naved and cross-beamed Imperial Hall, where coronation banquets took place from 1349 to 1531. Built as the successor to the Carolingian Royal Hall, today it contains exact replicas of the imperial crown jewels, true in size and material to the originals, presently in the Vienna Secular Treasury. On the walls are the Charlemagne frescoes, painted in the 19th century by Alfred Rethel, illustrating the victory of the Christian Franks over the Germanic heathens.

Am Markt. ✆ **0241/4-32-73-10.** Admission 1.50€ ($1.35) adults, 1€ (90¢) children and students. Daily 9am–1pm and 2–6:30pm. Closed sometimes for official events. Bus: 4 or 11.

**Suermondt Ludwig Museum** ★ The impressive collection of medieval German sculpture, one of the finest in the land, includes a *Madonna in Robes* (1420) from the Swabian school and a *Virgin and Child* from the 14th-century Tournai school. The second landing has a good collection of primitive Flemish and German works, along with 17th-century Dutch and Flemish paintings. Look for works by Van Dyck and Jordaens. The museum also has modern works, especially from the 1920s and 1930s.

Wilhelmstrasse 18. ✆ **0241/47-98-00.** Admission 3€ ($2.70) adults, 1.50€ ($1.35) children. Tues and Thurs–Fri 11am–6pm; Wed 11am–8pm; Sat–Sun 11am–5pm. Bus: 3, 4, or 13.

## WHERE TO STAY

**Am Marschiertor** ★ *Finds* This charming hotel stands in the center of Aachen, not far from the Hauptbahnhof and next to the medieval town gate for which it's named. The hotel is quiet, with a courtyard and a view over the Altstadt and cathedral. The lobby and connecting hall are attractive, with antique furniture. The recently refurbished rooms have a cozy atmosphere, and each—generally medium in size—is well appointed and well maintained with bathrooms containing shower-tub combinations.

Wallstrasse 1–7, 52064 Aachen. ✆ **0241/3-19-41-43.** Fax 0241/3-19-44. www.lodging-germany.com/aachen/ammarschiertor.htm. 50 units. 75€–95€ ($67–$84.85) double. Rates include buffet breakfast. AE, DC, MC, V. Parking 8.50€ ($7.60), opposite the hotel. Bus: 1, 11, or 21. **Amenities:** Breakfast room; lounge. *In room:* TV, hair dryer, safe.

**Aquis Grana City Hotel** ★ Aquis Grana City Hotel is your best bet in the town center. The comfortable rooms offer all the modern extras and range from spacious to medium. All units contain bathrooms with shower-tub combinations. The staff is very alert to all your needs. Housekeeping rates an A+.

Büchel 32, 52016 Aachen. ✆ **0241/44-30.** Fax 0241/44-31-37. www.hotel-aquisgrana.de. 99 units. 115€–135€ ($102.70–$120.55) double; from 150€ ($133.95) suite. Children up to 10 stay free in parents' room. Rates include buffet breakfast. AE, DC, MC, V. Parking 8€ ($7.15). Bus: 1, 11, or 21. **Amenities:** Restaurant; lounge; pool; health club; spa facilities; sauna; room service; laundry/dry cleaning. *In room:* TV, minibar, hair dryer.

**Hotel Benelux** *Value* The warm and inviting Benelux is within walking distance of many major attractions. It's a small family-run hotel, tastefully decorated and personalized. Americans from the Southwest will feel at home in the lobby/reception area—it has probably the only cactus collection in Aachen. Rooms range from small to medium. All units come equipped with bathrooms containing shower-tub combinations.

Franzstrasse 21–23 (5-min. walk from the Hauptbahnhof), 52064 Aachen. ✆ **0241/400-03-0.** Fax 0241/400-03-500. www.aachen-tourist.de/Benelux/benelux.htm. 33 units. 97€–133€ ($86.60–$118.75) double. Rates include continental breakfast. AE, DC, MC, V. Parking 8€ ($7.15). Bus: 1, 11, or 21. **Amenities:** Restaurant; lounge; fitness center; sauna; room service. *In room:* TV, minibar, hair dryer.

## WHERE TO DINE

**La Bécasse** ★★ GERMAN/FRENCH This modern restaurant, full of greenery, serves a pleasing combination of light, modern French specialties and traditional German recipes. Although not in the same league as Restaurant Gala (see below), La Bécasse is a discreetly classy place. Christof Lang, who realized early his "calling" of reproducing the fine foods of France, has been the owner since 1981. The food is imported every day from the wholesale markets at Rungis, outside Paris. Try his ragout of fish or his cassoulet.

Hanbrucherstrasse 1 (just outside the Altstadt by the Westpark). ✆ **0241/7-44-44.** Reservations recommended. Main courses 25€–34€ ($22.35–$30.35); fixed-price 6-course menu 60€ ($53.60). DC, MC, V. Daily 6:30–10:30pm; Tues–Fri noon–2:30pm. Bus: 15, 25, or 35.

**Ratskeller** WESTPHALIAN/GERMAN This is a charming, old-fashioned restaurant that's beloved by many. The less-expensive section is the Postwagen, a pub-like setting that serves platters and drinks in the afternoon. But we prefer the majesty of the brick-and-stone Ratskeller, where a sense of medievalism is enhanced by solid, conservative fare, such as sauerkraut with wurst; minestrone or potato soup; grilled steaks; fricassée of sole; and fresh berries and pastries for dessert.

Am Markt (in the Rathaus). ✆ **0241/3-50-01.** Reservations recommended. In Postwagen Pub, platters 8€–23€ ($7.15–$20.55); in Ratskeller Restaurant, main courses 11€–22€ ($9.80–$19.65). AE, DC, DISC, MC, V. Postwagen Pub daily 10am–11pm; Ratskeller Restaurant daily 11:30am–3pm and 6–10pm. Bus: 2, 11, or 25.

**Restaurant Elisenbrunnen** FISH/FRENCH/WESTPHALIAN This stately restaurant occupies the Elisenbrunnen Rotunda, built in 1838 to commemorate the visit of a local potentate, Queen Elisen. Today it shares the same site as the city tourist office. It specializes in regional dishes (such as Westphalian green cabbage with Mattwurst [pork sausage]); French specialties (choucroute garnie [sauerkraut accompanied by 3 or 4 pork products such as pork chops and ham] or chateaubriand with béarnaise sauce); and fresh fish. On warm days, you can dine on a large, well-maintained terrace in the shade of the Kaiserdom and the Rathaus.

Friedrich-Wilhelm-Platz 14. ✆ **0241/297-72.** Reservations recommended. Main courses 9€–24.50€ ($8.05–$21.90); fixed-price lunch 24€ ($21.45). AE, DC, MC, V. Daily 11am–11pm. Bus 15, 25, or 55.

**Restaurant Gala** ★★ GERMAN The best dining place in Aachen is the elegant Restaurant Gala, which is loosely linked to one of the country's busier casinos. Light plays merrily through the crystal-draped decor onto the oak-paneled walls. Some of the paintings are Salvador Dalí originals. (The restaurant is named for his former wife.) The Gala can soothe the frayed nerves of the most inveterate gamblers. The kitchen turns out modern, lighter interpretations of regional food, including gamecock in calvados-and-mustard sauce or filet of venison in blood sauce. Ingredients are trucked in daily from the Rungis markets near Paris. The wine list is encyclopedic; the French desserts are delectable.

Monheimsallee 44. ✆ **0241/15-30-13.** Reservations required. Main courses 18€–30€ ($16.05–$26.80); fixed-price menu 60€–80€ ($53.60–$71.45). AE, DC, MC, V. Tues–Sat 6:30–10pm. Bus: 13.

## AACHEN AFTER DARK

For information about what's happening in Aachen, pick up a copy of the booklet *Tourist-Information,* published and given away free by the tourist information office. Alternatively, you can buy a copy of a glossy-looking magazine, *Klenkes,* a monthly publication that's available in news kiosks around the city for 2€ ($1.80) each. For any local sports, entertainment, or cultural event, you can purchase tickets either from the establishment's ticket office or by contacting the tourist office's ticket booth (✆ **02451/180-2965**).

**THE PERFORMING ARTS** Classical concerts are presented in the town's convention center, **Kongresszentrum Eurogress,** Mondheimsallee 52

(✆ **0241/91-31-0;** bus: 57), by the local symphony orchestra and by visiting chamber orchestras. The **Theater Aachen** (formerly known as the Stadtheater), Theaterplatz (✆ **02451/4784244;** bus: 33, 34, or 57), hosts opera, theater, and dance recitals. Ticket prices in both places are around 10.50€ to 90€ ($9.40–$80.35). If you understand German and want to see experimental theater and plays by Bertolt Brecht, head for the small and rather cramped **Aachener Kultur und Theater Initiative,** Gasborn 9–11 (✆ **0241/2-74-58;** bus:166). Tickets are 13€ to 45€ ($11.60–$40.20).

**BARS & CAFES** There are at least a half-dozen bars in or around Aachen's Marktplatz. One of the most appealing is the **Martesa Keller,** Martesastrasse (no phone; bus: 13). This cozy, convivial, wood-paneled place offers live music, usually jazz, on most nights (usually Wed–Sat, beginning around 8:30pm), and a bar that opens every night at 6pm. More youth-oriented is the **Café Kittel,** Pontstrasse 39 (✆ **0241/3-65-60;** bus: 13), which somewhat resembles a greenhouse; its menu concentrates on beer, wine, sandwiches, and quiche. Open Monday to Thursday 10am to 2am, Friday and Saturday 10:30am to 3am, and Sunday 11am to 2am.

**DANCE CLUBS** Friday and Saturday nights, **Rotation,** Pontstrasse 135 (no phone; bus: 13), keeps the dance music cranking until 6am. Other nights, the music provides a background for drinking and socializing. There's no cover charge, and no food served. Open Sunday to Thursday 3pm to 2am.

**LIVE MUSIC** It's Irish in conception, but **Wild Rover,** Hirschgraben 13 (✆ **0241/3-54-53;** bus: 4 or 33), is a rock club first and foremost. The bands that take the stage nightly range from mainstream to punk. It's open daily 8pm to 2am, with a 3€ ($2.70) cover Sunday to Thursday, and a 4€ ($3.55) cover Friday and Saturday. A worthy competitor is the **Exil-Bar,** Schlosstrasse 2 (✆ **0241/51-23-45;** bus: 33, 34, or 57), where live music, including jazz and rock, is presented within a small, smoke-filled, and decidedly bohemian venue every night 6pm to 1am. A final nightlife venue is the **Domkeller,** Hof 1 (✆ **0241/3-42-65;** bus: 1, 11, or 21), which offers live blues or jazz on some nights, and lots of hubbub every night. Open Monday to Thursday 11am to 1am and to 2am Friday and Saturday.

## 9 Cologne (Köln) ★★★

27km (17 miles) N of Bonn, 40km (25 miles) S of Düsseldorf, 188km (117 miles) NW of Frankfurt

Cologne (Köln), the largest city in the Rhineland, is so rich in antiquity that every time a new foundation is dug, the excavators come up with archaeological finds. Devastating though the World War II bombing was—nearly all the buildings of the Altstadt were damaged—reconstruction brought to light a period of Cologne's history that had been a mystery for centuries. Evidence showed that Cologne was as important and powerful during the early Christian era as it was during Roman times and the Middle Ages.

Cologne traces its beginnings to 38 B.C., when Roman legions set up camp here. As early as A.D. 50, the emperor Claudius gave it municipal rights as capital of a Roman province. In the early Christian era, a bishopric was founded here and a number of saints were martyred, including the patron of the city, St. Ursula. During the Middle Ages, as Cologne became a center for international trade, Romanesque and Gothic churches were built with prosperous merchants' gold. Today there is much to see from every period of the city's 2,000-year history—from the old Roman towers to the modern opera house. But Cologne is also a bustling modern city, with a lively population. It's also increasingly becoming the fine-art capital of Germany.

## ESSENTIALS

**GETTING THERE** **By Plane** Cologne and Bonn share the same airport, **Flughafen Köln/Bonn Konrad Adenauer,** 14km (9 miles) southeast of Cologne. Flights come from most major European cities. For complete information, call ✆ **02203/40-40-01.** Bus 170 from the airport to the center of Cologne operates every 30 minutes 6:05am to 7:35am, every 15 minutes to 8:35pm, and then every 30 minutes to 11:05pm. Travel time takes 20 minutes, and the fare is 5€ ($4.45) per person. A taxi, suitable for up to four passengers, costs from 31€ ($27.70).

**By Train** The **Cologne Hauptbahnhof** is in the heart of the city, next to the cathedral. For schedules, call ✆ **01805/99-66-33.** This depot has frequent rail connections to all major German cities and many continental destinations. There are 17 trains per day from Berlin (trip time: 5½ hr.), 31 from Frankfurt (trip time: 2½ hr.), and 25 from Hamburg (trip time: 4½ hr.).

**By Bus** Cologne is linked to several major cities, including Frankfurt, by bus. For complete information and schedules, call **Deutsche Touring GmbH** (✆ **069/790350;** www.deutsche-touring.com). Regional bus service to nearby cities such as Trier (see chapter 15) is provided by **Regionalverkehr Köln GmbH** at Euskirchen (✆ **02251/12-44-12**).

**By Car** Cologne is easily reached from major German cities. It's connected north and south by the A3 Autobahn and east and west by the A4 Autobahn.

**VISITOR INFORMATION** For tourist information, go to the **Köln Tourismus Office,** Unter Fettenhennen 19 (Am Dom) (✆ **0221/19433;** www.willkommeninkoeln.de), a few steps from the cathedral. November to April, it's open Monday to Saturday 8am to 9pm and Sunday 9:30am to 7pm; May to October, Monday to Saturday 8am to 10:30pm, Sunday 9:30am to 10pm.

**GETTING AROUND** For 1.40€ to 8.10€ ($1.25–$7.25) per single ride, depending on where you're going, you can purchase a ticket allowing you to travel on Cologne's excellent **bus, tram, U-Bahn,** and **S-Bahn** connections. A day ticket, the Kölner Tageskarte, which costs 7.25€ ($6.45), will allow you to travel throughout the city's transportation network from 9am to 3am. For information about public transportation, call ✆ **0221/547-3333.**

For a taxi, call ✆ **0221/28-82** for a recorded message and then press 1 in reply. The meter will start at 2€ ($1.80) and rise 1.30€ ($1.15) per kilometer for rides between 6am and 10pm and 1.30€ ($1.25) per kilometer for rides between 10pm and 6am.

## EXPLORING THE CITY

One of the best panoramas over the ancient city of Cologne is available from within one of the cars of the Rhein-Seilbahn, the first and only cable car in Europe that was designed to span a major river. The Rhein-Seilbahn stretches between a point near the zoo, in the district of Cologne-Riehl, to the Rheinpark in Cologne-Deutz, a total of about 915m (3,000 ft.). From the air, you'll get a good view of the busy river traffic along the Rhine. The cable car operates April to October, Monday to Friday 11am to 6pm, Saturday and Sunday 10am to 6pm. A one-way ticket costs 4€ ($3.55) for adults, 2€ ($1.80) for children; a

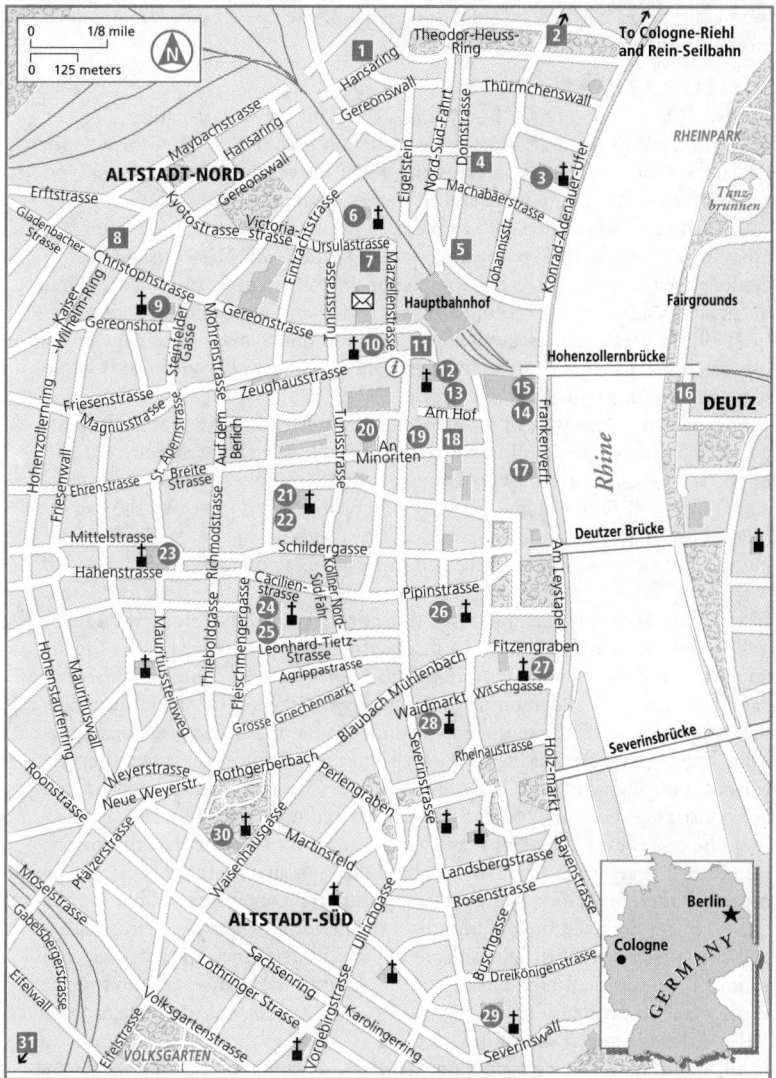


**ATTRACTIONS ●**

Cologne Cathedral (Dom) **12**
Gross St. Martin Church **21**
Kölner Philharmonie **15**
Museum für Angewandte Kunst **19**
Museum Ludwig **14**
Museum Schnütgen **25**
Oper der Stadt Köln **17**
Römisch-Germanische Museum **13**
St. Andreas Church **10**
St. Aposteln Church **23**
St. Cecilia's Church (Cäcilienkirche) **24**
St. Georg Church **28**
St. Gereon Church **9**
St. Kunibert Church **3**
St. Maria im Kapitol Church **26**
St. Maria Lyskirchen **27**
St. Pantaleon Church **30**
St. Severin Church **29**
St. Ursula Church **6**
Schauspielhaus **22**
Wallraf-Richartz Museum/ Fondation Corboud **20**

**ACCOMMODATIONS ■**

Antik-Hotel Bristol **8**
Brandenberger Hof **5**
Coellner Hof **1**
Dom-Hotel **18**
Excelsior Hotel Ernst **11**
Grandhotel Schloss Bensberg **2**
Hopper Hotel St. Antonius **4**
Hotel Cristall **7**
Hotel Im Wasserturm **31**
Hyatt Regency **16**

Church
Information
Post Office
S-Bahn

round-trip ticket costs 5€ ($4.45) for adults, 2.50€ ($2.25) for children. For more information, call ✆ **0221/76-20-06.**

## THE TOP ATTRACTIONS

**Kölner Dom (Cologne Cathedral)** ★★★ This majestic structure is one of the world's great cathedrals—the spiritual and geographical heart of the city. It's the largest Gothic cathedral in Germany. From the top of the south tower, you get panoramic views of the city and surrounding area.

Construction began in 1248, in order to house the relics of the three Magi brought to Cologne in 1164 by Archbishop Reinald von Dassel, chancellor to Frederick Barbarossa. After the completion of the chancel, south tower, and north-side aisles (around 1500), work was halted and not resumed until 1823. In 1880, the great enterprise was completed, and unlike many time-consuming constructions that change styles in midstream, the final result was in the Gothic style, true to the original plans.

For the best overall view of the cathedral, stand back from the south transept, where you can get an idea of its actual size and splendor. Note that there are no important horizontal lines—everything is vertical. The west side (front) is dominated by two towering spires, perfectly proportioned and joined by the narrow facade of the nave. The first two stories of the towers are square, gradually merging into the octagonal form of the top three stories and tapering off at the top with huge finials. There is no great rose window, so characteristic of Gothic architecture, between these spires—nothing detracts from the lofty vertical lines.

Entering through the west doors (main entrance), you are immediately caught up in the cathedral's grandeur. Although this portion of the church is somewhat bare, the clerestory and vaulting give a feeling of the size of the edifice. The towering windows on the south aisles include the Bavarian windows, donated by King Ludwig I of Bavaria in 1848. Like most windows in the nave, they are colored with pigments that have been burned on rather than stained. In the north aisles are the stained-glass Renaissance windows (1507–09).

In the center of the transept is an elegant bronze-and-marble altar that can be seen from all parts of the cathedral. Behind the high altar, in the chancel, is ***The Shrine of the Three Magi*** ★★★, the most important and valuable object in the cathedral. It's designed in gold and silver in the form of a triple-naved basilica and decorated with relief figures depicting the life of Christ, the Apostles, and various Old Testament prophets. Across the front of the chancel are two rows of **choir stalls** ★ divided into richly carved partitions. The oak choir dates from 1310 and is the largest extant in Germany.

Surrounding the chancel are nine chapels, each containing important works of religious art. The Chapel of the Cross, beneath the organ loft, shelters the oldest full-size cross in the Occident, the painted, carved oak cross of Archbishop Gero (969–76). Directly across the chancel, behind the altar in Our Lady's Chapel, is the famous ***Altar of the City Patrons*** ★★★ painted by Stephan Lochner (1400–51). When closed, this tryptych masterpiece shows the *Annunciation,* and when opened, it reveals the *Adoration of the Magi* in the center, flanked by St. Ursula, the patron saint of Cologne, and St. Gereon.

English-language tours are given Monday to Saturday at 10:30am and 2:30pm, and Sunday at 2:30pm. German-language tours are conducted Monday to Saturday at 11am, 12:30, 2, and 3:30pm, and every Sunday at 2 and 3:30pm. Tours last about an hour and cost 4€ ($3.55) for adults and 1.50€ ($1.35) for children and students.

Domkloster. ✆ **0221/92584720.** Treasury and cathedral tower each 2.50€ ($2.25) adults, 1.50€ ($1.35) children. Cathedral itself is free. Cathedral daily 7am–7pm, except during religious services. Cathedral tower daily 9am–5pm. Treasury Mon–Sat 9am–5pm; Sun and holidays 12:30–5pm. U-Bahn: Hauptbahnhof.

**Museum für Angewandte Kunst (Museum of Applied Art)** This is a showcase for the arts and crafts of Germany dating from the Middle Ages, with the 20th century prominently featured. This museum is one of the best of its kind in Germany.

An der Rechtsschule. ✆ **0221/22123860.** Admission 4€ ($3.55) adults, 1.50€ ($1.35) children 6–12, free for children 5 and under. Tues–Sun 11am–5pm; Wed 11am–8pm. U-Bahn: Hauptbahnhof.

**Museum Ludwig** ★★★ This stunningly upgraded museum is the home of one of the world's largest collections of the works of Pablo Picasso, topped only by the Picassos in Paris and Barcelona. Irene Ludwig, widow of the late German art patron, Peter Ludwig, for whom the museum is named, donated 774 works of Picasso to the museum. The donation includes 49 unique works, 29 ceramics, 37 works in paper, 15 relief plates, and 681 graphic prints. Up to now, these works have been on loan to the museum.

In 1976, Ludwig first gave more than 300 works of art to Cologne to form the basis of this museum. Some of these paintings are the most celebrated and reproduced Picassos in the world, including *Harlequin with Folded Hands* from 1923 and the disturbingly forceful *Woman with Artichoke* from 1941.

The museum is also home to a great collection of modern art from Dalí to Lichtenstein and Warhol. The American Pop Art collection that also includes Roy Lichtenstein, Rauschenberg, and Jasper Johns, rivals the Guggenheim in New York. Our two favorites are Dalí's *Railway Station at Perpignan* and Ed Kienholz's *Portable War Memorial.*

Museum Ludwig is also the home of **Agfa-Historama,** which chronicles the art of photography for the past century and a half, with works by all the greats. This collection of historic photographs and cameras is the largest in the world.

Bischofsgartenstrasse 1. ✆ **0221/2212-2382.** www.museenkoeln.de/ludwig/. Admission 7.70€ ($6.90) adults, 4.10€ ($3.65) students and children. Mon 10am–8pm, Tues–Fri 10am–6pm, Sat–Sun 11am–6pm. U-Bahn: Hauptbahnhof.

**Museum Schnütgen** ★★ This is Cologne's best collection of religious art and sculpture. It's all displayed in an original setting, St. Cecilia's Church (Cäcilienkirche), which is a fine example of Rhenish-Romanic architecture. The works displayed include several medieval ivories, woodwork, and tapestries, including one showing rosy-cheeked Magi bringing gifts to the Christ child (1470). There are also many Madonnas, of all sizes and descriptions, carved in stone, wood, and metal.

Cäcilienstrasse 29. ✆ **0221/221-23-620.** Admission 2.50€ ($2.25) adults, 1.50€ ($1.35) children. Tues–Fri 10am–5pm; Sat–Sun 11am–5pm. U-Bahn: Neumarkt.

**Römisch-Germanisches Museum (Roman-Germanic Museum)** The most compelling treasure in this museum is the Dionysos-Mosaik, from the 3rd century A.D., discovered in 1941 when workers were digging an air-raid shelter. This elaborately decorated and colored mosaic was once the floor of an *oecus* (main room) of a large Roman villa. It depicts Dionysus, the Greek god of wine. On the second floor of the museum is an unusual collection of Roman antiquities found in the Rhine Valley, including Roman glass from the 1st through 4th centuries, as well as pottery, marble busts, and jewelry.

Roncalliplatz 4. ✆ **0221/2212-4428.** Admission 2.55€ ($2.50) adults, 1.30€ ($1.25) children, free for children 5 and under. Tues–Sun 10am–5pm. U-Bahn: Hauptbahnhof.

**Wallraf-Richartz Museum/Foundation Corboud** ★★★ This is Cologne's oldest museum, begun in the 19th century with a collection of Gothic works by local artists, still one of the main attractions. The Wallraf-Richartz shows art from 1300 to 1900 A.D. Several well-known works from churches are exhibited as well, including the triptych of the *Madonna with the Vetch Flower* (1410). The painting collection represents nearly every period and school, from the Dutch and Flemish masters to the French impressionists. Stephan Lochner's *Madonna in the Rose Garden* (1450) is a fine example of the German Gothic style as are his frightening *Last Judgment* and Dürer's *Drummer and Piper.* The museum also houses Germany's largest collection of works by Wilhelm Leibl as well as paintings by Max Ernst, Paul Klee, and Ernst Ludwig Kirchner.

Martinstrasse 39. ✆ **0221/221-21119.** Admission 5.10€ ($4.55) adults, 2.60€ ($2.30) children and students. Tues 10am–8pm; Wed–Fri 10am–6pm; Sat–Sun 11am–6pm. U-Bahn: Hauptbahnhof.

## CHURCHES

Cologne has 12 important Romanesque churches, all within the medieval city wall. Devastated during World War II, they have been almost completely restored and again recapture Cologne's rich early medieval heritage. **St. Panteleon,** Am Pantaleonsberg 2 (U-Bahn: Poststrasse), built in 980, has the oldest cloister arcades remaining in Germany. **St. Gereon,** Gereonsdriesch 2–4 (U-Bahn: Christophestrasse), is elliptically shaped, with a decagon between its two towers. It contains the tomb of St. Gereon and other martyrs, and its crypt still has mosaics from the 11th century. **St. Severin,** Severinstrasse (U-Bahn: Severinstrasse), originated as a late–4th century memorial chapel; the present church dates from the 13th to the 15th centuries.

The church of **St. Ursula** (1135), Ursulaplatz (U-Bahn: Hauptbahnhof), is on the site of a Roman graveyard. Legend has it that St. Ursula, patron saint of Cologne, was martyred in Cologne with her 11,000 virgin companions in about 451. **St. Maria im Kapitol,** Kasinostrasse 6 (U-Bahn: Heumarkt), is on the site where Plectrudis, wife of Pippin (dim figures of the Dark Ages, who are significant because Plectrudis in one of the few women who had political power in the area, due to being the daughter of an important land owner), built a church in the early 8th century. The cloverleaf choir of the present structure was modeled on that of the Church of the Nativity in Bethlehem. **St. Aposteln,** Neumarkt 30 (U-Bahn: Neumarkt), and **Gross St. Martin,** on the Rhine in the Altstadt (U-Bahn: Heumarkt), also have the cloverleaf choir design.

**St. Georg,** Am Waidmarkt (U-Bahn: Poststrasse), the only remaining Romanesque pillared basilica in the Rhineland, contains an impressive forked crucifix from the early 14th century. **St. Cecilia's (Cäcilienkirche),** Cäcilienstrasse 29 (U-Bahn: Neumarkt), is the site of the Schnütgen Museum for sacred art (see above). **St. Andreas,** near the cathedral (U-Bahn: Hauptbahnhof), contains a wealth of late Romanesque architectural sculpture. The remaining two Romanesque churches are on the Rhine: **St. Kunibert,** Kunibertskloster 2 (U-Bahn: Hauptbahnhof), and **St. Maria Lyskirchen,** Am Lyskirchen 12 (U-Bahn: Heumarkt), both of 13th-century origin.

## SHOPPING

Shopping is not taken quite as seriously here as in Düsseldorf—with one exception. Increasingly, Cologne is emerging as the capital of contemporary art in Germany, and the city lately seems to be brimming with galleries.

### *Fun Fact* Cologne Water

The very word *cologne* has been a part of the common language since the introduction to the world many years ago of the scented water called *eau de cologne (Kölnisch Wasser).* **Eau de Cologne,** Glockengasse 4711 (✆ **0221/9-25-04-50;** U-Bahn: Neumarkt), sells the scented water first developed at this address by Italian chemist Giovanni Maria Farina in 1709. Originally employed to hide the stench of aristocrats who rarely bathed, cologne is now simply a sweet-smelling tradition and a cheap way to take home a little piece of Cologne. The smallest 25-milliliter flacon costs a mere 4€ ($3.55).

**ART GALLERIES** We'll recommend the major ones to get you started, but there are many more than we can list here. The gallery that launched Cologne as a European art mecca is **Galerie der Spiegel,** Richartstrasse 10 (✆ **0221/25-55-52;** U-Bahn: Hauptbahnhof). Established amid the ruins of the wartime bombings in 1945, it was a focal point for the contemporary art that evolved from the shattered dreams of the postwar years. Since then, it has managed to hold its own against rising competition. You might want to walk along **St. Apernstrasse** (U-Bahn: Neumarkt), where many leading art galleries are located. **Galerie Greve,** Drususgasse 1-5 (✆ **0221/2-57-10-12;** U-Bahn: Dom Hauptbahnhof), changes its exhibits every season, specializing in international postwar avant-garde painting. Another excellent gallery for both modern and experimental art is **Galerie Werner,** Gertrudenstrasse 24 (✆ **0221/9-25-46-20;** U-Bahn: Neumarkt), which sells contemporary European, particularly German, painters.

**OUTDOOR MARKETS** If you're interested in the kitschy artifacts that pour out of estate sales, be alert to the flea markets in Cologne's inner city. The most appealing are held within the **Alter Markt** (U-Bahn: Hauptbahnhof), at irregular intervals throughout the year, usually at least once a month (ask at the tourist office). More regular are the outdoor food and vegetable markets, the largest of which is held on the **Wilhelmsplatz,** in the Nippes district (U-Bahn: Florastrasse), Saturdays 8am to at least 2pm.

## WHERE TO STAY

### VERY EXPENSIVE

**Dom Hotel** ★★★ This is an old-world hotel right across from the cathedral. Few hotels in Germany have been so consistently awarded the official government five stars or maintained such a standard of excellence. We prefer the Excelsior Hotel Ernst (see below), but there are many clients who will stay nowhere else but the Dom. The hotel's location, in the shadow of the cathedral, assures it a steady clientele. In summer, the side portico overlooking the square is filled with cafe tables. Rooms have all modern conveniences and an interesting collection of period furniture. Try for one of the corner units, which are the most spacious and have the best views. All units contain neatly kept bathrooms containing shower-tub combinations. To reach the hotel by car, drive into the square to the side of the Dom's flying buttresses.

Domkloster 2A, 50667 Köln. ✆ **800/543-4300** in the U.S., or 0221/2-02-40. Fax 0221/2-02-44-44. www.lemeridien-hotels.com. 125 units. 424€–443€ ($378.65–$395.60) double. AE, DC, MC, V. Parking 15€ ($13.40). U-Bahn: Hauptbahnhof. **Amenities:** Restaurant; lounge; fitness center; Jacuzzi; sauna; massage; room service; babysitting; laundry/dry cleaning. *In room:* TV, minibar, hair dryer.

**Excelsior Hotel Ernst** ★★★ In spite of increased competition, notably from the Hyatt Regency, Cologne's longtime prestige hotel continues to hold its own as the premier address in Cologne. Founded in 1863, the hotel is known for its Empire-style lobby. The public areas contain old-master paintings, including an original work by Van Dyck. The breakfast room has a Gobelin tapestry. Rooms are spacious with bathrooms containing shower-tub combinations.

Domplatz, 50667 Köln. ✆ **0221/27-01.** Fax 0221/13-51-50. www.excelsiorhotelernst.de. 152 units. 280€–380€ ($250.05–$339.35) double; from 515€ ($459.90) suite. Rates include continental breakfast. AE, DC, MC, V. Parking 18€ ($16.05). U-Bahn: Hauptbahnhof. **Amenities:** Restaurant; bar; fitness center; whirlpool; steam room; hairdresser; room service; babysitting; laundry/dry cleaning. *In room:* A/C, TV, minibar, hair dryer, safe.

**Grandhotel Schloss Bensberg** ★★★ The most romantic place to stay in the area is this restored baroque castle constructed 300 years ago at a point 14km (9 miles) from Cologne. Crowning a hill, it offers panoramic views of the city. This is life on a grand scale, fit for a German prince—indeed, it was a prince, Jan Wellem, who built the castle in the first place.

After lavish renovations, it has been successfully transformed and elegantly furnished with all the modern amenities. Rooms vary in size—after all, this is a castle—but all of them are handsomely equipped with such extras as three phones. Our favorite is number 307 with its panorama of Cologne and its black marble bathroom with Jacuzzi. All of the accommodations come with modern tub-and-shower combos. The atmosphere is more intimate and friendly than some drafty castle might suggest. It features special grace notes such as a collection of 10,000 wines in the cellar, a state-of-the-art spa, and 66,000 lights around the pool imitating a night sky.

Even if you're not a guest, consider a reservation for lunch for dinner. Your choices are the Vendôme, run by a two-star Michelin chef, Joachim Wissler, with a formal French cuisine; the Enoteca, a rustic Italian bistro with freshly made pasta, or Jan Wellem, with its finely honed international cuisine.

Kadettenstrasse, 51429 Bergisch Gladbach. ✆ **02204/420.** Fax 02204/42888. www.schlossbensberg.com. 120 units. 250€–310€ ($223.25–$276.85) double, from 410€ ($366.15) suite. AE, DC, MC, V. **Amenities:** 3 restaurants; bar; pool; business center; room service; babysitting; laundry/valet. *In room:* TV, minibar, hair dryer, safe.

**Hotel im Wasserturm** ★★★ There's nothing quite like this place in all of Germany. The tallest water tower in Europe was converted into an 11-story deluxe hotel-in-the-round, at a cost of $75 million. Lying southwest of the city center, a mile from the Cathedral, this is one of the most avant-garde and daring reincarnations of an existing structure in all of Germany. If you think living in a water tower is not your idea of a good time, check it out anyway. The design and decor are ingenious, from the Warhol paintings to the tiled lobby with stunning dark woodwork. The structure is 19th century, but everything else is contemporary. Rooms come in unusual configurations, but each is cleverly designed for comfort, flair, and convenience. Original art and exquisite carpeting fill the spacious rooms, and the bathrooms are deluxe, tiled in mosaics and containing such extras as triptych mirrors, robes, and, deep tubs with power showers.

Kaygasse 2, Köln 50676. ✆ **0221/20080.** Fax 0221/2008888. www.hotel-im-wasserturm.de. 88 units. 200€–305€ ($178.60–$272.35) double; from 350€ ($312.55) suite. AE, DC, MC, V. **Amenities:** Restaurant; bar; room service; babysitting; laundry/dry cleaning. *In room:* A/C, TV, minibar, hair dryer, safe.

**Hyatt Regency** ★★ This is the most spectacular and up-to-date hotel in Cologne. It's an architectural triumph: a mixture of reddish granite, huge expanses of glass, and a facade that combines Art Deco and neo-Aztec styles. The lobby is dramatic, with a 4m (12-ft.) waterfall. Rooms are stylishly furnished and come with walk-in closets. Many have views of the Rhine and the cathedral on the other side. Bathrooms have private phones, deep tubs with showers, robes, and deluxe toiletries. To get to the Alstadt from here, you can take the Hohenzollernbrücke, a bridge across the Rhine.

Kennedy-Ufer 2A (across the Rhine from the Alstadt, a short walk from the train station), 50679 Cologne-Deutz. ✆ **800/228-1234** in the U.S., or 0221/8281234. Fax 0221/8281370. www.hyattregency.de. 305 units. 190€–390€ ($169.65–$348.25) double; from 310€ ($276.85) suite. AE, DC, MC, V. Parking 13€ ($11.60). Tram: 1 or 2. **Amenities:** 2 restaurants; bar; pool; fitness center; whirlpool; sauna; solarium; steam room; room service; massage; babysitting; laundry/dry cleaning. *In room:* A/C, TV, dataport, video games, minibar, coffeemaker, hair dryer, safe.

## MODERATE

**Antik-Hotel Bristol** ★★ The Bristol is exceptional in that each of its rooms is furnished with genuine antiques, either regal or rustic. There's a different antique bed in almost every room, ranging from French baroque and rococo to something reminiscent of High Rhenish ecclesiastical art; the oldest four-poster dates from 1742. Bathrooms include shower-tub combinations. The Bristol stands in a little park, with lots of greenery, flowers, and fountains. It's near an U-Bahn stop and within walking distance of the cathedral.

Kaiser-Wilhelm-Ring 48, 50672 Köln. ✆ **0221/12-01-95.** Fax 0221/13-14-95. www.antik-hotel-bristol.com. 44 units. 110€–174€ ($98.25–$155.40) double; 195€–245€ ($174.15–$218.80) suite. Rates include buffet breakfast. AE, DC, MC, V. Parking 13€ ($11.60). Closed Dec 23–Jan 2. U-Bahn: Christophstrasse. **Amenities:** Breakfast room; bar; room service; massage; babysitting; laundry/dry cleaning. *In room:* TV, minibar, hair dryer, safe.

**Hopper Hotel St. Antonius** Named after a statue of St. Antonius that stands in this hotel's garden (the owners bought it during a holiday in Portugal), this hotel rises five very modern floors from a location in the heart of Cologne's historic core. You'll register in a lobby sheathed with slabs of gray stone and floored with stone mosaics. The same colors are repeated within the very contemporary-looking bedrooms, with wooden floors, marble-sheathed bathrooms with tub and shower, and teakwood furniture. This is a well-selected and popular choice with an articulate staff and lots of comfort and style.

Dagobertstrasse 32, 50668 Köln. ✆ **0221/1-66-00.** Fax 0221/166-0166. www.hopper.de. 54 units. 140€–160€ ($125–$142.90) double, 210€ ($187.55) suite. AE, DC, MC, V. U-Bahn: Ebertplatz or Dom/Hauptbahnhof. **Amenities:** Restaurant; bar; room service (during opening hours of restaurant) laundry. *In room:* TV, dataport, minibar, safe.

## INEXPENSIVE

**Brandenburger Hof** In this family-style hotel, all rooms are small, warm, and equipped with running water, and there's a well-kept bathroom with combination tub and shower on each floor. A full breakfast, including orange juice and eggs, is served in a cozy room or, in summer, in the garden. The hotel is about 3 blocks from the river and within walking distance of the cathedral.

Brandenburgerstrasse 2–4 (behind the Hauptbahnhof), 50668 Köln. ✆ **0221/12-28-89.** Fax 0221/13-53-04. www.brandenburgerhof.de. 45 units, 28 with bath. 50€ ($44.65) double without bath; 70€ ($62.50) double with bath; 72€ ($64.30) triple without bath; 85€ ($75.90) quad without bath. Rates include continental breakfast. No credit cards. Free parking. U-Bahn: Hauptbahnhof. **Amenities:** Breakfast room; lounge.

**Coellner Hof** *Value* Set within a 10-minute walk north of the cathedral, this six-story, turn-of-the-century building houses a well-maintained, comfortable hotel that has received well-deserved praise from several readers. Public areas are distinguished looking, and some, including the dining room, are richly paneled. Each room is decorated in a conservative, solid style that evokes a baronial German home (*landhaus*). The less recently renovated of the bedrooms evoke the same *landhaus* style, although—at least within the bedrooms—that style is slowly being replaced with a crisp, comfortable, and clean modern international style that's soothing in its use of neutral, monochromatic colors and dark hardwoods. Bathrooms are larger than the norm in government-rated three-star hotels, and each comes with a small, tiled bathroom with tub-and-shower combination.

Hansaring 100, D-50670 Köln. ✆ **0221/16-660.** Fax 0221/1666-166. www.coellnerhof.de. 79 units. 105€ ($93.75) double. On selected weekends (Fri–Sun nights, inclusive) doubles 76€ ($67.85). Rates include breakfast. AE, DC, MC, V. U-Bahn: Ebertplatz. **Amenities:** Bar; restaurant; receptionist; laundry. *In room:* TV, hairdryer.

## WHERE TO DINE

### VERY EXPENSIVE

**Hanse Stube** ★★ FRENCH One of Cologne's best restaurants, Hanse Stube offers top-drawer cuisine and service. The food here is better than that served in the dining room of the Dom Hotel. Prodigious talent and imagination go into shaping the cuisine. Of the chef's appetizers, none are better than the salmon on truffled potato salad blended harmoniously with a Pommery mustard sauce. Unusual and tasty main courses include breast of guinea fowl stuffed with herbs, or medallions of venison with savoy cabbage and a sweet corn potato rösti (hash brown potatoes).

On the ground floor of the Excelsior Hotel Ernst, Domplatz. ✆ **0221/27-01.** Reservations recommended. Main courses 28€–35€ ($25–$31.25); fixed-price lunch 35€ ($31.25). AE, DC, MC, V. Daily noon–3pm and 6–11pm. U-Bahn: Hauptbahnhof.

### EXPENSIVE

**Börsen Restaurant Maître** ★★★ CONTINENTAL/MEDITERRANEAN This busy place, which serves Cologne's financial community, offers not only great food but also a glimpse of everyday Cologne life, particularly at lunch. Seasonally adjusted fixed-price meals feature classic, conservative dishes made from fresh ingredients. The restaurant offers a choice of different dining areas. In the Börsen-Stube, which has the same hours as the main restaurant, main courses range from 12.50€ to 21€ ($11.15–$18.75). The Börsen Schanke, open Monday to Friday 10am to 9:30pm, is a beer restaurant that serves local dishes, sometimes on its terrace. Meals range from 8€ to 18€ ($7.15–$16.05).

Unter Sachsenhausen 10–26 (near the stock exchange, a short walk from the cathedral). ✆ **0221/13-30-21.** Reservations recommended. Main courses 25€–30€ ($22.35–$26.80); fixed-price menu 42€–80€ ($37.50–$71.45). AE, DC, MC, V. Mon–Fri noon–2:30pm; Mon–Sat 6–11pm. U-Bahn: Hauptbahnhof.

**Le Moissonnier** ★ FRENCH This charming brasserie is steeped in the aesthetic and culinary traditions of the early 20th century, with mirrors, cove moldings, dark paneling against ocher-colored walls, bentwood chairs, and tiled floors. Here you'll enjoy the carefully crafted cuisine of the restaurant's namesake, Vincent Moissonnier. Menu items change with the season and the inspiration of the chef but are likely to include risotto with almonds and truffle oil; carpaccio of turbot; and a house specialty that combines braised filet of goose breast with tarragon and strips of goose liver, and is served with prosciutto-studded mashed potatoes. Salads and fresh fish are all delicious, as are the sauerkraut and a Toulouse-inspired version of cassoulet loaded with pork, small sausages, and white beans.

Krefelder Strasse 25. ✆ **0221/72-94-79.** Reservations recommended. Main courses 20€–29€ ($17.85–$25.90); midday plat du jour 12.50€ ($11.15). V. Tues–Sat noon–1:45pm and 7–10:45pm. U-Bahn: Hansaring.

### MODERATE

**Brauhaus im Walfisch** GERMAN/FRENCH Brauhaus im Walfisch isn't easy to find, but it's a good choice for atmospheric dining. This step-gabled inn with a black-and-white timbered facade dates from 1626. More importantly, it serves excellent food. There are many German specialties, often influenced by French cuisine. You might try the sole meunière or venison for two.

Salzgasse 13 (on a narrow street set back from the Rhine, near Heumarkt [Haymarket]). ✆ **0221/2-57-78-79.** Reservations required. Main courses 9.80€–16.50€ ($8.75–$14.75). AE, DC, MC, V. Daily 11am–midnight. U-Bahn: Heumarkt.

**Das Kleine Stapelhäuschen** ★ GERMAN This is one of the most popular wine taverns in Cologne. It's housed in an office building and opens onto the old fish-market square and the Rhine. The two-story dining room and service bar are antique in style. Provincial cabinets hold a varied wine collection. A wide cantilevered wooden staircase leads to mezzanine tables. Though the wine is the main reason for coming here (it's that special), the cuisine is also excellent. A specialty is Rheinischer sauerbraten with almonds, raisins, and potato dumplings. Desserts are appropriately luscious.

Fischmarkt 1–3 (a few minutes from the cathedral). ✆ **0221/2-57-78-62.** Reservations recommended. Main courses 7.80€–25€ ($6.95–$22.35). AE, MC, V. Daily noon–11:30pm. Closed Dec 22–Jan 10. U-Bahn: Heumarkt.

**Ratskeller** GERMAN This busy and very traditional restaurant occupies a trio of dining rooms in the cellar of Cologne's landmark city hall. It welcomes the city's political, business, and journalistic communities during the lunch hour. Menu items are conservative German, particularly Rhenish (from the Rheinland region), specialties and include generous portions of sauerbraten, *Schweinshaxen* (roast leg of pork), and *Kalbshaxen* (roast leg of veal). Any of these might be preceded with steaming bowls of Leberknoedel (liver dumplings) soup or goulash, salads, and marinated herring in cream sauce with onions. During warm weather, tables spill out into a courtyard that's protected from the roar of traffic. Look for a lavish lunch buffet every Sunday and a dinner buffet every Saturday. The price of each of those is 22€ ($19.65) per person.

Rathausplatz 1 (in the Rathaus). ✆ **0221/2-57-69-29.** Reservations recommended. Main courses 13€–24€ ($11.60–$21.45). AE, DC, MC, V. Mon–Sat noon–11pm; Sun 11am–3pm. U-Bahn: Heumarkt.

## COLOGNE AFTER DARK

One of Germany's major cultural centers, Cologne offers a variety of fine arts and nightlife options. Many clubs stay open into the early morning hours. You can pick up a copy of *Stadt Revue* or *Kölner* for 2€ ($1.80) each to find out what's happening in the city. If you're interested in attending a sports, entertainment-related, or cultural venue within Cologne, you can always head to the box office. More convenient, however, is the well-orchestrated services of **Köln-Ticket,** Roncalliplatz 4, next to the cathedral (✆ **0221/28-01;** U-Bahn: Hauptbahnhof), which has many different event tickets for sale. Depending on the ticket, the service charge for this convenience is around 4€ ($3.55).

### THE PERFORMING ARTS

The most impressive grouping of theater space in Cologne is within the **Schauspielhaus,** Offenbachplatz (✆ **0221/221-28-400;** U-Bahn: Neumarkt), the site

## Beer Taverns

Some of the best inexpensive places to eat (and drink) in Cologne are beer taverns. **Alt-Köln am Dom,** Trankgasse 7–9 (✆ **0221/13-74-71;** U-Bahn: Hauptbahnhof), is a re-creation of a group of old taverns, including one done in the Gothic style. You can come here for a beer or a good hot meal. Some of the upper-floor tables provide box-seat views of the cathedral. On the face of the building is a mechanical clock; when it chimes the hours, a parade of figures emerges and disappears. The favorite main dishes include Wiener schnitzel, *Schweinshaxen* (roast leg of pork), and a platter of sausage specialties with spicy mustard. Try also the braised beef Rhineland-style. Main courses cost 7.50€ to 16€ ($6.70–$14.30). American Express, Diners Club, MasterCard, and Visa are accepted. It's open daily 11am to midnight (kitchen closes at 11:30pm).

Come to **Bräuhaus Sion,** Unter Taschenmacher 5 (✆ **0221/2-57-85-40;** U-Bahn: Heumarkt; tram: 5 or 7), if you want a traditional local Bräuhaus where the beer is good, the wood paneling a little smoky with time and frequent polishing, and the food portions inexpensive and generous. The main courses are traditional and filling Westphalian fare, such as pigs' knuckles with sauerkraut and the inevitable bratwurst with savoy cabbage and fried potatoes. But the best traditional dish to order is *kölsch Kaviar* (blood sausage with onion rings). You can also ask for *halve Hahn,* which translates as "half rooster." On tap is the famed local beer, Kölsch, a light brew with an alcohol content of about 3%. It's served in *Stangen* (rods) about 7 inches tall. Main courses are 6.50€ to

of three theaters, each with its own agenda and schedule. Performances range from the avant-garde to the classic. **Der Keller,** Kleingedankstrasse 6 (✆ **0221/31-80-59;** U-Bahn: Ulrepsorte), hosts contemporary plays, usually in German, and dance performances. Tickets are 10€ to 26€ ($8.95–$23.20) each; call either the number listed above or **Köln-Ticket** (✆ **0221/28-01**) for schedules and show times.

If your German is fluent and you're interested in absorbing some of the counterculture trends sweeping the country's literature and politics scene, you might be interested in the **Theater Kaiserhof,** Hohenzollenring (✆ **0221/139-2772;** U-Bahn: Rudolfplatz). Performances are sometimes comic, sometimes obscure, sometimes trenchant, sometimes grotesque, sometimes satirical, and often a combination of all of the above. Most shows begin at 8pm. Tickets cost 22€ to 54€ ($19.65–$48.20).

**Kölner Philharmonie** This architectural showcase was completed during the late 1980s. The concert hall features a soaring roof, enviable acoustics, and some of the finest classical music along the country's western tier. The building is the home of two separate orchestras, the **Gürzenich Kölner Philharmoniker** and the **Westdeutscher Rundfunk Orchestra.** Pop and jazz programs are also presented. Performances are given almost every night at 8pm, except Monday. Bischofsgartenstrasse 1. ✆ **0221/20-40-80.** Tickets 4.10€–66.45€ ($4–$65). AE, DC, MC, V. U-Bahn: Hauptbahnhof.

17.50€ ($5.80–$15.65). No credit cards are accepted. It's open daily 10am to 11:30pm, but closed Christmas Eve.

**Früh am Dom** ★, Am Hof 12–14 (✆ **0221/261-30;** U-Bahn: Hauptbahnhof), is the best all-around choice for economy and hearty portions. Well-cooked meals are served on scrubbed wooden tables, with a different German specialty offered every day of the week. They have a menu for tourists, in English. A favorite dish is a Cologne specialty of cured smoked knuckle of pork cooked in root-vegetable broth and served with sauerkraut and potato purée; apple purée and dumplings go well with this dish. Also sample a glass of Früh-Kölsch—a top-fermented brew with a dry, inimitable taste and a 1,000-year-old tradition. In summer, there's a beer garden. Meals cost 12€ to 30€ ($10.70–$26.80). No credit cards are accepted. The tavern is open 8am to midnight; hot meals are served 11:30am to 11:30pm.

The venerable, beer-soaked **Haus Töller,** Weyerstrasse 96 (✆ **0221/2-40-91-87;** U-Bahn: Barbarossaplatz), a 15-minute walk south of the cathedral, has thrived as a brew house since 1876 by selling copious portions of two-fisted Teutonic food and foaming mugs of a local brew, Seon. No one will mind if you just want to spend a few hours drinking (the beer is very, very good), but if you want a meal, menu items include a local specialty, *Schinkenhempsel* (roast leg of pork), served with sauerkraut and roast potatoes. Main courses are 9.50€ to 17€ ($8.50–$15.20); a mug of Seon will set you back .60€ (55¢). No credit cards are accepted. It's open Monday to Saturday 5pm to midnight.

**Oper der Städt Köln** This is the leading opera house of the Rhineland, known for its exciting productions and innovative repertory of classical and contemporary works. Performances take place almost every evening except Tuesday, usually at 7:30pm. Dance programs are also presented. The box office is open 9am to 6pm Monday to Friday and Saturday 9am to 2pm. Offenbachplatz. ✆ **0221/22128400.** Tickets 12€–60€ ($10.70–$53.60). AE, DC, MC, V. U-Bahn/S-Bahn: Neumarkt.

## THE CLUB & MUSIC SCENE

**DANCE CLUBS** Live bands (Tues, Thurs, and Sat) and DJs (Mon, Wed, Fri, and Sun) play for dancers at **MTC,** Zulpicher Strasse 10 (✆ **0221/240-41-88;** U-Bahn: Zulpicherplatz), open 10pm to 3am. Cover is 4€ to 10€ ($3.55–$8.95).

One of the city's most dramatic and surreal nightlife options is **E-Werk,** Schanzenstrasse 28 (✆ **0221/96-27-90;** U-Bahn: Keupstrasse), a combination of a disco and a large concert hall. It's housed within what used to be an electrical power plant. Recorded music alternates with live acts. The Backstreet Boys have played here. It's open every Friday and Saturday night at 10pm.

**JAZZ CLUBS** **Klimperkasten** (also known as **Papa Joe's Biersalon**), Alter Markt 50–52 (✆ **0221/258-2132;** U-Bahn: Hauptbahnhof), is a small and intimate jazz and piano bar open from 11am to 2am, with live music every night beginning around 8pm. The jazz is also hot at **Papa Joe's Jazzlokal,** Buttermarkt 37 (✆ **0221/257-7931;** U-Bahn: Heumarkt). Sunday, when the music begins at 3:30pm and lasts until 1am, is the best day to come. The club is also open for live jazz Monday to Saturday 7pm to 2am. Surprisingly, there's never a cover.

**LIVE-MUSIC CLUBS** Several times a week, usually at 8pm on Wednesday and Saturday, but with frequent exceptions, the **Underground,** Vogelsanger Strasse 200 (✆ **0221/54-39-66;** U-Bahn: Venloerstrasse Gürtel), hosts rock groups that include relatively unknown local acts as well as high-profile bands. There's a disco on other nights. This place, in the words of a spokesperson, is "very alternative. If you're 40, you're probably too old to appreciate the music here." A food stand inside prepares pastas, burgers, and breakfast items for late-night (or early morning) hunger pangs. Cover is 6€ to 10€ ($5.35–$8.95).

**Prime Club** (formerly known as Luxor), Luxemburgstrasse 40 (✆ **0221/924-460;** U-Bahn: Barbarossa Platz), offers some kind of live music most nights of the week, except Monday. You'll never know what to expect here. The management books unknown, inexperienced bands, some of whom show great promise. Hours vary, but usually music starts at around 9pm. Cover ranges from 5€ to 15€ ($4.45–$13.40).

A final contender in Cologne's live-music sweepstakes is **Kantine,** Kempenorstrasse 135 (✆ **0221/9728636;** U-Bahn: Lohsestrasse), whose musical style, hours, and free-form scheduling policies are similar to those at Prime Club. Kantine also has a beer garden. Cover ranges from 5€ to 15€ ($4.45–$13.40).

## BARS

A 110-year-old bar, **Päffgen Bräuhaus,** Friesenstrasse 64–66 (✆ **0221/13-54-61;** U-Bahn: Friesenplatz), serves its Kölsch brand of beer, along with regional cuisine. Seating is available indoors and out. Open daily 10am to midnight. **Altstadt Päffgen,** Heumarkt 62 (✆ **0221/2-57-77-65;** U-Bahn: Heumarkt), also serves the local brew with German dishes. Open Tuesday to Sunday noon to midnight. **Broadway,** Ehrenstrasse 11 (✆ **0221/92-57-57-20;** U-Bahn: Neumarkt), is a cafe and bar associated with an arts-conscious movie theater. It's decorated with playbills and memorabilia from theater productions of yesteryear. Drinks, coffee, tea, sandwiches, and simple platters of snack food are served. Open daily 10am to 1am.

In a somewhat different setting is **Museum Pub,** Zulpicher Platz 9 (✆ **0221/23-20-98;** U-Bahn: Zulpicherplatz), which sells foaming mugs of beer to thirsty students. Rock and punk music are usually blaring from the stereo. This place might remind you of student dives in the Latin Quarter of Paris. Open Sunday to Thursday 6pm to 1am, and Friday and Saturday 6pm till 3am.

Students who have rediscovered the styles of the 1960s and 1970s lounge about amid a decor of lava lamps, futuristic televisions, and other memorabilia at **Hallmackenreuthur,** Brusseler Platz 9 (✆ **0221/51-79-70;** U-Bahn: Rudolfplatz). This is a place to drink, eat a late breakfast (until 4pm), or have a plate of pasta (6–11pm). It's open daily 11am to 1am. A holdover from Cologne's leftist days is **Hotelux,** Von Sandt Platz 10 (✆ **0221/241136**). Both its food and scarlet decor are self-consciously Soviet. You can eat platters of Russian food, drink Russian beer or more than two-dozen brands of Russian vodka, and sit within a garden whose greenery is thankfully apolitical. It's open daily 6pm to 1am. The most sophisticated rendezvous for hip straights and a few gays in Cologne today is called **Gloria,** Apostelnstrasse 11 (✆ **0221/254433;** U-Bahn: Neumarkt). If there's music playing, there's a cover of 5€ ($4.45). Open Sunday to Thursday 9am to 1am, Friday and Saturday 9am to 3am.

### GAY NIGHTLIFE

Cologne offers more diversions and distractions for gay men and women than any other city in the Rhineland. Head either to the Marienplatz area or the "Bermuda Triangle" (see below). A good gay bar for men and women is **Quo Vadis Pub,** near Marienplatz at Pipinstrasse 7 (✆ **0221/258-1414;** U-Bahn: Heumarkt), open daily noon to midnight during the week and 11am to 1am on the weekend. Another gay bar in the Marienplatz area is **Chains,** Stephansstrasse 4 (✆ **0221/23-87-30;** U-Bahn: Neumarkt), open 10pm to 2 or 3am. Also see the listing for Gloria, above.

If you want to do as the Kölners do, consider a walk through what locals call **"the Bermuda Triangle,"** formed by the locations of the three bar/clubs listed below. Visited as an ensemble, they provide plenty of insight into the lifestyle of the gay Rhineland. The first is **Schampanja,** Mauritiuswall 43 (✆ **0221/240-95-44;** U-Bahn: Neumarkt), a small pub that sometimes books live bands (often punk). Nearby, along the same street, is **The Park,** Mauritiuswall 84 (✆ **0221/21-33-57;** U-Bahn: Neumarkt), a cafe-style rendezvous point where table-hopping is a way of life. It's open daily 8am to 3am, but gay life is most visible in the late evening. A near neighbor at the opposite end of the Bermuda Triangle is **Café Huber,** Schaafenstrasse 51 (✆ **0221/240-6530;** U-Bahn: Zurticherplatz), where men drink, smoke, talk, and generally enjoy each other's company. It's open nightly 7pm until around 3am, depending on business.

Pay a visit to **Checkpoint,** Pipinstrasse 7 (✆ **0221/925-76868;** U-Bahn: Zurticherplatz), a privately owned dispenser of information that performs some of its functions in cooperation with the city's official tourism authorities. It's open daily 5 to 9pm and has a staff that's ready, willing, and able to tell you what's up in gay Cologne. They'll even sell you memorabilia.

The first weekend in July is devoted to the city's **Gay Pride Parade,** when as many as 500,000 spectators line the parade route for a glimpse of the floats and marchers. For specifics on the parade, contact Checkpoint (see above).

### DRAG ACTS

Cologne isn't prudish when it comes to admiring the female figure, even if that figure isn't biologically female. For the most sophisticated drag acts in the Rhineland, head for the **Bar of the Hotel Timp,** Heumarkt 25 (✆ **0221/258-1409;** U-Bahn: Heumarkt). This tiny spot opens at 10pm and presents drag acts every night from 1:30 to 4am (it stays open to 5 or 6am). The cover of 8€ to 13€ ($7.15–$11.60) gets you views of such camp heroines as the divine Marlene Dietrich, several European starlets, and even Leni Riefenstahl, the controversial *Wünderkind* of German movies during the Hitler regime. Those who want a good table should get here early. The Hotel Timp's most appealing competitor is **Star-Treff,** Alte Wallgasse (✆ **0221/25-50-63;** U-Bahn: Friesenplatz), which offers at least one, and sometimes two, shows a night, usually beginning at 7:45pm and 10:45pm, and stays open to 4am. Call in advance for the schedule. Cover is 8€ to 11€ ($7.15–$9.80).

## 10 Düsseldorf ★

40km (25 miles) N of Köln, 230km (143 miles) NW of Frankfurt

Düsseldorf is a wealthy city—the richest in Germany. It's big and commercial, full of banks and industrial offices and skyscrapers, but it's also refreshingly clean. Düsseldorf got its start as a settlement on the right bank of the Rhine, but today it's spread out on both sides—the older part on the right and the modern, commercial, and industrial part on the left. Five bridges connect the two sections, the most impressive being the Oberkassel. Parks and esplanades line the riverbanks. After 85% of the right bank was destroyed in World War II, the city could easily have grown into just another ugly manufacturing town, but Düsseldorf followed a modern trend in reconstruction, and today it's the most elegant metropolis in the Rhine Valley.

## ESSENTIALS

**GETTING THERE** **By Plane** **Düsseldorf International Airport,** 6km (4 miles) north of the city, has regularly scheduled connections to 14 German, 47 European, and 132 international airports. You can fly from Frankfurt to Düsseldorf on Lufthansa in just 45 minutes or from Munich or Berlin in an hour. For flight information, call ✆ **0211/421-22-23.**

The airport is linked to the **GermanRail** network. Transfer to the Düsseldorf main rail station is via S-Bahn 7, offering service daily 4:03am to 12:30am, with trains every 20 minutes (trip time: 12 min.). One-way fare is 1.75€ ($1.55). For information, call ✆ **0211/3680596.** Regular airport buses also connect the airport with Bonn and Cologne. A taxi ride to central Düsseldorf takes about 20 to 30 minutes and costs from 15€ ($13.40), depending on traffic.

**By Train** The main train station, the **Düsseldorf Hauptbahnhof,** on Konrad-Adenauer-Platz in the southeastern sector, offers frequent connections to all major cities. The trip time to Frankfurt is about 2½ hours; to Munich, about 7 hours. For information, call ✆ **01805/99-66-33.** Düsseldorf also has extensive regional rail links; for information on regional trains or trams, call ✆ **0211/5-82-28.** Luggage-storage facilities are available at the Hauptbahnhof.

**By Bus** Access to Düsseldorf is a lot easier by rail than by bus. The region's largest carriers are **Bandroch GmbH** (✆ **0211/353-862**) and **Adorf GmbH** (✆ **0211/320-771**), most of whose buses service small towns within the Rhineland that don't necessarily have railway stations of their own. Buses usually pull into Düsseldorf at the northern edge of the Bahnhofplatz.

**By Car** Access to Düsseldorf is by the A3 Autobahn north and south or the A46 east and west.

**VISITOR INFORMATION** For information, go to the **Verkehrsverein,** Konrad-Adenauer-Platz (✆ **0211/17-20-20,** followed by 0 after the recorded message in German), opposite the railway station. It's open Monday to Saturday 8am to 8pm and Sunday and national holidays 4 to 8pm. The office also has a hotel reservations service, which charges a one-time booking fee of 3€ ($2.70), along with a deposit that equals the price of the first night's accommodation. For the tourist office's room reservation services, call ✆ **0211/172-0226** Monday to Saturday 8am to 8pm, Sunday 2 to 6pm.

**GETTING AROUND** Düsseldorf is a big, sprawling city, so you'll probably want to rely on public transportation. The city and environs are served by a network of **S-Bahn railways** that fan out to the suburbs, along with **buses, trams (Strassenbahn),** and a **U-Bahn** system. Ask at the tourist office (✆ **0211/17-20-20**) about purchasing a **Tagesnetzkarte,** a whole day visitor's ticket, for 5.60€ ($5.50).

Taxi meters begin at 2.60€ ($2.30), after which you'll be billed between 1.30€ and 1.50€ ($1.15–$1.35) per kilometer, depending on the time of day. To call for a taxi in Düsseldorf, dial ✆ **0211/3-33-33.**

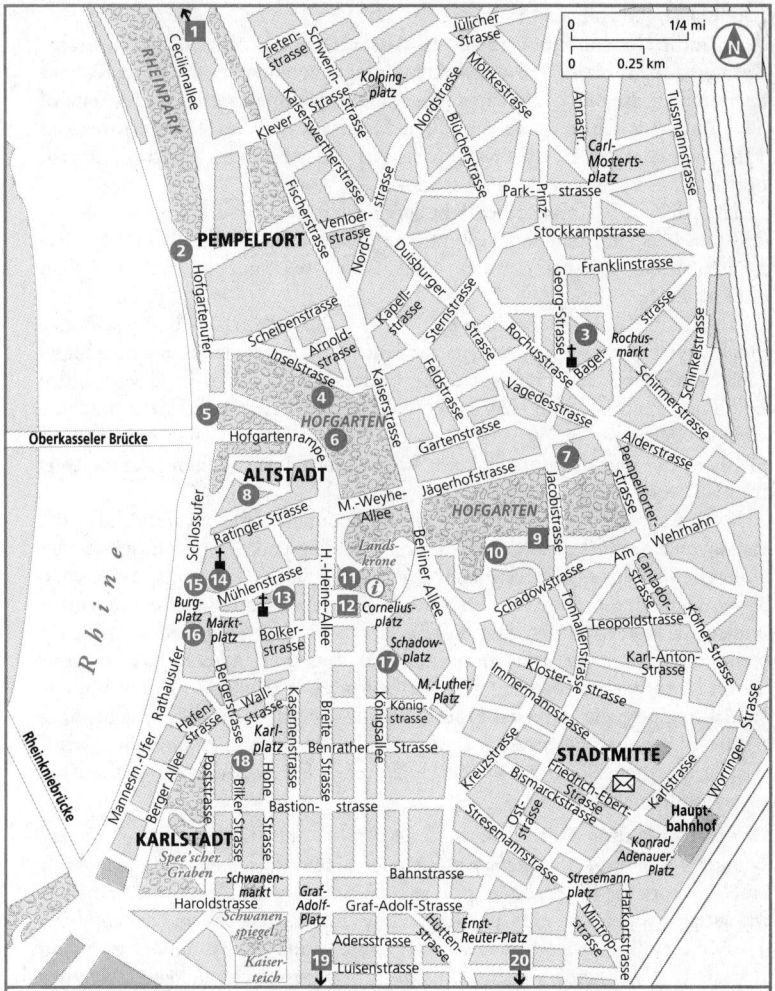

Church
Information
Post Office
S-Bahn

**ATTRACTIONS ●**

Deutsche Oper an Rhein **11**
Goethe-Museum Düsseldorf **7**
Heinrich-Heine-Institut **18**
Hofgarten **4**
Königsallee **17**
Kunst Halle Düsseldorf **8**
Kunstmuseum Düsseldorf **2**
K2O Kunstsammlung Am Grabbeplatz **8**
Rathaus (Town Hall) **16**
St. Andreas Church **13**
St. Lambertus Church **14**
St. Rochus Church **3**
Schauspielhaus **10**
Schlossturm **15**
Thyssen-House **6**
Tonhalle (Düsseldorf Symphony Orchestra) **5**

**ACCOMMODATIONS ■**

Ashley's Garden **1**
Fürstenhof **19**
Hotel Grosser Kurfürst **9**
Steigenberger Park-Hotel **12**
Wurms Hotel **20**

## EXPLORING THE CITY

As in most German cities, there's an **Altstadt,** with a marketplace, a Gothic **Rathaus (Town Hall),** and a few old buildings and churches. Near the Rathaus on Burgplatz are two of the city's most famous landmarks, the twisted spire of **St. Lambertus Church** and the round **Schlossturm (Castle Tower),** both of 13th-century origin. A short walk to the east takes you to **St. Andreas Church,** one of the most important in Düsseldorf.

The Altstadt has been called "the longest bar in the world" because of the 200-plus bars and restaurants found here. The favorite drink here is a top-fermented Altbier (old beer), a dark, mellow brew that must be consumed soon after it's made.

A walk up **Königsallee,** called the "Kö" by Düsseldorfers, will give visitors a quick overview of the city and its residents. This street flanks an ornamental canal, shaded by trees and crossed by bridges. One bank is lined with office buildings, the other with elegant shops, cafes, and restaurants. Here you'll see women dressed in the very latest styles. Düsseldorf is the fashion center of Germany. It's known for its Fashion Weeks, which attract designers and buyers from all over Europe.

If you walk up the Kö toward the Trident Fountain at the northern end of the canal, you'll reach the **Hofgarten,** a huge rambling park. Here you can wander along the walks or sit and relax amid shade trees, gardens, fountains, and statues, almost forgetting you're in the very center of the city. Among the monuments is one to the poet Heinrich Heine. The Hofgarten is a good central point for seeing the city's major attractions—nearly all museums and cultural attractions are on its perimeter. Towering over the Hofgarten is Düsseldorf's most impressive skyscraper, the **Thyssen-House.** Residents call it the Dreischeibenhaus ("three-slice house"), because it actually looks like three huge monoliths sandwiched together. Northeast of the Hofgarten is **St. Rochus,** one of the city's finest modern churches.

**Goethe-Museum Düsseldorf** The Anton and Katharina Kippenberg Foundation sponsors this literary museum dedicated to Goethe's life and work. It emerged from the Kippenbergs' private collection of some 35,000 items, including autographs, books, busts, paintings, coins, medals, plaques, and china. About 1,000 pieces of the collection are shown in the permanent exhibition, including first drafts of well-known poems. The displays present a chronology of Goethe's life and work. There are also exhibits on various topics of the Goethe era.

Schloss-Jägerhof (in the Jägerhof Castle at the Hofgarten), Jacobistrasse 2. ✆ **0211/8-99-62-62.** Admission 2€ ($1.80) adults, 1€ (90¢) children. Tues–Fri and Sun 11am–5pm; Sat 1–5pm. Tram: 707. Bus: 722.

**Heinrich-Heine-Institut** Heinrich Heine (1797–1856) was Germany's greatest lyric poet. More than 10,000 volumes, as well as the manuscript bequest of this Düsseldorf-born poet, are found here. Born into a Jewish family, Heine nominally converted to Christianity so that he could attend law school. He was the author of the famous *Die Lorelei,* and his poems were put to music by Schubert, Schumann, and Hugo Wolf. His work was prohibited during the Nazi era, during which *Die Lorelei* was officially attributed to an unknown author.

In the Altstadt, you visit the house where Heine was born. It's at Bölkerstrasse 53 and is marked by a plaque.

Bilkerstrasse 12–14. ✆ **0211/899-2902.** Admission 2€ ($1.80) adults, 1€ (90¢) children and students, free for children under 10. Tues–Fri and Sun 11am–5pm; Sat 1–5pm. Tram: 704 or 707.

**K20 Kunstsammlung am Grabbeplatz** This architecturally impressive museum has an outstanding collection of modern art, including works by many major French, German, and American artists. There is an especially large collection of works by Julius Bissier and also 16 works by Paul Klee—the Klee exhibition is rotated at regular intervals since all of it cannot be shown at the same time. Six temporary exhibitions of contemporary art are hosted in the large exhibition hall every year.

Grabbeplatz 5 (opposite the Kunsthalle). ✆ **0211/8381-130.** www.kunstsammlung.de. Admission 6.50€ ($5.80) adults, 4.50€ ($4) children over 6 and students, free for children 5 and under. Tues–Sun 10am–6pm (until 8pm Fri). U-Bahn: Heinrich-Heine-Allee.

**Kunsthalle Düsseldorf** The Kunst Halle Düsseldorf is devoted to contemporary art from the Rhineland and throughout Europe. No other museum in the city keeps up with changing trends in art as well as this one. Visiting exhibits of every shape and size, often bizarre, are displayed here. This museum should not be confused with the Kunstmuseum Düsseldorf (see below).

Grabbeplatz 4 (across from the Kunstsammlung Nordrhein-Westfalen, west of the Hofgarten). ✆ **0211/899-6240.** Entrance 6€ ($5.35) adults, 4€ ($3.55) for students and children over 10. Tues–Sat 11am–6pm (Fri until 9pm). U-Bahn: Heinrich-Heine-Allee.

**Kunstmuseum Düsseldorf** This is one of the largest and most comprehensive museums in the Rhineland. The painting collection includes works by Rubens, Caspar David Friedrich, and the Die Brücke and Der Blaue Reiter schools. The sculpture collection ranges from the late Middle Ages to the 20th century. There are also some 80,000 prints and drawings, as well as early Persian bronzes and ceramics, a glass collection, textiles from late antiquity to the present, and a design collection.

Ehrenhof 5. ✆ **0211/8-99-24-60.** Admission 2.50€ ($2.25) adults, 1.50€ ($1.35) students and children, 5€ ($4.45) family ticket. Tues–Sun 11am–6pm. Tram: 701, 706, 711, or 715.

**Kunstsammlung nordrhein-Westfalen** This architecturally impressive museum has an outstanding collection of modern art, including works by many major French, German, and American artists. There is an especially large collection of works by Julius Bissier and also 6 works by Paul Klee—the Klee exhibition is rotated at regular intervals since all of it cannot be shown at the same time. Six temporary exhibitions of contemporary art are hosted in the large exhibition hall every year.

Grabbeplatz 5 (opposite the Kunsthalle) ✆ 0211/8-38-10. Admission 6€ ($5.35) adults, 4.10€ ($3.65) children over 6 and students, free for children 5 and under. Tues–Sun 10am–6pm (until 8pm Fri). U-Bahn: Heinrich-Heine-Allee.

## SHOPPING

Düsseldorf is a city of high fashion and high prices. Many chic Europeans visit the city just to shop for what's new and hot. The best and trendiest fashions are sold on the opulent east side of the Königsallee. The two largest concentrations of designer shops are found at the **Kö Galerie,** Königsallee 60, and the **Kö Center,** Königsallee 30. Each gallery has some 100 shops. Those not interested in dishing out lots of euros for designer duds should head for the more recently opened **Schadow Arcade,** off Schadowplatz, at the end of the Kö. Fashion here isn't so *haute,* but neither are the prices. Shoppers spend some 500 million euros in the shops on Schadowstrasse annually—more than is spent on any other street in the country.

**ANTIQUES** Düsseldorf's historic core contains a fine selection of antiques stores. **Lothar Heubel,** Bastionstrasse 17 (✆ **0211/134-103;** U-Bahn: Heinrich-Heine-Allee), specializes in Asian and African antiques, including jewelry, ceramics, and Chinese items from the Han, Ming, and Tang dynasties, mixed in with a handful of antiques from Provence and the south of France.

**DEPARTMENT STORES** **Carsch Haus,** Heinrich-Heine-Platz (✆ **0211/8-39-70;** U-Bahn: Heinrich-Heine-Allee), carries a good selection of fashions, as well as quality home furnishings, jewelry, and other items.

**DESIGNER CLOTHING & ACCESSORIES** Designer shopping in Düsseldorf is limited only by your bank account. **Ritterskamp,** Trinkausstrasse 7 (✆ **0211/32-99-94**), caters to both sexes, with designers such as Richard Tyler, Gianfranco Ferre, and Donna Karan. **Bogner Shop,** Königsallee 6–8 (✆ **0211/13-42-22**), carries functional sportswear that's meant for action on the golf course, tennis court, and ski slopes. The designers have their workshop on the second floor.

**Chanel,** Kö Center (✆ **0211/32-59-35**), offers the company's complete line of products, from clothing to cosmetics and fragrances. Also in Kö Center, German designer **Jil Sander** (✆ **0211/32-84-44**) has set up one of her many shops selling women's fashions. For strictly German fashions, check the racks of women's clothing and accessories at **MCM (Modern Creations Munich),** Steinstrasse 5 (✆ **0211/32-23-50**).

Need shoes and accessories to go with your newly purchased outfits? Head for **Anena,** Kö Center (✆ **0211/32-73-03**), where one stop gives you access to the products of Calvin Klein, Jil Sander, Sonia Rykiel, Prada, Donna Karan, and other designers. Shoes and more shoes fill the racks at **Walter Steiger Schuhe,** Kö Galerie (✆ **0211/13-41-04**), the German designer of high-quality, high-fashion footwear. Choose from luggage, handbags, shoes, and other accessories at **Etienne Aigner,** Kö Galerie (✆ **0211/3-23-09-55**). In the boutique of **Louis Vuitton,** Kö Center (✆ **0211/32-32-30**), leather accessories, luggage, and handbags are sold.

**DINNERWARE & KITCHEN ACCESSORIES** A diversity of items and styles can be found at **Georg Jensen,** Kö Galerie (✆ **0211/32-42-81**), the shop of the German designer who redefines silver flatware, bowls, candle sticks, coffee pots, and much more.

**FURNITURE & DECORATIVE ACCESSORIES** One of Düsseldorf's largest purveyors of Art Deco furniture and art objects is **Arts Decoratifs,** Hohestrasse 20 (✆ **0211/32-45-53;** U-Bahn: Heinrich-Heine-Allee). Look for lamps, vases, paperweights, and high quality, prewar costume jewelry, some of which could make good souvenirs.

**JEWELRY & WATCHES** Located in the heart of the designer shopping district, **Wempe Juwelier,** Königsallee 14 (✆ **0211/32-72-87**), is one of a chain of 23 shops scattered throughout Düsseldorf that carry Swiss watches and jewelry designs in gold, silver, and precious stones.

## WHERE TO STAY

### VERY EXPENSIVE

**Steigenberger Park-Hotel** ★★ This traditional deluxe German hotel has been completely modernized and re-equipped to meet modern demands. Its central location, overlooking the Hofgarten park, is virtually unbeatable, which may explain why it attracts so many conventions and groups. The Steigenberger maintains a high level of service in the old-world style. All rooms, refitted to the latest standards, are cozy and comfortable. Bathrooms have makeup mirrors, robes, and shower-tub combinations.

Corneliusplatz 1 (at the beginning of Königsallee, next to the German Opera), 40213 Düsseldorf 1. ✆ **800/223-5652** in the U.S. and Canada, or 0211/1-38-10. Fax 0211/13-81-592. www.steigenberger.de. 133 units. 260€–380€ ($232.20–$339.35) double; 565€–995€ ($504.55–$888.55) suite. Rates include buffet breakfast. AE, DC, MC, V. Free parking. Tram: 78 or 79. Bus: 778. **Amenities:** 2 restaurants; bar; lounge; room service; babysitting; laundry/dry cleaning. *In room:* TV, minibar, hair dryer, safe.

## MODERATE

**Ashley's Garden** ★★ Posh, upscale, distinguished, and very quiet, this hotel occupies what was built in 1938 as a stately looking villa in the wealthy residential suburb of Golzheim, 5km (3 miles) north of the city center. Set within a 5-minute walk of both the Rhine and the Düsseldorf Fairgrounds (*Messe*), it's completely outfitted, in both the bedrooms and the public areas, with English antiques and yard upon yard of Laura Ashley fabrics. The overall look of Ashley's Garden is that of an English country house, an ambience that's enhanced by the 24-hour availability of light snacks and aperitifs in the lobby. Terraces overlook a pleasant garden. Bedrooms are exceedingly comfortable, beautifully furnished, and spacious for the most part. Each comes with a midsize tiled bathroom with tub-and-shower combination.

Karl-Kleppe-Strasse 20. 40474 Düsseldorf Ortsteil Golzheim. ✆ **0211/516-1710.** Fax 0211/45-32-99. www.ashleysgarden.de. 189€ ($168.80) double. AE, DC, MC, V. U-Bahn: Reeserplatz. **Amenities:** Bar; lounge; Restaurant Km 747 (a name that indicates the number of kilometers from the hotel to the source of the nearby Rhine); concierge; room service; laundry. *In room:* A/C, minibar, TV.

**Fürstenhof** This hotel is a good, safe choice in the center of town. It's modern but not glaringly so. It opens onto a tree-filled square. Rooms are handsomely furnished, each ranging in size from medium to spacious. All units contain bathrooms with shower-tub combinations. Nonsmoking rooms are available, and half the breakfast room is reserved for nonsmoking guests.

Fürstenplatz 3, 40215 Düsseldorf 1. ✆ **0211/38-64-60.** Fax 0211/37-90-62. 43 units. 75€–200€ ($67–$178.60) double. Rates include buffet breakfast. AE, DC, MC, V. Closed Dec 24–Jan 2. Tram: 701, 707, or 708. Bus: 725. **Amenities:** Breakfast room; lounge; health club; sauna; laundry/dry cleaning. *In room:* TV, minibar, hair dryer.

**Hotel Grosser Kurfürst** *Value* Although this modern hotel has some expensive rooms, it's a bargain overall—at least by the pricey standards of Düsseldorf. Rooms are small and sparsely furnished, though well organized. Bathrooms are also small and have shower-tub combinations. Breakfast is the only meal served, but several restaurants are nearby.

Kurfürstenstrasse 18, 40211 Düsseldorf. ✆ **0211/173370.** Fax 0211/16-25-97. 22 units. 90€–110€ ($80.35–$98.25) double. Rates include continental breakfast. AE, MC, V. Closed Dec 22–Jan 4. Tram: 709 or 719. **Amenities:** Breakfast room; lounge; sauna; solarium. *In room:* TV.

## INEXPENSIVE

**Wurms Hotel** The Wurms Hotel, set in a five-story stucco building, is a good budget choice. The small rooms are done in dark wood offset by bright bedspreads and curtains. Bathrooms are a bit plain but spotlessly maintained with showers. A few rooms—rented only to singles—are without private bathrooms. The buffet breakfast is the only meal served. The hotel is a short walk from the central landmark square, Graf-Adolf-Platz.

Scheurenstrasse 23 (near Graf-Adolf-Strasse, about 4 blocks from the Hauptbahnhof), 40215 Düsseldorf. ✆ **0211/37-50-01.** Fax 0211/37-50-03. www.hotel-wurms.de. 27 units, 24 with shower and toilet.

45€–60€ ($40.20–$53.60) single without bath, 80€–165€ ($71.45–$147.35) double with shower and toilet. Rates include buffet breakfast. MC, V. Parking 8€ ($7.15). Tram: 734, 741, or 752. Bus: 835. **Amenities:** Breakfast room; lounge; room service. *In room:* TV.

## WHERE TO DINE

### VERY EXPENSIVE

**Im Schiffchen** ★★ FRENCH/SEAFOOD The chefs at Im Schiffchen deliver a refined, brilliantly realized repertoire of the finest cuisine you'll find in any city along the Rhine. The ingredients that go into the meals are unimpeachably authentic—every tomato, every onion, every fish or piece of meat seems to have been thoroughly evaluated for quality before purchasing. The menu is ever-changing, based on seasonal variations, but you might find homemade goose-liver paté with green peppercorns, a delectable Norwegian salmon in Vouvray sauce, or lobster cooked in chamomile tea. We could return again and again for the pike-perch cooked aromatically in puff pastry. The desserts are luscious; try the granulated fruit mélange with almond cream.

Kaiserswerther Markt 9 (on the outskirts of the city, at Kaiserswerth). ✆ **0211/40-10-50.** Reservations required. Main courses 35€–55€ ($31.25–$49.10); fixed-priced 4-course menu 98€–110€ ($87.50–$98.25). AE, DC, MC V. Tues–Sat 7–10pm. Tram: 79 to Klemensplatz.

**Victorian Restaurant** ★★★ FRENCH/GERMAN This is the finest restaurant in the city center. The decor features sparkling crystal, black-leather banquettes, and masses of flowers. The food represents the best of both traditional and modern schools. Examples include heavenly deep-fried zucchini flowers stuffed with lobster mousse and flavored with a sauce of champagne vinegar and coriander, apple salad with slices of goose liver, and three-vegetable purée. The delectable desserts change with the inspiration of the pastry chef but might include terrine of oranges served with raspberry liqueur and fresh mint.

Nearby is the **Bistro im Victorian,** with a minimalist interior design. The kitchen area is wide open, so you can watch as the fresh ingredients are whipped into meals. Patrons can even discuss their food wishes with the chef himself. Meals in the Bistro begin at 22€ ($19.65).

Königstrasse 3A. ✆ **0211/8-65-50-22.** Reservations required for the restaurant, recommended for the bistro. Main courses 25€–40€ ($22.35–$35.70); fixed-price lunch 26€–42€ ($23.20–$37.50); fixed-price menu (lunch or dinner) 72€–90€ ($64.30–$80.35). AE, DC, MC, V. Mon–Sat noon–2:30pm and 7pm–midnight. Tram: 709 or 719. Bus: 834.

### EXPENSIVE

**De' Medici** ★ FRENCH/ITALIAN De' Medici is elegantly modern, serving two cuisines, French and Italian, which are blended harmoniously. The chefs make it their goal to startle and amaze diners with zesty flavors. The oversize menu lists an array of tried-and-true dishes, with concessions to whatever was available in the market that day. The marinated sweetbreads over sautéed eggplant or medallions of veal in puff pastry are both unusual and excellent.

Amboss-Strasse 3 (on the outskirts, at Oberkassel). ✆ **0211/59-41-51.** Reservations required. Main courses 15€–29€ ($13.40–$25.90). AE, DC, MC, V. Mon–Fri noon–2:30pm; Mon–Sat 6pm–midnight (last orders 10:30pm). U-Bahn: Amboss-Strasse.

**Restaurant Savini** ★ ITALIAN/INTERNATIONAL If you don't mind the trip outside the center, this restaurant offers the finest Italian dining in Düsseldorf. The white-walled dining room has tastefully colored banquettes. The creative Italian cuisine uses produce that comes fresh from the market and is deftly handled in the kitchen. Menu items include carpaccio of beef with warm king prawns, black spaghetti with scallops, or sea bass with risotto of mushrooms. The restaurant also has one of the best Italian wine cellars in Germany.

Stromstrasse 47, Unterbilk. ✆ **0211/39-39-31.** Reservations recommended. Main courses 16€–33€ ($14.30–$29.45); fixed-price menu 29€–55€ ($25.90–$49.10). AE, MC, V. Tues–Fri noon–3pm; Mon–Sat 6–11pm. Closed 3 weeks in July. Tram: 704 or 709 to Unterbilk.

**Rheinturm—Top 180 Restaurant** ★ INTERNATIONAL Most people come here for the view. This futuristic restaurant is set atop the spool-shaped summit of the city's tallest tower, affording a 360° panorama of Düsseldorf's buildings and parks. The competently prepared menu items include grills, game dishes, fish, and soups. Try the slices of smoked duck breast with creamy savoy cabbage or rolls of salmon stuffed with turbot filling and served in Riesling-and-saffron sauce. Vegetarian courses are also featured. A trip to the tower's observation lookout costs 3.20€ ($2.85) for adults, 2.50€ ($2.25) for those 13 to 17, and 1.60€ ($1.45) for children 6 to 12. Kids 5 and under go free. The tower is open daily 10am to 11:30pm.

Stromstrasse 20. ✆ **0211/84-85-80.** Reservations recommended. Main courses 17.50€–24.50€ ($15.65–$21.90); fixed-price 4-course dinner 47.50€ ($42.40). AE, DC, MC, V. Daily noon–2:30pm and 6:30–11pm. Tram: 704, 709, or 719. Bus: 725.

## MODERATE

**Zum Csikos** *Finds* HUNGARIAN When you tire of Germanic cookery, Zum Csikos makes a refreshing change of pace. The restaurant's name translates as "Hungarian cowboy." It's set on three levels of a narrow town house originally built in 1697. Candlelight gives the place (and the diners) a mellow glow. The home-style Hungarian food is well prepared, and the portions are hefty. The beef goulash is excellent as is the chopped liver. The restaurant follows the Hungarian tradition of late-night closings.

Andreastrasse 9. ✆ **0211/32-97-71.** Reservations recommended. Main courses 10€–20€ ($8.95–$17.85). AE, DC, MC. Daily 6pm–2am. Closed July. U-Bahn: Opernhaus.

## INEXPENSIVE

**Im Alten Bierhause** RHINELAND This place is actually more of a wine tavern than a restaurant. The building dates from 1641. Style connoisseurs will recognize it as typical of the Rhine's left bank (as opposed to the right, the left bank has more of a bohemian aura). Traditional German specialties are served here. The house specialty is *Speck-Pfannenkuchen,* a bacon pancake; a similar version is made with marmalade. On Sunday the beer drinkers pile in at 11am. The specialty of the house is a local dark and foamy brew called Altbier.

Alt-Niederkassel 75 (on the outskirts). ✆ **0211/55-12-72.** Reservations required. Main courses 8€–18€ ($7.15–$16.05). No credit cards. Tues–Sat 3–11pm; Sun 11am–11pm. Closed 3 weeks in July (dates vary). Bus: 834.

**Zum Schiffchen** ★ RHINELAND If you want the most traditional and atmospheric place to dine, come here before anywhere else. Zum Schiffchen, in the heart of the Altstadt, is Düsseldorf's oldest restaurant. A golden model ship on top of the step-gabled building (which dates from 1628) reminds you of its location, near the river. The interior follows the tavern tradition of scrubbed wooden tables and rustic artifacts. Good, hefty portions of regional cuisine are the rule here. The menu is large, and the service by the blue-aproned waiters (called *Köbesse*) is rather hectic. Zum Schiffchen is the perfect place to sample

Düsseldorf's local beer. Over the years, the restaurant has attracted a host of famous diners ranging from Napoléon and Heinrich Heine to Arthur Miller.

Hafenstrasse 5 (a block from the Rhine). ✆ **0211/13-24-21.** Reservations required. Main courses 8.80€–22€ ($7.85–$19.65). AE, DC, MC, V. Mon–Sat 11:30am–midnight. Tram: 705.

**Zum Schlüssel** GERMAN This establishment is as Germanic as the Rhine. Zum Schlüssel is located on the original site of the famous Gatzweilers Alt brewery. The decor is that of a classic German Gasthaus, with the aura of a country inn. The service is courteous and swift. The food has both aroma and taste, and there's plenty of it; sample the *Eisbein* (pigs' knuckles) or a huge bowl of soup. Wash it all down with the house beer, Gatzweilers Alt.

Gatzweilers beer hall, Bölkerstrasse 43–47. ✆ **0211/32-61-55.** Reservations recommended. Main courses 9€–25€ ($8.05–$22.35). AE, DC, MC, V. Sun–Thurs 11am–midnight; Fri–Sat 11am–1am. U-Bahn: Heinrich-Heine-Allee.

## DÜSSELDORF AFTER DARK

The place to go for nightlife in Düsseldorf is the **Altstadt.** This .8 sq. km (½ sq. mile) of narrow streets and alleyways, between Königsallee and the Rhine River, is jam-packed with restaurants, discos, art galleries, boutiques, nightclubs, and some 200 song-filled beer taverns. Düsseldorfers refer to a night cruising the Altstadt as an *Altstadttbummel.*

**THE PERFORMING ARTS** Classical music has long had an illustrious association with this city, once home to Brahms, Mendelssohn, and Schumann (though there are no specific tourist sites relating to them in Dusseldorf). However, because of that fact, it's not surprising that both the **Düsseldörfer Sinfonie** and its home, **Tonhalle,** Ehrenhof 2 (box office ✆ **0211/8-99-61-23;** U-Bahn: Tonhalle), are world-famous. The Tonhalle is perhaps Germany's most successful modern concert hall after Berlin's Philharmonie. The highly regarded orchestra gives about a dozen concerts a year, with tickets running 10.35€ to 52€ ($9.25–$46.45). **Deutsche Oper am Rhein,** Heinrich-Heine-Allee 16A (✆ **0211/8-90-82-11;** U-Bahn: Heinrich-Heine-Allee), is one of the city's renowned opera and ballet companies. Tickets are 10.35€ ($9.25).

The city's most dramatic venue, **Schauspielhaus,** Gustav-Gründgens-Platz (✆ **0211/36-99-11;** U-Bahn: Heinrich-Heine-Allee), is outstanding and is known all over Germany. The production and acting here are first-rate. Performances (in German) take place September to June, and tickets cost 10€ to 42€ ($8.95–$37.50).

**BARS & BEER HALLS** The oldest brewery-bar in the city is **Bräuerei Schumacher,** Oststrasse 123 (✆ **0211/326004;** U-Bahn: Oststrasse), a popular establishment that serves only beer that's brewed by the company that owns it. It's open Sunday to Thursday 10am to midnight, Friday and Saturday 10am to 1am. The brewery **Bräuerei zum Uerige,** Berger Strasse 1 (✆ **0211/86-69-90;** U-Bahn: Heinrich-Heine-Allee), serves traditional German dishes along with its house brews. Open Sunday to Thursday 10am to midnight and Friday and Saturday 10am to 1am. Two other breweries, each serving beer brewed on the premises, are **Bräuerei im Suchschen,** Ratingerstrasse 28 (✆ **0211/137-470;** U-Bahn: Heinrich-Heine-Allee), and **Bräuerei zum Schlüssel,** Bölkerstrasse 43 (✆ **0211/326-155;** U-Bahn: Heinrich-Heine-Allee), both of which also offer platters of German food. Purists in Düsseldorf are quick to point out that the **Bräuerei zum Uel,** Rattingerstrasse 16 (✆ **0211/32-53-69;** U-Bahn: Heinrich-Heine-Allee), is not technically a brewery at all, because beer is not brewed on the premises. Nonetheless, students flock here for the house beers and international dishes. It's open Monday to Saturday 10am to 1am, and Sunday noon to 1am.

Angel images fill every nook and cranny of **Engelchen** (German for "little angel"), Kurzestrasse 15 (✆ **0211/32-73-56;** U-Bahn: Heinrich-Heine-Allee), where an alternative arts crowd gathers for conversation and coffee, beer, or mixed drinks. It's open Monday to Friday 11am to 2am and weekends 3pm to 5am. **N.T. Pub,** Königsallee 27 (✆ **0211/138-000;** U-Bahn: Königsallee), is a conveniently located and convivial pub. It serves cafe-style platters and drinks every day 9am until after midnight, except on Sunday when they close at 11pm.

**DANCE CLUBS** Two hot dance spots, **Tor 3,** Ronsdorferstrasse 143 (✆ **0211/7-33-64-97**), and **Stahlwerk,** Ronsdorferstrasse 134 (✆ **0211/7-30-86-81**), face each other across the street (U-Bahn: Ronsdorferstrasse). Both intersperse recorded dance music with live acts from throughout Europe. Both draw a mixed, fashion-conscious crowd, are open Friday and Saturday from 10pm to about 5am, and charge a cover of 5€ to 15€ ($4.45–$13.40).

**JAZZ CLUBS** At the small and smoked-filled **Em Pootzke,** Mertensgasse 6 (✆ **0211/32-69-73;** U-Bahn: Heinrich-Heine-Allee), there's no cover and no food, just nightly live jazz and drinking 9pm to 1am.

**LIVE-MUSIC CLUBS** A popular piano bar, **Bei Tino,** Königsallee 21 (✆ **0211/32-64-63;** U-Bahn: Königsallee), has music noon to 3am nightly; guests are often allowed to play the piano. **McLaughlin's Irish Pub,** Kurzestrasse 11 (✆ **0211/32-46-11;** U-Bahn: Heinrich-Heine-Allee), serves Guinness and Murphy's with stew and pies, and presents touring Irish bands on the weekend. It's open Sunday to Thursday 11am to 1am and Friday and Saturday 11am to 3am. Another pub with a brogue, **Irish Pub Bei Fatties,** Hunsruckenstrasse 13 (✆ **0211/13-31-81;** U-Bahn: Heinrich-Heine-Allee), hosts live blues, rock, jazz, and Irish music on Friday and Saturday. It's open Monday to Friday 2:30pm until 3am, Saturday 1pm to 3am, and Sunday noon to 3am.

**GAY CLUBS** The centerpiece of gay life in Düsseldorf is the **Café Rosa Mond,** Oberbilker Allee 310 (✆ **0211/992-377;** U-Bahn: Oberbilke). It functions as a cafe, a bar, and an organizer of gay-themed entertainment, which changes virtually every night of the week. The staff can direct you to other gay-friendly venues. It's open nightly 8pm to 3am or later.

# 15

# The Mosel Valley

Those returning from Germany singing the praises of the Rhine as the most scenic German river have probably not yet toured the Mosel Valley. The Mosel meanders in a snake-like path through the mountains west of the Rhineland, passing town after town whose sole purpose seems to be to beautify the riverbanks. Nearly every village and hill has its own castle or fortress, often surrounded by vineyards.

The Mosel (*Moselle* in French) begins in the hills of France, but its most scenic portion is the last 193km (120 miles) before it enters the Rhine at Koblenz. Visitors to the area enjoy the lively landscapes, the legend-rich countryside, and, of course, the wines. Many of the rich and full-bodied Mosel wines are superior to those of the Rhine Valley.

If you enter Germany via France or Luxembourg, the Mosel route is a good way to begin your tour of the German countryside. You'll arrive first at the major city of **Trier** with its significant Roman ruins before weaving through the Hunsrück and Eifel mountains.

## 1 Cochem ★

92km (57 miles) NE of Trier, 51km (32 miles) SW of Koblenz

This medieval town, located in one of the best wine regions of the Mosel Valley, is crowded against the left bank of the river by a huge vineyard-covered hill. Because of its large number of inns, Cochem is your best choice for an overnight stopover between Koblenz and Trier.

The town is a typical wine village, with tastings and festivals. But the biggest attraction is **Reichsburg Cochem** ★ (✆ **02671/1787**), a huge castle at the top of the mound behind the town. The original 1027 structure was almost completely destroyed by Louis XIV's army in 1689. It has since been restored according to the original ground plans, and its medieval ramparts and turrets create a dramatic backdrop for the town (one which—at least to children—will evoke Walt Disney's Sleeping Beauty Castle). This single site is the most celebrated and photographed along the Mosel River. To reach the castle, follow the steep footpath from the center of town; the 15-minute walk is well worth it for the rewarding views of the town and the Mosel below. Although you can visit the grounds anytime, the interior of the castle is open daily mid-March to November 9am to 6pm. Guided tours are conducted at regular intervals. Admission is 4.10€, ($4) for adults and 2.05€, ($2) for children and students.

### ESSENTIALS

**GETTING THERE** **By Train** The Cochem Bahnhof is on the Wasserbillig–Trier–Koblenz rail line, with frequent service between these connecting cities. For information, call ✆ **01805/99-66-33.**

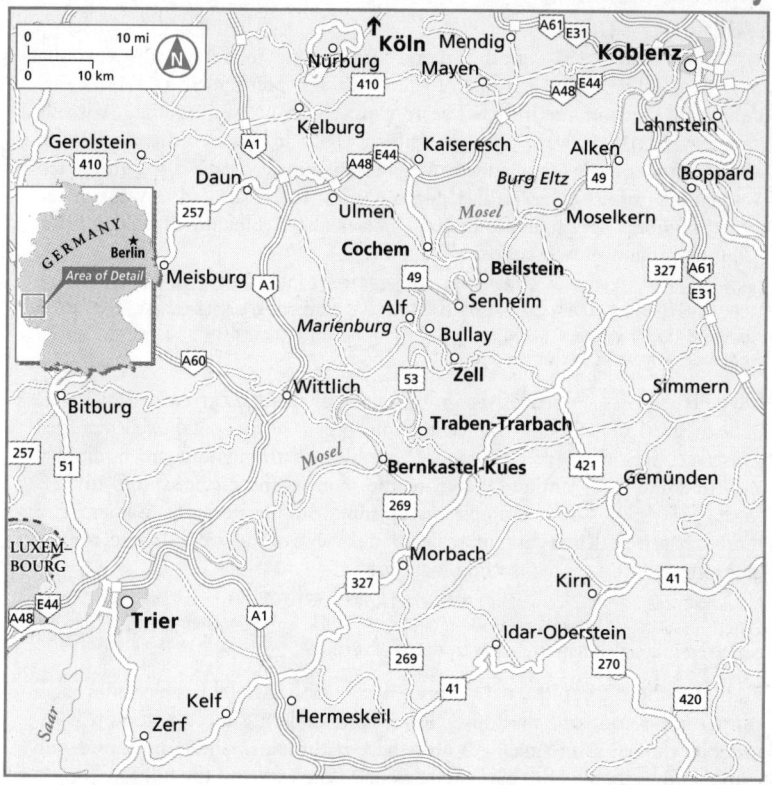


**By Bus** Regional bus service along the Mosel is provided by **RMV Rhein Mosel Verkehrsgesellschaft** (✆ **02671/8976**) and by **Moselbahn, GmbH** (✆ **0651/147750**).

**By Car** Access is via the A48 Autobahn on the Koblenz–Trier express highway; exit either at Ulmen or at Kaisersesch.

**By Boat** Boat rides on the Mosel River operate between Trier and Cochem. Contact **Mosel Personen Schiffahrt Gebrüder Kolb,** Briedern/Mosel (✆ **02673/1515**).

**VISITOR INFORMATION** For tourist information, contact the **Verkehrsamt,** Endertplatz 1 (✆ **02671/60040**), open Monday to Friday 9am to 5pm; May to October, also Saturday 10am to 3pm and Sunday 10am to noon.

**SPECIAL EVENTS** During the first week of June, **Mosel-Wein-Woche** begins, celebrating the region's wines with tasting booths and a street fair. A similar **Weinfest** takes place the last weekend of August. For information on either of these events, contact the tourist office (see above) or the **Weingut Winzerhof** (✆ **02671/72-97**) for details on dates, activities, and accommodations.

**SHOPPING** **Die Geschenkidee Heimes,** Herrenstrasse 13 (✆ **02671/9-11-22**), located on the town's main street, sells locally produced arts and crafts.

## WHERE TO STAY

**Alte Thorschenke** ★ Both a hotel and a wine restaurant, the centrally located Alte Thorschenke is one of the oldest and best-known establishments along either side of the Mosel. The romantically conceived building, with its timbers and towers, was originally built in 1332. It became a hotel in 1960, when a modern wing was added. Most rooms are reached via a cantilevered wooden staircase that has creaked for centuries (there's also an elevator in the rear). Six rooms have four-poster beds. There's also a romantic Napoléon suite. All units contain shower-tub combinations.

Brückenstrasse 3, 56812 Cochem. ✆ **02671/70-59.** Fax 02671/42-02. www.castle-thorschenke.com 40 units. 110€–125€ ($98.25–$111.65) double; 155€ ($138.40) suite. Rates include buffet breakfast. AE, DC, MC, V. Parking 6€ ($5.35) in garage. Closed Jan 5–Mar 15. **Amenities:** Restaurant; bar; room service; laundry/dry cleaning. *In room:* TV, minibar, hair dryer.

**Burg Hotel** *Value* Parts of the ground floor of this cozy riverside hotel were built in the 1500s. Today, the feeling you'll get is one of solid, well-managed conservatism and discreet prosperity. Furnishings throughout are traditional and, in some cases, antique. Seven of the rooms—those priced 46€ to 72€ ($41.10–$64.30)—are in a simple nearby annex. Rooms in the main house have more expansive balconies and more panoramic views of the river. All units contain bathrooms with shower-tub combinations.

Moselpromenade 23, 56812 Cochem. ✆ **02671/71-17.** Fax 02671/83-36. 43 units. 65€–130€ ($58.05–$116.10) double. Rates include buffet breakfast. AE, DC, MC, V. Free parking. **Amenities:** 2 restaurants; bar; pool; sauna; solarium; room service; laundry/dry cleaning. *In room:* TV.

**Flair Hotel am Rosenhügel** This centrally located hotel has balconies and a sun terrace overlooking the Mosel. Rooms are modern, simple, and quite comfortable, though a bit small. All units have bathrooms containing shower-tub combinations. Some offer panoramic views of the castle on the hill.

Valwigerstrasse 57, 56812 Cochem-Cond. ✆ **02671/9-76-30.** Fax 02671/97-63-63. 23 units. 96€ ($85.75) double. Rates include buffet breakfast. MC, V. Free parking. Closed Dec 15–Jan 3. **Amenities:** Breakfast room; lounge. *In room:* TV.

**Lohspeicher** This inn is good for an overnight stopover, although it's better known for serving the best food within Cochem than it is for rooms. A former warehouse, this generously proportioned 1832 building with hand-hewn beams has been renovated into a delightful and centrally located hotel and restaurant. Rooms, though generally a bit small, are comfortably furnished, all with bathrooms containing shower-tub combinations. Excellent Rhinelander cuisine is presented in the dining room. Snail soup may not be your thing, but connoisseurs flock here to sample it. The snails are some of the fattest and most delectable in Germany. Fresh fish and game such as venison in autumn round out the menu. Meals cost approximately 28€ to 45€ ($25-$40.20).

Obergasse 1, 56812 Cochem. ✆ **02671/39-76.** Fax 02671/17-72. 9 units. 78€–88€ ($69.65–$78.60) double. Rates include continental breakfast. AE, MC, V. Parking 4.40€ ($3.95). Closed Feb. **Amenities:** Restaurant; lounge; room service. *In room:* A/C, TV.

---

*Fun Fact* **Thunderbird, It's Not**

Mosel wines have the lowest alcoholic content (about 9%) of any white wine in the world. Because of this, they are best enjoyed in their youth.

---

*Moments* **Wine Tasting with the Baron**

Guests of the Alte Thorschenke can visit the 500-year-old **Castle of Baron von Landensberg** in Eller, about 7km (4½ miles) from Cochem. Here in the old cellars, you can taste some of the best wines produced along the banks of the Mosel. To arrange a visit if you're not staying at the hotel, call ✆ **02675/277.**

## WHERE TO DINE

The restaurant at Lohspeicher (see above) serves some of the best food in the area.

**Parkhotel Landenberg** GERMAN/INTERNATIONAL Parkhotel Landenberg offers a pleasing panoramic view over the Mosel. Delectable regional specialties include venison, wild boar, and fish—all best enjoyed with a good bottle of white Mosel wine from the hotel's own cellar.

Sehler Anlagen 1 (about 1.5km/1 mile from the Bahnhof), 56812 Cochem-Sehl. ✆ **02671/71-10.** Fax 02671/83-79. Reservations recommended. Main courses 10€–27€ ($8.95–$24.10). AE, MC, V. Daily noon–1:30pm and 6–9pm. Closed Jan 5–Mar 15.

**Weissmühle im Enterttal** GERMAN/FRENCH Set within Cochem's suburb of Enterttal, this respected restaurant is sought out by locals because of its fine cuisine. You can dine within either the Müllerstube, a woodsy, antique-looking room that might remind you of an inn high in the Swiss Alps, or the brighter, sunnier, and larger Sommerrestaurant. A trademark dish is fresh trout from the small nearby lake, stuffed with herbs, baked, and kept warm at your table with a hot stone.

Endertstrasse 1. ✆ **02671/89-55.** Fax 02671/82-07. Reservations recommended. Main courses 14€–25€ ($12.50–$22.35); fixed-price menu 25€–35€ ($22.35–$31.25). DC, MC, V. Daily noon–2pm and 6–9pm. From Cochem's center, drive toward the Autobahn, following the signs for Koblenz/Trier; the inn is on the left of the road, 1.5km (1 mile) northwest of Cochem.

## A SIDE TRIP TO BURG ELTZ

**Burg Eltz** ★★ (✆ **02672/95-05-00**), a stately castle on the north bank of the Mosel, is set above the village of Moselkern and surrounded by woodlands. It lies 29km (18 miles) northeast of Cochem and 29km (18 miles) southwest of Koblenz. Access is by the A48 and A61 Autobahns and Route 49. A parking lot, Antoniuskapelle, less than 1.5km (1 mile) from the castle, can be reached via Münstermaifeld. A bus runs to the castle every 5 minutes.

This is one of the few medieval castles in the region still intact. The original structure, built from the 12th to the 17th centuries, has been preserved in all its glory—the romance of the Middle Ages really comes alive here. The castle houses four separate residences, with original medieval furnishings, including some fine old paintings and tapestries. A treasury contains works by goldsmiths and silversmiths, armor, weapons, and other objects acquired by the family over the centuries. The castle is open daily April to November 1, 9:30am to 5:30pm. Admission is 5€ ($4.45) for adults and 3€ ($2.70) for children. There are two small self-service restaurants in the castle.

# 2 Beilstein

11km (7 miles) E of Cochem, 111km (69 miles) W of Mainz

This unspoiled medieval wine town on the east bank of the Mosel has an unusual marketplace hewn right into the rocky hillside. Above the town stands the former cloister church and the ruins of the 12th-century **Metternich Castle.**

## ESSENTIALS

**GETTING THERE** **By Train** The nearest rail station is at Cochem (see above).

**By Bus** Service from Cochem and other points along the Mosel is available from **RMV Rhein Mosel Verkehrsgesellschaft** (✆ **02671/8976;** www.rmv-bus.de) and from **Moselbahn, GmbH** (✆ **0651/147750**).

**By Car** Access by car is via the A48 Autobahn on the Koblenz–Trier run; exit at Kaisersesch.

**VISITOR INFORMATION** The nearest information office is at Cochem (see above).

## WHERE TO STAY & DINE

**Haus Burgfrieden** This hotel's simple but comfortable rooms are outfitted in an uncluttered modern style. They aren't very spacious, but the maintenance is good. All units contain neatly kept bathrooms equipped with shower-tub combinations. On the premises is a dining room featuring international cuisine.

Im Muhlental 63 (a 5-min. walk west of the town center), 56814 Beilstein. ✆ **02673/9-36-39.** Fax 02673/93-63-88. www.hotel-burgfrieden.de. 39 units. 64€–78€ ($57.15–$69.65) double. Rates include buffet breakfast. No credit cards. Free parking. Closed Nov–Feb. **Amenities:** Restaurant; lounge; room service. *In room:* TV.

**Haus Lipmann** ★ *Finds* You can sample the wines that made Beilstein famous at its favorite inn, Haus Lipmann, in the town center. Time has been kind to this 1795 timbered building. The five guest rooms are located in its main house. They're all small, cozy, and very inviting, with tiny bathrooms and showers.

For six generations, the same family has tended the vast riverside vineyards that have won them acclaim. Try their Ellenzer Goldbäumchen or their Beilsteiner Schlossberg. In summer, the most popular place at the inn for drinking and dining is the vine-covered terrace with a statue of Bacchus, overlooking the Mosel. You can also try the antique-filled tavern or the wood-paneled Rittersaal, with its collection of old firearms and pewter. In the cooler months, fires burn in the tall walk-in fireplace and the tiny open hearth.

Marktplatz 3, 56814 Beilstein. ✆ **02673/15-73.** Fax 02673/15-21. 5 units. 85€ ($75.90) double. Rates include continental breakfast. No credit cards. Free parking. Closed Nov 1–Mar 15. **Amenities:** Restaurant; bar; room service. *In room:* TV.

# 3 Zell

69km (43 miles) NE of Trier, 105km (65 miles) W of Mainz, 35km (22 miles) S of Cochem

This old town, stretching along the east bank of the Mosel, is best known for its excellent wine, Schwarze Katze ("Black Cat"). The grape is king here, as you'll quickly realize if you visit during the annual autumn wine festival. Nearby, on the left bank of the Mosel, 8km (5 miles) from Zell, stands the little wine village of **Alf.** The surroundings are idyllic, especially if you climb up to the Marienburg. From here, you get a fine view overlooking the Mosel and the vineyards of Zell.

## ESSENTIALS

**GETTING THERE** **By Train** The nearest rail station is at Bullay, some 4km (2½ miles) away. For information, call ✆ **01805/99-66-33.**

**By Bus** Regional bus service is provided by **RMV Rhein Mosel Verkehrsgesellschaft GmbH** (✆ **02671/8976;** www.rmv-bus.de), and by **Moselbahn GmbH** (✆ **0651/147750**).

**By Car** Access by car is via the A1 Autobahn north and south or Route 53 east and west.

**VISITOR INFORMATION** Check with **Tourist-Information,** in the Rathaus, Balduinstrasse 44 (✆ **06542/7-01-22**), Monday to Friday 9am to 5pm.

## WHERE TO STAY & DINE

**Weinhaus Mayer** This five-story, rustic, balconied building in the center of town thrives as both a hotel and a wine house. It offers small, simply furnished rooms in the century-old main building. Some have a view of the Mosel. Cheaper rooms are in a less desirable annex on the same street. All units contain bathrooms with shower-tub combinations. The in-house restaurant serves only dinner.

Balduinstrasse 15, 56856 Zell. ✆ **06542/45-30** (Apr–Nov) or **06542/57-76** (Dec–Mar). Fax 06542/6-11-60. 30 units. 70€–82€ ($62.50–$73.25) double. Rates include continental breakfast. V. Free parking. Closed Dec–Mar. **Amenities:** Restaurant; lounge; room service. *In room:* TV, minibar.

**Zur Post** This hotel sits directly on the river. Its small rooms are carpeted, with French doors opening onto balconies. The owner takes pride in looking after her guests and ensuring their comfort. On the inviting sun terrace you can enjoy a glass of Mosel wine while watching the river traffic go by. Or you can sample the local wine in the warmly decorated Weinstube.

Schlossstrasse 21, 56856 Zell. ✆ **06542/42-17.** Fax 06542/4-16-93. 16 units. 68€ ($60.70) double. Rates include continental breakfast. AE, DC, MC, V. Free parking. Closed Feb–mid-Mar. **Amenities:** Restaurant; lounge. *In room:* TV, hair dryer.

# 4 Traben-Trarbach

60km (37 miles) NE of Trier, 103km (64 miles) W of Mainz, 18km (11 miles) SW of Zell

Thanks to their central location on the Mosel, halfway between Koblenz and Trier, the twin towns of Traben and Trarbach have become the wine capitals of the Mosel Valley. Their garden-like promenades on both banks of the river are viewpoints for annual international speedboat and water-skiing competitions. The **July wine festival** attracts visitors from all over Europe to the old wine cellars and taverns of the towns.

Traben-Trarbach is also proud of its historic attractions. Above Trarbach, on the east bank of the river, are the remains of the 14th-century **Grevenburg Castle,** the scene of hard-fought battles to gain control of its strategic position. On the opposite bank, above Traben, are the ruins of **Mont Royal,** a late–17th century fortress built by the invading Louis XIV. You can wander about these testimonials to faded grandeur at any time, without charge. Another attraction, just south of town, is the spa resort, **Bad Wildstein,** with its thermal springs.

## ESSENTIALS

**GETTING THERE** **By Train** Rail passengers for Traben-Trarbach can arrive either at Trier or Bullay, then go the rest of the way by bus. Call ✆ **01805/99-66-33** for schedules and times.

**By Bus** Regional bus service among the Mosel River towns is provided by **RMV Rhein Mosel Verkehrsgesellschaft** (✆ **06571/7141;** www.rmv-bus.de) and by **Moselbahn GmbH** (✆ **0651/147750**).

**By Car** Access by car is via the A48 Autobahn (Trier–Koblenz); exit at Wittlich.

**VISITOR INFORMATION** For tourist information, contact the **Kurverwaltung und Verkehrsamt,** Bahnstrasse 22, Traben (✆ **06541/83980**), open Monday to Friday 8am to noon and 1 to 5pm; May to October, also Saturday 1 to 4pm.

## WHERE TO STAY & DINE

**Hotel Moseltor** ★ *Finds* You'll find this hotel on the outskirts of town at Im Otsteil Trarbach. Inside this masterpiece of 19th-century fieldstone masonry, a charming combination of new construction and antique elements creates a warm mixture of comfort and convenience. The inviting rooms have neatly kept bathrooms containing shower-tub combinations.

Chef George Bauer's reputation for light cuisine has spread so widely that German urbanites come here for gastronomic weekends (meals cost approximately 25€–35€/$22.35–$31.25). The hotel is open year-round, but the restaurant is closed in February.

Moselstrasse 1, 56841 Traben-Trarbach. ✆ **06541/65-51.** Fax 06541/49-22. www.moseltor.de. 11 units. 77€–128€ ($68.75–$114.30) double. Rates include continental breakfast. AE, DC, MC, V. Parking 7€ ($6.25) in garage. **Amenities:** Restaurant; lounge; room service. *In room:* TV, hair dryer, safe.

**Romantik Jugendstilhotel Bellevue** ★★ This Art Nouveau castle, right on the riverbank, is one of the finest hotels along the Mosel. It was designed in 1903 by the noted architect Bruno Moehring and features elaborate timberwork, a domed tower, a high-pitched roof, gables, and dormers. The cozy rooms are often furnished with antiques. All units contain neatly kept bathrooms with shower-tub combinations. The Clauss-Feist Restaurant is a romantic spot for both breakfast and dinner, with stained-glass windows and an old-German ambience. There's a cozy fireplace as well as an ivy-covered terrace for dining outside.

Am Moselufer, 56841 Traben-Trarbach. ✆ **06541/70-30.** Fax 06541/70-34-00. www.bellevuehotel.de. 60 units. 130€–150€ ($116.10–$133.95) double. Rates include buffet breakfast. AE, DC, MC, V. Free outdoor parking; 8€ ($7.15) in garage. **Amenities:** Restaurant; bar; pool; spa; sauna; room service; massage; babysitting; laundry/dry cleaning. *In room:* TV, minibar, hair dryer, safe.

# 5 Bernkastel-Kues ★

48km (30 miles) NE of Trier, 113km (70 miles) W of Mainz

In a valley full of wine towns, Bernkastel stands out as the most colorful. Its old Marktplatz is surrounded by half-timbered buildings dating from as early as 1608. In the center of the square stands the 17th-century **St. Michael's Fountain,** which flows with wine during the annual September wine festival. Like Traben-Trarbach, this town is split into twin villages on opposite banks of the Mosel.

## ESSENTIALS

**GETTING THERE** **By Train** The nearest rail station is the Wittlich Hauptbahnhof, 20km (12½) miles west, with a bus or taxi connection to Bernkastel-Kues. For information, call ✆ **01805/99-66-33.**

**By Bus** Regional bus service along the Mosel River is provided by **RMV Rhein Mosel Verkehrsgesellschaft** (✆ **06571/7141;** www.rmv-bus.de) and by **Moselbahn, GmbH** (✆ **0651/147750**).

**By Car** Access by car is via the A48 Autobahn on the Koblenz–Trier run; exit at Wittlich.

**VISITOR INFORMATION** Contact **Tourist-Information,** Gestade 5, in Bernkastel (✆ **06531/40-23-24**), open May to October, Monday to Friday

8:30am to 5pm, Saturday 10am to 5pm, and Sunday 10am to 1pm; November to April, Monday to Thursday 8:30am to 12:30pm and 1 to 5pm, and Friday 8:30am to 12:30pm and 1 to 3:30pm.

## WHERE TO STAY

**Doctor Weinstuben** This intricately half-timbered building in the town center dates from 1652. Today it's the most visually interesting hotel in Bernkastel. Transformed into a tavern in 1830, it still has many of its original woodcarvings. Its public areas are traditional, and the cozy but often too-small rooms are furnished in a simple, modern style with bathrooms containing shower-tub combinations. Look for the 100-year-old plant called "Blue Rain."

Hebegasse 5, 54470 Bernkastel-Kues. ✆ **06531/96650.** Fax 06531/62-96. www.gastroline.de/doctor-weinstuben. 20 units. 67€–98€ ($59.85–$87.50) double. AE, DC, MC, V. Free parking. **Amenities:** Restaurant; bar; lounge. *In room:* TV.

**Moselpark** ★★ This is a government-rated four-star hotel, the best in the area and also one of the largest. Many of its rivals are mere inns with only a few bedrooms. This hotel also boasts the widest range of leisure facilities and activities in the area, including a fitness studio, dance bar, and large swimming pool. The three-story hotel, built in 1983, was last renovated in 1998. Bedrooms are midsize to spacious and are exceedingly comfortable and well maintained, each coming with a tub-and-shower combination. You can virtually spend a week on the grounds, treating the place like a resort. Many distractions are right on the grounds, everything from a Bierstube to a massage parlor.

Im Kurpark, Bernkastel-Kues 54470. ✆ **06531/5080.** Fax 06531/5086. www.moselpark.de. 143 units. 115€–125€ ($102.70–$111.65) double, 125€–135€ ($111.65–$120.55) suite. AE, DC, MC, V. Free parking. **Amenities:** Restaurant; cafe; Bierstube; wine tasting; dance club; indoor and outdoor pools; 4 indoor and 2 outdoor tennis courts; fitness center; bike rental; horseback riding; room service; massages; babysitting; laundry/dry cleaning. *In room:* TV, hair dryer, safe.

**Zur Post** ★ Even though relatively modest, this is the wine-growing town's finest inn. This centrally located hotel was once a stopover for horseback riders on the local postal routes. The well-maintained but small rooms have both traditional and modern furnishings. Bathrooms are both tiny and tidy, containing shower-tub combinations. Public areas include an elegantly crafted stairwell flanked by half-timbered walls and a paneled, beamed dining room.

Gestade 17, 54470 Bernkastel-Kues. ✆ **06531/9-67-00.** Fax 06531/96-70-50. 42 units. 90€–143€ ($80.35–$127.70) double. Rates include buffet breakfast. AE, DC, MC, V. Free parking. Closed Jan. **Amenities:** 3 restaurants; lounge; room service. *In room:* TV, minibar.

## WHERE TO DINE

**Waldhotel Sonnora** ★★★ CONTINENTAL One of the most gastronomically spectacular restaurants in Germany is located 18km (11 miles) west of

### *Moments* For a Grand Panorama

On a rocky promontory, 3km (1¾ miles) to the southeast of the town, stands **Burg Landshut.** Once the domain of the archbishops of Trier, the property dates from the 11th century but long ago fell into ruins. You don't come here for these ruins but for one of the grandest **panoramas** ★★ in the entire Rhineland and Mosel areas. Even the steepest slopes on the way to this belvedere are covered with vines.

Bernkastel-Kues. Containing only 11 tables, it tends to be fully booked up to 3 months in advance on weekends, and 2 weeks in advance for weeknights. (***Hint:*** If you want to dine here on short notice, consider lunch instead of dinner, when demand for its tables is less intense.) If you're lucky enough to snare a reservation for dinner, it's best to opt for an overnight in one of the hotel's 20 bedrooms. Doubles (ranging from simple to elaborate, though all are conservative) cost from 90€ to 200€ ($80.35–$178.60). Each has TV and telephone, and most contain minibars.

Menu items are elaborate and concocted from hyper-upscale ingredients through the supervision of master chef Helmut Thieltges. His charming wife, Ulrike, supervises the dining room. Your meal might include rolls of young hen layered with Périgord truffles and served with macaroni and foie gras; or lobster braised in coconut milk, served with a curry-flavored cream sauce. More pungent, but memorably savory, might be a tart concocted from tartar of beef with Iranian caviar or a roasted rack of venison in wine sauce served with a purée of braised exotic mushrooms. The restaurant has one of the most comprehensive wine lists in the Mosel valley, with vintages from the region, the rest of Europe, and the world.

Auf dem Eichelfeld, D-54518 Dreis. ✆ **06578/98220.** Reservations essential. Main courses 30€–42€ ($26.80–$37.50); fixed-price menu 95€–115€ ($84.85–$102.70). AE, MC, V. Wed–Sun noon–2pm and 7–9pm. Closed Jan and 3 weeks in late July–early Aug.

## 6 Trier (Treves) ★★

124km (77 miles) SW of Koblenz, 143km (89 miles) SW of Bonn, 193km (120 miles) SW of Frankfurt

As the Romans spread over Europe, they established satellite capitals for ruling their distant colonies. Augusta Treverorum (Trier) was founded under Augustus in 16 B.C. It eventually became known as Roma Secunda—the second Rome. For nearly 5 centuries, well into the Christian era, Trier remained one of Europe's political, cultural, and ecclesiastical power centers.

But this city, Germany's oldest, actually dates back much farther. In 2000 B.C., according to legend, the Assyrians established a colony here, and archaeological findings indicate a pre-Roman Celtic civilization. The buildings and monuments still standing today, however, date from Roman and later periods.

Trier is an important gateway, lying only 10km (6 miles) from Luxembourg on the western frontier of Germany, where the Ruwer and Saar rivers meet the Mosel. The city is rich not only in art and tradition, but also, because of its location, in wine—it's one of Germany's largest exporters.

### ESSENTIALS

**GETTING THERE** **By Train** **Trier Hauptbahnhof** is on the Wasserbillig–Trier–Koblenz "Moselbahn" line and also the Trier–Saarbrücken line. Trier has frequent regional connections. There are 20 trains per day to Koblenz (trip time: 1 hr. 20 min.), 20 trains to Cologne (trip time: 2 hr. 25 min.), and 20 trains to Saarbrücken (trip time: 1 hr. 20 min.). For information, call ✆ **01805/99-66-33.**

**By Bus** Buses between Trier and Bullay run along the Mosel River, leaving from the main station in Trier at Bussteig 3. Service is provided by **RMV Rhein Mosel Verkehrsgesellschaft** (✆ **02671/8976;** www.rmv-bus.de) and by **Moselbahn, GmbH** (✆ **0651/147750**).

**By Boat** Boat rides on the Mosel River operate between Trier and Cochem (see section 1, earlier in this chapter). Contact **Mosel Personen Schiffahrt Gebrüder Kolb,** Briedern/Mosel (✆ **02673/1515**).

**By Car** Access by car to Trier is via the A1 Autobahn north and south, the A48 east, and Route 51 from the north.

**VISITOR INFORMATION** Contact **Tourist-Information,** An der Porta Nigra (✆ **0651/97-80-80;** www.trier.de), open Friday to Saturday 9am to 6:30pm, Saturday 9am to 4:30pm, and Sunday 9am to 3:30pm.

**GETTING AROUND** Most of Trier's attractions are within walking distance of each another, and few visitors need to take the bus. Bus tickets (purchased on the bus) cost 1.35€ ($1.20) within zone 1 (the city). For information, call ✆ **0651/71-72-73.**

**SHOPPING** Trier has a new wine-tasting and information center, **Haus des Weines,** Margaretengasschen 2A (✆ **0651/978-0834**), where you can purchase the finest selection of Mosel wines not only in Trier but in the entire valley. There is a large array of "products of the grape," along with various gifts, souvenirs, and accessories. From Easter to October, hours are Monday to Saturday 10am to 6pm, Sunday 10am to 4pm. In the off-season, it is open Monday to Friday 10am to 6pm, Saturday 10am to 4pm.

## SEEING THE SIGHTS

Every day May to October, the tourist office (see above) conducts a 2-hour **walking tour** that departs from the office at 1:30pm. The cost is 5€ ($4.45) per adult, 2€ ($1.80) for children 6 to 14.

### EXPLORING THE ROMAN RUINS

When the last Roman prefect departed from Trier in about A.D. 400, he left behind a vast collection of monuments from the centuries of Roman domination. **Porta Nigra (Black Gate)** ★★ (✆ **0651/75424**) is the best-preserved Roman structure in Germany, the only survivor of the great wall that once surrounded Trier. The huge sandstone blocks, assembled without mortar, were held together with iron clamps—the marks can still be seen. From outside the gate, the structure appeared to be simply two arched entrances between rounded towers leading directly into the town, but intruders soon discovered that the arches opened into an inner courtyard where they were at the mercy of the town's defenders. During the Middle Ages, the Greek hermit Simeon, later canonized, chose the east tower as his retreat. After his death, the archbishop turned the gate into a huge double church. When Napoléon came this way, however, he ordered all the architectural changes to be removed and the original Roman core restored. Porta Nigra is open daily, April to October, 9am to 6pm; November and January to March, 9am to 5pm; and December, 10am to 4pm. Admission is 3.10€ ($2.75) for adults and 1€ (90¢) for children.

The Imperial Palace district, stretching along the site of the former medieval wall of the city, begins with the Roman building known today as the **Basilica,** Basilikaplatz (✆ **0651/72468**). Although much of the structure has been demolished, the huge hall that remains—believed to be the throne room—gives some idea of the grandeur of the original palace. The two tiers of windows are arranged within high-rising arches in which fragments of the original wall paintings can be seen. Five large heating chambers outside the walls sent warm air through the hollow floor, in the unique method of Roman central heating. Today the Basilica serves as the main Protestant church in the city. It's open Monday to Saturday 9am to 6pm and Sunday 11am to 6pm. Admission is free.

Next to the Basilica stands the 17th-century **Kurfürstliches Palais (Electoral Palace)** (✆ **0651/94-94-218**), built in the German Renaissance style as

*Fun Fact* **Local Boy**

Karl Marx was born and grew up in Trier; his birthplace is now a museum. As a young man, he traveled down the Mosel Valley and was so shocked by the exploitation of vineyard workers that he decided to write an article about their plight. Thus began his career.

a residence for the archbishop-electors, the town's governors. The palace cannot be entered because its interior is used for city offices, but the adjoining **Palastgarten (Palace Gardens)** ★, full of ponds, flowers, and rococo statues, are always open and free.

The **Imperial Baths** ★★ (Kaiserthermen; ✆ **0651/44262**), at the south end of Palastgarten, were erected in the early-4th century by Constantine I. Of the huge complex, only the ruins of the hot baths remain. These were among the largest in the Roman empire, and although never completed, they were used in connection with the Imperial Palace. The older **Baths of St. Barbara** (Barbarathermen; ✆ **0651/762280**) are located on Südallee, near a Roman bridge. They're open daily 9am to 6pm, and admission to both is 2.10€ ($1.90) and .70€ (65¢) for children.

The **Amphitheater,** Amphitheaterplatz (✆ **0651/73010**), is the oldest Roman construction in Trier, dating from A.D. 100. The stone seats, arranged in three circles separated by broad promenades, held at least 20,000 people. The ruins are open daily 9am to 6pm; admission is 2.10€ ($1.90).

A **collective ticket,** which grants admission to the amphitheater, the two sets of Roman baths, and the Porta Nigra, costs 5€ ($4.45) for adults and 2€ ($1.80) for children under 18 and is available from the Tourist Office.

**Dom (Cathedral)** ★ From the outside, this cathedral, with its rough-hewn stonework, looks more like a fortress than a church. This is the third church to stand on the site of the former 4th-century palace of the Empress Helena, mother of Constantine. It was begun in 1035 in Romanesque style. The later Gothic and baroque additions only helped to pull the ecclesiastical architecture into a timeless unity. The interior combines baroque decoration with Gothic vaulting and archways. On the south aisle is a magnificent tympanum depicting Christ between the Virgin and St. Peter. The Treasury Museum contains many important works of art, including the 10th-century St. Andrew's Altar, an unusual portable altar made of wood and covered with gold and ivory.

Domfriehof (north of the Palace Gardens and Basilica). ✆ **0651/7-58-01.** Cathedral free; Treasury 2€ ($1.80). Cathedral Apr–Oct, daily 6am–6pm; Nov–Mar, daily 6am–4:30pm. Treasury Apr–Oct, Mon–Sat 10am–5pm; Nov–Mar, Mon–Sat 10am–noon and 2–4:30pm.

**Karl-Marx-Haus** This old burgher's house is where Karl Marx (1818–83) was born and where he lived until he finished school in 1835. The museum has exhibits on Marx's personal history, volumes of poetry, original letters, and photographs with personal dedications. There's also a collection of rare first editions and international editions of his works, as well as exhibits on the development of socialism in the 19th century. In the vicinity of the museum is a study center, **Studienzentrum Karl-Marx-Haus,** Johannestrasse 28 (same phone), for research on Marx and Engels.

Brückenstrasse 10. ✆ **0651/97-06-80.** Admission 2€ ($1.80) adults, 1€ (90¢) children. Apr–Oct, Mon 1–6pm, Tues–Sun 10am–6pm; Nov–Mar, Mon 2–5pm, Tues–Sun 10am–1pm and 2–5pm. Bus: 1, 2, 3, or 4.

**Liebfrauenkirche** ★ This parish church, separated from the cathedral by a narrow passageway, is more pleasing aesthetically than its older neighbor. Begun in 1235, it was among the first examples of French Gothic architecture. The ground plan is in the shape of a Greek cross, creating a circular effect with all points equidistant from the central high altar. The structure is supported by 12 circular columns, rather than the typical open buttresses. The interior is bathed in sunlight, which streams through the high transoms. Although its restoration after the war changed some of the effect of the central construction, it's still unique among German churches.

Some of the church's more important works of art are now in the **Bischöfliches Museum,** Windstrasse 8 (✆ **0651/7-10-52-55**). The sepulcher of Bishop Karl von Metternich, who represented the archbishopric during the Thirty Years' War, is among the most interesting of those remaining. The museum is open Monday to Saturday 9am to 1pm and 2 to 5pm, Sunday 1 to 5pm; admission is 1.50€ ($1.35) for adults and .50€ (45¢) for children.

Liebfrauenstrasse 2. ✆ **0651/75-801.** Free admission. Daily 7:30am–noon and 2–6pm.

**Rheinisches Landesmuseum** ★★ This is one of the outstanding museums of Roman antiquities north of the Alps. Numerous reliefs from funerary monuments show daily life in Roman times. The museum's most popular exhibit is the *Mosel Ship,* a sculpture of a wine-bearing vessel crowning a big burial monument of the 3rd century A.D. Also on display are many mosaics and frescoes, ceramics, glassware, a 2,700-year-old Egyptian casket complete with mummy, an outstanding numismatic collection, and prehistoric and medieval art and sculpture.

Weimarer Allee 1 (between the Imperial Baths and the Basilica, at the edge of the Palace Gardens). ✆ **0651/9-77-40.** Admission 5.50€ ($4.90) adults, 1.50€ ($1.35) children. Tues–Fri 9:30am–5pm; Sat–Sun 10:30am–5pm. Bus: 2, 6, 16, 26, or 30.

## BOAT TOURS

Trier owes much of its majesty to the river that nurtured its medieval commerce. You can take a day cruise for a waterside view of its historic banks. Easter to October, boats depart daily at 9:15am from the city docks (Zurlauben) for a 4-hour trip along the river to **Bernkastel** (see section 5, earlier in this chapter), passing vineyards, wine hamlets, historic churches, and semiruined fortresses en route. Participants spend 2 hours exploring Bernkastel before returning on the same boat to Trier, arriving back at 7:40pm. The cost is 25€ ($22.35) per person.

### *Moments* Trailing Bacchus into the Underground

Since medieval times, Trier has served as a warehouse and distribution center for thousands of liters of wine fermented in its underground cellars. At least 40 of these cellars lie beneath the streets of the city and surrounding suburbs and hamlets. The oldest and most venerable of these is **Vereinigte Hospitien,** Krahnen Ufer Strasse 19 (✆ **0651/94-50**), which only accepts visitors who phone in advance for a reservation. Be warned that if it's inconvenient for the staff to receive you, they'll be quick to tell you. The quickest way to arrange a tour of this cellar, or any of its competitors, is to enlist the aid of the tourist office. The staff there knows which group of vintners is receptive to visits, and they'll make suggestions as to the best spots for drop-ins.

If you don't want to spend so much time on the river, you can take a shorter, hour-long excursion to the nearby historic hamlet of **Pfalzel.** Boats depart from Trier's docks daily Easter to October at 11am, 12:30, 2, 3:15, and 4:30pm. One-way costs 4€ ($3.55); round-trip is 7€ ($6.25). You can prolong your excursion with a walk along the riverbanks in Pfalzel or return on the next boat, almost immediately after your arrival.

For information on either of these excursions, contact the tourist office (see above) or the boat operator **Gebrüder Kolb** (✆ **0651/2-63-17** in Trier, or **02673/15-15** at its corporate headquarters in the nearby town of Briedern).

## WHERE TO STAY

### EXPENSIVE

**Dorint Porta Nigra** ★ The six-story Dorint Porta Nigra combines style, comfort, and location, making it one of the two leading choices in Trier (the other is the Ramada; see below). Most rooms have sitting areas and ornately tiled bathrooms with shower-tub combinations. All were freshly renovated in 1999.

Porta-Nigra-Platz 1 (across from the Roman ruins), 54292 Trier. ✆ **0651/2-70-10.** Fax 0651/2-70-11-70. www.dorint.de. 106 units. 145€–158€ ($129.50–$141.10) double; 260€ ($232.20) suite. Rates include buffet breakfast. AE, DC, MC, V. Parking 8.20€ ($7.30). Bus: 3. **Amenities:** 2 restaurants; bar; cafe; room service; babysitting; laundry/dry cleaning. *In room:* TV, minibar, hair dryer, safe.

**Ramada Hotel Trier** ★ This is the most important hotel built in Trier in many a year. It's located in the heart of the sightseeing zone, near the old Roman monuments. It may be too sleek and impersonal for some tastes, but it's serviceable in every way. Rooms are spacious, with streamlined modern furnishings and bathrooms containing shower-tub combinations.

Kaiserstrasse 29, 54290 Trier. ✆ **800/854-7854** in the U.S., or 0651/9-49-50. Fax 0651/9-49-56-66. www.ramada-hotels.com/trier. 130 units. 92€–112.50€ ($82.15–$100.45) double; 122€–134.50€ ($108.95–$120.10) suite. AE, DC, MC, V. Parking 5.50€ ($4.90) outdoors; 8.50€ ($7.60) in garage. Bus: 1, 2, or 12. **Amenities:** Restaurant; lounge; room service; babysitting; laundry/dry cleaning. *In room:* A/C, TV, dataport, minibar, hair dryer, safe.

### MODERATE

**Kessler** *Value* The sunny Kessler is managed by an English speaker who does everything he can to make your stay pleasant. Rooms are small but attractively maintained and furnished in a clean, modern style, all with neatly kept bathrooms containing shower-tub combinations. The breakfast is very good.

Brückenstrasse 23 (next to the Karl-Marx-Haus), 54290 Trier. ✆ **0651/97-81-70.** Fax 0651/9-78-17-97. www.hotel-kessler-trier.de. 22 units. 72€–128€ ($64.30–$114.30) double; 92€–165€ ($82.15–$147.35) triple. Rates include buffet breakfast. AE, MC, V. Parking 2.50€ ($2.25) outside; 10€ ($8.95) in garage. Bus: 1, 2, 3, or 4. **Amenities:** Restaurant; bar; room service; laundry/dry cleaning. *In room:* TV, minibar, hair dryer.

**Petrisberg** Petrisberg is beautifully situated at a point where a forest, a vineyard, and a private park meet. Each room has a view of the greenery outside. All units contain neat furnishings and bathrooms equipped with shower-tub combinations. The ground-floor Weinstube is the gathering place for many locals, particularly on weekends.

Sickingenstrasse 11 (a 10-min. walk from the Altstadt), 54296 Trier. ✆ **0651/46-40.** Fax 0651/4-64-50. www.hotelpetrisberg.de. 37 units. 82€–88€ ($73.25–$78.60) double. Rates include buffet breakfast. MC, V. Free outdoor parking; 5€ ($4.45) in garage. Bus: 6. **Amenities:** Restaurant; lounge. *In room:* TV.

**Römischer Kaiser** ★ This small, century-old building is now a hotel offering cozily furnished rooms in a prime location. Renovation in the mid-'90s restored the building to its original beauty as a 19th-century patrician house. Because of the hotel's location, visitors touring the area often drop in for a meal.

Am Porta Nigra Platz 6, 54292 Trier. ✆ **0651/9-77-00.** Fax 0651/97-70-99. 43 units. 98€–108€ ($87.50–$96.45) double. Rates include buffet breakfast. AE, DC, MC, V. Free parking. Bus: 1, 2, 3, or 4. **Amenities:** Restaurant; lounge. *In room:* TV, minibar.

**Villa Hügel** ★★ *Kids* This lovely, white, Art Nouveau villa, built in 1914, offers more style and ambience than some of the more expensive hotels, such as the Ramada. The windows overlook either a private garden with old trees or the city. Rooms are spacious and high-ceilinged, all containing bathrooms with shower-tub combinations. Four double rooms are so large that they're almost suites, making them favorites with families.

Bernhardstrasse 14, 54295 Trier. ✆ **0651/3-30-66.** Fax 0651/3-79-58. 30 units. 97€–133€ ($86.60–$118.75) double. Rates include buffet breakfast. AE, DC, MC, V. Free outdoor parking; 9€ ($8.05) in garage. Bus: 2 or 8. **Amenities:** Restaurant; lounge; pool; sauna; room service; babysitting; laundry/dry cleaning. *In room:* TV, minibar, hair dryer.

## INEXPENSIVE

**Hotel Monopol** If you're seeking inexpensive lodging, try the four-story Monopol. It's a completely updated, century-old hotel with a cooperative staff. Its rooms are both good-size and well maintained, although completely sterile in decor. Rooms with shower or tub also contain some nice extras such as extra bed linen, comfortable chairs, a writing desk, and toiletries in the bathroom.

Bahnhofsplatz 7 (across from the Hauptbahnhof), 54292 Trier. ✆ **0651/71-40-90.** Fax 0651/7-14-09-10. 35 units, 24 with shower or tub. 69€ ($61.60) double without shower or tub; 82€ ($73.25) double with shower or tub. Rates include buffet breakfast. No credit cards. Parking 3€ ($2.70). Bus: 1, 2, or 12. **Amenities:** Breakfast room; lounge. *In room:* TV.

## WHERE TO DINE

**Palais Kesselstatt** ★ GERMAN/INTERNATIONAL This is the most unusual and interesting restaurant in Trier. The pink-sided baroque building was originally the residence of the count of Kesselstatt. Inside, the three high-ceilinged dining rooms include the former chapel and the Kaminstube (chimney area), which has an enormous fireplace. Menu items are made with fresh ingredients and change with the seasons. They might include fresh greens with slices of duck breast in herb vinaigrette, consommé with strips of filet steak, filet of turbot with prawns in a vegetable sauce, and a dessert specialty of Bavarian cream with strawberry sorbet, served with fresh marinated strawberries.

The restaurant prides itself on stocking only Rieslings produced in nearby vineyards—an excellent selection. Anyone interested in sampling the region's legendary wines in a less formal setting can head for the Weinstube where you can get wine and simple platters of traditional German and international food.

Liebfrauenstrasse 10 (next to the cathedral). ✆ **0651/4-02-04.** Reservations recommended. Main dining room, main courses 16.80€–22€ ($15–$19.65); fixed-price menu 32€ ($28.60); Weinstube platters 9€–11.50€ ($8.05–$10.25); wine 3.30€–5.90€ ($2.95–$5.25) per glass. AE, MC, V. Restaurant Tues–Sun 11:30am–2pm and 6–9:30pm. Weinstube, daily 10am–midnight. Bus: 1.

**Pfeffermühle** ★★ FRENCH This is clearly the best restaurant in Trier. Siegberg and Angelika Walde use fresh ingredients and maintain a bright, well-decorated dining room with a river view. Their nouvelle French cuisine is delectable. Try the assorted fish, cooked à point, with homemade noodles, followed by petit fours. The list of Mosel wines is extensive. In summer, guests can enjoy their meals on a terrace.

Zurlaubener Ufer 76, Zurlauben. ✆ **0651/2-61-33.** Reservations required. Main courses 22€–26€ ($19.65–$23.20); fixed-price menu 42€–62€ ($37.50–$55.35). MC, V. Tues–Sat noon–2pm; Mon–Sat 6:30–9:30pm. Closed Dec 24–Jan 4. Bus: 5.

**Zum Domstein** *Finds* RHINELAND Charming Zum Domstein is permeated with an old-time sense of bounty. It overlooks the flower stands and the fountain of Trier's central plaza. Ask for one of the wine tastings, which will get you either three glasses of wine (from the Mosel, the Ruwer, and the Saar) for a total of 3.20€ to 8€ ($2.85–$7.15); or a half-dozen very small glasses showcasing separate regional vintages for a total of 6€ ($5.35). In addition, at least 10 regional whites and six regional and French reds are sold by the glass, while hundreds more, in bottles, are stored within the cellars.

The food here is as tempting as the wine; a typically savory offering is a platter of filet of trout in a Riesling sauce or knuckle of lamb with vegetables. All the dishes are redolent with old-fashioned flavors; some are even said to have been enjoyed by the Romans, often with rich sauces. In winter, you'll want to find a spot near the huge tiled stove.

You might also want to look at the **Römischer Weinkeller,** originally built around A.D. 326. Original Roman artifacts, many connected with food and cooking, decorate the room. Dishes here are prepared according to recipes attributed to Marcus Gavius Apicius, said to have been the foremost chef at the court of the emperor Tiberius. Fixed-price menus in the cellar range from 14€ to 28€ ($12.50–$25).

Hauptmarkt 5. ✆ **0651/7-44-90.** Reservations recommended. Main courses 12€–15€ ($10.70–$13.40); fixed-price menu 22€–28€ ($19.65–$25). MC, V. Daily 9am–11:30pm, with hot food served daily 11:30am–2pm and 6–9:30pm. Bus: 1, 2, or 12.

## TRIER AFTER DARK

The cathedral hosts a series of free **organ recitals** in May, June, August, and September. Contact the tourist office (see earlier in this section) for schedules.

**TUFA** (✆ **0651/718-24-12**) presents theater, established touring bands, and the occasional disco. One student hangout, **Blaues Blut,** Pferdermarkt (✆ **0651/4-12-57**), features blue lights and tables covered in imported Turkish tile; outside, the terrace includes some of the only shade trees in the entire city (short-sighted architectural designers removed the rest). Open Monday to Friday 9:30 am to 1am and Saturday to Sunday 10am to 2am. Thursday to Saturday there's dancing and DJs. A club with a beer garden, **Exhaus,** Zurmainer Strasse 114 (✆ **0651/2-51-91**), has both dancing and bands, usually Wednesday to Saturday. Days vary, but the hours are 8pm to 2am. Call to see what's scheduled. Cover is 3€ to 10€ ($2.70–$8.95).

The subterranean **Dive,** Judengasse 21 (✆ **0651/44424**), is aptly named. On one level is a bar with a plastic-like surreal "beachfront," evocative of Miami in the '50s. Below is a dance club with blaring music and a hip crowd of locals, mainly from 22 to 35 years of age. Open Monday and Friday to Saturday from 9pm to 3am, and on Thursday from 9am to 2am. There's a cover of 3€ ($2.70). The aptly named **Irish Pub,** Jakobstrasse 10 (✆ **0651/4-95-39**), serves toasted sandwiches, along with Guinness and Harp. Many evenings you'll find an Irish, English, or German band entertaining a rowdy drinking crowd.

The area's nightlife hotspot is **Riverside,** a complex of bars and restaurants, about 1.5km (1 mile) north of the town center. The most popular place here is **Disco Riverside,** Zur Mainer Strasse 173 (✆ **0651/2-10-06**), which draws a high-energy crowd of local dance enthusiasts Wednesday to Sunday, beginning around 10:30pm. Cover is 8€ ($7.15) and usually includes the first drink.

# 16

# Bremen, Lower Saxony & North Hesse

The area between Frankfurt and Hamburg is Germany's most neglected tourist destination, yet it holds many discoveries. Some of Germany's best-preserved medieval towns, as well as some major spas, lie in the flatlands and rolling hills of Lower Saxony and North Hesse. The character of the area ranges widely, from the bustle of the port of Bremen to the isolation of the Lüneburg Heath.

Here you'll also find the beautiful Harz Mountains, perhaps the country's last stronghold of paganism, still a land of legends and fanciful names. It is said that the last bear was killed in the Harz in 1705, the last lynx in 1817, but there are still wildcats, badgers, deer, and foxes, as well as many limestone caves. The beech trees that grow in the Harz range have unusual size and great beauty, and walnut trees abound.

## 1 Bremen ★★

119km (74 miles) SW of Hamburg, 122km (76 miles) NW of Hannover

Bremen, Germany's oldest coastal city, is second only to Hamburg among German ports. As soon as you arrive at "this ancient town by the gray river," you see how closely Bremen is tied to the sea. The sights and smells of coffee, cacao, tropical fruit, lumber, and tobacco give the city an international flavor.

Bremen grew from a little fishing settlement on a sandy slope on the right bank of the river. It was already a significant port when it was made an episcopal see in 787. In the 11th century, under the progressive influence of Archbishop Adalbert, Bremen became known as the "Rome of the North." During the Middle Ages, it was one of the strongest members of the Hanseatic League, and in 1646 it became a free imperial city. It remains one of Europe's most important ports.

### ESSENTIALS

**GETTING THERE** **By Plane** The **Bremen Flughaven** (✆ **0421/55950**) lies only 3km (2 miles) southeast of the city center (take S-Bahn 5). It is used mainly as a commuter airport for flights within Germany.

**By Train** Bremen has excellent rail connections with leading German cities. Its **Hauptbahnhof** lies on major rail lines, including Hamburg–Bremen–Osnabrück–Münster and Hannover–Bremen–Bremerhaven. Thirty trains arrive daily from Hamburg (trip time: 1 hr.), 35 trains from Hannover (trip time: 1 hr.), 13 trains from Berlin (trip time: 5 hr.), and 50 trains from Frankfurt (trip time: 4 hr. 15 min.). For information, call ✆ **01805/99-66-33.**

**By Bus** Rail travel to Bremen is far more efficient, but the city does have some bus links to other towns. Call ✆ **0421/5596416** for information. The bus station is in front of the railway station.

**By Car** Access by car is via the A7 Autobahn east and west and the A27 north and south.

**VISITOR INFORMATION** Contact the **Bremen Tourist Center,** Tourist-Information am Bahnhofsplatz (✆ **0421/308000**). There's also a second branch at **Liebfrauenkircher Hof,** near Markplatz. Both are open Monday to Wednesday 9:30am to 6:30pm, Thursday and Friday 9:30am to 8pm, and Saturday and Sunday 9:30am to 4pm.

**GETTING AROUND** For information about public transportation within Bremen, call ✆ **0421/55-96-333.** A single ticket, good for one trip on the city's network of buses and trams, costs 1.85€ ($1.65) to most destinations. For 5€ ($4.45), two adults and up to five children may ride all day on the network. The meter on local taxis begins at 1.90€ ($1.70).

## EXPLORING THE CITY

### ORGANIZED TOURS

Bremen has both bus and walking tours of its historic sites. **Bus tours,** conducted in both German and English, depart from the Hauptbahnhof daily at 10:30am. They cost 15€ ($13.40) for adults and 8€ ($7.15) for children under 12. **Walking tours** depart every day at 2pm, last 2 hours, and cost 5€ ($4.45). The combination of a morning bus tour with an afternoon walking tour offers a broadly comprehensive overview of Bremen. Tickets should be reserved in advance, then picked up at the tourist office (see "Visitor Information," above).

The city also sponsors **boat trips** around the harbor. They depart from the jetty in front of the Martinikirche every day March to October. You can reach the jetty from Marktplatz by walking southwest along Böttcherstrasse for about 3 minutes. Tours depart at 11:45am, 1:30, and 3:15pm. The cost is 8€ ($7.15) for adults and 4€ ($3.55) for children under 14. For more information, call the tourist office (see above).

### THE TOP ATTRACTIONS

The main sights center around **Marktplatz** ★★, the "parlor" of Bremen life for more than 1,000 years. The 9m (30-ft.) statue (1404) of the city's protector, Roland, bears the "sword of justice" and a shield decorated with an imperial eagle. Local legend has it that as long as the statue stands in the Marketplace, Bremen will survive as a free city. During World War II, when this area was hard hit by Allied bombs, extensive measures were taken to protect the statue.

Across the square from the Rathaus stands another example of a happy merger of Gothic and Renaissance architecture, the **Schötting,** a 16th-century guild hall used by the chamber of commerce. Somewhat in contrast to these ancient masterpieces is the **Haus der Bürgerschaft,** home of Bremen's Parliament. The 1966 structure was scaled down to fit in with its surroundings. Even though it's a maze of glass, concrete, and steel, it doesn't look entirely out of place.

**Dom St. Petri (St. Peter's Cathedral)** ★★ St. Peter's, set back from the square, towers majestically over all other buildings in the Altstadt. Originally designed in 1043 as the archbishop's church, it was rebuilt in the 13th, 16th, and 19th centuries. There's a 12th-century bronze baptismal font in one of the Romanesque crypts. In the Bleikeller (Lead Cellar), there's a bizarre collection of mummified corpses of workers who fell from the roof during the construction. Their bodies were discovered in 1695.

You can also visit the **Dom Museum** (✆ **0421/365-04-11**), which displays artifacts found during the large-scale restoration of the cathedral, including

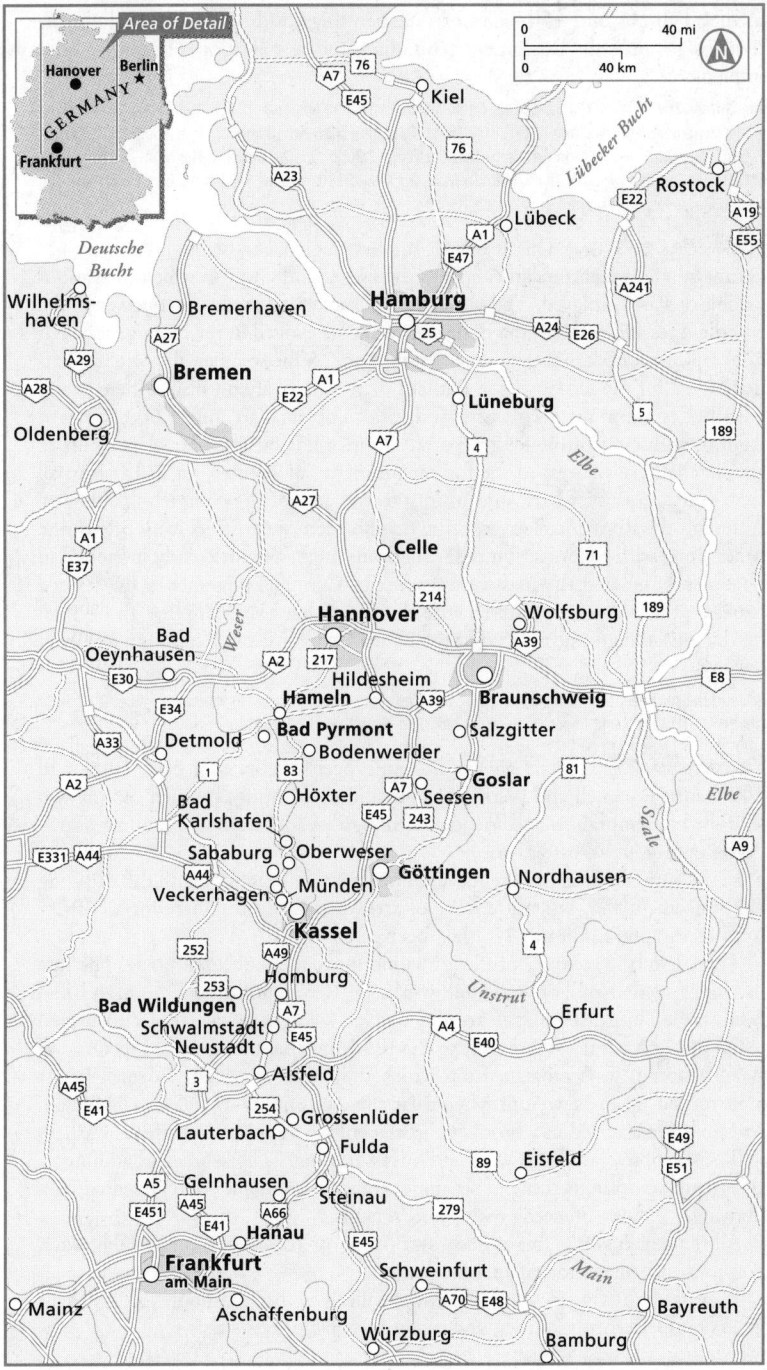
Area of Detail
Hanover
Berlin
GERMANY
Frankfurt
0 40 mi
0 40 km
N
Kiel
Lübecker Bucht
Rostock
Lübeck
Deutsche Bucht
Wilhelms-haven
Bremerhaven
Hamburg
Bremen
Lüneburg
Oldenberg
Elbe
Celle
Hannover
Wolfsburg
Weser
Bad Oeynhausen
Hildesheim
Hameln
Braunschweig
Bad Pyrmont
Salzgitter
Detmold
Bodenwerder
Goslar
Höxter
Seesen
Bad Karlshafen
Sababurg
Oberweser
Göttingen
Nordhausen
Veckerhagen
Münden
Kassel
Homburg
Unstrut
Bad Wildungen
Schwalmstadt
Neustadt
Erfurt
Alsfeld
Grossenlüder
Lauterbach
Fulda
Eisfeld
Gelnhausen
Steinau
Hanau
Frankfurt am Main
Schweinfurt
Main
Mainz
Aschaffenburg
Würzburg
Bamberg
Bayreuth

medieval tombs and 15th-century wall paintings. Other exhibits include the remains of an early Romanesque building and a collection of historic altar implements.

Sandstrasse 10–12. ✆ **0421/36-50-40.** Cathedral free; museum and tower 2.50€ ($2.25) adults, 1€ (90¢) students, seniors, and children; tower .70€ (65¢). Cathedral Mon–Fri 10am–5pm, Sat 10am–1:30pm, Sun 2–5pm. Museum May–Oct Mon–Fri 10am–5pm, Sat 10am–1:30pm, Sun 2–5pm; Nov–Apr Mon–Fri 11am–4pm, Sat 10am–noon, Sun 2–5pm. Cellar and tower May–Oct Mon–Fri 10am–5pm, Sat 10am–noon; closed Nov–Apr and holidays. Bus: 30, 31, or 34.

**Focke-Museum** ★ This is one of the best regional museums in this area of Germany, and we particularly applaud the user-friendly way in which the various exhibitions are displayed. The glory days of Bremen as a maritime power in the Middle Ages and through the Renaissance era are evoked in the main gallery. For safekeeping and because they were deteriorating in the weather, the original statues carved for the facade of the Rathaus or town hall are on display here, along with Ecclesiastical art, secular art, and various objets d'art, much of it retrieved from town houses of the long departed Bremen aristocracy. Lots of portraits of fat merchants also attest to the former prosperity of Bremen. In addition to all that, you can wander back into history to the days of the conquering Romans. Although the Roman collection is the richest, there are artifacts from prehistoric times along with Saxon antiquities. Americans might be particularly interested in documents showing the massive transport of German emigrants to the United States on the steamers operated by the Norddeutscher Lloyd Shipline. In the park on the museum grounds is a typical thatched farmhouse once common to Lower Saxony.

Schwachhauser Heerstrasse 240. ✆ **0421/3613575.** Admission 3.50€ ($3.15) for adults, 1.50€ ($1.35) for children 6–18. Free 5 and under. Open Mon–Sat 10am–6pm. S. Bahn: Focke Museum.

**Kunsthalle** ★ This art gallery has long been celebrated for its 19th- and 20th-century French and German art, including paintings by such old masters as Rubens, Rembrandt, and Tiepolo, although its collection also embraces such 20th-century artists as Picasso.

In the summer of 2001, the museum made world headlines with the stunning announcement that a treasure trove of art, which had hung here for a century until its disappearance in 1945, had been returned.

The tale of the recovery of the art would make the plot for a movie. The rare paintings, worth millions, include works by Rembrandt and Dürer, and had been stashed in a castle for safekeeping by Nazi soldiers. Soviet troops uncovered the works and handed them over to the KGB. In time they were shipped to the Baku Museum in Azerbaijan from which they were eventually stolen. The art later turned up in New York when a Japanese businessman and an Azerbaijani wrestler were arrested in a Brooklyn apartment where the stolen art was stashed.

The star of the purloined works is Dürer's drawing, "The Women's Bathhouse," showing a voluptuous scene of six nude women. Rembrandt is represented by a drawing, "Woman Standing with Raised Hands."

All the stolen works can be seen on display on Tuesdays. On any other days, you must call ahead for an appointment.

Even without these works, the Kuntshalle is worth a 2-hour visit, with its works by Delacroix, Courbet, and many French Impressionists.

Der Kunstverein in Bremen, Am Wall. 207. ✆ **049/421-329080.** Admission 5€ ($4.45) adults, 2€ ($1.80) students and children. Tues–Sun 10am–5pm. Bus: 1, 4, or 6.

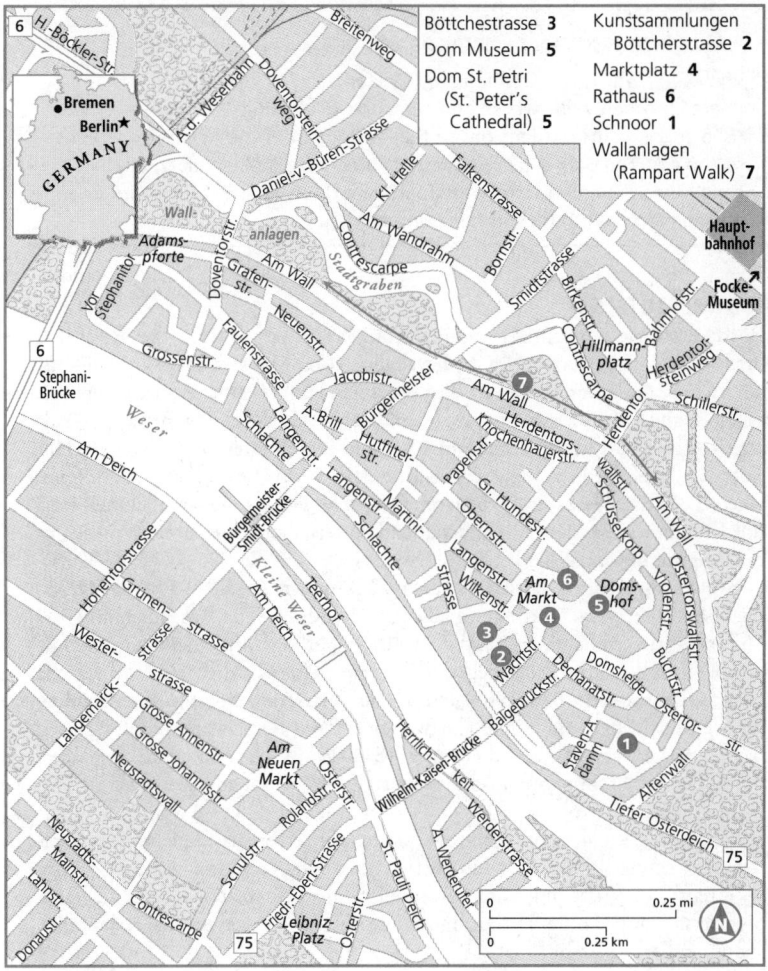


**Rathaus** ★ The 560-year-old Rathaus has seen several periods of transformation. Outside, at the west end, is one of the more recent additions, a sculpture of Bremen's visitors from the land of Grimm—the Bremen town musicians. The donkey, dog, cat, and cock are stacked, pyramid style, in a constant pose for the ever-present cameras. The original Gothic foundations of the Rathaus remain basically unchanged, but the upper section reflects the 17th-century Weser Renaissance style in the facade; the tall windows alternate with relief statues of Charlemagne and the electors of the Holy Roman Empire. The upper hall, part of the original structure, contains a beautifully carved early 17th-century oak staircase. A mural of *The Judgment of Solomon* (1537) reminds us that the hall was originally a council chamber and courtroom. Below the lower hall lies the historic wine cellar, the "good Ratskeller of Bremen" (see "Where to Dine," below).

Marktplatz. ✆ **0421/36-10.** Admission 2.50€ ($2.25) adults, 1.50€ ($1.35) children and students. For tours, inquire at the tourist office (see "Visitor Information," above). Tours generally begin Mon–Sat 11am, noon, 3, and 4pm; Sun 11am and noon. Tram: 1, 2, 3, or 5. Bus: 30, 31, or 34.

### *Moments* Rampart Promenade

This walk, which the Germans call **Wallanlagen** ★ (tram: 4, 5, or 6) is a peaceful green park where the ramparts protecting this Hanseatic city used to stand. Its gardens divide the Altstadt from the newer extensions of the city. The park is just a few short blocks from Marktplatz, along the canal (once Bremen's crown-shaped moat). Its major attraction is an ancient windmill that's still functioning.

## MORE SIGHTS

**Böttcherstrasse** ★ (tram: 4), running from Marktplatz to the Weser River, is a brick-paved reproduction of a medieval alley, complete with shops, restaurants, a museum, and galleries. The street was designed to present a picture of Bremen life, past and present. It was the brainchild of a wealthy Bremen merchant, Ludwig Roselius, and was dedicated in 1926 and rebuilt after World War II. This artery is one of Bremen's biggest attractions. Try to visit around noon, 3, or 6pm, when the Meissen bells strung between two gables set up a chorus of chimes for a full 15 minutes. Besides fine handcraft and pottery shops, the street also contains buildings of historical significance.

**Kunstsammlungen Böttcherstrasse** ★, Böttcherstrasse 8–10 (✆ **0421/33-65-066;** tram: 4), consists of two adjoining buildings. The Roselius House is a 16th-century merchant's home with a collection of medieval objets d'art and furniture. Next door, the Paula-Becker-Modersohn House is dedicated to Bremen's outstanding painter (1876–1907) and contains many of her best works, including paintings, drawings, and prints. The two upper floors house works of the sculptor, painter, and architect Bernhard Hoetger (1874–1949). The museum is open Tuesday to Sunday 11am to 6pm. Admission is 5€ ($4.45) for adults and 3€ ($2.70) for children aged 7 to 16.

**Schnoor** (tram: 4, 5, or 6), the old quarter of Bremen, has undergone restoration. The cottages of this east-end district, once homes of simple fishermen, have been rented to artists and artisans in an effort to revive many old arts and crafts. Sightseers visit not only for the atmosphere but also for the unusual restaurants, shops, and art galleries.

## SHOPPING

Bremen has thrived on business and commerce since it was founded. Today, you'll find lots of shopping options along two streets, **Obernstrasse** and **Sögestrasse,** as well as dozens of boutique-inspired gift shops in the **Schnoor.** The city's cutest stuffed teddy bears, available in all sizes and degrees of fuzziness, are sold at **Bärenhaus,** Stabendanstrasse 9 (✆ **0421/33-78-419;** tram: 4, 5, or 6), for prices that begin at 14€ ($12.50) for your garden-variety bear and can go much, much higher. Next door is **Rapunzel,** Schnoor 17 (same phone), an emporium for gift items, as well as T-shirts, souvenirs, books, and marionettes modeled after figures from the Brothers Grimm.

The best shop for women's fashions is **Roland Kleidung,** Sögestrasse 18–20 (✆ **0421/1-25-36;** tram: 4, 5, or 6), although the town's largest department store, **Karstadt,** Obernstrasse 1 (✆ **0421/3-07-10;** tram: 4, 5, or 6), also stocks an impressive selection of less expensive garments. Antiques, including some brass fixtures salvaged from old ships, are sold at **Antikitäten B&M,** Fedelhörn 19 (✆ **0421/328282;** tram: 10). Two art galleries that contain sometimes riveting modern art are **Gallery Hubert,** Sögestrasse at Pelzstrasse 4 (✆ **0421/1-65-55-44;** tram: 4, 5, or 6); and **Art Gallery,** Böttcherstrasse 8–20 (✆ **0421/33-88-20;** tram: 4, 5, or 6), both of which represent artists from the region and throughout middle Europe.

Shoes are the best buy in Bremen, and **Leder-Koopman,** Georgstrasse 56 (✆ **0471/30-28-29;** tram: 4, 5, or 6), is the best representative of the trade. The company has been making quality wallets, belts, bags, and other leather products for 100 years. Visit their shop to admire a level of craftsmanship that has become a rare commodity, and chances are you won't leave empty-handed. Bargain hunters swarm over the city's riverfront **flea markets.** The Weserflohmarkt is held at the Schlactel and Weser promenade every Saturday 8am to 5pm; on Sunday, the action shifts to Burgerweide 8am to 2pm.

## WHERE TO STAY

### VERY EXPENSIVE

**Park Hotel Bremen** ★★★ This hotel is without question the most outstanding and charming in Bremen. It occupies an enviable site, in a park whose meandering lakes, exotic trees, and zoo are the pride of the city. It's also just a short ride from the center of town. The hotel's terra-cotta dome and evenly proportioned side wings were rebuilt in 1955 to emulate a turn-of-the-20th-century pleasure pavilion. Rooms are generally spacious and well appointed, with large windows overlooking the park. All units contain immaculate bathrooms with shower-tub combinations.

Im Burgerpark, 28209 Bremen. ✆ **0421/3-40-80.** Fax 0421/3-40-86-02. www.park-hotel-bremen.de. 150 units. 205€–275€ ($183.05–$245.60) double; 320€–850€ ($285.75–$759.05) suite. Rates include buffet breakfast. AE, DC, MC, V. Free parking in front of the hotel; 18€ ($16.05) in the garage. Tram: 5 or 6. Bus: 26. **Amenities:** 3 restaurants; bar; bicycles; room service; babysitting; laundry/dry cleaning. *In room:* TV, minibar, hair dryer, safe.

### MODERATE

**Hotel Munte am Stadtwald** ★ You'll think you're in the country at this brick hotel because it fronts directly on one of Bremen's biggest parks. The handsome rooms range from medium to spacious, all containing neatly kept bathrooms with shower-tub combinations. The public rooms are inviting and comfortable, often filled with greenery to make them more home-like. The hotel is bright and friendly, with a helpful personnel. For such a reasonably priced hotel, the swimming pool, sauna, steam bath, and solarium come as an added luxury.

Parkallee 299 (in the Burgerpark, about 2.5km/1½ miles from the center), 28213 Bremen. ✆ **0421/2-20-20.** Fax 0421/22-02-609. www.hotel-munte.de. 134 units. 111€ ($99.10) ground-floor double, 139€ ($124.15) upper-floor double. Rates include buffet breakfast. AE, DC, MC, V. Free outdoor parking; 6€ ($5.35) in garage. Bus: 22 or 23. **Amenities:** 2 restaurants; lounge; pool; sauna; steam room; room service; laundry/dry cleaning. *In room:* TV, minibar, hair dryer.

**Hotel zur Post** ★ Hotel zur Post offers top-notch facilities and comfort, as well as Bremen's leading restaurant. Rooms are first-rate and slightly larger than average. All units contain tidily kept bathrooms with shower-tub combinations. Its proximity to the Hauptbahnhof makes it an ideal choice for train passengers.

Bahnhofsplatz 11, 28195 Bremen. ✆ **800/528-1234** in the U.S. and Canada, or 0421/3-05-90. Fax 0421/3-05-95-91. 183 units. 132€–166€ ($117.90–$148.25) double; from 196€ ($175.05) suite. Rates include buffet breakfast. AE, DC, MC, V. Parking 10€ ($8.95). Tram: 1, 5, 6, or 10. **Amenities:** 2 restaurants; bar; pool; fitness center; salon; room service; babysitting; laundry/dry cleaning. *In room:* TV, minibar, hair dryer, safe.

### INEXPENSIVE

**Hotel Buthman Garni** *Finds* This is an old but restored Bürger house on a tranquil side street within an easy walk of both the rail station and the Altstadt or old town. For nearly half a century, the helpful Buthman family has operated this inn in the center of Bremen. Many frugally minded locals from the countryside, in Bremen on business or a holiday, guard this as a cherished address kind to their pocketbooks. The bedrooms are cozy and midsize, each with traditional furnishings and a small bathroom with shower. We prefer to retreat to number 5 on the upper floor, enjoying its high-ceilinged comfort and its snugness away from the bustle of the city.

Löningstrasse 29, 28195 Bremen. ✆ **0421/326397.** Fax 0421/3398816. www.hotel-buthmann.de. 10 units. 69€–89€ ($61.60–$79.50) double. AE, DC, MC, V. **Amenities:** Breakfast room. *In room:* TV.

**Hotel Mercure Columbus** *Value* Mercure Columbus offers attractive and tasteful rooms, all with private bathrooms containing shower-tub combinations. An elegant recent renovation has set a higher standard for this hotel, putting it on the same footing as Munte am Stadtwald or Hotel zur Post (see above).

Bahnhofsplatz 5–7, 28195 Bremen. ✆ **0421/3-01-20.** Fax 0421/1-53-69. www.mercurehotel.de. 148 units. 121€–131€ ($108.05–$117) double; 141€ ($125.90) suite. Rates include buffet breakfast. AE, DC, MC, V. Parking 8€ ($7.15). Tram: 1, 5, 6, or 10. **Amenities:** Breakfast room; bar; lounge; sauna; solarium; room service; babysitting; laundry/dry cleaning. *In room:* TV, minibar, hair dryer.

**Hotel Tulip Inn Schaper-Siedenburg** Near the train station, this hotel is short on style but big on comfort and maintenance—all at an affordable price. The five-story building features colorful murals depicted on the walls of its multistory atrium. It's in a business section of town with a lot of noise and traffic, but if you ask for a room on the inner side of the atrium, you'll find accommodations more peaceful. Rooms are in a rather minimalist style with modern furniture and small tiled bathrooms with shower. The marketplace and the historic sections of Altstadt or old town are within an easy walk.

Bahnhofstrasse 7, 28195 Bremen. ✆ **0421/3087-0.** Fax 0421/3087-88. www.schaper-siedenburg.de/hotelzimmer_eng.html. 88 units. 90€–120€ ($80.35–$107.15) double. AE, DC, MC, V. **Amenities:** Laundry. *In room:* TV,minibar; coffeemaker, hair dryer, safe.

**Residence** Residence advertises itself as an Art Deco hotel. The elegant public areas have high ceilings with polished crisscrossed timbers and chandeliers. Rooms are comfortably furnished but small, all equipped with bathrooms containing shower-tub combinations.

Hohenlohestrasse 42, 28209 Bremen. ✆ **0421/34-87-10.** Fax 0421/34-23-22. www.hotelresidence.de. 30 units. 88€–118€ ($78.60–$105.35) double. Rates include buffet breakfast. AE, DC, MC, V. Free outdoor parking; 7€ ($6.25) in garage. Tram: 4, 5, 6, or 10. **Amenities:** 2 restaurants; bar; sauna; solarium; room service; laundry/dry cleaning. *In room:* TV, minibar, hair dryer.

## WHERE TO DINE

As a seaport, Bremen has developed its own style of cooking, concentrating much of its effort, naturally, on seafood from Scandinavia and the North Sea.

### VERY EXPENSIVE

**L'Orchidée** ★★★ FRENCH/MODERN GERMAN L'Orchidée, on the 6th floor of the Hotel zur Post (see above), offers an elegantly sophisticated gold, cream, and black decor to go with its candles, silverware, and fine porcelain. Year after year this hotel restaurant emerges at the top in Bremen. Veteran chefs watch over a well-trained kitchen crew, and the service is sophisticated and skillful. The dishes are simply delicious. Try the terrine of smoked eel and shrimp followed either by filet of turbot with lobster or breast of pigeon in a red wine sauce. The desserts are made fresh daily, and the wine list is extensive.

In the Hotel zur Post, Bahnhofsplatz 11. ✆ **0421/3-05-90.** Reservations required. Main courses 25€–31€ ($22.35–$27.70); fixed-price dinner 66€ ($58.95) for 5 courses, 82€ ($73.25) for 7 courses. AE, DC, MC, V. Tues–Sat 6:30–10pm. Closed 2 weeks at Easter and 4 weeks sometime in summer. Tram: 1, 5, 6, or 10.

## EXPENSIVE

**Grashoff's Bistro** ★★ *Finds* GERMAN This restaurant is well managed, charming, and concerned with quality and ambience. Its only real flaw is that it's never open for dinner—instead, it caters to mobs of office workers and shoppers at lunchtime. You'll get a distinct sense of the arts here, and a few memories of Paris as well, thanks to dozens of framed pictures hung edge-to-edge across the cream-colored, bistro-inspired walls. Menu items include a succulent version of spaghetti with lobster; flank steak in a pepper sauce; an oft-changing roster of fresh fish; and desserts such as crème brûlée, fresh pastries, and tarts.

Contrescarpe 80. ✆ **0421/1-47-40.** Reservations recommended. Main courses 20€–23.50€ ($17.85–$21). DC, MC, V. Mon–Fri 10am–7pm; Sat 10am–3pm. Tram: 4, 5, or 6.

**Meierei im Burgerpark** ★ CONTINENTAL This lovely restaurant, in the center of a city park, is managed by the Park Hotel (see above). Locals often combine a meal here with a promenade in the park. The restaurant occupies what was originally a local aristocrat's summerhouse, sheathed in lacy gingerbread and ringed with ornate verandas. It contains four dining rooms furnished in Hanseatic style. The food doesn't match the refined cuisine of the Park Restaurant, but we like the setting. Typical, and very good, dishes include fresh fish, consommé with scallops and saffron, fried breast of duck filled with herbs, sautéed squab with forest mushroom risotto, and medallions of monkfish with orange butter and basil sauce. Coffee and pastries are served every afternoon.

Im Burgerpark. ✆ **0421/3-40-86-19.** Reservations required. Main courses 19€–22€ ($16.95–$19.65). AE, DC, MC, V. Tues–Sun noon–2:30pm and 6:30–10pm. Tram: 6.

**Pappagallo** ★ ITALIAN This is the best Italian restaurant in Bremen; it's a welcome break from a steady diet of north German cuisine. It occupies a Tuscan-style manor originally built by a local industrialist in 1842. Its interior is decorated in a radically modern style that might have been inspired by Milanese minimalism. The angularity is offset by succulent food prepared in sophisticated but time-tested ways. The menu changes every 2 weeks and reflects whatever is in season. Examples might include Sicily-inspired spaghetti Norma, rich with eggplant and mozzarella and herbs; spaghetti with fresh artichoke hearts and asparagus tips; risotto with scampi; and pasta with Parma ham and asparagus.

Goetheplatz 4 (near the town center). ✆ **0421/32-79-63.** Reservations recommended. Main courses 17.50€–24€ ($15.65–$21.45). DC, MC, V. Mon–Fri noon–2:30pm; Mon–Sat 6–11pm. Tram: 2 or 3.

## MODERATE

**Ratskeller** ★ GERMAN/INTERNATIONAL This Ratskeller is one of Germany's most celebrated—and certainly one of the best. It's traditional for friends to gather in the evening over a good bottle of Mosel or Rhine wine (no beer is served). Appetizers include an assortment of smoked fish as well as creamy fish soup flavored with saffron; main courses often include fried pike-perch in a basil sauce and chicken ragout Bremen-style (in a crayfish sauce with calves' sweetbreads, tongue, mushrooms, sausages, and a vegetable risotto). The outstanding wine list is one of the longest lists of German vintages in the world. Some of the decorative kegs have contained wine for nearly 200 years. There's also a less formal bistro, with a limited list of less expensive traditional dishes that include *Laubskaus* and simple platters of fresh fish.

Am Markt (in the Rathaus). ✆ **0421/32-16-76.** Reservations recommended. Main courses 8€–24.30€ ($7.15–$21.70) in the Ratskeller Restaurant; 10€–21€ ($8.95–$18.75) in the Ratskeller Bistro. Fixed-price menu 39€–41€ ($34.85–$36.60) in the restaurant. AE, DC, MC, V. Restaurant daily noon–2:30pm and 7–10:30pm; bistro daily 11am–midnight. Tram: 1, 3, 5, 24, or 25.

### INEXPENSIVE

**Alte Gilde** CONTINENTAL Alte Gilde is located in one of the most ornately decorated houses in Bremen. In spite of the new building surrounding it, the 17th-century structure, with its gilt gargoyles and sea serpents, clings tenaciously to the past. The restaurant is in the vaulted cellar. The chef prepares many fresh fish dishes, as well as pork steak a la Kempinski, with poached eggs and béarnaise sauce—a lot of diners still go for this grandmotherly favorite.

Ansgaritorstrasse 24 (entrance on Hutfilterstrasse). ✆ **0421/17-17-12.** Reservations recommended. Main courses 5.80€–19.50€ ($5.20–$17.40); fixed-price lunch 14€–23€ ($12.50–$20.55); fixed-price dinner 15.50€–23€ ($13.85–$20.55). AE, DC, MC, V. Mon–Sat 11am–3pm and 7–10:30pm. Tram: 2 or 3. Bus: 6, 25, or 26.

## BREMEN AFTER DARK

Bremen nightlife offers a full range of activities. Many pubs and clubs, including those geared toward the gay community, are located in the **Ostertorsteinweg** district (tram: 10).

**THE PERFORMING ARTS** Classical concerts, opera, and dance performances by visiting companies are held in the **Theater am Goetheplatz** complex, Am Goetheplatz 1–3 (✆ **0421/365-3333;** tram: 2 or 3). Call for a list of scheduled performers, ticket prices, and available seating. One of its stages, Schauspielhaus (✆ **0421/3-65-30**), houses a theatrical company that occasionally performs in English. Tickets are 10€ to 24€ ($8.95–$21.45) during the September-to-June season. Opera and other musical performances are scheduled in the **Musiktheater,** Am Goetheplatz (✆ **0421/3-65-33-33;** tram: 2 or 3), where tickets are 10€ to 32€ ($8.95–$28.60). Experimental theater and modern dance can be found in the **Concordia,** Schwachauser Heerstrasse (✆ **0421/365-30;** tram: 1), where a seat costs 14€ to 25€ ($12.50–$22.35). To attend productions of the Bremen Shakespeare Company, head for the **Theater am Leibnitzplatz,** Friedrich-Ebert-Strasse (✆ **0421/50-03-33;** tram: 6), where tickets are 13€ to 25€ ($11.60–$22.35).

**BARS** An early evening bar, **Achims Beck Haus,** Carl-Ronning-Strasse 1 (✆ **0421/1-55-55;** tram: 4, 5, or 6), is a gathering place for drinks and simple pub fare. Open Monday to Thursday 10am to 11:30pm and Friday and Saturday 10am to 2am. An art-scene hangout with a large street-front terrace and a sometimes-rowdy clientele, **Litfass,** Ostertorsteinweg 22 (✆ **0421/70-32-92;** tram: 2 or 3), has the longest bar in town. It serves breakfast, snacks, coffee, and beer. Open Sunday to Thursday 10am to 2am; Friday and Saturday 10am to 4am.

**CASINO** Bremen's centrally located casino, **Bremer Spielbank,** 3 Boettcher Strasse 385 (✆ **0421/329-000;** tram: 4, 5, or 6), contains roulette and blackjack tables. Admission is 2€ ($1.80), and a passport is required, as are jackets and ties for men. Open daily 3pm to 3am.

**DANCE CLUBS** The place to dance is **Delight,** Am Liebfrauenkirchhof 23 (no phone; tram: 4, 5, or 6), a basement club where the DJs play house and hip-hop. Weekends generally bring theme parties. The club opens at 10pm Wednesday and Thursday and 11pm Friday and Saturday; there's no set closing time. On weeknights, the cover is 5€ to 8€ ($4.45–$7.15); on theme nights, it can be as much as 13€ ($11.60). The club is closed in August. In winter, **Modernes,** Neustadtwall 28 (✆ **0421/50-55-53;** tram: 1 or 8), is a movie house during the week, with dancing and live music on the weekend. The rest of the year, bands usually play 7 to 11pm; afterwards, it's a dance club. The cover charge is 5€ ($4.45) when there's just dancing; when there's live music, it's 10€ to 20€ ($8.95–$17.85). Twice monthly, there's a free show.

**GAY CLUBS** Much of the gay nightlife in and around Bremen is diverted into the clubs of nearby Hamburg, but there are still a few good spots. **Thealit,** Im Krummen Arm 1 (✆ **0421/70-16-32;** tram: 10), is the leading lesbian gathering place in town. It offers platters of German and international food every Monday to Saturday 6pm to 1am. Another gay bar of note, mostly for men, is **Rat und Tat,** Theodor-Körner-Strasse 1 (✆ **0421/70-00-08;** tram: 10).

**LIVE MUSIC** For music in a bar setting, check out the band line-up at **Aladin's,** Hannoverschestrasse 11 (✆ **0421/43-51-50;** bus: 40), which also houses a two-room disco and a bar with rock-'n'-roll memorabilia. Open Wednesday to Saturday 10pm to 7am; cover is 4€ to 5€ ($3.55–$4.45). **Moments,** Vordem Stein Tor 65 (no phone; tram: 2, 3, or 10), hosts live rhythm and blues and jazz for a crowd of loyal regulars. Cover is 3.60€ to 5.60€ ($3.20–$5). The place functions as a disco on some nights; cover is then 5.50€ ($4.90). The **Club Kernerwahl,** Kernerwahl 1 (✆ **0421/70-58-52;** tram: 2, 3, or 10), also has live music (and usually no cover charge). Both Moments and Kernerwahl are open Tuesday to Sunday 8pm until dawn.

**VARIETY** Popular with children and adults, the ambitious puppet theater **Theatrium,** Bleicherstrasse 28 (✆ **0421/361-61-81;** tram: 2 or 3), produces entertaining interpretations of books, plays, and movies, ranging from classical works to Woody Allen. Tickets cost 10€ to 20€ ($8.95–$17.85). In the same building, **Theater im Schnoor** (✆ **0421/32-60-54**) presents cabaret and underground theater productions. Tickets are 8€ to 19€ ($7.15–$16.95).

## 2 Lüneburg ★★

124km (77 miles) NE of Hannover, 132km (82 miles) E of Bremen, 55km (34 miles) SE of Hamburg

Motorists driving south from Scandinavia through the Baltic port of Lübeck often find themselves on the Old Salt Road leading to the Hanseatic city of Lüneburg. This was the route over which the "white gold" of Lüneburg's salt mines was transported to the Scandinavian countries during the Middle Ages. Because of its heavy salt deposits, Lüneburg became a spa, which it remains today. In the **Kurpark** is a bathing house where visitors can take brine mud baths. In the **spa gardens,** there are indoor swimming pools, sauna baths, and tennis courts.

Lüneburg is also the ideal starting point for excursions into the **Lüneburg Heath,** which is especially beautiful in late summer, when the heather is in bloom.

### ESSENTIALS

**GETTING THERE** **By Train** The **Lüneburg Bahnhof** lies on two major rail lines, the Hamburg–Hannover line and the Lüneburg–Lübeck–Kiel–Flensburg line, with frequent connections. For information call ✆ **01805/99-66-33.**

**By Bus** Long-distance bus service into Lüneberg is provided by **KVG GmbH** (✆ **04131/87-20-80**) or **VOG GmbH** (✆ **04131/88-07-0**). The bus station is in front of the railway station.

**By Car** Access is Route 4 from Hamburg.

**VISITOR INFORMATION** **Lüneburg Tourist Information** is in the Rathaus, Am Markt 1 (✆ **04131/207-6620**). It's open Monday to Friday 10am to 7pm (to 6pm November to April) and Saturday and Sunday 10am to 4pm.

## EXPLORING THE AREA

Although most buildings in this 1,000-year-old city are from its most prosperous period, the 15th and 16th centuries, a total of 7 centuries of architecture are represented here. The **Rathaus** ★★, Am Markt 1, reached along Auf der Meere, is a perfect example of several trends in architecture and design. You enter through a Gothic doorway into a Renaissance hall. The Great Council Room is the building's most outstanding feature, with sculptures and bas reliefs by Albert von Soest (1566–84). Daily guided tours are conducted all year at 11am, 12:30, and 3pm. The cost is 3€ ($2.70) for adults and 2€ ($1.80) for children and students. For information, call ✆ **04131/30-92-30.**

To understand Lüneberg's role as "the Salt City," visit the **Deutsches Salzmuseum,** Sülfmeisterstrasse 1 (✆ **04131/450-65**). Inside, a series of exhibits explore life in the Middle Ages and the role of salt in the region's economy and culture. Entrance is 4€ ($3.55) for adults, 2.70€ ($2.40) for children. Open May to September Monday to Friday 9am to 5pm, Saturday and Sunday 10am to 5pm. Off-season daily 10am to 5pm.

## SHOPPING

The heath area is known for its craftspeople. Some of the best local arts and crafts are on sale at the tourist office (see above). The town's largest department store is **Karstadt,** Am Markt (✆ **04131/3040**). The main shopping streets are **Bäckerstrasse** and **Grapengiesserstrasse,** both lying in pedestrian zones. There's also an abundance of antiques stores, the best of which are **H. Beckhaus,** Am Markt 5 (✆ **04131/3-11-61**), and **Brüning,** Auf der Altstadt 16 (✆ **04131/40-23-03**).

## WHERE TO STAY

**Bremer Hof** The logo of this hotel is an illustration of the animal musicians of Bremen, who, with their noise, frightened away robbers. The facade looks like something out of the 16th century. Rooms are modern and sunny, but a bit small. All units have bathrooms, some with shower only and some with shower-tub combinations. A 400-year-old wine cellar is open on weekends.

Lünestrasse 13 (a 2-min. walk from Marktplatz), 21335 Lüneburg. ✆ **04131/22-40.** Fax 04131/22-42-24. www.bremer-hof.de. 53 units. 87€–122€ ($77.70–$108.95) double. Rates include buffet breakfast. AE, DC, MC, V. Parking 4.50€ ($4). Bus: 3. **Amenities:** Restaurant; bar; lounge; room service; laundry/dry cleaning. *In room:* TV, hair dryer.

**Hotel Bargenturm** This three-story hotel at the edge of Lüneburg's historic center is one of the most modern in town. Its concrete walls and large expanses of glass make no concessions to the antique architecture of other parts of the city. Rooms are decorated with a no-nonsense comfortable modernity. All contain neatly kept bathrooms with shower-tub combinations. The staff is multilingual and efficient.

Lambertiplatz, 21335 Lüneburg. ✆ **04131/72-90.** Fax 04131/72-94-99. www.hotel-bargenturm.de. 40 units. 101€ ($90.20) double; 113€ ($100.90) junior suite. DC, MC, V. Parking 5€ ($4.45). **Amenities:** Restaurant; bar; room service. *In room:* TV, minibar, hair dryer, safe.

## WHERE TO DINE

**Ratskeller** GERMAN/CONTINENTAL The Ratskeller serves satisfying but unspectacular meals in a town not known for its restaurants. The varied

## The Lüneburg Heath

The **Lüneburg Heath** ★ (in German, *Lüneburger Heide*) is one of the major attractions of northern Germany. The heath covers nearly 775 sq. km (300 sq. miles) and includes many beautiful spots. The sandy soil is mainly covered with brush and heather, although there are a few oak and beech forests in the northern valleys. Toward late summer, the flowering heath turns from green to purple; August and September are the most beautiful months. The best way to approach the heath is via the old town of Lüneburg, the area's transportation hub.

You'll find dramatic, windswept, and bleakly evocative scenery in the **Naturschützpark Lüneburger Heide** ★★, a 260 sq. km (100-sq.-mile) sanctuary for plants and wildlife. Its highest point is the Wilsederberg, a low-lying peak only 168m (550 ft.) above sea level, accessible via a network of footpaths from the hamlet of Wilsede. This reserve, in the center of the heath, is a peaceful, pastoral scene of shepherds, sheep, and undulating hills. Strict laws enforce the maintenance of the thatch-roofed houses and rural atmosphere. One of the park's most charming hamlets is **Undeloh,** which has a good hotel, the **Heiderose,** Gästehaus Heideschmiede, Wilseder Strasse 13 (✆ **04131/477-10**), renting doubles for 85€ to 89€ ($75.90–$79.50), including breakfast. There are also a number of villages—listed on only the most detailed of maps—that post ZIMMER FREI (Room for Rent) signs. These accommodations might be on a heath farm or even a horse farm.

For information, contact **Fremdenverkehrsverbund Lüneburger Heide e.V.** Barkhausenstrasse 35, Lüneburg (✆ **04131/7-37-30**), the park's administrative headquarters, which can furnish maps and information on horseback riding and cycling. Open Monday to Friday 8am to 6pm. To reach the park from Lüneberg, drive 35km (22 miles) west, following the signs to Salzhausen. After you cross the bridge over the A7 Autobahn, follow the brown-and-white signs to the park. The tourist office (see above) compiles a list of places every summer where you can rent a bike.

menu includes game and regional specialties, according to the season. You can always count on good home-style cooking in a pleasant setting, backed up by a fine wine list. Parts of the decor date from 1328.

Am Markt 1 (on the market square). ✆ **04131/3-17-57.** Reservations recommended. Main courses 18€–28€ ($16.05–$25); fixed-price 4-course menu 23€–33€ ($20.55–$29.45). AE, MC, V. Thurs–Tues 11am–10pm. Closed Jan 6–20. Bus: 3.

## LÜNEBURG AFTER DARK

Students make this a rowdier place with a later nightlife than most other small towns. Bars are located along the river on **Am Stintmarkt.** The two most popular places for drinking and dancing are **Fun,** Aufdenbloecken 3 (✆ **04131/850-882**), and **Garage,** Auf der Hude 72 (✆ **04131/3-58-79**). Both places have DJs playing varied styles of popular music on weekends from 10pm to around 4am. Both also have a cover charge ranging from 4€ to 6€ ($3.55–$5.35).

Another important nightlife area is the **Schroederstrasse,** which is lined chock-a-block with bars and *nacht-cafés,* some of which provide live music. Locals like to duck in and out of as many bars as possible along this street during the course of an evening. Three of the best are **Max Bar,** Schroederstrasse 6 (✆ **04131/73-25-05**); **Café Central,** Schroederstrasse 1 (✆ **04131/40-50-99**); and **Lillienthal,** Schroederstrasse 5 (✆ **04131/40-11-44**).

## 3 Celle ★★

45km (28 miles) NE of Hannover, 111km (69 miles) SE of Bremen, 117km (73 miles) S of Hamburg

The well-preserved town of Celle stands at the edge of a silent expanse of moorland, looking like something out of a picture book. Its ancient half-timbered houses were untouched by the war, and the legends carved on their beams seem to live on today. Most of the houses date from the 16th and 17th centuries—the oldest was built in 1526—but they're in such good condition that they could have been constructed in the 1900s.

### ESSENTIALS

**GETTING THERE** **By Train** **Celle Hauptbahnhof** is on the Hamburg–Hannover rail line, with frequent connections to major German cities. Forty trains arrive daily from Hannover (trip time: 20–30 min.), and the same number pull in from Hamburg (trip time: 1 hr. 10 min.–1 hr. 30 min.). For information, call ✆ **01805/99-66-33.**

**By Bus** Long-distance bus connections, from cities such as Hannover, are provided by **Winkermann GmbH** (✆ **05143/98820**) and **Lempke & Koschick GmbH** (✆ **05143/46980**). Buses arrive in front of the main railway station.

**By Car** Access by car is via the A7 Autobahn north and south, or Route 214.

**VISITOR INFORMATION** Contact the **Verkehrsverein,** Markt 6 (✆ **05141/12-12**), open mid-October to March, Monday to Friday 9am to 5pm and Saturday 10am to 1pm; and April to mid-October, Monday to Friday 9am to 7pm and Saturday 10am to 4pm.

### SEEING THE SIGHTS

**Bomann Museum** For a picture of 16th- to 20th-century everyday life in Celle and the surrounding countryside, visit this fine regional museum. Included is a complete 16th-century farmhouse, as well as rooms from old cottages, period costumes, and Hannoverian uniforms from 1803 to 1866. In the portrait gallery of the Brunswick-Lüneburg dukes, you can see pictures of the electors, later kings of England and Hannover.

Schlossplatz 7. ✆ **05141/1-23-72.** Admission 2.50€ ($2.25) adults, 1.50€ ($1.35) children. Tues–Sun 10am–5pm. Bus: 2, 3, or 4.

**Herzogschloss** One of the landmarks of the town, the Herzogschloss is a square Renaissance castle, with a tower at each corner, surrounded by a moat. It once was the palace of the dukes of Brunswick and Lüneburg. The palace's bizarre 16th-century chapel was designed by Martin de Vos, with galleries and elaborate ornamentation. The pride of the castle, and of the town, is its baroque theater, the oldest in Germany (1674), still in regular use today. Call the tourist office (see above) to arrange for a tour given by an English-speaking guide.

West of the Altstadt. ✆ **05141/1-23-73.** Admission 4€ ($3.55) adults, 2€ ($1.80) children. Tours Apr–Oct Tues–Sun at noon, 1, 2, 3, and 4pm; Nov–Mar Tues–Sun at 11am and 3pm. Bus: 2, 3, or 4.

## WHERE TO STAY

**Fürstenhof Celle** ★★ This hotel, quite sophisticated for such a provincial town, is by far the best in Celle. It's a small-scale 17th-century manor house flanked by timbered wings. The brick courtyard in front of the salmon-colored mansion is shaded by a towering chestnut tree. The older and more traditional rooms are in the main house; more modern rooms are in an annex beyond the rear courtyard. Rooms range from medium to spacious, and all are equipped with bathrooms containing shower-tub combinations.

Hannoverschestrasse 55, 29221 Celle (at the edge of town). ✆ **05141/20-10.** Fax 05141/20-11-20. www.fuerstenhof.de. 76 units. 165€–180€ ($147.35–$160.75) double; 230€–255€ ($205.40–$227.70) suite. AE, DC, MC, V. Parking 8€ ($7.15). Bus: 3, 5, or 10. **Amenities:** 3 restaurants; 2 bars; pool; sauna; salon; room service; babysitting; laundry/dry cleaning. *In room:* TV, minibar, hair dryer, safe.

**Hotel Celler Hof** ★ *Value* Celler Hof is on the street where tournaments were once held. The old-world 1890 architecture of the hotel and its neighboring timbered houses renders the interior furnishings incongruously modern, though they are quite pleasing. Rooms, ranging from medium to spacious, have recently been renovated to a high standard. All units contain neatly kept bathrooms with shower-tub combinations. Many have a view of the castle. No dinner is served.

Stechbahn 11, 29221 Celle. ✆ **05141/2-80-61.** Fax 05141/2-80-65. www.fuerstenhof.de. 49 units. 90€–160€ ($80.35–$142.90) double. Rates include buffet breakfast. AE, DC, MC, V. Parking 6€ ($5.35). Bus: 3, 5, or 10. **Amenities:** Bar; cafe; lounge; laundry/dry cleaning. *In room:* TV, minibar, hair dryer.

**Hotel Schifferkrug** This is an old-time favorite. The brick-and-timber walls of this comfortable hotel have witnessed more than 3 centuries of innkeeping tradition. The small- to medium-size rooms have lace curtains and eiderdowns—old-fashioned comfort just like at Grandma's. All units have neatly kept bathrooms containing shower-tub combinations.

Speicherstrasse 9, 29221 Celle. ✆ **05141/374-776.** Fax 05141/374-7788. www.schifferkrug-celle.de. 12 units. 65€–85€ ($58.05–$75.90) double. Rates include buffet breakfast. V. Free parking. Bus: 3, 5, or 10. **Amenities:** 2 restaurants; bar; room service; laundry/dry cleaning. *In room:* TV

## WHERE TO DINE

In addition to the restaurants below, you can stop in at **Café Kiess,** Grosserplan 16–17 (✆ **05141/22540**), which serves coffee, pastries, drinks, and platters of hearty German food with democratic, and rather conservative, aplomb every day 8am to 7pm. **Alex's Antik Café,** Schuhstrasse 6 (✆ **05141/21-75-40**), is open Tuesday to Saturday 8:30am to 6pm, and Sunday 9am to 6pm. The youth and arts cultures hang out here.

**Historischer Ratskeller** ★ GERMAN Historischer Ratskeller is plusher than the typical Ratskeller and has better fare. Attentive waiters are constantly passing by, carrying silver platters heaped with spicy, flavorful German dishes, such as roast venison with juniperberries, pork schnitzels, and filet steak with a cognac-cream sauce and peppercorns.

Markt 14. ✆ **05141/2-90-99.** Reservations recommended. Main courses 8.50€–22.50€ ($7.60–$20.10); fixed-price menu 25€–35€ ($22.35–$31.25). AE, MC, V. Wed–Mon noon–3pm and 6–10pm. Bus: 3, 5, or 10.

**Restaurant Endtenfang** ★★★ FRENCH/GERMAN Celle's most prestigious and stylish restaurant occupies an appealingly old-fashioned dining room on the street level of this previously recommended hotel. Service is efficient, helpful, and friendly. The menu focuses on game dishes, including two succulent versions of duck. (The word "Endtenfang," from an old regional dialect, means "the hunting reserve for duck-shooting.") Traditional adornments include a pepper-cream sauce, cabbage roulade, a potato and pear gratin, and fresh mushrooms, along with slices of red apples. Other main courses include halibut sautéed with fresh coriander and veal liver cooked with baby onions. The small dumplings that accompany many dishes are light and feathery. Desserts are quite imaginative, and the wine list is the finest in the area.

In the Fürstenhof Celle, Hannoverschestrasse 55. ✆ **05141/20-10.** Reservations recommended. Main courses 29€–34€ ($25.90–$30.35). AE, DC, MC, V. Mon–Sat noon–2pm and 6:30–10pm.

**Ringhotel Celler Tor** GERMAN/INTERNATIONAL The Celler Tor is a cliché of German charm, with its gabled red-tile roof and banks of geraniums. When local residents want to celebrate a special occasion, they head here, knowing they can get a great selection of *gutbürgerlich* fare—that is, food fondly remembered from childhood. In season, that means wild game, such as ragout of stag with mushrooms. You can also get good shrimp and rice dishes.

The Celler Tor also rents 70 good rooms. A double costs 190€ to 260€ ($169.65–$232.20) including buffet breakfast; eight suites are also available, at 285€ to 335€ ($254.50–$299.15) each. Facilities include two pools, a workout room, a sauna, a solarium, and massage facilities.

Scheuener Strasse 2 (about 3km/2 miles outside town), 29229 Celle-Gross Hehlen. ✆ **05141/59-00.** Fax 05141/59-04-90. www.celler-tor.de. Reservations recommended. Main courses 14€–24.50€ ($12.50–$21.90); fixed-price menu 27.50€–46€ ($24.55–$41.10). AE, DC, MC, V. Daily noon–3pm and 6–10pm. Bus: 8.

## 4 Hannover

122km (76 miles) SE of Bremen, 151km (94 miles) S of Hamburg, 288km (179 miles) W of Berlin

This modest little city south of Hamburg still basks in the glow of Expo 2000 when it was visited by more foreigners than ever before. It remains one of Germany's hubs of industry, transportation, and commerce, and its annual industrial trade fair is still the largest such fair in the world, attracting producers and buyers from around the globe.

Even with a big money investment in its inner city, Hannover is hardly a city of grace and beauty, although it does have patches of beauty, including one of the finest baroque gardens in the world. In spite of certain idyllic sections, including the 2.5km (1½ mile) manmade lake, the Maschsee, and the encircling Eilenriede Forest, Hanover is a mere shadow of its former self. The royal court checked out in the early 19th century, heading for greener fields and greater power in London.

### ESSENTIALS

**GETTING THERE By Plane** Hannover is served by **Hannover-Langenhagen International Airport,** 10km (6 miles) north of the city center. Many international airlines fly here. Flying time between Hannover and Munich is 1 hour 10 minutes; between Frankfurt and Hannover, 50 minutes. For flight

*Fun Fact* **The House of Hannover**

Every student of English history is aware of the role that Hannover played in the history of Great Britain. For more than 100 years, Britain was ruled by monarchs descended from the House of Hannover (or Hanover), who technically also ruled over the German city. The most notorious was George III, the occasionally insane king whose policies provoked the American Revolutionary War.

information, call ✆ **0511/9-77-12-23.** Shuttle buses run between the airport and the city every 20 minutes 5am to 11pm, depositing passengers at the Hauptbahnhof. The cost is 5€ ($4.45) each way.

**By Train** Hannover lies at the junction of an important network of rail lines linking Scandinavia to Italy and Paris to Moscow. Some 500 trains per day pass through, with frequent connections to major German and European cities. Nineteen trains arrive daily from Berlin (trip time: 1 hr. 35 min.), 40 trains from Frankfurt (trip time: 2 hr. 21 min. or 3 hr., depending on the train), and 40 trains from Hamburg (trip time: 1 hr. 11 min.–1 hr. 30 min.). For information, call ✆ **01805/99-66-33.**

**By Bus** Long-distance bus service to major German cities is offered by **Deutsche Touring Büro Hannover,** at the Hauptbahnhof (✆ **0511/32-94-19**).

**By Car** Access is via the A1 Autobahn north or south and from the A2 east and west.

**VISITOR INFORMATION** Contact **Hannover Tourist Information,** located at Ernst-August-Platz 2 (✆ **0511/16-84-97-00**). Here you can reserve hotel rooms (ask about special weekend packages), book sightseeing tours, obtain general information about the city, and purchase tickets for local events as well as for trains, trams, and buses. The office is open Monday to Friday 9am to 7pm and Saturday 9:30am to 3pm.

**GETTING AROUND** The local public-transport system includes commuter trains, an extensive underground network, trams, and buses operated by several companies. Service is frequent and extensive. For information and schedules, contact **Regionalverkehr Hannover GmbH** (✆ **0511/9-90-01-30**).

## EXPLORING THE CITY

**Market Church (Marktkirche),** the Gothic brick basilica on Marktplatz, is one of Hannover's oldest structures, built in the mid-14th century. **Altes Rathaus,** facing the square, dates from 1425. It was badly damaged in the war, but has been restored and now houses the civic archives.

**Herrenhäuser Garten (Royal Gardens of Herrenhäusen)** ★★ No matter where you go in Hannover, you won't be far from a park or garden. But make sure you don't miss this one, the only surviving example of Dutch/Low German early baroque-style gardening. Designers from France, the Netherlands, England, and Italy, as well as Germany, worked together to create this masterpiece of living art. **Grosse Garten,** from 1666, is the largest garden, consisting of a rectangle surrounded by a moat. Within the maze of walks and trees are examples of French baroque, rococo, and Low German rose and flower gardens. The Grosse Garten also contains one of the highest fountains in Europe, shooting jets of water 72m (236 ft.) into the air, and the world's only existing baroque hedge-theater (1692), where plays by Shakespeare, Molière, and Brecht are still performed, along with ballets and jazz concerts. The smaller 17th-century **Berggarten,** across Herrenhäuser Strasse from the Grosse Garten, is a botanical garden with houses containing rare orchids and other tropical flowers.

Herrenhäuser Strasse 4. ✆ **0511/16-84-75-76.** Admission 3€ ($2.70) adults, free for children. Apr–Sept daily 8am–7pm; Oct–Mar daily 8am–4:30pm. Waterworks display May–Sept Mon–Fri 11am–noon and 3–5pm, Sat–Sun and holidays 11am–noon and 2–5pm. U-Bahn: Herrenhäuser Gärten.

**Niedersächsisches Landesmuseum Hannover (Lower Saxony State Museum)** ★ The Landesmuseum is one of the most important regional museums in Germany. There are exhibits on northern European biology and geology, ethnomedicine and ethnobotany, and on the history of Lower Saxony from the Paleolithic Age up to the Middle Ages. The aquarium shows a world of exotic fish, amphibians, and reptiles. In the newly created Kindermuseum, children can learn about prehistoric times with activities like grinding corn or working stone tools.

The museum's art gallery contains treasures spanning 7 centuries. A highlight is Meister Bertram von Minden's *Passion Altar* (1390–1400). You'll also see paintings by Rembrandt, Van Dyck, and Rubens (his *Madonna*), as well as the *Four Times of Day* series by Caspar David Friedrich.

Willy-Brandt-Allee (near the Maschpark). ✆ **0511/9-80-75.** Admission 4€ ($3.55). Tues–Wed and Fri–Sun 10am–5pm; Thurs 10am–7pm. Tram: 1, 2, 4, 5, 6, 7, 8, or 11. Bus: 132 or 267.

**Rathaus** The "new" Rathaus is a large structure, built between 1901 and 1913. An inclined elevator—the only one in Europe other than the elevator at the Eiffel Tower—takes visitors up to the 10m (33-ft.) dome. The building is attractive because of its location in the Maschpark, by a small lake. It's just a short distance from the extensive artificial Maschsee, frequented by Hannoverians for its beach, boats, and restaurants.

Am Maschpark. ✆ **0511/1-68-45-333.** Elevator ride to dome 2€ ($1.80) adults, 1.50€ ($1.35) students and children. Rathaus and elevator open Apr–Oct Mon–Fri 9:30am–6pm, Sat–Sun 10am–6pm. U-Bahn: Markthalle. Tram: 3, 7, or 9. Bus: 120.

## SHOPPING

The oldest and largest flea market in Germany, **Flohmarkt** sprawls across Am Hohen Ufer (U-Bahn: Markthalle) every Saturday from 7am to 4pm. Stalls are set up along the banks of the Leine River. The city is hardly confined to flea markets, however. Hanover is one of the most fashion-conscious cities of the country, sometimes called "the Milan of Germany." It is the home of stylish clothing, and Hanoverians are among the most fashionably dressed of all Germans.

Your first destination might be the glassed-over **Galerie Luise,** a multilevel shopping mall at the corner of Luisenstrasse and Rathenaustrasse (bus: 120), with upscale shops for clothing and home furnishings. **Der Herrenausstatter Hemdenstube,** Georgstrasse 42 (✆ **0511/36-38-04**), and **Donna-Men,** Krämerstrasse 25 (✆ **0511/32-50-12**), are good choices for menswear. Her counterpart for women's clothing is **Donna,** Lilienplatz 1 (✆ **0511/32-58-75;** U-Bahn: Markthalle). **Terner,** Luisenstrasse 9 (✆ **0511/36-39-31;** tram: 5), and **Joop,** Karmarsch Strasse 18 (✆ **0511/36-78-97-30;** bus: 7), have three floors loaded with designer-inspired clothing for men, women, and children.

Souvenirs are sold at **Raachermantel,** Luisenstrasse 1 (✆ **0511/3-63-14-24;** tram: 5), which specializes in hand-carved figures, some inspired by German folklore and fairy tales.

## WHERE TO STAY

To escape the clutches of the city's pricey (and rather sterile) hotels, you might stay at a restaurant-hotel—either the Landhaus Ammann or the Georgenhof-Stern (see "Where to Dine," below).

### EXPENSIVE

**Forum Hotel Schweizerhof** ★ This is one of the most imaginatively designed hotels in Hannover, with a lot more charm and atmosphere than other leading contenders. It sits on a quiet street in the central business district. Inside you'll find illuminated Plexiglas columns and sweeping expanses of russet-colored marble. The hotel serves an affluent clientele, often including visiting celebrities. Rooms are spacious and elegantly furnished, all with immaculately kept bathrooms with shower-tub combinations.

Hinuberstrasse 6, 30175 Hannover. ✆ **0511/3-49-50.** Fax 0511/3-49-51-23. www.forum-hotel-schweizerhof.de. 203 units. 155€–180€ ($138.40–$160.75) double; 295€ ($263.45) suite. Rates include buffet breakfast. AE, DC, MC, V. Parking 14€ ($12.50). Tram: 16. **Amenities:** 3 restaurants; bar; room service; laundry/dry cleaning; private garden. *In room:* A/C, TV, minibar, hair dryer, safe.

**Kastens Hotel Luisenhof** ★★ This is the leading hotel in town. Its stately glass-and-stone facade is just minutes from the Hauptbahnhof in the city center. A series of modernizations have enhanced comfort while maintaining conservative good taste. The carefully renovated rooms are spacious, stylishly furnished, and impeccably kept, all with bathrooms containing shower-tub combinations. The English-speaking staff welcomes overseas visitors.

Luisenstrasse 1–3 (near the Hauptbahnhof), 30159 Hannover. ✆ **0511/3-04-40.** Fax 0511/3-04-48-07. www.kastens-luisenhof.de. 152 units. 140€–320€ ($125–$285.75) double; 230€–500€ ($205.40–$446.50) suite. Rates include buffet breakfast. AE, DC, MC, V. Parking 8€ ($7.15). Tram: 16. **Amenities:** Restaurant; bar; room service; laundry/dry cleaning. *In room:* TV, minibar, hair dryer, safe.

### MODERATE

**Hotel Königshof** ★ Both the skylights and the modernized crenellations on this hotel's mansard roof make it look like an updated feudal fortress. The hotel was built in 1984 above a glass-and-steel shopping arcade in the town center. Each plushly carpeted room has a couch that converts to a bed and a bathroom with a shower-tub combination. Only breakfast is served at the hotel, but there's an Italian restaurant across the street.

Königstrasse 12, 30175 Hannover. ✆ **0511/31-20-71.** Fax 0511/31-20-79. 82 units. 91€–225€ ($81.25–$200.95) double. Discounts for children under 16 in parents' room. Rates include buffet breakfast. AE, DC, MC, V. Parking 5.50€ ($4.90). Bus: 20 or 39. **Amenities:** Breakfast room; lounge. *In room:* TV.

**Loccumer Hof** *Value* This is one of the best economy finds in the city. The location is favored by train travelers because of its proximity to the train station. The utilitarian rooms and bathrooms are small, with shower-tub combinations. Service and frills are minimal, but the beds are comfortable and the hotel is well maintained. Overall, it's a good, clean and decent choice.

Kurt-Schumacher-Strasse 16 (near the Hauptbahnhof), 30159 Hannover. ✆ **0511/1-26-40.** Fax 0511/13-11-92. www.loccumerhof.de. 87 units. 114€–260€ ($101.80–$232.20) double. Higher rates during fairs. Rates include buffet breakfast. AE, DC, MC, V. Parking 7€ ($6.25). Tram: 16. **Amenities:** Restaurant; lounge. *In room:* TV, minibar.

## WHERE TO DINE

### VERY EXPENSIVE

**Georgenhof-Stern Restaurant** ★★ INTERNATIONAL This is Hannover's most famous restaurant, and it's well worth the price. It's in a country inn in a private park near the Herrenhäuser Gardens. International dishes of fresh seafood and game are featured. In summer, tables are set on the terrace, overlooking a garden and pond. The place also rents 14 clean and pleasant rooms, with traditional, handcrafted furniture. Doubles run 130€ to 280€ ($116.10–$250.05); buffet breakfast is included.

Herrenhauser Kirchweg 20, 30167 Hannover. ✆ **0511/70-22-44.** Fax 0511/70-85-59. Reservations required. Main courses 28€–50€ ($25–$44.65); fixed-price meal 45€–90€ ($40.20–$80.35). AE, DC, MC, V. Daily noon–2pm and 6–10pm. Tram: 4, 5, or 6.

**Landhaus Ammann** ★★★ INTERNATIONAL This is the only restaurant in Hannover that serves better food and has a more luxurious atmosphere than the Georgenhof-Stern. Service is discreet and efficient, but never stuffy. The chefs turn out a distinguished cuisine, backed up by the city's finest wine cellar. The menu is adjusted seasonally to take advantage of fresh produce. Typical dishes include sea bass with caviar sauce.

The place also rents 15 beautifully furnished rooms; a double costs 150€ to 330€ ($133.95–$294.70), including a buffet breakfast. The setting, near a park, is tranquil. Rooms, decorated in a traditional motif, have minibars, trouser presses, and hair dryers.

Hildesheimer Strasse 185. ✆ **0511/83-08-18.** Fax 0511/8-43-77-49. www.landhaus-ammann.de. Reservations required. Main courses 25€–35€ ($22.35–$31.25); fixed-price meal 60€–95€ ($53.60–$84.85). Daily noon–2pm and 7–10pm. AE, DC, MC, V. Tram: 5.

## EXPENSIVE

**Wichmann** ★ GERMAN This family-owned, white-walled, shuttered inn, with its slate walks and carefully tended flower beds, is on the eastern edge of Hannover. The garden serves as a pleasant setting for dining in the summer months. The place is an oasis of comfort. Cooking is German *gutbürgerlich*—wholesome and hearty. Try specialties such as fish terrine, rack of lamb, homemade noodles, and wine and cheese from all over Germany.

Hildesheimer Strasse 230, at Hannover-Döhren. ✆ **0511/83-16-71.** Reservations required. Main courses 21€–26€ ($18.75–$23.20); fixed-price dinner 55€ ($49.10) for 4 courses, 95€ ($84.85) for 7 courses. AE, MC, V. Mon–Sat noon–3pm and 6–11pm. Tram: 1 or 8.

## MODERATE

**Basil** ★★ ECLECTIC This is the hippest restaurant in Hannover, drawing a chic clientele to its dining room known for its modern cuisine, fresh ingredients, and alert wait staff. The setting is in a riding hall built in 1867 for the Royal Prussian military. Guests dine in an antique atmosphere under a vaulted ceiling. We prefer a table in the delightful garden where we've seen Hannover's most famous son, Chancellor Gerhard Schröder, dining in days gone by. Like Clichy (see below) where the food is only slightly better, Basil changes each menu at least every 3 weeks, and it's always in tune to what's fresh, good, and flavorful at the market. Recipes range from the coasts of the Mediterranean to Asia. We recently arrived in the middle of spring to enjoy a *Spargel* (asparagus menu). Had it been autumn, game dishes would have been featured. The accent of the menu is always on fish, as exemplified by the likes of sea bream in a zesty lime sauce with spring onions, or perhaps moist and tender trout stuffed with fresh spinach.

Dragonerstrasse 30A. ✆ **0511/622636.** Reservations required. Main courses 12€–22€ ($10.70–$19.65); fixed-price menu 32€–38€ ($28.60–$33.95). Mon–Sat 6:30–11pm. U-Bahn: U1 or U2 to Dragonerstrasse.

**Clichy Restaurant** ★★ CONTINENTAL/MEDITERRANEAN This haven of refined cuisine doesn't get the press that Landhaus Ammann and Georgenhof-Stern Restaurant enjoy, but it is the most consistently reliable dining choice in the city. For more than 2 decades, its guiding light, Ekkehard Reimann, has coddled his guests with fine cuisine backed up by a well-stocked cellar. A Hannover food critic recently wrote, "For the nonexperienced gourmet, a visit here will be unforgettable." We'd include gourmets in that appraisal as well. His daily specials depend on his shopping for the day and the season, as he believes in finely honed dishes fashioned from the best ingredients in any season. Year after year, his cooking lives up to a superb standard, and his dishes are marked by intense flavors and a precise technique.

Weissekreuzstrasse 31. ✆ **0511/312447.** Reservations required. Main courses 18€–30€ ($16.05–$26.80). AE, MC. Mon–Fri noon–2:30pm and daily 6:30–11pm. Tram: 3 or 7.

**Steuerndieb** *Finds* INTERNATIONAL In 1329, a stone-sided tower was erected about 1.5km (1 mile) east of central Hannover to guard the lumber produced in Eilenreide Forest. The tower's name, Steuerndieb, translates from the archaic German as "Stop, thieves!" Around 1850 a rustic restaurant was built on the site, and it has been known ever since for hearty and flavor-filled food. Many of the specialties are cooked over an open fire, and the restaurant offers a locally inspired menu that, unlike those of many other restaurants, features game year-round. Two popular dishes are venison with red cabbage, dumplings, and black-cherry sauce; and rabbit with black-pepper sauce and red cabbage.

The establishment also has a modern wing containing seven simple, white-walled rooms, each with private bath, TV, telephone, and view overlooking the forest. Doubles cost 130€ ($116.10), including a buffet breakfast.

Steuerndieb 1, Hannover-Bothfeld, 30655 Hannover. ✆ **0511/90-99-60.** Reservations not required. Main courses 13.50€–22€ ($12.05–$19.65); fixed-price menu 29.50€ ($26.35) for 3 courses, 52.50€ ($46.90) for 7 courses. AE, DC, MC, V. Daily 11am–3pm and 6–10pm. Tram: 3 or 7.

### INEXPENSIVE

**Altdeutsche Bierstube** GERMAN With a decor that has changed little since its original construction around 1860, this old-fashioned Bierstube remains stable and solid, despite the monumental changes that have transformed the society around it. The unpretentious food is hearty, wholesome, and filling, with the regular fare augmented by seasonal specialties. Three favorites include pork knuckles with sauerkraut, filet of beef, and mixed grills.

Lärchenstrasse 4. ✆ **0511/34-49-21.** Reservations required. Main courses 10€–23€ ($8.95–$20.55); fixed-price 3-course menu 25€ ($22.35). AE, DC, MC, V. Mon–Fri noon–2pm; Mon–Sat 6pm–1am. Closed holidays. U-Bahn: Lister Platz.

## HANNOVER AFTER DARK

*Hannover Vorschau,* a monthly newspaper devoted exclusively to the city's nightlife and cultural venues, is available for 2€ ($1.80) at news kiosks, but is usually given out free in the city's hotels.

**THE PERFORMING ARTS** The **Nieder Sächsische Stadtstheater Hannover GmbH,** Opernplatz 1 (✆ **0511/32-11-33,** or 0511/9999-1111 for tickets and information; U-Bahn: Kröpcke), built between 1845 and 1852, is the region's leading venue for ballet, concerts, and opera. Depending on the performance, tickets cost from 10€ to 40€ ($8.95–$35.70) each. Less formal, with popular as well as classical offerings, is the **N. D. R. Symphoniker,** Rudolf Benigsen Ufer 22 (✆ **0511/9-88-0;** bus: 2 or 6), an ugly postwar building whose charm derives from what goes on inside. You can hear poetry readings, jazz and rock-'n'-roll concerts, and chamber orchestras. Contact the theaters or the tourist office for schedules. Tickets cost 10€ to 28€ ($8.95–$25).

**BARS** Oddly, many of Hannover's most appealing bars are Irish pubs. They include **The Irish Pub,** Brüderstrasse 4 (✆ **0511/1-45-89;** U-Bahn: Hauptbahnhof), which won a 1998 award as the best Irish Pub in Germany, and its most visible competitor, **The Irish Harp,** Schwarzer Bär (✆ **0511/44-70-70;** U-Bahn: Hauptbahnhof), which has a beer garden in good weather. Both are open daily 5pm to 2am; serve both Guinness and Murphy's on tap, along with sandwiches, pies, fish and chips, and Irish stew; and occasionally book Irish music bands, for which there's a cover of 5€ to 8€ ($4.45–$7.15).

**DANCE CLUBS** The best place for mainstream dance is **Osho Disco,** Rauschplatz 7L (✆ **0511/34-22-17;** U-Bahn: Hauptbahnhof), a 14-year survivor of the club scene. It plays funk, house, and other dance music. It's open 10pm to "whenever," Wednesday to Sunday. Cover is 3€ to 5€ ($2.70–$4.45). One of its leading competitors is **Palo Palo,** Rauschplatz 8A (✆ **0511/33-10-73;** U-Bahn: Hauptbahnhof), where house, funk, blues, reggae, and old-fashioned Motown soul play every night 9:30pm until dawn, for a cover of 4€ to 6€ ($3.55–$5.35) per person.

**LIVE MUSIC** An alternative venue, **Café Glocksee,** Glockseestrasse 35 (✆ **0511/1-61-47-12;** tram: 10), stages hard-core, punk, and techno shows. Thursday concerts start at 9pm; cover is 10€ ($8.95). On Friday and Saturday, it's disco mania 11pm to 7am and again on Wednesday 6pm to 2am; cover is 2.50€ ($2.25).

**GAY CLUBS** **Schwul Sau,** Schaufeldstrasse 38 (✆ **0511/7-00-05-25;** tram: 6), hosts discos, theater performances, and private parties, attended by a crowd of gay and straight arts-conscious patrons. It's open Tuesday, Wednesday, and Friday 8pm to 3am, Saturday 9pm to at least 7am, and Sunday 3pm to 2am. Cover is 8€ to 10€ ($7.15–$8.95) for parties or theater events, and 4.10€ ($4) for dancing. There's no cover Tuesday, Wednesday, or Sunday. A hip and happening dance spot, **Men's Factory,** Engelbosteler Damm 7 (✆ **0511/70-24-87;** tram: 6), is open on Friday, for a mixed dance night, and Saturday, for gay dance night. Friday cover is 8€ ($7.15); Saturday, it's 5€ ($4.45).

**A CASINO** The **Spielbank,** Österstrasse 40 (✆ **0511/98-06-60;** U-Bahn: Kröpcke), has an impressive roster of blackjack, roulette, and baccarat. It's set within a modern building, with none of the Belle Epoque trappings or decorations you might have hoped for, and contains both a bar and a restaurant. Men are required to wear jackets and ties, and women are requested to dress appropriately. Open daily 3pm to 3am. Admission costs 2.50€ ($2.25), and you must show your passport to enter.

## 5 Hameln ★

45km (28 miles) SW of Hannover, 48km (30 miles) W of Hildesheim

Hameln (Hamelin in English) has many, many interesting buildings and a history dating from the 11th century, but its main claim to fame is the folktale about the Pied Piper, which has been immortalized by the Brothers Grimm, Goethe, and Robert Browning, among others. According to legend, in 1284 the town was infested by rats. Soon after, there appeared a piper who offered, for a fee, to lure the vermin into the Weser River. The rat-catcher successfully performed the service, but the stingy denizens of Hameln refused to pay, claiming that he was a sorcerer. So the piper reappeared the next Sunday and played a tune that lured all the town's children, except one lame boy, into a mysterious door in a hill. The children and the Pied Piper were never heard from again.

There is some historical basis for the story. It appears that, several centuries ago, for some unknown reason, the children of Hameln did indeed leave the town. The story of the Pied Piper is retold every summer Sunday at noon in a special performance at the **Hochzeitshaus (Wedding House)** on Osterstrasse. In the town shops, you can buy rat figures made of almost every conceivable material, including candy.

## ESSENTIALS

**GETTING THERE** **By Plane** The nearest major airport is Hannover-Langenhagen, 55km (34 miles) away.

**By Train** The **Hameln Bahnhof** lies on the Hannover–Hameln–Altenbeken line, with frequent connections. Depending on the train, trip time from Hannover ranges from 45 to 55 minutes. For information, call ✆ **01805/99-66-33.**

**By Bus** Local and regional bus service to nearby towns and Hannover is available from **RVH Regional Verkehr** (✆ **05151/811414**). Buses stop in front of the Hauptbahnhof.

**By Car** It takes 3 hours to reach Hameln from Frankfurt and 6 to 7 hours from Munich. From Frankfurt, head northeast along the A5 Autobahn, then north on the A7, and finally west on A27. From Munich, take the A9 Autobahn north to Nürnberg, the A3 west to Würzburg, then the A7 north toward Hannover, and finally A27 west to Hameln.

**VISITOR INFORMATION** Contact the **Verkehrsverein,** Deisterallee (✆ **05151/20-26-17**), open May to September, Monday to Friday 9am to 6pm, Saturday 9:30am to 12:30pm and 2 to 4pm, and Sunday 9:30am to 12:30pm; October to April, Monday to Friday 9am to 1pm and 2 to 5pm.

## EXPLORING THE TOWN

Hameln's most interesting building is the Gothic Münster, at the end of Bäckerstrasse, overlooking the Weser River. Other attractions include the Rattenfängerhaus (Rat-Catcher's House; see "Where to Dine," below), on Osterstrasse, with frescoes illustrating the Pied Piper legend, and the Hochzeitshaus (Wedding House) on Osterstrasse, with its three attractive gables. The finest houses in the town are built in what is known as Weser Renaissance style. You can admire these nicely sculpted late–16th century houses as you stroll along the pedestrians-only streets. One of the best examples of the Weser-Renaissance style, which can be enjoyed by looking at its facade, is Dempterscheshaus, built in 1607. This house, at Pferdemarkt, standing in the middle of town, has protruding bay windows called Utluchten in German. This patrician building is also characterized by fine chiseled stones and decorations of ornaments and coats-of-arms.

**SHOPPING** There are lots of opportunities to buy folkloric art objects here. One of the best bets for souvenir and gift hunting, **Renner,** Am Markt 6 (✆ **05151/9-44-20**), has some genuinely charming objects. Antiques that might become part of your family heirlooms are at **Antikitäten Bayer,** Bäckerstrasse 49 (✆ **05151/32-97**), and **Antiqutiäten Franke,** Wendenstrasse 4 (✆ **05151/44388**). You also might simply want to window-shop along the town's best shopping streets, the **Osterstrasse** and the **Bäckerstrasse.**

**NIGHTLIFE** The town's **Weserbergland Festhalle,** Rathausplatz (✆ **05151/91-62-20**), hosts an array of concerts, opera and ballet performances, and theatrical productions. Call the theater or the visitor information center (see above) for upcoming events and ticket information. Tickets are 8€ to 24€ ($7.15–$21.45).

## WHERE TO STAY

**Dorint Hotel Hameln** This hotel stands in a park with lots of trees but is within walking distance of the heart of the Altstadt, at the northern edge of the Burgergarten. It rises like a modern collection of building blocks, with oversize glass walls. Rooms are standard and functional, and all contain bathrooms with shower-tub combinations.

164er Ring 3, 31785 Hameln. ✆ **05151/79-20.** Fax 05151/79-21-91. www.dorint.de/hameln. 105 units. 135€–145€ ($120.55–$129.50) double. Rates include buffet breakfast. AE, DC, MC, V. Parking 4.50€ ($4). Bus: 1 or 2. **Amenities:** Restaurant; bar; pool; health club; sauna; solarium; room service; massage; babysitting; laundry/dry cleaning. *In room:* TV, minibar, hair dryer.

**Hotel zur Börse** This balconied hotel within the walls of the Altstadt can be identified by the four peaks of its modern roofline. The interior is refreshingly uncluttered. Rooms are spacious and well maintained with bathrooms equipped with shower-tub combinations.

Osterstrasse 41A, 31785 Hameln. ✆ **05151/70-80.** Fax 05151/2-54-85. 31 units. 87€ ($77.70) double. Rates include buffet breakfast. AE, DC, MC, V. Parking 6.20€ ($5.55). Bus: 1 or 2. **Amenities:** Restaurant; lounge; room service. *In room:* TV, hair dryer.

**Komfort-Hotel Garni Christinenhof** The gabled windows of this half-timbered, 300-year-old building overlook a cobblestoned street in the middle of the Altstadt. Despite the antique facade, much of the hotel's interior is streamlined and modern, with many conveniences. All units contain neatly kept bathrooms with shower-tub combinations. Rooms are well furnished, though small.

Alte Markstrasse 18, 31785 Hameln. ✆ **05151/9-50-80.** Fax 05151/4-36-11. 30 units. 185€–220€ ($165.20–$196.45) double. Rates include buffet breakfast. AE, MC, V. Free parking. Closed Dec 20–Jan 6. Bus: 1 or 2. **Amenities:** Breakfast room; lounge; pool; sauna; solarium; laundry/dry cleaning. *In room:* TV, minibar, hair dryer.

## WHERE TO DINE

**Klütturm** GERMAN/FRENCH Even the lovely decor here takes second place to the restaurant's panoramic view of the Altstadt. The cooking is traditional, with special care lavished on the dessert wagon, whose confections change every day. In season, the cook will prepare game dishes, and throughout the year you'll find an aromatically seasoned rack of baby lamb with fresh vegetables, a tender entrecôte of beef with escargots, and Barbary duckling with an orange-pepper sauce. Adjacent to the restaurant is a stone-sided tower, with 99 steps, built in the 1820s. It can be climbed, without charge, as part of your dining experience. From the top, panoramic views extend out over the surrounding landscapes.

Auf dem Klütberg. ✆ **05151/6-16-44.** Reservations recommended. Main courses 7€–40€ ($6.25–$35.70). AE, MC, V. Wed–Mon 11:30am–2:30pm and 6–10pm. Closed Jan–Feb 10.

**Rattenfängerhaus** GERMAN Rattenfängerhaus (Rat-Catcher's House) dates from 1603. A meal here is practically like eating in a museum. The place is a little too touristy and crowded for some tastes, but it's an enduring favorite nonetheless. You can order traditional German dishes, including various kinds of schnitzels, roasted goose, or filets of salmon with hollandaise sauce. Souvenirs of the Pied Piper are offered.

Osterstrasse 28. ✆ **05151/38-88.** Reservations recommended. Main courses 9€–18€ ($8.05–$16.05). AE, DC, MC, V. Daily 11am–2:30pm and 6–11pm. Bus: 1 or 2.

## 6 Bad Pyrmont

72km (45 miles) SW of Hannover, 48km (30 miles) SE of Bielefeld

This attractive spa has enjoyed a good reputation for more than 2,000 years. Its springs vary from the brine variety in the fields to the medicinal iron waters on the southern side of the valley of the Weser Hills. In the center of town you can drink a medicinal cocktail from the fountain at the Hyllige Born spring. Another popular pastime is taking mud baths. But Bad Pyrmont is a good place to vacation even if you don't come to take the waters. Horseback riding in the hills, hiking, tennis, and swimming, as well as concerts and shows, make the resort a lively place.

## ESSENTIALS

**GETTING THERE** **By Train** The nearest airport is at Hannover, where there are good rail connections to Bad Pyrmont. There are frequent trains throughout the day on the Hannover–Paderborn main line. For information, call ✆ **01805/99-66-33.**

**By Bus** Regional buses run between Hameln (see above) and Bad Pyrmont. The service is provided by **RVH Busline Hameln** (✆ **05151/8-11-11**).

**By Car** From Hannover, Route 217 leads southwest to Bad Pyrmont.

**VISITOR INFORMATION** Go to **Kur- und Verkehrsverein,** Europaplatz 1 (✆ **05281/94-05-11**), open Monday to Friday 9am to 5pm and Saturday 10am to 12:30pm.

**SHOPPING** There aren't many shops in this quiet town, but **Hildebrandt,** Hauptallee 3 (✆ **05281/60-99-25**), has an appealing collection of German handicrafts.

## EXPLORING THE TOWN

The **Kurpark (Spa Park)** ★ is among the most beautiful in Germany, with little temples, flowering trees, and even a palm garden, an unusual touch in this temperate climate. The concert house in the Kurpark has shows during the busy summer. At night, the central promenade is glamorously lit, giving the spa a festive air, while guests sit at sidewalk tables drinking beer.

After a stroll through town in the day, you can visit **Festung und Schloss Pyrmont,** Schloss Strasse (✆ **05281/94-92-48**), the town castle, built in 1792. It displays antiques and paintings. Open Tuesday to Sunday 10am to 5pm; admission is 2€ ($1.80).

## WHERE TO STAY

**Bergkurpark** ★ Bergkurpark is not the most distinguished hotel at Bad Pyrmont (that honor goes to the Steigenberger—see below), but it is the most glamorous architecturally. Its entryway has a thatched roof covering a hewn stone and stucco facade with half-rounded picture windows—very dramatic. The hotel rents singles, twin-bedded rooms, and a few suites; all are very comfortable, and all contain bathrooms with shower-tub combinations. Your room might be in a modern block with private terraces overlooking a park.

Ockelstrasse 11, 31812 Bad Pyrmont. ✆ **05281/40-01.** Fax 05281/40-04. www.bergkurpark.de. 49 units. 96€–170€ ($85.75–$151.80) double; 190€ ($169.65) suite. Rates include continental breakfast. AE, MC, V. Parking 3€ ($2.70). Bus: 3. **Amenities:** 2 restaurants; bar; pool; fitness center; sauna; room service; babysitting; laundry/dry cleaning; private park. *In room:* TV, minibar, hair dryer, safe.

**Park-Hotel Rasmusen** This gracefully renovated villa stands on a traffic-free promenade in the center of Bad Pyrmont. The spacious rooms are well furnished, and many have balconies overlooking the promenade. All units have bathrooms containing shower-tub combinations. The staff is pleasant.

Hauptallee 8, 31812 Bad Pyrmont. ✆ **05281/9-30-64.** Fax 05281/60-68-72. 12 units. 180€ ($160.75) double. Rates include continental breakfast. AE, MC, V. Free parking in lot; 5€ ($4.45) in garage. Closed Jan. **Amenities:** Restaurant; lounge; room service. *In room:* TV, hair dryer.

**Steigenberger Bad Pyrmont** ★★★ This venerable 19th-century monument is the premier hotel in the spa, drawing people from all over the world. It's the only hotel in town with direct (covered) access to the spa. The calm and quiet rooms have a conservative modern gloss. They're the most comfortable in town. All have neatly kept bathrooms containing shower-tub combinations. This retreat is well suited to repairing the wear and tear of urban life. Nothing even comes near the Steigenberger for service.

Heiligenangerstrasse 2–4 (in the garden adjacent to the spa), 31812 Bad Pyrmont. ✆ **800/223-5652** in the U.S. and Canada, or 05281/15-02. Fax 05281/15-20-20. www.steigenberger.com. 154 units. 208€–228€ ($185.75–$203.60) double; 293€–378€ ($261.65–$337.55) suite. Rates include breakfast. AE, DC, MC, V. Parking 9€ ($8.05). **Amenities:** Restaurant; 2 bars; pool; health spa; whirlpool; sauna; room service; babysitting; laundry/dry cleaning. *In room:* TV, minibar, hair dryer, safe.

## WHERE TO DINE

**Restaurant Bergkurpark** INTERNATIONAL This restaurant is part of one of the town's finest hotels (see above). In summer, diners like to eat on the beautiful terrace. Otherwise, food is served in an elegantly decorated restaurant with large, comfortable chairs. We were impressed by the size and cleanliness of the kitchen, which turns out a reliable array of international specialties, with an emphasis on fresh produce. Try the medallions of veal with morel cream sauce, or salmon with a dill and morel sauce.

In the Hotel Bergkurpark, Ockelstrasse 11. ✆ **05281/40-01.** Main courses 12€–30€ ($10.70–$26.80); fixed-price lunch 15€ ($13.40). AE, MC, V. Daily 11:30am–2:30pm and 6:30–9pm.

# 7 Goslar ★★

90km (56 miles) SE of Hannover, 43km (27 miles) S of Braunschweig, 60km (37 miles) SE of Hildesheim

In spite of Goslar's growth, the old portion of the town looks just as it did hundreds of years ago. This ancient Hanseatic and imperial town at the foot of the Harz Mountains owed its early prosperity to the Harz silver mines, which were worked as early as 968. The 600-year-old streets are still in use today, as are the carved, half-timbered houses.

For hikers and other outdoor enthusiasts, Goslar is a good starting point for day trips and excursions into the **Harz Mountains** ★★, where some of the area's best ski resorts and several spas are found. Bus tours into the Harz Mountains can be booked at the tourist office (see below).

The legends and folklore associated with the Harz Mountains are perhaps more intriguing than the mountains themselves. Walpurgis Eve (the famous Witches' Sabbath), is still celebrated each year on the night of April 30. The mountain on which the witches supposedly danced in olden times was the **Brocken,** whose granite top has been flattened by erosion. The area around the Brocken is now a national park.

## ESSENTIALS

**GETTING THERE** **By Plane** The nearest major airport is in Hannover.

**By Train** The **Goslar Bahnhof** is on the Hannover–Hildesheim–Goslar–Bad Harzburg rail line, with frequent connections. It takes about 1½ hours to get to Goslar from Hannover. For information, call ✆ **01805/99-66-33.**

**By Bus** Long-distance bus service to Goslar is available through **Reisebüro Bokermann** (✆ **05321/25138**). Regional bus service to all parts of the city and nearby towns is offered by **Regionalbus Braunschweig GmbH,** Geschaftstelle, Goslar (✆ **05321/34310**).

**By Car** Access is via the A7 Autobahn north and south; exit at either Seesen or Rüden.

**VISITOR INFORMATION** Contact the **Kur- und Fremdenverkehrs-Gesellschaft,** Markt 7 (✆ **05321/7-80-60**), open November to April, Monday to Friday 9am to 5pm and Saturday 9:30am to 2pm; May to October, Monday to Friday 9am to 6pm, Saturday 9:30am to 4pm, and Sunday 9:15am to 2:15pm.

## SEEING THE SIGHTS

To best explore this 1,000-year-old town or **Altstadt** ★★★, park your car, put on a pair of comfortable shoes, and set out on foot through the Altstadt, which has more than 1,000 half-timbered buildings from the 15th to the 18th centuries. Don't miss any of the numerous attractions that await you. The impressive **Rathaus** ★ on the Marktplatz was built in 1450. The portico, with Gothic cross-vaulting, opening on to the Marktplatz, was used by merchants for centuries. Above this is the citizens' meeting hall and the councilmen's meeting chamber, lavishly decorated in the early 1300s with a cycle of 55 paintings depicting biblical and heathen iconography and believed to incorporate the zinc miners returning home from the Rammelsberg mines.

**Marktplatz** ★, in front of the Rathaus, was for a long time the town's hub of activity. In the center of the large square is a 13th-century fountain with two bronze basins and the German imperial eagle at the top. Many visitors view the performance of the town's **Glockenspiel** here as the highlight of their visit. Every day at noon, 3, and 6pm (there's a smaller version of the spectacle at 9am), a procession of mechanized miners, representing the silver trade of long ago, traipses out of the innards of the clock tower.

The churches of Goslar provide a look into the architectural history of the area. Many of the oldest—five had already been built by 1200—have been expanded and altered from their original Romanesque style to their current Gothic appearance. The Romanesque **Marktkirche,** just behind the Rathaus, has 700-year-old stained-glass windows and a 16th-century bronze baptismal font. From Marktplatz, take Rosentorstrasse north to reach the 11th-century **Jakobikirche,** later transformed into a Gothic masterpiece, complete with baroque altars. The church contains a *Pietà* by Hans Witten (1520). Farther down the street, the **Neuwerkkirche,** in a garden, has retained its purely Romanesque basilica, and its well-preserved sanctuary contains a richly decorated choir and stucco reliefs. It was originally constructed as a Cistercian convent in the late 1100s.

The 12th-century **Frankenberg Kirche,** on Bergstrasse, was completely remodeled in the 1700s. Over the elaborate baroque pulpit and altars hangs the intricately carved Nun's Choir Gallery, bedecked with gilded saints and symbols.

One of the reminders that Goslar was once a free imperial and Hanseatic city is the **Breites Tor (Broad Gate),** a three-towered town gate with walls up to 4m (13 ft.) thick. From here you can follow the old town fortifications to the **Kaiserpfalz,** Kaiserbleek 6 (✆ **05321/311-96-93**), a Romanesque palace that was the ruling seat of the emperors in the 11th and 12th centuries. You can view the 19th-century murals that cover its walls and visit the Ulrichskapelle, where the heart of Heinrich III was placed inside a large sarcophagus. The site is open April to October, daily 10am to 5pm; off-season, daily 10am to 4pm. Admission is 4.50€ ($4) for adults and 2.50€ ($2.25) for children.

For a quick and less exhausting look at the history of Goslar, visit the **Goslarer Museum,** at the corner of Abzuchstrasse and Königstrasse (✆ **05321/433-94**), which has displays of the architecture of the early town and several relics of the past. The museum also contains a large geological collection from the Harz Mountains. It's open April to October, Tuesday to Sunday 10am to

### *Finds* Into the Depths of an Ancient Mine

Just outside Goslar, about 1.5km (1 mile) south of the town center (follow the signs), you can explore an ancient mine. As early as the 3rd century A.D., lead, zinc, copper, silver, tin, and a little gold were being mined here. The **Rammelsberger Bergbaumuseum,** Bergtal 19 (✆ **05321/75-00**), conducts guided tours at hourly intervals, on foot or on a small underground train. The museum is open daily 9am to 6pm. Walking tours cost 5.50€ ($4.90) for adults and 2.50€ ($2.25) for children; the train is 8.50€ ($7.60) for adults and 5.50€ ($4.90) for children. For more information, call either the museum or the tourist office in Goslar (✆ **05321/7-80-60**).

5pm; November to March, Tuesday to Sunday 10am to 4pm. Admission is 3€ ($2.70) for adults and 1.50€ ($1.35) for children.

## WHERE TO STAY

**Dorint-Harzhotel Kreuzeck** ★ About 14km (9 miles) from Goslar is a well-rated, comfortable hotel set on a small lake with beautiful mountain scenery. The hotel offers country hospitality and exceptional food, and you may want to drive here for a meal even if you can't stay. Rooms, which range from medium to spacious, are comfortable and tranquil; the best in the area. All units have neatly kept bathrooms containing shower-tub combinations. Numerous ski lifts are in the vicinity, as well as a 30km (18½-mile) cross-country ski course. Ice-skating rinks are also nearby, and guests can enjoy an old-fashioned ride in a horse-drawn sleigh. In summer, available activities include sailing, windsurfing, hiking, tennis, and cycling.

Am Kreuzeck 1–4, 38644 Goslar-Hahnenklee. ✆ **05325/7-40.** Fax 05325/7-48-39. www.dorint.de. 104 units. 105€–115€ ($93.75–$102.70) double. Rates include buffet breakfast. AE, DC, MC, V. Free outdoor parking; 4.50€ ($4) in garage. Bus: 2434 from Goslar. Take the A7 Autobahn and exit at Seesen. **Amenities:** Restaurant; lounge; activity center; room service. *In room:* TV, minibar, hair dryer.

**Goldene Krone** *Value* This 300-year-old, recently renovated village inn comes complete with a friendly innkeeper, Herr Dietmar Pflug, who attends to the rooms and the meals. If you enjoy local color, this is a real find. Rooms are small and simple but home-like and clean, with bathrooms containing shower-tub combinations; they're a great value for the price.

Breitestrasse 46 (near the Breites Tor), 38640 Goslar. ✆ **05321/3-44-90.** Fax 05321/34-49-50. www.touronline.de/harz/hotel/goldkrone. 17 units. 85€–105€ ($75.90–$93.75) double. Rates include buffet breakfast. AE, DC, MC, V. Free parking. Bus: A or B. **Amenities:** Restaurant; bar; lounge; laundry/dry cleaning. *In room:* TV.

**Hotel Der Achtermann** ★ This hotel is a bustling but somewhat dowdy government-rated three-star hotel whose extras rival those of four-star hotels nearby. Just after World War II, one of the round-sided 500-year-old watchtowers in the city's wraparound fortifications was enlarged with a white-sided extension, thereby creating an intriguing but rather cumbersome-looking amalgam of old and new architecture. Rooms are well furnished and comfortable, except for a handful that are a bit too small (most, however, are spacious). All units contain tidy bathrooms with shower-tub combinations.

Rosentorstrasse 20, 38640 Goslar. ✆ **05321/7000-0.** Fax 05321/7000-999. www.der-achtermann.de. 152 units. 125€–182€ ($111.65–$162.55) double. Rates include breakfast. AE, DC, MC, V. **Amenities:** Breakfast room; lounge; pool; spa; sauna; room service; massage; laundry/dry cleaning. *In room:* TV, hair dryer.

**Kaiserworth** ★★ The Kaiserworth is a big, old-fashioned hotel, right in the heart of town. The building dates from 1494 and is a sightseeing attraction in itself. The exterior is Gothic, with an arched arcade across the front, topped by a turreted oriel window facing Marktplatz. The large rooms are designed for comfort; the corner rooms are big enough to be suites. All rooms contain shower-tub combinations. Rooms 102, 106, 110, 202, and 206 offer the best views of the nearby Glockenspiel performance outside.

Markt 3, 38640 Goslar. ✆ **05321/70-90.** Fax 05321/2-11-14. www.kaiserworth.de. 66 units. 101€–169€ ($90.20–$150.90) double. Rates include buffet breakfast. AE, DC, MC, V. Parking 6€ ($5.35). Bus: A or B. **Amenities:** 2 restaurants; bar; room service; laundry/dry cleaning. *In room:* TV, hair dryer.

## WHERE TO DINE

**Die Worth** ★ NORTH GERMAN This is the most rustic and also the most attractive dining room in Goslar. The restaurant is in a Gothic stone crypt with vaulted ceiling and arches, stained-glass windows, wrought-iron lanterns, and trestle tables. The food is good, and the portions are hearty, although all the recipes are very familiar. In season, roast game is featured with wild mushrooms, mashed apples, and berries. Rump steak is always an excellent choice, as is the more unusual *Harzer Blaubeer Schmandschnitzel,* a local recipe that combines pork schnitzel with blueberry-flavored cream sauce.

In the Kaiserworth, Markt 3. ✆ **05321/70-90.** Main courses 9.10€–24.75€ ($8.15–$22.10); fixed-price lunch 16€ ($14.30). AE, DC, MC, V. Daily noon–2:30pm and 6–11pm. Bus: A or B.

**Goldene Krone** INTERNATIONAL/NORTH GERMAN It seems like everyone in town knows about this historic Weinstube. The decor is rustic and cozy, and you'll feel at home with the polite service. In addition to the standard north German dishes, occasional international dishes appear on the changing seasonal menu.

The Goldene Krone also has 17 rooms for rent, all with showers, TVs, and phones. Doubles are 85€ to 105€ ($75.90–$93.75).

Breitestrasse 46 (on the eastern edge of Goslar), 38640 Goslar. ✆ **05321/3-44-90.** Fax 05321/34-49-50. Reservations recommended. Main courses 16€–20€ ($14.30–$17.85); fixed-price meal 13€–18€ ($11.60–$16.05) at lunch, 25€ ($22.35) at dinner. AE, MC, V. Daily 11:30am–2pm and 6–9pm. Bus: A or B.

# 8 Göttingen

132km (82 miles) S of Hannover, 47km (29 miles) NE of Kassel, 109km (68 miles) SW of Braunschweig

Heinrich Heine pronounced Göttingen "famed for its sausages and university." The university in this Gothic town is one of the oldest and most respected in Germany. It was established in 1737 by George II, king of England and elector of Hannover. In time, Göttingen became the most popular university town in Europe. The university suffered relatively little damage during World War II.

Medieval romanticism and lively student life make Göttingen worth a day's visit. By making a slight detour, you can explore the university town before dipping into the fairy-tale country of the upper Weser Valley. Göttingen is halfway between Bonn and Berlin.

## ESSENTIALS

**GETTING THERE** **By Train** Göttingen has frequent daily rail connections from Munich (trip time: 6 hr.), from Frankfurt (2½ hr.), and from Hannover (1 hr.). It lies on the major Kassel–Bebra–Göttingen–Hannover line, with frequent connections in all directions. For information, call ✆ **01805/99-63-33.**

**By Bus** Long-distance bus connection, from such cities as Hannover, is provided by **Winkermann GmbH** (✆ **05143/98820**) and **Lempke & Koschick GmbH** (✆ **05143/46980**). Buses arrive in front of the main railway station. Regional bus service to other parts of Lower Saxony is offered by **Regionalbus Braunsweig** (✆ **0551/5-06-84-22**).

**By Car** Access is via the A7 Autobahn, which runs north to Hannover and Hamburg.

**VISITOR INFORMATION** Contact **Tourist-Information,** Altes Rathaus, Markt 9 (✆ **0551/499-80-31**), open November to March, Monday to Friday 9:30am to 6pm and Saturday 10am to 1pm; April to October, Monday to Friday 9:30am to 6pm and Saturday and Sunday 10am to 4pm.

**GETTING AROUND** A network of buses run throughout the city from 6am to around 10:30pm. Their main junction point is at the corner of the Judenstrasse and Friedrichstrasse, at the edge of the Altstadt. Fare is 1.50€ ($1.35), with a four-ticket package priced at 5€ ($4.45).

## SEEING THE SIGHTS

In the center of Göttingen, you can wander down narrow streets, looking at wide-eaved, half-timbered houses. Many of the facades are carved and painted, and some bear marble plaques noting the famous people who lived inside, such as the more than 40 Nobel Prize winners who temporarily made their home here.

**Altes Rathaus** (bus: 4, 8, 10, 11, or 14) was originally built for trade purposes around 1270, but it wasn't completed until 1443. Its highlights are the open arcade, the Gothic heating system, and the Great Hall, in which the people of Göttingen once received princes and dignitaries, held courts of law, and gave feasts. **Marktplatz,** in front of the Town Hall, is the most interesting section of Göttingen. Here, since 1910, stands the "most-kissed girl in the world," the smiling statue of the Ganseliesel on the market fountain. By tradition, every student who attains a degree must plant a kiss on the lips of the little goose-girl.

**Stadtisches Museum,** Ritterplan 7–8 (✆ **0551/4-00-28-45;** bus: 3, 8, or 9), chronicles the history and culture of southern Lower Saxony. The most interesting exhibits are in the Göttingen history wing on the second floor. Surprisingly, the museum takes an uncompromising look at the town's Nazi past—most German towns tend to conceal it. Everything is here, from Hitlerjugend memorabilia to pages ripped from the local Nazi-run newspaper. The museum is open Tuesday to Friday 10am to 5pm and Saturday and Sunday 10am to 1pm. Admission is 1.50€ ($1.35) for adults and .50€ (45¢) for children.

## SHOPPING

The commercial heart of town is **Wenderstrasse** and **Grönestrasse,** both of which feature pedestrian malls during most of the shopping day. Here, you'll find an appealing roster of cafes and delicatessens selling sausages and cakes, as well as purveyors of the German-style good life. If you want souvenirs, the local tourist office (see above) sells T-shirts, cigarette lighters, beer mugs, and posters. Antiques are found at **Bohm,** Barfusserstrasse 12 (✆ **0551/5-78-86**). Junkier, dustier, less pretentious, and a lot less expensive is **Brocante,** Kurzestrasse 16 (no phone), where the accumulated treasures and debris of estate sales are displayed in an appealingly disorganized jumble. For the works of local and international painters and sculptors, try **Galerie Apex,** Burgstrasse 46 (✆ **0551/4-68-86**).

## WHERE TO STAY

**Central Hotel** *Finds* Although this quiet hotel on a pedestrian walkway is centrally located, as its name indicates, its best feature is the imaginative care the designers have used to decorate the rooms. For example, one room is flamboyantly wallpapered and curtained in vivid yellow and white tones, and another seems to be covered in pink silk. Each unit comes with a small, tiled bathroom with shower.

Judenstrasse 12 (near the university), 37073 Göttingen. ✆ **0551/5-71-57.** Fax 0551/5-71-05. 35 units. 80€–110€ ($71.45–$98.25) double; 150€ ($133.95) suite. Rates include buffet breakfast. AE, DC, MC, V. Parking 4.10€ ($4). Bus: 4, 8, 10, 11, or 14. **Amenities:** Breakfast room; lounge. *In room:* TV.

**Eden-Hotel** ★ The centrally located Eden-Hotel offers comfortable rooms with private tub or shower. The Eden is the second best choice in town, after Gebhards (see below). Rooms are provided with more amenities than most in this price range. The visiting businessperson finds a great deal of comfort here in the health club and pool, and so can the vacationer. Its restaurant offers a varied cuisine, ranging from Northern German to Italian, so you might want to check it out even if you're not a guest here.

Reinhauser Landstrasse 22A, 37083 Göttingen (near the new Rathaus). ✆ **0551/7-60-07.** Fax 0551/7-67-61. www.eden-hotel.de. 99 units. 92€–125€ ($82.15–$111.65) double. Rates include buffet breakfast. AE, MC, V. Parking 6€ ($5.35). **Amenities:** 2 restaurants; bar; pool; health club; sauna; solarium; room service; laundry/dry cleaning. *In room:* TV, minibar, hair dryer, safe.

**Romantik Gebhards Hotel** ★★ Gebhards is the best hotel in town. It's housed in a grand building that evokes a Tuscan villa, with a modern balconied annex built onto the back. The renovated interior offers high-ceilinged public areas and a pleasant bar area. Rooms are well designed and furnished. The cheapest double has a toilet and shower; the most expensive is an apartment with a complete private bathroom with a shower-tub combination.

Goethe-Allee 22–23 (in front of the Bahnhof), 37073 Göttingen. ✆ **0551/4-96-80.** Fax 0551/4-96-81-10. 60 units. 130€–170€ ($116.10–$151.80) double; 200€–220€ ($178.60–$196.45) suite. Rates include buffet breakfast. AE, DC, MC, V. Free parking. Bus: 4, 8, 10, 11, or 14. **Amenities:** Restaurant; bar; room service; laundry/dry cleaning. *In room:* TV, minibar, hair dryer.

## WHERE TO DINE

**Ratskeller** ★ NORTH GERMAN This 600-year-old restaurant lies in the historic cellar of the Altes Rathaus. This is the best place to eat in town, although Göttingen is not known for its restaurants. The menu is varied and extensive, with the longest list of soups and hors d'oeuvres in the region. The chef also prepares the best *Tafelspitz* (boiled beef) in the area. Specialties include Old German Farmer's Plate (chicken breast and pork steak with fried potatoes and roast onions) or fresh trout au bleu with parsley potatoes.

Markt 9. ✆ **0551/5-64-33.** Reservations recommended. Main courses 9€–22.50€ ($8.05–$20.10). AE, DC, MC, V. Daily 11:30am–midnight. Closed Christmas Eve. Bus: 4, 8, 10, 11, or 14.

**Zum Schwarzen Bären (The Black Bear)** NORTH GERMAN This fine restaurant is housed in a black-and-white timbered building (ca. 1500). It still has the original stained-glass leaded windows. Inside, the ambience is tavern style, with a ceramic stove in the corner and dining rooms with intimate booths. The innkeeper wisely recommends the brook trout from the Harz Mountains or *Bärenpfanne* (various filets with Spätzle).

Kurzestrasse 12. ✆ **0551/5-82-84.** Reservations required. Main courses 8€–16.60€ ($7.15–$14.80); fixed-price lunch 18€ ($16.05); fixed-price dinner 25€ ($22.35). AE, MC, V. Tues–Sun noon–2pm; Tues–Sat 6–10pm. Bus: 4, 8, 10, 11, or 14.

## GÖTTINGEN AFTER DARK

Pick up a copy of *Universitätsstadt Göttingen Informationsheft* for a complete rundown of entertainment listings.

**THE PERFORMING ARTS** The local symphony orchestra and boys choir are very active, and an annual Handel music festival is held in June. Information on schedules, venues, and tickets is available by calling ✆ **0551/5-67-71** or by contacting the tourist office (see above). Tickets are 8€ to 20€ ($7.15–$17.85).

For 100 years, the **Deutsches Theater,** Theaterplatz 11 (✆ **0551/4-96-90**), has been staging classical and contemporary drama. Its counterpart, the **Junges Theater,** Hospitalstrasse 6 (✆ **0551/49-50-15**), has produced experimental works for 40 years. Performances of both are held Tuesday to Sunday, with tickets costing 9€ to 14€ ($8.05–$12.50) for adults and 7€ to 10€ ($6.25–$8.95) for students. The box office is open Monday to Saturday 11am to 1pm and 6 to 8:30pm.

**BARS** **The Ratskeller** (see above) has already been recommended as the place to dine in this university center. Its beer cellar is also the most evocative spot to have a beer, or many beers if you'd like to drink as the locals do in this 600-year-old establishment. More half liters are consumed here than at any other place in town. As you lift a mug here, you can imagine that you're standing in the footsteps of previous patrons such as Otto von Bismarck, the Brothers Grimm (they were former faculty members at the university), or, more ominously, Werner Heisenberg, head of the German A-bomb project. A small cafe with indoor and outdoor seating, **Schroeder's Kneipe,** Judenstrasse 29 (✆ **0551/5-56-47**), serves beer, wine, and coffee, as well as chocolate and other sweets. It also has pinball. Open daily 10:30am to 2am. One of the more offbeat social centers of Göttingen is **KAZ (Kommunikations Aktions-Zentrum),** Hospitalstrasse 6 (✆ **0551/5-30-62**), where everyone from senior citizens to anarchists meet for drinks in one of the two on-premises pubs. One also serves traditional German cuisine; the other offers sandwiches. Within the complex, political forums, local discussion groups, and cultural associations meet regularly. Opening hours change with the seasons and the scheduling of volunteers and group discussion leaders, but in most cases, the center is open Monday to Thursday, noon to 2am, Friday noon to 4am, and Saturday 11am to 1am. A jazz soundtrack sets the mood at **Café Kadenz,** Judenstrasse 17 (✆ **0551/4-72-08**), where a mellow crowd meets for beer, wine, coffee, and perhaps a light meal or snack. Hours are Monday to Saturday 10am to 1am, Sunday 11am to midnight.

**LIVE MUSIC** Performance jazz is featured 1 night a week at the excellent **Blue Note,** Wilhelmsplatz 3 (✆ **0551/4-69-07**); on other nights, musicians explore blues, salsa, African, reggae, and other Caribbean forms. Open Sunday to Thursday 8pm to 2am; Friday and Saturday to 3am. Cover for most bands is 8€ to 16€ ($7.15–$14.30). Popular with locals and students, **Irish Pub,** Mühlenstrasse 4 (✆ **0551/4-56-64**), hosts live music every night of the week, from local rockers to visiting Irish folk bands. The pub serves Guinness, Kilkenny, and hard cider. There's never a cover, and it's open nightly 5pm to 2am.

**STUDENT TAVERNS** A visit to Göttingen is traditionally capped by going to one of the student taverns, such as the cramped but convivial **Zum Altdeutschen,** Prinzenstrasse 16 (✆ **0551/5-65-45**), open daily 4pm to 1am; or **Irish Pub** (see above).

**GAY CLUBS** **Café Kabale,** Geismarlandstrasse 19 (✆ **0551/48-58-30**), is where lesbians gather. It's open Monday to Friday 2pm to 2am, Saturday and

Sunday 10am to 2am. **Café Protz** and **Faces,** Nikolaikirchhofstrasse 11 (✆ **0551/5-76-99**), offer a cafe and a bar setting, respectively, that are popular with gay men. Café Protz is open 10am to 2am daily; Faces, daily 5pm to 2am.

## 9 Bad Wildungen

43km (27 miles) SW of Kassel, 160km (100 miles) NE of Frankfurt am Main

Bad Wildungen is more than 700 years old. Its healing mineral springs have long attracted northern Europeans to the rolling hills and deep forests of the Waldeck region, southwest of Kassel. Thousands of annual visitors come here seeking treatment for kidney and gallbladder disorders or simply for rest and relaxation and the numerous cultural activities.

### ESSENTIALS

**GETTING THERE** **By Train** There's frequent service on the Kassel–Fritzlar line from Kassel. For information, call ✆ **01805/99-66-33.** The nearest airport is at Frankfurt am Main, 160km (100 miles) away.

**By Bus** Bus service in the region is provided by **B.K.W. GmbH** (call ✆ **05621/802810** for information).

**By Car** From Kassel, take Route 49 southwest, then go west on Route 253.

**VISITOR INFORMATION** For information, contact the **Kurverwaltung,** Langemarckstrasse 2 (✆ **05621/704113**), open Monday to Friday 8am to 4:30pm and Saturday 8:30am to noon.

### SIGHTS & ACTIVITIES

Rising above the Altstadt is the massive tower of the 14th-century **Stadtkirche** (✆ **05621/40-11**), the most impressive (and oldest) structure in the town, with interesting Hallenkirch architecture. It was restored in 1995. The highlight of the church is its remarkable **Niederwildungen Altarpiece,** one of the best examples of early German painting. Painted in 1403 by Master Konrad von Soest, the wing-paneled altarpiece contains a large, dramatic scene of the crucifixion, flanked by six smaller scenes from the life of Christ. The work shows a French influence in the use of delicate colors and figures, made even more vivid by the use of actual gold. The church is open daily 10:30am to noon and 2 to 5pm.

The **spa gardens** augment the town's natural wooded surroundings with carefully planted flowers from all parts of the world, as well as with several attractive buildings, including two band shells where outdoor concerts are frequently given. The grounds are dotted with lawn chairs. The modern horseshoe-shaped arcade houses the George-Viktor Spring, plus several exclusive shops and a small auditorium.

**SHOPPING** Bad Wildungen's shops carry fashion suitable for Germany's most sophisticated cities. Shops line either side of the Brunnenallee. One of the most appealing is **Manhenke,** Brunnenallee 28 (✆ **05621/960253**), which sells clothes and accessories for both men and women.

### WHERE TO STAY

**Maritim Badehotel** ★ The Maritim Badehotel is located in the center of the town's clinical and cultural activities. No hotel in Bad Wildungen comes close to this one for comfort, style, amenities, and facilities. This place evokes the grandeur of another era. Large and rambling, it branches out in two great wings from the circular domed entrance. The renovated rooms are large, comfortable, sunlit, and airy, all with views of the Waldeck woodlands and spa gardens. All are equipped with neatly kept bathrooms containing shower-tub combinations.

Dr.-Marc-Strasse 4 (at the entrance to the gardens, in the Kurpark), 34537 Bad Wildungen. ✆ **05621/79-99.** Fax 05621/79-97-99. www.maritim.de. 230 units. 137€–157€ ($122.35–$140.20) double; 207€–340€ ($184.85–$303.60) suite. Rates include buffet breakfast. AE, DC, MC, V. Parking 8€ ($7.15). **Amenities:** Restaurant; lounge; pool; sauna; room service; massage; babysitting; laundry/dry cleaning. *In room:* TV, minibar, hair dryer, safe.

**Treff Hotel Quellenhof** This white-sided hotel has a mansard roof and Art Nouveau gables. Rooms are international in decor and carefully outfitted. All rooms come equipped with neatly kept bathrooms containing shower-tub combinations.

Brunnenallee 54 (across the street from the Kurpark), 35437 Bad Wildungen. ✆ **05621/80-70.** Fax 05621/80-75-00. 112 units. 93€–148€ ($83.05–$132.15) double. AE, DC, MC, V. **Amenities:** Restaurant; bar; whirlpool; sauna; solarium; room service; babysitting; laundry/dry cleaning; casino. *In room:* TV, minibar, hair dryer.

## WHERE TO DINE

The hotel dining rooms enjoy a culinary monopoly in Bad Wildungen; there is no major independent restaurant.

**Park Restaurant** INTERNATIONAL Stylish, airy, and international, this is the showcase restaurant of the Treff Hotel (see above). Though it's a top place to dine, its prices are affordable. The immaculately clean interior is outfitted with lots of green plants. The staff is alert and well trained. Menu items include well-prepared salads, roasted meats, pastas, pastries, and such traditional German dishes as sauerbraten and *Rostbraten* (roast beef).

In the Treff Hotel Quellenhof, Brunnenallee 54. ✆ **05621/80-70.** Reservations recommended. Main courses 10€–24€ ($8.95–$21.45). AE, DC, MC, V. Daily 11am–2pm and 6–10pm.

## BAD WILDUNGEN AFTER DARK

The tourist office keeps a list of special events, which are staged almost every week. Concerts and theater usually take place in the **Neues Kurhaus** in the town center or at the **Kursaal** in Reinhaltshausen, not far from Bad Wildungen. For tickets, call ✆ **05621/70-47-73.**

**Spielbank,** Brunnenallee 54 (✆ **05621/96-00-56**), located in the Treff Hotel (see above), is the resort's only casino. It's minor league as Germany's casinos go. Open daily 2:30 to 11pm, with an entrance fee of 1€ (90¢). Bring your passport. Men must wear sportsjackets.

Nighttime diversions in Bad Wildungen revolve around the **Brunnenallee** and its extension, the **Brunnenstrasse,** in the form of lively bars and cafes that stay open until around 2am. Some of the best include the **Warsteiner Ecke,** Brunnenstrasse 66 (✆ **05621/74172**) and the **Ratskeller,** Marktplatz (✆ **05621/71855**). The most earthy and rowdy of the town's beer halls is **Bräuhaus,** Frankenbergerstrasse 2 (✆ **05621/74150**), open Monday to Friday 6 to 11pm, Saturday noon to 11pm, and Sunday 8:30am to 4pm.

# 10 The Fairy-Tale Road ★★

To tour the Fairy-Tale Road (Märchenstrasse) is to take a trip though the land made immortal by the Brothers Grimm. German folklore survived in rural areas at least until the mid-19th century, and much of its charm is still visible and nostalgically remembered today. The Grimm brothers were the earliest scholars of their country's folklore; they traveled to far-flung corners of Germany in the early 19th century to record the tales they heard. Their compendium, *Kinder- und Hausmärchen* (*Grimm's Fairy Tales*), is the world's second most frequently translated book, after the Bible.

Today, you can follow the Fairy-Tale Road, a 595km (370-mile) route from Hanau, near Frankfurt, where the Brothers Grimm were born, to Bremen, where the "Town Musicians of Bremen" lived. The route goes through some of the prettiest medieval villages in the country, all listed on the German Tourist Office's maps of the road. In some towns, marionette shows (in German, but universal in appeal) are given in summer, and museums keep the legends alive, including the one in Ziegenhain in the Schwalm Valley, where costumes that might have been worn by Little Red Riding Hood and her grandmother are displayed.

A car is necessary to complete this tour, as the public transportation in this area is not adequate for what we've outlined.

## DAY 1

Begin in **Hanau,** 20km (12½) miles east of Frankfurt on the River Main, where Jakob (1785–1863) and Wilhelm (1786–1859) Grimm were born. Appropriately, the Fairy-Tale Road starts at a monument to the story-telling brothers at Neustadter Marktplatz. The memorial, erected in 1898, is about all that will interest you in this traffic-clogged suburb of Frankfurt. Hanau was heavily bombed in World War II.

From Hanau, go along B43 about 20km (12 miles) northeast to **Gelnhausen,** where the remains of the imperial palace evoke memories of the emperor, Friedrich Barbarossa, and his lover, Beautiful Gela. Barbarossa constructed the castle here on an island in the 12th century.

Continue another 20km (12 miles) to **Steinau an der Strasse,** where the Grimm brothers spent their carefree youth. Visit the Amtshaus, the Renaissance palace, and see a performance at the fairy-tale puppet theater. (Performances are held most Saturdays and Sundays at 3pm, though performances are not always guaranteed. All tickets sell for 5€/$4.45. For more information, call **Steinauer Marionettentheater** [Steinau Marionette Theater], Kumpen 2; ✆ **06663/245.**) Half-timbered buildings line cobblestone streets. The surrounding woods might have been the home of Snow White. In the center of the main square is a memorial fountain honoring the brothers.

Continue north another 32km (20 miles) on B40, following the signs to **Fulda,** noted for its baroque architecture, as exemplified by the bishops' palace on Schlossstrasse, overlooking the city. The prince-bishops were guardians of the tomb of St. Boniface, the apostle of Germany. Fulda's cathedral dates from 1704, and pilgrims still worship at the tomb of St. Boniface, in a crypt beneath the main altar. Consider staying overnight in Fulda.

**Romantik Hotel Goldener Karpfen,** Simpliziusbrunner 1 (✆ **0661/8-68-00;** fax 0661/8680100; www.hotel-goldener-karpfen.com), in Fulda, was built in the baroque era, but the facade is of a later date. Try to arrive for afternoon tea in the hotel's elegant lounge. The hotel rents 50 cozy and comfortable rooms; a double goes for 145€ to 230€ ($129.50–$205.40). The hotel also serves some of the best food in town. Meals range from 25€ to 47€ ($22.35–$41.95).

## DAY 2

Leave Fulda in the morning and take B254 into the Vogelsberg Mountains, going via Grossenlüder to **Lauterbach,** 24km (15 miles) northeast of Fulda. The town is known for its medieval half-timbered houses and its two castles, Eisenbach and Riedesel. In one of the Grimms' tales, the Little Scalawag loses his sock in Lauterbach. After your visit, follow Route 254 northwest to **Alsfeld,** a town of half-timbered houses and cobblestone streets. Its 1512 Altes Rathaus is a showpiece.

Follow the route along the Schwalm River, which the Germans call *Rotkäppchenland,* or Little Red Riding Hood country. Signs point to **Neustadt,** with its circular tower, from which Rapunzel might have let down her golden tresses. Continue north through Schwalmstadt for 29km (18 miles) to **Homberg.**

From Homberg, follow the signs for 39km (24 miles) north to **Kassel,** where you'll want to spend the night. The Waldeck Region and the Reinhards Forest around Kassel were the birthplace of many legends and tales about witches, sleeping princesses, strange beasts, and magic spells. These tales had a profound influence on the Grimm brothers, who lived in Kassel from 1798 to 1830. The **Bruder Grimm Museum,** at Schone Aussicht 2, contains letters, portraits, and mementos.

**Schloss Hotel Wilhelmshöhe** ★, Schlosspark 8 (✆ **0561/3-08-80;** 0561/3-08-8428), in Kassel, is not an old castle but a completely modern structure directly across the street from former imperial palaces. The 105-room hotel has many private terraces with views of the rolling castle park and its buildings, which were once a summer residence for the landgraves and electors of Hessen-Kassel. Later the area became the summer residence of Kaiser Wilhelm II. Doubles cost 129€ ($115.20), and meals begin at 25€ ($22.35).

## DAY 3

Leaving Kassel, go along B3 for some 16km (10 miles) north to **Münden** (known more properly as Hannoversch-Münden). The Fulda and Werra rivers meet here. In the town center are some 700 half-timbered houses built in many styles. Also in Münden is the tombstone of the much-maligned Doctor Eisenbart (a Grimm character), who is remembered every year at a folk festival.

**Jagshaus Heede,** Hermannshager Strasse 81 (✆ **05541/23-95**), in Hann-Münden, is inside the town's nature preserve. The 18-room hotel is an enlarged former private house. There's a cafe-style sun terrace on the premises, as well as a children's playground. The dining room serves conservative German cuisine and offers generous portions; fixed-price meals cost 14€ to 24.50€ ($12.50–$21.90); double rooms rent for 66€ ($58.95) each.

From Münden you can detour from the Fairy-Tale Road, taking the Autobahn (E45) to Göttingen (see section 8, "Göttingen," earlier in this chapter), where you may want to spend the night.

## DAY 4

Return to the Fairy-Tale Road by going back to Münden and then heading north on Route 80. About 10km (6 miles) north of Münden in the village of Veckerhagen, go left and follow the signs to **Sababurg.**

Right outside the village of Sababurg lies **Dornröschenschloss Sababurg,** Hofgeismar (✆ **05671/80-80**), a park and castle said to be the setting of the Sleeping Beauty legend. You'll almost start to believe the tale when you see the Italianate turrets of the castle. The park is said to be the oldest zoological garden in the world. The wilderness of ancient oak and beech trees, along with the tall ferns, adds to the fairy-tale atmosphere of the area. In the castle courtyard, where sweet-smelling briar roses still bloom, you half expect to see the prince coming to awaken Sleeping Beauty. The castle here has an excellent restaurant.

After viewing the castle, take the road back to the Weser Valley village of Oberweser and make a left turn onto B80 heading north. After some 13km (8 miles) you reach the spa of **Bad Karlshafen,** a resort noted for its baroque buildings.

**Hotel zum Schwan,** Conradistrasse 3, Bad Karlshafen (✆ **05672/10-44;** 05672/1046), is an elegant 32-room spa hotel situated beside the main bathhouse, opposite the town pond. Built in 1765, it has the baroque facade of a palace, with an entrance terrace overlooking the river. Excellent meals are served here, with many regional dishes featured, costing 25.55€ ($22.80) and up. If you'd like to spend the night, you can rent an attractively furnished double for 107€ ($95.55).

Continue on Route 80 north (which becomes Route 83) to **Höxter,** the easternmost town in Westphalia. Among its many Renaissance and baroque buildings, the town's most visited attraction is Dechanei (the Deanery). You can take Corveyer Allee from Höxter for about 3km (2 miles) to Corvey, one of the oldest Benedictine abbeys in Germany, planned by Charlemagne and constructed by his son, Ludwig the Pious, in 822.

Follow the Weser River north for some 32km (20 miles) to the town of **Bodenwerder,** the birthplace of Lügen Baron, known as the "Liar Baron" von Münchhausen. He's honored by the **Münchhausen Museum,** filled with mementos of his fanciful life. Lügen Baron von Münchhausen (1720-97) was one of the most colorful characters who ever lived along the Fairy Tale Road. He was called the Liar Baron because it is said that he told the biggest whoppers of anyone in Germany. The baron himself did not write his tall tales down in a book: he merely told them. An acquaintance of his (a name lost to history) recorded many of his tales and published them in a book which became one of the best-selling children's books of all time (issued over the years under various titles). The imaginative baron and his exploits were also the inspiration for Terry Gilliam's extravagant 1988 film, *The Adventures of Baron Munchhausen,* starring John Neville and Eric Idle.

He grew up around the Rathaus, or town hall, at which the **Münchhausen-Erinnerungszimmer** (Münchhausen Memorial Room) has been installed. The museum is filled with mementos of the life of the baron. The museum is open April to October only, daily from 10am to noon and 2 to 5pm, charging 1€ (90¢).

After Bodenwerder, head northwest on Route 83 for Hameln (see section 5, "Hameln," earlier in this chapter), where you'll want to spend the night.

## DAY 5

After a night in Hameln, take Route 83 northwest to the Autobahn (E30) and continue west beyond Osnabrück until you connect with the E37 Autobahn heading northeast to **Bremen** (see the first section of this chapter), the final stop of the trip.

# 17

# Hamburg

Hamburg has many faces. A walk down the neon-lit Reeperbahn at night will revive those old memories of "Sin-City Europe." A ride around Alster Lake in the center city will reveal the elegance of its finest parks and buildings. A stroll along one of Hamburg's many canals will show you why this city has been called the "Venice of the North." Contrasts are evident wherever you look in Hamburg. Amid the steel-and-glass structures of the modern city is the old baroque Hauptkirche St. Michaelis. A Sunday-morning visit to the Altona fish market will give you a good look at early shoppers mingling with late-night partyers.

Hamburg has had to be flexible to recover from the many disasters of its 1,200-year history. This North Sea port was almost totally destroyed during World War II. But out of the rubble of the old, the industrious Hamburgers rebuilt a larger and more beautiful city, with huge parks, impressive buildings, and important cultural institutions. Hamburg is today the greenest city in Europe, with nearly 50% of its surface area marked with water, woodlands, farmland, and some 1,400 parks and gardens. Green is, in fact, the city's official color.

Hamburg, the second-largest city of Germany, lies on the Elbe River, 109km (68 miles) from the North Sea, 285km (177 miles) northwest of Berlin, 119km (74 miles) northeast of Bremen, and 150km (93 miles) north of Hannover.

## 1 Orientation

### ARRIVING

**BY PLANE** The **Airport Hamburg-Fuhlsbüttel,** Paul-Baumer-Platz 1–3, is 8km (5 miles) north of the city center. It's served by many scheduled airlines and charter companies, with regular flights to major German airports and many European and intercontinental destinations. **Lufthansa** (✆ **01803/80-38-03**) offers flights to Hamburg from most major German cities, and many national carriers fly into Hamburg, including Air France from Paris and British Airways from London. United Airlines, Delta, and Lufthansa offer direct flights from the United States. For flight information in Hamburg, call ✆ **040/507-50.**

An ultra-modern terminal and passenger pier at the airport has a roof shaped like an enormous aircraft wing. This terminal contains an array of interesting shops and boutiques—even a branch of Harrods of London—as well as restaurants and other establishments.

The Hamburger Verkehrsverbund (HVV) **Air Express bus 110** runs every 10 minutes, linking the airport with the city's rapid-transit rail network (both U-Bahn and S-Bahn). A bus departs for the airport from the Hauptbahnhof every 20 minutes 5:40am to 9:30pm daily. Airport buses heading for the Hauptbahnhof leave daily 6:20am to 10:42pm. The one-way fare is 4.35€ ($3.90) for adults and 2.05€ ($1.85) for children under 12. A taxi from the airport to the city costs about 18€ ($16.05), with a trip time of about 25 minutes, depending on traffic.

**BY TRAIN** There are two major rail stations, the centrally located **Hamburg Hauptbahnhof,** Hachmannplatz 10 (✆ **040/39-18-30-46**), and **Hamburg-Altona** (✆ **040/3918-2387**), in the western part of the city. Most trains arrive at the Hauptbahnhof, although trains from the north of Germany, including Westerland and Schleswig, pull into Altona. The two stations are connected by train and S-Bahn. Hamburg has frequent train connections with all major German cities, as well as frequent continental connections. From Berlin, 15 trains arrive daily (trip time: 2 hr. 30 min.), 37 from Bremen (trip time: 54 min.–1 hr. 16 min.), and 33 from Hannover (trip time: 1 hr. 30 min.). For information, call ✆ **01805/99-66-33.**

**BY BUS** Because of Hamburg's location astride most of the rail lines of north Germany, the majority of passengers arrive by train. But if the bus appeals to you, call **Central Omnibus** (✆ **040/24-75-75**). From their headquarters across from the railway station, they'll supply information on fares and schedules for the buses that funnel passengers in from other cities. Information about short-haul buses from surrounding towns and villages is available from **Hamburger Verkehrsverbund** (✆ **040/32880**).

**BY FERRY** Ferry service links Harwich, England, and the St. Pauli Landungsbrücken in Hamburg (trip time: 20 hr.). For information, call **Scandinavian Seaways,** Van-der-Smissenstrasse (✆ **040/38-90-30**).

**BY CAR** The A1 Autobahn reaches Hamburg from the south and west, the A7 from the north and south, the A23 from the northwest, and the A24 from the east. Road signs and directions to Hamburg are frequently posted.

## VISITOR INFORMATION

For visitors to Hamburg, information is offered at several centers. **Tourist-Information,** Hauptbahnhof, Kirchenallee exit (✆ **040/30-05-12-01**), is open daily 7am to 11pm; and **Port Information,** St. Pauli Landungsbrücken (✆ **040/30-05-12-00**), is open daily 10am to 7pm.

## CITY LAYOUT

Hamburg is a showplace of modern architecture; historic structures stand side by side with towering steel-and-glass buildings. The 12 sq. km (4½ sq. miles) of parks and gardens are a vital part of the city, as are the 57 sq. km (22 sq. miles) of rivers and lakes. The city is not compact and can't be easily covered on foot. Many sections of interest are far apart; you'll have to depend on public transportation or taxis.

The **Alster** is the perfect starting point for a pleasurable exploration of Hamburg. This lake, rimmed by the city's most significant buildings, sparkles with the white sails of small boats and ripples with the movement of motor launches. The lake is divided by the Lombard and John F. Kennedy bridges into the **Binnenalster (Inner Alster)** and the larger **Aussenalster (Outer Alster).** The Binnenalster is flanked on the south and the west by the **Jungfernstieg,** one of Europe's best-known streets and Hamburg's most vital artery and shopping district. For landlubbers, the best view of the Alster is from this "maiden's path."

From the Hauptbahnhof, on the eastern fringe of the heart of town, in the vicinity of the Binnenalster, two major shopping streets fan out in a southwesterly direction, toward St. Petri Church and the Rathaus. They are **Spitalerstrasse** (reserved for pedestrians) and **Mönckebergstrasse,** paralleling it to the south. These streets contain some of the city's finest stores. Stay on Mönckebergstrasse to reach **Rathausmarkt,** which is dominated by the Rathaus, a Renaissance-style city hall palace.

The center of Hamburg offers fine opportunities for walking; for example, the eastern shoreline of the Binnenalster opens onto **Ballindamm,** which contains many elegant stores. At the foot of this lake is the Jungfernstieg, already mentioned, and along its western shoreline is yet another main artery, the Neuer Jungfernstieg. At the intersection of the Jungfernstieg and Neuer Jungfernstieg is one of the more fascinating streets of Hamburg, the **Colonnaden,** a colonnade of shops and cafes. In this neighborhood stands the Hamburgische Staatsoper, the famous modern opera house.

## NEIGHBORHOODS IN BRIEF

**Central Hamburg** This is the commercial and shopping district of Hamburg, seat of many of its finest hotels and restaurants. The district centers around Binnenalster and the Rathaus (City Hall). Boat rides on the Alster lakes are a major attraction. Many historic buildings that withstood World War II stand here, including St. Petri, the oldest surviving structure.

**The Harbor** The Port of Hamburg is the world's fifth-largest harbor, stretching for nearly 40km (25 miles) along the Elbe River. More than 1,500 ships from all over the world call each month. Since 1189, this has been one of the busiest centers for trade on the Continent, making Hamburg one of Germany's wealthiest cities.

**St. Pauli** This is the nightlife center of Hamburg, with lots of erotica. The district is split by its famous street, the Reeperbahn, neon-lit and dazzling, offering all sorts of nighttime pleasures—cafes, sex shows, bars, discos, and music halls.

**Altona** Formerly a city in its own right, this western district is now integrated into Greater Hamburg. It was once populated mainly by Jews and Portuguese. Today it's the scene of Hamburg's famous Fischmarkt, which takes place at dawn every Sunday.

**Pösseldorf** Northwest of Aussenalster, this is a tree-filled residential district, with many villas dating from the 1800s. Many exemplary Jugendstil buildings can still be seen here. The district is largely occupied by upwardly mobile professionals, including a lot of media stars.

## GETTING AROUND

*A word to the wise:* Park your car and use public transportation in this busy city. Practically all public transportation services in the Hamburg area—the **U-Bahn** (subway), **S-Bahn** (city rail), **A-Bahn** (commuter rail), buses, and harbor ferries—are run by **Hamburger Verkehrsverbund (HVV),** Steinstrasse 12. For information, call ✆ **040/32880** or visit www.hvv.de. Tickets are sold at Automats and railroad ticket counters.

**BY PUBLIC TRANSPORTATION** Hamburg's **U-Bahn,** one of the best in Germany, serves the entire central area and connects with the **S-Bahn** surface trains in the suburbs. This network is the fastest means of getting around, but buses offer a good alternative. The advantage of surface travel, of course, is that you get to see more of the city.

Fares for both U-Bahn and the bus are 1.40€ to 2.60€ ($1.25–$2.30), depending on the distance. You buy your ticket from the driver or from vending machines at stops and stations. If you plan to make a day of it, you can purchase a **day ticket** for unlimited use of public transportation services for 4.50€ ($4).

There are also discount cards that offer free travel on all public transport in Hamburg, as well as free admission to 11 Hamburg museums and a 30% discount on city tours, guided tours of the port, and lake cruises. A 1-day card goes for 7€ ($6.25) for individuals or 13.50€ ($12.05) for families. A 3-day card costs 13.50€ ($12.05) for individuals and 23€ ($20.55) for families. You can get these cards at some hotels, at major U-bahn stations, and at the tourist office.

**BY TAXI** Taxis are available at all hours; call ✆ **040/44-10-11** or 040/66-66-66. Taxi meters begin at 1.50€ ($1.35) and vary between 1.30€ ($1.15) and 1.60€ ($1.45) per kilometer after that.

## *FAST FACTS:* Hamburg

*American Express* The Amex office in Hamburg is at Ballindamm 39 (✆ **040/30-90-80;** U-Bahn: Jungfernstieg) and is open Monday to Friday 9am to 5pm and Saturday 10am to 1pm.

*Bookstores* **Frensche,** Landesbank Galerie, Spitalerstrasse 26C (✆ **040/32-75-85;** U-Bahn: Hauptbahnhof), is a good English-language bookstore with a large selection of books and tapes. It's open Monday to Wednesday 10am to 7pm; Thursday to Friday 10am to 7:30pm; Saturday 10am to 4pm.

*Business Hours* Most **banks** are open Monday to Friday 8:30am to 12:30pm and 1:30 to 3:30pm (many until 5:30pm on Thurs). Most **businesses** and **stores** are open Monday to Friday 9am to 6pm and Saturday 9am to 2pm (4 or 6pm on the 1st Sat of the month).

*Car Rentals* We don't recommend that you rent a car for touring Hamburg, but an automobile is ideal for the environs. Rentals are available at **Avis,** Drehbahn 15–25 (✆ **040/34-16-51;** U-Bahn: Gansemarkt), or at **Hertz,** Kirchenallee 34–36 (✆ **040/2-80-12-01-03;** U-Bahn: Hauptbahnhof).

*Consulates* See "Embassies & Consulates" in "Fast Facts: Germany," in chapter 3.

*Currency Exchange* The most convenient place for recent arrivals to exchange foreign currency for euros is the **ReiseBank** at the Hauptbahnhof (✆ **040/32-34-83**), which is open daily 7:30am to 10pm. The same bank maintains a branch at the Altona Station (✆ **040/390-3770**), open Monday and Wednesday to Friday 7:30am to 7:30pm, and Tuesday and Saturday 9am to 2pm and 2:45 to 5pm. There's also a branch in Terminal 4 of Hamburg's airport (✆ **040/5075-3374**), open daily 6:30am to 10pm.

*Doctor or Dentist* Ask at the British and American consulates or go to **Allgemeines Krankenhaus,** Lohmühlen Strasse 5, 20099 Hamburg (✆ **040/28-90-11;** U-Bahn: Stadthaus Brücke), where you'll find an English-speaking staff.

*Drugstores* Pharmacies that stock foreign drugs include **Internationale Apotheke,** Ballindamm 39 (✆ **040/30-96-060;** U-Bahn: Jungfernstieg), open Monday to Friday 8am to 7pm and Saturday 9am to 3:30pm. **Roth's**

**Alte Englische Apotheke,** Jungfernstieg 48 (✆ **040/34-39-06;** U-Bahn: Jungfernstieg), is open Monday to Friday 8:30am to 6:30pm and Saturday 9am to 2pm.

*Emergencies* Dial ✆ **110** for the police or an ambulance or emergency doctor or dentist; ✆ **112** for the fire brigade; and ✆ **01805/10-11-12** for the German Automobile Association (ADAC).

*Laundry/Dry Cleaning* Your hotel reception desk can often recommend a laundry or dry-cleaning place nearby. If not, try **Express Wasch-Center,** Friedrichstrasse 30 (✆ **040/3-19-14-34;** S-Bahn: Reeperbahn), for both laundry and dry cleaning. Open Monday to Friday 9:30am to 9pm and Saturday 9:30am to 5pm.

*Post Office* The post office at the Hauptbahnhof, Hachmannplatz 13, is convenient. You can make long-distance calls here far cheaper than at your hotel. Telegrams, telexes, and faxes can also be sent. It's open Monday to Friday 8am to 8pm, Saturday 8am to 6pm, and Sunday 10am to 4pm. A branch office located at the airport is open Monday to Friday 6:30am to 9pm, Saturday 8am to 6pm, and Sunday 10am to 6pm. For information on either post office call ✆ **01802/3333.**

*Restrooms* See "Fast Facts: Germany" in chapter 3. There are several decent public facilities in the center of Hamburg.

*Safety* Hamburg, like all big cities of the world, has its share of crime. The major crimes that tourists encounter are pickpocketing and purse and camera snatching. Most robberies occur in the big tourist areas, such as the Reeperbahn and the area around the Hauptbahnhof, which can be dangerous at night, but much less so than in Frankfurt or Munich.

*Telegrams/Telex/Fax* These can be sent from the post office at the Hauptbahnhof, Hachmannplatz 13 (✆ **040/3-25-51-60**).

*Transit Information* For U-Bahn and S-Bahn rail information, call the Hauptbahnhof, Hachmannplatz 10 (✆ **01805/99-66-33**).

## 2 Where to Stay

Hamburg is an expensive city with an abundance of first-class hotels but a limited number of budget accommodations, especially in the center of the city. During a busy convention period, you may have trouble finding a room. A department within **Hamburg's Tourist Information Office (Tourismus Centrale),** Steinstrasse 7 (✆ **040/30-05-13-00;** fax 040/30-05-13-33), in the Hauptbahnhof, at Kirchenallee in the Wandelhalle, can book accommodations. Rooms from more than 200 hotels in all price categories are available. There's a fee of 3€ ($2.70) per reservation. You can use this agency on a last-minute basis, but no more than 7 days in advance of the time you'll need the room. Hotel-booking desks can also be found at the airport in Arrival Hall A.

### NEAR THE HAUPTBAHNHOF

#### VERY EXPENSIVE

**Kempinski Hotel Atlantic Hamburg** ★★★ This sumptuous hotel, the Kempinski chain's flagship, is one of the two great hotels of the north. It's in a central location filled with trees and imposing villas and was one of the few buildings in the neighborhood to escape the bombs of World War II. Michael

Jackson, Prince, and Madonna cast their votes for this hotel, but we still think Vier Jahreszeiten (see below) is number one. Most rooms are very spacious with high ceilings. Bathrooms are large, with shower-tub combinations.

An der Alster 72 (near the Aussenalster), 20099 Hamburg. ✆ **800/426-3135** in the U.S., or 040/2-88-80. Fax 040/24-71-29. www.kempinski.atlantic.de. 267 units. 212€–270€ ($189.30–$241.10) double; from 302€ ($269.70) suite. AE, DC, MC, V. Parking 15€ ($13.40). U-Bahn: Hauptbahnhof. **Amenities:** Restaurant; 2 bars; pool; sauna; solarium; room service; babysitting; laundry/dry cleaning. *In room:* A/C, TV, minibar, hair dryer, safe.

## EXPENSIVE

**Aussen Alster** ★ Small and exclusive, and on a quiet residential street, Aussen Alster attracts actors, advertising directors, executives, writers, and artists. Its stylish, ultra-modern interior was designed by one of Germany's most famous architects. Hamburg film producer Klaus Feddermann and his partner, Burkhardt Stoelck, manage the place with panache. Rooms are medium-size, white-walled, angular, and consciously simple. Everything is designed for style and comfort, from the luxurious beds to the immaculate bathrooms with shower-tub combinations.

Schmilinskystrasse 11 (a 5-min. walk from the rail station and a 3-min. walk from the Alster), 20099 Hamburg. ✆ **040/24-15-57.** Fax 040/2-80-32-31. 27 units. 120€–145€ ($107.15–$129.50) double. Rates include buffet breakfast. AE, DC, MC, V. Closed Dec 22–27. U-Bahn: Hauptbahnhof. **Amenities:** Restaurant; bar; sauna; solarium; room service; babysitting; laundry/dry cleaning. *In room:* TV, hair dryer, safe.

**Europäischer Hof** ★ Europäischer Hof is the largest privately owned hotel in Hamburg. It lacks the atmosphere of the Maritim Hotel Reichshof or the chic of Aussen Alster hotel (see below and above, respectively), but it has its supporters, especially among business clients. The well-furnished and medium-size rooms have soundproof windows; most have tiny Art Deco dressing rooms, fax ports, and fine carpets that make for a welcoming ambience. All units contain neatly kept bathrooms with shower-tub combinations.

Kirchenallee 45 (across from the Hauptbahnhof), 20099 Hamburg. ✆ **040/24-82-48.** Fax 040/24-82-47-09. www.europaischer-hof.de. 320 units. 133€–183€ ($118.75–$163.40) double. Rates include buffet breakfast. AE, DC, MC, V. Parking 15€ ($13.40). U-Bahn: Hauptbahnhof. **Amenities:** 3 restaurants; bar; pool; fitness center; sauna; solarium; room service; babysitting; laundry/dry cleaning. *In room:* TV, minibar, hair dryer, safe.

**Maritim Hotel Reichshof** ★ When this long-venerated hotel was built in 1910, it was the largest hotel in Europe. In World War II, it lost most of its upper floors, but the landmark Art Nouveau lobby remained intact. The Reichshof is a favorite with business travelers, so more than half its rooms are classified as singles. Rooms are medium to spacious, comfortable, and have double glazing; those on the top floor open onto good views of the city. Bathrooms are small but have up-to-date plumbing and shower-tub combinations.

Kirchenallee 34–36 (across from the Hauptbahnhof), 20099 Hamburg. ✆ **040/24-83-30.** Fax 040/24-83-38-88. www.maritim.de. 303 units. 164€–226€ ($146.45–$201.80) double; from 245€ ($218.80) suite. Rates include buffet breakfast. AE, DC, MC, V. Parking 12€ ($10.70). U-Bahn: Hauptbahnhof. **Amenities:** Restaurant; bar; lounge; pool; sauna; room service; babysitting; laundry/dry cleaning. *In room:* TV, minibar, hair dryer, safe.

**Prem Hotel** ★★ This beautifully located mansion-hotel is called the "white house on the Alster." It attracts a well-heeled clientele. The glistening facade overlooks the lake, and the rear faces a quiet garden with umbrella-covered tables. The reception salons show off a personalized collection of French antiques and reproductions. Rooms, most furnished with Louis XV–style pieces, are well cared for, with luxury beds. Garden-facing rooms are much quieter than those on the Alster. Half the bathrooms are well equipped with big mirrors, marble tubs, and showers. The rest are a bit cramped with shower stalls and fewer extras.

# Hamburg Accommodations & Dining

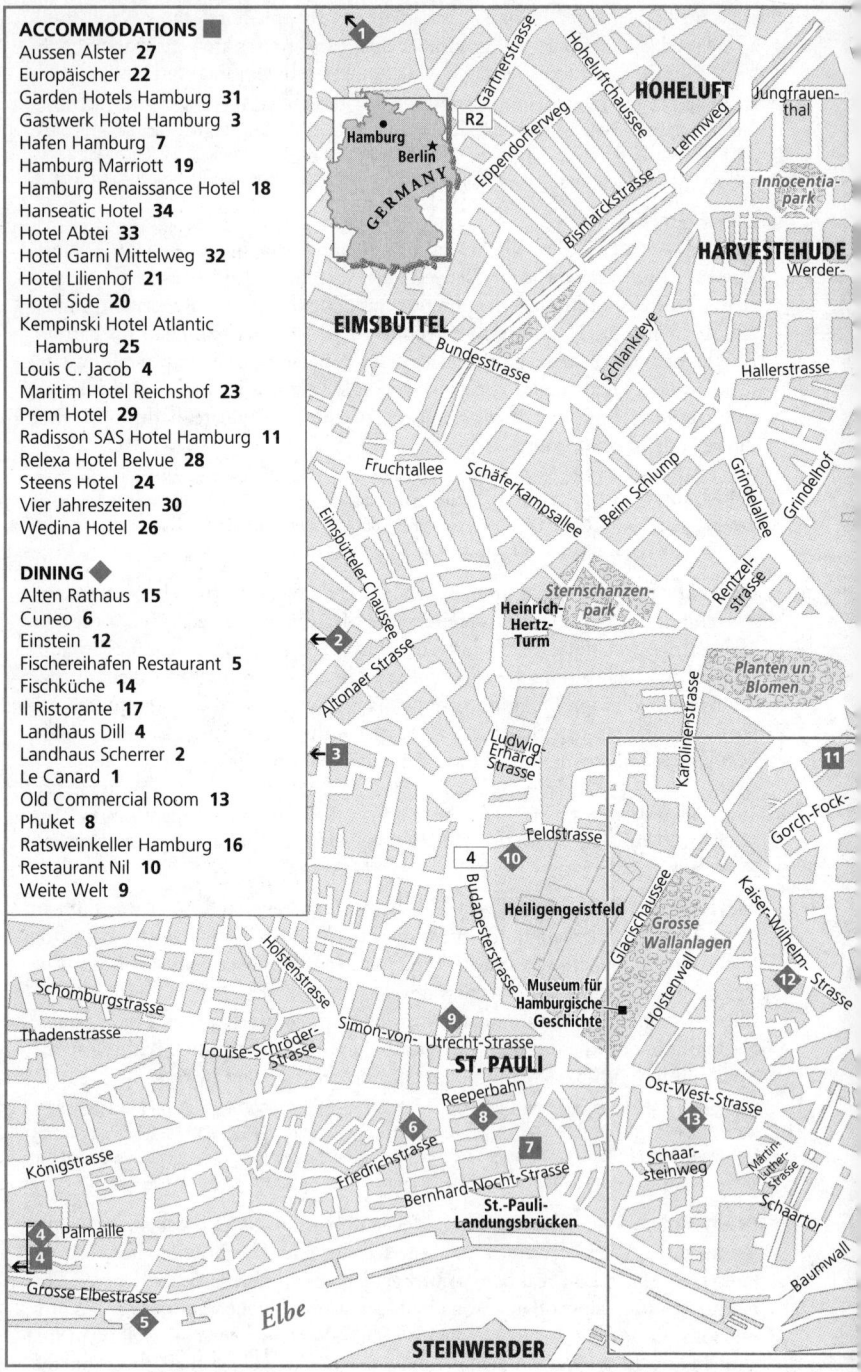

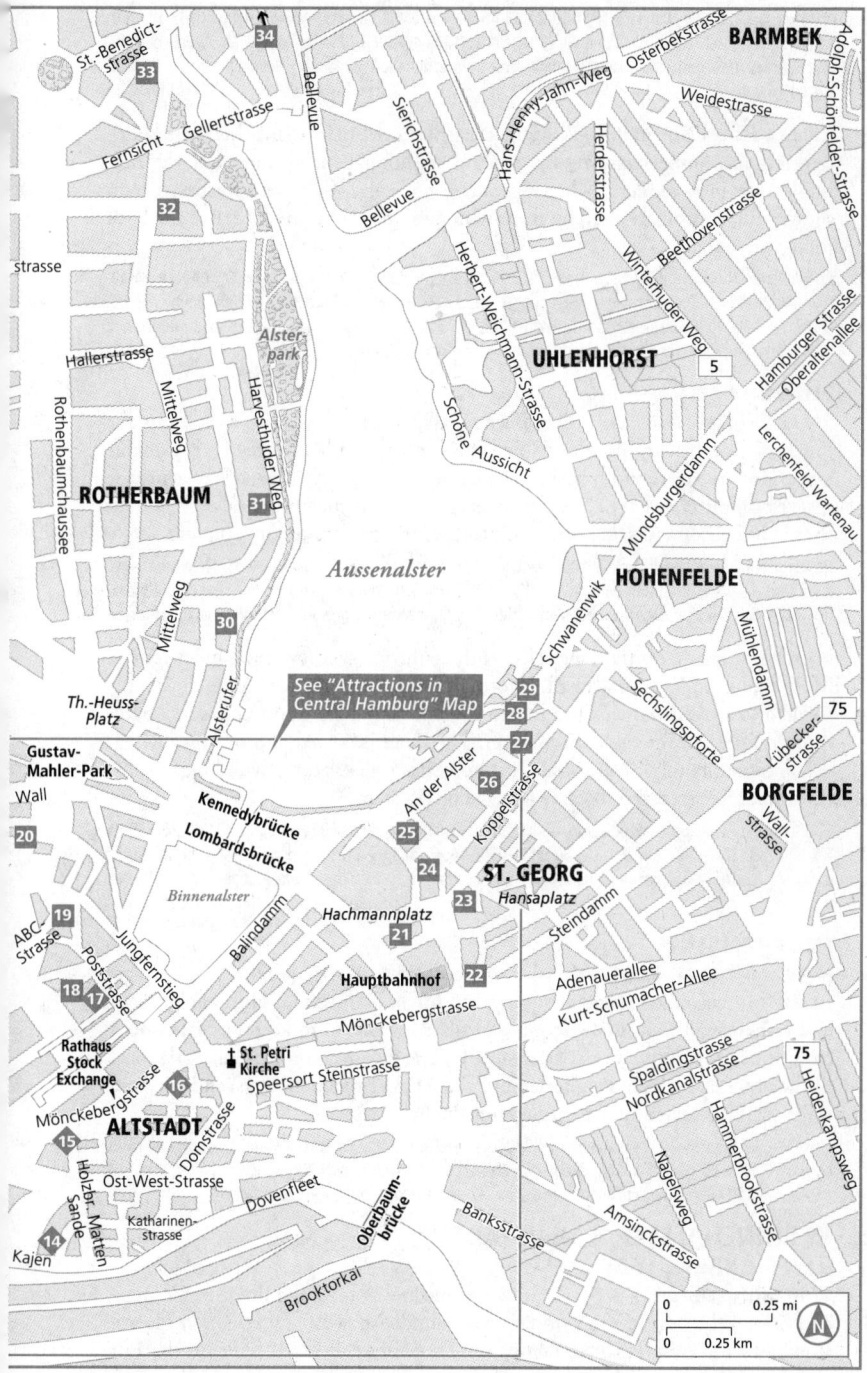
BARMBEK
UHLENHORST
ROTHERBAUM
HOHENFELDE
BORGFELDE
ST. GEORG
ALTSTADT
Aussenalster
Binnenalster
Alsterpark
See "Attractions in Central Hamburg" Map
St.-Benedict-strasse
Fernsicht
Gellertstrasse
Bellevue
Sierichstrasse
Hans-Henny-Jahn-Weg
Osterbekstrasse
Weidestrasse
Adolph-Schönfelder-Strasse
Herderstrasse
Beethovenstrasse
Winterhuder Weg
Herbert-Weichmann-Strasse
Hamburger Strasse
Oberaltenallee
Hallerstrasse
Mittelweg
Harvestuder Weg
Rothenbaumchaussee
Schöne Aussicht
Mundsburgerdamm
Lerchenfeld
Wartenau
Schwanenwik
Mühlendamm
Th.-Heuss-Platz
Alsterufer
Sechslingspforte
Lübecker-strasse
Gustav-Mahler-Park
Wall
Kennedybrücke
Lombardsbrücke
An der Alster
Koppelstrasse
Wall-strasse
Hachmannplatz
Hansaplatz
Steindamm
ABC-Strasse
Jungfernstieg
Poststrasse
Balmdamm
Hauptbahnhof
Adenauerallee
Kurt-Schumacher-Allee
Mönckebergstrasse
Rathaus
Stock Exchange
St. Petri Kirche
Speersort
Steinstrasse
Spaldingstrasse
Nordkanalstrasse
Heidenkampsweg
Hammerbrookstrasse
Nagelsweg
Domstrasse
Holzbr.-Matten
Sande
Ost-West-Strasse
Dovenfleet
Oberbaum-brücke
Bankstrasse
Amsinckstrasse
Katharinen-strasse
Kajen
Brooktorkai
0 0.25 mi
0 0.25 km
N

An der Alster 9, 20099 Hamburg. ✆ **040/24-83-40-40.** Fax 040/2-80-38-51. www.hotel-prem.de. 54 units. 115€–200€ ($102.70–$178.60) double; 230€–300€ ($205.40–$267.90) suite. AE, DC, MC, V. Free parking. Bus: 6. **Amenities:** Restaurant; lounge; sauna; room service; massage; laundry/dry cleaning. *In room:* TV, minibar, hair dryer, safe.

**Relexa Hotel Bellevue** ★ Many theatrical celebrities make this their Hamburg choice. Some larger rooms contain traditional furnishings, but the new singles are in a modern, often Scandinavian style. All have bathrooms with shower-tub combinations. The front windows open onto the lake, but the back rooms are quieter.

An der Alster 14 (facing the Alster, a short ride from the Hauptbahnhof), 20099 Hamburg. ✆ **040/28-44-40.** Fax 040/28-44-42-22. www.relexa-hotel.de. 92 units. 135€–185€ ($120.55–$165.20) double; 200€ ($178.60) suite. Rates include buffet breakfast. AE, DC, MC, V. Parking 8€ ($7.15). Bus: 6. **Amenities:** 2 restaurants; bar; room service; laundry/dry cleaning. *In room:* TV, minibar, hair dryer, safe.

### MODERATE

**Steens Hotel** *Value* *Kids* Despite its classy location, a short walk from the much more expensive Atlantic Hotel, this century-old house charges reasonable rates. Rooms are carefully maintained but short on style. Each has a private shower; all but two have a private toilet. Breakfast is the only meal served. This simple but clean and safe hotel is a great option for families on a budget.

Holzdamm 43 (near the Alster), 20099 Hamburg. ✆ **040/24-46-42.** Fax 040/2-80-35-93. www.steens-hotel.com. 11 units, 2 without bath. 90€–100€ ($80.35–$89.30) double. Rates include continental breakfast. AE, MC, V. U-Bahn: Hauptbahnhof. **Amenities:** Breakfast room; lounge. *In room:* TV, minibar, hair dryer.

**Wedina** This recently remodeled 18th-century town house is a quiet retreat. Most rooms open onto a small, informal Tuscan-style garden. All are tastefully styled and range from small to medium, each with a good bed and a tidy bathroom with a shower-tub combination. The hotel is owned and run by an English-speaking family. *Be warned:* This hotel has no elevator. If you lodge on the third floor, be prepared to carry luggage up 55 steps.

Gurlittstrasse 23 (near the lake, a 5-min. walk from the Hauptbahnhof), 20099 Hamburg. ✆ **040/280-8900.** Fax 040/2-80-38-94. www.wedina.de. 60 units. 95€–145€ ($84.85–$129.50) double. Rates include buffet breakfast. AE, DC, MC, V. Parking 10€ ($8.95). Bus: 6. **Amenities:** Breakfast room; lounge. *In room:* TV, hair dryer.

### INEXPENSIVE

**Hotel Lilienhof** ★ *Value* This unpretentious five-story hotel is a good place to stay for convenience and economy, but forget grand style. The simple, clean, and rather small rooms have double-insulated windows to keep out some noise from the heavy traffic on the street below. The quieter rooms overlook the back of the hotel. None contain a toilet, but some have private showers, and adequate toilet facilities are scattered throughout the hallways.

Ernst-Merck-Strasse 4, 20099 Hamburg. ✆ **040/24-10-87.** Fax 040/2-80-18-15. 24 units, none with private bath. 62€ ($55.35) double without shower; 75€ ($67) double with shower. Rates include buffet breakfast. AE, DC, MC, V. U-Bahn: Hauptbahnhof. **Amenities:** Breakfast room; lounge. *In room:* TV.

## IN BINNENALSTER & NEUSTADT

### VERY EXPENSIVE

**Vier Jahreszeiten** ★★★ This warm, mellow hotel is the finest in Germany and one of the best in the world. It was founded in 1897 by Friedrich Haerlin (today it's run by a Japanese company). Its position is ideal, right on the Binnenalster. Built in the baronial style, it evokes the grand Edwardian hotels. Antiques are used profusely throughout. Despite the large size, personal service is a hallmark. Although no two rooms are alike, they are all beautiful, with period furnishings, Oriental rugs, and all the modern luxuries, including bedside controls, double glazing on the windows, and bathrooms containing shower-tub combinations. This is a hotel for connoisseurs.

Neuer Jungfernstieg 9–14 (on the Binnenalster), 20354 Hamburg. ✆ **800/223-6800** in the U.S. and Canada, or 040/3-49-40. Fax 040/34-94-2600. www.hvj.de. 158 units. 255€–325€ ($227.70–$290.25) double; from 385€ ($343.80) suite. AE, DC, MC, V. Parking 17€ ($15.20). U-Bahn: Hauptbahnhof. **Amenities:** 3 restaurants; 2 bars; health club; sauna; room service; massage; babysitting; laundry/dry cleaning. *In room:* A/C, TV, minibar, hair dryer, safe.

## EXPENSIVE

**Hamburg Marriott** ★ This traditionally styled hotel is one of the finest in Hamburg. It was built on the site of the old Gänsemarkt, where geese were sold in the Middle Ages. The hotel is also near the Hanse Viertel shopping complex. The fashionable surrounding area is filled with boutiques, wine bars, shops, and restaurants. Rooms range from small to medium. The lower price listed below is for standard rooms; the higher for studios. Lavish suites are also available. One hundred rooms are reserved for nonsmokers. All units contain neatly kept bathrooms with shower-tub combinations.

ABC Strasse 52, 20354 Hamburg. ✆ **800/228-9290** in the U.S., or 040/35-05-0. Fax 040/35-05-17-77. www.marriott-hotels.com. 277 units. 153€–217€ ($136.65–$193.80) double; from 249€ ($222.35) suite. AE, DC, MC, V. Parking 18€ ($16.05). U-Bahn: Gänsemarkt. **Amenities:** Restaurant; bar; pool; fitness center; whirlpool; sauna; car rental; salon; room service; babysitting; laundry/dry cleaning. *In room:* A/C, TV, minibar, hair dryer, safe.

**Hamburg Renaissance Hotel** ★★ A 19th-century building, this nine-story hotel offers 20th-century comforts. From the sunken, antique-furnished lobby to the carpeted bar area, you'll be welcomed by the staff and serenaded by a resident pianist. Rooms range from well-appointed doubles to sumptuously upholstered suites. Most are quite spacious, with paired queen-size beds, plus large bathrooms with robes, makeup mirrors, phones, and shower-tub combinations. The hotel was constructed behind the facade of a historic building, and the entire complex was designed with connections to the Hanse Viertel Galerie Passage, Europe's longest shopping arcade.

Grosse Bleichen, Hanse-Viertel, 20354 Hamburg. ✆ **800/228-9290** in the U.S. and Canada, or 040/34-91-80. Fax 040/34-91-89-19. www.renaissancehotels.com. 205 units. 191€–246€ ($170.55–$219.70) double; from 261€ ($233.05) suite. AE, DC, MC, V. Parking 13€ ($11.60). U-Bahn: Jungfernstieg. **Amenities:** Restaurant; bar; pool; fitness center; sauna; room service; massage; babysitting; laundry/dry cleaning. *In room:* A/C, TV, minibar, hair dryer, safe.

**Hotel Side** ★★ Angular, offbeat, and postmodern, this is one of Hamburg's newest hotels, opened in the spring of 2001 and already a favorite address of media and fashion people. It rises 11 stone- and glass-sheathed floors above the street, with an additional four stories underground. Rooms are built around a central atrium, in a dramatic, cream, white and brown color scheme that was created by Matteo Thun, the well-known designer of Milan. He even designed the ashtrays for the hotel. The top two stories are devoted to suites, all encased in an architectural "box" that seems to float over the structure below. Guests can enjoy a terrace on the 8th floor that opens onto panoramic views of Hamburg. Bedrooms are efficiently organized with secret closets and storage space, and each contains deep upholsteries of a tasteful modern design, along with luxurious bathrooms with tub-and-shower combination.

49 Drehnbahn, D-20354 Hamburg. ✆ **040/309-990.** Fax 040/3099-9399. www.side-hamburg.de. 178 units. 205€–330€ ($183.05–$294.70) double; 430€–875€ ($384–$781.40) suite. Surcharge of 25€–50€ ($22.35–$44.65) during trade fairs. Parking 13€ ($11.60). AE, DC, MC, V. U-Bahn: Gänsemarkt or

Stephansplatz. **Amenities:** Restaurant; bar; indoor pool; health club/exercise room; sauna/steam room; 24-hr. room service; babysitting; laundry/dry cleaning. *In room:* A/C, TV, dataport, minibar, hair dryer, safe.

**Radisson SAS Hotel Hamburg** ★ *Kids* This 32-story high-rise hotel is of real architectural interest. It looks like a collection of narrow black lines banded together vertically. Although it's very professionally run and has many winning features, we'd rank it under the Hamburg Renaissance or the Marriott. The medium-size rooms are beautifully appointed, many with paneled walls; all contain neatly kept bathrooms with shower-tub combinations. One floor is reserved for nonsmokers. Since the hotel lies within sight of the botanical gardens and has a large breakfast buffet, it is good for families with children.

Marseillerstrasse 2 (in the Planten und Blomen Park), 20355 Hamburg. ✆ **040/3-50-20.** Fax 040/35-02-35-30. www.radisson.com/hamburgde. 560 units. 145€–193€ ($129.50–$172.35) double; from 280€ ($250.05) suite; business class 175€–240€ ($156.30–$214.30) double. AE, DC, MC, V. Parking 13€ ($11.60). Bus: 102. **Amenities:** 3 restaurants; 2 bars; cafe; pool; fitness center; sauna; solarium; room service; babysitting; laundry/dry cleaning. *In room:* A/C, TV, minibar, hair dryer, safe.

## MODERATE

**Hafen Hamburg** ★ This Hamburg landmark, constructed in the Wilhelmian style, offers panoramic views of the river and the harbor traffic. This hotel attracts the commercial traveler who's not on an expense account. The functionally furnished rooms are unusually spacious. If they're within your budget, book the more expensive harbor-view rooms. Each comes with a well-equipped private bathroom with a shower-tub combination.

Seewartenstrasse 9, 20459 Hamburg. ✆ **040/31-11-30.** Fax 040/31-11-3-755. www.hotel-hamburg.de. 340 units. 100€–120€ ($89.30–$107.15) double. AE, DC, MC, V. Parking 7€ ($6.25). U-Bahn: Landungsbrücke. **Amenities:** Restaurant; bar; fitness center nearby; sauna; laundry/dry cleaning. *In room:* A/C, TV, minibar, hair dryer, safe.

## IN HARVESTEHUDE

**Garden Hotels Hamburg** ★ *Kids* *Finds* This hotel dates from 1791, and over the years it has entertained many luminaries, including King Christian VIII of Denmark in 1824. The location, however, isn't for everyone. It stands in the Hamburg-Harvestehude district on the western sector of the Outer Alster Lake, about a mile from the historic heart of town and some 10km (6 miles) from the airport. This feature makes it attractive to families (who can afford the hotel) with kids since you can go boating in the Outer Alster Lake. Families also appreciate the helpfulness of the friendly staff and the hotel pool. Modern art and well-chosen antiques add to the sophisticated comfort of the rooms. Most are generous-size, and the luxurious bathrooms have shower-tub combinations.

Magdalenenstrasse 60 (1.5km/1 mile from the center), 20148 Hamburg. ✆ **040/41-40-40.** Fax 040/4-14-04-20. www.gardenhotels.de. 59 units. 135€–215€ ($120.55–$192) double; from 230€ ($205.40) suite. AE, DC, MC, V. Parking 10€ ($8.95). U-Bahn: Hallerstrasse. **Amenities:** Breakfast room; bar; pool; fitness center; room service; babysitting; laundry/dry cleaning. *In room:* TV, minibar, hair dryer, safe.

**Hotel Abtei** ★ This suburban hotel is small, choice, and engaging, with a discreet and well-trained staff. It occupies a 19th-century villa that was once an opulent private residence. The high-ceilinged rooms retain many aspects of a private home, including antique furniture and, in many cases, the building's original elaborate plasterwork and parquet floors. Each room contains its own stereo system. Bathrooms contain shower-tub combinations and robes.

Abteistrasse 14 (5km/3 miles north of the center), Harvestehude, 20149 Hamburg. ✆ **040/44-29-05.** Fax 040/44-98-20. 11 units. 180€–260€ ($160.75–$232.20) double. AE, MC, V. U-Bahn: Klosterstern. **Amenities:** Restaurant; lounge; room service; laundry/dry cleaning. *In room:* TV, minibar, hair dryer, safe.

**Hotel Garni Mittelweg** ★ *Finds* A real discovery, this stylishly-decorated family hotel lies in the upscale Poseldorf, within an easy stroll of the Aussenalster. The place is imbued with a country charm. Once the town house of a wealthy merchant and his family in the 19th century, the hotel has been tastefully converted to receive guests, with modern amenities added. Bedrooms are attractively furnished and comfortable, each with a small bathroom containing a tub bath or shower.

Mittelweg 59, Hamburg 20149. ✆ **040/414-1010.** Fax 040/4141-0120. www.hotel-mittelweg.de. 39 units. 110€–155€ ($98.25–$138.40). AE, DC, MC, V. Parking 10€ ($8.95). S-Bahn: Dammtor. **Amenities:** Room service, babysitting. *In room:* TV, minibar, safe.

## IN WINTERHUDE

**Hanseatic Hotel** ★★ *Finds* This hotel, on the banks of the Alster River, close to the Winterhude Market, is the smallest and most delightful place to stay in Hamburg. In summer, a little flower garden blooms in the front. The town house, painted a soothing white, was built around 1930. The interior evokes an English gentlemen's club, complete with prints of horses, chintz upholstery, and leather-bound books. Rooms, ranging from small to medium, are furnished in a one-of-a-kind manner, containing many antiques. All units are equipped with tidily kept bathrooms containing shower-tub combinations. Breakfast is the only meal served, but there's a bistro next door and other restaurants in the vicinity.

Sierichstrasse 150, 22299 Hamburg-Winterhude. ✆ **040/48-57-72.** Fax 040/48-57-73. 14 units. 164€–210€ ($146.45–$187.55) double. MC, V. U-Bahn: Hudt Wackerstrasse. Ferry: Alster. **Amenities:** Bar; lounge; room service; babysitting. *In room:* TV, minibar, hair dryer.

## IN NIENSTEDTEN

**Louis C. Jacob** ★★★ Lying outside the city center along the Elbe, this tranquil deluxe hotel compares to the Vier Jahreszeiten and Kempinski Hotel Atlantic Hamburg (see above). In summer, you can sit out under linden trees 2 centuries old and enjoy views of the river traffic. Built in 1791 as a guesthouse, it has been brought up to modernity after a major overhaul. The owners believe in spectacular luxury and coddling their guests. The hotel owns one of the biggest private art collections in the north of Germany. The medium to spacious rooms are elegantly appointed and decorated, with walk-in closets and state-of-the-art bathrooms, each with plush towels, toiletries, and a shower-tub combination.

Elbchaussee 401, 22609 Hamburg. ✆ **040/82-25-50.** Fax 040/82255444. www.hotel-jacob.de. 85 units. 225€–370€ ($200.95–$330.40) double; from 350€ ($312.55) suite. AE, DC, MC, V. Parking 18€ ($16.05). Lies 13km (8 miles) west via Elbchaussee. **Amenities:** Restaurant; lounge; room service; babysitting; laundry/dry cleaning. *In room:* TV, minibar, hair dryer, safe.

## IN BAHRENFELD

**Gastwerk Hotel Hamburg** ★★ *Finds* In one of the most stunning rescues of a decaying industrial building in Hamburg, an old public gasworks has been recycled and given new life as a modern boutique hotel. Developers preserved as much of the industrial structure—they call it "culture"—as was possible when they converted it into a comfortable hotel with a mixture of contemporary and traditional design. Bedrooms range from luxurious suites—one designed by Terence Conran—to classic loft spaces with exposed brick walls and mahogany furnishings. All the rooms, both public and private, are imbued with a light, intimate feeling. Bedrooms are midsize to spacious, and are inviting and beautifully maintained, each with a balcony and an immaculate tiled bathroom with tub and shower. The former gasworks were redesigned with all the amenities you'd expect from a good hotel, everything from an on-site health club to bedrooms designed for those with disabilities. The food is excellent at the on-site Porters Restaurant.

Forum Altes Gastwerk, Daimlerstrasse 67, 22761 Hamburg. ✆ **040/89-06-20.** Fax 040/890-62-20. www.gastwerk-hotel.de. 100 units. 110€–140€ ($98.25–$125) double; 145€–195€ ($129.50–$174.15) suite. AE, MC, V. U-Bahn: Bahrenseld. **Amenities:** Restaurant; coffee shop; health club; sauna; babysitting laundry/dry cleaning. *In room:* A/C, TV, minibar.

## 3 Where to Dine

Hamburg life is tied to the sea, and that includes the cuisine: lobster from Helgoland; shrimp from Büsum; turbot, plaice, and sole from the North Sea; and huge quantities of fresh oysters. Of course, there's also the traditional meat dish, *Stubenküchen* (hamburger steak), and the favorite sailor's dish, *Labskaus,* made with beer, onions, cured meat, potatoes, herring, and pickles. The *Aalsuppe* (eel soup) is the best known of all Hamburg's typical dishes. To locate the restaurants in this section, see the "Hamburg Accommodations & Dining" map on p. 590–591.

### IN BINNENALSTER & NEUSTADT

#### EXPENSIVE

**Fischküche** ★ SEAFOOD Breezy and unpretentious, this restaurant prides itself on specializing exclusively in fish. It's in a modern building, with a dining room brightly outfitted in bold colors and extravagant chandeliers. Menu items include a changing array of seafood, brought in fresh daily and priced with an eye for good value. Choices vary with the day's catch but might include several different preparations of clear or creamy fish soup, marinated crabmeat salad, flounder with spaghetti and lemon-butter sauce, codfish with potatoes and onion, and filet of monkfish in a mustard-herb sauce. It's hardly haute cuisine, but locals flock here for the robust specialties and no-nonsense service.

Kajen 12 (a 1-min. walk from the Elbe). ✆ **040/36-56-31.** Reservations recommended. Main courses 14.50€–31.50€ ($12.95–$28.15). AE, DC, MC, V. Mon–Fri noon–3pm and 6–11pm; Sat 6pm–midnight. U-Bahn: Rödingsmarkt.

**Il Ristorante** ★ ITALIAN/INTERNATIONAL The most fashionable Italian restaurant in Hamburg is located in the heart of town in a very modern building. The atmosphere is luxurious and formal, and only the freshest ingredients find their way into the kitchen. Even such simple dishes as carrot-and-celery soup have great flavor. After some well-chosen Italian wine, consider the perfectly prepared crayfish in a saffron sauce or the marinated salmon with green asparagus mousse. Mellow balsamic vinegar and aromatic fresh herbs lend zest and flavor to many dishes. Impeccably trained waiters provide smooth service.

Grosse Bleichen 16. ✆ **040/34-33-35.** Reservations required. Main courses 16.50€–25€ ($14.75–$22.35); fixed-price menu 32€ ($28.60) for 3 courses, 45€ ($40.20) for 5 courses. AE, DC, MC. Daily noon–midnight. U-Bahn: Jungfernstieg.

#### MODERATE

**Eisenstein** INTERNATIONAL The food available here is representative of the wide range of cultures that Hamburgers have been exposed to, thanks to the city's role as a great port. The menu lists specialties from Thailand, Japan (including sushi and sashimi), southern France, and Italy, as well as traditional and very fresh versions of the North German cuisine that Hamburg excels in—particularly fresh Atlantic Sea fish prepared virtually any way you want. The setting is a solid-looking, much-restored factory and former warehouse whose soaring, russet-colored brick walls envelop diners in a cozy womb against the sometimes gray weather outside. The clientele is artsy, hip, and stylish; the staff is cooperative; and the food is surprisingly flavorful, considering its diversity.

Friedensallee 9. ✆ **040/3904-606.** Reservations recommended. Main courses 16.50€–19.80€ ($14.75–$17.70); fixed-price lunch 12€ ($10.70); fixed-price dinner 30€ ($26.80). No credit cards. Daily noon–3pm and 6pm–midnight. U-Bahn: Altona Bahnhof.

**Ratsweinkeller Hamburg** ★ HAMBURG/INTERNATIONAL The city takes pride in the distinguished Ratsweinkeller Hamburg, in business since 1896. The overall theme is suggested at the entrance, where you'll find a stone statue of Bacchus. The main dining hall has high vaulted ceilings, wood-paneled columns, and large stained-glass windows. The 15€ ($13.40) menu is one of the best values in town, and even more wallet-friendly are the large portions, which make appetizers unnecessary. One excellent dish is the halibut steak in curry sauce. The fresh sole *bonne femme* is heavenly and served in large portions; the Hamburg crab soup is the best in the city. At the quarter hour, the chime of the great-grandfather clock resounds throughout the chambers.

Grosse Johannisstrasse 2. ✆ **040/36-41-53.** Reservations required. Main courses 12€–35€ ($10.70–$31.25); fixed-price menu 30€–50€ ($26.80–$44.65). AE, DC, MC, V. Mon–Sat 11am–10:30pm; Sun 11am–4pm. Closed holidays. U-Bahn: Rathausmarkt.

### INEXPENSIVE

**Alten Rathaus** NORTHERN GERMAN This restaurant occupies a carefully preserved mid–19th century building set close to the mouth of the Elbe, in the most historic part of the Altstadt. The upper floors are a preferred meeting place for civic associations, and a faithful clientele has been coming here for years. Surprisingly for Hamburg, no fish is served. Instead, the chefs prepare some of the town's best grilled meats, along with Argentine beef dishes and some savory chicken and turkey offerings. Finish with the Tyrolean apple pie or vanilla ice cream in a hot strawberry sauce.

Börsenbrücke 10 (in the Altstadt). ✆ **040/3751-89-07.** Reservations recommended. Main courses 14.50€–19€ ($12.95–$16.95). AE, MC, V. Mon–Sat noon–3pm and 6–10pm. U-Bahn: Rathausmarkt.

## IN ALTONA

### EXPENSIVE

**Fischereihafen Restaurant** ★★ SEAFOOD Fischereihafen, established some 4 decades ago, is the best seafood restaurant in town, if you prefer true local fare to the internationally oriented cuisine of other restaurants. Every day, the staff buys only the freshest fish and shellfish at the Hamburg auction hall. The menu changes daily, depending on what seafood is available. The second floor is said to be full of "fish and VIPs"—the latter have included the likes of Helmut Kohl and Tina Turner. Appetizers include filet of sole and lobster or a plate of fresh oysters, and the house special is turbot with salmon mousse dotted with truffles. Picture windows open onto a view of the Elbe.

Grosse Elbstrasse 143 (a 10-min. taxi ride from the wharf area of Landungsbrücken). ✆ **040/38-18-16.** Reservations required. Main courses 15€–35€ ($13.40–$31.25); fixed-price 4-course menu 26€ ($23.20); "Hamburg menu" 34€ ($30.35). AE, DC, MC, V. Sun–Thurs 11:30am–10:30pm; Fri–Sat 11:30am–10pm. S-Bahn: Königstrasse.

**Landhaus Scherrer** ★★★ CONTINENTAL Once a brewery, the Landhaus is now a citadel of gastronomy on the Elbe at Altona. It has gained a reputation for impeccable service and imaginatively prepared cuisine. The chef's superbly precise, inventive cookery combines the flavors of the home region of northern

Germany with those of lands farther afield. The result is an often stunning culinary achievement. Specialties are fresh seafood as well as excellent meat. An unusual variation might be roast goose with rhubarb in cassis sauce. Dessert might be praline cream or one of 30 types of pastry loading down the sweets trolley. Because of its location in a country house surrounded by trees, this place is also popular for wedding receptions.

Elbchaussee 130. ✆ **040/8-80-13-25.** Reservations required. Main courses 22€–35€ ($19.65–$31.25); fixed-price menu 96€ ($85.75) or 108€ ($96.45), depending on which one, with how many courses/what type of ingredients, you choose. AE, DC, MC, V. Mon–Sat noon–2:30pm and 6:30–10:30pm. Bus 135.

**Le Canard** ★★★ CONTINENTAL Le Canard is one of the best restaurants in Germany. Virtually every restaurant critic in the country has lauded the unusual *cuisine moderne* of its imaginative owner/chef, Josef Viehhauser. The unpretentious decor is made more alluring by soft lighting. The lobster soup is the city's finest, and the iced soup of potatoes—a kind of vichyssoise—comes graced with caviar. The crisp fried duck with a Bordeaux sauce is the best we've had in Hamburg, but we were especially drawn to an unusual concoction as an appetizer—a terrine of Roquefort with gazpacho jelly and olive bread. Pigeon with chanterelles is a delectable choice, or you can have your chanterelles with a perfectly sautéed turbot. The place isn't so trendy that they're afraid to serve an old-fashioned *Salzburger Nockerl* for dessert.

Elbchaussee 139, Ottensen (southwest of Hamburg's center). ✆ **040/8-80-50-57.** Reservations required. Main courses 27€–31€ ($24.10–$27.70); fixed-price menu 78€–108€ ($69.65–$96.45). AE, DC, MC, V. Mon–Sat noon–2:30pm and 7–10:30pm. Bus 115.

### MODERATE

**Landhaus Dill** ★★ CONTINENTAL This restaurant is imbued with a country charm, its windows opening onto views of the River Elbe. Although it's close to the street, the terrace is ideal to sit out and enjoy a warm Hamburg night. The young chefs are completely at ease with their recipes, which, for diversity, skip across the border from Austria to Germany, with heavy inspiration found west in France. Our last visit proved that the high-quality seasonal meat and fish specialties were just as exquisite as when we first discovered this place a long time back. Nothing is finer than the lobster salad which the maître d' prepares at your table. After that celestial beginning, you can go on to sample the halibut schnitzel or the savory scampi. The rack of lamb appears elegantly on your plate just fresh from the oven where it was roasted tender and is served with aromatic fresh herbs. Desserts are luscious in the Austrian tradition.

Elbachaussee 94. ✆ **040/390-5077.** Reservations required. Main courses 18€–28€ ($16.05–$25). AE, DC, MC, V. Tues–Sun noon–10:30pm. U-Bahn: Altona.

## IN ST. PAULI

### MODERATE

**Cuneo** ITALIAN Good Italian food at reasonable prices is what you'll find here. Behind an unprepossessing facade, unchanged since 1905, the restaurant opens onto crowded rooms that look like an art director's concept of a Greenwich Village restaurant in the 1930s. Grilled fish is one of the best items on the menu, but you can also order pizza, carpaccio, spaghetti with pesto, gnocchi with Gorgonzola, and Venetian-style liver.

Davidstrasse 11. ✆ **040/31-25-80.** Reservations required. Main courses 10€–19€ ($8.95–$16.95). MC, V. Mon–Sat 6:30pm–1:30am. Closed 2 weeks in July. U-Bahn: St. Pauli.

**Old Commercial Room** *Finds* NORTHERN GERMAN This restaurant, founded in 1643, is so tied into Hamburg maritime life that many residents consider it the premier sailors' stopover. It's the best place in town for *Labskaus* (sailor's hash), prepared with devotion by the chef; if you order it, you're given a numbered certificate proclaiming you a genuine Labskaus-eater. You can also order many traditional north German dishes. The restaurant's name, along with that of the street, speaks of the historic mercantile links between Hamburg and England.

Englische Planke 10 (at the foot of St. Michaelis). ✆ **040/36-63-19.** Reservations required. Main courses 12€–35€ ($10.70–$31.25); fixed-price menu 30€–45€ ($26.80–$40.20). AE, DC, MC, V. Daily noon–midnight. Closed Dec 24. U-Bahn: St. Pauli.

**Phuket** ★ THAI A town as cosmopolitan as Hamburg is bound to have more than one Thai restaurant, and in this case, Phuket, in the heart of St. Pauli, is *not* to be confused with a less-interesting restaurant with the same name on Adolph-Schönfelder-Strasse, in another part of Hamburg. This one, the one we prefer, occupies a single street-level dining room. The food here is attractively presented and beautifully seasoned, especially if you like very hot and spicy dishes. You face a nightly array of duck, rabbit, beef, and shrimp dishes. The coconut chicken soup is always our favorite opener. The chicken in red wine sauce is a perennial favorite—and justifiably so—as are the fiery hot fresh fish dishes that take you back to Southeast Asia in their authentic taste.

Taubenstrasse 23. ✆ **040/315-854.** Reservations required. Main courses 11€–15€ ($9.80–$13.40). AE, DC, MC, V. Daily 5pm–midnight. Metro: St. Pauli.

**Restaurant Nil** INTERNATIONAL Even though the name of this restaurant refers to Egypt's River Nile, don't imagine a decor influenced either by the desert or the Arab world. What you get is upscale French bistro, replete with mirrors, oiled mahogany, and polished brass. The name refers to the bounty provided by the Nile, as interpreted by North German tastes, and the cooking is superb. Clients derive from the worlds of publishing and the arts, with lots of cultural movers and shakers, many of whom have adopted this place as their preferred culinary hangout. Dishes include a carpaccio of beef with a black olive marinade and shiitake mushrooms; saltimbocca of ham and calves' liver prepared with artichoke hearts; braised leg of turkey stuffed with sautéed leeks and served with noodles in an orange-flavored whisky sauce; and beef bourguignonne with braised shallots, mushrooms, and mashed potatoes.

Neuer Pferdemarkt 5. ✆ **040/4397-823.** Reservations recommended. Main courses 10€–18€ ($8.95–$16.05); fixed-price menu 30€–42€ ($26.80–$37.50). AE, DC, MC, V. Mon–Fri noon–2:30pm; Sun–Thurs 6–11pm; Fri–Sat 6pm–midnight. U-Bahn: Feldstrasse.

**Weite Welt** ★ SEAFOOD In German, the name of this restaurant translates as "wide world," and the fish dishes served here are said to cross the continents of Europe and Asia. The location is unsavory in the St. Pauli district near the live sex shows presented nightly on the Reeperbahn's Grosse Freiheit. Yet this is a fine and decent place suitable to take your grandmother provided you cover her eyes as she makes her way through the district. Here in the rear of a former fish canning factory, this first-class bistro and bar serves some of the finest fish dishes we've sampled in Hamburg. Fresh fish arrives at least three times a week, and the chefs are experts at preparing it so that the maximum flavor is retained. Often theme dining is the order of the day (would you like to sample the same menu served the doomed passengers on their last supper before the *Titanic* hit an iceberg?). The wine list is amazingly long, some 40 pages, documenting a cellar of some 50,000 bottles. The place gets really crowded on weekends.

Grosse Freiheit 70. ✆ **040/319-1214.** Reservations required. Main courses 9€–28€ ($8.05–$25). V. Sun–Thurs 6pm–1am; Fri–Sat 6pm–3am. U-Bahn: St. Pauli.

## 4 Seeing the Sights

Before you tour the city, you can get a good overall view of Hamburg from the tower of the finest baroque church in northern Germany, **Hauptkirche St. Michaelis** ★, Krayenkamp 4C, Michaeliskirchplatz (✆ **040/3767-8100;** U-Bahn: Rüdingsmarkt or St. Pauli). Take the elevator or climb the 449 steps to enjoy the sweeping view from the top of the hammered-copper tower. The crypt is one of the largest in Europe and contains the tombs of such famous citizens as composer Carl Philipp Emanuel Bach and the church's builder, Ernst Georg Sonnin. Hours are daily April to September, 9am to 6pm; October to March, 10am to 5pm. Entrance to the church is free, but to use the stairs or elevator costs 2.50€ ($2.25). A combined ticket for the tower and crypt costs 3€ ($2.70).

The **Altstadt** actually has little left of the old architecture, but there are a few sights among the canals (fleets) that run through this section from the Alster to the Elbe. The largest of the old buildings is the **Rathaus,** Rathausplatz (✆ **040/42-83-10;** U-Bahn: Rathausmarkt), which is modern compared with many of Germany's town halls. This Renaissance-style structure was built in the late 19th century on a foundation of 3,780 pinewood piles. It has a sumptuous 647-room interior and can be visited on guided tours costing 1.50€ ($1.35). Tours in English are given Monday to Thursday, hourly 10:15am to 3:15pm; Friday to Sunday 10:15am to 1:15pm; no tours during official functions. The Rathaus's 49m (160-ft.) clock tower overlooks Rathausmarkt and the **Alster Fleet,** the city's largest canal. A visit to the Rathaus can be combined with a stop at the 16th-century **Hamburg Stock Exchange,** Adolphsplatz 1 (✆ **040/3-61-30-20**), which is back-to-back with the Rathaus. Free guided tours are offered Tuesday and Thursday at 11am and noon.

A few blocks away is **St. Petri Kirche,** Mönckebergstrasse (✆ **040/32-57-400;** U-Bahn: Rathausmarkt), built in the 12th century and renovated in 1842. The lion-head knocker on the main door is the oldest piece of art in Hamburg, dating from 1342. The church is open Monday to Friday 10am to 6pm, Saturday 9am to 5pm, and Sunday 9am to noon and 1 to 5pm.

The nearby 14th-century Gothic **Jacobikirche,** Jakobikirchhof 22, entrance on Steinstrasse (✆ **040/32-77-44;** U-Bahn: Mönckebergstrasse), was damaged in World War II but has been restored. It contains several medieval altars, pictures, and sculptures, as well as one of the largest baroque organs in the world (Arp-Schnitger, 1693). The church is open Monday to Saturday 10am to 5pm, Sunday 10am to noon. Guided tours in English can be arranged.

### THE TOP ATTRACTIONS

**Carl Hagenbeck's Tierpark** ★★ *Kids* Hamburg's zoo, one of Europe's best, was founded in 1848 and today is home to about 2,100 animals. The unfenced paddocks and beautifully landscaped park are world famous. There are sea lion and dolphin shows, rides on elephants and camels, a train ride through "fairyland," and a spacious children's playground. A restaurant serves well-prepared fixed-price menus at 9€ to 14€ ($8.05–$12.50) 11:30am to closing time.

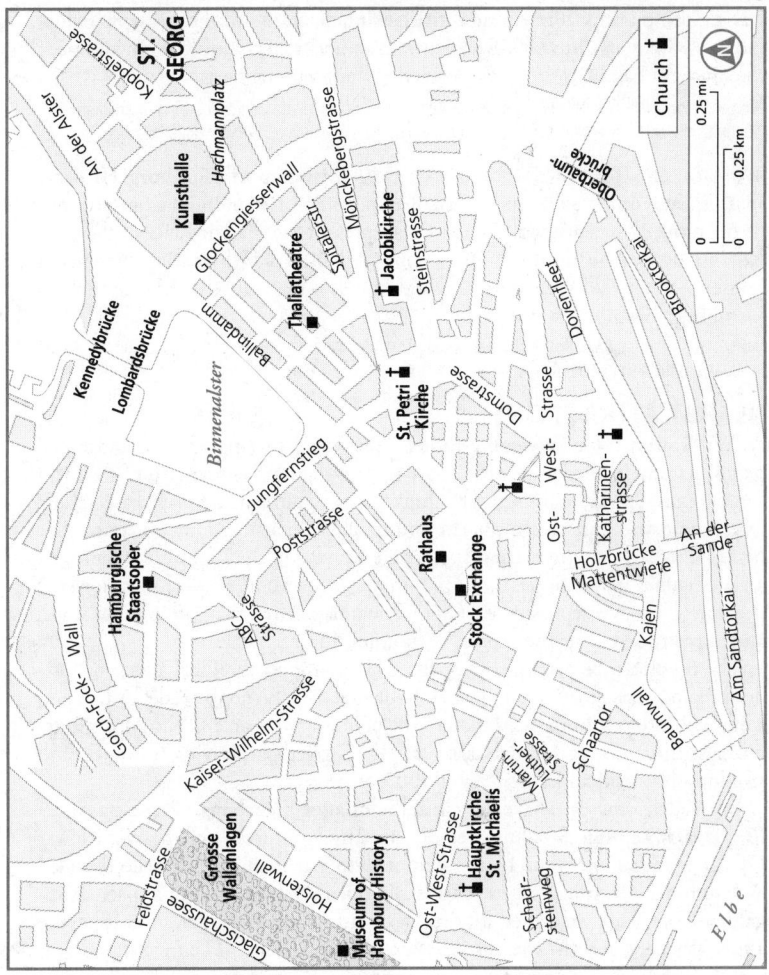


Hagenbeckallee at Steilingen (in the northwest suburbs). ✆ **040/5-40-00-10.** Admission 11.50€ ($10.25) adults, 8.50€ ($7.60) children. Free for children under 6. Spring–fall daily 9am–6pm; winter daily 9am–5pm. U-Bahn: Hagenbeck's Tierpark.

**Kunsthalle** ★★ This is the leading art museum in northern Germany. Be sure to see the outstanding **altarpiece** painted for the St. Petri Church in 1379 by Master Bertram, Hamburg's first painter known by name and a leading 14th-century German master. The 24 scenes on the wing panels depict the biblical story of humankind from creation to the flight into Egypt. Particularly interesting is the panel showing the creation of the animals, in which a primitive Christ-like figure is surrounded by creatures. As a sardonic note, one little fox is chewing the neck of the lamb next to it. The museum also contains works by Master Francke, a Dominican monk. The altar of St. Thomas Becket (1424) is the first known work to depict Becket's murder in Canterbury cathedral.

The museum collection also includes the distinctive visions of Philipp Otto Runge and Carl David Friedrich, German impressionists Max Liebermann and

Lovis Corinth, and 20th-century artists Munch, Andy Warhol, Joseph Beuys, Picasso, Kirchner, Otto Dix, Beckmann, Kandinsky, and Paul Klee. In addition, the museum has an entire wing devoted to contemporary art.

Glockengiesser Wall. ✆ **040/42-85-42-612.** Admission 7.50€ ($6.70) adults, 5€ ($4.45) children, 11€ ($9.80) family pass. Tues–Wed and Fri–Sun 10am–6pm; Thurs 10am–9pm. U-Bahn: Hauptbahnhof.

**Museum für Hamburgische Geschichte (Museum of Hamburg History)** In this museum, you'll find a detailed portrait of Hamburg from the 8th through the 20th centuries. Scale models represent the changing face of the port. Reconstructions of various rooms—from the hall of a 17th-century merchant's house to an air-raid shelter from World War II—illustrate the different eras in Hamburg's history.

Holsten Wall 24. ✆ **040/42841-2380.** Admission 4€ ($3.55) adults, 1.50€ ($1.35) children, 8.50€ ($7.60) family ticket. Tues–Sun 10am–6pm; Mon 1–5pm. U-Bahn: St. Pauli. Bus: 112.

## NEARBY ATTRACTIONS

At **Willkomm-Höft (Welcome Point),** every ship that passes this landscaped peninsula is welcomed in its own language, as well as in German, from sunrise to sunset (8am–8pm in summer). The ships' national anthems are played as a salute. The station was founded in the late spring of 1952, at the point where a sailor first catches sight of the soaring cranes and slipways of the Port of Hamburg. As a vessel comes in, you'll see the Hamburg flag on a 40m (130-ft.) mast lowered in salute. The ship replies by dipping its own flag. More than 50 arriving ships, and as many departing ones, pass Willkomm-Höft each day.

The point can be reached by car from Hamburg via the Elbchaussee or Ostdorfer Landstrasse to Wedel in half an hour. You can also go to Wedel by S-Bahn; a bus will take you from the station to the point, or you can enjoy the 15-minute walk. In the summer, you can take a HADAG riverboat, leaving from St. Pauli Landungsbrücken, an hour's ferry ride.

In Wedel, you can have lunch at **Schulauer Fährhaus,** Parnastrasse 29 (✆ **04103/92-000;** S-Bahn: Wedel), attractively situated on the wide lower Elbe. The restaurant is run by the sons of Otto Friedrich Behnke, who founded Willkomm-Höft. It has large enclosed and open verandas, as well a spacious tea garden. Guests are welcomed for breakfast, lunch, tea, or dinner. Fish dishes are a specialty here, and the wine list is modest but interesting. The restaurant's own bakery turns out a tempting array of goodies. Children, especially, will delight in watching the ships go by as they eat. Main courses run 11€ to 20€ ($9.80–$17.85). It's open daily from 9am to 10pm. MasterCard, Visa, and American Express are accepted.

In the cellars of the Schulauer Fährhaus is the **Buddelschiff-Museum** (✆ **04103/92000**), where more than 200 little vessels are carefully preserved in bottles. The museum is open March to October, daily 10am to 6pm; off-season, Wednesday, Saturday, and Sunday 10am to 6pm. Admission is 1.50€ ($1.35) for adults and free for children.

## GARDENS & PARKS

The major zoo is the **Carl Hagenbeck's Tierpark** (see above), but Hamburg also has many other "green lungs."

**Alsterpark** lies on the northwest banks of Alster Lake, spread across 72 well-manicured hectares (175 acres). Beautiful shade trees and cultivated gardens greet you at every turn. From many places, you'll also have a panoramic view of the Hamburg skyline. Enter on Harvestehuderweg.

The **Hirschpark** (S-Bahn: Blankensee) is the deer park of Hamburg. Its main entrance is at Mühlenberg. The park is landscaped and has a game enclosure. You can visit the Hirschparkhaus for an old-fashioned tea with pastries.

**Stadtpark** (U-Bahn: Borgweg, in Winterhude), spread across some 182ha (450 acres) north of the center, has some 32km (20 miles) of footpaths and numerous recreational facilities. These include a planetarium, sunbathing areas (Hamburgers often prefer their sun sans attire), and open-air pools. Music concerts are often staged here in summer. For your own safety, avoid this place when darkness falls.

Finally, **Wallringpark** (U-Bahn: Stefansplatz), is actually a quartet of beautifully maintained parks and gardens, including the flower garden Planten und Blomen, the Alter Botanischer Garten, and the Kleine and Grosse (big and little) Wallanlagen parks, with many recreational facilities. A miniature railway connects all four. The entire complex is also a popular leisure park, with a roller-skating rink, playgrounds, greenhouses filled with tropical plants, restaurants, and an ice-skating rink in winter. A particular highlight is the illuminated-fountain concert, with classical or pop music, at the onset of darkness—10pm June to August, earlier as the summer wanes. The largest Japanese garden in Europe is in **Planten und Blomen.** Here, rock gardens, flowering plants, miniature trees, and winding pathways attract garden enthusiasts.

## ESPECIALLY FOR KIDS

Although Hamburg is known for its X-rated entertainment, the city is actually also a good place for a family vacation.

**Carl Hagenbeck's Tierpark** (✆ **040/54000147**) is one of Europe's great zoos (see above), and many other parks in Hamburg have amusements for children—the **Wallringpark** has a roller-skating rink. Boat tours of the Alster and more lengthy tours of the Port of Hamburg will also delight kids. Also see the "Nearby Attractions" section above for more ideas.

Language is often not a problem for children, so they may enjoy the children's theater, **Theater für Kinder,** Max-Brauer-Allee 76 (✆ **040/38-25-38;** U-Bahn: Altona). All tickets cost 20€ to 33€ ($17.85–$29.45); call for show times.

## BOAT TOURS

You can tour Hamburg by water, on both the Inner and the Outer Alster, experiencing all the charm of the Alsterpark, the villas, and the sailing boats set against the panorama of towers and church spires. **ATG-Alster-Touristik,** Am Anleger Jungfernstieg (✆ **040/3-57-42-40;** www.alstertouristik.de), has daily departures about every 30 minutes 10am to 6pm, with trips lasting 50 minutes. November to March, tours depart daily at 10:30am, noon, and 1:30pm. The ships leave from the Jungfernstieg quayside (U-Bahn: Jungfernstieg). Cassettes with a description of the tour in English, plus a brochure in four languages (including English), are available from the captain. Trips cost 8€ ($7.15) for adults and 4€ ($3.55) for children under 16.

**HADAG Seetouristik und Fahrdienst AG,** Bei den St. Pauli, Fischmarkt 28 (✆ **040/3-11-70-70**), also conducts tours through the watery channels of Hamburg, in a comfortable heated pleasure boat. Tours are conducted in both German and English. They depart at hourly intervals every day April to October, 9am to 6pm, November to March, 10:30am to 3:30pm. Boats leave from the Landungsbrücken, Pier 3. The fare is 8.15€ ($7.30) for adults and 4.50€ ($4) for children under 14.

## 5 Sports & Outdoor Pursuits

### BOATING

A paddle on the Aussenalster (Outer Alster Lake) can be one of the most relaxing and charming warm-weather activities in Hamburg. **H. Pieper** (✆ **040/24-75-78**) and **Alfred Seebeck** (✆ **040/24-76-52**) rent rowboats, paddleboats, one-occupant sailing dinghies, and small catamarans; prices begin at 11€ to 18€ ($9.80–$16.05) per hour. Each of these boat-rental outfits is open only April to late September, daily 10am to 8pm.

### GOLF

Hamburg has many golf clubs, including **Golf Club auf der Wendlohe,** Oldesloerstrasse 251 (✆ **040/5-50-50-14**), and **Hamburger Golf-Club Falkenstein,** In de Bargen 59 (✆ **040/81-21-77**). Greens fees range from 40€ to 45€ ($35.70–$40.20) for 18 holes.

### JOGGING

Our favorite route, either for long promenades or jogging, is the pedestrian walkway that circumnavigates the Alster lakes. The total perimeter of the larger of the two lakes measures about 6km (4 miles); that of the more congested Binnenalster, about 1.5km (1 mile). Equally suitable for jogging and pedestrian rambles are the public parks flanking the northwestern edge of the inner city.

### SPECTATOR SPORTS

For information about soccer matches and other spectator events, contact the **Hamburger Sportbund (Hamburg Sports Association),** Schäferkampsallee 1, 20357 Hamburg (✆ **040/41-90-80**).

### SWIMMING

The rivers and lakes in Hamburg are being cleaned up, and there are many swimming pools. Two of the most popular are the **Alster-Schwimmhalle,** Ifflandstrasse 21 (✆ **040/22-30-12;** U-Bahn: Lohmühlenstrasse), and the **Holthusenbad,** Goernestrasse 21 (✆ **040/47-47-54;** U-Bahn: Eppendorfer Baum). The latter has the advantage of artificial waves, thermal baths, and steam baths. Alster-Schwimmhalle charges 7.80€ ($6.95) for all day; Holthusenbad, 9€ ($8.05) for all day.

### TENNIS

Not surprisingly, the country that gave the world Steffi Graf and Boris Becker has no lack of tennis facilities. For names and addresses of tennis facilities, as well as information about upcoming tournaments, contact the **Deutscher Tennis Bund,** Hallerstrasse 89 (✆ **040/4-11-78-0**).

Hamburg is also the Home of the **Hamburg Tennis Masters Series,** one of the nine Masters Series events that rank just below the Grand Slams. Previously known as the "German Open," it is also a major warm-up for the famous French Open, the only Grand Slam event to be played on clay. The Hamburg tournament is also played on clay (usually in May).

## 6 Shopping

Hamburg is a city of merchants. In general, stores are open Monday to Friday 9am to 6:30pm (some until 8pm on Thurs) and on Saturday 9am to 2pm (until 4 or 6pm on *langer Samstag,* the 1st Sat of the month). Unfortunately, the interesting shops are not concentrated in one location. Two of the oldest and most prestigious shopping streets, **Grosse Bleichen** and **Neuer Wall,** run parallel to the canals, connected transversely by Jungfernstieg and Ufer Strasse on the Binnenalster. Less expensive shopping streets are Spitalstrasse and Mönckebergstrasse.

Hamburg has nine major shopping malls. The glass-roofed **Hanse Viertel Galerie Passage** is some 200m (220 yd.) long. There's a scattering of upscale cafes here and even a stand-up seafood bar where glasses of beer or Sekt (sparkling wine) are served at tiny tables.

**Mönckebergstrasse** (U-Bahn: Hauptbahnhof), a street connecting the main station with the Rathaus, is the city's traditional shopping district. Here you'll find big department stores such as **Karstadt,** Mönckebergstrasse 16 (✆ **040/30940**), part of a chain that carries many of the same brands and items as the other leading department stores, all competitively priced. The store is open Monday to Friday 9am to 8pm and Saturday 9am to 4pm. A thrifty alternative, **Kaufhof,** Mönckebergstrasse 3 (✆ **040/33-30-70**), carries less-expensive items than the surrounding department stores and also offers better deals on merchandise markdowns. Bargain hunters combing the store are apt to find good values. Hours are Monday to Friday 9:30am to 8pm and Saturday 9:30am to 4pm. More fashionable and upscale than any of the three mentioned above is **Alsterhaus,** Jungfernstieg 22 (✆ **040/359011**), which some New Yorkers have compared favorably to Bloomingdale's (same hours as Karstadt).

If you walk down Bergstrasse to the second part of the city center, you pass along **Jungfernstieg,** with tourist boats of the Alster Fleet on the right and a teeming shopping street on the other side. About a block farther along you come to the **Hamburger Hof,** the elegant entrance to one of the most attractive chains of shopping galleries in Europe. At the end of Jungfernstieg, you can cross Gänsemarkt to **Gänsemarkt Passage,** another shopping gallery, with stores on three levels.

An upmarket and youthfully fashionable shopping area is in **Eppendorf** (U-Bahn: Eppendorfer Baum), Hamburg's oldest village, first mentioned in written history in 1140. Many prosperous and avant-garde Hamburgers live in the stately area's 19th-century homes and apartments. The shopping district, from Klosterstern to Eppendorfer Markt, has exclusive boutiques selling fashions from Paris, Milan, and New York; colorful shops with odds and ends for your home; antiques shops; and places where you can not only make purchases but watch goldsmiths, hatmakers, potters, and weavers at work.

The Hamburg **Fischmarkt (fish market),** between Hexenberg and Grosse Elbstrasse (U-Bahn: Landungsbrücken), is held every Sunday from 5am in summer or 7am otherwise. Flowers, fruit, vegetables, plants, and pets are also for sale at this traditional market, in existence since 1703. It sometimes seems that the fish are just an afterthought nowadays. The nearby taverns are open to serve Fischmarkt visitors and vendors. **Seifarth and Company,** Robert-Koch Strasse 19 (✆ **040/5-24-00-27;** U-Bahn: Lattenkamp), is an upscale shop dealing in seafood, among other items. It smokes its own salmon, runs one of the leading mail-order caviar businesses in Europe, has one of the Continent's largest selections of tea, imports paté and champagne from France, and stocks lobsters and Alaskan king crab. Everything can be shipped or ordered by mail.

One of the densest concentrations of antiques in Hamburg lies within the **Antik-Center,** Klosterwall 9–21 (✆ **040/32-62-85;** U-Bahn: Steinstrasse or Hauptbahnhof), a covered passageway loaded with more than 35 dealers and the accumulated loot of estate sales throughout England, Germany, and to a lesser degree, France. It's been compared to Portobello Road in London by aficionados of the trade who value the sheer volumes of objects that glint, sparkle, and evoke the values and aesthetics of other places and other times.

**Jil Sander,** Neuer Wall 43 (✆ **040/55-30-21-73;** U-Bahn: Damtor), is the best place to go for chic women's styling. Jil Sander burst upon Europe's fashion scene from her native city of Hamburg and has taken special efforts to make this three-floor store the flagship of her increasingly successful operation. Part of the success of her designs derives from their wearability—they are appropriate for the office, the boardroom, or cocktail hour. Another popular choice for women's fashions is **Escada Boutique,** Neuer Wall 32 (✆ **040/36-32-96;** U-Bahn: Hauptbahnhof), owned by the German design company of the same name. This store carries the firm's complete collection of women's sports, evening, business, and knit wear, plus accessories that include hats, bags, gloves, and shoes. A less-expensive division of Escada, **Laural Boutique,** Neuer Wall 41 (✆ **040/3-74-32-70;** U-Bahn: Hauptbahnhof), appeals to an active, younger clientele with alternative takes on casual day and elegant evening wear. If you think that hats have gone out of style, think again. **Monika Flac,** Bleichenhof Passage 35, off Grosse Bleichen (✆ **040/34-54-37;** U-Bahn: Hauptbahnhof), sells all kinds of hats, from serious garden party varieties festooned with cabbage roses to perky numbers that might have been favored by the late Jacqueline Onassis, as well as Homburgs and Stetson-style hats for men.

For high-fashion men's clothing, go to **Thomas-i-Punkt,** Gänsemarkt 24 (✆ **040/7-80-98-80;** U-Bahn: Hauptbahnhof), where you'll find suits, jackets, shirts, shoes, and belts carrying the exclusive Omen label. Ties, handkerchiefs, and other accessories are also available. Shoes, well-made and fashionably styled, are sold to both men and women at **Prange Schuhhaus,** Jungfernstieg 38 (✆ **040/34-31-51;** U-Bahn: Jungfernstieg).

One of the city's leading hairdressers, for both men and women, is **Marlies Müller** at Neuer Wall 61 (✆ **040/4-44-00-40;** U-Bahn: Damtor). Besides hair styling and beauty treatments, a large perfume and cosmetic selection is also offered here.

**Brahmfeld & Gutruf,** Jungfernstieg 12 (✆ **040/34-61-03;** U-Bahn: Jungfernstieg), is one of Germany's oldest jewelers, founded in 1743.

One of Hamburg's biggest selections of books, mostly in German but with lots of English-language texts as well, can be found at **Thalia Buchhandlung,** Spitalerstrasse 8 (✆ **040/3-02-07-01;** U-Bahn: Hauptbahnhof). A smaller branch of the same outfit, mostly with German-language titles, is at Hermannstrasse 18–20 (✆ **040-3-02-07-01;** U-Bahn: Jungfernstieg).

A store with a nautical nature, **Binikowski,** Lokstedter Weg 68 (✆ **040/46-28-52;** U-Bahn: Eppendorfer Baum), established in 1955, is the place to find a *Buddelschiffe* (ship in a bottle), as well as ship models and clocks. **Captain's Cabin,** St. Pauli Landungsbrücken (✆ **040/31-63-73;** S-Bahn: Landungsbrücken), stocks ship models, telescopes, barometers, figureheads, lamps, nautical clothing for the whole family, prints, posters, and more.

If you've ever fancied yourself as someone who looks best in silk, you might pay a visit to Hamburg's **Haus des Osten,** Jungfernstieg 7 (✆ **040/34-36-80;** U-Bahn: Jungfernstieg), which sells only silk clothing imported from Asia (usually China). There's an appealing collection of shirts and neckties for men, in all degrees of flamboyance and discretion. And for women, check out the kimonos, skirts, jumpers, undergarments, and scarves that fill the medium-size premises of this well-stocked store.

## 7 Hamburg After Dark

To find out what's happening in Hamburg, pick up a copy of *Hamburger Vorschau* for 1.30€ ($1.15). Published once a month, it's available at various tourist offices, most hotels, and most newsstands.

### THE PERFORMING ARTS

**Hamburgische Staatsoper (Hamburg State Opera)** This modern opera house was built after the bombings of World War II. Its acoustics and technical facilities are among the most advanced in the world. The venue is the home of the **Hamburg State Opera** and also the **Hamburg Ballet,** directed by Californian John Neumeier. For tickets, head for the ticket office at Grosstheaterstrasse 34. Grosstheaterstrasse 34. ✆ **040/35-68-80-0.** Tickets 5€–75€ ($4.45–$67). U-Bahn: Stefansplatz or Damtor.

**Musikhalle** This survivor of Germany's romantic age lies a few steps away from the Staatsoper, with which it shares some facilities and staff members. The building was painstakingly restored after World War II. It hosts concerts by the **Hamburg Symphony,** the **Hamburg Philharmonic,** the **NDR Symphony,** and the renowned **Monteverdi-Chor,** known for its interpretations of baroque and Renaissance music. Touring orchestras also perform here. In most cases, tickets don't exceed 38€ ($33.95). For tickets, call either the number listed below, or the number listed for the Staatsoper (see above). Johannes-Brahms-Platz. ✆ **040/34-69-20.** U-Bahn: Stefansplatz or Damtor.

**THEATER** Hamburg is blessed with more than 40 theaters, but for most of these, a good knowledge of German is necessary. An exception, the **English Theatre of Hamburg,** Lerchenfeld 14 (✆ **040/2-27-70-89;** www.englishtheatre.de; U-Bahn: Mundsburg), is the only English-speaking theater in the northern part of Germany. Tickets are 11€ to 26€ ($9.80–$23.20). Performances are Monday to Saturday at 7:30pm; a matinee is presented on Tuesday and Friday at 11am.

If you understand German, try the **Deutsches Schauspielhaus** ★, Kirchenallee 39 (✆ **040/24-87-10;** U-Bahn: Hauptbahnhof). It's one of the outstanding theaters in the German-speaking world, performing both the classics and modern plays.

Other theaters are the cutting-edge **Thaliatheater,** Alstertor (✆ **040/32-81-44-44;** U-Bahn: Jungfernstieg), and the **Kammerspiele,** Hartungstrasse 9–11 (✆ **040/41-33-4444;** U-Bahn: Hallerstrasse). Both stage a wide range of plays as well as musical shows. A new production usually opens every month. Tickets at these theaters range from 10€ to 42€ ($8.95–$37.50). Small ensemble performances such as *Evening with Marlene Dietrich* are the specialty of the

---

**Tips Ticket-Buying Tips**

Tickets to sporting events, including soccer matches, are best acquired through the **Hamburger Sportbund (Handburg Sports Association),** Schäferkampsallee 1, 20357 Hamburg (✆ **040/419080**). **Theater-Kasse Reckewell,** Einkaufcentrum shopping mall on Osterfer Landstrasse (✆ **040/80-10-13**), can arrange virtually everything else. A third option, for cultural (not necessarily sporting) events, is to contact Hamburg's Tourist Information Office (**Tourismus Centrale**), in the "Wendelhalle" of the city's main railway station (✆ **040/30-13-00**).

---

**Schmidt Theater,** Spielbudenplatz 24 (✆ **040/31-77-880;** S-Bahn: Reeperbahn). Its companion, **Schmidts Tivoli,** Spielbudenplatz 27–28 (same phone), hosts musicals and other popular performances. Tickets are 15€ to 55€ ($13.40–$49.10). All of these are closed on Monday.

Two of Hamburg's busiest theaters are the **Neue Flora Theater,** Stresemannstrasse 159A (✆ **01805/4444;** U-Bahn: Altona), and the **Operettenhaus,** Spielbudenplatz 1 (same phone; S-Bahn: Reeperbahn), which have enjoyed an unprecedented success with *Phantom of the Opera* (at the Neue Flora), and *Cats* (at the Operettenhaus). Performances have run within these theaters for 9 and 13 years, respectively, with only vague hints that they might be nearing the ends of their runs. The cost of seeing either of these shows is 60€ to 115€ ($53.60–$102.70), depending on your seat and the night you attend.

**Hansa Theater,** Steindamm 17 (✆ **040/24-14-14;** U-Bahn: Hauptbahnhof), is a north German variety show that claims to be intelligible to all foreigners. The humor is so broad that that may be true. Each show includes international attractions such as acrobats, clowns, dancers, magicians, and aerialists. There are special tables for smoking and drinking. Two shows are performed daily Monday to Saturday at 4 and 8pm and Sunday at 3 and 7pm. Prices are 21€ to 41€ ($18.75–$36.60).

## THE CLUB & MUSIC SCENE

### JAZZ

**Cotton Club** The legendary Cotton Club is the oldest (some 36 years) and best established of the Hamburg jazz clubs. Jazz and Dixieland bands come here from throughout Europe and the United States. Open Friday and Saturday 8pm to 1am and Monday to Thursday 8pm to midnight; September to April, also open Sunday 11pm to 3am. Alter Steinweg 10. ✆ **040/34-38-78.** Cover 4€–15€ ($3.55–$13.40). S-Bahn: Stadthausbrücke.

### ROCK

**Club Grosse Freiheit (Grosse Freiheit 36)** This club, now world-famous, is where the Beatles performed in their earliest days. Today, it's a free-for-all venue whose acts change almost nightly, and whose guests in the recent past have included Prince and Willie Nelson. Even the civic and municipal authorities of Hamburg view it as one of their preeminent cultural treasures. For recorded information about upcoming acts, call ✆ **040/3177-7811.** Grosse Freiheit 36. ✆ **040/3177780.** Cover 4€–20€ ($3.55–$17.85). S-Bahn: Reeperbahn.

**Fabrik** This cultural center is similar in style to the Markthalle (see below). Originally it was an old ammunition depot (ca. 1830), until it burned down; later, it was reconstructed in the same style. Open 8pm to midnight (later on Sat and Sun), Fabrik is a nightclub beloved by those who survived the 1970s more or less intact. It offers a mixed program likely to feature African bands, jazz, and blues. Barnerstrasse 36 (5 min. from Bahnhof Altona). ✆ **040/39-10-70.** Cover 8€–25€ ($7.15–$22.35). U-Bahn: Altona.

**Finnegan's Wake** This place is as Irish as it sounds. English speakers flock here for Guinness and Harp on tap as well as shepherd's pie, chili, and sandwiches (food is available until 9pm). Every Thursday to Saturday, there's live music of some sort. The pub is open Sunday to Thursday 11am to 1am and Friday and Saturday 11am to 4am. Börsenbrücke 4. ✆ **040/3-74-34-33.** Cover 4€ ($3.55) Fri–Sat; free admission Mon–Thurs. U-Bahn: Hauptbahnhof.

### *Fun Fact* Johnny & the Moondogs Invade Hamburg

No one had ever heard of the "Fab Four" or the Beatles in late 1959 and early 1960 when a mangy-looking group called "Johnny & the Moondogs" invaded Hamburg. At that time, the city was called the Las Vegas of Europe, and in its post-war atmosphere, sex, drugs, and alcohol ruled the night.

John Lennon, Paul McCartney, and Stu Sutcliffe (a friend of John's from his art college) formed the group. Stu couldn't play a note but was in anyway once he'd purchased a bass guitar with the money he'd won in an art show. The Moondogs had been booked for a grueling 8-hour-a-night gig in the dingy cellar of the still functioning Grosse Freiheit 36 (see above).

The basement lounge was reserved for untried, unproven acts. The big stage upstairs was for the rock stars with track records. Today, entertainers ranging from Ziggy Marley to Matchbox Twenty perform upstairs on the big stage right over the same cellar where the not-yet Beatles struggled to find an audience.

Although not yet world famous, and virtually unknown in America, the Liverpudlians still attracted the press in Hamburg. Their harshest critics compared them to a "musical tortilla"—that is, cold, flat, and foreign. Many young Hamburgers were more turned on by their "girlish hairdos" than by "their new fangled music."

Still managed by Alan Williams, the Moondogs dressed in leather. When they became The Beatles in 1960, their new manager, Brian Epstein, insisted that they dress in suits and ties, startling apparel for a rock 'n' roll band of the 1960s.

Their gig ended when the police discovered that George was underaged. He was deported to England. A year later, in 1961, they were to return to the club in Hamburg, where they made their first record, and then only as a back-up recording for their friend, Tony Sheridan.

The rather lackluster recording of "My Bonnie" was originally intended only for German release. At the end of their second Hamburg gig, Stu Sutcliffe, making the worst financial decision of his life, decided to stay behind in Hamburg to paint and to be with a German girlfriend he'd fallen in love with. He would soon die of a brain hemorrhage, and Ringo Starr loomed on the Beatle horizon, to take his place.

The city of Hamburg will always be remembered as a launching pad for the Beatles in those halcyon days before the group learned their "troubles are here to stay."

**Kaiserkeller** Kaiserkeller functions both as a stage for live music by not-terribly-famous bands and as a disco. Long-time aficionados of the Reeperbahn scene remember it, along with the now-defunct Star Club, whose empty premises stand across the street, as an early venue for performances by the Fab Four. The place has a different musical theme on different nights of the week (Sun is oldies night). Open nightly 10pm to 4 or 5am. Grosse Freiheit 36 (in the cellar of the Grosse Freiheit concert hall). ✆ **040/317-7780.** Cover 8€–27€ ($7.15–$24.10). S-Bahn: Reeperbahn.

## *Moments* The Reeperbahn: A Walk on the Wild Side

Commercialized sex flourishes in many towns, but hardworking, entrepreneurial Hamburg has succeeded better than almost anywhere else at transforming it into a tourist attraction. The place where it all hangs out is the St. Pauli district (U-Bahn: St. Pauli; S-Bahn: Reeperbahn), just east of the center. St. Pauli's midsection—the "genital-zone," as it's sometimes called—is the Reeperbahn, a half-mile thoroughfare whose name literally translates as "rope street," referring to the massive amounts of hempen rope produced here during the 18th and 19th centuries for ships in Germany's biggest harbor.

In the 19th century, most forms of entertainment, including theaters, were banned from the city's more respectable medieval core. As one resident of the district remarked, "Bourgeois Protestants don't know how to have fun." Consequently, this neighborhood near the great port developed entertainment options of its own, and sailors from around the world were safely channeled into a neighborhood where their recreational activities were out of sight (and out of mind) of the city's sober business establishment. Hamburg's first theater opened on the Reeperbahn in 1842. By the 1860s, the question, "Whatch'a doing, sailor?" became the unofficial motto of an army of prostitutes who set up shop (with the legal sanction of municipal authorities) in the district.

The city's official line is that the Reeperbahn is Hamburg's second greatest attraction and asset (the first is the port itself). The authorities see their policies as a rare instance of civic and moral enlightenment unparalleled in any other city, except for Amsterdam's more sanitized sex scene. They make frequent references to their requirement that every officially sanctioned working girl submit to a medical examination every 2 weeks—and pay income tax on her profits. Hamburg's most talked-about police station, Davidwache, at the corner of the Davidstrasse and the Reeperbahn, provides highly visible and omnipresent police protection.

What are the rules of the game and what should you do to survive such an "in-your-face" neighborhood? Throw your sense of scheduling to the wind and take a nap on the day of your visit. Mornings in St. Pauli are burned-out, unenthusiastic times, when virtually everyone is recovering from the bacchanals of the night before. Midafternoons perk up a bit. But regardless of the fogs that roll in from the Baltic and the damp chill that's an inseparable part of the Hamburg experience, by 8pm the district's bars and theaters (legitimate and otherwise) are roaring away. Between midnight and 5am, you'll find thousands of women and female wanna-bes (men in drag) strutting their stuff along the turf. German enterprise has honored these women (and their reputation for a good time) by naming one of Hamburg's native beers in their honor—the famous "St. Pauli Girl."

There's a distinct pecking order among the working girls, based on the neighborhood, or street, where they're headquartered. The most exclusive and expensive area is **Herberstrasse,** where plate-glass windows allow the women to display their charms to window shoppers.

By city ordinance, this street is only open to men over the age of 18. Less-expensive rents can be found on the streets near Herbertstrasse: Gunterstrasse, Erichstrasse, Friedrichstrasse, Davidstrasse, and Gerhardstrasse. Lots of the women here are from the Eastern Bloc, and lately there's been a distressing trend for runaway teenagers to join their ranks. Cross-dressers, transsexuals, and "shemales" ply their trade here, too.

If it's erotic theater you're looking for, you'll have to move a few blocks away to **Grosse Freiheit,** a street whose name appropriately translates as "Great Freedom." Any act of sexual expression, with every conceivable permutation except those that involve animals (bestiality is one of the few things expressly forbidden) is shown in these theaters. Be it joyful, be it disgusting, it's all here, often performed by artists whose barely concealed boredom sometimes permeates the setting in ways that anywhere else would be embarrassing, but here seems merely surreal.

You aren't likely to be solicited at a performance—municipal regulations forbid prostitution, or overt solicitation, inside erotic theaters. But there's nothing to prevent a member of the audience from suddenly deciding to be a performer—it's been known to happen, if rarely. And there's nothing that prevents performers setting up an off-premises rendezvous. In any event, *caveat emptor.*

Off-the-record theaters include **Safari,** Grosse Freiheit 24 (✆ **040/31-32-33;** S-Bahn: Reeperbahn), where you're likely to find the press agent for the city of Hamburg entertaining foreign travel writers. Expect to pay a fixed price of around 23€ ($20.55) for one beer.

If you're subject to sudden fits of guilt in places like this, municipal and religious authorities made provisions long ago. There always seems to be a church nearby, such as the early 18th-century **Kirche St. Joseph,** at 5 Grosse Freiheit. There's also a branch office of the Salvation Army, whose members are ready, willing, and able to fortify your resolve with a cup of coffee and some religious boosterism.

The district also contains the **Erotic Art Museum,** Nobistor 10A (✆ **040/31-74-757;** www.erotic-art-museum.hamburg.de). This institution is privately owned and funded, and closed to anyone under 16. It manages to present its displays in a way that's both academic and titillating, and it has a street-level gift shop featuring sexual toys and enhancements. Open daily 10am to midnight; entrance is 8€ ($7.15) adults, 5€ ($4.45) students.

Hamburg gay life is centered west of the city's medieval core, within the St.-Georg district (see below). **Absolut,** Hans-Albers-Platz (✆ **040/317-3400**), is a St. Pauli bar that caters to a mixed/gay/lesbian crowd. **Orange,** Grosse Freiheit 34 (✆ **040/31-42-36**), is mainly for lesbians. In the general free-for-all permissiveness that reigns in this neighborhood, however, sexual pigeonholing of visitors into specific gender preferences seems unnecessary.

**Logo** Because of its position near Hamburg's university, this club attracts lots of college students, although many Big Chill survivors in their 40s and 50s gravitate here as well. It's a small, informal place that often features rock bands. Sometimes well-known singers appear in concert. Open daily 8pm (live music begins at 9pm) to 2 or 3am. Audiences often sit on the floor. Grindelallee 5. ✆ **040/4-10-56-58.** Cover 5€–15€ ($4.45–$13.40). U-Bahn: Damtor.

**Markthalle** This is one of the most visible live music venues in Hamburg, with a special emphasis on up-and-coming British groups and sometimes heavy metal and high-volume electronics. The building functioned early in the 20th century as a covered marketplace. Inside is an amphitheater with a stage and a large area for standing or sitting on notoriously uncomfortable benches. Performances usually begin at 8pm, with the ticket office opening about an hour before. Klosterwall 49. ✆ **040/33-94-91.** Cover 10€–20€ ($8.95–$17.85). U-Bahn: Hauptbahnhof.

## EROTIC SHOWS

See "The Reeperbahn: A Walk on the Wild Side" box, above.

## DRAG SHOWS

**Pulverfass** The best-known drag show in town, Pulverfass is usually featured on the "Hamburg by Night" tours, which are escorted bus tours that take travelers on a tour of a few night clubs. This place is not for the timid. You might find the shows downright vulgar, especially if you know German. Female impersonators from all over Europe appear here. There are shows nightly (for which you need reservations) at 8:30 and 11:30pm, and also at 2:30am Friday and Saturday. Within the same building, with a view of the stage, there's a restaurant, **Teatro-Café,** which is open daily 6am to 3am, and where French- and German-inspired fixed-price menus cost 25€ ($22.35) each. Pulverteich 12. ✆ **040/24-97-91.** Cover 14€–17€ ($12.50–$15.20); first drink 13€ ($11.60), second at normal bar rate. U-Bahn: Steindamm.

## DANCE CLUBS

**After Shave** After Shave features funk, soul, jazz, and fusion. It's a place for dancing and for meeting people, and it attracts the 20-to-30 age group. The dance music is wide-ranging, featuring the latest imports but no hard rock or heavy metal. On Tuesday, jazz is featured exclusively. Open 11pm to 4am Thursday, to 5am Friday, and to 6am Saturday. Spielbudenplatz 7. ✆ **040/3-19-32-15.** Cover 5€–8€ ($4.45–$7.15). S-Bahn: Reeperbahn.

**Mojo Club** Although located on the Reeperbahn, this nightclub and disco is devoted not to sex but to soul music and acid jazz. It attracts a crowd of mainly straight couples in their 30s. One local TV station called it "the best night club in Germany," but we think that's a bit of an exaggeration. Reeperbahn 1. ✆ **040/3-19-19-99.** Cover 8€ ($7.15). S-Bahn: Reeperbahn.

**Molotow** This is the place to dance to funk—George Clinton and Bootsy Collins have been elevated to god status here. Say you've seen Parliament-Funkadelic, and you may make lifelong friends. It opens Wednesday at 9pm, Thursday to Saturday at 11pm, and Sunday at 9pm; closing time depends on the energy of the dancers. Spielbudenplatz 5. ✆ **040/31-08-45.** Cover 2.50€–10€ ($2.25–$8.95). S-Bahn: Reeperbahn.

**Top of the Town** This eagle's nest attracts a relatively youthful crowd, many of whom show up without jackets or neckties to dance, drink, and talk. A DJ spins out danceable tunes. This club isn't nearly as wild and crazy as those within less-restrictive parts of town, such as the Reeperbahn. Nonetheless, it can be fun, and there's a gorgeous panorama of North Germany's most dynamic city spread out in front of you. Open every night except Sunday, 9:30pm to around 4am. On the 26th floor of the Radisson SAS Hotel Hamburg, Marseiller Strasse 2. ✆ **040/35020.** Cover 5€ ($4.45) Fri–Sat only; no cover for guests of the hotel. Bus: 102.

## GAY CLUBS

Hamburg, like Berlin, is one of the major gay havens of Europe, with a particularly dense concentration of gay boutiques and cafes along the Lange Reihe in St. Pauli. A little journal, ***Dorn Rosa,*** distributed at most gay and lesbian bars, lists (in German) the clubs, restaurants, bars, and events that cater to a gay, lesbian, and bisexual clientele.

**Café Gnosa** More than any other eatery in Hamburg, this comes the closest to fulfilling the need for an official "gay restaurant." Set near the railway station, on a street noted for its gay clientele, it's open Tuesday to Sunday 11am to 1am and Monday 6pm to 1am. Platters of food range from 3.40€ to 10.50€ ($3.05–$9.40) and feature all-day breakfasts, steaks, fish, salads, and all kinds of coffee and drinks. Café Gnosa's bar is one of the most frequented gay bars in the area of the Hauptbahnhof and is quite cruisy. Lange Reihe 93. ✆ **040/24-30-34.** U-Bahn: Hauptbahnhof.

**Frauenkneipe** This bar is a major rendezvous point in Hamburg for women only—men are told to do their drinking elsewhere. The clientele is mainly lesbian, though there are a lot of straight women here, too. On the first Sunday of every month, there's ballroom dancing, with a 2.50€ ($2.25) cover, and Friday is disco night, with a cover of 4€ ($3.55). On other nights, this a good place to visit for a drink. Open Wednesday to Monday 8pm to 1am. Stresemannstrasse 60. No phone. Cover 2.50€–6€ ($2.25–$5.35). U-Bahn: Altona.

**Pit Club-Saloon/Tom's Bar** This is the best-established and most popular gay men's bar in Hamburg, known to virtually every gay male in town. Begin your night in the street-level disco, work your way up to a watering hole one floor above, and end your evening in the cellar, where leather is optional but encouraged. Women, if they come here at all (which is rare), usually remain in the street-level disco. At least one part of this place is open every night 10:30pm until dawn; every Wednesday to Sunday, additional sections open for greater space. Pulverteich 17. ✆ **040/280-30-56.** Cover 2.50€ ($2.25) for cellar leather bar; 5€ ($4.45) for street-level disco and first-floor "jeans bar." U-Bahn: Hauptbahnhof.

## THE BAR SCENE

**Bar Hamburg** This is one of the chicest bars in north Germany, attracting the likes of Bryan Adams or Mick Jagger if they're in town. It lies between the elegant Kempinski Hotel Atlantic and the red-light district near the train station. In bars, it is said to have sparked "a power lounge revolution." Decorated with "chocolate ice cream colored" leather sofas and plastic wood, it attracts Hamburg's most beautiful models (of either sex), artists, media types, and interior designers. From 7pm nightly until "indecently late," patrons sip drinks and dig into tasty snacks. Some of the best DJs in Hamburg keep you entertained. Rautenbergstrasse 6–8. ✆ **040/280-54-880.** No cover. U-Bahn: Hauptbahnhof.

**Bayrisch Zell** This beer hall, clearly an imitation of Munich's famed Hofbräuhaus, is one of the most popular places in the St. Pauli district. It may be on the Reeperbahn, but you could take your great-aunt here, especially if she likes to dance the polka. The place attracts couples young and old and has plenty of seats (1,200) for all. It also has good food, with meals ranging from 5€ to 12€ ($4.45–$10.70). If someone catches your fancy from across the room, call him or her from your table—that's what those phones are for. Open 7pm to 3am daily. Reeperbahn 110. ✆ **040/31-42-81.** No cover Mon–Thurs; 5€ ($4.45) Fri–Sat, including 1st drink. S-Bahn: Reeperbahn.

**Café Schone Aussichten** On most nights, the 300-seat beer garden is booked for private parties, but on Thursday nights, it is one of the hottest after-hour rendezvous in Hamburg. It's open from 8pm to 2am and serves beerhall type food. Gorch-Fock-Wall 4. ✆ **040/34-01-13.** No cover. U-Bahn: Gansemarkt.

**Gröninger Braukeller** Gröninger has been making and selling beer here since 1750; today the site consists of two brewpubs flanking a traditional German restaurant. One of the pubs opens at 11am, the other at 5pm, and both close at 1am. If you get hungry, the brewery restaurant serves meals 11:30am to 11:30pm. Ost-West-Strasse 47. ✆ **040/33-13-81.** No cover. U-Bahn: Messberg.

**La Paloma** This bar in the heart of the Reeperbahn has nothing to do with the sex trade going on around it. Instead, it's an artists' hangout where the wall space is used for art exhibitions. It's open Tuesday to Thursday 7pm to 1am, and Friday and Saturday 7pm to 4am. Gerhardstrasse 2, at the corner of Friedrichstrasse. ✆ **040/31-45-12.** No cover. S-Bahn: Reeperbahn.

**Schwenders** This is one of Hamburg's most venerated wine houses. The place today often attracts some 400 or more patrons to its Belle Epoque setting, filled with nooks and crannies, even though there's room for only 200 to sit down. Musical entertainment might be anything from a Viennese operetta to cabaret, sometimes performed by local (often amateur, or temporarily out-of-work) musicians. Deli cold cuts and excellent cheese will do if you want something to eat with your drinks. Live classical music is played October to March. The bar is open daily 4pm to 3am. Grossneumarkt 1. ✆ **040/34-54-23.** No cover. U-Bahn: Rödingsmarkt.

**Shamrock** The oldest Irish pub in Hamburg, the Shamrock has been in business for nearly 2 decades. It's a popular hangout for students and a transient English-speaking crowd that comes to soak up the Guinness, Kilkenney, Harp, and hard cider on tap. Open Sunday to Thursday 1pm to 2am and Friday and Saturday 5pm to 4am. Feldstrasse 40. ✆ **040/4-39-76-78.** No cover. U-Bahn: Altona.

## A CASINO

**Spielbank Hamburg** This casino offers roulette, blackjack, and baccarat, played according to international rules. You can also enjoy a drink at the bar, taking in the panoramic view over the roofs and lakes of Hamburg. The minimum stake for roulette is 2€ ($1.80), for blackjack 5€ ($4.45). Men should wear jackets and ties. Everyone needs a passport to get in. The casino is open daily 3pm to 3am. In the Hotel Inter-Continental, Fontenay 10. ✆ **040/44-70-44.** Cover 2.50€ ($2.25). U-Bahn: Stephansplatz.

# 18

# Schleswig-Holstein

In this region of Germany, you can walk along the dunes and hear the roaring sea break fiercely on the rocks, or you can lie on a tranquil beach while tiny waves lap at your feet. Sound inconsistent? Not in Schleswig-Holstein. Germany's northernmost province borders both the turbulent, chilly North Sea and the smooth, gentle Baltic. And between these two bodies of water are rolling groves and meadows, lakes and ponds, and little fishing villages with thatched cottages. Fashionable seaside resorts dot both shorelines and nearby islands. Even in the coldest weather you can swim in heated seawater at the resorts of Westerland and Helgoland. In Kiel, you can wander around the harbor and explore Schleswig, with its Viking memories.

If you're flying, Hamburg is a good gateway to the region. After that, go to Lübeck, which is easily reached from Hamburg by train or by car, via the A1 Autobahn. Roads are only overcrowded in July and August. Where the trains end, local buses wait to take you the rest of the way, linking small towns and villages.

## 1 Lübeck ★★★

92km (57 miles) SE of Kiel, 66km (41 miles) NE of Hamburg

It is said that nothing testifies to the wealth of an old European city as much as the size and number of its church spires. If this is so, Lübeck is rich indeed, for no fewer than seven towering steeples punctuate the skyline of this city. Lübeck was made a free imperial city in 1226. From the 13th century on, it was the capital of the Hanseatic League, the association of merchants that controlled trade along the Baltic as far as Russia.

Today Lübeck is a city of high-gabled houses, massive gates, and strong towers. The Hanseatic merchants decorated their churches with art treasures and gilded their spires to show off their wealth. Many of these survivors of nearly 900 years of history stand side by side with postwar housing developments, and the neon lights of the business district shine on the streets and narrow passageways of bygone days.

Lübeck has had several famous sons, notably Thomas Mann and Willy Brandt. As a young man, Brandt, who later became West German chancellor and won the Nobel Peace Prize in 1971, opposed the Nazis so vehemently that he had to flee on a boat to Norway. Thomas Mann's novel *Buddenbrooks,* set in his hometown, catapulted the 27-year-old author to international fame in 1902. In 1929, he won the Nobel Prize for literature.

Lübeck's other claim to fame is that it's the world capital of marzipan. According to legend, Lübeckers, riding out a long siege, ran out of flour and started grinding almonds to make bread. So delighted were they with the results that they've been doing it ever since. To sample marzipan on its home turf, go to the Niederegger shop across from the Rathaus.

## ESSENTIALS

**GETTING THERE** **By Train** The **Lübeck Hauptbahnhof** lies on major rail lines linking Denmark and Hamburg, and also on the Hamburg–Lüneburg–Lübeck–Kiel–Flensburg and the Lübeck–Rostock–Stralsund lines, with frequent connections. From Hamburg, 40 trains arrive daily (trip time: 40 min.), and from Berlin, 7 (trip time: 4 hr. 40 min.). For information, call ✆ **01805/99-66-33.**

**By Bus** Long-distance bus service to such cities as Berlin, Kiel, and Flensburg is provided by **Autokraft GmbH** (✆ **0451/888-28-28**).

**By Ferry** Ferryboat service from the region around Lübeck to Denmark lies astride the main railway lines between Hamburg and Copenhagen, and is therefore among the busiest in Europe. Service is offered by **ScandLines** (✆ **04371/86-51-61**), which has boats leaving across the sound every 30 minutes, 24 hours a day, every day of the year. The port on the German side is in Puttgarden; the one on the Danish side is in Roødbyhaven, a 2-hour train ride from Copenhagen. The trip takes about 75 minutes. Railway cars, trucks, and conventional automobiles are all taken on board. Round-trip transport for a car with up to four passengers averages 30€ ($26.80), with slight variations depending on the season.

**TT Saga Line** operates between the German port of Travemünde and the Swedish port of Trelleborg. Call ✆ **04502/80181** for bookings and departure times. And for transport by boat between Lübeck and the faraway Baltic port of Helsinki, **Finn Lines** (✆ **0451/1507443**) provides occasional service, usually favored by vacationers during mid-summer.

**By Car** Access to Lübeck is via the A1 Autobahn north and south.

**VISITOR INFORMATION** For tourist information, contact the **Lübeck-Informations-Zentrum,** Breitestrasse 62 (✆ **0451/1-22-81-06**), Monday to Friday 9:30am to 6pm and Saturday and Sunday 10am to 2pm; or the **Touristbüro Beckergrube,** Beckergrube 95 (✆ **0451/1-22-1909**), Monday to Friday 8am to 4pm.

**GETTING AROUND** The Altstadt and the attractions outlined below can be reached by taking bus 5, 6, 7, 11, 14, or 16. Fare is 2€ ($1.80).

**SPECIAL EVENTS** Lübeck is the center of the **Schleswig-Holstein Music Festival,** with performances between the end of June and August every year. For more information, contact ✆ **0451/389-570.** At the **Christmas market,** held mainly during the 3 weeks before Christmas, vendors from all over northwestern Germany descend on the town to sell their wares—many of them handmade. You can pick up deals on one-of-a-kind items from toys to pottery.

## EXPLORING THE CITY

Lübeck's **Altstadt** ★★★ is surrounded by the Trave River and its connecting canals, giving it an island-like appearance. It suffered heavily during World War II, when about one-fifth of the city was leveled. Today, damaged buildings have been restored or reconstructed, and Lübeck still offers a wealth of historic attractions.

Just across the west bridge from the Altstadt, the **Holstentor (Holsten Gate)** ★★ is the first monument to greet visitors emerging from the Bahnhof. At one time it was the main town entrance, built in the 15th century as much to awe visitors with the power and prestige of Lübeck as to defend it against intruders. To the outside world, the towers look simple and defiant, rather like part of a great palace. But on the city side, they contain a wealth of decoration, with windows, arcades, and rich terra-cotta friezes. Within the gate is the

**Museum Holstentor** (✆ **0451/1-22-41-29**), housing a model of Lübeck as it appeared in the mid-17th century. The museum is open Tuesday to Sunday 10am to 5pm (to 4pm in winter). Admission is 2.50€ ($2.25) for adults, 1.50€ ($1.35) for students, and .50€ (45¢) for children 17 and under.

The **Der Salzspeicher (Salt Lofts)** viewed from the riverside, near the Holstentor, are among Lübeck's most attractive sights. In the 16th century, these buildings were used to store the salt from Lüneburg before it was shipped to Scandinavia. Each of the six buildings is slightly different, reflecting trends in Renaissance gabled architecture.

The **Rathaus** ★, Rathausplatz (✆ **0451/1221005**), traces its origins from 1230. It has been rebuilt several times, but there are remains of the original structure in the vaulting and Romanesque pillars in the cellar and the Gothic south wall. The towering walls have been made with open-air medallions to relieve the pressure on the Gothic-arcaded ground floor and foundations. Tours are conducted Monday to Friday at 11am, noon, and 3pm, costing 2.50€ ($2.25) for adults and 1.50€ ($1.35) for children.

**Marienkirche (St. Mary's Church)** (✆ **0451/30-77-00**), across Marktplatz from the Rathaus, is the most outstanding church in Lübeck, possibly in northern Germany. Built on the highest point in the Altstadt, it has flying buttresses and towering windows that leave the rest of the city's rooftops at its feet. Some of its greatest art treasures were bombed and destroyed in 1942, but after the fire was put out, an earlier painted decoration on the walls and clerestory was discovered. The bells fell in a World War II air raid and embedded themselves in the floor of the church, where they remain to this day. Organ concerts take place during the summer months, carrying on the tradition established by St. Mary's best-known organist and composer, Dietrich Buxtehude (1668–1707).

**Buddenbrookhaus,** Mengstrasse 4 (✆ **0451/122-41-92**), near Marienkirche, is the house where the grandparents of Thomas Mann (1875–1955) lived. It's a big, solid stone structure with a gabled roof and a recessed doorway. Above a leaded-glass fan over the heavy double doors is the date 1758. This is the house Mann described as the home of the family in *Buddenbrooks.* The museum also highlights Thomas's brother, Heinrich Mann (1871–1950), author of *Professor Unrat,* the source of the movie *The Blue Angel.* The house is open daily 10am to 5pm; admission is 4€ ($3.55) for adults, 2€ ($1.80) for students, and is free for children under 14.

It's estimated that within an area of 5 sq. km (2 sq. miles) around the Marktplatz stand 1,000 medieval houses. Nearby is **Petersgrube,** the finest street in Lübeck, lined with restored houses. A walk through the old streets of Lübeck reveals a continuing use of brick (the city insisted on this after fires in the 13th century). The effect is one of unity among all the houses, churches, shops, and guildhalls.

**Haus der Schiffergesellschaft (Seamen's Guild House)** ★, on Breitestrasse, is one of the last of the elaborate guild houses of Hanseatic Lübeck, built in 1535 in Renaissance style, with stepped gables and High Gothic blind windows. It's worth seeing just for the medieval furnishings and the beamed ceilings in the main hall, now a restaurant (see "Where to Dine," below).

**Museen Behnhaus/Drägerhaus,** Königstrasse 9–11 (✆ **0451/122-41-48**), was formed from two patrician houses, both entered on Königstrasse, north of Glockengiesser Strasse. Like many such houses in the town, they are tall and narrow, constructed that way to avoid heavy taxes based on frontage. The museum displays mostly German impressionists and paintings from around 1900. There is an outstanding collection of German Romantic and "Nazarene" paintings and drawings, especially by Johann Friedrich Overbeck and his school. The Behnhaus has a permanent exhibition of contemporary paintings, including Schumacher, Schultze, Rainer, Antes, and Kirkeby, along with such 20th-century artists as Kirchner, Beckmann, Lehmbruck, and Barlach. Both houses are open April to September, Tuesday to Sunday 10am to 5pm; October to March, Tuesday to Sunday 10am to 4pm. Admission is 2.50€ ($2.25) for adults, 1.50€ ($1.35) for children 6 to 18, and free for children under 6.

You can take an excursion boat around **Lübeck Harbor,** departing from Trave Landing, right in front of the Jensen hotel. In season, departures are every half hour, 10am to 6pm.

## SHOPPING

Lübeck is a center for antiques stores. Two of the best are **Antique Center im Engelshof,** Engelsgrube 40 (✆ **0451/7-23-38**), and its competitor, **Antiquitäten Gunter Bannow,** Fleischhauerstrasse 87 (✆ **0451/7-73-38**). Both carry antique silver, crystal, porcelain, books, pewter, and English, Danish, and German furniture; any article can be shipped to your home. If you're in the market for antique books, head for the town's largest repository of antique books and folios, **Von Lingelsheim,** Breitestrasse 42 (✆ **0451/7-47-43**), which has everything from obscure volumes of Romantic poetry to arcane Protestant treatises. And if you're looking for souvenirs that celebrate Lübeck's rich maritime traditions, head for the town's most interesting handcrafts shop, **Kunsthaus Lübeck,** Königstrasse 20 (✆ **0451/7-57-00**), where tin, pewter, woodcarvings, pottery, and antique books will help you remember your visit. **Breitestrasse,** a pedestrian walkway throughout most of the day, is the main shopping street in town. Much of Lübeck's Altstadt is banned to cars, which makes for a pleasant afternoon of wandering.

**J.G. Niederegger,** Breitestrasse 98 (✆ **0451/5-30-10;** bus: 5, 7, 11, 14, or 16), sells that "sweetest of all sweetmeats," famous Lübeck marzipan. It's been across from the main entrance to the Rathaus since 1806. On the ground floor, you can purchase pastries to take away, or you can go upstairs to a pleasant cafe, where you can order dessert and the best brewed coffee in Lübeck. Ask for their pastry specialty, a nut torte resting under a huge slab of fresh marzipan. You'll pay around 29€ ($25.90) per kilo for the marzipan, which is about 14€ ($12.50) per pound. Open 9am to 6pm daily, no credit cards.

## WHERE TO STAY

### EXPENSIVE

**Radisson SAS Senator Hotel Lübeck** ★★ This hotel is the best in town. It's well laid out and well run. Although the bulk of its clients are businesspeople, it has equal appeal to other visitors. The soundproof and medium-size rooms are well kept and attractively furnished. The sleekly maintained bathrooms come with a basket of toiletries and shower-tub combinations.

Willy-Brandt-Allee 6 (on the banks of the river, connected to the Altstadt by pedestrian bridge), 23554 Lübeck. ✆ **800/333-3333** in the U.S., or 0451/14-20. Fax 0451/1-42-22-22. www.radisson.com/luebeck.de. 224 units. 130€–180€ ($116.10–$160.75) double; 210€ ($187.55) for a suite. AE, DC, MC, V. Parking 10€ ($8.95). Bus: 12. **Amenities:** 3 restaurants; bar; pool; health club; sauna; solarium; steam room; room service; massage; babysitting; laundry/dry cleaning. *In room:* A/C, TV, minibar, hair dryer, safe.

**Scandic Hotel** ★ This hotel is first-class. It's close to the ferry docks, and, as a result, attracts many Scandinavians as well as businesspeople. The medium-size rooms are well maintained. Half are nonsmoking. There are also accommodations for people with allergies. All units have bathrooms with shower-tub combinations.

Travemünder Allee 3 (near the Burgtor entrance of the Old Town), 23568 Lübeck. ✆ **0451/3-70-60.** Fax 0451/3-70-66-66. www.scandic-hotels.com. 158 units. 136€–162€ ($121.45–$144.65) double; 263€–276€ ($234.85–$246.45) suite. AE, DC, MC, V. Free outdoor parking; 8€ ($7.15) in garage. Bus: 12. **Amenities:** Restaurant; lounge; pool; health club; sauna; room service; babysitting; laundry/dry cleaning. *In room:* A/C, TV, minibar, hair dryer, safe.

### MODERATE

**Hotel Excelsior** This is a good, functional hotel and not a lot more. It's in a symmetrical baroque building with splendid proportions and an entirely renovated and modernized interior. It's especially convenient if you're traveling to Lübeck by rail. Rooms are small to medium and have a shower or bath.

Hansestrasse 3 (near Lindenplatz, opposite the central bus station and next to the train station), 23558 Lübeck. ✆ **0451/8-80-90.** Fax 0451/88-09-99. www.hotel-excelsior-luebeck.de. 61 units. 78€–108€ ($69.65–$96.45) double; 118€–138€ ($105.35–$123.25) suite. Rates include buffet breakfast. AE, DC, MC, V. Free outdoor parking; 6€ ($5.35) underground. Bus: 11 or 12. **Amenities:** Breakfast room; lounge; room service; laundry. *In room:* TV, dataport, minibar, hair dryer.

**Jensen** *Value* The Jensen is one of Lübeck's best moderately priced hotels, a good value if your expectations aren't too high. The small to medium rooms are modestly furnished in modern style and were recently renovated and had their plumbing upgraded. Some have fine views of the Hanseatic architecture across the canal. The buffet breakfast is served in a delightful room with picture windows overlooking the canal.

An der Obertrave 4–5 (near the Holstentor), 23552 Lübeck. ✆ **0451/70-24-90.** Fax 0451/7-33-86. www.ringhotel-jensen.de. 42 units. 85€–108€ ($75.90–$96.45) double; from 150€ ($133.95) suite. Rates include buffet breakfast. AE, DC, MC, V. Parking 6€ ($5.35). Bus: 1, 3, or 11. **Amenities:** Restaurant; lounge; room service, babysitting. *In room:* TV, minibar, hair dryer.

**Kaiserhof** ★ *Value* The Kaiserhof, frankly, could probably demand a higher price for its rooms, as it ranks up near the top with the Radisson SAS Senator Hotel Lübeck (see above). Two former patrician town houses outside the city center on a tree-lined boulevard have been remodeled into this hotel. The owner has created a fashionable yet home-like environment. Rooms come in various shapes and sizes and are individually furnished. Some overflow guests are housed in a more sterile but still quite comfortable annex. Bathrooms are compact and have shower-tub combinations.

Kronsforder Allee 11–13, 23560 Lübeck. ✆ **0451/70-33-01.** Fax 0451/79-50-83. www.kaiserhof-luebeck.de. 60 units. 121€–149€ ($108.05–$133.05) double; 202€–225€ ($180.40–$200.95) suite. Rates include buffet breakfast. AE, DC, MC, V. Free outdoor parking. Bus: 2, 7, 10, 16, or 32. **Amenities:** Breakfast room; lounge; pool; health club; sauna; steam room; room service; laundry/dry cleaning. *In room:* TV, dataport, minibar, hair dryer, safe.

**Mövenpick Hotel** *Kids* This long-established hotel provides great value for the money, and kids stay free. It stands by a canal, near the major attractions. Rooms are compact and furnished in a somewhat bland motel style. Bathrooms have shower-tub combinations. Rooms for nonsmokers are available.

Willy-Brandt-Allee 1–5 (across from the Holstentor), 23554 Lübeck. ✆ **800/111-2222** in the U.S., or 0451/1-50-40. Fax 0451/1-50-41-11. 197 units. 115€–135€ ($102.70–$120.55) double; 140€–185€ ($125–$165.20) suite. Children under 16 stay free in parents' room. AE, DC, MC, V. Parking 6€ ($5.35). Bus: 1, 3, or 11. **Amenities:** Restaurant; bar; 2 pools; car rental; room service; babysitting; laundry/dry cleaning. *In room:* TV, minibar, hair dryer.

## WHERE TO DINE

**Das Schabbelhaus** ★★ NORTHERN GERMAN/ITALIAN A classic example of Hanseatic architecture on a medieval street, the Schabbelhaus is installed in two patrician buildings from the 16th and 17th centuries. A wooden staircase and balcony lead to two rooms devoted to Thomas Mann memorabilia. In the restaurant, ceiling-high studio windows overlook the small gardens. It's easy to get the impression that the setting competes with the food, but that's not entirely true. Although the cuisine isn't quite as good as the Wullenwever's (see below), it's skillfully prepared with fresh ingredients. Begin with Lübecker crab soup, the finest in town, and follow with one of the fresh fish items from the Baltic. If you wish, the chef will prepare a steak to your specifications.

Mengstrasse 48–52. ✆ **0451/7-20-11.** Reservations recommended. Main courses 12€–20€ ($10.70–$17.85); fixed-price 4-course menu 34€ ($30.35); menu for two including wine 87€ ($77.70). AE, MC, V. Mon–Sat noon–3pm and 6–11pm. Bus: 5, 7, 11, 12, 14, or 16.

**Haus der Schiffergesellschaft** ★ NORTHERN GERMAN Entering this restaurant, with ship models and other nautical memorabilia, is like going inside a museum of Hanseatic architecture. The restaurant was once patronized exclusively by sailors. Today, good food (and lots of it) is served on scrubbed-oak plank tables with high-backed wooden booths carved with the coats of arms of Baltic merchants. Often, you must share a table. One of the most expensive items is an elaborate sole meunière (about ½ kg/1 lb.) with salad. Many regional dishes are featured, such as baked black pudding with slices of apple and lamb's lettuce. Try the roast pork with fruit, pickled fried herring with home-fried potatoes, or Baltic plaice flavored with bacon. You might want to have a drink in the cocktail bar of the historical Gotteskeller (open Mon–Saturday 6pm–2am).

Breitestrasse 2. ✆ **0451/7-67-76.** Reservations required. Main courses 9.20€–26€ ($8.20–$23.20). No credit cards. Daily 10am–midnight. Bus: 1 or 2.

**Historischer Weinkeller** ★★ INTERNATIONAL You'll find this first-class restaurant and 12th-century wine cellar in the basement of Holy Ghost Hospital. This is the number-three dining spot in town, topped only by the Wullenwever, which has better (and more expensive) food, and Das Schabbelhaus, which has a more refined atmosphere. You might begin with North Sea shrimp served with a quail egg and caviar or assorted fish in aspic. Soups can include mussel-cream soup with Pernod or clear soup prepared with Baltic fish. For a main dish, try filet of cod gratinée with sauerkraut or poached haddock in a mustard sauce. North Sea sole is never better than when it's sautéed simply in butter. A few meat dishes are also featured.

In the basement is a potato cellar, where the potato-based menu items include baked potatoes and potato soufflé, served along with simple meat or fish selections. Main courses here cost 7€ to 14€ ($6.25–$12.50).

Heiligen-Geist-Hospital, Koberg 8. ✆ **0451/7-62-34.** Reservations recommended. Main courses 9€–30€ ($8.05–$26.80). AE, MC, V. Daily noon–midnight. Bus: 1 or 3.

**Wullenwever** ★★★ FRENCH/CONTINENTAL Roy Petermann, in his elegant 16th-century house, has established himself as one of the finest chefs in northern Germany. Scion of a distinguished culinary family, Petermann has brought a refined and imaginative cuisine to sleepy Lübeck. Chandeliers and oil paintings enhance the ambience, and in summer, tables overflow onto a flower-filled courtyard. Using only the best and freshest produce, his dishes have subtle depths of flavor and texture. Game is featured in the autumn, and seafood is always available. One recent memorable creation is baked pike-perch filets in a red wine sauce.

Beckergrube 71. ✆ **0451/70-43-33.** Reservations required, as far in advance as possible. Main courses 19€–33€ ($16.95–$29.45); fixed-price menu 59€–69€ ($52.70–$61.60). AE, DC, MC, V. Tues–Sat noon–2:30pm and 7–11pm. Closed 2 weeks in Mar and Oct. Bus: 12.

**Zimmermann's Lübecker Hanse** ★ FRENCH/GERMAN This is one of the most praised restaurants of Lübeck. It has an authentically weathered exterior, with dark paneling inside. French food, regional meals, and lots of fresh seafood are offered. You might want to confine yourself to the *plats du jour;* they are invariably fresh and well prepared. Fresh fish from the Baltic is another good choice. In season, wild game is featured.

Am Kolk 3–7. ✆ **0451/7-80-54.** Reservations recommended. Main courses 12€–24.50€ ($10.70–$21.90); fixed-price lunch 17€–20€ ($15.20–$17.85); fixed-price dinner 22€–34€ ($19.65–$30.35). AE, DC, MC, V. Mon–Fri noon–2pm and 7–11pm. Closed Jan 1–6. Bus: 1, 3, or 11.

## LÜBECK AFTER DARK

Two newsletters, ***Piste*** and ***Szene Journal,*** free at most hotels, have news of local happenings.

Lübeck is known for its organ concerts, and about two a week are presented in various churches in the summer. The tourist office (see above) will provide complete details, or check with **Musik und Kongresshallen Lübeck,** Willy-Brandt-Allee 10 (✆ **0451/79-04-00**), about the many concert and theater opportunities in town. The most important theater venue is **Theater Combinale,** Huxstrasse 115 (✆ **0451/7-88-17;** bus: 11). Its plays range between the experimental and the classic. Performances are on Friday and Saturday August to June. Tickets are 10€ to 18€ ($8.95–$16.05) for adults and 8€ to 12€ ($7.15–$10.70) for students and children.

**Finnegan,** Mengstrasse 42 (✆ **0451/7-11-10;** bus: 12), won a 1997 award from Guinness as the best Irish pub in northern Germany. Naturally, there's Guinness on tap, as well as Kilkenny, other kinds of beers, and five or six whiskies. On Wednesday night, visiting bands play Irish music from 8pm to midnight. The pub is open Monday to Thursday 5pm to 1am and Friday and Saturday 6pm to either 3 or 4am.

**Bräuberger,** Alfstrasse 36 (✆ **0451/7-14-44;** bus: 12), is a restaurant and pub located in the oldest cellar in Lübeck, dating from 1225. Its beer, Zwickel, is brewed on the premises, and it also serves regional dishes and Bavarian specialties. Open Monday to Friday 5pm to 1am and Saturday 6pm to 2am. Large mugs of beer are 2.80€ ($2.50) each. Don't overlook this place for a hearty, traditional platter of German food as an accompaniment for your beer. Platters cost 7.50€ to 10.50€ ($6.70–$9.40) each.

## 2 Kiel ★

88km (55 miles) SE of the Danish border at Flensburg, 97km (60 miles) N of Hamburg, 92km (57 miles) NW of Lübeck

Everything about this city reflects the importance the sea has played in its growth and prosperity. Its perfect natural harbor at the end of a 16km (10-mile) extension of the Baltic Sea made Kiel a center for commerce with other northern European countries. The opening of the Kiel Canal in 1895 connected the Baltic with the North Sea and Western trade.

Although Kiel celebrated its 750th anniversary in 1992, there is little in the way of streets or buildings to make the casual visitor believe that the town was ever anything other than a modern city. Almost all its buildings were destroyed in World War II, after which the town was rebuilt in an admirable modern style. Kielers are proud of their broad streets, spacious squares, and green parks in the heart of town. Stretches of sandy beach in nearby resorts make this port a Baltic vacation spot as well.

### ESSENTIALS

**GETTING THERE** **By Plane** **Lufthansa** has flights from Frankfurt to Kiel Sunday to Friday. There are also daily flights from Munich and Hamburg. Call ✆ **800/645-3880** for flight information. In Kiel, call the airport at ✆ **0431/32-36-56.**

**By Train** The **Kiel Hauptbahnhof** is on two major rail lines, the Neumünster–Hamburg and the Flensburg–Kiel–Lübeck–Lüneburg lines, with frequent connections. From Hamburg, there are 40 trains daily (trip time: 1 hr. 10 min.). For information, call ✆ **01805/99-66-33.**

**By Bus** Long-distance bus service to Berlin and Flensburg, as well as local and regional service, is provided by **Autokraft GmbH,** in Kiel (✆ **0431/66-60**). Buses pull into the Bahnhofplatz. The tourist office (see below) will provide you with schedules.

**By Ferry** Service between Kiel and Oslo, Norway, is provided by **Color Line GmbH,** in Kiel (✆ **0431/73000**). **Stena Line,** in Kiel (✆ **0431/9099**), offers service between Kiel and Gothenburg (Göteborg), Sweden.

**By Car** To reach Kiel from Hamburg, head north along the A7 Autobahn; from Lübeck, take Route 76 west.

**VISITOR INFORMATION** Contact **Tourist Information Kiel,** Andreas-Gayk-Strasse 31 (✆ **0431/67-91-00;** www.kiel-tourist.de). It's open October to April, Monday to Friday 9am to 6pm; May and August to September, Monday to Saturday 9am to 6:30pm; and daily 9am to 6:30pm in June and July.

**GETTING AROUND** Most attractions in Kiel center around the harbor, reached by bus 8 or 18. Fare is 2€ ($1.80).

**SPECIAL EVENTS** **Kieler Woche (Kiel Week),** held each June, celebrates the port's close ties to the sea. This week of special events, held for more than 100 years, includes a spectacular regatta in which more than 1,500 yachts race on the water of the Kieler Förde. In 1936 and 1972, the Olympic yacht races were held on the waters at Schilksee. For information, call the **Kieler Wochenbüro** at ✆ **0431/901-24-02.**

## EXPLORING THE HARBOR & BEYOND

For the best overall look at the city and the harbor, go to the top of the Rathaus's 107m (350-ft.), century-old tower, much of which was restored after the devastating bombs of World War II. May to September, guided tours are offered Wednesday at noon and 6pm, and Sunday at noon, for 2€ ($1.80) per person. For an even closer view over the harbor, take a stroll along the **Hindenburgufer (Hindenburg Embankment)** ★, which stretches for 3km (2 miles) along the west side of the fjord, opposite the shipyards. Perches along this embankment are especially favored by spectators during regattas. Call tourist information for additional details.

If you'd like to go to the beach, take a short steamer trip to one of the nearby Baltic towns, such as Laboe, 16km (10 miles) to the north. Besides the beach, the town's main attraction is the restored World War II submarine **U-Boot 995,** Strandstrasse 92, Kiel-Laboe (✆ **04343/42700;** bus: 100 from the Kiel Hauptbahnhof). May to October, you can tour it every day 9:30am to 6pm (to 4pm Nov–Apr). Admission is 2.10€ ($1.90) adults, 1.50€ ($1.35) students and children.

The open-air **Schleswig-Holsteinisches Freilichtmuseum** ★★, Alte Hamburger Landstrasse (✆ **0431/659660;** bus: 502), lies 6km (4 miles) south of Kiel. Farms and rustic country homes, dating from the 16th to the 19th centuries, have been assembled here, and craftspeople operate shops while working animals perform their tasks. A half-timbered inn serves tasty lunches to visitors. The site is open November to March, Sundays and holidays 11am to 5pm; April to October, Tuesday to Sunday 9am to 6pm (July–Sept, also Mon 9am–6pm). Admission is 4.50€ ($4) for adults, 2.50€ ($2.25) for children 6 and over, and free for children under 6.

## WHERE TO STAY

**Hotel Kieler Yacht Club** ★ *Finds* This yacht club offers unusually fine guest facilities. It's in an old classical building, standing back from the harbor, with an adjoining contemporary motel annex. Rooms are comfortable but unexciting. For style, we prefer those in the main building. All units have neatly arranged bathrooms with shower-tub combinations.

Hindenburgufer 70, 24105 Kiel. ✆ **0431/8-81-30.** Fax 0431/8-81-34-44. www.yachtclub.bestwestern.de. 58 units. 132€–172€ ($117.90–$153.60) double. Rates include buffet breakfast. AE, DC, MC, V. Parking 8€ ($7.15). Bus: 8 or 18. **Amenities:** Restaurant; bar; pool; health club; room service. *In room:* TV, minibar, hair dryer.

**Hotel Wiking** The Wiking, in the center of town, offers well-furnished rooms for reasonable prices. The dark facade is ornamented with balconies painted a vividly contrasting white. Rooms are a bit small but are well maintained, each equipped with a comfortable bed, plus a compact bathroom with shower stalls.

Schützenwall 1–3, 24114 Kiel. ✆ **0431/66-10-90.** Fax 0431/66-109-66. www.hotel-wiking.de. 42 units. 85€–100€ ($75.90–$89.30) double. Rates include continental breakfast. AE, DC, MC, V. Parking 6€ ($5.35). Bus: 8 or 18. **Amenities:** Restaurant; lounge; sauna; solarium. *In room:* TV, safe.

**Maritim-Bellevue** ★ The Maritim-Bellevue is a well-appointed convention hotel opening onto the shore promenade of the Baltic. Its most serious rival, to which it plays second fiddle, is the Steigenberger Conti-Hansa (see below). The most expensive doubles are the luxurious corner rooms, but all—even the medium-size ones—are well furnished and beautifully maintained. All units contain bathrooms with shower-tub combinations.

Bismarckallee 2, 24105 Kiel. ✆ **0431/3-89-40.** Fax 0431/33-84-90. www.maritim.de. 89 units. 135€–186€ ($120.55–$166.10) double; 350€ ($312.55) suite. Rates include buffet breakfast. AE, DC, MC, V. Parking 9€ ($8.05). Bus: 8 or 18. **Amenities:** 2 restaurants; bar; room service; babysitting; laundry/dry cleaning. *In room:* TV, minibar.

**Steigenberger Conti-Hansa** ★★ Conti-Hansa, located between the edge of the harbor and a well-groomed city park, is Kiel's premier hotel. It's well maintained, modern, and solidly comfortable. The medium-size rooms are outfitted in streamlined contemporary furniture; most look out over the harbor or the park. All have bathrooms with shower-tub combinations.

Schlossgarten 7, 24103 Kiel. ✆ **800/223-5652** in the U.S. and Canada, or 0431/431-511-50. Fax 0431/511-5444. www.steigenberger.de. 166 units. 155€–190€ ($138.40–$169.65) double; 200€–355€ ($178.60–$317) suite. Rates include buffet breakfast. AE, DC, MC, V. Parking 11€ ($9.80). Bus: 1 or 12. **Amenities:** 2 restaurants; bar; sauna; solarium; car rental; room service; babysitting; laundry/dry cleaning. *In room:* A/C, TV, minibar, hair dryer, safe.

## WHERE TO DINE

**Kieler Yacht Club** CONTINENTAL The food here is solid and reliable, though not dazzling. The main attraction, naturally, is seafood. Try the filet of haddock with mustard sauce and potatoes. Other chef's specialties are saddle of venison with savoy cabbage, roasted lamb in wine sauce with herbs, and an assortment of meal-size salads. The bar, a local hangout, attracts the yachting set.

Hindenburgufer 70. ✆ **0431/8-81-34-42.** Reservations recommended. Main courses 15€–24€ ($13.40–$21.45); fixed-price menu 23€ ($20.55). AE, DC, MC, V. Daily noon–3pm and 6–10:30pm. Bus: 8 or 18.

**Restaurant im Schloss** ★ CONTINENTAL The most elegant formal restaurant in Kiel offers superb cuisine, service, and wine. The Schloss, a stone building overlooking the harbor, looks like a museum set in a park. If you reserve, you can get one of the window tables opening onto the water. The cuisine has a creative and lighthearted style, using the freshest of produce. Many fish dishes are from the north German seas. Try, for example, terrine of salmon and zander in cream sauce, followed by filet of lamb breast brushed with white bread crumbs and baked with fresh herbs.

Am Oslokai. ✆ **0431/9-11-55.** Reservations required. Main courses 14€–26€ ($12.50–$23.20); fixed-price menu 24€ ($21.45) for 3 courses, 51€ ($45.55) for 7 courses. AE, DC, MC, V. Year-round, Tues–Fri 11am–3pm; Mon–Sat 6–10:30pm. Sept–May also Sun noon–3:30pm. Bus: 1.

**Restaurant Jakob** CONTINENTAL Set on the lobby level of one of Kiel's most comfortable hotels, this restaurant boasts views over the harbor and a plush, modern decor. You might begin your meal with a crêpe filled with Jacob mussels served on red lentils, or a soup—perhaps lobster soup with cognac. Main dishes range from the mundane (strips of turkey breast in a curry-and-yogurt sauce) to the sublime (saddle of boar with a juniperberry sauce). Try the filet of pork medallions coated in bacon and served with a mustard sauce, or the calves' liver with asparagus and hollandaise. Dessert might be a slice of apricot cake with ice cream.

In the Steigenberger Conti-Hansa Hotel, Schlossgarten 7. ✆ **0431/5-11-54-07.** Reservations recommended. Main courses 12.50€–21€ ($11.15–$18.75); fixed-price menu 29€ ($25.90). AE, DC, MC, V. Daily noon–2:30pm and 6–9:30pm. Bus: 1 or 12.

## KIEL AFTER DARK

It's worthwhile to take a stroll after dark through the salt air and fog of this seafaring city, admiring the Hanseatic architecture and the ever-present sense of gloomy nostalgia. Along the way, you can stop at any of the small bars of the Altstadt. One of the most visible old-fashioned nightlife options in Kiel is **Klosterbräurei,** Alter Markt (✆ **0431/906-290**), which brews and serves, on-site, a medium-dark beer that locals compare to the better-known Düsseldorfer. Most clients come just for the beer, but if you're hungry, head for the self-service cafeteria, also on site, for heaping platters of sauerkraut, sausage, salads, and prepared meats (try the pig on a spit, rotating behind glass for your viewing pleasure), sold by the kilo. Expect to pay around 5€ to 12.90€ ($4.45–$11.50) for a platter.

A bar, **Hemingway,** Alter Markt (✆ **0431/96812**), named in honor of Papa, is the hippest in town, drawing a chic young crowd to its precincts nightly. An even younger and much less chic crowd can be found nightly at **Traumfabrik,** Graseg 19 (✆ **0431/548106**), devouring pizzas fresh from the oven or else dancing to loud, blaring recorded music.

Newer, and more intently geared to the developing (and sometimes cutting-edge) musical tastes of the under-25 crowd, is **Mex Musik Halle,** Eichhof Strasse 1 (✆ **0431/122-9944**). It's open Friday, Saturday, and Sunday 11pm until dawn. Entrance costs 5€ ($4.45) per person.

# 3 Schleswig ★

48km (30 miles) NW of Kiel, 34km (21 miles) S of Flensburg

This one-time Viking stronghold on the Schlei (an arm of the Baltic) is Schleswig-Holstein's oldest town, with some 1,200 years of history. Everything here is steeped in legend, even the seagulls. According to tradition, the birds nesting on Seagull Island in the middle of the Schlei are actually the fellow conspirators of Duke Abel, who in 1250 murdered his own brother, King Eric. The crime was discovered when the king's body, weighted with chains, washed ashore from the Schlei. The duke went mad, eventually died, and was impaled and buried in the Tiergarten. But his followers became seagulls, doomed to nest forever on Seagull Island. Today this sleepy town is visited mainly for its memories.

## ESSENTIALS

**GETTING THERE** **By Train** The **Schleswig Bahnhof** is on the Flensburg–Neumünster–Hamburg and Westerland–Hamburg rail lines, with frequent connections. Trains from Hamburg arrive daily (trip time: 2 hr. 20 min.). For information, call ✆ **01805/99-66-33.**

**By Bus** Long-distance bus service to and from Hamburg, Flensburg, and Kiel is provided by **Autokraft GmbH** in Kiel (✆ **0431/71070**).

**By Car** Access by car is via the A7 Autobahn north or south.

**VISITOR INFORMATION** For information, contact **Tourist-Information,** Plessenstrasse 7 (✆ **04621/98-16-16**). Hours are May to September, Monday to Friday 9am to 12:30pm and 1:30 to 5:30pm, Saturday 9am to noon; October to April, Monday to Thursday 9am to 12:30pm and 1:30 to 5pm, and Friday 9am to 12:30pm.

**GETTING AROUND** A network of buses fan out from Königstrasse and Plessenstrasse, in the town center. Fare is 1€ to 5€ (90¢–$4.45). Buses operate every day 6am to 10pm.

## EXPLORING THE TOWN

**Dom St. Petri (St. Peter's Cathedral)** ★ The jewel of Schleswig is St. Peter's Cathedral, a brick Romanesque-Gothic Hallenkirche (hall church) begun in the 12th century. Its towering spire makes the rest of the Altstadt seem like so many dollhouses by comparison. Inside is the outstanding 16th-century *Bordesholm Altarpiece,* a powerful work carved in oak by Hans Bruggeman for the convent at Bordesholm. Its elaborately carved Gothic panels contain nearly 400 figures. The cathedral and cloisters also possess art treasures, including the *Blue Madonna* by J. Ovens and 13th-century frescoes.

Süderdomstrasse 1. ✆ **04621/96-30-54.** Free admission. May–Sept, Mon–Thurs and Sat 9am–5pm, Fri 9am–3pm, Sun 1–5pm; Oct–Apr, Mon–Thurs and Sat 9:30am–4pm, Fri 10am–3pm, Sun 1–4pm. Bus: 1, 2, 3, 4, or 5.

**Schloss Gottorf** A dam and a bridge connect this castle, located on a small island, with the town. As you walk around the harbor, the panorama of the Altstadt and the widening bay opens up behind you. The castle is the largest in Schleswig-Holstein. The foundations date from the original 13th-century ducal palace; the present structure was built mainly in the 16th and 17th centuries and has been reconditioned since 1948 to house two museums.

The **Archäologisches Landesmuseum (Provincial Museum of Archeology)** ★ (✆ **04621/81-33-00**) has a most remarkable exhibit (in a separate building): the **Nydam Boat** ★★★, a 4th-century ship found in the Nydam marshes in 1863. In the same room are artifacts and weapons discovered with the ship and Viking corpses preserved in the moor, all adding up to one of the major archaeological finds in northern Germany.

**Schleswig-Holstein State Museum (Schleswig-Holstein State Museum)** ★ (✆ **04621/81-32-22**), also housed in the castle, contains an exceptional collection of fine and applied art from medieval times to the 20th century, including painting, sculpture, furniture, textiles, and weapons. Outstanding are the late Gothic King's Hall, the 17th-century ducal living rooms with rich stucco ceilings, and the Renaissance chapel with a private pew for the ducal family, decorated with intricate and elaborate carvings and inlays. Two buildings east of the castle house collections of contemporary art, including outstanding works of German expressionism and modern sculpture, plus the ethnological collection of implements and tools used by farmers, artisans, and fishermen.

On a small island in the Burgsee, a bay at the west end of the Schlei. ✆ **04621/8130.** Admission (including both museums) 4.60€ ($4.10) adults, 2.50€ ($2.25) children. Mar–Oct daily 9am–5pm; Nov–Feb daily 9:30am–4pm. Bus: 1, 2, 3, 4, or 5.

**Wikinger Museum Haithabu** Haithabu was one of the most prominent settlements of northern Europe during the Viking era. This Viking Museum, opened in 1985, contains the finds of archaeological excavations of the Viking-age town of Haithabu. Exhibits cover all aspects of daily life. There's even a Viking long ship. In summer, you can reach this site by a scenic, 20-minute boat ride. Departures are from Stadthafen, the town quay in Schleswig, south of the cathedral. After you dock, it's a 10-minute walk to the museum. In winter you'll have to take a 3km (2-mile) walk from the rail station.

Durchwahl, 2.5km (1½ miles) from Schleswig. ✆ **04621/81-33-00.** Admission 3€ ($2.70). Mar 10–Oct daily 9am–5pm; Nov–Mar 9 Tues–Sun 10am–4pm.

## WHERE TO STAY

**Hotel Waldschlösschen** ★ This elegant country hotel, finer than any of the in-town properties, is equipped with every convenience to make your stay interesting and comfortable. Rooms range from small to medium, each with a compact bathroom with shower-tub combination. Outside, there's a rock garden, a gabled house, an elongated annex, and lots of trees.

Kolonnenweg 152 (1.5km/1 mile southwest of town), 24837 Schleswig-Pulverholz. ✆ **04621/38-30.** Fax 04621/38-31-05. www.hotel-waldschloesschen.de. 117 units. 84€–120€ ($75–$107.15) double; 189€ ($168.80) suite. Rates include buffet breakfast. AE, DC, MC, V. Free parking. **Amenities:** Restaurant; bar; pool; health club; whirlpool; sauna; solarium; bowling alley; room service; babysitting; laundry/dry cleaning. *In room:* TV, minibar, hair dryer, safe.

**Strandhalle** *Value* Strandhalle may not be as good as the Waldschlösschen, but it has many winning features, especially for those who'd like to stay within Schleswig and absorb the atmosphere of this ancient town. Actually, this hotel is more of a holiday resort—right on the water, with its own rowboats available. The owners maintain an informal atmosphere. Rooms are small but neatly kept, each with a small, somewhat cramped bathroom with shower stall. Nonetheless, the hotel is good value for the area. Ask for a room opening on the water, with a view of the yacht harbor.

Strandweg 2, 24837 Schleswig. ✆ **04621/90-90.** Fax 04621/90-91-00. www.hotel-strandhalle.de. 25 units. 93€–115€ ($83.05–$102.70) double. Rates include buffet breakfast. AE, DC, MC, V. Parking 7.50€ ($6.70). Bus: 1, 2, 3, 4, or 5. **Amenities:** Breakfast room; lounge; pool; boat rental. *In room:* TV, minibar, hair dryer.

## WHERE TO DINE

**Olschewski's** CONTINENTAL This cozy, well-managed restaurant is the best in town, superior to any of the hotel dining rooms. You can dine in either a glass-sided modern extension or an unpretentious dining room with views of the Schlei. Your choices may include fresh salad in almost any season, cream of tomato soup, salmon with a tangy cream base or a Riesling sauce, filet of lamb with rosemary, or a perfectly cooked roast goose.

Hafenstrasse 40 (near the waterfront). ✆ **04621/2-55-77.** Reservations required Fri–Sat. Main courses 12€–25€ ($10.70–$22.35). AE, MC, V. Wed–Mon 11:30am–2:30pm; Wed–Sun 5:30–9:30pm. Bus: 1, 2, 3, 4, or 5.

## SCHLESWIG AFTER DARK

If you're looking for action, head for **Lollfuss,** running parallel to the Schlei between Schloss Gottorf and a north-side residential area. Many places here are cafes during the day and bars at night. The best and most popular pub of the lot is **Patio,** Lollfuss 3 (✆ **04621/2-99-99;** bus: 1 or 2), an intimate two-story structure that usually stays open until midnight or 1am (considered very late in this small town). It also has Schleswig's most popular outdoor terrace. If you get hungry, you'll find pastas, salads, pizzas, and steaks for 3.90€ to 12.40€ ($3.50–$11.05).

## 4 The Island of Sylt ★★

20km (13 miles) W of the German/Danish border, 193km (120 miles) NW of Hamburg

The long, narrow island of Sylt (pronounced *Zoolt*) and its capital, Westerland, form the northernmost point of Germany. Sylt lies in the North Sea off the coasts of Denmark and Schleswig-Holstein. It's the largest island of the Frisian archipelago, which stretches from Denmark to the Netherlands. The "Watt" is the name given to the eastern coast, facing the mainland. Pounding winter storms seem to take more and more of the coastline each year, and there are those who think that Sylt will one day disappear into the sea.

People come here to breathe the iodine-rich air and enjoy the rain-soaked North sea climate the Germans call *Reizklima.* Sylt is today the most exclusive resort in Germany, and its hotel prices reflect its lofty status. Sylt also has a sizable gay and lesbian population, and is often called "The Fire Island of Europe." In the 1960s, Sylt became famous for "the rich and the naked," when the entire island was reportedly an ongoing bacchanalian frenzy. But it's quieted down since then. Temperatures in midsummer are usually in the low to mid-20°s C (low 70°s F), but rain can come at any minute, and winds on the beach are a constant. This has given rise to the Sylt "mink," or yellow oilskin, which chic visitors wear to protect themselves from the elements.

The spa here has facilities for the treatment of everything from heart disease to skin irritations. The basic therapy is sunshine, pure air, and seawater, but in recent years mud baths have also become a method of treatment. Some of the more remote sections of the dunes have been turned into nudist beaches for purists in the art of sunshine therapy. In addition to bathing, there are facilities in and around Westerland for horseback riding, surfing, golf, and tennis, as well as more sedentary entertainment, such as theater and concerts.

### ESSENTIALS

**GETTING THERE** **By Plane** The nearest international airport is at Hamburg (see chapter 17). From there you can fly to the regional **Westland Airport** (✆ **04651/92-06-12**). There's also regularly scheduled air service from Berlin, Munich, and Frankfurt.

**By Train** The only link between the mainland and the island of Sylt is the railroad causeway running from the mainland town of Niebüll. If you wish to bring your car to the island, you'll have to load it on the train at Niebüll for the slow ride (see "By Car," below). No advance booking is necessary—you just arrive and take your chances. Passengers are carried free.

**Westerland Bahnhof** lies on the Westerland–Hamburg and the Westerland–Lübeck lines, with frequent connections. Seventeen trains arrive from Hamburg daily (trip time: 2 hr. 40 min.–3 hr. 20 min., depending on the train). For information, call ✆ **01805/99-66-33.**

**By Car-Ferry** An alternative way of reaching Sylt is to take a car-ferry between the Danish port of Havneby, on the island of Roømo (which is easily accessible via highway from Germany) and the German port of List, at the northern tip of Sylt. There are at least a dozen daily crossings between those points in summer, with a much-reduced schedule in winter. Reservations for your car are possible. For information, call the **Roømo–Sylt Line.** In List (Germany), its number is ✆ **04651/870475.**

**By Bus** The few buses that pull into Sylt are forced to ride the flatcars on the rail line across the Hindenburg Causeway for the final stretch of their journey.

## A Disappearing Playground

Scientists warn that the western coast of Sylt is one of the most fragile ecosystems in Germany and may one day be reclaimed by the sea. The entire island is little more than a strip, only 550m (1,800 ft.) wide at its narrowest point, that's composed mostly of sand and very little rock. As such, it presents little resistance—especially after it's been stripped of its tenacious salt grasses—to the onslaught of erosion and deterioration. The sand dunes, warmed by the Gulf Stream, are forever shifting, and the winds sweeping in from the North Sea can move them by as much as a dozen feet in only a year. (Locals call these "wandering" sand dunes *Wanderdunen*.) Although the winter months in general, and storms at any time of the year, are highly destructive, it's during strong south winds that most erosion takes place, and on some mornings after violent storms, huge amounts of sand migrate from the beachfront out into the North Sea.

In the 1970s, a series of *Tetrapoden* (four-legged concrete structures that look like giant jacks) were built on the sands of Westerland and Hornum beaches, in an unsuccessful attempt to hold back erosion. (They were later judged useless, and their construction discontinued.)

Today, everyone's favorite solution is one of the simplest: Whenever funds are allocated by the municipal budget, you'll see one or more barges moored offshore, pumping sand from deepwater sites back onto beaches of Sylt. There are also severe penalties for anyone removing salt grasses and scrub from the beachfronts, and severe restrictions against building new houses on any land that's deemed as fragile.

A Frisan we met took us for a day's walk to view the desert-like, forlorn beauty of the sand dunes. Deep, windless ridges were everywhere. "Look, the wind, the rain, and the sea are taking my island from me," the man said with a kind of despair. "One day—not in my time, perhaps—but one day it will be gone. The wind is actually blowing Sylt away. The crashing tides are claiming our coast."

If there is an air of desperation about the Germans who love and frolic in this North Sea playground, it may be because they know they won't be here forever.

Many passengers prefer to get off their bus in Niebühl and transfer onto one of the passenger trains that make the frequent crossings to Westerland from other parts of Germany and Europe. Rail fare between Niebühl and Westerland costs 12€ ($10.70) per person, round-trip. The ride takes between 30 and 45 minutes each way.

**By Car** Construction of a conventional bridge from the mainland of Schleswig-Holstein to Sylt has never really been feasible. Therefore, cars headed to Sylt are loaded onto flatcars at the mainland railway junction of Niebühl and hauled out across the *Hindenburg Damm* (Hindenburg Causeway) to the railway station of Westerland, on Sylt. Drivers remain in their cars, with the doors locked, eventually arriving at Westerland 30 to 40 minutes later. For information on these and all other (conventional) trains between the German mainland and Sylt, call the

**Deutsche Bahn** information service in Westerland at ✆ **01805/99-66-33.** Trains depart at 30-minute intervals daily 5am to 10pm. No reservations are accepted for hauling your car across. Round-trip transport for most cars costs 75€ ($67).

Access to Niebühl is possible via the A7 Autobahn north or south.

**VISITOR INFORMATION** For information, contact the **Fremdenverkehrszentrale,** Am Bundesbahnhof Westerland (✆ **04651/99-80**). It's open May to October daily 9am to 8pm; November to April Monday to Saturday 9am to 7pm.

**SHOPPING** Few other holiday destinations in Germany are as frenetic about clothing as Sylt. Garments are removed and put on again with abandon on this island with fickle weather and an extremely clothes-conscious population. You'll find impressive inventories of expensively casual clothing on Sylt—items that are artfully simple, easy to don, easy to doff, and easy to look at. The island's best shopping streets are the **Friedrichstrasse,** in Westerland, and the **Stroewae,** in Kampen, both lined with boutiques associated with the great names of European fashion.

In Westerland, look for menswear at **The Camel Store,** Friedrichstrasse 32 (✆ **04651/8-25-00**), and **Heising,** Friedrichstrasse 22 (✆ **04651/29-536**); and women's wear at **Marco Polo,** Strandstrasse 3–5 (✆ **04651/61-11**), or at any of the dozens of chic hole-in-the-wall boutiques.

The island's art galleries reflect the tastes and preoccupations of big-city Hamburg. One of the most interesting emporiums for dramatic modern art is **Galerie Sprotte,** Altdorfstrasse 1 (✆ **04651/4-24-13**), whose exhibition space is mostly devoted to the stylized and often riveting paintings of long-time Sylt resident Siegvard Sprotte. His renderings of the landscapes of Sylt have been influenced by everything from 16th-century Flemish portraits to early 20th-century impressionism.

## WHERE TO STAY

**Hotel Clausen** This four-story building is from 1950 but was radically modernized in 1992. Today, its congenial English-speaking owners occupy the upper (fourth) floor. On the building's lower stories is a series of small but tidily maintained rooms, each fitted with a quality mattress on a good bed. Bathrooms are also small and have shower stalls. Breakfast is the only meal served, but many restaurants are nearby.

Friedrichstrasse 20 (in Westerland's pedestrian zone, a 3-min. walk from the beach), 25980 Westerland/Sylt. ✆ **04651/9-22-90.** Fax 04651/2-80-07. 19 units. 95€–140€ ($84.85–$125) double; 160€ ($142.90) suite. Rates include buffet breakfast. AE, MC, V. Parking 5€ ($4.45). Closed Jan 7–21. **Amenities:** Breakfast room; lounge. *In room:* TV.

**Hotel Miramar** ★ This hotel, on a bluff just above the beach, is the second best accommodation at Westerland, just below Stadt Hamburg (see below). The Miramar is surrounded by an arched veranda, and its public areas are graced with enormous arched windows with views of the sea. An octagonal light, left over from the building's 1903 construction, illuminates the salon from above. The high-ceilinged rooms are quite comfortable and were recently renovated; each comes with a luxurious bed and a recently renewed bathroom equipped with shower-tub combinations.

Friedrichstrasse 43, 25980 Westerland/Sylt. ✆ **04651/85-50.** Fax 04651/ 85-52-22. www.hotel-miramar.de. 93 units. 155€–350€ ($138.40–$312.55) double; 245€–640€ ($218.80–$571.50) suite. Rates include buffet breakfast. AE, DC, MC, V. **Amenities:** Restaurant; bar; pool; health club; sauna; room service; massage; babysitting; laundry/dry cleaning. *In room:* TV, minibar, hair dryer, safe.

**Stadt Hamburg** ★★★ This is the best hotel on the island, though it looks more like a well-appointed country home than a hotel. The gleaming white entrance is reached through a white picket fence, and its rear windows overlook a well-kept lawn. Each spacious room is individually furnished, with home-like touches. Mattresses and linens are the island's finest, and the bathrooms are state of the art, with toiletries and shower-tub combinations.

Strandstrasse 2 (next to the casino), 25980 Westerland/Sylt. ✆ **04651/85-80.** Fax 04651/85-82-20. www.relaischateaux.com/stadthamburg. 78 units. 165€–285€ ($147.35–$254.50) double; 306€–393€ ($273.25–$350.95) suite. AE, MC, V. Parking 7€ ($6.25). **Amenities:** Restaurant; bar; lounge; room service; sauna; laundry/dry cleaning. *In room:* TV, hair dryer, safe.

**Wunschmann Hotel** This hotel is in the heart of the tourist belt of Westerland, yet only minutes from the sand dunes. Rooms are in a complex of modern buildings (with more than two dozen boutiques), but the hotel's interior exudes old-world tranquility. The medium-size and one-of-a-kind rooms are cheerful, with neatly kept bathrooms with shower-tub combinations.

Andreas-Dirks-Strasse 4, 25980 Westerland/Sylt. ✆ **04651/50-25.** Fax 04651/50-28. www.hotel-wuenschmann.de. 36 units. 107€–240€ ($95.55–$214.30) double; 306€–393€ ($273.25–$350.95) suite. AE, V. Parking 7€ ($6.25). Closed mid-Nov–mid-Dec. **Amenities:** Restaurant; lounge; sauna; room service; massage; babysitting; laundry/dry cleaning. *In room:* TV, hair dryer, safe.

## WHERE TO DINE

**Alte Friesenstube** *Finds* NORTHERN GERMAN/FRISIAN This restaurant is refreshingly down-to-earth amid the pretentiousness of Sylt. The thatched building housing this place was constructed in 1648. The menus are written on the wall in a German dialect, but someone will assist you in deciphering the offerings, which include regional pork, fish, and beef dishes. Especially popular is duck with orange sauce and a local saltwater fish (*Panfische*) with roasted potatoes and mustard sauce. No one puts on airs, and the kitchen hardly follows trendy recipes, sticking instead to the robust fare the islanders have been eating for decades.

Gaadt 4, Westerland. ✆ **04651/12-28.** Reservations required. Main courses 17€–20€ ($15.20–$17.85). AE. Tues–Sun 11:30am–2:30pm and 6–10:30pm. Closed Jan.

**Hardy auf Sylt** INTERNATIONAL/NORTHERN GERMAN This round, thatched restaurant offers a nostalgic interior featuring furniture dating from about 1890. Finely worked columns, old oil portraits, beautiful glass lamps, and skillfully wrought candlesticks combine to create a relaxed, intimate feeling. The menu is adjusted seasonally. There's a fine selection of French and German wines.

Norderstrasse 65, Westerland. ✆ **04651/2-27-75.** Reservations required. Main courses 14€–18€ ($12.50–$16.05). No credit cards. Tues–Sun 6pm–midnight. Closed Jan 15–Feb 15 and Nov 30–Dec 20.

**Jörg Müller** ★★★ CONTINENTAL/FRENCH The most elegant dining on the island is here. The brick building that contains this restaurant is almost a landmark in itself, thanks to its thatched roof, steep gables, and Frisian architecture. Menu items change with the seasons and feature a blend of contemporary Continental cuisine with imaginative variations of French recipes, which might include lobster salad with herb-flavored vinaigrette sauce, sliced and braised goose liver with segments of glazed apples, or roast salt-marsh lamb flavored with herbs and served with ratatouille-flavored cream sauce. You can also enjoy local oysters with compote of red shallots and champagne sauce or halibut baked in fennel. For dessert, you might order a compote of fresh fruits with pistachio nuts or feuilleté of chocolate served with both light- and dark-chocolate mousse.

Süderstrasse 8 (a 5-min. walk from the center of Westerland). ✆ **04651/2-77-88.** Reservations required. Main courses 28€–40€ ($25–$35.70); fixed-price menu 80€–100€ ($71.45–$89.30). AE, DC, MC, V. Thurs–Mon 11:30am–2pm; Wed–Mon 6–10pm. Closed Nov 25–Dec 18.

**Restaurant Stadt Hamburg** ★★ GERMAN/FRISIAN Top-rate cuisine is offered here in an attractive setting. The menu is so wide-ranging it may be hard to make up your mind. The smoothest beginning is the cream of lobster soup. Many seafood specialties are featured, such as pan-fried fresh North Sea sole and turbot medallions in saffron sauce with zucchini. Another good dish is the rack of lamb (raised on the salty grasslands of the island). For dessert, try homemade *rote Grütze*—berries and cherries topped with vanilla ice cream.

Strandstrasse 2, Westerland. ✆ **04651/85-80.** Reservations recommended. Main courses 22€–29.50€ ($19.65–$26.35); fixed-price dinner 38€–72€ ($33.95–$64.30). AE, MC, V. Daily 6–10pm. Bus: Centrale Omnibus Bahnhof.

**Web Christel** *Value* NORTHERN GERMAN Favored by local residents for its reasonable prices and cozy ambience, this restaurant occupies a century-old Frisian house set in the center of Westerland, opposite its more glamorous (and more expensive) rival, Jörg Müller. Menu items include a wide selection of fish, such as classic versions of turbot in an herb-butter-mustard sauce, and sole prepared in the meuniére style or grilled and served with hollandaise sauce. Roast duck with two different sauces is also available. The staff is warm and polite.

Süderstrasse 11 (opposite Jörg Müller), Westerland. ✆ **04651/2-29-00.** Reservations recommended. Main courses 15.10€–28.10€ ($13.50–$25.10); fixed-price menu 24.30€–50.60€ ($21.70–$45.20). No credit cards. Fri–Wed 5–11pm.

## SYLT AFTER DARK

**Disco Pony,** Strowae, in Kampen (✆ **04651/42182**), where both indoor and outdoor bar areas encompass views of the sea and the scrub-covered coastline that flanks it, attracts, for the most part, a clientele under 40. It's open nightly around 10:30pm. (It's closed on Mon–Tues Oct–April.)

Also in Kampen, its major competitor is **Club Rotes Kliff,** Alte Dorfstrasse (✆**04651/43400**), distinguished by its hip but not necessarily young crowd.

If you're in Westerland, the hot spot is **Compass,** Friedrichstrasse 42 (✆ **04651/23513**), drawing a young crowd in their 20s and 30s. This is a typical island dance club, but lacking the chic of the two Kampen clubs above. Compass doesn't heat up until the weekend.

Unless you're a hard-core gambler, the island's bars, cafes, and restaurants are more interesting than its casino, **Spielbank Westerland,** Strandstrasse (✆ **04561/230450**), which, ironically, occupies the same premises as Westerland's Rathaus (town hall). There's no maximum limit on how much you can bet, so the activities around the baccarat, roulette, and blackjack tables can get intense, depending on the crowd. Entrance costs 2.50€ ($2.25) per person. Men are encouraged to wear neckties. Hours are daily 3pm until at least 3am. You must present a passport to enter. On the premises is a sophisticated bar, open during the same hours as the gaming tables.

# 19

# A Scenic Drive Along the Baltic

The Baltic coast is saltier and windier and has a more international outlook than other regions of the former East Germany. Throughout the Cold War, this windswept seaside was a playground for the factory workers and bureaucrats of the now-defunct DDR. For centuries before that, the region thrived as the site of the busy ports of the Hanseatic League, whose lore still permeates the land.

Other cultural influences came from the Swedish, Latvian, Lithuanian, and Polish ports with which for many centuries the League did much of its trading. Since reunification, the Baltic Coast has slowly emerged as a hot spot for Germany's beach-loving throngs, and the entire coastline has benefited from a major restoration of its historic structures, many of which were decaying.

The region is best visited by car, on any of several different driving routes. The ideal departure point for this exploration is Lübeck (see chapter 18). From Lübeck, drive east along Highway 105 (also known as E22). En route, you'll traverse the frontier that separated West from East Germany for more than 45 years and enter the medieval principality of Mecklenburg-West Pomerania. Your first stop will be Wismar.

## 1 Wismar ★

60km (37 miles) E of Lübeck, 53km (33 miles) W of Rostock

Wismar was once an elegant city of the Hanseatic League, the medieval capital of Mecklenburg-West Pomerania. The city became prominent in the early 1200s because of its port facilities. For long periods of its history it was part of the overseas empire of Sweden. Wismar contains the largest market square in Germany—1 hectare (2½ acres). It's surrounded by elegant buildings with architectural styles ranging from 14th-century North German Gothic to 19th-century Romanesque revival. The square's focal point, and one of the town's most frequently photographed objects, is an elaborate wrought-iron fountain imported from Holland in the early 1600s. The silent filmmaker Friedrich Wilhelm Murnau used the twisting streets of Wismar's Altstadt as the backdrop for his classic vampire film, *Nosferatu.*

Unfortunately, your drive into this town's charming core will be dampened by a view of the socialist regime's endless concrete-sided suburbs. Sites to watch for in the historic city center include the pillared and gabled **Rathaus, Markt 1** built on the town's main square in the neoclassical style in 1819. Most of the Rathaus is not open to the public, but a small-scale museum in its basement, **Museum am Rathaus Keller** (✆ **03841/282350**) contains exhibitions that celebrate the history of Wismar. Open daily from 10am to 6pm, it charges 1€ (90¢) for adults, .50€ (45¢) for students and persons under 18. Children under 14 enter free. A very old house on the square, **Alter Schwede (The Old Swede),** constructed around 1380, functions as a restaurant (see "Where to Dine," below). The town's most famous church is the **St. Nikolaikirche**, Hinter dem Chor (✆ **03841/21-01-43**), a Gothic brick structure whose high altar dates from 1430. It's open May to October, Monday to Saturday 10am to noon and 1 to 6pm, and Sunday 1 to 5pm; in the off-season Saturday 11am to 3pm and Sunday 1 to 4pm only. Admission is free.

For tourist information in Wismar, contact **Wismar-Informationen,** Am Markt 11 (✆ **03841/1-94-33**), open year-round daily 9am to 6pm.

## WHERE TO STAY

Most visitors come to Wismar only for the day, moving on to overnight accommodations in either Rostock or Schwerin. However, if you need a place to stay, try the below.

**Steigenberger Hotel Stadt Hamburg** This well-managed hotel, recently renovated, is the best in town. It has three floors, three restaurants, an English-speaking staff, and a desirable location on the main (and most historic) square in Wismar. The no-frills rooms are comfortable and contemporary. Each is rather boxy, but all are fitted with comfortable mattresses and bathrooms containing shower-tub combinations.

Am Markt 24, 23966 Wismar. ✆ **03841/23-90.** Fax 03841/23-92-39. www.hotel-stadt-hamburg-wismar.de. 102 units. 104€ ($92.85) double, 162€–230€ ($144.65–$205.40) suite. Rates include buffet breakfast. AE, DC, MC, V. **Amenities:** Restaurant; bar; health club; sauna; room service (7am–10:30pm); laundry/dry cleaning. *In room:* TV, minibar.

## WHERE TO DINE

**Historische Restaurant Zum Weinberg** GERMAN One of the oldest and most historic restaurants in the province of Mecklenberg occupies a site directly behind Town Hall, within a baroque building from 1710 whose foundations, and the decor of a central hallway, date to 1557. Inside, a staff will proudly showcase a mostly regional menu of savory, time-tested dishes. These include Mecklenberg-style potato soup, onion soup, a medley of salads; marinated herring with cream sauce served with coarse black bread; baked knuckle of pork with bacon-flavored gravy; and fried duck. There's even a main course of braised kale, a tough green leafy vegetable, in this case flavored with strips of bacon fat and pork. The dining room, suitable for 100 guests at a time, is a woodsy, antique-looking place little changed for many generations.

Hintern Rathaus 3. ✆ **03841/28-35-50.** Reservations recommended. Main courses 8€–16€ ($7.15–$14.30). AE, MC, V. Daily 11am–11:30pm.

**Restaurant Alter Schwede** GERMAN Constructed in 1380, this building is one of the oldest and most historically evocative in Wismar, so well-known that many Germans drive from other parts of the Baltic just to see it. Its name, "The Old Swede," refers to the Swedish invasions of the 1600s, but luckily for sightseers, the building functions as a restaurant. In the high-ceilinged dining room, an old-time staff bustles back and forth, carrying steaming platters of traditional Germanic food. Menu items include sauerbraten with red cabbage and potatoes, a marinated pork roast known as *Rippenbraten,* all kinds of wursts, salmon roasted in orange sauce, and lots of fish from the Baltic.

Am Markt 20. ✆ **03841/28-35-52.** Reservations recommended in summer. Main courses 12€–16.50€ ($10.70–$14.75); fixed-price lunch 10€–40€ ($8.95–$35.70); fixed-price dinner 19€–40€ ($16.95–$35.70). AE, MC, V. Daily 11:30am–11:30pm.

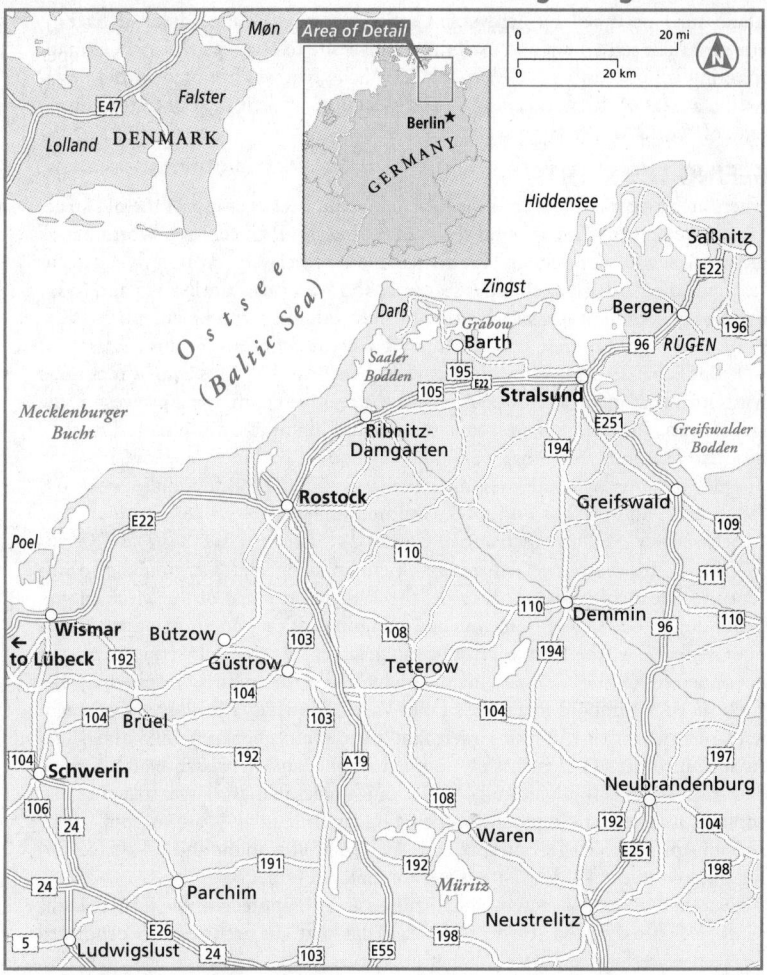


## FROM WISMAR TO SCHWERIN

To detour inland (south) toward the present-day capital of Mecklenburg–West Pomerania, drive out of Wismar along the main southbound artery (Hwy. 106) until you reach Schwerin.

## 2 Schwerin

30km (19 miles) S of Wismar

Lying inland from the Baltic coast, this town at the southwestern corner of Lake Schwerin is set in a fertile, well-irrigated district of "lakelets." Schwerin is the industrial and cultural center of an important agricultural district, but it has more to offer visitors than just commerce.

This is a city of ancient history and well-entrenched civic pride. It was originally established in the 11th century by Slavs, who fortified a settlement on the island now occupied by Schwerin Castle. Henry the Lion, duke of Saxony, annexed their settlement and used the strategic site to establish the first German-speaking colony east of the Elbe. In 1358, Schwerin was honored with a designation as seat of the ducal court of Mecklenburg, a title it held until the closing days of World War I.

## SEEING THE SIGHTS

There aren't many historic buildings in Schwerin, because most of the old structures were destroyed by fire and replaced during the 19th century. Worth a look are the **Arsenal,** set beside the Pfaffenteich (an artificial reservoir in the city center), and the **Kollegiengebäude,** seat of civic government until 1945 and today a site of government offices. (Neither of these buildings can be visited.)

Also of some interest is the **Marstall (Royal Stables),** Schloss Strasse 17 (✆ **0385/51-29-25**), site of the city's **Technische Museum (Technical Museum)** that incorporates examples of the region's engineering prowess of the last century, including planes, cars, railway and highway triumphs, and to-scale models of famous ships that were built or moored within the region. It's open Tuesday to Saturday 10am to 6pm, and charges 2€ ($1.80) for adults, 1€ (90¢) for students and persons under 18. Children under 6 enter free.

**Schweriner Schloss (Schwerin Castle)** ★, Lennestrasse 1 (✆ **0385/56-57-38**), is the most spectacular monument in town and a triumph of 19th-century civic architecture. This castle, the 19th-century seat of the Mecklenburg grand dukes, was spared from fires and bombings. It's set on an island that separates a small lake (the Burgsee) from a much larger lake (the Schweriner See), and is connected to the German mainland by a pair of bridges. Inspired by the Château de Chambord in France's Loire Valley, Schweriner Schloss is a pentagonal structure of many domes, towers, and turrets, built between 1843 and 1857. Its style incorporates elements of Gothic, baroque, and Renaissance architecture. The castle's chapel (built around 1560) is much older than the larger structure that contains it. The castle-museum is open Tuesday to Sunday 10am to 5pm (closes at 6pm Apr 15–Oct 14). Entrance costs 4€ ($3.55) for adults and 2.50€ ($2.25) for children under 14. Entrance is free for children under 6.

Even if the castle is closed, you'll still be able to appreciate the formal 18th-century **Schlossgarten** (castle park) that flanks it. Its architects incorporated terraced waterfalls, a battery of heroic statues, and a network of canals that divide the garden into a series of interconnected rectangles. Entrance to the gardens is possible anytime, and there's no admission fee.

On the mainland, a pair of imposing buildings stands in the former Alter Garten parade grounds. These include the neoclassical **Mecklenburgisches Staatstheater** (✆ **0385/530-0123**), where dramas, comedies, and operas are sometimes performed, and also the well-recommended **Staatliches Museum Schwerin-Kunstsammlunger (National Museum)** ★, Alter Garten 3, Werderstrasse (✆ **0385/59-580**), in a neoclassical building resembling a Roman temple, completed in 1785. Inside you'll find a worthy collection of 16th-century Dutch and Flemish paintings, as well as 18th-century paintings from France and the German-speaking world. Specific examples include *Drinking Boy* and *Boy Holding a Flute* by Frans Hals, and *Home Concert* by Frans van Mieris. There are also German medieval collections, including porcelain (especially Dresden china), 18th-century court paintings, and works by such modern artists as Max Liebermann. It's open Tuesday to Sunday 10am to 5pm. Admission is 4€ ($3.55) adults, 2€ ($1.80) students and children.

Schwerin's **Dom** ★, Am Marktplatz (✆ **0385/56-50-14**), was begun around 1248. The cathedral is a fine example of brick medieval architecture, designed in the Lübeck Hanseatic Gothic style. Highlights include a Gothic altarpiece, probably carved in Lübeck around 1480. If you'd like a panoramic view of the town, you can climb 200 steep and winding steps to the top of the 98m- (320-ft.-) high tower. The Dom is open June to September, Monday 10am to 1pm, Tuesday to Saturday 10am to 1pm and 2 to 5pm, and Sunday noon to 5pm. Other months, hours are Monday 10am to 4pm, Tuesday to Saturday 11am to noon and 2:30 to 4:30pm, and Sunday 2:30 to 4:30pm. You can enter the church free, but it costs 1€ (90¢) to climb the tower stairs.

Several interesting trips are possible from Schwerin. You can take a boat trip across the Schweriner See. Boats operate between May and late September, with departures every 30 minutes every one of those days between 10am and 6pm for cruises upon the water, without any particular destination. A 1-hour cruise costs 8€ ($7.15); a 90-minute cruise costs 9.50€ ($8.50). If you're feeling athletic and very robust, hike for a few miles along the lake's southern shore. (The lake's total circumference is about 80km/50 miles.) Information on attractions in and around the town can be obtained at the **City Tourist Office (Schwerin-Information),** Am Markt 10 (✆ **0385/592-52-13**). May to September, it's open Monday to Friday 9am to 7pm; Saturday and Sunday 10am to 6pm. October to April, it's open Monday to Friday 9am to 6pm; Saturday 10am to 4pm, Sunday 10am to 2pm.

## WHERE TO STAY

**Best Western Hotel Plaza Schwerin** This hotel is recommendable in many respects, despite its unappetizing location in a sea of Sputnik-era apartment blocks. Set close to the lake and built in a four-story format in 1992, it's popular with vacationers and business travelers. Most of the contemporary rooms are spacious, and all are designed for standard comfort with decent beds and compact little bathrooms with shower stalls.

Am Grünen Tal (near Schloss Schwerin, 5 min. east from the center by car), 19063 Schwerin. ✆ **800/528-1234** in the U.S., or 0385/3-99-20. Fax 0385/3-99-21-88. 79 units. 85€–102€ ($75.90–$91.10) double; 153€ ($136.65) suite. Rates include breakfast. AE, DC, MC, V. Free parking. Tram: 1 or 2. **Amenities:** Restaurant; lounge; sauna; solarium, room service; babysitting; laundry/dry cleaning. *In room:* TV, minibar, hair dryer, safe.

**Crowne Plaza Hotel Schwerin** ★★ Built in 1994 as a Holiday Inn, and upgraded 4 years later to a more upscale Crowne Plaza; this hotel rises five floors above the shoreline of a freshwater lake (the Ostdorfer See). It's part of a modern office and residential compound. Rooms are modern and convenient, although rather boxy and furnished in a completely functional way, but the beds are comfortable. All units come equipped with bathrooms containing shower-tub combinations. Some overlook the lake, others a verdant public park. Two of the five floors are reserved strictly for nonsmokers.

Bleicher Ufer 23 (a 15-min. walk west of the town center), 19053 Schwerin. ✆ **0385/5-75-50.** Fax 0385/5-75-57-77. www.crowneplaza.com. 100 units. 144€–154€ ($128.60–$137.50) Mon–Fri, 113€–123€ ($100.90–$109.85) Sat–Sun double; 219€ ($195.55) for a suite throughout the week. Rates include breakfast. AE, DC, MC, V. Tram: 1 or 2. Bus: 10. **Amenities:** Restaurant; bar; health club; sauna; room service (7am–11pm); babysitting; laundry/dry cleaning. *In room:* TV, minibar, hair dryer, safe.

**Hotel Nordlicht** *Finds* This inexpensive establishment is more like a B&B than a conventional hotel. It's across from a freshwater pond the *Pfaffenteich,* which is encircled by walkways. The hotel, built in 1991, consists of only five rooms furnished in a simple but modern style, each with a comfortable bed and a cramped bath with a shower stall.

Apothekerstrasse 2 (1km/½ mile from Marktplatz), 19055 Schwerin. ✆ **0385/55-81-50.** Fax 0385/5-57-43-83. www.hotel-nordlicht.m-vp.de. 5 units. 59€–64€ ($52.70–$57.15) double. Rates include continental breakfast. AE, MC, V. Free parking. Bus: 10 or 11. **Amenities:** Restaurant; cafe. *In room:* TV.

## WHERE TO DINE

**Primavera** ★ ITALIAN This restaurant, in the above-recommended Hotel Plaza Schwerin, is consistently voted the best in the Mecklenburg area. The menu changes with the season. Italian dishes are featured, along with a small regional menu. The service is impeccable, and the food is always good. The fresh fish is often from the North Sea. Arrive early for dinner and enjoy music in the piano bar beginning at 6pm.

In the Hotel Plaza Schwerin, Am Grünen Tal. ✆ **0385/3-99-20.** Reservations recommended. Main courses 12€–18€ ($10.70–$16.05); fixed-price lunch 14€ ($12.50); fixed-price dinner 19€ ($16.95). AE, DC, MC, V. Daily 11:30am–midnight. Tram: Zum Zoo.

**Weinhaus Uhle** ★ *Finds* INTERNATIONAL This wine house in the oldest part of town is set in a building dating from 1751. It's mostly decorated in Jugendstil (German Art Nouveau), but the second floor incorporates a traditional Rittersaal (Knight's Hall) with large and ornate windows, metal replicas of knights, and heraldic coats of arms. The chef's specialty is a savory Mecklenburger Ente (duck). A savory version of chateaubriand can be prepared for a minimum of 3 diners at a time. A host of other regional dishes, as well as an international mixed grill, are also offered. A pianist plays every Friday and Saturday night during the dinner hour.

Schusterstrasse 13–15 (near the castle and the cathedral). ✆ **0385/56-29-56.** Reservations recommended. Main courses 11€–18.50€ ($9.80–$16.50); fixed-price lunch or dinner 13€ ($11.60). Daily noon–11pm.

## A SIDE TRIP TO GÜSTROW

From Schwerin, strike out in a northeasterly direction along a secondary road (Rte. 104, but be aware that some sections along this road might also be called Rte. 192). Follow the signs to Brüel and then to the historic town of Güstrow, a distance of 69km (43 miles). En route, you'll pass through villages that haven't really changed very much since the days of the East German regime.

**Güstrow** holds one of the district's architectural gems, **Schloss Güstrow,** Franz Parr Platz 1 (✆ **03843/7520**), which rises in imposing 16th-century splendor amid formal French gardens. Inside is a museum that showcases life during the Middle Ages, displaying hunting trophies, religious artwork, and household artifacts set off within a series of high-ceilinged rooms that include a banqueting hall. It's open Tuesday to Sunday from 9am to 5pm. Entrance costs 3€ ($2.70) for adults. Students and persons under 18 pay .50€ (45¢) each. Also of interest is the town's cathedral, the **Dom** (Am Domplatz; ✆ **03843/682433**), whose decorative highlights include statues of the Apostles, sculptured in oak around 1530. Entrance is free. Opening hours are mid-October to mid-May, Tuesday to Sunday 9am to noon and 2 to 4pm; mid-May to mid-October, daily 10am to 5pm.

For information in Güstrow, contact the **Tourist Information Office (Güstrow-Information),** Domstrasse 9 (✆ **03843/68-10-23**). It's open May to September, Monday to Friday 9am to 7pm and Saturday and Sunday 9:30am to 1pm; October to April, Monday to Friday 9:30am to 6pm, and Saturday 9:30am to 1pm. (It's closed Sun in winter.)

Continue from Güstrow north along Autobahn 19 for another 42km (26 miles) into the heart of Rostock, one of the Baltic coast's most historic seaports. To get to Rostock from Schwerin, take Route 106 north to Wismar, and then take Route 105 (E22) east.

## 3 Rostock

117km (73 miles) NE of Lübeck, 282km (175 miles) NE of Berlin

Rostock is set on a wide and navigable estuary of the Warnow River. Throughout the Cold War, it was the largest and busiest seaport in East Germany, built on a scale to rival Hamburg. The town still bustles with maritime activity, though its importance has declined since reunification. Today visitors come to Rostock to wander its reconstructed Alstadt, which contains major sections of the town's medieval wall, and to visit the town's museums and churches.

During the 13th and 14th centuries, Rostock was one of the most important cities of the Hanseatic League, trading and competing with ports in Sweden, Denmark, Estonia, Poland, and Lithuania. Its university (founded in 1419) was the first in any city along the Baltic, and its wealth and strategic location soon provoked the envy of the Scandinavians. Danes and Swedes occupied the city twice, first during the Thirty Years' War (1618–48) and again from 1700 to 1721. Later, the French, under Napoléon, occupied the town for about a decade until 1813. During World War II, Rostock was blasted by British bombers. The monuments and houses lining its principal street, Lange Strasse (Long Street), were completely demolished. Some historic buildings were restored, at great expense, from piles of little more than rubble.

### SEEING THE SIGHTS

Some noteworthy historic buildings stand on Neuer Platz (also known as Ernst-Thalmann-Platz). Among the most prominent is the **Rathaus,** Neuer Markt (✆ **0381/3810**), which manages to incorporate three late–13th- and early-14th-century houses and seven towers into a brick structure linked by an arcaded gallery. Its interior is devoted to municipal offices.

Beginning at the Rathaus's base and extending westward for several historic blocks is Rostock's most photographed street, **Kröpeliner-Strasse,** a pedestrians-only walkway lined with shops and restored buildings constructed between 1500 and around 1850. It runs parallel to the more banal, and much less charming, Lange Strasse, Rostock's principal street. Of particular interest is the **step-gabled presbytery** (ca. 1480), from what used to be a hospital, at Kröpeliner-Strasse 82. The street ends at one of the most instantly recognizable features in town, the **Kröpeliner Tor**, Kröpeliner Strasse (✆ **0381/454177**) a 14th-century brick gatehouse whose interior contains a small-scale museum devoted to the history and culture of the town. It's open year-round Wednesday to Sunday 10am to 6pm, charging 3€ ($2.70) for adults, 1.50€ ($1.35) students and persons under 18. Children under 6, free.

Among the buildings that survived war damage is the **St-Marien-Kirche (St. Mary's Church)**, Am Ziegenmarkt (✆ **0381/4-92-33-96**), set on a narrow side street off Lange Strasse. It's one of the finest (and largest) ecclesiastical structures of the Baltic world. It began in the 1200s as a Romanesque Hallenkirche (hall church) and was enlarged and modified around 1398 into a cross-shaped basilica. The huge tower wasn't completed until the late 1700s. Inside the church are an enormous organ dating from 1770 and an astronomical clock originally built in the late 1400s and reconfigured in 1643. The Marien-Kirche is open Monday to Saturday 10am to 5pm. Sunday worship is at 10am, after which the church closes for the rest of the day, except for the period from July to September, when it remains open every Sunday from 11:45am to 5pm. Admission for adults is 1€ (90¢); .50€ (45¢) for students and kids under 18.

Other churches to be seen include the **Heilig-Kreuz-Kirche (Church of the Holy Cross),** a Gothic Hallenkirche with three naves (or aisles), built of brick in the 14th century. In the Cistercian convent associated with this church is the **Kultur-Historisches Museum** ★, Universitätsplatz (✆ **0381/203590**), containing medieval religious paintings and sacred art. It's open Tuesday to Sunday 10am to 6pm. Entrance costs 2€ ($1.80) for adults, 1€ (90¢) for children.

**Schiffahrtsmuseum (Navigational Museum)** ★, August-Bebel-Strasse 1, at the corner of Richard-Wagner-Strasse (✆ **0381/25-20-60**), contains exhibits related to the nautical history of one of Germany's most important seaports, beginning with the Vikings and focusing on the great maritime developments of the 19th and early 20th centuries. It's open Tuesday to Sunday 10am to 6pm. Admission is 3€ ($2.70) for adults; 1€ (90¢) for students and persons under 18, free for children under 6.

Rostock's **tourist office,** 3 Neuer Markt (✆ **0381/19433**), is open October to May, Monday to Friday 10am to 5pm and Saturday 10am to 4pm; June to September, Monday to Friday 10am to 7pm and Saturday and Sunday 10am to 4:30pm. The tourist office can provide information on any boat tours that might be offered at the time of your visit.

## WHERE TO STAY

**Courtyard by Marriott** ★ With a chain-linked name like this, you'd expect to encounter such a hotel near the airport outside Atlanta. Not so in Rostock. An up-to-date and modern hotel has been created within an 1800s mansion in the historic Altstadt, convenient to most of the city's attractions. The location, though most central, is still tranquil at this four-story hotel. Most of its guests are business travelers, but it's also ideal for the sightseer as well. Of all the hotels in the area, this one has the greatest number of amenities, with luxuries once unheard of in a hotel in the old East Germany. Bedrooms are attractively furnished and midsize, each with tiled bathrooms and shower-tub combinations.

Kropeliner/Schwaansche Strasse 6, 18055 Rostock. ✆ **0381/49700.** Fax 0381/497-0700. www.courtyard.com. 150 units. 80€–110€ ($71.45–$98.25) double; from 155€ ($138.40) suite. AE, DC, MC, V. Free parking. Tram: 11 or 12. **Amenities:** Restaurant; bar; sauna; car rental desk; room service; babysitting; laundry/dry cleaning. *In room:* A/C, TV, minibar, hair dryer, iron.

**Hotel Verdi** Small-scale and cozy, this family-run hotel occupies a much-modernized baroque house, painted yellow, in the city's historic core, immediately adjacent to one of the city's tallest churches, Petri Kirche. Bedrooms are comfortable but unfrilly, each equipped with a writing desk, comfortable beds, a small bathroom with shower, and a contemporary, uncontroversial, international-looking decor. No meals are served other than breakfast, although the staff will direct you to any of several nearby restaurants.

Wollenweberstrasse 28, D-18055 Rostock. ✆ **0381/252-240.** Fax 0381/252-2429. www.hotel-verdi.de. 11 units. 70€–83€ ($62.50–$74.10) double; 77€–87€ ($68.75–$77.70) suites for 2 with kitchen; 102€–127€ ($91.10–$113.40) suites for 4 with kitchen. Parking 7€ ($6.25). AE, MC, V. Tram: 11 or 12. **Amenities:** Laundry service. *In-room:* TV, minibar.

**Steigenberger Hotel Sonne** ★ One of Germany's most prestigious hotel chains has invaded Rostock to give Courtyard by Marriott a race for supremacy. So far, they're in a neck-and-neck battle. Both are ideal for business travelers or sightseers. Steigenberger has exceptional style for the area and the best service by a well-trained staff in town. Set almost in the exact center of town, most of its bedrooms open onto views of the rooftops of the old city. Bedrooms are midsize to spacious, with gleaming modern bathrooms with tub/shower combinations. The dining facilities are more extensive here than at Courtyard by Marriott, including two restaurants, a bar, and a cafe, each offering regional, vegetarian, and international dishes. Rooms are spread across five well-groomed floors.

Neuer Markt 2, 18055 Rostock. ✆ **0381/49730.** Fax 0381/4973351. www.hotel-sonne-rostock.de. 134 units. 100€–175€ ($89.30–$156.30) double; 150€–304€ ($133.95–$271.45) suite. AE, DC, MC, V. Free parking. Tram: 11 or 12. **Amenities:** 2 restaurants; bar/lounge; cafe; sauna; steambath; on-site massage; solarium; fitness center; babysitting; laundry/dry cleaning. *In room:* A/C, TV, minibar, hairdryer, safe.

## WHERE TO DINE

**Mond und Sterne** *Value* NORTHERN GERMAN/FISH/GAME This restaurant packs them in because of its well-prepared cuisine and its no-frills, rib-sticking food, rich with Baltic tradition. The decor is inspired by the old Hanseatic League, with timber beams and brass lighting fixtures. The restaurant offers steaming bowls of *Leberknödel* (liver dumplings) soup and goulash soup, platters of fried pork or veal schnitzels, and several preparations of herring and cod. A house specialty is a *Kontor Pfanne,* combining steaks of pork, veal, and beef into one pan that's carried directly to your table, accompanied with vegetables, bacon, herb-flavored butter, and potatoes. Another chef's specialty is *Edelfischteller Mond und Stern,* a platter of four Baltic fish, sautéed and then served with potatoes and chives. This traditional Baltic dish, popular in Denmark as well, is associated with civic and regional culinary pride.

Strandstrasse 85 (on the harbor). ✆ **0381/4-59-03-44.** Reservations recommended. Main courses 8.90€–15€ ($7.95–$13.40). AE, MC, V. Daily 11am–3:30pm and 5pm–midnight. Tram: Lange Strasse.

**Zur Kogge** *Finds* GERMAN Set immediately adjacent to the harbor, this is the oldest sailors' pub and restaurant in Rostock. It's decorated with all kinds of nautical marine items, either placed on shelves or hanging from the ceiling. Friday and Saturday, there's live music—the German version of New England sea chanteys. Naturally, fish specialties are the chef's best items. Try the *Mecklenburger Fischsuppe* (fish soup) or the various versions of smoked fish.

Wokrenterstrasse 27 (on the harbor). ✆ **0381/4-93-44-93.** Reservations required at night. Main courses 7.90€–14.30€ ($7.05–$12.75). MC, V. Daily 11:30am–11pm. Tram: Lange Strasse.

## FROM ROSTOCK TO STRALSUND

To continue our tour of Germany's Baltic coast from Rostock, drive northeast from the center of town along the E22 highway (also called Rte. 105), heading for the next major destination, Stralsund, about 72km (45 miles) away. Off the highway at any of about five different junctions are some half-dozen seafront towns, each permeated with the scents and salt air of the Baltic. Many are attractive and, to an increasing degree, open for resort business.

Consider breaking up your trip with a visit to one of the best of these towns, **Ribnitz-Damgarten,** about 26km (16 miles) northeast of Rostock, right beside the E22 highway. Its architectural highlight is the **Rostocker Tor,** an imposing tower that symbolized the town for many generations. Most visitors opt for only a brief exploration of Ribnitz before continuing on their journey. The **Tourist Information Office** in Ribnitz-Damgarten is at Am Markt 1 (✆ **03821/2201**). It's open Monday to Friday 9am to 5pm.

From Ribnitz, continue driving east along E22/Route 105 until you reach Stralsund.

## 4 Stralsund ★

72km (45 miles) NE of Rostock

Stralsund has one of the best natural harbors in the Baltic. The town is separated from the island of Rügen by a narrow sea channel, the Strait of Bodden, and makes its living mainly from shipyards, fishing fleets, and, to an increasing degree, tourism. Stralsund boasts a picturesque network of canals, coves, and lakes, as well as more half-timbered 19th-century houses and a more intact sense of history than many other cities on Germany's Baltic coast.

During the 1200s, it was rivaled in the Hanseatic League only by Lübeck and enjoyed a rich trade with many of the other cities around the Baltic basin. Perhaps because of its success, the town has been invaded repeatedly throughout its long history, by armies from Denmark, Sweden, Holland, Napoleonic France, Prussia, and, in May 1945, the Soviet Union. By the mid-1960s, much of the inner core of Stralsund had been faithfully rebuilt by the Communist local government, though some historic structures remain.

Many visitors use Stralsund as the takeoff point for the flat and sandy Baltic island of Rügen (see the next section below), which is joined to Stralsund by a 2km (1¼-mile) bridge.

### SEEING THE SIGHTS

Buildings of historic interest include a series of medieval defenses whose ramparts are best viewed on the town's western edge. Also important is the 13th-century **Rathaus** ★, Alter Markt (✆ **03831/25-20**), one of the most imposing examples of the North German secular brick Gothic architecture. Under reconstruction at this writing, it cannot be visited.

Stralsund's other attractions are mostly ecclesiastical buildings. **St. Nikolaikirche** ★, Alter Markt (✆ **03831/29-71-99**), with an entrance on Badenstrasse, whose design was based on models in Lübeck, has a very high nave that was built in the 13th and 14th centuries in the Hallenkirche style. This is the most beautiful church in town. It's open year-round Monday to Friday 10am to 5pm; Saturday 10am to 4pm, Sunday from around the end of Sunday services (around noon) to 4pm. Entrance is free. Also of interest is the **Marienkirche** ★, Neuer Markt (✆ **03831/29-89-65**), with an entrance on Bleistrasse. It was begun in the late 1200s and had a soaring tower added to it in the mid-1400s. Open Monday to Saturday 10am to 5pm; Sunday 11:30am to noon, and 2 to 4pm. If you don't mind climbing 349 steps, you'll be rewarded with a view of the old town, the coastline, and Rügen Island. It costs 2€ ($1.80) for adults to climb the tower, 1€ (90¢) for students and persons under 18. Another church, the **Jacobikirche** on Böttcherstrasse (✆ **0381/29-04-46**), was transformed into a three-nave basilica in the 14th century. It has a high altar with baroque mountings and paintings by J. H. Tischbein, one of the foremost ecclesiastical artists of his day. Today, it's used for a changing array of art exhibitions, concerts, and theatrical productions that change every season. A recent, much-applauded production was *Jesus Christ Superstar.* The gothic, brick-sided **Heiligengeistkirche (Church of the Holy Ghost),** on Wasserstrasse (✆ **03831/29-04-46**), is noteworthy for its severely dignified, somewhat plain decor, and an inner courtyard that's ringed with wooden galleries. It's open daily from 8am to noon, and from 3 to 5pm. Admission is free.

Stralsund's cultural museum, **Kulturhistorisches Museum,** Mönchstrasse 25–27 (✆ **03831/28790**), contains medieval sacred art and Stralsund-related historical exhibits. It's open Tuesday to Sunday 10am to 5pm (till 6pm between

June and Sept). Depending on what special exhibition is on view at the time of your arrival, admission costs 2.50€ to 7€ ($2.25–$6.25) for adults and 1.50€ to 3.50€ ($1.35–$3.15) for students and persons under 18. There's also the **Deutsches Museum für Meereskunde und Fischerei (Oceanographic Museum and Aquarium)** ★, Mönchstrasse 25 (✆ **03831/26500**), in a complex of buildings originally part of a 15th-century abbey, the Katharinenkloster. The museum features exhibitions pertaining to the sea life of the Baltic and the distillation of its seawater into salt during the Middle Ages. A very large 42,000l (11,000 gal.) aquarium, containing exhibitions of tropical fish, is housed in the cloister's medieval crypt. The complex is open November to April, Tuesday to Sunday 10am to 5pm; May, June, September, and October, daily 10am to 5pm; and July and August, Monday to Thursday 9am to 6pm and Friday to Sunday 10am to 5pm. Admission 4.50€ ($4) for adults and 3€ ($2.70) for students and persons under 18. Children under 6 enter free.

For more information, contact the **tourist office,** Alter Markt 9 at Ossenreierstrasse (✆ **03831/2-46-90**). It's open Monday to Friday 10am to 6pm, Saturday 9am to 4pm, and Sunday 10am to 2pm. It's closed Sundays between October and April.

## WHERE TO STAY

**An den Bleichen Garni** *Value* This 1993 hotel is a three-story, family-run establishment similar to many that have blossomed across Germany's eastern region since reunification. Rooms and bathrooms are rather small but still quite comfortable; everything is neatly maintained by the hardworking on-site owners. Rooms come equipped with neatly kept bathrooms containing shower-tub combinations. No meals are served other than breakfast, but many restaurants are within a short walk.

An den Bleichen 45 (a 10-min. walk west of the historic center), 18435 Stralsund. ✆ **03831/39-06-75.** Fax 03831/39-21-53. 23 units. 66€–72€ ($58.95–$64.30) double. Rates include buffet breakfast. AE, MC, V. Bus: 6. **Amenities:** Breakfast room; bar; lounge. *In room:* TV.

**Dorint im Hanseldom Stralsund** ★★ The finest hotel in town is known primarily for its leisure and recreation park, linked directly to the hotel. This is Northern Germany's largest center for fitness, sport, recreation, and health. The hotel is a first-class operation bringing refined comfort and elegance to this area of Germany. To emphasize the resort's coastal location, every room has a red-and white-striped lighthouse standing 2m (6 ft.) tall that encases a TV and minibar. Each midsize to spacious bedroom offers a maritime decor, with a small bathroom with tub-and-shower combination. The hotel restaurant, Vineta, is excellent, with many regional dishes of the Mediterranean. The hotel has a beauty center called Light of Fez, evocative of the Sahara. The guarantee is that if you check in ugly, you'll emerge beautiful. Beauty treatments range from a "mental relaxation zone" to a Moorish bathhouse. The location of the hotel is a 10-minute walk from the historic center of town.

Grünhuger Bogen 18–20, 18437 Stralsund. ✆ **03831/3773-0.** Fax 03831/3773-100. www.dorint.de/stralsund. 114 units. 100€–120€ ($89.30–$107.15) double, 160€–205€ ($142.90–$183.05) suite. AE, DC, MC, V. Bus: 3. **Amenities:** Restaurant; bar; health spa; room service; babysitting; laundry/dry cleaning. *In room:* TV, minibar, hair dryer; safe.

**Schlosspark-Hotel Hohendorf** ★★ *Value* One of our favorite stopovers along the Baltic is this historic 18th-century castle converted into an elegant country hotel that's set adjacent to the marshlands north of the city. It was designed by Karl Friedrich Schinkel, a legendary name among Prussian architects. Much of the old glamor has been retained in its conversion to a hotel of first-class comfort. Rooms tend to be a bit smallish, but each has been carefully and comfortably decorated in a traditional style; each accommodation different. Each bedroom comes with a well-kept bathroom with all modern fixtures, including a tub and shower. Completely renovated in 1993, the castle stands on 2.8 hectares (7 acres) of landscaped parkland, about 1.6km (1 mile) from the Baltic. The restaurant here serves an excellent regional cuisine, and in summer, there is also an outdoor café.

Am Park 7, 18445 Hohendorf. ✆ **038323/2500.** Fax 038323/25061. www.schlosspark-hotel-hohendorf.de. 42 units. 75€–85€ ($67–$75.90) double, 100€ ($89.30) suite. AE, MC, V. Bus: (marked) Hohendorf. **Amenities:** Restaurant; outdoor cafe; 2 tennis courts; sauna; solarium; bike rentals; room service; on-site massage; babysitting; laundry/dry cleaning. *In room:* TV.

## WHERE TO DINE

**Hansekeller** GERMAN Noted for its fine 15th-century architecture, and capped with brick and masonry vaults, this is one of the most atmospheric restaurants in town (you can see part of the kitchen from the dining room). The venue is cozy and comfortable, with leather banquettes and antique statues, some which might have functioned as the sculpted prows of sailing ships, fastened to the very old brick and masonry walls. Many of the locals here opt for the kind of food they remember from their childhoods. Examples include marinated filets of herring in cream sauce, served with coarse black pumpernickel bread; filet of turbot or sole served with a mustard-flavored herb sauce; and roasted cutlets—either lamb or pork—with sauerkraut. In late autumn and winter, look for game dishes, especially venison.

Mönchstrasse 48. ✆ **03831/703840.** Reservations recommended. Main courses 15€–25€ ($13.40–$22.35). AE, MC, V. Daily 11am–midnight. Bus: 6.

**Wulflamstuben** ★ *Finds* NORTHERN GERMAN This restaurant, established in 1991 within the historic walls of a town monument (the Wulflamhaus), dates from 1370. It's set on the ground floor and features a carefully preserved decor of ornate carvings and old-fashioned engravings of local folklore and architecture. In many ways, this place is a civic showcase of the town's culinary bounty. The focus is almost exclusively on the food of Mecklenburg and Lower Pomerania. Menu items include *Stralsunder Aal Suppe* (eel soup in the style of Stralsund), *Eisbein* (pigs' knuckles), stuffed goose in the style of Mecklenburg, and roast duckling stuffed with apples, black bread, and plums. There's also a choice of fish from local waters.

Alter Markt 5 (within the Wulflamhaus). ✆ **03831/29-15-33.** Reservations recommended. Main courses 9€–15€ ($8.05–$13.40). DC, MC, V. Daily 11am–11pm. Bus: 3.

## 5 Rügen ★

4km (2½ miles) NE of Stralsund

Rügen is the largest island in Germany, but in many ways, it's more Scandinavian than German in its climate, flavor, and feel. Riddled with saltwater lagoons and radically indented coves and harbors, it lies just off the northwestern coast of what used to be Pomeranian Prussia, joined to the town of Stralsund by an interconnected string, 3km (2 miles) long, of dikes, small islets, and bridges. (There's no toll.) From north to south, the island of Rügen stretches 51km (32 miles), covering a landmass of 927 sq. km (358 sq. miles)—mostly scrubland, windswept forests, and dunes.

Don't come here for monuments or museums; nature is the main attraction, as well as seaside bathing (often nude) in summer. Highlights include geological features such as the chalk cliffs of Stubbenkammer and the Königstuhl Rock on the island's northeastern tip. Kap (Cape) Arkona, a Baltic Gibraltar, is the most northerly point of what used to be East Germany.

## EXPLORING THE ISLAND

Of architectural interest is **Schloss Spyker (Spycher Castle),** Schlossallee, 18551 Spyker (✆ **038302/5-33-83;** fax 038302/53-386), a baronial building now functioning (somewhat erratically) as a restaurant and hotel. The island's most unusual building is the **Jagdschloss Granitz (Granitz Hunting Lodge),** in the village of Binz (✆ **038393/22-63**), an ornate neofeudal castle built in 1836 by Prince Wilhelm Malte I of Putbus. One of its most unusual features is a corkscrew-inspired stone staircase winding gracefully up 154 steps to the top of the building's massive central tower. The lodge is open October to April, Tuesday to Sunday 10am to 4pm; May to September, daily 9am to 6pm. Admission costs 3€ ($2.70) for adults and 1.50€ ($1.35) for children.

Although the island's capital is Bergen, most of the population is centered around the seasonal coastal resorts of Ostseebad Göhren, Ostseebad Baabe, Ostseebad Sellin, and Ostseebad Binz, all of which lie on the island's eastern edge. Of the above-mentioned villages, Ostseebad Binz (referred to locally simply as Binz) is the most interesting and most charming. Of special interest to bird-watchers are the shores of the island's vast inland sea, beautiful **Jasmunder Bodden.**

For **tourist information** on the island, go to the office at Markt 23 in Bergen (✆ **03838/25-60-95**). Most of the year, it's open Monday to Friday 10am to 6pm. (In July and Aug, it's open Mon–Sat 9am–7pm.)

## WHERE TO STAY & DINE

**Hotel Nordperd** Set on a low cliff above the water, this four-story, four-star hotel is one of the best on the island. Originally built as a private home in 1809, and enlarged throughout its lifetime with two modern annexes from the mid-1980s, it offers modern design and simple comfort. Many rooms have coastal views; all have streamlined furniture. Rooms come equipped with bathrooms containing shower-tub combinations. There's a restaurant on the premises that offers well-prepared regional food even when virtually everything else on Rügen is closed (this is the last place to close at the end of the season and the first place to open in the still-chilly spring). There's access to a private beach, which guests navigate via a set of stairs leading down along the cliff face to the water.

Nordperdstrasse 11, 18586 Göhren-Rügen. ✆ **038308/70.** Fax 038308/71-60. www.tc-hotels.de. 95 units. 73€–105€ ($65.20–$93.75) double. Rates include buffet breakfast. AE, DC, MC, V. Closed: Dec–March. **Amenities:** Restaurant; lounge; room service (7am–10pm). *In room:* TV.

**Steigenberger Resort Hotel Rügen** ★ *Kids* One of the grander choices on the island is this member of a first-class and deluxe chain hotel. The resort stands on its own 35 hectares (85 acre) site adjacent to Jasmund National Park, renowned for its chalk cliffs. It offers more facilities than anything else on island. Rooms are attractively furnished, with good-size bathrooms spotlessly maintained with shower-tub combinations. The children's center makes it a good choice for families. Don't come here imagining convenient access to a beach, however. The nearest one is 6.5km (4 miles) away, accessible via free shuttle buses

### *Moments* Storming the Gibraltar of the Baltic

The coast of Rügen contains some of the island's finest scenic beauty. To get to Kap (or Cape) Arkona, the Baltic Gibraltar, go northeast from Bergen on Route 96, until you come to a small secondary road signposted Kap Arkona. A lighthouse (*Leuchtturm Arkona)* stands at the cape, next to a restored watchtower, which you can climb for a view of the Danish island of Moen. Inside, there's a small museum, showcasing the role of the lighthouse and its construction. It's open daily from 10am to 6pm. Entrance costs 1.50€ ($1.35) for adults, .75€ (65¢) for persons under 18 and students. Free for children under 6. Near the lighthouse stand the ruins of the ancient fortress of Jarosmarburg, constructed by the Slavs but destroyed by invading Vikings in 1168. All around the cape, chalky cliffs rise to 51m (170 ft.) above the water.

After viewing the cape, drive back to Route 96, but instead of returning immediately to Bergen, follow this route east (it's signposted) to another end of the line, the towering chalky cliffs of Stubbenkammer, which lie 10km (6 miles) north of the small port of Sassnitz. Stubbenkammer is one of the most photographed sights on the island. From here, a steep trail leads down to a Baltic Beach.

that go back and forth at 20-minute intervals, as needed. This is very much an escape-from-urban-stress kind of hotel, with lots of focus on the isolated location and appreciation of the lonely, windswept Baltic topography it occupies.

Neddesitz 4, 18551 Sagard-Rügen. ✆ **038302/95.** Fax 038302/966-20. www.ruegen.steigenberger.de. 145 units. 66€–130€ ($58.95–$116.10) double; 90€–150€ ($80.35–$133.95) suite. Discounts granted for stays of 3 nights or more. AE, DC, MC, V. **Amenities:** 4 restaurants; 2 bars; 2 pools (1 indoor, 1 outdoor, both interconnected); fitness center; steam room; children's center; room service; massage; babysitting; laundry/dry cleaning. *In room:* A/C, TV, minibar, hair dryer.

**Vier Jahreszeiten** An elegant, stately, and white-painted resort that was originally built as a private villa around 1900, this landmark hotel enjoys a tranquil location at the beach along the *Schmachter See* (Schmacht Lake) and is set against the backdrop of the Granitz Woods. Rooms are brightly furnished and generally spacious, each with windows opening onto views of the woods, and each renovated in 2001–02. Each comes with a well-appointed, midsize bathroom with tub-and-shower combination, and most contain at least some of the old-fashioned furniture that decorated its rooms many generations ago The hotel restaurant is elegantly appointed and serves some of the best food on the island. Consider dining here even if you're not a guest of the hotel.

Zeppelinstrasse 8, 18609 Binz-Rügen. ✆ **038393/500.** Fax 038393/504-30. www.hotel-vier-jahreszeiten.de. 77 units. 80€–165€ ($71.45–$147.35) double; 180€–220€ ($160.75–$196.45) suite. Rates include breakfast. AE, MC, V. **Amenities:** Restaurant; bar; pool; tennis court; fitness center; sauna; solarium; room service. *In room:* TV, hair dryer.

# Appendix A: Germany in Depth

This appendix will introduce you to Germany's history, artistic and cultural traditions, and cuisine. We've also recommend some books in chapter 3, "Planning Your Trip to Germany," beginning on p. 59 to help you get even better acquainted with this fascinating country.

## 1 History 101

### EARLY DAYS

"A large build, very strong in the attack, but not suitable to the same extent for heavy work" was how Tacitus, the Roman historian, described the Teutons in A.D. 60. The Romans had been trying to push the borders of their empire up to the Rhineland, with mixed success, since 9 B.C., but the Teutonic tribes fought back ferociously. The first recognized German national hero was Arminius, who led his tribe (the Cherusci) in defeating three Roman legions near modern-day Bielefeld in A.D. 9.

After the deterioration of the Roman Empire, the Franks ruled much of what we now know as Germany. In 800, a Frankish king, Charlemagne, extended the Carolingian Empire from the Pyrenees to Saxony and Bavaria. His rule marks the high point of cultural and political development of that period. He divided the empire into counties, each with an administrator directly responsible to him, and promoted education, scholarship, and the revival of Greek and Roman culture.

### THE HOLY ROMAN EMPIRE

After Charlemagne's death, the Carolingian Empire fell apart. In 843, the Treaty of Verdun granted the empire's eastern territory to Louis the German, marking the beginning of German history.

#### Dateline

- **9 B.C.–A.D. 9** Romans attempt to conquer Teutonic tribes.
- **486** Clovis founds Frankish kingdom, ruling from Paris.
- **496** Franks are converted to Christianity.
- **800** Pope crowns Charlemagne in Rome.
- **962** Pope crowns Otto I as Holy Roman Emperor.
- **1152–90** Frederick Barbarossa's reign leads to a greater centralization of power, but his invasion of Italy is beaten back by the Lombard League.
- **1158** Munich founded by Henry the Lion, duke of Saxony.
- **1241** Hanseatic League founded to protect the trade of such cities as Bremen, Hamburg, and Lübeck.
- **1432** Maximilian I, "last of the German knights," becomes Holy Roman Emperor, marking the beginning of the hegemony of the Hapsburgs.
- **1456** Johannes Guttenberg prints the first book in Europe using movable type.
- **1517** Martin Luther nails his "Ninety-Five Theses" to a church door in Wittenberg, beginning the Protestant Reformation in Germany.
- **1618–48** Thirty Years' War devastates Germany, as Protestant forces defeat Catholic Hapsburgs.
- **1740–86** Prussian might grows under Frederick the Great in the Age of Enlightenment.

*continues*

In 962, the pope officially recognized Otto I as Emperor of what was later called the Holy Roman Empire. This new political entity was formed both to impose unity on the European political world and to create a bulwark against the invasion of non-Christian tribes. It claimed direct links both to the grandeur of ancient Rome and to the more contemporary might of the Church.

Unity, however, did not prevail. The empire splintered into a bickering alliance of dukedoms, bishoprics, and principalities. The emperor's authority was often dependent on German nobles and the pope. A capital city that could have served as a center of power was never established—the monarch would simply move from one city to another, mustering an army and collecting revenue wherever he could—so the possibilities for dynastic intrigues were endless. In subsequent jockeying, the church itself was a voracious competitor for power. This power struggle broke out into open conflict in 1076, when Pope Gregory VII excommunicated the emperor Henry IV, who was forced to stand barefoot in the snow outside Canossa, humiliated, awaiting a repeal.

To strengthen their position as the Holy Roman Empire declined, the emperors turned to alliances with the wealthy, independent trading ports to the north and east, under the federation of the Hanseatic League. Such German cities as Hamburg, Lübeck, and Bremen grew in both economic and political power. Eventually the league controlled trade as far as Novgorod in Russia.

## THE REFORMATION & THE RELIGIOUS WARS

When an Augustinian monk, Martin Luther, nailed his theological and political complaints to a church door in Wittenberg in 1517, he set off a political and religious wildfire that

- **1806** Armies of Napoléon invade Prussia, which is incorporated briefly into the French Empire.
- **1813** Prussians defeat Napoléon at Leipzig.
- **1815** At the Congress of Vienna, the German Confederation of 39 independent states is created.
- **1862** Otto von Bismarck (1815–98) becomes prime minister of Prussia.
- **1870–71** Germany invades and defeats France in the Franco-Prussian War.
- **1871** Wilhelm I is crowned emperor of the newly created German Empire; Bismarck becomes chancellor.
- **1890** Bismarck is dismissed by Kaiser Wilhelm II, who launches an aggressive foreign policy.
- **1907** Russia, Great Britain, and France form the Triple Entente, against the Triple Alliance of Germany, Austria-Hungary, and Italy.
- **1914** Assassination of Archduke Franz Ferdinand launches World War I.
- **1918** Germany is forced to sign the Treaty of Versailles, accepting responsibility for starting World War I.
- **1923** Hitler's "Beer Hall Putsch," a rightist revolt, fails in Munich.
- **1925** Hitler publishes *Mein Kampf.*
- **1926** Germany is admitted to the League of Nations, in the heyday of the Weimar Republic.
- **1933** Hitler becomes chancellor.
- **1934** President von Hindenburg dies and Hitler declares himself Führer (leader) of the Third Reich.
- **1935** Nürnberg Laws deprive Jews of citizenship and forbid marriage between Jews and non-Jewish Germans.
- **1936** Summer Olympic Games held in Berlin; Winter Games held at Garmisch-Partenkirchen; Germany militarizes the Rhineland in violation of the Treaty of Versailles; and Hitler signs agreements with Italy and Japan to form the Axis.
- **1938** Germany occupies Austria and the Sudetenland in Czechoslovakia.
- **1939** Hitler signs a non-aggression pact with the Soviet Union in August and invades Poland on September 1, launching World War II. After a Blitzkrieg, Hitler and Stalin carve up Poland.

spread across the landscape of Europe. He was not the first religious reformer; in the early 15th century, John Wyclif had translated the Bible into English, and Jan Hus of Prague had become a martyr to his beliefs at the Council of Constance. However, the fragmented political situation in Germany played into Luther's hands: For every prince who condemned him, he could find one to protect him. Luther's Reformation fanned the flames around Germany's political factions. The new conflict between Catholics and Protestants set the stage for the devastation of the Thirty Years' War (1618–48), which only entrenched the divided sensibilities of the splintered German nation.

The only powerful German state to emerge from these conflicts was the little kingdom of Prussia, in the northeast on the Baltic Sea. The rise of Prussian power continued throughout the 18th century until, led by that talented soldier and patron of the Enlightenment, Frederick the Great, Prussia became a major kingdom, with Berlin as its capital.

## NAPOLÉON ARRIVES

After the French Revolution, Napoléon and his new political ideas swept across Europe. The left bank of the Rhine came under French control. Under these pressures, the Holy Roman Empire officially came to an end in 1806. Around the same time, Napoléon's armies invaded Prussia, making it, for a brief time, a part of the French Empire. But Napoléon was defeated at Leipzig in 1813, and 2 years later, Britain and Prussia crushed him forever at the Battle of Waterloo.

## BISMARCK & PRUSSIA

The Congress of Vienna (1814–15) redrew the map of Germany after Napoléon's defeat, giving more territory to Prussia, but making Austria the leader in a German Confederation.

- **1940** Nazi troops overrun Denmark, then take Norway in fierce fighting. The Low Countries, Belgium, and France fall to Hitler. Hitler's Battle of Britain fails to bomb London into submission.
- **1941** Hitler orders the invasion of the Soviet Union in June, ending the Hitler-Stalin pact. The Nazi empire, at its peak, stretches from the Sahara Desert to the Arctic Circle. Hitler declares war on America after the Japanese attack Pearl Harbor.
- **1942–43** War starts to go against the Germans, with significant defeats in Stalingrad and North Africa.
- **1944** Eisenhower conducts the invasion of Normandy: The reconquest of Europe has begun. The Third Reich's final major offensive, the Battle of the Bulge, fails in December.
- **1945** Allies cross the Rhine, as Soviets advance toward Berlin. Hitler commits suicide. The Third Reich endures not for 1,000 years, but for 12. Germany sues for peace.
- **1945** The Yalta Conference divides Germany into zones of occupation. Germany is in ruins.
- **1948–49** The Soviet Union attempts to exclude the Allies from Berlin by blockade; the city is saved by a massive airlift.
- **1949** Soviets establish the German Democratic Republic (East Germany); Konrad Adenauer becomes chancellor of newly established Federal Republic of Germany (West Germany).
- **1950** West Germany's "economic miracle" begins to take hold.
- **1958** West Germany becomes a founding member of the European Economic Community (now European Union).
- **1961** The Berlin Wall divides the city.
- **1972** Summer Olympic Games in Munich are marred by a terrorist attack that kills 11 Israeli athletes.
- **1985** West Germany joins the Group of Seven (G7) organization of the world's greatest industrial powers.
- **1989** Refugees from East Germany flood into West Germany; Communist power collapses in the east, and the Berlin Wall comes down.

*continues*

During this time, there was a rising spirit of nationalism, exploited to good effect by Prince Otto von Bismarck when he became Prussia's prime minister in 1862. Prussia triumphed in the Austro-Prussian War of 1866, and after the subsequent Franco-Prussian War (1870–71), when Prussia laid siege to Paris, Bismarck succeeded in his goal of unification. Wilhelm I was made emperor of all Germany in 1871, and a strong, unified Germany at last took shape. Under Bismarck's leadership, Germany adopted an advanced social welfare system and brought its military and industrial production, as well as technical and scientific achievements, to new heights.

- **1990** East Germany and West Germany unite.
- **1991** Berlin is chosen as the capital of the united Germany.
- **1992** Unemployment and disillusionment sweep across the former East Germany as unification costs mount.
- **1995** Bundestag approves German participation in the NATO Bosnia mission.
- **1997** German government and private companies tally up the cost of rebuilding eastern Germany: $1 trillion U.S. dollars to date.
- **1998** Chancellor Kohl is defeated in election, bowing to Gerhard Schroeder.
- **1999** The German seat of government is returned to Berlin.
- **2000** Christian Democrats shaken by political scandals; Germany pledges $5.2 billion to aid Nazi victims.
- **2001** Chancellor Schroeder presides over restoration of German power in Europe and the country's change from deutschmark to euro.
- **2002** Germany abandons its post-war backseat military role and declares a more "muscular" policy. It also participates in U.S.-led strikes against terrorist bases.

## WORLD WAR I

By 1907, Europe was divided into two armed camps: the Triple Alliance (Germany, Austria-Hungary, and Italy) and the Triple Entente (France, Great Britain, and Russia). The match that ignited the powder keg was struck at Sarajevo in 1914, with the assassination of Archduke Franz Ferdinand, heir to the throne of the Austro-Hungarian Empire. The subsequent German invasion of France launched the bloodiest war the world had ever seen. A new and particularly demoralizing form of battle known as "trench warfare" produced staggering casualties. On August 8, 1918, the Triple Entente (also known as "the Allies"), now joined by the United States, penetrated German lines, and the German high command realized that the situation was hopeless.

In an attempt to get more favorable treatment from the Allies, the Germans voluntarily declared a parliamentary democracy, ending the reign of the kaiser. Despite that concession, in 1918 Germany was forced to sign the humiliating Treaty of Versailles, which demanded the surrender of strategic territories including Alsace-Lorraine, just west of the Rhine. The Allies—especially the French—also demanded huge monetary reparations.

## WEIMAR REPUBLIC

In 1919, the National Assembly met in Weimar to draw up a new constitution, which at the time was hailed as the most progressive in the world. But in defeated and humiliated postwar Germany, extremists from both the left and the right launched savage attacks against the inexperienced and idealistic government. The enormous payments demanded by the Allies crippled the German economy. When reparations from Germany couldn't be made, France retaliated by occupying the Ruhr, one of Germany's most valuable industrial resources. Inflation—perhaps the worst in history—destroyed what was left of the German economy.

## THE RISE OF NAZISM

This was just the right climate for the rise of Adolf Hitler and the Nazi Party. The Nazis believed in the superiority of the Aryan race and blamed non-Aryan elements, particularly Jews, for Germany's woes. At first Hitler's anti-Semitic, nationalist ideas failed to gain popular support, even with right-wingers. Nazi membership in the *Reichstag* (parliament) dropped from 25 in 1925 to only a dozen following the elections of 1928.

In 1932, Hitler lost the electoral race for president against the compromise candidate of the democratic parties, war hero Paul von Hindenburg. Nevertheless, Hitler's power increased, and on January 30, 1933, Hindenburg submitted to right-wing pressure and appointed him chancellor. Upon Hindenburg's death in 1934, Hitler declared himself *Führer* (leader) of a new German empire he called the "Third Reich." Protected by hastily drafted laws and regulations, he made his power absolute.

The horrors of unchecked Nazi rule lasted until 1945. The Gestapo, or secret police, launched one of the most notorious reigns of terror in history. Anyone whom the Nazis considered enemies, or simply undesirables—which included Communists, Social Democrats, homosexuals, political dissidents, Gypsies, and many others—were persecuted. Jews were disenfranchised, terrorized, deprived of property, and forced into ghettos and concentration camps.

On June 30, 1934, Hitler disposed of any opposing elements in his own party in the "Night of Long Knives," when hundreds were massacred, including Ernst Röhm, chief of his notorious Brownshirts. Heinrich Himmler's black-shirted *Schutzstaffel* (SS) became a powerful political force. Surrounded by adoring fans (or, at best, passive witnesses), Hitler now viewed his empire as a worthy successor to those of Charlemagne and Bismarck.

In 1936, Hitler remilitarized the Rhineland and signed agreements with Japan and fascist Italy, forming the Axis alliance. In 1938, he enforced the *Anschluss* (annexation) of Austria and marched triumphantly into the country of his birth. That same year, he occupied the German-speaking Sudetenland in Czechoslovakia, an act the other Western powers could not summon the will to oppose.

## WORLD WAR II

In late August 1939, Hitler signed a non-aggression pact with the Soviet Union that gave him free reign to launch an invasion of Poland, which he did on September 1. France and Britain, honoring their agreements with Poland, declared war on Germany. Germany scored early victories, and in one of the most stunning campaigns of the 20th century, invaded and occupied France in June 1940. In 1941, Hitler turned on the Soviet Union. Meeting at the Berlin suburb of Wannsee in 1942, the Nazi leadership formulated the implementation of the "final solution" to the "Jewish Question," the systematic extermination of millions of Jews. The mass murders of homosexuals, Gypsies, Communists, Slavs, and other undesirables were less systematic but also numbered in the millions.

Following Japan's attack on Pearl Harbor, Germany declared war on the United States on December 11, 1942. But after defeats in North Africa in 1942 and at Stalingrad in 1943, the recurrent theme became one of Nazi retreat. The D-Day landings along the coast of Normandy on June 6, 1944, began the steady advance of the Allied armies from the west, while Soviet armies relentlessly marched toward Berlin from the east. Hitler committed suicide in Berlin in April 1945. His country, along with much of Europe, lay in ruins.

## DIVISION OF GERMANY

At war's end, Germany and its capital city were divided. The nation shrank in size, losing long-held territories (among them East Prussia and Upper Silesia). The United States, Great Britain, France, and Soviet Union divided the country into four zones of occupation. Berlin, in the heart of the Soviet district, was also divided among the four powers. In the late 1940s, the Soviet Union tried to cut off all Allied access to Berlin, but a massive U.S.-sponsored airlift into the beleaguered city thwarted the attempt. In 1949, the Soviets established the German Democratic Republic (DDR) in their zone. In response, the Federal Republic of Germany was established in the American, British, and French zones. In 1961, the DDR sealed off its borders and erected the Berlin Wall, a stark symbol of the Cold War itself.

Throughout the 1960s, the financial world buzzed with the talk of an economic miracle in Germany. Led by Ludwig Erhard, the economist, this miracle was called *Wirtschaftswunder,* and it saw Germany rise to become the fourth largest economy in the world.

This era of prosperity also saw the rise of a young German leader, Willy Brandt. Along with his Social-Liberal Coalition, Brandt, as chancellor, brought about long-overdue reform, an overhaul of education, and much improvement in industrial relations. His controversial Eastern policy (*Ostpolitik*) improved relations with Soviet-dominated East Germany and other Communist countries to the east of Germany. His efforts in normalizing relations with the GDR brought Brandt the Nobel Prize of 1971.

The 1972 Summer Olympic Games were meant to show the entire world the bold new face of a radically rebuilt Munich. However, the terrorist attack on the Israeli athletes, and the collective murder of 11 of them, revived recollection of the recent past and left behind ambivalent memories.

Helmut Schmidt became chancellor in 1974, as West Germany continued to amaze the world with its economic muscle. Problems such as mounting unemployment remained, however, and in 1982, Helmut Kohl became the new German leader, pursuing welfare cuts, a tight-fisted money policy, and military cooperation with America. The Kohl era saw the rise of the Green Party as a political force, with the stated goals of disarmament and of protecting a fragile environment.

## FALL OF THE WALL & UNIFICATION

1989 was a year of change and turmoil. In the wake of the collapse of Communist power across eastern Europe, the Berlin Wall also fell. The following year was perhaps the most significant in postwar German history. The two German nations announced economic unification in July, followed by total unification—with its thousands of inherent problems and headaches—on October 3, 1990. In 1991, Parliament voted to quit Bonn, seat of the West German government, and reestablish the once-mighty capital of Berlin.

After the first heady period of reunification, disillusionment set in, especially in eastern Germany, which was riddled with unemployment and unrealized expectations. Resentment against immigrant workers led in some instances to violent neo-Nazi marches, bombings, and physical assaults. However, most Germans rose up in revulsion to condemn the ultra-rightists and the sporadic violence.

Psychological and emotional differences between the two zones were almost overwhelming, as were the vast disparities in industrial development. As the influential newspaper *Frankfurter Rundschau* editorialized, "The terms of east and west are not so much geographical expressions as they are descriptions of states of mind."

## GERMANY TODAY

Political scandal dominated headlines in Germany in 2000. The reputation of the Christian Democrat party was tarnished when former Chancellor Helmut Khol admitted to receiving more than $1 million in illicit donations. In the waning weeks of 1999, Germany sealed a historic agreement that resolved one of the gravest injustices left over from World War II, formally pledging to pay $5.2 billion in belated compensation to hundreds of thousands of Nazi-era slave workers and other victims of the Third Reich.

As the 21st century began, Germany, despite the enormous costs of reunification, is an economic powerhouse in the center of Europe. As a member of the European Union, NATO, and the G7 group of the world's industrial powers, Germany's influence extends throughout Europe and across the globe.

Chancellor Gerhard Schroeder is hailed as the most successful politician of Europe. He's already changed the political landscape of the country, governing as a center-right leader on a center-left ticket. As Germany moves deeper into the 21st century, Berlin has become the center of an undivided Continent. Of the three major European powers, including France and Great Britain, Germany appears to be the most dynamic. In fact, of all the members of the European Union, Germany more actively pursued the abandonment of national currencies such as it own historic Deutschmark and the adoption of the euro as the standard unit of currency for all EU countries. Many other countries, such as Great Britain, even though a member of the EU, still hold back. But many German economists have stated that the adoption of a single currency for Europe will lead to prosperity for all in a future "United States of Europe."

Homosexuals, once persecuted by the Nazis and sent to death camps along with Jews and Gypsies, moved significantly forward in post-millennium Germany. In 2001, in spite of fierce opposition from some conservatives, same-sex partners won legal status in Germany. The law, announced in Germany's unofficial gay capital of Berlin, allows Gay couples to register their unions at government offices and requires a court decision for divorce. Same-sex couples will also receive inheritance and health insurance rights given to married spouses.

In the aftermath of World War II, Germany had become an economic giant, but remained a military midget. Because of its aggression in Hitler's war, Germany remained timid about any strong show of military force anywhere in the world. But Schroder, in 2001, announced a major change in military policy for Germany: In Berlin, he claimed that in the future, Germany would pursue a "more muscular policy." He pronounced as "irrevocably passed" the day when Germany would be economically powerful but militarily timid. The Chancellor stated from the Bundestag that now that Germany was reunited, it had to take on more responsibilities in the international community. As proof of his stated goal, Germany sent troops to aid the United States in its military strikes against terrorist bases in Taliban-controlled Afghanistan following the terrorist attacks against the United States on September 11, 2001.

# 2 In Pursuit of Musical Excellence

## MUSIC

Music is an important and pervasive facet of German life. German disunity over the centuries actually helped foster German music. The many small principalities and bishoprics that split up the German-speaking world meant that there were many courts to offer opportunities to musicians, both composers and instrumentalists. As a result, the German-speaking nations produced more composers of indisputable greatness than any other.

Today, the musical scene in Germany is as vibrant as ever. Every major city has an opera house and an orchestra, many of them world-renowned. New composers are encouraged, and productions are often at the cutting edge.

**MUSIC FESTIVALS** Major music festivals take place in the summer, but music lovers can pretty well take their pick all year of what they want to hear. The most famous festival, of course, is the **Bayreuth Festival,** instituted by Richard Wagner, which made the town of Bayreuth a musical landmark (unfortunately, tickets are very hard to come by). But all major cities, including Munich and Berlin, have music festivals throughout the year. Contact German tourist offices, within the country and abroad, for the latest information and dates.

Since reunification, **Dresden** has emerged as a major center for music. The Dresden Music Festivals, held each year at the end of May and the beginning of June, bring together not only local ensembles but prominent German and international artists. The Dresden Festival of Contemporary Music is presented in October. And a Dixieland Festival, a tradition since 1971, transforms Dresden into a city of jazz in May.

Other world-class festivals include the **Mozart Festival** at **Würzburg** in June, the **Berliner Festwochen** in September, and the **Jazz-Fest Berlin** in November.

**MUSICAL MUSEUMS** The true devotee of German music may want to visit cities and towns where the masters lived and wrote their music. Some of the homes of former composers have been turned into museums, such as the home of **Franz Liszt** in **Weimar** and of **Richard Wagner** in **Bayreuth.** To see where the great **Beethoven** lived, head for **Bonn.** Considering how many famous musicians lived and composed in Germany, however, the country has surprisingly few museums devoted to these great artists. Blame it on wartime devastation.

## A HISTORY OF GERMAN MUSIC

**BAROQUE MUSIC** The greatest composer of the baroque era was **Johann Sebastian Bach** (1685–1750), who was a supreme master of all musical forms of his time. Bach produced many church cantatas, especially for St. Thomas's Lutheran Church in Leipzig (see chapter 5), where he served as cantor. His compositions were technically outstanding, vigorous, and profound. Little of his music was published during his lifetime, but after his death, his influence steadily grew, especially that of his organ works. The musical tradition in his large family was maintained by two of his talented sons, Carl Philipp Emanuel Bach (1714–88) and Johann Christian Bach (1735–82). The Brandenburg Concertos are highly recommended.

Bach's contemporary **George Frideric Handel** (1685–1759) was another great composer. He first rose to prominence as musician of the court of Hannover, a post that he left to become composer at the court of St. James of England. He was a leading composer of operas and instrumental music for the court. Listen to his oratorio: *Messiah.*

**THE CLASSICAL PERIOD** **Wolfgang Amadeus Mozart** (1756–91), although an Austrian, cannot be omitted from any discussion of German music. His operas, with their contemporary themes and lively musical characterizations, paved the way for later composers. **Franz Joseph Haydn** (1732–1809), another Austrian, also exerted great influence on German music, especially instrumental music. Listen to: Mozart's *The Marriage of Figaro* and *Don Giovanni,* Haydn's "Drum Roll" Symphony no. 103.

**THE 19TH CENTURY & ROMANTICISM** The 19th century was rich in musical genius. **Ludwig van Beethoven** (1770–1827) ushered in romanticism. His works included symphonies, piano concertos, piano sonatas, quartets, and many others. He greatly expanded and developed the orchestra. Tragically, he completely lost his hearing in 1819. However, the chamber music he wrote after this event shows an even greater depth and complexity than his previous compositions. Listen to: Symphony no. 5 and no. 9.

Other great composers of the era include **Franz Schubert** (1797–1828), **Felix Mendelssohn** (1809–47), **Robert Schumann** (1810–56), and **Johannes Brahms** (1833–97). Listen to: Schubert's *Lieder,* Mendelssohn's *Overture to "A Midsummer Night's Dream,"* Schumann's "Scenes from Childhood," and Brahms's *German Requiem.*

The giant of the 19th-century opera world was **Richard Wagner** (1813–83). His theories of musical drama exerted a tremendous influence on everyone who followed him, even his detractors. His influence can best be heard in the music of the later romantic composer **Richard Strauss** (1864–1949). Strauss's operas carry Wagner's ideas of character development to greater psychological depth. Listen to: Wagner's *The Ring of the Nibelungs,* Strauss's *Salome* and *Elektra.*

**THE 20TH CENTURY** Musical experimentation flourished in early–20th century Germany. Austrian-born **Arnold Schoenberg** (1874–1951) developed the 12-tone system of musical structure. **Kurt Weill** (1900–50) and **Paul Hindemith** (1895–1963) tried to reach a more popular audience. During the Nazi era, many composers fled Germany. Others, like **Hans Pfitzner** (1869–1949) and **Richard Strauss** (1864–1949), remained in an uneasy relationship with the Nazis. Listen to: Schoenberg's *Five Pieces for Orchestra,* Weill's *Threepenny Opera,* Hindemith's *Mathis der Maler.* The music of Pfitzner is still heard around the world in such operas as *Palestrina* from 1917 and *Das Herz* from 1931. The compositions of Richard Strauss remain among the most frequently played around the globe, especially his operas such as *Salome* (1905) and *Elektra* (1909).

Today, at the end of the 20th century, important composers such as **Karlheinz Stockhausen** (b. 1928) and **Hans Werner Henze** (b. 1926) carry on the traditions of Germany's musical past. Listen to: Stockhausen's *Gesang der Jünglinge* (*Song of the Youths*). Henze continues to win cultural awards around the world, honored for such compositions as *The English Cat* in 1980 and *La Cubana* in 1973

## 3 A Taste of Germany

Traditional Germans like to eat but don't like to count calories. Cholesterol-conscious Americans may recoil at the sight of heavy dumplings, *wurst* (sausages), and pastries. The beer that often accompanies meals is not in the "light" category, and helpings of food are not small. And even the heaviest meals do not keep many Germans from their cake and coffee break, considered a compulsory afternoon event.

However, Germans get German cooking at home, and so more and more restaurants are offering foreign foods and *neue Küche* (cuisine moderne). Young people are becoming increasingly health conscious and are eschewing the rich fare of their parents. Young chefs trained in Switzerland, France, or Italy are returning to Germany to open continental restaurants. Italians, many of whom originally came to Germany as "guest workers," have stayed to open up trattorie. Even health-food shops are beginning to pop up.

## REGIONAL SPECIALTIES

Every region has its own specialties, ranging from *Aalsuppe* (eel soup) in Hamburg to *Zwiebelbrot* (onion bread) in the Black Forest.

- **Bavaria & Franconia:** In southern Germany, you can feast on such hearty fare as *Leberkäs* (a chilled mold of minced pork, beef, and liver); lots of *Knödel* (dumplings or soaked bread); gigantic *Haxen* (pork or veal trotters, most often consumed with sauerkraut); *Rostbratwürste* (small finger sausages); and *Leberknödel* (large liver dumplings in a clear broth). *Schweinwürstl mit Kraut* (pork sausages with sauerkraut) is another unforgettable local dish.
- **Lower Saxony & Schleswig-Holstein:** Here in northwest Germany, with its maritime tradition, one of the most typical local dishes is *Aalsuppe*—sweet-and-sour eel soup flavored with bacon, vegetables, and sometimes even pears and prunes (or perhaps other fruits). The eternal sailor's favorite is *Labskaus,* a ground-together medley of pork, salt herring, and beef, along with potatoes and beets. The traditional topping is a fried egg and a side dish of cucumbers. *Bruntes Huhn* is salt beef on a bed of diced vegetables, a robust winter favorite. *Rollmops,* pickled herring rolled in sour cream, is another local specialty, as is *Finkenwerder Scholle* (plaice) and oysters, raw or baked with cheese.
- **Berlin:** During those cold nights in old Prussia, Berliners took comfort in their soups, notably *Kohlsuppe* (cabbage soup) and *Erbensuppe* (pea soup), along with dark bread, especially Westphalia pumpernickel. *Hase im Topf* is a delicious rabbit paté. Other favorites are *Bratwurst,* a pork sausage; and *Regensburger,* a spicy pork sausage. For dessert, Berliners like *Kugelhupf,* a marvelous coffeecake, and *Käsekuchen,* or cheesecake. But probably the most typical Berlin delicacy is *Eisbein,* pigs' knuckles.
- **Hassen & Westphalia:** Famed for its hams, this region of Germany eats food guaranteed to put hair on your chest. To go totally native, sample their *Sulperknochen,* made from the pig's trotters (feet), ears, and tail, and served

### The Best of the Wurst

The German love affair with *wurst* (sausage) dates from the dawn of history. Every region of Germany has its own specialty, but everybody's favorite seems to be bratwurst from Nürnberg, made of seasoned and spiced pork. Germans often take their wurst with a bun and a dab of mustard (often smoky). White sausage, called *Weisswurst,* is a medley of veal, calves' brains, and spleen. Tradition has it that this sausage should be eaten only between midnight and noon. *Bauernwurst* (farmer's sausage) and *Knockwurst* are variations of the frankfurter, which originated (naturally) in Frankfurt. (Oddly enough, small frankfurters, which are called wieners or Vienna sausages in the United States, and *Wienerwurst* in Germany, are known simply as frankfurters in Austria.) *Leberwurst* (made from liver) is a specialty of Hesse. *Rinderwurst* and *Blutwurst* (beef sausage and blood sausage) are specialties of Westphalia and are often consumed with *Steinhager* (corn brandy).

traditionally with peas pudding and pickled cabbage. Or try *Tüttchen,* a ragout of herb-flavored calf's head and calf's brains. Not into any of the above? You might settle for the local favorite *Pickert,* sweet potato cakes flavored with raisins.

- **Baden-Württemberg:** Here in southern Germany, in the region centered around Stuttgart, you can begin with such dishes as *Schneckensuppe* (snail soup), *Spätzle* (egg-based pasta), or perhaps *Maultaschen* (ravioli stuffed with ground meat, spinach, and calf's brains). A dish beloved in the area and widely consumed is *Geschnetzeltes* (slices of veal in a cream sauce). The favorite local dish in Stuttgart itself is *Gaisburger Marsch,* a beef stew. Another commonly served dish is *Rostbraten,* braised beef, invariably accompanied by *Sauerkraut,* or else *Linsen mit Saiten,* lentil stew cooked with sausages.
- **Saxony & Thuringia:** In eastern Germany, you can feast on everything from *Linsensuppe mit Thüringer Rotwurst* (lentil soup with Thuringian sausages) to *Rinderzunge in Rosinen-Sauce* (calf's tongue in grape sauce). *Kartoffelsuppe* (potato soup) remains a favorite of the district, as does a baked appetizer, *Quarkkeulchen,* made from curd, boiled potatoes, flour, sugar, and raisins, topped with cinnamon and served with applesauce. Each city in the district also has its own popular local dishes. Leipzig, for example, has its *Leipziger Allerlei,* a blend of carrots, peas, asparagus, cauliflower, mushrooms, crayfish, ox tails, bits of veal, and dumplings.
- **Rhineland:** The food of the Rhineland, embracing such cities as Düsseldorf and Cologne, is hearty and robust, designed to put hair on your chest, even if you're a woman. It's the type of cuisine containing specialties that have made Germans the subject of good-natured ridicule, especially in their neighboring country France. For example, Rhinelanders love a dish called *Saumagen,* which is stuffed pork belly with pickled cabbage. *Schweinepfeffer* is also beloved. This is a highly seasoned and spicy pork ragout that's thickened with pig blood. After that feast, it's on to *Hämchen,* pork trotters with pickled cabbage and potatoes, or else *Sauerbraten.* Of all the Rhineland dishes, *Sauerbraten* enjoys the most favor in other European coutries and in the United States. The hunk of beef is marinated in wine vinegar and spices. The late Konrad Adenauer, post-war chancellor of Germany, was a Rhinelander, and one of his favorite foods was *Reibekukchen,* small potato pancakes with a blueberry or apple sauce. Taverns along the Rhine fill up when *Federweisser,* their partially fermented new wine, comes in. They drink it while devouring onion tarts.

## BEER & WINE

**BEER** For variety and quality, German beer is unmatched. The world's oldest brewery is in Bavaria, but other regions in Germany have proud beer-making traditions. Export beers and the rather more bitter *Pils,* the most popular type of beer, are also produced in Berlin, Hamburg, the Ruhr, Hesse, and Stuttgart. *Altbier,* a very early product of the brewer's art, can be found today all over Germany. *Berliner Weisse* is made from wheat, like a Bavarian white beer, but with a dash of raspberry or woodruff syrup. Dark and sweet, malt beer contains hardly any alcohol, whereas "March beer" is also dark but considerably stronger.

In Germany, if you go into a beer hall and ask the bartender for *ein Bier,* you'll probably get the standard stock beer, *Vollbier,* which is 4% alcohol. More potent is *Export* at 5%, or *Bockbier* at 6%. *Helles Bier* is light, and brewed from malt

### *Fun Fact* O' Zapfstisl ("The Barrel Is Tapped")

Much of the world seems to think that the Germans invented beer, but the drink actually has been around for thousands of years, at least since the days of ancient Egypt and Babylon. But if the Germans didn't exactly invent beer, they certainly perfected the process of making it. Just ask them!

At Weilhenstephan, a former Benedictine monastery 30km (18 miles) northeast of Munich in Old Bavaria, stands the oldest brewery in the world. It dates from the year 1040, although there is evidence that a hop garden already existed near the grounds of the monastery in A.D. 768. The monks here brought beer to the masses in Europe. Even today, the oldest brewery within Munich itself, Augustiner, reflects brewing's monastic heritage.

Over the centuries, monks brewed a strong beer for consumption during the fasting period of Lent, during which they were technically supposed to drink only water. The story goes that the pope heard about this custom and ordered that the beer be transported to Rome for him to sample. When the pope finally tasted the beer (which didn't have preservatives back then) after its long journey, he couldn't imagine why anyone would want to drink it and decreed that the beer was strong enough punishment for the Bavarian monks to drink it during Lent. Today, all Munich breweries brew this strong beer during Lent. The beer always ends with an "ator" in its name; *Salvator* and *Triumphator* are the best-known brands. "Ator" in German means a strong beer. By long-standing tradition, the names of German Doppelbock beers (strong beers) end with an "ator" suffix.

To go into a German beer hall and ask simply for a beer would brand you a beer illiterate. Connoisseurs specify the type of beer they want

dried and baked by the local brewery, or *Brauerei.* When the malt has been darkly roasted and fermented for much longer, it becomes *dunkles Bier,* or dark beer. *Pils,* or *Pilsener,* beers are light and contain more hops. Dortmund has earned a reputation in this field. (See the "O' Zapfstisl ('The Barrel Is Tapped')" box for more information.)

Many inns today actually brew their own beer. In summer, Germans, particularly Bavarians, flock to beer gardens to enjoy their local brews, which are sometimes accompanied by white or red radishes and crisp pretzels.

**WINE** Germany has produced delightful wines for centuries, but sometime in the 1970s, German wine became the butt of jokes. The postwar German economic miracle had led to a boom in wine production. Many new vineyards sprung up suddenly, and quality was not always their first priority. Cheap, cloyingly sweet table wines flooded the market. One label in particular, Liebfraumilch, began to sully the reputation of the entire industry; the mere mention of its name to anyone in the know met with a knowing titter or contemptuous sneer. These days, however, German viticulture has been saved by smaller producers producing excellent, unique wines.

and often the brewery. The following is a bit of beer vocabulary. *Dunkel* is a generic designation for all dark beers. *Doppelbock* is an extra dark beer with a 6% alcoholic content. *Hell,* believe it or not, is the name for light-colored beers. Many Germans, especially the citizens of Bamberg, like their beer "smoked." If that appeals to you, request *Rauchbier.* In nearby Bayreuth, Richard Wagner's old hometown, locals prefer a "steam beer" known as *Dampfbier.* The denizens of Düsseldorf and Frankfurt can often be heard requesting *Alt,* a brown, barley-malt brew. *Kölsch* is a light beer drunk mainly in Cologne in tall fluted glasses. *Hefe-Weizen* is a yeasty wheat beer consumed often with a squeeze of lemon. Finally, *Starkbierzet* is a powerful beer served when the barrels are opened after the post-Lenten celebrations in March. It has the highest alcohol content of them all.

What to consume with this brew? Germans prefer white and red radishes, chives on buttered bread, cold sausages, and, you guessed it, pretzels. What about a main course? One old Bavarian who starts drinking beer at 7 in the morning (and has ever since he was 16) says there is only one "acceptable" dish—ox from the spit with a potato and cucumber salad. Many Germans, especially Bavarians, see nothing wrong with drinking beer in the morning, often along with a hearty second breakfast of white sausage.

Although beer festivals are common around the world, none has ever equaled Munich's renowned **Oktoberfest.** This massive celebration lasts 16 days and lures some 7 million visitors yearly, when some 5.7 million liters (1½ million gallons) of beer are consumed. Of course, if you attend the right beer party in Germany, any night can be Oktoberfest.

Good German wine is renowned for its natural lightness and its delicate balance of sweetness and acidity. Most vineyards flourish on steep hillsides, protected from harsh winds by wooded neighboring hills, especially on the banks of the Rhine and the Mosel rivers and their many tributaries. The vineyards profit from the warmth reflected off the sunlit water. The slow maturing of the grapes gives German wines their typical fresh, fruity acidity.

Germany does produce red wine, but as a rule it's better to stick to white or perhaps a rosé. The words *trocken* (dry) or *halbtrocken* (semidry) are often given on the labels; look for them if you want to escape anything sweet. This avoidance, however, should not extend to the delicious dessert wines, which resemble nectar as opposed to syrup.

The overload of information on a German wine label is often puzzling to foreigners, but it's not really that hard to decipher. First of all, the grape variety should be indicated. Legally, German wines are only required to contain 85% of the declared variety. The classic is *Riesling,* which can range widely in taste from fruity to spicy. Other grapes include *Weisburgunder,* used to make dry wines, often with an aroma of melon or pear, and *Scheurebe,* which produces delicious, high-quality wine with the aroma of red currant. No grape reference on the label often means a poorly blended, inferior quality wine.

The term "vintage" refers to when the grapes were grown (not harvested). The question of origin is also something to keep an eye on. It's best if the label gives a single vineyard, but these can only be distinguished from the less specific vineyard zones if you are in the know or can consult a pocket guide, such as Johnson's.

Next, check for the level of ripeness. German law distinguishes between *Tafelwein* (table wine) and *Qualitatswein* (quality wine). QbA on a bottle means the wine is made from the approved grape varieties, which will give it the particular and traditional taste of its region. QmP refers to *Qualitatswein mit Pradikat* (wine with distinction) and carries one of six special attributes. These, in order of ascending price, are *Kabinett, Spätlese, Auslese, Berrenauslese* (BA), *Eiswein,* and the exclusive *Trockenbeerenauslese* (TBA).

As a classification, *Kabinett* was first used by Eberbach Abbey in 1712 to denote quality. This wine is especially good as an apertif with light snacks or veal. The mildly sweet and fruity *Auslese* from the Mosel-Saar-Ruwer region and the rich *Spätlese* are well-suited to richer dishes such as duck, smoked fowl and oysters. Those *trocken* and *halbtrocken* Rieslings from the Rheingau and Mosel-Saar-Ruwer are perfect with pork, sausages, and sauerkraut as well as with mild cheeses. A fuller-bodied Riesling *Spätlese* and *Auslese Trocken* from Rheingau or Pfalz goes excellently with wild boar and lobster. The rarest vintages, those sweet wines carrying the BA and TBA designations, are best left for anything oily or pungent in flavor, such as goose-liver paté or rich cheeses. They are also wonderful with desserts.

Many foreign visitors tour one of the wine-growing districts. Since reunification, a number of wine districts have emerged in eastern Germany; however, the traditional German wine country, stretching from the middle Rhine at Bonn down to Lake Constance on the Swiss border, is still the most charming, with its classic scenery of imposing castle ruins, elegant spas, and Brothers Grimm villages replete with spires and black-and-white gabled houses.

# Appendix B: Useful Terms & Phrases

## 1 Glossary

### GENERAL TERMS

**Altes Rathaus** Old town hall (kept as an historical monument, but not used anymore as the headquarters/offices of the city's officials)
**Altstadt** Old part of a city or town
**Anlage** Park area
**Apotheke** Pharmacy
**Auf Wiedersehen** Goodbye
**Bad** Spa (also bath)
**Bahn** Railroad, train
**Bahnhof** Railroad station
**Berg** Mountain
**Bergbahn** Funicular (cable railway)
**Bitte** Please
**Brücke** Bridge
**Brunnen** Spring or well
**Burg** Fortified castle
**Damm** Dike, embankment
**Danke** Thank you
**Diet** A policy meeting of church officials
**Dom** Cathedral
**Domplatz** Cathedral square
**Drogerie** Shop selling cosmetics, sundries
**Fleet** Canal
**Gasse** Lane
**Gastarbeiter** Foreign worker
**Gasthof** Inn
**Gemütlichkeit (adj. gemütlich)** Comfort, coziness, friendliness
**Graben** Moat
**Gutbürgerliche Küche** German home-cooking
**Hallo** Hello
**Hauptbahnhof** Main railroad station
**Hotelgarni** Hotel that serves no meals or serves breakfast only
**Insel** Island
**Jugendstil** Art Nouveau
**Kaufhaus** Department store
**Kloster** Monastery
**Kneipe** Bar for drinking, may serve snacks
**Konditorei** Cafe for coffee and pastries
**Kunst** Art
**Marktplatz** Market square
**Messegelände** Exhibition center, fairgrounds
**Neue Küche** Cuisine moderne
**Neues Rathaus** New town hall (the seat of current city business)
**Neustadt** New part of city or town
**Oper** Opera
**Platz** Square
**Rathaus** Town or city hall
**Ratskeller** Restaurant in Rathaus cellar serving traditional German food
**Reisebüro** Travel agency
**Schauspielhaus** Theater for plays
**Schloss** Palace, castle
**See** Lake (der See) or sea (die See)
**Seilbahn** Cable car
**Spielbank** Casino
**Stadt** Town, city
**Stadtbahn** (S-Bahn) Commuter railroad
**Steg** Footbridge
**Strasse** Street
**Strassenbahn** Streetcar, tram
**Tor** Gateway
**Turm** Tower
**Ufer** Shore, riverbank
**Untergrundbahn** (U-Bahn) Subway, underground transportation system in a city

**Verkehrsamt** Tourist office
**Weg** Road
**Weinstube** Wine bar or tavern serving meals

## ART & ARCHITECTURE TERMS

**Apse** Domed or arched area at the altar end of a church
**Baroque** Ornate, decorated style of art and architecture in the 18th century; characterized by elaborate gilding and ornamentation
**Bauhaus** Style of functional design for architecture and objects, originating in the early 20th century in Germany
**Biedermeier** Solid, bourgeois style of furniture design and interior decoration in the mid-19th century
**Chancel** Part of a church that contains the altar, with seats for the clergy and choir
**Cloister** Covered walkway, usually enclosed by columns, around a quadrangle
**Finial** An ornament at the top of a column or some upper extremity in Gothic architecture
**Nave** The central part of a church
**Reliquary** A container or shrine for sacred relics
**Retable** A raised shelf above an altar for a cross
**Rococo** A highly decorative development of baroque style
**Transept** The part of a Gothic cross-shaped church at right angles to the nave
**Vault** An arched structure of masonry forming a ceiling or roof

# 2 Menu Terms

## SOUPS (SUPPEN)

**Erbsensuppe** Pea soup
**Gemüsesuppe** Vegetable soup
**Gulaschsuppe** Goulash soup
**Kartoffelsuppe** Potato soup
**Linsensuppe** Lentil soup
**Nudelsuppe** Noodle soup

## MEATS AND POULTRY (WURST, FLEISCH & GEFLÜGEL)

**Aufschnitt** Cold cuts
**Brathuhn** Roasted chicken
**Bratwurst** Grilled sausage
**Beefsteak or Rindfleisch** Hamburger steak
**Eisbein** Pigs' knuckles
**Ente** Duck
**Frankfurter** Hotdog
**Gans** Goose
**Geflügel** Poultry
**Kalb** Veal
**Kassler Rippchen** Pork chops
**Lamm** Lamb
**Leber** Liver
**Ragout** Stew
**Rinderbraten** Roast beef
**Rindfleisch** Beef
**Schinken** Ham
**Schnitzel** Cutlet
**Schweinebraten** Roast pork
**Truthahn** Turkey
**Wiener Schnitzel** Breaded veal cutlet
**Wurst** Sausage

## FISH (FISCH)

**Forelle** Trout
**Hecht** Pike
**Karpfen** Carp
**Krebs** Crayfish
**Lachs** Salmon
**Makrele** Mackerel
**Muschel** Mussel
**Rheinsalm** Rhine salmon
**Schellfisch** Haddock
**Seezunge** Sole

## EGGS (EIER)

**Eier in der Schale** Boiled eggs
**Mit Speck** With bacon
**Rühreier** Scrambled eggs
**Spiegeleier** Fried eggs
**Verlorene Eier** Poached eggs

## SALADS (SALAT)

**Gemischter Salat** Mixed salad
**Gurkensalat** Cucumber salad
**Rohkostplatte** Raw vegetable platter

## SANDWICHES (BELEGTE BROTE)

**Aufschnitt mit Brot** Cold cuts sandwich (a sandwich Germans are more fond of ordering than a specific type, such as roast beef or bologna)
**Brotaufstrich** Meat paste sandwich (a very popular sandwich in Germany)
**Entebrot** Chicken sandwich
**Eierbrot** Egg sandwich
**Käsebrot** Cheese sandwich
**Schinkenbrot** Ham sandwich
**Schwarzbrot mit Butter** Pumpernickel with butter sandwich
**Speckbrot** Bacon sandwich
**Tomatenbrot** Tomato sandwich
**Wurstbrot** Sausage sandwich

## VEGETABLES (GEMÜSE)

**Artischocken** Artichokes
**Blumenkohl** Cauliflower
**Bohnen** Beans
**Bratkartoffeln** Fried potatoes
**Champignon** Mushroom
**Erbsen** Peas
**Grüne Bohnen** Green or string beans
**Gurken** Cucumbers
**Karotten** Carrots
**Kartoffel** Potato
**Kartoffelbrei** Mashed potatoes
**Kartoffelsalat** Potato salad
**Knödel** Dumplings
**Kohl** Cabbage
**Rettich** Radish
**Reis** Rice
**Rote Rüben** Beets
**Rotkraut** Red cabbage
**Salat** Lettuce
**Salzkartoffeln** Boiled potatoes
**Sellerie** Celery
**Spargel** Asparagus
**Spinat** Spinach
**Steinpilze** Boletus mushrooms
**Tomaten** Tomatoes
**Vorspeisen** Hors d'oeuvres

## DESSERTS (NACHTISCH)

**Apfel Reispudding** Apple rice pudding
**Apfelstrudel** Apple strudel
**Auflauf** Soufflé
**Bienenstich** Honey almond cake
**Blatterteiggebäck** Puff pastry
**Bratapfel** Baked apple
**Dolce di Castagne** Chestnut roll
**Eis** Ice cream
**Erdbeermeringue** Strawberry meringue
**Kaffeecreme** Coffee mousse
**Käse** Cheese
**Kirschenstrudel** Cherry strudel
**Kompott** Stewed fruit
**Obstkuchen** Fruit tart
**Obstsalat** Fruit salad
**Pfannkuchen** Sugared pancakes
**Pflaumenkompott** Stewed plums
**Schwarzwälder Kirschtorte** Black Forest cake
**Schlagsahne** Whipped cream
**Schokolademus** Chocolate mousse
**Topfenpalatschinken** Cottage cheese pancakes
**Torte** Pastry
**Zwetschkenknodel** Plum dumplings

## FRUITS (OBST)

**Ananas** Pineapple
**Apfel** Apple
**Apfelsine** Orange
**Banane** Banana
**Birne** Pear
**Erdbeeren** Strawberries
**Himberren** Raspberries
**Kirschen** Cherries
**Pfirsich** Peach
**Weintrauben** Grapes
**Zitrone** Lemon

## BEVERAGES (GETRÄNKE)

**Bier** Beer
**Coca-Cola** Coca-Cola (order a soda in Germany by it's specific name: Coke, Pepsi, Dr. Pepper, etc.)
**Ein dunkles** A dark beer
**Ein helles** A light beer
**Eine Tasse Kaffee** A cup of coffee
**Eine Tasse Tee** A cup of tea
**Eiskalt** Chilled
**Eistee** Ice tea
**Geist** Brandy
**Hiesse Schokolade** Hot chocolate
**Kaffee** Coffee
**Kaffee mit Milch/Zucker** Coffee with cream/sugar:
**Kaffee mit Suss-stoff** Coffee with artificial sweetener
**Kaffee Schwarz** Black coffee
**Koffeinfrei** Decaffeinated coffee
**Kräutertee** Herb tea
**Leicht** Light (wine)
**Likör** Liqueur
**Limonade** Lemonade
**Milch** Milk
**Mineralwasser** Mineral water
**Mit Eis** With ice
**Mit Wasser** With water
**Ohne Eis** Without ice
**Ohne Wasser** Without water
**Pur** Straight
**Rotwein** Red wine
**Saft** Juice
**Schaumwein** Sparkling wine
**Schnaps** Schnapps
**Schokolade** Chocolate
**Soda** Club soda
**Soda mit gas** Soda with gas (to make sure your club soda is carbonated, if that's what you want—the German word for carbonated is *Kohlensäure,* but Germans don't use this when ordering drinks)
**Süss** Sweet (wine)
**Tee mit Milch** Tea with cream
**Tee mit Zitrone** Tea with lemon
**Tomatensaft** Tomato juice
**Trocken** Dry (wine)
**Wasser** Water
**Weisswein** White wine

## CONDIMENTS & TABLE ITEMS (WÜRZE & TAFELGESCHIRR)

**Brot** Bread
**Brötchen** Rolls
**Butter** Butter
**Eis** Ice
**Essig** Vinegar
**Flasche** Bottle
**Gabel** Fork
**Glas** Glass
**Kalte pikante sosse** Ketchup
**Löffel** Spoon
**Messer** Knife
**Öl** Oil
**Pfeffer** Pepper
**Platte** Plate
**Sahne** Cream
**Salat Zubereitung** Salad dressing
**Salz** Salt
**Senf** Mustard
**Tasse** Cup
**Tischzeug** Napkin
**Zucker** Sugar

## COOKING TERMS

**Gebacken** Baked
**Gebraten** Fried
**Gedämpft** Steamed
**Gefüllt** Stuffed
**Gekocht** Boiled
**Geröstet** Roasted
**Gut durchgebraten** Well done
**Heiss** Hot
**Kaltes** Cold
**Mittep** Medium
**Nicht durchgebraten** Rare
**Paniert** Breaded
**Pochiert** Poached

# Index


**Aachen (Aix-la-Chapelle), 503–507**
**AARP, 43**
**Abbey Church (Berchtesgaden), 327**
**Abtai Kirche St. Maria (Amorbach), 240**
**Accommodations**
best luxury hotels, 13–14
best small inns and hotels, 14–15
tips on, 58
**Adventure trips, 49–53**
**After Shave (Hamburg), 612**
**Agfa-Historama (Cologne), 511**
**Agidienkirche (Erfurt), 163**
**Ägyptisches Museum (Berlin), 104**
**Airfares, 45–46**
**Airlines**
to Germany, 44
within Germany, 55
**Airport Hamburg-Fuhlsbüttel, 584**
**Air travel security measures, 44–45**
**Alamannen Museum (Weingarten), 378**
**Albertinum (Dresden), 181**
**Albrechtsburg Castle (Meissen), 194**
**Alexanderplatz (Berlin), 68, 72, 117**
**Allerheiligengeistkirche (Erfurt), 163**
**Alpengarten (Alpine Garden) (Pforzheim), 399**
**Alpine Road (Deutsche Alpenstrasse), 11, 326**
**Alpspitz region, 344**
**Alsfeld, 582**
**Alster Lake (Hamburg), 585**
**Alsterpark (Hamburg), 602**
**Alster-Schwimmhalle (Hamburg), 604**
**Altar of the Holy Blood (Rothenburg), 247**
**Alte Hofhaltung (Bamberg), 203–204**
**Alte Mälzerei (Regensburg), 222**
**Altenburg, 161**
**Alte Oper (Frankfurt), 459**
**Alte Pinakothek (Munich), 7, 298–299**
**Alte Residenztheater (Cuvilliés Theater) (Munich), 298, 302**
**Alter Schwede (Wismar), 633**
**Altes Museum (Berlin), 108**
**Altes Rathaus (Old Town Hall)**
Bamberg, 203
Göttingen, 576
Hannover, 563
Leipzig, 168
Lindau, 358
Munich, 295
Regensburg, 220
**Altes Residenztheater (Cuvilliés Theater) (Munich), 298, 302, 316**
**Altes Schloss (Meersburg), 9, 366**
**Altes Schloss and Württembergisches Landesmuseum (Stuttgart), 424**
**Altes Schloss Ermitage (Bayreuth), 198**
**Alt-Köln am Dom (Cologne), 518**
**Altmühltal Nature Park, 196**
**Altona (Hamburg), 586**
restaurants, 597–598
**Altstadt (Old Town)**
Düsseldorf, 524
Frankfurt, 438, 452–454
Goslar, 573
Hamburg, 600
Heidelberg, 412
Lübeck, 616
Munich, 270
Nürnberg, 208
Passau, 223
Quedlinburg, 176
**Amalienburg pavilion (Munich), 304**
**Ambiente, 38**
**American Express**
Berlin, 74
Frankfurt, 439
Hamburg, 587
Munich, 273
**Ammersee, 310**
**Amorbach, 239–240**
**Amphitheater (Trier), 542**
**Ancestral Gallery (Munich), 300**
**An der Hauptwache (Frankfurt), 453**
**Annweiler, 483**
**An Sibin (Frankfurt), 461**
**Antikensammlung (Museum of Antiquities) (Berlin), 108**
**Antikensammlungen (Munich), 304–305**
**Antik & Flohmarkt (Berlin), 133**
**Antiquarium (Munich), 300, 302**
**Antiques**
Bamberg, 204
Berlin, 128
Bonn, 497–498
Bremen, 552
Dresden, 183–184
Düsseldorf, 526
Göttingen, 576
Hamburg, 605–606
Hameln, 569
Leipzig, 170
Lübeck, 618
Lüneburg, 558
Meissen, 194
Munich, 311
**Aquarium, Berlin, 124**
**Archäologisches Landesmuseum (Schleswig), 626**
**Architecture, 22–29**
**Arkaden (Leipzig), 166**
**Arnstadt, 161**
**Arsenal (Schwerin), 636**
**Art and artists, 18–22**

**ARTCO Galerie für Zeitgenössische Kunst (Leipzig), 170**
**Art galleries**
Berlin, 128–129
Bremen, 552–553
Cologne, 513
Dresden, 183–184
Göttingen, 576
Leipzig, 170
Lindau, 359
Munich, 312
Sylt, 630
Weimar, 162
**Arts and crafts.** ***See*** **Handcrafts**
**Asamkirche (Munich), 305–306**
**Aschaffenburg, 463–465**
**Assmannshausen, 491–492**
**ATMs (automated-teller machines), 37**
**A Trane (Berlin), 139**
**Auerbachs Keller (Leipzig), 166, 172**
**Augsburg, 255–260**
**Augustiner Museum (Freiburg), 380**
**Augustusplatz (Leipzig), 170**
**Aussenalster (Hamburg), 585, 604**
**Automobilclub von Deutschland (AvD), 57–58**
**Autonomes Kulturzentrum Würzburg, 237**

**Bach, Johann Sebastian, 8, 151, 165, 169, 654**
Bachhaus (Eisenach), 164
Bach-Museum (Leipzig), 168
**Bachhaus (Eisenach), 164**
**Bad Bergzabern, 483**
**Bad Dürkheim, 482**
**Baden-Baden, 2, 13, 51, 400–407**
**Badenweiler, 385–388**
**Bad Godesberg, 502–503**
**Bad Homburg, 13, 51, 469–472**
**Bad Homburg Palace, 470**
**Bad Karlshafen, 583**
**Bad Kissingen, 51**
**Bad Mergentheim, 240–242**
**Bad Nauheim, 13, 472–474**
**Bad Pyrmont, 570–572**
**Bad Reichenhall, 12–13, 51, 333–336**
**Bad Reichenhall Casino, 336**
**Bad Reichenhaller Saltmuseum, 334**
**Bad Wiessee, 339–341**
**Bad Wildungen, 579–580**
**Bahrenfeld (Hamburg), accommodations, 595–596**
**Baiersbronn, 396**
**Balalaika (Frankfurt), 462**
**Ballet**
Berlin, 135
Düsseldorf, 530
Frankfurt, 460
Hamburg, 607
Munich, 316
Stuttgart, 429
**Ballindamm (Hamburg), 586**
**Ballooning, 325, 402**
**Baltic coast, 34, 633–646**
**Bamberg, 202–207**
**Bamberger Haus (Munich), 294**
**Bamberger Reiter (Bamberg), 204**
**Bamberg Symphony Orchestra, 207**
**Bar am Lützowplatz (Berlin), 142**
**Bar Hamburg, 613**
**Baroque, 26**
**Baroque art and artists, 20**
**Bars and pubs.** ***See also*** **Beer halls and taverns**
Aachen, 507
Baden-Baden, 407
Bad Reichenhall, 336
Berlin, 141–144
Bonn, 501
Bremen, 556
Cologne, 520–521
Dresden, 190–191
Düsseldorf, 530–531
Frankfurt, 462–463
Freiburg, 385
Göttingen, 578
Hamburg, 613–614
Hannover, 567
Heidelberg, 417–418
Kiel, 625
Koblenz, 495
Leipzig, 173
Lübeck, 622
Lüneburg, 559, 560
Munich, 320
Passau, 226
Stuttgart, 429
**Baselitz, Georg, 22**
**Basilica (Trier), 541**
**Baths of St. Barbara (Trier), 542**
**Bauhaus, 28, 29**
**Bauhaus-Archiv Museum für Gestaltung (Bauhaus Design Museum) (Berlin), 110**
**Bauhaus-Museum (Weimar), 154**
**Bauhaus Universität (Weimar), 152, 154**
**Bavaria Film Studio (Munich), 309**
**Bavarian Alps, 31, 324–355**
driving tours in, 326
outdoor activities, 324–325
**Bavarian Association of Arts & Crafts (Munich), 312**
**Bavarian Lion (Lindau), 358**
**Bavarian National Museum (Munich), 299**
**Bavarian State Ballet (Munich), 316**
**Bavarian State Opera (Munich), 316**
**Bayerischen Staatsoper (Munich), 316**
**Bayerischer Hof Night Club (Munich), 318**
**Bayerischer Kunstgewerbeverein (Munich), 312**
**Bayerisches Nationalmuseum (Munich), 299**
**Bayerisches Staatsschauspiel (Munich), 316**
**Bayreuth, 197–202**
**Bayreuther Festspiele, 198**
**Bayrisch Zell (Hamburg), 613**
**Beaches**
Baltic Coast, 633
Bodensee (Lake Constance), 359, 366, 368, 370
Kiel, 622, 623
Konstanz, 370
Lake Titisee, 389
Lindau, 359
Munich, 310
Sylt, 628, 629
**The Beatles, 609**
**Beautiful Fountain (Nürnberg), 209**
**Beckmann, Max, 21, 108, 110**
**Beer, 657–658.** ***See also*** **Breweries**
types of, 659
**Beer gardens**
Augsburg, 260
Berlin, 141–142
Dresden, 187, 188
Munich, 294–295
**Beer halls and taverns.** ***See also*** **Bars and pubs**
Bad Wildungen, 580
best, 16

**Beer halls and taverns *(cont.)***
Cologne, 518–519
Dresden, 187
Düsseldorf, 530–531
Göttingen, 578
Hamburg, 613–614
Munich, 317–318
Ulm, 229
Weimar, 154, 162
Wiesbaden, 469
**Beethoven, Ludwig van, 169, 495, 655**
Festival (Bonn), 501
House (Bonn), 497, 501
**Begine Café Bistro Bar Exklusiv für Frauen (Berlin), 140**
**Beheiztes Freibad (Meersburg), 366**
**Beilstein, 535–536**
**Belchen, 383**
**Belvedere (Charlottenburg Palace, Berlin), 106**
**Belvedere Palace (Weimar), 156**
**Berchtesgaden, 327–333**
**Berchtesgadener Land, 324**
**Berchtesgaden National Park, 6, 52, 324**
**Berggarten (Hannover), 563**
**Berggruen Collection: Picasso and His Era (Berlin), 112–113**
**Berg Kolber, 351**
**Berg Laber, 351**
**Berlin, 30, 64–150**
accommodations, 1, 76–90
family-friendly, 80
arriving in, 64–67
average daytime temperature and rainfall, 38
beer gardens and wine cellars, 141–144
Berlin-Mitte, 69, 72
accommodations, 86–90
restaurants, 97–103
sights and attractions, 117–119
biking, 74, 126
boat tours, 125
business hours, 74
cabarets, 136–137
cafes, 144
car rentals, 73
casino, 145
Charlottenburg, 68
restaurants, 95–96
sights and attractions, 104, 106
club and music scene, 136–139
cuisine, 656
currency exchange, 74
dance clubs, 137–138
doctors and dentists, 74
drag shows, 139
driving in, 73
drugstores, 74–75
emergencies, 75
finding an address, 67
Frommer's favorite experiences in, 112
gay and lesbian travelers, 140–141
Grunewald, 69
accommodations, 85–86
restaurants, 96–97
hot lines, 75
Internet access, 75
Kurfürstendamm (Ku'damm), 67, 68, 112
accommodations, 77–83
restaurants, 91–94
shopping, 127
layout of, 67–68
lost property, 75
maps, 68
neighborhoods of, 68–71
nightlife and entertainment, 134–145
current listings, 134
outdoor activities, 126–127
parking, 73
parks and zoo, 123–124
performing arts, 134–136
post offices, 75
restaurants, 1, 90–103
family-friendly, 91
restrooms, 76
safety, 76
saunas, 126
shopping, 127–134
sights and attractions, 103–125
for kids, 123
spectator sports, 126
suggestions for first-time visitors, 103
taxis, 73
Tiergarten, 69, 123
museums, 110, 112
picnicking in, 112
restaurant near, 95
tours, 124–125
transportation, 72–74
visitor information, 67
walking tours, 124
what's new in, 1, 3
**Berlin.de website, 55**
**Berliner Dom (Berlin), 120–121**
**Berliner Ensemble (Berlin), 136**
**Berliner Festwochen, 39–40**
**Berliner Markthalle, 127**
**Berliner Philharmonisches Orchester (Berlin), 134**
**Berliner Trödelmarkt (Berlin), 133**
**Berliner Zinnfiguren (Berlin), 133**
**Berlin-Mitte, 69, 72**
accommodations, 86–90
restaurants, 97–103
sights and attractions, 117–119
**Berlin Philharmonic Orchestra, 134**
**Berlin-Schönefeld Airport, 64, 65**
**Berlin-Tegel Airport, 64, 65**
**Berlin-Tempelhof Airport, 64, 65**
**Berlin Wall, 109, 652**
**Berlin Zoo-Aquarium, 123–124**
**Bernkastel, 543**
**Bernkastel-Kues, 2, 538–540**
**Bethmann Park (Frankfurt), 456**
**Beuys, Josef, 22, 116, 602**
**Biergarten, 3**
**Biergarten Chinesischer Turm (Munich), 294–295**
**Big Eden (Berlin), 137**
**Biking**
Berlin, 74, 126
best, 12
Franconia, 196–197
Konstanz, 370
Lindau, 359
Meersburg, 366
Munich, 12, 273, 310
Neckar Valley, 410
Potsdam, 146
Romantic Road, 230
Rothenburg, 246
tours, 49
**Bildergalerie (Potsdam), 148**
**Binnenalster (Hamburg), 585**
accommodations, 592–594
restaurants, 596–597
**Birkenkopf, 424**
**Bischöfliches Museum (Trier), 543**
**Black Forest, Upper, 383**

**Black Forest (Schwarzwald), 32, 379–407**
**Black Gate (Trier), 541**
**Black September (1972; Munich), 308**
**Blaue Reiter group, 21**
**Blue Angel (Frankfurt), 461**
**BMW Museum (Munich), 308**
**Boating**
Hamburg, 604
Lindau, 359
Munich, 311
Titisee, 389
**Boat tours and cruises, 3, 58**
Berlin, 125
Bremen, 548
Danube River, 223
to Germany, 48–49
Hamburg, 603
Königssee, 330, 331
Konstanz, 369
Neckar Valley, 413
Rhine River, 478
Titisee, 389
Trier, 543–544
**Bockenheim, 482**
***Bodensee* (airship), 363**
**Bodensee (Lake Constance), 12, 31, 356–378**
beaches, 359, 366, 368, 370
**Bodensee Festival (Konstanz), 371**
**Bodensee Symphony Orchestra (Konstanz), 371**
**Bodenwerder, 583**
**Bomann Museum (Celle), 560**
**Bonn, 495–501**
**Bonn Symphony Orchestra, 501**
**Books, recommended, 59–60**
**Bookshops, Berlin, 129**
**Bookstores**
Frankfurt, 439
Hamburg, 587
Munich, 273, 312
Stuttgart, 426
**Botanischer Garten (Botanical Garden) (Big Bend National Park), 123**
**Böttcherstrasse (Bremen), 552**
**Brandenburg Gate (Berlin), 118**
**Brandt, Willy, 615, 652**
**Bräuerei Schumacher (Düsseldorf), 530**
**Bräuhaus Sion (Cologne), 518**
**Brecht, Bertolt, 101, 136, 255, 259, 507, 563**
Brecht-Weigel-Museum (Berlin), 118
**Brecht-Weigel-Museum (Berlin), 118**
**Breites Tor (Goslar), 573**
**Breitestrasse (Lübeck), 619**
**Bremen, 2, 547–557, 583**
accommodations, 553–554
gay clubs, 557
nightlife and entertainment, 556–557
organized tours, 548
restaurants, 554–556
shopping, 552–553
sights and attractions, 548–552
transportation, 548
traveling to, 547–548
visitor information, 548
**Bremer Spielbank, 556**
**Breweries, 658**
Düsseldorf, 530
Miltenberg, 238
tours, 49
**Broad Gate (Goslar), 573**
**Brocken, 572**
**Bröhan Museum (Berlin), 104**
**Brücke Museum (Berlin; opening in 2003), 21, 106**
**Bruder Grimm Museum (Kassel), 582**
**Buchenwald Concentration Camp and Memorial Site (near Weimar), 158**
**Buchinger Clinic (Überlingen), 375**
**Buddelschiff-Museum (Hamburg), 602**
**Buddenbrookhaus (Lübeck), 618**
**Burgberg Schloss (Quedlinburg), 176**
**Burg Eberbach, 420**
**Burg Eltz (near Moselkern), 9, 535**
**Burg Landeck (near Klingenmünster), 483**
**Burg Landshut (near Bernkastel-Kues), 539**
**Burgraves' Castle (Nürnberg), 211**
**Burg Trifels (Annweiler), 483**
**Business hours, 60**
**Bus tours**
Berlin, 124–125
Bremen, 548
Dresden, 182–183
Munich, 309–310
Obersalzberg, 333
Romantic Road, 230
**Bus travel, 58**

**Cabarets. *See* Nightclubs and cabarets**
**Cable cars**
Bad Wiessee, 339
Zugspitze, 346
**Cäcilienkirche (Cologne), 512**
**Cafe Aedes (Berlin), 144**
**Café/Bistro Leysieffer (Berlin), 144**
**Café Gnosa (Hamburg), 613**
**Café Karin (Frankfurt), 462–463**
**Café Keese (Berlin), 137**
**Café Laumer (Frankfurt), 463**
**Café-Restaurant in der Schirn (Frankfurt), 463**
**Café Ruhestörung (Nürnberg), 217**
**Café Schone Aussichten (Hamburg), 614**
**Café Silberstein (Berlin), 144**
**Cafe Wintergarten in Literaturhaus Berlin, 144**
**Calendar of events, 38–39**
**Calw, 396–398**
**Cape Arkona, 646**
**Caracalla-Therme (Baden-Baden), 401**
**Carl Hagenbeck's Tierpark (Hamburg), 600–601, 603**
**Car rentals, 57**
insurance, 41
**Carry-on baggage restrictions, 45**
**Cartoon (Nürnberg), 217**
**Car travel. *See also* Driving tours and scenic drives**
to Germany, 47
within Germany, 57–58
**Casinos**
Baden-Baden, 402
Bad Homburg, 472
Bad Reichenhall, 336
Bad Wildungen, 580
Berlin, 145
Bremen, 556
Garmisch-Partenkirchen, 349
Hamburg, 614
Hannover, 568
Konstanz, 371–372
Lindau, 361
Sylt, 632
Wiesbaden, 469
**Cassiopeia Therme (Badenweiler), 386**
**Castle Mill (Meersburg), 366**
**Castle of Baron von Landensberg (near Cochem), 535**

**Castles and palaces**
Albrechtsburg Castle (Meissen), 194
Alte Hofhaltung (Bamberg), 203–204
Altes Schloss (Meersburg), 366
Altes Schloss Ermitage (Bayreuth), 198
Bad Homburg Palace, 470
Belvedere Palace (Weimar), 156
best, 8–9
Bonn, 502
Burgberg Schloss (Quedlinburg), 176
Bürgeln Castle (Badenweiler), 386–387
Burg Eltz (near Moselkern), 535
Burg Landeck (near Klingenmünster), 483
Burg Landshut (near Bernkastel-Kues), 539
Burg Trifels (Annweiler), 483
Cecilienhof palace (Potsdam), 148–149
Dornröschenschloss Sababurg, 582
Eberbach Castle, 420
Festung und Schloss Pyrmont (Bad Pyrmont), 571
Frankenstein Schloss, 482
Friedrich IV's palace (Heidelberg), 412
Gottorf Castle (Schleswig), 626
Grevenburg Castle (Traben-Trarbach), 537
Güstrow Castle, 638
Hambach Castle, 483
Heidelberg Castle, 410, 412
Herrenchiemsee, 264
Hirschhorn Castle, 419
Hohenschwangau, 263–266
Hohes Schloss (Füssen), 261
Johannisburg Castle (Aschaffenburg), 464
Kaiserburg (Nürnberg), 211
Kaiserpfalz (Goslar), 573
Königliches Schloss Berchtesgaden, 328
Linderhof, 264
Montfort Castle (Langenargen), 361
Neue Residenz (Bamberg), 204
Neues Palais (Potsdam), 148
Neues Schloss (Bayreuth), 200
Neues Schloss (Meersburg), 366, 368
Neues Schloss (Stuttgart), 424
Neuschwanstein, 263–266
Nymphenburg Palace (Munich), 9, 264, 302, 304
Reichsburg Cochem, 532
Residenz (Munich), 300
Residenz (Schloss und Gartenverwaltung Würzburg), 234
Sans Souci Palace (Potsdam), 147
Schwerin Castle, 636
Sigmaringen Palace, 228
Spycher Castle (Rügen), 645
Tiefurt Palace (Weimar), 156
Wartburg Palace (Eisenach), 164
Weikersheim Castle, 242–243
Wildenberg Castle (near Amorbach), 240
Wittumspalais (Weimar), 157
**Castle Tower (Düsseldorf), 524**
**Cathedral of Our Lady (Munich), 306**
**Cathedrals (Dom)**
Aachen, 10, 504
Augsburg, 256
Bamberg, 204
Berlin, 66, 120–121
best, 10
Bremen, 548, 550
Cologne, 25, 510–511
Erfurt, 163
Frankfurt, 454–455
Freiburg, 25, 380, 382
Güstrow, 638
Mainz, 23, 485
Meissen, 193–194
Munich, 306
Passau, 223–224
Regensburg, 218
Schleswig, 626
Schwerin, 637
Speyer, 23–24, 476
Trier, 542
Ulm, 227
Ulm Münster, 25
Worms, 23, 480
Würzburg, 233
**Cathedral Square (Aachen), 504**
**Catholic Court Church (Dresden), 181**
**Cecilienhof palace (Potsdam), 148–149**
**Celle, 26, 560–562**
**Cézanne, Paul, 112, 113, 300**
**Channel Tunnel (Chunnel), 47**
**Chapel of Our Lord (Creglingen), 244**
**Chapel of St. Anne (Füssen), 261**
**Chapel of St. Bartholomew (Königssee), 331**
**Charlemagne, 10, 210, 435, 503, 505, 551, 583, 647**
relics of (Aachen), 504
**Charlottenburg (Berlin), 68**
restaurants, 95–96
sights and attractions, 104, 106
**Charlottenhof palace (Potsdam), 149**
**Château of Belvedere (Weimar), 156**
**Checkpoint Charlie (Berlin), 68**
Museum Haus am, 116
**Chez Nous (Berlin), 139**
**Chiemsee, 336–338**
**Children's Festival (Dinkelsbühl), 251**
**China. *See* Porcelain and china**
**Chip (Berlin), 138**
**Chorgestühl (Ulm), 227**
**Christmas Fair (Mainz), 40**
**Christmas market, Lübeck, 616**
**Christmas Village (Rothenburg), 247**
**Chunnel (Channel Tunnel), 47**
**Church of Our Lady (Dresden), 180**
**Church of Our Lady (Koblenz), 493**
**Church of Our Lady of the Fir Trees (Triberg), 392**
**Church of St. Jacob (Rothenburg), 247**
**Church of St. Nicholas (Nikolaikirche) (Berlin), 119–120**
**Church of St. Severi (Erfurt), 163**
**Church of St. Ulrich and St. Afra (Augsburg), 256**
**Church of the Cross (Dresden), 181**
**Church of the Holy Cross (Rostock), 640**

**Church of the Holy Ghost (Stralsund), 642**
**C-Keller Galerie (Weimar), 162**
**Clärchen's Ballhaus (Berlin), 138**
**Classical concerts. *See* Concerts**
**Classical music. *See* Concerts; Music festivals**
**Club Grosse Freiheit (Hamburg), 608**
**Club Paradise (Berlin), 126**
**Cochem, 11, 12, 532–535**
**Cologne (Köln), 2, 507–521**
accommodations, 513–516
bars and pubs, 520–521
gay nightlife, 521
nightlife and entertainment, 517–521
restaurants, 516–517
shopping, 512–513
sights and attractions, 8, 508–512
transportation, 508
traveling to, 508
visitor information, 508
**Cologne Cathedral, 10, 510**
**Concerts**
Augsburg, 260
Baden-Baden, 407
Bamberg, 207
Berlin, 134–136
Bonn, 501
Dresden, 189–190
Freiburg, 385
Garmisch-Partenkirchen, 350
Hamburg, 607
Hameln, 569
Konstanz, 371
Leipzig, 173
Lübeck, 621
Mainz, 488
Meersburg, 368
Munich, 317
Stuttgart, 429
Weimar, 162
Wiesbaden, 466, 469
**Congress Hall (Berlin), 120**
**Connection Disco (Berlin), 140**
**Constance (Konstanz), 368–372**
**Constance, Lake (Bodensee), 12, 31, 356–378**
beaches, 359, 366, 368, 370
**Cooky's (Frankfurt), 460**
**Corbusier House (Berlin), 120**
**Cotton Club (Hamburg), 608**
**Couven Museum (Aachen), 504**
**Crafts. *See* Handcrafts**
**Cranach, Lucas, the Elder, 19, 151, 152, 154, 156, 157, 175, 193, 196, 299, 454, 465**
House (Weimar), 152
**Credit cards, 37**
**Creglingen, 243–244**
**Cross-country skiing, 325**
**Cuckoo clocks, 247, 352, 391–393, 403**
**Currency and currency exchange, 36–37**
**Customs regulations, 35–36**
**Cuvilliés, François, the Younger, 317**
**Cuvilliés, Jean François de, the Elder, 27, 302, 306, 317**
**Cuvilliés Theater (Altes Residenztheater) (Munich), 298, 302, 316**

**Dachau Concentration Camp Memorial Site, 7, 323**
**Dachgarten (Berlin), 145**
**Dadaism, 21**
**Dahlem (Berlin), 68**
**Dahlemer Museen (Berlin), 108**
**Dallmayr (Munich), 314**
**Dance clubs and discos**
Aachen, 507
Bad Homburg, 472
Berlin, 137–138
Bonn, 501
Bremen, 556–557
Cologne, 519
Dresden, 191
Düsseldorf, 531
Frankfurt, 460–461
Hamburg, 612
Hannover, 568
Koblenz, 495
Konstanz, 372
Leipzig, 173
Mainz, 488
Nürnberg, 217
Regensburg, 222
Trier, 546
Tübingen, 432
**Danube Bicycle Path, 196**
**Danube River, 3, 196**
cruises, 223
**Das Gewandhaus (Leipzig), 173**
**Deidesheim, 482**
**Denkmal der März Gefallenen (Weimar), 157**
**Department stores**
Berlin, 130–131
Düsseldorf, 526
Frankfurt, 457–458
Hamburg, 605
Heidelberg, 414
Munich, 313
Nürnberg, 213
Stuttgart, 426
**Der Blaue Reiter group, 21**
**Der Jazzkeller (Frankfurt), 461**
**Der Salzspeicher (Lübeck), 617**
**Deutsche Alpenstrasse (Alpine Road), 11, 326**
**Deutsche Bücherei (Leipzig), 170**
**Deutsche Guggenheim Berlin, 112**
**Deutsche Oper am Rhein (Düsseldorf), 530**
**Deutsche Oper Berlin, 135**
**Deutsches Eck, 493**
**Deutsches Filmmuseum (Frankfurt), 455**
**Deutsches Historisches Museum (Berlin), 118**
**Deutsches Museum (Munich), 7, 298, 299–300, 309**
**Deutsches Museum für Meereskunde und Fischerei (Stralsund), 643**
**Deutsches Nationaltheater (Weimar), 162**
**Deutsches Salzmuseum (Lüneburg), 558**
**Deutsches Schauspielhaus (Hamburg), 607**
**Deutsche Staatsoper (Berlin), 135**
**Deutsches Theater (Göttingen), 578**
**Deutsches Theater (Munich), 316**
**Deutsches Uhrenmuseum (Triberg), 392**
**Deutsches Weintor (Schweigen-Rechtenbach), 484**
**Deutsche Weinstrasse (German Wine Road), 482–484**
**Deutschordenschloss (Bad Mergentheim), 241**
**Deutschordensmuseum (Bad Mergentheim), 241**
**Die Brücke, 21, 106**
**Diebsturm (Lindau), 358**
**Die Sammlung Berggruen: Picasso und Seine Zeit (Berlin), 112–113**

**Die Stachelschweine (Berlin), 136**
**Dimitroff, Georgi, 168**
**Dinkelsbühl, 11, 251–252**
**Diözesan Museum (Mainz), 485**
**Diozesanmuseum St. Ulrich (Regensburg), 219**
**Disabilities, travelers with, 41–42**
**Dix, Otto, 21, 181, 602**
**Dom.** ***See*** **Cathedrals**
**Domberg (Erfurt), 163**
**Dom Museum (Bremen), 548, 550**
**Dom Museum (Frankfurt), 454**
**Domschatzmuseum (Regensburg), 218**
**Donauwörth, 254–255**
**Dornburg, 161**
**Dornier Museum (Meersburg), 366**
**Dornröschenschloss Sababurg, 582**
**Drag shows**
Berlin, 139
Cologne, 521
Hamburg, 612
**Dreifaltigkeitskirke (Speyer), 477**
**Dreikönigskeller (Frankfurt), 461**
**Dresden, 30, 177–193, 654**
accommodations, 184–187
bus tours, 182–183
gay bars and clubs, 192
nightlife, 189–192
restaurants, 187–189
shopping, 183–184
side trip to the Spreewald and Sorb Country, 192–193
sights and attractions, 7, 180–182
transportation, 180
traveling to, 178
visitor information, 178, 180
what's new in, 1–2
**Dresden Philharmonic, 189**
**Driver's licenses, 58**
**Driving rules, 57**
**Driving tours and scenic drives**
along the Neckar, 6
Baltic coast, 633
Bavarian Alps, 326
best, 11
Deutsche Weinstrasse (German Wine Road), 482–484
Fairy-Tale Road (Märchenstrasse), 6, 33, 580–583
**Drug laws, 60**
**Drugstores, 60**
**Dürer, Albrecht, 19, 110, 156, 168, 182, 196, 208, 211, 213, 215, 258, 298, 299, 512, 550**
German Renaissance and, 210
House (Nürnberg), 210
**Düsseldorf, 521–531**

**Eagle's Nest (Kehlstein) (Obersalzberg), 331–333**
**Eastern Germany, 151**
**Eberbach, 419–420**
**Eberbach Castle, 420**
**Eckbauer, 6, 324, 344**
**Eichwald (Lindau), 359**
**Eigen & Art Gerd Harry Lybke (Berlin), 130**
**Eisenach, 164–165**
**Elbe River, 3**
**Elderhostel, 43**
**Elder Travelers, 43**
**Electoral Palace (Trier), 541–542**
**Electricity, 60**
**Elsheimer, Adam, 20, 454**
**Embassies and consulates, 61**
**Emergencies, 61**
**Englischer Garten (Munich), 270, 307, 311**
**English Theater (Frankfurt), 460**
**English Theatre of Hamburg, 607**
**Entry requirements, 35**
**Eppendorf (Hamburg), 605**
**Erfurt, 162–164**
**Ernst, Max, 21, 110, 128, 497, 512**
**Erotic Art Museum (Hamburg), 611**
**Erotik-Museum (Berlin), 113**
**Escorted tours, 48**
**E.T.A. Hoffmann Haus (Bamberg), 204**
**E.T.A. Hoffman Theater (Bamberg), 207**
**Ethnologisches Museum (Berlin), 108**
**Euro, 37**
**Europa Center (Berlin), 120**
**Europäische Wochen (European Weeks) Festival (Passau), 225–226**
**Expedia, 54**
**Expressionism, 21**

**Fabrik (Hamburg), 608**
**Fahrkirche Maria Krönung (Stuppach), 242**
**Fairy-Tale Road (Märchenstrasse), 6, 33, 580–583**
**Falls of Todtnau, 383**
**Families with children**
accommodations
Berlin, 80
Munich, 278
restaurants, Berlin, 91
**Far Out (Berlin), 138**
**Fasching, 38–39**
**Fashions (clothing)**
Baden-Baden, 403
Bavarian Alps, 340, 342, 346–347
Berlin, 131
Bremen, 552
Düsseldorf, 526
Frankfurt, 458
Hamburg, 606
Konstanz, 370
Munich, 313–314
Stuttgart, 425
Sylt, 630
**Fernsehturm (Stuttgart), 424–425**
**Fernsehturm (TV tower) (Berlin), 117**
**Festivals and special events, 38–39**
**Festspielhaus (Bayreuth), 197, 198, 200**
**Festung Ehrenbreitstein (near Koblenz), 493**
**Festung Marienberg (Würzburg), 233**
**Festung und Schloss Pyrmont (Bad Pyrmont), 571**
**Feuerwehrmuseum (Creglingen), 244**
**Figurentheater (Rothenburg), 250**
**Filmmuseum Berlin, 113**
**Fingerhutmuseum (Thimble Museum) (Creglingen), 243–244**
**Finnegan's Wake (Hamburg), 608**
**Fire-Brigade Museum (Creglingen), 244**

**Fischmarkt (Hamburg), 605**
**Fisher's Quarter (Ulm), 227**
**Fishing, in the Bavarian Alps, 325**
**Five Rivers Bicycle Path, 197**
**Flea markets**
Berlin, 133
Bonn, 498
Bremen, 553
Hannover, 564
Stuttgart, 425
**Flughafen Frankfurt/Main, 434**
**Focke-Museum (Bremen), 550**
**Food (cuisine), 655–660**
Munich, 314
**Franconia, 30–31, 196–197**
cuisine, 656
**Franconian Weeks' Festival (Bayreuth), 200**
**Frankenberg Kirche (Goslar), 573**
**Frankenstein Schloss, 482**
**Frankenwald, 196**
**Frankfurt, 434–474**
accommodations, 440–445
average daytime temperature and rainfall, 38
bars and cafes, 462–463
brief description of, 32–33
car rentals, 439
currency exchange, 439
emergencies, 440
gay and lesbian bars and clubs, 461–462
layout of, 435, 438
live-music clubs, 461
nightlife and entertainment, 459–463
performing arts, 459–460
restaurants, 445–452
shopping, 456–459
side trips from, 463–474
sights and attractions, 452–456
street maps, 438
taxis, 439
transportation, 438–439
traveling to, 434–435
visitor information, 435
**Frankfurt Book Fair, 40**
**Frankfurter Goethe-Museum, 453**
**Frankfurter Hof (Mainz), 488**
**Frankfurt Municipal Opera, 459**
**Franziskanerkirche (Überlingen), 375**
**Franz Josef Strauss International Airport (Munich), 267**
**Franz-Liszt-Museum (Bayreuth), 200**
**Frauenchiemsee (Fraueninsel), 336, 337**
**Frauenkirche (Dresden), 180**
**Frauenkirche (Munich), 306**
**Frauenkneipe (Hamburg), 613**
**Freiburg Cathedral, 380**
**Freiburg im Breisgau, 379–385**
**Freiburg Wine Tasting, 39**
**Freilichtmuseum Schwarzwälder (Triberg), 392**
**Freudenstadt, 393–396**
**Friedrich, Caspar David, 20, 106, 181, 525, 564, 601**
**Friedrichsbad (Baden-Baden), 402**
**Friedrichshafen, 362–365**
**Friedrichstadt-Palast (Berlin), 137**
**Friedrichswerdersche Kirche-Schinkelmuseum (Berlin), 113–114**
**Frommers.com, 54**
**Früh am Dom (Cologne), 519**
**Fuggerei (Augsburg), 256–258**
**Fulda, 581**
**Fürstenbaumuseum (Würzburg), 234**
**Füssen, 260–263**
arriving in, 267, 270

**Galerie Brusberg (Berlin), 128**
**Galerie für Angewandte Kunst München (Munich), 312**
**Galerie für Zeitgenössiche Kunst (Leipzig), 170**
**Galerie Luise (Hannover), 564**
**Galerie Pels-Leusden and Villa Grisebach Auktionen (Berlin), 128–129**
**Galeries Lafayette (Berlin), 130**
**Galerie Wohnmaschine (Berlin), 130**
**Gardens**
Alpengarten (Alpine Garden) (Pforzheim), 399
Bad Wildungen, 579
Botanical Garden (Berlin), 123
Englischer Garten (Munich), 307
Grosser Garten (Dresden), 181
Hamburg, 602–603
Herrenhäuser Garten (Hannover), 563
Krautergarten (Reichenau), 373
Linderhof Palace, 354
Palastgarten (Trier), 542
Palmengarten (Frankfurt), 456
Schwerin, 636
**Garmisch-Partenkirchen, 53, 343–350**
**Gasoline, 57**
**Gastroscout.com, 55**
**Gaststätte Hoeck (Wilhelm Hoeck) (Berlin), 143**
**Gaststätte zum Flaucher (Munich), 295**
**Gay and lesbian travelers, 653**
Berlin, 140–141
Bonn, 501
Bremen, 557
Cologne, 521
Dresden, 192
Düsseldorf, 531
Frankfurt, 461–462
Göttingen, 578–579
Hamburg, 611, 613
Hannover, 568
information and resources, 42–43
Leipzig, 174
Munich, 322
Nürnberg, 217
Regensburg, 222
Stuttgart, 429
**Gay Pride Parade (Cologne), 521**
**Gedenkstätte Buchenwald (near Weimar), 158**
**Geigenbau-und-Heimatmuseum (Mittenwald), 342**
**Gelnhausen, 581**
**Gemäldegalerie (Berlin), 7, 110**
**Gemäldegalerie Alte Meister (Dresden), 182**
**Gemäldegalerie Neue Meister (Dresden), 181**
**Georgenkirche (Dinkelsbühl), 251**
**German Bicycle Museum (Neckarsulm), 410**

**German Clock Museum (Triberg), 392**
**German Film Museum (Frankfurt), 455**
**Germanic National Museum (Nürnberg), 211**
**Germanisches Nationalmuseum (Nürnberg), 211**
**German Museum of Masterpieces of Science and Technology (Munich), 299–300**
**German National Tourist Board, 54**
**GermanRail, tourist passes, 56–57**
**GermanRail (DB Rail), 55**
**German Renaissance, 19, 207–208, 412**
Dürer and, 210
**German State Opera (Berlin), 135**
**German Wine Gate (Schweigen-Rechtenbach), 484**
**Gewandhaus Orchestra (Leipzig), 173**
**Gipsformerei der Staatlichen Museen Preussischer Kulturbesitz (Berlin), 134**
**Glasmuseum (Glass Museum) (Passau), 224**
**Gleisweiler, 483**
**Glockenspiel (Goslar), 573**
**Glossary, 661–665**
**Glyptothek (Munich), 305**
**Godesberg Castle, 502**
**Goethe, Johann Wolfgang von, 8, 14, 16, 32, 59, 151, 161, 166, 172, 190, 326, 492**
Frankfurter Goethe-Museum, 453
Gartenhaus (Weimar), 154
Goethe-Haus (Frankfurt), 453
Goethe-Museum Düsseldorf, 524
Goethe-Schiller Mausoleum (Weimar), 158
Nationalmuseum (Weimar), 154, 157
Park (Weimar), 152
**Goethe Park (Weimar), 152**
**Goethe-Schiller Mausoleum (Weimar), 158**
**Golf, 49–50**
Baden-Baden, 402–403
Frankfurt, 456
Hamburg, 604
**Goslar, 572–575**
**Goslarer Museum (Goslar), 573–574**
**Gothic architecture, 24–25**
**Gothic painting and sculpture, 18–19**
**Göttingen, 575–579**
**Grand Circle Travel, 43**
**Granitz Hunting Lodge (Rügen), 645**
**Great Hall of Mirrors (Neues Schloss), 337**
**Great House (Meersburg), 366**
**Green Vaults (Dresden), 181**
**Greenwich Bar–a.k.a. Cookie's (Berlin), 142**
**Greth (Überlingen), 375**
**Grevenburg Castle (Traben-Trarbach), 537**
**Grimm brothers, 580–581**
Bruder Grimm Museum (Kassel), 582
**Grips-Theater (Berlin), 123**
**Gröninger Braukeller (Hamburg), 614**
**Gropius, Walter, 28–30, 69, 115, 120, 154, 155, 157, 424**
**Grosse Freiheit (Hamburg), 611**
**Grosse Freiheit 36 (Hamburg), 608**
**Grosse Garten (Hannover), 563**
**Grosser Garten (Dresden), 181**
**Gross St. Martin (Cologne), 512**
**Grosz, George, 21**
**Grünes Gewölbe (Dresden), 181**
**Grunewald (Berlin), 69**
accommodations, 85–86
restaurants, 96–97
**Grunewald (Munich), jogging, 126**
**Grünewald, Matthis, 19, 242, 380, 454, 465**
**Gun Park (Heidelberg), 412**
**Güstrow, 638**
**Gutach Falls (near Triberg), 391**
**Gutenberg Museum (Mainz), 7–8, 485**

**Hackesche Höfe (Berlin), 72**
**Haidhausen (Munich), accommodations, 282–283**
**Hallenkirche (Hall Churches), 24, 25**
**Hall of Mirrors Building (Heidelberg), 412**
**Hall of the Swan Knight (Hohenschwangau), 264**
**Hambach Castle, 483**
**Hamburg, 2, 584–614**
accommodations, 588–596
bars, 613–614
boat tours and cruises, 603
brief description of, 33–34
business hours, 587
car rentals, 587
currency exchange, 587
doctors and dentists, 587
drugstores, 587–588
emergencies, 588
gardens and parks, 602–603
gay clubs, 611, 613
for kids, 603
layout of, 585–586
neighborhoods, 586
nightlife and entertainment, 607–614
performing arts, 607–608
post office, 588
restaurants, 596–600
safety, 588
shopping, 604–606
sights and attractions, 600–603
sports and outdoor activities, 604
taxis, 587
transportation, 586–587
traveling to, 584–585
visitor information, 585
**Hamburg Ballet, 607**
**Hamburgische Staatsoper (Hamburg), 607**
**Hamburg State Opera, 607**
**Hamburg Stock Exchange, 600**
**Hamburg Summer, 39**
**Hameln, 26, 568–570**
**Hanau, 581**
**Handcrafts, 17. *See also* Cuckoo clocks; Porcelain and china; Woodcarvings**
Berlin, 110
Cochem, 533
Freudenstadt, 394
Germanisches Nationalmuseum (Nürnberg), 211
Heidelberg, 413–414
Heimatmuseum (Freudenstadt), 394
Heimatmuseum (Ravensburg), 377

Kunstgewerbemuseum (Berlin), 110
Lübeck, 619
Munich, 312
Nürnberg, 212
Triberg, 391–392
Ulmer Museum, 227–228
**Handel, George Frideric, 654**
**Handwerkerhof (Nürnberg), 209, 212–213**
**Hang gliding, 325**
**Hann-Münden, 582**
**Hannover, 562–568**
**Hannoversch-Münden, 582**
**Hansa Theater (Hamburg), 608**
**Hansaviertel (Berlin), 69, 120**
**Hanseatic League, 547, 615, 633, 639, 642, 648**
**Harry's New York Bar (Berlin), 142**
**Harvestehude (Hamburg), accommodations, 594–595**
**Harvey's Cafe Bar (Frankfurt), 461–462**
**Harz Mountains, 547, 572**
**Hauptkirche St. Michaelis (Hamburg), 600**
**Hauptmarkt (Nürnberg), 209**
**Hauptwache (Frankfurt), 453, 457**
**Haus der Bürgerschaft (Bremen), 548**
**Haus der Geschichte der Bundesrepublik Deutschland (Bonn), 497**
**Haus der Schiffergesellschaft (Lübeck), 618**
**Haus der Wannsee-Konferenz (Berlin), 121–122**
**Haus des Weines (Trier), 541**
**Haus Thalheim (Eberbach), 419**
**Haus Töller (Cologne), 519**
**Haus zum Cavazzen (Lindau), 359**
**Haydn, Franz Joseph, 654–655**
**Health concerns, 40–41**
**Health insurance, 40–41**
**Heathen's Wall (Lindau), 359**
**Heidelberg, 32, 39, 408–418**
accommodations, 414–415
nightlife, 417–418
restaurants, 416–417
shopping, 413–414
sights and attractions, 410, 412–413
student drinking clubs, 417–418
traveling to, 410
visitor information, 410
**Heidelberg Castle, 9, 410, 412**
**Heilbronn, 420–421**
**Heiligengeistkirche (Stralsund), 642**
**Heiliggeistkirche (Heidelberg), 413**
**Heilig-Kreuz-Kirche (Rostock), 640**
**Heimatmuseum (Berchtesgaden), 328**
**Heimatmuseum (Freudenstadt), 394**
**Heimatmuseum (Oberammergau), 351**
**Heimatmuseum (Ravensburg), 377**
**Heimatmuseum (Reichenau), 373**
**Heimatmuseum (Überlingen), 375**
**Heine, Heinrich, 117, 496, 524, 575**
Heinrich-Heine-Institut (Düsseldorf), 524
**Hellabrunn Zoo (Munich), 307, 309**
**Herberstrasse (Hamburg), 610–611**
**Herb Garden (Reichenau), 373**
**Herder, Johann Gottfried, 154**
**Herkules Keule (Dresden), 192**
**Hermitage (Bayreuth), 198**
**Herrenchiemsee, 264**
**Herrenchiemsee (Herreninsel), 336, 337–338**
**Herrenhäuser Garten (Hannover), 563**
**Herrgottskirche (Creglingen), 244**
**Hertie (Munich), 313**
**Herzogschloss (Celle), 560**
**Hesse, Hermann, 396**
Haus (Calw), 397
**Hessisches Staatstheater (Wiesbaden), 469**
**Hiking, 50–52. *See* Walks and hikes**
Bavarian Alps, 3, 6, 51, 324, 344–346
Berchtesgaden National Park, 52
Black Forest, 393
Franconia, 196
**Hindenburgufer (Hindenburg Embankment) (Kiel), 623**
**Hinterzarten, 390**
**Hirschgarten (Munich), 295**
**Hirschhorn, 419**
**Hirschhorn Castle, 419**
**Hirschpark (Hamburg), 603**
**Historical Museum (Dresden), 182**
**Historischer Garten (Frankfurt), 454–455**
**Historischer Weinkeller (Berlin), 141**
**Historisches Museum (Frankfurt), 455**
**Historisches Museum der Pfalz (Speyer), 476**
**History of Germany, 647–653**
**Hitler, Adolf, 116, 119, 159, 164, 168, 208, 318, 327, 473, 651**
Obersalzberg, 2, 331–333
**Höchster Porzellan Manufacture GmbH (Frankfurt), 458–459**
**Hochzeitshaus (Hameln), 568**
**Hofbräuhaus am Platzl (Munich), 318**
**Hofburg Repertory Theater (Bamberg), 207**
**Hoffmann, E. T. A., Haus (Bamberg), 204**
**Hofgarten (Düsseldorf), 524**
**Hofgarten (Munich), 302**
**Hohenschwangau Castle (near Füssen), 9, 263–266**
**Hohes Schloss (Füssen), 261**
**Holbein, Hans**
the Elder, 256, 258, 259, 358
the Younger, 19, 255
**Hölderlinturm (Tübingen), 431**
**Holidays, 38**
**Holocaust, 52, 114, 122, 481, 497**
**Holstentor (Holsten Gate) (Lübeck), 616**
**Holthusenbad (Hamburg), 604**
**Holy Roman Empire, 647–648**
**Holzschittschule (Woodcarving School) (Oberammergau), 352**
**Homberg, 582**
**Horse-drawn sled and sleigh rides, 325, 339, 574**
**Horse racing, 402**
**Hot-air ballooning, 325, 402**
**Hotelguide Germany IHA Hotel Association, 54**
**House of Hannover, 562**
**Höxter, 583**

Imperial Baths (Trier), 542
Imperial Hall (Frankfurt), 454
Information sources, 34–35
Insurance, 40–41
Interhostel, 43
International Film Festival (Berlin), 38
International Gay & Lesbian Travel Association (IGLTA), 42
International May Festival (Wiesbaden), 39, 469
Internet access
  Berlin, 75
  Frankfurt, 440
  Munich, 274
Isar River, rafting, 311
Isartor (Isar Gate) (Munich), 298
Island of Sylt, 628–632

Jacobikirche (Hamburg), 600
Jacobikirche (Stralsund), 642
Jagdschloss Granitz (Rügen), 645
Jagdschloss Schachen (Garmisch-Partenkirchen), 345
Jagshaus Heede (Hann-Münden), 582
Jakobikirche (Goslar), 573
Jasmunder Bodden, 645
Jazz
  Berlin, 40, 139
  Cologne, 519–520
  Dresden, 191
  Düsseldorf, 531
  Freiburg, 385
  Göttingen, 578
  Hamburg, 608
  Heidelberg, 418
  Leipzig, 166, 174
  Munich, 319–320
  Würzburg, 237
Jazzclub (Bamberg), 207
Jewelry
  Berlin, 132
  Düsseldorf, 526
  Frankfurt, 458
  Hamburg, 606
  Munich, 314–315
  Schmuckmuseum (Pforzheim), 399
  Stuttgart, 425
Jewish Cemetery (Berlin), 122
Jewish Cemetery (Worms), 481
Jewish Museum Berlin, 114
Jewish quarter
  Speyer, 477–478
  Worms, 480–481
Jewish War Memorial (Berlin), 118
Jews, 52
J.G. Niederegger (Lübeck), 619
Jimmy's Bar (Frankfurt), 463
Joe's Wirthaus zum Löwen (Berlin), 141
Jogging
  Berlin, 126
  Frankfurt, 456
  Hamburg, 604
  Munich, 311
Johannapark (Leipzig), 170
Judenfriedhof (Worms), 481
Jüdischer Friedhof (Berlin), 122
Jüdisches Museum Berlin, 114
Jugendstil (German Art Nouveau), 28–29, 104, 224, 473, 586
July wine festival (Traben-Trarbach), 537
Junges Theater (Göttingen), 578
Jungfernstieg (Hamburg), 585
Justizgebäude (Justice Palace) (Nürnberg), 208, 210

K 20 Kunstsammlung am Grabbeplatz (Düsseldorf), 525
KaDeWe (Kaufhaus des Westens) (Berlin), 131
Kaiserburg (Nürnberg), 211
Kaiserburg Museum (Nürnberg), 211
Kaiserdom (Imperial Cathedral) (Bamberg), 204
Kaiserdom (Imperial Cathedral) (Speyer), 10, 476
Kaiserkeller (Hamburg), 609
Kaiserpfalz (Goslar), 573
Kaisersaal (Frankfurt), 454
Kaiser-Wilhelm Gedächtniskirche (Kaiser Wilhelm Memorial Church) (Berlin), 114–115
  accommodations near, 83–85
  restaurants near, 94–95
Kaiser Wilhelms Bad (Bad Homburg), 469–470
Kammerspiele (Hamburg), 607
Kandinsky, Wassily, 7, 21, 28, 154, 228, 300, 305, 602
Kap Arkona, 646
Karl-Marx-Haus (Trier), 542
Karlsplatz (Munich), 270
Karlstor (Munich), 298
Karmelitenklosterkirche (Ravensburg), 377
Kassel, 582
Käthe-Kollwitz-Museum (Berlin), 115
Käthe-Kruse-Puppen-Museum (Donauwörth), 255
Katholische Hofkirche (Dresden), 181
Katzenbuckl, 420
Kaufhaus (Freiburg), 382
Kaufhaus Schrill (Berlin), 133
Kaufhof (Munich), 313
Kayaking, 325
KAZ (Kommunikations Aktions-Zentrum) (Göttingen), 578
Kehlstein (Eagle's Nest) (Obersalzberg), 331–333
Kellertheater (Leipzig), 173
Kiefer, Anselm, 22, 156
Kiel, 622–625
Kieler Woche (Kiel Week), 623
Kinderzeche (Dinkelsbühl), 251
Kirchner, Ernst, 21, 106, 110, 425, 454, 497, 512, 602
Kit Kat Klub (Berlin), 140
Klee, Paul, 110, 113, 154, 228, 300, 305, 425, 512, 525, 602
Kleinhesseloher See, 311
Klimt, Gustav, 181, 305
Klingenmünster, 483
Klosterbräurei (Kiel), 625
Kloster Ettal, 355
Kloster Maulbronn, 399
Knaack-Klub (Berlin), 139
*Kneipen*, in Berlin, 112, 143–144
Knight's Hall (Rittersaal) (Weikersheim), 242–243
Koblenz, 492–495
Kollegiengebäude (Schwerin), 636
Köln. *See* Cologne
Kölner Dom, 510
Kölner Philharmonie (Cologne), 518

Komische Oper Berlin, 135–136
Kongresshalle (Augsburg), 260
Kongresshalle (Berlin), 120
Königliches Schloss Berchtesgaden, 328
Königsallee (Düsseldorf), 524
Königshaus (Leipzig), 168
Königssee, 3, 330–331
Konstanz (Constance), 368–372
Konstanz Casino, 371–372
Konstanz Stadttheater (Meersburg), 368
Konzerthaus (Freiburg), 385
Konzerthaus Berlin, 136
Kornhaus (Ravensburg), 376–377
KPM (Königliche Porzellan-Manufaktur) (Berlin), 129
Krämerbrücke (Erfurt), 163
Krautergarten (Reichenau), 373
Kreuzberg (Berlin), 69
Kreuzkirche (Dresden), 181
Kriminal Museum (Rothenburg), 246
Kröpeliner-Strasse (Rostock), 639
Kröpeliner Tor (Rostock), 639
Kultur-Historisches Museum (Rostock), 640
Kulturhistorisches Museum (Stralsund), 642–643
Kulturpalast (Dresden), 189–190
Kultur Rathaus (Dresden), 191
Kumpelnest 3000 (Berlin), 140
Kunstgewerbemuseum (Museum of Decorative Arts) (Berlin), 110
Kunsthalle (Bremen), 2, 550
Kunsthalle (Hamburg), 8, 601–602
Kunsthalle Düsseldorf, 525
Kunstlerhaus Mouson Turm (Frankfurt), 459
Kunstmuseum Bonn, 497
Kunstmuseum Düsseldorf, 525
Kunstring Meissen (Munich), 312
Kunstsammlungen Böttcherstrasse (Bremen), 552
Kunstsammlungen zu Weimar, 154–155
Kunstsammlung Nordrhein-Westfalen (Düsseldorf), 21
Kunstsammlung Nordrhein-Westfalen (Düsseldorf), 525
Kunst-und Kulturgeschichtliche Sammlungen (Regensburg), 219
Kurfürstendamm (Ku'damm) (Berlin), 67, 68, 112
  accommodations, 77–83
  restaurants, 91–94
  shopping, 127
Kurfürstliches Palais (Trier), 541–542
Kurgarten (Baden-Baden), 401
Kurhaus (Baden-Baden), 407
Kurhaus (Wiesbaden), 466, 469
Kurpark (Bad Pyrmont), 571
Kurpark (Wiesbaden), 466
Kurpfälzisches Museum (Heidelberg), 413
Kurvenstar (Berlin), 142
KZ-Gedenkstätte Dachau, 323

La Gata (Frankfurt), 462
Lake Constance Wine Festival (Meersburg), 365
Landesmuseum Mainz, 485–486
Langenargen, 361
Langenargen Stadtmuseum, 362
La Paloma (Hamburg), 614
Lapidarium (Mainz), 485
Lauterbach, 581–582
La Vie en Rose (Berlin), 139
Leipzieger Oper, 172
Leipzig, 30, 165–177
  accommodations, 170–171
  gay bars and clubs, 174
  nightlife, 172–174
  restaurants, 172
  shopping, 170
  side trips from, 174–177
  sights and attractions, 166–170
  special events, 166
  transportation, 166
  traveling to, 165–166
  visitor information, 166
Leipziger Jazztages, 166
Leipziger Stadtfest, 166
Leipziger Strassen Musikfestival, 166
Leipzig University Tower, 170
Lenz die Bar (Berlin), 140–141
Lenzkirch, 383
Lesbian travelers. *See* Gay and lesbian travelers
Lichtentaler Allee (Baden-Baden), 401
Liebermann, Max, 108, 181, 601, 636
Liebfrauenkirche (Koblenz), 493
Liebfrauenkirche (Ravensburg), 377
Liebfrauenkirche (Trier), 543
Liebighaus (Frankfurt), 453
Liederhalle (Stuttgart), 424
Lighthouses, Lindau, 358
Limburg, Monastery of (Bad Dürkheim), 482
Lindau, 11, 12, 356–362
Lindenhofbad (Lindau), 359
Linderhof, 264
Linderhof Palace, 354–355
Liquor laws, 61
Liszt, Franz
  House (Weimar), 155–156
  Museum (Bayreuth), 200
Live-music clubs
  Aachen, 507
  Berlin, 139
  Bonn, 501
  Bremen, 557
  Cologne, 519–520
  Frankfurt, 461
  Göttingen, 578
  Hannover, 568
  Heidelberg, 418
  Koblenz, 495
  Leipzig, 174
Lochgefängnis (Nürnberg), 211–212
Lochner, Stephan, 18, 510, 512
Logo (Hamburg), 612
Loni-Ubler-Haus (Nürnberg), 216
Lore Berlin, 142–143
Loretta im Garten (Pupasch) (Berlin), 141–142
Love Parade (Berlin), 135
Lower Saxony, 33
Lower Saxony State Museum (Hannover), 564
Lübeck, 34, 615–622
Lübeck Harbor, 618
Lucky's Manhattan (Frankfurt), 462
Ludwig Beck am Rathauseck (Munich), 313
Ludwig I, King of Bavaria, 302, 304, 327, 334, 464, 510

**Ludwig II, "Mad" King, 9, 28, 197, 304, 315, 326, 336**
biographical sketch of, 264
Neues Schloss (Herrenchiemsee), 337–338
Neuschwanstein, 263–266
Schloss Linderhof, 354–355
**Luna (Frankfurt), 463**
**Lüneburg, 557–560**
**Lüneburg Heath, 12, 557, 559**
**Luther, Martin, 174, 175, 479, 480, 648–649**
Lutherhaus (Eisenach), 164
**Lutherhalle Wittenberg, 175**
**Lutter und Wegner 1811 (Berlin), 144**

**Mach I (Nürnberg), 217**
**Macke, August, 21, 497**
**Mail and post offices, 61**
**Mainau Island, 12, 368, 369–370**
**Mainfränkisches Fortress (Würzburg), 233**
**Mainfränkisches Museum (Würzburg), 233–234**
**Mainz, 484–488**
**Mangturm (Lindau), 358**
**Mann, Thomas, 159, 354, 387, 615, 620**
Buddenbrookhaus (Lübeck), 618
**Märchenstrasse (Fairy-Tale Road), 6, 33, 580–583**
**Maria-Einsiedel, 310**
**Marienbrücke (behind Neuschwanstein Castle), 263**
**Marienkirche (Berlin), 117–118**
**Marienkirche (Lübeck), 617–618**
**Marienkirche (Stralsund), 642**
**Marienkirche (Würzburg), 233**
**Marienplatz (Munich), 270, 295**
**Marionette and puppet theaters, 250, 309, 557, 581**
**Marionettes and puppets, 250, 309, 403, 414**
**Market Church (Hannover), 563**
**Markets.** ***See also*** **Flea markets**
Berlin, 133
Bonn, 498
Cologne, 513
Hamburg, 605
Heidelberg, 413
Munich, 295
Würzburg, 232
**Markgräfliches Opernhaus (Bayreuth), 200**
**Märkisches Museum (Berlin), 115**
**Markthalle (Hamburg), 612**
**Marktkirche (Goslar), 573**
**Marktkirche (Hannover), 563**
**Marktplatz**
Bad Mergentheim, 241
Berchtesgaden, 327
Bremen, 548
Freudenstadt, 394
Goslar, 573
Göttingen, 576
Heidelberg, 413
Passau, 224
Schwäbisch Hall, 433
Tübingen, 430
Weikersheim, 243
Weimar, 152
**Marstall (Schwerin), 636**
**Marstallmuseum (Munich), 304**
**Martin-Gropius-Bau (Berlin), 115**
**Marx, Karl, 495, 542**
Karl-Marx-Haus (Trier), 542
Studienzentrum Karl-Marx-Haus (Trier), 542
**Matthäuskirche (Munich), 306**
**Maulbronn, 399**
**Mäuseturm (Mouse Tower), 489**
**Maximilianstrasse (Munich), 270**
**Max-Joseph-Platz (Munich), 270**
**Mecklenburgisches Staatstheater (Schwerin), 636**
**Medical insurance, 40–41**
**Meersburg, 365–368**
**Mehlsack Tower (Ravensburg), 377**
**Meissen, 10, 193–195**
**Meissener Porzellan (Berlin), 129**
**Meistertrunk festival (Rothenburg), 246**
**Memorial Church, Kaiser Wilhelm (Berlin), 114**
accommodations near, 83–85
restaurants near, 94–95
**Menzel, Adolph von, 106, 110**
**Mephisto Bar (Leipzig), 166, 173**
**Mercedes-Benz Museum (Stuttgart), 425**
**Metropole (Berlin), 138**
**Michaeliskirche (Erfurt), 163**
**Michaelskirche (Munich), 26, 306**
**Michaelskirche (Schwäbisch Hall), 433**
**Miltenberg, 238–239**
**Mitsukoshi (Frankfurt), 459**
**Mittelzell, 373**
**Mittenwald, 11, 341–343**
**Mobility International USA, 42**
**Mojo Club (Hamburg), 612**
**Molotow (Hamburg), 612**
**Monastery of Limburg (Bad Dürkheim), 482**
**Monet, Claude, 106, 181, 305, 454**
**Money matters, 36–37**
**Monteverdi-Chor (Hamburg), 607**
**Montfort Castle (Langenargen), 361**
**Mont Royal (Traben-Trarbach), 537**
**Moritzbastei (Leipzig), 174**
**Mosel River, boat tours, 533, 543–544**
**Mosel Valley, 11, 532–546**
brief description of, 33
**Mosel-Wein-Woche (Cochem), 533**
**Moss Rehab Hospital, 42**
**Mozart, Wolfgang Amadeus, 165, 169, 257, 259, 302, 309, 654**
Festival (Augsburg), 260
Festival (Würzburg), 39, 232, 234
**Mr. Dorian's Club (Frankfurt), 462**
**Münchener Marionetten Theater (Munich), 309**
**Münchhausen-Erinnerungszimmer (Bodenwerder), 583**
**Münchhausen Museum (Bodenwerder), 583**

**Münchner Kammerspiele (Munich), 316**
**Münchner Philharmoniker (Munich), 317**
**Münchner Poupenstuben und Zinnfiguren Kabinette (Munich), 315**
**Münchner Stadtmuseum (Munich), 305, 309**
**Münden, 582**
**Munich, 267–323**
accommodations, 2, 275–283
family-friendly, 278
bars and cafes, 320–322
beer gardens, 294–295
beer halls, 317
biking, 273
brief description of, 31
business hours, 274
churches, 305–307
currency exchange, 274
doctors and dentists, 274
drugstores, 274
finding addresses in, 270
Frommer's favorite experiences, 298
gay clubs, 322
Internet access, 274
for kids, 309
accommodations, 278
neighborhoods, 270–271
nightclubs, 318–319
nightlife and entertainment, 315–322
organized tours, 309–310
performing arts, 315–317
post office, 274
restaurants, 2, 283–294
safety, 275
Schwabing, 270, 271
accommodations, 282
restaurants, 292–293
shopping, 311–315
side trips from, 323
sights and attractions, 7, 294–310
sports and outdoor activities, 310–311
taxis, 273
transportation, 271–273
walking tours, 310
**Munich Philharmonic Orchestra, 317**
**Munich Tourist Office, 55**
**Municipal Museum (Munich), 305**
**Münster (Überlingen), 375**
**Münster Kirche Sankt Johannes (Bad Mergentheim), 241**
**Münsterplatz (Aachen), 504**
**Münster St. Maria and Markus (Reichenau), 373**
**Museen Behnhaus/Drägerhaus (Lübeck), 618**
**Museen de Stadt Regensburg, 219**
**Museum am Rathaus Keller (Wismar), 633**
**Museum Berlinische Galerie (Berlin), 115**
**Museum der Bildenden Künste (Leipzig), 168**
**Museum Europäischer Kulturen (Berlin), 109**
**Museum für Angewandte Kunst (Cologne), 511**
**Museum für Angewandte Kunst (Frankfurt), 455**
**Museum für Gegenwart (Berlin), 115–116**
**Museum für Hamburgische Geschichte (Hamburg), 602**
**Museum für Indische Kunst (Berlin), 108**
**Museum für Moderne Kunst (Frankfurt), 455**
**Museum für Neue Kunst (Freiburg), 382**
**Museum für Ostasiatische Kunst (Berlin), 108**
**Museum Haus am Checkpoint Charlie (Berlin), 116**
**Museum Holstentor (Lübeck), 617**
**Museum in der Runden Ecke (Leipzig), 168–169**
**Museum Ludwig (Cologne), 2, 8, 20, 511**
**Museum of Antiquities (Munich), 304–305**
**Museum of Applied Art (Cologne), 511**
**Museum of Applied Arts (Frankfurt), 455**
**Museum of Contemporary Art (Berlin), 115–116**
**Museum of Decorative Arts (Berlin), 110**
**Museum of Far Eastern Art (Berlin), 108**
**Museum of Folklore (Überlingen), 375**
**Museum of Füssen, 261**
**Museum of Hamburg History (Hamburg), 602**
**Museum of Islamic Art (Berlin), 109**
**Museum of Modern Art (Frankfurt), 455**
**Museum of Musical Instruments (Leipzig), 169**
**Museum of the Palatinate (Heidelberg), 413**
**Museum Quarter (Munich), 271**
**Museum Schnütgen (Cologne), 511**
**Museumsinsel (Museum Island) (Berlin), 68, 72, 106, 108–109**
**Music, 653–655.** ***See also*** **Concerts; Jazz; Live-music clubs; Music festivals**
**Musical museums, 654**
**Music festivals, 654**
Augsburg, 260
Bayreuth, 39, 198, 200
Berlin, 40
Dresden, 654
Freiburg, 385
Garmisch-Partenkirchen, 350
Heidelberg, 417
Konstanz, 371, 372
Leipzig, 166
Lübeck, 616
Passau, 225–226
Wiesbaden, 466, 469
Würzburg, 39, 232, 234
**Musikalischer Sommer Festival (Baden-Baden), 407**
**Musikhalle (Hamburg), 607**
**Musikinstrumenten-Museum (Leipzig), 169**

**Nacht Leben (Frankfurt), 460–461**
**Napoléon Bonaparte, 118, 168, 240, 258, 541, 639, 649**
**Nasch Markt (Leipzig), 166, 168**
**Naturschützpark Lüneburger Heide (Lüneburg), 559**
**Navigational Museum (Rostock), 640**
**Nazi Germany, 168, 192, 208, 651.** ***See also*** **Hitler, Adolf**
Buchenwald Concentration Camp and Memorial Site (near Weimar), 158
**N. D. R. Symphoniker (Hannover), 567**
**Near East Museum (Berlin), 109**
**Neckar River, 6**

**Neckar Valley, 32**
boat tours, 413
Cycle Path, 12, 410
**Neoclassical architecture architecture, 27–28**
**Neubulach, 397**
**Neue Flora Theater (Hamburg), 608**
**Neue Nationalgalerie (Staatliche Museum zu Berlin), 20, 110, 112**
**Neue Pinakothek (Munich), 305**
**Neue Residenz (Bamberg), 204**
**Neuer Garten (Potsdam), 146**
**Neue Sachlichkeit (New Objectivity), 21**
**Neues Museum Weimar, 156**
**Neues Opernhaus (Leipzig), 172**
**Neues Palais (Potsdam), 148**
**Neues Rathaus, Leipzig, 168**
**Neues Rathaus (New City Hall), Munich, 295**
**Neues Schloss (Bayreuth), 200**
**Neues Schloss (Herrenchiemsee), 337–338**
**Neues Schloss (Meersburg), 366, 368**
**Neues Schloss (Stuttgart), 424**
**Neue Synagoge Berlin-Centrum Judaicum (Berlin), 66, 122**
**Neuleiningen, 482**
**Neuschwanstein (near Füssen), 9, 263–266**
**Neustadt, 582**
accommodations, 592–594
restaurants, 596–597
**Neustadt-an-der-Weinstrasse, 483**
**Neuweier, restaurants in, 407**
**Neuwerkkirche (Goslar), 573**
**New Lighthouse (Lindau), 358**
**New Synagogue (Berlin), 66, 122**
**Newton Bar (Berlin), 143**
**New Year's Day International Ski Jumping (Garmisch-Partenkirchen), 38**
**Niedersächsisches Landesmuseum Hannover, 564**
**Nieder Sächsische Stadtstheater Hannover, 567**
**Niederwald Monument, 489**
**Niederwildungen Altarpiece (Bad Wildungen), 579**
**Niederzell, 373**
**Nienstedten (Hamburg), accommodations, 595**
**Nightclubs and cabarets**
Berlin, 136–137
Bonn, 501
Bremen, 557
Dresden, 191–192
Frankfurt, 460
Munich, 318–319
Nürnberg, 216
Passau, 226
**Nightlife and entertainment**
Aachen, 506–507
Augsburg, 260
Baden-Baden, 407
Bad Homburg, 472
Bad Reichenhall, 336
Bad Wildungen, 580
Bamberg, 207
Berlin, 134–145
Bonn, 500–501
Bremen, 556–557
Cologne, 517–521
Dresden, 189–192
Düsseldorf, 530–531
Frankfurt, 459–463
Freiburg, 385
Garmisch-Partenkirchen, 349–350
Göttingen, 578–579
Hamburg, 607–614
Hameln, 569
Hannover, 567–568
Heidelberg, 417–418
Kiel, 625
Koblenz, 494–495
Konstanz, 371–372
Leipzig, 172–174
Lübeck, 621–622
Lüneburg, 559–560
Mainz, 488
Meersburg, 368
Munich, 315–322
Nürnberg (Nuremberg), 216–217
Passau, 225–226
Regensburg, 222
Rothenburg, 250
Schleswig, 627
Stuttgart, 429
Sylt, 632
Trier, 546
Tübingen, 432
Weimar, 161–162
Wiesbaden, 469
Worms, 482
Würzburg, 237–238
**Nikolaikirche (Berlin), 119–120**
**Nikolaikirche (Leipzig), 170**
**Nikolaiviertel (Nikolai Quarter) (Berlin), 68–69, 72, 112**
sights and attractions, 119–120
**Nikolausbrücke (Calw), 397**
**Nollendorfplatz (Berlin), 140**
**Nonntal (Berchtesgaden), 328**
**Nördlingen, 252–254**
**North Hesse, 33**
**November Jazz-Fest Berlin, 40**
**Nürnberg (Nuremberg), 31, 207–217**
accommodations, 213–215
nightlife and entertainment, 216–217
restaurants, 215–216
shopping, 212–213
sights and attractions, 209–212
transportation, 208–209
traveling to, 208
visitor information, 208
**Nydam Boat (Schleswig), 626**
**Nymphenburg Palace (Munich), 9, 264, 271, 298, 302, 304, 311**

**Oberammergau, 350–355**
**Obersalzberg, 2, 331–333**
**Obersee, Lake, 331**
**Oberzell, 373**
**Obletter (Nürnberg), 213**
**Oceanographic Museum and Aquarium (Stralsund), 643**
**Oktoberfest (Munich), 39, 267, 659**
**Old Castle and Württemberg Regional Museum (Stuttgart), 424**
**The Old Swede (Wismar), 633**
**Olympiapark (Munich), 271, 307, 311**
**Olympia Tower (Munich), 307**
**Olympic Stadium (Berlin), 116, 120**
**One Ninety East (Frankfurt), 461**
**Opera**
Bayreuth, 198, 200
Berlin, 135–136

Bonn, 501
Bremen, 556
Dresden, 189
Düsseldorf, 530
Frankfurt, 459, 460
Hamburg, 607
Leipzig, 172
Munich, 316
Nürnberg, 216
Worms, 482
**Oper der Stadt Bonn, 501**
**Operettenhaus (Hamburg), 608**
**Oper Frankfurt/Ballet Frankfurt, 460**
**Optical products, 17**
**Orangerie (Potsdam), 148**
**Orbitz, 54**
**Ottheinrich Building (Heidelberg), 412**
**Otto Kellnberger Holzhandlung (Munich), 312**
**Oxymoron (Berlin), 139**

**Package tours, 47–48**
**Palace Gardens (Trier), 542**
**Palaces. *See* Castles and palaces**
**Palais Vischer (Calw), 397**
**Palastgarten (Trier), 542**
**Palmengarten (Frankfurt), 456**
**Paragliding, 325**
**Partnachklamm, 12**
**Partnachklamm Gorge, 346**
**Passau, 222–226**
**Passion Play (Oberammergau), 350**
**Pentagonal Tower (Nürnberg), 211**
**Performing arts. *See also* Ballet; Concerts; Jazz; Live-music clubs; Music festivals; Nightclubs and cabarets; Opera; Theater**
Aachen, 506–507
Berlin, 134–136
Bonn, 500–501
Bremen, 556
Cologne, 517–519
Dresden, 189
Düsseldorf, 530
Frankfurt, 459–460
Göttingen, 578
Hamburg, 607–608
Hannover, 567
Heidelberg, 417
Koblenz, 494–495
Leipzig, 172–173
Munich, 315–317
Stuttgart, 429
**Pergamon Altar (Berlin), 109**
**Pergamon Museum (Berlin), 7, 109**
**Permoser, Balthazar, 20, 181, 182**
**Petersgrube (Lübeck), 618**
**Peterskirche (Erfurt), 163**
**Peterskirche (Munich), 306**
**Pfalzel, 544**
**Pforzheim, 398–400**
**Pharmaceutical Museum (Heidelberg), 412**
**Philatelie und Ansichtskarten (Munich), 313**
**Philharmonic Orchestra of Baden-Baden (Baden-Baden), 407**
**Philharmonie (Berlin), 120**
**Philographikon Galerie Rauhut (Munich), 311–312**
**Picasso, Pablo, 8, 110, 112–113, 128, 228, 300, 511, 550, 602**
**Picture Gallery (Berlin), 110**
**Picture Gallery (Potsdam), 148**
**Pilatushaus (Oberammergau), 351**
**Pinakothek der Moderne (Munich), 21, 22, 300**
**Pit Club-Saloon/Tom's Bar (Hamburg), 613**
**Planten und Blomen (Hamburg), 603**
**Platzl quarter (Munich), 270**
**Police, 61**
**Pompeianum (Aschaffenburg), 464**
**Porcelain and china, 16–17**
Berlin, 129
Dresden, 184
Frankfurt, 458–459
Meissen, 194
Munich, 312, 315
Nürnberg, 213
**Porcelain Chamber (Charlottenburg Palace, Berlin), 106**
**Porcelain Gallery (Munich), 302**
**Porcelain Museum (Meissen), 194**
**Porcelain Museum (Munich), 304**
**Porta Nigra (Trier), 541**
**Porta Praetoria (Regensburg), 219**
**Porzellan-Manufaktur (Meissen), 194**
**Porzellan-Manufaktur-Nymphenburg (near Munich), 315**
**Porzellansammlung (Munich), 304**
**Pösseldorf (Hamburg), 586**
**Potsdam, 30, 145–150**
side trip to Potsdam, 145–150
**Potsdamer Platz (Berlin), 72**
**Potsdamer Platz Arkaden (Berlin), 134**
**Predigerkirche (Erfurt), 163**
**Prenzlauer Berg (Berlin), 66**
**Presley, Elvis, 473**
**Priceline, 54**
**Prinoth (Munich), 313**
**Prinzknecht (Berlin), 141**
**Projekttheater Dresden, 191**
**Protestant Reformation, 648–649**
**Provincial Museum of Archeology (Schleswig), 626**
**Provincial Museum of the Central Rhineland (Mainz), 485**
**Prussia, 649–650**
**Prüss & Ochs Gallery (Berlin), 129**
**Pulse (Frankfurt), 462**
**Pulverfass (Hamburg), 612**
**Pump Room (Baden-Baden), 402**
**Puppet and marionette theaters, 250, 309, 557, 581**
**Puppets and marionettes, 250, 309, 403, 414**

**Quixo, 54**
**Quasimodo (Berlin), 139**
**Quedlinburg, 10, 175–177**

**Rafting, Isar River, 311**
**Rammelsberger Bergbaumuseum (Goslar), 574**
**Raphael, 110, 178, 182, 299**
**Raschi-Haus Museum (Worms), 481**
**Rathaus (Town Hall). *See also* Altes Rathaus (Old Town Hall)**
Aachen, 504–505
Augsburg, 258
Dresden, 181

**Rathaus (Town Hall)** *(cont.)*
Düsseldorf, 524
Goslar, 573
Hamburg, 600
Hannover, 564
Heilbronn, 420
Koblenz, 493
Lübeck, 617
Lüneburg, 558
Meersburg, 366
Passau, 224
Quedlinburg, 176
Rostock, 639
Rothenburg, 246–247
Stralsund, 642
Tübingen, 430
Überlingen, 375
Ulm, 227
Wasserburg, 361
Wismar, 633
**Ratskeller (Göttingen), 578**
**Ravensburg, 376–378**
**Reception Chamber (Charlottenburg Palace, Berlin), 106**
**Red Wine Festival (Assmannshausen), 39**
**Reeperbahn (Hamburg), 610–611**
**Reformation, 648–649**
**Regensburg, 196, 217–222**
**Regions of Germany, 30–34**
**Reichenau, 372–374**
**Reichenstrasse (Füssen), 261**
**Reichsburg Cochem, 12, 532**
**Reichsstadtmuseum (Rothenburg), 247**
**Reichstag (Berlin), 66, 119**
**Reingold (Berlin), 143**
**Reisa Efau (Dresden), 191–192**
**Rembrandt van Rijn, 110, 156, 168, 178, 182, 213, 299, 550, 564**
**Renaissance architecture, 25–26**
**Renaissance art, 19, 210**
**Residenz (Munich), 300**
**Residenz (Schloss und Gartenverwaltung Würzburg), 8–9, 27, 234**
**Residenz Museum (Munich), 300**
**Residenztheater im Schloss (Dresden), 190**
**Restaurant Olympiasee (Munich), 307–308**
**Restaurants**
best, 15–16
glossary of menu terms, 662–665
**Restrooms, 61**
**The Rheingau, 489–492**
**Rheingau-und Weinmuseum (Rüdesheim), 490**
**Rheinisches Landesmuseum (Trier), 543**
**Rhein-Mosel-Halle (Koblenz), 494**
**The Rhineland, 33, 475–531**
cuisine, 657
**Rhine River, 3**
cruises, 478
**Ribnitz, 641**
**Ribnitz-Damgarten, 641**
**Richard-Wagner-Museum (Wahnfried) (Bayreuth), 200**
**Riemenschneider, Tilman, 18–19, 204, 233, 234, 247, 299, 328, 413, 453**
**The Ries (Nördlingen), 252**
**Rieskrater-Museum (Nördlingen), 253**
**Rittersaal (Knight's Hall) (Weikersheim), 242–243**
**Rock Am *See* Festival (Konstanz), 372**
**Rock climbing, Baden-Baden, 402**
**Rococo architecture, 26**
**Rococo art and artists, 20**
**Roman Baths (Potsdam), 149**
**Romanesque architecture, 23**
**Romanesque art, 18**
**Roman-Germanic Museum (Cologne), 511–512**
**Roman sites and antiquities**
Aachen, 503
Augsburg, 255, 256
Badenweiler, 386
Berlin, 108, 109
Cologne, 507–508, 511–512
Frankfurt, 453, 455
Mainz, 485
Munich, 304
Potsdam, 149
Regensburg, 219
Trier, 540, 541–542
**Romantic architecture, 27–28**
**Romantic art and artists, 20**
**Romantic Road *(Romantische Strasse)*, 11, 31, 230–266. *See also* specific towns**
bus tours, 230
towns of, 230
**Römerbad (Lindau), 359**
**Römerberg (Frankfurt), 435, 454**
**Römerberg Square, 454**
**Römisch-Germanisches Museum (Cologne), 511–512**
**Rosenthal (Berlin), 129**
**Rosenthal Studio-Hause (Munich), 312**
**Roses (Berlin), 143**
**Rostock, 639–641**
**Rostocker Tor (Ribnitz-Damgarten), 641**
**Rothenburg, 10–11**
**Rothenburger Tor (Dinkelsbühl), 251**
**Rothenburg ob der Tauber, 244–250**
**Royal Castle Walk, 12**
**Royal Gardens of Herrenhäusen (Hannover), 563**
**Royal Stables (Schwerin), 636**
**Rübenmarkt (Nördlingen), 253**
**Rubens, Peter Paul, 20, 168, 178, 182, 258, 299, 525, 550, 564**
**Rüdesheim, 11, 489–491**
**Rügen, 644–646**
**Ruprecht-Karl-University (Heidelberg), 408**
**Rüstkammer (Dresden), 182**

**Sababurg, 582**
**Sachensplatz (Leipzig), 170**
**Sachsenhausen Concentration Camp (near Berlin), 121**
**Safari (Hamburg), 611**
**Safety, 61**
**Sailing (yachting), Lake Constance (Bodensee), 356**
**St. Andreas (Cologne), 512**
**St. Andreas Church (Düsseldorf), 524**
**St. Anne, Chapel of (Füssen), 261**
**St. Aposteln (Cologne), 512**
**St. Bartholomäus, Dom (Frankfurt), 454–455**
**St. Castor's (Koblenz), 493**
**St. Cecilia's (Cologne), 512**
**St. Georg (Cologne), 512**
**St. George, Stiftskirche (Reichenau), 373**
**St. Georgskirche (Nördlingen), 253**
**St. Gereon (Cologne), 512**
**St. Jakob (Wasserburg), 361**

**St. Jakobskirche (Rothenburg), 247**
**St. Joseph's Church (Hamburg), 611**
**St. Katarina (Nürnberg), 216**
**St. Kilian, Dom (Würzburg), 233**
**St. Killian's Church (Heilbronn), 420**
**St. Kunibert (Cologne), 512**
**St. Lambertus Church (Düsseldorf), 524**
**St.-Lorenz-Kirche (Nürnberg), 212**
**St. Mangkirche (Füssen), 261**
**St. Maria, Abtai Kirche (Amorbach), 240**
**St. Maria, Dom (Augsburg), 256**
**St. Maria and Markus, Münster (Reichenau), 373**
**St. Maria im Kapitol (Cologne), 512**
**St. Maria Lyskirchen (Cologne), 512**
**St. Mary's Church (Lübeck), 617–618**
**St. Mary's Church (Marienkirche) (Berlin), 117–118**
**St. Mary's Church (Rostock), 639**
**St. Matthew's Church (Munich), 306**
**St. Michaelis, Hauptkirche (Hamburg), 600**
**St. Michael's Church (Munich), 306**
**St. Michael's Fountain (Bernkastel-Kues), 538**
**St. Nicholas, Church of (Berlin), 119**
**St. Nikolaikirche (Stralsund), 642**
**St. Nikolaikirche (Wismar), 634**
**St. Panteleon (Cologne), 512**
**St. Pauli (Hamburg), 610–611**
restaurants, 598–600
**St. Peter, Dom (Worms), 10, 480**
**St. Peter and St. Alexander, Stiftskirche St. (Aschaffenburg), 464–465**
**St. Peter and St. Paul, Stiftskirche (Reichenau), 373**
**St. Peter's, Dom (Regensburg), 218**
**St. Peter's Cathedral (Bremen), 548, 550**
**St. Peter's Cathedral (Schleswig), 626**
**St. Peter's Church (Lindau), 358**
**St. Peter's Church (Munich), 306**
**St. Petri, Dom (Bremen), 548, 550**
**St. Petri, Dom (Schleswig), 626**
**St. Petri Kirche (Hamburg), 600**
**St. Rochus (Düsseldorf), 524**
**St.-Sebaldus-Kirche (Nürnberg), 212**
**St. Servatius, Stiftskirche (Quedlinburg), 176**
**St. Severi, Church of (Erfurt), 163**
**St. Severin (Cologne), 512**
**St. Stephen's Cathedral (Passau), 223–224**
**St. Stephen's Church (Regensburg), 219**
**St. Thomas Boys' Choir (Leipzig), 169**
**St. Thomas Church (Leipzig), 169**
**St. Ulrich and St. Afra, Church of (Augsburg), 256**
**St. Ursula (Cologne), 512**
**St. Zeno (Bad Reichenhall), 334**
**Salt Lofts (Lübeck), 617**
**Salzbergwerk Berchtesgaden, 328**
**Sammlung Berger (Amorbach), 240**
**Sankt Michaelerskirche (Pforzheim), 399**
**Sans Souci Palace (Potsdam), 8, 27, 147**
**Sans Souci Park (Potsdam), 145–146**
**Savignyplatz (Berlin), 68**
**Saxony, 30**
cuisine, 657
**Scenic drives.** ***See*** **Driving tours and scenic drives**
**Schaezlerpalais (Augsburg), 258**
**Schatzkammer (Munich), 302**
**Schaubühne am Lehniner Platz (Berlin), 136**
**Schaubühne Lindenfels (Leipzig), 174**
**Schauinsland, 383**
**Schauspielhaus (Cologne), 517**
**Schauspielhaus (Dresden), 190**
**Schauspielhaus (Düsseldorf), 530**
**Schauspielhaus (Leipzig), 173**
**Scheulenviertel (Berlin), 130**
**Scheune (Dresden), 191**
**Schiffahrtsmuseum (Rostock), 640**
**Schiller, Friedrich von**
Goethe-Schiller Mausoleum (Weimar), 158
Schillerhaus (Leipzig), 169
Schillerhaus (Weimar), 156
**Schillerhaus (Leipzig), 169**
**Schillerplatz (Stuttgart), 424**
**Schinkel, Karl Friedrich, 28, 106, 108, 113, 114, 121, 136, 149, 189, 644**
**Schinkel Pavillon (Charlottenburg Palace, Berlin), 106**
**Schleswig, 625–627**
**Schleswig-Holstein, 615–632**
brief description of, 34
cuisine, 656
**Schleswig-Holsteinisches Freilichtmuseum (Kiel), 623**
**Schleswig-Holstein Music Festival (Lübeck), 616**
**Schleswig-Holstein State Museum (Schleswig), 626**
**Schloss Belvedere (Weimar), 156**
**Schloss Bürgeln (Badenweiler), 386**
**Schloss Cecilienhof (Potsdam), 148–149**
**Schloss Charlottenburg (Berlin), 104**
**Schloss Charlottenhof (Potsdam), 149**
**Schlossfest-Spiele festival (Heidelberg), 417**
**Schlossgarten (Schwerin), 636**
**Schloss Gottorf (Schleswig), 626**
**Schloss Güstrow, 638**
**Schloss Hambach, 483**
**Schloss Johannisburg (Aschaffenburg), 464**
**Schlosskirche (Friedrichshafen), 362, 363**
**Schlosskirche (Wittenberg), 175**
**Schloss Linderhof (near Oberammergau), 9, 354–355**
**Schloss Miltenburg (Miltenberg), 238**

Schlossmuseum (Weimar), 156
Schloss Nymphenburg (Munich), 9, 264, 302, 304, 311
Schlossplatz (Berchtesgaden), 327
Schloss Sigmaringen, 228
Schloss Spyker (Rügen), 645
Schloss Tiefurt (Weimar), 156
Schlossturm (Düsseldorf), 524
Schloss Veitshöchheim, 234–235
Schloss Wartburg (Eisenach), 8, 164
Schloss Weikersheim, 242
Schluchsee, 383
Schlüter, Andreas, 20, 104, 118, 470
Schmidts Tivoli (Hamburg), 608
Schmidt Theater (Hamburg), 608
Schmuckmuseum (Pforzheim), 399
Schnoor (Bremen), 552
Schönbusch Park (Aschaffenburg), 464
Schöneberg (Berlin), 69
Schöneberg Rathaus (Berlin), 116–117
Schötting (Bremen), 548
Schulemuseum (Friedrichshafen), 363
Schwabing (Munich), 270, 271
  accommodations, 282
  restaurants, 292–293
Schwäbisch Hall, 432–433
Schwarzwald. *See* Black Forest
Schwarzwald Hochstrasse, 379
Schwarzwald-Museum of Triberg, 391–392
Schweigen-Rechtenbach, 483
Schwenders (Hamburg), 614
Schwerin, 635–638
Schweriner Schloss (Schwerin), 636
Schwimmbad Titisee, 389
Schwitters, Kurt, 21
Schwules Museum (Berlin), 140
SchwuZ (Berlin), 141
Seagull Island (Schleswig), 625
Seamen's Guild House (Lübeck), 618
Seasons, 37–38
Security measures, air travel, 44–45
Seebuck, 383
Seepromenade (Friedrichshafen), 363
Seestrasse, 389
Semper Opera House (Dresden), 189
Senior travelers, 43–44
S.E.Z. Landsberger (Berlin), 126
Shamrock (Hamburg), 614
Shopping, best, 16–17
Shopping arcades, Berlin, 134
Siegessäule (Berlin), 123
Sinfonie an der Regnitz (Bamberg), 207
Singer's Hall (Neuschwanstein), 265
Sinkkasten (Frankfurt), 461
Skiing
  Bavarian Alps, 324, 325
  near Munich, 311
SO36 (Berlin), 138
Soccer
  Hamburg, 604
  Munich, 311
Society for Accessible Travel and Hospitality, 42
Sony Center am Potsdamer Platz (Berlin), 119
Sorb Country, 192–193
Spandau (Berlin), 69
Spandauer Zitadelle (Spandau Citadel) (Berlin), 122–123
Spa Park (Bad Homburg), 469
Spas, 6
  Bad Homburg, 469–470
  Bad Pyrmont, 570
  best, 12–13
  types of, 50–51
  Wiesbaden, 465–466
Special events and festivals, 38–39
Speer, Albert, 208
Speyer, 475–479
Spielbank Berlin, 145
Spielbank Garmisch-Partenkirchen, 349
Spielbank Hamburg, 614
Spielbank Im Kurpark (Bad Homburg), 472
Spielbank Westerland (Sylt), 632
Spielbank Wiesbaden, 469
Spielzeugmuseum (Munich), 309
Spielzeugmuseum (Nürnberg), 212
Spreewald, 192–193
Spycher Castle (Rügen), 645
Squirrel (Munich), 312
Staatliche Museum zu Berlin (Neue Nationalgalerie), 110, 112
Staatliches Museum Schwerin-Kunstsammlunger, 636
Staatsgalerie (Stuttgart), 20, 425
Staatsoper (Stuttgart), 429
Staats Operette (Dresden), 190
Staatstheater (Stuttgart), 429
Stachelschweine, Die (Berlin), 136
Städel Gallery (Frankfurt), 454
Stadtgarten (Lindau), 359
Stadtheater (Koblenz), 494
Städtische Bühnen (Nürnberg), 216
Städtische Bühnen/Schauspiel (Frankfurt), 459
Stadtische Galerie im Lenbachhaus (Munich), 7, 305
Stadtisches Museum (Göttingen), 576
Städtisches Spiel und Festhaus (Worms), 482
Stadtkirche (Bad Wildungen), 579
Stadtkirche (Freudenstadt), 394
Stadtkirche (Pforzheim), 399
Stadtkirche (Wittenberg), 175
Stadtkirche St. Peter und Paul (Weimar), 157
Stadtmauer (Überlingen), 375
Stadtmuseum (Nördlingen), 253
Stadtmuseum Dresden, 182
Stadtpark (Hamburg), 603
Stadttheater Company (Passau), 225
Stadttheater Konstanz, 371
Stadttheater Passau, 225
Starclub (Nürnberg), 217
Starnbergersee, 310
State Gallery of Stuttgart, 425

**State Theater (Munich), 316**
**Steinau an der Strasse, 581**
**Stiftskirche (Berchtesgaden), 327**
**Stiftskirche (Tübingen), 431**
**Stiftskirche St. George (Reichenau), 373**
**Stiftskirche St. Peter and St. Alexander (Aschaffenburg), 464–465**
**Stiftskirche St. Peter and St. Paul (Reichenau), 373**
**Stiftskirche St. Servatius (Quedlinburg), 176**
**St-Marien-Kirche (Rostock), 639**
**The Story of Berlin, 117**
**Stoss, Veit, 196, 208, 211, 212, 328**
**Stralsund, 641, 642–644**
**Strauss, Johann, Festival, 350**
**Strauss, Richard, 655**
**Street Music Festival (Leipzig), 166**
**Studentclub Kasseturm (Weimar), 162**
**Studentenkarzer (Student Jail) (Heidelberg), 413**
**Studienzentrum Karl-Marx-Haus (Trier), 542**
**Stuppach, 242**
**Stuppacher Madonna, 242**
**Stuttgart, 32, 422–429**
accommodations, 426–427
nightlife and entertainment, 429
restaurants, 428–429
shopping, 425–426
sights and attractions, 424–425
transportation, 424
traveling to, 422
visitor information, 422, 424
**Stuttgart Ballet (Stuttgart), 429**
**Südhaus Dance Theatre (Regensburg), 222**
**Suermondt Ludwig Museum (Aachen), 505**
**Swimming**
Baden-Baden, 403
Bavarian Alps, 325
Berlin, 126–127
Hamburg, 604
Lake Constance, 356
Munich, 310
Titisee, 389
**Sylt, 6–7, 628–632**

**Tacheles (Berlin), 130**
**Taunus Therme (Bad Homburg), 470**
**Taxes, 61–62**
**Technical Museum (Schwerin), 636**
**Technik-Museum (Speyer), 476**
**Technisches Museum (Pforzheim), 399**
**Technisches Museum (Schwerin), 636**
**Tegernsee Ducal palace (near Bad Wiessee), 340**
**Telephone, 62**
**Television Tower (Stuttgart), 424–425**
**Tennis, 311, 403, 456, 604**
Berlin, 127
**Thaliatheater (Hamburg), 607**
**Theater**
Aachen, 507
Baden-Baden, 407
Bamberg, 207
Berlin, 136
Bremen, 556, 557
Dresden, 190
Frankfurt, 459, 460
Hamburg, 603, 607–608
Koblenz, 494
Konstanz, 371
Leipzig, 173, 174
Lübeck, 621
Meersburg, 368
Nürnberg, 216
puppet, 250, 557, 581
Wiesbaden, 469
Worms, 482
**Theater am Goetheplatz (Baden-Baden), 407**
**Theater am Goetheplatz (Bremen), 556**
**Theater Combinale (Lübeck), 621**
**Theater der Stadt (Heidelberg), 417**
**Theater der Stadt Frankfurt, 459**
**Theater des Westens (Berlin), 136**
**Theater für Kinder (Hamburg), 603**
**Theater im Schaarfrichter-Haus (Passau), 226**
**Theater Junge Generation (Dresden), 190**
**Theatinerkirche (Munich), 306–307**
**Theatrium (Bremen), 557**
**Thermen (Berlin), 126**
**Thick Tower (Heidelberg), 412**
**Thieves' Tower (Lindau), 358**
**Thimble Museum (Fingerhutmuseum) (Creglingen), 243–244**
**Thomaskirche (Leipzig), 169**
**Thomasknasbenchor (Leipzig), 169**
**Thuringia**
brief description of, 30
cuisine, 657
**Thuringian Forest, 161**
**Thyssen-House (Düsseldorf), 524**
**Tiefurt Palace (Weimar), 156**
**Tiergarten (Berlin), 69, 123**
museums, 110, 112
picnicking in, 112
restaurant near, 95
**Tigerpalast (Frankfurt), 460**
**Times Bar (Berlin), 143**
**Time zone, 62**
**Tipping, 63**
**Titian, 110, 182**
**Titisee, 383, 388–391**
**Tom's Bar (Berlin), 141**
**Top of the Town (Hamburg), 612–613**
**Torhalle (Frauenchiemsee), 337**
**Tourist information, 34–35**
**Tours**
biking, 49
escorted, 48
package, 47
**Tower Restaurant (Munich), 307**
**Town Hall. *See* Rathaus**
**Toy Museum (Nürnberg), 212**
**Toys**
Heidelberg, 414
Munich, 315
Nürnberg, 212, 213
Spielzeugmuseum (Munich), 309
Stuttgart, 426
**Traben-Trarbach, 537–538**
**Train travel**
to Germany, 46–47
within Germany, 55–57
tourist passes, 56–57
**Travelocity, 54**
**Tresor Globus (Berlin), 138**
**Triberg, 391–393**
**Triebhaus (Nürnberg), 217**
**Trier (Treves), 33, 540–546**
**Trinity Church (Speyer), 477**
**Trinkhalle (Baden-Baden), 402**
**Tübingen, 32, 430–432**

**Turm Katzenbuckl (Katzenbuckl), 420**
**TV tower (Fernsehturm) (Berlin), 117**

**Überlingen, 374–376**
**U-Boot 995 (Kiel), 623**
**Ulm, 226–229**
**Ulmer Museum, 227–228**
**Ulm Münster, 10, 227**
**Undeloh, 559**
**Universität Leipzig, 170**
**Unter den Linden (Berlin), 68, 112, 117**
**Upper Black Forest, 11**

**Van Eyck, Jan, 110, 168, 454**
**Van Gogh, Vincent, 106, 113, 181, 305**
**Vantage Deluxe World Travel, 43**
**Veitshöchheim Palace, 234–235**
**Vereinigte Hospitien (Trier), 543**
**Veste Oberhaus (Passau), 223**
**Victory Column (Berlin), 123**
**Viktualienmarkt (Munich), 295**
**Vineyards, 6**
**Visitor information, 34–35**
**Vocabulary, 661–665**
**Völkerschlachdenkmal (Leipzig), 170**

**Wagner, Richard, 168, 197, 264, 655**
Bayreuther Festspiele, 198
Festival (Bayreuth), 39
Festspielhaus (Bayreuth), 198, 200
Richard-Wagner-Museum (Wahnfried) (Bayreuth), 200
**Wahnfried (Richard-Wagner-Museum) (Bayreuth), 200**
**Waldwirtschaft Grosshesselöhe (Munich), 318**
**Walhalla, 219**
**Walks and hikes, best, 12**
**Wallach (Munich), 313**
**Wallanlagen (Bremen), 552**
**Wallberg Road (Bad Wiessee), 339**
**Wallfahrtkirche Maria in der Tannen (Triberg), 392**
**Wallfahrtskirche (Birnau), 367**
**Wallraf-Richartz Museum/Foundation Corboud (Cologne), 8, 512**
**Wallringpark (Hamburg), 603**
**Walpurgis Festivals., 39**
**Wank, 345**
**Wannsee (Berlin), 127**
**Warhol, Andy, 112, 116, 300, 387, 452, 455, 511, 602**
**Wartburg Palace (Eisenach), 164**
**Wasserburg, 361**
**Watteau, Jean Antoine, 106, 454**
**Websites, travel-planning and booking, 53–55**
**Wedding House (Hameln), 568**
**Wehsener Porzellan (Dresden), 184**
**Weihnachtsdorf (Rothenburg), 247**
**Weihnachtsland am Zwinger (Dresden), 184**
**Weikersheim, 242–243**
**Weimar, 151–165**
accommodations, 159–160
nightlife, 161–162
restaurants, 160–161
shopping, 158–159
side trips from, 162–165
sights and attractions, 152–158
traveling to, 152
visitor information, 152
**Weimar Republic, 650**
**Weinfest (Cochem), 533**
**Weingarten, 378**
**Weingarten Basilica, 378**
**Weinstrasse, Deutsche (German Wine Road), 482–484**
**Welcome Point (Wedel), 602**
**Werkbund Archiv (Berlin), 115**
**Werkraum (Munich), 316**
**Wertheim (Berlin), 131**
**Weserbergland Festhalle (Hameln), 569**
**Weser Renaissance, 26, 551, 569**
**White-water rafting, 325**
**Wieland, Christoph Martin, 154**
**Wiesbaden, 13, 51, 465–469**
**Wieskirche (near Füssen), 27**
**Wieskirche (near Steingaden), 261**
**Wikinger Museum Haithabu (Schleswig), 626–627**
**Wild at Heart (Berlin), 139**
**Wildenberg Castle (near Amorbach), 240**
**Wildpark Bad (Bad Mergentheim), 241**
**Wilhelmine, Margravine, 198**
**Willkomm-Höft (Wedel), 602**
**Wilsederberg, 559**
**Wine Road (Deutsche Weinstrasse), 482–484**
**Wines and vineyards, 658–660**
Cochem, 533, 535
Freiburg Wine Tasting, 39
Heilbronn, 421
July wine festival (Traben-Trarbach), 537
Lake Constance Wine Festival (Meersburg), 365
Meissen, 194
Munich, 315
Red Wine Festival (Assmannshausen), 39
Reichenau, 373
Rüdesheim, 489–490
Trier, 541, 543
Würzburg, 232
**Wine Vat Building (Heidelberg), 412**
**Winter Dom (Hamburg), 40**
**Wintergarten (Berlin), 136–137**
**Winter Garten Variété (Berlin), 137**
**Winterhude (Hamburg), accommodations, 595**
**Winter sports, 52–53**
**Wismar, 633–635**
**Wittenberg, 174–175**
**Wittumspalais (Weimar), 157**
**Woodcarvings, 109, 209, 227**
Bad Wiessee, 340
Munich, 312–313
Oberammergau, 351, 352
**Woodcarving School (Holzschittschule) (Oberammergau), 352**
**World War I, 650**
**World War II, 651**
**Worms, 479–484**
***Wurst* (sausage), 656**
**Würzburg, 31, 230–237**

**Zavelstein, 397**
**Zell, 536–537**
**Zeltmusik festival (Freiburg), 385**
**Zeppelinfeld arena (Nürnberg), 208**
**Zeppelin-Museum (Friedrichshafen), 363**
**Zeughaus (Überlingen), 375**
**Zimmermann, Dominikus, 27, 261**
**Zimmermann, Johann Baptist, 27, 261, 302, 306**
**Zoologischer Garten Berlin, 123–124**
accommodations near, 83–85
restaurants near, 94–95
**Zoologischer Garten Leipzig, 170**
**Zoos**
Berlin, 123–124
accommodations near, 83–85
restaurants near, 94–95
Hamburg, 600–601
Leipzig, 170
Munich, 307, 309
**Zugspitze, 6, 345–346**
**Zugspitzplatt, 324**
**Zum Roten Ochsen (Heidelberg), 417–418**
**Zum Sepp'l (Heidelberg), 418**
**Zwinger (Dresden), 7, 182**

# HIT THE ROAD WITH FROMMER'S DRIVING TOURS!

**Frommer's Britain's Best-Loved Driving Tours**
**Frommer's California's Best-Loved Driving Tours**
**Frommer's Florida's Best-Loved Driving Tours**
**Frommer's France's Best-Loved Driving Tours**
**Frommer's Germany's Best-Loved Driving Tours**
**Frommer's Ireland's Best-Loved Driving Tours**
**Frommer's Italy's Best-Loved Driving Tours**
**Frommer's New England's Best-Loved Driving Tours**
**Frommer's Northern Italy's Best-Loved Driving Tours**
**Frommer's Scotland's Best-Loved Driving Tours**
**Frommer's Spain's Best-Loved Driving Tours**
**Frommer's Tuscany & Umbria's Best-Loved Driving Tours**

**Available at bookstores everywhere.**

## Frommer's® Complete Travel Guides

Alaska
Alaska Cruises & Ports of Call
Amsterdam
Argentina & Chile
Arizona
Atlanta
Australia
Austria
Bahamas
Barcelona, Madrid & Seville
Beijing
Belgium, Holland & Luxembourg
Bermuda
Boston
Brazil
British Columbia & the Canadian Rockies
Budapest & the Best of Hungary
California
Canada
Cancún, Cozumel & the Yucatán
Cape Cod, Nantucket & Martha's Vineyard
Caribbean
Caribbean Cruises & Ports of Call
Caribbean Ports of Call
Carolinas & Georgia
Chicago
China
Colorado
Costa Rica
Denmark
Denver, Boulder & Colorado Springs
England
Europe
European Cruises & Ports of Call
Florida
France
Germany
Great Britain
Greece
Greek Islands
Hawaii
Hong Kong
Honolulu, Waikiki & Oahu
Ireland
Israel
Italy
Jamaica
Japan
Las Vegas
London
Los Angeles
Maryland & Delaware
Maui
Mexico
Montana & Wyoming
Montréal & Québec City
Munich & the Bavarian Alps
Nashville & Memphis
Nepal
New England
New Mexico
New Orleans
New York City
New Zealand
Northern Italy
Nova Scotia, New Brunswick & Prince Edward Island
Oregon
Paris
Philadelphia & the Amish Country
Portugal
Prague & the Best of the Czech Republic
Provence & the Riviera
Puerto Rico
Rome
San Antonio & Austin
San Diego
San Francisco
Santa Fe, Taos & Albuquerque
Scandinavia
Scotland
Seattle & Portland
Shanghai
Singapore & Malaysia
South Africa
South America
South Florida
South Pacific
Southeast Asia
Spain
Sweden
Switzerland
Texas
Thailand
Tokyo
Toronto
Tuscany & Umbria
USA
Utah
Vancouver & Victoria
Vermont, New Hampshire & Maine
Vienna & the Danube Valley
Virgin Islands
Virginia
Walt Disney World® & Orlando
Washington, D.C.
Washington State

## Frommer's® Dollar-a-Day Guides

Australia from $50 a Day
California from $70 a Day
Caribbean from $70 a Day
England from $75 a Day
Europe from $70 a Day
Florida from $70 a Day
Hawaii from $80 a Day
Ireland from $60 a Day
Italy from $70 a Day
London from $85 a Day
New York from $90 a Day
Paris from $80 a Day
San Francisco from $70 a Day
Washington, D.C. from $80 a Day

## Frommer's® Portable Guides

Acapulco, Ixtapa & Zihuatanejo
Amsterdam
Aruba
Australia's Great Barrier Reef
Bahamas
Berlin
Big Island of Hawaii
Boston
California Wine Country
Cancún
Charleston & Savannah
Chicago
Disneyland®
Dublin
Florence
Frankfurt
Hong Kong
Houston
Las Vegas
London
Los Angeles
Los Cabos & Baja
Maine Coast
Maui
Miami
New Orleans
New York City
Paris
Phoenix & Scottsdale
Portland
Puerto Rico
Puerto Vallarta, Manzanillo & Guadalajara
Rio de Janeiro
San Diego
San Francisco
Seattle
Sydney
Tampa & St. Petersburg
Vancouver
Venice
Virgin Islands
Washington, D.C.

## Frommer's® National Park Guides

Banff & Jasper
Family Vacations in the National Parks
Grand Canyon
National Parks of the American West
Rocky Mountain
Yellowstone & Grand Teton
Yosemite & Sequoia/ Kings Canyon
Zion & Bryce Canyon

## Frommer's® Memorable Walks

Chicago
London
New York
Paris
San Francisco
Washington, D.C.

## Frommer's® Great Outdoor Guides

Arizona & New Mexico
New England
Northern California
Southern New England
Vermont & New Hampshire

## Suzy Gershman's Born to Shop Guides

Born to Shop: France
Born to Shop: Hong Kong, Shanghai & Beijing
Born to Shop: Italy
Born to Shop: London
Born to Shop: New York
Born to Shop: Paris

## Frommer's® Irreverent Guides

Amsterdam
Boston
Chicago
Las Vegas
London
Los Angeles
Manhattan
New Orleans
Paris
Rome
San Francisco
Seattle & Portland
Vancouver
Walt Disney World®
Washington, D.C.

## Frommer's® Best-Loved Driving Tours

Britain
California
Florida
France
Germany
Ireland
Italy
New England
Northern Italy
Scotland
Spain
Tuscany & Umbria

## Hanging Out™ Guides

Hanging Out in England
Hanging Out in Europe
Hanging Out in France
Hanging Out in Ireland
Hanging Out in Italy
Hanging Out in Spain

## The Unofficial Guides®

Bed & Breakfasts and Country Inns in:
- California
- Great Lakes States
- Mid-Atlantic
- New England
- Northwest
- Rockies
- Southeast
- Southwest

Best RV & Tent Campgrounds in:
- California & the West
- Florida & the Southeast
- Great Lakes States
- Mid-Atlantic
- Northeast
- Northwest & Central Plains
- Southwest & South Central Plains
- U.S.A.

Beyond Disney
Branson, Missouri
California with Kids
Chicago
Cruises
Disneyland®
Florida with Kids
Golf Vacations in the Eastern U.S.
Great Smoky & Blue Ridge Region
Inside Disney
Hawaii
Las Vegas
London
Mid-Atlantic with Kids
Mini Las Vegas
Mini-Mickey
New England and New York with Kids
New Orleans
New York City
Paris
San Francisco
Skiing in the West
Southeast with Kids
Walt Disney World®
Walt Disney World® for Grown-ups
Walt Disney World® with Kids
Washington, D.C.
World's Best Diving Vacations

## Special-Interest Titles

Frommer's Adventure Guide to Australia & New Zealand
Frommer's Adventure Guide to Central America
Frommer's Adventure Guide to India & Pakistan
Frommer's Adventure Guide to South America
Frommer's Adventure Guide to Southeast Asia
Frommer's Adventure Guide to Southern Africa
Frommer's Britain's Best Bed & Breakfasts and Country Inns
Frommer's Caribbean Hideaways
Frommer's Exploring America by RV
Frommer's Fly Safe, Fly Smart
Frommer's France's Best Bed & Breakfasts and Country Inns
Frommer's Gay & Lesbian Europe
Frommer's Italy's Best Bed & Breakfasts and Country Inns
Frommer's New York City with Kids
Frommer's Ottawa with Kids
Frommer's Road Atlas Britain
Frommer's Road Atlas Europe
Frommer's Road Atlas France
Frommer's Toronto with Kids
Frommer's Vancouver with Kids
Frommer's Washington, D.C., with Kids
Israel Past & Present
The New York Times' Guide to Unforgettable Weekends
Places Rated Almanac
Retirement Places Rated

America Online Keyword: Travel

**Booked seat 6A, open return.**

**Rented red 4-wheel drive.**

**Reserved cabin, no running water.**

**Discovered space.**

With over 700 airlines, 50,000 hotels, 50 rental car companies and 5,000 cruise and vacation packages, you can create the perfect getaway for you. Choose the car, the room, even the ground you walk on.

**Travelocity.com**
A Sabre Company
**Go Virtually Anywhere.**

Travelocity.® Travelocity.com® and the Travelocity skyline logo are trademarks and/or servicemarks of Travelocity.com L.P., and Sabre® is a trademark of an affiliate of Sabre Inc. © 2003 Travelocity.com L.P. All rights reserved.

America Online Keyword: Trave

# You Need A Vacation.

700 Airlines, 50,000 Hotels, 50 Rental Car Companies, And A Million Ways To Save Money.

Travelocity.com
A Sabre Company
**Go Virtually Anywhere.**

Travelocity,® Travelocity.com® and the Travelocity skyline logo are trademarks and/or servicemarks of Travelocity.com L.P. and Sabre® is a trademark of an affiliate of Sabre Inc. © 2002 Travelocity.com L.P. All rights reserved.